STUDIES OF ECONOMIES IN TRANSFORMATION

*ИССЛЕДОВАНИЯ ЭКОНОМИЧЕСКИХ СИСТЕМ НА СТАДИИ ТРАНСФОРМАЦИИ*

# Statistical Handbook 1996

## States of the Former USSR

# Статистический сборник, 1996 год

## Государства бывшего Советского Союза

**21**

The World Bank
Washington, D.C.

Всемирный Банк
Вашингтон, Округ Колумбия

First printing December 1996

Papers in the Studies of Economies in Transformation series present the results of policy analysis and research on the states of the former USSR. The papers have been prepared by World Bank staff and consultants and issued by the World Bank's Europe and Central Asia Department III under the supervision of Constantine Michalopoulos. In light of the worldwide interest in the problems and prospects of these countries, dissemination of these findings is encouraged for discussion and comment.



For a copy of *Update* describing new publications, contact the Distribution Unit, Office of the Publisher, The World Bank, 1818 H Street, N.W., Washington, D.C. 20433, U.S.A., or from Publications, The World Bank, 66, avenue d'Iéna, 75116 Paris, France.

ISSN: 1014-997X

# *Contents*

# *Содержание*

# *Country Tables**

Population, Labor Force, and Employment
1-1 Population and employment
1-2 Employment by sector
1-3 Registered unemployment

National Accounts
2-1 Gross domestic product at current prices
2-1A Distribution of gross domestic product at current prices
2-2 Gross domestic product at constant prices
2-2A Growth rates of gross domestic product at constant prices
2-2B Implicit price deflators for gross domestic product

Balance of Payments and Foreign Trade
3-1 Balance of payments at current prices in US dollars
3-2A Imports by commodity group in US dollars
3-2B Imports by commodity group in national currency
3-3A Exports by commodity group in US dollars
3-3B Exports by commodity group in national currency
3-4A Geographical distribution of foreign trade in US dollars
3-4B Geographical distribution of foreign trade in national currency

Government Finance
4-1 General government budget revenue
4-2 General government budget expenditure by economic type

Agriculture
5-1 Agricultural production at current prices
5-2 Agricultural production at constant prices
5-3 Production and average yield of major agricultural crops
5-4 Main aggregates of animal husbandry

Industry and Energy
6-1 Industrial production by sector at current prices
6-2 Industrial production by sector at constant prices
6-3 Primary energy supply
6-4 Final energy consumption

Price Indices and Wages
7-1 Price indices and exchange rates
7-2 Monthly nominal wages by sector

Household Incomes and Expenditure
8-1 Money income and expenditure of the population

---

* This is a standard list of tables for which data are presented for most of the countries. In this year's edition, there are exceptions where certain types of data are presented according to a different classification or where the table has been omitted because of lack of data or obsolete data. Refer to the country pages preceding each set of country tables for an exact list of tables presented for each country.

# *Статистические таблицы страны**

Население, трудовые ресурсы и занятость
1-1 Население и занятость
1-2 Численность занятого населения по секторам
1-3 Численность зарегистрированных безработных

Национальные счета
2-1 Валовой внутренний продукт в текущих ценах
2-1A Распределение ВВП в текущих ценах
2-2 Валовой внутренний продукт в постоянных ценах
2--2A Валовой внутренний продукт - темпы прироста
2--2B Дефляторы валового внутреннего продукта

Платежный баланс и внешняя торговля
3-1 Платежный баланс в текущих ценах
3-2A Импорт по товарным группам в долларах США
3-2B Импорт по товарным группам в национальной валюте
3-3A Экспорт по товарным группам в долларах США
3-3B Импорт по товарным группам в национальной валюте
3-4A Географическое распределение внешней торговли в долларах США
3-4B Географическое распределение внешней торговли в национальной валюте

Государственные финансы
4-1 Доходы госбюджета
4-2 Расходы госбюджета по экономическим типам

Сельскохозяйственная статистика
5-1 Сельскохозяйственная продукция
5-2 Сельскохозяйственная продукция в постоянных ценах
5-3 Производство и урожайность важнейших с/х культур
5-4 Основные показатели животноводства

Статистика промышленности и энергетики
6-1 Промышленное производство по отраслям
6-2 Промышленное производство в постоянных ценах
6-3 Ресурсы первичных видов энергии
6-4 Конечное потребление энергии

Цены и заработная плата
7-1 Индексы цен и валютный курс
7-2 Среднемесячная заработная плата по отраслям

Доходы и расходы домашних хозяйств
8-1 Денежные доходы и расходы населения

---

* Настоящий перечень представляет собой стандартный набор таблиц для большинства стран. Для отдельных стран некоторые из таблиц были опущены вследствие отсутствия данных или наличия только устаревших сведений.

# *Foreword*

The statistics in this volume present information on the economic and social developments in the countries of the former Soviet Union during the period of transition from planned to market economies. As economies adjust to new conditions, so do their statistical systems. The path to reform is neither easy nor smooth, either for the economies or for the statistical systems. While this compilation of data reflects the considerable progress made by the statistical systems in compiling and presenting data for a market oriented economy, the areas where further efforts are needed are evident as well.

This is the Bank's fifth annual statistical handbook on the economies of the former Soviet Union. It presents data developed by national statistical offices, along with other government agencies involved in compiling statistics. The current edition is the first in which the statistical offices of all fifteen FSU states completed and submitted the set of tables. This has greatly enhanced the completeness of the data in the handbook.

As part of an ongoing effort to make the Bank's publications more accessible to policymakers and analysts in all member countries, the handbook is published as a bilingual English-Russian edition.

Michael Bruno
Vice President and Chief Economist
Development Economics

Johannes Linn
Vice President
Europe and Central Asia
Region

# *Предисловие*

Статистические данные, представленные в настоящем издании, дают информацию об экономическом и социальном развитии стран бывшего Советского Союза во время переходного периода от плановой к рыночной экономике. По мере преобразования экономик этих стран претерпевают изменения и их статистические системы. И в экономике, и в статистике эти реформы сопряжены с трудностями. Собранные в этом сборнике данные наглядно отражают как значительный прогресс, достигнутый в сборе и представлении статистической информации в рыночных условиях, так и те области, где предстоит еще много сделать.

Настоящая публикация является пятым ежегодным изданием статистического сборника по экономике стран бывшего Советского Союза. В ней представлены данные национальных статистических ведомств и других правительственные организаций, занимающихся сбором статистической информации. Следует отметить, что впервые данные для предлагаемого сборника были предоставлены центральными статистическими ведомствами всех без исключения пятнадцати государств бывшего Советского Союза. Это значительно повысило полноту представляемой информации..

Чтобы сделать представленную информацию более доступной для сотрудников государственного аппарата и ученых-аналитиков всех странах-членов, сборник издается параллельным текстом на русском и английском языках.

Майкл Бруно
Вице-президент и Главный экономист
Экономика развивающихся стран

Йоханнес Линн
Вице-президент
Регион Европы и
Центральной Азии

# *Abstract*

This statistical handbook, the fifth in the series, represents a major compilation of data on the economies of the fifteen independent states of the former Soviet Union. Beginning with the 1993 edition and continuing this year, the data has been supplied primarily by the national statistical agencies of the countries of the former Soviet Union based on a standard set of tables provided by the Bank. These tables include population and labor force statistics, national accounts and foreign trade data, government finance statistics, data on agricultural and industrial production, information on prices and wages, as well as household income and expenditure statistics. The country tables present data mostly in monetary or physical units. For the purposes of cross-country comparison, a set of comparative tables has been included where the data are presented primarily as indices or percentages.

The data presented in the Handbook are used extensively by Bank staff for economic and sectoral analyses of these countries. In an effort to make the Bank's data and analysis more accessible to policymakers and analysts in the new independent states of the former Soviet Union, the Handbook is published as a bilingual English-Russian edition.

# *Резюме*

Настоящее, пятое по счету, издание статистического сборника представляет собой обширное собрание данных по экономике пятнадцати независимых государств, ранее входивших в состав Советского Союза. Начиная с 1993 года Всемирный Банк получает информацию, представленную стандартным набором таблиц, непосредственно от центральных статистических ведомств соответствующих стран. Эти таблицы содержат данные по населению и трудовым ресурсам, национальным счетам и внешней торговле, государственным финансам, статистику сельского хозяйства и промышленности, информацию о ценах и заработной плате, а также показатели денежных доходов и расходов населения. В страновых таблицах данные представлены преимущественно в денежном или натуральном выражении. В сборник включен также набор сравнительных таблиц для межстрановых сопоставлений. Данные в них представлены преимущественно в форме индексов или процентных соотношений.

Собранные данные лежат в основе проводимого Всемирным Банком анализа как экономики в целом, так и отдельных ее секторов по каждой из рассматриваемых стран. Преследуя цель сделать публикуемую информацию более доступной для пользователей в независимых государствах бывшего Советского Союза, настоящий сборник издается параллельно на русском и английском языках.

# Acknowledgments

The publication of this handbook is the result of the joint efforts of many professionals from different countries and their contribution is hereby gratefully acknowledged.

First and foremost, special thanks are extended to the statisticians in the fifteen states of the former Soviet Union for their hard work on the preparation and timely submission of the tables for their respective countries. In spite of the difficult circumstances under which they collect and process data, the progress they have made in reforming their statistical systems is clearly demonstrated by the greater availability and higher quality of the data in this volume.

The handbook was compiled under the general supervision of Misha V. Belkindas by staff of the Development Data Group at the International Economics Department in close cooperation with the staff of the Country Departments III and IV, Europe and Central Asia Region. The principal compilers of the handbook were Andrei Roudoi and Vesselina Hekimova. Gregory Kisunko prepared the comparative tables. Olga Ivanova provided essential methodological guidance and reviewed the handbook. Timothy E. Heleniak provided general guidance. Asieh Kehyari updated the FSU database and assisted with data processing. Afsaneh Farzin, Victor Gabor, Zhicheng Li, Mark Davis, Barbara Ossovicka, and Gero Verheyen helped in verifying data for the publication. Staff at the relevant World Bank resident missions helped to ensure timely data submission and provided supplementary country data. Bessie Smith provided desktop publishing assistance. Shaida Badiee and Constantine Michalopoulos provided guidance and comments.

# *От составителей*

Настоящий статистический сборник явился результатом работы многих специалистов из разных стран, вклад которых должен быть отмечен по достоинству.

Прежде всего особую благодарность мы приносим сотрудникам центральных статистических ведомств пятнадцати государств бывшего Советского Союза за их усилия по своевременной подготовке статистических таблиц. Очевидным является прогресс в реформировании статистических систем, которого им, несмотря на сложные условия, удалось достичь. Это нашло выражение в настоящей публикации в увеличении представительности статистических данных и их более высоком качестве.

Сборник был составлен сотрудниками Группы данных развития Департамента Мировой Экономики Всемирного банка под общим руководством Миши В. Белкиндаса совместно с сотрудниками Департаментов III и IV , Региона Европы и Центральной Азии. Основными составителями сборника были Весселина Хекимова и Андрей Рудой. Сравнительные таблицы подготовил Грегори Кисунько. Ольга Иванова осуществляла методологическое руководство и рецензирование сборника. Тимоти Е. Хелениак координировал работу. Асье Кехьяри работала над обновлением базы данных по странам бывшего Советского Союза и осуществляли системное обеспечение издания. Афсане Фарзин, Виктор Габор, Зиченг Ли, Марк Давис, Барбара Оссовицка и Геро Верхейен помогали в проверке данных. Подготовку публикации к печати осуществила Бесси Смит. Составители благодарят Шейду Бади и Константина Микалопулоса за поддержку, советы и замечания.

# *Abbreviations*

| | |
|---|---|
| BoP | balance of payments |
| CB | Central Bank |
| c.i.f. | cost of insurance and freight |
| CIS | Commonwealth of Independent States |
| DRS | Debt Reporting System (World Bank) |
| f.o.b. | free on board |
| FSU | former Soviet Union |
| GDP | gross domestic product |
| GFS | government finance statistics |
| GNFS | goods and nonfactor services |
| GNP | gross national product |
| ha | hectare |
| IMF | International Monetary Fund |
| MPS | material product system |
| MUV | manufacture unit value |
| NMP | net material product (a socialist concept) |
| NCV | net caloric value |
| SDRs | special drawing rights |
| SNA | system of national accounts |
| TOE | tons of oil equivalents |
| .. | data not available |
| 0.0 or 0 | negligible |

# *Сокращения*

| | |
|---|---|
| ПБ | платежный баланс |
| ЦБ | Центральный банк |
| сиф | стоимость страхования и фрахта |
| СНГ | Содружество Независимых Государств |
| СДО | система долговой отчетности МБРР |
| фоб | франко-борт |
| ВВП | валовый внутренний продукт |
| ГФС | государственная финансовая статистика |
| ТНУ | товары и непроизводственные услуги |
| ВНП | валовый национальный продукт |
| га | гектар |
| МВФ | Международный валютный фонд |
| БНХ | баланс народного хозяйства |
| СЕИ | стоимость единичного изделия |
| ЧМП | чистый материальный продукт |
| ЧКЦП | чистая калорийная ценность продукта |
| СПЗ | специальные права заимствования |
| СНС | Система национальных счетов |
| СНГ | Содружество независимых государств |
| ТНЭ | тонна нефтяного эквивалента |
| .. | данные отсутствуют |
| 0.0 или 0 | небольшая величина |

# *Introduction*

The World Bank collects data from each of its member countries to support the economic and sectoral analyses it needs for its lending operations. The Bank has developed a basic set of tables, covering most aspects of an economy, as an organizing framework. The makeup of the tables was based on data known to be collected by the statistical agencies of the states of the former Soviet Union and data that the Bank needed for its policy dialogue with these countries. Since 1993, the basic data presented in these tables have been prepared by the national statistical offices of the fifteen newly independent states using the same standard set of tables.

This year, the World Bank sent the Statistical Agencies in each country the data reported for that country in last year's edition and asked that they make any necessary corrections to the data for previous years as well as update the tables with data for 1995. Once received at the Bank, the data were verified for internal consistency and methodological accuracy. Although an effort was made to ensure consistency among the tables, in some instances complete consistency could not be achieved because of the different data sources used in compiling the tables. Deviations from the intended scope or coverage are documented in the country notes that follow each set of country tables.

The data presented in this volume are mostly those provided by the national statistical agencies of the relevant countries and might differ from data published by international organizations which sometimes make certain adjustments based on alternative information sources.

The country tables are preceded by a set of comparative tables designed to facilitate cross-country comparisons. Both the comparative tables and the country tables use the same underlying data. Technical notes following the country tables explain the methodology used in preparing the tables.

The transformation of statistical systems, like that of economic systems, takes time. Statistical measures that are less than optimal will thus have to suffice for policy and analytical purposes until fully developed measures can be put in place. For example, many of the new countries are experiencing difficulties in developing systems to measure activity in the newly emerging private sector. The private sector now comprises many more economic agents than existed in the formerly planned economies, where production was concentrated in a few large enterprises. To measure private activity, the statistical agencies need to introduce sample surveys to collect appropriate statistics. But doing so would require a register of business activity, which is lacking in most of the countries this handbook covers.

The sectoral and macroeconomic statistics in its "raw" format essentially undercount the growing private sector. In addition, the "old" system for collecting data from state enterprises does not produce reliable statistics. The number of nonresponses is increasing, and there are incentives for enterprises to underreport earnings. The hidden economy, also present in the USSR, is growing and is not always captured by data collection or adjustment mechanisms in the newly independent states. Moreover, the family budget surveys do not capture the new sources of income that have appeared. The gaps caused by these deficiencies in data collection must be filled through estimations to provide a more reliable basis for policymaking.

Despite the deficiencies in data collection, the data in the tables are mostly published as submitted by the central statistical offices of the fifteen countries; no attempt was made to adjust or to reestimate the indicators. Therefore, the data should be treated with more than the usual degree of caution.

The handbook is divided into eight sections. Section one contains population and employment data. Previously most people were employed in the state sector, but now a variety of new private and semi private or "mixed" forms of ownership have emerged. Because the existence of open, registered unemployment has only recently been officially acknowledged in the former Soviet Union, no system for measuring unemployment based on a nationally representative sample survey is yet in place. Unemployment is usually measured based on registers from the unemployment bureaus at which those out of work and looking for work register in most states. This is an example of an interim statistical measure - one between having no statistics and having statistics consistent with a market economy and international practice.

Section two contains a set of macroeconomic indicators. For the first time it presents only one set of national accounts - gross domestic product (GDP) calculated according to the System of National Accounts (SNA). The estimates of net material product (NMP) calculated in the former Soviet Union according to the Material Product System (MPS) are not presented in the handbook anymore. All FSU countries are gradually adopting the System of National Accounts, and most of the countries have abandoned the Material Product System altogether.

Section three presents balance of payments and foreign trade statistics. Statistics on foreign trade are those most affected by the breakup of the Soviet Union and the transformation of the statistical system. Measurement of foreign trade is subject to great uncertainty for several reasons: the need to measure movements of goods among the states of the former Soviet Union as foreign trade; the existence of only rudimentary customs services in some of the states; the entry into foreign trade of many new economic agents; the incentives for firms to avoid reporting foreign trade; and the introduction of new currencies and the rapid changes in exchange rates. Nevertheless, the data on exports and imports are presented, for the first time this year, with a breakdown according to UN harmonized trade system as well as by origin and destination. It should be noted that the national trade/BoP data might differ from those published by international organizations which often use additional data sources like partner countries' statistics to adjust national figures.

Section four reports data on general government budget revenues and expenditures. The general government budget consists of the consolidated budgets of the state (or national), local, and municipal governments. Government budget statistics is one of the weakest area of statistics in many transitional economies, and again international organizations data might differ from national ones because the former are compiled using additional data sources.

Section five reports agricultural production statistics, including summary data on the two major subsectors of agriculture - crops and animal husbandry. As more and more agricultural activity has shifted from the large state and collective farms into private hands, measuring agricultural production has become increasingly difficult. Furthermore, the constant price data in most countries are still calculated at obsolete 1983 "all-Union average" prices which distort substantially recent developments in agricultural production.

The same holds true for the data on industrial production presented in section six. This section also gives data on the production and uses of major energy products.

Section seven contains tables on prices, exchange rates, and wages. Producer and consumer price indices compilation methodology and techniques have only recently been introduced in the states of the former Soviet Union. Previously, inflation was measured based on the list prices that were assigned to products disguising the true inflation in the economy.

The final section contains data on household budgets showing the changes in income and expenditures that people are experiencing during the economic transformation. These data again should be treated with reservation due to biased samples in household surveys and probable underreporting of income by the respondents.

# *Введение*

В основе анализа экономики страны в целом и ее отдельных секторов, необходимого для предоставления кредитов, лежит получение данных от каждой страны, являющейся членом Всемирного Банка. В качестве организующего начала выступает разработанный в Банке базисный набор таблиц, отражающий основные аспекты экономики. При разработке таблиц принималась во внимание как конкретная статистическая практика стран бывшего Советского Союза, так и потребности Банка в данных, необходимых для ведения диалога по поводу экономической политики с этими странами. Начиная с 1993 г. данные, представляемые в этих таблицах, подготавливаются национальными статистическими органами пятнадцати новых независимых государств с использованием единого стандартного набора таблиц.

В этом году Банк направил в статистические ведомства всех стран таблицы из прошлогоднего издания с просьбой внести необходимые изменения в данные за предшествующие годы, а также предоставить данные за 1995 г. Поступив в Банк, полученные данные проверяются на внутреннюю непротиворечивость и методологическую аккуратность. Несмотря на то, что в процессе подготовки таблиц делалось все возможное для обеспечения взаимного соответствия между отдельными таблицами, в некоторых случаях, когда использовались различные источники данных, этого добиться не удалось. Все отклонения от заданного стандарта представления данных документированы в примечаниях, помещенных после таблиц каждого странового раздела.

Данные, приведенные в настоящем издании, в основном предоставлены национальными статистическими службами, и поэтому могут отличаться от данных, публикуемых международными организациями, которые иногда вводят определенные поправки, основанные на альтернативных источниках информации.

Собственно страновые таблицы предварены набором сравнительных таблиц, призванных облегчить межстрановые сопоставления. Сравнительные и страновые таблицы базируются на одной и той же информации. Методология составления таблиц объясняется в примечаниях, которые помещены в конце каждого странового раздела.

Преобразование статистических систем, также как и экономических, требует времени, поэтому пока, в отсутствие полностью разработанных новых показателей, для выработки экономической политики и в аналитических целях приходится пользоваться иногда и не самыми оптимальными показателями. Так, одна из основных трудностей, с которой столкнулись многие из рассматриваемых стран, - это разработка системы оценок экономической деятельности в возникающем частном секторе. Частный сектор в этих странах представлен гораздо большим числом экономических агентов, чем было в условиях централизованного планирования, когда производство было сконцентрировано на относительно небольшом числе крупных предприятий. Для измерения экономической деятельности в частном секторе статистическим службам потребуется ввести систему выборочных обследований в целях сбора соответствующей статистики. Для этого, в свою очередь, необходим регистр предприятий, который все еще отсутствует в большинстве рассматри-ваемых стран.

Таким образом, растущий частный сектор недооценивается в прямой статистической отчетности. К тому же "старая" система сбора данных путем сплошной отчетности государственных предприятий тоже не дает надежных показателей. Растет число предприятий, не сообщающих необходимые данные, кроме того, существуют стимулы занижать отчетность. Скрытая экономика, существовавшая и в Советском Союзе, расширяется в новых независимых государствах, но не всегда учитывается при сборе данных и досчетах. Кроме того, обследования семейных бюджетов не улавливают новые, прежде не существовавшие источники доходов. Недостатки в системе сбора данных заставляют вводить поправки, заполнять пустоты оценками, с тем чтобы обеспечить более надежную статистическую базу для выработки экономической политики.

Несмотря на указанные недостатки в сборе данных, в большинстве случаев данные в таблицах публикуются в том виде, как они были получены из центральных статистических органов пятнадцати рассматриваемых стран, и не делалось попытки скорректировать или заново оценить представленные показатели. Так что рассматривать эти данные следует с определенной поправкой на их надежность.

Справочник состоит из восьми разделов. В первом разделе содержатся данные о населении, занятости и безработице. Если раньше основная часть населения была занята в государственном секторе, сейчас появились разнообразные формы частной и смешанной собственности. Существование открытой, регистрируемой безработицы лишь недавно было признано официально, так что система оценки масштабов безработицы путем проведения представительных выборочных обследований для всей экономики пока отсутствует. В большинстве стран лица, потерявшие и/или ищущие работу, регистри-руются государственными службами занятости. Именно данные этих служб являются основой для определения масштабов безработицы. Это - один из примеров временного, промежуточного показателя при переходе от системы, когда безработица не измерялась вообще, к системе, когда она будет измеряться в соответствии с требованиями рыночной экономики и международных стандартов.

Во втором разделе приводятся макроэкономические показатели. В этом издании они впервые представлены только одним вариантом национальных счетов - Валовым внутренним продуктом (ВВП), рассчитанным в соответствии с Системой Национальных Счетов (СНС). Оценки Чистого материального продукта (ЧМП), рассчитывавшегося в Советском Союзе в соответствии с системой Материальных Балансов Народного Хозяйства (БНХ), больше не приводятся: все государства бывшего Советского Союза постепенно переходят на Систему Национальных Счетов и в большинстве из них расчеты по БНХ уже не осуществляются.

Третий раздел содержит статистику платежного баланса и внешней торговли. Внешнеторговая статистика больше всех была затронута распадом Советского Союза и преобразованием статистических систем. Оценки внешней торговли являются наименее надежными по целому ряду причин: возникновение необходимости учитывать движение товаров между странами, входившими в СССР, в качестве внешней торговли; отсутствие развитой таможенной службы во некоторых странах; резкое увеличение численности экономических агентов; стремление избежать отчета о внешнеэкономической деятельности; наконец, введение новых национальных валют и быстро меняющиеся валютные курсы. Тем не менее, в этом году впервые данные по товарной структуре экспорта и импорта приводятся в соответствии с Гармонизированной товарной номенклатурой. Также приведены данные по географической структуре внешней торговли. Следует еще раз отметить, что национальные данные по платежному балансу и внешней торговле могут отличаться от данных, публикуемых международными организациями, которые в своих оценках нередко используют дополнительные источники информации, например, внешнеторговую статистику стран-партнеров.

В четвертом разделе приводятся данные о доходах и расходах консолидированного государственного бюджета. Консолидированный государственный бюджет объединяет бюджеты центральных и местных органов управления. Надо отметить, что статистика государственных финансов остается слабым местом во многих странах, проводящих реформы, и опять-таки данные международных организаций могут отличаться от данных, представляемых национальными статистическими службами.

Пятый раздел посвящен статистике сельского хозяйства, в том числе двум его основным составляющим - растениеводству и животноводству. По мере все большего сосредоточения сельскохозяйственной деятельности в частных хозяйствах, оценка сельскохозяйственного производства становится все более трудной задачей. Следует также учесть, что во многих странах данные в постоянных ценах все еще рассчитываются в устаревших среднесоюзных ценах 1983 г., что ведет к существенному искажению динамики сельскохозяйственного производства в последние годы.

То же самое можно отнести и к статистике промышленности, помещенной в шестом разделе. В этом же разделе содержатся данные о производстве и потреблении основных энергоресурсов.

В седьмом разделе представлены данные о ценах, валютных курсах и заработной плате. Новые, более надежные методы построения индексов цен лишь недавно были введены в статистическую практику стран бывшего Советского Союза. До этого инфляция оценивалась на основе прейскурантных цен, что затушевывало истинные размеры инфляции в экономике.

Заключительный раздел посвящен балансам доходов и расходов населения, отражающим структурные изменения в переходный период. К этим данным также следует относиться с осторожностью, поскольку весьма вероятно смещение оценок в данных обследования домашних хозяйств, а также занижение респондентами данных о получаемых доходах.

# *Comparative Tables*

1. Population, labor force and employment
2. National accounts
3. Foreign trade: geographical distribution
4. Government finance
5. Industry and agriculture

# *Сравнительные таблицы*

1. Население, трудовые ресурсы и занятость
2. Национальные счета
3. Внешняя торговля: географическое распределение
4. Государственные финансы
5. Статистика промышленности и сельского хозяйства

**Table 1. Population, labor force, and employment (percent unless otherwise noted)**

**Таблица 1. Население, трудовые ресурсы , и занятость (в процентах, если другое не указано)**

| | Armenia | Azerbaijan | Belarus | Estonia | Georgia | Kazakstan | Kyrgyz Republic | Latvia | Lithuania | Moldova | Russia | Tajikistan | Turkmenistan | Ukraine | Uzbekistan | |
|---|---|---|---|---|---|---|---|---|---|---|---|---|---|---|---|---|
| **Population** | | | | | | | | | | | | | | | | **Население** |
| Total population, 1995 (thousands) | 3,766 | 7,444 | 10,297 | 1,484 | 5,411 | 16,607 | 4,451 | 2,502 | 3,715 | 4,339 | 147,609 | 5,757 | 4,478 | 51,728 | 22,467 | Население - всего, 1995 (тысяч) |
| Average annual growth rate, 1990-95 | 1.0 | 0.9 | 0.2 | -1.1 | -0.0 | -0.0 | 0.5 | -1.3 | -0.0 | -0.1 | -0.1 | 1.9 | 4.1 | -0.0 | 2.1 | Среднегодовые темпы роста, 1990-95 |
| Female, 1995 | 51.6 | 50.8 | 53.3 | 53.4 | 52.4* | 51.4 | 50.7 | 53.7 | 52.8 | 52.2 | 53.0* | 50.2* | 50.4 | 53.5 | 50.4 | Женщины, 1995 |
| Urban, 1995 | 67.3 | 52.9 | 68.6 | 69.9 | 55.6* | 55.8 | 35.0 | 69.0 | 67.9 | 46.1 | 72.9 | 28.6* | 44.5 | 67.9 | 38.6 | Городское, 1995 |
| **Age structure, 1995** | | | | | | | | | | | | | | | | **Возрастная структура, 1995** |
| Below working age | 30.1 | 35.1 | 23.6 | 21.9 | 25.6 | 32.1 | 39.9 | 20.3 | 23.2 | 28.3 | 22.9* | 46.0* | .. | 21.8 | 43.0 | Моложе трудоспособного возраста |
| Working age | 55.6 | 53.9 | 55.6 | 57.1 | 55.6 | 55.6 | 50.3 | 57.0 | 56.8 | 55.8 | 56.8* | 46.7* | 50.2 | 55.5 | 49.3 | Лица в трудоспособном возрасте |
| Above working age | 14.3 | 11.0 | 20.9 | 21.0 | 18.8 | 12.3 | 9.8 | 22.6 | 20.0 | 15.8 | 43.2* | 7.3* | .. | 22.8 | 7.7 | Старше трудоспособного возраста |
| **Sectoral shares of employment, 1995** | | | | | | | | | | | | | | | | **Структура занятости по секторам, 1995** |
| Agriculture | 33.9 | 31.3 | 19.8 | .. | 29.8 | 22.0 | 42.0 | 18.0 | 23.7 | 45.6* | 15.4* | 54.5* | 44.2 | 22.5 | 45.8 | Сельское хозяйство |
| Industry | 30.8 | 19.6 | 34.5 | .. | 20.5 | 22.2 | 19.3 | 25.1 | 28.2 | 19.2* | 37.0* | 16.8* | 19.2 | 30.5 | 18.4 | Промышленность |
| Services | 35.4 | 49.1 | 45.8 | .. | 49.7 | 55.8 | 38.7 | 56.9 | 48.1 | 35.2* | 47.6* | 83.2* | 36.6 | 47.0 | 35.8 | Услуги |
| **Labor resources, as share of the population, 1995** | 54.9 | 57.0 | 57.4 | .. | 56.1 | 55.1 | 51.4 | .. | 56.0 | 45.1 | 57.6* | 48.3* | .. | 58.1 | 49.9 | **Трудовые ресурсы в процентах к населению, 1995** |

* 1994

## Table 2. National accounts and gross domestic product (percent)
## Таблица 2. Национальные счета и валовый внутренний продукт (в процентах)

| | Armenia* | Azerbaijan | Belarus | Estonia | Georgia | Kazakstan | Kyrgyz Republic | Latvia | Lithuania | Moldova | Russia | Tajikistan | Turkmenistan | Ukraine | Uzbekistan | |
|---|---|---|---|---|---|---|---|---|---|---|---|---|---|---|---|---|
| **Distribution of current GDP, 1995** | | | | | | | | | | | | | | | | **Распределение ВВП в текущих ценах, 1995** |
| **by sector of origin** | | | | | | | | | | | | | | | | **по отраслям происхождения** |
| Agriculture | 43.5 | 26.8 | 12.0 | 6.7 | 45.6 | 12.2 | 40.4 | 8.5 | 9.5 | .. | 9.2 | 21.7 | 34.9 | 13.6 | 28.5 | Сельское хозяйство |
| Industry | 35.8 | 24.4 | 31.2 | 24.8 | 20.9 | 29.5 | 22.1 | .. | 30.8 | .. | 35.8 | 43.2 | 39.6 | 43.7 | 24.2 | Промышленность |
| Other | 20.8 | 49.4 | 51.9 | 56.5 | 31.9 | .. | .. | 49.6 | 59.7 | .. | 53.7 | .. | .. | 38.4 | .. | Услуги |
| **by expenditure category** | | | | | | | | | | | | | | | | **по категориям использования** |
| Consumption | 105.8 | 89.9 | 79.6 | .. | 114.1 | 75.9 | 89.9 | 80.1 | 83.6 | 75.2 | 64.6 | .. | .. | 69.8 | 74.6 | Конечное потребление |
| Gross domestic investment | 23.5 | 19.7 | 25.2 | .. | 1.1 | 23.7 | 15.7 | 21.9 | 19.2 | 29.8 | 28.1 | .. | .. | 34.3 | 29.6 | Валовые внутренние инвестиции |
| Resource balance | -33.8 | -11.4 | -4.7 | .. | -15.3 | -2.3 | -5.7 | -2.1 | -2.8 | -5.0 | 5.5 | .. | .. | -4.0 | -4.2 | Сальдо ресурсов |
| **GDP, growth rates** | | | | | | | | | | | | | | | | **Темпы роста ВВП** |
| 1991 | -11.7 | -0.7 | -1.2 | -11.0 | .. | -8.2 | -8.1 | -10.4 | .. | .. | -5.0 | .. | .. | .. | -0.5 | 1991 |
| 1992 | -41.8 | -22.6 | -9.6 | .. | .. | -3.6 | -15.8 | -34.9 | .. | .. | -14.5 | .. | .. | .. | -11.1 | 1992 |
| 1993 | -8.6 | -23.1 | -10.6 | -8.5 | .. | -9.6 | -16.3 | -14.9 | -30.4 | .. | -8.7 | .. | .. | .. | -2.3 | 1993 |
| 1994 | 5.5 | -19.7 | -12.6 | -2.7 | .. | -18.0 | -20.1 | 0.6 | 1.0 | .. | -12.6 | .. | .. | .. | -4.2 | 1994 |
| 1995 | .. | -17.2 | -10.1 | 2.9 | .. | -4.4 | -6.3 | -1.6 | 2.6 | .. | -4.3 | .. | .. | .. | -1.3 | 1995 |
| **GDP, growth rates by sector of origin** | | | | | | | | | | | | | | | | |
| **Agriculture** | | | | | | | | | | | | | | | | **Сельское хозяйство** |
| 1991 | -2.3 | .. | -3.2 | -6.5 | .. | -22.6 | -14.3 | -2.0 | .. | .. | -3.7 | .. | .. | .. | .. | 1991 |
| 1992 | -8.6 | .. | -14.4 | .. | .. | 28.7 | -5.0 | -29.0 | .. | .. | -9.0 | .. | .. | .. | .. | 1992 |
| 1993 | -5.8 | -16.3 | -10.4 | -13.8 | .. | -6.9 | -8.6 | -19.4 | -6.8 | .. | -4.0 | .. | .. | .. | 1.5 | 1993 |
| 1994 | 3.1 | -12.8 | -14.9 | -10.7 | .. | -21.2 | -8.6 | -15.6 | -5.5 | .. | -9.0 | .. | 42.4 | .. | -3.4 | 1994 |
| 1995 | .. | -5.0 | -7.4 | -1.8 | .. | -24.7 | -1.9 | -2.1 | 18.1 | .. | -5.9 | .. | 2.5 | .. | 2.3 | 1995 |
| **Industry** | | | | | | | | | | | | | | | | **Промышленность** |
| 1991 | -11.6 | .. | 0.8 | -6.0 | .. | -0.5 | 0.0 | .. | .. | .. | -7.0 | .. | .. | .. | .. | 1991 |
| 1992 | -65.9 | .. | -5.5 | .. | .. | -24.2 | -26.4 | .. | .. | .. | -21.0 | .. | .. | .. | .. | 1992 |
| 1993 | 4.2 | -25.1 | -11.7 | -21.9 | .. | -14.9 | -25.2 | .. | -41.1 | .. | -13.6 | .. | .. | .. | -5.3 | 1993 |
| 1994 | 14.3 | -27.1 | -20.3 | -3.6 | .. | -25.0 | -37.3 | .. | -7.3 | .. | -20.0 | .. | -29.7 | .. | -11.0 | 1994 |
| 1995 | .. | -34.6 | -13.8 | 2.7 | .. | -16.2 | -8.4 | .. | 6.1 | .. | -5.3 | .. | -8.9 | .. | -4.0 | 1995 |
| **Other** | | | | | | | | | | | | | | | | **Услуги** |
| 1991 | -10.9 | .. | -4.0 | -19.0 | .. | -0.5 | -7.5 | -11.8 | .. | .. | -2.0 | .. | .. | .. | .. | 1991 |
| 1992 | -11.1 | .. | -13.7 | .. | .. | -6.3 | -9.3 | -15.1 | .. | .. | -7.0 | .. | .. | .. | .. | 1992 |
| 1993 | -31.5 | -13.7 | -8.4 | 1.9 | .. | -1.3 | -46.3 | 6.6 | -24.2 | .. | -3.6 | .. | .. | .. | -0.9 | 1993 |
| 1994 | 13.0 | -9.8 | 0.0 | -1.3 | .. | -10.1 | -17.1 | 8.7 | 8.6 | .. | -3.1 | .. | -53.7 | .. | 1.3 | 1994 |
| 1995 | .. | -18.5 | -6.5 | 3.8 | .. | .. | .. | -0.9 | -2.5 | .. | -3.7 | .. | .. | .. | .. | 1995 |
| **Growth of implicit GDP deflators** | | | | | | | | | | | | | | | | **Темпы роста дефляторов ВВП** |
| 1991 | 79.4 | 83.2 | 103.5 | 158.0 | .. | 103.6 | 135.4 | 156.2 | 156.2 | .. | 128.6 | .. | .. | .. | 90.7 | 1991 |
| 1992 | 569.4 | 1,066.5 | 1,077.5 | .. | .. | 1,333.7 | 851.3 | 976.0 | 976.0 | .. | 1490.0 | .. | .. | .. | 711.1 | 1992 |
| 1993 | 1,399.5 | 747.6 | 1,097.1 | 83.2 | .. | 1270.7 | 763.1 | 71.5 | 71.5 | .. | 888.1 | .. | .. | .. | 1075.4 | 1993 |
| 1994 | 4,070.6 | 1,326.9 | 1,966.7 | 40.2 | .. | 1649.4 | 180.9 | 38.3 | 38.3 | .. | 307.5 | .. | .. | .. | 1229.3 | 1994 |
| 1995 | .. | 608.8 | 646.3 | 34.0 | .. | 148.8 | 38.5 | 17.4 | 17.4 | .. | 183.8 | .. | .. | .. | 366.0 | 1995 |

* GDP distribution is shown for 1994.

**Table 3. Foreign trade: geographical distribution (percent)**

**Таблица 3. Внешняя торговля: географическое распределение (в процентах)**

| | Armenia | Azerbaijan | Belarus | Estonia | Georgia | Kazakstan | Kyrgyz Republic | Latvia | Lithuania | Moldova | Russia | Tajikistan | Turkmenistan | Ukraine | Uzbekistan | |
|---|---|---|---|---|---|---|---|---|---|---|---|---|---|---|---|---|
| **Intra-CIS exports,1995** | 100.0 | 100.0 | 100.0 | 100.0 | 100.0 | 100.0 | 100.0 | 100.0 | 100.0 | 100.0 | 100.0 | 100.0 | 100.0 | 100.0 | 100.0 | **Экспорт в СНГ, 1995** |
| Armenia | .. | .. | 0.1 | 0.0 | 19.5 | 0.0 | .. | 0.0 | 0.1 | 0.6 | 0.9 | .. | 14.3 | 0.1 | 0.0 | Армения |
| Azerbaijan | .. | .. | 0.2 | 0.4 | 13.1 | 0.9 | 0.8 | 0.4 | 0.5 | 1.2 | 0.6 | 0.4 | 5.4 | 0.6 | 0.3 | Азербайджан |
| Belarus | 0.5 | 1.2 | .. | 10.0 | 2.2 | 2.2 | 1.9 | 11.4 | 25.4 | 5.7 | 20.6 | 0.9 | 0.2 | 7.1 | 2.5 | Беларусь |
| Georgia | 1.6 | 19.1 | 0.1 | 0.0 | .. | 0.0 | 0.3 | 0.0 | 0.7 | 0.0 | 0.3 | .. | 5.7 | 0.2 | 0.1 | Грузия |
| Kazakhstan | 0.1 | 7.7 | 2.6 | 2.0 | 1.9 | .. | 24.8 | 3.1 | 3.0 | 1.8 | 17.0 | 2.8 | 13.7 | 0.9 | 18.6 | Казахстан |
| Kyrgyz Republic | 0.0 | 0.4 | 0.2 | 0.1 | 0.5 | 2.8 | .. | 0.4 | 0.2 | 0.1 | 0.7 | 1.0 | 0.7 | 0.1 | 5.3 | Кыргызская Республика |
| Moldova | 0.0 | 1.4 | 2.4 | 0.8 | 0.2 | 0.1 | 0.4 | 0.9 | 1.2 | .. | 2.9 | .. | 0.3 | 2.2 | 0.2 | Молдова |
| Russia | 52.9 | 45.4 | 71.3 | 70.2 | 48.6 | 79.9 | 38.9 | 66.2 | 48.2 | 77.1 | .. | 37.9 | 7.2 | 83.6 | 45.6 | Россия |
| Tajikistan | 0.1 | 1.5 | 0.2 | 0.3 | 0.3 | 1.6 | 3.1 | 0.3 | 0.2 | 0.0 | 1.3 | .. | 0.6 | 0.1 | 12.2 | Таджикистан |
| Turkmenistan | 41.0 | 6.1 | 0.1 | 0.1 | 7.1 | 1.9 | 0.8 | 0.2 | 0.4 | 0.3 | 0.7 | 0.9 | .. | 3.7 | 11.7 | Туркменистан |
| Ukraine | 0.2 | 15.3 | 20.7 | 15.0 | 5.9 | 4.6 | 3.1 | 14.3 | 17.7 | 12.6 | 49.1 | 3.7 | 49.5 | .. | 3.5 | Украина |
| Uzbekistan | .. | 1.8 | 2.0 | 1.1 | 0.6 | 6.1 | 26.0 | 2.7 | 2.3 | 0.6 | 5.8 | 52.5 | 2.3 | 1.5 | .. | Узбекистан |
| **Intra-CIS imports,1995** | 100.0 | 100.0 | 100.0 | 100.0 | 100.0 | 100.0 | 100.0 | 100.0 | 100.0 | 100.0 | 100.0 | 100.0 | 100.0 | 100.0 | 100.0 | **Импорт из СНГ, 1995** |
| Armenia | .. | .. | 0.0 | .. | 7.3 | 0.1 | 0.2 | 0.0 | .. | .. | 0.6 | 0.0 | 8.4 | 0.0 | 0.0 | Армения |
| Azerbaijan | .. | .. | 0.1 | 0.1 | 28.1 | 1.0 | 0.9 | 0.1 | 0.3 | 1.0 | 0.8 | 0.0 | 9.8 | 0.5 | 0.1 | Азербайджан |
| Belarus | 0.6 | 2.1 | .. | 3.3 | 0.6 | 3.1 | 1.4 | 11.2 | 9.2 | 8.9 | 15.4 | 0.1 | 0.8 | 4.0 | 4.0 | Беларусь |
| Georgia | 18.5 | 8.3 | 0.1 | 0.1 | .. | 0.1 | 0.1 | 0.0 | 0.0 | 0.0 | 0.4 | .. | 3.0 | 0.1 | 0.0 | Грузия |
| Kazakhstan | 0.0 | 7.7 | 1.5 | 1.0 | 0.1 | .. | 31.8 | 1.6 | 1.1 | 0.4 | 20.2 | 5.6 | 4.2 | 0.8 | 17.3 | Казахстан |
| Kyrgyz Republic | 0.0 | 0.8 | 0.1 | .. | .. | 1.2 | .. | 0.0 | 0.0 | 0.1 | 0.7 | 0.6 | 0.5 | 0.1 | 2.7 | Кыргызская Республика |
| Moldova | 0.0 | 1.9 | 1.0 | 0.4 | 0.1 | 0.2 | 0.1 | 1.3 | 0.7 | .. | 4.7 | .. | 0.4 | 0.6 | 0.2 | Молдова |
| Russia | 40.5 | 38.7 | 80.6 | 85.6 | 32.0 | 71.1 | 32.4 | 76.9 | 78.9 | 48.9 | .. | 28.5 | 12.9 | 81.6 | 57.2 | Россия |
| Tajikistan | 0.0 | 0.0 | 0.1 | 1.0 | .. | 0.5 | 1.4 | 0.2 | 0.3 | .. | 1.2 | .. | 0.3 | 0.1 | 5.8 | Таджикистан |
| Turkmenistan | .. | 22.5 | 0.0 | 0.6 | 26.8 | 9.2 | 5.3 | 0.2 | 0.1 | 0.1 | 0.4 | 12.0 | .. | 11.7 | 7.8 | Туркменистан |
| Ukraine | 0.0 | 14.7 | 15.5 | 5.6 | 4.6 | 3.3 | 1.4 | 8.2 | 7.7 | 40.2 | 48.9 | 0.5 | 55.9 | .. | 4.9 | Украина |
| Uzbekistan | .. | 3.4 | 1.0 | 2.3 | 0.4 | 10.3 | 25.1 | 0.5 | 1.7 | 0.4 | 6.6 | 52.6 | 3.8 | 0.6 | .. | Узбекистан |
| **Extra-CIS exports,1995** | 100.0 | 100.0 | 100.0 | 100.0 | 100.0 | 100.0 | 100.0 | 100.0 | 100.0 | 100.0 | 100.0 | 100.0 | 100.0 | 100.0 | 100.0 | **Экспорт за пределы СНГ, 1995** |
| Industrial countries | 52.0 | 34.6 | 38.5 | 79.3 | 24.8 | 57.8 | 33.4 | 77.7 | 70.1 | 36.6 | 58.8 | 82.9 | 67.2 | 44.7 | 35.6 | Развитые страны |
| Eastern Europe | 0.4 | 2.9 | 43.3 | 18.5 | 10.2 | 11.5 | 6.7 | 19.8 | 25.5 | 55.4 | 17.8 | 11.3 | 2.8 | 18.5 | 4.9 | Восточная Европа |
| Other countries | 47.6 | 9.1 | 18.2 | 2.2 | 65.0 | 30.7 | 59.9 | 2.5 | 4.4 | 8.0 | 23.4 | 5.8 | 29.2 | 36.7 | 59.4 | Остальные страны |
| **Extra-CIS imports,1995** | 100.0 | 100.0 | 100.0 | 100.0 | 100.0 | 100.0 | 100.0 | 100.0 | 100.0 | 100.0 | 100.0 | 100.0 | 100.0 | 100.0 | 100.0 | **Импорт из-за пределов СНГ,1995** |
| Industrial countries | 62.0 | 23.3 | 59.5 | 89.0 | 35.6 | 57.3 | 45.8 | 76.8 | 75.3 | 50.9 | 67.2 | 90.2 | 52.0 | 65.8 | 38.3 | Развитые страны |
| Eastern Europe | 4.5 | 7.5 | 31.3 | 6.9 | 24.9 | 10.2 | 6.0 | 20.1 | 21.9 | 43.2 | 16.0 | 3.8 | 3.6 | 19.6 | 14.4 | Восточная Европа |
| Other countries | 33.6 | 33.4 | 9.2 | 4.1 | 39.4 | 32.5 | 48.3 | 3.0 | 2.8 | 5.9 | 16.8 | 6.0 | 44.4 | 14.5 | 47.4 | Остальные страны |

## Comparative tables

## Сравнительные таблицы

### Table 4. Government finance (percent)
### Таблица 4. Государственные финансы (в процентах)

| | Armenia | Azerbaijan | Belarus | Estonia | Georgia | Kazahstan | Kyrgyz Republic | Latvia | Lithuania | Moldova | Russia | Tajikistan | Turkmenistan | Ukraine | Uzbekistan | |
|---|---|---|---|---|---|---|---|---|---|---|---|---|---|---|---|---|
| **Current revenue shares by source** | | | | | | | | | | | | | | | | **Доли текущих доходов по источникам поступления** |
| Tax revenue | | | | | | | | | | | | | | | | Налоговые доходы |
| 1991 | 96.5 | 74.2 | .. | 88.6 | 71.2 | 88.1 | .. | 87.5 | 93.6 | 86.4 | .. | 74.6 | 38.3 | .. | .. | 1991 |
| 1992 | 98.4 | 70.2 | 96.7 | 85.9 | 81.9 | 94.4 | .. | 95.9 | 94.7 | 97.4 | .. | 77.7 | 53.8 | .. | .. | 1992 |
| 1993 | 56.2 | 67.2 | .. | 76.1 | 71.5 | 64.3 | .. | 95.1 | 87.5 | 85.2 | .. | 82.3 | 75.5 | .. | .. | 1993 |
| 1994 | 68.7 | 46.8 | 96.9 | 93.9 | .. | 43.7 | .. | 93.4 | 93.2 | 95.6 | .. | 84.1 | 96.8 | .. | .. | 1994 |
| 1995 | .. | .. | 91.8 | 93.9 | .. | .. | .. | 88.8 | 96.1 | 98.3 | .. | .. | 98.1 | .. | .. | 1995 |
| Non tax revenue | | | | | | | | | | | | | | | | Неналоговые доходы |
| 1991 | 3.5 | 9.9 | .. | 11.4 | 28.8 | 11.9 | .. | 12.5 | 6.4 | 13.6 | .. | 25.4 | 61.7 | .. | .. | 1991 |
| 1992 | 1.6 | 6.4 | 3.3 | 14.1 | 18.1 | 5.6 | .. | 4.1 | 5.3 | 2.6 | .. | 22.3 | 46.2 | .. | .. | 1992 |
| 1993 | 43.8 | 3.2 | .. | 23.9 | 28.5 | 35.7 | .. | 4.9 | 12.5 | 14.8 | .. | 17.7 | 24.5 | .. | .. | 1993 |
| 1994 | 31.3 | 0.6 | 3.1 | 6.1 | .. | 56.3 | .. | 6.6 | 6.8 | 4.4 | .. | 15.9 | 3.2 | .. | .. | 1994 |
| 1995 | .. | .. | 8.2 | 6.1 | .. | .. | .. | 11.2 | 3.9 | 1.7 | .. | .. | 1.9 | .. | .. | 1995 |
| **Total expenditure as a percentage of GDP, 1995 *** | 21.8 | 22.5 | 32.8 | 28.7 | 4.9 | 23.7 | 29.3 | 41.9 | 27.9 | 31.1 | .. | 54.5 | 28.3 | .. | .. | **Расходы бюджета в процентах к ВВП, 1995*** |
| Current expenditure | 19.3 | 22.5 | 26.4 | 27.0 | 3.8 | .. | 27.4 | 40.0 | 23.7 | 27.7 | .. | 38.7 | 23.5 | .. | .. | Текущие расходы |
| Capital expenditure | 2.6 | .. | 6.4 | 1.7 | 1.1 | .. | 1.0 | 1.9 | 4.2 | 3.4 | .. | 15.8 | 4.7 | .. | .. | Капитальные расходы |
| **Surplus/deficit (-) as a percentage of GDP** | | | | | | | | | | | | | | | | **Превыш. доходов над расх./деф.(-) в процентах к ВВП** |
| 1991 | 1.6 | 3.0 | .. | 6.0 | .. | -7.7 | 3.8 | 4.7 | 2.6 | 0.0 | .. | 7.7 | 3.5 | .. | .. | 1991 |
| 1992 | -16.1 | 1.5 | -2.4 | 2.8 | .. | -7.4 | -18.1 | -2.8 | 257.2 | -4.7 | .. | -29.2 | -10.1 | .. | .. | 1992 |
| 1993 | -11.8 | -7.1 | .. | 3.7 | .. | 3.0 | -15.6 | -0.6 | 0.8 | -6.2 | .. | -23.4 | -4.4 | .. | .. | 1993 |
| 1994 | -6.1 | -10.7 | -3.5 | 2.5 | .. | .. | -5.2 | -4.2 | -1.8 | -4.8 | .. | -5.5 | -3.6 | .. | .. | 1994 |
| 1995 | .. | -5.3 | -2.8 | 2.7 | .. | .. | -12.2 | -3.4 | -2.0 | -4.9 | .. | .. | -0.8 | .. | .. | 1995 |

* Armenia and Tadjikistan - 1994. Georgia and Kazakstan - 1993.
Армения и Таджикистан - 1994. Грузия и Казахстан - 1993.

## Comparative tables

## Сравнительные таблицы

**Table 5. Industry and agriculture (percent unless otherwise noted)**

**Таблица 5. Статистика промышленности и сельского хозяйства (в процентах, если другое не указано)**

| | Armenia | Azerbaijan | Belarus | Estonia | Georgia* | Kazakstan | Kyrgyz Republic | Latvia | Lithuania | Moldova | Russia | Tajikistan** | Turkmenistan | Ukraine | Uzbekistan | |
|---|---|---|---|---|---|---|---|---|---|---|---|---|---|---|---|---|
| **Growth rates of industrial production** | | | | | | | | | | | | | | | | **Темпы роста промышленного производства** |
| 1991 | -7.7 | 4.9 | -1.0 | .. | -22.6 | -0.9 | -0.3 | -0.6 | .. | -11.1 | -8.0 | -3.6 | 4.8 | -4.8 | 1.5 | 1991 |
| 1992 | -48.2 | -23.7 | -9.4 | .. | -45.8 | -13.8 | -26.1 | -34.5 | .. | -29.5 | -18.0 | -24.3 | -14.9 | -6.4 | -6.7 | 1992 |
| 1993 | -10.7 | -7.0 | -10.0 | .. | -36.7 | -14.8 | 2.4 | -32.1 | .. | 0.3 | -14.1 | -7.8 | 5.4 | -8.0 | 3.6 | 1993 |
| 1994 | 5.0 | -22.7 | -17.1 | .. | -39.1 | -28.1 | -4.3 | -9.9 | .. | -30.2 | -20.9 | -25.4 | -25.0 | -27.3 | 1.6 | 1994 |
| 1995 | .. | -17.2 | -11.9 | .. | -9.8 | -10.4 | -20.5 | -3.7 | .. | -2.4 | .. | -5.1 | -7.0 | -12.0 | 0.2 | 1995 |
| **Shares of industrial production by sector, 1995** | | | | | | | | | | | | | | | | **Доли промышленного производства по отраслям, 1995** |
| Fuel-energy industry | 16.7 | 65.4 | 18.1 | 18.1 | 37.7 | 39.5 | 21.0 | .. | .. | .. | 29.0 | 20.7 | 55.3 | 24.2 | 28.5 | Топливно-энергетический комплекс |
| Metallurgy | 8.9 | 1.1 | 2.5 | .. | 13.5 | 26.7 | 10.4 | .. | .. | .. | 15.8 | 37.8 | 0.1 | 23.4 | 11.5 | Металлургия |
| Chemicals and petrochemicals | 4.2 | 5.4 | 14.3 | 8.0 | 6.6 | 3.9 | 0.2 | .. | .. | 0.5 | 8.1 | 5.0 | 2.9 | 7.4 | 5.5 | Химия и нефтехимия |
| Machinery and metalworking | 12.6 | 3.6 | 23.3 | 8.9 | 5.9 | 7.6 | 9.7 | .. | .. | 9.2 | 18.2 | 3.8 | 1.5 | 16.1 | 8.9 | Машиностроение и металлообработка |
| Forestry, woodworking, pulp and paper | 0.4 | 0.2 | 5.3 | 7.7 | 0.9 | 0.9 | 0.6 | .. | .. | 4.1 | 5.2 | 0.1 | 0.3 | 2.2 | 1.1 | Лесная, деревообр. и целлюл.-бумажн. |
| Construction materials | 3.4 | 1.5 | 5.1 | 3.8 | 2.2 | 3.9 | 3.7 | .. | .. | 3.8 | 4.9 | 1.3 | 3.7 | 3.9 | 6.6 | Пром. строит. материалов |
| Light industry | 4.0 | 9.5 | 8.0 | 10.6 | 3.1 | 2.4 | 17.7 | .. | .. | 5.4 | 2.5 | 16.9 | 16.2 | 2.8 | 19.9 | Легкая промышленность |
| Food processing | 22.8 | 10.0 | 17.0 | 28.2 | 17.7 | 10.4 | 20.9 | .. | .. | 52.8 | 12.2 | 6.7 | 6.0 | 17.1 | 9.3 | Пищевая промышленность |
| **Average yield of major crops, 1995 (kg per hectare)** | | | | | | | | | | | | | | | | **Средняя урожайность основных сельхоз. культур (кг/га), 1995** |
| Grain (cleanweight) | 1,460 | 1,450 | 2,040 | 1,688 | .. | 500 | 1,810 | 1,690 | 1,850 | 2,988 | 1,160 | 870 | 1,680 | 2,430 | 1,920 | Зерно (в весе после доработки) |
| Oilseeds | .. | .. | .. | .. | 190 | 300 | 460 | 310 | 1,360 | 1,267 | 910 | .. | .. | .. | 890 | Семена масличных культур |
| Cotton - raw | .. | 1,300 | .. | .. | .. | 2,030 | 2,240 | 0 | .. | .. | .. | 1,870 | 2,300 | .. | 2,640 | Хлопок - сырой |
| Sugarbeets | .. | 5,480 | 21,200 | 30,197 | 14,900 | 9,790 | 12,310 | 26,400 | 28,410 | 20,796 | 17,600 | .. | .. | 20,470 | 10,740 | Сахарная свекла |
| Potatoes | 13,120 | 9,750 | 13,100 | 14,559 | 12,900 | 8,350 | 9,900 | 13,500 | 12,800 | 6,800 | 11,700 | 10,800 | 3,420 | 9,623 | .. | Картофель |
| Fruit | .. | 3,120 | 3,330 | 3,882 | .. | 1,430 | 2,110 | .. | 3,590 | 4,345 | .. | .. | .. | .. | .. | Фрукты |
| Vegetables | 20,820 | 15,710 | 13,300 | 10,557 | 17,500 | 10,060 | 10,300 | 1,220 | 13,970 | 7,500 | 14,200 | 15,560 | 15,870 | 12,018 | 17,600 | Овощи |

# Armenia / Армения

1996 Population / Численность населения в 1996 году
(thousands / тыс. человек): 3,766

Area / Территория
(thousand square kilometers / тыс. кв. км.): 29.8

Capital city / Столица:
Yerevan / Ереван

**TABLE 1-1. Population and employment (thousands)**
**ТАБЛИЦА 1-1. Население и занятость (тысяч)**

| Population or employment category | 1990 | 1991 | 1992 | 1993 | 1994 | 1995 | Население или группы занятых |
|---|---|---|---|---|---|---|---|
| **Total population** | 3,575 | 3,649 | 3,722 | 3,740 | 3,753 | 3,766 | **Население - всего** |
| Males | 1,734 | 1,769 | 1,802 | 1,811 | 1,818 | 1,823 | Мужчины |
| Females | 1,841 | 1,880 | 1,920 | 1,929 | 1,935 | 1,943 | Женщины |
| Urban population | 2,485 | 2,516 | 2,536 | 2,533 | 2,533 | 2,535 | Городское |
| Rural population | 1,090 | 1,133 | 1,186 | 1,207 | 1,220 | 1,231 | Сельское |
| Population under working age | 1,152 | 1,168 | 1,180 | 1,172 | 1,177 | 1,132 | Моложе трудоспособного возраста |
| Working-age population | 1,975 | 2,010 | 2,044 | 2,056 | 2,063 | 2,095 | Лица в трудоспособном возрасте |
| Population over working age | 448 | 471 | 498 | 512 | 513 | 539 | Старше трудоспособного возраста |
| Economically Active Population, in non-working age | 86 | 85 | 83 | 83 | 81 | 81 | Экономически активное население в нетрудоспособном возрасте |
| Above working age | 84 | 84 | 82 | 82 | 80 | 80 | Старше трудоспособного возраста |
| Below working age | 3 | 2 | 1 | 1 | 1 | 1 | Моложе трудоспособного возраста |
| **Total labor resources** | 2,031 | 2,039 | 2,086 | 2,002 | 1,984 | 2,067 | **Трудовые ресурсы - всего** |
| **Total employment** | 1,630 | 1,671 | 1,578 | 1,543 | 1,488 | 1,455 | **Занятое население - всего** |
| State sector employees | 1,330 | 1,138 | 973 | 871 | 794 | 749 | Государственный сектор |
| Leased enterprise employees | .. | 13 | 3 | .. | .. | .. | Арендные предприятия |
| Joint-stock company employees | .. | 6 | 4 | 2 | .. | .. | Акционерные общества |
| Economic association employees | .. | 4 | .. | .. | .. | .. | Хозяйственные ассоциации |
| Social organization employees | .. | 14 | 31 | 9 | 7 | 7 | Общественные организации |
| Joint venture employees | .. | .. | 1 | 1 | 6 | 6 | Совместные предприятия |
| Collective farm workers | 54 | 12 | 1 | 1 | .. | .. | Колхозы |
| Cooperative workers | 127 | 153 | 145 | 132 | 154 | .. | Кооперативы |
| Individual labor activities | 6 | 10 | 7 | 9 | 19 | .. | ИТД |
| Private subsidiary agricultural workers | 114 | 60 | 59 | 50 | 25 | .. | Личные подсобные хозяйства |
| Private agricultural workers | .. | 262 | 354 | 410 | 462 | .. | Фермерские хозяйства |
| **Students** | 158 | 144 | 144 | 130 | 122 | 144 | **Учащиеся** |
| **Religious workers** | 0 | 0 | 0 | .. | .. | .. | **Служащие религиозного культа** |
| **Working age population not employed in the national economy** | 243 | 224 | 364 | 329 | 374 | 468 | **Лица в трудоспособном возрасте, не занятые в экономике** |
| Housewives | .. | .. | .. | .. | .. | .. | Домохозяйки |
| Military personnel | .. | .. | .. | .. | .. | .. | Военнослужащие |
| Unemployed | .. | .. | 29 | 87 | 106 | 106 | Безработные |
| **Labor force** | .. | .. | 1,607 | 1,630 | 1,593 | 1,562 | **Рабочая сила** |

## TABLE 1-2. Employment by sector (thousands)
## ТАБЛИЦА 1-2. Численность занятого населения по секторам (тысяч)

| Sector | 1990 | 1991 | 1992 | 1993 | 1994 | 1995 | Сектор |
|---|---|---|---|---|---|---|---|
| **Material sphere** | 1,156 | 1,208 | 1,165 | 1,133 | 1,077 | 1,057 | **Сфера материального производства** |
| **Agriculture and forestry** | 289 | 389 | 487 | 522 | 504 | 493 | **Сельское и лесное хозяйство** |
| Agriculture | 284 | 385 | 484 | 520 | 502 | 492 | Сельское хозяйство |
| Forestry | 5 | 4 | 3 | 3 | 2 | 1 | Лесное хозяйство |
| **Industry and construction** | 679 | 635 | 541 | 480 | 452 | 448 | **Промышленность и строительство** |
| Industry | 495 | 458 | 405 | 363 | 355 | 352 | Промышленность |
| Construction | 184 | 177 | 136 | 117 | 97 | 96 | Строительство |
| **Other** | 188 | 184 | 137 | 131 | 119 | 115 | **Другие отрасли** |
| Transport of goods | 46 | 42 | 32 | 28 | 30 | 28 | Грузовой транспорт |
| Road Maintenance | .. | .. | .. | .. | .. | .. | Дорожное хозяйство |
| Communication servicing material production | 3 | 3 | 3 | 3 | .. | .. | Связь |
| Wholesale trade | 82 | 82 | 59 | 56 | 64 | 63 | Оптовая торговля |
| Retail trade and catering | .. | .. | .. | .. | .. | .. | Розничная торговля и общепит |
| Material supply | 12 | 10 | 8 | 8 | .. | .. | Материально-техническое снабжение |
| Procurement | 7 | 6 | 6 | 6 | .. | .. | Заготовки |
| Information and computing services | 4 | 3 | 2 | 2 | 1 | 1 | Информационно-техническое обслуживание |
| Other sectors | 34 | 38 | 27 | 29 | 23 | 23 | Другие отрасли сферы материального пр. |
| **Nonmaterial sphere** | 474 | 463 | 413 | 411 | 410 | 398 | **Сфера нематериального производства** |
| Passenger transport | 25 | 23 | 19 | 16 | 25 | 22 | Пассажирский транспорт |
| Communication | 11 | 11 | 11 | 9 | .. | .. | Связь |
| Housing | 23 | 18 | 15 | 15 | 58 | 57 | Жилищное хозяйство |
| Public utilities and personal services | 43 | 52 | 46 | 45 | .. | .. | Комм. хоз. и бытовое обслуживание |
| Health care, social security, physical culture and sports | 94 | 88 | 85 | 83 | 84 | 82 | Здравоохранение, социальное обеспечение, физкультура и спорт |
| Education | 152 | 150 | 140 | 145 | 147 | 144 | Образование |
| Culture and art | 44 | 43 | 35 | 36 | 34 | 34 | Культура и искусство |
| Science and scientific research | 46 | 45 | 25 | 24 | 25 | 24 | Наука и научное обслуживание |
| Credit | .. | .. | .. | .. | .. | .. | Кредитование |
| Insurance | 8 | 8 | 8 | 8 | 8 | 7 | Страхование |
| General administration and defense | 28 | 25 | 29 | 30 | 29 | .. | Государственное управление и оборона |
| Private nonprofit institutions serving households | .. | .. | .. | .. | .. | .. | Общественные организации, обслуживающие домашние хозяйства |
| **Other, material and nonmaterial spheres** | 662 | 647 | 550 | 541 | 529 | 513 | **Остальные отрасли материального производства и нематериальной сферы** |
| **Total employment** | 1,630 | 1,671 | 1,578 | 1,543 | 1,488 | 1,456 | **Занятые - всего** |

## TABLE 1-3. Registered unemployment (thousands; end of month)
## ТАБЛИЦА 1-3. Численность зарегистрированных безработных (тысяч; на конец месяца)

| Year and mont | Total Всего | Males Мужчины | Females Женщины | Receiving benefits Получающие пособие | Год и месяц |
|---|---|---|---|---|---|
| **1994** | | | | | **1994** |
| January | 104.8 | 51.8 | 53.0 | 30.7 | Январь |
| February | 107.0 | 39.6 | 67.5 | 32.8 | Февраль |
| March | 108.6 | 39.9 | 68.7 | 24.1 | Март |
| April | 110.4 | 40.8 | 69.6 | 25.6 | Апрель |
| May | 111.5 | 40.8 | 70.7 | 24.3 | Май |
| June | 112.0 | 40.7 | 71.3 | 20.1 | Июнь |
| July | 112.8 | 44.1 | 68.7 | 17.4 | Июль |
| August | 114.0 | 43.9 | 70.1 | 16.9 | Август |
| September | 104.4 | 39.1 | 65.3 | 15.4 | Сентябрь |
| October | 99.7 | 34.5 | 65.2 | 15.5 | Октябрь |
| November | 89.5 | 30.7 | 58.8 | 17.3 | Ноябрь |
| December | 91.7 | 31.6 | 60.1 | 22.9 | Декабрь |
| **1995** | | | | | **1995** |
| January | 79.1 | 27.1 | 52.0 | 24.7 | Январь |
| February | 84.8 | 29.0 | 55.8 | 33.1 | Февраль |
| March | 88.4 | 28.9 | 59.5 | 41.4 | Март |
| April | 90.8 | 28.6 | 62.2 | 39.2 | Апрель |
| May | 92.7 | 27.2 | 65.5 | 50.9 | Май |
| June | .. | .. | .. | .. | Июнь |
| July | .. | .. | .. | .. | Июль |
| August | .. | .. | .. | .. | Август |
| September | .. | .. | .. | .. | Сентябрь |
| October | .. | .. | .. | .. | Октябрь |
| November | .. | .. | .. | .. | Ноябрь |
| December | .. | .. | .. | .. | Декабрь |
| **1996** | | | | | **1996** |
| January | .. | .. | .. | .. | Январь |
| February | .. | .. | .. | .. | Февраль |
| March | .. | .. | .. | .. | Март |
| April | .. | .. | .. | .. | Апрель |
| May | .. | .. | .. | .. | Май |
| June | .. | .. | .. | .. | Июнь |
| July | .. | .. | .. | .. | Июль |
| August | .. | .. | .. | .. | Август |
| September | .. | .. | .. | .. | Сентябрь |
| October | .. | .. | .. | .. | Октябрь |
| November | .. | .. | .. | .. | Ноябрь |
| December | .. | .. | .. | .. | Декабрь |

**TABLE 2-1. Gross domestic product at current prices (millions of national currency)**
**ТАБЛИЦА 2-1. Валовой внутренний продукт в текущих ценах (млн. национальной валюты)**

| Sector of origin or expenditure category | 1990 | 1991 | 1992 | 1993 | 1994 | 1995 | Отраслевое происхождение или вид расходов |
|---|---|---|---|---|---|---|---|
| **Gross domestic product by sector of origin** | | | | | | | **Валовой внутренний продукт по отраслевому происхождению** |
| **Agriculture and forestry** | 1,607 | 3,764 | 17,672 | 415,563 | 81,406 | .. | **Сельское и лесное хозяйство** |
| Agriculture | 1,593 | 3,751 | 17,608 | 415,033 | 81,304 | .. | Сельское хозяйство |
| Forestry | 14 | 13 | 64 | 530 | 102 | .. | Лесное хозяйство |
| **Industry and construction** | 4,808 | 7,422 | 22,429 | 218,028 | 67,003 | .. | **Промышленность и строительство** |
| Industry | 3,033 | 5,625 | 18,862 | 184,903 | 54,495 | .. | Промышленность |
| Construction | 1,774 | 1,796 | 3,567 | 33,125 | 12,508 | .. | Строительство |
| **Other** | 2,861 | 4,005 | 18,239 | 187,945 | 38,928 | .. | **Другие отрасли** |
| Transport | 511 | 538 | 2,883 | 25,709 | 3,225 | .. | Транспорт |
| Road maintenance | 79 | 88 | 255 | 1,225 | 253 | .. | Дорожное хозяйство |
| Communication | 138 | 193 | 1,472 | 21,846 | 4,360 | .. | Связь |
| Wholesale trade | 20 | 57 | 447 | 4,589 | 499 | .. | Оптовая торговля |
| Retail trade and catering | 397 | 598 | 578 | 12,978 | 7,924 | .. | Розничная торговля и общепит |
| Material supply | 70 | 82 | 465 | 2,538 | 815 | .. | Материально-техническое снабжение |
| Procurement | 38 | 45 | 165 | 1,525 | 316 | .. | Заготовки |
| Information and computing services | 20 | 15 | 50 | 371 | 27 | .. | Информационно-вычислительное обслуживание |
| Other sectors of material production | 71 | 70 | 216 | 4,400 | 663 | .. | Другие отрасли сферы материального пр. |
| Housing | 193 | 186 | 635 | 2,804 | 2,194 | .. | Жилищное хозяйство |
| Public utilities and personal services | 101 | 192 | 2,553 | 23,046 | 2,257 | .. | Ком. хоз. и бытовое обслуживание |
| Health care, social security, physical culture and sports | 217 | 362 | 1,517 | 15,641 | 2,749 | .. | Здравоохранение, социальное обеспечение, физкультура и спорт |
| Education | 398 | 712 | 2,927 | 27,099 | 2,982 | .. | Образование |
| Culture and art | 109 | 153 | 530 | 3,555 | 614 | .. | Культура и искусство |
| Science and scientific research | 226 | 259 | 712 | 3,969 | 588 | .. | Наука и научное обслуживание |
| Credit | 37 | 160 | 1,397 | 9,979 | 6,289 | .. | Кредитование |
| Insurance | 18 | 20 | 125 | 723 | 16 | .. | Страхование |
| General administration and defense | 200 | 255 | 1,190 | 24,579 | 3,145 | .. | Государственное управление и оборона |
| Private nonprofit institutions serving households | 16 | 20 | 121 | 1,369 | 12 | .. | Общественные организации, обслуживающие домашние хозяйства |
| **Imputed service charge of financial intermediaries** | -22 | -117 | -1,412 | -13,880 | -6,157 | .. | **Условно-исчисляемая стоимость услуг финансовых посредников** |
| **Total gross value added (GVA)** | 9,255 | 15,072 | 56,928 | 807,656 | 181,180 | .. | **Валовая добавленная стоимость (ВДС) - всего** |
| **Taxes on production and imports (TOPI)** | 1,843 | 1,282 | 5,629 | 51,344 | 10,789 | .. | **Налоги на производство и импорт (НПиИ)** |
| Other taxes on production (OTOP) | 323 | 74 | 141 | 915 | 2,799 | .. | Другие налоги на производство (ДНП) |
| **Subsidies on production and imports (SOPI)** | 714 | 342 | 379 | 7,974 | 2,120 | .. | **Субсидии на производство и импорт (СПиИ)** |
| Other subsidies on production (OSOP) | .. | .. | .. | .. | .. | .. | Другие субсидии на производство (ДСП) |
| **Total GDP at factor cost (GVA-OTOP+OSOP)** | 8,932 | 14,998 | 56,787 | 806,741 | 178,381 | .. | **Всего ВВП по фактр. стоимости (ВДС-ДНП+ДСП)** |
| **Net Indirect taxes (TOPI - SOPI)** | 1,129 | 940 | 5,250 | 43,370 | 8,669 | .. | **Чистые косвенные налоги (НПиИ-СПиИ)** |
| **Total GDP at market prices** | 10,061 | 15,938 | 62,037 | 850,111 | 187,050 | .. | **Всего ВВП в рыночных ценах** |
| **Gross domestic product by expenditure category** | | | | | | | **Валовой внутренний продукт по видам расходов** |
| **Consumption** | 6,733 | 12,079 | 69,909 | 940,934 | 197,956 | .. | **Потребление** |
| Private consumption | 4,892 | 9,130 | 58,403 | 785,371 | 176,379 | .. | Личное потребление |
| Government consumption | 1,842 | 2,949 | 11,506 | 155,563 | 21,577 | .. | Общественное потребление |
| **Gross domestic investment** | 4,745 | 6,339 | 1,011 | 83,290 | 43,867 | .. | **Валовые внутренние инвестиции** |
| Gross fixed investment | 4,461 | 4,537 | 10,588 | 105,088 | 37,855 | .. | Валовое накопление основного капитала |
| Change in stocks | 284 | 1,802 | -9,577 | -21,798 | 6,012 | .. | Изменения в запасах (МОС) |
| **Resource balance (net exports of GNFS)** | -1,139 | -3,088 | -13,298 | -210,387 | -63,178 | .. | **Сальдо ресурсов (чистый экспорт ТНФУ)** |
| Exports of goods and nonfactor services | 3,523 | 6,493 | 24,700 | 302,185 | 73,569 | .. | Экспорт товаров и нефакторных услуг |
| Imports of goods and nonfactor services | 4,662 | 9,581 | 38,008 | 512,572 | 136,747 | .. | Импорт товаров и нефакторных услуг |

**TABLE 2-1A. Distribution of gross domestic product at current prices (percent)**

**ТАБЛИЦА 2-1А. Распределение валового внутреннего продукта в текущих ценах ( % )**

| Sector of origin or expenditure category | 1990 | 1991 | 1992 | 1993 | 1994 | 1995 | Отраслевое происхождение или вид расходов |
|---|---|---|---|---|---|---|---|
| **Gross domestic product by sector of origin** | | | | | | | **ВВП по отраслевому происхождению** |
| **Agriculture and forestry** | 16.0 | 23.6 | 28.5 | 48.9 | 43.5 | .. | **Сельское и лесное хозяйство** |
| Agriculture | 15.8 | 23.5 | 28.4 | 48.8 | 43.5 | .. | Сельское хозяйство |
| Forestry | 0.1 | 0.1 | 0.1 | 0.1 | 0.1 | .. | Лесное хозяйство |
| **Industry and construction** | 47.8 | 46.6 | 36.2 | 25.6 | 35.8 | .. | **Промышленность и строительство** |
| Industry | 30.2 | 35.3 | 30.4 | 21.8 | 29.1 | .. | Промышленность |
| Construction | 17.6 | 11.3 | 5.8 | 3.9 | 6.7 | .. | Строительство |
| **Other** | 28.4 | 25.1 | 29.4 | 22.1 | 20.8 | .. | **Другие отрасли** |
| Transport | 5.1 | 3.4 | 4.6 | 3.0 | 1.7 | .. | Транспорт |
| Road maintenance | 0.8 | 0.6 | 0.4 | 0.1 | 0.1 | .. | Дорожное хозяйство |
| Communication | 1.4 | 1.2 | 2.4 | 2.6 | 2.3 | .. | Связь |
| Wholesale trade | 0.2 | 0.4 | 0.7 | 0.5 | 0.3 | .. | Оптовая торговля |
| Retail trade and catering | 3.9 | 3.8 | 0.9 | 1.5 | 4.2 | .. | Розничная торговля и общепит |
| Material supply | 0.7 | 0.5 | 0.7 | 0.3 | 0.4 | .. | Материально-техническое снабжение |
| Procurement | 0.4 | 0.3 | 0.3 | 0.2 | 0.2 | .. | Заготовки |
| Information and computing services | 0.2 | 0.1 | 0.1 | 0.0 | 0.0 | .. | Информационно-вычислительное обслуживание |
| Other sectors of material production | 0.7 | 0.4 | 0.3 | 0.5 | 0.4 | .. | Другие отрасли сферы матерл. произ. |
| Housing | 1.9 | 1.2 | 1.0 | 0.3 | 1.2 | .. | Жилищное хозяйство |
| Public utilities and personal services | 1.0 | 1.2 | 4.1 | 2.7 | 1.2 | .. | Ком. хоз. и бытовое обслуживание |
| Health care, social security, physical culture and sports | 2.2 | 2.3 | 2.4 | 1.8 | 1.5 | .. | Здравоохранение, социальное обеспечение, физкультура и спорт |
| Education | 4.0 | 4.5 | 4.7 | 3.2 | 1.6 | .. | Образование |
| Culture and art | 1.1 | 1.0 | 0.9 | 0.4 | 0.3 | .. | Культура и искусство |
| Science and scientific research | 2.3 | 1.6 | 1.1 | 0.5 | 0.3 | .. | Наука и научное обслуживание |
| Credit | 0.4 | 1.0 | 2.3 | 1.2 | 3.4 | .. | Кредитование |
| Insurance | 0.2 | 0.1 | 0.2 | 0.1 | 0.0 | .. | Страхование |
| General administration and defense | 2.0 | 1.6 | 1.9 | 2.9 | 1.7 | .. | Государственное управление и оборона |
| Private nonprofit institutions serving households | 0.2 | 0.1 | 0.2 | 0.2 | 0.0 | .. | Общественные организации, обслуживающие домашние хозяйства |
| **Imputed service charge of financial intermediaries** | -0.2 | -0.7 | -2.3 | -1.6 | -3.3 | .. | **Условно-исчисляемая стоимость услуг финансовых посредников** |
| **Total gross value added** | 92.0 | 94.6 | 91.8 | 95.0 | 96.9 | .. | **Валовая добавленная стоимость - всего** |
| **Total GDP at factor cost** | 88.8 | 94.1 | 91.5 | 94.9 | 95.4 | .. | **ВВП по фактор. стоимости - всего** |
| **Net indirect taxes** | 11.2 | 5.9 | 8.5 | 5.1 | 4.6 | .. | **Чистые косвенные налоги (НПиИ-СПиИ)** |
| **Total GDP at market prices** | 100.0 | 100.0 | 100.0 | 100.0 | 100.0 | .. | **ВВП в рын. ценах - всего** |
| **Gross domestic product by expenditure category** | | | | | | | **ВВП по видам расходов** |
| **Consumption** | 66.9 | 75.8 | 112.7 | 110.7 | 105.8 | .. | **Потребление** |
| Private consumption | 48.6 | 57.3 | 94.1 | 92.4 | 94.3 | .. | Личное потребление |
| Government consumption | 18.3 | 18.5 | 18.5 | 18.3 | 11.5 | .. | Общественное потребление |
| **Gross domestic investment** | 47.2 | 39.8 | 1.6 | 9.8 | 23.5 | .. | **Вал. внутр. инвестиции** |
| Gross fixed investment | 44.3 | 28.5 | 17.1 | 12.4 | 20.2 | .. | Вал. накопление осн. капитала |
| Change in stocks | 2.8 | 11.3 | -15.4 | -2.6 | 3.2 | .. | Изменения в запасах (МОС) |
| **Resource balance (net exports of GNFS)** | -11.3 | -19.4 | -21.4 | -24.7 | -33.8 | .. | **Сальдо ресурсов (чистый экспорт ТНФУ)** |
| Exports of goods and nonfactor services | 35.0 | 40.7 | 39.8 | 35.5 | 39.3 | .. | Экспорт товаров и нефакторных услуг |
| Imports of goods and nonfactor services | 46.3 | 60.1 | 61.3 | 60.3 | 73.1 | .. | Импорт товаров и нефакторных услуг |

# TABLE 2-2. Gross domestic product at constant prices (millions of national currency)
# ТАБЛИЦА 2-2. Валовой внутренний продукт в постоянных ценах (млн. национальной валюты)



| Sector of origin or expenditure category | 1990 | 1991 | 1992 | 1993 | 1994 | 1995 | Отраслевое происхождение или вид расходов |
|---|---|---|---|---|---|---|---|
| **Gross domestic product by sector of origin** | | | | | | | **Валовой внутренний продукт по отраслевому происхождению** |
| **Agriculture and forestry** | .. | 1,570 | 3,438 | 16,650 | 2,143 | .. | **Сельское и лесное хозяйство** |
| Agriculture | .. | 1,561 | 3,426 | 16,590 | 2,140 | .. | Сельское хозяйство |
| Forestry | .. | 9 | 12 | 60 | 3 | .. | Лесное хозяйство |
| **Industry and construction** | .. | 4,248 | 2,531 | 23,369 | 1,246 | .. | **Промышленность и строительство** |
| Industry | .. | 2,912 | 2,267 | 20,527 | 1,019 | .. | Промышленность |
| Construction | .. | 1,336 | 264 | 2,842 | 227 | .. | Строительство |
| **Other** | .. | 2,550 | 3,559 | 12,485 | 1,062 | .. | **Другие отрасли** |
| Transport | .. | 455 | 174 | 976 | 118 | .. | Транспорт |
| Road maintenance | .. | .. | .. | .. | .. | .. | Дорожное хозяйство |
| Communication | .. | 122 | 170 | 419 | 112 | .. | Связь |
| Wholesale trade | .. | 25 | 65 | 280 | 11 | .. | Оптовая торговля |
| Retail trade and catering | .. | 307 | 140 | 609 | 123 | .. | Розничная торговля и общепит |
| Material supply | .. | 38 | 45 | 349 | 14 | .. | Материально-техническое снабжение |
| Procurement | .. | 30 | 17 | 105 | 8 | .. | Заготовки |
| Information and computing services | .. | 12 | 10 | 44 | 1 | .. | Информационно-вычислительное обслуживание |
| Other sectors of material production | .. | 46 | 58 | 458 | 15 | .. | Другие отрасли сферы материального пр. |
| Housing | .. | 166 | 189 | 264 | 58 | .. | Жилищное хозяйство |
| Public utilities and personal services | .. | 112 | 255 | 1,109 | 99 | .. | Ком. хоз. и бытовое обслуживание |
| Health care, social security, and sports | .. | 225 | 326 | 1,331 | 61 | .. | Здравоохранение, социальное обеспечение, физкультура и спорт |
| Education | .. | 431 | 651 | 3,149 | 117 | .. | Образование |
| Culture and art | .. | 81 | 147 | 150 | 18 | .. | Культура и искусство |
| Science and research | .. | 163 | 152 | 675 | 21 | .. | Наука и научное обслуживание |
| Credit | .. | 117 | 756 | 1,445 | 153 | .. | Кредитование |
| Insurance | .. | .. | .. | 31 | 3 | .. | Страхование |
| General administration and defense | .. | 206 | 380 | 938 | 129 | .. | Государственное управление и оборона |
| Private nonprofit institutions serving households | .. | 14 | 24 | 153 | 1 | .. | Общественные организации, обслуживающие домашние хозяйства |
| **Imputed service charge of financial intermediaries** | .. | -87 | -769 | -1,202 | -156 | .. | **Условно-исчисляемая стоимость услуг финансовых посредников** |
| **Total gross value added (GVA)** | .. | 8,281 | 8,759 | 51,302 | 4,295 | .. | **Валовая добавленная стоимость (ВДС) -** |
| **Total GDP at factor cost (GVA-OTOP+OSOP)** | .. | .. | .. | .. | .. | .. | **Всего ВВП по фактр. стоимости (ВДС-ДНП+ДСП)** |
| **Net indirect taxes (TOPI-SOPI)** | .. | .. | .. | .. | .. | .. | **Чистые косвенные налоги (НПиИ-СПиИ)** |
| **Total GDP at market prices** | 8,209 | 8,886 | 9,268 | 56,692 | 4,485 | .. | **Всего ВВП в рыночных ценах** |
| **Gross domestic product by expenditure category** | | | | | | | **Валовой внутренний продукт по видам расходов** |
| **Consumption** | .. | 6,228 | 10,508 | 54,663 | 4,887 | .. | **Потребление** |
| Private consumption | .. | 4,378 | 7,891 | 42,272 | 4,135 | .. | Личное потребление |
| Government consumption | .. | 1,850 | 2,617 | 12,391 | 752 | .. | Общественное потребление |
| **Gross domestic investment** | .. | 3,995 | -468 | 8,354 | 902 | .. | **Валовые внутренние инвестиции** |
| Gross fixed investment | .. | 2,991 | 582 | 9,665 | 761 | .. | Валовое накопление основного капитала |
| Change in stocks | .. | 1,004 | -1,050 | -1,311 | 141 | .. | Изменения в запасах (МОС) |
| **Resource balance (net exports of GNFS)** | .. | -1,669 | -1,439 | -8,605 | -1,505 | .. | **Сальдо ресурсов (чистый экспорт ТНФУ)** |
| Exports of goods and nonfactor services | .. | .. | .. | .. | .. | .. | Экспорт товаров и нефакторных услуг |
| Imports of goods and nonfactor services | .. | .. | .. | .. | .. | .. | Импорт товаров и нефакторных услуг |

**TABLE 2-2A. Growth rates of gross domestic product at constant prices (percent)**
**ТАБЛИЦА 2-2A. Валовой внутренний продукт - темпы прироста в постоянных ценах ( % )**

| Sector of origin or expenditure category | 1990 | 1991 | 1992 | 1993 | 1994 | 1995 | Отраслевое происхождение или вид расходов |
|---|---|---|---|---|---|---|---|
| **Growth rate by sector of origin** | | | | | | | **Валовый внутренний продукт по отраслевому происхождению** |
| **Agriculture and forestry** | .. | -2.3 | -8.6 | -5.8 | 3.1 | .. | **Сельское и лесное хозяйство** |
| Agriculture | .. | -2.0 | -8.7 | -5.8 | 3.1 | .. | Сельское хозяйство |
| Forestry | .. | -37.1 | -4.0 | -5.7 | 13.2 | .. | Лесное хозяйство |
| **Industry and construction** | .. | -11.6 | -65.9 | 4.2 | 14.3 | .. | **Промышленность и строительство** |
| Industry | .. | -4.0 | -59.7 | 8.8 | 10.2 | .. | Промышленность |
| Construction | .. | -24.7 | -85.3 | -20.3 | 37.1 | .. | Строительство |
| **Other** | .. | -10.9 | -11.1 | -31.5 | 13.0 | .. | **Другие отрасли** |
| Transport | .. | -10.9 | -67.7 | -66.1 | -8.2 | .. | Транспорт |
| Road maintenance | .. | .. | .. | .. | .. | .. | Дорожное хозяйство |
| Communication | .. | -11.8 | -11.9 | -71.5 | 2.5 | .. | Связь |
| Wholesale trade | .. | .. | .. | .. | .. | .. | Оптовая торговля |
| Retail trade and catering | .. | -22.7 | -76.6 | 5.3 | 89.6 | .. | Розничная торговля и общепит |
| Material supply | .. | -46.0 | -44.9 | -24.9 | 10.3 | .. | Материально-техническое снабжение |
| Procurement | .. | -20.4 | -62.0 | -36.5 | 4.9 | .. | Заготовки |
| Information and computing services | .. | -39.7 | -34.6 | -12.7 | -46.1 | .. | Информационно-вычислительное обслуживание |
| Other sectors of material production | .. | -35.5 | -17.6 | 111.6 | -31.8 | .. | Другие отрасли сферы материального пр. |
| Housing | .. | -13.9 | 1.7 | -58.4 | 313.7 | .. | Жилищное хозяйство |
| Public utilities and personal services | .. | 11.4 | 32.8 | -56.6 | -14.1 | .. | Ком. хоз. и бытовое обслуживание |
| Health care, social security, and sports | .. | 3.7 | -10.0 | -12.3 | -22.0 | .. | Здравоохранение, социальное обеспечение, физкультура и спорт |
| Education | .. | 8.2 | -8.6 | 7.6 | -13.6 | .. | Образование |
| Culture and art | .. | -25.8 | -4.0 | -71.7 | 1.3 | .. | Культура и искусство |
| Science and research | .. | -28.0 | -41.4 | -5.1 | 5.8 | .. | Наука и научное обслуживание |
| Credit | .. | 214.5 | 373.7 | 3.5 | 206.6 | .. | Кредитование |
| Insurance | .. | .. | .. | -75.2 | -17.0 | .. | Страхование |
| General administration and defense | .. | 2.8 | 49.3 | -21.2 | 5.0 | .. | Государственное управление и оборона |
| Private nonprofit institutions serving households | .. | -11.9 | 17.6 | 26.0 | -85.4 | .. | Общественные организации, обслуживающие домашние хозяйства |
| **Imputed service charge of financial intermediaries** | .. | 302.8 | 557.3 | -14.9 | -88.8 | .. | **Условно-исчисляемая стоимость услуг финансовых посредников** |
| **Total gross value added** | .. | -10.5 | -41.9 | -9.9 | 6.4 | .. | **Валовая добавленная стоимость (ВДС) - всего** |
| **Total GDP at factor cost** | .. | .. | .. | .. | .. | .. | **Всего ВВП по фактр. стоимости (ВДС-ДНП+ДСП)** |
| **Net indirect taxes** | .. | .. | .. | .. | .. | .. | **Чистые косвенные налоги (НПиИ-СПиИ)** |
| **Total GDP at market prices** | .. | -11.7 | -41.8 | -8.6 | 5.5 | .. | **Всего ВВП в рыночных ценах** |
| | | | | | | | |
| **Growth rate by expenditure category** | | | | | | | **Валовой внутренний продукт по видам расходов** |
| **Consumption** | .. | -7.5 | -13.0 | -21.8 | 3.9 | .. | **Потребление** |
| Private consumption | .. | -10.5 | -13.6 | -27.6 | 5.3 | .. | Личное потребление |
| Government consumption | .. | 0.4 | -11.3 | 7.7 | -3.3 | .. | Общественное потребление |
| **Gross domestic investment** | .. | -15.8 | -107.4 | 726.3 | 116.6 | .. | **Валовые внутренние инвестиции** |
| Gross fixed investment | .. | -33.0 | -87.2 | -8.7 | 44.8 | .. | Валовое накопление основного капитала |
| **Exports of goods and nonfactor services** | .. | .. | .. | .. | .. | .. | **Экспорт товаров и нефакторных услуг** |
| **Imports of goods and nonfactor services** | .. | .. | .. | .. | .. | .. | **Импорт товаров и нефакторных услуг** |

## TABLE 2-2B. Implicit price deflators for gross domestic product (percentage change)
## ТАБЛИЦА 2-2B. Дефляторы валового внутреннего продукта (темпы прироста в %)

| Sector of origin or expenditure category | 1990 | 1991 | 1992 | 1993 | 1994 | 1995 | Отраслевое происхождение или вид расходов |
|---|---|---|---|---|---|---|---|
| **Price deflators by sector of origin** | | | | | | | **Дефляторы по отраслевому происхождению или виду расходов** |
| **Agriculture and forestry** | .. | 139.7 | 414.0 | 2,395.9 | 3,698.7 | .. | **Сельское и лесное хозяйство** |
| Agriculture | .. | 140.3 | 414.0 | 2,401.7 | 3,699.3 | .. | Сельское хозяйство |
| Forestry | .. | 38.9 | 430.0 | 783.5 | 3,300.0 | .. | Лесное хозяйство |
| **Industry and construction** | .. | 74.7 | 786.2 | 833.0 | 5,277.4 | .. | **Промышленность и строительство** |
| Industry | .. | 93.2 | 732.0 | 800.8 | 5,247.9 | .. | Промышленность |
| Construction | .. | 34.5 | 1,251.2 | 1,065.6 | 5,410.1 | .. | Строительство |
| **Other** | .. | 57.1 | 412.5 | 1,405.4 | 3,565.5 | .. | **Другие отрасли** |
| Transport | .. | 18.3 | 1,556.9 | 2,534.1 | 2,633.1 | .. | Транспорт |
| Road maintenance | .. | .. | .. | .. | .. | .. | Дорожное хозяйство |
| Communication | .. | 58.2 | 765.8 | 5,113.7 | 3,792.9 | .. | Связь |
| Wholesale trade | .. | .. | .. | .. | .. | .. | Оптовая торговля |
| Retail trade and catering | .. | 94.9 | 313.1 | 2,031.0 | 6,342.3 | .. | Розничная торговля и общепит. |
| Material supply | .. | 114.7 | 932.2 | 627.2 | 5,721.4 | .. | Материально-техническое снабжение |
| Procurement | .. | 49.0 | 872.4 | 1,352.0 | 3,850.0 | .. | Заготовки |
| Information and computing services | .. | 27.5 | 404.0 | 743.4 | 2,600.0 | .. | Информационно-вычислительное обслуживание |
| Other sectors of material production | .. | 53.0 | 273.1 | 860.7 | 4,320.0 | .. | Другие отрасли сферы матерл. произ. |
| Housing | .. | 12.0 | 235.9 | 962.1 | 3,682.8 | .. | Жилищное хозяйство |
| Public utilities and personal services | .. | 71.4 | 901.2 | 1,978.0 | 2,179.8 | .. | Ком. хоз. и бытовое обслуживание |
| Health care, social security, and sports | .. | 60.9 | 365.4 | 1,075.1 | 4,406.6 | .. | Здравоохранение, социальное обеспечение, физкультура и спорт |
| Education | .. | 65.2 | 349.6 | 760.6 | 2,448.7 | .. | Образование |
| Culture and art | .. | .. | .. | .. | .. | .. | Культура и искусство |
| Science and research | .. | 59.1 | 368.1 | 488.1 | 2,700.0 | .. | Наука и научное обслуживание |
| Credit | .. | 36.4 | 84.8 | 590.6 | 4,010.5 | .. | Кредитование |
| Insurance | .. | .. | .. | 2,232.9 | 433.3 | .. | Страхование |
| General administration and defense | .. | 23.5 | 213.3 | 2,520.4 | 2,338.0 | .. | Государственное управление и оборона |
| Private nonprofit institutions serving households | .. | 45.7 | 405.8 | 795.0 | 1,100.0 | .. | Общественные организации, обслуживающие домашние хозяйства |
| **Imputed service charge of financial intermediaries** | .. | 34.5 | 83.6 | 1,054.7 | 3,846.8 | .. | **Условно-исчисляемая стоимость услуг финансовых посредников** |
| **Total gross value added** | .. | 82.0 | 549.9 | 1,474.3 | 4,118.4 | .. | **Валовая добавленная стоимость (ВДС) - всего** |
| **Total GDP at factor cost** | .. | .. | .. | .. | .. | .. | **ВВП по факторной стоимости (ВДС-ДНП+ДСП)** |
| **Net indirect taxes** | .. | .. | .. | .. | .. | .. | **Чистые косвенные налоги (НПИ-СПИ)** |
| **Total GDP at market prices** | .. | 79.4 | 569.4 | 1,399.5 | 4,070.6 | .. | **ВВП в рыночных ценах** |
| **Price deflators by expenditure category** | | | | | | | **Дефляторы по виду расходов** |
| **Consumption** | .. | 94.0 | 565.3 | 1,621.3 | 3,950.7 | .. | **Конечное потребление** |
| Private consumption | .. | 108.5 | 640.1 | 1,757.9 | 4,165.5 | .. | Личное потребление |
| Government consumption | .. | 59.4 | 339.6 | 1,155.5 | 2,769.3 | .. | Общественное потребление |
| **Gross domestic investment** | .. | 58.7 | -316.0 | 897.0 | 4,763.3 | .. | **Валовые внутренние инвестиции** |
| Gross fixed investment | .. | 51.7 | 1,719.2 | 987.3 | 4,874.4 | .. | Валовое накопление основного капитала |
| **Exports of goods and nonfactor services** | .. | .. | .. | .. | .. | .. | **Экспорт товаров и нефакторных услуг** |
| **Imports of goods and nonfactor services** | .. | .. | .. | .. | .. | .. | **Импорт товаров и нефакторных услуг** |

**TABLE 3-1. Balance of payments at current prices (millions of U.S. dollars)**
**ТАБЛИЦА 3-1. Платежный баланс в текущих ценах (в миллионах долларов США)**

| Item | 1990 | 1991 | 1992 | 1993 | 1994 | 1995 | Статьи |
|---|---|---|---|---|---|---|---|
| Exports of goods and services (including workers' remittances) | .. | .. | .. | 173.7 | 240.1 | 314.0 | Экспорт товаров и услуг (включая денежные переводы рабочих) |
| Exports of goods and nonfactor services | .. | .. | .. | 173.5 | 229.0 | 300.0 | Экспорт товаров и нефакт. услуг |
| Merchandise (FOB) | .. | .. | .. | 156.2 | 215.4 | 271.0 | Товары (ФОБ) |
| Nonfactor services | .. | .. | .. | 17.3 | 13.7 | 29.0 | Нефакторные услуги |
| Shipment | .. | .. | .. | .. | .. | 14.0 | Перевозки |
| Travel | .. | .. | .. | .. | .. | 1.0 | Поездки |
| Other | .. | .. | .. | 17.3 | 10.1 | 14.0 | Другие |
| Imports of goods and nonfactor services | .. | .. | .. | 294.2 | 434.3 | 726.0 | Импорт товаров и нефакт. услуг |
| Merchandise (FOB) | .. | .. | .. | 254.2 | 393.6 | 674.0 | Товары (ФОБ) |
| Nonfactor services | .. | .. | .. | 40.1 | 40.7 | 52.0 | Нефакторные услуги |
| Shipment | .. | .. | .. | 35.7 | 32.2 | 43.0 | Перевозки |
| Travel | .. | .. | .. | 0.4 | 0.8 | 3.0 | Поездки |
| Other | .. | .. | .. | 4.0 | 7.7 | 6.0 | Другие |
| Resource balance | .. | .. | .. | -120.8 | -205.3 | -426.0 | Сальдо ресурсов |
| Net factor income | .. | .. | .. | -1.3 | -4.0 | -13.0 | Чистый факторный доход |
| Factor receipts | .. | .. | .. | .. | .. | 2.0 | Факторные поступления |
| Factor payments | .. | .. | .. | 1.3 | 4.0 | 15.0 | Факторные платежи |
| Total interest due | .. | .. | .. | .. | .. | .. | Общая сумма процента к оплате |
| Other factor payments and discrepancy | .. | .. | .. | .. | .. | .. | Другие факторные платежи и стат. погр. |
| Net current transfers | .. | .. | .. | 55.2 | 105.0 | 160.0 | Чистые текущие трансферты |
| Current receipts | .. | .. | .. | 56.3 | 106.3 | 162.0 | Текущие поступления |
| Workers remittances | .. | .. | .. | 0.2 | 11.1 | 12.0 | Денежные переводы рабочих |
| Other current transfers | .. | .. | .. | 56.1 | 95.2 | 150.0 | Другие текущие трансферты |
| Current payments | .. | .. | .. | 1.1 | 0.8 | 2.0 | Текущие платежи |
| Current account balance before official grants | .. | .. | .. | -66.8 | -103.8 | -279.0 | Сальдо текущего счета до офиц. безвозмезд. трансфертов |
| Official capital grants | .. | .. | .. | 5.1 | 5.8 | 8.0 | Официальные кап. безвозмезные трансферты |
| Current account balance after official grants | .. | .. | .. | -61.7 | -98.0 | -271.0 | Сальдо текущего счета после офиц. безвозмезд. трансфертов |
| Long Term Capital Inflows | .. | .. | .. | 99.1 | 63.3 | 204.0 | Долгосрочные притоки капитала |
| Direct investment | .. | .. | .. | .. | .. | .. | Прямые инвестиции |
| Net long term borrowing | .. | .. | .. | .. | .. | .. | Чистые долгосрочные займы |
| Disbursements | .. | .. | .. | .. | .. | .. | Поступления |
| Repayments due | .. | .. | .. | .. | .. | .. | Сумма, подлежащая погашению |
| Other long-term inflows (net) | .. | .. | .. | 99.1 | 8.0 | 204.0 | Другие долгосрочные притоки (чистые) |

(continued on next page)

## TABLE 3-1. Balance of payments at current prices (millions of U.S. dollars)
## ТАБЛИЦА 3-1. Платежный баланс в текущих ценах (в миллионах долларов США)

| Item | 1990 | 1991 | 1992 | 1993 | 1994 | 1995 | Статьи |
|---|---|---|---|---|---|---|---|
| Adjustment to Scheduled Debt Service | .. | .. | .. | .. | .. | .. | Регулирование долга |
| Debt service not paid | .. | .. | .. | .. | .. | .. | Невыплаченный долг |
| Interest not paid | .. | .. | .. | .. | .. | .. | Невыплаченный процент |
| Principal not paid | .. | .. | .. | .. | .. | .. | Невыплаченная сумма основного долга |
| Arrears reductions/prepayments(-) | .. | .. | .. | .. | .. | .. | Погашение просроченных платежей/выплаты авансом (-) |
| Total Other items (Net) | .. | .. | .. | -8.6 | 22.2 | -29.0 | Общие другие статьи (чистые) |
| Net short-term capital | .. | .. | .. | .. | .. | -12.0 | Чистый краткосрочный капитал |
| Capital flows not elsewhere included | .. | .. | .. | .. | .. | .. | Потоки капитала, не указанные выше |
| Errors and omissions | .. | .. | .. | 15.9 | 14.6 | 41.0 | Ошибки и пропуски |
| Changes in net reserves | .. | .. | .. | -44.6 | 27.2 | 96.0 | Изменения в чистых резервах |
| Net credit from IMF | .. | .. | .. | .. | 23.6 | 46.0 | Чистый кредит МВФ |
| Reserve changes not elsewhere included | .. | .. | .. | -44.6 | 3.6 | 50.0 | Изменения резервов, не указанных выше |
| Escrow account | .. | .. | .. | .. | .. | .. | Счет депонирования |
| Gross reserves (excluding gold) | .. | .. | .. | .. | .. | 50.0 | Общие резервы (исключая золото) |
| Gross reserves (including gold) | .. | .. | .. | .. | .. | 42.0 | Общие резервы (включая золото) |
| Nominal official exchange rate (annual average) (rf) | .. | .. | .. | .. | .. | .. | Номинальный официальный или рыночный курс (среднегодовой) |
| Nominal official exchange rate (end-of-year) (ae) | .. | .. | .. | .. | .. | .. | Номинальный официальный или рыночный курс (на конец года) |
| Manufacture unit value (percent change) | .. | .. | .. | .. | .. | .. | Средний индекс цен на продукцию обр. пром.,% |
| Index of real effective exchange rate (IMF) | .. | .. | .. | .. | .. | .. | Индекс реального эффективного валютного курса (МВФ) |
| Total factor payments | .. | .. | .. | -1.3 | -4.2 | -13.0 | Общая сумма факторных платежей |
| Government interest | .. | .. | .. | -1.3 | -4.2 | -13.0 | Процент, выплачиваемый органами гос. управления |
| Private sector interest | .. | .. | .. | .. | .. | .. | Процент выплачиваемый частным сектором |
| Profits on direct foreign investment | .. | .. | .. | .. | .. | .. | Прибыль от прямых иностранных инвестиций |
| Official capital grants | .. | .. | .. | 5.1 | 5.7 | 8.0 | Официальные капитальные безвозмездные трансферты |
| For budgetary financing | .. | .. | .. | 5.1 | 5.7 | 8.0 | На бюджетное финансирование |
| To extrabudgetary entities | .. | .. | .. | .. | .. | .. | На внебюджетное финансирование |
| Government net long term borrowing | .. | .. | .. | .. | .. | 151.0 | Чистые долгосрочные государственные займы |
| Disbursements | .. | .. | .. | .. | .. | 151.0 | Поступления |
| Repayments | .. | .. | .. | .. | .. | .. | Погашения |
| Private net long term borrowing | .. | .. | .. | .. | .. | 2.0 | Чистые долгосрочные частные займы |
| Disbursements | .. | .. | .. | .. | .. | 2.0 | Поступления |
| Repayments | .. | .. | .. | .. | .. | .. | Погашения |

## TABLE 3-2A. Imports by commodity group (millions of U.S. dollars)
## ТАБЛИЦА 3-2А . Импорт по товарным группам (млн. долларов США)

| Commodity group | 1990 | 1991 | 1992 | 1993 | 1994 | 1995 | Товарные группы |
|---|---|---|---|---|---|---|---|
| TOTAL | .. | .. | .. | .. | 393.8 | 673.9 | ВСЕГО |
| I - Live animals; animal products | .. | .. | .. | .. | 46.1 | 63.3 | I - Живые животные и продукты животноводства |
| II - Vegetable products | .. | .. | .. | .. | 64.3 | 85.6 | II - Продукты растительного происхождения |
| III - Animal or vegetable fats and oils and their cleavage products; prepared edible fats; animal or vegetable waxes | .. | .. | .. | .. | 11.9 | 25.1 | III - Жиры и масла растительного и животного происхождения, воски |
| IV - Prepared foodstuffs; beverages, spirits and vinegar; tobacco and manufactured tobacco substitutes | .. | .. | .. | .. | 32.4 | 51.5 | IV -Продукция пищевой промышленности, алкогольные и безалкогольные напитки, табак и его заменители |
| V - Mineral products | .. | .. | .. | .. | 161.0 | 224.7 | V - Минеральные продукты |
| VI - Products of the chemical or allied industries | .. | .. | .. | .. | 9.1 | 55.4 | VI - Продукция химической промышленности |
| VII - Plastics and articles thereof; rubber and articles thereof | .. | .. | .. | .. | 1.0 | 4.0 | VII - Пластмассы и изделия из них |
| VIII - Raw hides and skins, leather, furskins and articles thereof; saddlery and harness; travel goods, handbags and similar containers; articles of animal gut | .. | .. | .. | .. | 0.2 | 0.3 | VIII - Кожевенное сырьё, кожи, пушнина, меховое сырьё и изделия из них |
| IX - Wood and articles of wood; wood charcoal; cork and articles of cork; manufactures of straw, of esparto or of other plaiting materials; basketware and wickerwork | .. | .. | .. | .. | 0.4 | 0.9 | IX - Древесина и изделия из древесины, древесный уголь |
| X - Pulp of wood or of other fibrous cellulosic material; waste and scrap of paper or paperboard; paper and paperboard and articles thereof | .. | .. | .. | .. | 2.7 | 8.1 | X - Бумажная масса, бумажные и картонные отходы, макулатура, бумага, картон и изделия из них |
| XI - Textiles and textile articles | .. | .. | .. | .. | 8.6 | 7.8 | XI - Текстиль и текстильные изделия |
| XII - Footwear, headgear, umbrellas, sun umbrellas, walking sticks, seat sticks, whips, riding crops and parts thereof; prepared feathers and articles made therewith; artificial flowers; articles of human hair | .. | .. | .. | .. | 0.3 | 0.9 | XII - Обувь, головные уборы, зонты, трости и пр. |

**TABLE 3-2A. Imports by commodity group (millions of U.S. dollars)**
**ТАБЛИЦА 3-2A . Импорт по товарным группам (млн. долларов США)**

| Commodity group | 1990 | 1991 | 1992 | 1993 | 1994 | 1995 | Товарные группы |
|---|---|---|---|---|---|---|---|
| XIII - Articles of stone, plaster, cement, asbestos, mica and similar materials; ceramic products; glass and glassware | .. | .. | .. | .. | 0.8 | 2.5 | XIII - Изделия из камня, гипса, цемента |
| XIV - Natural or cultured pearls, precious or semi-precious stones, precious metals, metals clad with precious metal and articles thereof; imitation jewellery; coin | .. | .. | .. | .. | 31.8 | 62.4 | XIV - Жемчуг, драгоценные и полудрагоценные камни, драгоценные металлы, бижутерия, монеты |
| XV - Base metals and articles of base metal | .. | .. | .. | .. | 3.6 | 15.9 | XV - Неблагородные металлы и изделия из них |
| XVI - Machinery and mechanical appliances; electrical equipment; parts thereof; sound recorders and reproducers, television image and sound recorders and reproducers, and parts and accessories of such articles | .. | .. | .. | .. | 8.0 | 49.6 | XVI - Машины, оборудование, механизмы, их части и принадлежности; звуковая и теле-аппаратура, их части и принадлежности |
| XVII - Vehicles, aircraft, vessels and associated transport equipment | .. | .. | .. | .. | 2.0 | 6.4 | XVII - Средства наземного, воздушного и водного транспорта |
| XVIII - Optical, photographic, cinematograp-hic, measuring, checking, precision, medical or surgical instruments and apparatus; clocks and watches; musical instruments; parts and accessories thereof | .. | .. | .. | .. | 2.9 | 5.8 | XVIII - Приборы, аппараты оптические, медицинские, измерительные и пр.; музыкальные инструменты; часы; их части и принадлежности |
| XIX - Arms and ammunition; parts and accessories thereof | .. | .. | .. | .. | .. | .. | XIX - Оружие и боеприпасы, их части и принадлежности |
| XX - Miscellaneous manufactured articles | .. | .. | .. | .. | 6.7 | 3.2 | XX - Разные промышленные товары |
| XXI - Works of art, collectors' pieces, and antiques | .. | .. | .. | .. | 0.0 | 0.6 | XXI - Произведения искусства, предметы антиквариата |
| XXII - Services | .. | .. | .. | .. | .. | .. | XXII - Услуги |

## TABLE 3-2B Imports by commodity group (millions of national currency)

## ТАБЛИЦА 3-2B. Импорт по товарным группам (млн. национальной валюты)



| Commodity group | 1990 | 1991 | 1992 | 1993 | 1994 | 1995 | Товарные группы |
|---|---|---|---|---|---|---|---|
| TOTAL | .. | .. | .. | .. | 1,128,237.0 | 2,733,338.0 | ВСЕГО |
| I - Live animals; animal products | .. | .. | .. | .. | 13,207.6 | 25,674.5 | I - Живые животные и продукты животноводства |
| II - Vegetable products | .. | .. | .. | .. | 18,421.9 | 34,719.4 | II - Продукты растительного происхождения |
| III - Animal or vegetable fats and oils and their cleavage products; prepared edible fats; animal or vegetable waxes | .. | .. | .. | .. | 3,409.4 | 10,180.6 | III - Жиры и масла растительного и животного происхождения, воски |
| IV - Prepared foodstuffs; beverages, spirits and vinegar; tobacco and manufactured tobacco substitutes | .. | .. | .. | .. | 9,282.6 | 20,888.4 | IV -Продукция пищевой промышленности, алкогольные и безалкогольные напитки, табак и его заменители |
| V - Mineral products | .. | .. | .. | .. | 46,126.5 | 91,138.3 | V - Минеральные продукты |
| VI - Products of the chemical or allied industries | .. | .. | .. | .. | 2,607.2 | 22470.2 | VI - Продукция химической промышленности |
| VII - Plastics and articles thereof; rubber and articles thereof | .. | .. | .. | .. | 286.5 | 1,622.4 | VII - Пластмассы и изделия из них |
| VIII - Raw hides and skins, leather, furskins and articles thereof; saddlery and harness; travel goods, handbags and similar containers; articles of animal gut | .. | .. | .. | .. | 57.3 | 121.7 | VIII - Кожевенное сырьё, кожи, пушнина, меховое сырьё и изделия из них |
| IX - Wood and articles of wood; wood charcoal; cork and articles of cork; manufactures of straw, of esparto or of other plaiting materials; basketware and wickerwork | .. | .. | .. | .. | 114.6 | 365.0 | IX - Древесина и изделия из древесины, древесный уголь |
| X - Pulp of wood or of other fibrous cellulosic material; waste and scrap of paper or paperboard; paper and paperboard and articles thereof | .. | .. | .. | .. | 773.5 | 3,285.4 | X - Бумажная масса, бумажные и картонные отходы, макулатура, бумага, картон и изделия из них |
| XI - Textiles and textile articles | .. | .. | .. | .. | 2,463.9 | 3,163.7 | XI - Текстиль и текстильные изделия |
| XII - Footwear, headgear, umbrellas, sun umbrellas, walking sticks, seat sticks, whips, riding crops and parts thereof; prepared feathers and articles made therewith; artificial flowers; articles of human hair | .. | .. | .. | .. | 85.9 | 365.0 | XII - Обувь, головные уборы, зонты, трости и пр. |

## TABLE 3-2B Imports by commodity group (millions of national currency)
## ТАБЛИЦА 3-2B. Импорт по товарным группам (млн. национальной валюты)

| Commodity group | 1990 | 1991 | 1992 | 1993 | 1994 | 1995 | Товарные группы |
|---|---|---|---|---|---|---|---|
| XIII - Articles of stone, plaster, cement, asbestos, mica and similar materials; ceramic products; glass and glassware | .. | .. | .. | .. | 229.3 | 1,014.0 | XIII - Изделия из камня, гипса, цемента |
| XIV - Natural or cultured pearls, precious or semi-precious stones, precious metals, metals clad with precious metal and articles thereof; imitation jewellery; coin | .. | .. | .. | .. | 9,110.7 | 25,309.4 | XIV - Жемчуг, драгоценные и полудрагоценные камни, драгоценные металлы, бижутерия, монеты |
| XV - Base metals and articles of base metal | .. | .. | .. | .. | 1031.4 | 6,449.0 | XV - Неблагородные металлы и изделия из них |
| XVI - Machinery and mechanical appliances; electrical equipment; parts thereof; sound recorders and reproducers, television image and sound recorders and reproducers, and parts and accessories of such articles | .. | .. | .. | .. | 2,292.0 | 20,117.8 | XVI - Машины, оборудование, механизмы, их части и принадлежности; звуковая и теле-аппаратура, их части и принадлежности |
| XVII - Vehicles, aircraft, vessels and associated transport equipment | .. | .. | .. | .. | 573.1 | 2,595.8 | XVII - Средства наземного, воздушного и водного транспорта |
| XVIII - Optical, photographic, cinematograp-hic, measuring, checking, precision, medical or surgical instruments and apparatus; clocks and watches; musical instruments; parts and accessories thereof | .. | .. | .. | .. | 830.8 | 2,311.9 | XVIII - Приборы, аппараты оптические, медицинские, измерительные и пр.; музыкальные инструменты; часы; их части и принадлежности |
| XIX - Arms and ammunition; parts and accessories thereof | .. | .. | .. | .. | 1,919.5 | 1,297.9 | XIX - Оружие и боеприпасы, их части и принадлежности |
| XX - Miscellaneous manufactured articles | .. | .. | .. | .. | 0.0 | 243.4 | XX - Разные промышленные товары |
| XXI - Works of art, collectors' pieces, and antiques | .. | .. | .. | .. | .. | .. | XXI - Произведения искусства, предметы антиквариата |
| XXII - Services | .. | .. | .. | .. | .. | .. | XXII - Услуги |

## TABLE 3-3A. Exports by commodity group (millions of U.S. dollars)
## ТАБЛИЦА 3-3А. Экспорт по товарным группам (млн. долларов США)

| Commodity group | 1990 | 1991 | 1992 | 1993 | 1994 | 1995 | Товарные группы |
|---|---|---|---|---|---|---|---|
| TOTAL | .. | .. | .. | .. | 215.5 | 270.9 | ВСЕГО |
| I - Live animals; animal products | .. | .. | .. | .. | 0.0 | 0.1 | I - Живые животные и продукты животноводства |
| II - Vegetable products | | | .. | .. | 0.7 | 0.9 | II - Продукты растительного происхождения |
| III - Animal or vegetable fats and oils and their cleavage products; prepared edible fats; animal or vegetable waxes | | | .. | .. | 0.0 | 0.0 | III - Жиры и масла растительного и животного происхождения, воски |
| IV - Prepared foodstuffs; beverages, spirits and vinegar; tobacco and manufactured tobacco substitutes | | | .. | .. | 12.9 | 12.6 | IV -Продукция пищевой промышленности, алкогольные и безалкогольные напитки, табак и его заменители |
| V - Mineral products | | | .. | .. | 17.8 | 28.8 | V - Минеральные продукты |
| VI - Products of the chemical or allied industries | | | .. | .. | 3.9 | 14.5 | VI - Продукция химической промышленности |
| VII - Plastics and articles thereof; rubber and articles thereof | | | .. | .. | 7.9 | 10.8 | VII - Пластмассы и изделия из них |
| VIII - Raw hides and skins, leather, furskins and articles thereof; saddlery and harness; travel goods, handbags and similar containers; articles of animal gut | | | .. | .. | 0.8 | 1.4 | VIII - Кожевенное сырьё, кожи, пушнина, меховое сырьё и изделия из них |
| IX - Wood and articles of wood; wood charcoal; cork and articles of cork; manufactures of straw, of esparto or of other plaiting materials; basketware and wickerwork | | | .. | .. | 0.0 | 0.2 | IX - Древесина и изделия из древесины, древесный уголь |
| X - Pulp of wood or of other fibrous cellulosic material; waste and scrap of paper or paperboard; paper and paperboard and articles thereof | | | .. | .. | 0.4 | 0.8 | X - Бумажная масса, бумажные и картонные отходы, макулатура, бумага, картон и изделия из них |
| XI - Textiles and textile articles | | | .. | .. | 15.8 | 15.2 | XI - Текстиль и текстильные изделия |
| XII - Footwear, headgear, umbrellas, sun umbrellas, walking sticks, seat sticks, whips, riding crops and parts thereof; prepared feathers and articles made therewith; artificial flowers; articles of human hair | | | .. | .. | 15.9 | 5.4 | XII - Обувь, головные уборы, зонты, трости и пр. |

**TABLE 3-3A. Exports by commodity group (millions of U.S. dollars)**
**ТАБЛИЦА 3-3А. Экспорт по товарным группам (млн. долларов США)**

| Commodity group | 1990 | 1991 | 1992 | 1993 | 1994 | 1995 | Товарные группы |
|---|---|---|---|---|---|---|---|
| XIII - Articles of stone, plaster, cement, asbestos, mica and similar materials; ceramic products; glass and glassware | .. | .. | .. | .. | 12.7 | 2.1 | XIII - Изделия из камня, гипса, цемента |
| XIV - Natural or cultured pearls, precious or semi-precious stones, precious metals, metals clad with precious metal and articles thereof; imitation jewellery; coin | .. | .. | .. | .. | 75.2 | 89.6 | XIV - Жемчуг, драгоценные и полудрагоценные камни, драгоценные металлы, бижутерия, монеты |
| XV - Base metals and articles of base metal | .. | .. | .. | .. | 9.4 | 30.5 | XV - Неблагородные металлы и изделия из них |
| XVI - Machinery and mechanical appliances; electrical equipment; parts thereof; sound recorders and reproducers, television image and sound recorders and reproducers, and parts and accessories of such articles | .. | .. | .. | .. | 30.9 | 39.1 | XVI - Машины, оборудование, механизмы, их части и принадлежности; звуковая и теле-аппаратура, их части и принадлежности |
| XVII - Vehicles, aircraft, vessels and associated transport equipment | .. | .. | .. | .. | 1.7 | 11.4 | XVII - Средства наземного, воздушного и водного транспорта |
| XVIII - Optical, photographic, cinematographic, measuring, checking, precision, medical or surgical instruments and apparatus; clocks and watches; musical instruments; parts and accessories thereof | .. | .. | .. | .. | 4.0 | 3.8 | XVIII - Приборы, аппараты оптические, медицинские, измерительные и пр.; музыкальные инструменты; часы; их части и принадлежности |
| XIX - Arms and ammunition; parts and accessories thereof | .. | .. | .. | .. | .. | .. | XIX - Оружие и боеприпасы, их части и принадлежности |
| XX - Miscellaneous manufactured articles | .. | .. | .. | .. | 5.5 | 3.4 | XX - Разные промышленные товары |
| XXI - Works of art, collectors' pieces, and antiques | .. | .. | .. | .. | 0.0 | 0.3 | XXI - Произведения искусства, предметы антиквариата |
| XXII - Services | .. | .. | .. | .. | .. | .. | XXII - Услуги |

**TABLE 3-3B. Exports by Commodity Group (millions of national currency)**
**ТАБЛИЦА 3-3B. Экспорт по товарным группам (млн. национальной валюты)**

| Commodity group | 1990 | 1991 | 1992 | 1993 | 1994 | 1995 | Товарные группы |
|---|---|---|---|---|---|---|---|
| TOTAL | .. | .. | .. | .. | 61,740.7 | 109,877.0 | ВСЕГО |
| I - Live animals; animal products | .. | .. | .. | .. | 0.0 | 40.6 | I - Живые животные и продукты животноводства |
| II - Vegetable products | .. | .. | .. | .. | 200.5 | 365.0 | II - Продукты растительного происхождения |
| III - Animal or vegetable fats and oils and their cleavage products; prepared edible fats; animal or vegetable waxes | .. | .. | .. | .. | 0.0 | 0.0 | III - Жиры и масла растительного и животного происхождения, воски |
| IV - Prepared foodstuffs; beverages, spirits and vinegar; tobacco and manufactured tobacco substitutes | .. | .. | .. | .. | 3,695.8 | 5,110.6 | IV -Продукция пищевой промышленности, алкогольные и безалкогольные напитки, табак и его заменители |
| V - Mineral products | .. | .. | .. | .. | 5,099.7 | 11,681.3 | V - Минеральные продукты |
| VI - Products of the chemical or allied industries | .. | .. | .. | .. | 1,117.3 | 5,881.2 | VI - Продукция химической промышленности |
| VII - Plastics and articles thereof; rubber and articles thereof | .. | .. | .. | .. | 2,263.3 | 4,380.5 | VII - Пластмассы и изделия из них |
| VIII - Raw hides and skins, leather, furskins and articles thereof; saddlery and harness; travel goods, handbags and similar containers; articles of animal gut | .. | .. | .. | .. | 229.2 | 567.7 | VIII - Кожевенное сырьё, кожи, пушнина, меховое сырьё и изделия из них |
| IX - Wood and articles of wood; wood charcoal; cork and articles of cork; manufactures of straw, of esparto or of other plaiting materials; basketware and wickerwork | .. | .. | .. | .. | 0.0 | 81.1 | IX - Древесина и изделия из древесины, древесный уголь |
| X - Pulp of wood or of other fibrous cellulosic material; waste and scrap of paper or paperboard; paper and paperboard and articles thereof | .. | .. | .. | .. | 114.6 | 324.5 | X - Бумажная масса, бумажные и картонные отходы, макулатура, бумага, картон и изделия из них |
| XI - Textiles and textile articles | .. | .. | .. | .. | 4,526.7 | 6,165.1 | XI - Текстиль и текстильные изделия |
| XII - Footwear, headgear, umbrellas, sun umbrellas, walking sticks, seat sticks, whips, riding crops and parts thereof; prepared feathers and articles made therewith; artificial flowers; articles of human hair | .. | .. | .. | .. | 4,555.4 | 2,190.1 | XII - Обувь, головные уборы, зонты, трости и пр. |

## TABLE 3-3B. Exports by Commodity Group (millions of national currency)
## ТАБЛИЦА 3-3B. Экспорт по товарным группам (млн. национальной валюты)

| Commodity group | 1990 | 1991 | 1992 | 1993 | 1994 | 1995 | Товарные группы |
|---|---|---|---|---|---|---|---|
| XIII - Articles of stone, plaster, cement, asbestos, mica and similar materials; ceramic products; glass and glassware | .. | .. | .. | .. | 3,638.5 | 851.8 | XIII - Изделия из камня, гипса, цемента |
| XIV - Natural or cultured pearls, precious or | .. | .. | .. | .. | 21,544.8 | 36,341.8 | XIV - Жемчуг, драгоценные и |
| semi-precious stones, precious metals, metals clad with precious metal and articles thereof; imitation jewellery; coin | | | | | 2,693.1 | 12,370.8 | полудрагоценные камни, драгоценные металлы, бижутерия, монеты |
| XV - Base metals and articles of base metal | .. | .. | .. | .. | 8,852.8 | 15,859.0 | XV - Неблагородные металлы и изделия из них |
| XVI - Machinery and mechanical appliances; electrical equipment; parts thereof; sound recorders and reproducers, television image and sound recorders and reproducers, and parts and accessories of such articles | .. | .. | .. | .. | .. | .. | XVI - Машины, оборудование, механизмы, их части и принадлежности; звуковая и теле-аппаратура, их части и принадлежности |
| XVII - Vehicles, aircraft, vessels and associated transport equipment | .. | .. | .. | .. | 487.2 | 4,623.8 | XVII - Средства наземного, воздушного и водного транспорта |
| XVIII - Optical, photographic, cinematographic, measuring, checking, precision, medical or surgical instruments and apparatus; clocks and watches; musical instruments; parts and accessories thereof | .. | .. | .. | .. | 1,146.0 | 1,541.3 | XVIII - Приборы, аппараты оптические, медицинские, измерительные и пр.; музыкальные инструменты; часы; их части и принадлежности |
| XIX - Arms and ammunition; parts and accessories thereof | .. | .. | .. | .. | .. | .. | XIX - Оружие и боеприпасы, их части и принадлежности |
| XX - Miscellaneous manufactured articles | .. | .. | .. | .. | 1,575.8 | 1,379.0 | XX - Разные промышленные товары |
| XXI - Works of art, collectors' pieces, and antiques | .. | .. | .. | .. | 0.0 | 121.7 | XXI - Произведения искусства, предметы антиквариата |
| XXII - Services | .. | .. | .. | .. | .. | .. | XXII - Услуги |

**TABLE 3-4A. Geographical distribution of foreign trade (millions of U.S. dollars)**
**ТАБЛИЦА 3-4A. Географическое распределение внешней торговли (млн. долларов США)**

| Country or country group | Exports Экспорт 1990 | 1991 | 1992 | 1993 | 1994 | 1995 | Imports Импорт 1990 | 1991 | 1992 | 1993 | 1994 | 1995 | Страна или группа стран |
|---|---|---|---|---|---|---|---|---|---|---|---|---|---|
| **Total trade** | .. | .. | .. | 156.1 | 215.5 | 270.9 | .. | .. | .. | 254.1 | 393.8 | 673.9 | **Всего** |
| **CIS countries** | .. | .. | .. | 126.5 | 157.9 | 167.2 | .. | .. | .. | 168.1 | 205.5 | 334.0 | **Страны СНГ** |
| Armenia | .. | .. | .. | .. | .. | .. | .. | .. | .. | .. | .. | .. | Армения |
| Azerbaijan | .. | .. | .. | .. | .. | .. | .. | .. | .. | .. | .. | .. | Азербайджан |
| Belarus | .. | .. | .. | 1.9 | 0.7 | 0.9 | .. | .. | .. | 1.2 | 0.4 | 1.9 | Беларусь |
| Georgia | .. | .. | .. | 3.2 | 2.9 | 2.7 | .. | .. | .. | 19.5 | 17.8 | 61.9 | Грузия |
| Kazakstan | .. | .. | .. | 1.4 | 0.9 | 0.1 | .. | .. | .. | 1.2 | 0.1 | 0.1 | Казахстан |
| Kyrgyz Republic | .. | .. | .. | 0.0 | .. | 0.0 | .. | .. | .. | 0.0 | .. | 0.0 | Киргизстан |
| Moldova | .. | .. | .. | 0.1 | 0.0 | 0.0 | .. | .. | .. | 0.1 | 0.1 | 0.1 | Молдова |
| Russia | .. | .. | .. | 58.5 | 83.9 | 88.5 | .. | .. | .. | 77.9 | 112.2 | 135.1 | Россия |
| Tajikistan | .. | .. | .. | 0.1 | 0.0 | 0.1 | .. | .. | .. | 0.2 | 0.0 | 0.0 | Таджикистан |
| Turkmenistan | .. | .. | .. | 57.0 | 65.7 | 68.6 | .. | .. | .. | 64.1 | .. | .. | Туркменистан |
| Ukraine | .. | .. | .. | 0.3 | 0.1 | 0.3 | .. | .. | .. | 0.1 | 0.1 | 0.1 | Украина |
| Uzbekistan | .. | .. | .. | .. | .. | .. | .. | .. | .. | .. | .. | .. | Узбекистан |
| **Non-CIS countries** | .. | .. | .. | 29.7 | 57.7 | 103.7 | .. | .. | .. | 85.9 | 188.3 | 339.9 | **Остальной мир** |
| **Europe** | .. | .. | .. | 18.9 | 38.8 | 53.7 | .. | .. | .. | 39.1 | 42.6 | 111.3 | **Европа** |
| Austria | .. | .. | .. | .. | .. | .. | .. | .. | .. | .. | .. | 2.1 | Австрия |
| Belgium | .. | .. | .. | 14.9 | 25.9 | 30.8 | .. | .. | .. | 2.9 | 1.4 | 15.6 | Бельгия |
| Bulgaria | .. | .. | .. | 1.0 | 0.0 | 0.1 | .. | .. | .. | 0.2 | 0.9 | 4.6 | Болгария |
| Czech Republic | .. | .. | .. | 0.0 | 0.1 | 0.2 | .. | .. | .. | 1.0 | 0.1 | 6.3 | Чешская Республика |
| Denmark | .. | .. | .. | .. | .. | .. | .. | .. | .. | .. | .. | 4.9 | Дания |
| Estonia | .. | .. | .. | 0.1 | 0.0 | 0.0 | .. | .. | .. | 0.4 | 0.3 | 0.1 | Эстония |
| Finland | .. | .. | .. | 0.0 | .. | 0.0 | .. | .. | .. | .. | 0.4 | 0.7 | Финляндия |
| Former Yugoslavia | .. | .. | .. | .. | .. | .. | .. | .. | .. | 0.1 | 0.2 | 0.2 | Быв. Югославия |
| France | .. | .. | .. | 1.3 | 0.4 | 0.2 | .. | .. | .. | 0.9 | 10.7 | 16.3 | Франция |
| Germany | .. | .. | .. | 0.3 | 6.6 | 10.1 | .. | .. | .. | 0.3 | 6.9 | 11.3 | Германия |
| Hungary | .. | .. | .. | .. | .. | .. | .. | .. | .. | .. | .. | 0.2 | Венгрия |
| Iceland | .. | .. | .. | .. | .. | .. | .. | .. | .. | .. | .. | .. | Исландия |
| Ireland | .. | .. | .. | .. | 1.2 | 0.5 | .. | .. | .. | .. | .. | 1.7 | Ирландия |
| Italy | .. | .. | .. | .. | .. | 0.1 | .. | .. | .. | 31.1 | 8.9 | 22.4 | Италия |
| Latvia | .. | .. | .. | 0.1 | 0.1 | .. | .. | .. | .. | 0.2 | 0.5 | 0.0 | Латвия |
| Lithuania | .. | .. | .. | 0.1 | 0.2 | 0.1 | .. | .. | .. | 0.3 | 0.7 | 2.0 | Литва |
| Netherlands | .. | .. | .. | 0.1 | 0.7 | 5.3 | .. | .. | .. | 0.3 | 8.3 | 6.0 | Нидерланды |
| Norway | .. | .. | .. | .. | .. | .. | .. | .. | .. | .. | .. | 1.1 | Норвегия |
| Poland | .. | .. | .. | 0.3 | 0.4 | 0.0 | .. | .. | .. | 0.8 | 0.2 | 0.4 | Польша |
| Romania | .. | .. | .. | .. | .. | .. | .. | .. | .. | .. | .. | 1.4 | Румыния |
| Slovak Republic | .. | .. | .. | .. | .. | .. | .. | .. | .. | .. | .. | .. | Словацкая Республика |
| Spain | .. | .. | .. | .. | .. | .. | .. | .. | .. | 0.1 | .. | .. | Испания |

TABLE 3-4A. Geographical distribution of foreign trade (millions of U.S. dollars)
ТАБЛИЦА 3-4А. Географическое распределение внешней торговли (млн. долларов США)

| Country or country group | Exports Экспорт 1990 | 1991 | 1992 | 1993 | 1994 | 1995 | Imports Импорт 1990 | 1991 | 1992 | 1993 | 1994 | 1995 | Страна или группа стран |
|---|---|---|---|---|---|---|---|---|---|---|---|---|---|
| Sweden | .. | .. | .. | .. | .. | .. | .. | .. | .. | .. | .. | .. | Швеция |
| Switzerland | .. | .. | .. | 0.4 | 2.5 | 3.1 | .. | .. | .. | 0.3 | 2.4 | 6.3 | Швейцария |
| United Kingdom | .. | .. | .. | .. | 0.5 | 1.3 | .. | .. | .. | 0.2 | 0.5 | 2.1 | Великобритания |
| Other Europe | .. | .. | .. | 0.3 | 0.1 | 1.9 | .. | .. | .. | .. | 0.0 | 5.6 | Остальные страны Европы |
| **Asia** | .. | .. | .. | 7.1 | 15.1 | 38.9 | .. | .. | .. | 19.6 | 48.9 | 110.2 | **Азия** |
| Afghanistan | .. | .. | .. | .. | .. | .. | .. | .. | .. | .. | .. | .. | Афганистан |
| China | .. | .. | .. | .. | .. | 0.0 | .. | .. | .. | .. | 1.6 | 0.4 | Китай |
| India | .. | .. | .. | .. | .. | 0.1 | .. | .. | .. | 0.1 | 1.8 | 0.2 | Индия |
| Iraq | .. | .. | .. | .. | .. | .. | .. | .. | .. | .. | .. | .. | Ирак |
| Japan | .. | .. | .. | .. | .. | .. | .. | .. | .. | .. | .. | .. | Япония |
| Korea, Dem. People's Rep. | .. | .. | .. | .. | .. | .. | .. | .. | .. | .. | .. | .. | КНДР |
| Korea, Rep. of | .. | .. | .. | .. | .. | .. | .. | .. | .. | .. | 1.4 | 0.2 | Южная Корея |
| Mongolia | .. | .. | .. | .. | .. | .. | .. | .. | .. | .. | .. | .. | МНР |
| Syrian Arab Republic | .. | .. | .. | 0.9 | 0.2 | 0.3 | .. | .. | .. | 0.1 | 0.0 | 0.6 | Сирия |
| Turkey | .. | .. | .. | 0.3 | 0.2 | 2.6 | .. | .. | .. | .. | 0.5 | 2.6 | Турция |
| Viet Nam | .. | .. | .. | .. | .. | .. | .. | .. | .. | .. | .. | .. | Вьетнам |
| Other Asia | .. | .. | .. | 5.9 | 14.7 | 35.9 | .. | .. | .. | 19.4 | 43.4 | 106.2 | Остальные страны Азии |
| **America** | .. | .. | .. | 3.5 | 3.6 | 0.6 | .. | .. | .. | 27.1 | 96.6 | 115.5 | **Сев. и Южная Америка** |
| Canada | .. | .. | .. | .. | .. | .. | .. | .. | .. | .. | 0.2 | 0.2 | Канада |
| Cuba | .. | .. | .. | .. | .. | .. | .. | .. | .. | .. | .. | .. | Куба |
| United States | .. | .. | .. | 0.2 | 0.4 | 0.6 | .. | .. | .. | 26.9 | 96.1 | 114.4 | США |
| Other America | .. | .. | .. | 3.3 | 3.2 | .. | .. | .. | .. | 0.2 | 0.2 | 0.9 | Остальные |
| **Africa** | .. | .. | .. | 0.2 | 0.2 | 10.5 | .. | .. | .. | 0.0 | 0.1 | 3.0 | **Африка** |
| Egypt | .. | .. | .. | .. | .. | 0.3 | .. | .. | .. | .. | .. | 0.0 | Египет |
| Libya | .. | .. | .. | 0.2 | 0.1 | .. | .. | .. | .. | .. | 0.1 | .. | Ливия |
| Other Africa | .. | .. | .. | .. | 0.1 | 10.2 | .. | .. | .. | .. | .. | 3.0 | Остальные |
| **Rest of the World** | .. | .. | .. | .. | .. | .. | .. | .. | .. | .. | .. | .. | **Прочие страны мира** |
| Australia | .. | .. | .. | .. | .. | .. | .. | .. | .. | .. | .. | .. | Австралия |

**TABLE 3-4B. Geographical distribution of foreign trade (millions of local currency)**

**ТАБЛИЦА 3-4B. Географическое распределение внешней торговли (миллионов национальной валюты)**

| Country or country group | Exports Экспорт | | | | | | Imports Импорт | | | | | | Страна или группа стран |
|---|---|---|---|---|---|---|---|---|---|---|---|---|---|
| | 1990 | 1991 | 1992 | 1993 | 1994 | 1995 | 1990 | 1991 | 1992 | 1993 | 1994 | 1995 | |
| **Total trade** | .. | .. | .. | .. | 61,830.1 | 109,952.1 | .. | .. | .. | .. | 113,002.7 | 273,341.8 | **Всего** |
| **CIS countries** | .. | .. | .. | .. | 45,290.3 | 67,901.7 | .. | .. | .. | .. | 58,975.2 | 135,450.1 | **Страны СНГ** |
| Armenia | .. | .. | .. | .. | .. | .. | .. | .. | .. | .. | .. | .. | Армения |
| Azerbaijan | .. | .. | .. | .. | .. | .. | .. | .. | .. | .. | .. | .. | Азербайджан |
| Belarus | .. | .. | .. | .. | 200.8 | 365.0 | .. | .. | .. | .. | 114.8 | 770.6 | Беларусь |
| Georgia | .. | .. | .. | .. | 832.0 | 1,107.3 | .. | .. | .. | .. | 5,106.8 | 2,906.6 | Грузия |
| Kazakhstan | .. | .. | .. | .. | 258.2 | 649.0 | .. | .. | .. | .. | 23.0 | 36.5 | Казахстан |
| Kyrgyz Republic | .. | .. | .. | .. | .. | 2.8 | .. | .. | .. | .. | .. | 16.2 | Киргизстан |
| Moldova | .. | .. | .. | .. | 2.9 | 0.4 | .. | .. | .. | .. | 34.4 | 40.6 | Молдова |
| Russia | .. | .. | .. | .. | 24,070.9 | 35,895.6 | .. | .. | .. | .. | 32,178.7 | 54,796.6 | Россия |
| Tajikistan | .. | .. | .. | .. | 0.3 | 40.6 | .. | .. | .. | .. | .. | 12.2 | Таджикистан |
| Turkmenistan | .. | .. | .. | .. | 18,849.3 | 27,894.2 | .. | .. | .. | .. | 19,979.7 | 52,444.1 | Туркменистан |
| Ukraine | .. | .. | .. | .. | 1,061.5 | 1,825.2 | .. | .. | .. | .. | 1,520.6 | 2,190.2 | Украина |
| Uzbekistan | .. | .. | .. | .. | 14.3 | 121.7 | .. | .. | .. | .. | 17.2 | 36.5 | Узбекистан |
| **Non-CIS countries** | .. | .. | .. | .. | 16,539.8 | 42,050.4 | .. | .. | .. | .. | 53,527.6 | 137,891.8 | **Остальной мир** |
| **Europe** | .. | .. | .. | .. | 11,117.4 | 21,784.0 | .. | .. | .. | .. | 11,684.6 | 45,143.3 | **Европа** |
| Austria | .. | .. | .. | .. | .. | 1.6 | .. | .. | .. | .. | .. | 851.8 | Австрия |
| Belgium | .. | .. | .. | .. | 7,430.7 | 12,492.5 | .. | .. | .. | .. | 387.3 | 6,327.4 | Бельгия |
| Bulgaria | .. | .. | .. | .. | 5.7 | 36.5 | .. | .. | .. | .. | 258.2 | 1,865.8 | Болгария |
| Czech Republic | .. | .. | .. | .. | 28.7 | 81.1 | .. | .. | .. | .. | 28.7 | 2,555.3 | Чешская Республика |
| Denmark | .. | .. | .. | .. | | .. | .. | .. | .. | .. | .. | 1,987.4 | Дания |
| Estonia | .. | .. | .. | .. | 8.6 | 8.1 | .. | .. | .. | .. | 86.1 | 24.3 | Эстония |
| Finland | .. | .. | .. | .. | .. | 12.2 | .. | .. | .. | .. | 114.8 | 283.9 | Финляндия |
| Former Yugoslavia | .. | .. | .. | .. | .. | .. | .. | .. | .. | .. | 57.4 | 81.1 | Быв. Югославия |
| France | .. | .. | .. | .. | 114.8 | 81.1 | .. | .. | .. | .. | 3,069.8 | 6,611.3 | Франция |
| Germany | .. | .. | .. | .. | 1,893.5 | 4,090.5 | .. | .. | .. | .. | 1,979.6 | 4,583.3 | Германия |
| Hungary | .. | .. | .. | .. | .. | .. | .. | .. | .. | .. | .. | 81.1 | Венгрия |
| Iceland | .. | .. | .. | .. | .. | .. | .. | .. | .. | .. | .. | .. | Исландия |
| Ireland | .. | .. | .. | .. | 344.3 | 202.8 | .. | .. | .. | .. | .. | 689.5 | Ирландия |
| Italy | .. | .. | .. | .. | .. | 40.6 | .. | .. | .. | .. | 2,564.9 | 9,085.4 | Италия |
| Latvia | .. | .. | .. | .. | 28.7 | .. | .. | .. | .. | .. | 143.5 | 162.2 | Латвия |
| Lithuania | .. | .. | .. | .. | 57.4 | 28.4 | .. | .. | .. | .. | 200.8 | 811.2 | Литва |
| Netherlands | .. | .. | .. | .. | 200.8 | 2,149.7 | .. | .. | .. | .. | 2,381.3 | 2,433.6 | Нидерланды |
| Norway | .. | .. | .. | .. | .. | .. | .. | .. | .. | .. | .. | 446.2 | Норвегия |
| Poland | .. | .. | .. | .. | 114.8 | 3.7 | .. | .. | .. | .. | 57.4 | 162.2 | Польша |
| Romania | .. | .. | .. | .. | .. | .. | .. | .. | .. | .. | .. | 567.8 | Румыния |
| Slovak Republic | .. | .. | .. | .. | .. | .. | .. | .. | .. | .. | .. | .. | Словацкая Республика |
| Spain | .. | .. | .. | .. | .. | .. | .. | .. | .. | .. | .. | .. | Испания |

**TABLE 3-4B. Geographical distribution of foreign trade (millions of local currency)**

**ТАБЛИЦА 3-4B. Географическое распределение внешней торговли (миллионов национальной валюты)**

| Country or country group | Exports Экспорт 1990 | 1991 | 1992 | 1993 | 1994 | 1995 | Imports Импорт 1990 | 1991 | 1992 | 1993 | 1994 | 1995 | Страна или группа стран |
|---|---|---|---|---|---|---|---|---|---|---|---|---|---|
| Sweden | .. | .. | .. | .. | .. | .. | .. | .. | .. | .. | .. | .. | Швеция |
| Switzerland | .. | .. | .. | .. | 717.3 | 1,257.4 | .. | .. | .. | .. | 200.0 | 2,555.3 | Швейцария |
| United Kingdom | .. | .. | .. | .. | 143.5 | 527.3 | .. | .. | .. | .. | 143.5 | 851.8 | Великобритания |
| Other Europe | .. | .. | .. | .. | 28.7 | 770.6 | .. | .. | .. | .. | 11.5 | 2,271.4 | Остальные страны Европы |
| **Asia** | .. | .. | .. | .. | 4,332.2 | 15,764.2 | .. | .. | .. | .. | 14,128.4 | 44,676.8 | **Азиа** |
| Afghanistan | .. | .. | .. | .. | .. | .. | .. | .. | .. | .. | .. | .. | Афганистан |
| China | .. | .. | .. | .. | .. | 1.6 | .. | .. | .. | .. | 464.8 | 162.2 | Китай |
| India | .. | .. | .. | .. | .. | 25.3 | .. | .. | .. | .. | 516.4 | 81.1 | Индия |
| Iraq | .. | .. | .. | .. | .. | .. | .. | .. | .. | .. | .. | .. | Ирак |
| Japan | .. | .. | .. | .. | .. | .. | .. | .. | .. | .. | .. | .. | Япония |
| Korea, Dem. People's Rep. | .. | .. | .. | .. | .. | .. | .. | .. | .. | .. | .. | .. | КНДР |
| Korea, Rep. of | .. | .. | .. | .. | .. | .. | .. | .. | .. | .. | 401.7 | 81.1 | Южная Корея |
| Mongolia | .. | .. | .. | .. | .. | .. | .. | .. | .. | .. | .. | .. | МНР |
| Syrian Arab Republic | .. | .. | .. | .. | 57.4 | 121.7 | .. | .. | .. | .. | 10.0 | 243.4 | Сирия |
| Turkey | .. | .. | .. | .. | 57.4 | 1,054.6 | .. | .. | .. | .. | 154.9 | 1,054.6 | Турция |
| Viet Nam | .. | .. | .. | .. | .. | .. | .. | .. | .. | .. | .. | .. | Вьетнам |
| Other Asia | .. | .. | .. | .. | 4,217.4 | 14,561.0 | .. | .. | .. | .. | 12,580.6 | 43,054.4 | Остальные |
| **America** | .. | .. | .. | .. | 1,032.8 | 243.4 | .. | .. | .. | .. | 27,685.9 | 46,846.8 | **Америка** |
| Canada | .. | .. | .. | .. | .. | .. | .. | .. | .. | .. | 57.4 | 81.1 | Канада |
| Cuba | .. | .. | .. | .. | .. | .. | .. | .. | .. | .. | .. | .. | Куба |
| United States | .. | .. | .. | .. | 114.8 | 243.4 | .. | .. | .. | .. | 27,571.1 | 46,400.6 | США |
| Other America | .. | .. | .. | .. | 918.1 | .. | .. | .. | .. | .. | 57.4 | 365.0 | Остальные |
| **Africa** | .. | .. | .. | .. | 57.4 | 4,258.9 | .. | .. | .. | .. | 2,869.0 | 1,224.9 | **Африка** |
| Egypt | .. | .. | .. | .. | .. | 121.7 | .. | .. | .. | .. | .. | 8.1 | Египет |
| Libya | .. | .. | .. | .. | 28.7 | .. | .. | .. | .. | .. | 2,869.0 | .. | Ливия |
| Other Africa | .. | .. | .. | .. | 28.7 | 4,137.2 | .. | .. | .. | .. | .. | 1,216.8 | Остальные |
| **Rest of the World** | .. | .. | .. | .. | .. | .. | .. | .. | .. | .. | .. | .. | **Прочие страны** |
| Australia | .. | .. | .. | .. | .. | .. | .. | .. | .. | .. | .. | .. | Австралия |

## TABLE 4-1. General government budget revenue (millions of national currency)
## ТАБЛИЦА 4-1. Доходы государственного бюджета (млн. национальной валюты)

| Type of revenue | 1990 | 1991 | 1992 | 1993 | 1994 | 1995 | Вид доходов |
|---|---|---|---|---|---|---|---|
| **Total revenue and grants** | 4,143 | 4,628 | 12,699 | 197,953 | 29,496 | .. | **Всего доходов и безвозм. поступл.** |
| Grants | 718 | 1,303 | 0 | 0 | 0 | .. | Безвозмездные поступления |
| Total Revenue | 3,425 | 3,325 | 12,699 | 197,953 | 29,496 | .. | Всего доходов |
| **Current revenue** | 3,425 | 3,326 | 12,699 | 197,953 | 29,496 | .. | **Текущие доходы** |
| Tax revenue | 3,021 | 3,209 | 12,499 | 111,329 | 20,268 | .. | Доход от налогов |
| Taxes on income and profits | 523 | 693 | 5,542 | 49,084 | 13,025 | .. | Налоги на доходы и прибыль |
| Individual | 106 | 172 | 1,423 | 12,567 | 2,290 | .. | Физические лица |
| Corporate | 417 | 521 | 4,119 | 36,517 | 10,735 | .. | Предприятия и организации |
| Social security contributions | 317 | .. | .. | .. | .. | .. | Отчисление на соцстрах. |
| Taxes on payroll or work force | 126 | .. | 31 | .. | .. | .. | Налоги на заработную плату и рабочую силу |
| Taxes on the use of labor force | .. | .. | .. | .. | .. | .. | Плата за трудовые ресурсы |
| Taxes on increases in wages and salaries | .. | .. | .. | .. | .. | .. | Налог с прироста средств на оплату труда |
| Other payroll/work force taxes | .. | .. | .. | .. | .. | .. | Другие налоги на зарплату и рабочую силу |
| Taxes on property | 1 | 2 | 30 | 314 | 527 | .. | Налоги на собственность |
| Taxes on immovable property | 1 | 2 | 13 | 272 | 523 | .. | Налоги на недвижимое имущество |
| Buildings | 1 | 2 | 4 | 28 | 10 | .. | Налог с владельцев строении |
| Land | .. | .. | 9 | 244 | 513 | .. | Земельныи налог |
| Estate, inheritance, and gift taxes | .. | .. | .. | .. | | .. | Налоги на наследство, подарки |
| Other property taxes | .. | .. | 17 | 42 | 4 | .. | Другие налоги на имущество |
| Domestic taxes on goods and services | 1,640 | 1,121 | 5,028 | 48,382 | 5,768 | .. | Внутренние налоги на товары и услуги |
| General sales, turnover, or value-added taxes | 1,464 | 1,083 | 4,131 | 39,209 | 4,923 | .. | Налог с продаж. с оборота или на добав. стоим. |
| Excises | .. | .. | 892 | 9,173 | 845 | .. | Акцизы |
| Profits of fiscal monopolies | .. | .. | .. | .. | .. | .. | Прибыли фискальных монополий |
| Taxes on specific services | 81 | 5 | 5 | .. | .. | .. | Налоги на особые услуги |
| Taxes on use of goods or permission to use goods or to perform activities | 95 | 33 | .. | .. | .. | .. | Налоги на пользование товарами или лицензии на пользование товарами и занятие деятельностью |
| Other taxes on goods and services | .. | .. | .. | .. | .. | .. | Другие налоги на товары и услуги |
| Taxes on international trade and transactions | 31 | 37 | .. | .. | .. | .. | Налоги на внешнюю торговлю и операции |
| Import duties | .. | .. | .. | .. | .. | .. | Импортные пошлины |
| Export duties | .. | .. | .. | .. | .. | .. | Экпортные пошлины |
| Other | 31 | 38 | .. | .. | .. | .. | Другие |
| Other taxes | 383 | 1,357 | 1,868 | 13,549 | 948 | .. | Прочие налоги |
| Nontax revenue | 404 | 116 | 200 | 86,624 | 9,228 | .. | Неналоговые доходы |
| **Capital revenue** | .. | .. | .. | .. | .. | .. | **Капитальные доходы** |

**TABLE 4-2. General government budget expenditure by economic type (millions of national currency)**
**ТАБЛИЦА 4-2. Расходы государственного бюджета по экономическим типам (млн. национальной валюты)**

| Type of expenditure or debt holder | 1990 | 1991 | 1992 | 1993 | 1994 | 1995 | Всего расходов |
|---|---|---|---|---|---|---|---|
| **Total expenditure by economic type** | 3,578 | 4,371 | 22,656 | 298,017 | 40,832 | .. | **Всего расходов по экономическим типам** |
| **Current expenditure** | 2,252 | 3,281 | 17,983 | 239,093 | 36,024 | .. | **Текущие расходы** |
| Expenditure on goods and services | 996 | 611 | 6,199 | 60,278 | 5,767 | .. | Расходы на товары и услуги |
| Wages and salaries | 522 | 387 | 4,284 | 40,386 | 3,247 | .. | Заработная плата |
| Employer contributions | 336 | .. | 90 | .. | 2,520 | .. | Отчисление на социальное страхование |
| Other Purchases of goods and services | 139 | 224 | 1,825 | 19,892 | .. | .. | Другие покупки товаров и услуг |
| Interest payments | 0 | 0 | 0 | .. | .. | .. | Выплаты процентов |
| Domestic debt | 0 | 0 | 0 | .. | .. | .. | По внутреннему долгу |
| Foreign debt | .. | .. | .. | .. | .. | .. | По внешнему долгу |
| Subsidies and other current transfers | 753 | 1,233 | 1,427 | 10,297 | 948 | .. | Субсидии на другие текущие трансферты |
| Subsidies | 632 | 339 | 1,009 | 8,087 | 760 | .. | Субсидии |
| Agricultural subsidies | 140 | 0 | 0 | .. | .. | .. | Субсидии на сельское хозяйство |
| Other current transfers | 121 | 894 | 418 | 2,210 | 188 | .. | Другие текущие трансферты |
| Other | 503 | 1,437 | 10,357 | 168,518 | 29,309 | .. | Прочие расходы |
| **Capital expenditure** | 1,327 | 1,090 | 4,673 | 58,924 | 4,808 | .. | **Капитальные расходы** |
| Acquisition of fixed capital assets | 217 | 261 | 1,785 | 9,786 | 638 | .. | Приобретение основного капитала |
| Capital transfers | 1,103 | 826 | 2,888 | 49,138 | 4,170 | .. | Капитальные трансферты |
| Other | 6 | 3 | 0 | .. | .. | .. | Другие капитальные расходы |
| **Surplus/deficit (-)** | 565 | 257 | -9,957 | -100,064 | -11,336 | .. | **Превыш. доходов над расходами/дефицит(-)** |
| **Financing by type of debt holder** | .. | .. | .. | .. | .. | .. | **Финансирование по типам кредиторов** |
| **Foreign (net)** | .. | .. | .. | -38,667 | -3,536 | .. | **Зарубежные кредиторы (сальдо)** |
| From international development institutions | .. | .. | .. | .. | .. | .. | Международные организации |
| From foreign governments | .. | .. | .. | -38,667 | -3,536 | .. | Правительства иностранных государств |
| Other borrowing abroad | .. | .. | .. | .. | .. | .. | Другие зарубежные кредиторы |
| **Domestic (net)** | .. | .. | -20,882 | -61,397 | -7,800 | .. | **Внутренние кредиторы (сальдо)** |
| From monetary authorities | .. | .. | -20,882 | -37,300 | -7,800 | .. | Органы денежного обращения |
| From deposit money banks | .. | .. | .. | -12,000 | .. | .. | Депозитные денежные банки |
| Other domestic borrowing | .. | .. | .. | -12,097 | .. | .. | Другие внутренние кредиторы |
| *Memo items:* | | | | | | | *Справочно:* |
| Extrabudgetary surplus/ Deficit (-) not included above | .. | .. | -10,925 | .. | .. | .. | Превышение доходов над расходами/дефицит (-) по внебюджетным фондам, не включенным выше |
| Total surplus/deficit (-) including extrabudgetary accounts | 565 | 257 | -20,882 | -100,064 | -11,336 | .. | Итого превышение доходов над расходами/дефицит, включая счета внебюджетных фондов |

**TABLE 5-1. Agricultural production (millions of national currency, current prices)** **ARMENIA**

**ТАБЛИЦА 5-1. Сельскохозяйственная продукция (млн. нац. валюты, текущие цены)**

| Item | 1990 | 1991 | 1992 | 1993 | 1994 | 1995 | Статьи |
|---|---|---|---|---|---|---|---|
| **Total gross agricultural production** | 1,792 | 5,887 | 42,791 | 8,404,164 | 141,100 | 332,900 | **Валовая продукция сельского хозяйства - всего** |
| **Crops** | 980 | 3,416 | 24,000 | 4,706,171 | 84,600 | 227,900 | **Продукция растениеводства** |
| Grains | .. | .. | .. | .. | .. | .. | Зерно |
| Potatoes | .. | .. | .. | .. | .. | .. | Картофель |
| Vegetables | .. | .. | .. | .. | .. | .. | Овощи |
| Fruits (excluding grapes) | .. | .. | .. | .. | .. | .. | Фрукты (без винограда) |
| Grapes | .. | .. | .. | .. | .. | .. | Виноград |
| Tobacco | .. | .. | .. | .. | .. | .. | Табак |
| Cotton | .. | .. | .. | .. | .. | .. | Хлопок |
| Sugarbeets | .. | .. | .. | .. | .. | .. | Сахарная свекла |
| Oilseeds | .. | .. | .. | .. | .. | .. | Семена масличных культур |
| Other | .. | .. | .. | .. | .. | .. | Прочие |
| **Animal husbandry** | 812 | 2,471 | 18,791 | 3,697,993 | 56,500 | 105,000 | **Продукция животноводства** |
| Livestock | .. | .. | .. | .. | .. | .. | Мясное животноводство |
| Cattle | .. | .. | .. | .. | .. | .. | Крупный рогатый скот |
| Pigs | .. | .. | .. | .. | .. | .. | Свиньи |
| Sheep and goats | .. | .. | .. | .. | .. | .. | Овцы и козы |
| Poultry | .. | .. | .. | .. | .. | .. | Птица |
| Other | .. | .. | .. | .. | .. | .. | Прочие |
| Milk | .. | .. | .. | .. | .. | .. | Молоко |
| Eggs | .. | .. | .. | .. | .. | .. | Яйца |
| Wool | .. | .. | .. | .. | .. | .. | Шерсть |
| Other livestock | .. | .. | .. | .. | .. | .. | Прочая |
| **Agricultural services** | .. | .. | .. | .. | .. | .. | **Сельскохозяйственные услуги** |

**TABLE 5-2. Agricultural production (millions of constant national currency)**

**ТАБЛИЦА 5-2. Сельскохозяйственная продукция в постоянных ценах (млн. национальной валюты)**

| Item | 1990 | 1991 | 1992 | 1993 | 1994 | 1995 | Статьи |
|---|---|---|---|---|---|---|---|
| **Total gross agricultural production** | 988 | 1,101 | 11,238 | 10,687 | 11,029 | 11,547 | **Валовая продукция сельского хозяйства - всего** |
| **Crops** | 446 | 591 | 680 | 672 | 688 | 722 | **Продукция растениеводства** |
| Grains | 31 | 35 | 38 | 38 | 28 | 32 | Зерно |
| Potatoes | 41 | 60 | 62 | 78 | 80 | 82 | Картофель |
| Vegetables | 131 | 216 | 153 | 185 | 136 | 142 | Овощи |
| Fruits (excluding grapes) | 101 | 85 | 90 | 36 | 90 | 103 | Фрукты (без винограда) |
| Grapes | 56 | 92 | 65 | 62 | 98 | 71 | Виноград |
| Tobacco | 1 | 1 | 1 | 1 | 0 | 0 | Табак |
| Cotton | .. | .. | .. | .. | .. | .. | Хлопок |
| Sugarbeets | .. | .. | .. | .. | .. | .. | Сахарная свекла |
| Oilseeds | .. | .. | .. | .. | .. | .. | Семена масличных культур |
| Other | 80 | 103 | 271 | 272 | 256 | 292 | Прочие |
| **Animal husbandry** | 542 | 510 | 444 | 397 | 415 | 433 | **Продукция животноводства** |
| Livestock | 196 | 265 | 231 | 153 | 171 | 178 | Мясное животноводство |
| Cattle | .. | .. | .. | .. | .. | .. | Крупный рогатый скот |
| Pigs | .. | .. | .. | .. | .. | .. | Свиньи |
| Sheep and goats | .. | .. | .. | .. | .. | .. | Овцы и козы |
| Poultry | .. | .. | .. | .. | .. | .. | Птица |
| Other | .. | .. | .. | .. | .. | .. | Прочие |
| Milk | 169 | 160 | 148 | 151 | 165 | 170 | Молоко |
| Eggs | 50 | 48 | 23 | 18 | 18 | 19 | Яйца |
| Wool | 24 | 20 | 17 | 15 | 15 | 13 | Шерсть |
| Other livestock | 103 | 17 | 24 | 59 | 48 | 54 | Прочая |
| **Agricultural services** | .. | .. | .. | .. | .. | .. | **Сельскохозяйственные услуги** |

**TABLE 5-3. Production and average yield of major agricultural crops**

**ТАБЛИЦА 5-3. Производство и урожайность важнейших сельскохозяйственных культур**

| Crop | 1990 | 1991 | 1992 | 1993 | 1994 | 1995 | Сельскохозяйственные культуры |
|---|---|---|---|---|---|---|---|
| **Production (thousands of tons)** | | | | | | | **Производство (тыс. тонн)** |
| Grain - Cleanweight | 254 | 299 | 292 | 304 | 229 | 255 | Зерно в чистом весе |
| Winter wheat | 155 | 169 | 131 | 201 | 136 | 186 | Пшеница - озимая |
| Spring wheat | 1 | 2 | 3 | 8 | 11 | 14 | яровая |
| Coarse grain | 271 | 304 | 310 | 316 | 238 | 263 | Зерно в физическом весе |
| Rye | 1 | 1 | 1 | 0 | 0 | 1 | Рожь |
| Corn | 0 | 1 | 4 | 4 | 5 | 4 | Кукуруза |
| Winter barley | 18 | 14 | 9 | 5 | 3 | 4 | Ячмень - озимый |
| Spring barley | 77 | 102 | 142 | 79 | 63 | 82 | яровой |
| Oats | 2 | 3 | 2 | 1 | 1 | .. | Овес |
| Millet | .. | .. | .. | .. | .. | .. | Просо |
| Rice | .. | .. | .. | .. | .. | .. | Рис |
| Flax | .. | .. | .. | .. | .. | .. | Лен |
| Oilseeds | .. | .. | .. | .. | .. | .. | Семена масличных культур |
| Cotton (raw) | .. | .. | .. | .. | .. | .. | Хлопок - сырец |
| Cotton fiber | .. | .. | .. | .. | .. | .. | волокно |
| Sugarbeets | .. | .. | .. | .. | .. | .. | Сахарная свекла |
| Potatoes | 213 | 275 | 322 | 414 | 417 | 428 | Картофель |
| Pulses | 3 | 2 | 3 | 4 | 5 | 5 | Бобовые |
| Vegetables | 390 | 444 | 497 | 417 | 424 | 451 | Овощи |
| Fruit | 300 | 359 | 275 | 184 | 340 | 300 | Фрукты |
| Grapes | 144 | 191 | 142 | 135 | 212 | 154 | Виноград |
| Other | 156 | 168 | 133 | 49 | 128 | 146 | Прочие |
| Corn (silage and greenchop) | 285 | 199 | 94 | 21 | 8 | 17 | Кукуруза (на силос и зеленый корм) |
| Hay | 694 | 657 | 720 | 692 | 722 | 847 | Сено |
| **Average yield (kilograms per hectare)** | | | | | | | **Ср. урожайность (кг с га)** |
| Grain | 1,840 | 1,960 | 1,620 | 1,480 | 1,300 | 1,460 | Зерно |
| Winter wheat | 2,130 | 2,160 | 1,790 | 1,930 | 1,660 | 1,780 | Пшеница - озимая |
| Spring wheat | 860 | 1,330 | 1,140 | 790 | 730 | 1,000 | яровая |
| Coarse grain | 1,960 | 1,990 | 1,710 | 1,530 | 1,350 | 1,500 | Зерно в физическом весе |
| Rye | 1,350 | 1,490 | 940 | 390 | 500 | 830 | Рожь |
| Corn | 1,670 | 2,520 | 3,230 | 3,380 | 3,190 | 1,810 | Кукуруза |
| Winter barley | 2,600 | 2,110 | 1,750 | 17,200 | 1,610 | 1,700 | Ячмень - озимый |
| Spring barley | 1,550 | 1,780 | 1,620 | 1,010 | 970 | 1,220 | яровой |
| Oats | 870 | 1,380 | 1,190 | 740 | 710 | 990 | Овес |
| Millet | .. | .. | .. | .. | .. | .. | Просо |
| Rice | .. | .. | .. | .. | .. | .. | Рис |
| Flax | .. | .. | .. | .. | .. | .. | Лен |
| Oilseeds | .. | .. | .. | .. | .. | .. | Семена масличных культур |
| Cotton (raw) | .. | .. | .. | .. | .. | .. | Хлопок - сырец |
| Cotton fiber | .. | .. | .. | .. | .. | .. | волокно |
| Sugarbeets | .. | .. | .. | .. | .. | .. | Сахарная свекла |
| Potatoes | 9,480 | 12,000 | 11,100 | 13,400 | 13,130 | 13,120 | Картофель |
| Pulses | 2,250 | 1,740 | 1,490 | 1,790 | 2,270 | 2,210 | Бобовые |
| Vegetables | 21,100 | 19,100 | 19,300 | 21,370 | 20,580 | 20,820 | Овощи |
| Fruit | .. | .. | .. | .. | .. | .. | Фрукты |
| Grapes | 5,780 | 7,680 | 5,960 | 5,440 | 8,360 | 6,780 | Виноград |
| Other | 4,260 | 4,680 | 4,610 | 1,680 | 3,690 | 4,330 | Прочие |
| Corn (silage and greenchop) | 13,400 | 13,000 | 16,200 | 13,160 | 11,070 | 24,930 | Кукуруза (на силос и зеленый корм) |
| Hay | 2,770 | 3,360 | 3,790 | 3,920 | 3,780 | 4,600 | Сено |

## TABLE 5-4. Main aggregates of animal husbandry
## ТАБЛИЦА 5-4. Основные показатели животноводства

| Type of livestock or product | 1990 | 1991 | 1992 | 1993 | 1994 | 1995 | Направление животноводства или вид продукции |
|---|---|---|---|---|---|---|---|
| **Livestock (thousands of heads)** | | | | | | | **Поголовье скота (тысяч голов)** |
| Cattle | 640 | 567 | 499 | 502 | 504 | 508 | Крупный рогатый скот |
| of which: Cows | 251 | 251 | 258 | 270 | 276 | 277 | в том числе коровы |
| Pigs | 311 | 224 | 84 | 82 | 82 | 80 | Свиньи |
| Sheep and goats | 1,186 | 1,023 | 873 | 736 | 636 | 604 | Овцы и козы |
| of which: Goats | 14 | 17 | 19 | 26 | 31 | 33 | в том числе козы |
| Horses | 7 | 7 | 9 | 11 | 12 | 13 | Лошади |
| Other | 2 | 3 | 4 | 5 | 6 | 6 | Прочие |
| **Animal husbandry products** | | | | | | | **Продукция животноводства** |
| Meat (thousands of tons) | 145 | 133 | 111 | 81 | 79 | 82 | Мясо (тысяч тонн) |
| Beef | 60 | 55 | 56 | 52 | 50 | 51 | Говядина |
| Pork | 23 | 26 | 25 | 7 | 9 | 7 | Свинина |
| Lamb | 20 | 19 | 18 | 18 | 16 | 15 | Баранина |
| Poultry | 42 | 33 | 12 | 4 | 4 | 9 | Птица |
| Other | 0 | 0 | 0 | 0 | .. | .. | Прочие виды мяса |
| Milk (thousands of tons) | 432 | 412 | 395 | 390 | 415 | 428 | Молоко (тысяч тонн) |
| Eggs (millions) | 518 | 485 | 253 | 189 | 191 | 198 | Яйца (миллионов штук) |
| Wool (thousands of tons) | 3 | 2 | 2 | 2 | 2 | 2 | Шерсть (тысяч тонн) |

**TABLE 6-1. Industrial production by sector (millions of national currency)** 

**ТАБЛИЦА 6-1. Промышленное производство по отраслям (млн. национальной валюты)**

| Sector | 1990 | 1991 | 1992 | 1993 | 1994 | 1995 | Отрасли |
|---|---|---|---|---|---|---|---|
| **All industry** | 7,302 | 12,861 | 63,935 | 494,370 | 93,264 | 172,007 | **Вся промышленность** |
| **Heavy industry** | 4,474 | 7,359 | 44,581 | 359,036 | 71,799 | 115,378 | **Тяжелая промышленность** |
| Fuel and energy | 252 | 529 | 6,448 | 30,914 | 13,572 | 28,773 | Топливно-энергетическая промышленноть |
| Electricity | 252 | 529 | 6,448 | 30,914 | 13,572 | 28,773 | Электроэнергетика |
| Fuels | .. | .. | .. | .. | .. | .. | Топливная промышленность |
| Ferrous and nonferrous metallurgy | 236 | 438 | 2,195 | 19,324 | 5,265 | 15,302 | Металлургия |
| Chemicals and petrochemical industry | 291 | 570 | 4,729 | 16,086 | 5,369 | 7,244 | Химическая и нефтехимическая пром. |
| Machine building and metalworking | 2,392 | 3,105 | 17,093 | 104,311 | 18,762 | 21,609 | Машиностроение и металлообработка |
| Forestry, woodworking, and pulp and paper | 154 | 221 | 586 | 4,394 | 666 | 627 | Лесная, деревообрабатывающая и целлюлозо-бумажная промышленность |
| Construction materials | 344 | 539 | 2,059 | 16,937 | 4,260 | 5,874 | Промышленность строительных материалов |
| **Light industry** | 1,795 | 2,836 | 8,229 | 54,814 | 6,197 | 6,925 | **Легкая промышленность** |
| Textiles | 709 | 1,092 | 3,829 | 24,336 | 2,469 | 2,761 | Текстильная |
| Clothing | 758 | 1,223 | 2,257 | 8,202 | 1,485 | 2,286 | Швейная |
| Leather and shoes | 328 | 522 | 2,141 | 22,275 | 2,243 | 1,878 | Кожевенная и обувная |
| **Food industry** | 963 | 2,531 | 9,809 | 72,724 | 14,178 | 39,266 | **Пищевая промышленность** |
| Processed foods | 650 | 1,737 | 8,334 | 62,393 | 12,188 | 37,323 | Пищевкусовая |
| Meat and dairy products | 292 | 766 | 1,392 | 8,214 | 1,818 | 1,648 | Мясная и молочная |
| Fish | 20 | 28 | 83 | 2,117 | 172 | 295 | Рыбная |

## TABLE 6-2. Industrial production by sector in constant prices
## ТАБЛИЦА 6-2. Промышленное производство по отраслям в постоянных ценах

| Sector | 1990 | 1991 | 1992 | 1993 | 1994 | 1995 | Отрасли |
|---|---|---|---|---|---|---|---|
| **Industrial production** | | | | | | | **Промышленное производство** |
| **All industry** | 208,811 | 192,733 | 99,836 | 89,153 | 93,645 | .. | **Вся промышленность** |
| **Heavy industry** | 153,161 | 141,827 | 71,764 | 66,884 | 71,799 | .. | **Тяжелая промышленность** |
| Fuel and energy | 28,618 | 26,414 | 23,060 | 15,427 | 13,572 | .. | Топливно-энергетическая промышленноть |
| Electricity | 28,618 | 26,414 | 23,060 | 15,427 | 13,572 | .. | Электроэнергетика |
| Fuels | .. | .. | .. | .. | .. | .. | Топливная промышленность |
| Ferrous and nonferrous metallurgy | 20,540 | 18,260 | 4,949 | 3,677 | 5,265 | .. | Металлургия |
| Chemicals and petrochemicals | 12,306 | 13,388 | 7,257 | 4,448 | 5,369 | .. | Химическая и нефтехимическая пром. |
| Machine building and metalworking | 43,358 | 38,632 | 18,118 | 20,166 | 18,762 | .. | Машиностроение и металлообработка |
| Forestry, woodworking, and pulp and paper | 2,331 | 2,114 | 9,955 | 801 | 666 | .. | Лесная, деревообрабатывающая и целлюлозо-бумажная промышленность |
| Construction materials | 19,576 | 17,422 | 5,314 | 4,395 | 4,260 | .. | Промышленность строительных материалов |
| **Light industry** | 18,552 | 17,957 | 10,092 | 9,073 | 6,777 | .. | **Легкая промышленность** |
| Textiles | 13,482 | 10,731 | 5,322 | 4,343 | 2,470 | .. | Текстильная |
| Clothing | 2,393 | 2,699 | 1,641 | 1,277 | 2,065 | .. | Швейная |
| Leather and shoe | 4,294 | 4,676 | 3,194 | 3,452 | 2,243 | .. | Кожевенная и обувная |
| **Food industry** | 39,161 | 34,031 | 16,709 | 12,064 | 14,178 | .. | **Пищевая промышленность** |
| Processed foods | 22,299 | 22,700 | 12,372 | 10,083 | 12,188 | .. | Пищевкусовая |
| Meat and dairy products | 15,929 | 10,736 | 3,235 | 1,682 | 1,818 | .. | Мясная и молочная |
| Fish | 933 | 595 | 502 | 299 | 172 | .. | Рыбная |
| **Growth in production by sector (in percent)** | | | | | | | **Рост производства по отраслям** |
| **All industry** | -7.5 | -7.7 | -48.2 | -10.7 | 5.0 | .. | **Вся промышленность** |
| **Heavy industry** | -9.2 | -7.4 | -49.4 | -6.8 | 7.3 | .. | **Тяжелая промышленность** |
| Power and fuels | -14.6 | -7.7 | -12.7 | -33.1 | -12.0 | .. | Топливно-энергетическая промышленноть |
| Electricity | -14.6 | -7.7 | -12.7 | -33.1 | -12.0 | .. | Электроэнергетика |
| Fuels | .. | .. | .. | .. | .. | .. | Топливная промышленность |
| Ferrous and nonferrous metallurgy | -20.1 | -11.1 | -72.9 | -25.7 | 43.2 | .. | Металлургия |
| Chemicals and petrochemicals | -38.4 | 8.8 | -45.8 | -38.7 | 20.7 | .. | Химическая и нефтехимическая пром. |
| Machine building and metalworking | -6.3 | -10.9 | -53.1 | 11.3 | -7.0 | .. | Машиностроение и металлообработка |
| Forestry, woodworking, and pulp and paper | -6.5 | -9.3 | 370.9 | -92.0 | -16.9 | .. | Лесная, деревообрабатывающая и целлюлозо-бумажная промышленность |
| Construction materials | -13.6 | -11.0 | -69.5 | -17.3 | -3.1 | .. | Промышленность строительных материалов |
| **Light industry** | 6.7 | -3.2 | -43.8 | -10.1 | -25.3 | .. | **Легкая промышленность** |
| Textiles | -0.9 | -20.4 | -50.4 | -18.4 | -43.1 | .. | Текстильная |
| Clothing | 18.8 | 12.8 | -39.2 | -22.2 | 61.7 | .. | Швейная |
| Leather and shoe | -0.7 | 8.9 | -31.7 | 8.1 | -35.0 | .. | Кожевенная и обувная |
| **Food industry** | -19.6 | -13.1 | -50.9 | -27.8 | 17.5 | .. | **Пищевая промышленность** |
| Processed foods | -19.2 | 1.8 | -45.5 | -18.5 | 20.9 | .. | Пищевкусовая |
| Meat and dairy products | -23.9 | -32.6 | -69.9 | -48.0 | 8.1 | .. | Мясная и молочная |
| Fish | 2.6 | -36.2 | -15.6 | -40.4 | -42.5 | .. | Рыбная |

## TABLE 6-3. Primary energy supply (million tons oil equivalent) — ARMENIA

## ТАБЛИЦА 6-3. Ресурсы первичных видов энергии (млн. тонн нефтяного эквивалента)

| Item | | 1990 | 1991 | 1992 | 1993 | 1994 | 1995 | Статьи | |
|---|---|---|---|---|---|---|---|---|---|
| **Primary production** | | | | | | | | **Производство первичной энергии** | |
| Coal and lignite (hard and brown) | | .. | .. | .. | .. | .. | .. | Уголь каменный и бурый | |
| Crude oil | | .. | .. | .. | .. | .. | .. | Нефть | |
| Gas | | .. | .. | .. | .. | .. | .. | Газ | |
| Nuclear | | .. | .. | .. | .. | .. | 303.7 | Атомная энергия | |
| Hydro/geothermal | | 0.1 | 1546.3 | 3044.3 | 4292.3 | 3514.2 | 1918.8 | Гидро-геотермальная | |
| Other | | .. | 7985.5 | 5976.2 | 2018.8 | 2159.1 | 3338.3 | Другие виды | |
| Total | | 0.1 | 9531.8 | 9020.5 | 6311.1 | 5673.3 | 5560.8 | Всего | |
| **Energy trade** | | | | | | | | **Торговля энергией** | |
| Coal and lignite | Exports | .. | .. | .. | .. | .. | .. | Уголь каменный и бурый | Экспорт |
| | Imports | 0.4 | .. | .. | .. | .. | .. | | Импорт |
| | Net imports | 0.4 | .. | .. | .. | .. | .. | | Чистый импорт |
| Oil/oil product | Exports | .. | .. | .. | .. | .. | .. | Нефть и нефтепродукты | Экспорт |
| | Imports | 4.1 | .. | .. | .. | .. | .. | | Импорт |
| | Net imports | 4.1 | .. | .. | .. | .. | .. | | Чистый импорт |
| Gas | Exports | .. | .. | .. | .. | .. | .. | Газ | Экспорт |
| | Imports | 4.4 | .. | .. | .. | .. | .. | | Импорт |
| | Net imports | 4.4 | .. | .. | .. | .. | .. | | Чистый импорт |
| Electricity | Exports | 0.1 | .. | .. | .. | .. | .. | Электричество | Экспорт |
| | Imports | 0.1 | .. | .. | .. | .. | .. | | Импорт |
| | Net imports | 0.0 | .. | .. | .. | .. | .. | | Чистый импорт |
| **Total net imports** | | 8.9 | .. | .. | .. | .. | .. | **Чистый импорт энергии-всего** | |
| **Total stock changes** | | 0.2 | .. | .. | .. | .. | .. | **Изменение запасов-всего** | |
| **Total primary energy supply** | | 9.2 | .. | .. | .. | .. | .. | **Ресурсы первичной энергии-всего** | |
| Coal and lignite | | 0.4 | .. | .. | .. | .. | .. | Уголь каменный и бурый | |
| Oil/oil products | | 4.1 | .. | .. | .. | .. | .. | Нефть и нефтепродукты | |
| Gas | | 4.4 | .. | .. | .. | .. | .. | Газ | |
| Nuclear | | .. | .. | .. | .. | .. | .. | Атомная энергия | |
| Hydro/geothermal | | 0.1 | .. | .. | .. | .. | .. | Гидро-геотермальная энергия | |
| Other | | 0.2 | .. | .. | .. | .. | .. | Другие виды | |
| **Total primary energy requirement (equals total primary energy supply)** | | 9.2 | .. | .. | .. | .. | .. | **Потребность в первичной энергии-всего (равно ресурсам первичной энергии)** | |

**TABLE 6-4. Final energy consumption (million tons oil equivalent)**
**ТАБЛИЦА 6-4. Конечное потребление энергии ( млн. тонн нефтяного эквивалента )**

| | 1991 | 1992 | 1993 | 1994 | 1995 | |
|---|---|---|---|---|---|---|
| **Final energy consumption** | 8,724 | 6,244 | 3,823 | 3,236 | 3,049 | **Конечное потребление энергии** |
| Coal & Lignite | .. | .. | .. | .. | .. | Уголь каменный и бурый |
| Oil Products | .. | .. | .. | .. | .. | Нефтепродукты |
| Gas | .. | .. | .. | .. | .. | Газ |
| Electricity | .. | .. | .. | .. | .. | Электроэнергия |
| Heat | .. | .. | .. | .. | .. | Тепло |
| Other | .. | .. | .. | .. | .. | Другие виды |
| Of which: | | | | | | В том числе |
| **Industry** | 3,202 | 1,807 | 966 | 958 | 723 | **Промышленность** |
| Coal & Lignite | .. | .. | .. | .. | .. | Уголь каменный и бурый |
| Oil Products | .. | .. | .. | .. | .. | Нефтепродукты |
| Gas | .. | .. | .. | .. | .. | Газ |
| Electricity | .. | .. | .. | .. | .. | Электроэнергия |
| Heat | .. | .. | .. | .. | .. | Тепло |
| Other | .. | .. | .. | .. | .. | Другие виды |
| **Agriculture** | 2,181 | 1,278 | 496 | 385 | 332 | **Сельское хозяйство** |
| Coal & Lignite | .. | .. | .. | .. | .. | Уголь каменный и бурый |
| Oil Products | .. | .. | .. | .. | .. | Нефтепродукты |
| Gas | .. | .. | .. | .. | .. | Газ |
| Electricity | .. | .. | .. | .. | .. | Электроэнергия |
| Heat | .. | .. | .. | .. | .. | Тепло |
| Other | .. | .. | .. | .. | .. | Другие виды |
| **Transport** | 421 | 329 | 269 | 298 | 273 | **Транспорт** |
| Oil Products | .. | .. | .. | .. | .. | Нефтепродукты |
| Other | .. | .. | .. | .. | .. | Другие виды |
| **Households** | 2,260 | 2,423 | 1,357 | 970 | 541 | **Домашние хозяйства** |
| Coal & Lignite | .. | .. | .. | .. | .. | Уголь каменный и бурый |
| Oil Products | .. | .. | .. | .. | .. | Нефтепродукты |
| Gas | .. | .. | .. | .. | .. | Газ |
| Electricity | .. | .. | .. | .. | .. | Электроэнергия |
| Heat | .. | .. | .. | .. | .. | Тепло |
| Other | .. | .. | .. | .. | .. | Другие виды |

## TABLE 7-1. Price indices and exchange rates
## ТАБЛИЦА 7-1. Индексы цен и обменный курс

| Year and month | National currency per U.S. dollar<br>Единиц нац. валюты за 1 доллар США | National currency per 100 Russian rubles<br>Единиц нац. валюты за 100 российских рублей | Consumer price index (as a percent of the previous month)<br>Индекс потребительских цен (в % к предыдущему месяцу) | Producer price index (as a percent of the previous month)<br>Индекс цен производителей (в % к предыдущему месяцу) | Consumer price index (as a percent of the previous December)<br>Индекс потребительских цен (в % к декабрю прошлого года) | Producer price index (as a percent of the previous December)<br>Индекс цен производителей (в % к декабрю прошлого года) | Год и месяц |
|---|---|---|---|---|---|---|---|
| **1993** | | | | | | | **1993** |
| January | 484.2 | .. | 133.4 | 110.2 | 133.4 | 110.2 | Январь |
| February | 568.6 | .. | 141.7 | 149.2 | 189.0 | 164.4 | Февраль |
| March | 660.6 | .. | 116.6 | 142.5 | 220.4 | 234.3 | Март |
| April | 571.8 | .. | 113.7 | 125.7 | 250.7 | 294.5 | Апрель |
| May | 890.1 | .. | 124.2 | 120.6 | 311.4 | 355.2 | Май |
| June | 1,074.8 | .. | 128.7 | 114.3 | 400.9 | 406.0 | Июнь |
| July | 1,029.0 | .. | 111.4 | 125.0 | 446.5 | 507.5 | Июль |
| August | 985.6 | .. | 124.6 | 126.3 | 556.3 | 639.6 | Август |
| September | 1,219.4 | .. | 114.5 | 108.1 | 637.0 | 690.6 | Сентябрь |
| October | 1,880.4 | .. | 155.6 | 115.2 | 990.9 | 794.1 | Октябрь |
| November | 2,593.6 | .. | 537.8 | 130.7 | 5,329.3 | 1,040.3 | Ноябрь |
| December | 8,658.3 | .. | 206.3 | 142.2 | 10,996.2 | 1,477.3 | Декабрь |
| **1994** | | | | | | | **1994** |
| January | 92.6 | 6.5 | 182.5 | 251.7 | 182.5 | 251.7 | Январь |
| February | 130.2 | 7.7 | 118.5 | 150.4 | 216.3 | 378.6 | Февраль |
| March | 202.6 | 11.6 | 144.5 | 186.9 | 313.5 | 707.9 | Март |
| April | 274.6 | 14.5 | 157.1 | 149.4 | 490.8 | 1,054.8 | Апрель |
| May | 317.7 | 17.2 | 156.5 | 125.0 | 768.0 | 1,318.5 | Май |
| June | 313.7 | 16.5 | 109.1 | 124.8 | 838.0 | 1,648.1 | Июнь |
| July | 310.1 | 15.7 | 98.2 | 107.5 | 822.9 | 1,779.9 | Июль |
| August | 319.1 | 15.3 | 103.7 | 100.0 | 853.0 | 1,779.9 | Август |
| September | 342.3 | 16.2 | 106.3 | 104.2 | 906.8 | 1,851.1 | Сентябрь |
| October | 365.2 | 10.9 | 111.3 | 118.4 | 1,009.3 | 2,184.3 | Октябрь |
| November | 409.3 | 12.8 | 114.7 | 104.3 | 1,157.9 | 2,271.7 | Ноябрь |
| December | 412.3 | 11.6 | 160.8 | 137.7 | 1,861.9 | 3,134.9 | Декабрь |

**TABLE 7-1. Price indices and exchange rates**

**ТАБЛИЦА 7-1. Индексы цен и обменный курс**

| Year and month | National currency per U.S. dollar<br>Единиц нац. валюты за 1 доллар США | National currency per 100 Russian rubles<br>Единиц нац. валюты за 100 российских рублей | Consumer price index (as a percent of the previous month)<br>Индекс потребительских цен (в % к предыдущему месяцу) | Producer price index (as a percent of the previous month)<br>Индекс цен производителей (в % к предыдущему месяцу) | Consumer price index (as a percent of the previous December)<br>Индекс потребительских цен (в % к декабрю прошлого года) | Producer price index (as a percent of the previous December)<br>Индекс цен производителей (в % к декабрю прошлого года) | Год и месяц |
|---|---|---|---|---|---|---|---|
| **1995** | | | | | | | **1995** |
| January | 406.3 | 9.4 | 103.9 | 103.8 | 103.9 | 103.8 | Январь |
| February | 405.0 | 8.9 | 100.7 | 106.1 | 104.7 | 110.1 | Февраль |
| March | 404.4 | 8.2 | 101.2 | 102.1 | 106.0 | 112.3 | Март |
| April | 408.1 | 7.9 | 107.1 | 101.1 | 113.6 | 113.6 | Апрель |
| May | 408.9 | 8.0 | 107.8 | 100.5 | 122.4 | 114.1 | Май |
| June | 409.1 | 8.5 | 100.6 | 101.2 | 123.2 | 115.5 | Июнь |
| July | 407.8 | 8.2 | 95.4 | 113.6 | 117.5 | 131.2 | Июль |
| August | 409.2 | 9.2 | 97.9 | 98.6 | 115.1 | 129.4 | Август |
| September | 407.6 | 9.0 | 99.9 | 104.7 | 115.0 | 135.5 | Сентябрь |
| October | 400.2 | 8.7 | 104.0 | 101.1 | 119.6 | 137.0 | Октябрь |
| November | 402.4 | 8.7 | 102.7 | 102.6 | 122.9 | 140.5 | Ноябрь |
| December | 402.6 | 8.5 | 107.6 | .. | 132.2 | .. | Декабрь |
| **1996** | | | | | | | **1996** |
| January | 402.0 | 8.4 | 103.6 | 105.6 | 103.6 | 105.6 | Январь |
| February | 402.7 | 8.2 | 103.4 | 104.7 | 107.1 | 110.6 | Февраль |
| March | 403.4 | 8.2 | 100.2 | 100.4 | 107.3 | 111.0 | Март |
| April | 405.5 | 8.2 | 99.6 | 97.9 | 106.9 | 108.7 | Апрель |
| May | 406.7 | 8.2 | 100.1 | 98.0 | 106.9 | 106.5 | Май |
| June | 409.2 | 8.1 | 98.7 | .. | 105.6 | .. | Июнь |
| July | .. | .. | .. | .. | .. | .. | Июль |
| August | .. | .. | .. | .. | .. | .. | Август |
| September | .. | .. | .. | .. | .. | .. | Сентябрь |
| October | .. | .. | .. | .. | .. | .. | Октябрь |
| November | .. | .. | .. | .. | .. | .. | Ноябрь |
| December | .. | .. | .. | .. | .. | .. | Декабрь |

## TABLE 7-2. Monthly nominal wages by sector
## ТАБЛИЦА 7-2. Среднемесячная денежная зарплата по отраслям

| Sector | 1990 | 1991 | 1992 | 1993 | 1994 | 1995 | Сектора |
|---|---|---|---|---|---|---|---|
| **Nominal wages** | | | | | | | **Средняя номинальная заработная плата** |
| **Economy average** | 241.3 | 344.6 | 1,403.0 | 11,736.0 | 1,612.0 | 6,371.0 | **По народному хозяйству** |
| **Material sphere** | 267.0 | 378.5 | 1,521.8 | 12,882.0 | 2,102.0 | 8,825.0 | **Отрасли сферы материального производства** |
| Industry | 264.1 | 345.7 | 1,616.0 | 12,926.0 | 2,302.0 | 8,643.0 | Промышленность |
| Construction | 410.0 | 524.2 | 1,845.6 | 17,966.0 | 1,428.0 | 13,131.0 | Строительство |
| Agriculture | 190.7 | 349.5 | 1,024.5 | 9,062.0 | 1,008.0 | 5,157.0 | Сельское хозяйство |
| Transport | 247.6 | 323.1 | 1,292.2 | 9,766.0 | 4,406.0 | 10,278.0 | Транспорт |
| Communications | 212.7 | 357.6 | 1,514.4 | 13,624.0 | 2,595.0 | 11,653.0 | Связь |
| Trade (retail and wholesale) | 170.2 | 231.7 | 756.0 | 14,405.0 | 882.0 | 4,662.0 | Торговля (оптовая и розничная) |
| Other | 174.6 | 290.3 | 1,201.8 | 9,988.0 | 790.0 | 4,167.0 | Прочие отрасли материального производства |
| **Nonmaterial sphere** | 186.1 | 280.5 | 1,213.8 | 10,029.0 | 1,006.0 | 3,804.0 | **Отрасли непроизводственной сферы** |
| Municipal services | 180.5 | 261.4 | 1,171.0 | 8,871.5 | 1,186.0 | 5,488.0 | Жилкомхоз и бытовое обслуживание |
| Science, research and development | 262.3 | 350.9 | 1,405.1 | 12,699.0 | 1,512.0 | 4,532.0 | Наука и научное обслуживание |
| Education | 165.5 | 260.6 | 1,188.0 | 7,353.0 | 726.0 | 2,859.0 | Образование |
| Culture | 134.1 | 219.4 | 875.1 | 7,847.0 | 712.0 | 2,580.0 | Культура |
| Arts | 162.4 | 239.9 | .. | .. | 793.0 | 2,502.0 | Искусство |
| Health care, social security, and sports | 154.4 | 253.6 | 1,111.2 | 9,029.0 | ɓ83.0 | 3,755.0 | Здравоохр., соц.обсл., физк. и спорт |
| Banking, finance, credit, insurance | 304.2 | 708.7 | 2,502.0 | 36,223.0 | 6,566.0 | 18,781.0 | Кредитование, страхование, банк. дело |
| Government | 295.8 | 397.2 | 1,583.3 | 20,290.0 | 1,089.0 | 4,328.0 | Управление |

**TABLE 8-1. Money income and expenditure of the population (millions of national currency)**
**ТАБЛИЦА 8-1. Денежные доходы и расходы населения (млн. национальной валюты)**

| Type of income or expenditure | 1990 | 1991 | 1992 | 1993 | 1994 | 1995 | Вид доходов или расходов |
|---|---|---|---|---|---|---|---|
| **Income** | | | | | | | **Доходы** |
| **Total labor income** | 5,665 | 7,928 | 28,418 | 266,158 | 229,168 | .. | **Всего трудовых доходов** |
| Regular wages | 5,150 | 6,578 | 22,819 | 207,106 | 159,084 | .. | Заработная плата |
| Wages paid by cooperatives | 758 | 949 | 1,520 | 5,055 | .. | .. | Заработная плата в кооперативах |
| Other wages and compensation | 172 | 272 | 1,266 | 13,202 | 29,554 | .. | Прочие доходы типа заработной платы |
| Income paid by collective farms | 141 | 169 | 71 | 44 | .. | .. | Доходы от колхозов |
| Income from sale of farm products | 202 | 909 | 4,262 | 45,806 | 40,530 | .. | Доходы от продажи продукции колхозов |
| **Total transfer receipts** | 2,292 | 6,735 | 13,280 | 128,855 | 314,891 | .. | **Всего трансфертных поступлений** |
| Pensions and allowances | 852 | 1,595 | 5,484 | 39,682 | 62,542 | .. | Пенсии и пособия |
| Scholarships | 36 | 97 | 494 | 2,562 | 1,726 | .. | Стипендии |
| Income from the financial system (insurance, interest, etc.) | 693 | 3,390 | 759 | 5,862 | 2,935 | .. | Доходы из финансовой системы (страховые возмещения, проценты и т.д.) |
| Other income | 712 | 1,653 | 6,543 | 80,749 | 247,688 | .. | Прочие виды доходов |
| **Total income** | 7,958 | 14,663 | 41,698 | 395,013 | 544,059 | 2,645,477 | **Всего доходов** |
| **Expenditure** | | | | | | | **Расходы** |
| **Total purchases** | 4,982 | 8,076 | 19,619 | 145,776 | 229,991 | .. | **Всего покупок товаров и услуг** |
| Retail goods | 4,495 | 7,265 | 15,845 | 118,293 | 158,882 | 2,090,000 | Товары в розничной торговле |
| Services | 488 | 811 | 3,773 | 27,483 | 71,109 | 519,190 | Услуги |
| Rent and utilities | 114 | 151 | 439 | 3,229 | 19,075 | .. | Квартирная плата и коммунальные платежи |
| Transport and communications | 243 | 338 | 2,136 | 19,680 | 39,602 | .. | Транспорт и связь |
| Health and other services | 109 | 186 | 748 | 4,574 | .. | .. | Здравоохранение и другие виды услуг |
| Cooperatives | 21 | 136 | 450 | .. | .. | .. | Кооперативы |
| **Transfers and savings** | 1,883 | 4,500 | 7,931 | 104,300 | 225,553 | 208,243 | **Трансферты и сбережения** |
| Taxes, fees, dues, and other | 593 | 706 | 1,762 | 10,494 | 23,483 | 66,650 | Налоги, сборы, пошлины и др. |
| Savings | 1,039 | 3,507 | -333 | 34,739 | 10,185 | 141,216 | Сбережения |
| Other | 251 | 287 | 6,502 | 59,067 | 191,885 | 877 | Прочие |
| **Total expenditure** | 6,865 | 12,577 | 27,550 | 250,076 | 455,544 | 2,817,433 | **Всего расходов** |
| **Income less expenditure** | 1,093 | 2,086 | 14,148 | 144,937 | 88,515 | -171,956 | **Доходы за вычетом расходов** |

# *Country Notes: Armenia*

**General Notes:** Unless otherwise indicated, data were supplied by the Statistics, State Register, and Analysis Administration of the Republic of Armenia.

**Currency:** The dram was introduced on November 22, 1993. The conversion factor at the time of introduction was 1 dram per 200 Russian rubles. Unless otherwise indicated, data up to 1993 are in rubles, and in drams for 1994 and 1995.

**Table 1-1:** End year population. Data for 1995 are estimates.

**Table 1-2:** Transport of goods includes road maintenance. Insurance is included with credit. Wholesale trade includes retail trade and catering. For 1994 and 1995, communication servicing material production is included with transportation of goods and communication in the non-material sphere is included with passenger transport. Data for 1995 are estimates.

**Table 2-1:** Statistical discrepancy between GDP by expenditure category and total GDP by industrial origin at market prices is as follows:

| Year | Statistical discrepancy |
|---|---|
| 1990 | -278 mln. rubles |
| 1991 | 607 mln. rubles |
| 1992 | 4416 mln. rubles |
| 1993 | 36274 mln. rubles |
| 1994 | 8405 mln. drams |

**Table 2-2:** Data are in previous year prices, in rubles up to 1993 and in drams for 1994. The conversion factor of 1 dram per 200 rubles was used to create a base for calculation of the 1994 GDP in constant 1993 drams.

**Tables 3-4A and 3-4B:** The category Other Asia includes trade with Iran as follows:

| 1993 | 1994 | 1995 |
|---|---|---|
| Exports | | |
| $ 5.5 mln. | $ 14.6 mln. | $ 35.0 mln. |
| .. | 4,189 mln. drams | 14,196 mln. drams |
| Imports | | |
| $ 15.8 mln. | $ 42.5 mln. | $ 89.8 mln. |
| .. | 12,193 mln. drams | 36,423 mln. drams |

**Table 5-2:** Data are in 1983 rubles.

**Table 5-4:** Meat production is given in live weight.

**Table 6-1:** Data for 1995 are preliminary.

**Table 6-2:** Data are in 1994 drams.

**Table 6-3:** For 1991-1994, primary energy production is measured in kilowatt-hours.

**Table 7-1:** Producer Price Index as a percent of the previous December was calculated by World Bank staff.

**Table 7-2:** For 1992 and 1993 Culture includes Art.

**Table 8-1:** The cash savings of the population are included with Other transfers and savings for 1994 and with Savings for 1995.

# *Комментарии к таблицам: Армения*

**Общее замечание:** За исключением особо отмеченных случаев, данные были получены из Государственного комитета по статистике, государственному регистру и анализу Республики Армения.

**Национальная валюта:** Национальная валюта Армении - драм, была введена 22 ноября 1993 г. Коэффициент пересчета на дату введения был 1 драм за 200 рублей. За исключением особо отмеченных случаев, данные до 1994 г. представлены в рублях, а с 1994 г. - в драмах.

**Таблица 1-1:** Численность населения дана на конец года. Данные за 1995 г. - предварительные.

**Таблица 1-2:** Грузовой транспорт включает также дорожное хозяйство. Кредитование включает страхование. Оптовая торговля включает также розничную торговлю и общественное питание. За 1994-1995 гг. связь в части обслуживания материального производства включена в грузовой транспорт, а связь в сфере нематериального производства - в пассажирский транспорт. Данные за 1995 г. - предварительные.

**Таблица 2-1:** Статистическое расхождение между ВВП по производству и ВВП по видам расходов составляет:

| Год | Статистическое расхождение |
|---|---|
| 1990 | -278 млн. рублей |
| 1991 | 607 млн. рублей |
| 1992 | 4416 млн. рублей |
| 1993 | 36274 млн. рублей |
| 1994 | 8405 млн. драмов |

**Таблица 2-2:** Данные приведены в ценах предыдущего года в рублях до 1993 г. включительно и в драмах за 1994 г. ВВП за 1994 г. в драмах 1993 г. рассчитан на основе коэффициента пересчета на дату введения драма.

**Таблицы 3-4А и 3-4В:** Торговля с остальными странами Азии включает торговлю с Ираном, которая составляет:

| 1993 | 1994 | 1995 |
|---|---|---|
| Экспорт | | |
| $ 5,5 млн. | $ 14,6 млн. | $ 35,0 млн. |
| ... | 4,189 млн. драмов | 14,196 млн. драмов |
| Импорт | | |
| $ 15,8 млн. | $ 42,5 млн. | $ 89,8 млн. |
| ... | 12,193 млн. драмов | 36,423 млн. драмов |

**Таблица 5-2:** Данные приведены в рублях, в ценах 1983 г.

**Таблица 5-4:** Производство мяса приводится в живом весе.

**Таблица 6-1:** За 1995 г. приведены предварительные данные.

**Таблица 6-2:** Данные приведены в драмах, в ценах 1994 г.

**Таблица 6-3:** За 1991-1994 гг. производство первичной энергии дано в млн. киловатт-часов.

**Таблица 7-1:** Индекс цен производителей в процентах к декабрю прошлого года рассчитан сотрудниками Всемирного Банка.

**Таблица 7-2:** За 1992-1993 гг. культура включает также искусство.

**Таблица 8-1:** Наличные денежные средства населения включены в прочие трансферты и сбережения за 1994 г., а за 1995 г. - в сбережения.

# Azerbaijan / Азербайджан

1996 Population / Численность населения в 1996 году
(thousands / тыс. человек.): 7,535

Area / Территория
(thousand square kilometers / тыс. кв. км.): 86.6

Capital city / Столица :
Baku / Баку

**Country Tables:** Tables 3-2B, 3-3B, 3-4B, 5-1, 5-2 and 6-3 are not included because there are either no or no recent data available.

**Статистические таблицы страны:** Таблицы 3-2В, 3-3В, 3-4В, 5-1, 5-2 и 6-3 не включены ввиду полного отсутствия данных либо их отсутствия за последние годы.

## TABLE 1-1. Population and employment (thousands)
## ТАБЛИЦА 1-1. Население и занятость (тысяч)

| Population or employment category | 1990 | 1991 | 1992 | 1993 | 1994 | 1995 | Население или группы занятых |
|---|---|---|---|---|---|---|---|
| **Total population** | 7,117 | 7,175 | 7,266 | 7,333 | 7,392 | 7,444 | **Население - всего** |
| Males | 3,474 | 3,505 | 3,553 | 3,593 | 3,628 | 3,660 | Мужчины |
| Females | 3,643 | 3,670 | 3,713 | 3,740 | 3,764 | 3,784 | Женщины |
| Urban population | 3,843 | 3,858 | 3,893 | 3,909 | 3,926 | 3,936 | Городское |
| Rural population | 3,274 | 3,317 | 3,373 | 3,424 | 3,466 | 3,508 | Сельское |
| Population under working age | 2,489 | 2,525 | 2,562 | 2,582 | 2,596 | 2,610 | Моложе трудоспособного возраста |
| Working-age population | 3,909 | 3,917 | 3,945 | 3,962 | 3,985 | 4,012 | Лица в трудоспособном возрасте |
| Population over working age | 719 | 733 | 759 | 789 | 811 | 822 | Старше трудоспособного возраста |
| Economically Active Population, in non-working age | 157 | 157 | 157 | 165 | 152 | 152 | Экономически активное население в нетрудоспособном возрасте |
| Above working age | 145 | 145 | 145 | 154 | 141 | 141 | Старше трудоспособного возраста |
| Below working age | 12 | 12 | 12 | 11 | 11 | 11 | Моложе трудоспособного возраста |
| **Total labor resources** | 4,266 | 4,304 | 4,333 | 4,280 | 4,249 | 4,245 | **Трудовые ресурсы - всего** |
| **Total employment** | 2,908 | 3,047 | 2,922 | 2,917 | 2,851 | 2,837 | **Занятое население - всего** |
| State sector employees | 2,173 | 1,984 | 1,836 | 1,842 | 1,724 | 1,647 | Государственный сектор |
| Leased enterprise employees | .. | 58 | 92 | 87 | 84 | 85 | Арендные предприятия |
| Joint-stock company employees | .. | 7 | 10 | 10 | 6 | 5 | Акционерные общества |
| Economic association employees | .. | 1 | .. | .. | .. | .. | Хозяйственные ассоциации |
| Social organization employees | .. | 93 | 25 | 13 | 16 | 15 | Общественные организации |
| Joint venture employees | .. | 1 | 2 | 2 | 6 | 7 | Совместные предприятия |
| Collective farm workers | 334 | 332 | 373 | 339 | 318 | 318 | Колхозы |
| Cooperative workers | 61 | 81 | 49 | 29 | 18 | 18 | Кооперативы |
| Individual labor activities | 3 | 3 | 3 | 3 | 5 | 5 | ИТД |
| Private subsidiary agricultural workers | 218 | 341 | 351 | 338 | 333 | 333 | Личные подсобные хозяйства |
| Private agricultural workers | .. | .. | 2 | 4 | 7 | 7 | Фермерские хозяйства |
| **Students** | 306 | 313 | 297 | 267 | 251 | 230 | **Учащиеся** |
| **Religious workers** | .. | .. | .. | .. | .. | 5 | **Служащие религиозного культа** |
| **Working age population not employed in the national economy** | 1,052 | 944 | 1,114 | 1,096 | 1,147 | 1,173 | **Лица в трудоспособном возрасте, не занятые в экономике** |
| Housewives | .. | .. | .. | .. | .. | .. | Домохозяйки |
| Military personnel | .. | .. | .. | .. | .. | .. | Военнослужащие |
| Unemployed | .. | 4 | 6 | 20 | 24 | 28 | Безработные |
| **Labor force** | 2,908 | 3,051 | 2,928 | 2,937 | 2,875 | 2,865 | **Рабочая сила** |

## TABLE 1-2. Employment by sector (thousands)
## ТАБЛИЦА 1-2. Численность занятого населения по секторам (тысяч)

| Sector | 1990 | 1991 | 1992 | 1993 | 1994 | 1995 | Сектор |
|---|---|---|---|---|---|---|---|
| **Material sphere** | 2,108 | 2,196 | 2,162 | 2,092 | 2,008 | 2,002 | **Сфера материального производства** |
| **Agriculture and forestry** | 899 | 978 | 1,014 | 944 | 899 | 888 | **Сельское и лесное хозяйство** |
| Agriculture | 894 | 972 | 1,009 | 939 | 895 | 883 | Сельское хозяйство |
| Forestry | 5 | 5 | 5 | 5 | 4 | 5 | Лесное хозяйство |
| **Industry and construction** | 721 | 705 | 655 | 604 | 565 | 555 | **Промышленность и строительство** |
| Industry | 469 | 459 | 429 | 392 | 374 | 370 | Промышленность |
| Construction | 252 | 246 | 226 | 212 | 192 | 185 | Строительство |
| **Other** | 489 | 514 | 492 | 544 | 543 | 558 | **Другие отрасли** |
| Transport of goods | 143 | 131 | 121 | 111 | 105 | 116 | Грузовой транспорт |
| Road Maintenance | .. | .. | .. | .. | .. | .. | Дорожное хозяйство |
| Communication servicing material production | .. | .. | .. | .. | .. | .. | Связь |
| Wholesale trade | .. | .. | .. | .. | .. | .. | Оптовая торговля |
| Retail trade and catering | 289 | 312 | 312 | 351 | 366 | 367 | Розничная торговля и общепит |
| Material supply | .. | .. | .. | .. | .. | .. | Материально-техническое снабжение |
| Procurement | .. | .. | .. | .. | .. | .. | Заготовки |
| Information and computing services | 7 | 6 | 3 | 3 | 4 | 3 | Информационно-техническое обслуживание |
| Other sectors | 50 | 64 | 56 | 78 | 69 | 73 | Другие отрасли сферы материального пр. |
| **Nonmaterial sphere** | 801 | 852 | 761 | 825 | 844 | 835 | **Сфера нематериального производства** |
| Passenger transport | 73 | 85 | 76 | 85 | 86 | 73 | Пассажирский транспорт |
| Communication | .. | .. | .. | .. | .. | .. | Связь |
| Housing | 100 | 110 | 71 | 86 | 91 | 92 | Жилищное хозяйство |
| Public utilities and personal services | .. | .. | .. | .. | .. | .. | Комм. хоз. и бытовое обслуживание |
| Health care, social security, physical culture and sports | 170 | 179 | 167 | 178 | 174 | 175 | Здравоохранение, социальное обеспечение, физкультура и спорт |
| Education | 338 | 355 | 347 | 380 | 394 | 395 | Образование |
| Culture and art | .. | .. | .. | .. | .. | .. | Культура и искусство |
| Science and scientific research | 58 | 59 | 41 | 34 | 37 | 37 | Наука и научное обслуживание |
| Credit | 11 | 10 | 11 | 13 | 13 | 13 | Кредитование |
| Insurance | .. | .. | .. | .. | .. | .. | Страхование |
| General administration and defense | 51 | 53 | 48 | 50 | 49 | 50 | Государственное управление и оборона |
| Private nonprofit institutions serving households | .. | .. | .. | .. | .. | .. | Общественные организации, обслуживающие домашние хозяйства |
| **Other, material and nonmaterial spheres** | 1,290 | 1,365 | 1,153 | 1,369 | 1,387 | 1,393 | **Остальные отрасли материального производства и нематериальной сферы** |
| **Total employment** | 2,908 | 3,047 | 2,922 | 2,917 | 2,851 | 2,837 | **Занятые - всего** |

## TABLE 1-3. Registered unemployment (thousands; end of month)
## ТАБЛИЦА 1-3. Численность зарегистрированных безработных (тысяч; на конец месяца)

| Year and m | Total<br>Всего | Males<br>Мужчины | Females<br>Женщины | Receiving benefits<br>Получающие пособие | Год и месяц |
|---|---|---|---|---|---|
| **1994** | | | | | **1994** |
| January | 20.2 | .. | .. | 4.6 | Январь |
| February | 20.9 | .. | .. | 4.9 | Февраль |
| March | 21.3 | 8.3 | 13.0 | 4.9 | Март |
| April | 21.8 | .. | .. | 4.7 | Апрель |
| May | 22.0 | .. | .. | 4.7 | Май |
| June | 22.4 | 8.8 | 13.6 | 4.4 | Июнь |
| July | 22.7 | .. | .. | 4.2 | Июль |
| August | 23.0 | .. | .. | 3.4 | Август |
| September | 23.3 | 9.1 | 14.2 | 3.3 | Сентябрь |
| October | 23.5 | .. | .. | 3.3 | Октябрь |
| November | 24.0 | .. | .. | .. | Ноябрь |
| December | 23.6 | 9.2 | 14.4 | 3.5 | Декабрь |
| **1995** | | | | | **1995** |
| January | 24.0 | .. | .. | 3.7 | Январь |
| February | 24.6 | .. | .. | 4.1 | Февраль |
| March | 25.0 | 9.8 | 15.2 | 4.4 | Март |
| April | 25.4 | .. | .. | 4.6 | Апрель |
| May | 26.0 | .. | .. | 5.0 | Май |
| June | 26.5 | 10.6 | 15.9 | 5.3 | Июнь |
| July | 26.9 | .. | .. | 5.3 | Июль |
| August | 27.3 | .. | .. | 4.1 | Август |
| September | 27.5 | 11.0 | 16.5 | 3.7 | Сентябрь |
| October | 27.5 | .. | .. | 3.5 | Октябрь |
| November | 27.7 | .. | .. | 3.2 | Ноябрь |
| December | 28.3 | 11.4 | 16.9 | 3.0 | Декабрь |
| **1996** | | | | | **1996** |
| January | 28.1 | .. | .. | 2.8 | Январь |
| February | 28.7 | .. | .. | 3.0 | Февраль |
| March | 29.1 | 11.8 | 17.3 | 3.1 | Март |
| April | 29.5 | .. | .. | 3.3 | Апрель |
| May | 29.7 | .. | .. | 3.3 | Май |
| June | .. | .. | .. | .. | Июнь |
| July | .. | .. | .. | .. | Июль |
| August | .. | .. | .. | .. | Август |
| September | .. | .. | .. | .. | Сентябрь |
| October | .. | .. | .. | .. | Октябрь |
| November | .. | .. | .. | .. | Ноябрь |
| December | .. | .. | .. | .. | Декабрь |

**TABLE 2-1. Gross domestic product at current prices (millions of national currency)**
**ТАБЛИЦА 2-1. Валовой внутренний продукт в текущих ценах (млн. национальной валюты)**

| Sector of origin or expenditure category | 1990 | 1991 | 1992 | 1993 | 1994 | 1995 | Отраслевое происхождение или вид расходов |
|---|---|---|---|---|---|---|---|
| **Gross domestic product by sector of origin** | | | | | | | **Валовой внутренний продукт по отраслевому происхождению** |
| **Agriculture and forestry** | 388.7 | 814.4 | 6,280.4 | 42,562 | 605,996 | 2,837,056 | **Сельское и лесное хозяйство** |
| Agriculture | 387.6 | 812.5 | 6,241.8 | 42,244 | 603,921 | 2,827,387 | Сельское хозяйство |
| Forestry | 1.1 | 1.9 | 38.6 | 318 | 2,075 | 9,669 | Лесное хозяйство |
| **Industry and construction** | 446.2 | 798.9 | 8,844.7 | 50,886 | 448,394 | 2,581,027 | **Промышленность и строительство** |
| Industry | 322.8 | 630.0 | 7,082.9 | 39,127 | 309,639 | 2,306,855 | Промышленность |
| Construction | 123.4 | 168.9 | 1,761.8 | 11,759 | 138,755 | 274,172 | Строительство |
| **Other** | 503.8 | 904.1 | 7,517.6 | 65,996.6 | 801,196 | 5,221,254 | **Другие отрасли** |
| Transport | 98.6 | 137.0 | 1,025.4 | 10,059 | 204,357 | 2,523,196 | Транспорт |
| Road maintenance | 6.0 | 12.2 | 47.5 | 315 | 2,755 | 33,910 | Дорожное хозяйство |
| Communication | 14.3 | 15.9 | 180.1 | 2,158 | 22,934 | 102,607 | Связь |
| Wholesale trade | 4.1 | 4.9 | 32.8 | 367 | 9,048 | 413,224 | Оптовая торговля |
| Retail trade and catering | 31.8 | 68.0 | 972.5 | 5,402 | 63,355 | .. | Розничная торговля и общепит |
| Material supply | 12.4 | 29.5 | 256.6 | 2,291 | 41,279 | 306,757 | Материально-техническое снабжение |
| Procurement | 7.7 | 12.7 | 117.4 | 391 | 3,737 | 15,553 | Заготовки |
| Information and computing services | 2.0 | 1.2 | 6.2 | 99 | 350 | 2,586 | Информационно-вычислительное обслуживание |
| Other sectors of material production | 13.4 | 23.3 | 71.6 | 633 | 4,021 | 29,690 | Другие отрасли сферы материального пр. |
| Housing | 28.1 | 38.2 | 220.5 | 1,109 | 19,416 | 71,508 | Жилищное хозяйство |
| Public utilities and personal services | 33.3 | 59.6 | 977.1 | 6,307 | 65,159 | 255,577 | Ком. хоз. и бытовое обслуживание |
| Health care, social security, physical culture and sports | 34.4 | 59.3 | 636.6 | 4,497 | 34,480 | 139,455 | Здравоохранение, социальное обеспечение, физкультура и спорт |
| Education | 73.7 | 151.2 | 1,508.6 | 9,563 | 101,543 | 384,838 | Образование |
| Culture and art | 17.4 | 16.7 | 137.3 | 1,016 | 15,673 | 67,490 | Культура и искусство |
| Science and scientific research | 17.3 | 21.9 | 56.9 | 877 | 11,605 | 47,499 | Наука и научное обслуживание |
| Credit | 3.2 | 6.4 | 568.7 | 10,653 | 103,767 | 432,693 | Кредитование |
| Insurance | 1.0 | 1.6 | 3.2 | 624 | 1,184 | .. | Страхование |
| General administration and defense | 101.9 | 240.0 | 687.3 | 9,415 | 96,018 | 392,271 | Государственное управление и оборона |
| Private nonprofit institutions serving households | 3.4 | 4.5 | 11.3 | 220 | 515 | 2,400 | Общественные организации, обслуживающие домашние хозяйства |
| **Imputed service charge of financial intermediaries** | .. | -1.1 | -610.0 | -10,045 | -91,383 | -375,211 | **Условно-исчисляемая стоимость услуг финансовых посредников** |
| **Total gross value added (GVA)** | 1,338.7 | 2,516.3 | 22,032.7 | 149,400 | 1,764,203 | 10,264,126 | **Валовая добавленная стоимость (ВДС) - всего** |
| **Taxes on production and imports (TOPI)** | 267.7 | 309.1 | 3,224.1 | 22,518 | 118,444 | 604,074 | **Налоги на производство и импорт (НПиИ)** |
| Other taxes on production (OTOP) | 45.3 | 22.6 | 82.1 | 2,050 | 13,221 | .. | Другие налоги на производство (ДНП) |
| **Subsidies on production and imports (SOPI)** | 95.1 | 135.2 | 1,074.2 | 12,786 | 68,622 | 299,967 | **Субсидии на производство и импорт (СПиИ)** |
| Other subsidies on production (OSOP) | .. | .. | .. | .. | .. | .. | Другие субсидии на производство (ДСП) |
| **Total GDP at factor cost (GVA-OTOP+OSOP)** | 1,293.4 | 2,493.7 | 21,950.7 | 147,350 | 1,750,982 | 10,264,126 | **Всего ВВП по фактр. стоимости (ВДС-ДНП+ДСП)** |
| **Net Indirect taxes (TOPI - SOPI)** | 172.6 | 173.9 | 2,149.9 | 9,732 | 49,822 | 304,107 | **Чистые косвенные налоги (НПиИ-СПиИ)** |
| **Total GDP at market prices** | 1,466.0 | 2,667.6 | 24,100.6 | 157,082 | 1,800,804 | 10,568,233 | **Всего ВВП в рыночных ценах** |
| **Gross domestic product by expenditure category** | | | | | | | **Валовой внутренний продукт по видам расходов** |
| **Consumption** | 1,028.7 | 1,875.4 | 19,656.0 | 150,457 | 1,872,651 | 9,497,092 | **Потребление** |
| Private consumption | 900.3 | 1,618.9 | 17,916.6 | 128,084 | 1,588,880 | 8,162,878 | Личное потребление |
| Government consumption | 128.4 | 256.5 | 1,739.4 | 22,373 | 283,771 | 1,334,214 | Общественное потребление |
| **Gross domestic investment** | 389.2 | 82.7 | -4,345.0 | 34,222 | 286,890 | 2,085,332 | **Валовые внутренние инвестиции** |
| Gross fixed investment | 297.1 | 305.9 | 1,079.8 | 32,897 | 491,957 | 1,303,166 | Валовое накопление основного капитала |
| Change in stocks | 92.1 | -223.2 | -5,424.8 | 1,325 | -205,067 | 782,166 | Изменения в запасах (МОС) |
| **Resource balance (net exports of GNFS)** | 67.7 | 118.9 | 7,617.5 | -29,148 | -286,154 | -1,206,625 | **Сальдо ресурсов (чистый экспорт ТНФУ)** |
| Exports of goods and nonfactor services | 643.0 | 1,219.9 | 20,775.6 | 90,216 | 1,196,712 | 3,041,751 | Экспорт товаров и нефакторных услуг |
| Imports of goods and nonfactor services | 575.2 | 1,101.0 | 13,158.1 | 119,364 | 1,482,866 | 4,248,376 | Импорт товаров и нефакторных услуг |

**TABLE 2-1A. Distribution of gross domestic product at current prices (percent)**
**ТАБЛИЦА 2-1А. Распределение валового внутреннего продукта в текущих ценах ( % )**

| Sector of origin or expenditure category | 1990 | 1991 | 1992 | 1993 | 1994 | 1995 | Отраслевое происхождение или вид расходов |
|---|---|---|---|---|---|---|---|
| **Gross domestic product by sector of origin** | | | | | | | **ВВП по отраслевому происхождению** |
| **Agriculture and forestry** | 26.5 | 30.5 | 26.1 | 27.1 | 33.7 | 26.8 | **Сельское и лесное хозяйство** |
| Agriculture | 26.4 | 30.5 | 25.9 | 26.9 | 33.5 | 26.8 | Сельское хозяйство |
| Forestry | 0.1 | 0.1 | 0.2 | 0.2 | 0.1 | 0.1 | Лесное хозяйство |
| **Industry and construction** | 30.4 | 29.9 | 36.7 | 32.4 | 24.9 | 24.4 | **Промышленность и строительство** |
| Industry | 22.0 | 23.6 | 29.4 | 24.9 | 17.2 | 21.8 | Промышленность |
| Construction | 8.4 | 6.3 | 7.3 | 7.5 | 7.7 | 2.6 | Строительство |
| **Other** | 34.4 | 33.9 | 31.2 | 42.0 | 44.5 | 49.4 | **Другие отрасли** |
| Transport | 6.7 | 5.1 | 4.3 | 6.4 | 11.3 | 23.9 | Транспорт |
| Road maintenance | .. | 0.5 | 0.2 | 0.2 | 0.2 | 0.3 | Дорожное хозяйство |
| Communication | 1.0 | 0.6 | 0.7 | 1.4 | 1.3 | 1.0 | Связь |
| Wholesale trade | 0.3 | 0.2 | 0.1 | 0.2 | 0.5 | 3.9 | Оптовая торговля |
| Retail trade and catering | 2.2 | 2.5 | 4.0 | 3.4 | 3.5 | .. | Розничная торговля и общепит |
| Material supply | 0.8 | 1.1 | 1.1 | 1.5 | 2.3 | 2.9 | Материально-техническое снабжение |
| Procurement | 0.5 | 0.5 | 0.5 | 0.2 | 0.2 | 0.1 | Заготовки |
| Information and computing services | 0.1 | 0.0 | 0.0 | 0.1 | 0.0 | 0.0 | Информационно-вычислительное обслуживание |
| Other sectors of material production | 0.9 | 0.9 | 0.3 | 0.4 | 0.2 | 0.3 | Другие отрасли сферы матерл. произ. |
| Housing | 1.9 | 1.4 | 0.9 | 0.7 | 1.1 | 0.7 | Жилищное хозяйство |
| Public utilities and personal services | 2.3 | 2.2 | 4.1 | 4.0 | 3.6 | 2.4 | Ком. хоз. и бытовое обслуживание |
| Health care, social security, physical culture and sports | 2.3 | 2.2 | 2.6 | 2.9 | 1.9 | 1.3 | Здравоохранение, социальное обеспечение, физкультура и спорт |
| Education | 5.0 | 5.7 | 6.3 | 6.1 | 5.6 | 3.6 | Образование |
| Culture and art | 1.2 | 0.6 | 0.6 | 0.6 | 0.9 | 0.6 | Культура и искусство |
| Science and scientific research | 1.2 | 0.8 | 0.2 | 0.6 | 0.6 | 0.4 | Наука и научное обслуживание |
| Credit | 0.2 | 0.2 | 2.4 | 6.8 | 5.8 | 4.1 | Кредитование |
| Insurance | 0.1 | 0.1 | 0.0 | 0.4 | 0.1 | 0.0 | Страхование |
| General administration and defense | 6.9 | 9.0 | 2.9 | 6.0 | 5.3 | 3.7 | Государственное управление и оборона |
| Private nonprofit institutions serving households | 0.2 | 0.2 | 0.0 | 0.1 | 0.0 | 0.0 | Общественные организации, обслуживающие домашние хозяйства |
| **Imputed service charge of financial intermediaries** | 0.0 | 0.0 | -2.5 | -6.4 | -5.1 | -3.6 | **Условно-исчисляемая стоимость услуг финансовых посредников** |
| **Total gross value added** | 91.3 | 94.3 | 91.4 | 95.1 | 98.0 | 97.1 | **Валовая добавленная стоимость - всего** |
| **Total GDP at factor cost** | 88.2 | 93.5 | 91.1 | 93.8 | 97.2 | 97.1 | **ВВП по фактор. стоимости - всего** |
| **Net indirect taxes** | 11.8 | 6.5 | 8.9 | 6.2 | 2.8 | 2.9 | **Чистые косвенные налоги (НПиИ-СПиИ)** |
| **Total GDP at market prices** | 100.0 | 100.0 | 100.0 | 100.0 | 100.0 | 100.0 | **ВВП в рын. ценах - всего** |
| **Gross domestic product by expenditure category** | | | | | | | **ВВП по видам расходов** |
| **Consumption** | 70.2 | 70.3 | 81.6 | 95.8 | 104.0 | 89.9 | **Потребление** |
| Private consumption | 61.4 | 60.7 | 74.3 | 81.5 | 88.2 | 77.2 | Личное потребление |
| Government consumption | 8.8 | 9.6 | 7.2 | 14.2 | 15.8 | 12.6 | Общественное потребление |
| **Gross domestic investment** | 26.5 | 3.1 | -18.0 | 21.8 | 15.9 | 19.7 | **Вал. внутр. инвестиции** |
| Gross fixed investment | 20.3 | 11.5 | 4.5 | 20.9 | 27.3 | 12.3 | Вал. накопление осн. капитала |
| Change in stocks | 6.3 | -8.4 | -22.5 | 0.8 | -11.4 | 7.4 | Изменения в запасах (МОС) |
| **Resource balance (net exports of GNFS)** | 4.6 | 4.5 | 31.6 | -18.6 | -15.9 | -11.4 | **Сальдо ресурсов (чистый экспорт ТНФУ)** |
| Exports of goods and nonfactor services | 43.9 | 45.7 | 86.2 | 57.4 | 66.5 | 28.8 | Экспорт товаров и нефакторных услуг |
| Imports of goods and nonfactor services | 39.2 | 41.3 | 54.6 | 76.0 | 82.3 | 40.2 | Импорт товаров и нефакторных услуг |

**TABLE 2-2. Gross domestic product at constant prices (millions of national currency)**
**ТАБЛИЦА 2-2. Валовой внутренний продукт в постоянных ценах (млн. национальной валюты)**

| Sector of origin or expenditure category | 1990 | 1991 | 1992 | 1993 | 1994 | 1995 | Отраслевое происхождение или вид расходов |
|---|---|---|---|---|---|---|---|
| **Gross domestic product by sector of origin** | | | | | | | **Валовой внутренний продукт по отраслевому происхождению** |
| **Agriculture and forestry** | .. | .. | .. | 5,259 | 37,114 | 575,819 | **Сельское и лесное хозяйство** |
| Agriculture | .. | .. | .. | 5,223 | 36,837 | 573,850 | Сельское хозяйство |
| Forestry | .. | .. | .. | 36 | 277 | 1,969 | Лесное хозяйство |
| **Industry and construction** | .. | .. | .. | 6,621 | 37,092 | 293,384 | **Промышленность и строительство** |
| Industry | .. | .. | .. | 5,564 | 29,463 | 243,411 | Промышленность |
| Construction | .. | .. | .. | 1,057 | 7,629 | 49,973 | Строительство |
| **Other** | .. | .. | .. | 6,486 | 59,508 | 653,120 | **Другие отрасли** |
| Transport | .. | .. | .. | 794 | 10,982 | 178,687 | Транспорт |
| Road maintenance | .. | .. | .. | .. | .. | .. | Дорожное хозяйство |
| Communication | .. | .. | .. | .. | .. | .. | Связь |
| Wholesale trade | .. | .. | .. | 538 | 3,871 | 74,580 | Оптовая торговля |
| Retail trade and catering | .. | .. | .. | .. | .. | .. | Розничная торговля и общепит |
| Material supply | .. | .. | .. | 284 | 1,725 | 32,458 | Материально-техническое снабжение |
| Procurement | .. | .. | .. | 52 | 309 | 3,142 | Заготовки |
| Information and computing services | .. | .. | .. | 6 | 78 | 276 | Информационно-вычислительное обслуживание |
| Other sectors of material production | .. | .. | .. | 37 | 478 | 3,160 | Другие отрасли сферы материального пр. |
| Housing | .. | .. | .. | 114 | 854 | 15,644 | Жилищное хозяйство |
| Public utilities and personal services | .. | .. | .. | 924 | 5,614 | 51,130 | Ком. хоз. и бытовое обслуживание |
| Health care, social security, and sports | .. | .. | .. | 637 | 3,417 | 27,989 | Здравоохранение, социальное обеспечение, физкультура и спорт |
| Education | .. | .. | .. | 1,518 | 9,563 | 81,715 | Образование |
| Culture and art | .. | .. | .. | 106 | 843 | 12,600 | Культура и искусство |
| Science and research | .. | .. | .. | 18 | 824 | 9,354 | Наука и научное обслуживание |
| Credit | .. | .. | .. | 657 | 11,334 | 84,634 | Кредитование |
| Insurance | .. | .. | .. | .. | .. | .. | Страхование |
| General administration and defense | .. | .. | .. | 793 | 9,462 | 77,284 | Государственное управление и оборона |
| Private nonprofit institutions serving households | .. | .. | .. | 8 | 154 | 467 | Общественные организации, обслуживающие домашние хозяйства |
| **Imputed service charge of financial intermediaries** | .. | .. | .. | -702 | -9,910 | -75,290 | **Условно-исчисляемая стоимость услуг финансовых посредников** |
| **Total gross value added (GVA)** | .. | .. | .. | 17,664 | 123,804 | 1,447,033 | **Валовая добавленная стоимость (ВДС) -** |
| **Total GDP at factor cost (GVA-OTOP+OSOP)** | .. | .. | .. | .. | .. | .. | **Всего ВВП по фактр. стоимости (ВДС-ДНП+ДСП)** |
| **Net indirect taxes (TOPI - SOPI)** | .. | .. | .. | 869 | 2,404 | 44,032 | **Чистые косвенные налоги (НПиИ-СПиИ)** |
| **Total GDP at market prices** | 1,362 | 1,456 | 2,066 | 18,533 | 126,208 | 1,491,065 | **Всего ВВП в рыночных ценах** |
| **Gross domestic product by expenditure category** | | | | | | | **Валовой внутренний продукт по видам расходов** |
| **Consumption** | .. | .. | .. | 15,224 | 120,745 | 1,820,831 | **Потребление** |
| Private consumption | .. | .. | .. | 13,463 | 99,616 | 1,584,028 | Личное потребление |
| Government consumption | .. | .. | .. | 1,761 | 21,129 | 236,803 | Общественное потребление |
| **Gross domestic investment** | .. | .. | .. | 893 | 4,748 | 179,572 | **Валовые внутренние инвестиции** |
| Gross fixed investment | .. | .. | .. | 659 | 17,107 | 137,748 | Валовое накопление основного капитала |
| Change in stocks | .. | .. | .. | 234 | -12,359 | 41,824 | Изменения в запасах (МОС) |
| **Resource balance (net exports of GNFS)** | .. | .. | .. | -4,014 | -6,453 | -397,963 | **Сальдо ресурсов (чистый экспорт ТНФУ)** |
| Exports of goods and nonfactor services | .. | .. | .. | 10,144 | 86,692 | 1,003,216 | Экспорт товаров и нефакторных услуг |
| Imports of goods and nonfactor services | .. | .. | .. | 14,158 | 93,145 | 1,401,179 | Импорт товаров и нефакторных услуг |

## TABLE 2-2A. Growth rates of gross domestic product at constant prices (percent)
## ТАБЛИЦА 2-2A. Валовой внутренний продукт - темпы прироста в постоянных ценах ( % )



| Sector of origin or expenditure category | 1990 | 1991 | 1992 | 1993 | 1994 | 1995 | Отраслевое происхождение или вид расходов |
|---|---|---|---|---|---|---|---|
| **Growth rate by sector of origin** | | | | | | | **Валовый внутренний продукт по отраслевому происхождению** |
| **Agriculture and forestry** | .. | .. | .. | -16.3 | -12.8 | -5.0 | **Сельское и лесное хозяйство** |
| Agriculture | .. | .. | .. | -16.3 | -12.8 | -5.0 | Сельское хозяйство |
| Forestry | .. | .. | .. | -6.8 | -12.9 | -5.1 | Лесное хозяйство |
| **Industry and construction** | .. | .. | .. | -25.1 | -27.1 | -34.6 | **Промышленность и строительство** |
| Industry | .. | .. | .. | -21.4 | -24.7 | -21.4 | Промышленность |
| Construction | .. | .. | .. | -40.0 | -35.1 | -64.0 | Строительство |
| **Other** | .. | .. | .. | -13.7 | -9.8 | -18.5 | **Другие отрасли** |
| Transport | .. | .. | .. | -36.6 | -12.4 | -22.3 | Транспорт |
| Road maintenance | .. | .. | .. | .. | .. | .. | Дорожное хозяйство |
| Communication | .. | .. | .. | .. | .. | .. | Связь |
| Wholesale trade | .. | .. | .. | -46.5 | -32.9 | 3.0 | Оптовая торговля |
| Retail trade and catering | .. | .. | .. | .. | .. | .. | Розничная торговля и общепит |
| Material supply | .. | .. | .. | 10.7 | -24.7 | -21.4 | Материально-техническое снабжение |
| Procurement | .. | .. | .. | -55.7 | -21.1 | -15.9 | Заготовки |
| Information and computing services | .. | .. | .. | -2.4 | -21.5 | -21.1 | Информационно-вычислительное обслуживание |
| Other sectors of material production | .. | .. | .. | -48.3 | -24.5 | -21.4 | Другие отрасли сферы материального пр. |
| Housing | .. | .. | .. | -48.3 | -23.0 | -19.4 | Жилищное хозяйство |
| Public utilities and personal services | .. | .. | .. | -5.4 | -11.0 | -21.5 | Ком. хоз. и бытовое обслуживание |
| Health care, social security, and sports | .. | .. | .. | 0.1 | -24.0 | -18.8 | Здравоохранение, социальное обеспечение, физкультура и спорт |
| Education | .. | .. | .. | 0.6 | 0.0 | -19.5 | Образование |
| Culture and art | .. | .. | .. | .. | .. | .. | Культура и искусство |
| Science and research | .. | .. | .. | -68.4 | -6.0 | -19.4 | Наука и научное обслуживание |
| Credit | .. | .. | .. | 14.9 | 0.5 | -19.4 | Кредитование |
| Insurance | .. | .. | .. | .. | .. | .. | Страхование |
| General administration and defense | .. | .. | .. | 15.4 | 0.5 | -19.5 | Государственное управление и оборона |
| Private nonprofit institutions serving households | .. | .. | .. | -28.9 | -30.0 | -9.3 | Общественные организации, обслуживающие домашние хозяйства |
| **Imputed service charge of financial intermediaries** | .. | .. | .. | 15.1 | -1.3 | -17.6 | **Условно-исчисляемая стоимость услуг финансовых посредников** |
| **Total gross value added** | .. | .. | .. | -19.8 | -17.1 | -18.0 | **Валовая добавленная стоимость (ВДС) - всего** |
| **Total GDP at factor cost** | .. | .. | .. | .. | .. | .. | **Всего ВВП по фактр. стоимости (ВДС-ДНП+ДСП)** |
| **Net indirect taxes** | .. | .. | .. | -59.6 | -75.3 | -11.6 | **Чистые косвенные налоги (НПиИ-СПиИ)** |
| **Total GDP at market prices** | .. | -0.7 | -22.6 | -23.1 | -19.7 | -17.2 | **Всего ВВП в рыночных ценах** |
| **Growth rate by expenditure category** | | | | | | | **Валовой внутренний продукт по видам расходов** |
| **Consumption** | .. | .. | .. | -22.5 | -19.7 | -2.8 | **Потребление** |
| Private consumption | .. | .. | .. | -24.9 | -22.2 | -0.3 | Личное потребление |
| Government consumption | .. | .. | .. | 1.2 | -5.6 | -16.6 | Общественное потребление |
| **Gross domestic investment** | .. | .. | .. | .. | .. | .. | **Валовые внутренние инвестиции** |
| Gross fixed investment | .. | .. | .. | -39.0 | -48.0 | -72.0 | Валовое накопление основного капитала |
| **Exports of goods and nonfactor services** | .. | .. | .. | -51.2 | -3.9 | -16.2 | **Экспорт товаров и нефакторных услуг** |
| **Imports of goods and nonfactor services** | .. | .. | .. | 7.6 | -22.0 | -5.5 | **Импорт товаров и нефакторных услуг** |

## TABLE 2-2B. Implicit price deflators for gross domestic product (percentage change)
## ТАБЛИЦА 2-2В. Дефляторы валового внутреннего продукта (темпы прироста в %)

| Sector of origin or expenditure category | 1990 | 1991 | 1992 | 1993 | 1994 | 1995 | Отраслевое происхождение или вид расходов |
|---|---|---|---|---|---|---|---|
| **Price deflators by sector of origin** | | | | | | | **Дефляторы по отраслевому происхождению или виду расходов** |
| **Agriculture and forestry** | .. | .. | .. | 709.3 | 1,532.8 | 392.7 | **Сельское и лесное хозяйство** |
| Agriculture | .. | .. | .. | 708.8 | 1,539.4 | 392.7 | Сельское хозяйство |
| Forestry | .. | .. | .. | 783.1 | 649.1 | 391.1 | Лесное хозяйство |
| **Industry and construction** | .. | .. | .. | 668.6 | 1,108.9 | 779.7 | **Промышленность и строительство** |
| Industry | .. | .. | .. | 603.2 | 950.9 | 847.7 | Промышленность |
| Construction | .. | .. | .. | 1,012.5 | 1,718.8 | 448.6 | Строительство |
| **Other** | .. | .. | .. | 917.5 | 1,246.4 | 699.4 | **Другие отрасли** |
| Transport | .. | .. | .. | 1,478.3 | 1,994.8 | 1,388.5 | Транспорт |
| Road maintenance | .. | .. | .. | .. | .. | .. | Дорожное хозяйство |
| Communication | .. | .. | .. | .. | .. | .. | Связь |
| Wholesale trade | .. | .. | .. | 972.3 | 1,770.4 | 454.1 | Оптовая торговля |
| Retail trade and catering | .. | .. | .. | .. | .. | .. | Розничная торговля и общепит. |
| Material supply | .. | .. | .. | 706.7 | 2,293.0 | 845.1 | Материально-техническое снабжение |
| Procurement | .. | .. | .. | 652.7 | 1,109.4 | 395.0 | Заготовки |
| Information and computing services | .. | .. | .. | 1,555.0 | 348.7 | 837.0 | Информационно-вычислительное обслуживание |
| Other sectors of material production | .. | .. | .. | 1,610.0 | 741.2 | 839.6 | Другие отрасли сферы матерл. произ. |
| Housing | .. | .. | .. | 872.8 | 2,173.5 | 357.1 | Жилищное хозяйство |
| Public utilities and personal services | .. | .. | .. | 582.6 | 1,060.7 | 399.9 | Ком. хоз. и бытовое обслуживание |
| Health care, social security, and sports | .. | .. | .. | 605.9 | 909.1 | 398.2 | Здравоохранение, социальное обеспечение, физкультура и спорт |
| Education | .. | .. | .. | 530.0 | 961.8 | 371.0 | Образование |
| Culture and art | .. | .. | .. | 858.9 | 1,759.2 | 435.6 | Культура и искусство |
| Science and research | .. | .. | .. | 4,771.7 | 1,308.4 | 407.8 | Наука и научное обслуживание |
| Credit | .. | .. | .. | 1,616.5 | 826.0 | 411.3 | Кредитование |
| Insurance | .. | .. | .. | .. | .. | .. | Страхование |
| General administration and defense | .. | .. | .. | 1,087.3 | 914.8 | 407.6 | Государственное управление и оборона |
| Private nonprofit institutions serving households | .. | .. | .. | 2,648.8 | 234.4 | 413.9 | Общественные организации, обслуживающие домашние хозяиства |
| **Imputed service charge of financial intermediaries** | .. | .. | .. | 1,330.9 | 822.1 | 398.4 | **Условно-исчисляемая стоимость услуг финансовых посредников** |
| **Total gross value added** | .. | .. | .. | 745.8 | 1,325.0 | 609.3 | **Валовая добавленная стоимость (ВДС) - всего** |
| **Total GDP at factor cost** | .. | .. | .. | .. | .. | .. | **ВВП по факторной стоимости (ВДС-ДНП+ДСП)** |
| **Net indirect taxes** | .. | .. | .. | 1,019.9 | 1,972.5 | 590.6 | **Чистые косвенные налоги (НПИ-СПИ)** |
| **Total GDP at market prices** | .. | 83.2 | 1,066.5 | 747.6 | 1,326.9 | 608.8 | **ВВП в рыночных ценах** |
| **Price deflators by expenditure category** | | | | | | | **Дефляторы по виду расходов** |
| **Consumption** | .. | .. | .. | 888.3 | 1,450.9 | 421.6 | **Конечное потребление** |
| Private consumption | .. | .. | .. | 851.4 | 1,495.0 | 415.3 | Личное потребление |
| Government consumption | .. | .. | .. | 1,170.5 | 1,243.0 | 463.4 | Общественное потребление |
| **Gross domestic investment** | .. | .. | .. | 3,732.3 | 5,942.3 | 1,061.3 | **Валовые внутренние инвестиции** |
| Gross fixed investment | .. | .. | .. | 4,892.0 | 2,775.8 | 846.1 | Валовое накопление основного капитала |
| **Exports of goods and nonfactor services** | .. | .. | .. | 789.4 | 1,280.4 | 203.2 | **Экспорт товаров и нефакторных услуг** |
| **Imports of goods and nonfactor services** | .. | .. | .. | 743.1 | 1,492.0 | 203.2 | **Импорт товаров и нефакторных услуг** |

## TABLE 3-1. Balance of payments at current prices (millions of U.S. dollars)
## ТАБЛИЦА 3-1. Платежный баланс в текущих ценах (в миллионах долларов США)

| Item | 1990 | 1991 | 1992 | 1993 | 1994 | 1995 | Статьи |
|---|---|---|---|---|---|---|---|
| Exports of goods and services (including workers' remittances) | .. | .. | .. | .. | 818.8 | 820.1 | Экспорт товаров и услуг (включая денежные переводы рабочих) |
| Exports of goods and nonfactor services | .. | .. | .. | .. | 818.8 | 784.7 | Экспорт товаров и нефакт. услуг |
| Merchandise (FOB) | .. | .. | .. | .. | 681.7 | 612.3 | Товары (ФОБ) |
| Nonfactor services | .. | .. | .. | .. | 137.1 | 172.4 | Нефакторные услуги |
| Shipment | .. | .. | .. | .. | 89.5 | 76.2 | Перевозки |
| Travel | .. | .. | .. | .. | 33.8 | 70.2 | Поездки |
| Other | .. | .. | .. | .. | 13.8 | 26.0 | Другие |
| Imports of goods and nonfactor services | .. | .. | .. | .. | 1,095.4 | 1,289.9 | Импорт товаров и нефакт. услуг |
| Merchandise (FOB) | .. | .. | .. | .. | 851.2 | 985.4 | Товары (ФОБ) |
| Nonfactor services | .. | .. | .. | .. | 244.2 | 304.5 | Нефакторные услуги |
| Shipment | .. | .. | .. | .. | 109.9 | 92.1 | Перевозки |
| Travel | .. | .. | .. | .. | 123.3 | 145.6 | Поездки |
| Other | .. | .. | .. | .. | 11.0 | 66.8 | Другие |
| Resource balance | .. | .. | .. | .. | .. | .. | Сальдо ресурсов |
| Net factor income | .. | .. | .. | .. | .. | .. | Чистый факторный доход |
| Factor receipts | .. | .. | .. | .. | .. | .. | Факторные поступления |
| Factor payments | .. | .. | .. | .. | .. | .. | Факторные платежи |
| Total interest due | .. | .. | .. | .. | .. | .. | Общая сумма процента к оплате |
| Other factor payments and discrepancy | .. | .. | .. | .. | .. | .. | Другие факторные платежи и стат. погр. |
| Net current transfers | .. | .. | .. | .. | 76.0 | 110.8 | Чистые текущие трансферты |
| Current receipts | .. | .. | .. | .. | 84.1 | 129.3 | Текущие поступления |
| Workers remittances | .. | .. | .. | .. | .. | .. | Денежные переводы рабочих |
| Other current transfers | .. | .. | .. | .. | .. | .. | Другие текущие трансферты |
| Current payments | .. | .. | .. | .. | 8.1 | 18.5 | Текущие платежи |
| Current account balance before official grants | .. | .. | .. | .. | .. | .. | Сальдо текущего счета до офиц. безвозмезд. трансфертов |
| Official capital grants | .. | .. | .. | .. | .. | .. | Официальные кап. безвозмезные трансферты |
| Current account balance after official grants | .. | .. | .. | .. | .. | .. | Сальдо текущего счета после офиц. безвозмезд. трансфертов |
| Long Term Capital Inflows | .. | .. | .. | .. | .. | .. | Долгосрочные притоки капитала |
| Direct investment | .. | .. | .. | .. | 21.6 | 154.7 | Прямые инвестиции |
| Net long term borrowing | .. | .. | .. | .. | .. | .. | Чистые долгосрочные займы |
| Disbursements | .. | .. | .. | .. | .. | .. | Поступления |
| Repayments due | .. | .. | .. | .. | .. | .. | Сумма, подлежащая погашению |
| Other long-term inflows (net) | .. | .. | .. | .. | .. | .. | Другие долгосрочные притоки (чистые) |

(continued on next page)

**TABLE 3-1. Balance of payments at current prices (millions of U.S. dollars)**
**ТАБЛИЦА 3-1. Платежный баланс в текущих ценах (в миллионах долларов США)**

| Item | 1990 | 1991 | 1992 | 1993 | 1994 | 1995 | Статьи |
|---|---|---|---|---|---|---|---|
| Adjustment to Scheduled Debt Service | .. | .. | .. | .. | .. | .. | Регулирование долга |
| Debt service not paid | .. | .. | .. | .. | .. | .. | Невыплаченный долг |
| Interest not paid | .. | .. | .. | .. | .. | .. | Невыплаченный процент |
| Principal not paid | .. | .. | .. | .. | .. | .. | Невыплаченная сумма основного долга |
| Arrears reductions/prepayments(-) | .. | .. | .. | .. | .. | .. | Погашение просроченных платежей/выплаты авансом (-) |
| | | | | | | | |
| Total Other items (Net) | .. | .. | .. | .. | .. | .. | Общие другие статьи (чистые) |
| Net short-term capital | .. | .. | .. | .. | .. | .. | Чистый краткосрочный капитал |
| Capital flows not elsewhere included | .. | .. | .. | .. | .. | .. | Потоки капитала, не указанные выше |
| Errors and omissions | .. | .. | .. | .. | .. | .. | Ошибки и пропуски |
| | | | | | | | |
| Changes in net reserves | .. | .. | .. | .. | .. | .. | Изменения в чистых резервах |
| Net credit from IMF | .. | .. | .. | .. | .. | .. | Чистый кредит МВФ |
| Reserve changes not elsewhere included | .. | .. | .. | .. | .. | .. | Изменения резервов, не указанных выше |
| Escrow account | .. | .. | .. | .. | .. | .. | Счет депонирования |
| | | | | | | | |
| Gross reserves (excluding gold) | .. | .. | .. | .. | .. | .. | Общие резервы (исключая золото) |
| Gross reserves (including gold) | .. | .. | .. | .. | .. | .. | Общие резервы (включая золото) |
| | | | | | | | |
| Nominal official exchange rate (annual average) (rf) | .. | 0.17 | 0.17 | 91 | 1,149.8 | 4,417.5 | Номинальный официальный или рыночный курс (среднегодовой) |
| Nominal official exchange rate (end-of-year) (ae) | 0.06 | 0.06 | 0.16 | 118 | 4,182.0 | 4,440.0 | Номинальный официальный или рыночный курс (на конец года) |
| Manufacture unit value (percent change) | .. | .. | .. | .. | .. | .. | Средний индекс цен на продукцию обр. пром.,% |
| Index of real effective exchange rate (IMF) | .. | .. | .. | .. | .. | .. | Индекс реального эффективного валютного курса (МВФ) |
| | | | | | | | |
| Total factor payments | .. | .. | .. | .. | .. | .. | Общая сумма факторных платежей |
| Government interest | .. | .. | .. | .. | .. | .. | Процент, выплачиваемый органами гос. управления |
| Private sector interest | .. | .. | .. | .. | .. | .. | Процент выплачиваемый частным сектором |
| Profits on direct foreign investment | .. | .. | .. | .. | .. | .. | Прибыль от прямых иностранных инвестиций |
| | | | | | | | |
| Official capital grants | .. | .. | .. | .. | .. | .. | Официальные капитальные безвозмездные трансферты |
| For budgetary financing | .. | .. | .. | .. | .. | .. | На бюджетное финансирование |
| To extrabudgetary entities | .. | .. | .. | .. | .. | .. | На внебюджетное финансирование |
| | | | | | | | |
| Government net long term borrowing | .. | .. | .. | .. | .. | .. | Чистые долгосрочные государственные займы |
| Disbursements | .. | .. | .. | .. | .. | .. | Поступления |
| Repayments | .. | .. | .. | .. | .. | .. | Погашения |
| | | | | | | | |
| Private net long term borrowing | .. | .. | .. | .. | .. | .. | Чистые долгосрочные частные займы |
| Disbursements | .. | .. | .. | .. | .. | .. | Поступления |
| Repayments | .. | .. | .. | .. | .. | .. | Погашения |

**TABLE 3-2A. Imports by commodity group (millions of U.S. dollars)**
**ТАБЛИЦА 3-2A . Импорт по товарным группам (млн. долларов США)**

| Commodity group | 1990 | 1991 | 1992 | 1993 | 1994 | 1995 | Товарные группы |
|---|---|---|---|---|---|---|---|
| TOTAL | .. | .. | 939.8 | 549.9 | 777.9 | 667.6 | ВСЕГО |
| I - Live animals; animal products | .. | .. | 32.0 | 8.0 | 42.2 | 74.3 | I - Живые животные и продукты животноводства |
| II - Vegetable products | .. | .. | 106.5 | 79.5 | 78.4 | 51.5 | II - Продукты растительного происхождения |
| III - Animal or vegetable fats and oils and their cleavage products; prepared edible fats; animal or vegetable waxes | .. | .. | 32.9 | 24.3 | 23.0 | 54.5 | III - Жиры и масла растительного и животного происхождения, воски |
| IV - Prepared foodstuffs; beverages, spirits and vinegar; tobacco and manufactured tobacco substitutes | .. | .. | 40.4 | 29.6 | 61.4 | 96.8 | IV -Продукция пищевой промышленности, алкогольные и безалкогольные напитки, табак и его заменители |
| V - Mineral products | .. | .. | 66.2 | 108.9 | 259.3 | 100.8 | V - Минеральные продукты |
| VI - Products of the chemical or allied industries | .. | .. | 27.5 | 20.8 | 37.8 | 61.3 | VI - Продукция химической промышленности |
| VII - Plastics and articles thereof; rubber and articles thereof | .. | .. | 14.6 | 4.2 | 14.4 | 11.6 | VII - Пластмассы и изделия из них |
| VIII - Raw hides and skins, leather, furskins and articles thereof; saddlery and harness; travel goods, handbags and similar containers; articles of animal gut | .. | .. | 1.9 | 0.8 | 1.7 | 2.6 | VIII - Кожевенное сырьё, кожи, пушнина, меховое сырьё и изделия из них |
| IX - Wood and articles of wood; wood charcoal; cork and articles of cork; manufactures of straw, of esparto or of other plaiting materials; basketware and wickerwork | .. | .. | 17.2 | 3.2 | 6.0 | 5.1 | IX - Древесина и изделия из древесины, древесный уголь |
| X - Pulp of wood or of other fibrous cellulosic material; waste and scrap of paper or paperboard; paper and paperboard and articles thereof | .. | .. | 5.4 | 2.8 | 6.9 | 15.2 | X - Бумажная масса, бумажные и картонные отходы, макулатура, бумага, картон и изделия из них |
| XI - Textiles and textile articles | .. | .. | 52.4 | 16.0 | 18.1 | 11.4 | XI - Текстиль и текстильные изделия |
| XII - Footwear, headgear, umbrellas, sun umbrellas, walking sticks, seat sticks, whips, riding crops and parts thereof; prepared feathers and articles made therewith; artificial flowers; articles of human hair | .. | .. | 25.0 | 4.3 | 7.0 | 1.9 | XII - Обувь, головные уборы, зонты, трости и пр. |

**TABLE 3-2A. Imports by commodity group (millions of U.S. dollars)**
**ТАБЛИЦА 3-2A . Импорт по товарным группам (млн. долларов США)**

| Commodity group | 1990 | 1991 | 1992 | 1993 | 1994 | 1995 | Товарные группы |
|---|---|---|---|---|---|---|---|
| XIII - Articles of stone, plaster, cement, asbestos, mica and similar materials; ceramic products; glass and glassware | .. | .. | 10.4 | 3.9 | 7.1 | 8.0 | XIII - Изделия из камня, гипса, цемента |
| XIV - Natural or cultured pearls, precious or semi-precious stones, precious metals, metals clad with precious metal and articles thereof; imitation jewellery; coin | .. | .. | .. | .. | 0.4 | 0.0 | XIV - Жемчуг, драгоценные и полудрагоценные камни, драгоценные металлы, бижутерия, монеты |
| XV - Base metals and articles of base metal | .. | .. | 36.5 | 30.6 | 97.4 | 42.0 | XV - Неблагородные металлы и изделия из них |
| XVI - Machinery and mechanical appliances; electrical equipment; parts thereof; sound recorders and reproducers, television image and sound recorders and reproducers, and parts and accessories of such articles | .. | .. | 32.9 | 24.2 | 78.9 | 82.9 | XVI - Машины, оборудование, механизмы, их части и принадлежности; звуковая и теле-аппаратура, их части и принадлежности |
| XVII - Vehicles, aircraft, vessels and associated transport equipment | .. | .. | 34.2 | 21.3 | 22.7 | 36.6 | XVII - Средства наземного, воздушного и водного транспорта |
| XVIII - Optical, photographic, cinematographic, measuring, checking, precision, medical or surgical instruments and apparatus; clocks and watches; musical instruments; parts and accessories thereof | .. | .. | 2.4 | 1.1 | 4.0 | 3.9 | XVIII - Приборы, аппараты оптические, медицинские, измерительные и пр.; музыкальные инструменты; часы; их части и принадлежности |
| XIX - Arms and ammunition; parts and accessories thereof | .. | .. | .. | .. | .. | 6.8 | XIX - Оружие и боеприпасы, их части и принадлежности |
| XX - Miscellaneous manufactured articles | .. | .. | 14.2 | 14.3 | 11.3 | 7.1 | XX - Разные промышленные товары |
| XXI - Works of art, collectors' pieces, and antiques | .. | .. | .. | .. | 0.0 | 0.0 | XXI - Произведения искусства, предметы антиквариата |
| XXII - Services | .. | .. | .. | .. | .. | .. | XXII - Услуги |

## TABLE 3-3A. Exports by commodity group (millions of U.S. dollars)
## ТАБЛИЦА 3-3А. Экспорт по товарным группам (млн. долларов США)

| Commodity group | 1990 | 1991 | 1992 | 1993 | 1994 | 1995 | Товарные группы |
|---|---|---|---|---|---|---|---|
| TOTAL | .. | .. | 1,483.9 | 724.6 | 636.8 | 547.4 | ВСЕГО |
| I - Live animals; animal products | .. | .. | 0.7 | 0.4 | 0.7 | 0.6 | I - Живые животные и продукты животноводства |
| II - Vegetable products | .. | .. | 7.1 | 14.5 | 14.5 | 13.3 | II - Продукты растительного происхождения |
| III - Animal or vegetable fats and oils and their cleavage products; prepared edible fats; animal or vegetable waxes | .. | .. | 0.8 | 0.0 | 0.1 | 0.3 | III - Жиры и масла растительного и животного происхождения, воски |
| IV - Prepared foodstuffs; beverages, spirits and vinegar; tobacco and manufactured tobacco substitutes | .. | .. | 83.2 | 21.2 | 48.7 | 24.4 | IV -Продукция пищевой промышленности, алкогольные и безалкогольные напитки, табак и его заменители |
| V - Mineral products | .. | .. | 701.1 | 210.3 | 217.7 | 283.3 | V - Минеральные продукты |
| VI - Products of the chemical or allied industries | .. | .. | 41.0 | 22.1 | 22.8 | 19.6 | VI - Продукция химической промышленности |
| VII - Plastics and articles thereof; rubber and articles thereof | .. | .. | 31.5 | 14.4 | 10.3 | 13.6 | VII - Пластмассы и изделия из них |
| VIII - Raw hides and skins, leather, furskins and articles thereof; saddlery and harness; travel goods, handbags and similar containers; articles of animal gut | .. | .. | 3.1 | 1.5 | 0.9 | 1.6 | VIII - Кожевенное сырьё, кожи, пушнина, меховое сырьё и изделия из них |
| IX - Wood and articles of wood; wood charcoal; cork and articles of cork; manufactures of straw, of esparto or of other plaiting materials; basketware and wickerwork | .. | .. | 7.4 | 4.7 | 0.5 | 0.3 | IX - Древесина и изделия из древесины, древесный уголь |
| X - Pulp of wood or of other fibrous cellulosic material; waste and scrap of paper or paperboard; paper and paperboard and articles thereof | .. | .. | 6.0 | 3.8 | 3.6 | 0.7 | X - Бумажная масса, бумажные и картонные отходы, макулатура, бумага, картон и изделия из них |
| XI - Textiles and textile articles | .. | .. | 100.0 | 71.6 | 114.4 | 124.5 | XI - Текстиль и текстильные изделия |
| XII - Footwear, headgear, umbrellas, sun umbrellas, walking sticks, seat sticks, whips, riding crops and parts thereof; prepared feathers and articles made therewith; artificial flowers; articles of human hair | .. | .. | 0.5 | 0.1 | 0.7 | 0.7 | XII - Обувь, головные уборы, зонты, трости и пр. |

**TABLE 3-3A. Exports by commodity group (millions of U.S. dollars)**
**ТАБЛИЦА 3-3A. Экспорт по товарным группам (млн. долларов США)**

| Commodity group | 1990 | 1991 | 1992 | 1993 | 1994 | 1995 | Товарные группы |
|---|---|---|---|---|---|---|---|
| XIII - Articles of stone, plaster, cement, asbestos, mica and similar materials; ceramic products; glass and glassware | .. | .. | 3.9 | 2.3 | 1.0 | 1.5 | XIII - Изделия из камня, гипса, цемента |
| XIV - Natural or cultured pearls, precious or semi-precious stones, precious metals, metals clad with precious metal and articles thereof; imitation jewellery; coin | .. | .. | .. | .. | 0.0 | .. | XIV - Жемчуг, драгоценные и полудрагоценные камни, драгоценные металлы, бижутерия, монеты |
| XV - Base metals and articles of base metal | .. | .. | 69.0 | 85.5 | 105.2 | 17.5 | XV - Неблагородные металлы и изделия из них |
| XVI - Machinery and mechanical appliances; electrical equipment; parts thereof; sound recorders and reproducers, television image and sound recorders and reproducers, and parts and accessories of such articles | .. | .. | 105.1 | 89.3 | 89.4 | 39.4 | XVI - Машины, оборудование, механизмы, их части и принадлежности; звуковая и теле-аппаратура, их части и принадлежности |
| XVII - Vehicles, aircraft, vessels and associated transport equipment | .. | .. | 4.0 | 3.8 | 4.4 | 4.4 | XVII - Средства наземного, воздушного и водного транспорта |
| XVIII - Optical, photographic, cinematographic, measuring, checking, precision, medical or surgical instruments and apparatus; clocks and watches; musical instruments; parts and accessories thereof | .. | .. | 0.0 | 0.0 | 1.2 | 1.8 | XVIII - Приборы, аппараты оптические, медицинские, измерительные и пр.; музыкальные инструменты; часы; их части и принадлежности |
| XIX - Arms and ammunition; parts and accessories thereof | .. | .. | .. | .. | .. | .. | XIX - Оружие и боеприпасы, их части и принадлежности |
| XX - Miscellaneous manufactured articles | .. | .. | 12.7 | 2.2 | 0.5 | 0.2 | XX - Разные промышленные товары |
| XXI - Works of art, collectors' pieces, and antiques | .. | .. | .. | .. | 0.0 | 0.0 | XXI - Произведения искусства, предметы антиквариата |
| XXII - Services | .. | .. | .. | .. | .. | .. | XXII - Услуги |

**TABLE 3-4A. Geographical distribution of foreign trade (millions of U.S. dollars)**
**ТАБЛИЦА 3-4А. Географическое распределение внешней торговли (млн. долларов США)**

| Country or country group | Exports / Экспорт 1990 | 1991 | 1992 | 1993 | 1994 | 1995 | Imports / Импорт 1990 | 1991 | 1992 | 1993 | 1994 | 1995 | Страна или группа стран |
|---|---|---|---|---|---|---|---|---|---|---|---|---|---|
| **Total trade** | .. | .. | 1483.9 | 724.6 | 636.8 | 547.4 | .. | .. | 939.8 | 549.9 | 777.9 | 667.6 | **Всего** |
| **CIS countries** | .. | .. | 729.6 | 373.7 | 274.1 | 217.7 | .. | .. | 607.2 | 308.4 | 485.9 | 228.4 | **Страны СНГ** |
| Armenia | .. | .. | .. | .. | .. | .. | .. | .. | .. | .. | .. | .. | Армения |
| Azerbaijan | .. | .. | .. | .. | .. | .. | .. | .. | .. | .. | .. | .. | Азербайджан |
| Belarus | .. | .. | 29.3 | 14.9 | 7.6 | 2.7 | .. | .. | 34.7 | 8.2 | 7.9 | 4.7 | Беларусь |
| Georgia | .. | .. | 61.1 | 30.6 | 16.6 | 41.5 | .. | .. | 18.4 | 18.4 | 8.0 | 18.9 | Грузия |
| Kazakstan | .. | .. | 38.7 | 30.5 | 16.5 | 16.8 | .. | .. | 42.5 | 35.1 | 51.9 | 17.6 | Казахстан |
| Kyrgyz Republic | .. | .. | 2.7 | 1.3 | 2.2 | 0.8 | .. | .. | 0.8 | 0.6 | 2.4 | 1.8 | Киргизстан |
| Moldova | .. | .. | 14.7 | 13.2 | 12.6 | 3.1 | .. | .. | 5.3 | 9.5 | 13.5 | 4.4 | Молдова |
| Russia | .. | .. | 347.6 | 185.2 | 139.7 | 98.9 | .. | .. | 25.5 | 127.0 | 117.5 | 88.3 | Россия |
| Tajikistan | .. | .. | 35.0 | 6.3 | 1.1 | 3.3 | .. | .. | 6.5 | 0.1 | 0.2 | 0.1 | Таджикистан |
| Turkmenistan | .. | .. | 55.1 | 39.3 | 17.1 | 13.2 | .. | .. | 26.6 | 54.6 | 95.6 | 51.4 | Туркменистан |
| Ukraine | .. | .. | 136.7 | 48.3 | 58.0 | 33.4 | .. | .. | 214.2 | 53.6 | 86.3 | 33.5 | Украина |
| Uzbekistan | .. | .. | 8.7 | 4.1 | 2.7 | 4.0 | .. | .. | 6.7 | 1.4 | 2.6 | 7.7 | Узбекистан |
| **Non-CIS countries** | .. | .. | 754.3 | 350.9 | 362.7 | 329.7 | .. | .. | 332.6 | 241.5 | 292.0 | 439.2 | **Остальной мир** |
| **Europe** | .. | .. | .. | .. | .. | .. | .. | .. | .. | .. | .. | .. | **Европа** |
| Austria | .. | .. | 33.6 | 5.6 | 9.5 | 3.5 | .. | .. | 8.3 | 7.5 | 0.9 | 3.6 | Австрия |
| Belgium | .. | .. | 3.7 | 0.3 | 1.0 | 0.7 | .. | .. | 5.8 | 0.1 | 8.9 | 8.8 | Бельгия |
| Bulgaria | .. | .. | 5.4 | 2.2 | 0.3 | 0.8 | .. | .. | 2.7 | 1.7 | 1.3 | 7.0 | Болгария |
| Czech Republic | .. | .. | 14.8 | 3.5 | 0.2 | 0.1 | .. | .. | 6.8 | 1.2 | 0.7 | 3.3 | Чешская Республика |
| Denmark | .. | .. | 4.8 | .. | .. | .. | .. | .. | .. | 0.0 | 0.5 | 3.7 | Дания |
| Estonia | .. | .. | 3.3 | 4.6 | 0.2 | 0.2 | .. | .. | 1.4 | 5.4 | 2.7 | 3.8 | Эстония |
| Finland | .. | .. | 1.0 | 5.5 | 3.6 | .. | .. | .. | 0.0 | 0.0 | 7.3 | 1.5 | Финляндия |
| Former Yugoslavia | .. | .. | 0.9 | 0.0 | .. | 0.2 | .. | .. | 3.3 | 0.3 | 0.2 | 0.6 | Быв. Югославия |
| France | .. | .. | 1.5 | 2.0 | 1.0 | 0.1 | .. | .. | 26.8 | 1.4 | 5.6 | 5.7 | Франция |
| Germany | .. | .. | 12.9 | 4.3 | 4.1 | 3.9 | .. | .. | 9.6 | 18.8 | 32.0 | 43.8 | Германия |
| Hungary | .. | .. | 5.7 | 0.8 | 0.4 | 0.3 | .. | .. | 4.4 | 1.3 | 4.1 | 1.6 | Венгрия |
| Iceland | .. | .. | .. | .. | .. | .. | .. | .. | .. | .. | .. | .. | Исландия |
| Ireland | .. | .. | .. | .. | 1.2 | .. | .. | .. | 4.8 | 4.6 | 1.4 | 0.3 | Ирландия |
| Italy | .. | .. | 19.0 | 13.3 | 0.1 | 26.5 | .. | .. | 4.8 | 8.7 | 3.9 | 2.5 | Италия |
| Latvia | .. | .. | 8.1 | 4.2 | 3.4 | 1.0 | .. | .. | 0.2 | 2.4 | 4.9 | 4.0 | Латвия |
| Lithuania | .. | .. | 5.2 | 6.2 | 3.7 | 6.4 | .. | .. | 1.8 | 5.0 | 4.7 | 4.5 | Литва |
| Netherlands | .. | .. | 0.2 | 0.1 | 0.0 | 0.0 | .. | .. | 3.0 | 1.2 | 1.3 | 3.2 | Нидерланды |
| Norway | .. | .. | .. | .. | .. | .. | .. | .. | 0.8 | .. | .. | 0.0 | Норвегия |
| Poland | .. | .. | 6.0 | 5.7 | 4.3 | 0.4 | .. | .. | 24.6 | 6.1 | 2.5 | 7.7 | Польша |
| Romania | .. | .. | 0.1 | 0.1 | .. | 0.1 | .. | .. | 0.0 | 0.0 | 0.2 | 0.3 | Румыния |
| Slovak Republic | .. | .. | .. | .. | .. | .. | .. | .. | .. | .. | .. | .. | Словацская Республика |
| Spain | .. | .. | 0.2 | .. | .. | 0.5 | .. | .. | 0.5 | 0.2 | .. | 0.9 | Испания |
| Sweden | .. | .. | .. | .. | 0.7 | 0.1 | .. | .. | 0.5 | 0.2 | 0.9 | 0.4 | Швеция |
| Switzerland | .. | .. | 2.4 | 3.2 | 4.0 | 28.3 | .. | .. | 0.7 | 9.7 | 2.4 | 3.3 | Швейцария |
| United Kingdom | .. | .. | 144.9 | 2.9 | 61.7 | 48.6 | .. | .. | 41.4 | 5.3 | 6.9 | 9.3 | Великобритания |

**TABLE 3-4A. Geographical distribution of foreign trade (millions of U.S. dollars)**
**ТАБЛИЦА 3-4А. Географическое распределение внешней торговли (млн. долларов США)**

| Country or country group | Exports Экспорт 1990 | 1991 | 1992 | 1993 | 1994 | 1995 | Imports Импорт 1990 | 1991 | 1992 | 1993 | 1994 | 1995 | Страна или группа стран |
|---|---|---|---|---|---|---|---|---|---|---|---|---|---|
| Other Europe | .. | .. | .. | .. | .. | .. | .. | .. | .. | .. | .. | .. | Остальные стараны Европы |
| **Asia** | .. | .. | .. | .. | .. | .. | .. | .. | .. | .. | .. | .. | **Азия** |
| Afghanistan | .. | .. | 4.0 | 2.5 | 1.1 | 0.4 | .. | .. | 2.3 | 2.4 | 1.2 | 0.1 | Афганистан |
| China | .. | .. | 0.3 | .. | 0.3 | 1.8 | .. | .. | 0.1 | 2.9 | 2.5 | 2.8 | Китай |
| India | .. | .. | .. | .. | .. | 0.0 | .. | .. | 0.4 | 0.2 | 0.8 | 0.5 | Индия |
| Iraq | .. | .. | .. | .. | .. | 0.1 | .. | .. | .. | .. | .. | .. | Ирак |
| Japan | .. | .. | 0.6 | .. | 0.1 | .. | .. | .. | .. | 0.3 | 0.2 | 1.3 | Япония |
| Korea, Dem. People's Rep. | .. | .. | 0.0 | 0.0 | .. | .. | .. | .. | 0.0 | 0.4 | 0.1 | 0.1 | КНДР |
| Korea, Rep. of | .. | .. | .. | .. | .. | .. | .. | .. | .. | .. | 14.2 | 2.4 | Южная Корея |
| Mongolia | .. | .. | 0.0 | .. | .. | .. | .. | .. | .. | .. | .. | .. | МНР |
| Syrian Arab Republic | .. | .. | .. | .. | .. | 0.1 | .. | .. | .. | 0.0 | 0.0 | 0.2 | Сирия |
| Turkey | .. | .. | 125.6 | 60.6 | 16.5 | 26.4 | .. | .. | 87.1 | 63.6 | 76.0 | 140.5 | Турция |
| Viet Nam | .. | .. | 0.0 | 0.1 | .. | 0.2 | .. | .. | 0.1 | 0.3 | .. | .. | Вьетнам |
| Other Asia | .. | .. | .. | .. | .. | .. | .. | .. | .. | .. | .. | .. | Остальные страны Азии |
| **America** | .. | .. | 39.5 | 3.4 | 0.0 | 1.1 | .. | .. | 27.2 | 22.0 | 11.6 | 14.1 | **Сев. и Южная Америка** |
| Canada | .. | .. | .. | .. | .. | .. | .. | .. | 2.1 | 0.1 | 0.0 | 0.7 | Канада |
| Cuba | .. | .. | .. | .. | .. | .. | .. | .. | .. | 0.0 | .. | .. | Куба |
| United States | .. | .. | 39.5 | 3.4 | 0.0 | 1.1 | .. | .. | 23.6 | 10.8 | 10.0 | 13.3 | США |
| Other America | .. | .. | .. | .. | .. | .. | .. | .. | 1.5 | 11.1 | 1.6 | 0.1 | Остальные |
| **Africa** | .. | .. | 0.9 | 0.0 | .. | 1.0 | .. | .. | 1.8 | 14.0 | 1.7 | 1.4 | **Африка** |
| Egypt | .. | .. | .. | .. | .. | .. | .. | .. | 1.7 | 0.1 | 0.0 | .. | Египет |
| Libya | .. | .. | .. | .. | .. | .. | .. | .. | .. | .. | .. | .. | Ливия |
| Other Africa | .. | .. | 0.9 | 0.0 | .. | 1.0 | .. | .. | 0.1 | 13.9 | 1.7 | .. | Остальные |
| **Rest of the World** | .. | .. | .. | .. | .. | .. | .. | .. | .. | .. | .. | .. | **Прочие страны мира** |
| Australia | .. | .. | 1.9 | 0.5 | 0.7 | 0.9 | .. | .. | 0.0 | .. | 0.3 | .. | Австралия |

## TABLE 4-1. General government budget revenue (millions of national currency)
## ТАБЛИЦА 4-1. Доходы государственного бюджета (млн. национальной валюты)

| Type of revenue | 1990 | 1991 | 1992 | 1993 | 1994 | 1995 | Вид доходов |
|---|---|---|---|---|---|---|---|
| **Total revenue and grants** | 482 | 1,044 | 7,275 | 53,596 | 477,156 | 1,816,700 | **Всего доходов и безвозм. поступл.** |
| Grants | 78 | 364 | .. | .. | .. | 232,000 | Безвозмездные поступления |
| Total Revenue | 405 | 680 | 7,275 | 53,596 | 477,156 | 1,584,700 | Всего доходов |
| **Current revenue** | 405 | 680 | 7,275 | 53,596 | 477,156 | .. | **Текущие доходы** |
| Tax revenue | 301 | 504 | 5,105 | 36,030 | 223,408 | .. | Доход от налогов |
| Taxes on income and profits | 106 | 191 | 1,798 | 16,745 | 123,875 | 541,000 | Налоги на доходы и прибыль |
| Individual | 23 | 60 | 454 | 3,758 | 35,212 | 114,000 | Физические лица |
| Corporate | 83 | 131 | 1,345 | 12,986 | 88,663 | 427,000 | Предприятия и организации |
| Social security contributions | .. | .. | .. | .. | .. | .. | Отчисление на соцстрах. |
| Taxes on payroll or work force | .. | | .. | .. | .. | .. | Налоги на заработную плату и рабочую силу |
| Taxes on the use of labor force | .. | .. | .. | .. | .. | .. | Плата за трудовые ресурсы |
| Taxes on increases in wages and salaries | .. | .. | .. | .. | .. | .. | Налог с прироста средств на оплату труда |
| Other payroll/work force taxes | .. | .. | .. | .. | .. | .. | Другие налоги на зарплату и рабочую силу |
| Taxes on property | .. | .. | .. | .. | .. | .. | Налоги на собственность |
| Taxes on immovable property | .. | .. | .. | .. | .. | .. | Налоги на недвижимое имущество |
| Buildings | .. | .. | .. | .. | .. | .. | Налог с владельцев строении |
| Land | .. | 1 | 18 | 336 | 2,179 | 4,000 | Земельныи налог |
| Estate, inheritance, and gift taxes | .. | .. | .. | .. | .. | .. | Налоги на наследство, подарки |
| Other property taxes | .. | .. | .. | .. | .. | .. | Другие налоги на имущество |
| Domestic taxes on goods and services | .. | .. | 2,184 | 12,507 | 64,426 | 153,100 | Внутренние налоги на товары и услуги |
| General sales, turnover, or value-added taxes | .. | .. | 2,184 | 6,349 | 32,829 | 89,000 | Налог с продаж. с оборота или на добав. стоим. |
| Excises | .. | .. | .. | .. | .. | .. | Акцизы |
| Profits of fiscal monopolies | .. | .. | .. | .. | .. | .. | Прибыли фискальных монополий |
| Taxes on specific services | .. | .. | .. | .. | .. | .. | Налоги на особые услуги |
| Taxes on use of goods or permission to use goods or to perform activities | .. | .. | .. | .. | .. | .. | Налоги на пользование товарами или лицензии на пользование товарами и занятие деятельностью |
| Other taxes on goods and services | .. | .. | .. | .. | .. | .. | Другие налоги на товары и услуги |
| Taxes on international trade and transactions | .. | 4 | 17 | 1,223 | 7,968 | 188,000 | Налоги на внешнюю торговлю и операции |
| Import duties | .. | .. | .. | .. | .. | .. | Импортные пошлины |
| Export duties | .. | .. | .. | .. | .. | .. | Экпортные пошлины |
| Other | .. | .. | .. | .. | .. | .. | Другие |
| Other taxes | .. | .. | .. | .. | .. | .. | Прочие налоги |
| Nontax revenue | .. | 67 | 465 | 1,740 | 2,646 | 142,500 | Неналоговые доходы |
| **Capital revenue** | .. | .. | .. | .. | .. | .. | **Капитальные доходы** |

## TABLE 4-2. General government budget expenditure by economic type (millions of national currency)
## ТАБЛИЦА 4-2. Расходы государственного бюджета по экономическим типам (млн. национальной валюты)



| Type of expenditure or debt holder | 1990 | 1991 | 1992 | 1993 | 1994 | 1995 | Всего расходов |
|---|---|---|---|---|---|---|---|
| **Total expenditure by economic type** | 482 | 964 | 6,907 | 64,796 | 669,805 | 2,377,600 | **Всего расходов по экономическим типам** |
| **Current expenditure** | 482 | 964 | 6,907 | 64,796 | 669,805 | 2,377,600 | **Текущие расходы** |
| Expenditure on goods and services | .. | .. | .. | .. | .. | .. | Расходы на товары и услуги |
| Wages and salaries | .. | 188 | 1,792 | 14,452 | 98,940 | .. | Заработная плата |
| Employer contributions | .. | .. | .. | .. | .. | .. | Отчисление на социальное страхование |
| Other Purchases of goods and services | .. | .. | .. | .. | .. | .. | Другие покупки товаров и услуг |
| Interest payments | .. | .. | .. | .. | .. | .. | Выплаты процентов |
| Domestic debt | .. | .. | .. | .. | .. | .. | По внутреннему долгу |
| Foreign debt | .. | .. | .. | .. | .. | .. | По внешнему долгу |
| Subsidies and other current transfers | .. | 140 | 629 | 6,605 | 51,568 | 232,000 | Субсидии на другие текущие трансферты |
| Subsidies | .. | .. | .. | .. | .. | .. | Субсидии |
| Agricultural subsidies | .. | .. | .. | .. | .. | .. | Субсидии на сельское хозяиство |
| Other current transfers | .. | .. | .. | .. | .. | .. | Другие текущие трансферты |
| Other | .. | 145 | 547 | 4,050 | 7,194 | 79 | Прочие расходы |
| **Capital expenditure** | .. | .. | .. | .. | .. | .. | **Капитальные расходы** |
| Acquisition of fixed capital assets | .. | .. | .. | .. | .. | .. | Приобретение основного капитала |
| Capital transfers | .. | .. | .. | .. | .. | .. | Капитальные трансферты |
| Other | .. | .. | .. | .. | .. | .. | Другие капитальные расходы |
| **Surplus/deficit (-)** | 0 | 80 | 368 | -11,199 | -192,649 | -560,900 | **Превыш. доходов над расходами/дефицит(-)** |
| **Financing by type of debt holder** | .. | .. | .. | .. | .. | .. | **Финансирование по типам кредиторов** |
| **Foreign (net)** | .. | .. | .. | .. | .. | 3,481,384 | **Зарубежные кредиторы (сальдо)** |
| From international development institutions | .. | .. | .. | .. | .. | 2,016,817 | Международные организации |
| From foreign governments | .. | .. | .. | .. | .. | 360,067 | Правительства иностранных государств |
| Other borrowing abroad | .. | .. | .. | .. | .. | 1,104,500 | Другие зарубежные кредиторы |
| **Domestic (net)** | 127 | 624 | 13,851 | 58,764 | 604,695 | 770,242 | **Внутренние кредиторы (сальдо)** |
| From monetary authorities | .. | .. | .. | .. | .. | .. | Органы денежного обращения |
| From deposit money banks | 127 | 624 | 13,851 | 58,764 | 604,695 | 770,242 | Депозитные денежные банки |
| Other domestic borrowing | .. | .. | .. | .. | .. | .. | Другие внутренние кредиторы |
| *Memo items:* | | | | | | | *Справочно:* |
| Extrabudgetary surplus/ Deficit (-) not included above | .. | .. | .. | .. | .. | .. | Превышение доходов над расходами/дефицит (-) по внебюджетным фондам, не включенным выше |
| Total surplus/deficit (-) including extrabudgetary accounts | 0 | 80 | 368 | -11,199 | -192,649 | -560,900 | Итого превышение доходов над расходами/дефицит, включая счета внебюджетных фондов |

## TABLE 5-3. Production and average yield of major agricultural crops
## ТАБЛИЦА 5-3. Производство и урожайность важнейших сельскохозяйственных культур

| Crop | 1990 | 1991 | 1992 | 1993 | 1994 | 1995 | Сельскохозяйственные культуры |
|---|---|---|---|---|---|---|---|
| **Production (thousands of tons)** | | | | | | | **Производство (тыс. тонн)** |
| Grain - Cleanweight | 1,414 | 1,291 | 1,285 | 1,100 | 988 | 881 | Зерно в чистом весе |
| Winter wheat | 877 | 900 | 900 | 805 | 701 | 597 | Пшеница - озимая |
| Spring wheat | .. | .. | .. | 1 | 1 | 1 | яровая |
| Coarse grain | .. | .. | .. | 1,148 | 1,039 | 921 | Зерно в физическом весе |
| Rye | .. | .. | .. | 1 | 3 | 1 | Рожь |
| Corn | 18 | 22 | .. | 14 | 14 | 12 | Кукуруза |
| Winter barley | 443 | .. | .. | 275 | 259 | 261 | Ячмень - озимый |
| Spring barley | 3 | .. | .. | 2 | 3 | 2 | яровой |
| Oats | 5 | .. | .. | 3 | 4 | 4 | Овес |
| Millet | .. | .. | .. | .. | .. | .. | Просо |
| Rice | .. | .. | .. | 1 | 1 | 4 | Рис |
| Flax | .. | .. | .. | .. | .. | .. | Лен |
| Oilseeds | .. | .. | .. | .. | .. | .. | Семена масличных культур |
| Cotton (raw) | 543 | 540 | 336 | 284 | 284 | 274 | Хлопок - сырец |
| Cotton fiber | 200 | 200 | 200 | .. | .. | .. | волокно |
| Sugarbeets | .. | .. | .. | 14 | 18 | 28 | Сахарная свекла |
| Potatoes | 185 | 180 | 156 | 152 | 150 | 155 | Картофель |
| Pulses | 12 | .. | 10 | 1 | 15 | 12 | Бобовые |
| Vegetables | 856 | 805 | 555 | 488 | 483 | 424 | Овощи |
| Fruit | 1,631 | 1,686 | 1,058 | 757 | 637 | 633 | Фрукты |
| Grapes | 1,196 | 1,126 | 607 | 411 | 314 | 309 | Виноград |
| Other | 435 | 560 | 451 | 346 | 323 | 324 | Прочие |
| Corn (silage and greenchop) | 900 | 800 | 600 | 462 | 360 | 182 | Кукуруза (на силос и зеленый корм) |
| Hay | .. | .. | .. | .. | .. | .. | Сено |
| **Average yield (kilograms per hectare)** | | | | | | | **Ср. урожайность (кг с га)** |
| Grain | 2,420 | 1,980 | 2,030 | 1,550 | 1,550 | 1,450 | Зерно |
| Winter wheat | 2,473 | 2,193 | 2,171 | 1,620 | 1,550 | 1,430 | Пшеница - озимая |
| Spring wheat | 1,449 | 916 | 1,100 | 790 | 720 | 860 | яровая |
| Coarse grain | .. | .. | .. | .. | 1,630 | 1,560 | Зерно в физическом весе |
| Rye | 1,668 | 1,318 | 1,469 | 880 | 1,340 | 1,370 | Рожь |
| Corn | .. | .. | 1,874 | 1,390 | 1,460 | 1,190 | Кукуруза |
| Winter barley | 2,466 | 1,955 | 2,025 | 1,490 | 1,650 | 1,590 | Ячмень - озимый |
| Spring barley | 927 | 676 | 949 | 500 | 900 | 670 | яровой |
| Oats | 1,514 | 1,536 | 1,829 | 1,200 | 1,340 | 1,120 | Овес |
| Millet | 476 | 247 | 319 | 70 | 640 | .. | Просо |
| Rice | 656 | 649 | 723 | 950 | 1,010 | 1,990 | Рис |
| Flax | .. | .. | .. | .. | .. | .. | Лен |
| Oilseeds | 3,519 | 2,335 | 2,059 | .. | .. | .. | Семена масличных культур |
| Cotton (raw) | 2,057 | 2,196 | 1,439 | 1,270 | 1,320 | 1,300 | Хлопок - сырец |
| Cotton fiber | 682 | 719 | 711 | .. | .. | .. | волокно |
| Sugarbeets | .. | .. | .. | 4,830 | 4,720 | 5,480 | Сахарная свекла |
| Potatoes | 7,779 | 8,013 | 8,270 | 7,810 | 8,260 | 9,750 | Картофель |
| Pulses | 1,947 | 1,835 | 701 | 3,050 | 3,600 | 2,036 | Бобовые |
| Vegetables | 19,959 | 18,896 | 16,691 | 15,800 | 15,350 | 15,710 | Овощи |
| Fruit | .. | .. | .. | .. | .. | 3,120 | Фрукты |
| Grapes | 7,646 | 7,534 | 4,585 | 3,250 | 3,050 | 3,260 | Виноград |
| Other | 3,231 | 4,376 | 3,675 | 3,090 | 2,980 | .. | Прочие |
| Corn (silage and greenchop) | 8,253 | 7,576 | 7,925 | 6,520 | 6,920 | 4,670 | Кукуруза (на силос и зеленый корм) |
| Hay | .. | .. | .. | .. | .. | .. | Сено |

## TABLE 5-4. Main aggregates of animal husbandry
## ТАБЛИЦА 5-4. Основные показатели животноводства

| Type of livestock or product | 1990 | 1991 | 1992 | 1993 | 1994 | 1995 | Направление животноводства или вид продукции |
|---|---|---|---|---|---|---|---|
| **Livestock (thousands of heads)** | | | | | | | **Поголовье скота (тысяч голов)** |
| Cattle | 1,832 | 1,826 | 1,731 | 1,621 | 1,633 | 1,682 | Крупный рогатый скот |
| of which: Cows | 711 | 734 | 735 | 712 | 743 | 772 | в том числе коровы |
| Pigs | 157 | 137 | 67 | 48 | 33 | 30 | Свиньи |
| Sheep and goats | 5,224 | 5,098 | 4,711 | 4,371 | 4,558 | 4,631 | Овцы и козы |
| of which: Goats | 195 | 194 | 190 | 168 | 184 | 210 | в том числе козы |
| Horses | 37 | 35 | 35 | 35 | 38 | 43 | Лошади |
| Other | 31 | 28 | 24 | 20 | 22 | 25 | Прочие |
| **Animal husbandry products** | | | | | | | **Продукция животноводства** |
| Meat (thousands of tons) | 176 | 154 | 113 | 93 | 84 | 76 | Мясо (тысяч тонн) |
| Beef | 74 | 63 | 50 | 44 | 43 | 38 | Говядина |
| Pork | 13 | 9 | 5 | 3 | 2 | 2 | Свинина |
| Lamb | 35 | 33 | 27 | 26 | 22 | 23 | Баранина |
| Poultry | 54 | 49 | 31 | 20 | 17 | 13 | Птица |
| Other | .. | .. | .. | .. | .. | .. | Прочие виды мяса |
| Milk (thousands of tons) | 970 | 948 | 850 | 799 | 784 | 827 | Молоко (тысяч тонн) |
| Eggs (millions) | 958 | 780 | 812 | 585 | 494 | 456 | Яйца (миллионов штук) |
| Wool (thousands of tons) | 11 | 11 | 10 | 10 | 9 | 9 | Шерсть (тысяч тонн) |

**TABLE 6-1. Industrial production by sector (millions of national currency)**

**ТАБЛИЦА 6-1. Промышленное производство по отраслям (млн. национальной валюты)**

| Sector | 1990 | 1991 | 1992 | 1993 | 1994 | 1995 | Отрасли |
|---|---|---|---|---|---|---|---|
| **All industry** | 1,369.8 | 2,745.8 | 25,118.5 | 123,012 | 1,137,755 | 8,855,950 | **Вся промышленность** |
| **Heavy industry** | 649.9 | 1,358.5 | 14,082.6 | 80,276 | 818,537 | 7,124,788 | **Тяжелая промышленность** |
| Fuel and energy | 193.7 | 507.4 | 6,854.7 | 36,490 | 570,898 | 5,794,943 | Топливно-энергетическая промышленноть |
| Electricity | 50.3 | 117.0 | 1,376.3 | 13,487 | 190,324 | 1,702,759 | Электроэнергетика |
| Fuels | 143.3 | 390.5 | 5,478.4 | 23,003 | 380,574 | 4,092,184 | Топливная промышленность |
| Ferrous and nonferrous metallurgy | 46.1 | 94.5 | 1,629.7 | 6,553 | 23,184 | 97,470 | Металлургия |
| Chemicals and petrochemical industry | 78.0 | 160.4 | 1,323.4 | 9,481 | 60,977 | 480,896 | Химическая и нефтехимическая пром. |
| Machine building and metalworking | 219.1 | 320.9 | 2,975.7 | 19,717 | 82,939 | 320,849 | Машиностроение и металлообработка |
| Forestry, woodworking, and pulp and paper in | 23.5 | 42.4 | 160.9 | 1,628 | 5,138 | 13,429 | Лесная, деревообрабатывающая и целлюлозо-бумажная промышленность |
| Construction materials | 37.9 | 64.3 | 411.6 | 6,172 | 34,164 | 135,361 | Промышленность строительных материалов |
| **Light industry** | 238.9 | 485.6 | 3,578.7 | 18,209 | 130,373 | 844,452 | **Легкая промышленность** |
| Textiles | 170.8 | 355.7 | 3,121.2 | 14,662 | 110,265 | 743,333 | Текстильная |
| Clothing | 43.6 | 86.6 | 262.4 | 2,092 | 11,847 | 59,757 | Швейная |
| Leather and shoes | 21.6 | 36.9 | 179.4 | 1,413 | 8,106 | 37,257 | Кожевенная и обувная |
| **Food industry** | 312.1 | 686.6 | 3,624.8 | 20,766 | 188,845 | 886,710 | **Пищевая промышленность** |
| Processed foods | 273.3 | 570.1 | 2,606.0 | 13,286 | 107,943 | 509,268 | Пищевкусовая |
| Meat and dairy products | 35.0 | 59.0 | 314.4 | 2,833 | 22,540 | 70,965 | Мясная и молочная |
| Fish | 3.8 | 9.3 | 42.0 | 186 | 1,517 | 6,630 | Рыбная |

**TABLE 6-2. Industrial production by sector in constant prices (bln. of national currency)**

**ТАБЛИЦА 6-2. Промышленное производство по отраслям в постоянных ценах (млрд. нац. валюты)**

| Sector | 1990 | 1991 | 1992 | 1993 | 1994 | 1995 | Отрасли |
|---|---|---|---|---|---|---|---|
| **Industrial production** | | | | | | | **Промышленное производство** |
| **All industry** | 18,589 | 19,499 | 14,878 | 13,837 | 10,696 | 8,856 | **Вся промышленность** |
| **Heavy industry** | .. | .. | .. | .. | .. | .. | **Тяжелая промышленность** |
| Fuel and energy | 9,123 | 8,885 | 7,277 | 6,862 | 6,238 | 5,795 | Топливно-энергетическая промышленноть |
| Electricity | 2,439 | 2,451 | 2,047 | 1,998 | 1,804 | 1,703 | Электроэнергетика |
| Fuels | 6,641 | 6,422 | 5,227 | 4,882 | 4,458 | 4,092 | Топливная промышленность |
| Ferrous and nonferrous metallurgy | 1,266 | 1,238 | 870 | 606 | 186 | 97 | Металлургия |
| Chemicals and petrochemicals | 2,073 | 2,154 | 986 | 861 | 573 | 481 | Химическая и нефтехимическая пром. |
| Machine building and metalworking | 836 | 917 | 714 | 683 | 494 | 321 | Машиностроение и металлообработка |
| Forestry, woodworking, and pulp and paper | 67 | 86 | 65 | 60 | 20 | 13 | Лесная, деревообрабатывающая и целлюлозо-бумажная промышленность |
| Construction materials | 309 | 343 | 329 | 331 | 214 | 135 | Промышленность строительных материалов |
| **Light industry** | 1,495 | 1,526 | 1,256 | 1,293 | 984 | 844 | **Легкая промышленность** |
| Textiles | 1,241 | 1,257 | 1,100 | 1,151 | 818 | 743 | Текстильная |
| Clothing | 122 | 133 | 126 | 124 | 108 | 60 | Швейная |
| Leather and shoe | 65 | 61 | 48 | 50 | 49 | 37 | Кожевенная и обувная |
| **Food industry** | 2,445 | 2,469 | 1,785 | 1,584 | 1,204 | 887 | **Пищевая промышленность** |
| Processed foods | 1,666 | 1,731 | 1,184 | 993 | 769 | 509 | Пищевкусовая |
| Meat and dairy products | 757 | 568 | 321 | 267 | 153 | 71 | Мясная и молочная |
| Fish | 39 | 37 | 23 | 12 | 10 | 6 | Рыбная |
| **Growth in production by sector (in percent)** | | | | | | | **Рост производства по отраслям** |
| **All industry** | .. | 4.9 | -23.7 | -7.0 | -22.7 | -17.2 | **Вся промышленность** |
| **Heavy industry** | .. | .. | .. | .. | .. | .. | **Тяжелая промышленность** |
| Power and fuels | .. | -2.6 | -18.1 | -5.7 | -9.1 | -7.1 | Топливно-энергетическая промышленноть |
| Electricity | .. | 0.5 | -16.5 | -2.4 | -9.7 | -5.6 | Электроэнергетика |
| Fuels | .. | -3.3 | -18.6 | -6.6 | -8.7 | -8.2 | Топливная промышленность |
| Ferrous and nonferrous metallurgy | .. | -2.2 | -29.7 | -30.3 | -69.3 | -47.8 | Металлургия |
| Chemicals and petrochemicals | .. | 3.9 | -54.2 | -12.7 | -33.4 | -16.1 | Химическая и нефтехимическая пром. |
| Machine building and metalworking | .. | 9.7 | -22.1 | -4.3 | -27.7 | -35.0 | Машиностроение и металлообработка |
| Forestry, woodworking, and pulp and paper | .. | 28.4 | -24.4 | -7.7 | -66.7 | -35.0 | Лесная, деревообрабатывающая и целлюлозо-бумажная промышленность |
| Construction materials | .. | 11.0 | -4.1 | 0.6 | -35.3 | -36.9 | Промышленность строительных материалов |
| **Light industry** | .. | 2.1 | -17.7 | 2.9 | -23.9 | -14.2 | **Легкая промышленность** |
| Textiles | .. | 1.3 | -12.5 | 4.6 | -28.9 | -9.2 | Текстильная |
| Clothing | .. | 9.0 | -5.3 | -1.6 | -12.9 | -44.4 | Швейная |
| Leather and shoe | .. | -6.2 | -21.3 | 4.2 | -2.0 | -24.5 | Кожевенная и обувная |
| **Food industry** | .. | 1.0 | -27.7 | -11.3 | -24.0 | -26.3 | **Пищевая промышленность** |
| Processed foods | .. | 3.9 | -31.6 | -16.1 | -22.6 | -33.8 | Пищевкусовая |
| Meat and dairy products | .. | -25.0 | -43.5 | -16.8 | -42.7 | -53.6 | Мясная и молочная |
| Fish | .. | -5.1 | -37.8 | -47.8 | -16.7 | -40.0 | Рыбная |

## TABLE 6-4. Final energy consumption (million tons oil equivalent) — AZERBAIJAN
## ТАБЛИЦА 6-4. Конечное потребление энергии ( млн. тонн нефтяного эквивалента )

| | 1991 | 1992 | 1993 | 1994 | 1995 | |
|---|---|---|---|---|---|---|
| **Final energy consumption** | .. | .. | .. | .. | .. | **Конечное потребление энергии** |
| Coal & Lignite | .. | .. | .. | .. | .. | Уголь каменный и бурый |
| Oil Products | 5.9 | 7.4 | 7.2 | 6.4 | 5.9 | Нефтепродукты |
| Gas | 16.8 | 10.2 | 8.7 | 8.1 | 5.3 | Газ |
| Electricity | 2.7 | 2.4 | 2.2 | 2.1 | 2.1 | Электроэнергия |
| Heat | 4.0 | 3.4 | 2.6 | 1.9 | 1.6 | Тепло |
| Other | .. | .. | .. | .. | .. | Другие виды |
| Of which: | | | | | | В том числе |
| **Industry** | .. | .. | .. | .. | .. | **Промышленность** |
| Coal & Lignite | .. | .. | .. | .. | .. | Уголь каменный и бурый |
| Oil Products | 3.0 | 4.0 | 4.2 | 3.5 | 3.4 | Нефтепродукты |
| Gas | 10.0 | 4.0 | 3.0 | 3.0 | 1.2 | Газ |
| Electricity | 1.8 | 1.5 | 1.3 | 1.3 | 1.2 | Электроэнергия |
| Heat | 3.3 | 2.8 | 2.1 | 1.6 | 1.3 | Тепло |
| Other | .. | .. | .. | .. | .. | Другие виды |
| **Agriculture** | .. | .. | .. | .. | .. | **Сельское хозяйство** |
| Coal & Lignite | .. | .. | .. | .. | .. | Уголь каменный и бурый |
| Oil Products | 0.6 | 1.5 | 1.2 | 1.0 | 0.9 | Нефтепродукты |
| Gas | 3.8 | 3.0 | 2.8 | 2.2 | 1.8 | Газ |
| Electricity | 0.6 | 0.6 | 0.6 | 0.5 | 0.5 | Электроэнергия |
| Heat | 0.3 | 0.3 | 0.2 | 0.1 | 0.1 | Тепло |
| Other | .. | .. | .. | .. | .. | Другие виды |
| **Transport** | .. | .. | .. | .. | .. | **Транспорт** |
| Oil Products | 1.8 | 1.5 | 1.3 | 1.2 | 1.1 | Нефтепродукты |
| Other | .. | .. | .. | .. | .. | Другие виды |
| **Households** | .. | .. | .. | .. | .. | **Домашние хозяйства** |
| Coal & Lignite | .. | .. | .. | .. | .. | Уголь каменный и бурый |
| Oil Products | 0.5 | 0.4 | 0.5 | 0.7 | 0.4 | Нефтепродукты |
| Gas | 3.0 | 3.2 | 2.9 | 2.9 | 2.3 | Газ |
| Electricity | 0.3 | 0.3 | 0.3 | 0.3 | 0.4 | Электроэнергия |
| Heat | 0.4 | 0.3 | 0.3 | 0.2 | 0.2 | Тепло |
| Other | .. | .. | .. | .. | .. | Другие виды |

## TABLE 7-1. Price indices and exchange rates
## ТАБЛИЦА 7-1. Индексы цен и обменный курс

| Year and month | National currency per U.S. dollar<br>Единиц нац. валюты за 1 доллар США | National currency per 100 Russian rubles<br>Единиц нац. валюты за 100 российских рублей | Consumer price index (as a percent of the previous month)<br>Индекс потребительских цен (в % к предыдущему месяцу) | Producer price index (as a percent of the previous month)<br>Индекс цен производителей (в % к предыдущему месяцу) | Consumer price index (as a percent of the previous December)<br>Индекс потребительских цен (в % к декабрю прошлого года) | Producer price index (as a percent of the previous December)<br>Индекс цен производителей (в % к декабрю прошлого года) | Год и месяц |
|---|---|---|---|---|---|---|---|
| **1993** | | | | | | | **1993** |
| January | .. | .. | 154.1 | 148.2 | 154.1 | 148.2 | Январь |
| February | .. | .. | 114.8 | 114.1 | 176.9 | 169.1 | Февраль |
| March | .. | .. | 112.3 | 125.7 | 198.7 | 212.6 | Март |
| April | .. | .. | 114.4 | 110.5 | 227.3 | 234.9 | Апрель |
| May | .. | .. | 126.5 | 105.4 | 287.4 | 247.6 | Май |
| June | .. | .. | 123.1 | 125.9 | 353.7 | 311.7 | Июнь |
| July | .. | .. | 109.7 | 113.1 | 387.9 | 352.5 | Июль |
| August | .. | .. | 113.0 | 112.5 | 438.1 | 396.6 | Август |
| September | .. | .. | 116.3 | 109.9 | 509.5 | 435.9 | Сентябрь |
| October | .. | .. | 122.0 | 148.1 | 621.8 | 645.6 | Октябрь |
| November | .. | .. | 136.2 | 194.5 | 847.3 | 1,255.6 | Ноябрь |
| December | .. | .. | 164.4 | 148.5 | 1,392.5 | 1,864.6 | Декабрь |
| **1994** | | | | | | | **1994** |
| January | 118.0 | 8.7 | 137.8 | 116.0 | 137.8 | 116.0 | Январь |
| February | 118.0 | 7.5 | 123.1 | 114.6 | 169.6 | 132.9 | Февраль |
| March | 174.2 | 10.0 | 124.9 | 128.1 | 211.8 | 170.3 | Март |
| April | 182.0 | 10.0 | 122.5 | 119.5 | 259.4 | 203.5 | Апрель |
| May | 1,100.0 | 58.8 | 143.3 | 117.1 | 371.9 | 238.3 | Май |
| June | 1,000.0 | 51.6 | 117.0 | 165.6 | 435.0 | 394.6 | Июнь |
| July | 980.0 | 48.0 | 111.5 | 193.4 | 485.1 | 763.2 | Июль |
| August | 1,200.0 | 56.0 | 105.9 | 103.6 | 513.7 | 790.7 | Август |
| September | 1,650.0 | 71.0 | 116.6 | 104.7 | 599.1 | 827.8 | Сентябрь |
| October | 2,200.0 | 73.4 | 133.5 | 238.6 | 800.0 | 1,975.2 | Октябрь |
| November | 3,300.0 | 103.1 | 152.0 | 168.8 | 1,215.9 | 3,334.1 | Ноябрь |
| December | 4,182.0 | 121.0 | 155.2 | 123.2 | 1,886.7 | 4,104.3 | Декабрь |

TABLE 7-1. Price indices and exchange rates

ТАБЛИЦА 7-1. Индексы цен и обменный курс

| Year and month | National currency per U.S. dollar<br>Единиц нац. валюты за 1 доллар США | National currency per 100 Russian rubles<br>Единиц нац. валюты за 100 российских рублей | Consumer price index (as a percent of the previous month)<br>Индекс потребительских цен (в % к предыдущему месяцу) | Producer price index (as a percent of the previous month)<br>Индекс цен производителей (в % к предыдущему месяцу) | Consumer price index (as a percent of the previous December)<br>Индекс потребительских цен (в % к декабрю прошлого года) | Producer price index (as a percent of the previous December)<br>Индекс цен производителей (в % к декабрю прошлого года) | Год и месяц |
|---|---|---|---|---|---|---|---|
| **1995** | | | | | | | **1995** |
| January | 4,290.0 | 109.0 | 127.8 | 127.6 | 127.8 | 127.6 | Январь |
| February | 4,375.0 | 102.0 | 112.5 | 210.3 | 143.8 | 268.3 | Февраль |
| March | 4,380.0 | 90.0 | 102.5 | 109.5 | 147.4 | 293.8 | Март |
| April | 4,405.0 | 87.0 | 105.6 | 124.4 | 155.7 | 365.5 | Апрель |
| May | 4,426.0 | 88.0 | 104.1 | 112.4 | 162.1 | 410.9 | Май |
| June | 4,453.0 | 99.0 | 99.4 | 113.3 | 161.1 | 465.5 | Июнь |
| July | 4,487.0 | 99.0 | 99.7 | 121.4 | 160.7 | 565.1 | Июль |
| August | 4,486.0 | 101.0 | 100.2 | 102.2 | 161.0 | 577.6 | Август |
| September | 4,435.0 | 99.0 | 105.4 | 104.7 | 169.6 | 604.7 | Сентябрь |
| October | 4,440.0 | 99.0 | 101.4 | 109.6 | 172.0 | 662.7 | Октябрь |
| November | 4,440.0 | 97.0 | 102.5 | 110.9 | 176.3 | 735.0 | Ноябрь |
| December | 4,440.0 | 95.0 | 104.7 | 101.0 | 184.6 | 742.3 | Декабрь |
| **1996** | | | | | | | **1996** |
| January | 4,445.0 | 95.0 | 102.1 | 102.3 | 102.1 | 102.3 | Январь |
| February | 4,438.0 | 92.0 | 103.1 | 101.8 | 105.3 | 104.1 | Февраль |
| March | 4,376.0 | 83.0 | 99.4 | 102.7 | 104.7 | 107.0 | Март |
| April | 4,363.0 | 85.0 | 100.5 | 100.9 | 105.2 | 108.0 | Апрель |
| May | 4,350.0 | 80.0 | 99.0 | 100.0 | 104.1 | 108.0 | Май |
| June | 4,315.0 | 82.0 | .. | .. | .. | .. | Июнь |
| July | 4,285.0 | 83.0 | .. | .. | .. | .. | Июль |
| August | 4,250.0 | 80.0 | .. | .. | .. | .. | Август |
| September | .. | .. | .. | .. | .. | .. | Сентябрь |
| October | .. | .. | .. | .. | .. | .. | Октябрь |
| November | .. | .. | .. | .. | .. | .. | Ноябрь |
| December | .. | .. | .. | .. | .. | .. | Декабрь |

## TABLE 7-2. Monthly nominal wages by sector
## ТАБЛИЦА 7-2. Среднемесячная денежная зарплата по отраслям

| Sector | 1990 | 1991 | 1992 | 1993 | 1994 | 1995 | Сектора |
|---|---|---|---|---|---|---|---|
| **Nominal wages** | | | | | | | **Средняя номинальная заработная плата** |
| **Economy average** | 19.5 | 31.8 | 270.3 | 2,184.7 | 15,325.3 | 58,702.8 | **По народному хозяйству** |
| **Material sphere** | 20.5 | 34.2 | 280.3 | 2,330.7 | 15,689.5 | 75,888.5 | **Отрасли сферы материального производства** |
| Industry | 21.9 | 40.0 | 388.3 | 3,109.2 | 21,009.0 | 95,556.7 | Промышленность |
| Construction | 29.1 | 45.3 | 367.5 | 3,277.8 | 22,366.2 | 98,872.5 | Строительство |
| Agriculture | 16.4 | 26.1 | 147.0 | 1,120.4 | 8,310.6 | 33,548.9 | Сельское хозяйство |
| Transport | 21.6 | 34.5 | 285.4 | 2,623.4 | 18,635.8 | 98,241.2 | Транспорт |
| Communications | 17.5 | 31.0 | 294.8 | 2,270.3 | 19,599.3 | 83,802.2 | Связь |
| Trade (retail and wholesale) | 15.1 | 22.9 | 162.8 | 1,163.8 | 7,647.1 | 37,518.7 | Торговля (оптовая и розничная) |
| Other | 14.9 | 26.0 | 173.4 | 1,644.4 | 8,129.6 | 60,572.0 | Прочие отрасли материального производства |
| **Nonmaterial sphere** | 17.3 | 26.9 | 252.1 | 1,945.9 | 13,396.8 | 44,429.8 | **Отрасли непроизводственной сферы** |
| Municipal services | 14.1 | 24.6 | 162.7 | 1,640.1 | 11,206.1 | 49,206.3 | Жилкомхоз и бытовое обслуживание |
| Science, research and development | 24.7 | 36.3 | 306.9 | 2,596.7 | 18,028.8 | 69,047.1 | Наука и научное обслуживание |
| Education | 17.7 | 25.6 | 257.1 | 2,021.6 | 14,038.3 | 46,412.3 | Образование |
| Culture | 12.5 | 29.3 | 202.5 | 1,502.0 | 10,480.5 | 33,442.6 | Культура |
| Arts | 17.6 | 33.7 | 165.7 | 1,376.8 | 7,751.6 | 24,161.2 | Искусство |
| Health care, social security, and sports | 13.2 | 22.7 | 240.6 | 1,294.0 | 9,982.6 | 26,303.6 | Здравоохр., соц.обсл., физк. и спорт |
| Banking, finance, credit, insurance | 27.1 | 61.4 | 675.7 | 6,431.0 | 33,316.8 | 169,063.8 | Кредитование, страхование, банк. дело |
| Government | 25.9 | 37.4 | 345.2 | 3,478.1 | 19,134.2 | 57,514.8 | Управление |

**TABLE 8-1. Money income and expenditure of the population (millions of national currency)**
**ТАБЛИЦА 8-1. Денежные доходы и расходы населения (млн. национальной валюты)**

| Type of income or expenditure | 1990 | 1991 | 1992 | 1993 | 1994 | 1995 | Вид доходов или расходов |
|---|---|---|---|---|---|---|---|
| **Income** | | | | | | | **Доходы** |
| **Total labor income** | 724 | 1,182 | 7,216 | 64,282 | 409,271 | 1,728,179 | **Всего трудовых доходов** |
| Regular wages | 562 | 880 | 6,112 | 56,521 | 352,531 | 1,431,830 | Заработная плата |
| Wages paid by cooperatives | 25 | 28 | 38 | 299 | 2,391 | 28,340 | Заработная плата в кооперативах |
| Other wages and compensation | 15 | 29 | 136 | 1,601 | 9,827 | 58,517 | Прочие доходы типа заработной платы |
| Income paid by collective farms | 77 | 126 | 510 | 3,224 | 29,243 | 146,350 | Доходы от колхозов |
| Income from sale of farm products | 70 | 148 | 458 | 2,936 | 17,670 | 91,482 | Доходы от продажи продукции колхозов |
| **Total transfer receipts** | 251 | 834 | 2,191 | 71,231 | 806,670 | 3,452,281 | **Всего трансфертных поступлений** |
| Pensions and allowances | 123 | 352 | 1,674 | 21,693 | 130,321 | 515,220 | Пенсии и пособия |
| Scholarships | 6 | 16 | 71 | 401 | 1,946 | .. | Стипендии |
| Income from the financial system (insurance, interest, etc.) | 81 | 276 | 169 | 524 | 16,673 | 2,937,963 | Доходы из финансовой системы (страховые возмещения, проценты и т.д.) |
| Other income | 42 | 192 | 277 | 48,613 | 657,731 | -902 | Прочие виды доходов |
| **Total income** | 975 | 2,017 | 9,407 | 135,513 | 1,215,942 | 5,180,460 | **Всего доходов** |
| **Expenditure** | | | | | | | **Расходы** |
| **Total purchases** | 677 | 1,225 | 5,913 | 83,739 | 833,156 | 4,230,990 | **Всего покупок товаров и услуг** |
| Retail goods | 607 | 1,126 | 5,182 | 75,984 | 767,699 | 3,654,375 | Товары в розничной торговле |
| Services | 71 | 100 | 731 | 7,755 | 65,457 | 576,616 | Услуги |
| Rent and utilities | 16 | 18 | 76 | 2,545 | 5,391 | 88,768 | Квартирная плата и коммунальные платежи |
| Transport and communications | 36 | 57 | 434 | 3,075 | 24,708 | 368,879 | Транспорт и связь |
| Health and other services | 16 | 21 | 172 | 2,071 | 34,038 | 45,772 | Здравоохранение и другие виды услуг |
| Cooperatives | 3 | 4 | 49 | 64 | 1,320 | 73,198 | Кооперативы |
| **Transfers and savings** | 253 | 650 | 1,670 | 13,130 | 133,187 | 569,099 | **Трансферты и сбережения** |
| Taxes, fees, dues, and other | 85 | 102 | 631 | 5,748 | 36,272 | 212,194 | Налоги, сборы, пошлины и др. |
| Savings | 153 | 535 | 995 | 7,382 | 78,065 | 54,977 | Сбережения |
| Other | 15 | 14 | 44 | 0 | 18,850 | 301,928 | Прочие |
| **Total expenditure** | 930 | 1,876 | 7,583 | 96,869 | 966,343 | 4,800,089 | **Всего расходов** |
| **Income less expenditure** | 45 | 141 | 1,824 | 38,644 | 249,600 | 380,371 | **Доходы за вычетом расходов** |

# *Country Notes: Azerbaijan*

**General notes:** Data were supplied by the State Statistical Committee of the Republic of Azerbaijan.

**Currency:** Unless otherwise indicated, data are in manats. The new national currency, manat, was introduced on January 1, 1994 with the conversion factor 1 manat = 10 rubles.

**Table 1-1:** The sums of employment categories do not equal the totals.

**Table 2-1:** In 1995, transport includes road maintenance; wholesale trade includes retail trade and catering; and credit includes insurance. The statistical discrepancy between total GDP by industrial origin at market prices and total GDP by expenditure category is as follows:

| Year | Statistical discrepancy (mln. manats) |
|---|---|
| 1990 | -20 |
| 1991 | 591 |
| 1992 | 1,172 |
| 1993 | 1,551 |
| 1994 | -72,583 |
| 1995 | 192,437 |

**Table 2-2:** Data are in previous year prices. Transport includes road maintenance; wholesale trade includes retail trade and catering; and credit includes insurance. The statistical discrepancy between total GDP by industrial origin and GDP by expenditure category is as follows:

| Year | Statistical discrepancy (mln. manats) |
|---|---|
| 1993 | 6,430 |
| 1994 | 7,168 |
| 1995 | -111,375 |

**Tables 3-2A and 3-3A:** Because of trade undistributed by categories, for most years the sums of exports and imports do not equal the totals.

**Table 3-4A:** Sums of trade flows do not always equal totals because of trade undistributed by country of origin.

**Table 6-2:** Data are in billions of 1995 manats. Discrepancies between the sums of components and the totals may be a result of rescaling.

**Table 7-1:** Exchange rates are shown for the end of the month. Data are from CIS Statistical Committee publications.

**Table 8-1:** In 1995, pensions and allowances include scholarships.

# Комментарии к таблицам: Азербайджан

**Общее замечание:** Данные были получены из Государственного Статистического Комитета Республики Азербайджан.

**Национальная валюта:** За исключением особо отмеченных случаев, данные приведены в манатах. Национальная валюта, манат, была введена 1 января 1994 г. с коэффициентом пересчета 1 манат = 10 рублей.

**Таблица 1-1:** Суммы занятых по категориям не равны приведенным итоговым величинам.

**Таблица 2-1:** В 1995 г. транспорт включает дорожное хозяйство, оптовая торговля включает розничную торговлю и общепит, кредитование включает страхование. Статистическое расхождение между ВВП по производству в рыночных ценах и ВВП по видам расходов составляет:

| Год | Статистическое расхождение (млн. манатов) |
|---|---|
| 1990 | -20 |
| 1991 | 591 |
| 1992 | 1172 |
| 1993 | 1551 |
| 1994 | -72583 |
| 1995 | 192434 |

**Таблица 2-2:** Данные приведены в ценах предыдущего года. Транспорт включает дорожное хозяйство, оптовая торговля включает розничную торговлю и общепит, кредитование включает страхование. Статистическое расхождение между ВВП по производству в рыночных ценах и ВВП по видам расходов составляет:

| Год | Статистическое расхождение (млн. манатов) |
|---|---|
| 1993 | 6430 |
| 1994 | 7168 |
| 1995 | -111375 |

**Таблицы 3-2А и 3-3А**: Из-за торговли нераспределенной по товарным группам, для большинства лет суммы объемов экспорта и импорта не равны соответствующим приведенным итоговым величинам.

**Таблица 3-4А:** Суммы объемов торговли не всегда равны приведенным итоговым величинам из-за торговли нераспределенной по странам.

**Таблица 6-2:** Данные приведены в миллиардах манатов в ценах 1995 г. Расхождения между суммами компонентов и приведенными итоговыми величинами могут быть результатом пересчета в эти цены.

**Таблица 7-1:** Валютные курсы приводятся на конец месяца. Данные получены из публикаций Статкомитета СНГ.

**Таблица 8-1:** В 1995 г. пенсии и пособии включают стипендии.

# Belarus / Беларусь

1996 Population / Численность населения в 1996 году
(thousands / тыс. человек.): 10,312

Area / Территория
(thousand square kilometers / тыс. кв. км.): 207.6

Capital city / Столица:
Minsk / Минск

**Country Tables:** Table 6-4 is not included because there are no recent data available.

**Статистические таблицы страны:** Таблица 6-4 не включена ввиду отсутствия данных за последние годы.

## TABLE 1-1. Population and employment (thousands)
## ТАБЛИЦА 1-1. Население и занятость (тысяч)



| Population or employment category | 1990 | 1991 | 1992 | 1993 | 1994 | 1995 | Население или группы занятых |
|---|---|---|---|---|---|---|---|
| **Total population** | 10,211 | 10,213 | 10,233 | 10,298 | 10,319 | 10,297 | **Население - всего** |
| Males | 4,784 | 4,788 | 4,801 | 4,837 | 4,849 | 4,807 | Мужчины |
| Females | 5,427 | 5,425 | 5,432 | 5,461 | 5,470 | 5,490 | Женщины |
| Urban population | 6,762 | 6,844 | 6,915 | 6,988 | 7,037 | 7,061 | Городское |
| Rural population | 3,449 | 3,369 | 3,318 | 3,310 | 3,282 | 3,236 | Сельское |
| Population under working age | 2,503 | 2,501 | 2,493 | 2,489 | 2,468 | 2,425 | Моложе трудоспособного возраста |
| Working-age population | 5,706 | 5,681 | 5,677 | 5,703 | 5,720 | 5,722 | Лица в трудоспособном возрасте |
| Population over working age | 2,002 | 2,031 | 2,063 | 2,106 | 2,131 | 2,150 | Старше трудоспособного возраста |
| Economically Active Population, in non-working age | 372 | 443 | 416 | 348 | 354 | 346 | Экономически активное население в нетрудоспособном возрасте |
| Above working age | 360 | 417 | 400 | 339 | 346 | 339 | Старше трудоспособного возраста |
| Below working age | 12 | 25 | 16 | 9 | 8 | 7 | Моложе трудоспособного возраста |
| **Total labor resources** | 5,966 | 6,025 | 6,008 | 5,925 | 5,917 | 5,906 | **Трудовые ресурсы - всего** |
| **Total employment** | 5,149 | 5,020 | 4,887 | 4,824 | 4,696 | 4,405 | **Занятое население - всего** |
| State sector employees | 3,806 | 3,557 | 3,176 | 3,045 | 2,810 | 2,637 | Государственный сектор |
| Leased enterprise employees | 259 | 323 | 387 | 389 | 301 | 249 | Арендные предприятия |
| Joint-stock company employees | 6 | 19 | 33 | 54 | 238 | 270 | Акционерные общества |
| Economic association employees | .. | 9 | 1 | 2 | 6 | 31 | Хозяйственные ассоциации |
| Social organization employees | 54 | 53 | 43 | 43 | 39 | 35 | Общественные организации |
| Joint venture employees | 3 | 8 | 14 | 18 | 23 | 27 | Совместные предприятия |
| Collective farm workers | 641 | 614 | 665 | 633 | 593 | 546 | Колхозы |
| Cooperative workers | 317 | 321 | 399 | 414 | 393 | 265 | Кооперативы |
| Individual labor activities | 11 | 19 | 56 | 115 | 179 | 223 | ИТД |
| Private subsidiary agricultural workers | 52 | 96 | 105 | 105 | 105 | 113 | Личные подсобные хозяйства |
| Private agricultural workers | .. | 1 | 8 | 6 | 9 | 9 | Фермерские хозяйства |
| **Students** | 428 | 415 | 421 | 408 | 407 | 406 | **Учащиеся** |
| **Religious workers** | 2 | 3 | 4 | 4 | 5 | 5 | **Служащие религиозного культа** |
| **Working age population not employed in the national economy** | 387 | 587 | 696 | 689 | 809 | 1,090 | **Лица в трудоспособном возрасте, не занятые в экономике** |
| Housewives | .. | .. | .. | .. | .. | .. | Домохозяйки |
| Military personnel | .. | .. | .. | .. | .. | .. | Военнослужащие |
| Unemployed | .. | 2 | 24 | 66 | 101 | 131 | Безработные |
| **Labor force** | 5,149 | 5,022 | 4,911 | 4,890 | 4,798 | 4,536 | **Рабочая сила** |

**TABLE 1-2. Employment by sector (thousands)**
**ТАБЛИЦА 1-2. Численность занятого населения по секторам (тысяч)**

| Sector | 1990 | 1991 | 1992 | 1993 | 1994 | 1995 | Сектор |
|---|---|---|---|---|---|---|---|
| **Material sphere** | 3,876 | 3,733 | 3,634 | 3,528 | 3,378 | 3,114 | **Сфера материального производства** |
| **Agriculture and forestry** | 1,007 | 959 | 995 | 970 | 917 | 870 | **Сельское и лесное хозяйство** |
| Agriculture | 985 | 937 | 976 | 945 | 892 | 844 | Сельское хозяйство |
| Forestry | 22 | 22 | 19 | 25 | 25 | 26 | Лесное хозяйство |
| **Industry and construction** | 2,163 | 2,084 | 1,970 | 1,845 | 1,735 | 1,518 | **Промышленность и строительство** |
| Industry | 1,593 | 1,566 | 1,489 | 1,430 | 1,365 | 1,216 | Промышленность |
| Construction | 570 | 519 | 481 | 415 | 370 | 302 | Строительство |
| **Other** | 705 | 690 | 669 | 713 | 726 | 726 | **Другие отрасли** |
| Transport of goods | 225 | 219 | 214 | 201 | 193 | 178 | Грузовой транспорт |
| Road Maintenance | .. | .. | .. | .. | .. | .. | Дорожное хозяйство |
| Communication servicing material production | 13 | 13 | 13 | 13 | 13 | 14 | Связь |
| Wholesale trade | .. | .. | .. | .. | 41 | 45 | Оптовая торговля |
| Retail trade and catering | 328 | 325 | 318 | 395 | 374 | 388 | Розничная торговля и общепит |
| Material supply | 40 | 39 | 43 | 34 | 32 | 28 | Материально-техническое снабжение |
| Procurement | 14 | 14 | 14 | 13 | 12 | 11 | Заготовки |
| Information and computing services | 17 | 14 | 12 | 9 | 7 | 6 | Информационно-техническое обслуживание |
| Other sectors | 68 | 67 | 55 | 48 | 54 | 56 | Другие отрасли сферы материального пр. |
| **Nonmaterial sphere** | 1,273 | 1,287 | 1,253 | 1,296 | 1,318 | 1,291 | **Сфера нематериального производства** |
| Passenger transport | 82 | 81 | 81 | 71 | 69 | 72 | Пассажирский транспорт |
| Communication | 45 | 45 | 45 | 45 | 43 | 46 | Связь |
| Housing | 60 | 61 | 55 | 62 | 56 | 54 | Жилищное хозяйство |
| Public utilities and personal services | 108 | 116 | 125 | 97 | 115 | 121 | Комм. хоз. и бытовое обслуживание |
| Health care, social security, physical culture and sports | 268 | 272 | 270 | 279 | 285 | 287 | Здравоохранение, социальное обеспечение, физкультура и спорт |
| Education | 434 | 432 | 424 | 420 | 423 | 418 | Образование |
| Culture and art | 74 | 73 | 68 | 71 | 69 | 70 | Культура и искусство |
| Science and scientific research | 103 | 101 | 79 | 60 | 53 | 46 | Наука и научное обслуживание |
| Credit | 29 | 30 | 31 | 34 | 41 | 46 | Кредитование |
| Insurance | .. | .. | .. | .. | .. | .. | Страхование |
| General administration and defense | 49 | 55 | 55 | 60 | 63 | 66 | Государственное управление и оборона |
| Private nonprofit institutions serving households | .. | .. | .. | .. | .. | .. | Общественные организации, обслуживающие домашние хозяйства |
| **Other, material and nonmaterial spheres** | 1,978 | 1,977 | 1,922 | 2,009 | 2,044 | 2,017 | **Остальные отрасли материального производства и нематериальной сферы** |
| **Total employment** | 5,149 | 5,020 | 4,887 | 4,824 | 4,696 | 4,405 | **Занятые - всего** |

**TABLE 1-3. Registered unemployment (thousands; end of month)**

**ТАБЛИЦА 1-3. Численность зарегистрированных безработных (тысяч; на конец месяца)**

| Year and m | Total Всего | Males Мужчины | Females Женщины | Receiving benefits Получающие пособие | Год и месяц |
|---|---|---|---|---|---|
| **1994** | | | | | **1994** |
| January | 72.5 | .. | .. | 36.8 | Январь |
| February | 76.7 | .. | .. | 40.3 | Февраль |
| March | 81.8 | 30.2 | 51.6 | 43.2 | Март |
| April | 85.6 | .. | .. | 45.9 | Апрель |
| May | 86.9 | .. | .. | 45.4 | Май |
| June | 88.0 | 32.4 | 55.6 | 45.3 | Июнь |
| July | 90.4 | .. | .. | 47.1 | Июль |
| August | 97.4 | .. | .. | 51.0 | Август |
| September | 99.5 | 36.2 | 63.3 | 52.0 | Сентябрь |
| October | 99.8 | .. | .. | 51.5 | Октябрь |
| November | 101.5 | .. | .. | 51.6 | Нолбрь |
| December | 101.2 | 36.7 | 64.5 | 52.2 | Декабрь |
| **1995** | | | | | **1995** |
| January | 107.0 | .. | .. | 54.4 | Январь |
| February | 108.9 | .. | .. | 56.1 | Февраль |
| March | 109.2 | 41.4 | 67.8 | 56.1 | Март |
| April | 109.2 | .. | .. | 56.1 | Апрель |
| May | 109.7 | .. | .. | 55.5 | Май |
| June | 111.2 | 41.2 | 70.0 | 55.1 | Июнь |
| July | 114.9 | .. | .. | 55.9 | Июль |
| August | 118.5 | .. | .. | 59.6 | Август |
| September | 120.2 | 42.7 | 77.5 | 61.1 | Сентябрь |
| October | 123.3 | .. | .. | 62.6 | Октябрь |
| November | 127.0 | .. | .. | 64.7 | Ноябрь |
| December | 131.0 | 46.7 | 84.3 | 68.7 | Декабрь |
| **1996** | | | | | **1996** |
| January | 143.2 | .. | .. | 76.5 | Январь |
| February | 156.7 | .. | .. | 84.5 | Февраль |
| March | 166.5 | 64.4 | 102.1 | 87.9 | Март |
| April | 172.2 | .. | .. | 89.1 | Апрель |
| May | 175.1 | .. | .. | 88.9 | Май |
| June | .. | .. | .. | .. | Июнь |
| July | .. | .. | .. | .. | Июль |
| August | .. | .. | .. | .. | Август |
| September | .. | .. | .. | .. | Сентябрь |
| October | .. | .. | .. | .. | Октябрь |
| November | .. | .. | .. | .. | Ноябрь |
| December | .. | .. | .. | .. | Декабрь |

## TABLE 2-1. Gross domestic product at current prices (millions of national currency)
## ТАБЛИЦА 2-1. Валовой внутренний продукт в текущих ценах (млн. национальной валюты)

| Sector of origin or expenditure category | 1990 | 1991 | 1992 | 1993 | 1994 | 1995 | Отраслевое происхождение или вид расходов |
|---|---|---|---|---|---|---|---|
| **Gross domestic product by sector of origin** | | | | | | | **Валовой внутренний продукт по отраслевому происхождению** |
| **Agriculture and forestry** | 9,883 | 17,438 | 207,460 | 1,690,248 | 2,417,790 | 14,268,542 | **Сельское и лесное хозяйство** |
| Agriculture | 9,824 | 17,285 | 204,635 | 1,642,660 | 2,324,443 | 13,422,496 | Сельское хозяйство |
| Forestry | 59 | 153 | 2,825 | 47,588 | 93,347 | 846,046 | Лесное хозяйство |
| **Industry and construction** | 19,598 | 41,027 | 398,417 | 3,697,738 | 5,904,773 | 36,978,369 | **Промышленность и строительство** |
| Industry | 16,251 | 34,523 | 334,683 | 2,931,627 | 4,851,800 | 30,396,015 | Промышленность |
| Construction | 3,347 | 6,504 | 63,734 | 766,111 | 1,052,973 | 6,582,354 | Строительство |
| **Other** | 12,121 | 25,279 | 279,515 | 4,632,150 | 8,871,389 | 61,528,067 | **Другие отрасли** |
| Transport | 2,348 | 3,735 | 66,362 | 937,909 | 1,750,842 | 12,565,229 | Транспорт |
| Road maintenance | .. | .. | .. | .. | .. | .. | Дорожное хозяйство |
| Communication | 427 | 733 | 6,879 | 109,010 | 202,474 | 2,072,506 | Связь |
| Wholesale trade | .. | .. | .. | .. | .. | .. | Оптовая торговля |
| Retail trade and catering | 1,490 | 4,006 | 44,842 | 864,614 | 1,798,071 | 10,972,272 | Розничная торговля и общепит |
| Material supply | 376 | 836 | 10,508 | 169,504 | 743,801 | 3,587,518 | Материально-техническое снабжение |
| Procurement | 149 | 462 | 5,220 | 74,879 | 87,064 | 381,505 | Заготовки |
| Information and computing services | 103 | 155 | 769 | 13,370 | 17,545 | 168,681 | Информационно-вычислительное обслуживание |
| Other sectors of material production | 296 | 535 | 3,435 | 44,241 | 81,986 | 811,028 | Другие отрасли сферы материального пр. |
| Housing | 654 | 1,028 | 9,856 | 141,751 | 296,370 | 4,321,108 | Жилищное хозяйство |
| Public utilities and personal services | 903 | 1,633 | 26,950 | 285,807 | 582,347 | 6,297,455 | Ком. хоз. и бытовое обслуживание |
| Health care, social security, physical culture and sports | 925 | 2,260 | 26,473 | 321,923 | 525,268 | 4,077,162 | Здравоохранение, социальное обеспечение, физкультура и спорт |
| Education | 877 | 2,367 | 29,888 | 399,834 | 598,144 | 5,278,923 | Образование |
| Culture and art | 217 | 402 | 6,440 | 70,599 | 76,041 | 550,204 | Культура и искусство |
| Science and scientific research | 1,297 | 2,110 | 6,971 | 75,975 | 140,552 | 1,187,373 | Наука и научное обслуживанис |
| Credit | 139 | 1,226 | 14,252 | 870,227 | 1,324,543 | 5,012,694 | Кредитование |
| Insurance | 37 | 62 | 686 | 12,175 | 15,433 | 157,870 | Страхование |
| General administration and defense | 1,797 | 3,485 | 18,858 | 229,727 | 616,441 | 3,968,008 | Государственное управление и оборона |
| Private nonprofit institutions serving households | 86 | 244 | 1,126 | 10,605 | 14,467 | 118,531 | Общественные организации, обслуживающие домашние хозяйства |
| **Imputed service charge of financial intermediaries** | .. | -1,336 | -15,796 | -855,042 | -1,206,674 | -5,884,076 | **Условно-исчисляемая стоимость услуг финансовых посредников** |
| **Total gross value added (GVA)** | 41,602 | 82,408 | 869,596 | 9,165,094 | 15,987,278 | 106,890,902 | **Валовая добавленная стоимость (ВДС) - всего** |
| **Taxes on production and imports (TOPI)** | 9,745 | 11,491 | 176,953 | 1,985,513 | 3,253,013 | 19,941,707 | **Налоги на производство и импорт (НПиИ)** |
| Other taxes on production (OTOP) | 1,451 | 745 | 29,770 | 352,191 | 472,678 | 4,787,820 | Другие налоги на производство (ДНП) |
| **Subsidies on production and imports (SOPI)** | 7,163 | 7,248 | 102,817 | 1,022,588 | 1,106,297 | 3,523,169 | **Субсидии на производство и импорт (СПиИ)** |
| Other subsidies on production (OSOP) | .. | .. | .. | .. | .. | .. | Другие субсидии на производство (ДСП) |
| **Total GDP at factor cost (GVA-OTOP+OSOP)** | 40,151 | 81,663 | 839,826 | 8,812,903 | 15,514,600 | 102,103,082 | **Всего ВВП по фактр. стоимости (ВДС-ДНП+ДСП)** |
| **Net Indirect taxes (TOPI - SOPI)** | 2,582 | 4,243 | 74,136 | 962,925 | 2,146,716 | 16,418,538 | **Чистые косвенные налоги (НПиИ-СПиИ)** |
| **Total GDP at market prices** | 42,733 | 85,906 | 913,962 | 9,775,828 | 17,661,316 | 118,521,620 | **Всего ВВП в рыночных ценах** |
| **Gross domestic product by expenditure category** | | | | | | | **Валовой внутренний продукт по видам расходов** |
| **Consumption** | 30,265 | 57,657 | 605,449 | 7,680,865 | 14,897,526 | 94,313,718 | **Потребление** |
| Private consumption | 20,105 | 39,483 | 459,249 | 5,760,139 | 11,130,753 | 68,352,080 | Личное потребление |
| Government consumption | 10,160 | 18,174 | 146,200 | 1,920,726 | 3,766,773 | 25,961,638 | Общественное потребление |
| **Gross domestic investment** | 11,508 | 25,269 | 295,134 | 3,752,603 | 5,107,838 | 29,818,540 | **Валовые внутренние инвестиции** |
| Gross fixed investment | 9,533 | 19,267 | 234,626 | 3,049,591 | 5,165,515 | 29,789,525 | Валовое накопление основного капитала |
| Change in stocks | 1,975 | 6,002 | 60,508 | 703,012 | -57,677 | 29,015 | Изменения в запасах (МОС) |
| **Resource balance (net exports of GNFS)** | 960 | 2,980 | 13,379 | -1,657,640 | -2,344,048 | -5,610,638 | **Сальдо ресурсов (чистый экспорт ТНФУ)** |
| Exports of goods and nonfactor services | 19,889 | 32,070 | 548,035 | 6,514,670 | 12,644,222 | 50,646,122 | Экспорт товаров и нефакторных услуг |
| Imports of goods and nonfactor services | 18,929 | 29,090 | 534,656 | 8,172,310 | 14,988,270 | 56,256,760 | Импорт товаров и нефакторных услуг |

## TABLE 2-1A. Distribution of gross domestic product at current prices (percent)
## ТАБЛИЦА 2-1A. Распределение валового внутреннего продукта в текущих ценах ( % )

**BELARUS**

| Sector of origin or expenditure category | 1990 | 1991 | 1992 | 1993 | 1994 | 1995 | Отраслевое происхождение или вид расходов |
|---|---|---|---|---|---|---|---|
| **Gross domestic product by sector of origin** | | | | | | | **ВВП по отраслевому происхождению** |
| **Agriculture and forestry** | 23.1 | 20.3 | 22.7 | 17.3 | 13.7 | 12.0 | **Сельское и лесное хозяйство** |
| Agriculture | 23.0 | 20.1 | 22.4 | 16.8 | 13.2 | 11.3 | Сельское хозяйство |
| Forestry | 0.1 | 0.2 | 0.3 | 0.5 | 0.5 | 0.7 | Лесное хозяйство |
| **Industry and construction** | 45.9 | 47.8 | 43.6 | 37.8 | 33.4 | 31.2 | **Промышленность и строительство** |
| Industry | 38.0 | 40.2 | 36.6 | 30.0 | 27.5 | 25.6 | Промышленность |
| Construction | 7.8 | 7.6 | 7.0 | 7.8 | 6.0 | 5.6 | Строительство |
| **Other** | 28.4 | 29.4 | 30.6 | 47.4 | 50.2 | 51.9 | **Другие отрасли** |
| Transport | 5.5 | 4.3 | 7.3 | 9.6 | 9.9 | 10.6 | Транспорт |
| Road maintenance | .. | .. | .. | .. | .. | .. | Дорожное хозяйство |
| Communication | 1.0 | 0.9 | 0.8 | 1.1 | 1.1 | 1.7 | Связь |
| Wholesale trade | .. | .. | .. | .. | .. | .. | Оптовая торговля |
| Retail trade and catering | 3.5 | 4.7 | 4.9 | 8.8 | 10.2 | 9.3 | Розничная торговля и общепит |
| Material supply | 0.9 | 1.0 | 1.1 | 1.7 | 4.2 | 3.0 | Материально-техническое снабжение |
| Procurement | 0.3 | 0.5 | 0.6 | 0.8 | 0.5 | 0.3 | Заготовки |
| Information and computing services | 0.2 | 0.2 | 0.1 | 0.1 | 0.1 | 0.1 | Информационно-вычислительное обслуживание |
| Other sectors of material production | 0.7 | 0.6 | 0.4 | 0.5 | 0.5 | 0.7 | Другие отрасли сферы матерл. произ. |
| Housing | 1.5 | 1.2 | 1.1 | 1.5 | 1.7 | 3.6 | Жилищное хозяйство |
| Public utilities and personal services | 2.1 | 1.9 | 2.9 | 2.9 | 3.3 | 5.3 | Ком. хоз. и бытовое обслуживание |
| Health care, social security, physical culture and sports | 2.2 | 2.6 | 2.9 | 3.3 | 3.0 | 3.4 | Здравоохранение, социальное обеспечение, физкультура и спорт |
| Education | 2.1 | 2.8 | 3.3 | 4.1 | 3.4 | 4.5 | Образование |
| Culture and art | 0.5 | 0.5 | 0.7 | 0.7 | 0.4 | 0.5 | Культура и искусство |
| Science and scientific research | 3.0 | 2.5 | 0.8 | 0.8 | 0.8 | 1.0 | Наука и научное обслуживание |
| Credit | 0.3 | 1.4 | 1.6 | 8.9 | 7.5 | 4.2 | Кредитование |
| Insurance | 0.1 | 0.1 | 0.1 | 0.1 | 0.1 | 0.1 | Страхование |
| General administration and defense | 4.2 | 4.1 | 2.1 | 2.3 | 3.5 | 3.3 | Государственное управление и оборона |
| Private nonprofit institutions serving households | 0.2 | 0.3 | 0.1 | 0.1 | 0.1 | 0.1 | Общественные организации, обслуживающие домашние хозяйства |
| **Imputed service charge of financial intermediaries** | 0.0 | -1.6 | -1.7 | -8.7 | -6.8 | -5.0 | **Условно-исчисляемая стоимость услуг финансовых посредников** |
| **Total gross value added** | 97.4 | 95.9 | 95.1 | 93.8 | 90.5 | 90.2 | **Валовая добавленная стоимость - всего** |
| **Total GDP at factor cost** | 94.0 | 95.1 | 91.9 | 90.1 | 87.8 | 86.1 | **ВВП по фактор. стоимости - всего** |
| **Net indirect taxes** | 6.0 | 4.9 | 8.1 | 9.9 | 12.2 | 13.9 | **Чистые косвенные налоги (НПиИ-СПиИ)** |
| **Total GDP at market prices** | 100.0 | 100.0 | 100.0 | 100.0 | 100.0 | 100.0 | **ВВП в рын. ценах - всего** |
| **Gross domestic product by expenditure category** | | | | | | | **ВВП по видам расходов** |
| **Consumption** | 70.8 | 67.1 | 66.2 | 78.6 | 84.4 | 79.6 | **Потребление** |
| Private consumption | 47.0 | 46.0 | 50.2 | 58.9 | 63.0 | 57.7 | Личное потребление |
| Government consumption | 23.8 | 21.2 | 16.0 | 19.6 | 21.3 | 21.9 | Общественное потребление |
| **Gross domestic investment** | 26.9 | 29.4 | 32.3 | 38.4 | 28.9 | 25.2 | **Вал. внутр. инвестиции** |
| Gross fixed investment | 22.3 | 22.4 | 25.7 | 31.2 | 29.2 | 25.1 | Вал. накопление осн. капитала |
| Change in stocks | 4.6 | 7.0 | 6.6 | 7.2 | -0.3 | 0.0 | Изменения в запасах (МОС) |
| **Resource balance (net exports of GNFS)** | 2.2 | 3.5 | 1.5 | -17.0 | -13.3 | -4.7 | **Сальдо ресурсов (чистый экспорт ТНФУ)** |
| Exports of goods and nonfactor services | 46.5 | 37.3 | 60.0 | 66.6 | 71.6 | 42.7 | Экспорт товаров и нефакторных услуг |
| Imports of goods and nonfactor services | 44.3 | 33.9 | 58.5 | 83.6 | 84.9 | 47.5 | Импорт товаров и нефакторных услуг |

## TABLE 2-2. Gross domestic product at constant prices (millions of national currency)
## ТАБЛИЦА 2-2. Валовой внутренний продукт в постоянных ценах (млн. национальной валюты)

| Sector of origin or expenditure category | 1990 | 1991 | 1992 | 1993 | 1994 | 1995 | Отраслевое происхождение или вид расходов |
|---|---|---|---|---|---|---|---|
| **Gross domestic product by sector of origin** | | | | | | | **Валовой внутренний продукт по отраслевому происхождению** |
| **Agriculture and forestry** | 9,883 | 9,565 | 14,922 | 185,855 | 143,863 | 2,237,716 | **Сельское и лесное хозяйство** |
| Agriculture | 9,824 | 9,504 | 14,778 | 183,022 | 139,081 | 2,147,107 | Сельское хозяйство |
| Forestry | 59 | 61 | 144 | 2,833 | 4,782 | 90,609 | Лесное хозяйство |
| **Industry and construction** | 19,598 | 19,762 | 38,780 | 351,871 | 294,880 | 5,088,872 | **Промышленность и строительство** |
| Industry | 16,251 | 16,419 | 32,739 | 299,415 | 237,658 | 4,339,279 | Промышленность |
| Construction | 3,347 | 3,343 | 6,041 | 52,456 | 57,222 | 749,593 | Строительство |
| **Other** | 12,121 | 11,642 | 21,820 | 256,147 | 463,175 | 8,295,075 | **Другие отрасли** |
| Transport | 2,348 | 2,335 | 2,999 | 53,938 | 72,188 | 1,558,489 | Транспорт |
| Road maintenance | .. | .. | .. | .. | .. | .. | Дорожное хозяйство |
| Communication | 427 | 310 | 532 | 5,446 | 10,520 | 176,022 | Связь |
| Wholesale trade | .. | .. | .. | .. | .. | .. | Оптовая торговля |
| Retail trade and catering | 1,490 | 1,425 | 3,325 | 38,963 | 79,059 | 1,346,595 | Розничная торговля и общепит |
| Material supply | 376 | 402 | 713 | 9,471 | 30,000 | 657,907 | Материально-техническое снабжение |
| Procurement | 149 | 129 | 390 | 4,653 | 6,064 | 66,356 | Заготовки |
| Information and computing services | 103 | 81 | 133 | 606 | 1,128 | 14,661 | Информационно-вычислительное обслуживание |
| Other sectors of material production | 296 | 246 | 563 | 3,340 | 4,399 | 87,577 | Другие отрасли сферы материального пр. |
| Housing | 654 | 670 | 1,072 | 9,993 | 14,245 | 294,459 | Жилищное хозяйство |
| Public utilities and personal services | 903 | 893 | 1,480 | 26,695 | 27,538 | 535,091 | Ком. хоз. и бытовое обслуживание |
| Health care, social security, and sports | 925 | 931 | 2,282 | 27,002 | 32,662 | 536,049 | Здравоохранение, социальное обеспечение, физкультура и спорт |
| Education | 877 | 883 | 2,326 | 28,960 | 40,002 | 613,193 | Образование |
| Culture and art | 217 | 218 | 348 | 5,898 | 6,645 | 77,012 | Культура и искусство |
| Science and research | 1,297 | 1,285 | 1,618 | 5,635 | 6,653 | 127,235 | Наука и научное обслуживание |
| Credit | 139 | 145 | 1,297 | 16,374 | 108,622 | 1,568,757 | Кредитование |
| Insurance | 37 | 39 | 66 | 572 | 1,130 | 13,929 | Страхование |
| General administration and defense | 1,797 | 1,560 | 2,474 | 17,672 | 21,424 | 608,477 | Государственное управление и оборона |
| Private nonprofit institutions serving households | 86 | 90 | 202 | 929 | 896 | 13,266 | Общественные организации, обслуживающие домашние хозяйства |
| **Imputed service charge of financial intermediaries** | .. | .. | -1,416 | -18,197 | -106,709 | -1,429,909 | **Условно-исчисляемая стоимость услуг финансовых посредников** |
| **Total gross value added (GVA)** | 41,602 | 40,969 | 74,106 | 775,676 | 795,209 | 14,191,754 | **Валовая добавленная стоимость (ВДС) -** |
| **Total GDP at factor cost (GVA-OTOP+OSOP)** | 40,151 | 40,969 | 74,106 | 775,676 | 795,209 | 14,191,754 | **Всего ВВП по фактр. стоимости (ВДС-ДНП+ДСП)** |
| **Net indirect taxes (TOPI - SOPI)** | 2,582 | 1,251 | 3,512 | 40,953 | 59,369 | 1,690,175 | **Чистые косвенные налоги (НПиИ-СПиИ)** |
| **Total GDP at market prices** | 42,733 | 42,220 | 77,618 | 816,629 | 854,578 | 15,881,929 | **Всего ВВП в рыночных ценах** |
| **Gross domestic product by expenditure category** | | | | | | | **Валовой внутренний продукт по видам расходов** |
| **Consumption** | 30,265 | 28,254 | 51,734 | 583,023 | 685,154 | 12,443,801 | **Потребление** |
| Private consumption | 20,105 | 18,881 | 36,348 | 452,171 | 498,841 | 8,744,738 | Личное потребление |
| Government consumption | 10,160 | 9,373 | 15,386 | 130,852 | 186,313 | 3,699,063 | Общественное потребление |
| **Gross domestic investment** | 11,508 | 13,267 | 21,284 | 258,170 | 249,688 | 3,775,024 | **Валовые внутренние инвестиции** |
| Gross fixed investment | 9,533 | 9,956 | 15,782 | 198,408 | 252,563 | 3,770,826 | Валовое накопление основного капитала |
| Change in stocks | 1,975 | 3,311 | 5,502 | 59,762 | -2,875 | 4,198 | Изменения в запасах (МОС) |
| **Resource balance (net exports of GNFS)** | 960 | 699 | 4,600 | -24,564 | -80,264 | -336,896 | **Сальдо ресурсов (чистый экспорт ТНФУ)** |
| Exports of goods and nonfactor services | 19,889 | 19,661 | 21,181 | 339,597 | 652,757 | .. | Экспорт товаров и нефакторных услуг |
| Imports of goods and nonfactor services | 18,929 | 18,962 | 16,581 | 364,161 | 733,021 | .. | Импорт товаров и нефакторных услуг |

**TABLE 2-2A. Growth rates of gross domestic product at constant prices (percent)**
**ТАБЛИЦА 2-2A. Валовой внутренний продукт - темпы прироста в постоянных ценах ( % )**

| Sector of origin or expenditure category | 1990 | 1991 | 1992 | 1993 | 1994 | 1995 | Отраслевое происхождение или вид расходов |
|---|---|---|---|---|---|---|---|
| **Growth rate by sector of origin** | | | | | | | **Валовый внутренний продукт по отраслевому происхождению** |
| **Agriculture and forestry** | .. | -3.2 | -14.4 | -10.4 | -14.9 | -7.4 | **Сельское и лесное хозяйство** |
| Agriculture | .. | -3.3 | -14.5 | -10.6 | -15.3 | -7.6 | Сельское хозяйство |
| Forestry | .. | 3.4 | -5.9 | 0.3 | 0.5 | -2.9 | Лесное хозяйство |
| **Industry and construction** | .. | 0.8 | -5.5 | -11.7 | -20.3 | -13.8 | **Промышленность и строительство** |
| Industry | .. | 1.0 | -5.2 | -10.5 | -18.9 | -10.6 | Промышленность |
| Construction | .. | -0.1 | -7.1 | -17.7 | -25.3 | -28.8 | Строительство |
| **Other** | .. | -4.0 | -13.7 | -8.4 | 0.0 | -6.5 | **Другие отрасли** |
| Transport | .. | -0.6 | -19.7 | -18.7 | -23.0 | -11.0 | Транспорт |
| Road maintenance | .. | .. | .. | .. | .. | .. | Дорожное хозяйство |
| Communication | .. | -27.4 | -27.4 | -20.8 | -3.5 | -13.1 | Связь |
| Wholesale trade | .. | .. | .. | .. | .. | .. | Оптовая торговля |
| Retail trade and catering | .. | -4.4 | -17.0 | -13.1 | -8.6 | -25.1 | Розничная торговля и общепит |
| Material supply | .. | 6.9 | -14.7 | -9.9 | 77.0 | -11.5 | Материально-техническое снабжение |
| Procurement | .. | -13.4 | -15.6 | -10.9 | -19.0 | -23.8 | Заготовки |
| Information and computing services | .. | -21.4 | -14.2 | -21.2 | -15.6 | -16.4 | Информационно-вычислительное обслуживание |
| Other sectors of material production | .. | -16.9 | 5.2 | -2.8 | -0.6 | 6.8 | Другие отрасли сферы материального пр. |
| Housing | .. | 2.4 | 4.3 | 1.4 | 0.5 | -0.6 | Жилищное хозяйство |
| Public utilities and personal services | .. | -1.1 | -9.4 | -0.9 | -3.6 | -8.1 | Ком. хоз. и бытовое обслуживание |
| Health care, social security, and sports | .. | 0.6 | 1.0 | 2.0 | 1.5 | 2.1 | Здравоохранение, социальное обеспечение, физкультура и спорт |
| Education | .. | 0.7 | -1.7 | -3.1 | 0.0 | 2.5 | Образование |
| Culture and art | .. | 0.5 | -13.4 | -8.4 | -5.9 | 1.3 | Культура и искусство |
| Science and research | .. | -0.9 | -23.3 | -19.2 | -12.4 | -9.5 | Наука и научное обслуживание |
| Credit | .. | 4.3 | 5.8 | 14.9 | 24.8 | 18.4 | Кредитование |
| Insurance | .. | 5.4 | 6.5 | -16.6 | -7.2 | -9.7 | Страхование |
| General administration and defense | .. | -13.2 | -29.0 | -6.3 | -6.7 | -1.3 | Государственное управление и оборона |
| Private nonprofit institutions serving households | .. | 4.7 | -17.2 | -17.5 | -15.5 | -8.3 | Общественные организации, обслуживающие домашние хозяйства |
| **Imputed service charge of financial intermediaries** | .. | .. | 6.0 | 15.2 | 24.8 | 18.5 | **Условно-исчисляемая стоимость услуг финансовых посредников** |
| **Total gross value added** | .. | -1.5 | -10.1 | -10.8 | -13.2 | -11.2 | **Валовая добавленная стоимость (ВДС) - всего** |
| **Total GDP at factor cost** | .. | 2.0 | -9.3 | -7.6 | -9.8 | -8.5 | **Всего ВВП по фактр. стоимости (ВДС-ДНП+ДСП)** |
| **Net indirect taxes** | .. | -51.5 | -17.2 | -44.8 | -38.3 | -21.3 | **Чистые косвенные налоги (НПиИ-СПиИ)** |
| **Total GDP at market prices** | .. | -1.2 | -9.6 | -10.6 | -12.6 | -10.1 | **Всего ВВП в рыночных ценах** |
| **Growth rate by expenditure category** | | | | | | | **Валовой внутренний продукт по видам расходов** |
| **Consumption** | .. | -6.6 | -10.3 | -3.7 | -10.8 | -16.5 | **Потребление** |
| Private consumption | .. | -6.1 | -7.9 | -1.5 | -13.4 | -21.4 | Личное потребление |
| Government consumption | .. | -7.7 | -15.3 | -10.5 | -3.0 | -1.8 | Общественное потребление |
| **Gross domestic investment** | .. | 15.3 | -15.8 | -12.5 | -33.5 | -26.1 | **Валовые внутренние инвестиции** |
| Gross fixed investment | .. | 4.4 | -18.1 | -15.4 | -17.2 | -27.0 | Валовое накопление основного капитала |
| **Exports of goods and nonfactor services** | .. | .. | -34.0 | -38.0 | 0.2 | .. | **Экспорт товаров и нефакторных услуг** |
| **Imports of goods and nonfactor services** | .. | .. | -43.0 | -31.9 | -10.3 | .. | **Импорт товаров и нефакторных услуг** |

**TABLE 2-2B. Implicit price deflators for gross domestic product (percentage change)**

**ТАБЛИЦА 2-2B. Дефляторы валового внутреннего продукта (темпы прироста в %)**

| Sector of origin or expenditure category | 1990 | 1991 | 1992 | 1993 | 1994 | 1995 | Отраслевое происхождение или вид расходов |
|---|---|---|---|---|---|---|---|
| **Price deflators by sector of origin** | | | | | | | **Дефляторы по отраслевому происхождению или виду расходов** |
| **Agriculture and forestry** | .. | 82.3 | 1,290.3 | 809.4 | 1,580.6 | 537.6 | **Сельское и лесное хозяйство** |
| Agriculture | .. | 81.9 | 1,284.7 | 797.5 | 1,571.3 | 525.1 | Сельское хозяйство |
| Forestry | .. | 150.8 | 1,861.8 | 1,579.8 | 1,852.0 | 833.7 | Лесное хозяйство |
| **Industry and construction** | .. | 107.6 | 927.4 | 950.9 | 1,902.4 | 626.7 | **Промышленность и строительство** |
| Industry | .. | 110.3 | 922.3 | 879.1 | 1,941.5 | 600.5 | Промышленность |
| Construction | .. | 94.6 | 955.0 | 1,360.5 | 1,740.2 | 778.1 | Строительство |
| **Other** | .. | 117.1 | 1,181.0 | 1,708.4 | 1,815.3 | 641.7 | **Другие отрасли** |
| Transport | .. | 60.0 | 2,112.8 | 1,638.9 | 2,325.4 | 706.2 | Транспорт |
| Road maintenance | .. | .. | .. | .. | .. | .. | Дорожное хозяйство |
| Communication | .. | 136.5 | 1,193.0 | 1,901.7 | 1,824.7 | 1,077.4 | Связь |
| Wholesale trade | .. | .. | .. | .. | .. | .. | Оптовая торговля |
| Retail trade and catering | .. | 181.1 | 1,248.6 | 2,119.1 | 2,174.3 | 714.8 | Розничная торговля и общепит. |
| Material supply | .. | 108.0 | 1,373.8 | 1,689.7 | 2,379.3 | 445.3 | Материально-техническое снабжение |
| Procurement | .. | 258.1 | 1,238.5 | 1,509.3 | 1,335.8 | 474.9 | Заготовки |
| Information and computing services | .. | 91.4 | 478.2 | 2,106.3 | 1,455.4 | 1,050.5 | Информационно-вычислительное обслуживание |
| Other sectors of material production | .. | 117.5 | 510.1 | 1,224.6 | 1,763.7 | 826.1 | Другие отрасли сферы матерл. произ. |
| Housing | .. | 53.4 | 819.4 | 1,318.5 | 1,980.5 | 1,367.5 | Жилищное хозяйство |
| Public utilities and personal services | .. | 82.9 | 1,720.9 | 970.6 | 2,014.7 | 1,076.9 | Ком. хоз. и бытовое обслуживание |
| Health care, social security, and sports | .. | 142.7 | 1,060.1 | 1,092.2 | 1,508.2 | 660.6 | Здравоохранение, социальное обеспечение, физкультура и спорт |
| Education | .. | 168.1 | 1,185.0 | 1,280.6 | 1,395.3 | 760.9 | Образование |
| Culture and art | .. | .. | .. | .. | .. | .. | Культура и искусство |
| Science and research | .. | 64.2 | 330.8 | 1,248.3 | 2,012.6 | 833.2 | Наука и научное обслуживание |
| Credit | .. | 745.5 | 998.8 | 5,214.7 | 1,119.4 | 219.5 | Кредитование |
| Insurance | .. | 59.0 | 939.4 | 2,028.5 | 1,265.8 | 1,033.4 | Страхование |
| General administration and defense | .. | 123.4 | 662.2 | 1,199.9 | 2,777.3 | 552.1 | Государственное управление и оборона |
| Private nonprofit institutions serving households | .. | 171.1 | 457.4 | 1,041.6 | 1,514.6 | 793.5 | Общественные организации, обслуживающие домашние хозяиства |
| **Imputed service charge of financial intermediaries** | .. | .. | 1,015.5 | 4,598.8 | 1,030.8 | 311.5 | **Условно-исчисляемая стоимость услуг финансовых посредников** |
| **Total gross value added** | .. | 101.1 | 1,073.4 | 1,081.6 | 1,910.4 | 653.2 | **Валовая добавленная стоимость (ВДС) - всего** |
| **Total GDP at factor cost** | .. | 99.3 | 1,033.3 | 1,036.2 | 1,851.0 | 619.5 | **ВВП по факторной стоимости (ВДС-ДНП+ДСП)** |
| **Net indirect taxes** | .. | 239.2 | 2,010.9 | 2,251.3 | 3,515.9 | 871.4 | **Чистые косвенные налоги (НПИ-СПИ)** |
| **Total GDP at market prices** | .. | 103.5 | 1,077.5 | 1,097.1 | 1,966.7 | 646.3 | **ВВП в рыночных ценах** |
| **Price deflators by expenditure category** | | | | | | | **Дефляторы по виду расходов** |
| **Consumption** | .. | 104.1 | 1,070.3 | 1,217.4 | 2,074.3 | 657.9 | **Конечное потребление** |
| Private consumption | .. | 109.1 | 1,163.5 | 1,173.9 | 2,131.3 | 681.6 | Личное потребление |
| Government consumption | .. | 93.9 | 850.2 | 1,367.9 | 1,921.7 | 601.8 | Общественное потребление |
| **Gross domestic investment** | .. | 90.5 | 1,286.6 | 1,353.5 | 1,945.7 | 689.9 | **Валовые внутренние инвестиции** |
| Gross fixed investment | .. | 93.5 | 1,386.7 | 1,437.0 | 1,945.2 | 690.0 | Валовое накопление основного капитала |
| **Exports of goods and nonfactor services** | .. | 63.1 | 2,487.4 | 1,818.4 | 1,837.0 | .. | **Экспорт товаров и нефакторных услуг** |
| **Imports of goods and nonfactor services** | .. | 53.4 | 3,124.5 | 2,144.1 | 1,944.7 | .. | **Импорт товаров и нефакторных услуг** |

## TABLE 3-1. Balance of payments at current prices (millions of U.S. dollars)
## ТАБЛИЦА 3-1. Платежный баланс в текущих ценах (в миллионах долларов США)

| Item | 1990 | 1991 | 1992 | 1993 | 1994 | 1995 | Статьи |
|---|---|---|---|---|---|---|---|
| Exports of goods and services (including workers' remittances) | .. | .. | .. | .. | 2,771.4 | 5,019.4 | Экспорт товаров и услуг (включая денежные переводы рабочих) |
| Exports of goods and nonfactor services | .. | .. | .. | .. | 2,770.9 | 4,989.0 | Экспорт товаров и нефакт. услуг |
| Merchandise (FOB) | .. | .. | .. | .. | 2,519.6 | 4,375.2 | Товары (ФОБ) |
| Nonfactor services | .. | .. | .. | .. | 251.3 | 614.0 | Нефакторные услуги |
| Shipment | .. | .. | .. | .. | 183.7 | 301.9 | Перевозки |
| Travel | .. | .. | .. | .. | 38.6 | 23.2 | Поездки |
| Other | .. | .. | .. | .. | 29.0 | 289.0 | Другие |
| Imports of goods and nonfactor services | .. | .. | .. | .. | 3,240.0 | 5,387.0 | Импорт товаров и нефакт. услуг |
| Merchandise (FOB) | .. | .. | .. | .. | 3,041.0 | 5,035.0 | Товары (ФОБ) |
| Nonfactor services | .. | .. | .. | .. | 199.0 | 352.0 | Нефакторные услуги |
| Shipment | .. | .. | .. | .. | 75.0 | 99.0 | Перевозки |
| Travel | .. | .. | .. | .. | 74.0 | 87.0 | Поездки |
| Other | .. | .. | .. | .. | 50.0 | 166.0 | Другие |
| Resource balance | .. | .. | .. | .. | -469.5 | -398.0 | Сальдо ресурсов |
| Net factor income | .. | .. | .. | .. | -28.0 | -51.0 | Чистый факторный доход |
| Factor receipts | .. | .. | .. | .. | 0.5 | 1.9 | Факторные поступления |
| Factor payments | .. | .. | .. | .. | 29.0 | 52.9 | Факторные платежи |
| Total interest due | .. | .. | .. | .. | .. | .. | Общая сумма процента к оплате |
| Other factor payments and discrepancy | .. | .. | .. | .. | .. | .. | Другие факторные платежи и стат. погр. |
| Net current transfers | .. | .. | .. | .. | 26.4 | 78.6 | Чистые текущие трансферты |
| Current receipts | .. | .. | .. | .. | 50.9 | 108.0 | Текущие поступления |
| Workers remittances | .. | .. | .. | .. | .. | 28.5 | Денежные переводы рабочих |
| Other current transfers | .. | .. | .. | .. | .. | 78.7 | Другие текущие трансферты |
| Current payments | .. | .. | .. | .. | 25.0 | 29.0 | Текущие платежи |
| Current account balance before official grants | .. | .. | .. | .. | -471.1 | -370.3 | Сальдо текущего счета до офиц. безвозмезд. трансфертов |
| Official capital grants | .. | .. | .. | .. | .. | .. | Официальные кап. безвозмезные трансферты |
| Current account balance after official grants | .. | .. | .. | .. | .. | .. | Сальдо текущего счета после офиц. безвозмезд. трансфертов |
| Long Term Capital Inflows | .. | .. | .. | .. | 1,082.0 | 94.6 | Долгосрочные притоки капитала |
| Direct investment | .. | .. | .. | .. | 364.8 | 6.7 | Прямые инвестиции |
| Net long term borrowing | .. | .. | .. | .. | 693.4 | 80.6 | Чистые долгосрочные займы |
| Disbursements | .. | .. | .. | .. | .. | 176.9 | Поступления |
| Repayments due | .. | .. | .. | .. | .. | 96.3 | Сумма, подлежащая погашению |
| Other long-term inflows (net) | .. | .. | .. | .. | 23.8 | 7.3 | Другие долгосрочные притоки (чистые) |

(continued on next page)

## TABLE 3-1. Balance of payments at current prices (millions of U.S. dollars)
## ТАБЛИЦА 3-1. Платежный баланс в текущих ценах (в миллионах долларов США)

| Item | 1990 | 1991 | 1992 | 1993 | 1994 | 1995 | Статьи |
|---|---|---|---|---|---|---|---|
| Adjustment to Scheduled Debt Service | .. | .. | .. | .. | .. | .. | Регулирование долга |
| Debt service not paid | .. | .. | .. | .. | .. | .. | Невыплаченный долг |
| Interest not paid | .. | .. | .. | .. | .. | .. | Невыплаченный процент |
| Principal not paid | .. | .. | .. | .. | .. | .. | Невыплаченная сумма основного долга |
| Arrears reductions/prepayments(-) | .. | .. | .. | .. | .. | .. | Погашение просроченных платежей/выплаты авансом (-) |
| Total Other items (Net) | .. | .. | .. | .. | 490.0 | 375.0 | Общие другие статьи (чистые) |
| Net short-term capital | .. | .. | .. | .. | 407.7 | 352.1 | Чистый краткосрочный капитал |
| Capital flows not elsewhere included | .. | .. | .. | .. | .. | .. | Потоки капитала, не указанные выше |
| Errors and omissions | .. | .. | .. | .. | 82.3 | 23.0 | Ошибки и пропуски |
| Changes in net reserves | .. | .. | .. | .. | .. | .. | Изменения в чистых резервах |
| Net credit from IMF | .. | .. | .. | .. | .. | .. | Чистый кредит МВФ |
| Reserve changes not elsewhere included | .. | .. | .. | .. | .. | .. | Изменения резервов, не указанных выше |
| Escrow account | .. | .. | .. | .. | .. | .. | Счет депонирования |
| Gross reserves (excluding gold) | .. | .. | .. | .. | -89.3 | -100.2 | Общие резервы (исключая золото) |
| Gross reserves (including gold) | .. | .. | .. | .. | .. | .. | Общие резервы (включая золото) |
| Nominal official exchange rate (annual average) (rf) | .. | .. | .. | .. | .. | .. | Номинальный официальный или рыночный курс (среднегодовой) |
| Nominal official exchange rate (end-of-year) (ae) | .. | .. | .. | .. | .. | .. | Номинальный официальный или рыночный курс (на конец года) |
| Manufacture unit value (percent change) | .. | .. | .. | .. | .. | .. | Средний индекс цен на продукцию обр. пром.,% |
| Index of real effective exchange rate (IMF) | .. | .. | .. | .. | .. | .. | Индекс реального эффективного валютного курса (МВФ) |
| Total factor payments | .. | .. | .. | .. | .. | .. | Общая сумма факторных платежей |
| Government interest | .. | .. | .. | .. | .. | .. | Процент, выплачиваемый органами гос. управления |
| Private sector interest | .. | .. | .. | .. | .. | .. | Процент выплачиваемый частным сектором |
| Profits on direct foreign investment | .. | .. | .. | .. | .. | .. | Прибыль от прямых иностранных инвестиций |
| Official capital grants | .. | .. | .. | .. | .. | .. | Официальные капитальные безвозмездные трансферты |
| For budgetary financing | .. | .. | .. | .. | .. | .. | На бюджетное финансирование |
| To extrabudgetary entities | .. | .. | .. | .. | .. | .. | На внебюджетное финансирование |
| Government net long term borrowing | .. | .. | .. | .. | .. | 75.7 | Чистые долгосрочные государственные займы |
| Disbursements | .. | .. | .. | .. | .. | 185.6 | Поступления |
| Repayments | .. | .. | .. | .. | .. | 109.9 | Погашения |
| Private net long term borrowing | .. | .. | .. | .. | .. | 4.0 | Чистые долгосрочные частные займы |
| Disbursements | .. | .. | .. | .. | .. | 5.4 | Поступления |
| Repayments | .. | .. | .. | .. | .. | 0.5 | Погашения |

**TABLE 3-2A. Imports by commodity group (millions of U.S. dollars)**
**ТАБЛИЦА 3-2A . Импорт по товарным группам (млн. долларов США)**

| Commodity group | 1990 | 1991 | 1992 | 1993 | 1994 | 1995 | Товарные группы |
|---|---|---|---|---|---|---|---|
| TOTAL | .. | .. | .. | .. | .. | 5,563.6 | ВСЕГО |
| I - Live animals; animal products | .. | .. | .. | .. | .. | 62.9 | I - Живые животные и продукты животноводства |
| II - Vegetable products | .. | .. | .. | .. | .. | 207.2 | II - Продукты растительного происхождения |
| III - Animal or vegetable fats and oils and their cleavage products; prepared edible fats; animal or vegetable waxes | .. | .. | .. | .. | .. | 65.1 | III - Жиры и масла растительного и животного происхождения, воски |
| IV - Prepared foodstuffs; beverages, spirits and vinegar; tobacco and manufactured tobacco substitutes | .. | .. | .. | .. | .. | 306.9 | IV -Продукция пищевой промышленности, алкогольные и безалкогольные напитки, табак и его заменители |
| V - Mineral products | .. | .. | .. | .. | .. | 1,983.4 | V - Минеральные продукты |
| VI - Products of the chemical or allied industries | .. | .. | .. | .. | .. | 550.1 | VI - Продукция химической промышленности |
| VII - Plastics and articles thereof; rubber and articles thereof | .. | .. | .. | .. | .. | 271.9 | VII - Пластмассы и изделия из них |
| VIII - Raw hides and skins, leather, furskins and articles thereof; saddlery and harness; travel goods, handbags and similar containers; articles of animal gut | .. | .. | .. | .. | .. | 24.7 | VIII - Кожевенное сырьё, кожи, пушнина, меховое сырьё и изделия из них |
| IX - Wood and articles of wood; wood charcoal; cork and articles of cork; manufactures of straw, of esparto or of other plaiting materials; basketware and wickerwork | .. | .. | .. | .. | .. | 12.1 | IX - Древесина и изделия из древесины, древесный уголь |
| X - Pulp of wood or of other fibrous cellulosic material; waste and scrap of paper or paperboard; paper and paperboard and articles thereof | .. | .. | .. | .. | .. | 92.2 | X - Бумажная масса, бумажные и картонные отходы, макулатура, бумага, картон и изделия из них |
| XI - Textiles and textile articles | .. | .. | .. | .. | .. | 231.5 | XI - Текстиль и текстильные изделия |
| XII - Footwear, headgear, umbrellas, sun umbrellas, walking sticks, seat sticks, whips, riding crops and parts thereof; prepared feathers and articles made therewith; artificial flowers; articles of human hair | .. | .. | .. | .. | .. | 21.3 | XII - Обувь, головные уборы, зонты, трости и пр. |

**TABLE 3-2A. Imports by commodity group (millions of U.S. dollars)**
**ТАБЛИЦА 3-2A . Импорт по товарным группам (млн. долларов США)**

| Commodity group | 1990 | 1991 | 1992 | 1993 | 1994 | 1995 | Товарные группы |
|---|---|---|---|---|---|---|---|
| XIII - Articles of stone, plaster, cement, asbestos, mica and similar materials; ceramic products; glass and glassware | .. | .. | .. | .. | .. | 44.6 | XIII - Изделия из камня, гипса, цемента |
| XIV - Natural or cultured pearls, precious or semi-precious stones, precious metals, metals clad with precious metal and articles thereof; imitation jewellery; coin | .. | .. | .. | .. | .. | 28.4 | XIV - Жемчуг, драгоценные и полудрагоценные камни, драгоценные металлы, бижутерия, монеты |
| XV - Base metals and articles of base metal | .. | .. | .. | .. | .. | 522.2 | XV - Неблагородные металлы и изделия из них |
| XVI - Machinery and mechanical appliances; electrical equipment; parts thereof; sound recorders and reproducers, television image and sound recorders and reproducers, and parts and accessories of such articles | .. | .. | .. | .. | .. | 620.3 | XVI - Машины, оборудование, механизмы, их части и принадлежности; звуковая и теле-аппаратура, их части и принадлежности |
| XVII - Vehicles, aircraft, vessels and associated transport equipment | .. | .. | .. | .. | .. | 325.4 | XVII - Средства наземного, воздушного и водного транспорта |
| XVIII - Optical, photographic, cinematographic, measuring, checking, precision, medical or surgical instruments and apparatus; clocks and watches; musical instruments; parts and accessories thereof | .. | .. | .. | .. | .. | 124.7 | XVIII - Приборы, аппараты оптические, медицинские, измерительные и пр.; музыкальные инструменты; часы; их части и принадлежности |
| XIX - Arms and ammunition; parts and accessories thereof | .. | .. | .. | .. | .. | 0.5 | XIX - Оружие и боеприпасы, их части и принадлежности |
| XX - Miscellaneous manufactured articles | .. | .. | .. | .. | .. | 36.3 | XX - Разные промышленные товары |
| XXI - Works of art, collectors' pieces, and antiques | .. | .. | .. | .. | .. | 0.0 | XXI - Произведения искусства, предметы антиквариата |
| XXII - Services | .. | .. | .. | .. | .. | 17.0 | XXII - Услуги |

## TABLE 3-2B Imports by commodity group (millions of national currency)
## ТАБЛИЦА 3-2B. Импорт по товарным группам (млн. национальной валюты)

| Commodity group | 1990 | 1991 | 1992 | 1993 | 1994 | 1995 | Товарные группы |
|---|---|---|---|---|---|---|---|
| TOTAL | .. | .. | .. | .. | .. | 63,752,635.1 | ВСЕГО |
| I - Live animals; animal products | .. | .. | .. | .. | .. | 726,211.2 | I - Живые животные и продукты животноводства |
| II - Vegetable products | .. | .. | .. | .. | .. | 2,388,640.4 | II - Продукты растительного происхождения |
| III - Animal or vegetable fats and oils and their cleavage products; prepared edible fats; animal or vegetable waxes | .. | .. | .. | .. | .. | 751,539.2 | III - Жиры и масла растительного и животного происхождения, воски |
| IV - Prepared foodstuffs; beverages, spirits and vinegar; tobacco and manufactured tobacco substitutes | .. | .. | .. | .. | .. | 3,533,995.4 | IV -Продукция пищевой промышленности, алкогольные и безалкогольные напитки, табак и его заменители |
| V - Mineral products | .. | .. | .. | .. | .. | 22,705,501.5 | V - Минеральные продукты |
| VI - Products of the chemical or allied industries | .. | .. | .. | .. | .. | 6,225,738.8 | VI - Продукция химической промышленности |
| VII - Plastics and articles thereof; rubber and articles thereof | .. | .. | .. | .. | .. | 3,128,133.9 | VII - Пластмассы и изделия из них |
| VIII - Raw hides and skins, leather, furskins and articles thereof; saddlery and harness; travel goods, handbags and similar containers; articles of animal gut | .. | .. | .. | .. | .. | 287,090.4 | VIII - Кожевенное сырьё, кожи, пушнина, меховое сырьё и изделия из них |
| IX - Wood and articles of wood; wood charcoal; cork and articles of cork; manufactures of straw, of esparto or of other plaiting materials; basketware and wickerwork | .. | .. | .. | .. | .. | 139,421.4 | IX - Древесина и изделия из древесины, древесный уголь |
| X - Pulp of wood or of other fibrous cellulosic material; waste and scrap of paper or paperboard; paper and paperboard and articles thereof | .. | .. | .. | .. | .. | 1,061,701.7 | X - Бумажная масса, бумажные и картонные отходы, макулатура, бумага, картон и изделия из них |
| XI - Textiles and textile articles | .. | .. | .. | .. | .. | 2,664,833.4 | XI - Текстиль и текстильные изделия |
| XII - Footwear, headgear, umbrellas, sun umbrellas, walking sticks, seat sticks, whips, riding crops and parts thereof; prepared feathers and articles made therewith; artificial flowers; articles of human hair | .. | .. | .. | .. | .. | 245,165.3 | XII - Обувь, головные уборы, зонты, трости и пр. |

**TABLE 3-2B Imports by commodity group (millions of national currency)**
**ТАБЛИЦА 3-2В. Импорт по товарным группам (млн. национальной валюты)**

| Commodity group | 1990 | 1991 | 1992 | 1993 | 1994 | 1995 | Товарные группы |
|---|---|---|---|---|---|---|---|
| XIII - Articles of stone, plaster, cement, asbestos, mica and similar materials; ceramic products; glass and glassware | .. | .. | .. | .. | .. | 513,305.6 | XIII - Изделия из камня, гипса, цемента |
| XIV - Natural or cultured pearls, precious or semi-precious stones, precious metals, metals clad with precious metal and articles thereof; imitation jewellery; coin | .. | .. | .. | .. | .. | 327,195.6 | XIV - Жемчуг, драгоценные и полудрагоценные камни, драгоценные металлы, бижутерия, монеты |
| XV - Base metals and articles of base metal | .. | .. | .. | .. | .. | 6,011,578.9 | XV - Неблагородные металлы и изделия из них |
| XVI - Machinery and mechanical appliances; electrical equipment; parts thereof; sound recorders and reproducers, television image and sound recorders and reproducers, and parts and accessories of such articles | .. | .. | .. | .. | .. | 7,160,429.1 | XVI - Машины, оборудование, механизмы, их части и принадлежности; звуковая и теле-аппаратура, их части и принадлежности |
| XVII - Vehicles, aircraft, vessels and associated transport equipment | .. | .. | .. | .. | .. | 3,744,216.6 | XVII - Средства наземного, воздушного и водного транспорта |
| XVIII - Optical, photographic, cinematographic, measuring, checking, precision, medical or surgical instruments and apparatus; clocks and watches; musical instruments; parts and accessories thereof | .. | .. | .. | .. | .. | 1,439,161.4 | XVIII - Приборы, аппараты оптические, медицинские, измерительные и пр.; музыкальные инструменты; часы; их части и принадлежности |
| XIX - Arms and ammunition; parts and accessories thereof | .. | .. | .. | .. | .. | 6,114.9 | XIX - Оружие и боеприпасы, их части и принадлежности |
| XX - Miscellaneous manufactured articles | .. | .. | .. | .. | .. | 418,265.7 | XX - Разные промышленные товары |
| XXI - Works of art, collectors' pieces, and antiques | .. | .. | .. | .. | .. | 38.3 | XXI - Произведения искусства, предметы антиквариата |
| XXII - Services | .. | .. | .. | .. | .. | 193,324.1 | XXII - Услуги |

## TABLE 3-3A. Exports by commodity group (millions of U.S. dollars)



## ТАБЛИЦА 3-3A. Экспорт по товарным группам (млн. долларов США)

| Commodity group | 1990 | 1991 | 1992 | 1993 | 1994 | 1995 | Товарные группы |
|---|---|---|---|---|---|---|---|
| TOTAL | .. | .. | .. | .. | .. | 4,706.8 | ВСЕГО |
| I - Live animals; animal products | .. | .. | .. | .. | .. | 150.6 | I - Живые животные и продукты животноводства |
| II - Vegetable products | .. | .. | .. | .. | .. | 53.3 | II - Продукты растительного происхождения |
| III - Animal or vegetable fats and oils and their cleavage products; prepared edible fats; animal or vegetable waxes | .. | .. | .. | .. | .. | 4.1 | III - Жиры и масла растительного и животного происхождения, воски |
| IV - Prepared foodstuffs; beverages, spirits and vinegar; tobacco and manufactured tobacco substitutes | .. | .. | .. | .. | .. | 109.6 | IV -Продукция пищевой промышленности, алкогольные и безалкогольные напитки, табак и его заменители |
| V - Mineral products | .. | .. | .. | .. | .. | 576.5 | V - Минеральные продукты |
| VI - Products of the chemical or allied industries | .. | .. | .. | .. | .. | 647.5 | VI - Продукция химической промышленности |
| VII - Plastics and articles thereof; rubber and articles thereof | .. | .. | .. | .. | .. | 252.6 | VII - Пластмассы и изделия из них |
| VIII - Raw hides and skins, leather, furskins and articles thereof; saddlery and harness; travel goods, handbags and similar containers; articles of animal gut | .. | .. | .. | .. | .. | 55.2 | VIII - Кожевенное сырьё, кожи, пушнина, меховое сырьё и изделия из них |
| IX - Wood and articles of wood; wood charcoal; cork and articles of cork; manufactures of straw, of esparto or of other plaiting materials; basketware and wickerwork | .. | .. | .. | .. | .. | 99.4 | IX - Древесина и изделия из древесины, древесный уголь |
| X - Pulp of wood or of other fibrous cellulosic material; waste and scrap of paper or paperboard; paper and paperboard and articles thereof | .. | .. | .. | .. | .. | 55.5 | X - Бумажная масса, бумажные и картонные отходы, макулатура, бумага, картон и изделия из них |
| XI - Textiles and textile articles | .. | .. | .. | .. | .. | 627.4 | XI - Текстиль и текстильные изделия |
| XII - Footwear, headgear, umbrellas, sun umbrellas, walking sticks, seat sticks, whips, riding crops and parts thereof; prepared feathers and articles made therewith; artificial flowers; articles of human hair | .. | .. | .. | .. | .. | 49.9 | XII - Обувь, головные уборы, зонты, трости и пр. |

**TABLE 3-3A. Exports by commodity group (millions of U.S. dollars)**
**ТАБЛИЦА 3-3А. Экспорт по товарным группам (млн. долларов США)**

| Commodity group | 1990 | 1991 | 1992 | 1993 | 1994 | 1995 | Товарные группы |
|---|---|---|---|---|---|---|---|
| XIII - Articles of stone, plaster, cement, asbestos, mica and similar materials; ceramic products; glass and glassware | .. | .. | .. | .. | .. | 108.2 | XIII - Изделия из камня, гипса, цемента |
| XIV - Natural or cultured pearls, precious or semi-precious stones, precious metals, metals clad with precious metal and articles thereof; imitation jewellery; coin | .. | .. | .. | .. | .. | 36.7 | XIV - Жемчуг, драгоценные и полудрагоценные камни, драгоценные металлы, бижутерия, монеты |
| XV - Base metals and articles of base metal | .. | .. | .. | .. | .. | 295.3 | XV - Неблагородные металлы и изделия из них |
| XVI - Machinery and mechanical appliances; electrical equipment; parts thereof; sound recorders and reproducers, television image and sound recorders and reproducers, and parts and accessories of such articles | .. | .. | .. | .. | .. | 629.6 | XVI - Машины, оборудование, механизмы, их части и принадлежности; звуковая и теле-аппаратура, их части и принадлежности |
| XVII - Vehicles, aircraft, vessels and associated transport equipment | .. | .. | .. | .. | .. | 750.1 | XVII - Средства наземного, воздушного и водного транспорта |
| XVIII - Optical, photographic, cinematograp-hic, measuring, checking, precision, medical or surgical instruments and apparatus; clocks and watches; musical instruments; parts and accessories thereof | .. | .. | .. | .. | .. | 67.1 | XVIII - Приборы, аппараты оптические, медицинские, измерительные и пр.; музыкальные инструменты; часы; их части и принадлежности |
| XIX - Arms and ammunition; parts and accessories thereof | .. | .. | .. | .. | .. | 3.2 | XIX - Оружие и боеприпасы, их части и принадлежности |
| XX - Miscellaneous manufactured articles | .. | .. | .. | .. | .. | 131.3 | XX - Разные промышленные товары |
| XXI - Works of art, collectors' pieces, and antiques | .. | .. | .. | .. | .. | 0.0 | XXI - Произведения искусства, предметы антиквариата |
| XXII - Services | .. | .. | .. | .. | .. | 236.3 | XXII - Услуги |

**TABLE 3-3B. Exports by Commodity Group (millions of national currency)**
**ТАБЛИЦА 3-3B. Экспорт по товарным группам (млн. национальной валюты)**

| Commodity group | 1990 | 1991 | 1992 | 1993 | 1994 | 1995 | Товарные группы |
|---|---|---|---|---|---|---|---|
| TOTAL | .. | .. | .. | .. | .. | 54,035,810.9 | ВСЕГО |
| I - Live animals; animal products | .. | .. | .. | .. | .. | 1,733,338.0 | I - Живые животные и продукты животноводства |
| II - Vegetable products | .. | .. | .. | .. | .. | 613,515.3 | II - Продукты растительного происхождения |
| III - Animal or vegetable fats and oils and their cleavage products; prepared edible fats; animal or vegetable waxes | .. | .. | .. | .. | .. | 47,453.4 | III - Жиры и масла растительного и животного происхождения, воски |
| IV - Prepared foodstuffs; beverages, spirits and vinegar; tobacco and manufactured tobacco substitutes | .. | .. | .. | .. | .. | 1,258,493.2 | IV -Продукция пищевой промышленности, алкогольные и безалкогольные напитки, табак и его заменители |
| V - Mineral products | .. | .. | .. | .. | .. | 6,591,985.0 | V - Минеральные продукты |
| VI - Products of the chemical or allied industries | .. | .. | .. | .. | .. | 7,389,945.8 | VI - Продукция химической промышленности |
| VII - Plastics and articles thereof; rubber and articles thereof | .. | .. | .. | .. | .. | 2,893,802.0 | VII - Пластмассы и изделия из них |
| VIII - Raw hides and skins, leather, furskins and articles thereof; saddlery and harness; travel goods, handbags and similar containers; articles of animal gut | .. | .. | .. | .. | .. | 632,928.7 | VIII - Кожевенное сырьё, кожи, пушнина, меховое сырьё и изделия из них |
| IX - Wood and articles of wood; wood charcoal; cork and articles of cork; manufactures of straw, of esparto or of other plaiting materials; basketware and wickerwork | .. | .. | .. | .. | .. | 1,146,303.5 | IX - Древесина и изделия из древесины, древесный уголь |
| X - Pulp of wood or of other fibrous cellulosic material; waste and scrap of paper or paperboard; paper and paperboard and articles thereof | .. | .. | .. | .. | .. | 638,270.4 | X - Бумажная масса, бумажные и картонные отходы, макулатура, бумага, картон и изделия из них |
| XI - Textiles and textile articles | .. | .. | .. | .. | .. | 7,214,745.5 | XI - Текстиль и текстильные изделия |
| XII - Footwear, headgear, umbrellas, sun umbrellas, walking sticks, seat sticks, whips, riding crops and parts thereof; prepared feathers and articles made therewith; artificial flowers; articles of human hair | .. | .. | .. | .. | .. | 575,427.9 | XII - Обувь, головные уборы, зонты, трости и пр. |

**TABLE 3-3B. Exports by Commodity Group (millions of national currency)**
**ТАБЛИЦА 3-3B. Экспорт по товарным группам (млн. национальной валюты)**

| Commodity group | 1990 | 1991 | 1992 | 1993 | 1994 | 1995 | Товарные группы |
|---|---|---|---|---|---|---|---|
| XIII - Articles of stone, plaster, cement, asbestos, mica and similar materials; ceramic products; glass and glassware | .. | .. | .. | .. | .. | 1,245,390.0 | XIII - Изделия из камня, гипса, цемента |
| XIV - Natural or cultured pearls, precious or semi-precious stones, precious metals, metals clad with precious metal and articles thereof; imitation jewellery; coin | .. | .. | .. | .. | .. | 423,063.0 | XIV - Жемчуг, драгоценные и полудрагоценные камни, драгоценные металлы, бижутерия, монеты |
| XV - Base metals and articles of base metal | .. | .. | .. | .. | .. | 3,401,894.4 | XV - Неблагородные металлы и изделия из них |
| XVI - Machinery and mechanical appliances; electrical equipment; parts thereof; sound recorders and reproducers, television image and sound recorders and reproducers, and parts and accessories of such articles | .. | .. | .. | .. | .. | 7,219,805.6 | XVI - Машины, оборудование, механизмы, их части и принадлежности; звуковая и теле-аппаратура, их части и принадлежности |
| XVII - Vehicles, aircraft, vessels and associated transport equipment | .. | .. | .. | .. | .. | 8,641,256.3 | XVII - Средства наземного, воздушного и водного транспорта |
| XVIII - Optical, photographic, cinematographic, measuring, checking, precision, medical or surgical instruments and apparatus; clocks and watches; musical instruments; parts and accessories thereof | .. | .. | .. | .. | .. | 772,783.6 | XVIII - Приборы, аппараты оптические, медицинские, измерительные и пр.; музыкальные инструменты; часы; их части и принадлежности |
| XIX - Arms and ammunition; parts and accessories thereof | .. | .. | .. | .. | .. | 36,701.2 | XIX - Оружие и боеприпасы, их части и принадлежности |
| XX - Miscellaneous manufactured articles | .. | .. | .. | .. | .. | 1,515,984.4 | XX - Разные промышленные товары |
| XXI - Works of art, collectors' pieces, and antiques | .. | .. | .. | .. | .. | 125.2 | XXI - Произведения искусства, предметы антиквариата |
| XXII - Services | .. | .. | .. | .. | .. | 2,733,708.6 | XXII - Услуги |

**TABLE 3-4A. Geographical distribution of foreign trade (millions of U.S. dollars)**
**ТАБЛИЦА 3-4А. Географическое распределение внешней торговли (млн. долларов США)**

| Country or country group | Exports Экспорт 1990 | 1991 | 1992 | 1993 | 1994 | 1995 | Imports Импорт 1990 | 1991 | 1992 | 1993 | 1994 | 1995 | Страна или группа стран |
|---|---|---|---|---|---|---|---|---|---|---|---|---|---|
| **Total trade** | .. | .. | .. | .. | .. | 4,706.8 | .. | .. | .. | .. | .. | 5,563.6 | **Всего** |
| **CIS countries** | .. | .. | .. | .. | .. | 2,930.4 | .. | .. | .. | .. | .. | 3,676.8 | **Страны СНГ** |
| Armenia | .. | .. | .. | .. | .. | 2.7 | .. | .. | .. | .. | .. | 1.0 | Армения |
| Azerbaijan | .. | .. | .. | .. | .. | 6.2 | .. | .. | .. | .. | .. | 4.3 | Азербайджан |
| Belarus | .. | .. | .. | .. | .. | .. | .. | .. | .. | .. | .. | .. | Беларусь |
| Georgia | .. | .. | .. | .. | .. | 3.6 | .. | .. | .. | .. | .. | 3.0 | Грузия |
| Kazakstan | .. | .. | .. | .. | .. | 76.5 | .. | .. | .. | .. | .. | 56.0 | Казахстан |
| Kyrgyz Republic | .. | .. | .. | .. | .. | 5.9 | .. | .. | .. | .. | .. | 2.9 | Киргизстан |
| Moldova | .. | .. | .. | .. | .. | 70.9 | .. | .. | .. | .. | .. | 35.0 | Молдова |
| Russia | .. | .. | .. | .. | .. | 2,088.9 | .. | .. | .. | .. | .. | 2,965.0 | Россия |
| Tajikistan | .. | .. | .. | .. | .. | 5.3 | .. | .. | .. | .. | .. | 3.0 | Таджикистан |
| Turkmenistan | .. | .. | .. | .. | .. | 3.2 | .. | .. | .. | .. | .. | 0.8 | Туркменистан |
| Ukraine | .. | .. | .. | .. | .. | 607.2 | .. | .. | .. | .. | .. | 569.0 | Украина |
| Uzbekistan | .. | .. | .. | .. | .. | 60.0 | .. | .. | .. | .. | .. | 36.8 | Узбекистан |
| **Non-CIS countries** | .. | .. | .. | .. | .. | 1,776.4 | .. | .. | .. | .. | .. | 1,886.8 | **Остальной мир** |
| **Europe** | .. | .. | .. | .. | .. | 1,386.1 | .. | .. | .. | .. | .. | 1,589.6 | **Европа** |
| Austria | .. | .. | .. | .. | .. | 18.4 | .. | .. | .. | .. | .. | 45.3 | Австрия |
| Belgium | .. | .. | .. | .. | .. | 53.4 | .. | .. | .. | .. | .. | 43.6 | Бельгия |
| Bulgaria | .. | .. | .. | .. | .. | 15.9 | .. | .. | .. | .. | .. | 22.6 | Болгария |
| Czech Republic | .. | .. | .. | .. | .. | 15.4 | .. | .. | .. | .. | .. | 53.7 | Чешская Республика |
| Denmark | .. | .. | .. | .. | .. | 5.8 | .. | .. | .. | .. | .. | 24.1 | Дания |
| Estonia | .. | .. | .. | .. | .. | 19.0 | .. | .. | .. | .. | .. | 15.8 | Эстония |
| Finland | .. | .. | .. | .. | .. | 18.2 | .. | .. | .. | .. | .. | 38.3 | Финляндия |
| Former Yugoslavia | .. | .. | .. | .. | .. | 3.1 | .. | .. | .. | .. | .. | 0.2 | Быв. Югославия |
| France | .. | .. | .. | .. | .. | 22.8 | .. | .. | .. | .. | .. | 62.0 | Франция |
| Germany | .. | .. | .. | .. | .. | 267.8 | .. | .. | .. | .. | .. | 424.1 | Германия |
| Hungary | .. | .. | .. | .. | .. | 37.9 | .. | .. | .. | .. | .. | 88.0 | Венгрия |
| Iceland | .. | .. | .. | .. | .. | 0.0 | .. | .. | .. | .. | .. | 0.2 | Исландия |
| Ireland | .. | .. | .. | .. | .. | 1.4 | .. | .. | .. | .. | .. | 4.5 | Ирландия |
| Italy | .. | .. | .. | .. | .. | 60.8 | .. | .. | .. | .. | .. | 82.7 | Италия |
| Latvia | .. | .. | .. | .. | .. | 195.7 | .. | .. | .. | .. | .. | 57.8 | Латвия |
| Lithuania | .. | .. | .. | .. | .. | 146.4 | .. | .. | .. | .. | .. | 117.8 | Литва |
| Netherlands | .. | .. | .. | .. | .. | 76.2 | .. | .. | .. | .. | .. | 86.8 | Нидерланды |
| Norway | .. | .. | .. | .. | .. | 2.7 | .. | .. | .. | .. | .. | 10.4 | Норвегия |
| Poland | .. | .. | .. | .. | .. | 271.4 | .. | .. | .. | .. | .. | 197.4 | Польша |
| Romania | .. | .. | .. | .. | .. | 24.3 | .. | .. | .. | .. | .. | 5.0 | Румыния |
| Slovak Republic | .. | .. | .. | .. | .. | 40.0 | .. | .. | .. | .. | .. | 32.7 | Словацская Республика |
| Spain | .. | .. | .. | .. | .. | 3.5 | .. | .. | .. | .. | .. | 14.1 | Испания |
| Sweden | .. | .. | .. | .. | .. | 3.5 | .. | .. | .. | .. | .. | 41.6 | Швеция |

**TABLE 3-4A. Geographical distribution of foreign trade (millions of U.S. dollars)**
**ТАБЛИЦА 3-4А. Географическое распределение внешней торговли (млн. долларов США)**

| Country or country group | Exports Экспорт 1990 | 1991 | 1992 | 1993 | 1994 | 1995 | Imports Импорт 1990 | 1991 | 1992 | 1993 | 1994 | 1995 | Страна или группа стран |
|---|---|---|---|---|---|---|---|---|---|---|---|---|---|
| Switzerland | .. | .. | .. | .. | .. | 7.5 | .. | .. | .. | .. | .. | 16.7 | Швейцария |
| United Kingdom | .. | .. | .. | .. | .. | 38.8 | .. | .. | .. | .. | .. | 57.2 | Великобритания |
| Other Europe | .. | .. | .. | .. | .. | 36.2 | .. | .. | .. | .. | .. | 47.0 | Остальные страны Европы |
| **Asia** | .. | .. | .. | .. | .. | 189.8 | .. | .. | .. | .. | .. | 121.3 | **Азия** |
| Afghanistan | .. | .. | .. | .. | .. | 1.7 | .. | .. | .. | .. | .. | 0.6 | Афганистан |
| China | .. | .. | .. | .. | .. | 16.0 | .. | .. | .. | .. | .. | 16.7 | Китай |
| India | .. | .. | .. | .. | .. | 4.0 | .. | .. | .. | .. | .. | 11.8 | Индия |
| Iraq | .. | .. | .. | .. | .. | .. | .. | .. | .. | .. | .. | .. | Ирак |
| Japan | .. | .. | .. | .. | .. | 0.9 | .. | .. | .. | .. | .. | 20.8 | Япония |
| Korea, Dem. People's Rep. | .. | .. | .. | .. | .. | 5.6 | .. | .. | .. | .. | .. | 0.1 | КНДР |
| Korea, Rep. of | .. | .. | .. | .. | .. | 3.2 | .. | .. | .. | .. | .. | 7.3 | Южная Корея |
| Mongolia | .. | .. | .. | .. | .. | 6.0 | .. | .. | .. | .. | .. | 0.0 | МНР |
| Syrian Arab Republic | .. | .. | .. | .. | .. | 0.8 | .. | .. | .. | .. | .. | 0.9 | Сирия |
| Turkey | .. | .. | .. | .. | .. | 33.6 | .. | .. | .. | .. | .. | 7.6 | Турция |
| Viet Nam | .. | .. | .. | .. | .. | 12.9 | .. | .. | .. | .. | .. | 1.1 | Вьетнам |
| Other Asia | .. | .. | .. | .. | .. | 105.1 | .. | .. | .. | .. | .. | 54.4 | Остальные страны Азии |
| **America** | .. | .. | .. | .. | .. | 84.0 | .. | .. | .. | .. | .. | 152.3 | **Сев. и Южная Америка** |
| Canada | .. | .. | .. | .. | .. | 6.2 | .. | .. | .. | .. | .. | 4.9 | Канада |
| Cuba | .. | .. | .. | .. | .. | 2.5 | .. | .. | .. | .. | .. | 5.3 | Куба |
| United States | .. | .. | .. | .. | .. | 57.7 | .. | .. | .. | .. | .. | 97.2 | США |
| Other America | .. | .. | .. | .. | .. | 17.6 | .. | .. | .. | .. | .. | 44.9 | Остальные |
| **Africa** | .. | .. | .. | .. | .. | 113.5 | .. | .. | .. | .. | .. | 22.9 | **Африка** |
| Egypt | .. | .. | .. | .. | .. | 70.4 | .. | .. | .. | .. | .. | 0.4 | Египет |
| Libya | .. | .. | .. | .. | .. | 0.0 | .. | .. | .. | .. | .. | 0.1 | Ливия |
| Other Africa | .. | .. | .. | .. | .. | 43.1 | .. | .. | .. | .. | .. | 22.4 | Остальные |
| **Rest of the World** | .. | .. | .. | .. | .. | 3.0 | .. | .. | .. | .. | .. | 0.7 | **Прочие страны мира** |
| Australia | .. | .. | .. | .. | .. | 2.8 | .. | .. | .. | .. | .. | 0.6 | Австралия |

TABLE 3-4B. Geographical distribution of foreign trade (millions of national currency)

ТАБЛИЦА 3-4B. Географическое распределение внешней торговли (миллионов национальной валюты)

| Country or country group | Exports Экспорт 1990 | 1991 | 1992 | 1993 | 1994 | 1995 | Imports Импорт 1990 | 1991 | 1992 | 1993 | 1994 | 1995 | Страна или группа стран |
|---|---|---|---|---|---|---|---|---|---|---|---|---|---|
| **Total trade** | .. | .. | .. | .. | .. | 54,035,810.9 | .. | .. | .. | .. | .. | 63,752,635.1 | **Всего** |
| **CIS countries** | .. | .. | .. | .. | .. | 33,558,879.8 | .. | .. | .. | .. | .. | 42,105,783.0 | **Страны СНГ** |
| Armenia | .. | .. | .. | .. | .. | 30,850.4 | .. | .. | .. | .. | .. | 11,993.1 | Армения |
| Azerbaijan | .. | .. | .. | .. | .. | 71,936.7 | .. | .. | .. | .. | .. | 49,461.7 | Азербайджан |
| Belarus | .. | .. | .. | .. | .. | .. | .. | .. | .. | .. | .. | .. | Беларусь |
| Georgia | .. | .. | .. | .. | .. | 41,115.3 | .. | .. | .. | .. | .. | 34,585.6 | Грузия |
| Kazakstan | .. | .. | .. | .. | .. | 880,940.0 | .. | .. | .. | .. | .. | 645,564.2 | Казахстан |
| Kyrgyz Republic | .. | .. | .. | .. | .. | 68,122.8 | .. | .. | .. | .. | .. | 33,709.4 | Киргизстан |
| Moldova | .. | .. | .. | .. | .. | 816,761.7 | .. | .. | .. | .. | .. | 403,396.6 | Молдова |
| Russia | .. | .. | .. | .. | .. | 23,854,814.4 | .. | .. | .. | .. | .. | 33,908,254.6 | Россия |
| Tajikistan | .. | .. | .. | .. | .. | 60,984.7 | .. | .. | .. | .. | .. | 34,249.4 | Таджикистан |
| Turkmenistan | .. | .. | .. | .. | .. | 37,286.7 | .. | .. | .. | .. | .. | 9,355.4 | Туркменистан |
| Ukraine | .. | .. | .. | .. | .. | 7,004,822.8 | .. | .. | .. | .. | .. | 6,552,981.7 | Украина |
| Uzbekistan | .. | .. | .. | .. | .. | 691,243.7 | .. | .. | .. | .. | .. | 422,231.3 | Узбекистан |
| **Non-CIS countries** | .. | .. | .. | .. | .. | 20,476,931.0 | .. | .. | .. | .. | .. | 21,646,852.2 | **Остальной мир** |
| **Europe** | .. | .. | .. | .. | .. | 15,976,489.0 | .. | .. | .. | .. | .. | 18,228,467.9 | **Европа** |
| Austria | .. | .. | .. | .. | .. | 211,701.0 | .. | .. | .. | .. | .. | 518,063.0 | Австрия |
| Belgium | .. | .. | .. | .. | .. | 617,193.2 | .. | .. | .. | .. | .. | 499,373.5 | Бельгия |
| Bulgaria | .. | .. | .. | .. | .. | 183,617.5 | .. | .. | .. | .. | .. | 260,525.1 | Болгария |
| Czech Republic | .. | .. | .. | .. | .. | 177,116.0 | .. | .. | .. | .. | .. | 619,525.3 | Чешская Республика |
| Denmark | .. | .. | .. | .. | .. | 67,289.4 | .. | .. | .. | .. | .. | 276,543.6 | Дания |
| Estonia | .. | .. | .. | .. | .. | 219,351.4 | .. | .. | .. | .. | .. | 182,559.3 | Эстония |
| Finland | .. | .. | .. | .. | .. | 209,660.9 | .. | .. | .. | .. | .. | 440,682.1 | Финляндия |
| Former Yugoslavia | .. | .. | .. | .. | .. | 35,895.1 | .. | .. | .. | .. | .. | 1,898.3 | Быв. Югославия |
| France | .. | .. | .. | .. | .. | 262,578.4 | .. | .. | .. | .. | .. | 714,424.0 | Франция |
| Germany | .. | .. | .. | .. | .. | 3,088,061.9 | .. | .. | .. | .. | .. | 4,815,786.4 | Германия |
| Hungary | .. | .. | .. | .. | .. | 436,961.3 | .. | .. | .. | .. | .. | 1,014,568.6 | Венгрия |
| Iceland | .. | .. | .. | .. | .. | 269.3 | .. | .. | .. | .. | .. | 2,021.0 | Исландия |
| Ireland | .. | .. | .. | .. | .. | 15,887.2 | .. | .. | .. | .. | .. | 51,346.5 | Ирландия |
| Italy | .. | .. | .. | .. | .. | 700,880.4 | .. | .. | .. | .. | .. | 950,308.7 | Италия |
| Latvia | .. | .. | .. | .. | .. | 2,252,862.6 | .. | .. | .. | .. | .. | 666,716.7 | Латвия |
| Lithuania | .. | .. | .. | .. | .. | 1,686,100.4 | .. | .. | .. | .. | .. | 1,356,494.3 | Литва |
| Netherlands | .. | .. | .. | .. | .. | 877,588.8 | .. | .. | .. | .. | .. | 999,320.6 | Нидерланды |
| Norway | .. | .. | .. | .. | .. | 31,131.1 | .. | .. | .. | .. | .. | 120,159.3 | Норвегия |
| Poland | .. | .. | .. | .. | .. | 3,129,825.5 | .. | .. | .. | .. | .. | 2,272,440.5 | Польша |
| Romania | .. | .. | .. | .. | .. | 279,546.1 | .. | .. | .. | .. | .. | 58,015.9 | Румыния |
| Slovak Republic | .. | .. | .. | .. | .. | 461,416.6 | .. | .. | .. | .. | .. | 377,584.9 | Словацкая Республика |
| Spain | .. | .. | .. | .. | .. | 40,442.1 | .. | .. | .. | .. | .. | 162,332.3 | Испания |

**TABLE 3-4B. Geographical distribution of foreign trade (millions of national currency)**

**ТАБЛИЦА 3-4B. Географическое распределение внешней торговли (миллионов национальной валюты)**

| Country or country group | Exports Экспорт 1990 | 1991 | 1992 | 1993 | 1994 | 1995 | Imports Импорт 1990 | 1991 | 1992 | 1993 | 1994 | 1995 | Страна или группа стран |
|---|---|---|---|---|---|---|---|---|---|---|---|---|---|
| Sweden | .. | .. | .. | .. | .. | 40,305.5 | .. | .. | .. | .. | .. | 477,999.4 | Швеция |
| Switzerland | .. | .. | .. | .. | .. | 86,761.1 | .. | .. | .. | .. | .. | 192,669.8 | Швейцария |
| United Kingdom | .. | .. | .. | .. | .. | 447,121.4 | .. | .. | .. | .. | .. | 658,640.0 | Великобритания |
| Other Europe | .. | .. | .. | .. | .. | 416,926.0 | .. | .. | .. | .. | .. | 538,468.8 | Остальные страны Европы |
| **Asia** | .. | .. | .. | .. | .. | 2,188,276.9 | .. | .. | .. | .. | .. | 1,395,213.3 | **Азия** |
| Afghanistan | .. | .. | .. | .. | .. | 19,826.5 | .. | .. | .. | .. | .. | 7,049.7 | Афганистан |
| China | .. | .. | .. | .. | .. | 184,298.2 | .. | .. | .. | .. | .. | 192,075.1 | Китай |
| India | .. | .. | .. | .. | .. | 45,995.7 | .. | .. | .. | .. | .. | 136,632.4 | Индия |
| Iraq | .. | .. | .. | .. | .. | .. | .. | .. | .. | .. | .. | .. | Ирак |
| Japan | .. | .. | .. | .. | .. | 10,815.0 | .. | .. | .. | .. | .. | 236,177.3 | Япония |
| Korea, Dem. People's Rep. | .. | .. | .. | .. | .. | 64,186.5 | .. | .. | .. | .. | .. | 1,161.9 | КНДР |
| Korea, Rep. of | .. | .. | .. | .. | .. | 36,785.1 | .. | .. | .. | .. | .. | 84,476.1 | Южная Корея |
| Mongolia | .. | .. | .. | .. | .. | 69,171.1 | .. | .. | .. | .. | .. | 92.9 | МНР |
| Syrian Arab Republic | .. | .. | .. | .. | .. | 8,856.4 | .. | .. | .. | .. | .. | 10,355.8 | Сирия |
| Turkey | .. | .. | .. | .. | .. | 387,485.4 | .. | .. | .. | .. | .. | 87,764.3 | Турция |
| Viet Nam | .. | .. | .. | .. | .. | 148,498.2 | .. | .. | .. | .. | .. | 12,470.3 | Вьетнам |
| Other Asia | .. | .. | .. | .. | .. | 1,212,359.4 | .. | .. | .. | .. | .. | 626,957.5 | Остальные страны Азии |
| **America** | .. | .. | .. | .. | .. | 967,923.8 | .. | .. | .. | .. | .. | 1,749,415.5 | **Сев. и Южная Америка** |
| Canada | .. | .. | .. | .. | .. | 71,776.5 | .. | .. | .. | .. | .. | 56,319.0 | Канада |
| Cuba | .. | .. | .. | .. | .. | 29,115.6 | .. | .. | .. | .. | .. | 60,463.2 | Куба |
| United States | .. | .. | .. | .. | .. | 663,853.3 | .. | .. | .. | .. | .. | 1,115,964.9 | США |
| Other America | .. | .. | .. | .. | .. | 203,178.4 | .. | .. | .. | .. | .. | 516,669.2 | Остальные |
| **Africa** | .. | .. | .. | .. | .. | 1,309,696.6 | .. | .. | .. | .. | .. | 265,326.7 | **Африка** |
| Egypt | .. | .. | .. | .. | .. | 811,711.3 | .. | .. | .. | .. | .. | 4,291.0 | Египет |
| Libya | .. | .. | .. | .. | .. | 539.0 | .. | .. | .. | .. | .. | 815.6 | Ливия |
| Other Africa | .. | .. | .. | .. | .. | 497,447.0 | .. | .. | .. | .. | .. | 260,220.1 | Остальные |
| **Rest of the World** | .. | .. | .. | .. | .. | 34,544.1 | .. | .. | .. | .. | .. | 8,428.0 | **Прочие страны мира** |
| Australia | .. | .. | .. | .. | .. | 32,266.6 | .. | .. | .. | .. | .. | 7,150.3 | Австралия |

**TABLE 4-1. General government budget revenue (millions of national currency)**

**ТАБЛИЦА 4-1. Доходы государственного бюджета (млн. национальной валюты)**

| Type of revenue | 1990 | 1991 | 1992 | 1993 | 1994 | 1995 | Вид доходов |
|---|---|---|---|---|---|---|---|
| **Total revenue and grants** | .. | .. | 295,759 | .. | 6,492,566 | 35,467,949 | **Всего доходов и безвозм. поступл.** |
| Grants | .. | .. | 4,500 | .. | .. | .. | Безвозмездные поступления |
| Total Revenue | .. | .. | 291,259 | .. | 6,492,566 | 35,467,949 | Всего доходов |
| **Current revenue** | .. | .. | 286,244 | .. | 6,388,421 | 34,608,756 | **Текущие доходы** |
| Tax revenue | .. | .. | 276,858 | .. | 6,192,050 | 31,768,051 | Доход от налогов |
| Taxes on income and profits | .. | .. | 98,478 | .. | 2,464,983 | 11,634,219 | Налоги на доходы и прибыль |
| Individual | .. | .. | 21,949 | .. | 473,161 | 3,300,135 | Физические лица |
| Corporate | .. | .. | 76,529 | .. | 1,991,822 | 8,334,083 | Предприятия и организации |
| Social security contributions | .. | .. | 369 | .. | .. | .. | Отчисление на соцстрах. |
| Taxes on payroll or work force | .. | .. | 24,810 | .. | 412,632 | 2,785,963 | Налоги на заработную плату и рабочую силу |
| Taxes on the use of labor force | .. | .. | .. | .. | .. | .. | Плата за трудовые ресурсы |
| Taxes on increases in wages and salaries | .. | .. | .. | .. | .. | .. | Налог с прироста средств на оплату труда |
| Other payroll/work force taxes | .. | .. | 24,810 | .. | 412,632 | 2,785,963 | Другие налоги на зарплату и рабочую силу |
| Taxes on property | .. | .. | 3,348 | .. | 103,171 | 1,216,591 | Налоги на собственность |
| Taxes on immovable property | .. | .. | 1,797 | .. | 83,825 | 883,090 | Налоги на недвижимое имущество |
| Buildings | .. | .. | 1,785 | .. | 83,509 | 881,585 | Налог с владельцев строении |
| Land | .. | .. | 12 | .. | 316 | 1,505 | Земельныи налог |
| Estate, inheritance, and gift taxes | .. | .. | 1,363 | .. | 19,179 | 308,863 | Налоги на наследство, подарки |
| Other property taxes | .. | .. | 188 | .. | 167 | 24,638 | Другие налоги на имущество |
| Domestic taxes on goods and services | .. | .. | 145,016 | .. | 2,627,802 | 13,814,543 | Внутренние налоги на товары и услуги |
| General sales, turnover, or value-added taxes | .. | .. | 110,671 | .. | 1,780,052 | 9,933,911 | Налог с продаж. с оборота или на добав. стоим. |
| Excises | .. | .. | 33,477 | .. | 833,130 | 3,402,801 | Акцизы |
| Profits of fiscal monopolies | .. | .. | .. | .. | .. | .. | Прибыли фискальных монополий |
| Taxes on specific services | .. | .. | .. | .. | .. | .. | Налоги на особые услуги |
| Taxes on use of goods or permission to use goods or to perform activities | .. | .. | 121 | .. | 1,006 | 341,379 | Налоги на пользование товарами или лицензии на пользование товарами и занятие деятельностью |
| Other taxes on goods and services | .. | .. | 747 | .. | 13,614 | 136,452 | Другие налоги на товары и услуги |
| Taxes on international trade and transactions | .. | .. | 4,786 | .. | 583,462 | 1,864,577 | Налоги на внешнюю торговлю и операции |
| Import duties | .. | .. | 1,001 | .. | 146,623 | 1,065,034 | Импортные пошлины |
| Export duties | .. | .. | 2,105 | .. | 37,727 | 731,128 | Экпортные пошлины |
| Other | .. | .. | 1,680 | .. | 399,112 | 68,415 | Другие |
| Other taxes | .. | .. | 51 | .. | .. | 452,158 | Прочие налоги |
| Nontax revenue | .. | .. | 9,386 | .. | 196,371 | 2,840,705 | Неналоговые доходы |
| **Capital revenue** | .. | .. | 5,015 | .. | 104,145 | 859,193 | **Капитальные доходы** |

**TABLE 4-2. General government budget expenditure by economic type (millions of national currency)**
**ТАБЛИЦА 4-2. Расходы государственного бюджета по экономическим типам (млн. национальной валюты)**

| Type of expenditure or debt holder | 1990 | 1991 | 1992 | 1993 | 1994 | 1995 | Всего расходов |
|---|---|---|---|---|---|---|---|
| **Total expenditure by economic type** | .. | .. | 318,097 | .. | 7,109,663 | 38,816,632 | **Всего расходов по экономическим типам** |
| **Current expenditure** | .. | .. | 246,430 | .. | 5,680,378 | 31,284,587 | **Текущие расходы** |
| Expenditure on goods and services | .. | .. | 164,242 | .. | 3,912,266 | 27,113,886 | Расходы на товары и услуги |
| Wages and salaries | .. | .. | 35,680 | .. | 656,582 | 5,436,946 | Заработная плата |
| Employer contributions | .. | .. | 12,400 | .. | 209,132 | 1,764,757 | Отчисление на социальное страхование |
| Other Purchases of goods and services | .. | .. | 116,162 | .. | 3,046,552 | 19,912,183 | Другие покупки товаров и услуг |
| Interest payments | .. | .. | 5,945 | .. | 39,558 | 293,832 | Выплаты процентов |
| Domestic debt | .. | .. | 5,945 | .. | 39,558 | 184,803 | По внутреннему долгу |
| Foreign debt | .. | .. | .. | .. | .. | 109,029 | По внешнему долгу |
| Subsidies and other current transfers | .. | .. | 76,243 | .. | 1,728,554 | 3,876,869 | Субсидии на другие текущие трансферты |
| Subsidies | .. | .. | 46,688 | .. | 930,873 | 1,421,219 | Субсидии |
| Agricultural subsidies | .. | .. | 11,526 | .. | 30,255 | 58,756 | Субсидии на сельское хозяиство |
| Other current transfers | .. | .. | 29,555 | .. | 797,681 | 2,455,650 | Другие текущие трансферты |
| Other | .. | .. | .. | .. | .. | .. | Прочие расходы |
| **Capital expenditure** | .. | .. | 71,667 | .. | 1,429,285 | 7,532,045 | **Капитальные расходы** |
| Acquisition of fixed capital assets | .. | .. | 71,667 | .. | 1,429,285 | 7,532,045 | Приобретение основного капитала |
| Capital transfers | .. | .. | .. | .. | .. | .. | Капитальные трансферты |
| Other | .. | .. | .. | .. | .. | .. | Другие капитальные расходы |
| **Surplus/deficit (-)** | .. | .. | -22,338 | .. | -617,097 | -3,348,683 | **Превыш. доходов над расходами/дефицит(-)** |
| **Financing by type of debt holder** | .. | .. | 22,338 | .. | 617,097 | 3,348,683 | **Финансирование по типам кредиторов** |
| **Foreign (net)** | .. | .. | 9,433 | .. | 451,699 | 431,168 | **Зарубежные кредиторы (сальдо)** |
| From international development institutions | .. | .. | 9,433 | .. | .. | 1,038,879 | Международные организации |
| From foreign governments | .. | .. | .. | .. | .. | .. | Правительства иностранных государств |
| Other borrowing abroad | .. | .. | .. | .. | .. | -607,711 | Другие зарубежные кредиторы |
| **Domestic (net)** | .. | .. | 12,905 | .. | 165,398 | 2,917,515 | **Внутренние кредиторы (сальдо)** |
| From monetary authorities | .. | .. | 27,296 | .. | 9,619 | 485,034 | Органы денежного обращения |
| From deposit money banks | .. | .. | -13,740 | .. | 448,900 | 2,036,980 | Депозитные денежные банки |
| Other domestic borrowing | .. | .. | -651 | .. | -293,121 | 395,501 | Другие внутренние кредиторы |
| *Memo items:* | | | | | | | *Справочно:* |
| Extrabudgetary surplus/ Deficit (-) not included above | .. | .. | .. | .. | .. | .. | Превышение доходов над расходами/дефицит (-) по внебюджетным фондам, не включенным выше |
| Total surplus/deficit (-) including extrabudgetary accounts | .. | .. | .. | .. | .. | .. | Итого превышение доходов над расходами/дефицит, включая счета внебюджетных фондов |

**TABLE 5-1. Agricultural production (millions of national currency, current prices)** **BELARUS**

**ТАБЛИЦА 5-1. Сельскохозяйственная продукция (млн. нац. валюты, текущие цены)**

| Item | 1990 | 1991 | 1992 | 1993 | 1994 | 1995 | Статьи |
|---|---|---|---|---|---|---|---|
| **Total gross agricultural production** | 16,904 | 30,122 | 321,248 | 3,764,087 | 7,547,414 | 49,668,332 | **Валовая продукция сельского хозяйства - всего** |
| **Crops** | 6,084 | 14,015 | 166,915 | 1,799,700 | 4,387,104 | 23,642,000 | **Продукция растениеводства** |
| Grains | .. | .. | .. | .. | .. | .. | Зерно |
| Potatoes | .. | .. | .. | .. | .. | .. | Картофель |
| Vegetables | .. | .. | .. | .. | .. | .. | Овощи |
| Fruits (excluding grapes) | .. | .. | .. | .. | .. | .. | Фрукты (без винограда) |
| Grapes | .. | .. | .. | .. | .. | .. | Виноград |
| Tobacco | .. | .. | .. | .. | .. | .. | Табак |
| Cotton | .. | .. | .. | .. | .. | .. | Хлопок |
| Sugarbeets | .. | .. | .. | .. | .. | .. | Сахарная свекла |
| Oilseeds | .. | .. | .. | .. | .. | .. | Семена масличных культур |
| Other | .. | .. | .. | .. | .. | .. | Прочие |
| **Animal husbandry** | 10,819 | 16,107 | 154,333 | 1,964,387 | 3,160,310 | 26,026,332 | **Продукция животноводства** |
| Livestock | .. | .. | .. | .. | .. | .. | Мясное животноводство |
| Cattle | .. | .. | .. | .. | .. | .. | Крупный рогатый скот |
| Pigs | .. | .. | .. | .. | .. | .. | Свиньи |
| Sheep and goats | .. | .. | .. | .. | .. | .. | Овцы и козы |
| Poultry | .. | .. | .. | .. | .. | .. | Птица |
| Other | .. | .. | .. | .. | .. | .. | Прочие |
| Milk | .. | .. | .. | .. | .. | .. | Молоко |
| Eggs | .. | .. | .. | .. | .. | .. | Яйца |
| Wool | .. | .. | .. | .. | .. | .. | Шерсть |
| Other livestock | .. | .. | .. | .. | .. | .. | Прочая |
| **Agricultural services** | .. | .. | .. | .. | .. | .. | **Сельскохозяйственные услуги** |

## TABLE 5-2. Agricultural production (millions of constant national currency)
## ТАБЛИЦА 5-2. Сельскохозяйственная продукция в постоянных ценах (млн. национальной валюты)

| Item | 1990 | 1991 | 1992 | 1993 | 1994 | 1995 | Статьи |
|---|---|---|---|---|---|---|---|
| **Total gross agricultural production** | 11,847 | 11,267 | 10,308 | 10,693 | 9,157 | 8,723 | **Валовая продукция сельского хозяйства - всего** |
| **Crops** | 4,378 | 4,652 | 4,638 | 5,257 | 4,059 | 4,133 | **Продукция растениеводства** |
| Grains | 923 | 796 | 933 | 1,034 | 839 | 752 | Зерно |
| Potatoes | 1,642 | 1,713 | 1,714 | 2,226 | 1,576 | 1,817 | Картофель |
| Vegetables | 216 | 274 | 242 | 321 | 309 | 313 | Овощи |
| Fruits (excluding grapes) | 223 | 192 | 294 | 427 | 234 | 219 | Фрукты (без винограда) |
| Grapes | .. | .. | .. | .. | .. | .. | Виноград |
| Tobacco | .. | .. | .. | .. | .. | .. | Табак |
| Cotton | .. | .. | .. | .. | .. | .. | Хлопок |
| Sugarbeets | 76 | 59 | 57 | 81 | 55 | 60 | Сахарная свекла |
| Oilseeds | 57 | 47 | 51 | 28 | 27 | 36 | Семена масличных культур |
| Other | 1,241 | 1,571 | 1,347 | 1,140 | 1,019 | 936 | Прочие |
| **Animal husbandry** | 7,469 | 6,615 | 5,670 | 5,436 | 5,098 | 4,590 | **Продукция животноводства** |
| Livestock | 4,007 | 3,438 | 2,879 | 2,705 | 2,412 | 2,103 | Мясное животноводство |
| Cattle | 2,349 | 1,948 | 1,646 | 1,528 | 1,368 | 1,160 | Крупный рогатый скот |
| Pigs | 1,185 | 1,017 | 832 | 797 | 720 | 691 | Свиньи |
| Sheep and goats | 28 | 21 | 21 | 19 | 15 | 15 | Овцы и козы |
| Poultry | 445 | 452 | 380 | 361 | 309 | 237 | Птица |
| Other | .. | .. | .. | .. | .. | .. | Прочие |
| Milk | 2,955 | 2,700 | 2,332 | 2,213 | 2,184 | 2,010 | Молоко |
| Eggs | 350 | 356 | 335 | 340 | 326 | 323 | Яйца |
| Wool | 8 | 7 | 6 | 5 | 4 | .. | Шерсть |
| Other livestock | 149 | 114 | 118 | 173 | 172 | 154 | Прочая |
| **Agricultural services** | .. | .. | .. | .. | .. | .. | **Сельскохозяйственные услуги** |

## TABLE 5-3. Production and average yield of major agricultural crops



## ТАБЛИЦА 5-3. Производство и урожайность важнейших сельскохозяйственных культур

| Crop | 1990 | 1991 | 1992 | 1993 | 1994 | 1995 | Сельскохозяйственные культуры |
|---|---|---|---|---|---|---|---|
| **Production (thousands of tons)** | | | | | | | **Производство (тыс. тонн)** |
| Grain - Cleanweight | 7,035 | 6,296 | 7,230 | 7,508 | 6,095 | 5,502 | Зерно в чистом весе |
| Winter wheat | 353 | 221 | 304 | 316 | 185 | 358 | Пшеница - озимая |
| Spring wheat | 29 | 21 | 26 | 38 | 46 | 81 | яровая |
| Coarse grain | 8,236 | 7,199 | 7,972 | 8,766 | 7,116 | 6,157 | Зерно в физическом весе |
| Rye | 2,652 | 1,962 | 3,063 | 2,826 | 1,864 | 2,143 | Рожь |
| Corn | 24 | 28 | 3 | 6 | 1 | 3 | Кукуруза |
| Winter barley | 2 | 13 | 27 | 31 | 11 | 7 | Ячмень - озимый |
| Spring barley | 2,906 | 3,020 | 2,907 | 3,134 | 3,003 | 1,957 | яровой |
| Oats | 806 | 760 | 723 | 871 | 760 | 638 | Овес |
| Millet | 0 | 0 | 0 | 0 | 0 | 0 | Просо |
| Rice | .. | .. | .. | .. | .. | .. | Рис |
| Flax | 52 | 76 | 61 | 57 | 49 | 60 | Лен |
| Oilseeds | 0 | 0 | 0 | .. | .. | .. | Семена масличных культур |
| Cotton (raw) | .. | .. | .. | .. | .. | .. | Хлопок - сырец |
| Cotton fiber | .. | .. | .. | .. | .. | .. | волокно |
| Sugarbeets | 1,479 | 1,147 | 1,120 | 1,568 | 1,078 | 1,172 | Сахарная свекла |
| Potatoes | 8,590 | 8,958 | 8,984 | 11,644 | 8,241 | 9,504 | Картофель |
| Pulses | 252 | 257 | 169 | 193 | 155 | 187 | Бобовые |
| Vegetables | 749 | 918 | 838 | 1,047 | 1,029 | 1,031 | Овощи |
| Fruit | 373 | 311 | 480 | 807 | 396 | 383 | Фрукты |
| Grapes | .. | .. | .. | .. | .. | .. | Виноград |
| Other | .. | .. | .. | .. | .. | .. | Прочие |
| Corn (silage and greenchop) | 10,463 | 9,651 | 5,261 | 7,078 | 2,758 | 3,007 | Кукуруза (на силос и зеленый корм) |
| Hay | 2,083 | 2,581 | 2,020 | 1,713 | 1,959 | 1,508 | Сено |
| **Average yield (kilograms per hectare)** | | | | | | | **Ср. урожайность (кг с га)** |
| Grain | 2,660 | 2,420 | 2,680 | 2,770 | 2,240 | 2,040 | Зерно |
| Winter wheat | 2,830 | 2,590 | 2,880 | 2,680 | 2,220 | 2,540 | Пшеница - озимая |
| Spring wheat | 1,870 | 2,070 | 2,050 | 2,770 | 2,520 | 2,230 | яровая |
| Coarse grain | 3,110 | 2,760 | 2,950 | 3,230 | 2,616 | 2,287 | Зерно в физическом весе |
| Rye | 2,890 | 2,510 | 3,060 | 2,790 | 2,250 | 2,210 | Рожь |
| Corn | 3,210 | 3,460 | 2,390 | 1,200 | 530 | 2,450 | Кукуруза |
| Winter barley | 2,780 | 2,280 | 2,790 | 2,080 | 2,190 | 2,310 | Ячмень - озимый |
| Spring barley | 2,820 | 2,540 | 2,660 | 2,850 | 2,380 | 1,900 | яровой |
| Oats | 2,240 | 2,110 | 2,170 | 2,820 | 2,060 | 1,890 | Овес |
| Millet | .. | 1,780 | 1,490 | 1,250 | .. | .. | Просо |
| Rice | .. | .. | .. | .. | .. | .. | Рис |
| Flax | 350 | 630 | 490 | 590 | 590 | 610 | Лен |
| Oilseeds | .. | .. | .. | .. | .. | .. | Семена масличных культур |
| Cotton (raw) | .. | .. | .. | .. | .. | .. | Хлопок - сырец |
| Cotton fiber | .. | .. | .. | .. | .. | .. | волокно |
| Sugarbeets | 32,000 | 25,600 | 21,900 | 28,300 | 18,700 | 21,200 | Сахарная свекла |
| Potatoes | 13,500 | 13,700 | 11,500 | 15,500 | 11,800 | 13,100 | Картофель |
| Pulses | 1,460 | 1,740 | 1,430 | 1,950 | 1,480 | 1,570 | Бобовые |
| Vegetables | 17,800 | 17,400 | 13,000 | 15,800 | 14,100 | 13,300 | Овощи |
| Fruit | 3,190 | 2,680 | 4,160 | 6,990 | 3,460 | 3,330 | Фрукты |
| Grapes | .. | .. | .. | .. | .. | .. | Виноград |
| Other | .. | .. | .. | .. | .. | .. | Прочие |
| Corn (silage and greenchop) | 22,100 | 21,700 | 12,800 | 19,700 | 10,100 | 18,800 | Кукуруза (на силос и зеленый корм) |
| Hay | 2,480 | 2,890 | 2,390 | 2,310 | 2,270 | 2,486 | Сено |

**TABLE 5-4. Main aggregates of animal husbandry**
**ТАБЛИЦА 5-4. Основные показатели животноводства**

| Type of livestock or product | 1990 | 1991 | 1992 | 1993 | 1994 | 1995 | Направление животноводства или вид продукции |
|---|---|---|---|---|---|---|---|
| **Livestock (thousands of heads)** | | | | | | | **Поголовье скота (тысяч голов)** |
| Cattle | 6,975 | 6,577 | 6,221 | 5,851 | 5,403 | 5,054 | Крупный рогатый скот |
| of which: Cows | 2,362 | 2,314 | 2,220 | 2,199 | 2,180 | 2,137 | в том числе коровы |
| Pigs | 5,051 | 4,703 | 4,308 | 4,181 | 4,005 | 3,895 | Свиньи |
| Sheep and goats | 445 | 424 | 381 | 323 | 284 | 262 | Овцы и козы |
| of which: Goats | 42 | 44 | 45 | 51 | 54 | 58 | в том числе козы |
| Horses | 217 | 212 | 215 | 215 | 220 | 229 | Лошади |
| Other | 50,617 | 51,703 | 48,949 | 47,308 | 45,265 | 40,145 | Прочие |
| **Animal husbandry products** | | | | | | | **Продукция животноводства** |
| Meat (thousands of tons) | 1,758 | 1,590 | 1,441 | 1,242 | 1,138 | 995 | Мясо (тысяч тонн) |
| Beef | 977 | 887 | 840 | 693 | 654 | 543 | Говядина |
| Pork | 555 | 481 | 409 | 365 | 327 | 334 | Свинина |
| Lamb | 16 | 12 | 11 | 12 | 9 | 7 | Баранина |
| Poultry | 198 | 198 | 170 | 161 | 138 | 101 | Птица |
| Other | 12 | 12 | 11 | 11 | 10 | 10 | Прочие виды мяса |
| Milk (thousands of tons) | 7,457 | 6,812 | 5,885 | 5,584 | 5,510 | 5,070 | Молоко (тысяч тонн) |
| Eggs (millions) | 3,657 | 3,718 | 3,502 | 3,514 | 3,400 | 3,373 | Яйца (миллионов штук) |
| Wool (thousands of tons) | 958 | 772 | 682 | 583 | 459 | 396 | Шерсть (тысяч тонн) |

**TABLE 6-1. Industrial production by sector (millions of national currency)**
**ТАБЛИЦА 6-1. Промышленное производство по отраслям (млн. национальной валюты)**

| Sector | 1990 | 1991 | 1992 | 1993 | 1994 | 1995 | Отрасли |
|---|---|---|---|---|---|---|---|
| **All industry** | 41,742 | 91,924 | 1,266,582 | 17,561,860 | 30,521,725 | 131,022,000 | **Вся промышленность** |
| **Heavy industry** | 27,142 | 51,275 | 891,738 | 12,948,570 | 22,636,477 | 95,687,000 | **Тяжелая промышленность** |
| Fuel and energy | 2,990 | 6,653 | 200,065 | 3,968,980 | 6,714,779 | 23,674,000 | Топливно-энергетическая промышленноть |
| Electricity | 1,071 | 2,819 | 97,712 | 2,564,031 | 4,761,389 | 18,064,000 | Электроэнергетика |
| Fuels | 1,919 | 3,834 | 102,353 | 1,404,949 | 1,953,390 | 5,610,000 | Топливная промышленность |
| Ferrous and nonferrous metallurgy | 435 | 822 | 26,886 | 347,725 | 784,408 | 3,218,000 | Металлургия |
| Chemicals and petrochemical industry | 3,741 | 6,585 | 147,169 | 2,177,670 | 4,211,998 | 18,733,000 | Химическая и нефтехимическая пром. |
| Machine building and metalworking | 14,272 | 24,585 | 354,199 | 3,881,170 | 6,897,910 | 30,513,000 | Машиностроение и металлообработка |
| Forestry, woodworking, and pulp and paper industry | 1,845 | 4,394 | 58,425 | 790,284 | 1,403,999 | 6,924,000 | Лесная, деревообрабатывающая и целлюлозо-бумажная промышленность |
| Construction materials | 1,544 | 3,547 | 62,094 | 1,001,026 | 1,429,271 | 6,666,000 | Промышленность строительных материалов |
| **Light industry** | 7,172 | 17,623 | 166,759 | 1,984,490 | 3,174,259 | 10,455,000 | **Легкая промышленность** |
| Textiles | 4,353 | 10,842 | 100,013 | 1,082,716 | 1,793,456 | 5,729,000 | Текстильная |
| Clothing | 1,944 | 4,052 | 32,801 | 385,009 | 552,321 | 1,701,000 | Швейная |
| Leather and shoes | 729 | 1,677 | 19,235 | 330,286 | 676,117 | 2,911,000 | Кожевенная и обувная |
| **Food industry** | 6,200 | 23,026 | 165,019 | 2,300,603 | 4,150,955 | 22,281,000 | **Пищевая промышленность** |
| Processed foods | 2,355 | 7,812 | 67,079 | 977,338 | 1,896,986 | 8,962,000 | Пищевкусовая |
| Meat and dairy products | 3,760 | 15,060 | 97,143 | 1,218,008 | 2,208,308 | 13,105,000 | Мясная и молочная |
| Fish | 85 | 154 | 797 | 23,328 | 45,661 | 214,000 | Рыбная |

## TABLE 6-2. Industrial production by sector in constant prices
## ТАБЛИЦА 6-2. Промышленное производство по отраслям в постоянных ценах

| Sector | 1990 | 1991 | 1992 | 1993 | 1994 | 1995 | Отрасли |
|---|---|---|---|---|---|---|---|
| **Industrial production** | | | | | | | **Промышленное производство** |
| **All industry** | 5,523,880 | 5,468,641 | 4,954,589 | 4,459,136 | 3,696,624 | 3,256,726 | **Вся промышленность** |
| **Heavy industry** | 3,869,518 | 3,981,734 | 3,583,561 | 3,092,613 | 2,514,294 | 2,305,608 | **Тяжелая промышленность** |
| Fuel and energy | 1,452,628 | 1,393,070 | 911,068 | 648,192 | 482,255 | 462,965 | Топливно-энергетическая промышленноть |
| Electricity | 288,807 | 291,406 | 282,372 | 251,647 | 223,211 | 187,944 | Электроэнергетика |
| Fuels | 1,163,894 | 1,101,044 | 628,696 | 396,545 | 217,307 | 240,559 | Топливная промышленность |
| Ferrous and nonferrous metallurgy | 78,587 | 87,703 | 74,460 | 62,566 | 57,373 | 56,168 | Металлургия |
| Chemicals and petrochemicals | 794,408 | 741,183 | 632,229 | 554,489 | 461,335 | 502,394 | Химическая и нефтехимическая пром. |
| Machine building and metalworking | 1,264,969 | 1,329,482 | 1,231,100 | 1,265,018 | 1,086,650 | 862,800 | Машиностроение и металлообработка |
| Forestry, woodworking, and pulp and paper | 206,702 | 220,964 | 205,055 | 198,034 | 172,884 | 156,114 | Лесная, деревообрабатывающая и целлюлозо-бумажная промышленность |
| Construction materials | 280,111 | 294,117 | 262,941 | 200,217 | 142,555 | 112,191 | Промышленность строительных материалов |
| **Light industry** | 601,389 | 607,403 | 611,655 | 621,750 | 478,748 | 315,495 | **Легкая промышленность** |
| Textiles | 365,158 | 339,962 | 333,163 | 353,153 | 254,270 | 159,936 | Текстильная |
| Clothing | 87,394 | 98,841 | 104,969 | 122,079 | 94,245 | 74,359 | Швейная |
| Leather and shoe | 115,159 | 119,305 | 102,602 | 117,069 | 107,938 | 68,757 | Кожевенная и обувная |
| **Food industry** | 785,364 | 711,540 | 586,309 | 586,634 | 554,369 | 481,747 | **Пищевая промышленность** |
| Processed foods | 335,471 | 323,394 | 284,910 | 302,859 | 313,762 | 299,643 | Пищевкусовая |
| Meat and dairy products | 415,620 | 364,914 | 293,756 | 276,424 | 244,635 | 199,867 | Мясная и молочная |
| Fish | 7,783 | 7,674 | 5,034 | 5,089 | 4,041 | 3,495 | Рыбная |
| **Growth in production by sector (in percent)** | | | | | | | **Рост производства по отраслям** |
| **All industry** | 3.4 | -1.0 | -9.4 | -10.0 | -17.1 | -11.9 | **Вся промышленность** |
| **Heavy industry** | 4.5 | 2.9 | -10.0 | -13.7 | -18.7 | -8.3 | **Тяжелая промышленность** |
| Power and fuels | -1.2 | -4.1 | -34.6 | -28.9 | -25.6 | -4.0 | Топливно-энергетическая промышленноть |
| Electricity | 3.2 | 0.9 | -3.1 | -10.9 | -11.3 | -15.8 | Электроэнергетика |
| Fuels | -2.2 | -5.4 | -42.9 | -36.9 | -45.2 | 10.7 | Топливная промышленность |
| Ferrous and nonferrous metallurgy | 12.8 | 11.6 | -15.1 | -16.0 | -8.3 | -2.1 | Металлургия |
| Chemicals and petrochemicals | 3.8 | -6.7 | -14.7 | -12.3 | -16.8 | 8.9 | Химическая и нефтехимическая пром. |
| Machine building and metalworking | 3.4 | 5.1 | -7.4 | 2.8 | -14.1 | -20.6 | Машиностроение и металлообработка |
| Forestry, woodworking, and pulp and paper | 10.0 | 6.9 | -7.2 | -3.4 | -12.7 | -9.7 | Лесная, деревообрабатывающая и целлюлозо-бумажная промышленность |
| Construction materials | 14.2 | 5.0 | -10.6 | -23.9 | -28.8 | -21.3 | Промышленность строительных материалов |
| **Light industry** | 9.3 | 1.0 | 0.7 | 1.7 | -23.0 | -34.1 | **Легкая промышленность** |
| Textiles | -2.9 | -6.9 | -2.0 | 6.0 | -28.0 | -37.1 | Текстильная |
| Clothing | 6.0 | 13.1 | 6.2 | 16.3 | -22.8 | -21.1 | Швейная |
| Leather and shoe | 5.3 | 3.6 | -14.0 | 14.1 | -7.8 | -36.3 | Кожевенная и обувная |
| **Food industry** | 2.3 | -9.4 | -17.6 | 0.1 | -5.5 | -13.1 | **Пищевая промышленность** |
| Processed foods | 1.1 | -3.6 | -11.9 | 6.3 | 3.6 | -4.5 | Пищевкусовая |
| Meat and dairy products | 2.4 | -12.2 | -19.5 | -5.9 | -11.5 | -18.3 | Мясная и молочная |
| Fish | -2.5 | -1.4 | -34.4 | 1.1 | -20.6 | -13.5 | Рыбная |

## TABLE 6-3. Primary energy supply (million tons oil equivalent) BELARUS

## ТАБЛИЦА 6-3. Ресурсы первичных видов энергии (млн. тонн нефтяного эквивалента)

| Item | | 1990 | 1991 | 1992 | 1993 | 1994 | 1995 | Статьи | |
|---|---|---|---|---|---|---|---|---|---|
| **Primary production** | | | | | | | | **Производство первичной энергии** | |
| Coal and lignite (hard and brown) | | .. | .. | .. | .. | .. | .. | Уголь каменный и бурый | |
| Crude oil | | 2.938 | 2.946 | 2.860 | 2.867 | 2.860 | 2.763 | Нефть | |
| Gas | | 0.490 | 0.485 | 0.482 | 0.480 | 0.482 | 0.436 | Газ | |
| Nuclear | | .. | .. | .. | .. | .. | .. | Атомная энергия | |
| Hydro/geothermal | | 0.007 | 0.005 | 0.005 | 0.006 | 0.006 | 0.006 | Гидро-геотермальная | |
| Other | | 1.985 | 2.059 | 2.135 | 1.650 | 1.770 | 1.717 | Другие виды | |
| Total | | 5.420 | 5.495 | 5.482 | 5.003 | 5.118 | 4.922 | Всего | |
| **Energy trade** | | | | | | | | **Торговля энергией** | |
| Coal and lignite | Exports | 5.833 | .. | .. | .. | .. | 0.005 | Уголь каменный и бурый | Экспорт |
| | Imports | 7.804 | 1.331 | 1.081 | 0.677 | 0.781 | 1.000 | | Импорт |
| | Net imports | 1.971 | 1.331 | 1.081 | 0.677 | 0.781 | 0.995 | | Чистый импорт |
| Oil/oil product | Exports | 97.528 | 20.834 | 9.333 | 1.365 | 3.368 | 4.582 | Нефть и нефтепродукты | Экспорт |
| | Imports | 132.313 | 50.985 | 30.642 | 18.959 | 17.464 | 16.891 | | Импорт |
| | Net imports | 34.785 | 30.151 | 21.309 | 17.594 | 14.096 | 12.309 | | Чистый импорт |
| Gas | Exports | 27.979 | .. | .. | .. | .. | .. | Газ | Экспорт |
| | Imports | 45.976 | 18.012 | 20.675 | 18.751 | 16.442 | 15.561 | | Импорт |
| | Net imports | 17.997 | 18.012 | 20.675 | 18.751 | 16.442 | 15.561 | | Чистый импорт |
| Electricity | Exports | 1.540 | 0.107 | 0.050 | 0.042 | 0.003 | 0.004 | Электричество | Экспорт |
| | Imports | 4.604 | 4.613 | 3.220 | 1.993 | 1.244 | 2.023 | | Импорт |
| | Net imports | 3.064 | 4.506 | 3.170 | 1.951 | 1.241 | 2.019 | | Чистый импорт |
| **Total net imports** | | 57.817 | 54.000 | 46.235 | 38.973 | 32.560 | 30.884 | **Чистый импорт энергии-всего** | |
| **Total stock changes** | | -0.228 | 0.505 | 0.483 | 1.477 | 0.822 | -0.464 | **Изменение запасов-всего** | |
| **Total primary energy supply** | | 63.009 | 60.000 | 52.200 | 45.453 | 38.500 | 35.342 | **Ресурсы первичной энергии-всего** | |
| Coal and lignite | | 1.971 | 1.496 | 1.276 | 0.655 | 0.946 | 0.914 | Уголь каменный и бурый | |
| Oil/oil products | | 37.723 | 33.693 | 24.923 | 20.597 | 14.866 | 14.647 | Нефть и нефтепродукты | |
| Gas | | 18.487 | 18.661 | 21.175 | 19.670 | 17.006 | 16.046 | Газ | |
| Nuclear | | .. | .. | .. | .. | .. | .. | Атомная энергия | |
| Hydro/geothermal | | 0.007 | 0.005 | 0.005 | 0.006 | 0.006 | 0.006 | Гидро-геотермальная энергия | |
| Other | | 4.821 | 6.145 | 4.821 | 4.525 | 5.676 | 3.729 | Другие виды | |
| **Total primary energy requirement (equals total primary energy supply)** | | 63.009 | 60.000 | 52.200 | 45.453 | 38.500 | 35.342 | **Потребность в первичной энергии-всего (равно ресурсам первичной энергии)** | |

## TABLE 7-1. Price indices and exchange rates
## ТАБЛИЦА 7-1. Индексы цен и обменный курс

| Year and month | National currency per U.S. dollar<br>Единиц нац. валюты за 1 доллар США | National currency per Russian ruble<br>Единиц нац. валюты за 1 российский рубль | Consumer price index (as a percent of the previous month)<br>Индекс потребительских цен (в % к предыдущему месяцу) | Producer price index (as a percent of the previous month)<br>Индекс цен производителей (в % к предыдущему месяцу) | Consumer price index (as a percent of the previous December)<br>Индекс потребительских цен (в % к декабрю прошлого года) | Producer price index (as a percent of the previous December)<br>Индекс цен производителей (в % к декабрю прошлого года) | Год и месяц |
|---|---|---|---|---|---|---|---|
| **1993** | | | | | | | **1993** |
| January | 559.0 | 1.00 | 114.8 | 126.1 | 114.8 | 126.1 | Январь |
| February | 625.0 | 1.00 | 119.7 | 125.0 | 137.5 | 157.6 | Февраль |
| March | 878.0 | 1.08 | 128.1 | 138.6 | 176.1 | 218.4 | Март |
| April | 1,096.0 | 1.86 | 124.8 | 122.2 | 219.8 | 266.9 | Апрель |
| May | 1,566.0 | 2.00 | 119.7 | 113.2 | 263.0 | 302.2 | Май |
| June | 1,827.0 | 1.85 | 126.3 | 113.2 | 332.1 | 342.1 | Июнь |
| July | 2,000.0 | 1.84 | 123.3 | 121.2 | 409.3 | 414.4 | Июль |
| August | 2,821.0 | 2.23 | 125.1 | 125.8 | 512.1 | 521.4 | Август |
| September | 3,351.0 | 1.50 | 136.0 | 134.8 | 696.3 | 703.0 | Сентябрь |
| October | 4,186.0 | 2.90 | 144.6 | 156.0 | 1,006.5 | 1,096.6 | Октябрь |
| November | 6,030.0 | 4.43 | 143.2 | 171.6 | 1,440.9 | 1,881.8 | Ноябрь |
| December | 7,311.0 | 4.33 | 145.5 | 128.4 | 2,096.5 | 2,415.5 | Декабрь |
| **1994** | | | | | | | **1994** |
| January | 6,801.0 | 4.36 | 140.7 | 124.5 | 140.7 | 124.5 | Январь |
| February | 7,721.0 | 4.87 | 118.7 | 117.4 | 167.0 | 146.2 | Февраль |
| March | 16,044.0 | 7.13 | 110.2 | 112.0 | 184.0 | 163.6 | Март |
| April | 19,167.0 | 9.80 | 128.6 | 137.0 | 236.6 | 224.1 | Апрель |
| May | 20,176.0 | 10.46 | 128.7 | 132.5 | 304.5 | 296.8 | Май |
| June | 26,330.0 | 13.22 | 119.5 | 122.0 | 364.0 | 362.2 | Июнь |
| July | 27,577.0 | 13.44 | 126.6 | 117.5 | 461.0 | 425.5 | Июль |
| August | 3,260.0 | 1.63 | 153.4 | 142.5 | 707.3 | 606.4 | Август |
| September | 4,601.0 | 2.07 | 125.5 | 141.1 | 888.1 | 855.9 | Сентябрь |
| October | 6,577.0 | 2.19 | 125.7 | 141.6 | 1,116.2 | 1,212.2 | Октябрь |
| November | 7,843.0 | 2.49 | 140.5 | 128.4 | 1,568.6 | 1,556.1 | Ноябрь |
| December | 9,666.0 | 2.88 | 131.3 | 126.4 | 2,059.9 | 1,966.7 | Декабрь |

## TABLE 7-1. Price indices and exchange rates
## ТАБЛИЦА 7-1. Индексы цен и обменный курс

| Year and month | National currency per U.S. dollar<br>Единиц нац. валюты за 1 доллар США | National currency per Russian ruble<br>Единиц нац. валюты за 1 российский рубль | Consumer price index (as a percent of the previous month)<br>Индекс потребительских цен (в % к предыдущему месяцу) | Producer price index (as a percent of the previous month)<br>Индекс цен производителей (в % к предыдущему месяцу) | Consumer price index (as a percent of the previous December)<br>Индекс потребительских цен (в % к декабрю прошлого года) | Producer price index (as a percent of the previous December)<br>Индекс цен производителей (в % к декабрю прошлого года) | Год и месяц |
|---|---|---|---|---|---|---|---|
| **1995** | | | | | | | **1995** |
| January | 11,551.0 | 2.92 | 139.2 | 144.4 | 139.2 | 144.4 | Январь |
| February | 11,666.0 | 2.76 | 133.7 | 113.2 | 186.1 | 163.5 | Февраль |
| March | 11,643.0 | 2.49 | 120.0 | 109.5 | 223.3 | 179.1 | Март |
| April | 11,496.0 | 2.25 | 114.5 | 107.6 | 255.5 | 192.7 | Апрель |
| May | 11,501.0 | 2.23 | 103.4 | 101.7 | 264.3 | 195.9 | Май |
| June | 11,501.0 | 2.42 | 102.5 | 101.3 | 270.9 | 198.4 | Июнь |
| July | 11,507.0 | 2.51 | 105.2 | 102.4 | 285.0 | 203.1 | Июль |
| August | 11,518.0 | 2.59 | 103.0 | 105.2 | 293.4 | 213.5 | Август |
| September | 11,511.0 | 2.56 | 105.2 | 105.0 | 308.8 | 224.2 | Сентябрь |
| October | 11,513.0 | 2.55 | 103.4 | 102.1 | 319.4 | 228.8 | Октябрь |
| November | 11,505.0 | 2.52 | 103.7 | 102.7 | 331.1 | 235.1 | Ноябрь |
| December | 11,500.0 | 2.48 | 103.9 | 102.2 | 344.0 | 240.3 | Декабрь |
| **1996** | | | | | | | **1996** |
| January | 11,500.0 | 2.52 | 105.6 | 104.7 | 105.6 | 104.7 | Январь |
| February | 11,505.0 | 2.41 | 104.0 | 100.2 | 109.8 | 104.9 | Февраль |
| March | 11,500.0 | 2.37 | 102.0 | 100.6 | 112.0 | 105.6 | Март |
| April | 12,001.0 | 2.44 | 101.5 | 101.7 | 113.7 | 107.3 | Апрель |
| May | 12,494.0 | 2.49 | 100.6 | 100.9 | 114.4 | 108.3 | Май |
| June | .. | .. | .. | .. | .. | .. | Июнь |
| July | .. | .. | .. | .. | .. | .. | Июль |
| August | .. | .. | .. | .. | .. | .. | Август |
| September | .. | .. | .. | .. | .. | .. | Сентябрь |
| October | .. | .. | .. | .. | .. | .. | Октябрь |
| November | .. | .. | .. | .. | .. | .. | Ноябрь |
| December | .. | .. | .. | .. | .. | .. | Декабрь |

## TABLE 7-2. Monthly nominal wages by sector
## ТАБЛИЦА 7-2. Среднемесячная денежная зарплата по отраслям

| Sector | 1990 | 1991 | 1992 | 1993 | 1994 | 1995 | Сектора |
|---|---|---|---|---|---|---|---|
| **Nominal wages** | | | | | | | **Средняя номинальная заработная плата** |
| **Economy average** | 269.0 | 541.0 | 5,072.0 | 61,208.0 | 98,203.0 | 755,129.0 | **По народному хозяйству** |
| **Material sphere** | 282.0 | 562.0 | 5,257.0 | 63,893.0 | 101,971.0 | 767,826.0 | **Отрасли сферы материального производства** |
| Industry | 281.0 | 596.0 | 6,025.0 | 70,720.0 | 119,917.0 | 861,856.0 | Промышленность |
| Construction | 333.0 | 662.0 | 6,460.0 | 81,834.0 | 135,245.0 | 1,048,468.0 | Строительство |
| Agriculture | 251.0 | 468.0 | 3,949.0 | 47,503.0 | 62,780.0 | 468,313.0 | Сельское хозяйство |
| Transport | 298.0 | 570.0 | 5,655.0 | 71,190.0 | 115,385.0 | 935,745.0 | Транспорт |
| Communications | 224.0 | 485.0 | 4,817.0 | 60,755.0 | 94,679.0 | 919,400.0 | Связь |
| Trade (retail and wholesale) | 247.0 | 496.0 | 4,321.0 | 56,860.0 | 92,094.0 | 639,432.0 | Торговля (оптовая и розничная) |
| Other | 217.0 | 472.0 | 4,106.0 | 54,434.0 | 88,378.0 | 698,277.0 | Прочие отрасли материального производства |
| **Nonmaterial sphere** | 221.0 | 469.0 | 4,440.0 | 53,202.0 | 87,797.0 | 722,414.0 | **Отрасли непроизводственной сферы** |
| Municipal services | 207.0 | 430.0 | 4,407.0 | 52,038.0 | 84,437.0 | 735,849.0 | Жилкомхоз и бытовое обслуживание |
| Science, research and development | 343.0 | 635.0 | 4,488.0 | 58,763.0 | 96,880.0 | 815,598.0 | Наука и научное обслуживание |
| Education | 191.0 | 419.0 | 4,201.0 | 48,200.0 | 78,810.0 | 594,554.0 | Образование |
| Culture | 172.0 | 406.0 | 3,673.0 | 43,230.0 | 66,707.0 | 517,685.0 | Культура |
| Arts | 257.0 | 510.0 | 3,672.0 | 44,693.0 | 68,246.0 | 516,556.0 | Искусство |
| Health care, social security, and sports | 193.0 | 444.0 | 4,157.0 | 47,810.0 | 79,118.0 | 639,080.0 | Здравоохр., соц.обсл., физк. и спорт |
| Banking, finance, credit, insurance | 363.0 | 859.0 | 9,057.0 | 129,023.0 | 214,865.0 | 1,612,084.0 | Кредитование, страхование, банк. дело |
| Government | 344.0 | 577.0 | 5,604.0 | 74,745.0 | 123,611.0 | 1,176,016.0 | Управление |

**TABLE 8-1. Money income and expenditure of the population (millions of national currency)**
**ТАБЛИЦА 8-1. Денежные доходы и расходы населения (млн. национальной валюты)**

| Type of income or expenditure | 1990 | 1991 | 1992 | 1993 | 1994 | 1995 | Вид доходов или расходов |
|---|---|---|---|---|---|---|---|
| **Income** | | | | | | | **Доходы** |
| **Total labor income** | 19,170 | 35,379 | 293,550 | 4,037,362 | 6,385,581 | 42,071,438 | **Всего трудовых доходов** |
| Regular wages | 15,471 | 29,122 | 247,646 | 3,372,157 | 5,406,346 | 37,735,605 | Заработная плата |
| Wages paid by cooperatives | 658 | 626 | 1,933 | 36,759 | 28,129 | .. | Заработная плата в кооперативах |
| Other wages and compensation | 529 | 1,399 | 9,081 | 95,613 | 119,940 | .. | Прочие доходы типа заработной платы |
| Income paid by collective farms | 1,866 | 3,304 | 23,988 | 366,250 | 420,171 | 2,535,420 | Доходы от колхозов |
| Income from sale of farm products | 1,304 | 1,554 | 12,835 | 203,342 | 439,124 | 1,800,413 | Доходы от продажи продукции колхозов |
| **Total transfer receipts** | 5,273 | 12,150 | 114,607 | 2,068,420 | 4,500,218 | 33,246,313 | **Всего трансфертных поступлений** |
| Pensions and allowances | 3,482 | 8,137 | 74,066 | 891,733 | 1,420,760 | 12,744,219 | Пенсии и пособия |
| Scholarships | 117 | 327 | 2,749 | 26,181 | 41,706 | 270,291 | Стипендии |
| Income from the financial system (insurance, interest, etc.) | 1,087 | 1,446 | 18,504 | 231,361 | 253,485 | 2,471,583 | Доходы из финансовой системы (страховые возмещения, проценты и т.д.) |
| Other income | 587 | 2,240 | 19,288 | 919,145 | 2,784,267 | 17,760,220 | Прочие виды доходов |
| **Total income** | 24,443 | 47,529 | 408,157 | 6,105,782 | 10,885,799 | 75,317,751 | **Всего доходов** |
| **Expenditure** | | | | | | | **Расходы** |
| **Total purchases** | 20,196 | 35,927 | 316,512 | 4,670,693 | 9,069,479 | 51,178,358 | **Всего покупок товаров и услуг** |
| Retail goods | 18,386 | 33,149 | 297,116 | 4,232,712 | 8,156,754 | 44,032,272 | Товары в розничной торговле |
| Services | 1,810 | 2,778 | 19,396 | 437,981 | 912,725 | 7,146,086 | Услуги |
| Rent and utilities | 439 | 537 | 2,959 | 66,411 | 146,222 | 2,183,545 | Квартирная плата и коммунальные платежи |
| Transport and communications | 766 | 1,442 | 11,203 | 113,810 | 321,145 | 2,850,166 | Транспорт и связь |
| Health and other services | 536 | 748 | 5,062 | 256,140 | 445,358 | 2,112,375 | Здравоохранение и другие виды услуг |
| Cooperatives | 69 | 51 | 172 | 1,620 | .. | .. | Кооперативы |
| **Transfers and savings** | 4,422 | 10,448 | 59,802 | 962,117 | 1,219,069 | 21,359,961 | **Трансферты и сбережения** |
| Taxes, fees, dues, and other | 1,743 | 2,538 | 22,498 | 266,392 | 504,038 | 3,755,154 | Налоги, сборы, пошлины и др. |
| Savings | 1,664 | 6,324 | 27,514 | 305,221 | 589,312 | 16,758,539 | Сбережения |
| Other | 1,015 | 1,586 | 9,790 | 390,504 | 125,719 | 846,268 | Прочие |
| **Total expenditure** | 24,618 | 46,375 | 376,314 | 5,632,810 | 10,288,548 | 72,538,319 | **Всего расходов** |
| **Income less expenditure** | -175 | 1,154 | 31,843 | 472,972 | 597,251 | 2,779,432 | **Доходы за вычетом расходов** |

# *Country Notes: Belarus*

**General notes**: Data were supplied by the Ministry of Statistics and Analysis of the Republic of Belarus.

**Currency:** Unless otherwise indicated, data for 1994-1995 reflect 10-fold denomination of the rubel.

**Table 1-1:** The cooperative sector includes production cooperatives, customers' cooperatives and enterprises of collective and mixed ownership. The individual labor activities sector includes the individual labor and the private sectors.

**Table 1-2:** The sums of the sectors in the nonmaterial sphere do not equal the totals.

**Table 2-2:** Data are in previous year prices.

**Tables 3-2A, 3-2B, 3-3A, 3-3B:** Services are not included in the totals. The totals also include trade flows not distributed by categories.

**Table 5-2:** Data are in 1983 prices.

**Table 5-4:** Livestock data are presented as of the end of the year.

**Table 6-2:** Data are in January 1993 prices. Discrepancies between the sums of components and the totals might be a result of rescaling to those prices.

**Table 7-1:** Starting from August 1994 Exchange rates reflect 10-fold denomination of the Belorussian rubel.

# *Комментарии к таблицам: Беларусь*

**Общее замечание:** Данные были получены из Министерства Статистики и Анализа Республики Беларусь.

**Национальная валюта:** За исключением особо отмеченных случаев, данные за 1994-1995 гг. отражают десятикратную деноминацию рубеля.

**Таблица 1-1:** Кооперативный сектор включает производственные и потребительские кооперативы, а также предприятия коллективной и смешанной собственности. Индивидуально-трудовая деятельность включает индивидуальный трудовой и частный сектора.

**Таблица 1-2:** Суммы по секторам нематериальной сферы не равны итогу.

**Таблица 2-2:** Данные приведены в ценах предыдущего года.

**Таблицы 3-2A, 3-2B, 3-3A и 3-3B:** Услуги не включены в итог. Итог включает торговлю, не распределенную по категориям.

**Таблица 5-2:** Данные приведены в ценах 1983 г.

**Таблица 5-4:** Данные по поголовью скота приведены на конец года.

**Таблица 6-2:** Данные приведены в ценах января 1993 года. Расхождения между суммами компонентов и приведенными итоговыми величинами могут быть результатом пересчета в эти цены.

**Таблица 7-1:** Начиная с августа 1994 г. данные по валютным курсам отражают десятикратную деноминацию рубеля.

# Estonia / Эстония

1996 Population / Численность населения в 1996 году
(thousands / тыс. человек): 1,476

Area / Территория
(thousand square kilometers / тыс. кв. км.): 45.2

Capital city / Столица :
Tallinn / Таллинн

**Country Tables:** Tables 1-2, 6-2 and 8-1 are not included because there are no recent data available.

**Статистические таблицы страны**: Таблицы 1-2, 6-2 и 8-1 не включены ввиду отсутствия данных за последние годы.

## TABLE 1-1. Population and employment (thousands)
## ТАБЛИЦА 1-1. Население и занятость (тысяч)



| Population or employment category | 1990 | 1991 | 1992 | 1993 | 1994 | 1995 | Население или группы занятых |
|---|---|---|---|---|---|---|---|
| **Total population** | 1,571 | 1,566 | 1,544 | 1,517 | 1,499 | 1,484 | **Население - всего** |
| Males | 735 | 733 | 722 | 708 | 700 | 692 | Мужчины |
| Females | 836 | 833 | 822 | 808 | 799 | 792 | Женщины |
| Urban population | 1,122 | 1,117 | 1,095 | 1,068 | 1,051 | 1,037 | Городское |
| Rural population | 449 | 449 | 449 | 449 | 448 | 447 | Сельское |
| Population under working age | 372 | 368 | 358 | 345 | 334 | 325 | Моложе трудоспособного возраста |
| Working-age population | 880 | 875 | 862 | 846 | 855 | 848 | Лица в трудоспособном возрасте |
| Population over working age | 320 | 323 | 325 | 326 | 310 | 311 | Старше трудоспособного возраста |
| Economically Active Population, in non-working age | 84 | .. | .. | .. | .. | .. | Экономически активное население в нетрудоспособном возрасте |
| Above working age | 82 | .. | .. | .. | .. | .. | Старше трудоспособного возраста |
| Below working age | 2 | .. | .. | .. | .. | .. | Моложе трудоспособного возраста |
| **Total labor resources** | .. | .. | .. | .. | .. | .. | **Трудовые ресурсы - всего** |
| **Total employment** | 796 | 812 | .. | .. | .. | .. | **Занятое население - всего** |
| State sector employees | 677 | 578 | .. | .. | .. | .. | Государственный сектор |
| Leased enterprise employees | .. | 5 | .. | .. | .. | .. | Арендные предприятия |
| Joint-stock company employees | .. | 71 | .. | .. | .. | .. | Акционерные общества |
| Economic association employees | .. | .. | .. | .. | .. | .. | Хозяйственные ассоциации |
| Social organization employees | .. | .. | .. | .. | .. | .. | Общественные организации |
| Joint venture employees | .. | 6 | .. | .. | .. | .. | Совместные предприятия |
| Collective farm workers | 81 | 85 | .. | .. | .. | .. | Колхозы |
| Cooperative workers | 29 | 34 | .. | .. | .. | .. | Кооперативы |
| Individual labor activities | 1 | 6 | .. | .. | .. | .. | ИТД |
| Private subsidiary agricultural workers | .. | .. | .. | .. | .. | .. | Личные подсобные хозяйства |
| Private agricultural workers | 5 | 5 | 8 | .. | .. | .. | Фермерские хозяйства |
| **Students** | 62 | .. | .. | .. | .. | .. | **Учащиеся** |
| **Religious workers** | .. | .. | .. | .. | .. | .. | **Служащие религиозного культа** |
| **Working age population not employed in the national economy** | .. | .. | .. | .. | .. | .. | **Лица в трудоспособном возрасте, не занятые в экономике** |
| Housewives | .. | .. | .. | .. | .. | .. | Домохозяйки |
| Military personnel | .. | .. | .. | .. | .. | .. | Военнослужащие |
| Unemployed | .. | 1 | 15 | 16 | 13 | 16 | Безработные |
| **Labor force** | .. | .. | .. | .. | .. | .. | **Рабочая сила** |

## TABLE 1-3. Registered unemployment (thousands; end of month)
## ТАБЛИЦА 1-3. Численность зарегистрированных безработных (тысяч; на конец месяца)

| Year and month | Total Всего | Males Мужчины | Females Женщины | Receiving benefits Получающие пособие | Год и месяц |
|---|---|---|---|---|---|
| **1994** | | | | | **1994** |
| January | 16.9 | .. | .. | .. | Январь |
| February | 18.4 | .. | .. | .. | Февраль |
| March | 19.5 | 8.6 | 10.9 | .. | Март |
| April | 19.5 | .. | .. | .. | Апрель |
| May | 18.1 | .. | .. | .. | Май |
| June | 16.7 | 7.2 | 9.5 | .. | Июнь |
| July | 15.4 | .. | .. | .. | Июль |
| August | 13.7 | .. | .. | .. | Август |
| September | 12.4 | 5.1 | 7.3 | .. | Сентябрь |
| October | 11.8 | .. | .. | .. | Октябрь |
| November | 12.1 | .. | .. | .. | Ноябрь |
| December | 12.7 | 4.9 | 7.8 | .. | Декабрь |
| **1995** | | | | | **1995** |
| January | 15.1 | .. | .. | 14.2 | Январь |
| February | 16.1 | .. | .. | 14.4 | Февраль |
| March | 16.8 | 6.2 | 10.5 | 14.6 | Март |
| April | 16.8 | .. | .. | 14.9 | Апрель |
| May | 16.7 | .. | .. | 15.4 | Май |
| June | 15.5 | 5.5 | 10.0 | 14.8 | Июнь |
| July | 14.3 | .. | .. | 14.2 | Июль |
| August | 13.4 | .. | .. | 12.8 | Август |
| September | 13.2 | 4.2 | 9.1 | 12.1 | Сентябрь |
| October | 13.6 | .. | .. | 12.3 | Октябрь |
| November | 15.0 | .. | .. | 12.9 | Ноябрь |
| December | 15.6 | 5.1 | 10.5 | 13.6 | Декабрь |
| **1996** | | | | | **1996** |
| January | 17.2 | .. | .. | 15.1 | Январь |
| February | 18.6 | .. | .. | 17.6 | Февраль |
| March | 19.5 | 6.7 | 12.8 | 18.6 | Март |
| April | 19.8 | .. | .. | 18.3 | Апрель |
| May | 19.2 | .. | .. | 18.4 | Май |
| June | .. | .. | .. | .. | Июнь |
| July | .. | .. | .. | .. | Июль |
| August | .. | .. | .. | .. | Август |
| September | .. | .. | .. | .. | Сентябрь |
| October | .. | .. | .. | .. | Октябрь |
| November | .. | .. | .. | .. | Ноябрь |
| December | .. | .. | .. | .. | Декабрь |

## TABLE 2-1. Gross domestic product at current prices (millions of national currency)
## ТАБЛИЦА 2-1. Валовой внутренний продукт в текущих ценах (млн. национальной валюты)



| Sector of origin or expenditure category | 1990 | 1991 | 1992 | 1993 | 1994 | 1995 | Отраслевое происхождение или вид расходов |
|---|---|---|---|---|---|---|---|
| **Gross domestic product by sector of origin** | | | | | | | **Валовой внутренний продукт по отраслевому происхождению** |
| **Agriculture and forestry** | 1,246 | 2,745 | 1,560 | 2,060 | 2,500 | 2,781 | **Сельское и лесное хозяйство** |
| Agriculture | .. | 2,711 | .. | .. | .. | .. | Сельское хозяйство |
| Forestry | .. | 34 | .. | .. | .. | .. | Лесное хозяйство |
| **Industry and construction** | 3,732 | 7,705 | 4,223 | 6,152 | 8,060 | 10,299 | **Промышленность и строительство** |
| Industry | 3,161 | 6,592 | 3,620 | 4,851 | 6,380 | 8,360 | Промышленность |
| Construction | 570 | 1,113 | 603 | 1,301 | 1,680 | 1,939 | Строительство |
| **Other** | 3,000 | 6,059 | 6,438 | 11,587 | 15,754 | 23,429 | **Другие отрасли** |
| Transport | 513 | 962 | 1,715 | 2,456 | 2,482 | 3,698 | Транспорт |
| Road maintenance | .. | .. | .. | .. | .. | .. | Дорожное хозяйство |
| Communication | .. | 144 | .. | .. | .. | .. | Связь |
| Wholesale trade | .. | 656 | 1,773 | 3,359 | 4,763 | 6,805 | Оптовая торговля |
| Retail trade and catering | .. | 670 | .. | .. | .. | .. | Розничная торговля и общепит |
| Material supply | .. | .. | .. | .. | .. | .. | Материально-техническое снабжение |
| Procurement | .. | .. | .. | .. | .. | .. | Заготовки |
| Information and computing services | .. | .. | .. | .. | .. | .. | Информационно-вычислительное обслуживание |
| Other sectors of material production | 644 | 980 | .. | .. | .. | .. | Другие отрасли сферы материального пр. |
| Housing | 182 | 146 | .. | .. | .. | .. | Жилищное хозяйство |
| Public utilities and personal services | .. | .. | .. | .. | .. | .. | Ком. хоз. и бытовое обслуживание |
| Health care, social security, physical culture and sports | 399 | 288 | 195 | 507 | 952 | 1,364 | Здравоохранение, социальное обеспечение, физкультура и спорт |
| Education | 614 | 441 | 479 | 1,124 | 1,517 | 2,035 | Образование |
| Culture and art | .. | .. | .. | .. | .. | .. | Культура и искусство |
| Science and scientific research | .. | .. | .. | .. | .. | .. | Наука и научное обслуживание |
| Credit | 187 | .. | .. | .. | .. | .. | Кредитование |
| Insurance | 18 | 13 | .. | .. | .. | .. | Страхование |
| General administration and defense | 420 | 302 | 285 | 681 | 1,199 | 1,688 | Государственное управление и оборона |
| Private nonprofit institutions serving households | 23 | 17 | .. | .. | .. | .. | Общественные организации, обслуживающие домашние хозяйства |
| **Imputed service charge of financial intermediaries** | .. | .. | .. | .. | .. | .. | **Условно-исчисляемая стоимость услуг финансовых посредников** |
| **Total gross value added (GVA)** | 7,977 | 16,509 | 12,221 | 19,799 | 26,314 | 36,509 | **Валовая добавленная стоимость (ВДС) - всего** |
| **Taxes on production and imports (TOPI)** | .. | 2,520 | 1,157 | 2,477 | 4,076 | 5,305 | **Налоги на производство и импорт (НПиИ)** |
| Other taxes on production (OTOP) | .. | 304 | .. | .. | .. | .. | Другие налоги на производство (ДНП) |
| **Subsidies on production and imports (SOPI)** | .. | 410 | 220 | 216 | 287 | 311 | **Субсидии на производство и импорт (СПиИ)** |
| Other subsidies on production (OSOP) | .. | .. | .. | .. | .. | .. | Другие субсидии на производство (ДСП) |
| **Total GDP at factor cost (GVA-OTOP+OSOP)** | .. | 16,205 | 12,221 | 19,799 | 26,314 | 36,509 | **Всего ВВП по фактр. стоимости (ВДС-ДНП+ДСП)** |
| **Net Indirect taxes (TOPI - SOPI)** | .. | 2,110 | 937 | 2,261 | 3,789 | 4,994 | **Чистые косвенные налоги (НПиИ-СПиИ)** |
| **Total GDP at market prices** | 7,977 | 18,315 | 13,158 | 22,060 | 30,103 | 41,503 | **Всего ВВП в рыночных ценах** |
| **Gross domestic product by expenditure category** | | | | | | | **Валовой внутренний продукт по видам расходов** |
| **Consumption** | 6,195 | 11,602 | 9,345 | 17,011 | 24,468 | 33,399 | **Потребление** |
| Private consumption | 5,141 | 10,017 | 7,261 | 12,537 | 17,678 | 23,698 | Личное потребление |
| Government consumption | 1,054 | 1,585 | 2,084 | 4,474 | 6,790 | 9,701 | Общественное потребление |
| **Gross domestic investment** | 2,411 | 4,478 | 3,518 | 5,821 | 8,613 | 11,149 | **Валовые внутренние инвестиции** |
| Gross fixed investment | 1,895 | 3,573 | 2,755 | 5,280 | 7,827 | 10,375 | Валовое накопление основного капитала |
| Change in stocks | 516 | 905 | 763 | 541 | 786 | 774 | Изменения в запасах (МОС) |
| **Resource balance (net exports of GNFS)** | -629 | 2,235 | 772 | -928 | -3,235 | -3,595 | **Сальдо ресурсов (чистый экспорт ТНФУ)** |
| Exports of goods and nonfactor services | .. | .. | 7,893 | 15,197 | 23,799 | 31,327 | Экспорт товаров и нефакторных услуг |
| Imports of goods and nonfactor services | .. | .. | 7,121 | 16,125 | 27,034 | 34,922 | Импорт товаров и нефакторных услуг |

## TABLE 2-1A. Distribution of gross domestic product at current prices (percent)
## ТАБЛИЦА 2-1A. Распределение валового внутреннего продукта в текущих ценах ( % )

| Sector of origin or expenditure category | 1990 | 1991 | 1992 | 1993 | 1994 | 1995 | Отраслевое происхождение или вид расходов |
|---|---|---|---|---|---|---|---|
| **Gross domestic product by sector of origin** | | | | | | | **ВВП по отраслевому происхождению** |
| **Agriculture and forestry** | 15.6 | 15.0 | 11.9 | 9.3 | 8.3 | 6.7 | **Сельское и лесное хозяйство** |
| Agriculture | .. | 14.8 | .. | .. | .. | .. | Сельское хозяйство |
| Forestry | .. | 0.2 | .. | .. | .. | .. | Лесное хозяйство |
| **Industry and construction** | 46.8 | 42.1 | 32.1 | 27.9 | 26.8 | 24.8 | **Промышленность и строительство** |
| Industry | 39.6 | 36.0 | 27.5 | 22.0 | 21.2 | 20.1 | Промышленность |
| Construction | 7.1 | 6.1 | 4.6 | 5.9 | 5.6 | 4.7 | Строительство |
| **Other** | 37.6 | 33.1 | 48.9 | 52.5 | 52.3 | 56.5 | **Другие отрасли** |
| Transport | 6.4 | 5.3 | 13.0 | 11.1 | 8.2 | 8.9 | Транспорт |
| Road maintenance | .. | .. | .. | .. | .. | .. | Дорожное хозяйство |
| Communication | .. | 0.8 | .. | .. | .. | .. | Связь |
| Wholesale trade | .. | 3.6 | 13.5 | 15.2 | 15.8 | 16.4 | Оптовая торговля |
| Retail trade and catering | .. | 3.7 | .. | .. | .. | .. | Розничная торговля и общепит |
| Material supply | .. | .. | .. | .. | .. | .. | Материально-техническое снабжение |
| Procurement | .. | .. | .. | .. | .. | .. | Заготовки |
| Information and computing services | .. | .. | .. | .. | .. | .. | Информационно-вычислительное обслуживание |
| Other sectors of material production | 8.1 | 5.3 | .. | .. | .. | .. | Другие отрасли сферы матерл. произ. |
| Housing | 2.3 | 0.8 | .. | .. | .. | .. | Жилищное хозяйство |
| Public utilities and personal services | .. | .. | .. | .. | .. | .. | Ком. хоз. и бытовое обслуживание |
| Health care, social security, physical culture and sports | 5.0 | 1.6 | 1.5 | 2.3 | 3.2 | 3.3 | Здравоохранение, социальное обеспечение, физкультура и спорт |
| Education | 7.7 | 2.4 | 3.6 | 5.1 | 5.0 | 4.9 | Образование |
| Culture and art | .. | .. | .. | .. | .. | .. | Культура и искусство |
| Science and scientific research | .. | .. | .. | .. | .. | .. | Наука и научное обслуживание |
| Credit | 2.3 | .. | .. | .. | .. | .. | Кредитование |
| Insurance | 0.2 | 0.1 | .. | .. | .. | .. | Страхование |
| General administration and defense | 5.3 | 1.6 | 2.2 | 3.1 | 4.0 | 4.1 | Государственное управление и оборона |
| Private nonprofit institutions serving households | 0.3 | 0.1 | .. | .. | .. | .. | Общественные организации, обслуживающие домашние хозяйства |
| **Imputed service charge of financial intermediaries** | .. | .. | .. | .. | .. | .. | **Условно-исчисляемая стоимость услуг финансовых посредников** |
| **Total gross value added** | 100.0 | 90.1 | 92.9 | 89.8 | 87.4 | 88.0 | **Валовая добавленная стоимость - всего** |
| **Total GDP at factor cost** | .. | 88.5 | 92.9 | 89.8 | 87.4 | 88.0 | **ВВП по фактор. стоимости - всего** |
| **Net indirect taxes** | .. | 11.5 | 7.1 | 10.2 | 12.6 | 12.0 | **Чистые косвенные налоги (НПиИ-СПиИ)** |
| **Total GDP at market prices** | 100.0 | 100.0 | 100.0 | 100.0 | 100.0 | 100.0 | **ВВП в рын. ценах - всего** |
| **Gross domestic product by expenditure category** | | | | | | | **ВВП по видам расходов** |
| **Consumption** | .. | .. | .. | .. | .. | .. | **Потребление** |
| Private consumption | .. | .. | .. | .. | .. | .. | Личное потребление |
| Government consumption | .. | .. | .. | .. | .. | .. | Общественное потребление |
| **Gross domestic investment** | .. | .. | .. | .. | .. | .. | **Вал. внутр. инвестиции** |
| Gross fixed investment | .. | .. | .. | .. | .. | .. | Вал. накопление осн. капитала |
| Change in stocks | .. | .. | .. | .. | .. | .. | Изменения в запасах (МОС) |
| **Resource balance (net exports of GNFS)** | .. | .. | .. | .. | .. | .. | **Сальдо ресурсов (чистый экспорт ТНФУ)** |
| Exports of goods and nonfactor services | .. | .. | .. | .. | .. | .. | Экспорт товаров и нефакторных услуг |
| Imports of goods and nonfactor services | .. | .. | .. | .. | .. | .. | Импорт товаров и нефакторных услуг |

**TABLE 2-2. Gross domestic product at constant prices (millions of national currency)**
**ТАБЛИЦА 2-2. Валовой внутренний продукт в постоянных ценах (млн. национальной валюты)**

| Sector of origin or expenditure category | 1990 | 1991 | 1992 | 1993 | 1994 | 1995 | Отраслевое происхождение или вид расходов |
|---|---|---|---|---|---|---|---|
| **Gross domestic product by sector of origin** | | | | | | | **Валовой внутренний продукт по отраслевому происхождению** |
| **Agriculture and forestry** | 950 | 888 | 2,390 | 2,060 | 1,839 | 1,806 | **Сельское и лесное хозяйство** |
| Agriculture | .. | .. | .. | .. | .. | .. | Сельское хозяйство |
| Forestry | .. | .. | .. | .. | .. | .. | Лесное хозяйство |
| **Industry and construction** | 2,468 | 2,321 | 7,880 | 6,152 | 5,928 | 6,086 | **Промышленность и строительство** |
| Industry | 2,076 | .. | 6,804 | 4,851 | 4,691 | 4,807 | Промышленность |
| Construction | 392 | .. | 1,076 | 1,301 | 1,237 | 1,279 | Строительство |
| **Other** | 2,287 | 1,851 | 11,371 | 11,587 | 11,439 | 11,868 | **Другие отрасли** |
| Transport | 361 | .. | 2,339 | 2,456 | 2,395 | 2,415 | Транспорт |
| Road maintenance | .. | .. | .. | .. | .. | .. | Дорожное хозяйство |
| Communication | .. | .. | .. | .. | .. | .. | Связь |
| Wholesale trade | .. | .. | 2,881 | 3,359 | 3,410 | 3,559 | Оптовая торговля |
| Retail trade and catering | .. | .. | .. | .. | .. | .. | Розничная торговля и общепит |
| Material supply | .. | .. | .. | .. | .. | .. | Материально-техническое снабжение |
| Procurement | .. | .. | .. | .. | .. | .. | Заготовки |
| Information and computing services | .. | .. | .. | .. | .. | .. | Информационно-вычислительное обслуживание |
| Other sectors of material production | 488 | .. | .. | .. | .. | .. | Другие отрасли сферы материального пр. |
| Housing | 141 | .. | .. | .. | .. | .. | Жилищное хозяйство |
| Public utilities and personal services | .. | .. | .. | .. | .. | .. | Ком. хоз. и бытовое обслуживание |
| Health care, social security, and sports | .. | .. | 477 | 507 | 512 | 502 | Здравоохранение, социальное обеспечение, физкультура и спорт |
| Education | .. | .. | 1,077 | 1,124 | 1,135 | 1,166 | Образование |
| Culture and art | .. | .. | .. | .. | .. | .. | Культура и искусство |
| Science and research | .. | .. | .. | .. | .. | .. | Наука и научное обслуживание |
| Credit | .. | .. | .. | .. | .. | .. | Кредитование |
| Insurance | .. | .. | .. | .. | .. | .. | Страхование |
| General administration and defense | .. | .. | 654 | 681 | 688 | 696 | Государственное управление и оборона |
| Private nonprofit institutions serving households | .. | .. | .. | .. | .. | .. | Общественные организации, обслуживающие домашние хозяйства |
| **Imputed service charge of financial intermediaries** | .. | .. | .. | .. | .. | .. | **Условно-исчисляемая стоимость услуг финансовых посредников** |
| **Total gross value added (GVA)** | 5,774 | 5,109 | 21,641 | 19,799 | 19,206 | 19,760 | **Валовая добавленная стоимость (ВДС) - всего** |
| **Total GDP at factor cost (GVA-OTOP+OSOP)** | .. | .. | .. | .. | .. | .. | **Всего ВВП по фактр. стоимости (ВДС-ДНП+ДСП)** |
| **Net indirect taxes (TOPI-SOPI)** | .. | .. | 2,471 | 2,261 | 2,261 | 2,330 | **Чистые косвенные налоги (НПиИ-СПиИ)** |
| **Total GDP at market prices** | 5,774 | 5,139 | 24,112 | 22,060 | 21,468 | 22,090 | **Всего ВВП в рыночных ценах** |
| **Gross domestic product by expenditure category** | | | | | | | **Валовой внутренний продукт по видам расходов** |
| **Consumption** | .. | .. | .. | .. | .. | .. | **Потребление** |
| Private consumption | .. | .. | .. | .. | .. | .. | Личное потребление |
| Government consumption | .. | .. | .. | .. | .. | .. | Общественное потребление |
| **Gross domestic investment** | .. | .. | .. | .. | .. | .. | **Валовые внутренние инвестиции** |
| Gross fixed investment | .. | .. | .. | .. | .. | .. | Валовое накопление основного капитала |
| Change in stocks | .. | .. | .. | .. | .. | .. | Изменения в запасах (МОС) |
| **Resource balance (net exports of GNFS)** | .. | .. | .. | .. | .. | .. | **Сальдо ресурсов (чистый экспорт ТНФУ)** |
| Exports of goods and nonfactor services | .. | .. | .. | .. | .. | .. | Экспорт товаров и нефакторных услуг |
| Imports of goods and nonfactor services | .. | .. | .. | .. | .. | .. | Импорт товаров и нефакторных услуг |

ESTONIA

**TABLE 2-2A. Growth rates of gross domestic product at constant prices (percent)**

**ТАБЛИЦА 2-2А. Валовой внутренний продукт - темпы прироста в постоянных ценах ( % )**

| Sector of origin or expenditure category | 1990 | 1991 | 1992 | 1993 | 1994 | 1995 | Отраслевое происхождение или вид расходов |
|---|---|---|---|---|---|---|---|
| **Growth rate by sector of origin** | | | | | | | **Валовый внутренний продукт по отраслевому происхождению** |
| **Agriculture and forestry** | .. | -6.5 | .. | -13.8 | -10.7 | -1.8 | **Сельское и лесное хозяйство** |
| Agriculture | .. | .. | .. | .. | .. | .. | Сельское хозяйство |
| Forestry | .. | .. | .. | .. | .. | .. | Лесное хозяйство |
| **Industry and construction** | .. | -6.0 | .. | -21.9 | -3.6 | 2.7 | **Промышленность и строительство** |
| Industry | .. | .. | .. | -28.7 | -3.3 | 2.5 | Промышленность |
| Construction | .. | .. | .. | 20.9 | -4.9 | 3.4 | Строительство |
| **Other** | .. | -19.0 | .. | 1.9 | -1.3 | 3.8 | **Другие отрасли** |
| Transport | .. | .. | .. | 5.0 | -2.5 | 0.8 | Транспорт |
| Road maintenance | .. | .. | .. | .. | .. | .. | Дорожное хозяйство |
| Communication | .. | .. | .. | .. | .. | .. | Связь |
| Wholesale trade | .. | .. | .. | 16.6 | 1.5 | 4.4 | Оптовая торговля |
| Retail trade and catering | .. | .. | .. | .. | .. | .. | Розничная торговля и общепит |
| Material supply | .. | .. | .. | .. | .. | .. | Материально-техническое снабжение |
| Procurement | .. | .. | .. | .. | .. | .. | Заготовки |
| Information and computing services | .. | .. | .. | .. | .. | .. | Информационно-вычислительное обслуживание |
| Other sectors of material production | .. | .. | .. | .. | .. | .. | Другие отрасли сферы материального пр. |
| Housing | .. | .. | .. | .. | .. | .. | Жилищное хозяйство |
| Public utilities and personal services | .. | .. | .. | .. | .. | .. | Ком. хоз. и бытовое обслуживание |
| Health care, social security, and sports | .. | .. | .. | 6.3 | 1.0 | -2.0 | Здравоохранение, социальное обеспечение, физкультура и спорт |
| Education | .. | .. | .. | 4.4 | 1.0 | 2.7 | Образование |
| Culture and art | .. | .. | .. | .. | .. | .. | Культура и искусство |
| Science and research | .. | .. | .. | .. | .. | .. | Наука и научное обслуживание |
| Credit | .. | .. | .. | .. | .. | .. | Кредитование |
| Insurance | .. | .. | .. | .. | .. | .. | Страхование |
| General administration and defense | .. | .. | .. | 4.1 | 1.0 | 1.2 | Государственное управление и оборона |
| Private nonprofit institutions serving households | .. | .. | .. | .. | .. | .. | Общественные организации, обслуживающие домашние хозяйства |
| **Imputed service charge of financial intermediaries** | .. | .. | | .. | .. | .. | **Условно-исчисляемая стоимость услуг финансовых посредников** |
| **Total gross value added** | .. | -11.5 | .. | -8.5 | -3.0 | 2.9 | **Валовая добавленная стоимость (ВДС) - всего** |
| **Total GDP at factor cost** | .. | .. | .. | .. | .. | .. | **Всего ВВП по фактр. стоимости (ВДС-ДНП+ДСП)** |
| **Net indirect taxes** | .. | .. | .. | -8.5 | 0.0 | 3.1 | **Чистые косвенные налоги (НПиИ-СПиИ)** |
| **Total GDP at market prices** | .. | -11.0 | .. | -8.5 | -2.7 | 2.9 | **Всего ВВП в рыночных ценах** |
| **Growth rate by expenditure category** | | | | .. | .. | .. | **Валовой внутренний продукт по видам расходов** |
| **Consumption** | .. | .. | .. | .. | .. | .. | **Потребление** |
| Private consumption | .. | .. | .. | .. | .. | .. | Личное потребление |
| Government consumption | .. | .. | .. | .. | .. | .. | Общественное потребление |
| **Gross domestic investment** | .. | .. | .. | .. | .. | .. | **Валовые внутренние инвестиции** |
| Gross fixed investment | .. | .. | .. | .. | .. | .. | Валовое накопление основного капитала |
| **Exports of goods and nonfactor services** | .. | .. | .. | .. | .. | .. | **Экспорт товаров и нефакторных услуг** |
| **Imports of goods and nonfactor services** | .. | .. | .. | .. | .. | .. | **Импорт товаров и нефакторных услуг** |

**TABLE 2-2B. Implicit price deflators for gross domestic product (percentage change)**

**ТАБЛИЦА 2-2В. Дефляторы валового внутреннего продукта (темпы прироста в %)**

| Sector of origin or expenditure category | 1990 | 1991 | 1992 | 1993 | 1994 | 1995 | Отраслевое происхождение или вид расходов |
|---|---|---|---|---|---|---|---|
| **Price deflators by sector of origin** | | | | | | | **Дефляторы по отраслевому происхождению или виду расходов** |
| **Agriculture and forestry** | .. | 135.6 | .. | 53.2 | 35.9 | 13.3 | **Сельское и лесное хозяйство** |
| Agriculture | .. | .. | .. | .. | .. | .. | Сельское хозяйство |
| Forestry | .. | .. | .. | .. | .. | .. | Лесное хозяйство |
| **Industry and construction** | .. | 119.6 | .. | 86.6 | 36.0 | 24.5 | **Промышленность и строительство** |
| Industry | .. | .. | .. | 88.0 | 36.0 | 27.9 | Промышленность |
| Construction | .. | .. | .. | 78.4 | 35.8 | 11.6 | Строительство |
| **Other** | .. | 149.5 | .. | 76.6 | 37.7 | 43.3 | **Другие отрасли** |
| Transport | .. | .. | .. | 36.4 | 3.6 | 47.8 | Транспорт |
| Road maintenance | .. | .. | .. | .. | .. | .. | Дорожное хозяйство |
| Communication | .. | .. | .. | .. | .. | .. | Связь |
| Wholesale trade | .. | .. | .. | 62.5 | 39.7 | 36.9 | Оптовая торговля |
| Retail trade and catering | .. | .. | .. | .. | .. | .. | Розничная торговля и общепит. |
| Material supply | .. | .. | .. | .. | .. | .. | Материально-техническое снабжение |
| Procurement | .. | .. | .. | .. | .. | .. | Заготовки |
| Information and computing services | .. | .. | .. | .. | .. | .. | Информационно-вычислительное обслуживание |
| Other sectors of material production | .. | .. | .. | .. | .. | .. | Другие отрасли сферы матерл. произ. |
| Housing | .. | .. | .. | .. | .. | .. | Жилищное хозяйство |
| Public utilities and personal services | .. | .. | .. | .. | .. | .. | Ком. хоз. и бытовое обслуживание |
| Health care, social security, and sports | .. | .. | .. | 144.6 | 85.9 | 46.1 | Здравоохранение, социальное обеспечение, физкультура и спорт |
| Education | .. | .. | .. | 124.8 | 33.7 | 30.6 | Образование |
| Culture and art | .. | .. | .. | .. | .. | .. | Культура и искусство |
| Science and research | .. | .. | .. | .. | .. | .. | Наука и научное обслуживание |
| Credit | .. | .. | .. | .. | .. | .. | Кредитование |
| Insurance | .. | .. | .. | .. | .. | .. | Страхование |
| General administration and defense | .. | .. | .. | 129.5 | 74.3 | 39.2 | Государственное управление и оборона |
| Private nonprofit institutions serving households | .. | .. | .. | .. | .. | .. | Общественные организации, обслуживающие домашние хозяйства |
| **Imputed service charge of financial intermediaries** | .. | .. | .. | .. | .. | .. | **Условно-исчисляемая стоимость услуг финансовых посредников** |
| **Total gross value added** | .. | 133.9 | .. | 77.1 | 37.0 | 34.9 | **Валовая добавленная стоимость (ВДС) - всего** |
| **Total GDP at factor cost** | .. | .. | .. | .. | .. | .. | **ВВП по факторной стоимости (ВДС-ДНП+ДСП)** |
| **Net indirect taxes** | .. | .. | .. | 163.7 | 67.6 | 27.9 | **Чистые косвенные налоги (НПИ-СПИ)** |
| **Total GDP at market prices** | .. | 158.0 | .. | 83.2 | 40.2 | 34.0 | **ВВП в рыночных ценах** |
| **Price deflators by expenditure category** | | | | | | | **Дефляторы по виду расходов** |
| **Consumption** | .. | .. | .. | .. | .. | .. | **Конечное потребление** |
| Private consumption | .. | .. | .. | .. | .. | .. | Личное потребление |
| Government consumption | .. | .. | .. | .. | .. | .. | Общественное потребление |
| **Gross domestic investment** | .. | .. | .. | .. | .. | .. | **Валовые внутренние инвестиции** |
| Gross fixed investment | .. | .. | .. | .. | .. | .. | Валовое накопление основного капитала |
| **Exports of goods and nonfactor services** | .. | .. | .. | .. | .. | .. | **Экспорт товаров и нефакторных услуг** |
| **Imports of goods and nonfactor services** | .. | .. | .. | .. | .. | .. | **Импорт товаров и нефакторных услуг** |

## TABLE 3-1. Balance of payments at current prices (millions of U.S. dollars)
## ТАБЛИЦА 3-1. Платежный баланс в текущих ценах (в миллионах долларов США)

| Item | 1990 | 1991 | 1992 | 1993 | 1994 | 1995 | Статьи |
|---|---|---|---|---|---|---|---|
| Exports of goods and services (including workers' remittances) | .. | .. | 659 | 1,173 | 1,882 | 2,801 | Экспорт товаров и услуг (включая денежные переводы рабочих) |
| Exports of goods and nonfactor services | .. | .. | 659 | 1,146 | 1,845 | 2,738 | Экспорт товаров и нефакт. услуг |
| Merchandise (FOB) | .. | .. | 457 | 812 | 1,329 | 1,862 | Товары (ФОБ) |
| Nonfactor services | .. | .. | 202 | 335 | 516 | 876 | Нефакторные услуги |
| Shipment | .. | .. | 149 | 223 | 338 | 374 | Перевозки |
| Travel | .. | .. | 27 | 50 | 92 | 357 | Поездки |
| Other | .. | .. | 26 | 62 | 87 | 145 | Другие |
| Imports of goods and nonfactor services | .. | .. | 707 | 1,216 | 2,095 | 3,052 | Импорт товаров и нефакт. услуг |
| Merchandise (FOB) | .. | .. | 547 | 957 | 1,684 | 2,554 | Товары (ФОБ) |
| Nonfactor services | .. | .. | 159 | 259 | 411 | 498 | Нефакторные услуги |
| Shipment | .. | .. | 93 | 124 | 185 | 222 | Перевозки |
| Travel | .. | .. | 19 | 25 | 48 | 91 | Поездки |
| Other | .. | .. | 47 | 110 | 178 | 185 | Другие |
| Resource balance | .. | .. | -48 | -70 | -250 | -314 | Сальдо ресурсов |
| Net factor income | .. | .. | -13 | -14 | -30 | 3 | Чистый факторный доход |
| Factor receipts | .. | .. | 1 | 27 | 37 | 63 | Факторные поступления |
| Factor payments | .. | .. | 14 | 41 | 67 | 60 | Факторные платежи |
| Total interest due | .. | .. | 14 | 41 | 67 | 57 | Общая сумма процента к оплате |
| Other factor payments and discrepancy | .. | .. | 0 | 0 | 0 | 3 | Другие факторные платежи и стат. погр. |
| Net current transfers | .. | .. | 97 | 105 | 115 | 126 | Чистые текущие трансферты |
| Current receipts | .. | .. | 97 | 108 | 120 | 134 | Текущие поступления |
| Workers remittances | .. | .. | 0 | 0 | 0 | 0 | Денежные переводы рабочих |
| Other current transfers | .. | .. | 97 | 108 | 120 | 135 | Другие текущие трансферты |
| Current payments | .. | .. | 0 | 3 | 5 | 8 | Текущие платежи |
| Current account balance before official grants | .. | .. | 36 | 21 | -164 | -185 | Сальдо текущего счета до офиц. безвозмезд. трансфертов |
| Official capital grants | .. | .. | .. | .. | .. | .. | Официальные кап. безвозмезные трансферты |
| Current account balance after official grants | .. | .. | .. | .. | .. | .. | Сальдо текущего счета после офиц. безвозмезд. трансфертов |
| Long Term Capital Inflows | .. | .. | 117 | 283 | 218 | 276 | Долгосрочные притоки капитала |
| Direct investment | .. | .. | 80 | 156 | 212 | 202 | Прямые инвестиции |
| Net long term borrowing | .. | .. | 37 | 127 | 5 | 73 | Чистые долгосрочные займы |
| Disbursements | .. | .. | .. | .. | .. | .. | Поступления |
| Repayments due | .. | .. | .. | .. | .. | .. | Сумма, подлежащая погашению |
| Other long-term inflows (net) | .. | .. | -1 | 0 | 1 | 1 | Другие долгосрочные притоки (чистые) |

(continued on next page)

**TABLE 3-1. Balance of payments at current prices (millions of U.S. dollars)**
**ТАБЛИЦА 3-1. Платежный баланс в текущих ценах (в миллионах долларов США)**

| Item | 1990 | 1991 | 1992 | 1993 | 1994 | 1995 | Статьи |
|---|---|---|---|---|---|---|---|
| Adjustment to Scheduled Debt Service | .. | .. | .. | .. | .. | .. | Регулирование долга |
| Debt service not paid | .. | .. | .. | .. | .. | .. | Невыплаченный долг |
| Interest not paid | .. | .. | .. | .. | .. | .. | Невыплаченный процент |
| Principal not paid | .. | .. | .. | .. | .. | .. | Невыплаченная сумма основного долга |
| Arrears reductions/prepayments(-) | .. | .. | .. | .. | .. | .. | Погашение просроченных платежей/выплаты авансом (-) |
| Total Other items (Net) | .. | .. | -98 | -110 | -23 | 15 | Общие другие статьи (чистые) |
| Net short-term capital | .. | .. | -92 | -64 | -37 | -1 | Чистый краткосрочный капитал |
| Capital flows not elsewhere included | .. | .. | .. | .. | .. | .. | Потоки капитала, не указанные выше |
| Errors and omissions | .. | .. | -6 | -46 | 14 | 14 | Ошибки и пропуски |
| Changes in net reserves | .. | .. | -82 | -195 | -31 | -106 | Изменения в чистых резервах |
| Net credit from IMF | .. | .. | .. | .. | .. | .. | Чистый кредит МВФ |
| Reserve changes not elsewhere included | .. | .. | .. | .. | .. | .. | Изменения резервов, не указанных выше |
| Escrow account | .. | .. | .. | .. | .. | .. | Счет депонирования |
| Gross reserves (excluding gold) | .. | .. | .. | .. | 4,710 | .. | Общие резервы (исключая золото) |
| Gross reserves (including gold) | .. | .. | .. | .. | .. | .. | Общие резервы (включая золото) |
| Nominal official exchange rate (annual average) (rf) | .. | .. | 12.0789 | 13.2339 | 12.9698 | 11.4649 | Номинальный официальный или рыночный курс (среднегодовой) |
| Nominal official exchange rate (end-of-year) (ae) | .. | .. | 12.9120 | 13.8776 | 12.3904 | 11.4624 | Номинальный официальный или рыночный курс (на конец года) |
| Manufacture unit value (percent change) | .. | .. | .. | .. | .. | .. | Средний индекс цен на продукцию обр. пром.,% |
| Index of real effective exchange rate (IMF) | .. | .. | .. | 1.993 | 2.202 | 2.858 | Индекс реального эффективного валютного курса (МВФ) |
| Total factor payments | .. | .. | .. | .. | .. | .. | Общая сумма факторных платежей |
| Government interest | .. | .. | .. | .. | .. | .. | Процент, выплачиваемый органами гос. управления |
| Private sector interest | .. | .. | .. | .. | .. | .. | Процент выплачиваемый частным сектором |
| Profits on direct foreign investment | .. | .. | .. | .. | .. | .. | Прибыль от прямых иностранных инвестиций |
| Official capital grants | .. | .. | .. | .. | .. | .. | Официальные капитальные безвозмездные трансферты |
| For budgetary financing | .. | .. | .. | .. | .. | .. | На бюджетное финансирование |
| To extrabudgetary entities | .. | .. | .. | .. | .. | .. | На внебюджетное финансирование |
| Government net long term borrowing | .. | .. | .. | .. | .. | .. | Чистые долгосрочные государственные займы |
| Disbursements | .. | .. | .. | .. | .. | .. | Поступления |
| Repayments | .. | .. | .. | .. | .. | .. | Погашения |
| Private net long term borrowing | .. | .. | .. | .. | .. | .. | Чистые долгосрочные частные займы |
| Disbursements | .. | .. | .. | .. | .. | .. | Поступления |
| Repayments | .. | .. | .. | .. | .. | .. | Погашения |

## TABLE 3-2A. Imports by commodity group (millions of U.S. dollars)
## ТАБЛИЦА 3-2А . Импорт по товарным группам (млн. долларов США)

| Commodity group | 1990 | 1991 | 1992 | 1993 | 1994 | 1995 | Товарные группы |
|---|---|---|---|---|---|---|---|
| TOTAL | .. | .. | .. | 894.0 | 1,658.4 | 2,538.3 | ВСЕГО |
| I - Live animals; animal products | .. | .. | .. | 9.9 | 34.5 | 60.1 | I - Живые животные и продукты животноводства |
| II - Vegetable products | .. | .. | .. | 20.1 | 45.2 | 78.2 | II - Продукты растительного происхождения |
| III - Animal or vegetable fats and oils and their cleavage products; prepared edible fats; animal or vegetable waxes | .. | .. | .. | 10.5 | 20.1 | 31.3 | III - Жиры и масла растительного и животного происхождения, воски |
| IV - Prepared foodstuffs; beverages, spirits and vinegar; tobacco and manufactured tobacco substitutes | .. | .. | .. | 91.0 | 164.6 | 191.0 | IV -Продукция пищевой промышленности, алкогольные и безалкогольные напитки, табак и его заменители |
| V - Mineral products | .. | .. | .. | 139.0 | 234.0 | 291.5 | V - Минеральные продукты |
| VI - Products of the chemical or allied industries | .. | .. | .. | 57.4 | 125.4 | 203.5 | VI - Продукция химической промышленности |
| VII - Plastics and articles thereof; rubber and articles thereof | .. | .. | .. | 28.9 | 65.0 | 115.1 | VII - Пластмассы и изделия из них |
| VIII - Raw hides and skins, leather, furskins and articles thereof; saddlery and harness; travel goods, handbags and similar containers; articles of animal gut | .. | .. | .. | 6.0 | 14.6 | 20.0 | VIII - Кожевенное сырьё, кожи, пушнина, меховое сырьё и изделия из них |
| IX - Wood and articles of wood; wood charcoal; cork and articles of cork; manufactures of straw, of esparto or of other plaiting materials; basketware and wickerwork | .. | .. | .. | 6.9 | 23.1 | 39.4 | IX - Древесина и изделия из древесины, древесный уголь |
| X - Pulp of wood or of other fibrous cellulosic material; waste and scrap of paper or paperboard; paper and paperboard and articles thereof | .. | .. | .. | 18.5 | 43.9 | 84.8 | X - Бумажная масса, бумажные и картонные отходы, макулатура, бумага, картон и изделия из них |
| XI - Textiles and textile articles | .. | .. | .. | 94.3 | 171.0 | 263.6 | XI - Текстиль и текстильные изделия |
| XII - Footwear, headgear, umbrellas, sun umbrellas, walking sticks, seat sticks, whips, riding crops and parts thereof; prepared feathers and articles made therewith; artificial flowers; articles of human hair | .. | .. | .. | 9.0 | 26.2 | 33.3 | XII - Обувь, головные уборы, зонты, трости и пр. |

## TABLE 3-2A. Imports by commodity group (millions of U.S. dollars)



## ТАБЛИЦА 3-2A . Импорт по товарным группам (млн. долларов США)

| Commodity group | 1990 | 1991 | 1992 | 1993 | 1994 | 1995 | Товарные группы |
|---|---|---|---|---|---|---|---|
| XIII - Articles of stone, plaster, cement, asbestos, mica and similar materials; ceramic products; glass and glassware | .. | .. | .. | 10.9 | 29.8 | 53.9 | XIII - Изделия из камня, гипса, цемента |
| XIV - Natural or cultured pearls, precious or semi-precious stones, precious metals, metals clad with precious metal and articles thereof; imitation jewellery; coin | .. | .. | .. | 4.7 | 4.5 | 7.2 | XIV - Жемчуг, драгоценные и полудрагоценные камни, драгоценные металлы, бижутерия, монеты |
| XV - Base metals and articles of base metal | .. | .. | .. | 45.0 | 98.6 | 179.8 | XV - Неблагородные металлы и изделия из них |
| XVI - Machinery and mechanical appliances; electrical equipment; parts thereof; sound recorders and reproducers, television image and sound recorders and reproducers, and parts and accessories of such articles | .. | .. | .. | 158.5 | 327.1 | 547.3 | XVI - Машины, оборудование, механизмы, их части и принадлежности; звуковая и теле-аппаратура, их части и принадлежности |
| XVII - Vehicles, aircraft, vessels and associated transport equipment | .. | .. | .. | 127.0 | 142.6 | 201.3 | XVII - Средства наземного, воздушного и водного транспорта |
| XVIII - Optical, photographic, cinematographic, measuring, checking, precision, medical or surgical instruments and apparatus; clocks and watches; musical instruments; parts and accessories thereof | .. | .. | .. | 21.7 | 39.3 | 61.7 | XVIII - Приборы, аппараты оптические, медицинские, измерительные и пр.; музыкальные инструменты; часы; их части и принадлежности |
| XIX - Arms and ammunition; parts and accessories thereof | .. | .. | .. | 2.2 | 2.9 | 1.1 | XIX - Оружие и боеприпасы, их части и принадлежности |
| XX - Miscellaneous manufactured articles | .. | .. | .. | 26.2 | 46.0 | 74.2 | XX - Разные промышленные товары |
| XXI - Works of art, collectors' pieces, and antiques | .. | .. | .. | 6.3 | 0.0 | 0.0 | XXI - Произведения искусства, предметы антиквариата |
| XXII - Services | .. | .. | .. | .. | .. | .. | XXII - Услуги |

## TABLE 3-2B Imports by commodity group (millions of national currency)
## ТАБЛИЦА 3-2B. Импорт по товарным группам (млн. национальной валюты)

| Commodity group | 1990 | 1991 | 1992 | 1993 | 1994 | 1995 | Товарные группы |
|---|---|---|---|---|---|---|---|
| TOTAL | .. | .. | .. | 11,831.0 | 21,509.3 | 29,100.7 | ВСЕГО |
| I - Live animals; animal products | .. | .. | .. | 131.6 | 448.0 | 688.9 | I - Живые животные и продукты животноводства |
| II - Vegetable products | .. | .. | .. | 266.4 | 585.7 | 896.3 | II - Продукты растительного происхождения |
| III - Animal or vegetable fats and oils and their cleavage products; prepared edible fats; animal or vegetable waxes | .. | .. | .. | 138.8 | 261.2 | 359.2 | III - Жиры и масла растительного и животного происхождения, воски |
| IV - Prepared foodstuffs; beverages, spirits and vinegar; tobacco and manufactured tobacco substitutes | .. | .. | .. | 1,204.2 | 2,135.0 | 2,190.1 | IV -Продукция пищевой промышленности, алкогольные и безалкогольные напитки, табак и его заменители |
| V - Mineral products | .. | .. | .. | 1,840.1 | 3,034.7 | 3,341.5 | V - Минеральные продукты |
| VI - Products of the chemical or allied industries | .. | .. | .. | 759.6 | 1,627.1 | 2,332.9 | VI - Продукция химической промышленности |
| VII - Plastics and articles thereof; rubber and articles thereof | .. | .. | .. | 382.2 | 843.1 | 1,319.2 | VII - Пластмассы и изделия из них |
| VIII - Raw hides and skins, leather, furskins and articles thereof; saddlery and harness; travel goods, handbags and similar containers; articles of animal gut | .. | .. | .. | 79.5 | 189.0 | 229.3 | VIII - Кожевенное сырьё, кожи, пушнина, меховое сырьё и изделия из них |
| IX - Wood and articles of wood; wood charcoal; cork and articles of cork; manufactures of straw, of esparto or of other plaiting materials; basketware and wickerwork | .. | .. | .. | 91.2 | 299.8 | 452.1 | IX - Древесина и изделия из древесины, древесный уголь |
| X - Pulp of wood or of other fibrous cellulosic material; waste and scrap of paper or paperboard; paper and paperboard and articles thereof | .. | .. | .. | 244.2 | 570.3 | 972.6 | X - Бумажная масса, бумажные и картонные отходы, макулатура, бумага, картон и изделия из них |
| XI - Textiles and textile articles | .. | .. | .. | 1,247.5 | 2,217.3 | 3,022.1 | XI - Текстиль и текстильные изделия |
| XII - Footwear, headgear, umbrellas, sun umbrellas, walking sticks, seat sticks, whips, riding crops and parts thereof; prepared feathers and articles made therewith; artificial flowers; articles of human hair | .. | .. | .. | 119.7 | 339.8 | 381.7 | XII - Обувь, головные уборы, зонты, трости и пр. |

**TABLE 3-2B Imports by commodity group (millions of national currency)**
**ТАБЛИЦА 3-2B. Импорт по товарным группам (млн. национальной валюты)**

| Commodity group | 1990 | 1991 | 1992 | 1993 | 1994 | 1995 | Товарные группы |
|---|---|---|---|---|---|---|---|
| XIII - Articles of stone, plaster, cement, asbestos, mica and similar materials; ceramic products; glass and glassware | .. | .. | .. | 144.4 | 386.8 | 617.5 | XIII - Изделия из камня, гипса, цемента |
| XIV - Natural or cultured pearls, precious or semi-precious stones, precious metals, metals clad with precious metal and articles thereof; imitation jewellery; coin | .. | .. | .. | 62.1 | 57.7 | 82.4 | XIV - Жемчуг, драгоценные и полудрагоценные камни, драгоценные металлы, бижутерия, монеты |
| XV - Base metals and articles of base metal | .. | .. | .. | 594.9 | 1,278.5 | 2,061.7 | XV - Неблагородные металлы и изделия из них |
| XVI - Machinery and mechanical appliances; electrical equipment; parts thereof; sound recorders and reproducers, television image and sound recorders and reproducers, and parts and accessories of such articles | .. | .. | .. | 2,097.8 | 4,242.1 | 6,274.9 | XVI - Машины, оборудование, механизмы, их части и принадлежности; звуковая и теле-аппаратура, их части и принадлежности |
| XVII - Vehicles, aircraft, vessels and associated transport equipment | .. | .. | .. | 1,680.3 | 1,849.5 | 2,308.1 | XVII - Средства наземного, воздушного и водного транспорта |
| XVIII - Optical, photographic, cinematographic, measuring, checking, precision, medical or surgical instruments and apparatus; clocks and watches; musical instruments; parts and accessories thereof | .. | .. | .. | 286.9 | 509.4 | 707.5 | XVIII - Приборы, аппараты оптические, медицинские, измерительные и пр.; музыкальные инструменты; часы; их части и принадлежности |
| XIX - Arms and ammunition; parts and accessories thereof | .. | .. | .. | 29.4 | 37.7 | 12.1 | XIX - Оружие и боеприпасы, их части и принадлежности |
| XX - Miscellaneous manufactured articles | .. | .. | .. | 346.2 | 596.5 | 850.4 | XX - Разные промышленные товары |
| XXI - Works of art, collectors' pieces, and antiques | .. | .. | .. | 84.0 | 0.1 | 0.2 | XXI - Произведения искусства, предметы антиквариата |
| XXII - Services | .. | .. | .. | .. | .. | .. | XXII - Услуги |

**TABLE 3-3A. Exports by commodity group (millions of U.S. dollars)**
**ТАБЛИЦА 3-3A. Экспорт по товарным группам (млн. долларов США)**

| Commodity group | 1990 | 1991 | 1992 | 1993 | 1994 | 1995 | Товарные группы |
|---|---|---|---|---|---|---|---|
| TOTAL | .. | .. | .. | 803.7 | 1,304.9 | 1,835.2 | ВСЕГО |
| I - Live animals; animal products | .. | .. | .. | 88.5 | 100.2 | 141.2 | I - Живые животные и продукты животноводства |
| II - Vegetable products | .. | .. | .. | 8.5 | 22.5 | 22.7 | II - Продукты растительного происхождения |
| III - Animal or vegetable fats and oils and their cleavage products; prepared edible fats; animal or vegetable waxes | .. | .. | .. | 5.7 | 6.1 | 9.1 | III - Жиры и масла растительного и животного происхождения, воски |
| IV - Prepared foodstuffs; beverages, spirits and vinegar; tobacco and manufactured tobacco substitutes | .. | .. | .. | 86.0 | 160.2 | 128.1 | IV -Продукция пищевой промышленности, алкогольные и безалкогольные напитки, табак и его заменители |
| V - Mineral products | .. | .. | .. | 61.6 | 106.6 | 149.0 | V - Минеральные продукты |
| VI - Products of the chemical or allied industries | .. | .. | .. | 38.4 | 88.5 | 139.3 | VI - Продукция химической промышленности |
| VII - Plastics and articles thereof; rubber and articles thereof | .. | .. | .. | 11.9 | 23.3 | 49.0 | VII - Пластмассы и изделия из них |
| VIII - Raw hides and skins, leather, furskins and articles thereof; saddlery and harness; travel goods, handbags and similar containers; articles of animal gut | .. | .. | .. | 13.9 | 16.1 | 20.9 | VIII - Кожевенное сырьё, кожи, пушнина, меховое сырьё и изделия из них |
| IX - Wood and articles of wood; wood charcoal; cork and articles of cork; manufactures of straw, of esparto or of other plaiting materials; basketware and wickerwork | .. | .. | .. | 60.4 | 133.4 | 225.8 | IX - Древесина и изделия из древесины, древесный уголь |
| X - Pulp of wood or of other fibrous cellulosic material; waste and scrap of paper or paperboard; paper and paperboard and articles thereof | .. | .. | .. | 4.8 | 10.8 | 21.5 | X - Бумажная масса, бумажные и картонные отходы, макулатура, бумага, картон и изделия из них |
| XI - Textiles and textile articles | .. | .. | .. | 98.8 | 179.3 | 248.3 | XI - Текстиль и текстильные изделия |
| XII - Footwear, headgear, umbrellas, sun umbrellas, walking sticks, seat sticks, whips, riding crops and parts thereof; prepared feathers and articles made therewith; artificial flowers; articles of human hair | .. | .. | .. | 9.8 | 19.2 | 26.6 | XII - Обувь, головные уборы, зонты, трости и пр. |

**TABLE 3-3A. Exports by commodity group (millions of U.S. dollars)**
**ТАБЛИЦА 3-3А. Экспорт по товарным группам (млн. долларов США)**

| Commodity group | 1990 | 1991 | 1992 | 1993 | 1994 | 1995 | Товарные группы |
|---|---|---|---|---|---|---|---|
| XIII - Articles of stone, plaster, cement, asbestos, mica and similar materials; ceramic products; glass and glassware | .. | .. | .. | 15.3 | 22.2 | 27.9 | XIII - Изделия из камня, гипса, цемента |
| XIV - Natural or cultured pearls, precious or semi-precious stones, precious metals, metals clad with precious metal and articles thereof; imitation jewellery; coin | .. | .. | .. | 9.7 | 5.0 | 6.6 | XIV - Жемчуг, драгоценные и полудрагоценные камни, драгоценные металлы, бижутерия, монеты |
| XV - Base metals and articles of base metal | .. | .. | .. | 84.4 | 104.1 | 125.5 | XV - Неблагородные металлы и изделия из них |
| XVI - Machinery and mechanical appliances; electrical equipment; parts thereof; sound recorders and reproducers, television image and sound recorders and reproducers, and parts and accessories of such articles | .. | .. | .. | 61.8 | 121.2 | 239.4 | XVI - Машины, оборудование, механизмы, их части и принадлежности; звуковая и теле-аппаратура, их части и принадлежности |
| XVII - Vehicles, aircraft, vessels and associated transport equipment | .. | .. | .. | 85.8 | 99.2 | 127.4 | XVII - Средства наземного, воздушного и водного транспорта |
| XVIII - Optical, photographic, cinematographic, measuring, checking, precision, medical or surgical instruments and apparatus; clocks and watches; musical instruments; parts and accessories thereof | .. | .. | .. | 12.1 | 16.0 | 21.9 | XVIII - Приборы, аппараты оптические, медицинские, измерительные и пр.; музыкальные инструменты; часы; их части и принадлежности |
| XIX - Arms and ammunition; parts and accessories thereof | .. | .. | .. | 0.4 | 0.1 | 0.4 | XIX - Оружие и боеприпасы, их части и принадлежности |
| XX - Miscellaneous manufactured articles | .. | .. | .. | 41.4 | 70.8 | 104.4 | XX - Разные промышленные товары |
| XXI - Works of art, collectors' pieces, and antiques | .. | .. | .. | 4.5 | 0.1 | 0.2 | XXI - Произведения искусства, предметы антиквариата |
| XXII - Services | .. | .. | .. | .. | .. | .. | XXII - Услуги |

## TABLE 3-3B. Exports by Commodity Group (millions of national currency)
## ТАБЛИЦА 3-3B. Экспорт по товарным группам (млн. национальной валюты)

| Commodity group | 1990 | 1991 | 1992 | 1993 | 1994 | 1995 | Товарные группы |
|---|---|---|---|---|---|---|---|
| TOTAL | .. | .. | .. | 10,638.5 | 16,924.4 | 21,039.9 | ВСЕГО |
| I - Live animals; animal products | .. | .. | .. | 1,171.4 | 1,300.1 | 1,618.4 | I - Живые животные и продукты животноводства |
| II - Vegetable products | .. | .. | .. | 112.8 | 291.6 | 260.4 | II - Продукты растительного происхождения |
| III - Animal or vegetable fats and oils and their cleavage products; prepared edible fats; animal or vegetable waxes | .. | .. | .. | 74.8 | 78.9 | 103.9 | III - Жиры и масла растительного и животного происхождения, воски |
| IV - Prepared foodstuffs; beverages, spirits and vinegar; tobacco and manufactured tobacco substitutes | .. | .. | .. | 1,139.6 | 2,077.5 | 1,469.3 | IV -Продукция пищевой промышленности, алкогольные и безалкогольные напитки, табак и его заменители |
| V - Mineral products | .. | .. | .. | 814.7 | 1,382.9 | 1,708.1 | V - Минеральные продукты |
| VI - Products of the chemical or allied industries | .. | .. | .. | 508.6 | 1,148.0 | 1,596.9 | VI - Продукция химической промышленности |
| VII - Plastics and articles thereof; rubber and articles thereof | .. | .. | .. | 156.8 | 302.5 | 562.2 | VII - Пластмассы и изделия из них |
| VIII - Raw hides and skins, leather, furskins and articles thereof; saddlery and harness; travel goods, handbags and similar containers; articles of animal gut | .. | .. | .. | 184.5 | 208.6 | 239.4 | VIII - Кожевенное сырьё, кожи, пушнина, меховое сырьё и изделия из них |
| IX - Wood and articles of wood; wood charcoal; cork and articles of cork; manufactures of straw, of esparto or of other plaiting materials; basketware and wickerwork | .. | .. | .. | 800.5 | 1,730.1 | 2,589.4 | IX - Древесина и изделия из древесины, древесный уголь |
| X - Pulp of wood or of other fibrous cellulosic material; waste and scrap of paper or paperboard; paper and paperboard and articles thereof | .. | .. | .. | 63.4 | 139.6 | 246.3 | X - Бумажная масса, бумажные и картонные отходы, макулатура, бумага, картон и изделия из них |
| XI - Textiles and textile articles | .. | .. | .. | 1,307.5 | 2,324.8 | 2,846.6 | XI - Текстиль и текстильные изделия |
| XII - Footwear, headgear, umbrellas, sun umbrellas, walking sticks, seat sticks, whips, riding crops and parts thereof; prepared feathers and articles made therewith; artificial flowers; articles of human hair | .. | .. | .. | 130.3 | 249.2 | 305.1 | XII - Обувь, головные уборы, зонты, трости и пр. |

**TABLE 3-3B. Exports by Commodity Group (millions of national currency)**
**ТАБЛИЦА 3-3B. Экспорт по товарным группам (млн. национальной валюты)**

| Commodity group | 1990 | 1991 | 1992 | 1993 | 1994 | 1995 | Товарные группы |
|---|---|---|---|---|---|---|---|
| XIII - Articles of stone, plaster, cement, asbestos, mica and similar materials; ceramic products; glass and glassware | .. | .. | .. | 203.0 | 287.4 | 320.4 | XIII - Изделия из камня, гипса, цемента |
| XIV - Natural or cultured pearls, precious or semi-precious stones, precious metals, metals clad with precious metal and articles thereof; imitation jewellery; coin | .. | .. | .. | 127.8 | 64.9 | 75.3 | XIV - Жемчуг, драгоценные и полудрагоценные камни, драгоценные металлы, бижутерия, монеты |
| XV - Base metals and articles of base metal | .. | .. | .. | 1,116.6 | 1,350.1 | 1,438.3 | XV - Неблагородные металлы и изделия из них |
| XVI - Machinery and mechanical appliances; electrical equipment; parts thereof; sound recorders and reproducers, television image and sound recorders and reproducers, and parts and accessories of such articles | .. | .. | .. | 817.2 | 1,572.2 | 2,744.6 | XVI - Машины, оборудование, механизмы, их части и принадлежности; звуковая и теле-аппаратура, их части и принадлежности |
| XVII - Vehicles, aircraft, vessels and associated transport equipment | .. | .. | .. | 1,136.0 | 1,287.2 | 1,460.7 | XVII - Средства наземного, воздушного и водного транспорта |
| XVIII - Optical, photographic, cinematographic, measuring, checking, precision, medical or surgical instruments and apparatus; clocks and watches; musical instruments; parts and accessories thereof | .. | .. | .. | 160.7 | 207.3 | 250.5 | XVIII - Приборы, аппараты оптические, медицинские, измерительные и пр.; музыкальные инструменты; часы; их части и принадлежности |
| XIX - Arms and ammunition; parts and accessories thereof | .. | .. | .. | 5.4 | 1.8 | 4.6 | XIX - Оружие и боеприпасы, их части и принадлежности |
| XX - Miscellaneous manufactured articles | .. | .. | .. | 547.6 | 918.5 | 1,197.3 | XX - Разные промышленные товары |
| XXI - Works of art, collectors' pieces, and antiques | .. | .. | .. | 59.3 | 1.2 | 2.2 | XXI - Произведения искусства, предметы антиквариата |
| XXII - Services | .. | .. | .. | .. | .. | .. | XXII - Услуги |

## TABLE 3-4A. Geographical distribution of foreign trade (millions of U.S. dollars)
## ТАБЛИЦА 3-4А. Географическое распределение внешней торговли (млн. долларов США)

| Country or country group | Exports / Экспорт 1990 | 1991 | 1992 | 1993 | 1994 | 1995 | Imports / Импорт 1990 | 1991 | 1992 | 1993 | 1994 | 1995 | Страна или группа стран |
|---|---|---|---|---|---|---|---|---|---|---|---|---|---|
| **Total trade** | .. | .. | .. | 803.7 | 1,304.9 | 1,835.2 | .. | .. | .. | 894.0 | 1,658.4 | 2,538.3 | **Всего** |
| **CIS countries** | .. | .. | .. | 244.1 | 395.5 | 460.2 | .. | .. | .. | 192.8 | 339.6 | 477.7 | **Страны СНГ** |
| Armenia | .. | .. | .. | 0.7 | 0.8 | 0.2 | .. | .. | .. | 0.1 | 0.1 | 0.0 | Армения |
| Azerbaijan | .. | .. | .. | 3.7 | 3.0 | 1.7 | .. | .. | .. | 1.4 | 0.5 | 0.4 | Азербайджан |
| Belarus | .. | .. | .. | 9.1 | 26.7 | 45.9 | .. | .. | .. | 12.9 | 14.0 | 15.7 | Беларусь |
| Georgia | .. | .. | .. | 0.5 | 2.8 | 0.1 | .. | .. | .. | 0.3 | 0.4 | 0.6 | Грузия |
| Kazakstan | .. | .. | .. | 7.4 | 7.1 | 9.0 | .. | .. | .. | 2.0 | 3.1 | 5.0 | Казахстан |
| Kyrgyz Republic | .. | .. | .. | 0.4 | 0.1 | 0.5 | .. | .. | .. | 0.3 | 0.0 | 0.0 | Киргизстан |
| Moldova | .. | .. | .. | 2.3 | 2.9 | 3.7 | .. | .. | .. | 3.6 | 1.5 | 1.9 | Молдова |
| Russia | .. | .. | .. | 182.0 | 301.1 | 323.1 | .. | .. | .. | 153.6 | 279.1 | 408.9 | Россия |
| Tajikistan | .. | .. | .. | 3.0 | 3.9 | 1.4 | .. | .. | .. | 0.3 | 1.7 | 4.8 | Таджикистан |
| Turkmenistan | .. | .. | .. | 3.8 | 1.8 | 0.5 | .. | .. | .. | 2.7 | 3.4 | 2.7 | Туркменистан |
| Ukraine | .. | .. | .. | 28.6 | 40.0 | 68.9 | .. | .. | .. | 14.5 | 28.0 | 26.9 | Украина |
| Uzbekistan | .. | .. | .. | 2.6 | 5.3 | 5.2 | .. | .. | .. | 1.1 | 7.8 | 10.8 | Узбекистан |
| **Non-CIS countries** | .. | .. | .. | 559.6 | 909.4 | 1,375.0 | .. | .. | .. | 701.2 | 1,318.8 | 2,060.6 | **Остальной мир** |
| **Europe** | .. | .. | .. | 515.4 | 852.0 | 1,289.8 | .. | .. | .. | 611.9 | 1,167.0 | 1,859.8 | **Европа** |
| Austria | .. | .. | .. | 2.2 | 1.9 | 5.2 | .. | .. | .. | 2.2 | 10.4 | 17.1 | Австрия |
| Belgium | .. | .. | .. | 5.0 | 14.1 | 16.5 | .. | .. | .. | 9.4 | 23.1 | 38.9 | Бельгия |
| Bulgaria | .. | .. | .. | 2.1 | 1.3 | 1.2 | .. | .. | .. | 0.9 | 1.3 | 2.2 | Болгария |
| Czech Republic | .. | .. | .. | 4.9 | 3.0 | 2.7 | .. | .. | .. | 3.8 | 8.9 | 15.0 | Чешская Республика |
| Denmark | .. | .. | .. | 19.1 | 44.5 | 60.3 | .. | .. | .. | 23.2 | 43.8 | 70.6 | Дания |
| Estonia | .. | .. | .. | .. | .. | .. | .. | .. | .. | .. | .. | .. | Эстония |
| Finland | .. | .. | .. | 166.4 | 233.0 | 394.3 | .. | .. | .. | 249.6 | 495.9 | 826.8 | Финляндия |
| Former Yugoslavia | .. | .. | .. | 0.4 | 0.1 | 0.5 | .. | .. | .. | 0.2 | 1.8 | 1.7 | Быв. Югославия |
| France | .. | .. | .. | 2.4 | 5.9 | 13.9 | .. | .. | .. | 10.4 | 24.5 | 36.8 | Франция |
| Germany | .. | .. | .. | 64.3 | 88.9 | 132.5 | .. | .. | .. | 96.2 | 165.3 | 242.8 | Германия |
| Hungary | .. | .. | .. | 3.6 | 2.6 | 2.6 | .. | .. | .. | 3.8 | 6.4 | 12.9 | Венгрия |
| Iceland | .. | .. | .. | 0.4 | 1.5 | 3.8 | .. | .. | .. | 0.1 | 0.2 | 0.4 | Исландия |
| Ireland | .. | .. | .. | 0.4 | 0.4 | 4.0 | .. | .. | .. | 1.5 | 5.2 | 10.6 | Ирландия |
| Italy | .. | .. | .. | 5.2 | 11.5 | 15.5 | .. | .. | .. | 18.5 | 39.9 | 66.2 | Италия |
| Latvia | .. | .. | .. | 69.0 | 107.2 | 137.6 | .. | .. | .. | 20.2 | 24.1 | 50.3 | Латвия |
| Lithuania | .. | .. | .. | 29.7 | 70.7 | 86.2 | .. | .. | .. | 29.6 | 42.7 | 41.0 | Литва |
| Netherlands | .. | .. | .. | 32.6 | 41.1 | 85.5 | .. | .. | .. | 32.4 | 51.0 | 78.5 | Нидерланды |
| Norway | .. | .. | .. | 4.8 | 19.5 | 34.0 | .. | .. | .. | 4.2 | 10.5 | 21.3 | Норвегия |
| Poland | .. | .. | .. | 8.5 | 8.9 | 21.2 | .. | .. | .. | 3.6 | 10.0 | 15.0 | Польша |
| Romania | .. | .. | .. | 0.5 | 3.3 | 1.5 | .. | .. | .. | 0.3 | 0.3 | 0.2 | Румыния |
| Slovak Republic | .. | .. | .. | 0.3 | 1.7 | 1.5 | .. | .. | .. | 0.2 | 1.3 | 3.2 | Словацкая Республика |
| Spain | .. | .. | .. | 0.4 | 1.2 | 1.8 | .. | .. | .. | 2.1 | 4.2 | 11.0 | Испания |

TABLE 3-4A. Geographical distribution of foreign trade (millions of U.S. dollars)
ТАБЛИЦА 3-4A. Географическое распределение внешней торговли (млн. долларов США)

| Country or country group | Exports Экспорт 1990 | 1991 | 1992 | 1993 | 1994 | 1995 | Imports Импорт 1990 | 1991 | 1992 | 1993 | 1994 | 1995 | Страна или группа стран |
|---|---|---|---|---|---|---|---|---|---|---|---|---|---|
| Sweden | .. | .. | .. | 76.1 | 141.6 | 198.8 | .. | .. | .. | 79.7 | 147.3 | 215.0 | Швеция |
| Switzerland | .. | .. | .. | 2.8 | 5.9 | 4.8 | .. | .. | .. | 4.6 | 9.8 | 20.6 | Швейцария |
| United Kingdom | .. | .. | .. | 11.2 | 36.4 | 60.0 | .. | .. | .. | 13.1 | 35.4 | 56.1 | Великобритания |
| Other Europe | .. | .. | .. | 3.1 | 5.8 | 3.9 | .. | .. | .. | 2.1 | 3.7 | 5.6 | Остальные страны Европы |
| **Asia** | .. | .. | .. | 10.8 | 17.1 | 27.4 | .. | .. | .. | 54.2 | 90.7 | 109.8 | **Азия** |
| Afghanistan | .. | .. | .. | 0.3 | 0.0 | 0.2 | .. | .. | .. | 0.2 | 0.0 | 0.4 | Афганистан |
| China | .. | .. | .. | 2.0 | 4.1 | 1.4 | .. | .. | .. | 3.5 | 8.5 | 11.1 | Китай |
| India | .. | .. | .. | 0.0 | 0.5 | 0.3 | .. | .. | .. | 1.5 | 4.6 | 3.7 | Индия |
| Iraq | .. | .. | .. | .. | .. | .. | .. | .. | .. | .. | .. | .. | Ирак |
| Japan | .. | .. | .. | 3.5 | 5.9 | 8.8 | .. | .. | .. | 37.6 | 48.4 | 47.6 | Япония |
| Korea, Dem. People's Rep. | .. | .. | .. | 0.3 | .. | .. | .. | .. | .. | 0.1 | 0.2 | 0.3 | КНДР |
| Korea, Rep. of | .. | .. | .. | 0.0 | 0.2 | 0.5 | .. | .. | .. | 2.1 | 5.2 | 12.7 | Южная Корея |
| Mongolia | .. | .. | .. | .. | 0.1 | 0.1 | .. | .. | .. | .. | .. | .. | МНР |
| Syrian Arab Republic | .. | .. | .. | 0.1 | .. | 0.4 | .. | .. | .. | 0.0 | .. | 0.0 | Сирия |
| Turkey | .. | .. | .. | 2.1 | 0.2 | 9.1 | .. | .. | .. | 0.4 | 0.9 | 2.7 | Турция |
| Viet Nam | .. | .. | .. | 0.0 | 1.5 | 0.0 | .. | .. | .. | 0.5 | 0.1 | 0.0 | Вьетнам |
| Other Asia | .. | .. | .. | 2.5 | 4.6 | 6.6 | .. | .. | .. | 8.3 | 22.8 | 31.3 | Остальные страны Азии |
| **America** | .. | .. | .. | 18.7 | 29.8 | 49.7 | .. | .. | .. | 31.3 | 55.8 | 86.3 | **Сев. и Южная Америка** |
| Canada | .. | .. | .. | 1.3 | 1.9 | 2.1 | .. | .. | .. | 2.2 | 6.3 | 5.5 | Канада |
| Cuba | .. | .. | .. | .. | 0.2 | 0.1 | .. | .. | .. | 0.0 | 0.1 | 0.1 | Куба |
| United States | .. | .. | .. | 14.9 | 23.8 | 43.9 | .. | .. | .. | 24.4 | 41.4 | 62.0 | США |
| Other America | .. | .. | .. | 2.5 | 3.9 | 3.6 | .. | .. | .. | 4.7 | 8.0 | 18.7 | Остальные |
| **Africa** | .. | .. | .. | 14.4 | 10.2 | 8.0 | .. | .. | .. | 0.5 | 4.7 | 3.6 | **Африка** |
| Egypt | .. | .. | .. | 2.0 | 1.1 | 0.0 | .. | .. | .. | 0.0 | 0.3 | 0.1 | Египет |
| Libya | .. | .. | .. | .. | .. | .. | .. | .. | .. | 0.1 | 0.0 | .. | Ливия |
| Other Africa | .. | .. | .. | 12.4 | 9.1 | 8.0 | .. | .. | .. | 0.4 | 4.4 | 3.5 | Остальные |
| **Rest of the World** | .. | .. | .. | 0.1 | 0.3 | 0.1 | .. | .. | .. | 0.2 | 0.6 | 1.1 | **Прочие страны мира** |
| Australia | .. | .. | .. | 0.1 | 0.3 | 0.1 | .. | .. | .. | 0.1 | 0.2 | 0.9 | Австралия |

TABLE 3-4B. Geographical distribution of foreign trade (millions of national currency)

ТАБЛИЦА 3-4B. Географическое распределение внешней торговли (миллионов национальной валюты)

| Country or country group | Exports Экспорт 1990 | 1991 | 1992 | 1993 | 1994 | 1995 | Imports Импорт 1990 | 1991 | 1992 | 1993 | 1994 | 1995 | Страна или группа стран |
|---|---|---|---|---|---|---|---|---|---|---|---|---|---|
| **Total trade** | .. | .. | .. | 10,641.7 | 16,924.4 | 21,039.9 | .. | .. | .. | 11,847.8 | 21,509.3 | 29,100.7 | **Всего** |
| **CIS countries** | .. | .. | .. | 3,227.3 | 5,127.2 | 5,275.3 | .. | .. | .. | 2,567.4 | 4,404.0 | 5,475.6 | **Страны СНГ** |
| Armenia | .. | .. | .. | 9.2 | 10.0 | 2.2 | .. | .. | .. | 0.8 | 1.0 | 0.1 | Армения |
| Azerbaijan | .. | .. | .. | 48.6 | 39.0 | 19.6 | .. | .. | .. | 19.0 | 7.1 | 5.1 | Азербайджан |
| Belarus | .. | .. | .. | 121.0 | 345.9 | 526.2 | .. | .. | .. | 171.6 | 182.2 | 179.3 | Беларусь |
| Georgia | .. | .. | .. | 6.2 | 36.2 | 1.2 | .. | .. | .. | 3.3 | 4.9 | 6.9 | Грузия |
| Kazakstan | .. | .. | .. | 98.1 | 92.1 | 102.7 | .. | .. | .. | 26.8 | 39.7 | 57.5 | Казахстан |
| Kyrgyz Republic | .. | .. | .. | 5.0 | 1.1 | 5.5 | .. | .. | .. | 3.7 | 0.4 | 0.0 | Киргизстан |
| Moldova | .. | .. | .. | 30.9 | 37.0 | 41.9 | .. | .. | .. | 47.1 | 19.8 | 21.9 | Молдова |
| Russia | .. | .. | .. | 2,406.6 | 3,905.5 | 3,704.6 | .. | .. | .. | 2,033.3 | 3,620.0 | 4,687.6 | Россия |
| Tajikistan | .. | .. | .. | 40.2 | 50.4 | 15.6 | .. | .. | .. | 3.8 | 21.4 | 54.4 | Таджикистан |
| Turkmenistan | .. | .. | .. | 49.7 | 23.3 | 5.8 | .. | .. | .. | 35.8 | 43.7 | 31.1 | Туркменистан |
| Ukraine | .. | .. | .. | 378.0 | 518.3 | 790.0 | .. | .. | .. | 207.4 | 362.8 | 308.3 | Украина |
| Uzbekistan | .. | .. | .. | 33.8 | 68.4 | 60.0 | .. | .. | .. | 14.8 | 101.0 | 123.4 | Узбекистан |
| **Non-CIS countries** | .. | .. | .. | 7,414.3 | 11,797.2 | 15,764.6 | .. | .. | .. | 9,280.5 | 17,105.3 | 23,625.1 | **Остальной мир** |
| **Europe** | .. | .. | .. | 6,828.6 | 11,051.0 | 14,787.3 | .. | .. | .. | 8,098.0 | 15,135.7 | 21,322.6 | **Европа** |
| Austria | .. | .. | .. | 28.5 | 24.1 | 59.9 | .. | .. | .. | 29.7 | 134.6 | 196.3 | Австрия |
| Belgium | .. | .. | .. | 66.2 | 183.5 | 189.3 | .. | .. | .. | 124.5 | 299.2 | 446.3 | Бельгия |
| Bulgaria | .. | .. | .. | 27.1 | 16.8 | 13.7 | .. | .. | .. | 11.9 | 17.2 | 25.1 | Болгария |
| Czech Republic | .. | .. | .. | 68.1 | 38.9 | 31.3 | .. | .. | .. | 52.3 | 115.6 | 172.3 | Чешская Республика |
| Denmark | .. | .. | .. | 253.1 | 577.0 | 691.3 | .. | .. | .. | 307.4 | 568.4 | 809.3 | Дания |
| Estonia | .. | .. | .. | .. | .. | .. | .. | .. | .. | .. | .. | .. | Эстония |
| Finland | .. | .. | .. | 2,202.6 | 3,022.6 | 4,520.3 | .. | .. | .. | 3,304.4 | 6,432.4 | 9,479.2 | Финляндия |
| Former Yugoslavia | .. | .. | .. | 6.0 | 2.5 | 5.5 | .. | .. | .. | 1.9 | 23.6 | 18.2 | Быв. Югославия |
| France | .. | .. | .. | 31.7 | 76.9 | 160.0 | .. | .. | .. | 137.7 | 317.5 | 421.4 | Франция |
| Germany | .. | .. | .. | 851.4 | 1,153.7 | 1,518.7 | .. | .. | .. | 1,272.5 | 2,143.3 | 2,783.2 | Германия |
| Hungary | .. | .. | .. | 47.8 | 33.7 | 29.4 | .. | .. | .. | 49.7 | 82.4 | 147.9 | Венгрия |
| Iceland | .. | .. | .. | 5.8 | 19.6 | 43.1 | .. | .. | .. | 1.5 | 2.4 | 4.7 | Исландия |
| Ireland | .. | .. | .. | 5.2 | 5.8 | 46.1 | .. | .. | .. | 20.5 | 67.4 | 121.7 | Ирландия |
| Italy | .. | .. | .. | 69.4 | 148.6 | 177.6 | .. | .. | .. | 244.7 | 170.0 | 758.9 | Италия |
| Latvia | .. | .. | .. | 914.0 | 1,390.0 | 1,577.4 | .. | .. | .. | 267.4 | 313.1 | 577.1 | Латвия |
| Lithuania | .. | .. | .. | 395.8 | 916.9 | 988.7 | .. | .. | .. | 391.0 | 553.5 | 470.2 | Литва |
| Netherlands | .. | .. | .. | 431.4 | 532.8 | 980.6 | .. | .. | .. | 429.1 | 661.5 | 900.2 | Нидерланды |
| Norway | .. | .. | .. | 63.3 | 252.4 | 389.2 | .. | .. | .. | 55.9 | 136.3 | 244.2 | Норвегия |
| Poland | .. | .. | .. | 112.3 | 115.6 | 242.9 | .. | .. | .. | 48.1 | 130.3 | 172.3 | Польша |
| Romania | .. | .. | .. | 7.1 | 42.2 | 17.7 | .. | .. | .. | 4.3 | 3.7 | 2.3 | Румыния |
| Slovak Republic | .. | .. | .. | .. | 21.7 | 16.5 | .. | .. | .. | .. | 16.2 | 37.2 | Словацкая Республика |
| Spain | .. | .. | .. | 5.0 | 15.2 | 20.9 | .. | .. | .. | 27.2 | 54.9 | 125.7 | Испания |

TABLE 3-4B. Geographical distribution of foreign trade (millions of national currency)

ТАБЛИЦА 3-4B. Географическое распределение внешней торговли (миллионов национальной валюты)

| Country or country group | Exports Экспорт 1990 | 1991 | 1992 | 1993 | 1994 | 1995 | Imports Импорт 1990 | 1991 | 1992 | 1993 | 1994 | 1995 | Страна или группа стран |
|---|---|---|---|---|---|---|---|---|---|---|---|---|---|
| Sweden | .. | .. | .. | 1,011.4 | 1,836.7 | 2,279.6 | .. | .. | .. | 1,055.0 | 1,911.1 | 2,464.9 | Швеция |
| Switzerland | .. | .. | .. | 37.2 | 77.1 | 55.5 | .. | .. | .. | 61.2 | 127.4 | 236.8 | Швейцария |
| United Kingdom | .. | .. | .. | 148.0 | 471.8 | 688.2 | .. | .. | .. | 173.1 | 458.7 | 643.2 | Великобритания |
| Other Europe | .. | .. | .. | 40.2 | 74.9 | 43.9 | .. | .. | .. | 27.0 | 395.0 | 64.0 | Остальные страны Европы |
| **Asia** | .. | .. | .. | 145.1 | 223.0 | 314.1 | .. | .. | .. | 717.9 | 1,177.6 | 1,259.3 | **Азия** |
| Afghanistan | .. | .. | .. | 4.1 | 0.3 | 2.1 | .. | .. | .. | 2.1 | 0.8 | 4.0 | Афганистан |
| China | .. | .. | .. | 27.0 | 53.6 | 15.9 | .. | .. | .. | 46.6 | 110.0 | 127.1 | Китай |
| India | .. | .. | .. | 0.1 | 6.6 | 3.2 | .. | .. | .. | 19.7 | 59.2 | 42.6 | Индия |
| Iraq | .. | .. | .. | .. | .. | .. | .. | .. | .. | .. | .. | 0.0 | Ирак |
| Japan | .. | .. | .. | 46.8 | 76.0 | 101.3 | .. | .. | .. | 497.7 | 627.4 | 545.5 | Япония |
| Korea, Dem. People's Rep. | .. | .. | .. | 4.1 | .. | .. | .. | .. | .. | 0.7 | 2.1 | 3.2 | КНДР |
| Korea, Rep. of | .. | .. | .. | 0.6 | 2.3 | 5.3 | .. | .. | .. | 27.7 | 67.0 | 145.3 | Южная Корея |
| Mongolia | .. | .. | .. | .. | 1.0 | 0.9 | .. | .. | .. | .. | .. | .. | МНР |
| Syrian Arab Republic | .. | .. | .. | 1.3 | .. | 4.7 | .. | .. | .. | 0.0 | .. | 0.5 | Сирия |
| Turkey | .. | .. | .. | 27.7 | 2.1 | 104.9 | .. | .. | .. | 5.9 | 11.4 | 30.7 | Турция |
| Viet Nam | .. | .. | .. | 0.0 | 19.6 | 0.0 | .. | .. | .. | 6.1 | 1.9 | 0.4 | Вьетнам |
| Other Asia | .. | .. | .. | 33.4 | 61.5 | 75.8 | .. | .. | .. | 111.4 | 297.8 | 360.0 | Остальные страны Азии |
| **America** | .. | .. | .. | 246.9 | 386.2 | 570.2 | .. | .. | .. | 415.0 | 723.5 | 989.3 | **Сев. и Южная Америка** |
| Canada | .. | .. | .. | 16.8 | 24.6 | 24.4 | .. | .. | .. | 29.2 | 82.1 | 63.1 | Канада |
| Cuba | .. | .. | .. | .. | 2.7 | 1.1 | .. | .. | .. | 0.1 | 0.5 | 1.2 | Куба |
| United States | .. | .. | .. | 197.6 | 308.9 | 503.3 | .. | .. | .. | 322.4 | 536.4 | 710.6 | США |
| Other America | .. | .. | .. | 32.5 | 50.0 | 41.4 | .. | .. | .. | 63.3 | 104.5 | 214.4 | Остальные |
| **Africa** | .. | .. | .. | 192.0 | 132.9 | 92.1 | .. | .. | .. | 5.8 | 61.3 | 41.1 | **Африка** |
| Egypt | .. | .. | .. | 26.9 | 14.3 | 0.1 | .. | .. | .. | 0.6 | 3.9 | 1.2 | Египет |
| Libya | .. | .. | .. | 0.4 | 0.0 | 0.0 | .. | .. | .. | 0.9 | 0.5 | .. | Ливия |
| Other Africa | .. | .. | .. | 164.7 | 118.6 | 92.0 | .. | .. | .. | 4.3 | 56.9 | 39.9 | Остальные |
| **Rest of the World** | .. | .. | .. | 1.8 | 4.1 | 0.9 | .. | .. | .. | 2.5 | 7.2 | 12.8 | **Прочие страны мира** |
| Australia | .. | .. | .. | 1.7 | 3.8 | 0.9 | .. | .. | .. | 1.4 | 2.7 | 9.6 | Австралия |

## TABLE 4-1. General government budget revenue (millions of national currency)
## ТАБЛИЦА 4-1. Доходы государственного бюджета (млн. национальной валюты)

| Type of revenue | 1990 | 1991 | 1992 | 1993 | 1994 | 1995 | Вид доходов |
|---|---|---|---|---|---|---|---|
| **Total revenue and grants** | 2,847 | 7,054 | 4,538 | 10,667 | 10,859 | 13,070 | **Всего доходов и безвозм. поступл.** |
| Grants | 303 | 11 | 15 | .. | .. | .. | Безвозмездные поступления |
| Total Revenue | 2,545 | 7,043 | 4,523 | 10,667 | 10,859 | 13,070 | Всего доходов |
| **Current revenue** | 2,545 | 7,039 | 4,523 | 10,657 | 10,859 | 13,070 | **Текущие доходы** |
| Tax revenue | 2,026 | 6,237 | 3,887 | 8,107 | 10,197 | 12,278 | Доход от налогов |
| Taxes on income and profits | 886 | 2,567 | 1,577 | 2,869 | 3,426 | 2,772 | Налоги на доходы и прибыль |
| Individual | 337 | 1,194 | 857 | 1,832 | 2,388 | 1,722 | Физические лица |
| Corporate | 549 | 1,373 | 720 | 1,037 | 1,038 | 1,050 | Предприятия и организации |
| Social security contributions | .. | 1,530 | 1,170 | 2,600 | 2,507 | 4,104 | Отчисление на соцстрах. |
| Taxes on payroll or work force | .. | | .. | .. | .. | .. | Налоги на заработную плату и рабочую силу |
| Taxes on the use of labor force | .. | .. | .. | .. | .. | .. | Плата за трудовые ресурсы |
| Taxes on increases in wages and salaries | .. | .. | .. | .. | .. | .. | Налог с прироста средств на оплату труда |
| Other payroll/work force taxes | .. | .. | .. | .. | .. | .. | Другие налоги на зарплату и рабочую силу |
| Taxes on property | .. | 85 | .. | 28 | 124 | 44 | Налоги на собственность |
| Taxes on immovable property | .. | 85 | .. | 28 | 124 | 44 | Налоги на недвижимое имущество |
| Buildings | .. | .. | .. | .. | .. | .. | Налог с владельцев строении |
| Land | .. | 85 | .. | 28 | 124 | 44 | Земельныи налог |
| Estate, inheritance, and gift taxes | .. | .. | .. | .. | .. | .. | Налоги на наследство, подарки |
| Other property taxes | .. | .. | .. | .. | .. | .. | Другие налоги на имущество |
| Domestic taxes on goods and services | 1,050 | 1,998 | 1,108 | 2,491 | 4,077 | 5,304 | Внутренние налоги на товары и услуги |
| General sales, turnover, or value-added taxes | 1,033 | 1,232 | 903 | 1,994 | 3,309 | 4,112 | Налог с продаж. с оборота или на добав. стоим. |
| Excises | .. | 736 | 182 | 403 | 611 | 1,137 | Акцизы |
| Profits of fiscal monopolies | .. | .. | .. | .. | .. | .. | Прибыли фискальных монополий |
| Taxes on specific services | .. | .. | .. | 7 | .. | .. | Налоги на особые услуги |
| Taxes on use of goods or permission to use goods or to perform activities | .. | .. | .. | 7 | .. | .. | Налоги на пользование товарами или лицензии на пользование товарами и занятие деятельностью |
| Other taxes on goods and services | 17 | 30 | 23 | 80 | 157 | 55 | Другие налоги на товары и услуги |
| Taxes on international trade and transactions | 90 | 28 | 15 | 39 | 36 | 8 | Налоги на внешнюю торговлю и операции |
| Import duties | .. | .. | .. | .. | .. | .. | Импортные пошлины |
| Export duties | .. | .. | .. | .. | .. | .. | Экпортные пошлины |
| Other | .. | .. | .. | .. | .. | .. | Другие |
| Other taxes | .. | 29 | 17 | 80 | 27 | 46 | Прочие налоги |
| Nontax revenue | 519 | 802 | 636 | 2,550 | 662 | 792 | Неналоговые доходы |
| **Capital revenue** | .. | 4 | 0 | 10 | 0 | 0 | **Капитальные доходы** |

**TABLE 4-2. General government budget expenditure by economic type (millions of nationa** **ESTONIA**

**ТАБЛИЦА 4-2. Расходы государственного бюджета по экономическим типам (млн. национальной валюты)**

| Type of expenditure or debt holder | 1990 | 1991 | 1992 | 1993 | 1994 | 1995 | Всего расходов |
|---|---|---|---|---|---|---|---|
| **Total expenditure by economic type** | 2,660 | 5,946 | 4,176 | 9,857 | 10,120 | 11,932 | **Всего расходов по экономическим типам** |
| **Current expenditure** | .. | 5,201 | 3,835 | 8,637 | 8,802 | 11,210 | **Текущие расходы** |
| Expenditure on goods and services | .. | 735 | 1,558 | 5,435 | 4,749 | 6,036 | Расходы на товары и услуги |
| Wages and salaries | .. | 735 | 552 | 1,225 | 1,318 | 1,904 | Заработная плата |
| Employer contributions | .. | .. | 694 | 2,545 | 2,552 | 3,211 | Отчисление на социальное страхование |
| Other Purchases of goods and services | .. | .. | 312 | 1,665 | 879 | 921 | Другие покупки товаров и услуг |
| Interest payments | .. | 10 | .. | .. | 83 | 100 | Выплаты процентов |
| Domestic debt | .. | .. | .. | .. | 46 | 70 | По внутреннему долгу |
| Foreign debt | .. | .. | .. | .. | 37 | 30 | По внешнему долгу |
| Subsidies and other current transfers | .. | 346 | 545 | 875 | 1,135 | 1,360 | Субсидии на другие текущие трансферты |
| Subsidies | .. | 204 | 148 | 313 | 449 | 253 | Субсидии |
| Agricultural subsidies | .. | .. | .. | .. | .. | 109 | Субсидии на сельское хозяйство |
| Other current transfers | .. | 142 | 397 | 562 | 686 | 1,107 | Другие текущие трансферты |
| Other | .. | 4,110 | 1,732 | 2,327 | 2,835 | 3,714 | Прочие расходы |
| **Capital expenditure** | .. | 745 | 341 | 1,220 | 1,318 | 722 | **Капитальные расходы** |
| Acquisition of fixed capital assets | .. | 497 | 199 | 643 | 648 | 89 | Приобретение основного капитала |
| Capital transfers | .. | 248 | 142 | 577 | 670 | 633 | Капитальные трансферты |
| Other | .. | .. | .. | .. | .. | .. | Другие капитальные расходы |
| **Surplus/deficit (-)** | 187 | 1,108 | 362 | 810 | 739 | 1,138 | **Превыш. доходов над расходами/дефицит(-)** |
| **Financing by type of debt holder** | .. | .. | .. | .. | .. | .. | **Финансирование по типам кредиторов** |
| **Foreign (net)** | .. | .. | .. | .. | .. | .. | **Зарубежные кредиторы (сальдо)** |
| From international development institutions | .. | .. | .. | .. | .. | .. | Международные организации |
| From foreign governments | .. | .. | .. | .. | .. | .. | Правительства иностранных государств |
| Other borrowing abroad | .. | .. | .. | .. | .. | .. | Другие зарубежные кредиторы |
| **Domestic (net)** | .. | .. | .. | .. | .. | .. | **Внутренние кредиторы (сальдо)** |
| From monetary authorities | .. | .. | .. | .. | .. | .. | Органы денежного обращения |
| From deposit money banks | .. | .. | .. | .. | .. | .. | Депозитные денежные банки |
| Other domestic borrowing | .. | .. | .. | .. | .. | .. | Другие внутренние кредиторы |
| *Memo items:* | | | | | | | *Справочно:* |
| Extrabudgetary surplus/ Deficit (-) not included above | .. | -483 | -266 | .. | .. | .. | Превышение доходов над расходами/дефицит (-) по внебюджетным фондам, не включенным выше |
| Total surplus/deficit (-) including extrabudgetary accounts | 187 | 625 | 96 | .. | .. | .. | Итого превышение доходов над расходами/дефицит, включая счета внебюджетных фондов |

## TABLE 5-1. Agricultural production (millions of national currency, current prices)



## ТАБЛИЦА 5-1. Сельскохозяйственная продукция (млн. нац. валюты, текущие цены)

| Item | 1990 | 1991 | 1992 | 1993 | 1994 | 1995 | Статьи |
|---|---|---|---|---|---|---|---|
| **Total gross agricultural production** | 223 | 488 | 3,502 | 4,684 | 5,596 | 5,738 | **Валовая продукция сельского хозяйства - всего** |
| **Crops** | 77 | 227 | 1,787 | 2,038 | 2,682 | 2,438 | **Продукция растениеводства** |
| Grains | 25 | 79 | 544 | 702 | 432 | .. | Зерно |
| Potatoes | 18 | 64 | 559 | 463 | 970 | .. | Картофель |
| Vegetables | 10 | 21 | 156 | 146 | 224 | .. | Овощи |
| Fruits (excluding grapes) | 4 | 4 | 47 | 119 | 120 | .. | Фрукты (без винограда) |
| Grapes | .. | .. | .. | .. | .. | .. | Виноград |
| Tobacco | .. | .. | .. | .. | .. | .. | Табак |
| Cotton | .. | .. | .. | .. | .. | .. | Хлопок |
| Sugarbeets | .. | 0 | 2 | 1 | 5 | .. | Сахарная свекла |
| Oilseeds | .. | 0 | 6 | 4 | 5 | .. | Семена масличных культур |
| Other | 20 | 59 | 473 | 603 | 926 | .. | Прочие |
| **Animal husbandry** | 146 | 261 | 1,715 | 2,646 | 2,914 | 3,300 | **Продукция животноводства** |
| Livestock | 89 | 139 | 669 | 1,351 | 1,340 | .. | Мясное животноводство |
| Cattle | 41 | 57 | 241 | 710 | 528 | .. | Крупный рогатый скот |
| Pigs | 37 | 67 | 341 | 531 | 648 | .. | Свиньи |
| Sheep and goats | 2 | 2 | 11 | 33 | 28 | .. | Овцы и козы |
| Poultry | 8 | 12 | 72 | 61 | 127 | .. | Птица |
| Other | 1 | 1 | 4 | 16 | 9 | .. | Прочие |
| Milk | 48 | 96 | 801 | 1,029 | 1,191 | .. | Молоко |
| Eggs | 5 | 18 | 183 | 136 | 211 | .. | Яйца |
| Wool | 0 | 1 | 5 | 7 | 7 | .. | Шерсть |
| Other livestock | 4 | 7 | 57 | 123 | 165 | .. | Прочая |
| **Agricultural services** | .. | .. | .. | .. | .. | .. | **Сельскохозяйственные услуги** |

**TABLE 5-2. Agricultural production (millions of constant national currency)** **ESTONIA**

**ТАБЛИЦА 5-2. Сельскохозяйственная продукция в постоянных ценах (млн. национальной валюты)**

| Item | 1990 | 1991 | 1992 | 1993 | 1994 | 1995 | Статьи |
|---|---|---|---|---|---|---|---|
| **Total gross agricultural production** | 7,065 | 6,611 | 5,306 | 4,684 | 4,020 | .. | **Валовая продукция сельского хозяйства - всего** |
| **Crops** | 2,498 | 2,542 | 2,078 | 2,038 | 1,723 | .. | **Продукция растениеводства** |
| Grains | .. | 789 | 529 | 702 | 439 | .. | Зерно |
| Potatoes | .. | 509 | 575 | 463 | 484 | .. | Картофель |
| Vegetables | .. | 240 | 170 | 146 | 146 | .. | Овощи |
| Fruits (excluding grapes) | .. | 89 | 116 | 119 | 87 | .. | Фрукты (без винограда) |
| Grapes | .. | .. | .. | .. | .. | .. | Виноград |
| Tobacco | .. | .. | .. | .. | .. | .. | Табак |
| Cotton | .. | .. | .. | .. | .. | .. | Хлопок |
| Sugarbeets | .. | 0 | 2 | 1 | 3 | .. | Сахарная свекла |
| Oilseeds | .. | 3 | 6 | 4 | 5 | .. | Семена масличных культур |
| Other | .. | 912 | 680 | 603 | 560 | .. | Прочие |
| **Animal husbandry** | 4,567 | 4,069 | 3,228 | 2,646 | 2,297 | .. | **Продукция животноводства** |
| Livestock | .. | 2,290 | 1,733 | 1,351 | 1,066 | .. | Мясное животноводство |
| Cattle | .. | 809 | 780 | 710 | 475 | .. | Крупный рогатый скот |
| Pigs | .. | 1,185 | 781 | 531 | 472 | .. | Свиньи |
| Sheep and goats | .. | 41 | 47 | 33 | 25 | .. | Овцы и козы |
| Poultry | .. | 240 | 115 | 61 | 83 | .. | Птица |
| Other | .. | 15 | 10 | 16 | 11 | .. | Прочие |
| Milk | .. | 1,392 | 1,171 | 1,029 | 983 | .. | Молоко |
| Eggs | .. | 226 | 180 | 136 | 141 | .. | Яйца |
| Wool | .. | 6 | 9 | 7 | 6 | .. | Шерсть |
| Other livestock | .. | 155 | 135 | 123 | 101 | .. | Прочая |
| **Agricultural services** | .. | .. | .. | .. | .. | .. | **Сельскохозяйственные услуги** |

**TABLE 5-3. Production and average yield of major agricultural crops**

**ТАБЛИЦА 5-3. Производство и урожайность важнейших сельскохозяйственных культур**

| Crop | 1990 | 1991 | 1992 | 1993 | 1994 | 1995 | Сельскохозяйственные культуры |
|---|---|---|---|---|---|---|---|
| **Production (thousands of tons)** | | | | | | | **Производство (тыс. тонн)** |
| Grain - Cleanweight | 958 | 939 | 599 | 811 | 511 | 520 | Зерно в чистом весе |
| Winter wheat | 53 | 43 | 65 | 66 | 24 | 25 | Пшеница - озимая |
| Spring wheat | 12 | 19 | 25 | 40 | 33 | 52 | яровая |
| Coarse grain | 1,177 | 1,136 | 706 | 924 | 615 | 568 | Зерно в физическом весе |
| Rye | 178 | 127 | 153 | 122 | 41 | 58 | Рожь |
| Corn | .. | .. | .. | .. | .. | .. | Кукуруза |
| Winter barley | .. | .. | .. | .. | .. | .. | Ячмень - озимый |
| Spring barley | 600 | 623 | 301 | 477 | 339 | 279 | яровой |
| Oats | 93 | 107 | 44 | 85 | 58 | 80 | Овес |
| Millet | .. | .. | .. | .. | .. | .. | Просо |
| Rice | .. | .. | .. | .. | .. | .. | Рис |
| Flax | 2 | 3 | 1 | 1 | 0 | 0 | Лен |
| Oilseeds | .. | .. | .. | .. | .. | .. | Семена масличных культур |
| Cotton (raw) | .. | .. | .. | .. | .. | .. | Хлопок - сырец |
| Cotton fiber | .. | .. | .. | .. | .. | .. | волокно |
| Sugarbeets | .. | 1 | 8 | 5 | 11 | 13 | Сахарная свекла |
| Potatoes | 618 | 592 | 669 | 539 | 563 | 537 | Картофель |
| Pulses | .. | .. | .. | .. | .. | .. | Бобовые |
| Vegetables | 105 | 121 | 78 | 70 | 78 | 57 | Овощи |
| Fruit | 22 | 23 | 31 | 48 | 21 | 37 | Фрукты |
| Grapes | .. | .. | .. | .. | .. | .. | Виноград |
| Other | 22 | 23 | 31 | 48 | 21 | 37 | Прочие |
| Corn (silage and greenchop) | 57 | .. | .. | .. | .. | .. | Кукуруза (на силос и зеленый корм) |
| Hay | 589 | 800 | 776 | 668 | 730 | 778 | Сено |
| **Average yield (kilograms per hectare)** | | | | | | | **Ср. урожайность (кг с га)** |
| Grain | 2,410 | 2,250 | 1,410 | 2,160 | 1,597 | 1,688 | Зерно |
| Winter wheat | 2,500 | 2,480 | 2,420 | 2,010 | 1,543 | 1,905 | Пшеница - озимая |
| Spring wheat | 2,580 | 2,730 | 1,470 | 2,260 | 1,772 | 2,046 | яровая |
| Coarse grain | 2,960 | 2,720 | 1,670 | 2,460 | 1,920 | 1,844 | Зерно в физическом весе |
| Rye | 2,700 | 2,170 | 2,590 | 1,980 | 1,907 | 1,819 | Рожь |
| Corn | .. | .. | .. | .. | .. | .. | Кукуруза |
| Winter barley | .. | .. | .. | .. | .. | .. | Ячмень - озимый |
| Spring barley | 2,270 | 2,190 | 1,120 | 2,190 | 1,558 | 1,499 | яровой |
| Oats | 2,800 | 2,520 | 1,050 | 2,380 | 1,593 | 2,078 | Овес |
| Millet | .. | .. | .. | .. | .. | .. | Просо |
| Rice | .. | .. | .. | .. | .. | .. | Рис |
| Flax | 950 | 2,260 | 970 | 1,540 | 841 | 870 | Лен |
| Oilseeds | .. | .. | .. | .. | .. | .. | Семена масличных культур |
| Cotton (raw) | .. | .. | .. | .. | .. | .. | Хлопок - сырец |
| Cotton fiber | .. | .. | .. | .. | .. | .. | волокно |
| Sugarbeets | .. | 28,800 | 13,810 | 24,950 | 22,090 | 30,197 | Сахарная свекла |
| Potatoes | 13,600 | 11,340 | 14,450 | 12,640 | 14,096 | 14,559 | Картофель |
| Pulses | .. | .. | .. | .. | .. | .. | Бобовые |
| Vegetables | 16,600 | 18,140 | 12,390 | 12,840 | 15,849 | 10,557 | Овощи |
| Fruit | 2,390 | 2,340 | 3,130 | 5,100 | 2,169 | 3,882 | Фрукты |
| Grapes | .. | .. | .. | .. | .. | .. | Виноград |
| Other | 2,390 | 2,340 | 3,130 | 5,100 | 2,169 | 3,882 | Прочие |
| Corn (silage and greenchop) | 22,940 | .. | .. | .. | .. | .. | Кукуруза (на силос и зеленый корм) |
| Hay | 3,510 | 4,540 | 3,350 | 2,800 | 3,057 | 3,303 | Сено |

**TABLE 5-4. Main aggregates of animal husbandry**
**ТАБЛИЦА 5-4. Основные показатели животноводства**

| Type of livestock or product | 1990 | 1991 | 1992 | 1993 | 1994 | 1995 | Направление животноводства или вид продукции |
|---|---|---|---|---|---|---|---|
| **Livestock (thousands of heads)** | | | | | | | **Поголовье скота (тысяч голов)** |
| Cattle | 758 | 708 | 615 | 463 | 420 | 370 | Крупный рогатый скот |
| of which: Cows | 281 | 264 | 253 | 227 | 211 | 185 | в том числе коровы |
| Pigs | 960 | 799 | 541 | 424 | 460 | 449 | Свиньи |
| Sheep and goats | 140 | 143 | 124 | 83 | 62 | 50 | Овцы и козы |
| of which: Goats | 1 | 1 | 1 | 1 | 1 | 2 | в том числе козы |
| Horses | 9 | 8 | 7 | 5 | 5 | 5 | Лошади |
| Other | 6,537 | 5,538 | 3,418 | 3,226 | 3,130 | 2,911 | Прочие |
| **Animal husbandry products** | | | | | | | **Продукция животноводства** |
| Meat (thousands of tons) | 183 | 152 | 108 | 84 | 69 | 68 | Мясо (тысяч тонн) |
| Beef | 63 | 52 | 46 | 43 | 31 | 26 | Говядина |
| Pork | 95 | 75 | 50 | 35 | 30 | 35 | Свинина |
| Lamb | 3 | 3 | 2 | 1 | 1 | 1 | Баранина |
| Poultry | 22 | 22 | 10 | 5 | 7 | 6 | Птица |
| Other | 0 | 0 | 0 | 0 | 0 | 0 | Прочие виды мяса |
| Milk (thousands of tons) | 1,208 | 1,093 | 919 | 807 | 772 | 707 | Молоко (тысяч тонн) |
| Eggs (millions) | 547 | 560 | 456 | 346 | 359 | 142 | Яйца (миллионов штук) |
| Wool (thousands of tons) | 0 | 0 | 0 | 0 | 0 | 0 | Шерсть (тысяч тонн) |

## TABLE 6-1. Industrial production by sector (millions of national currency)
## ТАБЛИЦА 6-1. Промышленное производство по отраслям (млн. национальной валюты)

| Sector | 1990 | 1991 | 1992 | 1993 | 1994 | 1995 | Отрасли |
|---|---|---|---|---|---|---|---|
| **All industry** | 7,883 | 18,118 | 12,065 | 14,535 | 19,832 | 26,118 | **Вся промышленность** |
| **Heavy industry** | .. | .. | .. | .. | .. | .. | **Тяжелая промышленность** |
| Fuel and energy | 464 | 1,152 | 1,807 | 2,527 | 3,818 | 4,719 | Топливно-энергетическая промышленноть |
| Electricity | 322 | 752 | 1,298 | 1,845 | 2,900 | 3,530 | Электроэнергетика |
| Fuels | 142 | 400 | 509 | 682 | 918 | 1,189 | Топливная промышленность |
| Ferrous and nonferrous metallurgy | .. | .. | .. | .. | .. | .. | Металлургия |
| Chemicals and petrochemical industry | 511 | 1,250 | 891 | 976 | 1,502 | 2,102 | Химическая и нефтехимическая пром. |
| Machine building and metalworking | 1,114 | 2,245 | 976 | 1,133 | 1,663 | 2,332 | Машиностроение и металлообработка |
| Forestry, woodworking, and pulp and paper industry | 636 | 1,645 | 676 | 557 | 1,046 | 2,008 | Лесная, деревообрабатывающая и целлюлозо-бумажная промышленность |
| Construction materials | 343 | 627 | 461 | 539 | 923 | 983 | Промышленность строительных материалов |
| **Light industry** | 1,455 | 3,850 | 2,009 | 1,424 | 1,821 | 2,762 | **Легкая промышленность** |
| Textiles | 1,009 | 2,978 | 1,388 | 664 | 908 | 1,546 | Текстильная |
| Clothing | 245 | 491 | 378 | 549 | 643 | 901 | Швейная |
| Leather and shoes | 201 | 381 | 243 | 211 | 272 | 315 | Кожевенная и обувная |
| **Food industry** | 1,899 | 4,469 | 3,620 | 5,324 | 6,333 | 7,357 | **Пищевая промышленность** |
| Processed foods | 372 | 968 | 1,570 | 2,120 | 3,403 | 3,194 | Пищевкусовая |
| Meat and dairy products | 960 | 2,605 | 1,627 | 2,577 | 2,588 | 3,124 | Мясная и молочная |
| Fish | 567 | 896 | 423 | 627 | .. | 1,039 | Рыбная |

## TABLE 6-3. Primary energy supply (million tons oil equivalent) ESTONIA

## ТАБЛИЦА 6-3. Ресурсы первичных видов энергии (млн. тонн нефтяного эквивалента)

| Item | | 1990 | 1991 | 1992 | 1993 | 1994 | 1995 | Статьи | |
|---|---|---|---|---|---|---|---|---|---|
| **Primary production** | | | | | | | | **Производство первичной энергии** | |
| Coal and lignite (hard and brown) | | 5.01 | 4.43 | 4.22 | 3.00 | 3.30 | 2.90 | Уголь каменный и бурый | |
| Crude oil | | .. | .. | .. | .. | .. | .. | Нефть | |
| Gas | | .. | .. | .. | .. | .. | .. | Газ | |
| Nuclear | | .. | .. | .. | .. | .. | .. | Атомная энергия | |
| Hydro/geothermal | | .. | .. | .. | .. | .. | .. | Гидро-геотермальная | |
| Other | | 0.34 | 0.35 | 0.33 | 0.30 | 0.40 | 0.50 | Другие виды | |
| Total | | 5.34 | 4.77 | 4.55 | 3.30 | 3.70 | 3.40 | Всего | |
| **Energy trade** | | | | | | | | **Торговля энергией** | |
| Coal and lignite | Exports | 0.05 | 0.03 | 0.01 | 0.00 | 0.10 | 0.10 | Уголь каменный и бурый | Экспорт |
| | Imports | 0.75 | 0.76 | 0.61 | 0.40 | 0.50 | 0.40 | | Импорт |
| | Net imports | 0.70 | 0.74 | 0.60 | 0.40 | 0.40 | 0.30 | | Чистый импорт |
| Oil/oil product | Exports | 0.08 | 0.06 | 0.04 | 0.00 | 0.40 | 0.50 | Нефть и нефтепродукты | Экспорт |
| | Imports | 3.16 | 2.44 | 1.27 | 1.50 | 1.60 | 1.60 | | Импорт |
| | Net imports | 3.08 | 2.39 | 1.23 | 1.50 | 1.20 | 1.10 | | Чистый импорт |
| Gas | Exports | .. | .. | .. | .. | .. | .. | Газ | Экспорт |
| | Imports | 1.26 | 1.26 | 0.73 | 0.40 | 0.50 | 0.60 | | Импорт |
| | Net imports | 1.26 | 1.26 | 0.73 | 0.40 | 0.50 | 0.60 | | Чистый импорт |
| Electricity | Exports | 0.74 | 0.60 | 0.30 | 0.10 | 0.10 | 0.10 | Электричество | Экспорт |
| | Imports | 0.13 | 0.19 | 0.00 | .. | 0.00 | 0.00 | | Импорт |
| | Net imports | -0.61 | -0.41 | -0.30 | -0.10 | -0.10 | -0.10 | | Чистый импорт |
| **Total net imports** | | 4.43 | 3.98 | 2.26 | 2.20 | 2.00 | 1.90 | **Чистый импорт энергии-всего** | |
| **Total stock changes** | | -0.19 | -0.61 | 0.02 | 0.00 | 0.00 | 0.10 | **Изменение запасов-всего** | |
| **Total primary energy supply** | | 9.59 | 8.14 | 6.84 | 5.50 | 5.70 | 5.40 | **Ресурсы первичной энергии-всего** | |
| Coal and lignite | | 5.70 | 5.16 | 4.82 | 3.40 | 3.60 | 3.40 | Уголь каменный и бурый | |
| Oil/oil products | | 3.08 | 2.39 | 1.23 | 1.50 | 1.30 | 1.00 | Нефть и нефтепродукты | |
| Gas | | 1.26 | 1.26 | 0.73 | 0.40 | 0.50 | 0.60 | Газ | |
| Nuclear | | .. | .. | .. | .. | .. | .. | Атомная энергия | |
| Hydro/geothermal | | .. | .. | .. | .. | .. | .. | Гидро-геотермальная энергия | |
| Other | | -0.46 | -0.68 | 0.05 | 0.10 | 0.30 | 0.40 | Другие виды | |
| **Total primary energy requirement (equals total primary energy supply)** | | 9.59 | 8.14 | 6.84 | 5.50 | 5.70 | 5.40 | **Потребность в первичной энергии-всего (равно ресурсам первичной энергии)** | |

**TABLE 6-4. Final energy consumption (million tons oil equivalent)**
**ТАБЛИЦА 6-4. Конечное потребление энергии ( млн. тонн нефтяного эквивалента )**

| | 1991 | 1992 | 1993 | 1994 | 1995 | |
|---|---|---|---|---|---|---|
| **Final energy consumption** | 4.99 | 3.30 | 2.70 | 2.80 | 2.60 | **Конечное потребление энергии** |
| Coal & Lignite | 0.29 | 0.30 | 0.20 | 0.20 | 0.10 | Уголь каменный и бурый |
| Oil Products | 1.51 | 0.78 | 0.90 | 0.90 | 0.80 | Нефтепродукты |
| Gas | 0.28 | 0.12 | 0.10 | 0.10 | 0.10 | Газ |
| Electricity | 0.58 | 0.51 | 0.40 | 0.40 | 0.40 | Электроэнергия |
| Heat | 2.13 | 1.40 | 1.00 | 1.00 | 1.00 | Тепло |
| Other | 0.22 | 0.20 | 0.10 | 0.20 | 0.20 | Другие виды |
| Of which: | | | | | | В том числе |
| **Industry** | 1.94 | 1.04 | 0.50 | 0.90 | 0.70 | **Промышленность** |
| Coal & Lignite | 0.18 | 0.09 | 0.00 | 0.10 | 0.10 | Уголь каменный и бурый |
| Oil Products | 0.33 | 0.17 | 0.20 | 0.20 | 0.00 | Нефтепродукты |
| Gas | 0.15 | 0.07 | 0.00 | 0.00 | 0.00 | Газ |
| Electricity | 0.25 | 0.20 | 0.20 | 0.20 | 0.20 | Электроэнергия |
| Heat | 1.03 | 0.50 | 0.10 | 0.40 | 0.40 | Тепло |
| Other | 0.01 | 0.01 | 0.00 | 0.00 | 0.00 | Другие виды |
| **Agriculture** | 0.68 | 0.39 | 0.10 | 0.10 | 0.10 | **Сельское хозяйство** |
| Coal & Lignite | 0.00 | 0.00 | 0.00 | 0.00 | 0.00 | Уголь каменный и бурый |
| Oil Products | 0.15 | 0.08 | 0.10 | 0.10 | 0.10 | Нефтепродукты |
| Gas | 0.00 | 0.00 | 0.00 | 0.00 | 0.00 | Газ |
| Electricity | 0.17 | 0.15 | 0.00 | 0.00 | 0.00 | Электроэнергия |
| Heat | 0.35 | 0.16 | 0.00 | 0.00 | 0.00 | Тепло |
| Other | 0.01 | 0.00 | 0.00 | 0.00 | 0.00 | Другие виды |
| **Transport** | 0.78 | 0.44 | 0.30 | 0.50 | 0.60 | **Транспорт** |
| Oil Products | 0.72 | 0.40 | 0.30 | 0.40 | 0.50 | Нефтепродукты |
| Other | 0.07 | 0.04 | 0.00 | 0.10 | 0.10 | Другие виды |
| **Households** | 0.95 | 0.52 | 0.60 | 1.00 | 1.10 | **Домашние хозяйства** |
| Coal & Lignite | 0.04 | 0.03 | 0.00 | 0.00 | 0.00 | Уголь каменный и бурый |
| Oil Products | 0.20 | 0.10 | 0.10 | 0.20 | 0.20 | Нефтепродукты |
| Gas | 0.07 | 0.04 | 0.00 | 0.10 | 0.10 | Газ |
| Electricity | 0.08 | 0.06 | 0.10 | 0.10 | 0.10 | Электроэнергия |
| Heat | 0.48 | 0.24 | 0.40 | 0.50 | 0.50 | Тепло |
| Other | 0.09 | 0.06 | 0.00 | 0.10 | 0.20 | Другие виды |

## TABLE 7-1. Price indices and exchange rates
## ТАБЛИЦА 7-1. Индексы цен и обменный курс

| Year and month | National currency per U.S. dollar<br>Единиц нац. валюты за 1 доллар США | National currency per Russian ruble<br>Единиц нац. валюты за 1 российский рубль | Consumer price index (as a percent of the previous month)<br>Индекс потребительских цен (в % к предыдущему месяцу) | Producer price index (as a percent of the previous month)<br>Индекс цен производителей (в % к предыдущему месяцу) | Consumer price index (as a percent of the previous December)<br>Индекс потребительских цен (в % к декабрю прошлого года) | Producer price index (as a percent of the previous December)<br>Индекс цен производителей (в % к декабрю прошлого года) | Год и месяц |
|---|---|---|---|---|---|---|---|
| **1993** | | | | | | | **1993** |
| January | 12.94 | .. | 3.4 | 2.7 | 3.4 | 2.7 | Январь |
| February | 13.12 | .. | 1.7 | 6.3 | 5.1 | 9.2 | Февраль |
| March | 13.19 | .. | 3.6 | 1.2 | 8.9 | 10.5 | Март |
| April | 12.78 | .. | 2.3 | 3.9 | 11.4 | 14.8 | Апрель |
| May | 12.84 | .. | 1.7 | 1.3 | 13.3 | 16.3 | Май |
| June | 13.15 | .. | 1.3 | 2.1 | 14.8 | 18.7 | Июнь |
| July | 13.70 | .. | 2.6 | 1.2 | 17.8 | 20.2 | Июль |
| August | 13.59 | .. | 0.7 | 3.6 | 18.6 | 24.6 | Август |
| September | 13.00 | .. | 3.0 | 1.0 | 22.2 | 25.8 | Сентябрь |
| October | 13.08 | .. | 2.6 | 1.1 | 25.3 | 27.2 | Октябрь |
| November | 13.59 | .. | 4.0 | 4.5 | 30.3 | 32.9 | Ноябрь |
| December | 13.68 | .. | 4.1 | 3.1 | 35.6 | 37.1 | Декабрь |
| **1994** | | | | | | | **1994** |
| January | 13.94 | .. | 5.5 | 3.1 | 5.5 | 3.1 | Январь |
| February | 13.89 | .. | 5.2 | 4.9 | 10.9 | 8.2 | Февраль |
| March | 13.54 | .. | 8.9 | 4.2 | 20.8 | 12.7 | Март |
| April | 13.58 | .. | 3.1 | 1.0 | 24.6 | 13.9 | Апрель |
| May | 13.26 | .. | 1.1 | 1.6 | 26.0 | 15.8 | Май |
| June | 13.06 | .. | 0.7 | 1.3 | 26.8 | 17.3 | Июнь |
| July | 12.56 | .. | 2.8 | 0.6 | 30.4 | 18.0 | Июль |
| August | 12.51 | .. | 1.0 | 2.1 | 31.7 | 20.5 | Август |
| September | 12.41 | .. | 3.2 | 6.5 | 36.0 | 28.3 | Сентябрь |
| October | 12.17 | .. | 1.1 | 1.6 | 37.5 | 30.3 | Октябрь |
| November | 12.31 | .. | 1.6 | 0.2 | 39.7 | 30.6 | Ноябрь |
| December | 12.57 | .. | 1.4 | 1.7 | 41.7 | 32.8 | Декабрь |

## TABLE 7-1. Price indices and exchange rates
## ТАБЛИЦА 7-1. Индексы цен и обменный курс

| Year and month | National currency per U.S. dollar<br>Единиц нац. валюты за 1 доллар США | National currency per Russian ruble<br>Единиц нац. валюты за 1 российский рубль | Consumer price index (as a percent of the previous month)<br>Индекс потребительских цен (в % к предыдущему месяцу) | Producer price index (as a percent of the previous month)<br>Индекс цен производителей (в % к предыдущему месяцу) | Consumer price index (as a percent of the previous December)<br>Индекс потребительских цен (в % к декабрю прошлого года) | Producer price index (as a percent of the previous December)<br>Индекс цен производителей (в % к декабрю прошлого года) | Год и месяц |
|---|---|---|---|---|---|---|---|
| **1995** | | | | | | | **1995** |
| January | 12.26 | .. | 3.5 | 8.1 | 3.5 | 8.1 | Январь |
| February | 12.03 | .. | 2.9 | 1.8 | 6.5 | 10.1 | Февраль |
| March | 11.25 | .. | 2.4 | 0.8 | 9.0 | 10.9 | Март |
| April | 11.03 | .. | 1.0 | 0.1 | 10.2 | 11.1 | Апрель |
| May | 11.27 | .. | 2.6 | -0.2 | 13.1 | 10.9 | Май |
| June | 11.21 | .. | 2.3 | -0.4 | 15.6 | 10.5 | Июнь |
| July | 11.11 | .. | 1.7 | 0.0 | 17.7 | 10.5 | Июль |
| August | 11.56 | .. | 0.6 | 1.3 | 18.4 | 11.9 | Август |
| September | 11.70 | .. | 2.1 | 1.4 | 20.8 | 13.5 | Сентябрь |
| October | 11.32 | .. | 3.1 | 2.8 | 24.6 | 16.7 | Октябрь |
| November | 11.33 | .. | 1.4 | 1.0 | 26.3 | 17.8 | Ноябрь |
| December | 11.52 | .. | 2.0 | 3.4 | 28.9 | 21.8 | Декабрь |
| **1996** | | | | | | | **1996** |
| January | 11.69 | .. | 3.5 | 2.2 | 3.5 | 2.2 | Январь |
| February | 11.73 | .. | 3.3 | 0.8 | 6.9 | 3.1 | Февраль |
| March | 11.82 | .. | 1.6 | 1.2 | 8.6 | 4.4 | Март |
| April | .. | .. | 1.8 | -0.1 | 10.5 | 4.3 | Апрель |
| May | .. | .. | 0.6 | -0.1 | 11.1 | 4.3 | Май |
| June | .. | .. | .. | .. | .. | .. | Июнь |
| July | .. | .. | .. | .. | .. | .. | Июль |
| August | .. | .. | .. | .. | .. | .. | Август |
| September | .. | .. | .. | .. | .. | .. | Сентябрь |
| October | .. | .. | .. | .. | .. | .. | Октябрь |
| November | .. | .. | .. | .. | .. | .. | Ноябрь |
| December | .. | .. | .. | .. | .. | .. | Декабрь |

**TABLE 7-2. Monthly nominal wages by sector**

**ТАБЛИЦА 7-2. Среднемесячная денежная зарплата по отраслям**

| Sector | 1990 | 1991 | 1992 | 1993 | 1994 | 1995 | Сектора |
|---|---|---|---|---|---|---|---|
| **Nominal wages** | | | | | | | **Средняя номинальная заработная плата** |
| **Economy average** | 340.7 | 586.4 | 549.0 | 1,066.0 | 1,734.0 | .. | **По народному хозяйству** |
| **Material sphere** | 358.1 | 590.4 | 569.0 | 1,116.0 | 1,831.0 | .. | **Отрасли сферы материального производства** |
| Industry | 359.8 | 678.7 | 576.0 | 1,109.0 | 1,898.0 | .. | Промышленность |
| Construction | 454.4 | 717.6 | 647.0 | 1,264.0 | 2,047.0 | .. | Строительство |
| Agriculture | 257.0 | 681.6 | 388.0 | 641.0 | 1,010.0 | .. | Сельское хозяйство |
| Transport | 363.4 | 573.2 | 867.0 | 1,741.0 | 2,421.0 | .. | Транспорт |
| Communications | .. | .. | .. | .. | .. | .. | Связь |
| Trade (retail and wholesale) | .. | .. | 516.0 | 917.0 | 1,510.0 | .. | Торговля (оптовая и розничная) |
| Other | 246.4 | 457.9 | .. | .. | .. | .. | Прочие отрасли материального производства |
| **Nonmaterial sphere** | 213.8 | 501.1 | 549.0 | 959.0 | 1,610.0 | .. | **Отрасли непроизводственной сферы** |
| Municipal services | .. | .. | .. | .. | .. | .. | Жилкомхоз и бытовое обслуживание |
| Science, research and development | 392.1 | 553.8 | .. | .. | .. | .. | Наука и научное обслуживание |
| Education | 240.1 | 426.0 | 459.0 | 850.0 | 1,259.0 | .. | Образование |
| Culture | 243.7 | 462.4 | .. | .. | .. | .. | Культура |
| Arts | 373.3 | 409.2 | .. | .. | .. | .. | Искусство |
| Health care, social security, and sports | 252.1 | 459.5 | 415.0 | 818.0 | 1,402.0 | .. | Здравоохр., соц.обсл., физк. и спорт |
| Banking, finance, credit, insurance | 469.3 | 737.4 | 1,078.0 | 2,496.0 | 3,571.0 | .. | Кредитование, страхование, банк. дело |
| Government | 376.7 | 581.8 | 533.0 | 1,103.0 | 2,030.0 | .. | Управление |

# *Country Notes: Estonia*

**General notes:** Unless otherwise indicated the data were supplied by the Department of Statistics for the Republic of Estonia.

**Currency:** The Estonian kroon (EEK) was introduced on June 20, 1992. The conversion factor at the time of introduction was 10 rubles per 1 EEK. Unless otherwise indicated data are in rubles up to 1991, and in EEK starting with 1992.

**Table 2-1:** The sum of the subcategories within "Other" does not equal the total due to missing information. Data for 1995 are preliminary. For 1992-1995 storage and communication are included with transport, and retail trade is included with wholesale trade. For 1992-1995 the statistical discrepancy between total GDP by industrial origin at market prices and total GDP by expenditure category is as follows:

| Year | 1992 | 1993 | 1994 | 1995 |
|---|---|---|---|---|
| Statistical discrepancy (million EEK) | -477 | 156 | 257 | 550 |

**Table 2-2:** Data for 1992-1995 are in 1993 EEK, prior to this data are in 1987 rubles. Due to rescaling the sum of the components for Total gross value added for 1990 and 1991 does not equal the total. Data for 1995 are preliminary. For 1992-1995 storage and communication are included with transport, and retail trade is included with wholesale trade.

**Table 3-1:** The base for the index of real effective exchange rate is June of 1992.

**Tables 3-4A and 3-4B:** Former Yugoslavia includes Croatia, Macedonia, Slovenia, and Yugoslavia.

**Table 5-1:** Data for 1995 are preliminary.

**Table 5-2:** Data are in 1993 EEK.

**Table 7-1:** Percentage changes of the price indices with respect to the previous month (or previous December) are reported instead of the price indices as percentage of the previous month (or previous December).

# *Комментарии к таблицам: Эстония*

**Общее замечание:** За исключением особо отмеченных случаев, данные, используемые в таблицах, были получены из Департамента статистики Эстонской республики.

**Национальная валюта**: Национальная валюта Эстонии - эстонская крона - была введена 20 июня 1992 г. Коэффициент пересчета в эстонские кроны на дату введения был 10 рублей за крону. За исключением особо отмеченных случаев, данные приведены в рублях до 1991 г. включительно, и в эстонских кронах начиная с 1992 г.

**Таблица 2-1:** Сумма компонентов раздела Другие отрасли не совпадает с итогом вследствие отсутствия данных. За 1995 г. приведены предварительные данные. В 1992-1995 гг. транспорт включает также складирование и связь, а оптовая торговля включает также розничную торговлю. В 1992-1995 гг. статистическое расхождение между ВВП по производству в рыночных ценах и ВВП по видам расходов составляло:

| Год | 1992 | 1993 | 1994 | 1995 |
|---|---|---|---|---|
| Статистическое расхождение (млн. эст. крон) | -477 | 156 | 257 | 550 |

**Таблица 2-2:** Данные за 1992-1995 гг. приведены в ценах 1993 г. в кронах, за предшествующий период - в ценах 1987 г. в рублях. В 1990-1991гг. сумма компонентов раздела ВДС-всего не совпадает с итогом вследствие пересчета в цены 1987 г. За 1995 г. приведены предварительные данные. В 1992-1995 гг. транспорт включает также складирование и связь, а оптовая торговля включает также розничную торговлю.

**Таблица 3-1:** Индекс реального курса обмена (МВФ) рассчитан к июню 1992 г.

**Таблицы 3-4А и 3-4В**: Бывшая Югославия включает Македонию, Словению, Хорватию и Югославию.

**Таблица 5-1:** Данные за 1995 г. - предварительные.

**Таблица 5-2 :** Данные приведены в эстонских кронах в ценах 1993 г.

**Таблица 7-1:** Вместо индексов цен в процентах к предыдущему месяцу (или к декабрю прошлого года) приведены изменения индексов цен по отношению к предыдущему месяцу (или к декабрю прошлого года).

# Georgia / Грузия

1996 Population / Численность населения в 1996 году
(thousands / тыс. человек): 5,411

Area / Территория
(thousand square kilometers / тыс. кв. км.): 69.7

Capital city / Столица :
Tbilisi / Тбилиси

**Country Tables:** Tables 2-2 to 2-2B are not included because there are no data available.

**Статистические таблицы страны:** Таблицы с 2-2 по 2-2B не включены ввиду отсутствия данных.

## TABLE 1-1. Population and employment (thousands)
## ТАБЛИЦА 1-1. Население и занятость (тысяч)

| Population or employment category | 1990 | 1991 | 1992 | 1993 | 1994 | 1995 | Население или группы занятых |
|---|---|---|---|---|---|---|---|
| **Total population** | 5,422 | 5,420 | 5,405 | 5,387 | 5,369 | 5,411 | **Население - всего** |
| Males | 2,579 | 2,580 | 2,576 | 2,564 | 2,556 | .. | Мужчины |
| Females | 2,843 | 2,840 | 2,829 | 2,823 | 2,813 | .. | Женщины |
| Urban population | 3,029 | 3,024 | 3,005 | 2,995 | 2,985 | .. | Городское |
| Rural population | 2,393 | 2,396 | 2,400 | 2,392 | 2,384 | .. | Сельское |
| Population under working age | 1,417 | 1,408 | 1,382 | .. | .. | .. | Моложе трудоспособного возраста |
| Working-age population | 3,027 | 3,022 | 3,006 | .. | .. | .. | Лица в трудоспособном возрасте |
| Population over working age | 978 | 990 | 1,017 | .. | .. | .. | Старше трудоспособного возраста |
| Economically Active Population, in non-working age | 264 | 262 | 257 | 235 | 204 | 179 | Экономически активное население в нетрудоспособном возрасте |
| Above working age | 252 | 249 | 245 | 223 | 193 | 168 | Старше трудоспособного возраста |
| Below working age | 12 | 12 | 12 | 12 | 11 | 11 | Моложе трудоспособного возраста |
| **Total labor resources** | 3,176 | 3,161 | 3,138 | 3,104 | 3,065 | 3,036 | **Трудовые ресурсы - всего** |
| **Total employment** | 2,763 | 2,519 | 1,984 | 1,792 | 1,750 | 1,730 | **Занятое население - всего** |
| State sector employees | 2,087 | 1,891 | 1,376 | 1,160 | 979 | 810 | Государственный сектор |
| Leased enterprise employees | .. | .. | .. | 26 | 51 | 79 | Арендные предприятия |
| Joint-stock company employees | .. | .. | .. | 49 | 102 | 251 | Акционерные общества |
| Economic association employees | 78 | 72 | 50 | 66 | 89 | 100 | Хозяйственные ассоциации |
| Social organization employees | .. | .. | .. | 27 | 67 | 61 | Общественные организации |
| Joint venture employees | .. | .. | .. | 2 | 1 | 1 | Совместные предприятия |
| Collective farm workers | 200 | 154 | 85 | 61 | 48 | 36 | Колхозы |
| Cooperative workers | 137 | 109 | 62 | 27 | 48 | 40 | Кооперативы |
| Individual labor activities | 4 | 4 | 4 | 5 | 5 | 6 | ИТД |
| Private subsidiary agricultural workers | 225 | 252 | 341 | 345 | 357 | 340 | Личные подсобные хозяйства |
| Private agricultural workers | 31 | 36 | 66 | 24 | 3 | 6 | Фермерские хозяйства |
| **Students** | 209 | 201 | 203 | 208 | 182 | 200 | **Учащиеся** |
| **Religious workers** | 1 | 1 | 1 | 2 | 2 | 2 | **Служащие религиозного культа** |
| **Working age population not employed in the national economy** | 203 | 440 | 949 | 1,102 | 1,131 | 1,104 | **Лица в трудоспособном возрасте, не занятые в экономике** |
| Housewives | 203 | 438 | 916 | 1,051 | 1,042 | 1,019 | Домохозяйки |
| Military personnel | .. | .. | 14 | 24 | 24 | 24 | Военнослужащие |
| Unemployed | .. | 2 | 19 | 27 | 65 | 61 | Безработные |
| **Labor force** | 2,764 | 2,521 | 2,004 | 1,919 | 1,815 | 1,791 | **Рабочая сила** |

## TABLE 1-2. Employment by sector (thousands)
## ТАБЛИЦА 1-2. Численность занятого населения по секторам (тысяч)

| Sector | 1990 | 1991 | 1992 | 1993 | 1994 | 1995 | Сектор |
|---|---|---|---|---|---|---|---|
| **Material sphere** | 1,919 | 1,731 | 1,367 | 1,202 | 1,203 | 1,169 | **Сфера материального производства** |
| **Agriculture and forestry** | 707 | 677 | 649 | 562 | 545 | 516 | **Сельское и лесное хозяйство** |
| Agriculture | 695 | 666 | 640 | 553 | 539 | 510 | Сельское хозяйство |
| Forestry | 12 | 11 | 10 | 9 | 6 | 6 | Лесное хозяйство |
| **Industry and construction** | 840 | 723 | 490 | 428 | 341 | 354 | **Промышленность и строительство** |
| Industry | 560 | 497 | 355 | 303 | 277 | 264 | Промышленность |
| Construction | 281 | 225 | 135 | 125 | 64 | 90 | Строительство |
| **Other** | 372 | 331 | 228 | 212 | 317 | 299 | **Другие отрасли** |
| Transport of goods | 109 | 97 | 75 | 58 | 57 | 47 | Грузовой транспорт |
| Road Maintenance | .. | .. | .. | .. | .. | .. | Дорожное хозяйство |
| Communication servicing material production | 6 | 6 | 7 | 5 | 6 | 5 | Связь |
| Wholesale trade | 104 | 86 | 58 | 72 | 136 | 132 | Оптовая торговля |
| Retail trade and catering | 50 | 42 | 27 | 34 | 86 | 83 | Розничная торговля и общепит |
| Material supply | 18 | 17 | 9 | 6 | 3 | 3 | Материально-техническое снабжение |
| Procurement | 8 | 7 | 5 | 5 | 2 | 1 | Заготовки |
| Information and computing services | 4 | 4 | 5 | 2 | 1 | 1 | Информационно-техническое обслуживание |
| Other sectors | 74 | 73 | 44 | 30 | 26 | 27 | Другие отрасли сферы материального пр. |
| **Nonmaterial sphere** | 844 | 787 | 617 | 590 | 547 | 561 | **Сфера нематериального производства** |
| Passenger transport | 62 | 59 | 47 | 28 | 29 | 27 | Пассажирский транспорт |
| Communication | 20 | 20 | 17 | 16 | 13 | 13 | Связь |
| Housing | 33 | 26 | 13 | 8 | 7 | 8 | Жилищное хозяйство |
| Public utilities and personal services | 98 | 83 | 49 | 58 | 46 | 44 | Комм. хоз. и бытовое обслуживание |
| Health care, social security, physical culture and sports | 184 | 186 | 159 | 156 | 155 | 160 | Здравоохранение, социальное обеспечение, физкультура и спорт |
| Education | 251 | 235 | 185 | 177 | 190 | 200 | Образование |
| Culture and art | 59 | 55 | 53 | 45 | 26 | 28 | Культура и искусство |
| Science and scientific research | 73 | 63 | 42 | 41 | 36 | 36 | Наука и научное обслуживание |
| Credit | 12 | 12 | 12 | 12 | 10 | 10 | Кредитование |
| Insurance | .. | .. | .. | .. | .. | .. | Страхование |
| General administration and defense | 52 | 48 | 39 | 49 | 35 | 35 | Государственное управление и оборона |
| Private nonprofit institutions serving households | .. | .. | .. | .. | .. | .. | Общественные организации, обслуживающие домашние хозяйства |
| **Other, material and nonmaterial spheres** | 1,216 | 1,118 | 845 | 802 | 864 | 860 | **Остальные отрасли материального производства и нематериальной сферы** |
| **Total employment** | 2,763 | 2,519 | 1,984 | 1,792 | 1,750 | 1,730 | **Занятые - всего** |

## TABLE 1-3. Registered unemployment (thousands; end of month)

GEORGIA

## ТАБЛИЦА 1-3. Численность зарегистрированных безработных (тысяч; на конец месяца)

| Year and month | Total<br>Всего | Males<br>Мужчины | Females<br>Женщины | Receiving benefits<br>Получающие пособие | Год и месяц |
|---|---|---|---|---|---|
| **1994** | | | | | **1994** |
| January | 60.6 | .. | .. | 6.4 | Январь |
| February | 60.6 | .. | .. | 5.7 | Февраль |
| March | 62.2 | .. | .. | 5.4 | Март |
| April | 66.2 | .. | .. | 5.3 | Апрель |
| May | 77.4 | .. | .. | 5.0 | Май |
| June | 78.3 | .. | .. | 4.5 | Июнь |
| July | 77.5 | .. | .. | 6.4 | Июль |
| August | 80.0 | .. | .. | 4.9 | Август |
| September | 70.0 | .. | .. | 1.5 | Сентябрь |
| October | 70.1 | .. | .. | 1.0 | Октябрь |
| November | 70.1 | .. | .. | 0.8 | Ноябрь |
| December | 65.0 | .. | .. | 0.8 | Декабрь |
| **1995** | | | | | **1995** |
| January | 58.7 | .. | .. | 1.0 | Январь |
| February | 53.0 | .. | .. | 0.8 | Февраль |
| March | 50.8 | .. | .. | 1.0 | Март |
| April | 53.6 | .. | .. | 0.7 | Апрель |
| May | 57.1 | .. | .. | 0.5 | Май |
| June | 55.1 | .. | .. | 0.8 | Июнь |
| July | 57.0 | .. | .. | 0.9 | Июль |
| August | 54.1 | .. | .. | 1.0 | Август |
| September | 59.2 | .. | .. | 1.3 | Сентябрь |
| October | 52.5 | .. | .. | 1.3 | Октябрь |
| November | 57.4 | .. | .. | 2.1 | Ноябрь |
| December | 61.1 | .. | .. | 2.5 | Декабрь |
| **1996** | | | | | **1995** |
| January | 63.1 | .. | .. | 2.2 | Январь |
| February | 63.2 | .. | .. | 2.3 | Февраль |
| March | 60.7 | .. | .. | 2.4 | Март |
| April | 52.3 | .. | .. | 3.1 | Апрель |
| May | 45.5 | .. | .. | 3.4 | Май |
| June | 46.7 | .. | .. | 4.1 | Июнь |
| July | 48.4 | .. | .. | 4.9 | Июль |
| August | .. | .. | .. | .. | Август |
| September | .. | .. | .. | .. | Сентябрь |
| October | .. | .. | .. | .. | Октябрь |
| November | .. | .. | .. | .. | Ноябрь |
| December | .. | .. | .. | .. | Декабрь |

## TABLE 2-1. Gross domestic product at current prices (millions of national currency)
## ТАБЛИЦА 2-1. Валовой внутренний продукт в текущих ценах (млн. национальной валюты)

| Sector of origin or expenditure category | 1990 | 1991 | 1992 | 1993 | 1994 | 1995 | Отраслевое происхождение или вид расходов |
|---|---|---|---|---|---|---|---|
| **Gross domestic product by sector of origin** | | | | | | | **Валовой внутренний продукт по отраслевому происхождению** |
| **Agriculture and forestry** | 4,474 | 5,109 | 75,715 | 18,284,000 | 406,677,000 | 1,193 | **Сельское и лесное хозяйство** |
| Agriculture | 4,454 | 5,080 | 75,380 | 18,262,000 | 406,677,000 | 1,193 | Сельское хозяйство |
| Forestry | 20 | 29 | 335 | 22,000 | .. | .. | Лесное хозяйство |
| **Industry and construction** | 4,742 | 6,608 | 26,767 | 1,867,000 | 379,790,000 | 546 | **Промышленность и строительство** |
| Industry | 3,434 | 5,111 | 17,485 | 1,701,000 | 301,900,000 | 454 | Промышленность |
| Construction | 1,308 | 1,497 | 9,282 | 166,000 | 77,890,000 | 92 | Строительство |
| **Other** | 5,002 | 6,150 | 34,854 | 5,445,000 | 403,536,000 | 835 | **Другие отрасли** |
| Transport | 860 | 1,030 | 4,498 | 885,000 | 125,255,000 | 135 | Транспорт |
| Road maintenance | 141 | 145 | 325 | 56,000 | .. | .. | Дорожное хозяйство |
| Communication | 56 | 124 | 879 | 44,000 | .. | .. | Связь |
| Wholesale trade | 50 | 57 | 136 | 131,000 | 90,625,000 | 386 | Оптовая торговля |
| Retail trade and catering | 801 | 1,039 | 2,266 | 1,731,000 | .. | .. | Розничная торговля и общепит |
| Material supply | 86 | 114 | 1,005 | 39,000 | .. | .. | Материально-техническое снабжение |
| Procurement | 63 | 95 | 607 | 35,000 | .. | .. | Заготовки |
| Information and computing services | 32 | 22 | 21 | 1,000 | .. | .. | Информационно-вычислительное обслуживание |
| Other sectors of material production | 62 | 80 | 816 | 12,000 | .. | .. | Другие отрасли сферы материального пр. |
| Housing | 471 | 464 | 2,344 | 398,000 | .. | .. | Жилищное хозяйство |
| Public utilities and personal services | 347 | 418 | 2,927 | 442,000 | .. | .. | Ком. хоз. и бытовое обслуживание |
| Health care, social security, physical culture and sports | 389 | 647 | 2,520 | 247,000 | .. | .. | Здравоохранение, социальное обеспечение, физкультура и спорт |
| Education | 655 | 995 | 4,142 | 311,000 | .. | .. | Образование |
| Culture and art | 107 | 107 | 537 | 79,000 | .. | .. | Культура и искусство |
| Science and scientific research | 201 | 170 | 624 | 59,000 | .. | .. | Наука и научное обслуживание |
| Credit | 68 | 130 | 6,758 | 664,000 | .. | .. | Кредитование |
| Insurance | -8 | -101 | 53 | 6,000 | .. | .. | Страхование |
| General administration and defense | 609 | 608 | 4,338 | 298,000 | .. | .. | Государственное управление и оборона |
| Private nonprofit institutions serving households | 12 | 6 | 35 | 1,000 | .. | .. | Общественные организации, обслуживающие домашние хозяйства |
| **Imputed service charge of financial intermediaries** | -51 | -91 | -663 | -143,000 | .. | .. | **Условно-исчисляемая стоимость услуг финансовых посредников** |
| **Total gross value added (GVA)** | 14,167 | 17,776 | 136,673 | 25,453,000 | 1,190,003,000 | 2,574 | **Валовая добавленная стоимость (ВДС) - всего** |
| **Taxes on production and imports (TOPI)** | 2,277 | 2,477 | 9,661 | 1,578,000 | .. | .. | **Налоги на производство и импорт (НПиИ)** |
| Other taxes on production (OTOP) | .. | .. | .. | .. | .. | .. | Другие налоги на производство (ДНП) |
| **Subsidies on production and imports (SOPI)** | 1,479 | 1,107 | 8,039 | 72,000 | .. | .. | **Субсидии на производство и импорт (СПиИ)** |
| Other subsidies on production (OSOP) | .. | .. | .. | .. | .. | .. | Другие субсидии на производство (ДСП) |
| **Total GDP at factor cost (GVA-OTOP+OSOP)** | 14,167 | 17,776 | 136,673 | .. | 1,190,003,000 | .. | **Всего ВВП по фактр. стоимости (ВДС-ДНП+ДСП)** |
| **Net Indirect taxes (TOPI - SOPI)** | 798 | 1,370 | 1,622 | 1,506,000 | 228,918,000 | .. | **Чистые косвенные налоги (НПиИ-СПиИ)** |
| **Total GDP at market prices** | 14,965 | 19,146 | 138,295 | 26,959,000 | 1,418,921,000 | 2,616 | **Всего ВВП в рыночных ценах** |
| **Gross domestic product by expenditure category** | | | | | | | **Валовой внутренний продукт по видам расходов** |
| **Consumption** | 11,963 | 14,846 | 171,966 | 30,671,000 | 1,792,915,000 | 2,985 | **Потребление** |
| Private consumption | 10,548 | 13,334 | 160,076 | 29,705,000 | 1,738,704,000 | 2,865 | Личное потребление |
| Government consumption | 1,415 | 1,512 | 11,890 | 966,000 | 54,211,000 | 120 | Общественное потребление |
| **Gross domestic investment** | 4,585 | 5,400 | 48,214 | 304,000 | 18,448,000 | 30 | **Валовые внутренние инвестиции** |
| Gross fixed investment | 3,541 | 3,702 | 24,403 | 213,000 | 12,755,000 | 22 | Валовое накопление основного капитала |
| Change in stocks | 1,044 | 1,698 | 23,813 | 91,000 | 5,693,000 | 8 | Изменения в запасах (МОС) |
| **Resource balance (net exports of GNFS)** | -856 | -636 | -68,630 | -4,016,000 | -392,442,000 | -399 | **Сальдо ресурсов (чистый экспорт ТНФУ)** |
| Exports of goods and nonfactor services | 5,983 | 5,318 | 68,495 | 5,317,000 | 421,605,000 | 349 | Экспорт товаров и нефакторных услуг |
| Imports of goods and nonfactor services | 6,839 | 5,954 | 137,125 | 9,333,000 | 814,047,000 | 748 | Импорт товаров и нефакторных услуг |

**TABLE 2-1A. Distribution of gross domestic product at current prices (percent)**
**ТАБЛИЦА 2-1A. Распределение валового внутреннего продукта в текущих ценах ( % )**

| Sector of origin or expenditure category | 1990 | 1991 | 1992 | 1993 | 1994 | 1995 | Отраслевое происхождение или вид расходов |
|---|---|---|---|---|---|---|---|
| **Gross domestic product by sector of origin** | | | | | | | **ВВП по отраслевому происхождению** |
| **Agriculture and forestry** | 29.9 | 26.7 | 54.7 | 67.8 | 28.7 | 45.6 | **Сельское и лесное хозяйство** |
| Agriculture | 29.8 | 26.5 | 54.5 | 67.7 | 28.7 | 45.6 | Сельское хозяйство |
| Forestry | 0.1 | 0.2 | 0.2 | 0.1 | 0.0 | 0.0 | Лесное хозяйство |
| **Industry and construction** | 31.7 | 34.5 | 19.4 | 6.9 | 26.8 | 20.9 | **Промышленность и строительство** |
| Industry | 22.9 | 26.7 | 12.6 | 6.3 | 21.3 | 17.4 | Промышленность |
| Construction | 8.7 | 7.8 | 6.7 | 0.6 | 5.5 | 3.5 | Строительство |
| **Other** | 33.4 | 32.1 | 25.2 | 20.2 | .. | .. | **Другие отрасли** |
| Transport | 5.7 | 5.4 | 3.3 | 3.3 | 8.8 | 5.2 | Транспорт |
| Road maintenance | .. | .. | .. | .. | .. | .. | Дорожное хозяйство |
| Communication | 0.4 | 0.6 | 0.6 | 0.2 | .. | .. | Связь |
| Wholesale trade | .. | .. | .. | .. | .. | .. | Оптовая торговля |
| Retail trade and catering | 5.4 | 5.4 | 1.6 | 6.4 | .. | .. | Розничная торговля и общепит |
| Material supply | 0.6 | 0.6 | 0.7 | 0.1 | .. | .. | Материально-техническое снабжение |
| Procurement | 0.4 | 0.5 | 0.4 | 0.1 | .. | .. | Заготовки |
| Information and computing services | 0.2 | 0.1 | 0.0 | 0.0 | .. | .. | Информационно-вычислительное обслуживание |
| Other sectors of material production | 0.4 | 0.4 | 0.6 | 0.0 | .. | .. | Другие отрасли сферы матерл. произ. |
| Housing | 3.1 | 2.4 | 1.7 | 1.5 | .. | .. | Жилищное хозяйство |
| Public utilities and personal services | 2.3 | 2.2 | 2.1 | 1.6 | .. | .. | Ком. хоз. и бытовое обслуживание |
| Health care, social security, physical culture and sports | 2.6 | 3.4 | 1.8 | 0.9 | .. | .. | Здравоохранение, социальное обеспечение, физкультура и спорт |
| Education | 4.4 | 5.2 | 3.0 | 1.2 | .. | .. | Образование |
| Culture and art | 0.7 | 0.6 | 0.4 | 0.3 | .. | .. | Культура и искусство |
| Science and scientific research | 1.3 | 0.9 | 0.5 | 0.2 | .. | .. | Наука и научное обслуживание |
| Credit | 0.5 | 0.7 | 4.9 | 2.5 | .. | .. | Кредитование |
| Insurance | -0.1 | -0.5 | 0.0 | 0.0 | .. | .. | Страхование |
| General administration and defense | 4.1 | 3.2 | 3.1 | 1.1 | .. | .. | Государственное управление и оборона |
| Private nonprofit institutions serving households | 0.1 | 0.0 | 0.0 | 0.0 | .. | .. | Общественные организации, обслуживающие домашние хозяйства |
| **Imputed service charge of financial intermediaries** | -0.3 | -0.5 | -0.5 | -0.5 | .. | .. | **Условно-исчисляемая стоимость услуг финансовых посредников** |
| **Total gross value added** | 94.7 | 92.8 | 98.8 | 94.4 | 83.9 | 98.4 | **Валовая добавленная стоимость - всего** |
| **Total GDP at factor cost** | 94.7 | 92.8 | 98.8 | 0.0 | 83.9 | .. | **ВВП по фактор. стоимости - всего** |
| **Net indirect taxes** | 5.3 | 7.2 | 1.2 | 5.6 | 16.1 | .. | **Чистые косвенные налоги (НПиИ-СПиИ)** |
| **Total GDP at market prices** | 100.0 | 100.0 | 100.0 | 100.0 | 100.0 | 100.0 | **ВВП в рын. ценах - всего** |
| **Gross domestic product by expenditure category** | | | | | | | **ВВП по видам расходов** |
| **Consumption** | 79.9 | 77.5 | 124.3 | 113.8 | 126.4 | 114.1 | **Потребление** |
| Private consumption | 70.5 | 69.6 | 115.7 | 110.2 | 122.5 | 109.5 | Личное потребление |
| Government consumption | 9.5 | 7.9 | 8.6 | 3.6 | 3.8 | 4.6 | Общественное потребление |
| **Gross domestic investment** | 30.6 | 28.2 | 34.9 | 1.1 | 1.3 | 1.1 | **Вал. внутр. инвестиции** |
| Gross fixed investment | 23.7 | 19.3 | 17.6 | 0.8 | 0.9 | 0.8 | Вал. накопление осн. капитала |
| Change in stocks | 7.0 | 8.9 | 17.2 | 0.3 | 0.4 | 0.3 | Изменения в запасах (МОС) |
| **Resource balance (net exports of GNFS)** | -5.7 | -3.3 | -49.6 | -14.9 | -27.7 | -15.3 | **Сальдо ресурсов (чистый экспорт ТНФУ)** |
| Exports of goods and nonfactor services | 40.0 | 27.8 | 49.5 | 19.7 | 29.7 | 13.3 | Экспорт товаров и нефакторных услуг |
| Imports of goods and nonfactor services | 45.7 | 31.1 | 99.2 | 34.6 | 57.4 | 28.6 | Импорт товаров и нефакторных услуг |

## TABLE 3-1. Balance of payments at current prices (millions of U.S. dollars)
## ТАБЛИЦА 3-1. Платежный баланс в текущих ценах (в миллионах долларов США)

| Item | 1990 | 1991 | 1992 | 1993 | 1994 | 1995 | Статьи |
|---|---|---|---|---|---|---|---|
| Exports of goods and services (including workers' remittances) | .. | .. | 403 | 478 | 393 | 405 | Экспорт товаров и услуг (включая денежные переводы рабочих) |
| Exports of goods and nonfactor services | .. | .. | 353 | 433 | 393 | 401 | Экспорт товаров и нефакт. услуг |
| Merchandise (FOB) | .. | .. | 266 | 362 | 291 | 290 | Товары (ФОБ) |
| Nonfactor services | .. | .. | 87 | 71 | 102 | 111 | Нефакторные услуги |
| Shipment | .. | .. | 47 | 53 | 95 | 100 | Перевозки |
| Travel | .. | .. | 27 | 11 | 7 | 6 | Поездки |
| Other | .. | .. | 13 | 7 | 0 | 5 | Другие |
| Imports of goods and nonfactor services | .. | .. | 709 | 760 | 758 | 817 | Импорт товаров и нефакт. услуг |
| Merchandise (FOB) | .. | .. | 644 | 702 | 603 | 711 | Товары (ФОБ) |
| Nonfactor services | .. | .. | 65 | 58 | 155 | 106 | Нефакторные услуги |
| Shipment | .. | .. | 40 | 35 | 70 | 81 | Перевозки |
| Travel | .. | .. | 15 | 17 | 0 | 23 | Поездки |
| Other | .. | .. | 10 | 6 | 85 | 2 | Другие |
| Resource balance | .. | .. | -356 | -327 | -365 | -416 | Сальдо ресурсов |
| Net factor income | .. | .. | 36 | 31 | -13 | -61 | Чистый факторный доход |
| Factor receipts | .. | .. | 50 | 45 | 0 | 4 | Факторные поступления |
| Factor payments | .. | .. | 14 | 14 | 13 | 65 | Факторные платежи |
| Total interest due | .. | .. | .. | .. | .. | .. | Общая сумма процента к оплате |
| Other factor payments and discrepancy | .. | .. | .. | .. | .. | .. | Другие факторные платежи и стат. погр. |
| Net current transfers | .. | .. | 71 | 127 | .. | .. | Чистые текущие трансферты |
| Current receipts | .. | .. | 71 | 127 | .. | .. | Текущие поступления |
| Workers remittances | .. | .. | .. | .. | .. | .. | Денежные переводы рабочих |
| Other current transfers | .. | .. | 71 | 127 | .. | .. | Другие текущие трансферты |
| Current payments | .. | .. | .. | .. | .. | .. | Текущие платежи |
| Current account balance before official grants | .. | .. | -249 | -169 | -378 | -477 | Сальдо текущего счета до офиц. безвозмезд. трансфертов |
| Official capital grants | .. | .. | .. | .. | 68 | 114 | Официальные кап. безвозмезные трансферты |
| Current account balance after official grants | .. | .. | .. | .. | -310 | -363 | Сальдо текущего счета после офиц. безвозмезд. трансфертов |
| Long Term Capital Inflows | .. | .. | 65 | 159 | 103 | 21 | Долгосрочные притоки капитала |
| Direct investment | .. | .. | 2 | 2 | .. | .. | Прямые инвестиции |
| Net long term borrowing | .. | .. | 63 | .. | 76 | 21 | Чистые долгосрочные займы |
| Disbursements | .. | .. | 63 | .. | 84 | 85 | Поступления |
| Repayments due | .. | .. | .. | .. | 8 | 64 | Сумма, подлежащая погашению |
| Other long-term inflows (net) | .. | .. | .. | 157 | 27 | .. | Другие долгосрочные притоки (чистые) |

(continued on next page)

**TABLE 3-1. Balance of payments at current prices (millions of U.S. dollars)**
**ТАБЛИЦА 3-1. Платежный баланс в текущих ценах (в миллионах долларов США)**

| Item | 1990 | 1991 | 1992 | 1993 | 1994 | 1995 | Статьи |
|---|---|---|---|---|---|---|---|
| Adjustment to Scheduled Debt Service | .. | .. | .. | .. | .. | .. | Регулирование долга |
| Debt service not paid | .. | .. | .. | .. | .. | 301 | Невыплаченный долг |
| Interest not paid | .. | .. | .. | .. | .. | 45 | Невыплаченный процент |
| Principal not paid | .. | .. | .. | .. | .. | 256 | Невыплаченная сумма основного долга |
| Arrears reductions/prepayments(-) | .. | .. | .. | .. | .. | .. | Погашение просроченных платежей/выплаты авансом (-) |
| Total Other items (Net) | .. | .. | 408 | .. | 33 | 113 | Общие другие статьи (чистые) |
| Net short-term capital | .. | .. | .. | .. | .. | .. | Чистый краткосрочный капитал |
| Capital flows not elsewhere included | .. | .. | .. | .. | .. | .. | Потоки капитала, не указанные выше |
| Errors and omissions | .. | .. | 408 | .. | 33 | 113 | Ошибки и пропуски |
| Changes in net reserves | .. | .. | .. | .. | .. | .. | Изменения в чистых резервах |
| Net credit from IMF | .. | .. | .. | .. | .. | .. | Чистый кредит МВФ |
| Reserve changes not elsewhere included | .. | .. | .. | .. | .. | .. | Изменения резервов, не указанных выше |
| Escrow account | .. | .. | .. | .. | .. | .. | Счет депонирования |
| Gross reserves (excluding gold) | .. | .. | .. | .. | .. | .. | Общие резервы (исключая золото) |
| Gross reserves (including gold) | .. | .. | .. | .. | .. | .. | Общие резервы (включая золото) |
| Nominal official exchange rate (annual average) (rf) | 0.58 | 0.57 | 193.2 | 233.9 | 1,073,326.0 | 1.3 | Номинальный официальный или рыночный курс (среднегодовой) |
| Nominal official exchange rate (end-of-year) (ae) | .. | .. | .. | .. | 1,330,000.0 | 1.2 | Номинальный официальный или рыночный курс (на конец года) |
| Manufacture unit value (percent change) | .. | .. | .. | .. | .. | .. | Средний индекс цен на продукцию обр. пром.,% |
| Index of real effective exchange rate (IMF) | .. | .. | .. | .. | .. | .. | Индекс реального эффективного валютного курса (МВФ) |
| Total factor payments | .. | .. | .. | .. | .. | 17 | Общая сумма факторных платежей |
| Government interest | .. | .. | .. | .. | .. | 17 | Процент, выплачиваемый органами гос. управления |
| Private sector interest | .. | .. | .. | .. | .. | .. | Процент выплачиваемый частным сектором |
| Profits on direct foreign investment | .. | .. | .. | .. | .. | .. | Прибыль от прямых иностранных инвестиций |
| Official capital grants | .. | .. | .. | .. | .. | .. | Официальные капитальные безвозмездные трансферты |
| For budgetary financing | .. | .. | .. | .. | .. | .. | На бюджетное финансирование |
| To extrabudgetary entities | .. | .. | .. | .. | .. | .. | На внебюджетное финансирование |
| Government net long term borrowing | .. | .. | .. | .. | .. | 155 | Чистые долгосрочные государственные займы |
| Disbursements | .. | .. | .. | .. | .. | 172 | Поступления |
| Repayments | .. | .. | .. | .. | .. | 17 | Погашения |
| Private net long term borrowing | .. | .. | .. | .. | .. | .. | Чистые долгосрочные частные займы |
| Disbursements | .. | .. | .. | .. | .. | .. | Поступления |
| Repayments | .. | .. | .. | .. | .. | .. | Погашения |

## TABLE 3-2A. Imports by commodity group (millions of U.S. dollars)
## ТАБЛИЦА 3-2A . Импорт по товарным группам (млн. долларов США)

GEORGIA

| Commodity group | 1990 | 1991 | 1992 | 1993 | 1994 | 1995 | Товарные группы |
|---|---|---|---|---|---|---|---|
| TOTAL | .. | .. | .. | 238.5 | 327.4 | 379.0 | ВСЕГО |
| I - Live animals; animal products | .. | .. | .. | 4.8 | 4.3 | 10.9 | I - Живые животные и продукты животноводства |
| II - Vegetable products | .. | .. | .. | 4.9 | 4.2 | 24.5 | II - Продукты растительного происхождения |
| III - Animal or vegetable fats and oils and their cleavage products; prepared edible fats; animal or vegetable waxes | .. | .. | .. | 5.5 | 3.9 | 10.5 | III - Жиры и масла растительного и животного происхождения, воски |
| IV - Prepared foodstuffs; beverages, spirits and vinegar; tobacco and manufactured tobacco substitutes | .. | .. | .. | 20.9 | 18.0 | 76.2 | IV -Продукция пищевой промышленности, алкогольные и безалкогольные напитки, табак и его заменители |
| V - Mineral products | .. | .. | .. | 166.3 | 267.9 | 198.9 | V - Минеральные продукты |
| VI - Products of the chemical or allied industries | .. | .. | .. | 5.2 | 2.8 | 9.9 | VI - Продукция химической промышленности |
| VII - Plastics and articles thereof; rubber and articles thereof | .. | .. | .. | 0.9 | 4.3 | 5.1 | VII - Пластмассы и изделия из них |
| VIII - Raw hides and skins, leather, furskins and articles thereof; saddlery and harness; travel goods, handbags and similar containers; articles of animal gut | .. | .. | .. | 0.2 | 0.3 | 0.3 | VIII - Кожевенное сырьё, кожи, пушнина, меховое сырьё и изделия из них |
| IX - Wood and articles of wood; wood charcoal; cork and articles of cork; manufactures of straw, of esparto or of other plaiting materials; basketware and wickerwork | .. | .. | .. | 0.3 | 0.4 | 0.2 | IX - Древесина и изделия из древесины, древесный уголь |
| X - Pulp of wood or of other fibrous cellulosic material; waste and scrap of paper or paperboard; paper and paperboard and articles thereof | .. | .. | .. | 0.6 | 0.4 | 1.9 | X - Бумажная масса, бумажные и картонные отходы, макулатура, бумага, картон и изделия из них |
| XI - Textiles and textile articles | .. | .. | .. | 4.6 | 1.7 | 5.6 | XI - Текстиль и текстильные изделия |
| XII - Footwear, headgear, umbrellas, sun umbrellas, walking sticks, seat sticks, whips, riding crops and parts thereof; prepared feathers and articles made therewith; artificial flowers; articles of human hair | .. | .. | .. | 1.2 | 0.7 | 2.1 | XII - Обувь, головные уборы, зонты, трости и пр. |

**TABLE 3-2A. Imports by commodity group (millions of U.S. dollars)** **GEORGIA**

**ТАБЛИЦА 3-2A . Импорт по товарным группам (млн. долларов США)**

| Commodity group | 1990 | 1991 | 1992 | 1993 | 1994 | 1995 | Товарные группы |
|---|---|---|---|---|---|---|---|
| XIII - Articles of stone, plaster, cement, asbestos, mica and similar materials; ceramic products; glass and glassware | .. | .. | .. | 4.0 | 2.5 | 3.9 | XIII - Изделия из камня, гипса, цемента |
| XIV - Natural or cultured pearls, precious or semi-precious stones, precious metals, metals clad with precious metal and articles thereof; imitation jewellery; coin | .. | .. | .. | 3.2 | 0.1 | 0.7 | XIV - Жемчуг, драгоценные и полудрагоценные камни, драгоценные металлы, бижутерия, монеты |
| XV - Base metals and articles of base metal | .. | .. | .. | 3.9 | 1.3 | 2.4 | XV - Неблагородные металлы и изделия из них |
| XVI - Machinery and mechanical appliances; electrical equipment; parts thereof; sound recorders and reproducers, television image and sound recorders and reproducers, and parts and accessories of such articles | .. | .. | .. | 6.8 | 10.1 | 18.5 | XVI - Машины, оборудование, механизмы, их части и принадлежности; звуковая и теле-аппаратура, их части и принадлежности |
| XVII - Vehicles, aircraft, vessels and associated transport equipment | .. | .. | .. | 3.5 | 1.5 | 3.4 | XVII - Средства наземного, воздушного и водного транспорта |
| XVIII - Optical, photographic, cinematographic, measuring, checking, precision, medical or surgical instruments and apparatus; clocks and watches; musical instruments; parts and accessories thereof | .. | .. | .. | 0.3 | 1.5 | 1.9 | XVIII - Приборы, аппараты оптические, медицинские, измерительные и пр.; музыкальные инструменты; часы; их части и принадлежности |
| XIX - Arms and ammunition; parts and accessories thereof | .. | .. | .. | .. | 0.1 | 0.1 | XIX - Оружие и боеприпасы, их части и принадлежности |
| XX - Miscellaneous manufactured articles | .. | .. | .. | 1.4 | 1.3 | 1.8 | XX - Разные промышленные товары |
| XXI - Works of art, collectors' pieces, and antiques | .. | .. | .. | 0.0 | 0.0 | 0.0 | XXI - Произведения искусства, предметы антиквариата |
| XXII - Services | .. | .. | .. | .. | .. | .. | XXII - Услуги |

## TABLE 3-2B Imports by commodity group (millions of national currency)
## ТАБЛИЦА 3-2B. Импорт по товарным группам (млн. национальной валюты)

| Commodity group | 1990 | 1991 | 1992 | 1993 | 1994 | 1995 | Товарные группы |
|---|---|---|---|---|---|---|---|
| TOTAL | .. | .. | .. | 2,928,875.5 | 351,299,764.2 | 488.8 | ВСЕГО |
| I - Live animals; animal products | .. | .. | .. | 58,945.9 | 4,615,304.0 | 14.1 | I - Живые животные и продукты животноводства |
| II - Vegetable products | .. | .. | .. | 60,174.0 | 4,507,971.3 | 31.6 | II - Продукты растительного происхождения |
| III - Animal or vegetable fats and oils and their cleavage products; prepared edible fats; animal or vegetable waxes | .. | .. | .. | 67,542.2 | 4,185,973.4 | 13.5 | III - Жиры и масла растительного и животного происхождения, воски |
| IV - Prepared foodstuffs; beverages, spirits and vinegar; tobacco and manufactured tobacco substitutes | .. | .. | .. | 256,660.4 | 19,319,877.0 | 98.3 | IV -Продукция пищевой промышленности, алкогольные и безалкогольные напитки, табак и его заменители |
| V - Mineral products | .. | .. | .. | 2,042,230.5 | 287,544,169.4 | 256.6 | V - Минеральные продукты |
| VI - Products of the chemical or allied industries | .. | .. | .. | 63,858.1 | 3,005,314.2 | 12.8 | VI - Продукция химической промышленности |
| VII - Plastics and articles thereof; rubber and articles thereof | .. | .. | .. | 11,052.4 | 4,615,304.0 | 6.6 | VII - Пластмассы и изделия из них |
| VIII - Raw hides and skins, leather, furskins and articles thereof; saddlery and harness; travel goods, handbags and similar containers; articles of animal gut | .. | .. | .. | 2,456.1 | 321,998.0 | 0.4 | VIII - Кожевенное сырьё, кожи, пушнина, меховое сырьё и изделия из них |
| IX - Wood and articles of wood; wood charcoal; cork and articles of cork; manufactures of straw, of esparto or of other plaiting materials; basketware and wickerwork | .. | .. | .. | 3,684.1 | 429,330.6 | 0.3 | IX - Древесина и изделия из древесины, древесный уголь |
| X - Pulp of wood or of other fibrous cellulosic material; waste and scrap of paper or paperboard; paper and paperboard and articles thereof | .. | .. | .. | 7,368.2 | 429,330.6 | 2.5 | X - Бумажная масса, бумажные и картонные отходы, макулатура, бумага, картон и изделия из них |
| XI - Textiles and textile articles | .. | .. | .. | 56,489.8 | 1,824,655.1 | 7.2 | XI - Текстиль и текстильные изделия |
| XII - Footwear, headgear, umbrellas, sun umbrellas, walking sticks, seat sticks, whips, riding crops and parts thereof; prepared feathers and articles made therewith; artificial flowers; articles of human hair | .. | .. | .. | 14,736.5 | 751,328.6 | 2.7 | XII - Обувь, головные уборы, зонты, трости и пр. |

## TABLE 3-2B Imports by commodity group (millions of national currency) — GEORGIA
## ТАБЛИЦА 3-2B. Импорт по товарным группам (млн. национальной валюты)

| Commodity group | 1990 | 1991 | 1992 | 1993 | 1994 | 1995 | Товарные группы |
|---|---|---|---|---|---|---|---|
| XIII - Articles of stone, plaster, cement, asbestos, mica and similar materials; ceramic products; glass and glassware | .. | .. | .. | 49,121.6 | 2,683,316.3 | 5.0 | XIII - Изделия из камня, гипса, цемента |
| XIV - Natural or cultured pearls, precious or semi-precious stones, precious metals, metals clad with precious metal and articles thereof; imitation jewellery; coin | .. | .. | .. | 39,297.3 | 107,332.7 | 0.9 | XIV - Жемчуг, драгоценные и полудрагоценные камни, драгоценные металлы, бижутерия, монеты |
| XV - Base metals and articles of base metal | .. | .. | .. | 47,893.6 | 1,395,324.5 | 3.1 | XV - Неблагородные металлы и изделия из них |
| XVI - Machinery and mechanical appliances; electrical equipment; parts thereof; sound recorders and reproducers, television image and sound recorders and reproducers, and parts and accessories of such articles | .. | .. | .. | 83,506.7 | 10,840,597.7 | 23.9 | XVI - Машины, оборудование, механизмы, их части и принадлежности; звуковая и теле-аппаратура, их части и принадлежности |
| XVII - Vehicles, aircraft, vessels and associated transport equipment | .. | .. | .. | 42,981.4 | 1,609,989.8 | 4.4 | XVII - Средства наземного, воздушного и водного транспорта |
| XVIII - Optical, photographic, cinematographic, measuring, checking, precision, medical or surgical instruments and apparatus; clocks and watches; musical instruments; parts and accessories thereof | .. | .. | .. | 3,684.1 | 1,609,989.8 | 2.5 | XVIII - Приборы, аппараты оптические, медицинские, измерительные и пр.; музыкальные инструменты; часы; их части и принадлежности |
| XIX - Arms and ammunition; parts and accessories thereof | .. | .. | .. | .. | 107,332.7 | 0.1 | XIX - Оружие и боеприпасы, их части и принадлежности |
| XX - Miscellaneous manufactured articles | .. | .. | .. | 17,192.6 | 1,395,324.5 | 2.3 | XX - Разные промышленные товары |
| XXI - Works of art, collectors' pieces, and antiques | .. | .. | .. | 0.0 | 0.0 | 0.0 | XXI - Произведения искусства, предметы антиквариата |
| XXII - Services | .. | .. | .. | .. | .. | .. | XXII - Услуги |

**TABLE 3-3A. Exports by commodity group (millions of U.S. dollars)**
**ТАБЛИЦА 3-3А. Экспорт по товарным группам (млн. долларов США)**

| Commodity group | 1990 | 1991 | 1992 | 1993 | 1994 | 1995 | Товарные группы |
|---|---|---|---|---|---|---|---|
| TOTAL | .. | .. | .. | 226.7 | 155.7 | 154.4 | ВСЕГО |
| I - Live animals; animal products | .. | .. | .. | 0.1 | 0.0 | 0.4 | I - Живые животные и продукты животноводства |
| II - Vegetable products | .. | .. | .. | 55.7 | 20.0 | 19.8 | II - Продукты растительного происхождения |
| III - Animal or vegetable fats and oils and their cleavage products; prepared edible fats; animal or vegetable waxes | .. | .. | .. | 0.1 | 0.5 | 0.1 | III - Жиры и масла растительного и животного происхождения, воски |
| IV - Prepared foodstuffs; beverages, spirits and vinegar; tobacco and manufactured tobacco substitutes | .. | .. | .. | 22.8 | 11.6 | 19.2 | IV -Продукция пищевой промышленности, алкогольные и безалкогольные напитки, табак и его заменители |
| V - Mineral products | .. | .. | .. | 20.1 | 14.6 | 21.2 | V - Минеральные продукты |
| VI - Products of the chemical or allied industries | .. | .. | .. | 15.2 | 13.9 | 13.1 | VI - Продукция химической промышленности |
| VII - Plastics and articles thereof; rubber and articles thereof | .. | .. | .. | 1.7 | 3.7 | 1.8 | VII - Пластмассы и изделия из них |
| VIII - Raw hides and skins, leather, furskins and articles thereof; saddlery and harness; travel goods, handbags and similar containers; articles of animal gut | .. | .. | .. | 0.5 | 1.2 | 1.0 | VIII - Кожевенное сырьё, кожи, пушнина, меховое сырьё и изделия из них |
| IX - Wood and articles of wood; wood charcoal; cork and articles of cork; manufactures of straw, of esparto or of other plaiting materials; basketware and wickerwork | .. | .. | .. | 0.5 | 0.0 | 0.5 | IX - Древесина и изделия из древесины, древесный уголь |
| X - Pulp of wood or of other fibrous cellulosic material; waste and scrap of paper or paperboard; paper and paperboard and articles thereof | .. | .. | .. | 1.0 | 2.7 | 2.5 | X - Бумажная масса, бумажные и картонные отходы, макулатура, бумага, картон и изделия из них |
| XI - Textiles and textile articles | .. | .. | .. | 15.5 | 13.6 | 5.2 | XI - Текстиль и текстильные изделия |
| XII - Footwear, headgear, umbrellas, sun umbrellas, walking sticks, seat sticks, whips, riding crops and parts thereof; prepared feathers and articles made therewith; artificial flowers; articles of human hair | .. | .. | .. | 4.1 | 0.9 | 0.0 | XII - Обувь, головные уборы, зонты, трости и пр. |

**TABLE 3-3A. Exports by commodity group (millions of U.S. dollars)**
**ТАБЛИЦА 3-3А. Экспорт по товарным группам (млн. долларов США)**

| Commodity group | 1990 | 1991 | 1992 | 1993 | 1994 | 1995 | Товарные группы |
|---|---|---|---|---|---|---|---|
| XIII - Articles of stone, plaster, cement, asbestos, mica and similar materials; ceramic products; glass and glassware | .. | .. | .. | 0.6 | 0.7 | 0.9 | XIII - Изделия из камня, гипса, цемента |
| XIV - Natural or cultured pearls, precious or semi-precious stones, precious metals, metals clad with precious metal and articles thereof; imitation jewellery; coin | .. | .. | .. | 10.1 | 1.0 | 1.2 | XIV - Жемчуг, драгоценные и полудрагоценные камни, драгоценные металлы, бижутерия, монеты |
| XV - Base metals and articles of base metal | .. | .. | .. | 66.8 | 48.4 | 56.4 | XV - Неблагородные металлы и изделия из них |
| XVI - Machinery and mechanical appliances; electrical equipment; parts thereof; sound recorders and reproducers, television image and sound recorders and reproducers, and parts and accessories of such articles | .. | .. | .. | 8.1 | 18.1 | 7.5 | XVI - Машины, оборудование, механизмы, их части и принадлежности; звуковая и теле-аппаратура, их части и принадлежности |
| XVII - Vehicles, aircraft, vessels and associated transport equipment | .. | .. | .. | 3.0 | 3.0 | 3.0 | XVII - Средства наземного, воздушного и водного транспорта |
| XVIII - Optical, photographic, cinematographic, measuring, checking, precision, medical or surgical instruments and apparatus; clocks and watches; musical instruments; parts and accessories thereof | .. | .. | .. | 0.3 | 0.2 | 0.2 | XVIII - Приборы, аппараты оптические, медицинские, измерительные и пр.; музыкальные инструменты; часы; их части и принадлежности |
| XIX - Arms and ammunition; parts and accessories thereof | .. | .. | .. | .. | 0.0 | 0.0 | XIX - Оружие и боеприпасы, их части и принадлежности |
| XX - Miscellaneous manufactured articles | .. | .. | .. | 0.5 | 1.5 | 0.3 | XX - Разные промышленные товары |
| XXI - Works of art, collectors' pieces, and antiques | .. | .. | .. | 0.0 | 0.0 | 0.0 | XXI - Произведения искусства, предметы антиквариата |
| XXII - Services | .. | .. | .. | .. | .. | .. | XXII - Услуги |

## TABLE 3-3B. Exports by Commodity Group (millions of national currency)
## ТАБЛИЦА 3-3В. Экспорт по товарным группам (млн. национальной валюты)

| Commodity group | 1990 | 1991 | 1992 | 1993 | 1994 | 1995 | Товарные группы |
|---|---|---|---|---|---|---|---|
| TOTAL | .. | .. | .. | 2,783,966.4 | 167,224,269.8 | 198.8 | ВСЕГО |
| I - Live animals; animal products | .. | .. | .. | 1,228.0 | 0.0 | 0.5 | I - Живые животные и продукты животноводства |
| II - Vegetable products | .. | .. | .. | 684,018.3 | 21,466,530.0 | 25.5 | II - Продукты растительного происхождения |
| III - Animal or vegetable fats and oils and their cleavage products; prepared edible fats; animal or vegetable waxes | .. | .. | .. | 1,228.0 | 536,663.3 | 0.1 | III - Жиры и масла растительного и животного происхождения, воски |
| IV - Prepared foodstuffs; beverages, spirits and vinegar; tobacco and manufactured tobacco substitutes | .. | .. | .. | 279,993.1 | 12,450,587.4 | 24.8 | IV -Продукция пищевой промышленности, алкогольные и безалкогольные напитки, табак и его заменители |
| V - Mineral products | .. | .. | .. | 246,836.0 | 15,670,566.9 | 27.3 | V - Минеральные продукты |
| VI - Products of the chemical or allied industries | .. | .. | .. | 186,662.1 | 14,919,238.4 | 16.9 | VI - Продукция химической промышленности |
| VII - Plastics and articles thereof; rubber and articles thereof | .. | .. | .. | 20,876.7 | 3,971,308.1 | 2.3 | VII - Пластмассы и изделия из них |
| VIII - Raw hides and skins, leather, furskins and articles thereof; saddlery and harness; travel goods, handbags and similar containers; articles of animal gut | .. | .. | .. | 6,140.2 | 1,287,991.8 | 1.3 | VIII - Кожевенное сырьё, кожи, пушнина, меховое сырьё и изделия из них |
| IX - Wood and articles of wood; wood charcoal; cork and articles of cork; manufactures of straw, of esparto or of other plaiting materials; basketware and wickerwork | .. | .. | .. | 6,140.2 | 0.0 | 0.6 | IX - Древесина и изделия из древесины, древесный уголь |
| X - Pulp of wood or of other fibrous cellulosic material; waste and scrap of paper or paperboard; paper and paperboard and articles thereof | .. | .. | .. | 12,280.4 | 2,897,981.6 | 3.2 | X - Бумажная масса, бумажные и картонные отходы, макулатура, бумага, картон и изделия из них |
| XI - Textiles and textile articles | .. | .. | .. | 190,346.2 | 14,597,240.4 | 6.7 | XI - Текстиль и текстильные изделия |
| XII - Footwear, headgear, umbrellas, sun umbrellas, walking sticks, seat sticks, whips, riding crops and parts thereof; prepared feathers and articles made therewith; artificial flowers; articles of human hair | .. | .. | .. | 50,349.6 | 965,993.9 | 0.0 | XII - Обувь, головные уборы, зонты, трости и пр. |

## TABLE 3-3B. Exports by Commodity Group (millions of national currency)
## ТАБЛИЦА 3-3В. Экспорт по товарным группам (млн. национальной валюты)

| Commodity group | 1990 | 1991 | 1992 | 1993 | 1994 | 1995 | Товарные группы |
|---|---|---|---|---|---|---|---|
| XIII - Articles of stone, plaster, cement, asbestos, mica and similar materials; ceramic products; glass and glassware | .. | .. | .. | 7,368.2 | 751,328.6 | 1.2 | XIII - Изделия из камня, гипса, цемента |
| XIV - Natural or cultured pearls, precious or semi-precious stones, precious metals, metals clad with precious metal and articles thereof; imitation jewellery; coin | .. | .. | .. | 124,032.0 | 1,073,326.5 | 1.5 | XIV - Жемчуг, драгоценные и полудрагоценные камни, драгоценные металлы, бижутерия, монеты |
| XV - Base metals and articles of base metal | .. | .. | .. | 820,330.7 | 51,949,002.6 | 72.6 | XV - Неблагородные металлы и изделия из них |
| XVI - Machinery and mechanical appliances; electrical equipment; parts thereof; sound recorders and reproducers, television image and sound recorders and reproducers, and parts and accessories of such articles | .. | .. | .. | 99,471.2 | 19,427,209.7 | 9.7 | XVI - Машины, оборудование, механизмы, их части и принадлежности; звуковая и теле-аппаратура, их части и принадлежности |
| XVII - Vehicles, aircraft, vessels and associated transport equipment | .. | .. | .. | 36,841.2 | 3,219,979.5 | 3.9 | XVII - Средства наземного, воздушного и водного транспорта |
| XVIII - Optical, photographic, cinematographic, measuring, checking, precision, medical or surgical instruments and apparatus; clocks and watches; musical instruments; parts and accessories thereof | .. | .. | .. | 3,684.1 | 214,665.3 | 0.3 | XVIII - Приборы, аппараты оптические, медицинские, измерительные и пр.; музыкальные инструменты; часы; их части и принадлежности |
| XIX - Arms and ammunition; parts and accessories thereof | .. | .. | .. | .. | 0.0 | 0.0 | XIX - Оружие и боеприпасы, их части и принадлежности |
| XX - Miscellaneous manufactured articles | .. | .. | .. | 6,140.2 | 1,609,989.8 | 0.4 | XX - Разные промышленные товары |
| XXI - Works of art, collectors' pieces, and antiques | .. | .. | .. | 0.0 | 0.0 | 0.0 | XXI - Произведения искусства, предметы антиквариата |
| XXII - Services | .. | .. | .. | .. | .. | .. | XXII - Услуги |

**TABLE 3-4A. Geographical distribution of foreign trade (millions of U.S. dollars)**
**ТАБЛИЦА 3-4А. Географическое распределение внешней торговли (млн. долларов США)**

| Country or country group | Exports Экспорт 1990 | 1991 | 1992 | 1993 | 1994 | 1995 | Imports Импорт 1990 | 1991 | 1992 | 1993 | 1994 | 1995 | Страна или группа стран |
|---|---|---|---|---|---|---|---|---|---|---|---|---|---|
| **Total trade** | .. | .. | 87.0 | 226.7 | 155.7 | 154.4 | .. | .. | 175.9 | 238.5 | 327.4 | 378.9 | **Всего** |
| **CIS countries** | .. | .. | 76.8 | 175.1 | 117.1 | 96.7 | .. | .. | 159.2 | 165.1 | 268.2 | 154.0 | **Страны СНГ** |
| Armenia | .. | .. | 0.8 | 10.2 | 12.9 | 18.9 | .. | .. | 0.6 | 4.7 | 1.0 | 11.2 | Армения |
| Azerbaijan | .. | .. | 4.4 | 14.8 | 14.7 | 12.7 | .. | .. | 12.5 | 2.5 | 21.9 | 43.2 | Азербайджан |
| Belarus | .. | .. | 2.3 | 2.2 | 3.3 | 2.1 | .. | .. | 2.6 | 0.4 | 0.4 | 1.0 | Беларусь |
| Georgia | .. | .. | .. | .. | .. | .. | .. | .. | .. | .. | .. | .. | Грузия |
| Kazakstan | .. | .. | 3.6 | 12.9 | 9.0 | 1.8 | .. | .. | 2.8 | 1.7 | 0.4 | 0.1 | Казахстан |
| Kyrgyz Republic | .. | .. | 0.8 | 0.8 | 0.1 | 0.5 | .. | .. | 0.1 | 0.1 | 0.0 | .. | Киргизстан |
| Moldova | .. | .. | 0.4 | 0.4 | 0.2 | 0.2 | .. | .. | 0.3 | 0.1 | 0.0 | 0.2 | Молдова |
| Russia | .. | .. | 43.6 | 103.3 | 52.3 | 47.0 | .. | .. | 45.8 | 9.7 | 24.7 | 49.3 | Россия |
| Tajikistan | .. | .. | 0.7 | 0.7 | 0.3 | 0.3 | .. | .. | 0.2 | 0.0 | 0.1 | 0.0 | Таджикистан |
| Turkmenistan | .. | .. | 8.2 | 12.4 | 15.5 | 6.9 | .. | .. | 80.7 | 132.6 | 215.6 | 41.2 | Туркменистан |
| Ukraine | .. | .. | 10.3 | 12.7 | 6.1 | 5.7 | .. | .. | 12.4 | 13.2 | 3.8 | 7.1 | Украина |
| Uzbekistan | .. | .. | 1.7 | 4.7 | 2.7 | 0.6 | .. | .. | 1.2 | 0.0 | 0.3 | 0.6 | Узбекистан |
| **Non-CIS countries** | .. | .. | 10.2 | 51.6 | 38.6 | 57.7 | .. | .. | 16.7 | 73.4 | 59.2 | 224.9 | **Остальной мир** |
| **Europe** | .. | .. | 10.0 | 24.6 | 5.5 | 19.5 | .. | .. | 7.0 | 29.2 | 16.6 | 117.3 | **Европа** |
| Austria | .. | .. | 1.4 | 0.1 | 0.0 | 0.0 | .. | .. | 0.0 | 1.6 | 0.3 | 12.0 | Австрия |
| Belgium | .. | .. | .. | 0.1 | .. | 0.0 | .. | .. | 0.0 | 0.2 | 1.0 | 1.7 | Бельгия |
| Bulgaria | .. | .. | .. | 3.4 | 0.1 | 5.7 | .. | .. | 0.1 | 0.2 | 1.9 | 25.5 | Болгария |
| Czech Republic | .. | .. | 0.0 | 9.9 | 0.2 | 0.0 | .. | .. | 0.1 | 3.9 | 0.1 | 0.4 | Чешская Республика |
| Denmark | .. | .. | .. | 0.3 | 0.1 | 0.3 | .. | .. | .. | 0.0 | 0.2 | 1.9 | Дания |
| Estonia | .. | .. | 0.1 | 0.3 | 0.0 | 0.1 | .. | .. | 3.7 | 0.1 | 0.0 | 0.1 | Эстония |
| Finland | .. | .. | .. | 0.1 | .. | .. | .. | .. | .. | 0.0 | 0.0 | 0.0 | Финляндия |
| Former Yugoslavia | .. | .. | .. | 0.0 | .. | .. | .. | .. | 0.1 | 0.0 | 0.0 | 0.0 | Быв. Югославия |
| France | .. | .. | .. | 0.3 | 0.2 | 0.9 | .. | .. | 0.0 | 6.9 | 0.3 | 1.5 | Франция |
| Germany | .. | .. | 0.7 | 1.0 | 0.1 | 1.2 | .. | .. | 0.4 | 1.6 | 4.3 | 10.1 | Германия |
| Hungary | .. | .. | 0.4 | 0.0 | 1.3 | .. | .. | .. | .. | 0.1 | 0.1 | 1.0 | Венгрия |
| Iceland | .. | .. | .. | .. | .. | .. | .. | .. | .. | .. | .. | .. | Исландия |
| Ireland | .. | .. | .. | 0.0 | 0.1 | .. | .. | .. | 0.3 | .. | 0.0 | 0.2 | Ирландия |
| Italy | .. | .. | .. | 0.3 | 0.1 | 2.8 | .. | .. | 0.3 | 1.7 | 2.4 | 1.0 | Италия |
| Latvia | .. | .. | 0.3 | 0.6 | 0.1 | 0.0 | .. | .. | 1.2 | 1.1 | 0.0 | 0.0 | Латвия |
| Lithuania | .. | .. | 0.4 | 0.7 | 0.1 | 0.0 | .. | .. | 0.8 | 0.1 | 0.0 | 0.4 | Литва |
| Netherlands | .. | .. | 0.0 | 1.2 | 0.7 | 1.1 | .. | .. | .. | 6.2 | 0.8 | 4.4 | Нидерланды |
| Norway | .. | .. | .. | .. | .. | .. | .. | .. | .. | .. | 0.0 | 0.1 | Норвегия |
| Poland | .. | .. | 0.0 | 0.2 | 0.1 | 0.1 | .. | .. | 0.0 | 0.1 | 0.1 | 0.3 | Польша |
| Romania | .. | .. | .. | .. | .. | .. | .. | .. | 0.0 | 0.0 | 3.0 | 28.2 | Румыния |
| Slovak Republic | .. | .. | .. | .. | 0.1 | .. | .. | .. | .. | .. | 0.0 | 0.1 | Словацкая Республика |
| Spain | .. | .. | .. | 0.0 | .. | 0.0 | .. | .. | .. | 0.1 | 0.0 | 3.4 | Испания |

**TABLE 3-4A. Geographical distribution of foreign trade (millions of U.S. dollars)**
**ТАБЛИЦА 3-4А. Географическое распределение внешней торговли (млн. долларов США)**

| Country or country group | Exports Экспорт 1990 | 1991 | 1992 | 1993 | 1994 | 1995 | Imports Импорт 1990 | 1991 | 1992 | 1993 | 1994 | 1995 | Страна или группа стран |
|---|---|---|---|---|---|---|---|---|---|---|---|---|---|
| Sweden | .. | .. | 5.6 | 0.0 | .. | .. | .. | .. | .. | 0.1 | .. | 0.0 | Швеция |
| Switzerland | .. | .. | 1.0 | 0.4 | 2.1 | 6.1 | .. | .. | .. | 0.5 | 0.1 | 2.2 | Швейцария |
| United Kingdom | .. | .. | .. | 0.7 | 0.0 | 0.4 | .. | .. | 0.0 | 4.1 | 0.3 | 10.7 | Великобритания |
| Other Europe | .. | .. | 0.0 | 5.0 | 0.2 | 0.8 | .. | .. | .. | 0.6 | 1.6 | 12.0 | Остальные страны Европы |
| **Asia** | .. | .. | 0.2 | 25.7 | 29.4 | 37.2 | .. | .. | 7.4 | 39.3 | 37.0 | 88.9 | **Азия** |
| Afghanistan | .. | .. | 0.0 | 0.0 | .. | 0.0 | .. | .. | 0.0 | .. | .. | .. | Афганистан |
| China | .. | .. | .. | 1.5 | 1.0 | 0.7 | .. | .. | 0.0 | 2.9 | 0.1 | 0.1 | Китай |
| India | .. | .. | .. | .. | .. | 0.3 | .. | .. | 0.1 | .. | .. | 0.1 | Индия |
| Iraq | .. | .. | .. | .. | .. | .. | .. | .. | .. | .. | .. | 0.1 | Ирак |
| Japan | .. | .. | .. | 0.0 | 0.0 | 0.1 | .. | .. | 0.0 | 0.1 | 0.1 | 0.9 | Япония |
| Korea, Dem. People's Rep. | .. | .. | .. | .. | .. | .. | .. | .. | 0.1 | .. | .. | .. | КНДР |
| Korea, Rep. of | .. | .. | .. | .. | .. | .. | .. | .. | .. | 0.1 | .. | 0.0 | Южная Корея |
| Mongolia | .. | .. | .. | .. | .. | 0.2 | .. | .. | .. | .. | .. | 0.0 | МНР |
| Syrian Arab Republic | .. | .. | .. | 0.7 | .. | .. | .. | .. | 0.1 | 0.1 | .. | 0.3 | Сирия |
| Turkey | .. | .. | 0.2 | 21.9 | 23.6 | 34.9 | .. | .. | 7.1 | 34.5 | 35.1 | 80.2 | Турция |
| Viet Nam | .. | .. | .. | .. | .. | .. | .. | .. | 0.0 | .. | .. | .. | Вьетнам |
| Other Asia | .. | .. | .. | 1.6 | 4.8 | 1.0 | .. | .. | 0.0 | 1.6 | 1.7 | 7.2 | Остальные страны Азии |
| **America** | .. | .. | 0.0 | 1.3 | 3.7 | 1.0 | .. | .. | 2.3 | 3.1 | 5.0 | 18.5 | **Сев. и Южная Америка** |
| Canada | .. | .. | .. | .. | .. | 0.0 | .. | .. | .. | 0.4 | 0.2 | 0.0 | Канада |
| Cuba | .. | .. | .. | 0.6 | .. | .. | .. | .. | .. | .. | .. | .. | Куба |
| United States | .. | .. | 0.0 | 0.7 | 3.7 | 0.6 | .. | .. | 2.1 | 2.7 | 4.6 | 17.9 | США |
| Other America | .. | .. | .. | .. | .. | 0.4 | .. | .. | 0.2 | 0.0 | 0.2 | 0.6 | Остальные |
| **Africa** | .. | .. | .. | 0.0 | .. | .. | .. | .. | 0.0 | 0.2 | 0.0 | .. | **Африка** |
| Egypt | .. | .. | .. | .. | .. | .. | .. | .. | 0.0 | .. | .. | .. | Египет |
| Libya | .. | .. | .. | .. | .. | .. | .. | .. | .. | .. | .. | .. | Ливия |
| Other Africa | .. | .. | .. | 0.0 | .. | .. | .. | .. | 0.0 | 0.2 | 0.0 | .. | Остальные |
| | .. | .. | | | | | .. | .. | | | | | |
| **Rest of the World** | .. | .. | .. | .. | .. | .. | .. | .. | .. | 1.6 | 0.6 | 0.2 | **Прочие страны мира** |
| Australia | .. | .. | .. | .. | .. | .. | .. | .. | .. | 1.6 | 0.6 | 0.1 | Австралия |

## TABLE 3-4B. Geographical distribution of foreign trade (millions of national currency) — GEORGIA

## ТАБЛИЦА 3-4B. Географическое распределение внешней торговли (миллионов национальной валюты)

| Country or country group | Exports / Экспорт 1990 | 1991 | 1992 | 1993 | 1994 | 1995 | Imports / Импорт 1990 | 1991 | 1992 | 1993 | 1994 | 1995 | Страна или группа стран |
|---|---|---|---|---|---|---|---|---|---|---|---|---|---|
| **Total trade** | 3,276.2 | 5,336.4 | 16,762.5 | 2,783,966.8 | 167,224,269.8 | 199.2 | 3,836.9 | 5,386.5 | 34,002.2 | 2,928,875.5 | 351,299,764.3 | 488.9 | **Всего** |
| **CIS countries** | 2,840.6 | 5,169.4 | 14,802.5 | 2,150,298.2 | 125,686,533.6 | 124.8 | 3,057.0 | 4,365.2 | 30,756.6 | 2,026,266.0 | 287,866,167.5 | 198.5 | **Страны СНГ** |
| Armenia | 33.8 | 121.8 | 145.2 | 125,260.1 | 13,845,911.9 | 24.4 | 94.9 | 81.2 | 113.8 | 57,717.9 | 1,073,326.5 | 14.4 | Армения |
| Azerbaijan | 55.6 | 92.3 | 856.9 | 181,749.9 | 15,777,899.6 | 16.4 | 147.3 | 322.4 | 2,423.6 | 30,701.0 | 23,505,850.4 | 55.7 | Азербайджан |
| Belarus | 56.6 | 108.6 | 443.0 | 27,016.9 | 3,541,977.5 | 2.7 | 156.5 | 128.2 | 496.9 | 4,912.2 | 429,330.6 | 1.3 | Беларусь |
| Georgia | .. | .. | .. | .. | .. | .. | .. | .. | .. | .. | .. | .. | Грузия |
| Kazakstan | 261.9 | 329.8 | 689.7 | 158,417.2 | 9,659,938.5 | 2.3 | 59.3 | 74.0 | 545.5 | 20,876.7 | 429,330.6 | 0.1 | Казахстан |
| Kyrgyz Republic | 28.3 | 45.4 | 154.9 | 9,824.3 | 107,332.7 | 0.6 | 4.0 | 5.3 | 17.2 | 1,228.0 | 0.0 | .. | Киргизстан |
| Moldova | 39.9 | 48.1 | 72.2 | 4,912.2 | 214,665.3 | 0.3 | 228.6 | 36.1 | 57.5 | 1,228.0 | 0.0 | 0.3 | Молдова |
| Russia | 1,755.8 | 3,556.5 | 8,422.7 | 1,268,565.3 | 56,134,976.0 | 60.6 | 1,647.8 | 2,721.9 | 8,850.6 | 119,119.9 | 26,511,164.6 | 63.6 | Россия |
| Tajikistan | 47.7 | 83.5 | 124.9 | 8,596.3 | 321,998.0 | 0.4 | 13.2 | 11.1 | 45.0 | 0.0 | 107,332.7 | 0.0 | Таджикистан |
| Turkmenistan | 56.6 | 80.0 | 1,585.4 | 152,277.0 | 16,636,560.8 | 8.9 | 18.3 | 11.0 | 15,582.2 | 1,628,381.0 | 231,409,193.4 | 53.1 | Туркменистан |
| Ukraine | 371.5 | 548.1 | 1,981.3 | 155,961.1 | 6,547,291.7 | 7.4 | 571.2 | 906.8 | 2,397.6 | 162,101.3 | 4,078,640.7 | 9.2 | Украина |
| Uzbekistan | 132.9 | 155.2 | 326.2 | 57,717.9 | 2,897,981.6 | 0.8 | 115.8 | 67.1 | 226.9 | 0.0 | 321,998.0 | 0.8 | Узбекистан |
| **Non-CIS countries** | 435.6 | 167.0 | 1,960.0 | 633,668.6 | 41,537,736.2 | 74.4 | 779.9 | 1,021.3 | 3,245.6 | 901,381.0 | 63,433,596.8 | 290.4 | **Остальной мир** |
| **Europe** | 74.3 | 144.9 | 1,917.2 | 302,097.8 | 6,010,629.0 | 25.1 | 518.7 | 456.2 | 1,386.2 | 358,587.4 | 17,709,887.7 | 151.6 | **Европа** |
| Austria | .. | 0.6 | 278.3 | 1,228.0 | 0.0 | 0.0 | 14.2 | 6.5 | 0.2 | 19,648.6 | 321,998.0 | 15.5 | Австрия |
| Belgium | 0.6 | 1.7 | .. | 1,228.0 | .. | 0.0 | 2.6 | 31.0 | 6.5 | 2,456.1 | 1,073,326.5 | 2.2 | Бельгия |
| Bulgaria | 6.4 | 0.9 | .. | 41,753.4 | 107,332.7 | 7.4 | 38.7 | 15.4 | 25.9 | 2,456.1 | 2,039,320.4 | 32.9 | Болгария |
| Czech Republic | 0.2 | 1.2 | 4.9 | 121,576.0 | 214,665.3 | 0.0 | 35.6 | 28.1 | 27.2 | 47,893.6 | 107,332.7 | 0.5 | Чешская Республика |
| Denmark | 1.8 | .. | .. | 3,684.1 | 107,332.7 | 0.4 | 0.1 | 0.1 | .. | 0.0 | 214,665.3 | 2.5 | Дания |
| Estonia | 8.3 | 21.7 | 24.3 | 3,684.1 | 0.0 | 0.1 | 17.9 | 28.2 | 719.0 | 1,228.0 | 0.0 | 0.1 | Эстония |
| Finland | 0.1 | 0.2 | .. | 1,228.0 | .. | .. | 5.1 | 4.5 | .. | 0.0 | 0.0 | 0.0 | Финляндия |
| Former Yugoslavia | .. | 0.1 | .. | 0.0 | .. | .. | 17.9 | 14.9 | 14.6 | 0.0 | 0.0 | 0.0 | Быв. Югославия |
| France | .. | .. | .. | 3,684.1 | 214,665.3 | 1.2 | 45.5 | 27.3 | 3.6 | 84,734.8 | 321,998.0 | 1.9 | Франция |
| Germany | 0.2 | 5.1 | 134.2 | 12,280.4 | 107,332.7 | 1.5 | 116.8 | 84.6 | 83.7 | 19,648.6 | 4,615,304.0 | 13.0 | Германия |
| Hungary | 7.3 | 4.4 | 82.7 | 0.0 | 1,395,324.5 | .. | 16.4 | 15.4 | .. | 1,228.0 | 107,332.7 | 1.3 | Венгрия |
| Iceland | .. | .. | .. | .. | .. | .. | .. | .. | .. | .. | .. | .. | Исландия |
| Ireland | .. | .. | .. | 0.0 | 107,332.7 | .. | .. | .. | 60.0 | .. | 0.0 | 0.3 | Ирландия |
| Italy | .. | 0.0 | .. | 3,684.1 | 107,332.7 | 3.6 | 27.6 | 8.9 | 65.2 | 20,876.7 | 2,575,983.6 | 1.3 | Италия |
| Latvia | 22.9 | 44.5 | 58.6 | 7,368.2 | 107,332.7 | 0.0 | 79.0 | 103.1 | 224.7 | 13,508.4 | 0.0 | 0.0 | Латвия |
| Lithuania | 23.3 | 51.6 | 70.9 | 8,596.3 | 107,332.7 | 0.0 | 48.6 | 46.5 | 151.7 | 1,228.0 | 0.0 | 0.5 | Литва |
| Netherlands | .. | .. | 1.9 | 14,736.5 | 751,328.6 | 1.4 | 3.5 | 0.1 | .. | 76,138.5 | 858,661.2 | 5.7 | Нидерланды |
| Norway | .. | .. | .. | .. | .. | .. | .. | .. | .. | .. | 0.0 | 0.3 | Норвегия |
| Poland | 3.1 | 5.3 | 1.6 | 2,456.1 | 107,332.7 | 0.1 | 14.8 | 20.5 | 3.2 | 1,228.0 | 107,332.7 | 0.4 | Польша |
| Romania | 0.1 | 0.6 | .. | .. | .. | .. | 10.2 | 14.9 | 0.3 | 0.0 | 3,219,979.5 | 36.4 | Румыния |
| Slovak Republic | .. | .. | .. | .. | 107,332.7 | .. | .. | .. | .. | .. | 0.0 | 0.3 | Словацкая Республика |
| Spain | .. | .. | .. | 0.0 | .. | 0.0 | .. | .. | .. | 1,228.0 | 0.0 | 4.4 | Испания |

## TABLE 3-4B. Geographical distribution of foreign trade (millions of national currency) GEORGIA

## ТАБЛИЦА 3-4B. Географическое распределение внешней торговли (миллионов национальной валюты)

| Country or country group | Exports / Экспорт 1990 | 1991 | 1992 | 1993 | 1994 | 1995 | Imports / Импорт 1990 | 1991 | 1992 | 1993 | 1994 | 1995 | Страна или группа стран |
|---|---|---|---|---|---|---|---|---|---|---|---|---|---|
| Sweden | .. | .. | 1,074.6 | 0.0 | .. | .. | 6.5 | 0.1 | .. | 1,228.0 | .. | 0.0 | Швеция |
| Switzerland | .. | 3.5 | 185.1 | 4,912.2 | 2,253,985.7 | 7.9 | 5.4 | 2.2 | .. | 6,140.2 | 107,332.7 | 2.8 | Швейцария |
| United Kingdom | 0.0 | .. | .. | 8,596.3 | 0.0 | 0.5 | 8.4 | 2.0 | 0.4 | 50,349.6 | 321,998.0 | 13.8 | Великобритания |
| Other Europe | .. | 3.5 | 0.0 | 61,402.0 | 214,665.3 | 1.0 | 3.8 | 1.7 | .. | 7,368.2 | 1,717,322.4 | 15.5 | Ост. страны Европы |
| **Asia** | 68.5 | 19.3 | 38.4 | 315,606.3 | 31,555,799.1 | 48.0 | 182.3 | 463.7 | 1,414.0 | 482,619.6 | 39,713,080.7 | 114.7 | **Азия** |
| Afghanistan | .. | 2.2 | 4.3 | 0.0 | .. | 0.0 | .. | .. | 2.5 | .. | .. | .. | Афганистан |
| China | 4.8 | 9.9 | .. | 18,420.6 | 1,073,326.5 | 0.9 | 39.2 | 27.7 | 2.9 | 35,613.2 | 107,332.7 | 0.1 | Китай |
| India | 0.0 | 0.7 | .. | .. | .. | 0.4 | 63.7 | 35.1 | 11.7 | .. | .. | 0.1 | Индия |
| Iraq | .. | 0.0 | .. | .. | .. | .. | 0.8 | .. | .. | .. | .. | 0.1 | Ирак |
| Japan | .. | .. | .. | 0.0 | 0.0 | 0.1 | 13.1 | 0.5 | 1.4 | 1,228.0 | 107,332.7 | 1.2 | Япония |
| Korea, DPR | .. | .. | .. | .. | .. | .. | .. | .. | 12.0 | .. | .. | .. | КНДР |
| Korea, Rep. of | 1.0 | 0.1 | .. | .. | .. | .. | .. | .. | .. | 1,228.0 | .. | 0.0 | Южная Корея |
| Mongolia | 5.3 | 2.9 | .. | .. | .. | 0.3 | .. | .. | .. | .. | .. | 0.0 | МНР |
| Syrian Arab Republic | 2.7 | 0.0 | .. | 8,596.3 | .. | .. | 6.6 | 12.0 | 11.0 | 1,228.0 | .. | 0.4 | Сирия |
| Turkey | 5.0 | 0.7 | 34.1 | 268,940.8 | 25,330,505.4 | 45.0 | 0.2 | 367.6 | 1,369.5 | 423,673.8 | 37,673,760.2 | 103.5 | Турция |
| Viet Nam | 42.8 | 0.0 | .. | .. | .. | .. | 5.5 | 9.4 | 0.2 | .. | .. | .. | Вьетнам |
| Other Asia | 6.5 | 2.2 | .. | 19,648.6 | 5,151,967.2 | 1.3 | 41.6 | 10.6 | 2.7 | 19,648.6 | 1,824,655.1 | 9.3 | Ост. страны Азии |
| **America** | 11.6 | 2.7 | 4.4 | 15,964.5 | 3,971,308.1 | 1.3 | 40.9 | 88.4 | 436.9 | 38,069.3 | 5,366,632.5 | 23.9 | **Сев. и Южная Америка** |
| Canada | .. | .. | .. | .. | .. | 0.0 | 4.2 | 12.9 | .. | 4,912.2 | 214,665.3 | 0.0 | Канада |
| Cuba | 5.3 | 2.5 | .. | 7,368.2 | .. | .. | 0.0 | .. | .. | .. | .. | .. | Куба |
| United States | 0.1 | .. | 4.4 | 8,596.3 | 3,971,308.1 | 0.8 | 20.3 | 53.6 | 403.6 | 33,157.1 | 4,937,301.9 | 23.1 | США |
| Other America | 6.2 | 0.2 | .. | .. | .. | 0.5 | 16.4 | 21.9 | 33.3 | 0.0 | 214,665.3 | 0.8 | Остальные |
| **Africa** | 2.7 | 0.1 | .. | 0.0 | .. | .. | 6.4 | 1.2 | 8.5 | 2,456.1 | 0.0 | .. | **Африка** |
| Egypt | 0.4 | 0.6 | .. | .. | .. | .. | 11.6 | 0.8 | 0.1 | .. | 0.0 | .. | Египет |
| Libya | .. | 0.0 | .. | .. | .. | .. | .. | .. | .. | .. | .. | .. | Ливия |
| Other Africa | 2.7 | 0.1 | .. | 0.0 | .. | .. | 6.4 | 1.2 | 8.4 | 2,456.1 | 0.0 | .. | Остальные |
| **Rest of the World** | 278.5 | .. | .. | .. | .. | .. | 31.6 | 11.8 | .. | 20,877.5 | 643,995.9 | 0.2 | **Прочие страны мира** |
| Australia | .. | .. | .. | .. | .. | .. | .. | .. | .. | 19,648.6 | 643,995.9 | 0.1 | Австралия |

**TABLE 4-1. General government budget revenue (millions of national currency)**
**ТАБЛИЦА 4-1. Доходы государственного бюджета (млн. национальной валюты)**

| Type of revenue | 1990 | 1991 | 1992 | 1993 | 1994 | 1995 | Вид доходов |
|---|---|---|---|---|---|---|---|
| **Total revenue and grants** | 4,979 | 6,362 | 20,457 | 638,909 | .. | .. | **Всего доходов и безвозм. поступл.** |
| Grants | 931 | 2 | .. | .. | .. | .. | Безвозмездные поступления |
| Total Revenue | 4,048 | 6,360 | 20,457 | 638,909 | .. | .. | Всего доходов |
| **Current revenue** | 4,048 | 6,360 | 20,457 | 638,909 | .. | .. | **Текущие доходы** |
| Tax revenue | 3,777 | 4,527 | 16,745 | 456,614 | .. | .. | Доход от налогов |
| Taxes on income and profits | 794 | 2,016 | 8,336 | 189,527 | .. | .. | Налоги на доходы и прибыль |
| Individual | 278 | 520 | 1,719 | 1,169 | .. | .. | Физические лица |
| Corporate | 516 | 1,495 | 6,617 | 188,358 | .. | .. | Предприятия и организации |
| Social security contributions | 529 | .. | .. | .. | .. | .. | Отчисление на соцстрах. |
| Taxes on payroll or work force | 178 | .. | 10 | 4,746 | .. | .. | Налоги на заработную плату и рабочую силу |
| Taxes on the use of labor force | 123 | .. | .. | .. | .. | .. | Плата за трудовые ресурсы |
| Taxes on increases in wages and salaries | 1 | .. | .. | .. | .. | .. | Налог с прироста средств на оплату труда |
| Other payroll/work force taxes | 55 | 168 | 10 | 4,746 | .. | .. | Другие налоги на зарплату и рабочую силу |
| Taxes on property | 242 | 44 | 35 | 380 | .. | .. | Налоги на собственность |
| Taxes on immovable property | 16 | 15 | 10 | 217 | .. | .. | Налоги на недвижимое имущество |
| Buildings | 7 | 7 | 10 | 217 | .. | .. | Налог с владельцев строении |
| Land | 9 | 8 | .. | .. | .. | .. | Земельныи налог |
| Estate, inheritance, and gift taxes | .. | .. | .. | .. | .. | .. | Налоги на наследство, подарки |
| Other property taxes | 227 | 30 | 26 | 163 | .. | .. | Другие налоги на имущество |
| Domestic taxes on goods and services | 1,900 | 2,124 | 7,766 | 168,141 | .. | .. | Внутренние налоги на товары и услуги |
| General sales, turnover, or value-added taxes | 1,810 | 2,124 | 4,792 | 98,864 | .. | .. | Налог с продаж. с оборота или на добав. стоим. |
| Excises | .. | .. | 2,966 | 68,450 | .. | .. | Акцизы |
| Profits of fiscal monopolies | .. | .. | .. | .. | .. | .. | Прибыли фискальных монополий |
| Taxes on specific services | .. | .. | 8 | 826 | .. | .. | Налоги на особые услуги |
| Taxes on use of goods or permission to use goods or to perform activities | 90 | .. | .. | .. | .. | .. | Налоги на пользование товарами или лицензии на пользование товарами и занятие деятельностью |
| Other taxes on goods and services | .. | .. | .. | .. | .. | .. | Другие налоги на товары и услуги |
| Taxes on international trade and transactions | 27 | 93 | 377 | 90,448 | .. | .. | Налоги на внешнюю торговлю и операции |
| Import duties | .. | .. | .. | 1,430 | .. | .. | Импортные пошлины |
| Export duties | .. | .. | .. | 8,507 | .. | .. | Экпортные пошлины |
| Other | 27 | 93 | 377 | 80,510 | .. | .. | Другие |
| Other taxes | 106 | 81 | 220 | 3,373 | .. | .. | Прочие налоги |
| Nontax revenue | 271 | 1,834 | 3,712 | 182,296 | .. | .. | Неналоговые доходы |
| **Capital revenue** | .. | .. | .. | .. | .. | .. | **Капитальные доходы** |

**TABLE 4-2. General government budget expenditure by economic type (millions of national currency)**
**ТАБЛИЦА 4-2. Расходы государственного бюджета по экономическим типам (млн. национальной валюты)**

| Type of expenditure or debt holder | 1990 | 1991 | 1992 | 1993 | 1994 | 1995 | Всего расходов |
|---|---|---|---|---|---|---|---|
| **Total expenditure by economic type** | 4,786 | 5,940 | 45,453 | 1,332,791 | .. | .. | **Всего расходов по экономическим типам** |
| **Current expenditure** | 3,395 | 3,490 | 30,458 | 1,033,242 | .. | .. | **Текущие расходы** |
| Expenditure on goods and services | 1,009 | 1,757 | 11,615 | 304,696 | .. | .. | Расходы на товары и услуги |
| Wages and salaries | 728 | 1,185 | 7,053 | 150,846 | .. | .. | Заработная плата |
| Employer contributions | 51 | 252 | 1,146 | 18,382 | .. | .. | Отчисление на социальное страхование |
| Other Purchases of goods and services | 231 | 321 | 3,415 | 135,469 | .. | .. | Другие покупки товаров и услуг |
| Interest payments | .. | .. | .. | .. | .. | .. | Выплаты процентов |
| Domestic debt | .. | .. | .. | .. | .. | .. | По внутреннему долгу |
| Foreign debt | .. | .. | .. | .. | .. | .. | По внешнему долгу |
| Subsidies and other current transfers | 1,726 | 489 | 10,278 | 147,078 | .. | .. | Субсидии на другие текущие трансферты |
| Subsidies | 898 | 386 | 9,756 | 140,178 | .. | .. | Субсидии |
| Agricultural subsidies | 791 | 154 | 5,094 | 2,912 | .. | .. | Субсидии на сельское хозяиство |
| Other current transfers | 828 | 103 | 521 | 6,900 | .. | .. | Другие текущие трансферты |
| Other | 660 | 1,244 | 8,565 | 581,468 | .. | .. | Прочие расходы |
| **Capital expenditure** | 1,392 | 2,450 | 14,995 | 299,549 | .. | .. | **Капитальные расходы** |
| Acquisition of fixed capital assets | 81 | 64 | 2,052 | 109,604 | .. | .. | Приобретение основного капитала |
| Capital transfers | 1,242 | 2,294 | 12,392 | 168,542 | .. | .. | Капитальные трансферты |
| Other | 68 | 91 | 552 | 21,403 | .. | .. | Другие капитальные расходы |
| **Surplus/deficit (-)** | .. | .. | .. | .. | .. | .. | **Превыш. доходов над расходами/дефицит(-)** |
| **Financing by type of debt holder** | .. | .. | 27,300 | 1,120,541 | .. | .. | **Финансирование по типам кредиторов** |
| **Foreign (net)** | .. | .. | .. | .. | .. | .. | **Зарубежные кредиторы (сальдо)** |
| From international development institutions | .. | .. | .. | .. | .. | .. | Международные организации |
| From foreign governments | .. | .. | .. | .. | .. | .. | Правительства иностранных государств |
| Other borrowing abroad | .. | .. | .. | .. | .. | .. | Другие зарубежные кредиторы |
| **Domestic (net)** | .. | .. | 27,300 | 1,120,541 | .. | .. | **Внутренние кредиторы (сальдо)** |
| From monetary authorities | .. | .. | 27,300 | 1,120,541 | .. | .. | Органы денежного обращения |
| From deposit money banks | .. | .. | .. | .. | .. | .. | Депозитные денежные банки |
| Other domestic borrowing | .. | .. | .. | .. | .. | .. | Другие внутренние кредиторы |
| *Memo items:* | | | | | | | *Справочно:* |
| Extrabudgetary surplus/ Deficit (-) not included above | .. | .. | .. | .. | .. | .. | Превышение доходов над расходами/дефицит (-) по внебюджетным фондам, не включенным выше |
| Total surplus/deficit (-) including extrabudgetary accounts | .. | .. | .. | .. | .. | .. | Итого превышение доходов над расходами/дефицит, включая счета внебюджетных фондов |

**TABLE 5-1. Agricultural production (millions of national currency, current prices)**

**ТАБЛИЦА 5-1. Сельскохозяйственная продукция (млн. нац. валюты, текущие цены)**

| Item | 1990 | 1991 | 1992 | 1993 | 1994 | 1995 | Статьи |
|---|---|---|---|---|---|---|---|
| **Total gross agricultural production** | 5,199 | 6,630 | 108,593 | 25,318,000 | 678,000,000 | 1,851 | **Валовая продукция сельского хозяйства - всего** |
| **Crops** | 3,535 | 5,335 | 69,531 | 18,988,000 | 427,000,000 | 1,310 | **Продукция растениеводства** |
| Grains | 141 | 237 | 13,579 | 1,726,000 | 33,000,000 | 120 | Зерно |
| Potatoes | 99 | 169 | 6,749 | 702,000 | 24,000,000 | 82 | Картофель |
| Vegetables | 236 | 391 | 2,139 | 2,319,000 | 80,000,000 | 235 | Овощи |
| Fruits (excluding grapes) | 1,060 | 3,331 | 16,123 | 4,044,000 | 131,000,000 | 516 | Фрукты (без винограда) |
| Grapes | 569 | 850 | 19,121 | 3,589,000 | 152,000,000 | 323 | Виноград |
| Tobacco | 171 | 132 | 721 | 228,000 | 5,000,000 | 25 | Табак |
| Cotton | .. | .. | .. | .. | .. | .. | Хлопок |
| Sugarbeets | 4 | 0 | 27 | 0 | 0 | 2 | Сахарная свекла |
| Oilseeds | 0 | 0 | 0 | .. | 2,000,000 | 7 | Семена масличных культур |
| Other | 1,255 | 225 | 11,072 | 6,380,000 | 0 | 0 | Прочие |
| **Animal husbandry** | 1,664 | 1,295 | 39,062 | 6,330,000 | 251,000,000 | 541 | **Продукция животноводства** |
| Livestock | 961 | 633 | 18,626 | 4,092,000 | 127,000,000 | 248 | Мясное животноводство |
| Cattle | 331 | 211 | 7,298 | .. | 33,000,000 | 109 | Крупный рогатый скот |
| Pigs | 333 | 106 | 8,176 | .. | 36,000,000 | 102 | Свиньи |
| Sheep and goats | 60 | 67 | 2,052 | .. | 6,000,000 | 17 | Овцы и козы |
| Poultry | 196 | 220 | 1,049 | .. | 7,000,000 | 20 | Птица |
| Other | 41 | 28 | 51 | .. | 45,000,000 | 0 | Прочие |
| Milk | 469 | 443 | 16,236 | 1,527,000 | 114,000,000 | 258 | Молоко |
| Eggs | 133 | 78 | 2,274 | 209,000 | 8,000,000 | 32 | Яйца |
| Wool | 92 | 141 | 558 | 472,000 | 2,000,000 | 3 | Шерсть |
| Other livestock | 0 | 0 | 1,368 | 30,000 | 0 | 0 | Прочая |
| **Agricultural services** | .. | .. | .. | .. | .. | .. | **Сельскохозяйственные услуги** |

**TABLE 5-2. Agricultural production (millions of constant national currency)**

**ТАБЛИЦА 5-2. Сельскохозяйственная продукция в постоянных ценах (млн. национальной валюты)**

| Item | 1990 | 1991 | 1992 | 1993 | 1994 | 1995 | Статьи |
|---|---|---|---|---|---|---|---|
| **Total gross agricultural production** | 2,938 | 1,878 | 1,627 | 1,434 | 1,599 | 1,813 | **Валовая продукция сельского хозяиства - всего** |
| **Crops** | 2,005 | 1,508 | 1,107 | 969 | 1,117 | 1,289 | **Продукция растениеводства** |
| Grains | 76 | 66 | 60 | 47 | 55 | 60 | Зерно |
| Potatoes | 56 | 49 | 40 | 47 | 57 | 51 | Картофель |
| Vegetables | 82 | 111 | 96 | 120 | 138 | 147 | Овощи |
| Fruits (excluding grapes) | 613 | 808 | 533 | 456 | 666 | 797 | Фрукты (без винограда) |
| Grapes | 323 | 242 | 153 | 164 | 133 | 177 | Виноград |
| Tobacco | 42 | 38 | 20 | 11 | 8 | 13 | Табак |
| Cotton | .. | .. | .. | .. | .. | .. | Хлопок |
| Sugarbeets | 2 | 1 | 1 | 0 | 0 | 1 | Сахарная свекла |
| Oilseeds | 2 | 2 | 2 | 1 | 2 | 2 | Семена масличных культур |
| Other | 809 | 191 | 202 | 123 | 58 | 41 | Прочие |
| **Animal husbandry** | 933 | 370 | 520 | 465 | 482 | 524 | **Продукция животноводства** |
| Livestock | 543 | 184 | 271 | 240 | 259 | 289 | Мясное животноводство |
| Cattle | 185 | 60 | .. | .. | .. | .. | Крупный рогатый скот |
| Pigs | 184 | 30 | .. | .. | .. | .. | Свиньи |
| Sheep and goats | 34 | 19 | .. | .. | .. | .. | Овцы и козы |
| Poultry | 111 | 63 | .. | .. | .. | .. | Птица |
| Other | 29 | 11 | .. | .. | .. | .. | Прочие |
| Milk | 263 | 124 | 187 | 171 | 170 | 182 | Молоко |
| Eggs | 74 | 22 | 27 | 22 | 23 | 24 | Яйца |
| Wool | 53 | 40 | 35 | 31 | 29 | 28 | Шерсть |
| Other livestock | 0 | 0 | 0 | 1 | 1 | 1 | Прочая |
| **Agricultural services** | .. | .. | .. | .. | .. | .. | **Сельскохозяйственные услуги** |

**TABLE 5-3. Production and average yield of major agricultural crops**

**ТАБЛИЦА 5-3. Производство и урожайность важнейших сельскохозяйственных культур**

| Crop | 1990 | 1991 | 1992 | 1993 | 1994 | 1995 | Сельскохозяйственные культуры |
|---|---|---|---|---|---|---|---|
| **Production (thousands of tons)** | | | | | | | **Производство (тыс. тонн)** |
| Grain - Cleanweight | 700 | 600 | 500 | 410 | 481 | 515 | Зерно в чистом весе |
| Winter wheat | 300 | 200 | 200 | 113 | 100 | 135 | Пшеница - озимая |
| Spring wheat | .. | .. | .. | .. | .. | .. | яровая |
| Coarse grain | 700 | 600 | 500 | 425 | 493 | 520 | Зерно в физическом весе |
| Rye | .. | .. | .. | .. | .. | .. | Рожь |
| Corn | 300 | 200 | 200 | 243 | 343 | 344 | Кукуруза |
| Winter barley | 100 | 100 | 100 | 29 | 17 | 27 | Ячмень - озимый |
| Spring barley | .. | .. | .. | .. | .. | .. | яровой |
| Oats | .. | .. | .. | .. | .. | .. | Овес |
| Millet | .. | .. | .. | .. | .. | .. | Просо |
| Rice | .. | .. | .. | .. | .. | .. | Рис |
| Flax | .. | .. | .. | .. | .. | .. | Лен |
| Oilseeds | .. | .. | .. | .. | .. | .. | Семена масличных культур |
| Cotton (raw) | .. | .. | .. | .. | .. | .. | Хлопок - сырец |
| Cotton fiber | .. | .. | .. | .. | .. | .. | волокно |
| Sugarbeets | 31 | 18 | 24 | 13 | 8 | 11 | Сахарная свекла |
| Potatoes | 300 | 300 | 200 | 249 | 297 | 265 | Картофель |
| Pulses | .. | .. | .. | .. | .. | .. | Бобовые |
| Vegetables | 400 | 400 | 300 | 386 | 400 | 470 | Овощи |
| Fruit | 1,600 | 1,100 | 800 | 663 | 755 | 943 | Фрукты |
| Grapes | 700 | 500 | 300 | 352 | 285 | 380 | Виноград |
| Other | 900 | 600 | 500 | 311 | 470 | 563 | Прочие |
| Corn (silage and greenchop) | 500 | 400 | 100 | 31 | 21 | 15 | Кукуруза (на силос и зеленый корм) |
| Hay | .. | .. | .. | .. | .. | .. | Сено |
| **Average yield (kilograms per hectare)** | | | | | | | **Ср. урожайность (кг с га)** |
| Grain | 2,470 | 1,970 | 1,810 | 1,590 | 1,860 | .. | Зерно |
| Winter wheat | 2,820 | 2,090 | 1,690 | 1,360 | 1,300 | .. | Пшеница - озимая |
| Spring wheat | 1,510 | 1,350 | 1,480 | 660 | 1,010 | .. | яровая |
| Coarse grain | 2,560 | 2,060 | 1,900 | 1,650 | 1,910 | 2,010 | Зерно в физическом весе |
| Rye | 2,680 | 2,140 | 1,530 | 540 | 720 | 1,250 | Рожь |
| Corn | 2,520 | 2,120 | 2,320 | 2,170 | 2,480 | 2,410 | Кукуруза |
| Winter barley | 2,930 | 2,160 | 1,870 | 1,370 | 1,280 | 850 | Ячмень - озимый |
| Spring barley | 2,280 | 2,140 | 1,310 | 830 | 1,220 | .. | яровой |
| Oats | 1,320 | 1,180 | 1,090 | 720 | 880 | 810 | Овес |
| Millet | .. | .. | .. | .. | .. | .. | Просо |
| Rice | .. | .. | .. | .. | .. | .. | Рис |
| Flax | .. | .. | .. | .. | .. | .. | Лен |
| Oilseeds | 580 | 540 | 590 | 230 | 430 | 190 | Семена масличных культур |
| Cotton (raw) | .. | .. | .. | .. | .. | .. | Хлопок - сырец |
| Cotton fiber | .. | .. | .. | .. | .. | .. | волокно |
| Sugarbeets | 25,200 | 16,700 | 16,100 | 10,800 | 8,400 | 14,900 | Сахарная свекла |
| Potatoes | 10,600 | 11,000 | 9,500 | 11,600 | 12,300 | 12,900 | Картофель |
| Pulses | 480 | 480 | 510 | 450 | 620 | 610 | Бобовые |
| Vegetables | 11,100 | 10,500 | 11,400 | 14,100 | 14,300 | 17,500 | Овощи |
| Fruit | 14,140 | 11,430 | 9,400 | 4,250 | 4,610 | .. | Фрукты |
| Grapes | 6,760 | 6,120 | 4,070 | 4,730 | 3,760 | .. | Виноград |
| Other | 7,380 | 5,310 | 5,330 | 3,820 | 5,340 | .. | Прочие |
| Corn (silage and greenchop) | 9,500 | 7,300 | 4,600 | 2,300 | 2,700 | 2,700 | Кукуруза (на силос и зеленый корм) |
| Hay | .. | .. | .. | .. | .. | .. | Сено |

**TABLE 5-4. Main aggregates of animal husbandry**
**ТАБЛИЦА 5-4. Основные показатели животноводства**

| Type of livestock or product | 1990 | 1991 | 1992 | 1993 | 1994 | 1995 | Направление животноводства или вид продукции |
|---|---|---|---|---|---|---|---|
| **Livestock (thousands of heads)** | | | | | | | **Поголовье скота (тысяч голов)** |
| Cattle | 1,298 | 1,208 | 1,003 | 929 | 944 | 974 | Крупный рогатый скот |
| of which: Cows | 552 | 543 | 502 | 487 | 514 | 531 | в том числе коровы |
| Pigs | 880 | 733 | 476 | 365 | 367 | 353 | Свиньи |
| Sheep and goats | 1,618 | 1,470 | 1,192 | 958 | 793 | 725 | Овцы и козы |
| of which: Goats | 68 | 59 | 45 | 38 | 39 | 51 | в том числе козы |
| Horses | 20 | 18 | 17 | 20 | 21 | 24 | Лошади |
| Other | 21,760 | 20,167 | 11,211 | 11,856 | 12,290 | 13,021 | Прочие |
| **Animal husbandry products** | | | | | | | **Продукция животноводства** |
| Meat (thousands of tons) | 263 | 212 | 177 | 159 | 171 | 196 | Мясо (тысяч тонн) |
| Beef | 98 | 77 | 69 | 69 | 75 | 93 | Говядина |
| Pork | 91 | 83 | 80 | 64 | 67 | 71 | Свинина |
| Lamb | 23 | 16 | 14 | 15 | 17 | 18 | Баранина |
| Poultry | 49 | 34 | 13 | 11 | 12 | 13 | Птица |
| Other | 2 | 2 | 1 | 0 | 0 | 1 | Прочие виды мяса |
| Milk (thousands of tons) | 659 | 562 | 470 | 433 | 429 | 475 | Молоко (тысяч тонн) |
| Eggs (millions) | 769 | 638 | 297 | 243 | 251 | 269 | Яйца (миллионов штук) |
| Wool (thousands of tons) | 6 | 5 | 4 | 4 | 3 | 3 | Шерсть (тысяч тонн) |

**TABLE 6-1. Industrial production by sector (millions of national currency)**

**ТАБЛИЦА 6-1. Промышленное производство по отраслям (млн. национальной валюты)**

| Sector | 1990 | 1991 | 1992 | 1993 | 1994 | 1995 | Отрасли |
|---|---|---|---|---|---|---|---|
| **All industry** | 12,063 | 17,233 | 89,967 | 2,588,264 | 242,359,363 | 575 | **Вся промышленность** |
| **Heavy industry** | 4,712 | 6,745 | 53,669 | 1,889,151 | 178,775,893 | .. | **Тяжелая промышленность** |
| Fuel and energy | 422 | 738 | 13,630 | 512,985 | 91,362,853 | .. | Топливно-энергетическая промышленноть |
| Electricity | 287 | 514 | 10,540 | 337,386 | 75,258,876 | .. | Электроэнергетика |
| Fuels | 135 | 224 | 3,090 | 175,599 | 16,103,977 | .. | Топливная промышленность |
| Ferrous and nonferrous metallurgy | 454 | 793 | 14,552 | 498,032 | 32,763,637 | .. | Металлургия |
| Chemicals and petrochemical industry | 448 | 769 | 5,820 | 222,275 | 15,967,102 | .. | Химическая и нефтехимическая пром. |
| Machine building and metalworking | 1,730 | 2,012 | 10,270 | 471,532 | 14,405,303 | .. | Машиностроение и металлообработка |
| Forestry, woodworking, and pulp and paper industry | 401 | 622 | 1,384 | 16,497 | 2,162,589 | .. | Лесная, деревообрабатывающая и целлюлозо-бумажная промышленность |
| Construction materials | 618 | 684 | 3,440 | 49,190 | 5,365,906 | .. | Промышленность строительных материалов |
| **Light industry** | 2,555 | 3,537 | 10,011 | 178,495 | 7,538,157 | .. | **Легкая промышленность** |
| Textiles | 1,472 | 2,156 | 7,748 | 142,472 | 5,908,560 | .. | Текстильная |
| Clothing | 899 | 1,105 | 1,554 | 20,591 | 1,216,981 | .. | Швейная |
| Leather and shoes | 161 | 246 | 611 | 13,146 | 346,707 | .. | Кожевенная и обувная |
| **Food industry** | 4,508 | 6,422 | 22,273 | 479,969 | 42,848,803 | .. | **Пищевая промышленность** |
| Processed foods | 3,963 | 5,658 | 21,098 | 441,537 | 41,161,630 | .. | Пищевкусовая |
| Meat and dairy products | 438 | 669 | 1,081 | 34,274 | 1,559,169 | .. | Мясная и молочная |
| Fish | 107 | 96 | 94 | 4,158 | 128,004 | .. | Рыбная |

## TABLE 6-2. Industrial production by sector in constant prices

## ТАБЛИЦА 6-2. Промышленное производство по отраслям в постоянных ценах

GEORGIA

| Sector | 1990 | 1991 | 1992 | 1993 | 1994 | 1995 | Отрасли |
|---|---|---|---|---|---|---|---|
| **Industrial production** | | | | | | | **Промышленное производство** |
| **All industry** | 23,194 | 17,952 | 9,730 | 6,158 | 3,752 | 3,384 | **Вся промышленность** |
| **Heavy industry** | 8,416 | 6,497 | 3,365 | 2,183 | 1,280 | .. | **Тяжелая промышленность** |
| Fuel and energy | 592 | 543 | 343 | 281 | 191 | .. | Топливно-энергетическая промышленноть |
| Electricity | 350 | 328 | 285 | 255 | 176 | .. | Электроэнергетика |
| Fuels | 242 | 214 | 58 | 26 | 15 | .. | Топливная промышленность |
| Ferrous and nonferrous metallurgy | 1,162 | 794 | 439 | 232 | 115 | .. | Металлургия |
| Chemicals and petrochemicals | 938 | 887 | 339 | 294 | 86 | .. | Химическая и нефтехимическая пром. |
| Machine building and metalworking | 2,816 | 1,959 | 952 | 539 | 237 | .. | Машиностроение и металлообработка |
| Forestry, woodworking, and pulp and paper | 750 | 622 | 235 | 124 | 72 | .. | Лесная, деревообрабатывающая и целлюлозо-бумажная промышленность |
| Construction materials | 1,039 | 684 | 336 | 148 | 48 | .. | Промышленность строительных материалов |
| **Light industry** | 4,823 | 3,550 | 2,230 | 1,009 | 426 | .. | **Легкая промышленность** |
| Textiles | 3,076 | 2,156 | 1,473 | 608 | 170 | .. | Текстильная |
| Clothing | 1,439 | 1,118 | 581 | 352 | 237 | .. | Швейная |
| Leather and shoe | 267 | 246 | 103 | 30 | 11 | .. | Кожевенная и обувная |
| **Food industry** | 9,383 | 7,376 | 4,107 | 2,737 | 1,846 | .. | **Пищевая промышленность** |
| Processed foods | 7,937 | 6,612 | 3,835 | 2,579 | 1,745 | .. | Пищевкусовая |
| Meat and dairy products | 1,303 | 669 | 223 | 130 | 85 | .. | Мясная и молочная |
| Fish | 143 | 95 | 49 | 28 | 16 | .. | Рыбная |
| **Growth in production by sector (in percent)** | | | | | | | **Рост производства по отраслям** |
| **All industry** | -5.7 | -22.6 | -45.8 | -36.7 | -39.1 | -9.8 | **Вся промышленность** |
| **Heavy industry** | -6.1 | -22.8 | -48.2 | -35.1 | -41.4 | .. | **Тяжелая промышленность** |
| Power and fuels | -8.8 | -8.3 | -36.8 | -18.1 | -32.0 | .. | Топливно-энергетическая промышленноть |
| Electricity | -8.9 | -6.3 | -13.1 | -10.6 | -31.0 | .. | Электроэнергетика |
| Fuels | -8.7 | -11.6 | -73.0 | -54.9 | -42.3 | .. | Топливная промышленность |
| Ferrous and nonferrous metallurgy | -16.4 | -31.7 | -44.7 | -47.1 | -50.4 | .. | Металлургия |
| Chemicals and petrochemicals | 15.0 | -5.4 | -61.8 | -13.3 | -70.7 | .. | Химическая и нефтехимическая пром. |
| Machine building and metalworking | 35.2 | -30.4 | -51.4 | -43.4 | -56.0 | .. | Машиностроение и металлообработка |
| Forestry, woodworking, and pulp and paper | -3.1 | -17.1 | -62.2 | -47.2 | -41.9 | .. | Лесная, деревообрабатывающая и целлюлозо-бумажная промышленность |
| Construction materials | -6.2 | -34.2 | -50.9 | -55.9 | -67.6 | .. | Промышленность строительных материалов |
| **Light industry** | -7.6 | -26.4 | -37.2 | -54.7 | -57.8 | .. | **Легкая промышленность** |
| Textiles | -10.5 | -29.9 | -31.7 | -58.7 | -72.0 | .. | Текстильная |
| Clothing | -3.8 | -22.3 | -48.1 | -39.4 | -32.7 | .. | Швейная |
| Leather and shoe | -6.3 | -7.9 | -58.1 | -70.9 | -63.3 | .. | Кожевенная и обувная |
| **Food industry** | -4.4 | -21.4 | -44.3 | -33.4 | -32.6 | .. | **Пищевая промышленность** |
| Processed foods | -2.0 | -16.7 | -42.0 | -32.7 | -32.3 | .. | Пищевкусовая |
| Meat and dairy products | -15.5 | -48.7 | -66.6 | -41.8 | -34.6 | .. | Мясная и молочная |
| Fish | -17.3 | -33.6 | -48.6 | -42.6 | -42.9 | .. | Рыбная |

## TABLE 6-3. Primary energy supply (million tons oil equivalent) GEORGIA

## ТАБЛИЦА 6-3. Ресурсы первичных видов энергии (млн. тонн нефтяного эквивалента)

| Item | | 1990 | 1991 | 1992 | 1993 | 1994 | 1995 | Статьи | |
|---|---|---|---|---|---|---|---|---|---|
| **Primary production** | | | | | | | | **Производство первичной энергии** | |
| Coal and lignite (hard and brown) | | 0.4 | 0.3 | 0.1 | 0.1 | 0.1 | .. | Уголь каменный и бурый | |
| Crude oil | | 0.2 | 0.2 | 0.1 | 0.1 | 0.1 | .. | Нефть | |
| Gas | | 0.1 | 0.0 | 0.0 | 0.0 | 0.0 | .. | Газ | |
| Nuclear | | .. | .. | .. | .. | .. | .. | Атомная энергия | |
| Hydro/geothermal | | 2.5 | 2.5 | 2.3 | 2.4 | 2.2 | .. | Гидро-геотермальная | |
| Other | | .. | .. | .. | .. | 0.0 | .. | Другие виды | |
| Total | | 3.2 | 3.0 | 2.5 | 2.6 | 2.4 | .. | Всего | |
| **Energy trade** | | | | | | | | **Торговля энергией** | |
| Coal and lignite | Exports | 0.4 | 0.2 | 0.0 | 0.0 | 0.0 | .. | Уголь каменный и бурый | Экспорт |
| | Imports | 0.5 | 0.2 | 0.0 | 0.0 | 0.0 | .. | | Импорт |
| | Net imports | 0.1 | 0.0 | 0.0 | 0.0 | 0.0 | .. | | Чистый импорт |
| Oil/oil product | Exports | 1.3 | 0.0 | 0.0 | 0.0 | 0.0 | .. | Нефть и нефтепродукты | Экспорт |
| | Imports | 8.9 | 6.7 | 1.1 | 0.9 | 1.0 | .. | | Импорт |
| | Net imports | 7.6 | 6.7 | 1.1 | 0.9 | 1.0 | .. | | Чистый импорт |
| Gas | Exports | 0.0 | 0.0 | 0.0 | 0.0 | .. | .. | Газ | Экспорт |
| | Imports | 6.3 | 5.4 | 5.6 | 5.2 | 2.7 | .. | | Импорт |
| | Net imports | 6.3 | 5.4 | 5.6 | .. | 2.7 | .. | | Чистый импорт |
| Electricity | Exports | 0.4 | 0.3 | 0.2 | 0.1 | 0.0 | .. | Электричество | Экспорт |
| | Imports | 1.4 | 1.2 | 0.5 | 0.3 | 0.3 | .. | | Импорт |
| | Net imports | 1.0 | 0.9 | 0.3 | 0.2 | 0.3 | .. | | Чистый импорт |
| **Total net imports** | | 15.0 | 13.0 | 7.0 | 1.1 | 4.0 | .. | **Чистый импорт энергии-всего** | |
| **Total stock changes** | | -0.2 | 0.0 | 0.0 | 0.0 | 0.0 | .. | **Изменение запасов-всего** | |
| **Total primary energy supply** | | 18.0 | 16.0 | 9.5 | 3.7 | 6.4 | .. | **Ресурсы первичной энергии-всего** | |
| Coal and lignite | | 0.5 | .. | .. | .. | 0.1 | .. | Уголь каменный и бурый | |
| Oil/oil products | | 7.8 | .. | .. | .. | 1.1 | .. | Нефть и нефтепродукты | |
| Gas | | 0.0 | .. | .. | .. | 2.7 | .. | Газ | |
| Nuclear | | .. | .. | .. | .. | .. | .. | Атомная энергия | |
| Hydro/geothermal | | 2.5 | .. | .. | .. | 2.5 | .. | Гидро-геотермальная энергия | |
| Other | | 0.8 | .. | .. | .. | 0.0 | .. | Другие виды | |
| **Total primary energy requirement (equals total primary energy supply)** | | .. | .. | .. | .. | 6.4 | .. | **Потребность в первичной энергии-всего (равно ресурсам первичной энергии)** | |

## TABLE 6-4. Final energy consumption (million tons oil equivalent) GEORGIA
## ТАБЛИЦА 6-4. Конечное потребление энергии ( млн. тонн нефтяного эквивалента )

| | 1991 | 1992 | 1993 | 1994 | 1995 | |
|---|---|---|---|---|---|---|
| **Final energy consumption** | 15.6 | 9.9 | 8.3 | 6.2 | .. | **Конечное потребление энергии** |
| Coal & Lignite | 0.5 | 0.1 | 0.1 | 0.0 | .. | Уголь каменный и бурый |
| Oil Products | 3.8 | 0.7 | 0.3 | 0.3 | .. | Нефтепродукты |
| Gas | 4.7 | 4.1 | 3.4 | 3.2 | .. | Газ |
| Electricity | 3.9 | 3.1 | 2.6 | 1.9 | .. | Электроэнергия |
| Heat | .. | .. | .. | .. | .. | Тепло |
| Other | 2.7 | 1.9 | 1.9 | 0.8 | .. | Другие виды |
| Of which: | | | | | | В том числе |
| **Industry** | .. | .. | .. | .. | .. | **Промышленность** |
| Coal & Lignite | .. | .. | .. | .. | .. | Уголь каменный и бурый |
| Oil Products | .. | .. | .. | .. | .. | Нефтепродукты |
| Gas | .. | .. | .. | .. | .. | Газ |
| Electricity | .. | .. | .. | .. | .. | Электроэнергия |
| Heat | .. | .. | .. | .. | .. | Тепло |
| Other | .. | .. | .. | .. | .. | Другие виды |
| **Agriculture** | .. | .. | .. | .. | .. | **Сельское хозяйство** |
| Coal & Lignite | .. | .. | .. | .. | .. | Уголь каменный и бурый |
| Oil Products | .. | .. | .. | .. | .. | Нефтепродукты |
| Gas | .. | .. | .. | .. | .. | Газ |
| Electricity | .. | .. | .. | .. | .. | Электроэнергия |
| Heat | .. | .. | .. | .. | .. | Тепло |
| Other | .. | .. | .. | .. | .. | Другие виды |
| **Transport** | .. | .. | .. | .. | .. | **Транспорт** |
| Oil Products | .. | .. | .. | .. | .. | Нефтепродукты |
| Other | .. | .. | .. | .. | .. | Другие виды |
| **Households** | .. | .. | .. | .. | .. | **Домашние хозяйства** |
| Coal & Lignite | .. | .. | .. | .. | .. | Уголь каменный и бурый |
| Oil Products | .. | .. | .. | .. | .. | Нефтепродукты |
| Gas | .. | .. | .. | .. | .. | Газ |
| Electricity | .. | .. | .. | .. | .. | Электроэнергия |
| Heat | .. | .. | .. | .. | .. | Тепло |
| Other | .. | .. | .. | .. | .. | Другие виды |

**TABLE 7-1. Price indices and exchange rates**

**ТАБЛИЦА 7-1. Индексы цен и обменный курс**

| Year and month | National currency per U.S. dollar<br>Единиц нац. валюты за 1 доллар США | National currency per Russian ruble<br>Единиц нац. валюты за 1 российский рубль | Consumer price index (as a percent of the previous month)<br>Индекс потребительских цен (в % к предыдущему месяцу) 1) | Producer price index (as a percent of the previous month)<br>Индекс цен производителей (в % к предыдущему месяцу) | Consumer price index (as a percent of the previous December)<br>Индекс потребительских цен (в % к декабрю рошлого года) 1) | Producer price index (as a percent of the previous December)<br>Индекс цен производителей (в % к декабрю прошлого года) | Год и месяц |
|---|---|---|---|---|---|---|---|
| **1993** | | | | | | | **1993** |
| January | .. | .. | .. | .. | .. | .. | Январь |
| February | .. | .. | .. | .. | .. | .. | Февраль |
| March | .. | .. | .. | .. | .. | .. | Март |
| April | .. | .. | .. | .. | .. | .. | Апрель |
| May | .. | .. | .. | .. | .. | .. | Май |
| June | .. | .. | .. | .. | .. | .. | Июнь |
| July | .. | .. | .. | .. | .. | .. | Июль |
| August | 5,181.8 | 5.2 | .. | .. | .. | .. | Август |
| September | 11,739.5 | 10.6 | .. | .. | .. | .. | Сентябрь |
| October | 18,927.0 | 16.4 | .. | .. | .. | .. | Октябрь |
| November | 34,987.4 | 30.3 | .. | .. | .. | .. | Ноябрь |
| December | 71,085.9 | 60.6 | .. | .. | .. | .. | Декабрь |
| **1994** | | | | | | | **1994** |
| January | 144,415.0 | 99.2 | 251.3 | .. | 251.3 | .. | Январь |
| February | 196,779.0 | 103.6 | 134.6 | .. | 338.2 | .. | Февраль |
| March | 289,398.0 | 156.8 | 151.4 | .. | 512.0 | .. | Март |
| April | 659,267.0 | 329.0 | 183.0 | .. | 937.0 | .. | Апрель |
| May | 912,258.0 | 462.7 | 143.3 | .. | 1,342.7 | .. | Май |
| June | 794,333.0 | 409.1 | 95.0 | .. | 1,275.6 | .. | Июнь |
| July | 821,290.0 | 408.5 | 106.1 | .. | 1,353.4 | .. | Июль |
| August | 1,496,614.0 | 712.0 | 170.7 | .. | 2,310.3 | .. | Август |
| September | 2,110,000.0 | 942.0 | 310.9 | .. | 7,182.7 | .. | Сентябрь |
| October | 2,195,484.0 | 728.4 | 91.7 | .. | 6,586.5 | .. | Октябрь |
| November | 1,816,533.0 | 574.5 | 101.5 | .. | 6,685.3 | .. | Ноябрь |
| December | 1,443,548.0 | 387.3 | 91.9 | .. | 6,143.8 | .. | Декабрь |

## TABLE 7-1. Price indices and exchange rates
## ТАБЛИЦА 7-1. Индексы цен и обменный курс

| Year and month | National currency per U.S. dollar / Единиц нац. валюты за 1 доллар США | National currency per Russian ruble / Единиц нац. валюты за 1 российский рубль | Consumer price index (as a percent of the previous month) / Индекс потребительских цен (в % к предыдущему месяцу) 1) | Producer price index (as a percent of the previous month) / Индекс цен производителей (в % к предыдущему месяцу) | Consumer price index (as a percent of the previous December) / Индекс потребительских цен (в % к декабрю рошлого года) 1) | Producer price index (as a percent of the previous December) / Индекс цен производителей (в % к декабрю прошлого года) | Год и месяц |
|---|---|---|---|---|---|---|---|
| **1995** | | | | | | | **1995** |
| January | 1,290,161.0 | 299.2 | 113.1 | .. | 113.1 | .. | Январь |
| February | 1,300,000.0 | 288.0 | 100.8 | .. | 114.0 | .. | Февраль |
| March | 1,300,000.0 | 272.0 | 96.8 | .. | 110.4 | .. | Март |
| April | 1,300,000.0 | 241.7 | 99.0 | .. | 109.3 | .. | Апрель |
| May | 1,300,000.0 | 243.4 | 105.2 | .. | 114.9 | .. | Май |
| June | 1,300,000.0 | 257.6 | 98.9 | .. | 113.7 | .. | Июнь |
| July | 1,300,000.0 | 245.0 | 100.8 | .. | 114.6 | .. | Июль |
| August | 1,300,000.0 | 259.0 | 103.3 | .. | 118.4 | .. | Август |
| September | 1,300,000.0 | 248.3 | 104.1 | .. | 123.2 | .. | Сентябрь |
| October | 1.2732 | 0.00025 | 123.4 | .. | 152.0 | .. | Октябрь |
| November | 1.2553 | 0.00025 | 100.1 | .. | 152.2 | .. | Ноябрь |
| December | 1.2456 | 0.00025 | 103.4 | .. | 152.4 | .. | Декабрь |
| **1996** | | | | | | | **1996** |
| January | 1.2414 | 0.00024 | 102,5 | .. | 102,5 | .. | Январь |
| February | 1.2542 | 0.00024 | 103,0 | .. | 105,6 | .. | Февраль |
| March | 1.2598 | 0.00023 | 103,1 | .. | 108,8 | .. | Март |
| April | 1.2580 | 0.00023 | 101,7 | .. | 110,7 | .. | Апрель |
| May | 1.2589 | 0.00022 | 100,5 | .. | 111,3 | .. | Май |
| June | 1.2595 | 0.00022 | 100,4 | .. | 111,7 | .. | Июнь |
| July | 1.2591 | 0.00023 | 98,8 | .. | 110,4 | .. | Июль |
| August | .. | .. | .. | .. | .. | .. | Август |
| September | .. | .. | .. | .. | .. | .. | Сентябрь |
| October | .. | .. | .. | .. | .. | .. | Октябрь |
| November | .. | .. | .. | .. | .. | .. | Ноябрь |
| December | .. | .. | .. | .. | .. | .. | Декабрь |

**TABLE 7-2. Monthly nominal wages by sector**

**ТАБЛИЦА 7-2. Среднемесячная денежная зарплата по отраслям**

| Sector | 1990 | 1991 | 1992 | 1993 | 1994 | 1995 | Сектора |
|---|---|---|---|---|---|---|---|
| **Nominal wages** | | | | | | | **Средняя номинальная заработная плата** |
| **Economy average** | 214.0 | 270.3 | 1,518.0 | 27,950.0 | 6,151,600.0 | 15.7 | **По народному хозяйству** |
| **Material sphere** | .. | .. | .. | .. | .. | .. | **Отрасли сферы материального производства** |
| Industry | 249.0 | 333.4 | 1,858.2 | 41,153.0 | 9,641,100.0 | 21.3 | Промышленность |
| Construction | 334.4 | 393.8 | 2,199.7 | 45,955.0 | 12,550,500.0 | 40.3 | Строительство |
| Agriculture | 196.4 | 204.6 | 876.5 | 15,665.0 | 1,357,700.0 | 4.2 | Сельское хозяйство |
| Transport | 215.4 | 306.3 | 1,400.6 | 52,287.0 | 9,317,200.0 | 22.6 | Транспорт |
| Communications | 186.1 | 294.5 | 1,751.5 | 36,397.0 | 6,541,100.0 | 25.9 | Связь |
| Trade (retail and wholesale) | 160.0 | 232.1 | 982.8 | 11,569.0 | 2,673,700.0 | 23.1 | Торговля (оптовая и розничная) |
| Other | 188.1 | 130.4 | 1,817.8 | 13,587.0 | 4,962,600.0 | 17.4 | Прочие отрасли материального производства |
| **Nonmaterial sphere** | .. | .. | .. | .. | .. | .. | **Отрасли непроизводственной сферы** |
| Municipal services | 168.2 | 211.9 | 1,366.2 | 27,872.0 | 28,756,600.0 | 20.4 | Жилкомхоз и бытовое обслуживание |
| Science, research and development | 236.5 | 291.7 | 1,471.7 | 23,401.0 | 1,792,100.0 | 9.5 | Наука и научное обслуживание |
| Education | 156.9 | 229.8 | 1,200.0 | 13,181.0 | 1,177,800.0 | 5.4 | Образование |
| Culture | 144.4 | 211.7 | 932.4 | 18,503.0 | 1,073,300.0 | 3.9 | Культура |
| Arts | 147.9 | 221.6 | 1,016.7 | 21,470.0 | 1,829,100.0 | 5.8 | Искусство |
| Health care, social security, and sports | 133.9 | 205.1 | 989.1 | 14,983.0 | 995,100.0 | 5.8 | Здравоохр., соц.обсл., физк. и спорт |
| Banking, finance, credit, insurance | 329.7 | 514.8 | 5,049.4 | 64,294.0 | 5,114,800.0 | 29.3 | Кредитование, страхование, банк. дело |
| Government | 255.9 | 317.8 | 4,596.6 | 24,944.0 | 2,853,800.0 | 8.5 | Управление |

**TABLE 8-1. Money income and expenditure of the population (millions of national currency)**
**ТАБЛИЦА 8-1. Денежные доходы и расходы населения (млн. национальной валюты)**

| Type of income or expenditure | 1990 | 1991 | 1992 | 1993 | 1994 | 1995 | Вид доходов или расходов |
|---|---|---|---|---|---|---|---|
| **Income** | | | | | | | **Доходы** |
| **Total labor income** | 9,397 | 13,075 | 57,436 | 1,691,000 | 127,016,803 | 457 | **Всего трудовых доходов** |
| Regular wages | 7,297 | 10,907 | 32,774 | 1,437,000 | 43,219,008 | 129 | Заработная плата |
| Wages paid by cooperatives | 887 | 984 | 1,548 | 111,000 | .. | .. | Заработная плата в кооперативах |
| Other wages and compensation | 236 | 424 | 1,601 | 77,000 | 5,386,752 | 18 | Прочие доходы типа заработной платы |
| Income paid by collective farms | 607 | 600 | 1,542 | 66,000 | 18,816 | 35 | Доходы от колхозов |
| Income from sale of farm products | 1,257 | 1,145 | 21,519 | 111,000 | 78,392,227 | 276 | Доходы от продажи продукции колхозов |
| **Total transfer receipts** | 2,734 | 3,507 | 17,972 | 520,000 | 141,803,626 | 230 | **Всего трансфертных поступлений** |
| Pensions and allowances | 1,291 | 1,834 | 9,877 | 447,000 | 6,779,136 | 42 | Пенсии и пособия |
| Scholarships | 45 | 88 | 355 | 8,000 | 115,584 | 2 | Стипендии |
| Income from the financial system (insurance, interest, etc.) | 803 | 913 | 5,330 | 50,000 | 1,598,016 | 3 | Доходы из финансовой системы (страховые возмещения, проценты и т.д.) |
| Other income | 595 | 672 | 2,410 | 15,000 | 133,310,890 | 183 | Прочие виды доходов |
| **Total income** | 12,131 | 16,583 | 75,408 | 2,211,000 | 268,820,429 | 687 | **Всего доходов** |
| **Expenditure** | | | | | | | **Расходы** |
| **Total purchases** | 7,848 | 10,460 | 25,633 | 1,150,000 | 216,124,439 | 419 | **Всего покупок товаров и услуг** |
| Retail goods | 6,922 | 9,307 | 21,603 | 982,000 | 192,851,635 | 372 | Товары в розничной торговле |
| Services | 926 | 1,153 | 4,030 | 168,000 | 23,272,804 | 47 | Услуги |
| Rent and utilities | 164 | 169 | 1,368 | 57,000 | 6,566,884 | 10 | Квартирная плата и коммунальные платежи |
| Transport and communications | 409 | 533 | 1,328 | 61,000 | 287,616 | 31 | Транспорт и связь |
| Health and other services | 289 | 349 | 1,322 | 49,000 | 16,418,304 | 5 | Здравоохранение и другие виды услуг |
| Cooperatives | 64 | 102 | 12 | 1,000 | .. | .. | Кооперативы |
| **Transfers and savings** | 3,081 | 3,461 | 30,268 | 308,000 | 33,746,494 | 194 | **Трансферты и сбережения** |
| Taxes, fees, dues, and other | 1,279 | 1,203 | 2,719 | 125,000 | 3,847,870 | 12 | Налоги, сборы, пошлины и др. |
| Savings | 1,750 | 2,258 | 27,309 | 182,000 | 29,898,624 | 95 | Сбережения |
| Other | 52 | .. | 240 | 1,000 | .. | 87 | Прочие |
| **Total expenditure** | 10,929 | 13,921 | 55,901 | 1,458,000 | 249,870,933 | 613 | **Всего расходов** |
| **Income less expenditure** | 1,203 | 2,662 | 19,507 | 753,000 | 18,949,496 | 74 | **Доходы за вычетом расходов** |

# *Country Notes: Georgia*

**General notes:** Unless otherwise indicated, the data were supplied by the State Department for Socio-Economic Information of Georgia.

**Currency:** In August 1993 Georgia introduced the coupon and in September of 1995 - the lary. The conversion factor for the new national currency at the time of introduction was 1 lary per 1,000,000 coupons. Unless otherwise indicated, data are in rubles up to 1992, in coupons for 1993 and 1994, and in lary for 1995.

**Table 1-1:** The population figure for 1995 is from the CIS Statistical Bulletin No. 13, 1996.

**Table 1-3:** Data reflect the total unemployed population rather than just those registered as unemployed.

**Table 2-1:** The sum of the subcategories within "Other" does not equal the total due to missing information. Data for 1995 are preliminary, and total GDP at market prices is calculated as equal to the total GDP by expenditure category. For 1994-1995, communication is included with transport, and retail trade is included with wholesale trade. For 1990-1992 the statistical discrepancy between total GDP by industrial origin at market prices and total GDP by expenditure category is as follows:

| Year | 1990 | 1991 | 1992 |
|---|---|---|---|
| Statistical discrepancy (mln. rubles) | -727 | -464 | -13255 |

**Table 5-2:** All data are in 1983 rubles.

**Table 6-2:** All data are in 1982 rubles.

**Table 7-1:** The Consumer Price Index has been calculated using prevailing prices in the capital city of Tbilisi only. For 1996, the nation-wide CPI is as follows:

| Month | CPI as % of the previous month | CPI as % of the previous December |
|---|---|---|
| January | 102.6 | 102.6 |
| February | 103.6 | 106.3 |
| March | 102.9 | 109.4 |
| April | 101.2 | 110.7 |
| May | 100.4 | 111.1 |
| June | 100.8 | 112.0 |
| July | 98.6 | 110.4 |

# *Комментарии к таблицам: Грузия*

**Общее замечание:** За исключением особо отмеченнных случаев, все данные, используемые в таблицах, были получены из Департамента социально-экономической информации республики Грузия.

**Национальная валюта:** В августе 1993 г. в Грузии были введены купоны, а в сентябре 1995 г. была введена новая национальная валюта - лари. Коэффициент пересчета на дату введения был 1 лари за 1.000.000 купонов. За исключением особо отмеченных случаев, данные приведены в рублях до 1992 г. включительно, в купонах за 1993-1994 гг., и в лари за 1995 г.

**Таблица 1-1:** За 1995 г. численность населения приводится из Статистического Бюллетеня СНГ № 13, 1996.

**Таблица 1-3:** Данные учитывают численность всех безработных, а не только лиц, имеющих установленный статус безработного.

**Таблица 2-1:** Сумма компонентов раздела Другие отрасли не совпадает с итогом вследствие отсутствия данных по некоторым отраслям. За 1995 г. приведены предварительные данные, и ВВП в рыночных ценах расчитан на основе ВВП по видам расходов. За 1994-1995 гг. транспорт включает также связь, а оптовая торговля включает также розничную торговлю и общепит. В 1990-1992 гг. статистическое расхождение между ВВП по производству в рыночных ценах и ВВП по видам расходов составляло:

| Год | 1990 | 1991 | 1992 |
|---|---|---|---|
| Статистическое расхождение (млн. рублей) | -727 | -46 4 | -13255 |

**Таблица 5-2:** Все данные в рублях, в ценах 1983 г.

**Таблица 6-2:** Все данные приведены в рублях, в ценах 1982 г.

**Таблица 7-1:** Индекс потребительских цен приводится по г. Тбилиси. Национальный индекс потребительских цен рассчитывается с 1996 г. и составляет:

| Месяц | ИПЦ % к предыдуоему месяцу | ИПЦ % к декабрю прошлого года |
|---|---|---|
| Январь | 102.6 | 102.6 |
| Февраль | 103.6 | 106.3 |
| Март | 102.9 | 109.4 |
| Апрель | 101.2 | 110.7 |
| Май | 100.4 | 111.1 |
| Июнь | 100.8 | 112.0 |
| Июль | 98.6 | 110.4 |

# Kazakstan / Казахстан

1996 Population / Численность населения в 1996 году
(thousands / тыс. человек): 16,544

Area / Территория
(thousand square kilometers / тыс. кв. км.): 2,717.3

Capital city / Столица:
Almaty / Алматы

**Country Tables: :** Tables 3-2B, 3-3B and 3-4B are not included because there are no data available.

**Статистические таблицы страны:** Таблицы с 3-2B, 3-3B и 3-4B не включены ввиду отсутствия данных.

## TABLE 1-1. Population and employment (thousands)
## ТАБЛИЦА 1-1. Население и занятость (тысяч)

| Population or employment category | 1990 | 1991 | 1992 | 1993 | 1994 | 1995 | Население или группы занятых |
|---|---|---|---|---|---|---|---|
| **Total population** | 16,618 | 16,721 | 16,892 | 16,913 | 16,870 | 16,607 | **Население - всего** |
| Males | 8,057 | 8,116 | 8,204 | 8,218 | 8,199 | 8,068 | Мужчины |
| Females | 8,561 | 8,605 | 8,688 | 8,695 | 8,671 | 8,539 | Женщины |
| Urban population | 9,523 | 9,606 | 9,713 | 9,655 | 9,491 | 9,270 | Городское |
| Rural population | 7,095 | 7,115 | 7,179 | 7,258 | 7,379 | 7,337 | Сельское |
| Population under working age | 5,573 | 5,559 | 5,574 | 5,533 | 5,467 | 5,334 | Моложе трудоспособного возраста |
| Working-age population | 9,175 | 9,226 | 9,335 | 9,356 | 9,359 | 9,231 | Лица в трудоспособном возрасте |
| Population over working age | 1,870 | 1,936 | 1,983 | 2,024 | 2,044 | 2,042 | Старще трудоспособного возраста |
| Economically Active Population, in non-working age | 230 | 229 | 230 | 265 | 217 | 170 | Экономически активное население в нетрудоспособном возрасте |
| Above working age | 218 | 218 | 219 | 244 | 203 | 161 | Старше трудоспособного возраста |
| Below working age | 12 | 11 | 11 | 21 | 14 | 9 | Моложе трудоспособного возраста |
| **Total labor resources** | 9,262 | 9,331 | 9,368 | 9,380 | 9,240 | 9,153 | **Трудовые ресурсы - всего** |
| **Total employment** | 7,563 | 7,494 | 7,356 | 6,926 | 6,579 | 6,548 | **Занятое население - всего** |
| State sector employees | 5,912 | 5,686 | 5,231 | 4,486 | 3,415 | 3,039 | Государственный сектор |
| Leased enterprise employees | 484 | 673 | 344 | 168 | .. | .. | Арендные предприятия |
| Joint-stock company employees | 8 | 15 | 251 | 508 | .. | .. | Акционерные общества |
| Economic association employees | 121 | 127 | 12 | .. | .. | .. | Хозяйственные ассоциации |
| Social organization employees | 37 | 52 | 33 | 25 | .. | .. | Общественные организации |
| Joint venture employees | .. | 7 | 7 | 13 | 23 | 25 | Совместные предприятия |
| Collective farm workers | 260 | 258 | 268 | 247 | .. | .. | Колхозы |
| Cooperative workers | 241 | 185 | 98 | 43 | 344 | 159 | Кооперативы |
| Individual labor activities | 12 | 16 | 24 | 12 | 541 | 1,069 | ИТД |
| Private subsidiary agricultural workers | 275 | 310 | 337 | 349 | .. | .. | Личные подсобные хозяйства |
| Private agricultural workers | 1 | 5 | 39 | 49 | 69 | 102 | Фермерские хозяйства |
| **Students** | 759 | 763 | 734 | 701 | 671 | 625 | **Учащиеся** |
| **Religious workers** | .. | .. | 2 | 2 | 3 | 3 | **Служащие религиозного культа** |
| **Working age population not employed in the national economy** | 940 | 1,074 | 1,064 | 1,715 | 1,988 | 1,976 | **Лица в трудоспособном возрасте, не занятые в экономике** |
| Housewives | .. | .. | .. | .. | .. | .. | Домохозяйки |
| Military personnel | .. | .. | .. | .. | .. | .. | Военнослужащие |
| Unemployed | .. | 4 | 34 | 37 | 536 | 808 | Безработные |
| **Labor force** | .. | 7,498 | 7,390 | 6,963 | 7,118 | 7,359 | **Рабочая сила** |

## TABLE 1-2. Employment by sector (thousands)
## ТАБЛИЦА 1-2. Численность занятого населения по секторам (тысяч)

| Sector | 1990 | 1991 | 1992 | 1993 | 1994 | 1995 | Сектор |
|---|---|---|---|---|---|---|---|
| **Material sphere** | 5,405 | 5,307 | 5,187 | 4,752 | 4,673 | 4,687 | **Сфера материального производства** |
| **Agriculture and forestry** | 1,726 | 1,754 | 1,794 | 1,759 | 1,417 | 1,442 | **Сельское и лесное хозяйство** |
| Agriculture | 1,713 | 1,740 | 1,781 | 1,746 | 1,406 | 1,432 | Сельское хозяйство |
| Forestry | 14 | 14 | 13 | 13 | 11 | 10 | Лесное хозяйство |
| **Industry and construction** | 2,447 | 2,304 | 2,230 | 1,925 | 1,683 | 1,452 | **Промышленность и строительство** |
| Industry | 1,539 | 1,533 | 1,490 | 1,305 | 1,201 | 1,088 | Промышленность |
| Construction | 908 | 771 | 740 | 620 | 482 | 364 | Строительство |
| **Other** | 1,232 | 1,249 | 1,163 | 1,068 | 1,573 | 1,793 | **Другие отрасли** |
| Transport of goods | 510 | 508 | 484 | 448 | 424 | 390 | Грузовой транспорт |
| Road Maintenance | .. | .. | .. | 0 | .. | .. | Дорожное хозяйство |
| Communication servicing material production | .. | .. | .. | 0 | .. | .. | Связь |
| Wholesale trade | 561 | 551 | 533 | 482 | 847 | 1,035 | Оптовая торговля |
| Retail trade and catering | .. | .. | .. | 0 | .. | .. | Розничная торговля и общепит |
| Material supply | .. | .. | .. | 0 | .. | .. | Материально-техническое снабжение |
| Procurement | .. | .. | .. | 0 | .. | .. | Заготовки |
| Information and computing services | 21 | 20 | 14 | 11 | 10 | 6 | Информационно-техническое обслуживание |
| Other sectors | 140 | 170 | 132 | 127 | 292 | 362 | Другие отрасли сферы материального пр. |
| **Nonmaterial sphere** | 2,158 | 2,187 | 2,169 | 2,174 | 1,909 | 1,864 | **Сфера нематериального производства** |
| Passenger transport | 194 | 192 | 180 | 136 | 127 | 117 | Пассажирский транспорт |
| Communication | .. | .. | .. | 0 | .. | .. | Связь |
| Housing | 292 | 289 | 283 | 283 | 270 | 275 | Жилищное хозяйство |
| Public utilities and personal services | .. | .. | .. | 0 | .. | .. | Комм. хоз. и бытовое обслуживание |
| Health care, social security, physical culture and sports | 456 | 465 | 481 | 429 | 428 | 417 | Здравоохранение, социальное обеспечение, физкультура и спорт |
| Education | 1,022 | 1,036 | 871 | 837 | 826 | 818 | Образование |
| Culture and art | .. | .. | .. | 0 | .. | .. | Культура и искусство |
| Science and scientific research | .. | .. | 124 | 79 | .. | .. | Наука и научное обслуживание |
| Credit | 39 | 42 | 46 | 54 | 49 | 50 | Кредитование |
| Insurance | .. | .. | .. | 0 | .. | .. | Страхование |
| General administration and defense | 155 | 163 | 184 | 132 | 144 | 148 | Государственное управление и оборона |
| Private nonprofit institutions serving households | .. | .. | .. | .. | .. | .. | Общественные организации, обслуживающие домашние хозяйства |
| **Other, material and nonmaterial spheres** | 3,390 | 3,436 | 3,332 | 3,242 | 3,482 | 3,657 | **Остальные отрасли материального производства и нематериальной сферы** |
| **Total employment** | 7,563 | 7,494 | 7,356 | 6,926 | 6,582 | 6,551 | **Занятые - всего** |

## TABLE 1-3. Registered unemployment (thousands; end of month) KAZAKSTAN

## ТАБЛИЦА 1-3. Численность зарегистрированных безработных (тысяч; на конец месяца)

| Year and month | Total Всего | Males Мужчины | Females Женщины | Receiving benefits Получающие пособие | Год и месяц |
|---|---|---|---|---|---|
| **1994** | | | | | **1994** |
| January | 42.9 | .. | .. | 16.0 | Январь |
| February | 46.7 | .. | .. | 17.8 | Февраль |
| March | 48.1 | 17.5 | 30.6 | 18.5 | Март |
| April | 50.8 | .. | .. | 20.8 | Апрель |
| May | 51.1 | .. | .. | 21.0 | Май |
| June | 52.2 | 18.7 | 33.5 | 21.8 | Июнь |
| July | 53.6 | .. | .. | 23.5 | Июль |
| August | 56.2 | .. | .. | 25.2 | Август |
| September | 60.0 | 20.5 | 39.5 | 26.7 | Сентябрь |
| October | 62.5 | .. | .. | 27.6 | Октябрь |
| November | 66.7 | .. | .. | 29.8 | Ноябрь |
| December | 70.1 | 24.7 | 45.4 | 33.2 | Декабрь |
| **1995** | | | | | **1995** |
| January | 75.4 | .. | .. | 36.0 | Январь |
| February | 82.8 | .. | .. | 41.6 | Февраль |
| March | 85.7 | 32.9 | 52.8 | 44.6 | Март |
| April | 90.3 | .. | .. | 48.3 | Апрель |
| May | 92.5 | .. | .. | 49.2 | Май |
| June | 95.8 | 36.9 | 58.9 | 49.4 | Июнь |
| July | 98.3 | .. | .. | 52.3 | Июль |
| August | 103.1 | .. | .. | 54.0 | Август |
| September | 108.4 | 42.3 | 66.1 | 56.1 | Сентябрь |
| October | 116.1 | .. | .. | 58.9 | Октябрь |
| November | 127.8 | .. | .. | 65.0 | Ноябрь |
| December | 139.6 | 55.7 | 83.9 | 73.5 | Декабрь |
| **1996** | | | | | **1996** |
| January | 157.7 | .. | .. | 84.8 | Январь |
| February | 186.5 | .. | .. | 102.9 | Февраль |
| March | 205.7 | 84.7 | 121.0 | 116.7 | Март |
| April | 225.9 | .. | .. | 134.2 | Апрель |
| May | 235.9 | .. | .. | 140.6 | Май |
| June | 244.4 | 98.5 | 145.9 | 148.0 | Июнь |
| July | 255.8 | .. | .. | 154.6 | Июль |
| August | 264.7 | .. | .. | 156.3 | Август |
| September | .. | .. | .. | .. | Сентябрь |
| October | .. | .. | .. | .. | Октябрь |
| November | .. | .. | .. | .. | Ноябрь |
| December | .. | .. | .. | .. | Декабрь |

**TABLE 2-1. Gross domestic product at current prices (millions of national currency)**
**ТАБЛИЦА 2-1. Валовой внутренний продукт в текущих ценах (млн. национальной валюты)**

| Sector of origin or expenditure category | 1990 | 1991 | 1992 | 1993 | 1994 | 1995 | Отраслевое происхождение или вид расходов |
|---|---|---|---|---|---|---|---|
| **Gross domestic product by sector of origin** | | | | | | | **Валовой внутренний продукт по отраслевому происхождению** |
| **Agriculture and forestry** | 16,286 | 25,304 | 281,266 | 4,835 | 63,155 | 124,349 | **Сельское и лесное хозяйство** |
| Agriculture | 16,246 | 25,235 | 280,743 | 4,816 | 62,895 | 123,830 | Сельское хозяйство |
| Forestry | 40 | 69 | 524 | 19 | 261 | 519 | Лесное хозяйство |
| **Industry and construction** | 15,471 | 32,316 | 469,768 | 11,595 | 169,188 | 301,192 | **Промышленность и строительство** |
| Industry | 9,821 | 23,323 | 375,704 | 8,444 | 123,278 | 238,733 | Промышленность |
| Construction | 5,649 | 8,993 | 94,063 | 3,151 | 45,911 | 62,459 | Строительство |
| **Other** | 15,483 | 32,337 | 451,147 | 13,564 | 193,023 | 544,149 | **Другие отрасли** |
| Transport | 4,113 | 5,868 | 85,004 | 2,741 | 43,280 | 95,000 | Транспорт |
| Road maintenance | .. | .. | .. | .. | .. | .. | Дорожное хозяйство |
| Communication | 378 | 551 | 5,605 | 196 | 4,003 | 13,203 | Связь |
| Wholesale trade | 2,979 | 5,357 | 62,910 | 2,318 | 42,523 | 164,481 | Оптовая торговля |
| Retail trade and catering | .. | .. | .. | .. | .. | .. | Розничная торговля и общепит |
| Material supply | 444 | 1,020 | 29,078 | 484 | 5,016 | 6,917 | Материально-техническое снабжение |
| Procurement | 488 | 594 | 11,177 | 248 | 3,857 | 3,245 | Заготовки |
| Information and computing services | 99 | 136 | 784 | 31 | 272 | 967 | Информационно-вычислительное обслуживание |
| Other sectors of material production | 742 | 1,281 | 37,428 | 823 | 12,027 | 49,488 | Другие отрасли сферы материального пр. |
| Housing | 826 | 1,761 | 25,583 | 782 | 20,263 | 55,996 | Жилищное хозяйство |
| Public utilities and personal services | 1,128 | 3,402 | 48,402 | 1,069 | 19,600 | 46,326 | Ком. хоз. и бытовое обслуживание |
| Health care, social security, physical culture and sports | 328 | 2,762 | 18,997 | 892 | 6,685 | 22,780 | Здравоохранение, социальное обеспечение, физкультура и спорт |
| Education | 2,033 | 4,241 | 31,382 | 1,273 | 14,062 | 40,923 | Образование |
| Culture and art | 334 | 598 | 3,600 | 153 | 4,827 | 11,837 | Культура и искусство |
| Science and scientific research | 336 | 341 | 7,677 | 287 | 1,364 | 3,231 | Наука и научное обслуживание |
| Credit | 506 | 2,740 | 54,086 | 1,563 | 8,555 | ... | Кредитование |
| Insurance | .. | .. | .. | .. | .. | .. | Страхование |
| General administration and defense | 476 | 1,109 | 12,692 | 581 | 6,531 | 23,794 | Государственное управление и оборона |
| Private nonprofit institutions serving households | 273 | 577 | 16,741 | 124 | 159 | 997 | Общественные организации, обслуживающие домашние хозяйства |
| **Imputed service charge of financial intermediaries** | -425 | -2,163 | -51,808 | -1,666 | -10,410 | .. | **Условно-исчисляемая стоимость услуг финансовых посредников** |
| **Total gross value added (GVA)** | 46,815 | 87,795 | 1,150,373 | 28,328 | 414,957 | 969,690 | **Валовая добавленная стоимость (ВДС) - всего** |
| **Taxes on production and imports (TOPI)** | 4,962 | 5,983 | 82,197 | 2,146 | 21,442 | .. | **Налоги на производство и импорт (НПиИ)** |
| Other taxes on production (OTOP) | .. | .. | .. | .. | .. | .. | Другие налоги на производство (ДНП) |
| **Subsidies on production and imports (SOPI)** | 5,104 | 6,554 | 26,622 | 593 | 7,603 | .. | **Субсидии на производство и импорт (СПиИ)** |
| Other subsidies on production (OSOP) | .. | .. | .. | .. | .. | .. | Другие субсидии на производство (ДСП) |
| **Total GDP at factor cost (GVA-OTOP+OSOP)** | 46,815 | 87,795 | 1,150,373 | 28,328 | 414,957 | 969,690 | **Всего ВВП по фактр. стоимости (ВДС-ДНП+ДСП)** |
| **Net Indirect taxes (TOPI - SOPI)** | -142 | -571 | 55,575 | 1,553 | 13,839 | 50,032 | **Чистые косвенные налоги (НПиИ-СПиИ)** |
| **Total GDP at market prices** | 46,673 | 87,224 | 1,205,948 | 29,881 | 428,795 | 1,019,722 | **Всего ВВП в рыночных ценах** |
| **Gross domestic product by expenditure category** | | | | | | | **Валовой внутренний продукт по видам расходов** |
| **Consumption** | 34,429 | 72,146 | 779,368 | 24,013 | 389,911 | 773,494 | **Потребление** |
| Private consumption | 28,048 | 58,886 | 652,458 | 19,174 | 335,908 | 742,178 | Личное потребление |
| Government consumption | 6,381 | 13,259 | 126,911 | 4,840 | 54,003 | 31,316 | Общественное потребление |
| **Gross domestic investment** | 22,459 | 19,964 | 379,921 | 8,306 | 96,243 | 241,994 | **Валовые внутренние инвестиции** |
| Gross fixed investment | 18,767 | 26,257 | 367,174 | 9,498 | 85,345 | 186,995 | Валовое накопление основного капитала |
| Change in stocks | 3,692 | -6,294 | 12,747 | -1,191 | 10,898 | 54,999 | Изменения в запасах (МОС) |
| **Resource balance (net exports of GNFS)** | -10,872 | -10,349 | -16,077 | -1,935 | -43,620 | -22,985 | **Сальдо ресурсов (чистый экспорт ТНФУ)** |
| Exports of goods and nonfactor services | 3,712 | 24,462 | 892,512 | 10,950 | 137,353 | 355,560 | Экспорт товаров и нефакторных услуг |
| Imports of goods and nonfactor services | 14,584 | 34,811 | 908,589 | 12,885 | 180,973 | 378,545 | Импорт товаров и нефакторных услуг |

**TABLE 2-1A. Distribution of gross domestic product at current prices (percent)**
**ТАБЛИЦА 2-1А. Распределение валового внутреннего продукта в текущих ценах ( % )**

| Sector of origin or expenditure category | 1990 | 1991 | 1992 | 1993 | 1994 | 1995 | Отраслевое происхождение или вид расходов |
|---|---|---|---|---|---|---|---|
| **Gross domestic product by sector of origin** | | | | | | | **ВВП по отраслевому происхождению** |
| **Agriculture and forestry** | 34.9 | 29.0 | 23.3 | 16.2 | 14.7 | 12.2 | **Сельское и лесное хозяйство** |
| Agriculture | 34.8 | 28.9 | 23.3 | 16.1 | 14.7 | 12.1 | Сельское хозяйство |
| Forestry | 0.1 | 0.1 | 0.0 | 0.1 | 0.1 | 0.1 | Лесное хозяйство |
| **Industry and construction** | 33.1 | 37.0 | 39.0 | 38.8 | 39.5 | 29.5 | **Промышленность и строительство** |
| Industry | 21.0 | 26.7 | 31.2 | 28.3 | 28.7 | 23.4 | Промышленность |
| Construction | 12.1 | 10.3 | 7.8 | 10.5 | 10.7 | 6.1 | Строительство |
| **Other** | 33.2 | 37.1 | 37.4 | 45.4 | 45.0 | .. | **Другие отрасли** |
| Transport | 8.8 | 6.7 | 7.0 | 9.2 | 10.1 | 9.3 | Транспорт |
| Road maintenance | .. | .. | .. | .. | .. | .. | Дорожное хозяйство |
| Communication | 0.8 | 0.6 | 0.5 | 0.7 | 0.9 | 1.3 | Связь |
| Wholesale trade | 6.4 | 6.1 | 5.2 | 7.8 | 9.9 | 16.1 | Оптовая торговля |
| Retail trade and catering | .. | .. | .. | .. | .. | .. | Розничная торговля и общепит |
| Material supply | 1.0 | 1.2 | 2.4 | 1.6 | 1.2 | 0.7 | Материально-техническое снабжение |
| Procurement | 1.0 | 0.7 | 0.9 | 0.8 | 0.9 | 0.3 | Заготовки |
| Information and computing services | 0.2 | 0.2 | 0.1 | 0.1 | 0.1 | 0.1 | Информационно-вычислительное обслуживание |
| Other sectors of material production | 1.6 | 1.5 | 3.1 | 2.8 | 2.8 | 4.9 | Другие отрасли сферы матерл. произ. |
| Housing | 1.8 | 2.0 | 2.1 | 2.6 | 4.7 | 5.5 | Жилищное хозяйство |
| Public utilities and personal services | 2.4 | 3.9 | 4.0 | 3.6 | 4.6 | 4.5 | Ком. хоз. и бытовое обслуживание |
| Health care, social security, physical culture and sports | 0.7 | 3.2 | 1.6 | 3.0 | 1.6 | 2.2 | Здравоохранение, социальное обеспечение, физкультура и спорт |
| Education | 4.4 | 4.9 | 2.6 | 4.3 | 3.3 | 4.0 | Образование |
| Culture and art | 0.7 | 0.7 | 0.3 | 0.5 | 1.1 | 1.2 | Культура и искусство |
| Science and scientific research | 0.7 | 0.4 | 0.6 | 1.0 | 0.3 | 0.3 | Наука и научное обслуживание |
| Credit | 1.1 | 3.1 | 4.5 | 5.2 | 2.0 | .. | Кредитование |
| Insurance | .. | .. | .. | .. | .. | .. | Страхование |
| General administration and defense | 1.0 | 1.3 | 1.1 | 1.9 | 1.5 | 2.3 | Государственное управление и оборона |
| Private nonprofit institutions serving households | 0.6 | 0.7 | 1.4 | 0.4 | 0.0 | 0.1 | Общественные организации, обслуживающие домашние хозяйства |
| **Imputed service charge of financial intermediaries** | -0.9 | -2.5 | -4.3 | -5.6 | -2.4 | .. | **Условно-исчисляемая стоимость услуг финансовых посредников** |
| **Total gross value added** | 100.3 | 100.7 | 95.4 | 94.8 | 96.8 | 95.1 | **Валовая добавленная стоимость - всего** |
| **Total GDP at factor cost** | 100.3 | 100.7 | 95.4 | 94.8 | 96.8 | 95.1 | **ВВП по фактор. стоимости - всего** |
| **Net indirect taxes** | -0.3 | -0.7 | 4.6 | 5.2 | 3.2 | 4.9 | **Чистые косвенные налоги (НПиИ-СПиИ)** |
| **Total GDP at market prices** | 100.0 | 100.0 | 100.0 | 100.0 | 100.0 | 100.0 | **ВВП в рын. ценах - всего** |
| **Gross domestic product by expenditure category** | | | | | | | **ВВП по видам расходов** |
| **Consumption** | 73.8 | 82.7 | 64.6 | 80.4 | 90.9 | 75.9 | **Потребление** |
| Private consumption | 60.1 | 67.5 | 54.1 | 64.2 | 78.3 | 72.8 | Личное потребление |
| Government consumption | 13.7 | 15.2 | 10.5 | 16.2 | 12.6 | 3.1 | Общественное потребление |
| **Gross domestic investment** | 48.1 | 22.9 | 31.5 | 27.8 | 22.4 | 23.7 | **Вал. внутр. инвестиции** |
| Gross fixed investment | 40.2 | 30.1 | 30.4 | 31.8 | 19.9 | 18.3 | Вал. накопление осн. капитала |
| Change in stocks | 7.9 | -7.2 | 1.1 | -4.0 | 2.5 | 5.4 | Изменения в запасах (МОС) |
| **Resource balance (net exports of GNFS)** | -23.3 | -11.9 | -1.3 | -6.5 | -10.2 | -2.3 | **Сальдо ресурсов (чистый экспорт ТНФУ)** |
| Exports of goods and nonfactor services | 8.0 | 28.0 | 74.0 | 36.6 | 32.0 | 34.9 | Экспорт товаров и нефакторных услуг |
| Imports of goods and nonfactor services | 31.2 | 39.9 | 75.3 | 43.1 | 42.2 | 37.1 | Импорт товаров и нефакторных услуг |

# TABLE 2-2. Gross domestic product at constant prices (millions of national currency)
# ТАБЛИЦА 2-2. Валовой внутренний продукт в постоянных ценах (млн. национальной валюты)

| Sector of origin or expenditure category | 1990 | 1991 | 1992 | 1993 | 1994 | 1995 | Отраслевое происхождение или вид расходов |
|---|---|---|---|---|---|---|---|
| **Gross domestic product by sector of origin** | | | | | | | **Валовой внутренний продукт по отраслевому происхождению** |
| **Agriculture and forestry** | .. | 12,599 | 32,568 | 261,903 | 3,811 | 47,548 | **Сельское и лесное хозяйство** |
| Agriculture | .. | 12,558 | 32,503 | 261,371 | 3,795 | .. | Сельское хозяйство |
| Forestry | .. | 40 | 65 | 532 | 16 | .. | Лесное хозяйство |
| **Industry and construction** | .. | 15,397 | 24,487 | 399,673 | 8,696 | 141,734 | **Промышленность и строительство** |
| Industry | .. | 9,861 | 19,343 | 323,106 | 6,122 | 113,169 | Промышленность |
| Construction | .. | 5,536 | 5,144 | 76,567 | 2,575 | 28,565 | Строительство |
| **Other** | .. | 15,407 | 30,300 | 445,303 | 12,195 | .. | **Другие отрасли** |
| Transport | .. | 3,856 | 4,730 | 72,202 | 1,968 | 37,567 | Транспорт |
| Road maintenance | .. | .. | .. | .. | .. | .. | Дорожное хозяйство |
| Communication | .. | 379 | 509 | 5,380 | 195 | 3,810 | Связь |
| Wholesale trade | .. | 2,941 | 4,423 | 58,915 | 1,915 | 75,414 | Оптовая торговля |
| Retail trade and catering | .. | .. | .. | .. | .. | .. | Розничная торговля и общепит |
| Material supply | .. | 447 | 879 | 23,611 | 346 | .. | Материально-техническое снабжение |
| Procurement | .. | 423 | 606 | 7,042 | 216 | .. | Заготовки |
| Information and computing services | .. | 93 | 97 | 557 | 26 | 223 | Информационно-вычислительное обслуживание |
| Other sectors of material production | .. | 817 | 1,186 | 54,531 | 1,135 | .. | Другие отрасли сферы материального пр. |
| Housing | .. | 846 | 1,779 | 25,687 | 796 | 20,080 | Жилищное хозяйство |
| Public utilities and personal services | .. | 1,148 | 3,444 | 46,076 | 1,025 | 21,828 | Ком. хоз. и бытовое обслуживание |
| Health care, social security, and sports | .. | 313 | 2,880 | 18,023 | 850 | 6,494 | Здравоохранение, социальное обеспечение, физкультура и спорт |
| Education | .. | 2,112 | 4,179 | 30,422 | 1,211 | 13,823 | Образование |
| Culture and art | .. | 327 | 515 | 3,431 | 135 | 4,735 | Культура и искусство |
| Science and research | .. | 319 | 287 | 6,697 | 144 | 1,315 | Наука и научное обслуживание |
| Credit | .. | 544 | 2,981 | 61,897 | 1,461 | .. | Кредитование |
| Insurance | .. | .. | .. | .. | .. | .. | Страхование |
| General administration and defense | .. | 536 | 1,227 | 13,255 | 636 | 6,597 | Государственное управление и оборона |
| Private nonprofit institutions serving households | .. | 306 | 577 | 17,578 | 135 | 143 | Общественные организации, обслуживающие домашние хозяйства |
| **Imputed service charge of financial intermediaries** | .. | -428 | -2,687 | -67,138 | -1,466 | .. | **Условно-исчисляемая стоимость услуг финансовых посредников** |
| **Total gross value added (GVA)** | .. | 42,975 | 84,668 | 1,039,742 | 23,236 | 397,882 | **Валовая добавленная стоимость (ВДС) -** |
| **Total GDP at factor cost (GVA-OTOP+OSOP)** | .. | 42,975 | 84,668 | 1,039,742 | 23,236 | 397,882 | **Всего ВВП по фактр. стоимости (ВДС-ДНП+ДСП)** |
| **Net indirect taxes (TOPI - SOPI)** | .. | -130 | -551 | 50,230 | 1,274 | 12,012 | **Чистые косвенные налоги (НПиИ-СПиИ)** |
| **Total GDP at market prices** | .. | 42,844 | 84,117 | 1,089,972 | 24,511 | 409,894 | **Всего ВВП в рыночных ценах** |
| **Gross domestic product by expenditure category** | | | | | | | **Валовой внутренний продукт по видам расходов** |
| **Consumption** | .. | 37,212 | 63,644 | 741,932 | 20,782 | 281,509 | **Потребление** |
| Private consumption | .. | 30,712 | 51,027 | 618,548 | 16,128 | 269,910 | Личное потребление |
| Government consumption | .. | 6,500 | 12,616 | 123,384 | 4,655 | 11,599 | Общественное потребление |
| **Gross domestic investment** | .. | 11,086 | 19,139 | 275,564 | 7,044 | 86,347 | **Валовые внутренние инвестиции** |
| Gross fixed investment | .. | 13,841 | 18,368 | 330,096 | 6,475 | 63,431 | Валовое накопление основного капитала |
| Change in stocks | .. | -2,754 | 771 | -54,531 | 569 | 22,916 | Изменения в запасах (МОС) |
| **Resource balance (net exports of GNFS)** | .. | -6,000 | -4,174 | 21,434 | -3,294 | 20,692 | **Сальдо ресурсов (чистый экспорт ТНФУ)** |
| Exports of goods and nonfactor services | .. | 3,378 | 20,608 | 820,628 | 9,295 | 157,746 | Экспорт товаров и нефакторных услуг |
| Imports of goods and nonfactor services | .. | 9,378 | 24,782 | 799,195 | 12,590 | 137,055 | Импорт товаров и нефакторных услуг |

## TABLE 2-2A. Growth rates of gross domestic product at constant prices (percent)
## ТАБЛИЦА 2-2А. Валовой внутренний продукт - темпы прироста в постоянных ценах ( % )

| Sector of origin or expenditure category | 1990 | 1991 | 1992 | 1993 | 1994 | 1995 | Отраслевое происхождение или вид расходов |
|---|---|---|---|---|---|---|---|
| **Growth rate by sector of origin** | | | | | | | **Валовый внутренний продукт по отраслевому происхождению** |
| **Agriculture and forestry** | .. | -22.6 | 28.7 | -6.9 | -21.2 | -24.7 | **Сельское и лесное хозяйство** |
| Agriculture | .. | -22.7 | 28.8 | -6.9 | -21.2 | .. | Сельское хозяйство |
| Forestry | .. | 1.5 | -5.9 | 1.6 | -13.8 | .. | Лесное хозяйство |
| **Industry and construction** | .. | -0.5 | -24.2 | -14.9 | -25.0 | -16.2 | **Промышленность и строительство** |
| Industry | .. | 0.4 | -17.1 | -14.0 | -27.5 | -8.2 | Промышленность |
| Construction | .. | -2.0 | -42.8 | -18.6 | -18.3 | -37.8 | Строительство |
| **Other** | .. | -0.5 | -6.3 | -1.3 | -10.1 | .. | **Другие отрасли** |
| Transport | .. | -6.2 | -19.4 | -15.1 | -28.2 | -13.2 | Транспорт |
| Road maintenance | .. | .. | .. | .. | .. | .. | Дорожное хозяйство |
| Communication | .. | 0.2 | -7.5 | -4.0 | -0.2 | -4.8 | Связь |
| Wholesale trade | .. | -1.3 | -17.4 | -6.3 | -17.4 | 46.7 | Оптовая торговля |
| Retail trade and catering | .. | .. | .. | .. | .. | .. | Розничная торговля и общепит |
| Material supply | .. | 0.7 | -13.8 | -18.8 | -28.5 | .. | Материально-техническое снабжение |
| Procurement | .. | -13.4 | 2.0 | -37.0 | -13.0 | .. | Заготовки |
| Information and computing services | .. | -6.7 | -28.9 | -29.0 | -17.3 | -17.9 | Информационно-вычислительное обслуживание |
| Other sectors of material production | .. | 10.1 | -7.5 | 45.7 | 38.0 | .. | Другие отрасли сферы материального пр. |
| Housing | .. | 2.4 | 1.1 | 0.4 | 1.8 | -0.9 | Жилищное хозяйство |
| Public utilities and personal services | .. | 1.8 | 1.3 | -4.8 | -4.1 | 11.4 | Ком. хоз. и бытовое обслуживание |
| Health care, social security, and sports | .. | -4.5 | 4.3 | -5.1 | -4.7 | -2.8 | Здравоохранение, социальное обеспечение, физкультура и спорт |
| Education | .. | 3.9 | -1.5 | -3.1 | -4.8 | -1.7 | Образование |
| Culture and art | .. | .. | .. | .. | .. | .. | Культура и искусство |
| Science and research | .. | -4.8 | -15.7 | -12.8 | -49.8 | -3.6 | Наука и научное обслуживание |
| Credit | .. | 7.4 | 8.8 | 14.4 | -6.5 | .. | Кредитование |
| Insurance | .. | .. | .. | .. | .. | .. | Страхование |
| General administration and defense | .. | 12.6 | 10.6 | 4.4 | 9.6 | 1.0 | Государственное управление и оборона |
| Private nonprofit institutions serving households | .. | 11.9 | 0.0 | 5.0 | 9.0 | .. | Общественные организации, обслуживающие домашние хозяйства |
| **Imputed service charge of financial intermediaries** | .. | 0.7 | 24.2 | 29.6 | -12.0 | .. | **Условно-исчисляемая стоимость услуг финансовых посредников** |
| **Total gross value added** | .. | -8.2 | -3.6 | -9.6 | -18.0 | -4.1 | **Валовая добавленная стоимость (ВДС) - всего** |
| **Total GDP at factor cost** | .. | -8.2 | -3.6 | -9.6 | -18.0 | -4.1 | **Всего ВВП по фактр. стоимости (ВДС-ДНП+ДСП)** |
| **Net indirect taxes** | .. | -8.2 | -3.6 | -9.6 | -18.0 | -13.2 | **Чистые косвенные налоги (НПиИ-СПиИ)** |
| **Total GDP at market prices** | .. | -8.2 | -3.6 | -9.6 | -18.0 | -4.4 | **Всего ВВП в рыночных ценах** |
| **Growth rate by expenditure category** | | | | | | | **Валовой внутренний продукт по видам расходов** |
| **Consumption** | .. | 8.1 | -11.8 | -4.8 | -13.5 | -27.8 | **Потребление** |
| Private consumption | .. | 9.5 | -13.3 | -5.2 | -15.9 | -19.6 | Личное потребление |
| Government consumption | .. | 1.9 | -4.8 | -2.8 | -3.8 | -78.5 | Общественное потребление |
| **Gross domestic investment** | .. | -50.6 | -4.1 | -27.5 | -15.2 | -10.3 | **Валовые внутренние инвестиции** |
| Gross fixed investment | .. | -26.2 | -30.0 | -10.1 | -31.8 | -25.7 | Валовое накопление основного капитала |
| **Exports of goods and nonfactor services** | .. | -9.0 | -15.8 | -8.1 | -15.1 | .. | **Экспорт товаров и нефакторных услуг** |
| **Imports of goods and nonfactor services** | .. | -35.7 | -28.8 | -12.0 | -2.3 | .. | **Импорт товаров и нефакторных услуг** |

**TABLE 2-2B. Implicit price deflators for gross domestic product (percentage change)**
**ТАБЛИЦА 2-2B. Дефляторы валового внутреннего продукта (темпы прироста в %)**

| Sector of origin or expenditure category | 1990 | 1991 | 1992 | 1993 | 1994 | 1995 | Отраслевое происхождение или вид расходов |
|---|---|---|---|---|---|---|---|
| **Price deflators by sector of origin** | | | | | | | **Дефляторы по отраслевому происхождению или виду расходов** |
| **Agriculture and forestry** | .. | 100.8 | 763.6 | 823.1 | 1,557.0 | 161.5 | **Сельское и лесное хозяйство** |
| Agriculture | .. | 100.9 | 763.7 | 821.3 | 1,557.3 | .. | Сельское хозяйство |
| Forestry | .. | 69.6 | 709.8 | 1,678.9 | 1,498.7 | .. | Лесное хозяйство |
| **Industry and construction** | .. | 109.9 | 1,818.4 | 1,350.5 | 1,845.6 | 112.5 | **Промышленность и строительство** |
| Industry | .. | 136.5 | 1,842.3 | 1,206.6 | 1,913.8 | 111.0 | Промышленность |
| Construction | .. | 62.4 | 1,728.6 | 1,957.8 | 1,683.3 | 118.7 | Строительство |
| **Other** | .. | 109.9 | 1,388.9 | 1,423.0 | 1,482.9 | .. | **Другие отрасли** |
| Transport | .. | 52.2 | 1,697.3 | 1,798.1 | 2,099.5 | 152.9 | Транспорт |
| Road maintenance | .. | .. | .. | .. | .. | .. | Дорожное хозяйство |
| Communication | .. | 45.5 | 1,000.4 | 1,719.6 | 1,948.4 | 246.5 | Связь |
| Wholesale trade | .. | 82.1 | 1,322.4 | 1,867.6 | 2,120.4 | 131.6 | Оптовая торговля |
| Retail trade and catering | .. | .. | .. | .. | .. | .. | Розничная торговля и общепит. |
| Material supply | .. | 127.9 | 3,208.4 | 925.2 | 1,349.2 | .. | Материально-техническое снабжение |
| Procurement | .. | 40.5 | 1,744.8 | 1,664.0 | 1,684.6 | .. | Заготовки |
| Information and computing services | .. | 47.4 | 707.9 | 2,675.4 | 965.0 | .. | Информационно-вычислительное обслуживание |
| Other sectors of material production | .. | 56.9 | 3,056.9 | 654.3 | 959.4 | .. | Другие отрасли сферы матерл. произ. |
| Housing | .. | 108.2 | 1,337.8 | 1,421.9 | 2,445.3 | 178.9 | Жилищное хозяйство |
| Public utilities and personal services | .. | 196.2 | 1,305.3 | 1,060.3 | 1,812.2 | 112.2 | Ком. хоз. и бытовое обслуживание |
| Health care, social security, and sports | .. | 782.0 | 559.6 | 2,374.0 | 686.9 | 250.8 | Здравоохранение, социальное обеспечение, физкультура и спорт |
| Education | .. | 100.8 | 650.9 | 1,991.5 | 1,061.0 | 196.1 | Образование |
| Culture and art | .. | .. | .. | .. | .. | .. | Культура и искусство |
| Science and research | .. | 6.7 | 2,571.1 | 2,044.5 | 846.1 | 145.7 | Наука и научное обслуживание |
| Credit | .. | 404.0 | 1,714.1 | 1,162.6 | 485.4 | .. | Кредитование |
| Insurance | .. | .. | .. | .. | .. | .. | Страхование |
| General administration and defense | .. | 106.9 | 934.7 | 2,090.1 | 926.5 | 260.7 | Государственное управление и оборона |
| Private nonprofit institutions serving households | .. | 88.9 | 2,799.4 | 251.6 | 17.9 | .. | Общественные организации, обслуживающие домашние хозяйства |
| **Imputed service charge of financial intermediaries** | .. | .. | 1,828.2 | 1,141.0 | 610.3 | .. | **Условно-исчисляемая стоимость услуг финансовых посредников** |
| **Total gross value added** | .. | 104.3 | 1,258.7 | 1,262.2 | 1,685.8 | 143.7 | **Валовая добавленная стоимость (ВДС) - всего** |
| **Total GDP at factor cost** | .. | 104.3 | 1,258.7 | 1,262.2 | 1,685.8 | 143.7 | **Всего ВВП по фактр. стоимости (ВДС-ДНП+ДСП)** |
| **Net indirect taxes** | .. | 338.0 | -10,192.3 | 1,446.1 | 986.2 | 316.5 | **Чистые косвенные налоги (НПИ-СПИ)** |
| **Total GDP at market prices** | .. | 103.6 | 1,333.7 | 1,270.7 | 1,649.4 | 148.8 | **ВВП в рыночных ценах** |
| **Price deflators by expenditure category** | | | | | | | **Дефляторы по виду расходов** |
| **Consumption** | .. | 93.9 | 1,124.6 | -96.8 | 1,776.2 | 174.8 | **Конечное потребление** |
| Private consumption | .. | 91.7 | 1,178.6 | -96.9 | 1,982.8 | 175.0 | Личное потребление |
| Government consumption | .. | 104.0 | 905.9 | -96.1 | 1,060.2 | 170.0 | Общественное потребление |
| **Gross domestic investment** | .. | 80.1 | 1,885.0 | -97.0 | 1,266.3 | 180.3 | **Валовые внутренние инвестиции** |
| Gross fixed investment | .. | 89.7 | 1,899.0 | -97.1 | 1,218.1 | 194.8 | Валовое накопление основного капитала |
| **Exports of goods and nonfactor services** | .. | 624.1 | 4,231.0 | -98.7 | 1,377.6 | .. | **Экспорт товаров и нефакторных услуг** |
| **Imports of goods and nonfactor services** | .. | 271.2 | 3,566.3 | -98.4 | 1,337.5 | .. | **Импорт товаров и нефакторных услуг** |

## TABLE 3-1. Balance of payments at current prices (millions of U.S. dollars)
## ТАБЛИЦА 3-1. Платежный баланс в текущих ценах (в миллионах долларов США)

| Item | 1990 | 1991 | 1992 | 1993 | 1994 | 1995 | Статьи |
|---|---|---|---|---|---|---|---|
| Exports of goods and services (including workers' remittances) | .. | .. | .. | 4,134.4 | 3,961.7 | .. | Экспорт товаров и услуг (включая денежные переводы рабочих) |
| Exports of goods and nonfactor services | .. | .. | .. | 4,134.0 | 3,958.0 | .. | Экспорт товаров и нефакт. услуг |
| Merchandise (FOB) | .. | .. | .. | 3,324.0 | 3,285.0 | .. | Товары (ФОБ) |
| Nonfactor services | .. | .. | .. | 810.0 | 673.0 | .. | Нефакторные услуги |
| Shipment | .. | .. | .. | 726.0 | 557.0 | .. | Перевозки |
| Travel | .. | .. | .. | 48.0 | 44.0 | .. | Поездки |
| Other | .. | .. | .. | 36.0 | 72.0 | .. | Другие |
| Imports of goods and nonfactor services | .. | .. | .. | 4,848.0 | 4,397.0 | .. | Импорт товаров и нефакт. услуг |
| Merchandise (FOB) | .. | .. | .. | 4,528.0 | 4,129.0 | .. | Товары (ФОБ) |
| Nonfactor services | .. | .. | .. | 320.0 | 268.0 | .. | Нефакторные услуги |
| Shipment | .. | .. | .. | 197.0 | 159.0 | .. | Перевозки |
| Travel | .. | .. | .. | 41.0 | 15.0 | .. | Поездки |
| Other | .. | .. | .. | 82.0 | 94.0 | .. | Другие |
| Resource balance | .. | .. | .. | -714.0 | -439.0 | .. | Сальдо ресурсов |
| Net factor income | .. | .. | .. | 0.4 | 3.1 | .. | Чистый факторный доход |
| Factor receipts | .. | .. | .. | 0.4 | 3.7 | .. | Факторные поступления |
| Factor payments | .. | .. | .. | .. | 0.6 | .. | Факторные платежи |
| Total interest due | .. | .. | .. | .. | .. | .. | Общая сумма процента к оплате |
| Other factor payments and discrepancy | .. | .. | .. | .. | .. | .. | Другие факторные платежи и стат. погр. |
| Net current transfers | .. | .. | .. | 73.0 | 97.0 | .. | Чистые текущие трансферты |
| Current receipts | .. | .. | .. | 73.0 | 97.0 | .. | Текущие поступления |
| Workers remittances | .. | .. | .. | .. | .. | .. | Денежные переводы рабочих |
| Other current transfers | .. | .. | .. | 73.0 | 97.0 | .. | Другие текущие трансферты |
| Current payments | .. | .. | .. | .. | .. | .. | Текущие платежи |
| Current account balance before official grants | .. | .. | .. | -640.6 | -338.9 | .. | Сальдо текущего счета до офиц. безвозмезд. трансфертов |
| Official capital grants | .. | .. | .. | 605.0 | 1,179.0 | .. | Официальные кап. безвозмезные трансферты |
| Current account balance after official grants | .. | .. | .. | -35.6 | 840.1 | .. | Сальдо текущего счета после офиц. безвозмезд. трансфертов |
| Long Term Capital Inflows | .. | .. | .. | 2,062.0 | 1,675.0 | .. | Долгосрочные притоки капитала |
| Direct investment | .. | .. | .. | 228.0 | 519.0 | .. | Прямые инвестиции |
| Net long term borrowing | .. | .. | .. | 72.0 | 8.0 | .. | Чистые долгосрочные займы |
| Disbursements | .. | .. | .. | .. | .. | .. | Поступления |
| Repayments due | .. | .. | .. | .. | .. | .. | Сумма, подлежащая погашению |
| Other long-term inflows (net) | .. | .. | .. | 1,762.0 | 1,148.0 | .. | Другие долгосрочные притоки (чистые) |

(continued on next page)

## TABLE 3-1. Balance of payments at current prices (millions of U.S. dollars)
## ТАБЛИЦА 3-1. Платежный баланс в текущих ценах (в миллионах долларов США)

| Item | 1990 | 1991 | 1992 | 1993 | 1994 | 1995 | Статьи |
|---|---|---|---|---|---|---|---|
| Adjustment to Scheduled Debt Service | .. | .. | .. | .. | .. | .. | Регулирование долга |
| Debt service not paid | .. | .. | .. | .. | .. | .. | Невыплаченный долг |
| Interest not paid | .. | .. | .. | .. | .. | .. | Невыплаченный процент |
| Principal not paid | .. | .. | .. | .. | .. | .. | Невыплаченная сумма основного долга |
| Arrears reductions/prepayments(-) | .. | .. | .. | .. | .. | .. | Погашение просроченных платежей/выплаты авансом (-) |
| Total Other items (Net) | .. | .. | .. | -357.0 | 536.0 | .. | Общие другие статьи (чистые) |
| Net short-term capital | .. | .. | .. | .. | .. | .. | Чистый краткосрочный капитал |
| Capital flows not elsewhere included | .. | .. | .. | .. | .. | .. | Потоки капитала, не указанные выше |
| Errors and omissions | .. | .. | .. | -357.0 | 536.0 | .. | Ошибки и пропуски |
| Changes in net reserves | .. | .. | .. | -354.0 | -394.0 | .. | Изменения в чистых резервах |
| Net credit from IMF | .. | .. | .. | -20.0 | 9.0 | .. | Чистый кредит МВФ |
| Reserve changes not elsewhere included | .. | .. | .. | -334.0 | -403.0 | .. | Изменения резервов, не указанных выше |
| Escrow account | .. | .. | .. | .. | .. | .. | Счет депонирования |
| Gross reserves (excluding gold) | .. | .. | .. | -354.0 | -394.0 | .. | Общие резервы (исключая золото) |
| Gross reserves (including gold) | .. | .. | .. | .. | .. | .. | Общие резервы (включая золото) |
| Nominal official exchange rate (annual average) (rf) | .. | .. | .. | 2.4 | .. | .. | Номинальный официальный или рыночный курс (среднегодовой) |
| Nominal official exchange rate (end-of-year) (ae) | .. | .. | .. | 6.3 | .. | .. | Номинальный официальный или рыночный курс (на конец года) |
| Manufacture unit value (percent change) | .. | .. | .. | .. | .. | .. | Средний индекс цен на продукцию обр. пром.,% |
| Index of real effective exchange rate (IMF) | .. | .. | .. | .. | .. | .. | Индекс реального эффективного валютного курса (МВФ) |
| Total factor payments | .. | .. | .. | .. | .. | .. | Общая сумма факторных платежей |
| Government interest | .. | .. | .. | .. | .. | .. | Процент, выплачиваемый органами гос. управления |
| Private sector interest | .. | .. | .. | .. | .. | .. | Процент выплачиваемый частным сектором |
| Profits on direct foreign investment | .. | .. | .. | .. | .. | .. | Прибыль от прямых иностранных инвестиций |
| Official capital grants | .. | .. | .. | .. | .. | .. | Официальные капитальные безвозмездные трансферты |
| For budgetary financing | .. | .. | .. | .. | .. | .. | На бюджетное финансирование |
| To extrabudgetary entities | .. | .. | .. | .. | .. | .. | На внебюджетное финансирование |
| Government net long term borrowing | .. | .. | .. | .. | .. | .. | Чистые долгосрочные государственные займы |
| Disbursements | .. | .. | .. | .. | .. | .. | Поступления |
| Repayments | .. | .. | .. | .. | .. | .. | Погашения |
| Private net long term borrowing | .. | .. | .. | .. | .. | .. | Чистые долгосрочные частные займы |
| Disbursements | .. | .. | .. | .. | .. | .. | Поступления |
| Repayments | .. | .. | .. | .. | .. | .. | Погашения |

**TABLE 3-2A. Imports by commodity group (millions of U.S. dollars)**
**ТАБЛИЦА 3-2A . Импорт по товарным группам (млн. долларов США)**

| Commodity group | 1990 | 1991 | 1992 | 1993 | 1994 | 1995 | Товарные группы |
|---|---|---|---|---|---|---|---|
| TOTAL | .. | .. | .. | .. | 3,560.5 | 3,781.0 | ВСЕГО |
| I - Live animals; animal products | .. | .. | .. | .. | 27.4 | 28.7 | I - Живые животные и продукты животноводства |
| II - Vegetable products | .. | .. | .. | .. | 72.1 | 63.2 | II - Продукты растительного происхождения |
| III - Animal or vegetable fats and oils and their cleavage products; prepared edible fats; animal or vegetable waxes | .. | .. | .. | .. | 29.9 | 20.7 | III - Жиры и масла растительного и животного происхождения, воски |
| IV - Prepared foodstuffs; beverages, spirits and vinegar; tobacco and manufactured tobacco substitutes | .. | .. | .. | .. | 229.4 | 290.2 | IV -Продукция пищевой промышленности, алкогольные и безалкогольные напитки, табак и его заменители |
| V - Mineral products | .. | .. | .. | .. | 1,103.7 | 1,104.3 | V - Минеральные продукты |
| VI - Products of the chemical or allied industries | .. | .. | .. | .. | 272.5 | 324.1 | VI - Продукция химической промышленности |
| VII - Plastics and articles thereof; rubber and articles thereof | .. | .. | .. | .. | 76.4 | 124.1 | VII - Пластмассы и изделия из них |
| VIII - Raw hides and skins, leather, furskins and articles thereof; saddlery and harness; travel goods, handbags and similar containers; articles of animal gut | .. | .. | .. | .. | 9.0 | 4.4 | VIII - Кожевенное сырьё, кожи, пушнина, меховое сырьё и изделия из них |
| IX - Wood and articles of wood; wood charcoal; cork and articles of cork; manufactures of straw, of esparto or of other plaiting materials; basketware and wickerwork | .. | .. | .. | .. | 37.2 | 62.4 | IX - Древесина и изделия из древесины, древесный уголь |
| X - Pulp of wood or of other fibrous cellulosic material; waste and scrap of paper or paperboard; paper and paperboard and articles thereof | .. | .. | .. | .. | 46.3 | 91.0 | X - Бумажная масса, бумажные и картонные отходы, макулатура, бумага, картон и изделия из них |
| XI - Textiles and textile articles | .. | .. | .. | .. | 165.3 | 93.9 | XI - Текстиль и текстильные изделия |
| XII - Footwear, headgear, umbrellas, sun umbrellas, walking sticks, seat sticks, whips, riding crops and parts thereof; prepared feathers and articles made therewith; artificial flowers; articles of human hair | .. | .. | .. | .. | 74.1 | 33.8 | XII - Обувь, головные уборы, зонты, трости и пр. |

## TABLE 3-2A. Imports by commodity group (millions of U.S. dollars)
## ТАБЛИЦА 3-2A . Импорт по товарным группам (млн. долларов США)



| Commodity group | 1990 | 1991 | 1992 | 1993 | 1994 | 1995 | Товарные группы |
|---|---|---|---|---|---|---|---|
| XIII - Articles of stone, plaster, cement, asbestos, mica and similar materials; ceramic products; glass and glassware | .. | .. | .. | .. | 40.2 | 64.0 | XIII - Изделия из камня, гипса, цемента |
| XIV - Natural or cultured pearls, precious or semi-precious stones, precious metals, metals clad with precious metal and articles thereof; imitation jewellery; coin | .. | .. | .. | .. | 0.6 | 5.2 | XIV - Жемчуг, драгоценные и полудрагоценные камни, драгоценные металлы, бижутерия, монеты |
| XV - Base metals and articles of base metal | .. | .. | .. | .. | 263.6 | 310.3 | XV - Неблагородные металлы и изделия из них |
| XVI - Machinery and mechanical appliances; electrical equipment; parts thereof; sound recorders and reproducers, television image and sound recorders and reproducers, and parts and accessories of such articles | .. | .. | .. | .. | 719.7 | 759.9 | XVI - Машины, оборудование, механизмы, их части и принадлежности; звуковая и теле-аппаратура, их части и принадлежности |
| XVII - Vehicles, aircraft, vessels and associated transport equipment | .. | .. | .. | .. | 274.0 | 266.4 | XVII - Средства наземного, воздушного и водного транспорта |
| XVIII - Optical, photographic, cinematograp-hic, measuring, checking, precision, medical or surgical instruments and apparatus; clocks and watches; musical instruments; parts and accessories thereof | .. | .. | .. | .. | 56.7 | 80.9 | XVIII - Приборы, аппараты оптические, медицинские, измерительные и пр.; музыкальные инструменты; часы; их части и принадлежности |
| XIX - Arms and ammunition; parts and accessories thereof | .. | .. | .. | .. | 2.7 | 1.6 | XIX - Оружие и боеприпасы, их части и принадлежности |
| XX - Miscellaneous manufactured articles | .. | .. | .. | .. | 59.7 | 51.9 | XX - Разные промышленные товары |
| XXI - Works of art, collectors' pieces, and antiques | .. | .. | .. | .. | 0.0 | 0.0 | XXI - Произведения искусства, предметы антиквариата |
| XXII - Services | .. | .. | .. | .. | .. | .. | XXII - Услуги |

**TABLE 3-3A. Exports by commodity group (millions of U.S. dollars)**
**ТАБЛИЦА 3-3A. Экспорт по товарным группам (млн. долларов США)**

| Commodity group | 1990 | 1991 | 1992 | 1993 | 1994 | 1995 | Товарные группы |
|---|---|---|---|---|---|---|---|
| TOTAL | .. | .. | .. | .. | 3,231.3 | 4,974.4 | ВСЕГО |
| I - Live animals; animal products | .. | .. | .. | .. | 36.8 | 100.2 | I - Живые животные и продукты животноводства |
| II - Vegetable products | .. | .. | .. | .. | 118.8 | 407.6 | II - Продукты растительного происхождения |
| III - Animal or vegetable fats and oils and their cleavage products; prepared edible fats; animal or vegetable waxes | .. | .. | .. | .. | 0.6 | 2.8 | III - Жиры и масла растительного и животного происхождения, воски |
| IV - Prepared foodstuffs; beverages, spirits and vinegar; tobacco and manufactured tobacco substitutes | .. | .. | .. | .. | 43.5 | 59.8 | IV -Продукция пищевой промышленности, алкогольные и безалкогольные напитки, табак и его заменители |
| V - Mineral products | .. | .. | .. | .. | 1,091.1 | 1,384.8 | V - Минеральные продукты |
| VI - Products of the chemical or allied industries | .. | .. | .. | .. | 319.9 | 461.9 | VI - Продукция химической промышленности |
| VII - Plastics and articles thereof; rubber and articles thereof | .. | .. | .. | .. | 31.4 | 52.9 | VII - Пластмассы и изделия из них |
| VIII - Raw hides and skins, leather, furskins and articles thereof; saddlery and harness; travel goods, handbags and similar containers; articles of animal gut | .. | .. | .. | .. | 18.5 | 41.2 | VIII - Кожевенное сырьё, кожи, пушнина, меховое сырьё и изделия из них |
| IX - Wood and articles of wood; wood charcoal; cork and articles of cork; manufactures of straw, of esparto or of other plaiting materials; basketware and wickerwork | .. | .. | .. | .. | 0.4 | 2.0 | IX - Древесина и изделия из древесины, древесный уголь |
| X - Pulp of wood or of other fibrous cellulosic material; waste and scrap of paper or paperboard; paper and paperboard and articles thereof | .. | .. | .. | .. | 5.8 | 3.7 | X - Бумажная масса, бумажные и картонные отходы, макулатура, бумага, картон и изделия из них |
| XI - Textiles and textile articles | .. | .. | .. | .. | 99.2 | 127.2 | XI - Текстиль и текстильные изделия |
| XII - Footwear, headgear, umbrellas, sun umbrellas walking sticks, seat sticks, whips, riding crops and parts thereof; prepared feathers and articles made therewith; artificial flowers; articles of human hair | .. | .. | .. | .. | 3.5 | 3.6 | XII - Обувь, головные уборы, зонты, трости и пр. |

**TABLE 3-3A. Exports by commodity group (millions of U.S. dollars)**
**ТАБЛИЦА 3-3А. Экспорт по товарным группам (млн. долларов США)**

| Commodity group | 1990 | 1991 | 1992 | 1993 | 1994 | 1995 | Товарные группы |
|---|---|---|---|---|---|---|---|
| XIII - Articles of stone, plaster, cement, asbestos, mica and similar materials; ceramic products; glass and glassware | .. | .. | .. | .. | 18.3 | 19.8 | XIII - Изделия из камня, гипса, цемента |
| XIV - Natural or cultured pearls, precious or semi-precious stones, precious metals, metals clad with precious metal and articles thereof; imitation jewellery; coin | .. | .. | .. | .. | 1.5 | 11.5 | XIV - Жемчуг, драгоценные и полудрагоценные камни, драгоценные металлы, бижутерия, монеты |
| XV - Base metals and articles of base metal | .. | .. | .. | .. | 1,296.1 | 2,057.1 | XV - Неблагородные металлы и изделия из них |
| XVI - Machinery and mechanical appliances; electrical equipment; parts thereof; sound recorders and reproducers, television image and sound recorders and reproducers, and parts and accessories of such articles | .. | .. | .. | .. | 88.2 | 140.8 | XVI - Машины, оборудование, механизмы, их части и принадлежности; звуковая и теле-аппаратура, их части и принадлежности |
| XVII - Vehicles, aircraft, vessels and associated transport equipment | .. | .. | .. | .. | 30.8 | 56.7 | XVII - Средства наземного, воздушного и водного транспорта |
| XVIII - Optical, photographic, cinematographic, measuring, checking, precision, medical or surgical instruments and apparatus; clocks and watches; musical instruments; parts and accessories thereof | .. | .. | .. | .. | 5.4 | 10.2 | XVIII - Приборы, аппараты оптические, медицинские, измерительные и пр.; музыкальные инструменты; часы; их части и принадлежности |
| XIX - Arms and ammunition; parts and accessories thereof | .. | .. | .. | .. | 12.3 | 23.6 | XIX - Оружие и боеприпасы, их части и принадлежности |
| XX - Miscellaneous manufactured articles | .. | .. | .. | .. | 9.2 | 7.0 | XX - Разные промышленные товары |
| XXI - Works of art, collectors' pieces, and antiques | .. | .. | .. | .. | 0.0 | 0.0 | XXI - Произведения искусства, предметы антиквариата |
| XXII - Services | .. | .. | .. | .. | .. | .. | XXII - Услуги |

TABLE 3-4A. Geographical distribution of foreign trade (millions of U.S. dollars)
ТАБЛИЦА 3-4A. Географическое распределение внешней торговли (млн. долларов США)

| Country or country group | Exports Экспорт 1990 | 1991 | 1992 | 1993 | 1994 | 1995 | Imports Импорт 1990 | 1991 | 1992 | 1993 | 1994 | 1995 | Страна или группа стран |
|---|---|---|---|---|---|---|---|---|---|---|---|---|---|
| **Total trade** | .. | .. | .. | .. | 3,231.2 | 4,974.4 | .. | .. | .. | .. | 3,560.5 | 3,781.0 | **Всего** |
| **CIS countries** | .. | .. | .. | .. | 1,874.4 | 2,631.4 | .. | .. | .. | .. | 2,176.1 | 2,608.7 | **Страны СНГ** |
| Armenia | .. | .. | .. | .. | 1.0 | 0.2 | .. | .. | .. | .. | 1.3 | 2.7 | Армения |
| Azerbaijan | .. | .. | .. | .. | 46.3 | 22.4 | .. | .. | .. | .. | 11.7 | 24.9 | Азербайджан |
| Belarus | .. | .. | .. | .. | 43.9 | 57.2 | .. | .. | .. | .. | 64.1 | 79.8 | Беларусь |
| Georgia | .. | .. | .. | .. | 1.2 | 0.3 | .. | .. | .. | .. | 2.9 | 2.2 | Грузия |
| Kazakstan | .. | .. | .. | .. | .. | .. | .. | .. | .. | .. | .. | .. | Казахстан |
| Kyrgyz Republic | .. | .. | .. | .. | 59.9 | 73.3 | .. | .. | .. | .. | 104.0 | 30.8 | Киргизстан |
| Moldova | .. | .. | .. | .. | 3.2 | 2.5 | .. | .. | .. | .. | 8.1 | 5.6 | Молдова |
| Russia | .. | .. | .. | .. | 1,438.9 | 2,102.6 | .. | .. | .. | .. | 1,292.1 | 1,854.4 | Россия |
| Tajikistan | .. | .. | .. | .. | 9.5 | 40.8 | .. | .. | .. | .. | 17.9 | 12.1 | Таджикистан |
| Turkmenistan | .. | .. | .. | .. | 25.3 | 51.1 | .. | .. | .. | .. | 277.6 | 241.3 | Туркменистан |
| Ukraine | .. | .. | .. | .. | 128.0 | 121.4 | .. | .. | .. | .. | 119.8 | 86.7 | Украина |
| Uzbekistan | .. | .. | .. | .. | 117.2 | 159.6 | .. | .. | .. | .. | 276.6 | 268.2 | Узбекистан |
| **Non-CIS countries** | .. | .. | .. | .. | 1,356.8 | 2,343.0 | .. | .. | .. | .. | 1,384.4 | 1,172.3 | **Остальной мир** |
| **Europe** | .. | .. | .. | .. | 885.6 | 1,576.1 | .. | .. | .. | .. | 818.1 | 700.1 | **Европа** |
| Austria | .. | .. | .. | .. | 12.5 | 15.6 | .. | .. | .. | .. | 39.4 | 51.6 | Австрия |
| Belgium | .. | .. | .. | .. | 6.4 | 15.1 | .. | .. | .. | .. | 12.8 | 7.0 | Бельгия |
| Bulgaria | .. | .. | .. | .. | 12.3 | 5.7 | .. | .. | .. | .. | 16.5 | 7.4 | Болгария |
| Czech Republic | .. | .. | .. | .. | 70.6 | 26.7 | .. | .. | .. | .. | 29.5 | 22.4 | Чешская Республика |
| Denmark | .. | .. | .. | .. | 0.1 | .. | .. | .. | .. | .. | 5.0 | 2.6 | Дания |
| Estonia | .. | .. | .. | .. | 3.6 | 15.7 | .. | .. | .. | .. | 3.4 | 6.8 | Эстония |
| Finland | .. | .. | .. | .. | 16.6 | 50.5 | .. | .. | .. | .. | 15.9 | 31.3 | Финляндия |
| Former Yugoslavia | .. | .. | .. | .. | 0.7 | .. | .. | .. | .. | .. | 4.9 | 1.9 | Быв. Югославия |
| France | .. | .. | .. | .. | 7.2 | .. | .. | .. | .. | .. | 30.6 | 26.4 | Франция |
| Germany | .. | .. | .. | .. | 73.2 | 170.4 | .. | .. | .. | .. | 293.6 | 201.5 | Германия |
| Hungary | .. | .. | .. | .. | 49.0 | 8.4 | .. | .. | .. | .. | 31.2 | 21.4 | Венгрия |
| Iceland | .. | .. | .. | .. | .. | .. | .. | .. | .. | .. | 0.9 | 0.2 | Исландия |
| Ireland | .. | .. | .. | .. | 1.9 | 71.6 | .. | .. | .. | .. | 7.0 | 7.8 | Ирландия |
| Italy | .. | .. | .. | .. | 42.3 | 142.6 | .. | .. | .. | .. | 60.7 | 30.1 | Италия |
| Latvia | .. | .. | .. | .. | 14.5 | 33.2 | .. | .. | .. | .. | 10.4 | 11.5 | Латвия |
| Lithuania | .. | .. | .. | .. | 13.4 | 120.8 | .. | .. | .. | .. | 16.5 | 18.0 | Литва |
| Netherlands | .. | .. | .. | .. | 247.8 | 492.8 | .. | .. | .. | .. | 31.1 | 30.9 | Нидерланды |
| Norway | .. | .. | .. | .. | 2.4 | 1.2 | .. | .. | .. | .. | 1.7 | 0.1 | Норвегия |
| Poland | .. | .. | .. | .. | 55.7 | 38.0 | .. | .. | .. | .. | 23.4 | 20.8 | Польша |
| Romania | .. | .. | .. | .. | 11.0 | 0.5 | .. | .. | .. | .. | 17.0 | 2.3 | Румыния |
| Slovak Republic | .. | .. | .. | .. | 13.7 | 20.9 | .. | .. | .. | .. | 4.2 | 7.1 | Словацская Республика |
| Spain | .. | .. | .. | .. | 3.2 | 1.4 | .. | .. | .. | .. | 6.1 | 6.3 | Испания |
| Sweden | .. | .. | .. | .. | 10.0 | 2.8 | .. | .. | .. | .. | 11.7 | 16.5 | Швеция |

**TABLE 3-4A. Geographical distribution of foreign trade (millions of U.S. dollars)**
**ТАБЛИЦА 3-4А. Географическое распределение внешней торговли (млн. долларов США)**

| Country or country group | Exports Экспорт 1990 | 1991 | 1992 | 1993 | 1994 | 1995 | Imports Импорт 1990 | 1991 | 1992 | 1993 | 1994 | 1995 | Страна или группа стран |
|---|---|---|---|---|---|---|---|---|---|---|---|---|---|
| Switzerland | .. | .. | .. | .. | 130.0 | 186.7 | .. | .. | .. | .. | 65.2 | 57.3 | Швейцария |
| United Kingdom | .. | .. | .. | .. | 64.9 | 111.7 | .. | .. | .. | .. | 66.4 | 82.8 | Великобритания |
| Other Europe | .. | .. | .. | .. | 22.6 | 43.8 | .. | .. | .. | .. | 13.0 | 28.1 | Остальные страны Европы |
| **Asia** | .. | .. | .. | .. | 372.6 | 644.3 | .. | .. | .. | .. | 408.6 | 348.7 | **Азия** |
| Afghanistan | .. | .. | .. | .. | 1.8 | 3.2 | .. | .. | .. | .. | 0.3 | 0.1 | Афганистан |
| China | .. | .. | .. | .. | 148.9 | 294.2 | .. | .. | .. | .. | 69.8 | 34.2 | Китай |
| India | .. | .. | .. | .. | 11.8 | 48.5 | .. | .. | .. | .. | 10.6 | 14.0 | Индия |
| Iraq | .. | .. | .. | .. | 27.1 | 45.0 | .. | .. | .. | .. | 0.2 | .. | Ирак |
| Japan | .. | .. | .. | .. | 3.6 | 0.9 | .. | .. | .. | .. | 53.2 | 8.4 | Япония |
| Korea, Dem. People's Rep. | .. | .. | .. | .. | 60.1 | 91.6 | .. | .. | .. | .. | 0.7 | 0.1 | КНДР |
| Korea, Rep. of | .. | .. | .. | .. | 1.5 | 2.4 | .. | .. | .. | .. | 67.0 | 43.2 | Южная Корея |
| Mongolia | .. | .. | .. | .. | .. | .. | .. | .. | .. | .. | 22.4 | 60.7 | МНР |
| Syrian Arab Republic | .. | .. | .. | .. | .. | .. | .. | .. | .. | .. | 0.7 | .. | Сирия |
| Turkey | .. | .. | .. | .. | 49.1 | 70.8 | .. | .. | .. | .. | 87.2 | 123.9 | Турция |
| Viet Nam | .. | .. | .. | .. | 2.8 | 2.8 | .. | .. | .. | .. | .. | .. | Вьетнам |
| Other Asia | .. | .. | .. | .. | 65.9 | 84.9 | .. | .. | .. | .. | 96.5 | 64.1 | Остальные страны Азии |
| **America** | .. | .. | .. | .. | 91.8 | 109.7 | .. | .. | .. | .. | 143.2 | 118.6 | **Сев. и Южная Америка** |
| Canada | .. | .. | .. | .. | 12.9 | 2.4 | .. | .. | .. | .. | 15.0 | 7.9 | Канада |
| Cuba | .. | .. | .. | .. | .. | 0.2 | .. | .. | .. | .. | 9.3 | .. | Куба |
| United States | .. | .. | .. | .. | 75.1 | 44.7 | .. | .. | .. | .. | 109.3 | 72.5 | США |
| Other America | .. | .. | .. | .. | 3.8 | 62.4 | .. | .. | .. | .. | 9.6 | 38.2 | Остальные |
| **Africa** | .. | .. | .. | .. | 5.3 | 12.5 | .. | .. | .. | .. | 5.2 | 1.7 | **Африка** |
| Egypt | .. | .. | .. | .. | .. | 0.2 | .. | .. | .. | .. | 1.4 | 0.4 | Египет |
| Libya | .. | .. | .. | .. | .. | .. | .. | .. | .. | .. | .. | 0.1 | Ливия |
| Other Africa | .. | .. | .. | .. | 5.3 | 12.3 | .. | .. | .. | .. | 3.8 | 1.2 | Остальные |
| **Rest of the World** | .. | .. | .. | .. | 1.5 | 0.4 | .. | .. | .. | .. | 9.3 | 3.2 | **Прочие страны мира** |
| Australia | .. | .. | .. | .. | 0.2 | 0.1 | .. | .. | .. | .. | 7.5 | 2.9 | Австралия |

**TABLE 4-1. General government budget revenue (millions of national currency)**
**ТАБЛИЦА 4-1. Доходы государственного бюджета (млн. национальной валюты)**

| Type of revenue | 1990 | 1991 | 1992 | 1993 | 1994 | 1995 | Вид доходов |
|---|---|---|---|---|---|---|---|
| **Total revenue and grants** | 18,352 | 26,070 | 298,000 | 7,964 | 104,103 | 262,738 | **Всего доходов и безвозм. поступл.** |
| Grants | 6,053 | 6,033 | 21,000 | 413 | 1,514 | .. | Безвозмездные поступления |
| Total Revenue | 12,299 | 20,037 | 277,000 | 7,551 | 102,589 | .. | Всего доходов |
| **Current revenue** | 12,299 | 20,037 | 276,400 | 7,551 | 102,589 | .. | **Текущие доходы** |
| Tax revenue | 11,853 | 17,649 | 261,000 | 4,855 | 44,814 | 129,173 | Доход от налогов |
| Taxes on income and profits | 4,239 | 9,866 | 92,000 | 1,250 | 14,714 | 35,671 | Налоги на доходы и прибыль |
| Individual | 1,370 | 3,088 | 30,000 | .. | 107 | 401 | Физические лица |
| Corporate | 2,869 | 6,778 | 62,000 | 1,250 | 14,607 | 35,270 | Предприятия и организации |
| Social security contributions | 1,805 | .. | .. | .. | .. | .. | Отчисление на соцстрах. |
| Taxes on payroll or work force | .. | .. | .. | 743 | 8,150 | 25,802 | Налоги на заработную плату и рабочую силу |
| Taxes on the use of labor force | .. | .. | .. | .. | .. | .. | Плата за трудовые ресурсы |
| Taxes on increases in wages and salaries | .. | .. | .. | .. | .. | .. | Налог с прироста средств на оплату труда |
| Other payroll/work force taxes | .. | .. | .. | .. | .. | .. | Другие налоги на зарплату и рабочую силу |
| Taxes on property | .. | .. | .. | 32 | 287 | 2,059 | Налоги на собственность |
| Taxes on immovable property | .. | .. | .. | 18 | 287 | 2,059 | Налоги на недвижимое имущество |
| Buildings | .. | .. | .. | .. | 57 | .. | Налог с владельцев строении |
| Land | .. | .. | .. | 18 | 230 | 2,059 | Земельныи налог |
| Estate, inheritance, and gift taxes | .. | .. | .. | .. | .. | .. | Налоги на наследство, подарки |
| Other property taxes | .. | .. | .. | 13 | .. | .. | Другие налоги на имущество |
| Domestic taxes on goods and services | 4,925 | 5,897 | 72,000 | 1,318 | 12,979 | 39,567 | Внутренние налоги на товары и услуги |
| General sales, turnover, or value-added taxes | .. | .. | 72,000 | 1,159 | 10,798 | 33,259 | Налог с продаж. с оборота или на добав. стоим. |
| Excises | .. | .. | .. | 160 | 2,181 | 6,308 | Акцизы |
| Profits of fiscal monopolies | .. | .. | .. | .. | .. | .. | Прибыли фискальных монополий |
| Taxes on specific services | .. | .. | .. | .. | .. | .. | Налоги на особые услуги |
| Taxes on use of goods or permission to use goods or to perform activities | .. | .. | .. | .. | .. | .. | Налоги на пользование товарами или лицензии на пользование товарами и занятие деятельностью |
| Other taxes on goods and services | .. | .. | .. | .. | .. | .. | Другие налоги на товары и услуги |
| Taxes on international trade and transactions | .. | .. | 28,000 | 139 | 8,578 | 26,074 | Налоги на внешнюю торговлю и операции |
| Import duties | .. | .. | .. | 32 | 422 | 3,023 | Импортные пошлины |
| Export duties | .. | .. | .. | 77 | 5,264 | 9,145 | Экпортные пошлины |
| Other | .. | .. | 28,000 | 29 | 2,892 | 13,906 | Другие |
| Other taxes | 884 | 1,886 | 69,000 | 1,374 | 106 | .. | Прочие налоги |
| Nontax revenue | 446 | 2,388 | 15,400 | 2,696 | 57,775 | 128,231 | Неналоговые доходы |
| **Capital revenue** | .. | .. | 600 | .. | .. | .. | **Капитальные доходы** |

## TABLE 4-2. General government budget expenditure by economic type (millions of national currency)
## ТАБЛИЦА 4-2. Расходы государственного бюджета по экономическим типам (млн. национальной валюты)

| Type of expenditure or debt holder | 1990 | 1991 | 1992 | 1993 | 1994 | 1995 | Всего расходов |
|---|---|---|---|---|---|---|---|
| **Total expenditure by economic type** | 17,055 | 32,758 | 387,000 | 7,075 | .. | .. | **Всего расходов по экономическим типам** |
| **Current expenditure** | .. | .. | 306,000 | .. | .. | .. | **Текущие расходы** |
| Expenditure on goods and services | .. | .. | 212,000 | .. | .. | .. | Расходы на товары и услуги |
| Wages and salaries | .. | .. | 39,000 | .. | .. | .. | Заработная плата |
| Employer contributions | .. | .. | .. | .. | .. | .. | Отчисление на социальное страхование |
| Other Purchases of goods and services | .. | .. | 173,000 | .. | .. | .. | Другие покупки товаров и услуг |
| Interest payments | .. | .. | 33,000 | .. | .. | .. | Выплаты процентов |
| Domestic debt | .. | .. | .. | .. | .. | .. | По внутреннему долгу |
| Foreign debt | .. | .. | 33,000 | .. | .. | .. | По внешнему долгу |
| Subsidies and other current transfers | .. | .. | 61,000 | .. | .. | .. | Субсидии на другие текущие трансферты |
| Subsidies | .. | .. | 18,000 | .. | .. | .. | Субсидии |
| Agricultural subsidies | .. | .. | .. | .. | .. | .. | Субсидии на сельское хозяйство |
| Other current transfers | .. | .. | 43,000 | .. | .. | .. | Другие текущие трансферты |
| Other | .. | .. | .. | .. | .. | .. | Прочие расходы |
| **Capital expenditure** | .. | .. | 81,000 | .. | .. | .. | **Капитальные расходы** |
| Acquisition of fixed capital assets | .. | .. | 81,000 | .. | .. | .. | Приобретение основного капитала |
| Capital transfers | .. | .. | .. | .. | .. | .. | Капитальные трансферты |
| Other | .. | .. | .. | .. | .. | .. | Другие капитальные расходы |
| **Surplus/deficit (-)** | 1,297 | -6,688 | -89,000 | 890 | .. | .. | **Превыш. доходов над расходами/дефицит(-)** |
| **Financing by type of debt holder** | .. | .. | 89,000 | .. | .. | .. | **Финансирование по типам кредиторов** |
| **Foreign (net)** | .. | .. | 70,995 | .. | .. | .. | **Зарубежные кредиторы (сальдо)** |
| From international development institutions | .. | .. | .. | .. | .. | .. | Международные организации |
| From foreign governments | .. | .. | .. | .. | .. | .. | Правительства иностранных государств |
| Other borrowing abroad | .. | .. | .. | .. | .. | .. | Другие зарубежные кредиторы |
| **Domestic (net)** | .. | .. | 18,005 | .. | .. | .. | **Внутренние кредиторы (сальдо)** |
| From monetary authorities | .. | .. | .. | .. | .. | .. | Органы денежного обращения |
| From deposit money banks | .. | .. | -2,080 | .. | .. | .. | Депозитные денежные банки |
| Other domestic borrowing | .. | .. | 20,090 | .. | .. | .. | Другие внутренние кредиторы |
| *Memo items:* | | | | | | | *Справочно:* |
| Extrabudgetary surplus/ Deficit (-) not included above | .. | .. | 4,920 | .. | .. | .. | Превышение доходов над расходами/дефицит (-) по внебюджетным фондам, не включенным выше |
| Total surplus/deficit (-) including extrabudgetary accounts | 1,297 | -6,688 | -84,080 | .. | .. | .. | Итого превышение доходов над расходами/дефицит, включая счета внебюджетных фондов |

**TABLE 5-1. Agricultural production (millions of national currency, current prices)** **KAZAKSTAN**

**ТАБЛИЦА 5-1. Сельскохозяйственная продукция (млн. нац. валюты, текущие цены)**

| Item | 1990 | 1991 | 1992 | 1993 | 1994 | 1995 | Статьи |
|---|---|---|---|---|---|---|---|
| **Total gross agricultural production** | 21,797 | 35,749 | 407,006 | 7,466 | 111,627 | 203,893 | **Валовая продукция сель-ского хозяйства - всего** |
| **Crops** | 8,672 | 12,379 | 145,320 | 4,913 | 73,320 | 109,336 | **Продукция растениеводства** |
| Grains | .. | .. | .. | .. | .. | .. | Зерно |
| Potatoes | .. | .. | .. | .. | .. | .. | Картофель |
| Vegetables | .. | .. | .. | .. | .. | .. | Овощи |
| Fruits (excluding grapes) | .. | .. | .. | .. | .. | .. | Фрукты (без винограда) |
| Grapes | .. | .. | .. | .. | .. | .. | Виноград |
| Tobacco | .. | .. | .. | .. | .. | .. | Табак |
| Cotton | .. | .. | .. | .. | .. | .. | Хлопок |
| Sugarbeets | .. | .. | .. | .. | .. | .. | Сахарная свекла |
| Oilseeds | .. | .. | .. | .. | .. | .. | Семена масличных культур |
| Other | .. | .. | .. | .. | .. | .. | Прочие |
| **Animal husbandry** | 13,124 | 23,370 | 261,686 | 2,553 | 38,307 | 94,557 | **Продукция животноводства** |
| Livestock | .. | .. | .. | .. | .. | .. | Мясное животноводство |
| Cattle | .. | .. | .. | .. | .. | .. | Крупный рогатый скот |
| Pigs | .. | .. | .. | .. | .. | .. | Свиньи |
| Sheep and goats | .. | .. | .. | .. | .. | .. | Овцы и козы |
| Poultry | .. | .. | .. | .. | .. | .. | Птица |
| Other | .. | .. | .. | .. | .. | .. | Прочие |
| Milk | .. | .. | .. | .. | .. | .. | Молоко |
| Eggs | .. | .. | .. | .. | .. | .. | Яйца |
| Wool | .. | .. | .. | .. | .. | .. | Шерсть |
| Other livestock | .. | .. | .. | .. | .. | .. | Прочая |
| **Agricultural services** | .. | .. | .. | .. | .. | .. | **Сельскохозяйственные услуги** |

## TABLE 5-2. Agricultural production (millions of constant national currency)
## ТАБЛИЦА 5-2. Сельскохозяйственная продукция в постоянных ценах (млн. национальной валюты)

| Item | 1990 | 1991 | 1992 | 1993 | 1994 | 1995 | Статьи |
|---|---|---|---|---|---|---|---|
| **Total gross agricultural production** | 15,673 | 14,041 | 14,063 | 13,424 | 111,627 | 85,014 | **Валовая продукция сельского хозяйства - всего** |
| **Crops** | 6,118 | 4,883 | 5,716 | 5,120 | 73,320 | 57,857 | **Продукция растениеводства** |
| Grains | 3,690 | 1,689 | 3,834 | 2,845 | 33,259 | 19,550 | Зерно |
| Potatoes | 444 | 410 | 491 | 439 | 13,718 | 17,455 | Картофель |
| Vegetables | 366 | 307 | 320 | 415 | 7,584 | 7,396 | Овощи |
| Fruits (excluding grapes) | 190 | 77 | 109 | 61 | 701 | 198 | Фрукты (без винограда) |
| Grapes | 65 | 31 | 29 | 19 | 175 | 328 | Виноград |
| Tobacco | 24 | 24 | 20 | 21 | 24 | .. | Табак |
| Cotton | 236 | 207 | 171 | 142 | 1,992 | 8,564 | Хлопок |
| Sugarbeets | 58 | 37 | 66 | 43 | 495 | 539 | Сахарная свекла |
| Oilseeds | 70 | 45 | 70 | 44 | 606 | 784 | Семена масличных культур |
| Other | 975 | 2,056 | 606 | 1,091 | 14,766 | 3,043 | Прочие |
| **Animal husbandry** | 9,555 | 9,158 | 8,347 | 8,304 | 38,307 | 27,157 | **Продукция животноводства** |
| Livestock | 5,817 | 5,520 | 4,941 | 4,867 | 20,054 | 14,689 | Мясное животноводство |
| Cattle | 2,857 | 2,705 | 2,487 | 2,511 | 8,763 | .. | Крупный рогатый скот |
| Pigs | 816 | 775 | 623 | 586 | 3,705 | .. | Свиньи |
| Sheep and goats | 1,259 | 1,203 | 1,128 | 1,134 | 3,904 | .. | Овцы и козы |
| Poultry | 616 | 573 | 422 | 345 | 1,768 | .. | Птица |
| Other | 269 | 264 | 281 | 241 | 1,914 | 1,046 | Прочие |
| Milk | 2,246 | 2,211 | 2,096 | 2,220 | 13,427 | 9,124 | Молоко |
| Eggs | 401 | 390 | 341 | 315 | 2,926 | 2,038 | Яйца |
| Wool | 933 | 904 | 835 | 816 | 1,900 | 1,306 | Шерсть |
| Other livestock | 158 | 133 | 134 | 86 | .. | .. | Прочая |

## TABLE 5-3. Production and average yield of major agricultural crops



## ТАБЛИЦА 5-3. Производство и урожайность важнейших сельскохозяйственных культур

| Crop | 1990 | 1991 | 1992 | 1993 | 1994 | 1995 | Сельскохозяйственные культуры |
|---|---|---|---|---|---|---|---|
| **Production (thousands of tons)** | | | | | | | **Производство (тыс. тонн)** |
| Grain - Cleanweight | 28,488 | 11,992 | 29,772 | 21,631 | 16,454 | 9,505 | Зерно в чистом весе |
| Winter wheat | 1,966 | 1,298 | 1,743 | 1,934 | 884 | 622 | Пшеница - озимая |
| Spring wheat | 14,231 | 5,591 | 16,542 | 9,651 | 8,168 | 5,868 | яровая |
| Coarse grain | .. | .. | .. | 24,040 | 18,342 | 10,560 | Зерно в физическом весе |
| Rye | 889 | 506 | 568 | 889 | 264 | 84 | Рожь |
| Corn | 442 | 330 | 368 | 355 | 234 | 136 | Кукуруза |
| Winter barley | 118 | 105 | 125 | 119 | 25 | 19 | Ячмень - озимый |
| Spring barley | 9,185 | 3,307 | 9,357 | 7,790 | 5,472 | 2,189 | яровой |
| Oats | 681 | 265 | 831 | 906 | 822 | 250 | Овес |
| Millet | 1,077 | 287 | 562 | 294 | 130 | 39 | Просо |
| Rice | 653 | 590 | 543 | 479 | 283 | 183 | Рис |
| Flax | .. | .. | .. | .. | .. | .. | Лен |
| Oilseeds | 230 | 155 | 235 | 172 | 184 | 162 | Семена масличных культур |
| Cotton (raw) | 324 | 291 | 252 | 200 | 208 | 223 | Хлопок - сырец |
| Cotton fiber | 10 | 9 | .. | .. | .. | .. | волокно |
| Sugarbeets | 1,134 | 726 | 1,276 | 925 | 433 | 371 | Сахарная свекла |
| Potatoes | 2,324 | 2,143 | 2,570 | 2,296 | 2,040 | 1,720 | Картофель |
| Pulses | 176 | 75 | 148 | 108 | 52 | 29 | Бобовые |
| Vegetables | 1,136 | 955 | 985 | 808 | 781 | 780 | Овощи |
| Fruit | 301 | 98 | 169 | 85 | 100 | 97 | Фрукты |
| Grapes | 139 | 66 | 62 | 40 | 37 | 68 | Виноград |
| Other | 162 | 32 | 107 | .. | .. | .. | Прочие |
| Corn (silage and greenchop) | 44,104 | 14,238 | 24,748 | 19,202 | 15,837 | 4,404 | Кукуруза (на силос и зеленый корм) |
| Hay | 17,150 | 13,401 | 16,416 | 16,132 | 15,679 | 11,332 | Сено |
| **Average yield (kilograms per hectare)** | | | | | | | **Ср. урожайность (кг с га)** |
| Grain | 1,220 | 530 | 1,320 | 1,000 | 790 | 500 | Зерно |
| Winter wheat | 1,640 | 1,080 | 1,430 | 1,500 | 890 | 780 | Пшеница - озимая |
| Spring wheat | 1,110 | 460 | 1,310 | 800 | 700 | 500 | яровая |
| Coarse grain | 1,300 | 600 | 1,500 | 1,100 | 890 | 560 | Зерно в физическом весе |
| Rye | 1,160 | 900 | 910 | 1,500 | 820 | 480 | Рожь |
| Corn | 3,440 | 2,720 | 2,910 | 3,000 | 2,080 | 1,580 | Кукуруза |
| Winter barley | 2,240 | 1,600 | 2,060 | 1,900 | 970 | 870 | Ячмень - озимый |
| Spring barley | 1,390 | 500 | 1,650 | 1,100 | 910 | 460 | яровой |
| Oats | 1,780 | 520 | 1,820 | 1,700 | 1,280 | 510 | Овес |
| Millet | 1,380 | 340 | 560 | 600 | 360 | 160 | Просо |
| Rice | 5,250 | 4,980 | 4,490 | 4,300 | 2,760 | 1,930 | Рис |
| Flax | .. | .. | .. | .. | .. | .. | Лен |
| Oilseeds | 860 | 510 | 510 | 400 | 420 | 300 | Семена масличных культур |
| Cotton (raw) | 2,710 | 2,500 | 2,250 | 1,800 | 1,870 | 2,030 | Хлопок - сырец |
| Cotton fiber | 850 | 810 | .. | .. | .. | .. | волокно |
| Sugarbeets | 25,990 | 15,900 | 15,000 | 13,500 | 8,340 | 9,790 | Сахарная свекла |
| Potatoes | 11,290 | 9,890 | 10,400 | 9,400 | 9,350 | 8,350 | Картофель |
| Pulses | 1,110 | 500 | 1,060 | 900 | 490 | 440 | Бобовые |
| Vegetables | 15,440 | 12,100 | 11,400 | 10,600 | 10,390 | 10,060 | Овощи |
| Fruit | 4,190 | 1,460 | 2,220 | 1,200 | 1,490 | 1,430 | Фрукты |
| Grapes | 8,050 | 3,850 | 3,680 | 2,500 | 2,380 | 4,610 | Виноград |
| Other | .. | .. | .. | .. | .. | .. | Прочие |
| Corn (silage and greenchop) | 19,300 | 7,200 | 11,000 | 9,600 | 9,710 | 5,400 | Кукуруза (на силос и зеленый корм) |
| Hay | .. | .. | .. | .. | .. | .. | Сено |

## TABLE 5-4. Main aggregates of animal husbandry
## ТАБЛИЦА 5-4. Основные показатели животноводства

| Type of livestock or product | 1990 | 1991 | 1992 | 1993 | 1994 | 1995 | Направление животноводства или вид продукции |
|---|---|---|---|---|---|---|---|
| **Livestock (thousands of heads)** | | | | | | | **Поголовье скота (тысяч голов)** |
| Cattle | 9,757 | 9,592 | 9,576 | 9,347 | 8,073 | 6,860 | Крупный рогатый скот |
| of which: Cows | 3,368 | 3,490 | 3,623 | 3,687 | 3,397 | 3,045 | в том числе коровы |
| Pigs | 3,224 | 2,976 | 2,591 | 2,445 | 1,983 | 1,623 | Свиньи |
| Sheep and goats | 35,661 | 34,556 | 34,420 | 33,133 | 25,132 | 19,584 | Овцы и козы |
| of which: Goats | 983 | 997 | 1,044 | 1,095 | 897 | 859 | в том числе козы |
| Horses | 1,626 | 1,666 | 1,704 | 1,777 | 1,636 | 1,557 | Лошади |
| Other | .. | .. | .. | .. | .. | .. | Прочие |
| **Animal husbandry products** | | | | | | | **Продукция животноводства** |
| Meat (thousands of tons) | 1,560 | 1,524 | 1,258 | 1,312 | 1,207 | 985 | Мясо (тысяч тонн) |
| Beef | 710 | 724 | 596 | 662 | 642 | 548 | Говядина |
| Pork | 286 | 274 | 217 | 194 | 158 | 113 | Свинина |
| Lamb | 286 | 270 | 243 | 275 | 252 | 206 | Баранина |
| Poultry | 201 | 185 | 139 | 114 | 80 | 53 | Птица |
| Other | 77 | 72 | 62 | 67 | 75 | 65 | Прочие виды мяса |
| Milk (thousands of tons) | 5,642 | 5,555 | 5,265 | 5,577 | 5,296 | 4,619 | Молоко (тысяч тонн) |
| Eggs (millions) | 4,185 | 4,075 | 3,565 | 3,288 | 2,629 | 1,841 | Яйца (миллионов штук) |
| Wool (thousands of tons) | 108 | 104 | 96 | 95 | 75 | 58 | Шерсть (тысяч тонн) |

**TABLE 6-1. Industrial production by sector (millions of national currency)**
**ТАБЛИЦА 6-1. Промышленное производство по отраслям (млн. национальной валюты)**

| Sector | 1990 | 1991 | 1992 | 1993 | 1994 | 1995 | Отрасли |
|---|---|---|---|---|---|---|---|
| **All industry** | 34,738 | 85,436 | 1,301,988 | 22,951 | 340,993 | 621,563 | **Вся промышленность** |
| **Heavy industry** | 22,235 | 48,301 | 1,063,511 | 18,499 | 286,905 | 528,890 | **Тяжелая промышленность** |
| Fuel and energy | 4,521 | 10,627 | 375,263 | 6,902 | 139,105 | 245,586 | Топливно-энергетическая промышленноть |
| Electricity | 1,797 | 4,141 | 121,309 | 3,302 | 64,535 | 105,668 | Электроэнергетика |
| Fuels | 2,723 | 6,486 | 253,954 | 3,600 | 74,570 | 139,918 | Топливная промышленность |
| Ferrous and nonferrous metallurgy | 5,728 | 12,670 | 360,120 | 5,491 | 81,585 | 165,784 | Металлургия |
| Chemicals and petrochemical industry | 2,259 | 5,390 | 99,447 | 925 | 12,763 | 24,408 | Химическая и нефтехимическая пром. |
| Machine building and metalworking | 5,531 | 9,918 | 110,954 | 2,281 | 24,821 | 47,171 | Машиностроение и металлообработка |
| Forestry, woodworking, and pulp and paper industry | 964 | 1,788 | 15,731 | 541 | 3,563 | 5,760 | Лесная, деревообрабатывающая и целлюлозо-бумажная промышленность |
| Construction materials | 1,990 | 4,200 | 51,842 | 1,193 | 13,995 | 24,048 | Промышленность строительных материалов |
| **Light industry** | 5,402 | 15,798 | 83,673 | 1,323 | 12,906 | 14,809 | **Легкая промышленность** |
| Textiles | 3,299 | 11,008 | 58,125 | 838 | 8,439 | 10,809 | Текстильная |
| Clothing | 1,459 | 3,235 | 15,486 | 273 | 2,685 | 2,617 | Швейная |
| Leather and shoes | 635 | 1,541 | 7,545 | 208 | 1,740 | 1,342 | Кожевенная и обувная |
| **Food industry** | 5,640 | 19,014 | 126,041 | 2,612 | 33,783 | 64,338 | **Пищевая промышленность** |
| Processed foods | 2,275 | 4,900 | 56,505 | 1,120 | 15,314 | 33,338 | Пищевкусовая |
| Meat and dairy products | 3,189 | 13,730 | 67,255 | 1,424 | 17,416 | 29,175 | Мясная и молочная |
| Fish | 176 | 384 | 2,282 | 68 | 1,054 | 1,824 | Рыбная |

## TABLE 6-2. Industrial production by sector in constant prices
## ТАБЛИЦА 6-2. Промышленное производство по отраслям в постоянных ценах

| Sector | 1990 | 1991 | 1992 | 1993 | 1994 | 1995 | Отрасли |
|---|---|---|---|---|---|---|---|
| **Industrial production** | | | | | | | **Промышленное производство** |
| **All industry** | .. | .. | .. | .. | .. | .. | **Вся промышленность** |
| **Heavy industry** | .. | .. | .. | .. | .. | .. | **Тяжелая промышленность** |
| Fuel and energy | .. | .. | .. | .. | .. | .. | Топливно-энергетическая промышленноть |
| Electricity | .. | .. | .. | .. | .. | .. | Электроэнергетика |
| Fuels | .. | .. | .. | .. | .. | .. | Топливная промышленность |
| Ferrous and nonferrous metallurgy | .. | .. | .. | .. | .. | .. | Металлургия |
| Chemicals and petrochemicals | .. | .. | .. | .. | .. | .. | Химическая и нефтехимическая пром. |
| Machine building and metalworking | .. | .. | .. | .. | .. | .. | Машиностроение и металлообработка |
| Forestry, woodworking, and pulp and paper | .. | .. | .. | .. | .. | .. | Лесная, деревообрабатывающая и |
| | .. | .. | .. | .. | .. | .. | целлюлозо-бумажная промышленность |
| Construction materials | .. | .. | .. | .. | .. | .. | Промышленность строительных материалов |
| **Light industry** | .. | .. | .. | .. | .. | .. | **Легкая промышленность** |
| Textiles | .. | .. | .. | .. | .. | .. | Текстильная |
| Clothing | .. | .. | .. | .. | .. | .. | Швейная |
| Leather and shoe | .. | .. | .. | .. | .. | .. | Кожевенная и обувная |
| **Food industry** | .. | .. | .. | .. | .. | .. | **Пищевая промышленность** |
| Processed foods | .. | .. | .. | .. | .. | .. | Пищевкусовая |
| Meat and dairy products | .. | .. | .. | .. | .. | .. | Мясная и молочная |
| Fish | .. | .. | .. | .. | .. | .. | Рыбная |
| **Growth in production by sector (in percent)** | | | | | | | **Рост производства по отраслям** |
| **All industry** | -0.8 | -0.9 | -13.8 | -14.8 | -28.1 | -10.4 | **Вся промышленность** |
| **Heavy industry** | -2.1 | -1.2 | -10.9 | -15.7 | -21.5 | .. | **Тяжелая промышленность** |
| Power and fuels | -2.4 | 1.4 | -6.0 | -11.5 | -14.5 | -7.0 | Топливно-энергетическая промышленноть |
| Electricity | -1.4 | -0.9 | -6.2 | -4.4 | -15.2 | -1.6 | Электроэнергетика |
| Fuels | -3.0 | 2.5 | -5.9 | -14.8 | -14.0 | -12.3 | Топливная промышленность |
| Ferrous and nonferrous metallurgy | -3.8 | -1.4 | -6.6 | -15.9 | -20.6 | 11.9 | Металлургия |
| Chemicals and petrochemicals | -0.3 | -5.1 | -26.9 | -44.6 | -41.1 | 3.6 | Химическая и нефтехимическая пром. |
| Machine building and metalworking | -3.0 | 2.4 | -16.3 | -14.7 | -37.1 | -27.8 | Машиностроение и металлообработка |
| Forestry, woodworking, and pulp and paper | 1.4 | 2.7 | -14.4 | -8.7 | -44.9 | -42.8 | Лесная, деревообрабатывающая и целлюлозо-бумажная промышленность |
| Construction materials | -2.2 | 1.3 | -16.9 | -26.8 | -57.1 | -32.1 | Промышленность строительных материалов |
| **Light industry** | 1.5 | 2.5 | -21.0 | -11.7 | -44.3 | -60.1 | **Легкая промышленность** |
| Textiles | 0.2 | -1.2 | -21.5 | -12.2 | -39.7 | -55.4 | Текстильная |
| Clothing | 4.0 | 15.5 | -22.0 | -4.3 | -54.9 | -83.5 | Швейная |
| Leather and shoe | 2.0 | 4.8 | -16.6 | -17.4 | -56.3 | -76.4 | Кожевенная и обувная |
| **Food industry** | 2.2 | -6.1 | -24.9 | -11.7 | -23.9 | -37.3 | **Пищевая промышленность** |
| Processed foods | -0.7 | -7.4 | -17.6 | -15.6 | -18.8 | -39.3 | Пищевкусовая |
| Meat and dairy products | 0.8 | -6.8 | -34.1 | -12.7 | -31.6 | -36.9 | Мясная и молочная |
| Fish | -1.8 | 10.2 | -20.2 | -1.3 | -23.2 | -21.9 | Рыбная |

**TABLE 6-3. Primary energy supply (million tons oil equivalent)**

**ТАБЛИЦА 6-3. Ресурсы первичных видов энергии (млн. тонн нефтяного эквивалента)**

| Item | | 1990 | 1991 | 1992 | 1993 | 1994 | 1995 | Статьи | |
|---|---|---|---|---|---|---|---|---|---|
| **Primary production** | | | | | | | | **Производство первичной энергии** | |
| Coal and lignite (hard and brown) | | 131.4 | 130.4 | 126.5 | 111.9 | 104.6 | 83.3 | Уголь каменный и бурый | |
| Crude oil | | 21.7 | 22.0 | 21.9 | 19.6 | 18.5 | 17.9 | Нефть | |
| Gas | | 7.1 | 7.9 | 8.1 | 6.7 | 4.5 | 5.9 | Газ | |
| Nuclear | | .. | .. | .. | .. | .. | .. | Атомная энергия | |
| Hydro/geothermal | | .. | .. | .. | .. | .. | .. | Гидро-геотермальная | |
| Other | | .. | .. | .. | .. | .. | .. | Другие виды | |
| Total | | .. | .. | .. | .. | .. | .. | Всего | |
| **Energy trade** | | | | | | | | **Торговля энергией** | |
| Coal and lignite | Exports | .. | .. | .. | 34.5 | 22.5 | 13.0 | Уголь каменный и бурый | Экспорт |
| | Imports | .. | .. | .. | 4.7 | 0.2 | 1.2 | | Импорт |
| | Net imports | .. | .. | .. | -29.7 | -22.3 | -11.8 | | Чистый импорт |
| Oil/oil product | Exports | .. | .. | .. | 15.4 | 10.6 | 12.6 | Нефть и нефтепродукты | Экспорт |
| | Imports | .. | .. | .. | 10.4 | 3.9 | 2.4 | | Импорт |
| | Net imports | .. | .. | .. | -5.0 | -6.7 | -10.2 | | Чистый импорт |
| Gas | Exports | .. | .. | .. | 3.5 | 1.6 | 2.6 | Газ | Экспорт |
| | Imports | .. | .. | .. | 9.8 | 7.2 | 9.1 | | Импорт |
| | Net imports | .. | .. | .. | 6.3 | 5.5 | 6.6 | | Чистый импорт |
| Electricity | Exports | .. | .. | .. | .. | .. | .. | Электричество | Экспорт |
| | Imports | .. | .. | .. | 11705.8 | 13030.7 | 7392.7 | | Импорт |
| | Net imports | .. | .. | .. | 11705.8 | 13030.7 | 7392.7 | | Чистый импорт |
| **Total net imports** | | .. | .. | .. | .. | .. | .. | **Чистый импорт энергии-всего** | |
| **Total stock changes** | | .. | .. | .. | .. | .. | .. | **Изменение запасов-всего** | |
| **Total primary energy supply** | | .. | .. | .. | .. | .. | .. | **Ресурсы первичной энергии-всего** | |
| Coal and lignite | | .. | .. | .. | .. | .. | .. | Уголь каменный и бурый | |
| Oil/oil products | | .. | .. | .. | .. | .. | .. | Нефть и нефтепродукты | |
| Gas | | .. | .. | .. | .. | .. | .. | Газ | |
| Nuclear | | .. | .. | .. | .. | .. | .. | Атомная энергия | |
| Hydro/geothermal | | .. | .. | .. | .. | .. | .. | Гидро-геотермальная энергия | |
| Other | | .. | .. | .. | .. | .. | .. | Другие виды | |
| **Total primary energy requirement (equals total primary energy supply)** | | .. | .. | .. | .. | .. | .. | **Потребность в первичной энергии-всего (равно ресурсам первичной энергии)** | |

**TABLE 6-4. Final energy consumption (million tons oil equivalent)**
**ТАБЛИЦА 6-4. Конечное потребление энергии ( млн. тонн нефтяного эквивалента )**

| | 1991 | 1992 | 1993 | 1994 | 1995 | |
|---|---|---|---|---|---|---|
| **Final energy consumption** | .. | .. | .. | .. | .. | **Конечное потребление энергии** |
| Coal & Lignite | 77.3 | 78.2 | 73.7 | 64.7 | 61.0 | Уголь каменный и бурый |
| Oil Products | 16.5 | 15.4 | 13.5 | 10.3 | 8.5 | Нефтепродукты |
| Gas | 10.8 | 11.9 | 9.9 | 7.8 | 7.5 | Газ |
| Electricity | 101.6 | 96.9 | 89.2 | 79.4 | 73.5 | Электроэнергия |
| Heat | 106.2 | 113.0 | 100.7 | 81.7 | 71.0 | Тепло |
| Other | 0.4 | 0.3 | 0.3 | 0.3 | 0.3 | Другие виды |
| Of which: | | | | | | В том числе |
| **Industry** | .. | .. | .. | .. | .. | **Промышленность** |
| Coal & Lignite | .. | .. | 63.3 | 54.9 | 53.0 | Уголь каменный и бурый |
| Oil Products | .. | .. | 5.7 | 5.0 | 4.5 | Нефтепродукты |
| Gas | .. | .. | 8.2 | 5.5 | 5.7 | Газ |
| Electricity | 60.3 | 52.7 | 44.9 | 36.4 | 35.6 | Электроэнергия |
| Heat | 59.0 | 70.9 | 58.2 | 47.0 | 41.0 | Тепло |
| Other | .. | .. | 0.2 | 0.2 | 0.2 | Другие виды |
| **Agriculture** | .. | .. | .. | .. | .. | **Сельское хозяйство** |
| Coal & Lignite | .. | .. | 5.7 | 5.2 | 3.5 | Уголь каменный и бурый |
| Oil Products | .. | .. | 4.1 | 3.2 | 2.2 | Нефтепродукты |
| Gas | .. | .. | 0.4 | 0.3 | 0.2 | Газ |
| Electricity | 14.1 | 15.1 | 16.4 | 15.9 | 12.4 | Электроэнергия |
| Heat | .. | .. | .. | .. | .. | Тепло |
| Other | .. | .. | 0.0 | 0.0 | 0.0 | Другие виды |
| **Transport** | .. | .. | .. | .. | .. | **Транспорт** |
| Oil Products | .. | .. | 1.8 | 1.2 | 1.1 | Нефтепродукты |
| Other | .. | .. | 0.0 | 0.0 | 0.0 | Другие виды |
| **Households** | .. | .. | .. | .. | .. | **Домашние хозяйства** |
| Coal & Lignite | .. | .. | .. | .. | .. | Уголь каменный и бурый |
| Oil Products | .. | .. | .. | .. | .. | Нефтепродукты |
| Gas | .. | .. | .. | .. | .. | Газ |
| Electricity | .. | 9.1 | 9.1 | 9.3 | 8.1 | Электроэнергия |
| Heat | 35.6 | 38.0 | 48.1 | 27.0 | 21.5 | Тепло |
| Other | .. | .. | .. | .. | .. | Другие виды |

## TABLE 7-1. Price indices and exchange rates
## ТАБЛИЦА 7-1. Индексы цен и обменный курс

| Year and month | National currency per U.S. dollar / Единиц нац. валюты за 1 доллар США | National currency per Russian ruble / Единиц нац. валюты за 1 российский рубль | Consumer price index (as a percent of the previous month) / Индекс потребительских цен (в % к предыдущему месяцу) | Producer price index (as a percent of the previous month) / Индекс цен производителей (в % к предыдущему месяцу) | Consumer price index (as a percent of the previous December) / Индекс потребительских цен (в % к декабрю прошлого года) | Producer price index (as a percent of the previous December) / Индекс цен производителей (в % к декабрю прошлого года) | Год и месяц |
|---|---|---|---|---|---|---|---|
| **1993** | | | | | | | **1993** |
| January | 0.9 | 0.0020 | 132.9 | 116.0 | 132.9 | 116.0 | Январь |
| February | 1.1 | 0.0020 | 131.9 | 132.0 | 175.0 | 153.1 | Февраль |
| March | 1.3 | 0.0020 | 133.0 | 123.0 | 232.8 | 188.3 | Март |
| April | 1.5 | 0.0020 | 121.4 | 121.6 | 282.5 | 229.0 | Апрель |
| May | 1.8 | 0.0020 | 116.1 | 115.1 | 327.9 | 263.6 | Май |
| June | 2.2 | 0.0020 | 117.9 | 124.1 | 386.7 | 327.1 | Июнь |
| July | 2.1 | 0.0020 | 121.8 | 122.6 | 471.0 | 401.1 | Июль |
| August | 2.8 | 0.0028 | 129.1 | 126.7 | 608.0 | 508.1 | Август |
| September | 3.2 | 0.0030 | 129.0 | 120.6 | 784.1 | 612.8 | Сентябрь |
| October | 3.5 | 0.0030 | 138.2 | 128.3 | 1,083.7 | 786.2 | Октябрь |
| November | 4.6 | 0.0039 | 155.5 | 130.3 | 1,684.8 | 1,024.5 | Ноябрь |
| December | 5.8 | 0.0043 | 134.4 | 139.0 | 2,265.0 | 1,424.0 | Декабрь |
| **1994** | | | | | | | **1994** |
| January | 7.9 | 0.0055 | 142.6 | 144.9 | 142.6 | 144.9 | Январь |
| February | 11.4 | 0.0070 | 124.2 | 134.9 | 177.1 | 195.5 | Февраль |
| March | 16.7 | 0.0097 | 117.4 | 129.5 | 207.8 | 253.2 | Март |
| April | 23.6 | 0.0131 | 131.8 | 182.8 | 273.8 | 462.8 | Апрель |
| May | 35.6 | 0.0177 | 133.8 | 137.2 | 366.3 | 634.9 | Май |
| June | 41.7 | 0.0220 | 145.9 | 145.7 | 534.3 | 925.1 | Июнь |
| July | 44.7 | 0.0217 | 125.4 | 135.8 | 669.9 | 1,256.6 | Июль |
| August | 45.7 | 0.0209 | 113.3 | 113.2 | 759.2 | 1,422.7 | Август |
| September | 47.0 | 0.0210 | 109.7 | 116.8 | 832.4 | 1,661.9 | Сентябрь |
| October | 48.7 | 0.0165 | 120.1 | 113.1 | 1,000.0 | 1,879.9 | Октябрь |
| November | 51.0 | 0.0159 | 114.2 | 103.0 | 1,141.6 | 1,936.9 | Ноябрь |
| December | 53.5 | 0.0163 | 110.2 | 104.5 | 1,258.3 | 2,023.8 | Декабрь |

## TABLE 7-1. Price indices and exchange rates
## ТАБЛИЦА 7-1. Индексы цен и обменный курс

| Year and month | National currency per U.S. dollar<br>Единиц нац. валюты за 1 доллар США | National currency per Russian ruble<br>Единиц нац. валюты за 1 российский рубль | Consumer price index (as a percent of the previous month)<br>Индекс потребительских цен (в % к предыдущему месяцу) | Producer price index (as a percent of the previous month)<br>Индекс цен производителей (в % к предыдущему месяцу) | Consumer price index (as a percent of the previous December)<br>Индекс потребительских цен (в % к декабрю прошлого года) | Producer price index (as a percent of the previous December)<br>Индекс цен производителей (в % к декабрю прошлого года) | Год и месяц |
|---|---|---|---|---|---|---|---|
| **1995** | | | | | | | **1995** |
| January | 55.4 | 0.0148 | 108.9 | 105.9 | 108.9 | 105.9 | Январь |
| February | 58.7 | 0.0139 | 106.7 | 105.5 | 116.2 | 111.7 | Февраль |
| March | 60.5 | 0.0128 | 105.1 | 105.1 | 122.1 | 117.4 | Март |
| April | 62.1 | 0.0124 | 103.2 | 104.3 | 126.0 | 122.4 | Апрель |
| May | 63.1 | 0.0121 | 102.7 | 100.4 | 129.4 | 122.9 | Май |
| June | 63.5 | 0.0134 | 102.3 | 101.2 | 132.4 | 124.3 | Июнь |
| July | 62.6 | 0.0138 | 102.9 | 101.9 | 136.3 | 126.7 | Июль |
| August | 56.6 | 0.0130 | 102.1 | 106.7 | 139.2 | 135.2 | Август |
| September | 59.8 | 0.0134 | 102.4 | 97.8 | 142.4 | 132.2 | Сентябрь |
| October | 61.5 | 0.0136 | 104.1 | 103.7 | 148.2 | 137.1 | Октябрь |
| November | 63.3 | 0.0140 | 104.4 | 101.6 | 154.7 | 139.3 | Ноябрь |
| December | 64.0 | 0.0139 | 103.6 | 100.6 | 160.3 | 140.2 | Декабрь |
| **1996** | | | | | | | **1996** |
| January | 64.3 | 0.0138 | 104.1 | 103.6 | 104.1 | 103.6 | Январь |
| February | 65.2 | 0.0139 | 102.5 | 103.0 | 106.7 | 106.7 | Февраль |
| March | 65.2 | 0.0138 | 101.7 | 100.4 | 108.5 | 107.1 | Март |
| April | 65.5 | 0.0138 | 102.9 | 101.0 | 111.8 | 108.1 | Апрель |
| May | 66.4 | 0.0138 | 102.0 | 101.5 | 114.0 | 109.7 | Май |
| June | 66.8 | .. | 102.5 | 101.9 | 116.8 | 111.8 | Июнь |
| July | 67.0 | .. | 101.8 | 99.7 | 118.9 | 111.4 | Июль |
| August | 67.3 | .. | 100.7 | 101.3 | 119.7 | 112.8 | Август |
| September | .. | .. | .. | .. | .. | .. | Сентябрь |
| October | .. | .. | .. | .. | .. | .. | Октябрь |
| November | .. | .. | .. | .. | .. | .. | Ноябрь |
| December | .. | .. | .. | .. | .. | .. | Декабрь |

## TABLE 7-2. Monthly nominal wages by sector
## ТАБЛИЦА 7-2. Среднемесячная денежная зарплата по отраслям

| Sector | 1990 | 1991 | 1992 | 1993 | 1994 | 1995 | Сектора |
|---|---|---|---|---|---|---|---|
| **Nominal wages** | | | | | | | **Средняя номинальная заработная плата** |
| **Economy average** | 265.4 | 440.8 | 4,625.0 | 127.5 | 1,725.7 | 4,786.0 | **По народному хозяйству** |
| **Material sphere** | 287.0 | 467.0 | 5,100.0 | 138.0 | 1,980.0 | 5,432.0 | **Отрасли сферы материального производства** |
| Industry | 296.0 | 534.3 | 6,161.0 | 170.5 | 2,800.5 | 7,792.0 | Промышленность |
| Construction | 330.3 | 536.1 | 5,727.0 | 170.4 | 2,660.1 | 7,850.0 | Строительство |
| Agriculture | 292.4 | 413.6 | 4,834.0 | 100.5 | 1,038.2 | 2,392.0 | Сельское хозяйство |
| Transport | 302.7 | 492.8 | 5,797.0 | 181.6 | 2,407.7 | 6,808.0 | Транспорт |
| Communications | 227.5 | 388.9 | 3,726.0 | 119.8 | 1,821.4 | 5,875.0 | Связь |
| Trade (retail and wholesale) | 212.6 | 356.8 | 3,349.0 | 92.8 | 1,188.5 | 3,350.0 | Торговля (оптовая и розничная) |
| Other | 176.1 | 293.2 | 3,531.0 | 92.4 | 1,353.4 | 4,058.0 | Прочие отрасли материального производства |
| **Nonmaterial sphere** | 203.0 | 356.0 | 2,853.0 | 93.0 | 1,170.6 | 3,538.0 | **Отрасли непроизводственной сферы** |
| Municipal services | 198.9 | 336.7 | 3,283.0 | 101.7 | 1,581.3 | 4,628.0 | Жилкомхоз и бытовое обслуживание |
| Science, research and development | 320.2 | 476.0 | 4,459.0 | 119.3 | 1,469.9 | 4,483.0 | Наука и научное обслуживание |
| Education | 182.1 | 319.0 | 2,484.0 | 80.6 | 892.6 | 2,933.0 | Образование |
| Culture | 161.1 | 285.4 | 2,011.0 | 70.0 | 774.9 | 2,342.0 | Культура |
| Arts | 169.5 | 297.5 | 2,160.0 | 68.1 | 748.0 | 2,233.0 | Искусство |
| Health care, social security, and sports | 178.0 | 351.8 | 2,199.0 | 66.2 | 797.2 | 2,675.0 | Здравоохр., соц.обсл., физк. и спорт |
| Banking, finance, credit, insurance | 354.2 | 742.7 | 8,340.0 | 288.1 | 4,179.2 | 1,096.7 | Кредитование, страхование, банк. дело |
| Government | 334.7 | 474.2 | 4,665.0 | 139.4 | 1,775.0 | 4,475.0 | Управление |

## TABLE 8-1. Money income and expenditure of the population (millions of national currency)
## ТАБЛИЦА 8-1. Денежные доходы и расходы населения (млн. национальной валюты)

| Type of income or expenditure | 1990 | 1991 | 1992 | 1993 | 1994 | 1995 | Вид доходов или расходов |
|---|---|---|---|---|---|---|---|
| **Income** | | | | | | | **Доходы** |
| **Total labor income** | 26,697 | 44,478 | 455,361 | 7,824 | 83,870 | 215,064 | **Всего трудовых доходов** |
| Regular wages | 23,033 | 37,654 | 301,293 | 6,960 | 74,442 | 199,671 | Заработная плата |
| Wages paid by cooperatives | 1,167 | 1,712 | 20,496 | 496 | .. | 199 | Заработная плата в кооперативах |
| Other wages and compensation | 850 | 1,945 | 10,281 | 243 | 3,253 | 9,167 | Прочие доходы типа заработной платы |
| Income paid by collective farms | 702 | 1,701 | 8,919 | 210 | .. | 448 | Доходы от колхозов |
| Income from sale of farm products | 2,112 | 3,178 | 134,868 | 411 | 6,174 | 5,679 | Доходы от продажи продукции колхозов |
| **Total transfer receipts** | 5,606 | 16,231 | 97,712 | 2,819 | 37,733 | 74,923 | **Всего трансфертных поступлений** |
| Pensions and allowances | 3,430 | 13,467 | 81,340 | 1,802 | 23,454 | 52,839 | Пенсии и пособия |
| Scholarships | 184 | 546 | 2,878 | 52 | 675 | 2,632 | Стипендии |
| Income from the financial system (insurance, interest, etc.) | 1,286 | 1,329 | 9,598 | 263 | 1,992 | 7,656 | Доходы из финансовой системы (страховые возмещения, проценты и т.д.) |
| Other income | 706 | 889 | 3,896 | 702 | 11,612 | 11,796 | Прочие виды доходов |
| **Total income** | 32,303 | 60,709 | 553,073 | 10,643 | 121,602 | 289,987 | **Всего доходов** |
| **Expenditure** | | | | | | | **Расходы** |
| **Total purchases** | 24,039 | 41,237 | 297,461 | 5,487 | 69,470 | 121,454 | **Всего покупок товаров и услуг** |
| Retail goods | 21,512 | 35,591 | 261,209 | 4,601 | 50,633 | 67,710 | Товары в розничной торговле |
| Services | 2,527 | 5,646 | 36,252 | 886 | 18,837 | 53,744 | Услуги |
| Rent and utilities | 667 | 760 | 7,688 | 180 | 3,881 | 17,531 | Квартирная плата и коммунальные платежи |
| Transport and communications | 1,113 | 1,860 | 18,581 | 634 | 8,016 | 26,673 | Транспорт и связь |
| Health and other services | 636 | 2,300 | 9,723 | 42 | 6,941 | 9,539 | Здравоохранение и другие виды услуг |
| Cooperatives | 111 | 725 | 260 | 30 | .. | .. | Кооперативы |
| **Transfers and savings** | 6,349 | 11,011 | 120,010 | 2,105 | 34,453 | 139,304 | **Трансферты и сбережения** |
| Taxes, fees, dues, and other | 3,864 | 4,715 | 45,252 | 1,272 | 9,207 | 34,646 | Налоги, сборы, пошлины и др. |
| Savings | 2,274 | 6,061 | 74,735 | 830 | 4,703 | 7,717 | Сбережения |
| Other | 211 | 235 | 23 | 3 | 20,543 | 96,941 | Прочие |
| **Total expenditure** | 30,388 | 52,248 | 417,471 | 7,592 | 103,922 | 260,757 | **Всего расходов** |
| **Income less expenditure** | 1,915 | 8,461 | 135,602 | 3,051 | 17,680 | 29,230 | **Доходы за вычетом расходов** |

# *Country Notes: Kazakstan*

**General Note:** Unless otherwise indicated, the data were supplied by the State Committee for Statistics and Analysis of the Republic of Kazakstan.

**Currency:** The national currency, tenge, was introduced on November 15, 1993 with the conversion factor 1 tenge = 500 rubles. Unless otherwise indicated, data for 1990-1992 are in rubles and for 1993-1995 in tenge.

**Table 1-1:** Data are shown as of the beginning of the year. Prior to 1994, the unemployed are registered unemployed. For 1994-1995, all unemployed are included. Sums of items of total employment and total labor resources mostly do not add up to the respective totals.

**Table 2-1:** Data for 1991-1994 are preliminary estimates of the World Bank staff and the State Committee for Statistics and Analysis of the Republic of Kazakstan. Transport includes road maintenance. Wholesale trade includes retail trade and catering. In 1995 it also includes material supply, procurement, and information and computer services. Credit includes insurance. The statistical discrepancy between GDP by industrial origin and total GDP by expenditure category is as follows:

| Year | Statistical discrepancy |
|---|---|
| 1990 | 656.5 |
| 1991 | 5,463.8 |
| 1992 | 62,735.8 |
| 1993 | -504.2 |
| 1994 | -13,738.8 |
| 1995 | 27218.7 |

**Table 2-2:** Data are in previous year prices. See also notes to Table 2-1. In 1995 Wholesale trade includes also material supply and procurement. The statistical discrepancy between total GDP by industrial origin at market prices and total GDP by expenditure category is as follows:

| Year | Statistical discrepancy |
|---|---|
| 1991 | 545.4 |
| 1992 | 5,508.5 |
| 1993 | 51,041.3 |
| 1994 | -21.5 |
| 1995 | 21,345.8 |

**Table 5-2:** For 1990-1993 data are in millions of 1983 rubles. For 1994-1995, data are in millions of 1994 tenge. Data for 1995 are preliminary. In 1993, the sum of items of livestock does not equal the total.

**Table 6-1:** Data do not include households' production, which in 1995 the amounted to: in all industry - 24.3, in light industry - 1.7, and in food industry - 21.4 bln. tenge.

**Table 6-3:** Oil, coal and lignite are in millions of tons. Gas is in billions of cubic meters. Electricity is in millions of kilowatt-hours.

**Table 6-4:** Oil products, coal and lignite are in millions of tons. Gas is in billions of cubic meters. Electricity is in billions of kilowatt-hours. Heat is in millions of gigacalories. Other energy consumption is in thousands of tons of conventional fuel.

# *Комментарии к таблицам: Казахстан*

**Общее замечание:** За исключением особо отмеченных случаев, данные были получены из Государственного Комитета по Статистике и Анализу Республики Казахстан.

**Национальная валюта:** Тенге был введен 15 ноября 1993 г. с коэффициентом пересчета 1 тенге = 500 рублей. За исключением особо отмеченных случаев, данные за 1990-1992 гг. приведены в рублях, а за 1993-1995 гг. - в тенге.

**Таблица 1-1:** Данные приведены на начало года. До 1994 г. строка Безработные показывает только зарегестрированных безработных, а в 1994-1995 гг. - всех безработных. Суммы компонентов занятого населения и трудовых ресурсов, как правило, не равны приведенным итогам.

**Таблица 2-1:** Данные за 1991-1994 гг. являются предварительными оценками сотрудников Всемирного Банка и Государственного Комитета по Статистике и Анализу Республики Казахстан. Транспорт включает дорожное хозяйство. Оптовая торговля включает розничную торговлю и общепит. Кредитование включает страхование. Статистическое расхождение между ВВП по производству в рыночных ценах и ВВП по видам расходов составляет:

| Год | Статистическое расхождение |
|---|---|
| 1990 | 656,5 |
| 1991 | 5463,8 |
| 1992 | 62735,8 |
| 1993 | -504,2 |
| 1994 | -13738,8 |
| 1995 | 27218,7 |

**Таблица 2-2:** Данные приведены в ценах предыдущего года. См. комментарии к Таблице 2-1. В 1995 г. Оптовая торговля включает также материально-техническое снабжение и заготовки. Статистическое расхождение между ВВП по производству в рыночных ценах и ВВП по видам расходов составляет:

| Год | Статистическое расхождение |
|---|---|
| 1991 | 545,4 |
| 1992 | 5508,5 |
| 1993 | 51041,3 |
| 1994 | -21,5 |
| 1995 | 21345,8 |

**Таблица 5-2:** За 1990-1993 гг. данные приведены в миллионах рублей в ценах 1983 г., за 1994-1995 гг. - в миллионах тенге в ценах 1994 г. Данные за 1995 г. являются предварительными. В 1993 г. сумма компонентов по мясному животноводству не равна приведенной итоговой величине.

**Таблица 6-1:** Данные не включают производство в домашнем хозяйстве, объем которого составлял в 1995 г. 24,3 миллиарда тенге во всей промышленности, 1,7 миллиарда тенге - в легкой промышленности и 21,4 миллиарда тенге - в пищевой промышленности.

**Таблица 6-3:** Нефть и уголь приведены в миллионах тонн, газ - в миллиардах кубических метров, электричество в миллионах киловатт-часов.

**Таблица 6-4:** Нефтепродукты и уголь приведены в миллионах тонн, газ - в миллиардах кубических метров, электричество - в миллиардах киловатт-часов, тепло - в миллионах гигакалорий, конечное потребление других видов энергии - в тысячах тонн условного топлива.

# Kyrgyz Republic / Кыргызская Республика

1996 Population / Численность населения в 1996 году
(thousands / тыс. человек): 4,545

Area / Территория
(thousand square kilometers / тыс. кв. км.): 198.5

Capital city / Столица :
Bishkek / Бишкек

**Country Tables:** Tables 6-3 and 6-4 are not included because there are no data available.

**Статистические таблицы страны: :** Таблицы 6-3 и 6-4 не включены ввиду отсутствия данных.

## TABLE 1-1. Population and employment (thousands)
## ТАБЛИЦА 1-1. Население и занятость (тысяч)



| Population or employment category | 1990 | 1991 | 1992 | 1993 | 1994 | 1995 | Население или группы занятых |
|---|---|---|---|---|---|---|---|
| **Total population** | 4,335 | 4,390 | 4,452 | 4,469 | 4,430 | 4,451 | **Население - всего** |
| Males | 2,118 | 2,149 | 2,183 | 2,197 | 2,185 | 2,194 | Мужчины |
| Females | 2,217 | 2,241 | 2,269 | 2,272 | 2,245 | 2,257 | Женщины |
| Urban population | 1,648 | 1,668 | 1,681 | 1,662 | 1,572 | 1,558 | Городское |
| Rural population | 2,687 | 2,722 | 2,771 | 2,807 | 2,858 | 2,893 | Сельское |
| Population under working age | 1,714 | 1,740 | 1,767 | 1,777 | 1,771 | 1,774 | Моложе трудоспособного возраста |
| Working-age population | 2,185 | 2,211 | 2,239 | 2,243 | 2,219 | 2,239 | Лица в трудоспособном возрасте |
| Population over working age | 435 | 439 | 445 | 450 | 440 | 438 | Старше трудоспособного возраста |
| Economically Active Population, in non-working age | 50 | 50 | 72 | 82 | 84 | 85 | Экономически активное население в нетрудоспособном возрасте |
| Above working age | 47 | 47 | 65 | 74 | 75 | 77 | Старше трудоспособного возраста |
| Below working age | 3 | 3 | 7 | 8 | 8 | 8 | Моложе трудоспособного возраста |
| **Total labor resources** | 2,184 | 2,215 | 2,264 | 2,256 | 2,261 | 2,290 | **Трудовые ресурсы - всего** |
| **Total employment** | 1,748 | 1,754 | 1,836 | 1,681 | 1,645 | 1,641 | **Занятое население - всего** |
| State sector employees | 1,350 | 1,202 | 1,150 | 885 | 686 | 656 | Государственный сектор |
| Leased enterprise employees | .. | 93 | 45 | 22 | 12 | 7 | Арендные предприятия |
| Joint-stock company employees | .. | 11 | 44 | 144 | 150 | 140 | Акционерные общества |
| Economic association employees | .. | 0 | 1 | 2 | 0 | 14 | Хозяйственные ассоциации |
| Social organization employees | .. | 6 | 9 | 9 | 8 | 8 | Общественные организации |
| Joint venture employees | .. | 1 | 1 | 3 | 4 | 7 | Совместные предприятия |
| Collective farm workers | 178 | 194 | 169 | 173 | 166 | 37 | Колхозы |
| Cooperative workers | 33 | 21 | 52 | 36 | 25 | 30 | Кооперативы |
| Individual labor activities | 3 | 3 | 10 | 27 | 141 | 140 | ИТД |
| Private subsidiary agricultural workers | 184 | 208 | 224 | 210 | 201 | 200 | Личные подсобные хозяйства |
| Private agricultural workers | .. | 16 | 80 | 77 | 140 | 305 | Фермерские хозяйства |
| **Students** | 204 | 205 | 201 | 182 | 170 | 165 | **Учащиеся** |
| **Religious workers** | 0 | .. | 0 | 0 | 1 | 1 | **Служащие религиозного культа** |
| **Working age population not employed in the national economy** | 232 | 256 | 227 | 394 | 446 | 484 | **Лица в трудоспособном возрасте, не занятые в экономике** |
| Housewives | .. | .. | .. | .. | .. | .. | Домохозяйки |
| Military personnel | .. | .. | .. | .. | .. | .. | Военнослужащие |
| Unemployed | .. | .. | .. | .. | 71 | 100 | Безработные |
| **Labor force** | .. | .. | .. | .. | 1,716 | 1,741 | **Рабочая сила** |

**TABLE 1-2. Employment by sector (thousands)**
**ТАБЛИЦА 1-2. Численность занятого населения по секторам (тысяч)**

| Sector | 1990 | 1991 | 1992 | 1993 | 1994 | 1995 | Сектор |
|---|---|---|---|---|---|---|---|
| **Material sphere** | 1,261 | 1,281 | 1,319 | 1,214 | 1,213 | 1,207 | **Сфера материального производства** |
| **Agriculture and forestry** | 572 | 623 | 701 | 655 | 691 | 689 | **Сельское и лесное хозяйство** |
| Agriculture | 569 | 620 | 696 | 651 | 685 | 683 | Сельское хозяйство |
| Forestry | 3 | 3 | 4 | 4 | 6 | 6 | Лесное хозяйство |
| **Industry and construction** | 487 | 466 | 414 | 359 | 318 | 317 | **Промышленность и строительство** |
| Industry | 334 | 319 | 300 | 270 | 241 | 240 | Промышленность |
| Construction | 153 | 147 | 114 | 89 | 77 | 77 | Строительство |
| **Other** | 202 | 192 | 205 | 200 | 204 | 201 | **Другие отрасли** |
| Transport of goods | 57 | 55 | 54 | 54 | 44 | 43 | Грузовой транспорт |
| Road Maintenance | .. | .. | .. | .. | .. | .. | Дорожное хозяйство |
| Communication servicing material production | .. | .. | .. | .. | 3 | 3 | Связь |
| Wholesale trade | .. | .. | .. | .. | .. | .. | Оптовая торговля |
| Retail trade and catering | 115 | 111 | 107 | 88 | 113 | 112 | Розничная торговля и общепит |
| Material supply | .. | .. | .. | .. | 8 | 9 | Материально-техническое снабжение |
| Procurement | .. | .. | .. | .. | 6 | 5 | Заготовки |
| Information and computing services | 5 | 4 | 3 | 2 | 1 | 1 | Информационно-техническое обслуживание |
| Other sectors | 26 | 23 | 40 | 56 | 29 | 28 | Другие отрасли сферы материального пр. |
| **Nonmaterial sphere** | 487 | 474 | 517 | 467 | 432 | 434 | **Сфера нематериального производства** |
| Passenger transport | 37 | 39 | 40 | 32 | 28 | 30 | Пассажирский транспорт |
| Communication | .. | .. | . | .. | 10 | 10 | Связь |
| Housing | 45 | 44 | 42 | 36 | 33 | 32 | Жилищное хозяйство |
| Public utilities and personal services | .. | .. | .. | .. | .. | .. | Комм. хоз. и бытовое обслуживание |
| Health care, social security, physical culture and sports | 105 | 107 | 142 | 125 | 102 | 103 | Здравоохранение, социальное обеспечение, физкультура и спорт |
| Education | 216 | 213 | 217 | 199 | 169 | 170 | Образование |
| Culture and art | .. | .. | .. | .. | 16 | 15 | Культура и искусство |
| Science and scientific research | 35 | 27 | 14 | 11 | 8 | 8 | Наука и научное обслуживание |
| Credit | .. | .. | .. | .. | 8 | 8 | Кредитование |
| Insurance | 7 | 7 | 8 | 8 | 7 | .. | Страхование |
| General administration and defense | 43 | 37 | 54 | 56 | 58 | 58 | Государственное управление и оборона |
| Private nonprofit institutions serving households | .. | .. | .. | .. | .. | .. | Общественные организации, обслуживающие домашние хозяйства |
| **Other, material and nonmaterial spheres** | 689 | 666 | 722 | 668 | 636 | 635 | **Остальные отрасли материального производства и нематериальной сферы** |
| **Total employment** | 1,748 | 1,754 | 1,836 | 1,681 | 1,645 | 1,641 | **Занятые - всего** |

TABLE 1-3. Registered unemployment (thousands; end of month) KYRGYZ REPUBLIC

ТАБЛИЦА 1-3. Численность зарегистрированных безработных (тысяч; на конец месяца)

| Year and month | Total<br>Всего | Males<br>Мужчины | Females<br>Женщины | Receiving benefits<br>Получающие пособие | Год и месяц |
|---|---|---|---|---|---|
| **1994** | | | | | **1994** |
| January | 3.1 | 1.0 | 2.1 | 1.9 | Январь |
| February | 3.6 | 1.2 | 2.4 | 2.1 | Февраль |
| March | 4.1 | 1.4 | 2.7 | 2.6 | Март |
| April | 5.1 | 1.7 | 3.4 | 3.4 | Апрель |
| May | 6.1 | 2.0 | 4.1 | 3.9 | Май |
| June | 7.1 | 2.8 | 4.3 | 4.3 | Июнь |
| July | 8.3 | 3.3 | 5.0 | 4.9 | Июль |
| August | 9.0 | 3.3 | 5.7 | 5.5 | Август |
| September | 10.2 | 3.8 | 6.4 | 6.3 | Сентябрь |
| October | 11.0 | 4.1 | 6.9 | 6.6 | Октябрь |
| November | 11.9 | 4.7 | 7.2 | 7.0 | Ноябрь |
| December | 12.6 | 4.9 | 7.7 | 7.9 | Декабрь |
| **1995** | | | | | **1995** |
| January | 14.1 | 6.1 | 8.0 | 8.9 | Январь |
| February | 18.6 | 8.0 | 10.6 | 11.3 | Февраль |
| March | 22.3 | 9.6 | 12.7 | 14.4 | Март |
| April | 24.9 | 10.9 | 14.0 | 16.4 | Апрель |
| May | 28.0 | 12.3 | 15.7 | 18.7 | Май |
| June | 31.8 | 14.0 | 17.9 | 22.7 | Июнь |
| July | 36.0 | 15.2 | 20.7 | 24.3 | Июль |
| August | 38.3 | 16.2 | 22.2 | 25.9 | Август |
| September | 40.7 | 17.2 | 23.5 | 25.4 | Сентябрь |
| October | 43.2 | 17.7 | 25.5 | 26.8 | Октябрь |
| November | 46.1 | 18.8 | 27.4 | 28.4 | Ноябрь |
| December | 50.4 | 20.5 | 29.9 | 28.9 | Декабрь |
| **1996** | | | | | **1996** |
| January | .. | .. | .. | .. | Январь |
| February | .. | .. | .. | .. | Февраль |
| March | .. | .. | .. | .. | Март |
| April | .. | .. | .. | .. | Апрель |
| May | .. | .. | .. | .. | Май |
| June | .. | .. | .. | .. | Июнь |
| July | .. | .. | .. | .. | Июль |
| August | .. | .. | .. | .. | Август |
| September | .. | .. | .. | .. | Сентябрь |
| October | .. | .. | .. | .. | Октябрь |
| November | .. | .. | .. | .. | Ноябрь |
| December | .. | .. | .. | .. | Декабрь |

## TABLE 2-1. Gross domestic product at current prices (millions of national currency)
## ТАБЛИЦА 2-1. Валовой внутренний продукт в текущих ценах (млн. национальной валюты)

| Sector of origin or expenditure category | 1990 | 1991 | 1992 | 1993 | 1994 | 1995 | Отраслевое происхождение или вид расходов |
|---|---|---|---|---|---|---|---|
| **Gross domestic product by sector of origin** | | | | | | | **Валовой внутренний продукт по отраслевому происхождению** |
| **Agriculture and forestry** | 14.1 | 32.9 | 278.3 | 2,094.1 | 4,811.1 | 6,305.9 | **Сельское и лесное хозяйство** |
| Agriculture | 14.0 | 32.6 | 276.3 | 2,090.6 | 4,601.3 | 6,289.6 | Сельское хозяйство |
| Forestry | 0.1 | 0.2 | 2.1 | 3.4 | 209.8 | 16.3 | Лесное хозяйство |
| **Industry and construction** | 14.6 | 31.3 | 267.3 | 1,634.0 | 2,870.6 | 3,455.4 | **Промышленность и строительство** |
| Industry | 11.3 | 25.4 | 238.3 | 1,344.5 | 2,461.7 | 2,425.5 | Промышленность |
| Construction | 3.3 | 5.9 | 29.1 | 289.6 | 408.9 | 1,029.9 | Строительство |
| **Other** | 13.1 | 24.8 | 168.0 | 1,501.4 | 4,074.0 | .. | **Другие отрасли** |
| Transport | 1.6 | 2.4 | 17.2 | 172.9 | 378.4 | .. | Транспорт |
| Road maintenance | 0.3 | 0.3 | 1.6 | 12.7 | 53.7 | .. | Дорожное хозяйство |
| Communication | 0.5 | 0.8 | 2.3 | 22.8 | 115.3 | .. | Связь |
| Wholesale trade | 0.1 | 0.2 | 1.6 | 28.2 | 17.8 | .. | Оптовая торговля |
| Retail trade and catering | 1.6 | 3.7 | 24.4 | 321.7 | 1,144.6 | 1,469.1 | Розничная торговля и общепит |
| Material supply | 0.4 | 0.7 | 12.6 | 52.0 | 36.3 | 38.3 | Материально-техническое снабжение |
| Procurement | 0.2 | 0.3 | 2.4 | 12.9 | 10.5 | 7.1 | Заготовки |
| Information and computing services | 0.1 | 0.1 | 0.5 | 1.7 | 4.5 | 4.7 | Информационно-вычислительное обслуживание |
| Other sectors of material production | 0.6 | 0.8 | 10.4 | 71.4 | 76.2 | .. | Другие отрасли сферы материального пр. |
| Housing | 1.1 | 1.7 | 6.0 | 44.9 | 121.4 | .. | Жилищное хозяйство |
| Public utilities and personal services | 0.7 | 1.2 | 15.8 | 111.0 | 289.1 | .. | Ком. хоз. и бытовое обслуживание |
| Health care, social security, physical culture and sports | 1.3 | 3.0 | 16.4 | 124.2 | 324.3 | .. | Здравоохранение, социальное обеспечение, физкультура и спорт |
| Education | 2.1 | 3.7 | 24.6 | 149.5 | 555.5 | .. | Образование |
| Culture and art | 0.3 | 0.6 | 4.4 | 15.4 | 41.3 | .. | Культура и искусство |
| Science and scientific research | 0.2 | 0.3 | 1.8 | 10.9 | 32.1 | .. | Наука и научное обслуживание |
| Credit | 0.3 | 1.0 | 11.7 | 245.3 | 571.7 | .. | Кредитование |
| Insurance | 0.1 | 0.1 | 0.9 | 8.6 | 5.2 | .. | Страхование |
| General administration and defense | 1.5 | 3.4 | 11.9 | 90.9 | 268.7 | .. | Государственное управление и оборона |
| Private nonprofit institutions serving households | 0.2 | 0.5 | 1.5 | 4.4 | 27.5 | .. | Общественные организаций, обслуживающие домашние хозяйства |
| **Imputed service charge of financial intermediaries** | -0.2 | -0.7 | -6.3 | -123.3 | -276.5 | .. | **Условно-исчисляемая стоимость услуг финансовых посредников** |
| **Total gross value added (GVA)** | 41.6 | 88.3 | 707.5 | 5,106.1 | 11,479.2 | 14,436.7 | **Валовая добавленная стоимость (ВДС) - всего** |
| **Taxes on production and imports (TOPI)** | 2.6 | 6.2 | 67.2 | 449.3 | 1,178.9 | .. | **Налоги на производство и импорт (НПиИ)** |
| Other taxes on production (OTOP) | 1.0 | 1.2 | 12.8 | 111.3 | 377.6 | .. | Другие налоги на производство (ДНП) |
| **Subsidies on production and imports (SOPI)** | 0.4 | 0.7 | 20.6 | 89.4 | 61.2 | .. | **Субсидии на производство и импорт (СПиИ)** |
| Other subsidies on production (OSOP) | .. | .. | .. | .. | .. | .. | Другие субсидии на производство (ДСП) |
| **Total GDP at factor cost (GVA-OTOP+OSOP)** | 40.7 | 87.0 | 694.6 | 4,994.9 | 10,901.6 | .. | **Всего ВВП по фактр. стоимости (ВДС-ДНП+ДСП)** |
| **Net Indirect taxes (TOPI - SOPI)** | 2.1 | 5.5 | 46.6 | 359.9 | 1,117.7 | .. | **Чистые косвенные налоги (НПиИ-СПиИ)** |
| **Total GDP at market prices** | 42.8 | 92.6 | 741.3 | 5,354.7 | 12,019.2 | 15,606.1 | **Всего ВВП в рыночных ценах** |
| **Gross domestic product by expenditure category** | | | | | | | **Валовой внутренний продукт по видам расходов** |
| **Consumption** | 41.2 | 79.5 | 682.6 | 5,139.2 | 10,331.7 | 14,033.1 | **Потребление** |
| Private consumption | 30.5 | 59.3 | 524.2 | 4,053.1 | 7,899.9 | 10,507.4 | Личное потребление |
| Government consumption | 10.7 | 20.2 | 158.4 | 1,086.2 | 2,431.8 | 3,525.7 | Общественное потребление |
| **Gross domestic investment** | 10.4 | 14.2 | 147.7 | 624.8 | 2,413.6 | 2,450.4 | **Валовые внутренние инвестиции** |
| Gross fixed investment | 9.9 | 16.2 | 108.1 | 714.6 | 1,492.7 | 3,465.9 | Валовое накопление основного капитала |
| Change in stocks | 0.5 | -1.9 | 39.6 | -89.8 | 920.9 | -1,015.5 | Изменения в запасах (МОС) |
| **Resource balance (net exports of GNFS)** | -8.7 | -1.2 | -89.0 | -412.3 | -726.0 | -894.8 | **Сальдо ресурсов (чистый экспорт ТНФУ)** |
| Exports of goods and nonfactor services | 12.5 | 32.7 | 263.8 | 1,795.5 | 4,019.9 | 4,110.5 | Экспорт товаров и нефакторных услуг |
| Imports of goods and nonfactor services | 21.2 | 33.9 | 352.8 | 2,207.8 | 4,745.9 | 5,005.3 | Импорт товаров и нефакторных услуг |

**TABLE 2-1A. Distribution of gross domestic product at current prices (percent)**
**ТАБЛИЦА 2-1А. Распределение валового внутреннего продукта в текущих ценах ( % )**

| Sector of origin or expenditure category | 1990 | 1991 | 1992 | 1993 | 1994 | 1995 | Отраслевое происхождение или вид расходов |
|---|---|---|---|---|---|---|---|
| **Gross domestic product by sector of origin** | | | | | | | **ВВП по отраслевому происхождению** |
| **Agriculture and forestry** | 32.9 | 35.5 | 37.5 | 39.1 | 40.0 | 40.4 | **Сельское и лесное хозяйство** |
| Agriculture | 32.7 | 35.3 | 37.3 | 39.0 | 38.3 | 40.3 | Сельское хозяйство |
| Forestry | 0.2 | 0.2 | 0.3 | 0.1 | 1.7 | 0.1 | Лесное хозяйство |
| **Industry and construction** | 34.1 | 33.8 | 36.1 | 30.5 | 23.9 | 22.1 | **Промышленность и строительство** |
| Industry | 26.4 | 27.5 | 32.1 | 25.1 | 20.5 | 15.5 | Промышленность |
| Construction | 7.7 | 6.3 | 3.9 | 5.4 | 3.4 | 6.6 | Строительство |
| **Other** | 30.7 | 26.8 | 22.7 | 28.0 | 33.9 | .. | **Другие отрасли** |
| Transport | 3.6 | 2.6 | 2.3 | 3.2 | 3.1 | .. | Транспорт |
| Road maintenance | 0.8 | 0.4 | 0.2 | 0.2 | 0.4 | .. | Дорожное хозяйство |
| Communication | 1.2 | 0.8 | 0.3 | 0.4 | 1.0 | .. | Связь |
| Wholesale trade | 0.1 | 0.2 | 0.2 | 0.5 | 0.1 | .. | Оптовая торговля |
| Retail trade and catering | 3.6 | 4.0 | 3.3 | 6.0 | 9.5 | 9.4 | Розничная торговля и общепит |
| Material supply | 0.9 | 0.8 | 1.7 | 1.0 | 0.3 | 0.2 | Материально-техническое снабжение |
| Procurement | 0.4 | 0.3 | 0.3 | 0.2 | 0.1 | 0.0 | Заготовки |
| Information and computing services | 0.1 | 0.1 | 0.1 | 0.0 | 0.0 | 0.0 | Информационно-техническое обслуживание |
| Other sectors of material production | 1.4 | 0.9 | 1.4 | 1.3 | 0.6 | .. | Другие отрасли сферы матерл. произ. |
| Housing | 2.6 | 1.8 | 0.8 | 0.8 | 1.0 | .. | Жилищное хозяйство |
| Public utilities and personal services | 1.6 | 1.3 | 2.1 | 2.1 | 2.4 | .. | Ком. хоз. и бытовое обслуживание |
| Health care, social security, physical culture and sports | 3.1 | 3.3 | 2.2 | 2.3 | 2.7 | .. | Здравоохранение, социальное обеспечение, физкультура и спорт |
| Education | 5.0 | 4.0 | 3.3 | 2.8 | 4.6 | .. | Образование |
| Culture and art | 0.7 | 0.7 | 0.6 | 0.3 | 0.3 | .. | Культура и искусство |
| Science and scientific research | 0.5 | 0.3 | 0.2 | 0.2 | 0.3 | .. | Наука и научное обслуживание |
| Credit | 0.6 | 1.1 | 1.6 | 4.6 | 4.8 | .. | Кредитование |
| Insurance | 0.2 | 0.2 | 0.1 | 0.2 | 0.0 | .. | Страхование |
| General administration and defense | 3.6 | 3.6 | 1.6 | 1.7 | 2.2 | .. | Государственное управление и оборона |
| Private nonprofit institutions serving households | 0.5 | 0.6 | 0.2 | 0.1 | 0.2 | .. | Общественные организации, обслуживающие домашние хозяйства |
| **Imputed service charge of financial intermediaries** | -0.5 | -0.7 | -0.8 | -2.3 | -2.3 | .. | **Условно-исчисляемая стоимость услуг финансовых посредников** |
| **Total gross value added** | 97.2 | 95.4 | 95.4 | 95.4 | 95.5 | 92.5 | **Валовая добавленная стоимость - всего** |
| **Total GDP at factor cost** | 95.0 | 94.0 | 93.7 | 93.3 | 90.7 | 0.0 | **ВВП по фактор. стоимости - всего** |
| **Net indirect taxes** | 5.0 | 6.0 | 6.3 | 6.7 | 9.3 | 0.0 | **Чистые косвенные налоги (НПиИ-СПиИ)** |
| **Total GDP at market prices** | 100.0 | 100.0 | 100.0 | 100.0 | 100.0 | 100.0 | **ВВП в рын. ценах - всего** |
| **Gross domestic product by expenditure category** | | | | | | | **ВВП по видам расходов** |
| **Consumption** | 96.2 | 85.9 | 92.1 | 96.0 | 86.0 | 89.9 | **Потребление** |
| Private consumption | 71.2 | 64.1 | 70.7 | 75.7 | 65.7 | 67.3 | Личное потребление |
| Government consumption | 25.0 | 21.8 | 21.4 | 20.3 | 20.2 | 22.6 | Общественное потребление |
| **Gross domestic investment** | 24.2 | 15.4 | 19.9 | 11.7 | 20.1 | 15.7 | **Вал. внутр. инвестиции** |
| Gross fixed investment | 23.1 | 17.5 | 14.6 | 13.3 | 12.4 | 22.2 | Вал. накопление осн. капитала |
| Change in stocks | 1.1 | -2.1 | 5.3 | -1.7 | 7.7 | -6.5 | Изменения в запасах (МОС) |
| **Resource balance (net exports of GNFS)** | -20.4 | -1.3 | -12.0 | -7.7 | -6.0 | -5.7 | **Сальдо ресурсов (чистый экспорт ТНФУ)** |
| Exports of goods and nonfactor services | 29.2 | 35.3 | 35.6 | 33.5 | 33.4 | 26.3 | Экспорт товаров и нефакторных услуг |
| Imports of goods and nonfactor services | 49.6 | 36.6 | 47.6 | 41.2 | 39.5 | 32.1 | Импорт товаров и нефакторных услуг |

## TABLE 2-2. Gross domestic product at constant prices (millions of national currency)
## ТАБЛИЦА 2-2. Валовой внутренний продукт в постоянных ценах (млн. национальной валюты)

| Sector of origin or expenditure category | 1990 | 1991 | 1992 | 1993 | 1994 | 1995 | Отраслевое происхождение или вид расходов |
|---|---|---|---|---|---|---|---|
| **Gross domestic product by sector of origin** | | | | | | | **Валовой внутренний продукт по отраслевому происхождению** |
| **Agriculture and forestry** | 2,814.3 | 2,412.3 | 2,291.7 | 2,094.1 | 1,913.8 | 1,876.7 | **Сельское и лесное хозяйство** |
| Agriculture | .. | .. | .. | 2,090.6 | 1,910.3 | 1,873.2 | Сельское хозяйство |
| Forestry | .. | .. | .. | 3.4 | 3.5 | 3.5 | Лесное хозяйство |
| **Industry and construction** | 2,970.9 | 2,970.9 | 2,185.8 | 1,634.0 | 1,024.4 | 938.0 | **Промышленность и строительство** |
| Industry | .. | .. | .. | 1,344.4 | 859.4 | 635.9 | Промышленность |
| Construction | .. | .. | .. | 289.6 | 165.1 | 302.0 | Строительство |
| **Other** | 3,057.5 | 2,827.8 | 2,565.3 | 1,378.0 | 1,142.4 | .. | **Другие отрасли** |
| Transport | .. | .. | .. | 185.6 | 126.0 | .. | Транспорт |
| Road maintenance | .. | .. | .. | .. | .. | .. | Дорожное хозяйство |
| Communication | .. | .. | .. | .. | .. | .. | Связь |
| Wholesale trade | .. | .. | .. | .. | .. | .. | Оптовая торговля |
| Retail trade and catering | .. | .. | .. | 349.9 | 339.9 | 309.6 | Розничная торговля и общепит |
| Material supply | .. | .. | .. | 52.0 | 32.3 | 23.9 | Материально-техническое снабжение |
| Procurement | .. | .. | .. | 12.9 | 4.9 | 2.3 | Заготовки |
| Information and computing services | .. | .. | .. | 1.7 | 1.4 | 1.1 | Информационно-вычислительное обслуживание |
| Other sectors of material production | .. | .. | .. | 71.4 | 59.0 | 53.7 | Другие отрасли сферы материального пр. |
| Housing | .. | .. | .. | 44.9 | 42.0 | .. | Жилищное хозяйство |
| Public utilities and personal services | .. | .. | .. | 111.0 | 79.2 | .. | Ком. хоз. и бытовое обслуживание |
| Health care, social security, and sports | .. | .. | .. | 124.2 | 46.8 | .. | Здравоохранение, социальное обеспечение, физкультура и спорт |
| Education | .. | .. | .. | 149.5 | 147.4 | .. | Образование |
| Culture and art | .. | .. | .. | 15.4 | 13.0 | .. | Культура и искусство |
| Science and research | .. | .. | .. | 10.9 | 9.2 | .. | Наука и научное обслуживание |
| Credit | .. | .. | .. | 253.9 | 244.9 | 112.2 | Кредитование |
| Insurance | .. | .. | .. | .. | .. | .. | Страхование |
| General administration and defense | .. | .. | .. | 90.9 | 87.1 | .. | Государственное управление и оборона |
| Private nonprofit institutions serving households | .. | .. | .. | 4.4 | 4.2 | .. | Общественные организации, обслуживающие домашние хозяйства |
| **Imputed service charge of financial intermediaries** | -924.8 | -924.8 | -924.8 | -123.3 | -116.3 | .. | **Условно-исчисляемая стоимость услуг финансовых посредников** |
| **Total gross value added (GVA)** | 7,917.9 | 7,286.2 | 6,117.9 | 5,106.1 | 4,080.7 | 3,824.5 | **Валовая добавленная стоимость (ВДС) -** |
| **Total GDP at factor cost (GVA-OTOP+OSOP)** | .. | .. | .. | 5,106.1 | 4,080.7 | 3,824.5 | **Всего ВВП по фактр. стоимости (ВДС-ДНП+ДСП)** |
| **Net indirect taxes (TOPI - SOPI)** | .. | .. | .. | 248.6 | 198.6 | 186.2 | **Чистые косвенные налоги (НПиИ-СПиИ)** |
| **Total GDP at market prices** | 8,268.2 | 7,598.9 | 6,398.0 | 5,354.7 | 4,279.3 | 4,010.7 | **Всего ВВП в рыночных ценах** |
| **Gross domestic product by expenditure category** | | | | | | | **Валовой внутренний продукт по видам расходов** |
| **Consumption** | .. | .. | .. | 5,139.2 | 3,659.4 | 3,565.4 | **Потребление** |
| Private consumption | .. | .. | .. | 4,053.1 | 2,812.1 | 2,684.0 | Личное потребление |
| Government consumption | .. | .. | .. | 1,086.2 | 847.3 | 881.4 | Общественное потребление |
| **Gross domestic investment** | .. | .. | .. | 624.8 | 853.3 | 613.0 | **Валовые внутренние инвестиции** |
| Gross fixed investment | .. | .. | .. | 714.6 | 511.9 | 879.4 | Валовое накопление основного капитала |
| Change in stocks | .. | .. | .. | -89.8 | 341.4 | -266.4 | Изменения в запасах (МОС) |
| **Resource balance (net exports of GNFS)** | .. | .. | .. | -409.3 | -233.4 | -167.8 | **Сальдо ресурсов (чистый экспорт ТНФУ)** |
| Exports of goods and nonfactor services | .. | .. | .. | 1,795.5 | 1,948.5 | 1,441.8 | Экспорт товаров и нефакторных услуг |
| Imports of goods and nonfactor services | .. | .. | .. | 2,204.8 | 2,181.8 | 1,609.5 | Импорт товаров и нефакторных услуг |

**TABLE 2-2A. Growth rates of gross domestic product at constant prices (percent)**

**ТАБЛИЦА 2-2А. Валовой внутренний продукт - темпы прироста в постоянных ценах ( % )**

| Sector of origin or expenditure category | 1990 | 1991 | 1992 | 1993 | 1994 | 1995 | Отраслевое происхождение или вид расходов |
|---|---|---|---|---|---|---|---|
| **Growth rate by sector of origin** | | | | | | | **Валовый внутренний продукт по отраслевому происхождению** |
| **Agriculture and forestry** | .. | -14.3 | -5.0 | -8.6 | -8.6 | -1.9 | **Сельское и лесное хозяйство** |
| Agriculture | .. | .. | .. | .. | -8.6 | -1.9 | Сельское хозяйство |
| Forestry | .. | .. | .. | .. | 2.9 | 0.0 | Лесное хозяйство |
| **Industry and construction** | .. | 0.0 | -26.4 | -25.2 | -37.3 | -8.4 | **Промышленность и строительство** |
| Industry | .. | .. | .. | .. | -36.1 | -26.0 | Промышленность |
| Construction | .. | .. | .. | .. | -43.0 | 83.0 | Строительство |
| **Other** | .. | -7.5 | -9.3 | -46.3 | -17.1 | .. | **Другие отрасли** |
| Transport | .. | .. | .. | .. | -32.1 | .. | Транспорт |
| Road maintenance | .. | .. | .. | .. | .. | .. | Дорожное хозяйство |
| Communication | .. | .. | .. | .. | .. | .. | Связь |
| Wholesale trade | .. | .. | .. | .. | .. | .. | Оптовая торговля |
| Retail trade and catering | .. | .. | .. | .. | -2.9 | -8.9 | Розничная торговля и общепит |
| Material supply | .. | .. | .. | .. | -37.9 | -26.1 | Материально-техническое снабжение |
| Procurement | .. | .. | .. | .. | -62.4 | -52.8 | Заготовки |
| Information and computing services | .. | .. | .. | .. | -16.3 | -25.0 | Информационно-вычислительное обслуживание |
| Other sectors of material production | .. | .. | .. | .. | -17.5 | -9.0 | Другие отрасли сферы материального пр. |
| Housing | .. | .. | .. | .. | -6.4 | .. | Жилищное хозяйство |
| Public utilities and personal services | .. | .. | .. | .. | -28.7 | .. | Ком. хоз. и бытовое обслуживание |
| Health care, social security, and sports | .. | .. | .. | .. | -62.3 | .. | Здравоохранение, социальное обеспечение, физкультура и спорт |
| Education | .. | .. | .. | .. | -1.4 | .. | Образование |
| Culture and art | .. | .. | .. | .. | -15.8 | .. | Культура и искусство |
| Science and research | .. | .. | .. | .. | -15.0 | .. | Наука и научное обслуживание |
| Credit | .. | .. | .. | .. | -3.6 | -54.2 | Кредитование |
| Insurance | .. | .. | .. | .. | .. | .. | Страхование |
| General administration and defense | .. | .. | .. | .. | -4.2 | .. | Государственное управление и оборона |
| Private nonprofit institutions serving households | .. | .. | .. | .. | -4.3 | .. | Общественные организации, обслуживающие домашние хозяйства |
| **Imputed service charge of financial intermediaries** | .. | .. | .. | .. | .. | .. | **Условно-исчисляемая стоимость услуг финансовых посредников** |
| **Total gross value added** | .. | -8.0 | -16.0 | -16.5 | -20.1 | -6.3 | **Валовая добавленная стоимость (ВДС) - всего** |
| **Total GDP at factor cost** | .. | .. | .. | .. | -20.1 | -6.3 | **Всего ВВП по фактр. стоимости (ВДС-ДНП+ДСП)** |
| **Net indirect taxes** | .. | .. | .. | .. | -20.1 | -6.3 | **Чистые косвенные налоги (НПиИ-СПиИ)** |
| **Total GDP at market prices** | .. | -8.1 | -15.8 | -16.3 | -20.1 | -6.3 | **Всего ВВП в рыночных ценах** |
| **Growth rate by expenditure category** | | | | | | | **Валовой внутренний продукт по видам расходов** |
| **Consumption** | .. | .. | .. | .. | -28.8 | -2.6 | **Потребление** |
| Private consumption | .. | .. | .. | .. | -30.6 | -4.6 | Личное потребление |
| Government consumption | .. | .. | .. | .. | -22.0 | 4.0 | Общественное потребление |
| **Gross domestic investment** | .. | .. | .. | .. | 36.6 | -28.2 | **Валовые внутренние инвестиции** |
| Gross fixed investment | .. | .. | .. | .. | -28.4 | 71.8 | Валовое накопление основного капитала |
| **Exports of goods and nonfactor services** | .. | .. | .. | .. | 8.5 | -26.0 | **Экспорт товаров и нефакторных услуг** |
| **Imports of goods and nonfactor services** | .. | .. | .. | .. | -1.0 | -26.2 | **Импорт товаров и нефакторных услуг** |

**TABLE 2-2B. Implicit price deflators for gross domestic product (percentage change)**

**ТАБЛИЦА 2-2B. Дефляторы валового внутреннего продукта (темпы прироста в %)**

| Sector of origin or expenditure category | 1990 | 1991 | 1992 | 1993 | 1994 | 1995 | Отраслевое происхождение или вид расходов |
|---|---|---|---|---|---|---|---|
| **Price deflators by sector of origin** | | | | | | | **Дефляторы по отраслевому происхождению или виду расходов** |
| **Agriculture and forestry** | .. | 172.6 | 791.9 | 723.4 | 151.4 | 33.7 | **Сельское и лесное хозяйство** |
| Agriculture | .. | .. | .. | .. | 140.9 | 39.4 | Сельское хозяйство |
| Forestry | .. | .. | .. | .. | .. | .. | Лесное хозяйство |
| **Industry and construction** | .. | 114.5 | 1,061.3 | 717.6 | 180.2 | 31.5 | **Промышленность и строительство** |
| Industry | .. | .. | .. | .. | 186.4 | 33.1 | Промышленность |
| Construction | .. | .. | .. | .. | 147.7 | 37.7 | Строительство |
| **Other** | .. | 104.1 | 646.6 | 1,563.2 | 227.3 | .. | **Другие отрасли** |
| Transport | .. | .. | .. | .. | 222.3 | .. | Транспорт |
| Road maintenance | .. | .. | .. | .. | .. | .. | Дорожное хозяйство |
| Communication | .. | .. | .. | .. | .. | .. | Связь |
| Wholesale trade | .. | .. | .. | .. | .. | .. | Оптовая торговля |
| Retail trade and catering | .. | .. | .. | .. | 242.0 | 38.7 | Розничная торговля и общепит. |
| Material supply | .. | .. | .. | .. | 12.3 | 43.0 | Материально-техническое снабжение |
| Procurement | .. | .. | .. | .. | 115.7 | 44.2 | Заготовки |
| Information and computing services | .. | .. | .. | .. | 213.9 | 39.8 | Информационно-вычислительное обслуживание |
| Other sectors of material production | .. | .. | .. | .. | 29.2 | .. | Другие отрасли сферы матерл. произ. |
| Housing | .. | .. | .. | .. | 189.0 | .. | Жилищное хозяйство |
| Public utilities and personal services | .. | .. | .. | .. | 265.2 | .. | Ком. хоз. и бытовое обслуживание |
| Health care, social security, and sports | .. | .. | .. | .. | 593.0 | .. | Здравоохранение, социальное обеспечение, физкультура и спорт |
| Education | .. | .. | .. | .. | 276.8 | .. | Образование |
| Culture and art | .. | .. | .. | .. | 217.8 | .. | Культура и искусство |
| Science and research | .. | .. | .. | .. | 248.2 | .. | Наука и научное обслуживание |
| Credit | .. | .. | .. | .. | 141.7 | .. | Кредитование |
| Insurance | .. | .. | .. | .. | .. | .. | Страхование |
| General administration and defense | .. | .. | .. | .. | 208.5 | .. | Государственное управление и оборона |
| Private nonprofit institutions serving households | .. | .. | .. | .. | 550.4 | .. | Общественные организации, обслуживающие домашние хозяйства |
| **Imputed service charge of financial intermediaries** | .. | .. | .. | .. | .. | .. | **Условно-исчисляемая стоимость услуг финансовых посредников** |
| **Total gross value added** | .. | 130.7 | 854.5 | 764.8 | 181.3 | 34.2 | **Валовая добавленная стоимость (ВДС) - всего** |
| **Total GDP at factor cost** | .. | .. | .. | .. | 173.1 | .. | **ВВП по факторной стоимости (ВДС-ДНП+ДСП)** |
| **Net indirect taxes** | .. | .. | .. | .. | 288.7 | .. | **Чистые косвенные налоги (НПИ-СПИ)** |
| **Total GDP at market prices** | .. | 135.4 | 851.3 | 763.1 | 180.9 | 38.5 | **ВВП в рыночных ценах** |
| **Price deflators by expenditure category** | | | | | | | **Дефляторы по виду расходов** |
| **Consumption** | .. | .. | .. | .. | 182.3 | 39.4 | **Конечное потребление** |
| Private consumption | .. | .. | .. | .. | 180.9 | 39.4 | Личное потребление |
| Government consumption | .. | .. | .. | .. | 187.0 | 39.4 | Общественное потребление |
| **Gross domestic investment** | .. | .. | .. | .. | 182.9 | 41.3 | **Валовые внутренние инвестиции** |
| Gross fixed investment | .. | .. | .. | .. | 191.6 | 35.2 | Валовое накопление основного капитала |
| **Exports of goods and nonfactor services** | .. | .. | .. | .. | 106.3 | 38.2 | **Экспорт товаров и нефакторных услуг** |
| **Imports of goods and nonfactor services** | .. | .. | .. | .. | 117.2 | 43.0 | **Импорт товаров и нефакторных услуг** |

## TABLE 3-1. Balance of payments at current prices (millions of U.S. dollars)
## ТАБЛИЦА 3-1. Платежный баланс в текущих ценах (в миллионах долларов США)

| Item | 1990 | 1991 | 1992 | 1993 | 1994 | 1995 | Статьи |
|---|---|---|---|---|---|---|---|
| Exports of goods and services (including workers' remittances) | .. | .. | .. | 348.3 | 372.6 | 440.1 | Экспорт товаров и услуг (включая денежные переводы рабочих) |
| Exports of goods and nonfactor services | .. | .. | .. | 348.3 | 372.6 | 440.1 | Экспорт товаров и нефакт. услуг |
| Merchandise (FOB) | .. | .. | 284.8 | 339.6 | 340.0 | 408.9 | Товары (ФОБ) |
| Nonfactor services | .. | .. | .. | 8.7 | 32.6 | 31.2 | Нефакторные услуги |
| Shipment | .. | .. | .. | 2.2 | 14.3 | 15.6 | Перевозки |
| Travel | .. | .. | .. | 0.3 | 2.6 | 4.7 | Поездки |
| Other | .. | .. | .. | 6.2 | 15.7 | 10.9 | Другие |
| Imports of goods and nonfactor services | .. | .. | .. | 520.1 | 441.8 | 626.5 | Импорт товаров и нефакт. услуг |
| Merchandise (FOB) | .. | .. | 395.7 | 506.4 | 399.7 | 554.6 | Товары (ФОБ) |
| Nonfactor services | .. | .. | .. | 13.7 | 42.1 | 71.9 | Нефакторные услуги |
| Shipment | .. | .. | .. | 8.5 | 4.9 | 10.3 | Перевозки |
| Travel | .. | .. | .. | .. | 1.8 | 5.8 | Поездки |
| Other | .. | .. | .. | 5.2 | 35.4 | 55.8 | Другие |
| Resource balance | .. | .. | 234.0 | -171.8 | -69.2 | -186.4 | Сальдо ресурсов |
| Net factor income | .. | .. | -3.8 | -4.5 | -17.5 | -18.3 | Чистый факторный доход |
| Factor receipts | .. | .. | 0.0 | .. | .. | .. | Факторные поступления |
| Factor payments | .. | .. | 3.8 | 5.1 | 16.5 | .. | Факторные платежи |
| Total interest due | .. | .. | 0.0 | 5.1 | 16.5 | .. | Общая сумма процента к оплате |
| Other factor payments and discrepancy | .. | .. | 3.8 | 0.0 | 0.0 | .. | Другие факторные платежи и стат. погр. |
| Net current transfers | .. | .. | 14.5 | 28.8 | 15.4 | 58.0 | Чистые текущие трансферты |
| Current receipts | .. | .. | .. | .. | .. | .. | Текущие поступления |
| Workers remittances | .. | .. | .. | .. | .. | .. | Денежные переводы рабочих |
| Other current transfers | .. | .. | .. | .. | .. | .. | Другие текущие трансферты |
| Current payments | .. | .. | .. | .. | .. | .. | Текущие платежи |
| Current account balance before official grants | .. | .. | 244.7 | -147.5 | -71.3 | -146.7 | Сальдо текущего счета до офиц. безвозмезд. трансфертов |
| Official capital grants | .. | .. | .. | 85.9 | 45.7 | 17.8 | Официальные кап. безвозмезные трансферты |
| Current account balance after official grants | .. | .. | .. | -61.6 | -25.6 | -128.9 | Сальдо текущего счета после офиц. безвозмезд. трансфертов |
| Long Term Capital Inflows | .. | .. | -1.7 | 81.5 | 151.2 | .. | Долгосрочные притоки капитала |
| Direct investment | .. | .. | 0.0 | 10.0 | 44.9 | 190.5 | Прямые инвестиции |
| Net long term borrowing | .. | .. | -1.7 | 71.5 | 106.3 | .. | Чистые долгосрочные займы |
| Disbursements | .. | .. | 5.3 | 81.5 | 107.0 | .. | Поступления |
| Repayments due | .. | .. | 7.0 | 10.0 | 0.4 | .. | Сумма, подлежащая погашению |
| Other long-term inflows (net) | .. | .. | .. | .. | .. | .. | Другие долгосрочные притоки (чистые) |

(continued on next page)

## TABLE 3-1. Balance of payments at current prices (millions of U.S. dollars)
## ТАБЛИЦА 3-1. Платежный баланс в текущих ценах (в миллионах долларов США)

| Item | 1990 | 1991 | 1992 | 1993 | 1994 | 1995 | Статьи |
|---|---|---|---|---|---|---|---|
| Adjustment to Scheduled Debt Service | .. | .. | .. | .. | .. | .. | Регулирование долга |
| Debt service not paid | .. | .. | .. | .. | .. | .. | Невыплаченный долг |
| Interest not paid | .. | .. | .. | .. | .. | .. | Невыплаченный процент |
| Principal not paid | .. | .. | .. | .. | .. | .. | Невыплаченная сумма основного долга |
| Arrears reductions/prepayments(-) | .. | .. | .. | .. | .. | .. | Погашение просроченных платежей/выплаты авансом (-) |
| Total Other items (Net) | .. | .. | -45.5 | -15.6 | -74.9 | .. | Общие другие статьи (чистые) |
| Net short-term capital | .. | .. | -45.5 | -59.0 | 11.8 | .. | Чистый краткосрочный капитал |
| Capital flows not elsewhere included | .. | .. | 0.0 | 86.7 | -53.2 | .. | Потоки капитала, не указанные выше |
| Errors and omissions | .. | .. | .. | -43.3 | -33.5 | -160.8 | Ошибки и пропуски |
| Changes in net reserves | .. | .. | 147.4 | 144.5 | 13.6 | .. | Изменения в чистых резервах |
| Net credit from IMF | .. | .. | 0.0 | 61.8 | 13.8 | 46.6 | Чистый кредит МВФ |
| Reserve changes not elsewhere included | .. | .. | 147.4 | 82.7 | -0.2 | .. | Изменения резервов, не указанных выше |
| Escrow account | .. | .. | .. | .. | .. | .. | Счет депонирования |
| Gross reserves (excluding gold) | .. | .. | .. | .. | .. | .. | Общие резервы (исключая золото) |
| Gross reserves (including gold) | .. | .. | .. | .. | .. | .. | Общие резервы (включая золото) |
| Nominal official exchange rate (annual average) (rf) | .. | .. | .. | .. | .. | .. | Номинальный официальный или рыночный курс (среднегодовой) |
| Nominal official exchange rate (end-of-year) (ae) | .. | .. | .. | .. | .. | .. | Номинальный официальный или рыночный курс (на конец года) |
| Manufacture unit value (percent change) | .. | .. | .. | .. | .. | .. | Средний индекс цен на продукцию обр. пром.,% |
| Index of real effective exchange rate (IMF) | .. | .. | .. | .. | .. | .. | Индекс реального эффективного валютного курса (МВФ) |
| Total factor payments | .. | .. | .. | .. | .. | .. | Общая сумма факторных платежей |
| Government interest | .. | .. | .. | .. | .. | .. | Процент, выплачиваемый органами гос. управления |
| Private sector interest | .. | .. | .. | .. | .. | .. | Процент выплачиваемый частным сектором |
| Profits on direct foreign investment | .. | .. | .. | .. | .. | .. | Прибыль от прямых иностранных инвестиций |
| Official capital grants | .. | .. | .. | .. | .. | .. | Официальные капитальные безвозмездные трансферты |
| For budgetary financing | .. | .. | .. | .. | .. | .. | На бюджетное финансирование |
| To extrabudgetary entities | .. | .. | .. | .. | .. | .. | На внебюджетное финансирование |
| Government net long term borrowing | .. | .. | .. | .. | .. | .. | Чистые долгосрочные государственные займы |
| Disbursements | .. | .. | .. | .. | .. | .. | Поступления |
| Repayments | .. | .. | .. | .. | .. | .. | Погашения |
| Private net long term borrowing | .. | .. | .. | .. | .. | .. | Чистые долгосрочные частные займы |
| Disbursements | .. | .. | .. | .. | .. | .. | Поступления |
| Repayments | .. | .. | .. | .. | .. | .. | Погашения |

## TABLE 3-2A. Imports by commodity group (millions of U.S. dollars)



## ТАБЛИЦА 3-2А . Импорт по товарным группам (млн. долларов США)

| Commodity group | 1990 | 1991 | 1992 | 1993 | 1994 | 1995 | Товарные группы |
|---|---|---|---|---|---|---|---|
| TOTAL | .. | .. | .. | .. | .. | 522.3 | ВСЕГО |
| I - Live animals; animal products | .. | .. | .. | .. | .. | 3.1 | I - Живые животные и продукты животноводства |
| II - Vegetable products | .. | .. | .. | .. | .. | 28.9 | II - Продукты растительного происхождения |
| III - Animal or vegetable fats and oils and their cleavage products; prepared edible fats; animal or vegetable waxes | .. | .. | .. | .. | .. | 6.0 | III - Жиры и масла растительного и животного происхождения, воски |
| IV - Prepared foodstuffs; beverages, spirits and vinegar; tobacco and manufactured tobacco substitutes | .. | .. | .. | .. | .. | 60.3 | IV -Продукция пищевой промышленности, алкогольные и безалкогольные напитки, табак и его заменители |
| V - Mineral products | .. | .. | .. | .. | .. | 195.5 | V - Минеральные продукты |
| VI - Products of the chemical or allied industries | .. | .. | .. | .. | .. | 30.9 | VI - Продукция химической промышленности |
| VII - Plastics and articles thereof; rubber and articles thereof | .. | .. | .. | .. | .. | 8.0 | VII - Пластмассы и изделия из них |
| VIII - Raw hides and skins, leather, furskins and articles thereof; saddlery and harness; travel goods, handbags and similar containers; articles of animal gut | .. | .. | .. | .. | .. | 0.8 | VIII - Кожевенное сырьё, кожи, пушнина, меховое сырьё и изделия из них |
| IX - Wood and articles of wood; wood charcoal; cork and articles of cork; manufactures of straw, of esparto or of other plaiting materials; basketware and wickerwork | .. | .. | .. | .. | .. | 5.5 | IX - Древесина и изделия из древесины, древесный уголь |
| X - Pulp of wood or of other fibrous cellulosic material; waste and scrap of paper or paperboard; paper and paperboard and articles thereof | .. | .. | .. | .. | .. | 6.4 | X - Бумажная масса, бумажные и картонные отходы, макулатура, бумага, картон и изделия из них |
| XI - Textiles and textile articles | .. | .. | .. | .. | .. | 23.6 | XI - Текстиль и текстильные изделия |
| XII - Footwear, headgear, umbrellas, sun umbrellas, walking sticks, seat sticks, whips, riding crops and parts thereof; prepared feathers and articles made therewith; artificial flowers; articles of human hair | .. | .. | .. | .. | .. | 2.7 | XII - Обувь, головные уборы, зонты, трости и пр. |

TABLE 3-2A. Imports by commodity group (millions of U.S. dollars)
ТАБЛИЦА 3-2А . Импорт по товарным группам (млн. долларов США)

| Commodity group | 1990 | 1991 | 1992 | 1993 | 1994 | 1995 | Товарные группы |
|---|---|---|---|---|---|---|---|
| XIII - Articles of stone, plaster, cement, asbestos, mica and similar materials; ceramic products; glass and glassware | .. | .. | .. | .. | .. | 5.4 | XIII - Изделия из камня, гипса, цемента |
| XIV - Natural or cultured pearls, precious or semi-precious stones, precious metals, metals clad with precious metal and articles thereof; imitation jewellery; coin | .. | .. | .. | .. | .. | 0.5 | XIV - Жемчуг, драгоценные и полудрагоценные камни, драгоценные металлы, бижутерия, монеты |
| XV - Base metals and articles of base metal | .. | .. | .. | .. | .. | 36.2 | XV - Неблагородные металлы и изделия из них |
| XVI - Machinery and mechanical appliances; electrical equipment; parts thereof; sound recorders and reproducers, television image and sound recorders and reproducers, and parts and accessories of such articles | .. | .. | .. | .. | .. | 63.4 | XVI - Машины, оборудование, механизмы, их части и принадлежности; звуковая и теле-аппаратура, их части и принадлежности |
| XVII - Vehicles, aircraft, vessels and associated transport equipment | .. | .. | .. | .. | .. | 30.1 | XVII - Средства наземного, воздушного и водного транспорта |
| XVIII - Optical, photographic, cinematographic, measuring, checking, precision, medical or surgical instruments and apparatus; clocks and watches; musical instruments; parts and accessories thereof | .. | .. | .. | .. | .. | 4.2 | XVIII - Приборы, аппараты оптические, медицинские, измерительные и пр.; музыкальные инструменты; часы; их части и принадлежности |
| XIX - Arms and ammunition; parts and accessories thereof | .. | .. | .. | .. | .. | 1.2 | XIX - Оружие и боеприпасы, их части и принадлежности |
| XX - Miscellaneous manufactured articles | .. | .. | .. | .. | .. | 9.6 | XX - Разные промышленные товары |
| XXI - Works of art, collectors' pieces, and antiques | .. | .. | .. | .. | .. | .. | XXI - Произведения искусства, предметы антиквариата |
| XXII - Services | .. | .. | .. | .. | .. | 0.0 | XXII - Услуги |

**TABLE 3-2B Imports by commodity group (millions of national currency)**
**ТАБЛИЦА 3-2B. Импорт по товарным группам (млн. национальной валюты)**

| Commodity group | 1990 | 1991 | 1992 | 1993 | 1994 | 1995 | Товарные группы |
|---|---|---|---|---|---|---|---|
| TOTAL | .. | .. | .. | .. | .. | 5,668.5 | ВСЕГО |
| I - Live animals; animal products | .. | .. | .. | .. | .. | 33.0 | I - Живые животные и продукты животноводства |
| II - Vegetable products | .. | .. | .. | .. | .. | 316.4 | II - Продукты растительного происхождения |
| III - Animal or vegetable fats and oils and their cleavage products; prepared edible fats; animal or vegetable waxes | .. | .. | .. | .. | .. | 65.2 | III - Жиры и масла растительного и животного происхождения, воски |
| IV - Prepared foodstuffs; beverages, spirits and vinegar; tobacco and manufactured tobacco substitutes | .. | .. | .. | .. | .. | 656.3 | IV -Продукция пищевой промышленности, алкогольные и безалкогольные напитки, табак и его заменители |
| V - Mineral products | .. | .. | .. | .. | .. | 2,120.1 | V - Минеральные продукты |
| VI - Products of the chemical or allied industries | .. | .. | .. | .. | .. | 333.4 | VI - Продукция химической промышленности |
| VII - Plastics and articles thereof; rubber and articles thereof | .. | .. | .. | .. | .. | 86.4 | VII - Пластмассы и изделия из них |
| VIII - Raw hides and skins, leather, furskins and articles thereof; saddlery and harness; travel goods, handbags and similar containers; articles of animal gut | .. | .. | .. | .. | .. | 8.8 | VIII - Кожевенное сырьё, кожи, пушнина, меховое сырьё и изделия из них |
| IX - Wood and articles of wood; wood charcoal; cork and articles of cork; manufactures of straw, of esparto or of other plaiting materials; basketware and wickerwork | .. | .. | .. | .. | .. | 60.0 | IX - Древесина и изделия из древесины, древесный уголь |
| X - Pulp of wood or of other fibrous cellulosic material; waste and scrap of paper or paperboard; paper and paperboard and articles thereof | .. | .. | .. | .. | .. | 68.5 | X - Бумажная масса, бумажные и картонные отходы, макулатура, бумага, картон и изделия из них |
| XI - Textiles and textile articles | .. | .. | .. | .. | .. | 255.3 | XI - Текстиль и текстильные изделия |
| XII - Footwear, headgear, umbrellas, sun umbrellas, walking sticks, seat sticks, whips, riding crops and parts thereof; prepared feathers and articles made therewith; artificial flowers; articles of human hair | .. | .. | .. | .. | .. | 29.2 | XII - Обувь, головные уборы, зонты, трости и пр. |

## TABLE 3-2B Imports by commodity group (millions of national currency)
## ТАБЛИЦА 3-2B. Импорт по товарным группам (млн. национальной валюты)

| Commodity group | 1990 | 1991 | 1992 | 1993 | 1994 | 1995 | Товарные группы |
|---|---|---|---|---|---|---|---|
| XIII - Articles of stone, plaster, cement, asbestos, mica and similar materials; ceramic products; glass and glassware | .. | .. | .. | .. | .. | 59.3 | XIII - Изделия из камня, гипса, цемента |
| XIV - Natural or cultured pearls, precious or semi-precious stones, precious metals, metals clad with precious metal and articles thereof; imitation jewellery; coin | .. | .. | .. | .. | .. | 5.0 | XIV - Жемчуг, драгоценные и полудрагоценные камни, драгоценные металлы, бижутерия, монеты |
| XV - Base metals and articles of base metal | .. | .. | .. | .. | .. | 392.6 | XV - Неблагородные металлы и изделия из них |
| XVI - Machinery and mechanical appliances; electrical equipment; parts thereof; sound recorders and reproducers, television image and sound recorders and reproducers, and parts and accessories of such articles | .. | .. | .. | .. | .. | 690.9 | XVI - Машины, оборудование, механизмы, их части и принадлежности; звуковая и теле-аппаратура, их части и принадлежности |
| XVII - Vehicles, aircraft, vessels and associated transport equipment | .. | .. | .. | .. | .. | 325.4 | XVII - Средства наземного, воздушного и водного транспорта |
| XVIII - Optical, photographic, cinematograp-hic, measuring, checking, precision, medical or surgical instruments and apparatus; clocks and watches; musical instruments; parts and accessories thereof | .. | .. | .. | .. | .. | 45.4 | XVIII - Приборы, аппараты оптические, медицинские, измерительные и пр.; музыкальные инструменты; часы; их части и принадлежности |
| XIX - Arms and ammunition; parts and accessories thereof | .. | .. | .. | .. | .. | 13.0 | XIX - Оружие и боеприпасы, их части и принадлежности |
| XX - Miscellaneous manufactured articles | .. | .. | .. | .. | .. | 104.3 | XX - Разные промышленные товары |
| XXI - Works of art, collectors' pieces, and antiques | .. | .. | .. | .. | .. | .. | XXI - Произведения искусства, предметы антиквариата |
| XXII - Services | .. | .. | .. | .. | .. | 0.3 | XXII - Услуги |

## TABLE 3-3A. Exports by commodity group (millions of U.S. dollars)
## ТАБЛИЦА 3-3А. Экспорт по товарным группам (млн. долларов США)

| Commodity group | 1990 | 1991 | 1992 | 1993 | 1994 | 1995 | Товарные группы |
|---|---|---|---|---|---|---|---|
| TOTAL | .. | .. | .. | .. | .. | 408.9 | ВСЕГО |
| I - Live animals; animal products | .. | .. | .. | .. | .. | 7.0 | I - Живые животные и продукты животноводства |
| II - Vegetable products | .. | .. | .. | .. | .. | 27.3 | II - Продукты растительного происхождения |
| III - Animal or vegetable fats and oils and their cleavage products; prepared edible fats; animal or vegetable waxes | .. | .. | .. | .. | .. | 0.8 | III - Жиры и масла растительного и животного происхождения, воски |
| IV - Prepared foodstuffs; beverages, spirits and vinegar; tobacco and manufactured tobacco substitutes | .. | .. | .. | .. | .. | 84.4 | IV -Продукция пищевой промышленности, алкогольные и безалкогольные напитки, табак и его заменители |
| V - Mineral products | .. | .. | .. | .. | .. | 48.3 | V - Минеральные продукты |
| VI - Products of the chemical or allied industries | .. | .. | .. | .. | .. | 25.0 | VI - Продукция химической промышленности |
| VII - Plastics and articles thereof; rubber and articles thereof | .. | .. | .. | .. | .. | 2.0 | VII - Пластмассы и изделия из них |
| VIII - Raw hides and skins, leather, furskins and articles thereof; saddlery and harness; travel goods, handbags and similar containers; articles of animal gut | .. | .. | .. | .. | .. | 5.5 | VIII - Кожевенное сырьё, кожи, пушнина, меховое сырьё и изделия из них |
| IX - Wood and articles of wood; wood charcoal; cork and articles of cork; manufactures of straw, of esparto or of other plaiting materials; basketware and wickerwork | .. | .. | .. | .. | .. | 0.6 | IX - Древесина и изделия из древесины, древесный уголь |
| X - Pulp of wood or of other fibrous cellulosic material; waste and scrap of paper or paperboard; paper and paperboard and articles thereof | .. | .. | .. | .. | .. | 0.7 | X - Бумажная масса, бумажные и картонные отходы, макулатура, бумага, картон и изделия из них |
| XI - Textiles and textile articles | .. | .. | .. | .. | .. | 78.8 | XI - Текстиль и текстильные изделия |
| XII - Footwear, headgear, umbrellas, sun umbrellas, walking sticks, seat sticks, whips, riding crops and parts thereof; prepared feathers and articles made therewith; artificial flowers; articles of human hair | .. | .. | .. | .. | .. | 1.6 | XII - Обувь, головные уборы, зонты, трости и пр. |

**TABLE 3-3A. Exports by commodity group (millions of U.S. dollars)**
**ТАБЛИЦА 3-3А. Экспорт по товарным группам (млн. долларов США)**

| Commodity group | 1990 | 1991 | 1992 | 1993 | 1994 | 1995 | Товарные группы |
|---|---|---|---|---|---|---|---|
| XIII - Articles of stone, plaster, cement, asbestos, mica and similar materials; ceramic products; glass and glassware | .. | .. | .. | .. | .. | 9.2 | XIII - Изделия из камня, гипса, цемента |
| XIV - Natural or cultured pearls, precious or semi-precious stones, precious metals, metals clad with precious metal and articles thereof; imitation jewellery; coin | .. | .. | .. | .. | .. | 0.2 | XIV - Жемчуг, драгоценные и полудрагоценные камни, драгоценные металлы, бижутерия, монеты |
| XV - Base metals and articles of base metal | .. | .. | .. | .. | .. | 69.0 | XV - Неблагородные металлы и изделия из них |
| XVI - Machinery and mechanical appliances; electrical equipment; parts thereof; sound recorders and reproducers, television image and sound recorders and reproducers, and parts and accessories of such articles | .. | .. | .. | .. | .. | 30.0 | XVI - Машины, оборудование, механизмы, их части и принадлежности; звуковая и теле-аппаратура, их части и принадлежности |
| XVII - Vehicles, aircraft, vessels and associated transport equipment | .. | .. | .. | .. | .. | 7.5 | XVII - Средства наземного, воздушного и водного транспорта |
| XVIII - Optical, photographic, cinematographic, measuring, checking, precision, medical or surgical instruments and apparatus; clocks and watches; musical instruments; parts and accessories thereof | .. | .. | .. | .. | .. | 1.3 | XVIII - Приборы, аппараты оптические, медицинские, измерительные и пр.; музыкальные инструменты; часы; их части и принадлежности |
| XIX - Arms and ammunition; parts and accessories thereof | .. | .. | .. | .. | .. | 7.8 | XIX - Оружие и боеприпасы, их части и принадлежности |
| XX - Miscellaneous manufactured articles | .. | .. | .. | .. | .. | 1.9 | XX - Разные промышленные товары |
| XXI - Works of art, collectors' pieces, and antiques | .. | .. | .. | .. | .. | .. | XXI - Произведения искусства, предметы антиквариата |
| XXII - Services | .. | .. | .. | .. | .. | 3.1 | XXII - Услуги |

**TABLE 3-3B. Exports by Commodity Group (millions of national currency)**
**ТАБЛИЦА 3-3B. Экспорт по товарным группам (млн. национальной валюты)**

| Commodity group | 1990 | 1991 | 1992 | 1993 | 1994 | 1995 | Товарные группы |
|---|---|---|---|---|---|---|---|
| TOTAL | .. | .. | .. | .. | .. | 4,419.8 | ВСЕГО |
| I - Live animals; animal products | .. | .. | .. | .. | .. | 75.4 | I - Живые животные и продукты животноводства |
| II - Vegetable products | .. | .. | .. | .. | .. | 293.8 | II - Продукты растительного происхождения |
| III - Animal or vegetable fats and oils and their cleavage products; prepared edible fats; animal or vegetable waxes | .. | .. | .. | .. | .. | 9.2 | III - Жиры и масла растительного и животного происхождения, воски |
| IV - Prepared foodstuffs; beverages, spirits and vinegar; tobacco and manufactured tobacco substitutes | .. | .. | .. | .. | .. | 917.0 | IV -Продукция пищевой промышленности, алкогольные и безалкогольные напитки, табак и его заменители |
| V - Mineral products | .. | .. | .. | .. | .. | 515.7 | V - Минеральные продукты |
| VI - Products of the chemical or allied industries | .. | .. | .. | .. | .. | 270.1 | VI - Продукция химической промышленности |
| VII - Plastics and articles thereof; rubber and articles thereof | .. | .. | .. | .. | .. | 22.0 | VII - Пластмассы и изделия из них |
| VIII - Raw hides and skins, leather, furskins and articles thereof; saddlery and harness; travel goods, handbags and similar containers; articles of animal gut | .. | .. | .. | .. | .. | 59.5 | VIII - Кожевенное сырьё, кожи, пушнина, меховое сырьё и изделия из них |
| IX - Wood and articles of wood; wood charcoal; cork and articles of cork; manufactures of straw, of esparto or of other plaiting materials; basketware and wickerwork | .. | .. | .. | .. | .. | 6.3 | IX - Древесина и изделия из древесины, древесный уголь |
| X - Pulp of wood or of other fibrous cellulosic material; waste and scrap of paper or paperboard; paper and paperboard and articles thereof | .. | .. | .. | .. | .. | 7.7 | X - Бумажная масса, бумажные и картонные отходы, макулатура, бумага, картон и изделия из них |
| XI - Textiles and textile articles | .. | .. | .. | .. | .. | 851.6 | XI - Текстиль и текстильные изделия |
| XII - Footwear, headgear, umbrellas, sun umbrellas, walking sticks, seat sticks, whips, riding crops and parts thereof; prepared feathers and articles made therewith; artificial flowers; articles of human hair | .. | .. | .. | .. | .. | 17.4 | XII - Обувь, головные уборы, зонты, трости и пр. |

**TABLE 3-3B. Exports by Commodity Group (millions of national currency)**
**ТАБЛИЦА 3-3B. Экспорт по товарным группам (млн. национальной валюты)**

| Commodity group | 1990 | 1991 | 1992 | 1993 | 1994 | 1995 | Товарные группы |
|---|---|---|---|---|---|---|---|
| XIII - Articles of stone, plaster, cement, asbestos, mica and similar materials; ceramic products; glass and glassware | .. | .. | .. | .. | .. | 99.1 | XIII - Изделия из камня, гипса, цемента |
| XIV - Natural or cultured pearls, precious or semi-precious stones, precious metals, metals clad with precious metal and articles thereof; imitation jewellery; coin | .. | .. | .. | .. | .. | 1.9 | XIV - Жемчуг, драгоценные и полудрагоценные камни, драгоценные металлы, бижутерия, монеты |
| XV - Base metals and articles of base metal | .. | .. | .. | .. | .. | 747.4 | XV - Неблагородные металлы и изделия из них |
| XVI - Machinery and mechanical appliances; electrical equipment; parts thereof; sound recorders and reproducers, television image and sound recorders and reproducers, and parts and accessories of such articles | .. | .. | .. | .. | .. | 325.8 | XVI - Машины, оборудование, механизмы, их части и принадлежности; звуковая и теле-аппаратура, их части и принадлежности |
| XVII - Vehicles, aircraft, vessels and associated transport equipment | .. | .. | .. | .. | .. | 80.7 | XVII - Средства наземного, воздушного и водного транспорта |
| XVIII - Optical, photographic, cinematograp-hic, measuring, checking, precision, medical or surgical instruments and apparatus; clocks and watches; musical instruments; parts and accessories thereof | .. | .. | .. | .. | .. | 14.1 | XVIII - Приборы, аппараты оптические, медицинские, измерительные и пр.; музыкальные инструменты; часы; их части и принадлежности |
| XIX - Arms and ammunition; parts and accessories thereof | .. | .. | .. | .. | .. | 84.4 | XIX - Оружие и боеприпасы, их части и принадлежности |
| XX - Miscellaneous manufactured articles | .. | .. | .. | .. | .. | 20.7 | XX - Разные промышленные товары |
| XXI - Works of art, collectors' pieces, and antiques | .. | .. | .. | .. | .. | .. | XXI - Произведения искусства, предметы антиквариата |
| XXII - Services | .. | .. | .. | .. | .. | 33.5 | XXII - Услуги |

TABLE 3-4A. Geographical distribution of foreign trade (millions of U.S. dollars)
ТАБЛИЦА 3-4А. Географическое распределение внешней торговли (млн. долларов США)

| Country or country group | Exports Экспорт 1990 | 1991 | 1992 | 1993 | 1994 | 1995 | Imports Импорт 1990 | 1991 | 1992 | 1993 | 1994 | 1995 | Страна или группа стран |
|---|---|---|---|---|---|---|---|---|---|---|---|---|---|
| **Total trade** | .. | .. | .. | .. | .. | 408.9 | .. | .. | .. | .. | .. | 522.3 | **Всего** |
| **CIS countries** | .. | .. | .. | .. | .. | 269.2 | .. | .. | .. | .. | .. | 353.6 | **Страны СНГ** |
| Armenia | .. | .. | .. | .. | .. | 0.0 | .. | .. | .. | .. | .. | 0.6 | Армения |
| Azerbaijan | .. | .. | .. | .. | .. | 2.1 | .. | .. | .. | .. | .. | 3.3 | Азербайджан |
| Belarus | .. | .. | .. | .. | .. | 5.0 | .. | .. | .. | .. | .. | 5.0 | Беларусь |
| Georgia | .. | .. | .. | .. | .. | 0.7 | .. | .. | .. | .. | .. | 0.3 | Грузия |
| Kazakstan | .. | .. | .. | .. | .. | 66.8 | .. | .. | .. | .. | .. | 112.5 | Казахстан |
| Kyrgyz Republic | .. | .. | .. | .. | .. | .. | .. | .. | .. | .. | .. | .. | Киргизстан |
| Moldova | .. | .. | .. | .. | .. | 1.0 | .. | .. | .. | .. | .. | 0.2 | Молдова |
| Russia | .. | .. | .. | .. | .. | 104.8 | .. | .. | .. | .. | .. | 114.4 | Россия |
| Tajikistan | .. | .. | .. | .. | .. | 8.3 | .. | .. | .. | .. | .. | 4.8 | Таджикистан |
| Turkmenistan | .. | .. | .. | .. | .. | 2.2 | .. | .. | .. | .. | .. | 18.6 | Туркменистан |
| Ukraine | .. | .. | .. | .. | .. | 8.3 | .. | .. | .. | .. | .. | 5.0 | Украина |
| Uzbekistan | .. | .. | .. | .. | .. | 70.0 | .. | .. | .. | .. | .. | 88.9 | Узбекистан |
| **Non-CIS countries** | .. | .. | .. | .. | .. | 139.7 | .. | .. | .. | .. | .. | 168.7 | **Остальной мир** |
| **Europe** | .. | .. | .. | .. | .. | 50.0 | .. | .. | .. | .. | .. | 55.1 | **Европа** |
| Austria | .. | .. | .. | .. | .. | 1.7 | .. | .. | .. | .. | .. | 1.3 | Австрия |
| Belgium | .. | .. | .. | .. | .. | 0.2 | .. | .. | .. | .. | .. | 3.5 | Бельгия |
| Bulgaria | .. | .. | .. | .. | .. | 2.9 | .. | .. | .. | .. | .. | 3.0 | Болгария |
| Czech Republic | .. | .. | .. | .. | .. | 1.2 | .. | .. | .. | .. | .. | 0.3 | Чешская Республика |
| Denmark | .. | .. | .. | .. | .. | .. | .. | .. | .. | .. | .. | 1.9 | Дания |
| Estonia | .. | .. | .. | .. | .. | 0.1 | .. | .. | .. | .. | .. | 0.3 | Эстония |
| Finland | .. | .. | .. | .. | .. | 0.0 | .. | .. | .. | .. | .. | 1.3 | Финляндия |
| Former Yugoslavia | .. | .. | .. | .. | .. | 0.1 | .. | .. | .. | .. | .. | 0.1 | Быв. Югославия |
| France | .. | .. | .. | .. | .. | 3.6 | .. | .. | .. | .. | .. | 1.8 | Франция |
| Germany | .. | .. | .. | .. | .. | 2.1 | .. | .. | .. | .. | .. | 18.7 | Германия |
| Hungary | .. | .. | .. | .. | .. | 0.2 | .. | .. | .. | .. | .. | 1.0 | Венгрия |
| Iceland | .. | .. | .. | .. | .. | .. | .. | .. | .. | .. | .. | .. | Исландия |
| Ireland | .. | .. | .. | .. | .. | .. | .. | .. | .. | .. | .. | 0.1 | Ирландия |
| Italy | .. | .. | .. | .. | .. | 2.9 | .. | .. | .. | .. | .. | 1.7 | Италия |
| Latvia | .. | .. | .. | .. | .. | 2.3 | .. | .. | .. | .. | .. | 1.5 | Латвия |
| Lithuania | .. | .. | .. | .. | .. | 0.4 | .. | .. | .. | .. | .. | 1.7 | Литва |
| Netherlands | .. | .. | .. | .. | .. | 0.9 | .. | .. | .. | .. | .. | 1.5 | Нидерланды |
| Norway | .. | .. | .. | .. | .. | .. | .. | .. | .. | .. | .. | 1.7 | Норвегия |
| Poland | .. | .. | .. | .. | .. | 1.3 | .. | .. | .. | .. | .. | 1.9 | Польша |
| Romania | .. | .. | .. | .. | .. | 0.1 | .. | .. | .. | .. | .. | 0.1 | Румыния |
| Slovak Republic | .. | .. | .. | .. | .. | 0.8 | .. | .. | .. | .. | .. | 0.2 | Словацская Республика |
| Spain | .. | .. | .. | .. | .. | .. | .. | .. | .. | .. | .. | .. | Испания |
| Sweden | .. | .. | .. | .. | .. | .. | .. | .. | .. | .. | .. | 0.1 | Швеция |
| Switzerland | .. | .. | .. | .. | .. | 1.8 | .. | .. | .. | .. | .. | 1.2 | Швейцария |
| United Kingdom | .. | .. | .. | .. | .. | 27.4 | .. | .. | .. | .. | .. | 1.7 | Великобритания |

**TABLE 3-4A. Geographical distribution of foreign trade (millions of U.S. dollars)**
**ТАБЛИЦА 3-4А. Географическое распределение внешней торговли (млн. долларов США)**

| Country or country group | Exports Экспорт 1990 | 1991 | 1992 | 1993 | 1994 | 1995 | Imports Импорт 1990 | 1991 | 1992 | 1993 | 1994 | 1995 | Страна или группа стран |
|---|---|---|---|---|---|---|---|---|---|---|---|---|---|
| Other Europe | .. | .. | .. | .. | .. | .. | .. | .. | .. | .. | .. | 8.5 | Остальные страны Европы |
| **Asia** | .. | .. | .. | .. | .. | 84.3 | .. | .. | .. | .. | .. | 65.9 | **Азия** |
| Afghanistan | .. | .. | .. | .. | .. | 3.0 | .. | .. | .. | .. | .. | 3.0 | Афганистан |
| China | .. | .. | .. | .. | .. | 68.5 | .. | .. | .. | .. | .. | 6.3 | Китай |
| India | .. | .. | .. | .. | .. | 0.5 | .. | .. | .. | .. | .. | 0.6 | Индия |
| Iraq | .. | .. | .. | .. | .. | .. | .. | .. | .. | .. | .. | .. | Ирак |
| Japan | .. | .. | .. | .. | .. | 0.6 | .. | .. | .. | .. | .. | 7.2 | Япония |
| Korea, Dem. People's Rep. | .. | .. | .. | .. | .. | 0.5 | .. | .. | .. | .. | .. | 0.8 | КНДР |
| Korea, Rep. of | .. | .. | .. | .. | .. | 0.8 | .. | .. | .. | .. | .. | 2.5 | Южная Корея |
| Mongolia | .. | .. | .. | .. | .. | 0.9 | .. | .. | .. | .. | .. | .. | МНР |
| Syrian Arab Republic | .. | .. | .. | .. | .. | .. | .. | .. | .. | .. | .. | 0.0 | Сирия |
| Turkey | .. | .. | .. | .. | .. | 3.2 | .. | .. | .. | .. | .. | 38.3 | Турция |
| Viet Nam | .. | .. | .. | .. | .. | .. | .. | .. | .. | .. | .. | .. | Вьетнам |
| Other Asia | .. | .. | .. | .. | .. | 6.3 | .. | .. | .. | .. | .. | 7.2 | Остальные страны Азии |
| **America** | .. | .. | .. | .. | .. | 5.4 | .. | .. | .. | .. | .. | 47.7 | **Сев. и Южная Америка** |
| Canada | .. | .. | .. | .. | .. | 1.4 | .. | .. | .. | .. | .. | 5.9 | Канада |
| Cuba | .. | .. | .. | .. | .. | .. | .. | .. | .. | .. | .. | 22.7 | Куба |
| United States | .. | .. | .. | .. | .. | 4.0 | .. | .. | .. | .. | .. | 19.1 | США |
| Other America | .. | .. | .. | .. | .. | .. | .. | .. | .. | .. | .. | .. | Остальные |
| **Africa** | .. | .. | .. | .. | .. | .. | .. | .. | .. | .. | .. | .. | **Африка** |
| Egypt | .. | .. | .. | .. | .. | .. | .. | .. | .. | .. | .. | .. | Египет |
| Libya | .. | .. | .. | .. | .. | .. | .. | .. | .. | .. | .. | .. | Ливия |
| Other Africa | .. | .. | .. | .. | .. | .. | .. | .. | .. | .. | .. | .. | Остальные |
| **Rest of the World** | .. | .. | .. | .. | .. | .. | .. | .. | .. | .. | .. | .. | **Прочие страны мира** |
| Australia | .. | .. | .. | .. | .. | .. | .. | .. | .. | .. | .. | .. | Австралия |

**TABLE 3-4B. Geographical distribution of foreign trade (millions of national currency)**

**ТАБЛИЦА 3-4B. Географическое распределение внешней торговли (миллионов национальной валюты)**

| Country or country group | Exports Экспорт 1990 | 1991 | 1992 | 1993 | 1994 | 1995 | Imports Импорт 1990 | 1991 | 1992 | 1993 | 1994 | 1995 | Страна или группа стран |
|---|---|---|---|---|---|---|---|---|---|---|---|---|---|
| **Total trade** | .. | .. | .. | .. | .. | 4,419.8 | .. | .. | .. | .. | .. | 5,668.5 | **Всего** |
| **CIS countries** | .. | .. | .. | .. | .. | 2,909.8 | .. | .. | .. | .. | .. | 3,834.5 | **Страны СНГ** |
| Armenia | .. | .. | .. | .. | .. | 0.4 | .. | .. | .. | .. | .. | 6.5 | Армения |
| Azerbaijan | .. | .. | .. | .. | .. | 23.2 | .. | .. | .. | .. | .. | 35.3 | Азербайджан |
| Belarus | .. | .. | .. | .. | .. | 54.2 | .. | .. | .. | .. | .. | 54.7 | Беларусь |
| Georgia | .. | .. | .. | .. | .. | 7.5 | .. | .. | .. | .. | .. | 3.6 | Грузия |
| Kazakstan | .. | .. | .. | .. | .. | 721.7 | .. | .. | .. | .. | .. | 1,215.5 | Казахстан |
| Kyrgyz Republic | .. | .. | .. | .. | .. | .. | .. | .. | .. | .. | .. | .. | Киргизстан |
| Moldova | .. | .. | .. | .. | .. | 10.7 | .. | .. | .. | .. | .. | 2.5 | Молдова |
| Russia | .. | .. | .. | .. | .. | 1,134.0 | .. | .. | .. | .. | .. | 1,240.4 | Россия |
| Tajikistan | .. | .. | .. | .. | .. | 89.5 | .. | .. | .. | .. | .. | 52.3 | Таджикистан |
| Turkmenistan | .. | .. | .. | .. | .. | 23.8 | .. | .. | .. | .. | .. | 202.0 | Туркменистан |
| Ukraine | .. | .. | .. | .. | .. | 90.9 | .. | .. | .. | .. | .. | 53.6 | Украина |
| Uzbekistan | .. | .. | .. | .. | .. | 753.9 | .. | .. | .. | .. | .. | 968.1 | Узбекистан |
| **Non-CIS countries** | .. | .. | .. | .. | .. | 1,510.0 | .. | .. | .. | .. | .. | 1,834.0 | **Остальной мир** |
| **Europe** | .. | .. | .. | .. | .. | 541.8 | .. | .. | .. | .. | .. | 595.0 | **Европа** |
| Austria | .. | .. | .. | .. | .. | 18.9 | .. | .. | .. | .. | .. | 14.0 | Австрия |
| Belgium | .. | .. | .. | .. | .. | 2.3 | .. | .. | .. | .. | .. | 38.3 | Бельгия |
| Bulgaria | .. | .. | .. | .. | .. | 30.9 | .. | .. | .. | .. | .. | 32.2 | Болгария |
| Czech Republic | .. | .. | .. | .. | .. | 13.1 | .. | .. | .. | .. | .. | 3.0 | Чешская Республика |
| Denmark | .. | .. | .. | .. | .. | 0.0 | .. | .. | .. | .. | .. | 20.2 | Дания |
| Estonia | .. | .. | .. | .. | .. | 0.9 | .. | .. | .. | .. | .. | 2.7 | Эстония |
| Finland | .. | .. | .. | .. | .. | 0.5 | .. | .. | .. | .. | .. | 14.3 | Финляндия |
| Former Yugoslavia | .. | .. | .. | .. | .. | 0.9 | .. | .. | .. | .. | .. | 1.6 | Быв. Югославия |
| France | .. | .. | .. | .. | .. | 38.8 | .. | .. | .. | .. | .. | 19.5 | Франция |
| Germany | .. | .. | .. | .. | .. | 22.5 | .. | .. | .. | .. | .. | 201.9 | Германия |
| Hungary | .. | .. | .. | .. | .. | 2.0 | .. | .. | .. | .. | .. | 10.9 | Венгрия |
| Iceland | .. | .. | .. | .. | .. | .. | .. | .. | .. | .. | .. | .. | Исландия |
| Ireland | .. | .. | .. | .. | .. | .. | .. | .. | .. | .. | .. | 0.9 | Ирландия |
| Italy | .. | .. | .. | .. | .. | 31.7 | .. | .. | .. | .. | .. | 18.4 | Италия |
| Latvia | .. | .. | .. | .. | .. | 24.1 | .. | .. | .. | .. | .. | 16.4 | Латвия |
| Lithuania | .. | .. | .. | .. | .. | 4.6 | .. | .. | .. | .. | .. | 19.0 | Литва |
| Netherlands | .. | .. | .. | .. | .. | 9.5 | .. | .. | .. | .. | .. | 16.3 | Нидерланды |
| Norway | .. | .. | .. | .. | .. | .. | .. | .. | .. | .. | .. | 17.7 | Норвегия |
| Poland | .. | .. | .. | .. | .. | 14.6 | .. | .. | .. | .. | .. | 20.8 | Польша |
| Romania | .. | .. | .. | .. | .. | 1.7 | .. | .. | .. | .. | .. | 0.7 | Румыния |
| Slovak Republic | .. | .. | .. | .. | .. | 9.1 | .. | .. | .. | .. | .. | 2.4 | Словацская Республика |
| Spain | .. | .. | .. | .. | .. | .. | .. | .. | .. | .. | .. | .. | Испания |
| Sweden | .. | .. | .. | .. | .. | .. | .. | .. | .. | .. | .. | 0.9 | Швеция |
| Switzerland | .. | .. | .. | .. | .. | 19.5 | .. | .. | .. | .. | .. | 12.6 | Швейцария |

**TABLE 3-4B. Geographical distribution of foreign trade (millions of national currency)**

**ТАБЛИЦА 3-4B. Географическое распределение внешней торговли (миллионов национальной валюты)**

| Country or country group | Exports Экспорт 1990 | 1991 | 1992 | 1993 | 1994 | 1995 | Imports Импорт 1990 | 1991 | 1992 | 1993 | 1994 | 1995 | Страна или группа стран |
|---|---|---|---|---|---|---|---|---|---|---|---|---|---|
| United Kingdom | .. | .. | .. | .. | .. | 296.0 | .. | .. | .. | .. | .. | 18.0 | Великобритания |
| Other Europe | .. | .. | .. | .. | .. | 0.2 | .. | .. | .. | .. | .. | 92.3 | Остальные страны Европы |
| **Asia** | .. | .. | .. | .. | .. | 909.4 | .. | .. | .. | .. | .. | 716.3 | **Азия** |
| Afghanistan | .. | .. | .. | .. | .. | 32.5 | .. | .. | .. | .. | .. | 32.4 | Афганистан |
| China | .. | .. | .. | .. | .. | 737.9 | .. | .. | .. | .. | .. | 67.8 | Китай |
| India | .. | .. | .. | .. | .. | 5.7 | .. | .. | .. | .. | .. | 5.9 | Индия |
| Iraq | .. | .. | .. | .. | .. | .. | .. | .. | .. | .. | .. | .. | Ирак |
| Japan | .. | .. | .. | .. | .. | 6.1 | .. | .. | .. | .. | .. | 77.9 | Япония |
| Korea, Dem. People's Rep. | .. | .. | .. | .. | .. | 5.5 | .. | .. | .. | .. | .. | 8.5 | КНДР |
| Korea, Rep. of | .. | .. | .. | .. | .. | 8.7 | .. | .. | .. | .. | .. | 27.1 | Южная Корея |
| Mongolia | .. | .. | .. | .. | .. | 9.6 | .. | .. | .. | .. | .. | .. | МНР |
| Syrian Arab Republic | .. | .. | .. | .. | .. | .. | .. | .. | .. | .. | .. | 0.0 | Сирия |
| Turkey | .. | .. | .. | .. | .. | 34.8 | .. | .. | .. | .. | .. | 417.6 | Турция |
| Viet Nam | .. | .. | .. | .. | .. | .. | .. | .. | .. | .. | .. | .. | Вьетнам |
| Other Asia | .. | .. | .. | .. | .. | 68.6 | .. | .. | .. | .. | .. | 79.1 | Остальные страны Азии |
| **America** | .. | .. | .. | .. | .. | 58.8 | .. | .. | .. | .. | .. | 522.7 | **Сев. и Южная Америка** |
| Canada | .. | .. | .. | .. | .. | 15.5 | .. | .. | .. | .. | .. | 63.2 | Канада |
| Cuba | .. | .. | .. | .. | .. | .. | .. | .. | .. | .. | .. | 250.6 | Куба |
| United States | .. | .. | .. | .. | .. | 43.3 | .. | .. | .. | .. | .. | 208.9 | США |
| Other America | .. | .. | .. | .. | .. | .. | .. | .. | .. | .. | .. | .. | Остальные |
| **Africa** | .. | .. | .. | .. | .. | .. | .. | .. | .. | .. | .. | .. | **Африка** |
| Egypt | .. | .. | .. | .. | .. | .. | .. | .. | .. | .. | .. | .. | Египет |
| Libya | .. | .. | .. | .. | .. | .. | .. | .. | .. | .. | .. | .. | Ливия |
| Other Africa | .. | .. | .. | .. | .. | .. | .. | .. | .. | .. | .. | .. | Остальные |
| **Rest of the World** | .. | .. | .. | .. | .. | .. | .. | .. | .. | .. | .. | .. | **Прочие страны мира** |
| Australia | .. | .. | .. | .. | .. | .. | .. | .. | .. | .. | .. | .. | Австралия |

**TABLE 4-1. General government budget revenue (millions of national currency)**
**ТАБЛИЦА 4-1. Доходы государственного бюджета (млн. национальной валюты)**

| Type of revenue | 1990 | 1991 | 1992 | 1993 | 1994 | 1995 | Вид доходов |
|---|---|---|---|---|---|---|---|
| **Total revenue and grants** | 16.1 | 27.2 | 127.5 | 1,330 | 2,298 | 2,671 | **Всего доходов и безвозм. поступл.** |
| Grants | 4.6 | 9.7 | .. | 462 | 303 | 55 | Безвозмездные поступления |
| Total Revenue | 11.5 | 17.5 | 127.5 | 869 | 1,995 | 2,616 | Всего доходов |
| **Current revenue** | .. | .. | .. | .. | .. | .. | **Текущие доходы** |
| Tax revenue | 10.9 | 13.3 | 111.8 | 721 | 1,696 | 2,430 | Доход от налогов |
| Taxes on income and profits | 2.8 | 5.2 | 52.4 | 300 | 651 | 720 | Налоги на доходы и прибыль |
| Individual | 1.8 | 1.9 | 13.5 | 72 | 225 | 287 | Физические лица |
| Corporate | 1.0 | 3.3 | 38.9 | 229 | 426 | 433 | Предприятия и организации |
| Social security contributions | .. | .. | .. | .. | .. | .. | Отчисление на соцстрах. |
| Taxes on payroll or work force | .. | .. | .. | .. | .. | .. | Налоги на заработную плату и рабочую силу |
| Taxes on the use of labor force | .. | .. | .. | | .. | .. | Плата за трудовые ресурсы |
| Taxes on increases in wages and salaries | .. | .. | .. | .. | .. | .. | Налог с прироста средств на оплату труда |
| Other payroll/work force taxes | 0.0 | 0.0 | 0.0 | 0 | 0 | .. | Другие налоги на зарплату и рабочую силу |
| Taxes on property | .. | .. | .. | .. | .. | .. | Налоги на собственность |
| Taxes on immovable property | .. | .. | .. | .. | .. | .. | Налоги на недвижимое имущество |
| Buildings | .. | .. | .. | .. | .. | .. | Налог с владельцев строении |
| Land | .. | .. | .. | .. | .. | .. | Земельныи налог |
| Estate, inheritance, and gift taxes | .. | .. | .. | .. | .. | .. | Налоги на наследство, подарки |
| Other property taxes | .. | .. | .. | .. | .. | .. | Другие налоги на имущество |
| Domestic taxes on goods and services | 5.9 | 7.4 | 52.2 | 346 | 754 | 1,216 | Внутренние налоги на товары и услуги |
| General sales, turnover, or value-added taxes | 5.9 | 7.4 | 38.3 | 274 | 582 | 908 | Налог с продаж. с оборота или на добав. стоим. |
| Excises | .. | .. | 14.0 | 72 | 172 | 308 | Акцизы |
| Profits of fiscal monopolies | .. | .. | .. | .. | .. | .. | Прибыли фискальных монополий |
| Taxes on specific services | .. | .. | .. | .. | .. | .. | Налоги на особые услуги |
| Taxes on use of goods or permission to use goods or to perform activities | .. | .. | .. | .. | .. | .. | Налоги на пользование товарами или лицензии на пользование товарами и занятие деятельностью |
| Other taxes on goods and services | .. | .. | .. | .. | .. | .. | Другие налоги на товары и услуги |
| Taxes on international trade and transactions | .. | .. | .. | .. | .. | .. | Налоги на внешнюю торговлю и операции |
| Import duties | .. | .. | .. | .. | .. | .. | Импортные пошлины |
| Export duties | .. | .. | .. | .. | .. | .. | Экпортные пошлины |
| Other | .. | .. | .. | .. | .. | .. | Другие |
| Other taxes | 2.3 | 0.8 | 7.3 | 76 | 291 | 494 | Прочие налоги |
| Nontax revenue | 0.6 | 4.2 | 15.7 | 139 | 198 | 186 | Неналоговые доходы |
| **Capital revenue** | .. | .. | .. | 9 | 102 | 1 | **Капитальные доходы** |

**TABLE 4-2. General government budget expenditure by economic type (millions of national currency)**
**ТАБЛИЦА 4-2. Расходы государственного бюджета по экономическим типам (млн. национальной валюты)**

| Type of expenditure or debt holder | 1990 | 1991 | 1992 | 1993 | 1994 | 1995 | Всего расходов |
|---|---|---|---|---|---|---|---|
| **Total expenditure by economic type** | 15.9 | 23.7 | 261.9 | 2,163 | 2,927 | 4,580 | **Всего расходов по экономическим типам** |
| **Current expenditure** | 13.5 | 22.7 | 189.8 | 1,615 | 2,498 | 4,272 | **Текущие расходы** |
| Expenditure on goods and services | 6.9 | 12.6 | 99.0 | 584 | 1,561 | 2,676 | Расходы на товары и услуги |
| Wages and salaries | 2.7 | 5.6 | 47.9 | 281 | 885 | 1,529 | Заработная плата |
| Employer contributions | .. | .. | .. | .. | .. | .. | Отчисление на социальное страхование |
| Other Purchases of goods and services | 4.2 | 7.0 | 51.2 | 303 | 676 | 1,148 | Другие покупки товаров и услуг |
| Interest payments | .. | .. | 4.4 | 37 | 28 | 225 | Выплаты процентов |
| Domestic debt | .. | .. | .. | .. | .. | .. | По внутреннему долгу |
| Foreign debt | .. | .. | .. | .. | .. | .. | По внешншму долгу |
| Subsidies and other current transfers | 6.7 | 10.2 | 52.7 | 975 | 370 | 1,027 | Субсидии на другие текущие трансферты |
| Subsidies | .. | .. | .. | .. | .. | .. | Субсидии |
| Agricultural subsidies | .. | .. | .. | .. | .. | .. | Субсидии на сельское хозяиство |
| Other current transfers | .. | .. | .. | .. | .. | .. | Другие текущие трансферты |
| Other | .. | .. | 33.8 | 19 | 539 | 344 | Прочие расходы |
| **Capital expenditure** | 2.4 | 1.0 | 11.4 | 75 | 278 | 159 | **Капитальные расходы** |
| Acquisition of fixed capital assets | .. | .. | .. | .. | .. | .. | Приобретение основного капитала |
| Capital transfers | .. | .. | .. | .. | .. | .. | Капитальные трансферты |
| Other | .. | .. | .. | .. | .. | .. | Другие капитальные расходы |
| **Surplus/deficit (-)** | 0.2 | 3.5 | -134.4 | -833 | -629 | -1,909 | **Превыш. доходов над расходами/дефицит(-)** |
| **Financing by type of debt holder** | .. | .. | .. | .. | .. | .. | **Финансирование по типам кредиторов** |
| **Foreign (net)** | .. | .. | .. | .. | .. | .. | **Зарубежные кредиторы (сальдо)** |
| From international development institutions | .. | .. | .. | .. | .. | .. | Международные организации |
| From foreign governments | .. | .. | .. | .. | .. | .. | Правительства иностранных государств |
| Other borrowing abroad | .. | .. | .. | .. | .. | .. | Другие зарубежные кредиторы |
| **Domestic (net)** | .. | .. | .. | .. | .. | .. | **Внутренние кредиторы (сальдо)** |
| From monetary authorities | .. | .. | .. | .. | .. | .. | Органы денежного обращения |
| From deposit money banks | .. | .. | .. | .. | .. | .. | Депозитные денежные банки |
| Other domestic borrowing | .. | .. | .. | .. | .. | .. | Другие внутренние кредиторы |
| *Memo items:* | | | | | | | *Справочно:* |
| Extrabudgetary surplus/ Deficit (-) not included above | .. | .. | .. | .. | .. | .. | Превышение доходов над расходами/дефицит (-) по внебюджетным фондам, не включенным выше |
| Total surplus/deficit (-) including extrabudgetary accounts | .. | .. | .. | .. | .. | .. | Итого превышение доходов над расходами/дефицит, включая счета внебюджетных фондов |

## TABLE 5-1. Agricultural production (millions of national currency, current prices)



## ТАБЛИЦА 5-1. Сельскохозяйственная продукция (млн. нац. валюты, текущие цены)

| Item | 1990 | 1991 | 1992 | 1993 | 1994 | 1995 | Статьи |
|---|---|---|---|---|---|---|---|
| **Total gross agricultural production** | 20 | 43 | 363 | 2,991 | 6,933 | 9,571 | **Валовая продукция сельского хозяиства - всего** |
| **Crops** | 8 | 17 | 206 | 1,186 | 3,051 | 4,764 | **Продукция растениеводства** |
| Grains | 3 | 3 | 64 | .. | 889 | 1,267 | Зерно |
| Potatoes | 1 | 5 | 19 | .. | 523 | 1,042 | Картофель |
| Vegetables | 1 | 3 | 11 | .. | 497 | 677 | Овощи |
| Fruits (excluding grapes) | 0 | 1 | 3 | .. | 44 | 328 | Фрукты (без винограда) |
| Grapes | 0 | 0 | 1 | .. | 37 | 45 | Виноград |
| Tobacco | 2 | 5 | 92 | .. | 134 | 65 | Табак |
| Cotton | 0 | 1 | 14 | .. | 214 | 387 | Хлопок |
| Sugarbeets | .. | .. | 0 | .. | 43 | 61 | Сахарная свекла |
| Oilseeds | 0 | 0 | 0 | .. | 68 | 106 | Семена масличных культур |
| Other | 1 | 0 | 1 | .. | 601 | 786 | Прочие |
| **Animal husbandry** | 12 | 26 | 157 | 1,806 | 3,882 | 4,807 | **Продукция животноводства** |
| Livestock | 5 | 10 | 62 | .. | 1,634 | 2,213 | Мясное животноводство |
| Cattle | 2 | 2 | 23 | .. | 526 | 858 | Крупный рогатый скот |
| Pigs | 1 | 1 | 8 | .. | 175 | 508 | Свиньи |
| Sheep and goats | 1 | 1 | 14 | .. | 786 | 672 | Овцы и козы |
| Poultry | 0 | 1 | 5 | .. | 58 | 57 | Птица |
| Other | 2 | 5 | 12 | .. | 90 | 118 | Прочие |
| Milk | 2 | 4 | 32 | .. | 1,813 | 2,259 | Молоко |
| Eggs | 0 | 1 | 5 | .. | 133 | 144 | Яйца |
| Wool | 2 | 7 | 49 | .. | 113 | 123 | Шерсть |
| Other livestock | 2 | 5 | 10 | .. | 189 | 68 | Прочая |
| **Agricultural services** | .. | .. | .. | .. | .. | .. | **Сельскохозяйственные услуги** |

## TABLE 5-2. Agricultural production (thousands of constant national currency)
## ТАБЛИЦА 5-2. Сельскохозяйственная продукция в постоянных ценах (тысяч национальной валюты)

| Item | 1990 | 1991 | 1992 | 1993 | 1994 | 1995 | Статьи |
|---|---|---|---|---|---|---|---|
| **Total gross agricultural production** | 15,119 | 13,612 | 12,868 | 11,611 | 9,464 | .. | **Валовая продукция сельского хозяйства - всего** |
| **Crops** | 5,535 | 4,609 | 4,650 | 4,020 | 3,470 | .. | **Продукция растениеводства** |
| Grains | 865 | 795 | 880 | 843 | 582 | .. | Зерно |
| Potatoes | 350 | 310 | 345 | 295 | 298 | .. | Картофель |
| Vegetables | 775 | 635 | 570 | 346 | 351 | .. | Овощи |
| Fruits (excluding grapes) | 405 | 330 | 325 | 125 | 200 | .. | Фрукты (без винограда) |
| Grapes | 100 | 70 | 75 | 21 | 41 | .. | Виноград |
| Tobacco | 1,410 | 1,100 | 1,175 | 1,267 | 948 | .. | Табак |
| Cotton | 315 | 235 | 200 | 196 | 215 | .. | Хлопок |
| Sugarbeets | .. | 5 | 35 | 57 | 30 | .. | Сахарная свекла |
| Oilseeds | 25 | 10 | 10 | 12 | 24 | .. | Семена масличных культур |
| Other | 1,289 | 1,119 | 1,035 | 858 | 781 | .. | Прочие |
| **Animal husbandry** | 9,585 | 9,003 | 8,218 | 7,591 | 5,994 | .. | **Продукция животноводства** |
| Livestock | 4,690 | 4,555 | 4,240 | 3,751 | 2,904 | .. | Мясное животноводство |
| Cattle | 1,905 | 1,780 | 1,665 | 1,694 | 1,373 | .. | Крупный рогатый скот |
| Pigs | 515 | 475 | 460 | 346 | 261 | .. | Свиньи |
| Sheep and goats | 1,660 | 1,500 | 1,380 | 1,388 | 1,032 | .. | Овцы и козы |
| Poultry | 260 | 525 | 350 | 132 | 51 | .. | Птица |
| Other | 350 | 275 | 385 | 191 | 187 | .. | Прочие |
| Milk | 2,359 | 2,245 | 1,910 | 1,882 | 1,730 | .. | Молоко |
| Eggs | 210 | 310 | 285 | 186 | 97 | .. | Яйца |
| Wool | 2,000 | 1,595 | 1,470 | 1,361 | 1,042 | .. | Шерсть |
| Other livestock | 326 | 298 | 313 | 411 | 221 | .. | Прочая |
| **Agricultural services** | .. | .. | .. | .. | .. | .. | **Сельскохозяйственные услуги** |

## TABLE 5-3. Production and average yield of major agricultural crops
## ТАБЛИЦА 5-3. Производство и урожайность важнейших сельскохозяйственных культур

| Crop | 1990 | 1991 | 1992 | 1993 | 1994 | 1995 | Сельскохозяйственные культуры |
|---|---|---|---|---|---|---|---|
| **Production (thousands of tons)** | | | | | | | **Производство (тыс. тонн)** |
| Grain - Cleanweight | 1,503 | 1,374 | 1,517 | 1,508 | 996 | 913 | Зерно в чистом весе |
| Winter wheat | 464 | 398 | 559 | 688 | 376 | 424 | Пшеница - озимая |
| Spring wheat | 19 | 37 | 75 | 143 | 190 | 201 | яровая |
| Coarse grain | .. | .. | .. | .. | .. | .. | Зерно в физическом весе |
| Rye | 1,573 | 1,446 | 1,602 | 1,596 | 1,063 | 981 | Рожь |
| Corn | 406 | 365 | 281 | 184 | 129 | 116 | Кукуруза |
| Winter barley | 167 | 196 | 210 | 135 | 37 | 23 | Ячмень - озимый |
| Spring barley | 464 | 401 | 411 | 374 | 272 | 150 | яровой |
| Oats | 16 | 13 | 13 | 9 | 8 | 3 | Овес |
| Millet | .. | .. | .. | .. | .. | .. | Просо |
| Rice | 2 | 3 | 4 | 3 | 4 | 8 | Рис |
| Flax | .. | .. | .. | .. | .. | .. | Лен |
| Oilseeds | 10 | 5 | 6 | 7 | 14 | 20 | Семена масличных культур |
| Cotton (raw) | 81 | 63 | 52 | 49 | 54 | 75 | Хлопок - сырец |
| Cotton fiber | .. | .. | .. | .. | .. | .. | волокно |
| Sugarbeets | 2 | 13 | 135 | 220 | 114 | 107 | Сахарная свекла |
| Potatoes | 365 | 326 | 362 | 308 | 311 | 432 | Картофель |
| Pulses | 4 | 3 | 1 | 1 | 1 | 1 | Бобовые |
| Vegetables | 487 | 399 | 404 | 259 | 266 | 318 | Овощи |
| Fruit | 141 | 85 | 118 | 45 | 79 | 67 | Фрукты |
| Grapes | 43 | 29 | 31 | 9 | 18 | 20 | Виноград |
| Other | .. | .. | .. | .. | .. | .. | Прочие |
| Corn (silage and greenchop) | 2,735 | 2,474 | 2,089 | 1,460 | 821 | 445 | Кукуруза (на силос и зеленый корм) |
| Hay | 1,310 | 1,184 | 1,178 | 1,114 | 984 | 1,099 | Сено |
| **Average yield (kilograms per hectare)** | | | | | | | **Ср. урожайность (кг с га)** |
| Grain | 2,800 | 2,470 | 2,630 | 2,420 | 1,700 | 1,810 | Зерно |
| Winter wheat | 2,540 | 2,270 | 2,680 | 2,600 | 1,950 | 2,090 | Пшеница - озимая |
| Spring wheat | 1,710 | 2,010 | 1,890 | 1,940 | 1,360 | 1,460 | яровая |
| Coarse grain | 2,930 | 2,600 | 2,780 | 2,560 | 1,810 | 1,950 | Зерно в физическом весе |
| Rye | 2,100 | 1,550 | 1,760 | 2,240 | 1,830 | 1,970 | Рожь |
| Corn | 6,180 | 5,850 | 5,130 | 4,520 | 3,530 | 3,910 | Кукуруза |
| Winter barley | 3,230 | 2,530 | 2,680 | 2,380 | 1,700 | 1,730 | Ячмень - озимый |
| Spring barley | 2,160 | 1,880 | 2,220 | 2,090 | 1,470 | 1,370 | яровой |
| Oats | 2,650 | 2,460 | 2,970 | 2,780 | 2,210 | 1,470 | Овес |
| Millet | 990 | 940 | 630 | 810 | 740 | 650 | Просо |
| Rice | 1,790 | 1,550 | 1,870 | 1,110 | 1,420 | 1,750 | Рис |
| Flax | .. | .. | .. | .. | .. | .. | Лен |
| Oilseeds | 1,320 | 1,030 | 780 | 490 | 470 | 460 | Семена масличных культур |
| Cotton (raw) | 2,730 | 2,450 | 2,440 | 1,420 | 2,020 | 2,240 | Хлопок - сырец |
| Cotton fiber | .. | .. | .. | .. | .. | .. | волокно |
| Sugarbeets | 16,850 | 15,570 | 21,330 | 18,820 | 11,620 | 12,310 | Сахарная свекла |
| Potatoes | 13,600 | 13,660 | 12,380 | 10,760 | 8,970 | 9,900 | Картофель |
| Pulses | 1,410 | 1,300 | 1,060 | 950 | 1,150 | 890 | Бобовые |
| Vegetables | 19,600 | 17,970 | 15,340 | 13,970 | 11,520 | 10,300 | Овощи |
| Fruit | 4,120 | 2,590 | 3,540 | 1,420 | 2,010 | 2,110 | Фрукты |
| Grapes | 6,320 | 4,530 | 5,060 | 1,590 | 2,560 | 2,960 | Виноград |
| Other | .. | .. | .. | .. | .. | .. | Прочие |
| Corn (silage and greenchop) | 30,130 | 27,260 | 22,870 | 20,170 | 12,800 | 12,140 | Кукуруза (на силос и зеленый корм) |
| Hay | 5,070 | 4,600 | 4,600 | 4,520 | 3,760 | 4,499 | Сено |

**TABLE 5-4. Main aggregates of animal husbandry**
**ТАБЛИЦА 5-4. Основные показатели животноводства**

| Type of livestock or product | 1990 | 1991 | 1992 | 1993 | 1994 | 1995 | Направление животноводства или вид продукции |
|---|---|---|---|---|---|---|---|
| **Livestock (thousands of heads)** | | | | | | | **Поголовье скота (тысяч голов)** |
| Cattle | 1,205 | 1,190 | 1,122 | 1,062 | 920 | 869 | Крупный рогатый скот |
| of which: Cows | 506 | 519 | 515 | 511 | 481 | 471 | в том числе коровы |
| Pigs | 393 | 358 | 247 | 169 | 118 | 114 | Свиньи |
| Sheep and goats | 9,545 | 9,107 | 8,362 | 6,972 | 4,783 | 3,899 | Овцы и козы |
| of which: Goats | 428 | 418 | 380 | 350 | 293 | 376 | в том числе козы |
| Horses | 313 | 321 | 313 | 322 | 299 | 308 | Лошади |
| Other | 13,915 | 13,571 | 10,421 | 6,916 | 2,208 | 2,032 | Прочие |
| **Animal husbandry products** | | | | | | | **Продукция животноводства** |
| Meat (thousands of tons) | 254 | 229 | 228 | 214 | 197 | 176 | Мясо (тысяч тонн) |
| Beef | 91 | 88 | 88 | 88 | 82 | 74 | Говядина |
| Pork | 41 | 33 | 36 | 25 | 18 | 15 | Свинина |
| Lamb | 77 | 71 | 70 | 82 | 76 | 70 | Баранина |
| Poultry | 33 | 29 | 22 | 9 | 7 | 5 | Птица |
| Other | 12 | 9 | 12 | 10 | 14 | 12 | Прочие виды мяса |
| Milk (thousands of tons) | 1,185 | 1,131 | 961 | 946 | 872 | 864 | Молоко (тысяч тонн) |
| Eggs (millions) | 714 | 650 | 591 | 389 | 202 | 149 | Яйца (миллионов штук) |
| Wool (thousands of tons) | 39 | 37 | 34 | 31 | 21 | 15 | Шерсть (тысяч тонн) |

## TABLE 6-1. Industrial production by sector (millions of national currency)
## ТАБЛИЦА 6-1. Промышленное производство по отраслям (млн. национальной валюты)

| Sector | 1990 | 1991 | 1992 | 1993 | 1994 | 1995 | Отрасли |
|---|---|---|---|---|---|---|---|
| **All industry** | 33.8 | 75.3 | 576.6 | 3,305.6 | 6,569.5 | 7,004.9 | **Вся промышленность** |
| **Heavy industry** | 14.9 | 27.2 | 275.8 | 1,573.5 | 3,666.3 | 3,197.3 | **Тяжелая промышленность** |
| Fuel and energy | 1.7 | 3.4 | 52.4 | 499.4 | 1,643.6 | 1,471.6 | Топливно-энергетическая промышленноть |
| Electricity | 1.4 | 2.3 | 41.4 | 398.9 | 1,426.9 | 1,189.6 | Электроэнергетика |
| Fuels | 0.3 | 1.1 | 11.0 | 100.5 | 216.7 | 282.0 | Топливная промышленность |
| Ferrous and nonferrous metallurgy | 1.5 | 2.4 | 48.8 | 208.7 | 687.6 | 726.3 | Металлургия |
| Chemicals and petrochemical industry | 0.2 | 0.5 | 2.5 | 12.6 | 15.5 | 16.8 | Химическая и нефтехимическая пром. |
| Machine building and metalworking | 8.3 | 14.4 | 121.4 | 561.6 | 705.4 | 680.8 | Машиностроение и металлообработка |
| Forestry, woodworking, and pulp and paper industry | 0.5 | 1.3 | 11.3 | 40.7 | 50.1 | 40.7 | Лесная, деревообрабатывающая и целлюлозо-бумажная промышленность |
| Construction materials | 1.5 | 3.1 | 26.6 | 145.8 | 284.6 | 260.8 | Промышленность строительных материалов |
| **Light industry** | 9.3 | 28.2 | 172.4 | 948.4 | 1,320.3 | 1,240.7 | **Легкая промышленность** |
| Textiles | 6.9 | 22.8 | 146.6 | 784.6 | 1,116.2 | 1,090.2 | Текстильная |
| Clothing | 1.7 | 4.0 | 17.6 | 108.2 | 115.0 | 73.3 | Швейная |
| Leather and shoes | 0.7 | 1.4 | 8.1 | 55.5 | 89.1 | 77.2 | Кожевенная и обувная |
| **Food industry** | 8.4 | 19.9 | 91.3 | 628.1 | 950.1 | 1,465.3 | **Пищевая промышленность** |
| Processed foods | 6.2 | 10.8 | 60.8 | 415.1 | 632.3 | 1,239.3 | Пищевкусовая |
| Meat and dairy products | 2.2 | 6.1 | 30.4 | 212.0 | 316.1 | 224.8 | Мясная и молочная |
| Fish | 0.0 | 0.0 | 0.1 | 0.9 | 1.6 | 1.3 | Рыбная |

## TABLE 6-2. Industrial production by sector in constant prices
## ТАБЛИЦА 6-2. Промышленное производство по отраслям в постоянных ценах

| Sector | 1990 | 1991 | 1992 | 1993 | 1994 | 1995 | Отрасли |
|---|---|---|---|---|---|---|---|
| **Industrial production** | | | | | | | **Промышленное производство** |
| **All industry** | 33.80 | 33.70 | 24.90 | 25.50 | 24.40 | 19.40 | **Вся промышленность** |
| **Heavy industry** | 14.90 | 15.20 | 10.90 | 10.30 | 11.50 | 10.10 | **Тяжелая промышленность** |
| Fuel and energy | 1.70 | 1.80 | 1.40 | 1.50 | 1.70 | 1.66 | Топливно-энергетическая промышленноть |
| Electricity | 1.40 | 1.50 | 1.20 | 1.30 | 1.50 | 1.50 | Электроэнергетика |
| Fuels | 0.33 | 0.31 | 0.20 | 0.25 | 0.23 | 0.17 | Топливная промышленность |
| Ferrous and nonferrous metallurgy | 1.50 | 1.50 | 1.40 | 1.20 | 1.50 | 1.20 | Металлургия |
| Chemicals and petrochemicals | 0.23 | 0.24 | 0.16 | 0.07 | 0.04 | 0.03 | Химическая и нефтехимическая пром. |
| Machine building and metalworking | 8.30 | 8.50 | 5.40 | 5.00 | 3.80 | 3.20 | Машиностроение и металлообработка |
| Forestry, woodworking, and pulp and paper | 0.50 | 0.60 | 0.50 | 0.40 | 0.20 | 0.14 | Лесная, деревообрабатывающая и целлюлозо-бумажная промышленность |
| Construction materials | 1.50 | 1.50 | 1.00 | 0.70 | 0.90 | 0.70 | Промышленность строительных материалов |
| **Light industry** | 9.30 | 9.70 | 8.20 | 8.20 | 5.90 | 3.80 | **Легкая промышленность** |
| Textiles | 6.90 | 7.00 | 6.20 | 6.10 | 4.60 | 3.00 | Текстильная |
| Clothing | 1.70 | 2.10 | 1.50 | 1.50 | 0.70 | 0.40 | Швейная |
| Leather and shoe | 0.70 | 0.70 | 0.50 | 0.49 | 0.36 | 0.27 | Кожевенная и обувная |
| **Food industry** | 9.70 | 8.80 | 5.50 | 6.90 | 6.60 | 5.40 | **Пищевая промышленность** |
| Processed foods | 6.20 | 6.40 | 3.30 | 5.00 | 4.50 | 3.70 | Пищевкусовая |
| Meat and dairy products | 2.20 | 1.70 | 1.40 | 1.30 | 1.30 | 1.10 | Мясная и молочная |
| Fish | 0.03 | 0.02 | 0.02 | 0.01 | 0.01 | 0.01 | Рыбная |
| **Growth in production by sector (in percent)** | | | | | | | **Рост производства по отраслям** |
| **All industry** | -1.3 | -0.3 | -26.1 | 2.4 | -4.3 | -20.5 | **Вся промышленность** |
| **Heavy industry** | -3.7 | 2.0 | -28.3 | -5.5 | 11.7 | -12.2 | **Тяжелая промышленность** |
| Power and fuels | -6.9 | 5.9 | -22.2 | 7.1 | 13.3 | -2.4 | Топливно-энергетическая промышленноть |
| Electricity | -7.2 | 7.1 | -20.0 | 8.3 | 15.4 | 0.0 | Электроэнергетика |
| Fuels | -5.1 | -6.1 | -35.5 | 25.0 | -8.0 | -26.1 | Топливная промышленность |
| Ferrous and nonferrous metallurgy | 7.0 | 0.0 | -6.7 | -14.3 | 25.0 | -20.0 | Металлургия |
| Chemicals and petrochemicals | 3.2 | 4.3 | -33.3 | -56.3 | -42.9 | -25.0 | Химическая и нефтехимическая пром. |
| Machine building and metalworking | -1.6 | 2.4 | -36.5 | -7.4 | -24.0 | -15.8 | Машиностроение и металлообработка |
| Forestry, woodworking, and pulp and paper | -6.7 | 20.0 | -16.7 | -20.0 | -50.0 | -30.0 | Лесная, деревообрабатывающая и целлюлозо-бумажная промышленность |
| Construction materials | 2.1 | 0.0 | -33.3 | -30.0 | 28.6 | -22.2 | Промышленность строительных материалов |
| **Light industry** | -0.5 | 4.3 | -15.5 | 0.0 | -28.0 | -35.6 | **Легкая промышленность** |
| Textiles | -2.1 | 1.4 | -11.4 | -1.6 | -24.6 | -34.8 | Текстильная |
| Clothing | 4.5 | 23.5 | -28.6 | 0.0 | -53.3 | -42.9 | Швейная |
| Leather and shoe | 3.6 | 0.0 | -28.6 | -2.0 | -26.5 | -25.0 | Кожевенная и обувная |
| **Food industry** | 4.1 | -9.3 | -37.5 | 25.5 | -4.3 | -18.2 | **Пищевая промышленность** |
| Processed foods | 7.1 | 3.2 | -48.4 | 51.5 | -10.0 | -17.8 | Пищевкусовая |
| Meat and dairy products | -2.3 | -22.7 | -17.6 | -7.1 | 0.0 | -15.4 | Мясная и молочная |
| Fish | 0.0 | -33.3 | 0.0 | -50.0 | 0.0 | -20.0 | Рыбная |

## TABLE 7-1. Price indices and exchange rates
## ТАБЛИЦА 7-1. Индексы цен и обменный курс

| Year and month | National currency per U.S. dollar<br>Единиц нац. валюты за 1 доллар США | National currency per 100 Russian rubles<br>Единиц нац. валюты за 100 российских рублей | Consumer price index (as a percent of the previous month)<br>Индекс потребительских цен (в % к предыдущему месяцу) | Producer price index (as a percent of the previous month)<br>Индекс цен производителей (в % к предыдущему месяцу) | Consumer price index (as a percent of the previous December)<br>Индекс потребительских цен (в % к декабрю прошлого года) | Producer price index (as a percent of the previous December)<br>Индекс цен производителей (в % к декабрю прошлого года) | Год и месяц |
|---|---|---|---|---|---|---|---|
| **1993** | | | | | | | **1993** |
| January | .. | .. | 146.3 | 143.0 | 146.3 | 143.0 | Январь |
| February | .. | .. | 139.9 | 146.3 | 204.7 | 209.2 | Февраль |
| March | .. | .. | 124.4 | 130.0 | 254.6 | 272.0 | Март |
| April | .. | .. | 116.6 | 125.0 | 296.9 | 340.0 | Апрель |
| May | .. | .. | 121.4 | 134.3 | 360.4 | 456.6 | Май |
| June | .. | .. | 117.1 | 119.1 | 422.0 | 543.8 | Июнь |
| July | .. | .. | 116.5 | 111.2 | 491.7 | 604.7 | Июль |
| August | .. | .. | 119.6 | 118.3 | 588.0 | 715.3 | Август |
| September | .. | .. | 132.8 | 135.0 | 780.9 | 965.7 | Сентябрь |
| October | .. | .. | 133.1 | 113.4 | 1,039.4 | 1,095.1 | Октябрь |
| November | .. | .. | 121.9 | 114.0 | 1,267.0 | 1,248.4 | Ноябрь |
| December | 8.03 | 0.6440 | 115.7 | 117.6 | 1,466.0 | 1,468.1 | Декабрь |
| **1994** | | | | | | | **1994** |
| January | 9.10 | 0.5926 | 112.8 | 112.8 | 112.8 | 112.8 | Январь |
| February | 10.80 | 0.6814 | 116.9 | 110.7 | 131.9 | 124.9 | Февраль |
| March | 11.10 | 0.6740 | 107.4 | 113.0 | 141.6 | 141.1 | Март |
| April | 12.30 | 0.6758 | 104.9 | 102.8 | 148.6 | 145.1 | Апрель |
| May | 12.00 | 0.6313 | 103.5 | 103.3 | 153.8 | 149.8 | Май |
| June | 11.30 | 0.5693 | 103.5 | 103.9 | 159.1 | 155.7 | Июнь |
| July | 10.20 | 0.4371 | 102.8 | 104.6 | 163.6 | 162.8 | Июль |
| August | 10.48 | 0.4850 | 101.7 | 103.8 | 166.4 | 169.0 | Август |
| September | 10.50 | 0.4045 | 100.2 | 103.6 | 166.7 | 175.1 | Сентябрь |
| October | 10.60 | 0.3470 | 105.0 | 105.2 | 175.0 | 184.2 | Октябрь |
| November | 10.65 | 0.3295 | 103.2 | 100.7 | 180.6 | 185.5 | Ноябрь |
| December | 10.60 | 0.2985 | 103.6 | 103.7 | 187.2 | 192.4 | Декабрь |

## TABLE 7-1. Price indices and exchange rates
## ТАБЛИЦА 7-1. Индексы цен и обменный курс

| Year and month | National currency per U.S. dollar / Единиц нац. валюты за 1 доллар США | National currency per 100 Russian rubles / Единиц нац. валюты за 100 российских рублей | Consumer price index (as a percent of the previous month) / Индекс потребительских цен (в % к предыдущему месяцу) | Producer price index (as a percent of the previous month) / Индекс цен производителей (в % к предыдущему месяцу) | Consumer price index (as a percent of the previous December) / Индекс потребительских цен (в % к декабрю прошлого года) | Producer price index (as a percent of the previous December) / Индекс цен производителей (в % к декабрю прошлого года) | Год и месяц |
|---|---|---|---|---|---|---|---|
| **1995** | | | | | | | **1995** |
| January | 10.80 | 0.2697 | 107.1 | 102.6 | 107.1 | 102.6 | Январь |
| February | 10.80 | 0.2451 | 106.8 | 105.3 | 114.4 | 108.0 | Февраль |
| March | 10.90 | 0.2226 | 101.6 | 100.6 | 116.2 | 108.7 | Март |
| April | 10.90 | 0.2137 | 100.8 | 104.0 | 117.1 | 113.0 | Апрель |
| May | 10.96 | 0.2176 | 101.6 | 100.5 | 119.0 | 113.6 | Май |
| June | 10.60 | 0.2347 | 100.7 | 100.1 | 119.8 | 113.7 | Июнь |
| July | 10.53 | 0.2385 | 100.4 | 102.2 | 120.3 | 116.2 | Июль |
| August | 10.45 | 0.2360 | 99.7 | 104.1 | 120.0 | 121.0 | Август |
| September | 10.86 | 0.2418 | 102.5 | 102.4 | 123.0 | 123.9 | Сентябрь |
| October | 10.92 | 0.2424 | 101.1 | 100.8 | 124.3 | 124.9 | Октябрь |
| November | 11.00 | 0.2402 | 102.6 | 104.9 | 127.6 | 131.0 | Ноябрь |
| December | 11.20 | 0.2410 | 103.4 | 101.1 | 131.9 | 132.4 | Декабрь |
| **1996** | | | | | | | **1996** |
| January | 11.33 | 0.2401 | 103.6 | 102.7 | 103.6 | 102.7 | Январь |
| February | 11.40 | 0.2368 | 103.8 | 101.6 | 107.5 | 104.3 | Февраль |
| March | 11.35 | 0.2338 | 104.0 | 101.1 | 111.8 | 105.5 | Март |
| April | 11.65 | 0.2362 | 104.6 | 101.4 | 117.0 | 107.0 | Апрель |
| May | 12.50 | 0.2496 | 102.5 | 116.1 | 119.9 | 124.2 | Май |
| June | 12.20 | 0.2394 | 101.0 | 104.6 | 121.1 | 129.9 | Июнь |
| July | 12.20 | 0.2355 | .. | .. | .. | .. | Июль |
| August | 12.15 | 0.2272 | .. | .. | .. | .. | Август |
| September | 13.25 | 0.2456 | .. | .. | .. | .. | Сентябрь |
| October | .. | .. | .. | .. | .. | .. | Октябрь |
| November | .. | .. | .. | .. | .. | .. | Ноябрь |
| December | .. | .. | .. | .. | .. | .. | Декабрь |

## TABLE 7-2. Monthly nominal wages by sector
## ТАБЛИЦА 7-2. Среднемесячная денежная зарплата по отраслям

| Sector | 1990 | 1991 | 1992 | 1993 | 1994 | 1995 | Сектора |
|---|---|---|---|---|---|---|---|
| **Nominal wages** | | | | | | | **Средняя номинальная заработная плата** |
| **Economy average** | 219.2 | 349.1 | 11.5 | 83.8 | 231.8 | 368.2 | **По народному хозяйству** |
| **Material sphere** | 232.5 | 390.1 | 13.1 | 96.2 | 227.0 | 384.7 | **Отрасли сферы материального производства** |
| Industry | 263.7 | 428.5 | 16.0 | 124.8 | 388.3 | 571.3 | Промышленность |
| Construction | 273.9 | 421.4 | 14.8 | 122.0 | 375.2 | 583.6 | Строительство |
| Agriculture | 197.7 | 330.2 | 11.7 | 60.1 | 103.8 | 151.9 | Сельское хозяйство |
| Transport | 239.1 | 342.4 | 11.3 | 91.2 | 296.3 | 439.2 | Транспорт |
| Communications | 213.5 | 372.6 | 12.1 | 94.1 | 376.5 | 614.4 | Связь |
| Trade (retail and wholesale) | 204.9 | .. | 8.0 | 64.6 | 161.1 | 263.0 | Торговля (оптовая и розничная) |
| Other | 137.1 | 246.2 | 14.0 | 92.1 | 301.4 | 322.0 | Прочие отрасли материального производства |
| **Nonmaterial sphere** | 190.2 | 300.8 | 8.7 | 60.9 | 257.7 | 342.2 | **Отрасли непроизводственной сферы** |
| Municipal services | 179.8 | 280.6 | 9.6 | 71.2 | 274.2 | 384.9 | Жилкомхоз и бытовое обслуживание |
| Science, research and development | 301.4 | 411.5 | 11.4 | 83.3 | 283.7 | 445.5 | Наука и научное обслуживание |
| Education | 167.8 | 268.1 | 7.7 | 54.7 | 234.8 | 309.4 | Образование |
| Culture | 132.1 | 243.6 | 7.0 | 45.6 | 196.8 | 297.6 | Культура |
| Arts | 149.8 | 250.7 | 6.8 | 48.9 | 194.7 | 302.5 | Искусство |
| Health care, social security, and sports | 166.8 | 266.7 | 7.7 | 52.2 | 208.8 | 291.5 | Здравоохр., соц.обсл., физк. и спорт |
| Banking, finance, credit, insurance | 319.3 | 665.3 | 21.4 | 173.8 | 536.3 | 761.4 | Кредитование, страхование, банк. дело |
| Government | 297.3 | 393.5 | 14.0 | 90.2 | 310.3 | 468.3 | Управление |

**TABLE 8-1. Money income and expenditure of the population (millions of national currency)**
**ТАБЛИЦА 8-1. Денежные доходы и расходы населения (млн. национальной валюты)**

| Type of income or expenditure | 1990 | 1991 | 1992 | 1993 | 1994 | 1995 | Вид доходов или расходов |
|---|---|---|---|---|---|---|---|
| **Income** | | | | | | | **Доходы** |
| **Total labor income** | 4,755 | 8,043 | 40,340 | 1,382 | 3,450 | 5,214 | **Всего трудовых доходов** |
| Regular wages | 3,613 | 5,528 | 30,885 | 1,005 | 2,897 | 4,329 | Заработная плата |
| Wages paid by cooperatives | 139 | 204 | 2,606 | 77 | 162 | 169 | Заработная плата в кооперативах |
| Other wages and compensation | 140 | 323 | 1,458 | 42 | 117 | 169 | Прочие доходы типа заработной платы |
| Income paid by collective farms | 455 | 591 | 2,783 | 142 | 184 | 46 | Доходы от колхозов |
| Income from sale of farm products | 547 | 1,600 | 5,214 | 193 | 252 | 670 | Доходы от продажи продукции колхозов |
| **Total transfer receipts** | 1,284 | 3,012 | 17,436 | 1,209 | 4,247 | 4,880 | **Всего трансфертных поступлений** |
| Pensions and allowances | 818 | 2,257 | 15,160 | 481 | 939 | 1,446 | Пенсии и пособия |
| Scholarships | 44 | 95 | 581 | 16 | 42 | 40 | Стипендии |
| Income from the financial system (insurance, interest, etc.) | 293 | 373 | 435 | 8 | 58 | 31 | Доходы из финансовой системы (страховые возмещения, проценты и т.д.) |
| Other income | 129 | 287 | 1,260 | 704 | 3,208 | 3,363 | Прочие виды доходов |
| **Total income** | 6,039 | 11,055 | 57,776 | 2,591 | 7,697 | 10,094 | **Всего доходов** |
| **Expenditure** | | | | | | | **Расходы** |
| **Total purchases** | 5,031 | 8,095 | 36,537 | 2,072 | 6,268 | 8,092 | **Всего покупок товаров и услуг** |
| Retail goods | 4,560 | 6,960 | 29,612 | 1,796 | 5,335 | 6,672 | Товары в розничной торговле |
| Services | 471 | 1,135 | 6,925 | 276 | 933 | 1,420 | Услуги |
| Rent and utilities | 93 | 88 | 575 | 63 | 193 | 307 | Квартирная плата и коммунальные платежи |
| Transport and communications | 200 | 354 | 4,417 | 117 | 382 | 598 | Транспорт и связь |
| Health and other services | 158 | 435 | 1,887 | 96 | 358 | 515 | Здравоохранение и другие виды услуг |
| Cooperatives | 20 | 257 | 46 | .. | .. | .. | Кооперативы |
| **Transfers and savings** | 912 | 1,976 | 6,285 | 146 | 809 | 1,090 | **Трансферты и сбережения** |
| Taxes, fees, dues, and other | 599 | 852 | 4,782 | 128 | 695 | 1,021 | Налоги, сборы, пошлины и др. |
| Savings | 313 | 1,124 | 1,503 | 18 | 114 | 69 | Сбережения |
| Other | .. | .. | .. | .. | .. | .. | Прочие |
| **Total expenditure** | 5,943 | 10,071 | 42,822 | 2,218 | 7,077 | 9,182 | **Всего расходов** |
| **Income less expenditure** | 96 | 985 | 14,954 | 373 | 620 | 912 | **Доходы за вычетом расходов** |

# *Country Notes: Kyrgyz Republic*

**General Note:** Unless otherwise indicated, data were supplied by the National Statistical Committee of the Kyrgyz Republic.

**Currency:** The national currency, som, was introduced on May 10, 1993 with the conversion factor 1 som = 200 rubles. Unless otherwise indicated, data are in soms.

**Table 1-1:** Data on total employed population for 1992-1995 do not add up to the totals because not all private sector employees are included.

**Table 1-2:** Retail trade and catering include wholesale trade.

**Table 2-1:** For 1995 Retail trade includes Wholesale trade. The statistical discrepancy between total GDP by industrial origin at market prices and total GDP by expenditure category is as follows:

| Year | Statistical discrepancy (mln. of soms) |
|---|---|
| 1993 | 3.0 |
| 1995 | 17.4 |

**Table 2-2:** Data are millions of 1993 soms. Retail trade includes Wholesale trade.

**Tables 3-2A, 3-2B, 3-3A, and 3-3B:** Totals do not include services.

**Table 4-1:** Data are World Bank and IMF staff estimates.

**Table 4-2:** Data are World Bank and IMF staff estimates. For 1992-1995 the sum of current and capital expenditures is smaller than total expenditure because total expenditure also includes net lending. Amounts of some grants were not distributed across expenditure by economic type.

**Table 5-2:** Data are in thousands of 1983 soms.

**Table 6-2:** Data are in millions of 1990 soms.

**Table 7-1:** Exchange rates are shown for the end of the month. Data are from CIS Statistical Committee publications.

**Table 7-2:** Data are in rubles for 1990-1991 and in soms for 1992-1995.

**Table 8-1:** Data are in millions of rubles for 1990-1992 and in millions of soms for 1993-1995.

# Комментарии к таблицам: Кыргызская Республика

**Общее замечание:** За исключением особо отмеченных случаев, данные были получены из Национального Статистического Комитета Кыргызской Республики.

**Национальная валюта:** Национальная валюта, сом, была введена 10 мая 1993 года с коэффициентом пересчета 1 сом = 200 рублей. За исключением особо отмеченных случаев, данные приведены в сомах.

**Таблица 1-1:** В 1992-1995 гг. сумма компонентов занятого населения не совпадает с итогом, из-за того, что не включены все занятые в частном секторе.

**Таблица 1-2:** Розничная торговля и общепит включают оптовую торговлю.

**Таблица 2-1:** В 1995 г. розничная торговля включает оптовую. Статистическое расхождение между ВВП по производству в рыночных ценах и ВВП по видам расходов составляет:

| Год | Статистическое расхождение (млн. сомов). |
|---|---|
| 1993 | 3,0 |
| 1995 | 17,4 |

**Таблица 2-2:** Данные приведены в миллионах сомов в ценах 1993 г. Розничная торговля включает оптовую.

**Таблицы 3-2А, 3-2В, 3-3А и 3-3В:** Услуги не включены в итог.

**Таблица 4-1:** Данные рассчитаны сотрудниками Всемирного Банка и МВФ.

**Таблица 4-2:** Данные рассчитаны сотрудниками Всемирного Банка и МВФ. За 1992-1995 гг. сумма текущих и капитальных расходов меньше общей величины расходов из-за того, что общая величина расходов включает в себя также чистое кредитование. Некоторые виды безвозмездных поступлений не были распределены по видам расходов.

**Таблица 5-2:** Данные приведены в тысячах сомов в ценах 1983г.

**Таблица 6-2:** Данные приведены в миллионах сомов в ценах 1990 г.

**Таблица 7-1:** Валютные курсы приводятся на конец месяца. Данные получены из публикаций Статкомитета СНГ.

**Таблица 7-2:** Данные приведены в рублях за 1990-1991 гг. и в сомах за 1992-1995 гг.

**Таблица 8-1:** Данные приведены в миллионах рублей за 1990-1992 гг. и в миллионах сомов за 1993-1995 гг.

# Latvia / Латвия

1996 Population / Численность населения в 1996 году
(thousands / тыс. человек): 2,500

Area / Территория
(thousand square kilometers / тыс. кв. км.): 64.6

Capital city / Столица :
Riga / Рига

**Country Tables:** Table 8-1 is not included because there are no data available. Tables 1-2a, 6-1a, and 6-2a have replaced Tables 1-2, 6-1, and 6-2. They present data on employment, industrial production (in current and constant prices) and wages according to the ISIC system.

**Статистические таблицы страны:** Таблица 8-1 не включена ввиду отсутствия данных. В дополнительных таблицах 1-2a, 6-1a и 6-2a представлены данные о занятости, продукции промышленности (в текущих и постоянных ценах) согласно отраслевому разрезу ISIC.

## TABLE 1-1. Population and employment (thousands)



## ТАБЛИЦА 1-1. Население и занятость (тысяч)

| Population or employment category | 1990 | 1991 | 1992 | 1993 | 1994 | 1995 | Население или группы занятых |
|---|---|---|---|---|---|---|---|
| **Total population** | 2,668 | 2,657 | 2,606 | 2,566 | 2,530 | 2,502 | **Население - всего** |
| Males | 1,242 | 1,237 | 1,211 | 1,191 | 1,172 | 1,159 | Мужчины |
| Females | 1,426 | 1,420 | 1,395 | 1,375 | 1,358 | 1,343 | Женщины |
| Urban population | 1,847 | 1,836 | 1,791 | 1,776 | 1,747 | 1,726 | Городское |
| Rural population | 821 | 821 | 815 | 790 | 783 | 776 | Сельское |
| Population under working age | 574 | 570 | 554 | 539 | 525 | 509 | Моложе трудоспособного возраста |
| Working-age population | 1,533 | 1,522 | 1,484 | 1,457 | 1,437 | 1,427 | Лица в трудоспособном возрасте |
| Population over working age | 561 | 565 | 568 | 570 | 568 | 570 | Старше трудоспособного возраста |
| Economically Active Population, in non-working age | .. | .. | .. | .. | .. | .. | Экономически активное население в нетрудоспособном возрасте |
| Above working age | .. | .. | .. | .. | .. | .. | Старше трудоспособного возраста |
| Below working age | .. | .. | .. | .. | .. | .. | Моложе трудоспособного возраста |
| **Total labor resources** | .. | .. | .. | .. | .. | .. | **Трудовые ресурсы - всего** |
| **Total employment** | 1,409 | 1,397 | 1,345 | 1,245 | 1,205 | 1,189 | **Занятое население - всего** |
| State sector employees | 1,139 | 1,083 | 758 | 558 | 402 | .. | Государственный сектор |
| Leased enterprise employees | .. | .. | .. | .. | .. | .. | Арендные предприятия |
| Joint-stock company employees | .. | .. | .. | .. | .. | .. | Акционерные общества |
| Economic association employees | .. | .. | .. | .. | .. | .. | Хозяйственные ассоциации |
| Social organization employees | .. | .. | .. | .. | .. | .. | Общественные организации |
| Joint venture employees | .. | .. | .. | .. | .. | .. | Совместные предприятия |
| Collective farm workers | 152 | 144 | 168 | 101 | 58 | .. | Колхозы |
| Cooperative workers | 89 | 131 | 220 | 344 | 467 | .. | Кооперативы |
| Individual labor activities | 3 | 3 | 94 | 119 | 126 | .. | ИТД |
| Private subsidiary agricultural workers | 9 | 16 | 30 | 30 | 48 | .. | Личные подсобные хозяйства |
| Private agricultural workers | 17 | 20 | 75 | 93 | 104 | .. | Фермерские хозяйства |
| **Students** | 100 | 99 | 121 | 116 | 119 | 121 | **Учащиеся** |
| **Religious workers** | 1 | 1 | 1 | 1 | 1 | 1 | **Служащие религиозного культа** |
| **Working age population not employed in the national economy** | 125 | 131 | .. | .. | .. | .. | **Лица в трудоспособном возрасте, не занятые в экономике** |
| Housewives | .. | .. | .. | .. | .. | .. | Домохозяйки |
| Military personnel | .. | .. | .. | .. | .. | .. | Военнослужащие |
| Unemployed | 8 | 9 | 23 | 76 | 96 | 87 | Безработные |
| **Labor force** | 1,416 | 1,405 | 1,367 | 1,320 | 1,301 | 1,276 | **Рабочая сила** |

**TABLE 1-2a. Employment by sector according to ISIC ( thousands)**
**ТАБЛИЦА 1-2а. Численность занятого населения по секторам в соответсвии с МСПК (тысяч)**

| Sector | 1985 | 1990 | 1991 | 1992 | 1993 | 1994 | 1995 | Сектор |
|---|---|---|---|---|---|---|---|---|
| **Employed in all sectors of economic activity-** | .. | | | | | | | **Занято во всех секторах экономической деятельности** |
| **Total** | .. | 1,409 | 1,397 | 1,345 | 1,245 | 1,205 | 1,189 | **Всего** |
| Agriculture, hunting and forestry (A) | .. | 233 | 236 | 262 | 235 | 224 | 214 | Сельское хозяйство, охота, и лесное хозяйство (А) |
| Of which: | | | | | | | | В том числе: |
| agriculture and hunting (01) | .. | 218 | 219 | 249 | 223 | 209 | 201 | сельское хозяйство и охота (01) |
| forestry and logging (02) | .. | 15 | 17 | 13 | 12 | 15 | 13 | лесное хозяйство и лесорубство (02) |
| Fishing (B) | .. | 12 | 12 | 7 | 8 | 8 | 6 | Рыболовное хозяйство (Б) |
| Industry-Total (C+D+E) | .. | 391 | 371 | 340 | 287 | 253 | 228 | Промышленность-Всего (С+Д+Е) |
| Of which: | | | | | | | | В том числе: |
| mining and quarrying (C) | .. | 4 | 4 | 3 | 2 | 3 | 3 | горная промышленность и разработка карьеров (С) |
| manufacturing (D) | .. | 373 | 356 | 321 | 269 | 232 | 208 | обрабатывающая промышленность (Д) |
| electricity, thermal energy and water supply (E) | .. | 14 | 11 | 16 | 16 | 18 | 17 | электричество, тепловая энергия и водоснабжение (Е) |
| Construction (F) | .. | 136 | 130 | 89 | 68 | 62 | 71 | Строительство ( Ф) |
| Wholesale and retail trade; repair of motor vehicles, motorcycles and household goods (G) | .. | 109 | 119 | 138 | 155 | 162 | 164 | Оптовая и розничная торговля; ремонт автомобилей, мотоциклов и бытовой техники (Г) |
| Hotels and restaurants (H) | .. | 61 | 59 | 49 | 32 | 36 | 27 | Гостиницы и рестораны (Ч) |
| Transport and Communication (I) | .. | 106 | 107 | 105 | 108 | 106 | 105 | Транспорт и связь (И) |
| Financial inter mediation (J) | .. | 7 | 7 | 10 | 10 | 12 | 20 | Финансовое посредничество (Й) |
| Real estate, renting and business activities (K) | .. | 81 | 78 | 65 | 60 | 61 | 57 | Продажа недвижимости, аренда и деловая деятельность (К) |
| Public administration and defence: compulsory social security (L) | .. | 21 | 24 | 37 | 44 | 50 | 56 | Государственное управление и оборона; обязательное социальное страхование (Л) |
| Education (M) | .. | 101 | 94 | 101 | 94 | 92 | 104 | Образование (М) |
| Health and social work (N) | .. | 68 | 66 | 70 | 80 | 74 | 74 | Здравоохранение и социальное обеспечение (Н) |
| Other community, social and personal services (O) | .. | 83 | 94 | 72 | 64 | 65 | 63 | Другие общественные, социальные и персональные услуги (О) |

## TABLE 1-3. Registered unemployment (thousands; end of month) LATVIA

## ТАБЛИЦА 1-3. Численность зарегистрированных безработных (тысяч; на конец месяца)

| Year and month | Total<br>Всего | Males<br>Мужчины | Females<br>Женщины | Receiving benefits<br>Получающие пособие | Год и месяц |
|---|---|---|---|---|---|
| **1994** | | | | | **1994** |
| January | 80.7 | 38.3 | 42.4 | 40.7 | Январь |
| February | 84.4 | 40.4 | 44.0 | 38.5 | Февраль |
| March | 87.2 | 42.0 | 45.2 | 37.4 | Март |
| April | 87.5 | 42.4 | 45.1 | 35.9 | Апрель |
| May | 85.7 | 41.8 | 43.9 | 33.7 | Май |
| June | 85.1 | 41.4 | 43.7 | 33.7 | Июнь |
| July | 85.5 | 41.0 | 44.5 | 34.5 | Июль |
| August | 83.3 | 39.6 | 43.7 | 31.5 | Август |
| September | 81.0 | 38.5 | 42.5 | 37.9 | Сентябрь |
| October | 79.2 | 37.4 | 41.8 | 40.6 | Октябрь |
| November | 81.9 | 39.0 | 42.9 | 43.4 | Ноябрь |
| December | 83.9 | 40.4 | 43.5 | 42.7 | Декабрь |
| **1995** | | | | | **1995** |
| January | 85.7 | 41.7 | 44.0 | 42.0 | Январь |
| February | 86.5 | 42.3 | 44.2 | 40.3 | Февраль |
| March | 85.7 | 42.0 | 43.7 | 39.1 | Март |
| April | 83.5 | 41.1 | 42.4 | 35.6 | Апрель |
| May | 80.6 | 39.7 | 40.9 | 34.3 | Май |
| June | 77.9 | 38.0 | 39.9 | 34.4 | Июнь |
| July | 78.5 | 37.6 | 40.9 | 37.6 | Июль |
| August | 77.6 | 36.9 | 40.7 | 38.4 | Август |
| September | 76.6 | 36.3 | 40.3 | 36.8 | Сентябрь |
| October | 76.8 | 36.0 | 40.8 | 36.0 | Октябрь |
| November | 79.9 | 37.8 | 42.1 | 35.9 | Ноябрь |
| December | 83.2 | 39.7 | 43.5 | 34.8 | Декабрь |
| **1996** | | | | | **1996** |
| January | 83.8 | 40.2 | 43.6 | 35.2 | Январь |
| February | 86.3 | 41.7 | 44.6 | 35.2 | Февраль |
| March | 88.2 | 42.7 | 45.5 | 35.9 | Март |
| April | 89.8 | 43.5 | 46.3 | 34.6 | Апрель |
| May | 89.5 | 43.5 | 46.0 | 37.0 | Май |
| June | .. | .. | .. | .. | Июнь |
| July | .. | .. | .. | .. | Июль |
| August | .. | .. | .. | .. | Август |
| September | .. | .. | .. | .. | Сентябрь |
| October | .. | .. | .. | .. | Октябрь |
| November | .. | .. | .. | .. | Ноябрь |
| December | .. | .. | .. | .. | Декабрь |

**TABLE 2-1. Gross domestic product at current prices (thousands of national currency)**
**ТАБЛИЦА 2-1. Валовой внутренний продукт в текущих ценах (тысяч национальной валюты)**

| Sector of origin or expenditure category | 1990 | 1991 | 1992 | 1993 | 1994 | 1995 | Отраслевое происхождение или вид расходов |
|---|---|---|---|---|---|---|---|
| **Gross domestic product by sector of origin** | | | | | | | **Валовой внутренний продукт по отраслевому происхождению** |
| **Agriculture and forestry** | 12,690 | 30,535 | 161,650 | 155,516 | 170,122 | 200,667 | **Сельское и лесное хозяйство** |
| Agriculture | .. | .. | .. | 136,842 | 151,043 | 166,079 | Сельское хозяйство |
| Forestry | .. | .. | .. | 18,674 | 19,079 | 34,588 | Лесное хозяйство |
| **Industry and construction** | .. | .. | .. | .. | .. | .. | **Промышленность и строительство** |
| Industry | 21,930 | 53,150 | 280,005 | 409,708 | 458,689 | 518,199 | Промышленность |
| Construction | 5,850 | 8,020 | 47,310 | 56,603 | 107,324 | 157,781 | Строительство |
| **Other** | 19,230 | 45,800 | 445,965 | 708,685 | 1,071,603 | 1,170,873 | **Другие отрасли** |
| Transport | 6,545 | 10,270 | 166,445 | 307,651 | 370,154 | 414,608 | Транспорт |
| Road maintenance | .. | .. | .. | .. | .. | .. | Дорожное хозяйство |
| Communication | .. | .. | .. | .. | .. | .. | Связь |
| Wholesale trade | .. | .. | .. | .. | .. | .. | Оптовая торговля |
| Retail trade and catering | .. | .. | .. | .. | .. | .. | Розничная торговля и общепит |
| Material supply | .. | .. | .. | .. | .. | .. | Материально-техническое снабжение |
| Procurement | .. | .. | .. | .. | .. | .. | Заготовки |
| Information and computing services | .. | .. | .. | .. | .. | .. | Информационно-вычислительное обслуживание |
| Other sectors of material production | .. | .. | .. | .. | .. | .. | Другие отрасли сферы материального пр. |
| Housing | .. | .. | .. | .. | .. | .. | Жилищное хозяйство |
| Public utilities and personal services | .. | .. | .. | .. | .. | .. | Ком. хоз. и бытовое обслуживание |
| Health care, social security, physical culture and sports | .. | .. | .. | .. | .. | .. | Здравоохранение, социальное обеспечение, физкультура и спорт |
| Education | 1,580 | 3,740 | 29,460 | 58,089 | 96,051 | 119,532 | Образование |
| Culture and art | .. | .. | .. | .. | .. | .. | Культура и искусство |
| Science and scientific research | .. | .. | .. | .. | .. | .. | Наука и научное обслуживание |
| Credit | .. | .. | .. | .. | .. | .. | Кредитование |
| Insurance | .. | .. | .. | .. | .. | .. | Страхование |
| General administration and defense | .. | .. | .. | .. | .. | .. | Государственное управление и оборона |
| Private nonprofit institutions serving households | .. | .. | .. | .. | .. | .. | Общественные организации, обслуживающие домашние хозяйства |
| **Imputed service charge of financial intermediaries** | .. | .. | .. | .. | .. | .. | **Условно-исчисляемая стоимость услуг финансовых посредников** |
| **Total gross value added (GVA)** | 60,190 | 139,185 | 938,570 | 1,331,823 | 1,808,839 | 2,048,613 | **Валовая добавленная стоимость (ВДС) - всего** |
| **Taxes on production and imports (TOPI)** | 13,670 | 18,275 | 72,260 | 171,085 | 277,254 | .. | **Налоги на производство и импорт (НПиИ)** |
| Other taxes on production (OTOP) | 3,035 | 5,925 | 2,520 | 35,896 | 42,678 | .. | Другие налоги на производство (ДНП) |
| **Subsidies on production and imports (SOPI)** | 9,545 | 8,665 | 7,970 | 10,788 | 10,733 | .. | **Субсидии на производство и импорт (СПиИ)** |
| Other subsidies on production (OSOP) | 1,160 | 455 | 4,215 | 10,788 | 9,873 | .. | Другие субсидии на производство (ДСП) |
| **Total GDP at factor cost (GVA-OTOP+OSOP)** | 58,315 | 133,715 | 940,265 | 1,306,715 | 1,776,034 | .. | **Всего ВВП по фактр. стоимости (ВДС-ДНП+ДСП)** |
| **Net Indirect taxes (TOPI - SOPI)** | 4,125 | 9,610 | 64,290 | 160,297 | 266,521 | .. | **Чистые косвенные налоги (НПиИ-СПиИ)** |
| **Total GDP at market prices** | 62,440 | 143,325 | 1,004,555 | 1,467,012 | 2,042,555 | 2,360,718 | **Всего ВВП в рыночных ценах** |
| **Gross domestic product by expenditure category** | | | | | | | **Валовой внутренний продукт по видам расходов** |
| **Consumption** | 38,235 | 80,990 | 521,240 | 1,091,208 | 1,605,123 | 1,891,070 | **Потребление** |
| Private consumption | 32,890 | 66,250 | 395,880 | 767,122 | 1,194,520 | 1,401,980 | Личное потребление |
| Government consumption | 5,345 | 14,740 | 125,360 | 324,086 | 410,603 | 489,090 | Общественное потребление |
| **Gross domestic investment** | 25,030 | 48,345 | 414,225 | 134,615 | 390,810 | 518,116 | **Валовые внутренние инвестиции** |
| Gross fixed investment | 14,360 | 8,840 | 112,325 | 201,842 | 303,935 | 392,113 | Валовое накопление основного капитала |
| Change in stocks | 10,670 | 39,505 | 301,900 | -67,227 | 86,875 | 126,003 | Изменения в запасах (МОС) |
| **Resource balance (net exports of GNFS)** | -825 | 13,990 | 69,090 | 238,497 | 42,066 | -48,468 | **Сальдо ресурсов (чистый экспорт ТНФУ)** |
| Exports of goods and nonfactor services | 29,785 | 50,520 | 803,080 | 1,074,356 | 948,838 | 1,111,198 | Экспорт товаров и нефакторных услуг |
| Imports of goods and nonfactor services | 30,610 | 36,530 | 733,990 | 835,859 | 906,772 | 1,159,666 | Импорт товаров и нефакторных услуг |

**TABLE 2-1A. Distribution of gross domestic product at current prices (percent)**

**ТАБЛИЦА 2-1А. Распределение валового внутреннего продукта в текущих ценах ( % )**

| Sector of origin or expenditure category | 1990 | 1991 | 1992 | 1993 | 1994 | 1995 | Отраслевое происхождение или вид расходов |
|---|---|---|---|---|---|---|---|
| **Gross domestic product by sector of origin** | | | | | | | **ВВП по отраслевому происхождению** |
| **Agriculture and forestry** | 20.3 | 21.3 | 16.1 | 10.6 | 8.3 | 8.5 | **Сельское и лесное хозяйство** |
| Agriculture | .. | .. | .. | 9.3 | 7.4 | 7.0 | Сельское хозяйство |
| Forestry | .. | .. | .. | 1.3 | 0.9 | 1.5 | Лесное хозяйство |
| **Industry and construction** | .. | .. | .. | .. | .. | .. | **Промышленность и строительство** |
| Industry | 35.1 | 37.1 | 27.9 | 27.9 | 22.5 | 22.0 | Промышленность |
| Construction | 9.4 | 5.6 | 4.7 | 3.9 | 5.3 | 6.7 | Строительство |
| **Other** | 30.8 | 32.0 | 44.4 | 48.3 | 52.5 | 49.6 | **Другие отрасли** |
| Transport | 10.5 | 7.2 | 16.6 | 21.0 | 18.1 | 17.6 | Транспорт |
| Road maintenance | .. | .. | .. | .. | .. | .. | Дорожное хозяйство |
| Communication | .. | .. | .. | .. | .. | .. | Связь |
| Wholesale trade | .. | .. | .. | .. | .. | .. | Оптовая торговля |
| Retail trade and catering | .. | .. | .. | .. | .. | .. | Розничная торговля и общепит |
| Material supply | .. | .. | .. | .. | .. | .. | Материально-техническое снабжение |
| Procurement | .. | .. | .. | .. | .. | .. | Заготовки |
| Information and computing services | .. | .. | .. | .. | .. | .. | Информационно-вычислительное обслуживание |
| Other sectors of material production | .. | .. | .. | .. | .. | .. | Другие отрасли сферы матерл. произ. |
| Housing | .. | .. | .. | .. | .. | .. | Жилищное хозяйство |
| Public utilities and personal services | .. | .. | .. | .. | .. | .. | Ком. хоз. и бытовое обслуживание |
| Health care, social security, physical culture and sports | .. | .. | .. | .. | .. | .. | Здравоохранение, социальное обеспечение, физкультура и спорт |
| Education | 2.5 | 2.6 | 2.9 | 4.0 | 4.7 | 5.1 | Образование |
| Culture and art | .. | .. | .. | .. | .. | .. | Культура и искусство |
| Science and scientific research | .. | .. | .. | .. | .. | .. | Наука и научное обслуживание |
| Credit | .. | .. | .. | .. | .. | .. | Кредитование |
| Insurance | .. | .. | .. | .. | .. | .. | Страхование |
| General administration and defense | .. | .. | .. | .. | .. | .. | Государственное управление и оборона |
| Private nonprofit institutions serving households | .. | .. | .. | .. | .. | .. | Общественные организации, обслуживающие домашние хозяйства |
| **Imputed service charge of financial intermediaries** | .. | .. | .. | .. | .. | .. | **Условно-исчисляемая стоимость услуг финансовых посредников** |
| **Total gross value added** | 96.4 | 97.1 | 93.4 | 90.8 | 88.6 | 86.8 | **Валовая добавленная стоимость - всего** |
| **Total GDP at factor cost** | 93.4 | 93.3 | 93.6 | 89.1 | 87.0 | .. | **ВВП по фактор. стоимости - всего** |
| **Net indirect taxes** | 6.6 | 6.7 | 6.4 | 10.9 | 13.0 | .. | **Чистые косвенные налоги (НПиИ-СПиИ)** |
| **Total GDP at market prices** | 100.0 | 100.0 | 100.0 | 100.0 | 100.0 | 100.0 | **ВВП в рын. ценах - всего** |
| **Gross domestic product by expenditure category** | | | | | | | **ВВП по видам расходов** |
| **Consumption** | 61.2 | 56.5 | 51.9 | 74.4 | 78.6 | 80.1 | **Потребление** |
| Private consumption | 52.7 | 46.2 | 39.4 | 52.3 | 58.5 | 59.4 | Личное потребление |
| Government consumption | 8.6 | 10.3 | 12.5 | 22.1 | 20.1 | 20.7 | Общественное потребление |
| **Gross domestic investment** | 40.1 | 33.7 | 41.2 | 9.2 | 19.1 | 21.9 | **Вал. внутр. инвестиции** |
| Gross fixed investment | 23.0 | 6.2 | 11.2 | 13.8 | 14.9 | 16.6 | Вал. накопление осн. капитала |
| Change in stocks | 17.1 | 27.6 | 30.1 | -4.6 | 4.3 | 5.3 | Изменения в запасах (МОС) |
| **Resource balance (net exports of GNFS)** | -1.3 | 9.8 | 6.9 | 16.3 | 2.1 | -2.1 | **Сальдо ресурсов (чистый экспорт ТНФУ)** |
| Exports of goods and nonfactor services | 47.7 | 35.2 | 79.9 | 73.2 | 46.5 | 47.1 | Экспорт товаров и нефакторных услуг |
| Imports of goods and nonfactor services | 49.0 | 25.5 | 73.1 | 57.0 | 44.4 | 49.1 | Импорт товаров и нефакторных услуг |

# TABLE 2-2. Gross domestic product at constant prices (thousands of national currency)
# ТАБЛИЦА 2-2. Валовой внутренний продукт в постоянных ценах (тысяч национальной валюты)

| Sector of origin or expenditure category | 1990 | 1991 | 1992 | 1993 | 1994 | 1995 | Отраслевое происхождение или вид расходов |
|---|---|---|---|---|---|---|---|
| **Gross domestic product by sector of origin** | | | | | | | **Валовой внутренний продукт по отраслевому происхождению** |
| **Agriculture and forestry** | 277,537 | 271,851 | 192,898 | 155,516 | 131,191 | 128,442 | **Сельское и лесное хозяйство** |
| Agriculture | .. | .. | .. | 136,842 | 110,761 | 103,676 | Сельское хозяйство |
| Forestry | .. | .. | .. | 18,674 | 20,430 | 24,766 | Лесное хозяйство |
| **Industry and construction** | .. | .. | .. | .. | .. | .. | **Промышленность и строительство** |
| Industry | 1,072,251 | 1,069,795 | 583,081 | 409,708 | 376,330 | 354,635 | Промышленность |
| Construction | 460,307 | 273,430 | 112,126 | 56,603 | 63,113 | 73,588 | Строительство |
| **Other** | 887,458 | 782,930 | 664,556 | 708,685 | 770,272 | 763,717 | **Другие отрасли** |
| Transport | .. | .. | 285,823 | 307,651 | 349,707 | 349,028 | Транспорт |
| Road maintenance | .. | .. | .. | .. | .. | .. | Дорожное хозяйство |
| Communication | .. | .. | .. | .. | .. | .. | Связь |
| Wholesale trade | .. | .. | .. | .. | .. | .. | Оптовая торговля |
| Retail trade and catering | .. | .. | .. | .. | .. | .. | Розничная торговля и общепит |
| Material supply | .. | .. | .. | .. | .. | .. | Материально-техническое снабжение |
| Procurement | .. | .. | .. | .. | .. | .. | Заготовки |
| Information and computing services | .. | .. | .. | .. | .. | .. | Информационно-вычислительное обслуживание |
| Other sectors of material production | .. | .. | .. | .. | .. | .. | Другие отрасли сферы материального пр. |
| Housing | .. | .. | .. | .. | .. | .. | Жилищное хозяйство |
| Public utilities and personal services | .. | .. | .. | .. | .. | .. | Ком. хоз. и бытовое обслуживание |
| Health care, social security, and sports | .. | .. | .. | .. | .. | .. | Здравоохранение, социальное обеспечение, физкультура и спорт |
| Education | .. | .. | 62,102 | 58,089 | 59,032 | 59,555 | Образование |
| Culture and art | .. | .. | .. | .. | .. | .. | Культура и искусство |
| Science and research | .. | .. | .. | .. | .. | .. | Наука и научное обслуживание |
| Credit | .. | .. | .. | .. | .. | .. | Кредитование |
| Insurance | .. | .. | .. | .. | .. | .. | Страхование |
| General administration and defense | .. | .. | .. | .. | .. | .. | Государственное управление и оборона |
| Private nonprofit institutions serving households | .. | .. | .. | .. | .. | .. | Общественные организации, обслуживающие домашние хозяйства |
| **Imputed service charge of financial intermediaries** | .. | .. | .. | .. | .. | .. | **Условно-исчисляемая стоимость услуг финансовых посредников** |
| **Total gross value added (GVA)** | 2,701,053 | 2,401,399 | 1,554,304 | 1,331,823 | 1,342,148 | 1,321,777 | **Валовая добавленная стоимость (ВДС) -** |
| **Total GDP at factor cost (GVA-OTOP+OSOP)** | .. | .. | .. | .. | .. | .. | **Всего ВВП по фактр. стоимости (ВДС-ДНП+ДСП)** |
| **Net indirect taxes (TOPI - SOPI)** | 251,812 | 243,998 | 168,940 | 135,189 | 134,375 | 131,458 | **Чистые косвенные налоги (НПиИ-СПиИ)** |
| **Total GDP at market prices** | 2,952,865 | 2,645,397 | 1,723,244 | 1,467,012 | 1,476,523 | 1,453,235 | **Всего ВВП в рыночных ценах** |
| **Gross domestic product by expenditure category** | | | | | | | **Валовой внутренний продукт по видам расходов** |
| **Consumption** | 2,300,858 | 1,769,810 | 1,147,743 | 1,091,208 | 1,112,641 | 1,153,665 | **Потребление** |
| Private consumption | 1,983,432 | 1,467,824 | 828,832 | 767,122 | 791,545 | 822,618 | Личное потребление |
| Government consumption | 317,426 | 301,986 | 318,911 | 324,086 | 321,096 | 331,047 | Общественное потребление |
| **Gross domestic investment** | 1,167,856 | 955,795 | 576,940 | 134,615 | 207,264 | 153,130 | **Валовые внутренние инвестиции** |
| Gross fixed investment | 932,832 | 336,423 | 239,717 | 201,842 | 203,446 | 229,080 | Валовое накопление основного капитала |
| Change in stocks | 235,024 | 619,372 | 337,223 | -67,227 | 3,818 | -75,950 | Изменения в запасах (МОС) |
| **Resource balance (net exports of GNFS)** | -515,849 | -80,208 | -4,213 | 238,497 | 153,840 | 143,662 | **Сальдо ресурсов (чистый экспорт ТНФУ)** |
| Exports of goods and nonfactor services | 1,777,130 | 1,205,238 | 1,384,234 | 1,074,356 | 984,044 | 950,451 | Экспорт товаров и нефакторных услуг |
| Imports of goods and nonfactor services | 2,292,979 | 1,285,446 | 1,388,447 | 835,859 | 830,204 | 806,789 | Импорт товаров и нефакторных услуг |

TABLE 2-2A. Growth rates of gross domestic product at constant prices (percent)
ТАБЛИЦА 2-2A. Валовой внутренний продукт - темпы прироста в постоянных ценах ( % )



| Sector of origin or expenditure category | 1990 | 1991 | 1992 | 1993 | 1994 | 1995 | Отраслевое происхождение или вид расходов |
|---|---|---|---|---|---|---|---|
| **Growth rate by sector of origin** | | | | | | | **Валовый внутренний продукт по отраслевому происхождению** |
| **Agriculture and forestry** | .. | -2.0 | -29.0 | -19.4 | -15.6 | -2.1 | **Сельское и лесное хозяйство** |
| Agriculture | .. | .. | .. | .. | -19.1 | -6.4 | Сельское хозяйство |
| Forestry | .. | .. | .. | .. | 9.4 | 21.2 | Лесное хозяйство |
| **Industry and construction** | .. | .. | .. | .. | .. | .. | **Промышленность и строительство** |
| Industry | .. | -0.2 | -45.5 | -29.7 | -8.1 | -5.8 | Промышленность |
| Construction | .. | -40.6 | -59.0 | -49.5 | 11.5 | 16.6 | Строительство |
| **Other** | .. | -11.8 | -15.1 | 6.6 | 8.7 | -0.9 | **Другие отрасли** |
| Transport | .. | .. | .. | 7.6 | 13.7 | -0.2 | Транспорт |
| Road maintenance | .. | .. | .. | .. | .. | .. | Дорожное хозяйство |
| Communication | .. | .. | .. | .. | .. | .. | Связь |
| Wholesale trade | .. | .. | .. | .. | .. | .. | Оптовая торговля |
| Retail trade and catering | .. | .. | .. | .. | .. | .. | Розничная торговля и общепит |
| Material supply | .. | .. | .. | .. | .. | .. | Материально-техническое снабжение |
| Procurement | .. | .. | .. | .. | .. | .. | Заготовки |
| Information and computing services | .. | .. | .. | .. | .. | .. | Информационно-вычислительное обслуживание |
| Other sectors of material production | .. | .. | .. | .. | .. | .. | Другие отрасли сферы материального пр. |
| Housing | .. | .. | .. | .. | .. | .. | Жилищное хозяйство |
| Public utilities and personal services | .. | .. | .. | .. | .. | .. | Ком. хоз. и бытовое обслуживание |
| Health care, social security, and sports | .. | .. | .. | .. | .. | .. | Здравоохранение, социальное обеспечение, физкультура и спорт |
| Education | .. | .. | .. | -6.5 | 1.6 | 0.9 | Образование |
| Culture and art | .. | .. | .. | .. | .. | .. | Культура и искусство |
| Science and research | .. | .. | .. | .. | .. | .. | Наука и научное обслуживание |
| Credit | .. | .. | .. | .. | .. | .. | Кредитование |
| Insurance | .. | .. | .. | .. | .. | .. | Страхование |
| General administration and defense | .. | .. | .. | .. | .. | .. | Государственное управление и оборона |
| Private nonprofit institutions serving households | .. | .. | .. | .. | .. | .. | Общественные организации, обслуживающие домашние хозяйства |
| **Imputed service charge of financial intermediaries** | .. | .. | .. | .. | .. | .. | **Условно-исчисляемая стоимость услуг финансовых посредников** |
| **Total gross value added** | .. | -11.1 | -35.3 | -14.3 | 0.8 | -1.5 | **Валовая добавленная стоимость (ВДС) - всего** |
| **Total GDP at factor cost** | .. | .. | .. | .. | .. | .. | **Всего ВВП по фактр. стоимости (ВДС-ДНП+ДСП)** |
| **Net indirect taxes** | .. | -3.1 | -30.8 | -20.0 | -0.6 | -2.2 | **Чистые косвенные налоги (НПиИ-СПиИ)** |
| **Total GDP at market prices** | .. | -10.4 | -34.9 | -14.9 | 0.6 | -1.6 | **Всего ВВП в рыночных ценах** |
| **Growth rate by expenditure category** | | | | | | | **Валовой внутренний продукт по видам расходов** |
| **Consumption** | .. | -23.1 | -35.1 | -4.9 | 2.0 | 3.7 | **Потребление** |
| Private consumption | .. | -26.0 | -43.5 | -7.4 | 3.2 | 3.9 | Личное потребление |
| Government consumption | .. | -4.9 | 5.6 | 1.6 | -0.9 | 3.1 | Общественное потребление |
| **Gross domestic investment** | .. | -18.2 | -39.6 | -76.7 | 54.0 | -26.1 | **Валовые внутренние инвестиции** |
| Gross fixed investment | .. | -63.9 | -28.7 | -15.8 | 0.8 | 12.6 | Валовое накопление основного капитала |
| **Exports of goods and nonfactor services** | .. | -32.2 | 14.9 | -22.4 | -8.4 | -3.4 | **Экспорт товаров и нефакторных услуг** |
| **Imports of goods and nonfactor services** | .. | -43.9 | 8.0 | -39.8 | -0.7 | -2.8 | **Импорт товаров и нефакторных услуг** |

**TABLE 2-2B. Implicit price deflators for gross domestic product (percentage change)**
**ТАБЛИЦА 2-2B. Дефляторы валового внутреннего продукта (темпы прироста в %)**

| Sector of origin or expenditure category | 1990 | 1991 | 1992 | 1993 | 1994 | 1995 | Отраслевое происхождение или вид расходов |
|---|---|---|---|---|---|---|---|
| **Price deflators by sector of origin** | | | | | | | **Дефляторы по отраслевому происхождению или виду расходов** |
| **Agriculture and forestry** | .. | 145.7 | 646.1 | 19.3 | 29.7 | 20.5 | **Сельское и лесное хозяйство** |
| Agriculture | .. | .. | .. | .. | 36.4 | 17.5 | Сельское хозяйство |
| Forestry | .. | .. | .. | .. | -6.6 | 49.5 | Лесное хозяйство |
| **Industry and construction** | .. | .. | .. | .. | .. | .. | **Промышленность и строительство** |
| Industry | .. | 142.9 | 866.6 | 108.2 | 21.9 | 19.9 | Промышленность |
| Construction | .. | 130.8 | 1,338.5 | 137.0 | 70.1 | 26.1 | Строительство |
| **Other** | .. | 170.0 | 1,047.2 | 49.0 | 39.1 | 10.2 | **Другие отрасли** |
| Transport | .. | .. | 1,520.7 | 71.7 | 5.8 | 12.2 | Транспорт |
| Road maintenance | .. | .. | .. | .. | .. | .. | Дорожное хозяйство |
| Communication | .. | .. | .. | .. | .. | .. | Связь |
| Wholesale trade | .. | .. | .. | .. | .. | .. | Оптовая торговля |
| Retail trade and catering | .. | .. | .. | .. | .. | .. | Розничная торговля и общепит. |
| Material supply | .. | .. | .. | .. | .. | .. | Материально-техническое снабжение |
| Procurement | .. | .. | .. | .. | .. | .. | Заготовки |
| Information and computing services | .. | .. | .. | .. | .. | .. | Информационно-вычислительное обслуживание |
| Other sectors of material production | .. | .. | .. | .. | .. | .. | Другие отрасли сферы матерл. произ. |
| Housing | .. | .. | .. | .. | .. | .. | Жилищное хозяйство |
| Public utilities and personal services | .. | .. | .. | .. | .. | .. | Ком. хоз. и бытовое обслуживание |
| Health care, social security, and sports | .. | .. | .. | .. | .. | .. | Здравоохранение, социальное обеспечение, физкультура и спорт |
| Education | .. | .. | 687.7 | 110.8 | 62.7 | 23.4 | Образование |
| Culture and art | .. | .. | .. | .. | .. | .. | Культура и искусство |
| Science and research | .. | .. | .. | .. | .. | .. | Наука и научное обслуживание |
| Credit | .. | .. | .. | .. | .. | .. | Кредитование |
| Insurance | .. | .. | .. | .. | .. | .. | Страхование |
| General administration and defense | .. | .. | .. | .. | .. | .. | Государственное управление и оборона |
| Private nonprofit institutions serving households | .. | .. | .. | .. | .. | .. | Общественные организации, обслуживающие домашние хозяиства |
| **Imputed service charge of financial intermediaries** | .. | .. | .. | .. | .. | .. | **Условно-исчисляемая стоимость услуг финансовых посредников** |
| **Total gross value added** | .. | 160.1 | 941.8 | 65.6 | 34.8 | 15.0 | **Валовая добавленная стоимость (ВДС) - всего** |
| **Total GDP at factor cost** | .. | .. | .. | .. | .. | .. | **ВВП по факторной стоимости (ВДС-ДНП+ДСП)** |
| **Net indirect taxes** | .. | 140.4 | 866.2 | 211.6 | 67.3 | .. | **Чистые косвенные налоги (НПИ-СПИ)** |
| **Total GDP at market prices** | .. | 156.2 | 976.0 | 71.5 | 38.3 | 17.4 | **ВВП в рыночных ценах** |
| **Price deflators by expenditure category** | | | | | | | **Дефляторы по виду расходов** |
| **Consumption** | .. | 175.4 | 892.4 | 120.2 | 44.3 | 13.6 | **Конечное потребление** |
| Private consumption | .. | 172.2 | 958.2 | 109.4 | 50.9 | 12.9 | Личное потребление |
| Government consumption | .. | 189.9 | 705.3 | 154.4 | 27.9 | 15.5 | Общественное потребление |
| **Gross domestic investment** | .. | 136.0 | 1,319.4 | 39.3 | 88.6 | 79.4 | **Валовые внутренние инвестиции** |
| Gross fixed investment | .. | 70.7 | 1,683.2 | 113.4 | 49.4 | 14.6 | Валовое накопление основного капитала |
| **Exports of goods and nonfactor services** | .. | 150.1 | 1,284.1 | 72.4 | -3.6 | 21.3 | **Экспорт товаров и нефакторных услуг** |
| **Imports of goods and nonfactor services** | .. | 112.9 | 1,760.2 | 89.2 | 9.2 | 31.6 | **Импорт товаров и нефакторных услуг** |

**TABLE 3-1. Balance of payments at current prices (millions of U.S. dollars)**
**ТАБЛИЦА 3-1. Платежный баланс в текущих ценах (в миллионах долларов США)**

| Item | 1990 | 1991 | 1992 | 1993 | 1994 | 1995 | Статьи |
|---|---|---|---|---|---|---|---|
| Exports of goods and services (including workers' remittances) | .. | .. | 1,199.8 | 1,605.0 | 1,966.3 | 2,151.0 | Экспорт товаров и услуг (включая денежные переводы рабочих) |
| Exports of goods and nonfactor services | .. | .. | 1,191.1 | 1,587.8 | 1,934.0 | 2,080.0 | Экспорт товаров и нефакт. услуг |
| Merchandise (FOB) | .. | .. | 869.2 | 1,054.4 | 1,310.8 | 1,368.0 | Товары (ФОБ) |
| Nonfactor services | .. | .. | 321.9 | 533.3 | 623.2 | 712.0 | Нефакторные услуги |
| Shipment | .. | .. | 304.9 | 424.9 | 511.5 | 652.0 | Перевозки |
| Travel | .. | .. | 8.0 | 15.4 | 17.3 | 20.0 | Поездки |
| Other | .. | .. | 9.0 | 93.1 | 94.4 | 41.0 | Другие |
| Imports of goods and nonfactor services | .. | .. | 1,089.7 | 1,256.1 | 1,531.8 | 2,192.0 | Импорт товаров и нефакт. услуг |
| Merchandise (FOB) | .. | .. | 913.5 | 1,051.3 | 1,328.2 | 1,947.0 | Товары (ФОБ) |
| Nonfactor services | .. | .. | 176.2 | 204.8 | 203.5 | 245.0 | Нефакторные услуги |
| Shipment | .. | .. | 113.2 | 130.3 | 130.0 | 153.0 | Перевозки |
| Travel | .. | .. | 14.1 | 28.9 | 26.8 | 24.0 | Поездки |
| Other | .. | .. | 48.9 | 45.5 | 46.7 | 68.0 | Другие |
| Resource balance | .. | .. | 101.4 | 331.7 | 402.2 | -113.0 | Сальдо ресурсов |
| Net factor income | .. | .. | 1.4 | 7.2 | -1.2 | 19.0 | Чистый факторный доход |
| Factor receipts | .. | .. | 2.6 | 17.3 | 32.3 | 71.0 | Факторные поступления |
| Factor payments | .. | .. | 1.2 | 10.0 | 33.5 | 53.0 | Факторные платежи |
| Total interest due | .. | .. | 0.8 | .. | .. | .. | Общая сумма процента к оплате |
| Other factor payments and discrepancy | .. | .. | 0.4 | .. | .. | .. | Другие факторные платежи и стат. погр. |
| Net current transfers | .. | .. | 109.4 | 77.9 | 50.4 | 67.0 | Чистые текущие трансферты |
| Current receipts | .. | .. | 110.3 | 80.5 | 52.6 | 72.0 | Текущие поступления |
| Workers remittances | .. | .. | 0.0 | .. | .. | .. | Денежные переводы рабочих |
| Other current transfers | .. | .. | 110.3 | .. | .. | 36.0 | Другие текущие трансферты |
| Current payments | .. | .. | 0.9 | 2.6 | 2.1 | 5.0 | Текущие платежи |
| Current account balance before official grants | .. | .. | 212.2 | 416.8 | 451.5 | -27.0 | Сальдо текущего счета до офиц. безвозмезд. трансфертов |
| Official capital grants | .. | .. | 0.0 | .. | .. | .. | Официальные кап. безвозмезные трансферты |
| Current account balance after official grants | .. | .. | 212.2 | .. | .. | .. | Сальдо текущего счета после офиц. безвозмезд. трансфертов |
| Long Term Capital Inflows | .. | .. | 59.2 | 140.4 | 83.5 | .. | Долгосрочные притоки капитала |
| Direct investment | .. | .. | 0.8 | 49.6 | 202.2 | 245.0 | Прямые инвестиции |
| Net long term borrowing | .. | .. | 58.4 | .. | .. | .. | Чистые долгосрочные займы |
| Disbursements | .. | .. | .. | .. | .. | .. | Поступления |
| Repayments due | .. | .. | .. | .. | .. | .. | Сумма, подлежащая погашению |
| Other long-term inflows (net) | .. | .. | 0.0 | 90.8 | -118.6 | .. | Другие долгосрочные притоки (чистые) |

(continued on next page)

**TABLE 3-1. Balance of payments at current prices (millions of U.S. dollars)**
**ТАБЛИЦА 3-1. Платежный баланс в текущих ценах (в миллионах долларов США)**

| Item | 1990 | 1991 | 1992 | 1993 | 1994 | 1995 | Статьи |
|---|---|---|---|---|---|---|---|
| Adjustment to Scheduled Debt Service | .. | .. | 0.0 | .. | .. | .. | Регулирование долга |
| Debt service not paid | .. | .. | 0.0 | .. | .. | 101.0 | Невыплаченный долг |
| Interest not paid | .. | .. | 0.0 | .. | .. | .. | Невыплаченный процент |
| Principal not paid | .. | .. | 0.0 | .. | .. | .. | Невыплаченная сумма основного долга |
| Arrears reductions/prepayments(-) | .. | .. | 0.0 | .. | .. | .. | Погашение просроченных платежей/выплаты авансом (-) |
| Total Other items (Net) | .. | .. | -200.7 | .. | .. | .. | Общие другие статьи (чистые) |
| Net short-term capital | .. | .. | 0.0 | .. | .. | .. | Чистый краткосрочный капитал |
| Capital flows not elsewhere included | .. | .. | -106.2 | .. | .. | .. | Потоки капитала, не указанные выше |
| Errors and omissions | .. | .. | -94.5 | .. | .. | 699.0 | Ошибки и пропуски |
| Changes in net reserves | .. | .. | -70.7 | .. | .. | .. | Изменения в чистых резервах |
| Net credit from IMF | .. | .. | -27.9 | .. | .. | .. | Чистый кредит МВФ |
| Reserve changes not elsewhere included | .. | .. | -42.8 | .. | .. | .. | Изменения резервов, не указанных выше |
| Escrow account | .. | .. | 0.0 | .. | .. | .. | Счет депонирования |
| Gross reserves (excluding gold) | .. | .. | 0.0 | .. | .. | .. | Общие резервы (исключая золото) |
| Gross reserves (including gold) | .. | .. | 0.0 | .. | .. | .. | Общие резервы (включая золото) |
| Nominal official exchange rate (annual average) (rf) | .. | .. | .. | .. | .. | .. | Номинальный официальный или рыночный курс (среднегодовой) |
| Nominal official exchange rate (end-of-year) (ae) | .. | .. | .. | .. | .. | .. | Номинальный официальный или рыночный курс (на конец года) |
| Manufacture unit value (percent change) | .. | .. | .. | .. | .. | .. | Средний индекс цен на продукцию обр. пром.,% |
| Index of real effective exchange rate (IMF) | .. | .. | .. | .. | .. | .. | Индекс реального эффективного валютного курса (МВФ) |
| Total factor payments | .. | .. | .. | .. | .. | .. | Общая сумма факторных платежей |
| Government interest | .. | .. | .. | .. | .. | .. | Процент, выплачиваемый органами гос. управления |
| Private sector interest | .. | .. | .. | .. | .. | .. | Процент выплачиваемый частным сектором |
| Profits on direct foreign investment | .. | .. | .. | .. | .. | .. | Прибыль от прямых иностранных инвестиций |
| Official capital grants | .. | .. | .. | .. | .. | .. | Официальные капитальные безвозмездные трансферты |
| For budgetary financing | .. | .. | .. | .. | .. | .. | На бюджетное финансирование |
| To extrabudgetary entities | .. | .. | .. | .. | .. | .. | На внебюджетное финансирование |
| Government net long term borrowing | .. | .. | .. | .. | .. | .. | Чистые долгосрочные государственные займы |
| Disbursements | .. | .. | .. | .. | .. | .. | Поступления |
| Repayments | .. | .. | .. | .. | .. | .. | Погашения |
| Private net long term borrowing | .. | .. | .. | .. | .. | .. | Чистые долгосрочные частные займы |
| Disbursements | .. | .. | .. | .. | .. | .. | Поступления |
| Repayments | .. | .. | .. | .. | .. | .. | Погашения |

## TABLE 3-2A. Imports by commodity group (thousands of U.S. dollars)
## ТАБЛИЦА 3-2A . Импорт по товарным группам (тысяч долларов США)

| Commodity group | 1990 | 1991 | 1992 | 1993 | 1994 | 1995 | Товарные группы |
|---|---|---|---|---|---|---|---|
| TOTAL | .. | .. | .. | 963,961 | 1,241,491 | 1,817,721 | ВСЕГО |
| I - Live animals; animal products | .. | .. | .. | 9,302 | 28,004 | 31,322 | I - Живые животные и продукты животноводства |
| II - Vegetable products | .. | .. | .. | 17,796 | 36,360 | 55,871 | II - Продукты растительного происхождения |
| III - Animal or vegetable fats and oils and their cleavage products; prepared edible fats; animal or vegetable waxes | .. | .. | .. | 3,495 | 5,097 | 13,416 | III - Жиры и масла растительного и животного происхождения, воски |
| IV - Prepared foodstuffs; beverages, spirits and vinegar; tobacco and manufactured tobacco substitutes | .. | .. | .. | 32,011 | 63,839 | 97,686 | IV -Продукция пищевой промышленности, алкогольные и безалкогольные напитки, табак и его заменители |
| V - Mineral products | .. | .. | .. | 436,051 | 363,273 | 392,695 | V - Минеральные продукты |
| VI - Products of the chemical or allied industries | .. | .. | .. | 69,144 | 126,339 | 204,504 | VI - Продукция химической промышленности |
| VII - Plastics and articles thereof; rubber and articles thereof | .. | .. | .. | 17,237 | 36,032 | 68,892 | VII - Пластмассы и изделия из них |
| VIII - Raw hides and skins, leather, furskins and articles thereof; saddlery and harness; travel goods, handbags and similar containers; articles of animal gut | .. | .. | .. | 3,630 | 4,590 | 6,334 | VIII - Кожевенное сырьё, кожи, пушнина, меховое сырьё и изделия из них |
| IX - Wood and articles of wood; wood charcoal; cork and articles of cork; manufactures of straw, of esparto or of other plaiting materials; basketware and wickerwork | .. | .. | .. | 2,788 | 5,999 | 15,039 | IX - Древесина и изделия из древесины, древесный уголь |
| X - Pulp of wood or of other fibrous cellulosic material; waste and scrap of paper or paperboard; paper and paperboard and articles thereof | .. | .. | .. | 13,286 | 36,943 | 81,005 | X - Бумажная масса, бумажные и картонные отходы, макулатура, бумага, картон и изделия из них |
| XI - Textiles and textile articles | .. | .. | .. | 44,549 | 73,373 | 142,900 | XI - Текстиль и текстильные изделия |
| XII - Footwear, headgear, umbrellas, sun umbrellas, walking sticks, seat sticks, whips, riding crops and parts thereof; prepared feathers and articles made therewith; artificial flowers; articles of human hair | .. | .. | .. | 10,549 | 10,708 | 13,256 | XII - Обувь, головные уборы, зонты, трости и пр. |

**TABLE 3-2A. Imports by commodity group (thousands of U.S. dollars)**
**ТАБЛИЦА 3-2А . Импорт по товарным группам (тысяч долларов США)**

| Commodity group | 1990 | 1991 | 1992 | 1993 | 1994 | 1995 | Товарные группы |
|---|---|---|---|---|---|---|---|
| XIII - Articles of stone, plaster, cement, asbestos, mica and similar materials; ceramic products; glass and glassware | .. | .. | .. | 10,415 | 17,405 | 32,611 | XIII - Изделия из камня, гипса, цемента |
| XIV - Natural or cultured pearls, precious or semi-precious stones, precious metals, metals clad with precious metal and articles thereof; imitation jewellery; coin | .. | .. | .. | 937 | 951 | 2,056 | XIV - Жемчуг, драгоценные и полудрагоценные камни, драгоценные металлы, бижутерия, монеты |
| XV - Base metals and articles of base metal | .. | .. | .. | 42,695 | 62,048 | 116,724 | XV - Неблагородные металлы и изделия из них |
| XVI - Machinery and mechanical appliances; electrical equipment; parts thereof; sound recorders and reproducers, television image and sound recorders and reproducers, and parts and accessories of such articles | .. | .. | .. | 95,981 | 200,755 | 314,381 | XVI - Машины, оборудование, механизмы, их части и принадлежности; звуковая и теле-аппаратура, их части и принадлежности |
| XVII - Vehicles, aircraft, vessels and associated transport equipment | .. | .. | .. | 88,056 | 83,417 | 146,828 | XVII - Средства наземного, воздушного и водного транспорта |
| XVIII - Optical, photographic, cinematograp-hic, measuring, checking, precision, medical or surgical instruments and apparatus; clocks and watches; musical instruments; parts and accessories thereof | .. | .. | .. | 10,112 | 30,144 | 36,583 | XVIII - Приборы, аппараты оптические, медицинские, измерительные и пр.; музыкальные инструменты; часы; их части и принадлежности |
| XIX - Arms and ammunition; parts and accessories thereof | .. | .. | .. | 945 | 1,627 | 2,157 | XIX - Оружие и боеприпасы, их части и принадлежности |
| XX - Miscellaneous manufactured articles | .. | .. | .. | 12,505 | 22,163 | 43,235 | XX - Разные промышленные товары |
| XXI - Works of art, collectors' pieces, and antiques | .. | .. | .. | 5 | 23 | 19 | XXI - Произведения искусства, предметы антиквариата |
| XXII - Services | .. | .. | .. | .. | .. | .. | XXII - Услуги |

## TABLE 3-2B Imports by commodity group (thousands of national currency)
## ТАБЛИЦА 3-2B. Импорт по товарным группам (тысяч национальной валюты)

| Commodity group | 1990 | 1991 | 1992 | 1993 | 1994 | 1995 | Товарные группы |
|---|---|---|---|---|---|---|---|
| TOTAL | .. | .. | 541,520 | 639,247 | 694,588 | 959,636 | ВСЕГО |
| I - Live animals; animal products | .. | .. | .. | 6,013 | 15,766 | 16,566 | I - Живые животные и продукты животноводства |
| II - Vegetable products | .. | .. | .. | 11,698 | 20,391 | 29,447 | II - Продукты растительного происхождения |
| III - Animal or vegetable fats and oils and their cleavage products; prepared edible fats; animal or vegetable waxes | .. | .. | .. | 2,266 | 2,875 | 7,112 | III - Жиры и масла растительного и животного происхождения, воски |
| IV - Prepared foodstuffs; beverages, spirits and vinegar; tobacco and manufactured tobacco substitutes | .. | .. | .. | 21,090 | 35,631 | 51,530 | IV -Продукция пищевой промышленности, алкогольные и безалкогольные напитки, табак и его заменители |
| V - Mineral products | .. | .. | .. | 291,732 | 204,396 | 208,228 | V - Минеральные продукты |
| VI - Products of the chemical or allied industries | .. | .. | .. | 45,184 | 70,604 | 108,046 | VI - Продукция химической промышленности |
| VII - Plastics and articles thereof; rubber and articles thereof | .. | .. | .. | 11,354 | 20,059 | 36,361 | VII - Пластмассы и изделия из них |
| VIII - Raw hides and skins, leather, furskins and articles thereof; saddlery and harness; travel goods, handbags and similar containers; articles of animal gut | .. | .. | .. | 2,356 | 2,546 | 3,340 | VIII - Кожевенное сырьё, кожи, пушнина, меховое сырьё и изделия из них |
| IX - Wood and articles of wood; wood charcoal; cork and articles of cork; manufactures of straw, of esparto or of other plaiting materials; basketware and wickerwork | .. | .. | .. | 1,844 | 3,338 | 7,904 | IX - Древесина и изделия из древесины, древесный уголь |
| X - Pulp of wood or of other fibrous cellulosic material; waste and scrap of paper or paperboard; paper and paperboard and articles thereof | .. | .. | .. | 8,738 | 20,564 | 42,691 | X - Бумажная масса, бумажные и картонные отходы, макулатура, бумага, картон и изделия из них |
| XI - Textiles and textile articles | .. | .. | .. | 29,374 | 40,912 | 75,271 | XI - Текстиль и текстильные изделия |
| XII - Footwear, headgear, umbrellas, sun umbrellas, walking sticks, seat sticks, whips, riding crops and parts thereof; prepared feathers and articles made therewith; artificial flowers; articles of human hair | .. | .. | .. | 6,857 | 5,977 | 6,999 | XII - Обувь, головные уборы, зонты, трости и пр. |

**TABLE 3-2B Imports by commodity group (thousands of national currency)**
**ТАБЛИЦА 3-2B. Импорт по товарным группам (тысяч национальной валюты)**

| Commodity group | 1990 | 1991 | 1992 | 1993 | 1994 | 1995 | Товарные группы |
|---|---|---|---|---|---|---|---|
| XIII - Articles of stone, plaster, cement, asbestos, mica and similar materials; ceramic products; glass and glassware | .. | .. | .. | 6,851 | 9,703 | 17,202 | XIII - Изделия из камня, гипса, цемента |
| XIV - Natural or cultured pearls, precious or semi-precious stones, precious metals, metals clad with precious metal and articles thereof; imitation jewellery; coin | .. | .. | .. | 587 | 533 | 1,088 | XIV - Жемчуг, драгоценные и полудрагоценные камни, драгоценные металлы, бижутерия, монеты |
| XV - Base metals and articles of base metal | .. | .. | .. | 28,365 | 34,644 | 61,511 | XV - Неблагородные металлы и изделия из них |
| XVI - Machinery and mechanical appliances; electrical equipment; parts thereof; sound recorders and reproducers, television image and sound recorders and reproducers, and parts and accessories of such articles | .. | .. | .. | 63,119 | 111,812 | 165,748 | XVI - Машины, оборудование, механизмы, их части и принадлежности; звуковая и теле-аппаратура, их части и принадлежности |
| XVII - Vehicles, aircraft, vessels and associated transport equipment | .. | .. | .. | 59,569 | 46,512 | 77,152 | XVII - Средства наземного, воздушного и водного транспорта |
| XVIII - Optical, photographic, cinematograp-hic, measuring, checking, precision, medical or surgical instruments and apparatus; clocks and watches; musical instruments; parts and accessories thereof | .. | .. | .. | 6,512 | 16,847 | 19,344 | XVIII - Приборы, аппараты оптические, медицинские, измерительные и пр.; музыкальные инструменты; часы; их части и принадлежности |
| XIX - Arms and ammunition; parts and accessories thereof | .. | .. | .. | 616 | 912 | 1,142 | XIX - Оружие и боеприпасы, их части и принадлежности |
| XX - Miscellaneous manufactured articles | .. | .. | .. | 8,110 | 12,327 | 22,833 | XX - Разные промышленные товары |
| XXI - Works of art, collectors' pieces, and antiques | .. | .. | .. | 3 | 12 | 10 | XXI - Произведения искусства, предметы антиквариата |
| XXII - Services | .. | .. | .. | .. | .. | .. | XXII - Услуги |

## TABLE 3-3A. Exports by commodity group (thousands of U.S. dollars)
## ТАБЛИЦА 3-3A. Экспорт по товарным группам (тысяч долларов США)

| Commodity group | 1990 | 1991 | 1992 | 1993 | 1994 | 1995 | Товарные группы |
|---|---|---|---|---|---|---|---|
| TOTAL | .. | .. | .. | 1,000,878 | 989,724 | 1,304,536 | ВСЕГО |
| I - Live animals; animal products | .. | .. | .. | 62,395 | 29,221 | 59,929 | I - Живые животные и продукты животноводства |
| II - Vegetable products | .. | .. | .. | 17,016 | 9,919 | 7,289 | II - Продукты растительного происхождения |
| III - Animal or vegetable fats and oils and their cleavage products; prepared edible fats; animal or vegetable waxes | .. | .. | .. | 2,798 | 1,229 | 1,449 | III - Жиры и масла растительного и животного происхождения, воски |
| IV - Prepared foodstuffs; beverages, spirits and vinegar; tobacco and manufactured tobacco substitutes | .. | .. | .. | 68,946 | 86,571 | 145,076 | IV -Продукция пищевой промышленности, алкогольные и безалкогольные напитки, табак и его заменители |
| V - Mineral products | .. | .. | .. | 134,363 | 21,935 | 28,385 | V - Минеральные продукты |
| VI - Products of the chemical or allied industries | .. | .. | .. | 69,928 | 72,714 | 83,412 | VI - Продукция химической промышленности |
| VII - Plastics and articles thereof; rubber and articles thereof | .. | .. | .. | 6,067 | 8,845 | 13,492 | VII - Пластмассы и изделия из них |
| VIII - Raw hides and skins, leather, furskins and articles thereof; saddlery and harness; travel goods, handbags and similar containers; articles of animal gut | .. | .. | .. | 15,494 | 17,878 | 21,565 | VIII - Кожевенное сырьё, кожи, пушнина, меховое сырьё и изделия из них |
| IX - Wood and articles of wood; wood charcoal; cork and articles of cork; manufactures of straw, of esparto or of other plaiting materials; basketware and wickerwork | .. | .. | .. | 88,936 | 201,810 | 344,637 | IX - Древесина и изделия из древесины, древесный уголь |
| X - Pulp of wood or of other fibrous cellulosic material; waste and scrap of paper or paperboard; paper and paperboard and articles thereof | .. | .. | .. | 8,030 | 8,409 | 15,194 | X - Бумажная масса, бумажные и картонные отходы, макулатура, бумага, картон и изделия из них |
| XI - Textiles and textile articles | .. | .. | .. | 127,501 | 130,933 | 182,561 | XI - Текстиль и текстильные изделия |
| XII - Footwear, headgear, umbrellas, sun umbrellas, walking sticks, seat sticks, whips, riding crops and parts thereof; prepared feathers and articles made therewith; artificial flowers; articles of human hair | .. | .. | .. | 22,431 | 17,304 | 8,971 | XII - Обувь, головные уборы, зонты, трости и пр. |

**TABLE 3-3A. Exports by commodity group (thousands of U.S. dollars)**
**ТАБЛИЦА 3-3А. Экспорт по товарным группам (тысяч долларов США)**

| Commodity group | 1990 | 1991 | 1992 | 1993 | 1994 | 1995 | Товарные группы |
|---|---|---|---|---|---|---|---|
| XIII - Articles of stone, plaster, cement, asbestos, mica and similar materials; ceramic products; glass and glassware | .. | .. | .. | 13,777 | 12,968 | 26,002 | XIII - Изделия из камня, гипса, цемента |
| XIV - Natural or cultured pearls, precious or semi-precious stones, precious metals, metals clad with precious metal and articles thereof; imitation jewellery; coin | .. | .. | .. | 7,654 | 2,112 | 2,408 | XIV - Жемчуг, драгоценные и полудрагоценные камни, драгоценные металлы, бижутерия, монеты |
| XV - Base metals and articles of base metal | .. | .. | .. | 85,849 | 100,179 | 103,316 | XV - Неблагородные металлы и изделия из них |
| XVI - Machinery and mechanical appliances; electrical equipment; parts thereof; sound recorders and reproducers, television image and sound recorders and reproducers, and parts and accessories of such articles | .. | .. | .. | 72,444 | 91,655 | 113,719 | XVI - Машины, оборудование, механизмы, их части и принадлежности; звуковая и теле-аппаратура, их части и принадлежности |
| XVII - Vehicles, aircraft, vessels and associated transport equipment | .. | .. | .. | 125,330 | 98,398 | 83,189 | XVII - Средства наземного, воздушного и водного транспорта |
| XVIII - Optical, photographic, cinematographic, measuring, checking, precision, medical or surgical instruments and apparatus; clocks and watches; musical instruments; parts and accessories thereof | .. | .. | .. | 6,193 | 6,052 | 5,787 | XVIII - Приборы, аппараты оптические, медицинские, измерительные и пр.; музыкальные инструменты; часы; их части и принадлежности |
| XIX - Arms and ammunition; parts and accessories thereof | .. | .. | .. | 231 | 183 | 122 | XIX - Оружие и боеприпасы, их части и принадлежности |
| XX - Miscellaneous manufactured articles | .. | .. | .. | 34,774 | 44,595 | 57,810 | XX - Разные промышленные товары |
| XXI - Works of art, collectors' pieces, and antiques | .. | .. | .. | 1 | 71 | 4 | XXI - Произведения искусства, предметы антиквариата |
| XXII - Services | .. | .. | .. | .. | .. | .. | XXII - Услуги |

## TABLE 3-3B. Exports by Commodity Group (thousands of national currency)
## ТАБЛИЦА 3-3B. Экспорт по товарным группам (тысяч национальной валюты)

**LATVIA**

| Commodity group | 1990 | 1991 | 1992 | 1993 | 1994 | 1995 | Товарные группы |
|---|---|---|---|---|---|---|---|
| TOTAL | .. | .. | 572,666 | 675,611 | 553,437 | 688,413 | ВСЕГО |
| I - Live animals; animal products | .. | .. | .. | 42,383 | 16,318 | 31,629 | I - Живые животные и продукты животноводства |
| II - Vegetable products | .. | .. | .. | 11,239 | 5,490 | 3,852 | II - Продукты растительного происхождения |
| III - Animal or vegetable fats and oils and their cleavage products; prepared edible fats; animal or vegetable waxes | .. | .. | .. | 1,953 | 688 | 765 | III - Жиры и масла растительного и животного происхождения, воски |
| IV - Prepared foodstuffs; beverages, spirits and vinegar; tobacco and manufactured tobacco substitutes | .. | .. | .. | 45,287 | 48,562 | 76,688 | IV -Продукция пищевой промышленности, алкогольные и безалкогольные напитки, табак и его заменители |
| V - Mineral products | .. | .. | .. | 96,360 | 12,205 | 14,912 | V - Минеральные продукты |
| VI - Products of the chemical or allied industries | .. | .. | .. | 46,372 | 40,692 | 43,965 | VI - Продукция химической промышленности |
| VII - Plastics and articles thereof; rubber and articles thereof | .. | .. | .. | 4,159 | 4,936 | 7,114 | VII - Пластмассы и изделия из них |
| VIII - Raw hides and skins, leather, furskins and articles thereof; saddlery and harness; travel goods, handbags and similar containers; articles of animal gut | .. | .. | .. | 10,278 | 9,994 | 11,419 | VIII - Кожевенное сырьё, кожи, пушнина, меховое сырьё и изделия из них |
| IX - Wood and articles of wood; wood charcoal; cork and articles of cork; manufactures of straw, of esparto or of other plaiting materials; basketware and wickerwork | .. | .. | .. | 59,392 | 112,590 | 181,933 | IX - Древесина и изделия из древесины, древесный уголь |
| X - Pulp of wood or of other fibrous cellulosic material; waste and scrap of paper or paperboard; paper and paperboard and articles thereof | .. | .. | .. | 5,624 | 4,674 | 8,023 | X - Бумажная масса, бумажные и картонные отходы, макулатура, бумага, картон и изделия из них |
| XI - Textiles and textile articles | .. | .. | .. | 85,698 | 73,312 | 96,424 | XI - Текстиль и текстильные изделия |
| XII - Footwear, headgear, umbrellas, sun umbrellas, walking sticks, seat sticks, whips, riding crops and parts thereof; prepared feathers and articles made therewith; artificial flowers; articles of human hair | .. | .. | .. | 15,308 | 9,714 | 4,731 | XII - Обувь, головные уборы, зонты, трости и пр. |

## TABLE 3-3B. Exports by Commodity Group (thousands of national currency)
## ТАБЛИЦА 3-3B. Экспорт по товарным группам (тысяч национальной валюты)

| Commodity group | 1990 | 1991 | 1992 | 1993 | 1994 | 1995 | Товарные группы |
|---|---|---|---|---|---|---|---|
| XIII - Articles of stone, plaster, cement, asbestos, mica and similar materials; ceramic products; glass and glassware | .. | .. | .. | 9,459 | 7,258 | 13,701 | XIII - Изделия из камня, гипса, цемента |
| XIV - Natural or cultured pearls, precious or semi-precious stones, precious metals, metals clad with precious metal and articles thereof; imitation jewellery; coin | .. | .. | .. | 5,622 | 1,186 | 1,259 | XIV - Жемчуг, драгоценные и полудрагоценные камни, драгоценные металлы, бижутерия, монеты |
| XV - Base metals and articles of base metal | .. | .. | .. | 56,862 | 56,050 | 54,411 | XV - Неблагородные металлы и изделия из них |
| XVI - Machinery and mechanical appliances; electrical equipment; parts thereof; sound recorders and reproducers, television image and sound recorders and reproducers, and parts and accessories of such articles | .. | .. | .. | 48,114 | 51,177 | 60,038 | XVI - Машины, оборудование, механизмы, их части и принадлежности; звуковая и теле-аппаратура, их части и принадлежности |
| XVII - Vehicles, aircraft, vessels and associated transport equipment | .. | .. | .. | 84,830 | 55,204 | 43,849 | XVII - Средства наземного, воздушного и водного транспорта |
| XVIII - Optical, photographic, cinematographic, measuring, checking, precision, medical or surgical instruments and apparatus; clocks and watches; musical instruments; parts and accessories thereof | .. | .. | .. | 4,057 | 3,357 | 3,045 | XVIII - Приборы, аппараты оптические, медицинские, измерительные и пр.; музыкальные инструменты; часы; их части и принадлежности |
| XIX - Arms and ammunition; parts and accessories thereof | .. | .. | .. | 166 | 101 | 66 | XIX - Оружие и боеприпасы, их части и принадлежности |
| XX - Miscellaneous manufactured articles | .. | .. | .. | 23,134 | 24,991 | 30,471 | XX - Разные промышленные товары |
| XXI - Works of art, collectors' pieces, and antiques | .. | .. | .. | 1 | 41 | 2 | XXI - Произведения искусства, предметы антиквариата |
| XXII - Services | .. | .. | .. | .. | .. | .. | XXII - Услуги |

## TABLE 3-4A. Geographical distribution of foreign trade (thousands of U.S. dollars)
## ТАБЛИЦА 3-4А. Географическое распределение внешней торговли (тысяч долларов США)



| Country or country group | Exports / Экспорт 1990 | 1991 | 1992 | 1993 | 1994 | 1995 | Imports / Импорт 1990 | 1991 | 1992 | 1993 | 1994 | 1995 | Страна или группа стран |
|---|---|---|---|---|---|---|---|---|---|---|---|---|---|
| **Total trade** | .. | .. | .. | 1,000,878 | 989,724 | 1,304,536 | .. | .. | .. | 963,961 | 1,241,491 | 1,817,721 | **Всего** |
| **CIS countries** | .. | .. | .. | 478,388 | 422,336 | 499,172 | .. | .. | .. | 365,612 | 377,043 | 511,686 | **Страны СНГ** |
| Armenia | .. | .. | .. | 2,083 | 1,035 | 192 | .. | .. | .. | 60 | 13 | 11 | Армения |
| Azerbaijan | .. | .. | .. | 14,659 | 5,628 | 2,039 | .. | .. | .. | 8,276 | 1,129 | 587 | Азербайджан |
| Belarus | .. | .. | .. | 50,104 | 42,697 | 56,771 | .. | .. | .. | 34,545 | 37,919 | 57,251 | Беларусь |
| Georgia | .. | .. | .. | 1,204 | 498 | 234 | .. | .. | .. | 357 | 90 | 10 | Грузия |
| Kazakstan | .. | .. | .. | 22,379 | 19,111 | 15,315 | .. | .. | .. | 10,186 | 2,715 | 8,042 | Казахстан |
| Kyrgyz Republic | .. | .. | .. | 1,388 | 476 | 1,911 | .. | .. | .. | 305 | 292 | 37 | Киргизстан |
| Moldova | .. | .. | .. | 5,081 | 3,692 | 4,716 | .. | .. | .. | 4,152 | 3,185 | 6,484 | Молдова |
| Russia | .. | .. | .. | 299,178 | 278,340 | 330,316 | .. | .. | .. | 276,580 | 292,085 | 393,355 | Россия |
| Tajikistan | .. | .. | .. | 1,549 | 524 | 1,380 | .. | .. | .. | 498 | 841 | 870 | Таджикистан |
| Turkmenistan | .. | .. | .. | 11,541 | 1,991 | 1,213 | .. | .. | .. | 935 | 497 | 910 | Туркменистан |
| Ukraine | .. | .. | .. | 60,568 | 58,375 | 71,458 | .. | .. | .. | 28,626 | 37,566 | 41,780 | Украина |
| Uzbekistan | .. | .. | .. | 8,654 | 9,969 | 13,627 | .. | .. | .. | 1,092 | 711 | 2,349 | Узбекистан |
| **Non-CIS countries** | .. | .. | .. | 522,490 | 567,388 | 805,364 | .. | .. | .. | 457,703 | 772,528 | 1,306,035 | **Остальной мир** |
| **Europe** | .. | .. | .. | 446,212 | 519,458 | 763,469 | .. | .. | .. | 409,112 | 682,426 | 1,202,380 | **Европа** |
| Austria | .. | .. | .. | 2,361 | 20,536 | 3,563 | .. | .. | .. | 5,284 | 9,066 | 21,776 | Австрия |
| Belgium | .. | .. | .. | 14,609 | 4,565 | 11,868 | .. | .. | .. | 4,592 | 13,245 | 24,972 | Бельгия |
| Bulgaria | .. | .. | .. | 4,686 | 1,346 | 1,942 | .. | .. | .. | 1,690 | 4,036 | 3,930 | Болгария |
| Czech Republic | .. | .. | .. | 4,280 | 4,770 | 6,764 | .. | .. | .. | 4,133 | 12,089 | 14,429 | Чешская Республика |
| Denmark | .. | .. | .. | 9,109 | 15,515 | 26,315 | .. | .. | .. | 17,857 | 28,593 | 52,805 | Дания |
| Estonia | .. | .. | .. | 19,163 | 25,753 | 40,600 | .. | .. | .. | 30,691 | 43,729 | 91,660 | Эстония |
| Finland | .. | .. | .. | 19,495 | 23,893 | 42,053 | .. | .. | .. | 39,650 | 106,080 | 189,847 | Финляндия |
| Former Yugoslavia | .. | .. | .. | 1,389 | 1,832 | 735 | .. | .. | .. | 1,568 | 1,994 | 2,886 | Быв. Югославия |
| France | .. | .. | .. | 10,584 | 14,078 | 16,889 | .. | .. | .. | 6,130 | 18,876 | 28,235 | Франция |
| Germany | .. | .. | .. | 66,593 | 104,381 | 177,753 | .. | .. | .. | 94,407 | 168,757 | 280,741 | Германия |
| Hungary | .. | .. | .. | 6,262 | 4,640 | 2,503 | .. | .. | .. | 2,693 | 7,877 | 8,343 | Венгрия |
| Iceland | .. | .. | .. | 207 | 603 | 1,952 | .. | .. | .. | 25 | 90 | 191 | Исландия |
| Ireland | .. | .. | .. | 1,071 | 9,956 | 14,036 | .. | .. | .. | 579 | 2,868 | 5,779 | Ирландия |
| Italy | .. | .. | .. | 13,837 | 9,434 | 14,896 | .. | .. | .. | 8,412 | 22,324 | 42,177 | Италия |
| Latvia | .. | .. | .. | .. | .. | .. | .. | .. | .. | .. | .. | .. | Латвия |
| Lithuania | .. | .. | .. | 43,485 | 54,735 | 72,179 | .. | .. | .. | 86,919 | 73,851 | 100,568 | Литва |
| Netherlands | .. | .. | .. | 76,694 | 18,655 | 25,653 | .. | .. | .. | 10,261 | 19,382 | 55,461 | Нидерланды |
| Norway | .. | .. | .. | 3,040 | 6,397 | 22,581 | .. | .. | .. | 1,637 | 6,772 | 13,792 | Норвегия |
| Poland | .. | .. | .. | 29,871 | 16,015 | 32,417 | .. | .. | .. | 8,518 | 19,916 | 34,478 | Польша |
| Romania | .. | .. | .. | 715 | 360 | 232 | .. | .. | .. | 241 | 207 | 173 | Румыния |
| Slovak Republic | .. | .. | .. | .. | .. | 2,427 | .. | .. | .. | .. | .. | 6,452 | Словацская Республика |
| Spain | .. | .. | .. | 1,515 | 913 | 1,576 | .. | .. | .. | 2,519 | 5,670 | 7,852 | Испания |
| Sweden | .. | .. | .. | 63,273 | 68,440 | 121,208 | .. | .. | .. | 54,395 | 79,797 | 145,981 | Швеция |
| Switzerland | .. | .. | .. | 3,746 | 13,566 | 3,916 | .. | .. | .. | 6,513 | 6,428 | 16,195 | Швейцария |
| United Kingdom | .. | .. | .. | 48,589 | 96,127 | 118,387 | .. | .. | .. | 19,661 | 29,660 | 49,421 | Великобритания |

**TABLE 3-4A. Geographical distribution of foreign trade (thousands of U.S. dollars)**
**ТАБЛИЦА 3-4А. Географическое распределение внешней торговли (тысяч долларов США)**

| Country or country group | Exports / Экспорт 1990 | 1991 | 1992 | 1993 | 1994 | 1995 | Imports / Импорт 1990 | 1991 | 1992 | 1993 | 1994 | 1995 | Страна или группа стран |
|---|---|---|---|---|---|---|---|---|---|---|---|---|---|
| Other Europe | .. | .. | .. | 1,638 | 2,948 | 1,024 | .. | .. | .. | 737 | 1,119 | 4,236 | Остальные стараны Европы |
| **Asia** | .. | .. | .. | 52,804 | 24,341 | 15,925 | .. | .. | .. | 26,432 | 37,645 | 36,499 | **Азия** |
| Afghanistan | .. | .. | .. | 535 | 167 | 91 | .. | .. | .. | 108 | 65 | 203 | Афганистан |
| China | .. | .. | .. | 9,287 | 4,825 | 75 | .. | .. | .. | 889 | 1,415 | 1,766 | Китай |
| India | .. | .. | .. | 28 | 535 | 26 | .. | .. | .. | 3,018 | 3,354 | 3,310 | Индия |
| Iraq | .. | .. | .. | .. | .. | .. | .. | .. | .. | .. | .. | .. | Ирак |
| Japan | .. | .. | .. | 6,604 | 3,766 | 3,823 | .. | .. | .. | 10,500 | 15,404 | 10,553 | Япония |
| Korea, Dem. People's Rep. | .. | .. | .. | 4 | 1 | 862 | .. | .. | .. | 1,392 | 2,473 | 1,814 | КНДР |
| Korea, Rep. of | .. | .. | .. | 2 | 15 | 259 | .. | .. | .. | 286 | 931 | 2,548 | Южная Корея |
| Mongolia | .. | .. | .. | .. | 313 | 174 | .. | .. | .. | .. | .. | .. | МНР |
| Syrian Arab Republic | .. | .. | .. | 12 | 87 | 106 | .. | .. | .. | 4 | 4 | 11 | Сирия |
| Turkey | .. | .. | .. | 3,601 | 618 | 1,374 | .. | .. | .. | 4,817 | 2,281 | 1,826 | Турция |
| Viet Nam | .. | .. | .. | 166 | 95 | 859 | .. | .. | .. | 63 | 77 | 111 | Вьетнам |
| Other Asia | .. | .. | .. | 32,565 | 13,919 | 8,276 | .. | .. | .. | 5,355 | 11,641 | 14,377 | Остальные страны Азии |
| **America** | .. | .. | .. | 13,519 | 17,679 | 18,495 | .. | .. | .. | 20,457 | 46,239 | 49,513 | **Сев. и Южная Америка** |
| Canada | .. | .. | .. | 594 | 807 | 1,037 | .. | .. | .. | 1,097 | 1,155 | 2,937 | Канада |
| Cuba | .. | .. | .. | 54 | 95 | 10 | .. | .. | .. | 333 | 14,136 | 35 | Куба |
| United States | .. | .. | .. | 6,835 | 12,000 | 17,036 | .. | .. | .. | 13,807 | 24,633 | 35,185 | США |
| Other America | .. | .. | .. | 6,036 | 4,777 | 412 | .. | .. | .. | 5,220 | 6,315 | 11,356 | Остальные |
| **Africa** | .. | .. | .. | 9,537 | 5,747 | 7,246 | .. | .. | .. | 1,680 | 3,771 | 1,872 | **Африка** |
| Egypt | .. | .. | .. | .. | .. | .. | .. | .. | .. | .. | 38 | 53 | Египет |
| Libya | .. | .. | .. | .. | .. | .. | .. | .. | .. | .. | .. | .. | Ливия |
| Other Africa | .. | .. | .. | 9,529 | 5,478 | 5,007 | .. | .. | .. | 1,680 | 3,733 | 1,819 | Остальные |
| **Rest of the World** | .. | .. | .. | 418 | 163 | 229 | .. | .. | .. | 22 | 2,447 | 15,771 | **Прочие страны мира** |
| Australia | .. | .. | .. | 410 | 157 | 229 | .. | .. | .. | 16 | 1,666 | 15,382 | Австралия |

# TABLE 3-4B. Geographical distribution of foreign trade (thousands of national currency)
# ТАБЛИЦА 3-4B. Географическое распределение внешней торговли (тысяч национальной валюты)

| Country or country group | Exports / Экспорт 1990 | 1991 | 1992 | 1993 | 1994 | 1995 | Imports / Импорт 1990 | 1991 | 1992 | 1993 | 1994 | 1995 | Страна или группа стран |
|---|---|---|---|---|---|---|---|---|---|---|---|---|---|
| **Total trade** | .. | .. | 572,666 | 675,611 | 553,437 | 688,413 | .. | .. | 541,520 | 639,247 | 694,588 | 959,636 | **Всего** |
| **CIS countries** | .. | .. | 257,717 | 321,590 | 236,375 | 263,561 | .. | .. | 203,713 | 244,380 | 211,600 | 270,847 | **Страны СНГ** |
| Armenia | .. | .. | 1,663 | 1,356 | 578 | 102 | .. | .. | 151 | 26 | 7 | 6 | Армения |
| Azerbaijan | .. | .. | 8,398 | 10,305 | 3,177 | 1,085 | .. | .. | 2,361 | 5,396 | 630 | 302 | Азербайджан |
| Belarus | .. | .. | 26,935 | 34,394 | 23,889 | 29,893 | .. | .. | 19,852 | 26,483 | 21,085 | 30,303 | Беларусь |
| Georgia | .. | .. | 1,672 | 808 | 276 | 123 | .. | .. | 456 | 273 | 50 | 5 | Грузия |
| Kazakstan | .. | .. | 10,120 | 15,279 | 10,741 | 8,104 | .. | .. | 5,844 | 6,404 | 1,529 | 4,238 | Казахстан |
| Kyrgyz Republic | .. | .. | 1,247 | 958 | 269 | 1,008 | .. | .. | 299 | 213 | 163 | 20 | Киргизстан |
| Moldova | .. | .. | 3,872 | 3,509 | 2,060 | 2,478 | .. | .. | 2,028 | 2,831 | 1,771 | 3,422 | Молдова |
| Russia | .. | .. | 148,737 | 200,105 | 155,719 | 174,386 | .. | .. | 150,825 | 181,941 | 164,178 | 208,335 | Россия |
| Tajikistan | .. | .. | 688 | 1,059 | 294 | 734 | .. | .. | 64 | 335 | 464 | 459 | Таджикистан |
| Turkmenistan | .. | .. | 1,759 | 7,855 | 1,130 | 644 | .. | .. | 1,730 | 621 | 283 | 472 | Туркменистан |
| Ukraine | .. | .. | 47,092 | 40,091 | 32,727 | 37,738 | .. | .. | 19,420 | 19,095 | 21,037 | 22,049 | Украина |
| Uzbekistan | .. | .. | 5,534 | 5,871 | 5,515 | 7,266 | .. | .. | 683 | 762 | 403 | 1,236 | Узбекистан |
| **Non-CIS countries** | .. | .. | 314,614 | 354,021 | 317,062 | 424,852 | .. | .. | 272,801 | 303,623 | 430,841 | 688,789 | **Остальной мир** |
| **Europe** | .. | .. | 285,647 | 303,843 | 289,932 | 402,762 | .. | .. | 235,919 | 279,420 | 380,565 | 634,084 | **Европа** |
| Austria | .. | .. | 3,596 | 1,578 | 11,246 | 1,881 | .. | .. | 5,401 | 3,519 | 5,063 | 11,361 | Австрия |
| Belgium | .. | .. | 32,537 | 10,688 | 2,543 | 6,218 | .. | .. | 3,132 | 4,307 | 7,431 | 13,160 | Бельгия |
| Bulgaria | .. | .. | 1,626 | 3,098 | 754 | 1,017 | .. | .. | 1,424 | 1,016 | 2,265 | 2,073 | Болгария |
| Czech Republic | .. | .. | 3,808 | 2,893 | 2,672 | 3,576 | .. | .. | 4,091 | 2,636 | 6,768 | 7,618 | Чешская Республика |
| Denmark | .. | .. | 4,360 | 5,997 | 8,665 | 13,878 | .. | .. | 4,360 | 11,778 | 15,976 | 27,753 | Дания |
| Estonia | .. | .. | 7,557 | 13,060 | 14,360 | 21,429 | .. | .. | 34,667 | 25,249 | 24,412 | 48,507 | Эстония |
| Finland | .. | .. | 21,267 | 13,601 | 13,327 | 22,188 | .. | .. | 14,032 | 26,928 | 59,102 | 100,065 | Финляндия |
| Former Yugoslavia | .. | .. | 1,763 | 969 | 1,054 | 385 | .. | .. | 3,919 | 1,131 | 1,112 | 1,516 | Быв. Югославия |
| France | .. | .. | 7,009 | 6,991 | 7,845 | 8,839 | .. | .. | 4,676 | 5,216 | 10,521 | 14,891 | Франция |
| Germany | .. | .. | 45,492 | 44,548 | 58,271 | 93,662 | .. | .. | 81,176 | 63,679 | 94,011 | 147,825 | Германия |
| Hungary | .. | .. | 5,640 | 4,226 | 2,614 | 1,324 | .. | .. | 2,755 | 1,746 | 4,410 | 4,398 | Венгрия |
| Iceland | .. | .. | .. | 137 | 335 | 1,035 | .. | .. | .. | 14 | 51 | 101 | Исландия |
| Ireland | .. | .. | 60 | 691 | 5,478 | 7,378 | .. | .. | 14 | 377 | 1,616 | 3,078 | Ирландия |
| Italy | .. | .. | 4,337 | 9,025 | 5,290 | 7,868 | .. | .. | 3,349 | 4,881 | 12,416 | 22,212 | Италия |
| Latvia | .. | .. | .. | .. | .. | .. | .. | .. | .. | .. | .. | .. | Латвия |
| Lithuania | .. | .. | 20,711 | 28,870 | 30,694 | 38,148 | .. | .. | 17,028 | 61,228 | 41,243 | 53,246 | Литва |
| Netherlands | .. | .. | 42,832 | 55,071 | 10,402 | 13,546 | .. | .. | 18,946 | 6,563 | 10,852 | 29,223 | Нидерланды |
| Norway | .. | .. | 1,643 | 1,983 | 3,544 | 11,871 | .. | .. | 330 | 851 | 3,787 | 7,319 | Норвегия |
| Poland | .. | .. | 12,923 | 19,960 | 8,988 | 17,191 | .. | .. | 6,774 | 6,254 | 11,115 | 18,234 | Польша |
| Romania | .. | .. | 345 | 501 | 204 | 121 | .. | .. | 126 | 157 | 117 | 91 | Румыния |
| Slovak Republic | .. | .. | .. | .. | .. | 1,277 | .. | .. | .. | .. | .. | 3,403 | Словацкая Республика |
| Spain | .. | .. | 2,447 | 988 | 506 | 825 | .. | .. | 677 | 1,558 | 3,164 | 4,168 | Испания |
| Sweden | .. | .. | 43,063 | 43,781 | 38,114 | 64,067 | .. | .. | 20,548 | 33,806 | 44,494 | 76,957 | Швеция |
| Switzerland | .. | .. | 1,248 | 2,470 | 7,514 | 2,118 | .. | .. | 4,992 | 4,191 | 3,557 | 8,527 | Швейцария |

**TABLE 3-4B. Geographical distribution of foreign trade (thousands of national currency)**

**ТАБЛИЦА 3-4B. Географическое распределение внешней торговли (тысяч национальной валюты)**

| Country or country group | Exports Экспорт 1990 | 1991 | 1992 | 1993 | 1994 | 1995 | Imports Импорт 1990 | 1991 | 1992 | 1993 | 1994 | 1995 | Страна или группа стран |
|---|---|---|---|---|---|---|---|---|---|---|---|---|---|
| United Kingdom | .. | .. | 20,059 | 31,648 | 53,894 | 62,377 | .. | .. | 3,375 | 11,924 | 16,473 | 26,109 | Великобритания |
| Other Europe | .. | .. | 1,324 | 1,069 | 1,618 | 543 | .. | .. | 127 | 411 | 2,609 | 2,251 | Остальные стараны Европы |
| **Asia** | .. | .. | 20,789 | 35,345 | 13,920 | 8,451 | .. | .. | 13,552 | 12,579 | 20,981 | 19,225 | **Азия** |
| Afghanistan | .. | .. | 251 | 407 | 92 | 48 | .. | .. | .. | 61 | 38 | 109 | Афганистан |
| China | .. | .. | 6,059 | 7,070 | 2,807 | 38 | .. | .. | 1,290 | 285 | 785 | 932 | Китай |
| India | .. | .. | 117 | 18 | 295 | 13 | .. | .. | 1,928 | 1,895 | 1,882 | 1,752 | Индия |
| Iraq | .. | .. | .. | .. | .. | .. | .. | .. | .. | .. | .. | .. | Ирак |
| Japan | .. | .. | 4,091 | 4,423 | 2,125 | 2,018 | .. | .. | 4,201 | 2,773 | 8,556 | 5,515 | Япония |
| Korea, Dem. People's Rep. | .. | .. | .. | 3 | 1 | 458 | .. | .. | 245 | 505 | 1,387 | 957 | КНДР |
| Korea, Rep. of | .. | .. | 3 | 2 | 9 | 139 | .. | .. | 302 | 5 | 514 | 1,348 | Южная Корея |
| Mongolia | .. | .. | 28 | .. | 173 | 93 | .. | .. | 139 | .. | .. | .. | МНР |
| Syrian Arab Republic | .. | .. | 169 | 9 | 51 | 55 | .. | .. | .. | .. | 2 | 6 | Сирия |
| Turkey | .. | .. | 100 | 2,332 | 360 | 726 | .. | .. | 3,006 | 4,649 | 1,273 | 970 | Турция |
| Viet Nam | .. | .. | 0 | 114 | 52 | 460 | .. | .. | .. | 17 | 44 | 58 | Вьетнам |
| Other Asia | .. | .. | 9,971 | 20,967 | 7,955 | 4,403 | .. | .. | 2,441 | 2,389 | 6,500 | 7,578 | Остальные страны Азии |
| **America** | .. | .. | 5,863 | 8,692 | 9,845 | 9,729 | .. | .. | 21,080 | 11,258 | 25,803 | 26,069 | **Сев. и Южная Америка** |
| Canada | .. | .. | 307 | 377 | 448 | 548 | .. | .. | 4,552 | 502 | 641 | 1,552 | Канада |
| Cuba | .. | .. | 2,374 | 33 | 56 | 5 | .. | .. | 2,077 | 197 | 7,870 | 18 | Куба |
| United States | .. | .. | 2,120 | 4,338 | 6,721 | 8,960 | .. | .. | 14,079 | 7,648 | 13,771 | 18,596 | США |
| Other America | .. | .. | 1,062 | 3,944 | 2,620 | 216 | .. | .. | 372 | 2,911 | 3,521 | 5,903 | Остальные |
| **Africa** | .. | .. | 1,962 | 5,869 | 3,274 | 3,788 | .. | .. | 2,229 | 357 | 2,119 | 989 | **Африка** |
| Egypt | .. | .. | .. | .. | .. | .. | .. | .. | 9 | .. | 22 | 28 | Египет |
| Libya | .. | .. | .. | .. | .. | .. | .. | .. | .. | .. | .. | .. | Ливия |
| Other Africa | .. | .. | 1,622 | 5,860 | 3,127 | 2,624 | .. | .. | 2,220 | 357 | 2,097 | 961 | Остальные |
| **Rest of the World** | .. | .. | 353 | 272 | 91 | 122 | .. | .. | 21 | 9 | 1,373 | 8,422 | **Прочие страны мира** |
| Australia | .. | .. | 300 | 267 | 88 | 122 | .. | .. | .. | 9 | 930 | 8,217 | Австралия |

**TABLE 4-1. General government budget revenue (thousands of national currency)**
**ТАБЛИЦА 4-1. Доходы государственного бюджета (тысяч национальной валюты)**

| Type of revenue | 1990 | 1991 | 1992 | 1993 | 1994 | 1995 | Вид доходов |
|---|---|---|---|---|---|---|---|
| **Total revenue and grants** | 22,875 | 37,985 | .. | .. | 705,580 | 909,070 | **Всего доходов и безвозм. поступл.** |
| Grants | 265 | .. | .. | .. | 56,080 | 55,450 | Безвозмездные поступления |
| Total Revenue | 22,610 | 37,985 | 144,165 | 495,729 | 649,500 | 853,620 | Всего доходов |
| **Current revenue** | 22,595 | 37,955 | 144,165 | 495,729 | 647,300 | 831,040 | **Текущие доходы** |
| Tax revenue | 21,060 | 33,225 | 138,195 | 471,286 | 604,770 | 737,830 | Доход от налогов |
| Taxes on income and profits | 6,105 | 10,455 | 41,910 | 106,077 | 172,460 | 180,720 | Налоги на доходы и прибыль |
| Individual | .. | .. | .. | .. | 90,860 | 133,170 | Физические лица |
| Corporate | 6,105 | 10,455 | 41,910 | 106,077 | 81,600 | 47,550 | Предприятия и организации |
| Social security contributions | 405 | .. | .. | 143,475 | 180,610 | 211,970 | Отчисление на соцстрах. |
| Taxes on payroll or work force | 3,420 | .. | 27,410 | 57,250 | .. | .. | Налоги на заработную плату и рабочую силу |
| Taxes on the use of labor force | 590 | .. | .. | | .. | .. | Плата за трудовые ресурсы |
| Taxes on increases in wages and salaries | 35 | .. | 620 | 1,748 | .. | .. | Налог с прироста средств на оплату труда |
| Other payroll/work force taxes | 2,795 | 5,155 | 26,790 | 55,502 | .. | .. | Другие налоги на зарплату и рабочую силу |
| Taxes on property | 100 | 1,990 | 5,080 | 17,486 | 21,860 | 25,850 | Налоги на собственность |
| Taxes on immovable property | 20 | 1,990 | 1,930 | 10,574 | 12,400 | 15,060 | Налоги на недвижимое имущество |
| Buildings | 20 | 825 | .. | .. | .. | .. | Налог с владельцев строении |
| Land | .. | 1,165 | .. | .. | .. | .. | Земельныи налог |
| Estate, inheritance, and gift taxes | .. | .. | 3,120 | 6,912 | 9,460 | 10,790 | Налоги на наследство, подарки |
| Other property taxes | 80 | .. | 30 | .. | .. | .. | Другие налоги на имущество |
| Domestic taxes on goods and services | 10,700 | 14,410 | 56,165 | 114,640 | 206,430 | 276,510 | Внутренние налоги на товары и услуги |
| General sales, turnover, or value-added taxes | 10,620 | 9,035 | 33,520 | 95,378 | 174,250 | 219,860 | Налог с продаж. с оборота или на добав. стоим. |
| Excises | .. | 4,580 | 19,985 | 12,104 | 29,190 | 51,560 | Акцизы |
| Profits of fiscal monopolies | .. | .. | .. | .. | .. | .. | Прибыли фискальных монополий |
| Taxes on specific services | 15 | 10 | 10 | 558 | .. | .. | Налоги на особые услуги |
| Taxes on use of goods or permission to use goods or to perform activities | 15 | 30 | 10 | 68 | .. | .. | Налоги на пользование товарами или лицензии на пользование товарами и занятие деятельностью |
| Other taxes on goods and services | 50 | 755 | 2,640 | 6,532 | 2,990 | 5,090 | Другие налоги на товары и услуги |
| Taxes on international trade and transactions | 40 | 55 | 3,090 | 20,250 | 23,410 | 18,300 | Налоги на внешнюю торговлю и операции |
| Import duties | .. | .. | .. | .. | 23,410 | 18,300 | Импортные пошлины |
| Export duties | 35 | .. | .. | .. | .. | .. | Экпортные пошлины |
| Other | 5 | 55 | .. | .. | .. | .. | Другие |
| Other taxes | 290 | 1,160 | 4,540 | 12,108 | .. | 24,480 | Прочие налоги |
| Nontax revenue | 1,535 | 4,730 | 5,970 | 24,443 | 42,530 | 93,210 | Неналоговые доходы |
| **Capital revenue** | 15 | 30 | .. | .. | 2,200 | 22,580 | **Капитальные доходы** |

## TABLE 4-2. General government budget expenditure by economic type (ths. of national currency)
## ТАБЛИЦА 4-2. Расходы государственного бюджета по экономическим типам (тыс. национальной валюты)

| Type of expenditure or debt holder | 1989 | 1990 | 1991 | 1992 | 1993 | 1994 | 1995 | Всего расходов |
|---|---|---|---|---|---|---|---|---|
| **Total expenditure by economic type** | 16,275 | 21,880 | 31,270 | 172,510 | 504,379 | 791,680 | 989,100 | **Всего расходов по экономическим типам** |
| **Current expenditure** | 13,040 | 18,135 | 27,820 | 145,410 | 465,337 | 755,040 | 943,430 | **Текущие расходы** |
| Expenditure on goods and services | 2,600 | 2,965 | 8,760 | 88,815 | 196,804 | 272,200 | 422,010 | Расходы на товары и услуги |
| Wages and salaries | 1,640 | 1,895 | 5,020 | 44,745 | 92,539 | 131,700 | 203,900 | Заработная плата |
| Employer contributions | 100 | 120 | 1,530 | 14,785 | 33,784 | .. | .. | Отчисление на социальное страхование |
| Other Purchases of goods and services | 860 | 950 | 2,210 | 29,285 | 70,481 | 140,500 | 218,110 | Другие покупки товаров и услуг |
| Interest payments | .. | .. | .. | 1,370 | 3,596 | 8,910 | 27,290 | Выплаты процентов |
| Domestic debt | .. | .. | .. | 1,370 | 3,596 | .. | .. | По внутреннему долгу |
| Foreign debt | .. | .. | .. | .. | .. | .. | .. | По внешншму долгу |
| Subsidies and other current transfers | 8,425 | 10,780 | 4,990 | 11,650 | 21,487 | 426,130 | 482,670 | Субсидии на другие текущие трансферты |
| Subsidies | 6,425 | 8,535 | 4,615 | 7,110 | 14,749 | .. | 10,330 | Субсидии |
| Agricultural subsidies | 6,330 | 8,385 | 4,160 | 4,145 | 9,280 | .. | 8,680 | Субсидии на сельское хозяиство |
| Other current transfers | 2,000 | 2,245 | 375 | 4,540 | 6,738 | 426,130 | 472,340 | Другие текущие трансферты |
| Other | 2,015 | 4,390 | 14,070 | 43,575 | 243,450 | 47,800 | 11,460 | Прочие расходы |
| **Capital expenditure** | 3,235 | 3,745 | 3,450 | 27,100 | 39,042 | 36,640 | 45,670 | **Капитальные расходы** |
| Acquisition of fixed capital assets | .. | .. | .. | .. | .. | 30,360 | 40,310 | Приобретение основного капитала |
| Capital transfers | 3,235 | 3,745 | 3,450 | 27,100 | 39,042 | 5,560 | 5,110 | Капитальные трансферты |
| Other | .. | .. | .. | .. | .. | 120 | 250 | Другие капитальные расходы |
| **Surplus/deficit (-)** | 665 | 995 | 6,715 | -28,345 | -8,650 | -86,100 | -80,030 | **Превыш. доходов над расходами/дефицит(-)** |
| **Financing by type of debt holder** | .. | .. | .. | .. | .. | 86,100 | 80,030 | **Финансирование по типам кредиторов** |
| **Foreign (net)** | .. | .. | .. | .. | .. | 35,000 | 39,150 | **Зарубежные кредиторы (сальдо)** |
| From international development institutions | .. | .. | .. | .. | .. | .. | 970 | Международные организации |
| From foreign governments | .. | .. | .. | .. | .. | .. | .. | Правительства иностранных государств |
| Other borrowing abroad | .. | .. | .. | .. | .. | 35,000 | 38,180 | Другие зарубежные кредиторы |
| **Domestic (net)** | .. | .. | .. | 28,345 | 8,650 | 51,100 | 40,880 | **Внутренние кредиторы (сальдо)** |
| From monetary authorities | .. | .. | .. | 8,100 | 28 | 13,870 | -20,600 | Органы денежного обращения |
| From deposit money banks | .. | .. | .. | .. | .. | .. | .. | Депозитные денежные банки |
| Other domestic borrowing | .. | .. | .. | 20,245 | 8,622 | 37,230 | 61,480 | Другие внутренние кредиторы |
| *Memo items:* | | | | | | | | *Справочно:* |
| Extrabudgetary surplus/ Deficit (-) not included above | .. | .. | 230 | 170 | .. | .. | .. | Превышение доходов над расходами/дефицит (-) по внебюджетным фондам, не включенным выше |
| Total surplus/deficit (-) including extrabudgetary accounts | 665 | 995 | 6,945 | -28,175 | -8,650 | .. | .. | Итого превышение доходов над расходами/дефицит, включая счета внебюджетных фондов |

LATVIA

**TABLE 5-1. Agricultural production (thousands of national currency, current prices)**

**ТАБЛИЦА 5-1. Сельскохозяйственная продукция (тысяч нац. валюты, текущие цены)**

| Item | 1990 | 1991 | 1992 | 1993 | 1994 | 1995 | Статьи |
|---|---|---|---|---|---|---|---|
| **Total gross agricultural production** | 20,660 | 44,407 | 280,390 | 365,400 | 411,327 | 443,153 | **Валовая продукция сельского хозяйства - всего** |
| **Crops** | 7,107 | 16,936 | 121,970 | 162,117 | 170,704 | 202,031 | **Продукция растениеводства** |
| Grains | 1,642 | 3,912 | 41,820 | 47,794 | 45,545 | 39,383 | Зерно |
| Potatoes | 1,450 | 3,455 | 23,595 | 43,415 | 40,970 | 67,627 | Картофель |
| Vegetables | 583 | 1,389 | 20,940 | 28,455 | 34,950 | 71,526 | Овощи |
| Fruits (excluding grapes) | .. | .. | 2,495 | 4,029 | 5,955 | 8,738 | Фрукты (без винограда) |
| Grapes | .. | .. | .. | .. | .. | .. | Виноград |
| Tobacco | .. | .. | .. | .. | .. | .. | Табак |
| Cotton | .. | .. | .. | .. | .. | .. | Хлопок |
| Sugarbeets | 113 | 271 | 7,840 | 4,827 | 6,485 | 5,250 | Сахарная свекла |
| Oilseeds | .. | .. | .. | .. | .. | .. | Семена масличных культур |
| Other | 3,319 | 7,909 | 25,280 | 33,597 | 36,799 | 9,507 | Прочие |
| **Animal husbandry** | 13,553 | 27,471 | 158,420 | 203,283 | 240,623 | 241,122 | **Продукция животноводства** |
| Livestock | 7,300 | 14,807 | 88,103 | 105,107 | 133,035 | 136,445 | Мясное животноводство |
| Cattle | 3,350 | 6,785 | 39,240 | 33,258 | 50,735 | 49,800 | Крупный рогатый скот |
| Pigs | 3,096 | 6,263 | 41,116 | 58,759 | 66,300 | 74,760 | Свиньи |
| Sheep and goats | 128 | 275 | 1,420 | 1,195 | 1,470 | 570 | Овцы и козы |
| Poultry | 701 | 1,428 | 5,887 | 10,554 | 13,015 | 11,315 | Птица |
| Other | 25 | 56 | 440 | 1,341 | 1,515 | 0 | Прочие |
| Milk | 4,884 | 9,890 | 54,749 | 75,423 | 78,985 | 84,665 | Молоко |
| Eggs | 510 | 1,044 | 7,880 | 11,436 | 13,980 | 14,410 | Яйца |
| Wool | 20 | 47 | 250 | 1,082 | 525 | 60 | Шерсть |
| Other livestock | 839 | 1,683 | 7,438 | 10,235 | 14,098 | 5,542 | Прочая |
| **Agricultural services** | .. | .. | .. | .. | .. | .. | **Сельскохозяйственные услуги** |

**TABLE 5-2. Agricultural production (thousands of constant national currency)**

**ТАБЛИЦА 5-2. Сельскохозяйственная продукция в постоянных ценах (тысяч национальной валюты)**

| Item | 1990 | 1991 | 1992 | 1993 | 1994 | 1995 | Статьи |
|---|---|---|---|---|---|---|---|
| **Total gross agricultural production** | 13,715 | 13,181 | 11,115 | 8,620 | 6,857 | 6,428 | **Валовая продукция сельского хозяйства - всего** |
| **Crops** | 3,966 | 4,177 | 3,714 | 3,706 | 2,817 | 2,614 | **Продукция растениеводства** |
| Grains | 1,029 | 806 | 730 | 786 | 545 | 475 | Зерно |
| Potatoes | 971 | 902 | 1,116 | 1,216 | 1,005 | 880 | Картофель |
| Vegetables | 271 | 321 | 289 | 227 | 205 | 225 | Овощи |
| Fruits (excluding grapes) | 107 | 311 | 213 | 417 | 315 | 265 | Фрукты (без винограда) |
| Grapes | .. | .. | .. | .. | .. | .. | Виноград |
| Tobacco | .. | .. | .. | .. | .. | .. | Табак |
| Cotton | .. | .. | .. | .. | .. | .. | Хлопок |
| Sugarbeets | 113 | 97 | 119 | 77 | 60 | 65 | Сахарная свекла |
| Oilseeds | 5 | 10 | 5 | 5 | 5 | 10 | Семена масличных культур |
| Other | 1,470 | 1,730 | 1,242 | 978 | 680 | 694 | Прочие |
| **Animal husbandry** | 9,749 | 9,004 | 7,401 | 4,914 | 4,040 | 3,814 | **Продукция животноводства** |
| Livestock | 5,146 | 4,749 | 3,753 | 1,995 | 1,565 | 1,720 | Мясное животноводство |
| Cattle | 2,508 | 2,394 | 2,035 | 1,035 | 790 | 760 | Крупный рогатый скот |
| Pigs | 1,985 | 1,734 | 1,339 | 720 | 595 | 780 | Свиньи |
| Sheep and goats | 70 | 73 | 58 | 45 | 30 | 30 | Овцы и козы |
| Poultry | 564 | 528 | 303 | 185 | 144 | 150 | Птица |
| Other | 19 | 20 | 18 | 10 | 6 | 0 | Прочие |
| Milk | 3,751 | 3,450 | 3,041 | 2,640 | 2,285 | 1,870 | Молоко |
| Eggs | 392 | 364 | 292 | 185 | 150 | 200 | Яйца |
| Wool | 15 | 16 | 16 | 15 | 10 | 5 | Шерсть |
| Other livestock | 445 | 425 | 299 | 79 | 30 | 19 | Прочая |
| **Agricultural services** | .. | .. | .. | .. | .. | .. | **Сельскохозяйственные услуги** |

**TABLE 5-3. Production and average yield of major agricultural crops**
**ТАБЛИЦА 5-3. Производство и урожайность важнейших сельскохозяйственных культур**

| Crop | 1990 | 1991 | 1992 | 1993 | 1994 | 1995 | Сельскохозяйственные культуры |
|---|---|---|---|---|---|---|---|
| **Production (thousands of tons)** | | | | | | | Производство (тыс. тонн) |
| Grain - Cleanweight | 1,622 | 1,336 | 1,152 | 1,235 | 901 | 694 | Зерно в чистом весе |
| Winter wheat | 370 | 186 | 324 | 305 | 151 | 199 | Пшеница - озимая |
| Spring wheat | 2 | 4 | 8 | 33 | 48 | 45 | яровая |
| Coarse grain | .. | .. | .. | .. | .. | .. | Зерно в физическом весе |
| Rye | 324 | 146 | 295 | 341 | 113 | 71 | Рожь |
| Corn | 0 | 0 | 0 | 0 | 0 | 0 | Кукуруза |
| Winter barley | 4 | 3 | 7 | 10 | 4 | 13 | Ячмень - озимый |
| Spring barley | 693 | 762 | 426 | 446 | 477 | 271 | яровой |
| Oats | 176 | 177 | 60 | 74 | 89 | 73 | Овес |
| Millet | 0 | 0 | 0 | 0 | 0 | 0 | Просо |
| Rice | 0 | 0 | 0 | 0 | 0 | 0 | Рис |
| Flax | 3 | 4 | 1 | .. | .. | 1 | Лен |
| Oilseeds | 2 | 2 | 1 | .. | .. | .. | Семена масличных культур |
| Cotton (raw) | 0 | 0 | 0 | 0 | 0 | 0 | Хлопок - сырец |
| Cotton fiber | 0 | 0 | 0 | 0 | 0 | 0 | волокно |
| Sugarbeets | 439 | 378 | 463 | 298 | 228 | 250 | Сахарная свекла |
| Potatoes | 1,016 | 944 | 1,167 | 1,272 | 1,045 | 864 | Картофель |
| Pulses | 23 | 21 | 9 | 4 | 5 | 5 | Бобовые |
| Vegetables | 169 | 209 | 251 | 285 | 233 | 224 | Овощи |
| Fruit | 23 | 100 | 66 | 118 | 34 | 77 | Фрукты |
| Grapes | 0 | 0 | 0 | 0 | 0 | 0 | Виноград |
| Other | 23 | 100 | 66 | 118 | 34 | 77 | Прочие |
| Corn (silage and greenchop) | 967 | 785 | 318 | 138 | 27 | 13 | Кукуруза (на силос и зеленый корм) |
| Hay | 1,405 | 1,711 | 2,031 | 1,756 | 1,871 | 1,215 | Сено |
| **Average yield (kilograms per hectare)** | | | | | | | Ср. урожайность (кг с га) |
| Grain | 2,360 | 2,030 | 1,640 | 1,770 | 1,840 | 1,690 | Зерно |
| Winter wheat | 2,630 | 2,660 | 2,630 | 2,000 | 2,070 | 2,320 | Пшеница - озимая |
| Spring wheat | 2,030 | 2,530 | 1,500 | 2,040 | 2,230 | 1,860 | яровая |
| Coarse grain | .. | .. | .. | .. | .. | .. | Зерно в физическом весе |
| Rye | 2,480 | 2,110 | 2,240 | 1,820 | 1,810 | 1,770 | Рожь |
| Corn | 0 | 0 | 0 | 0 | 0 | 0 | Кукуруза |
| Winter barley | 2,940 | 2,700 | 2,200 | 1,930 | 1,840 | 1,720 | Ячмень - озимый |
| Spring barley | 2,260 | 1,920 | 1,230 | 1,650 | 1,810 | 1,380 | яровой |
| Oats | 2,140 | 1,910 | 860 | 1,520 | 1,650 | 1,610 | Овес |
| Millet | 0 | 0 | 0 | 0 | 0 | 0 | Просо |
| Rice | 0 | 0 | 0 | 0 | 0 | 0 | Рис |
| Flax | 250 | 410 | 190 | 110 | 260 | 550 | Лен |
| Oilseeds | 130 | 240 | 80 | 140 | 200 | 310 | Семена масличных культур |
| Cotton (raw) | 0 | 0 | 0 | 0 | 0 | 0 | Хлопок - сырец |
| Cotton fiber | 0 | 0 | 0 | 0 | 0 | 0 | волокно |
| Sugarbeets | 29,900 | 25,800 | 18,700 | 24,700 | 19,000 | 26,400 | Сахарная свекла |
| Potatoes | 12,700 | 11,500 | 12,000 | 14,500 | 13,000 | 13,500 | Картофель |
| Pulses | 2,160 | 2,300 | 1,290 | 1,570 | 1,630 | 1,600 | Бобовые |
| Vegetables | 14,200 | 15,100 | 12,400 | 14,800 | 12,800 | 1,220 | Овощи |
| Fruit | .. | .. | .. | .. | .. | .. | Фрукты |
| Grapes | 0 | 0 | 0 | 0 | 0 | 0 | Виноград |
| Other | 940 | 4,350 | 3,680 | 6,570 | 1,890 | 3,440 | Прочие |
| Corn (silage and greenchop) | 21,600 | 19,900 | 12,800 | 14,900 | 9,700 | 21,900 | Кукуруза (на силос и зеленый корм) |
| Hay | 3,890 | 4,270 | 2,910 | 2,220 | 2,580 | 2,960 | Сено |

**TABLE 5-4. Main aggregates of animal husbandry**
**ТАБЛИЦА 5-4. Основные показатели животноводства**

| Type of livestock or product | 1990 | 1991 | 1992 | 1993 | 1994 | 1995 | Направление животноводства или вид продукции |
|---|---|---|---|---|---|---|---|
| **Livestock (thousands of heads)** | | | | | | | **Поголовье скота (тысяч голов)** |
| Cattle | 1,439 | 1,383 | 1,144 | 678 | 551 | 537 | Крупный рогатый скот |
| of which: Cows | 535 | 531 | 482 | 351 | 312 | 292 | в том числе коровы |
| Pigs | 1,401 | 1,247 | 867 | 482 | 501 | 553 | Свиньи |
| Sheep and goats | 170 | 190 | 171 | 120 | 94 | 81 | Овцы и козы |
| of which: Goats | 5 | 6 | 6 | 6 | 7 | 9 | в том числе козы |
| Horses | 31 | 30 | 28 | 26 | 27 | 27 | Лошади |
| Other | 10,321 | 10,395 | 5,438 | 4,124 | 3,700 | 4,198 | Прочие |
| **Animal husbandry products** | | | | | | | **Продукция животноводства** |
| Meat (thousands of tons) | 309 | 296 | 247 | 193 | 136 | 123 | Мясо (тысяч тонн) |
| Beef | 125 | 132 | 120 | 107 | 68 | 48 | Говядина |
| Pork | 138 | 126 | 101 | 68 | 54 | 63 | Свинина |
| Lamb | 4 | 4 | 4 | 4 | 2 | 1 | Баранина |
| Poultry | 40 | 33 | 21 | 13 | 11 | 11 | Птица |
| Other | 1 | 1 | 1 | 1 | 1 | 0 | Прочие виды мяса |
| Milk (thousands of tons) | 1,893 | 1,741 | 1,479 | 1,157 | 1,001 | 948 | Молоко (тысяч тонн) |
| Eggs (millions) | 819 | 761 | 596 | 389 | 360 | 421 | Яйца (миллионов штук) |
| Wool (thousands of tons) | 0 | 0 | 0 | 0 | 0 | 0 | Шерсть (тысяч тонн) |

**TABLE 6-1a. Industrial production by sector according to ISIC (million lats)**
**ТАБЛИЦА 6-1а. Промышленное производство по отраслям в соответствии с системой МСПК (млн. лат)**

| Sector | 1990 | 1991 | 1992 | 1993 | 1994 | 1995 | Отрасли |
|---|---|---|---|---|---|---|---|
| **All industry** | 52.9 | 127.0 | 841.4 | 1,051.8 | 1,076.1 | 1,193.9 | **Вся промышленность** |
| **Mining and quarrying** | 0.4 | 0.5 | 2.8 | 3.6 | 6.0 | 6.6 | **Добывающая промышленность и разработка карьеров** |
| Peat | 0.2 | 0.2 | 2.3 | 2.6 | 4.7 | 4.6 | Добыча торфа |
| Quarrying | 0.2 | 0.3 | 0.5 | 1.0 | 1.3 | 2.0 | Разработка карьеров |
| **Manufacturing** | 51.0 | 122.2 | 730.6 | 829.1 | 860.1 | 965.3 | **Обрабатывающая промышленность** |
| Food and kindered products | 13.1 | 32.9 | 265.1 | 311.0 | 334.4 | 374.1 | Производство пищевых продуктов |
| Tobacco manufactures | 0.2 | 0.5 | 3.7 | 6.3 | 6.6 | 5.3 | Производство табачных изделий |
| Textile mill products | 7.0 | 18.8 | 67.5 | 56.6 | 53.3 | 58.5 | Производство текстильных изделий |
| Clothing and fur | 2.0 | 5.9 | 17.3 | 13.9 | 16.1 | 18.7 | Производство одежды; выделка и крашение меха |
| Leather and leather products | 1.1 | 4.8 | 25.4 | 26.2 | 16.3 | 11.6 | Дубление и выделка кожи; производство чемоданов, сумок шорно-седельных изделий и обуви |
| Wood and cork excluding furniture | 1.1 | 3.0 | 29.5 | 42.2 | 66.8 | 98.4 | Производство древесины и деревянных и пробковых изделий, кроме мебели; производство изделий из соломки и плетенки |
| Paper and allied products | 0.6 | 2.4 | 12.0 | 5.9 | 4.7 | 5.9 | Производство бумаги и изделий из бумаги |
| Printingng and publishing | 0.6 | 1.7 | 5.4 | 12.0 | 20.3 | 34.8 | Издательское дело , полиграфическая промышленность и воспроизведение печатных материалов |
| Petroleum and coal products | 0.0 | 0.1 | 1.0 | 16.4 | 0.4 | 1.0 | Производство кокса продуктов нефтеперегонки и ядерного топлива |
| Chemicals and allied products | 4.5 | 9.8 | 74.1 | 67.5 | 62.7 | 74.4 | Производство химических веществ и химических продуктов |
| Rubber and plastic products | 0.3 | 1.0 | 3.8 | 4.0 | 6.1 | 7.7 | Производство резиновых и пластмассовых изделий |
| Nonmetallic mineral products | 1.9 | 5.2 | 37.3 | 26.1 | 26.8 | 25.5 | Производство прочих неметаллических минеральных продуктов |
| Metallurgy | 0.7 | 1.0 | 21.1 | 41.2 | 37.8 | 30.3 | Металлургическая промышленность |
| Metalworking excluding production of machinery and equipment | 1.3 | 2.1 | 10.1 | 9.3 | 12.4 | 20.4 | Металлообрабатывающая промышленность, кроме производства машин и обордавания |
| Production of machinery and equipment not elsewhere classified | 3.9 | 8.0 | 42.2 | 40.7 | 40.1 | 47.3 | Производство машин и оборудования не включенных в другие категории |
| Electronic-computing equipment | 0.0 | 0.1 | 0.2 | 0.4 | 2.6 | 4.1 | Производство канцелярских, бухгалтерских и электронно-вычислительных машин |
| Electrical and electronic equipment not elsewhere classified | 1.4 | 2.5 | 21.6 | 25.5 | 22.8 | 22.3 | Производство электрических машин и аппаратуры, не включенных в другие категории |
| Radio and TV equipment | 5.1 | 8.1 | 22.3 | 17.8 | 18.1 | 15.6 | Производство оборудования и аппаратуры для радио, телевидения и связи |
| Medical, physiological, and biological research equipment | 0.2 | 0.2 | 0.6 | 1.7 | 2.7 | 3.6 | Производство медицинских приборов точных и оптических инструментов, научных и прочих часов |
| Motor vehicles and trailers | 0.7 | 1.9 | 29.3 | 42.5 | 25.8 | 19.6 | Производство автомобилей, прицепов и полуприцепов |
| Transportation equipment | 1.6 | 3.4 | 19.9 | 25.4 | 41.5 | 47.4 | Производство прочего транспортного оборудования |
| Furniture and fixtures, not elsewhere classified | 3.5 | 8.6 | 20.0 | 30.8 | 32.7 | 32.7 | Производство мебели; производство готовых изделий не включенных в другие категории |
| Recycling | 0.1 | 0.2 | 1.2 | 5.6 | 9.1 | 6.1 | Вторичная переработка |
| **Electric power, gas and water supply** | 1.5 | 4.3 | 108.0 | 219.1 | 210.0 | 222.0 | **Электроэнергия , газ и водоснабжение** |
| Electric power, gas, steam, and hot water | 1.4 | 4.0 | 105.4 | 213.3 | 201.5 | 211.3 | Снабжение электроэнергией, газом, паром и горячей водой |
| Water supply system | 0.1 | 0.3 | 2.6 | 5.8 | 8.5 | 10.2 | Сбор, очистка и распределение воды |

**TABLE 6-2a. Industrial production by sector in constant prices (real growth rates)**
**ТАБЛИЦА 6-2a. Промышленное производство по отраслям в постоянных ценах (темпы прироста)**

| Sector | 1990 | 1991 | 1992 | 1993 | 1994 | 1995 | Отрасли |
|---|---|---|---|---|---|---|---|
| **All industry** | 0.8 | -0.6 | -34.5 | -32.1 | -9.9 | -3.7 | **Вся промышленность** |
| **Mining and Quarrying** | -9.3 | -11.2 | -36.2 | -32.9 | 22.5 | -16.8 | **Добывающая промышленность и разработка карьеров** |
| Peat | -11.7 | -0.6 | -19.9 | -31.0 | 27.7 | -27.4 | Добыча торфа |
| Quarrying | -7.3 | -21.4 | -63.7 | -37.7 | 5.4 | 27.7 | Разработка карьеров |
| **Manufacturing** | 0.7 | -0.5 | -35.4 | -34.9 | -12.0 | -4.5 | **Обрабатывающая промышленность** |
| Food and kindered products | -2.9 | -9.9 | -27.3 | -35.5 | -7.8 | -2.7 | Производство пищевых продуктов |
| Tobacco manufactures | -6.5 | 11.9 | -41.2 | -25.8 | -19.2 | 0.4 | Производство табачных изделий |
| Textile mill products | -1.1 | -3.3 | -45.5 | -37.9 | -19.3 | -15.6 | Производство текстильных изделий |
| Clothing and fur | 1.5 | 0.0 | -40.2 | -52.2 | 13.5 | 7.5 | Производство одежды; выделка и крашение меха |
| Leather and leather products | -7.1 | 27.0 | -27.4 | -33.3 | -33.2 | -32.7 | Дубление и выделка кожи; производство чемоданов, сумок шорно-седельных изделии и обуви |
| Wood and cork excluding furniture | -1.5 | -2.8 | -12.2 | 0.4 | 27.8 | 21.4 | Производство древесины и деревянных и пробковых изделии, кроме мебели; производство изделии из соломки и плетенки |
| Paper and allied products | -2.7 | 28.2 | -53.0 | -58.3 | -26.5 | 46.9 | Производство бумаги и изделий из бумаги |
| Printingng and publishing | 36.6 | 13.7 | -11.7 | -2.2 | -10.7 | 14.1 | Издательское дело , полиграфическая промышленность и воспроизведение печатных материалов |
| Petrolium and coal products | -1.7 | -12.3 | -30.9 | -44.8 | 34.4 | 13.6 | Производство кокса продуктов нефтеперегонки и ядерного топлива |
| Chemicals and allied products | 3.8 | 14.4 | -28.0 | -31.1 | -37.8 | -0.5 | Производство химических веществ и химических продуктов |
| Rubber and plastic products | -20.1 | 5.3 | -27.6 | -46.1 | 0.9 | 18.2 | Производство резиновых и пластмассовых изделий |
| Nonmetallic mineral products | 0.1 | -8.7 | -46.4 | -69.2 | -32.4 | -14.1 | Производство прочих неметаллических минеральных продуктов |
| Metallurgy | -1.7 | -14.6 | -42.1 | 23.6 | 12.0 | -17.8 | Металлургическая промышленность |
| Metalworking excluding production of machinery and equipment | -8.8 | 9.1 | -43.1 | -32.0 | 61.5 | -5.1 | Металлообрабатывающая промышленность, кроме производства машин и оборудавания |
| Production of machinery and equipment not elsewhere classified | -1.3 | 3.0 | -43.3 | -41.7 | -16.1 | -6.7 | Производство машин и оборудования не включенных в другие категории |
| Electronic-computing equipment | -21.5 | 118.6 | -82.4 | -17.2 | - | 118.3 | Производство канцелярских, бухгалтерских и электронно-вычислительных машин |
| Electrical and electronic equipment not elsewhere classified | 0.4 | 10.6 | -49.3 | -35.0 | -39.0 | -0.5 | Производство электрических машин и аппаратуры, не включенных в другие категории |
| Radio and TV equipment | 6.1 | 3.9 | -53.1 | -57.5 | -32.3 | -43.8 | Производство оборудования и аппаратуры для радио, телевидения и связи |
| Medical, physiological, and biological research equipment | 8.5 | -2.1 | -33.4 | 25.5 | 28.7 | -46.7 | Производство медицинских приборов точных и оптических инструментов, научных и прочих часов |
| Motor vehicles and trailers | 11.4 | 10.8 | -2.5 | -32.0 | -40.5 | -31.7 | Производство автомобилей, прицепов и полуприцепов |
| Transportation equipment | 3.4 | 5.2 | -29.0 | -31.6 | 7.4 | 1.6 | Производство прочего транспортного оборудования |
| Furniture and fixtures, not elsewhere classified | 12.3 | 1.9 | -44.4 | -14.1 | -6.6 | -9.1 | Производство мебели; производство готовых изделий не включенных в другие категории |
| Recycling | -17.3 | -10.4 | -55.8 | -36.0 | 0.2 | -57.1 | Вторичная переработка |
| **Electric power, gas and water supply** | 11.6 | -2.6 | -23.5 | -19.8 | -2.0 | -0.2 | **Электроэнергия , газ и водоснабжение** |
| Electric power, gas, steam, and hot water | 13.1 | -4.2 | -23.5 | -19.8 | -2.2 | 0.2 | Снабжение электроэнергией, газом, паром и горячей -водой |
| Water supply system | -1.9 | 20.3 | -25.5 | -20.6 | 4.8 | -9.2 | Сбор, очистка и распределение воды |

TABLE 6-3. Primary energy supply (million tons oil equivalent)

ТАБЛИЦА 6-3. Ресурсы первичных видов энергии (млн. тонн нефтяного эквивалента)

LATVIA

| Item | | 1990 | 1991 | 1992 | 1993 | 1994 | 1995 | Статьи | |
|---|---|---|---|---|---|---|---|---|---|
| **Primary production** | | | | | | | | **Производство первичной энергии** | |
| Coal and lignite (hard and brown) | | .. | .. | .. | .. | .. | .. | Уголь каменный и бурый | |
| Crude oil | | .. | .. | .. | .. | .. | .. | Нефть | |
| Gas | | .. | .. | .. | .. | .. | .. | Газ | |
| Nuclear | | .. | .. | .. | .. | .. | .. | Атомная энергия | |
| Hydro/geothermal | | 0.387 | 0.282 | 0.216 | 0.200 | 0.284 | 0.260 | Гидро-геотермальная | |
| Other | | 0.453 | 0.841 | 0.850 | 0.900 | 0.735 | 0.657 | Другие виды | |
| Total | | 0.840 | 1.123 | 1.066 | 1.100 | 1.019 | 0.917 | Всего | |
| **Energy trade** | | | | | | | | **Торговля энергией** | |
| Coal and lignite | Exports | 0.002 | .. | .. | 0.000 | 0.066 | 0.006 | Уголь каменный и бурый | Экспорт |
| | Imports | 0.588 | 0.507 | 0.415 | 0.400 | 0.326 | 0.169 | | Импорт |
| | Net imports | 0.586 | 0.500 | 0.400 | 0.400 | 0.260 | 0.163 | | Чистый импорт |
| Oil/oil product | Exports | 22.614 | .. | .. | 0.900 | 0.011 | 0.068 | Нефть и нефтепродукты | Экспорт |
| | Imports | 27.271 | 3.224 | 2.630 | 3.300 | 2.496 | 2.103 | | Импорт |
| | Net imports | 4.657 | 3.200 | 2.600 | 2.400 | 2.485 | 2.035 | | Чистый импорт |
| Gas | Exports | 0.121 | .. | .. | .. | 0.000 | .. | Газ | Экспорт |
| | Imports | 2.665 | 2.458 | 1.744 | 0.900 | 0.941 | 1.000 | | Импорт |
| | Net imports | 2.544 | 2.500 | 1.700 | 0.900 | 0.941 | 1.000 | | Чистый импорт |
| Electricity | Exports | 0.036 | 0.243 | 0.296 | 0.000 | 0.071 | 0.034 | Электричество | Экспорт |
| | Imports | 0.344 | 0.607 | 0.643 | 0.200 | 0.228 | 0.218 | | Импорт |
| | Net imports | 0.308 | 0.364 | 0.347 | 0.200 | 0.157 | 0.194 | | Чистый импорт |
| **Total net imports** | | 8.095 | 6.600 | 5.000 | 3.900 | 3.889 | 3.290 | **Чистый импорт энергии-всего** | |
| **Total stock changes** | | 0.214 | .. | .. | -0.500 | 0.091 | 0.010 | **Изменение запасов-всего** | |
| **Total primary energy supply** | | 9.149 | 7.700 | 6.100 | 4.500 | 4.999 | 4.217 | **Ресурсы первичной энергии-всего** | |
| Coal and lignite | | 0.586 | 0.500 | 0.400 | 0.400 | 0.298 | 0.176 | Уголь каменный и бурый | |
| Oil/oil products | | 4.657 | 3.200 | 2.600 | 2.400 | 2.547 | 1.997 | Нефть и нефтепродукты | |
| Gas | | 2.544 | 2.500 | 1.700 | 0.900 | 0.958 | 1.011 | Газ | |
| Nuclear | | .. | .. | .. | .. | .. | .. | Атомная энергия | |
| Hydro/geothermal | | 0.387 | 0.282 | 0.216 | 0.200 | 0.284 | 0.260 | Гидро-геотермальная энергия | |
| Other | | 0.900 | 1.205 | 1.197 | 0.600 | 0.912 | 0.773 | Другие виды | |
| **Total primary energy requirement (equals total primary energy supply)** | | 9.149 | 7.700 | 6.100 | 4.500 | 4.999 | 4.217 | **Потребность в первичной энергии-всего (равно ресурсам первичной энергии)** | |

## TABLE 6-4. Final energy consumption (million tons oil equivalent)
## ТАБЛИЦА 6-4. Конечное потребление энергии ( млн. тонн нефтяного эквивалента )

| | 1991 | 1992 | 1993 | 1994 | 1995 | |
|---|---|---|---|---|---|---|
| **Final energy consumption** | 6.10 | 4.97 | 4.80 | 4.20 | 3.50 | **Конечное потребление энергии** |
| Coal & Lignite | 0.26 | 0.14 | 0.20 | 0.20 | 0.10 | Уголь каменный и бурый |
| Oil Products | 2.07 | 1.71 | 1.60 | 1.60 | 1.30 | Нефтепродукты |
| Gas | 0.63 | 0.66 | 0.40 | 0.30 | 0.30 | Газ |
| Electricity | 0.71 | 0.56 | 0.40 | 0.40 | 0.40 | Электроэнергия |
| Heat | 1.75 | 1.24 | 1.50 | 1.20 | 1.10 | Тепло |
| Other | 0.67 | 0.66 | 0.70 | 0.50 | 0.30 | Другие виды |
| Of which: | | | | | | В том числе |
| **Industry** | 1.60 | 1.26 | 0.90 | 0.90 | 0.90 | **Промышленность** |
| Coal & Lignite | 0.01 | 0.02 | 0.00 | 0.00 | 0.00 | Уголь каменный и бурый |
| Oil Products | 0.16 | 0.14 | 0.20 | 0.30 | 0.20 | Нефтепродукты |
| Gas | 0.35 | 0.33 | 0.20 | 0.30 | 0.10 | Газ |
| Electricity | 0.28 | 0.22 | 0.10 | 0.10 | 0.20 | Электроэнергия |
| Heat | 0.79 | 0.55 | 0.40 | 0.10 | 0.40 | Тепло |
| Other | 0.01 | 0.01 | 0.00 | 0.10 | 0.00 | Другие виды |
| **Agriculture** | 0.75 | 0.60 | 0.40 | 0.20 | 0.20 | **Сельское хозяйство** |
| Coal & Lignite | 0.01 | 0.01 | 0.00 | 0.00 | 0.00 | Уголь каменный и бурый |
| Oil Products | 0.13 | 0.11 | 0.20 | 0.10 | 0.10 | Нефтепродукты |
| Gas | 0.04 | 0.03 | 0.00 | 0.00 | 0.10 | Газ |
| Electricity | 0.13 | 0.12 | 0.10 | 0.00 | 0.00 | Электроэнергия |
| Heat | 0.10 | 0.04 | 0.00 | 0.00 | 0.00 | Тепло |
| Other | 0.35 | 0.29 | 0.10 | 0.10 | 0.00 | Другие виды |
| **Transport** | 1.05 | 0.92 | 0.80 | 0.80 | 0.50 | **Транспорт** |
| Oil Products | 0.95 | 0.86 | 0.70 | 0.80 | 0.50 | Нефтепродукты |
| Other | 0.10 | 0.06 | 0.10 | 0.00 | 0.00 | Другие виды |
| **Households** | 1.90 | 1.62 | 1.10 | 1.40 | 1.50 | **Домашние хозяйства** |
| Coal & Lignite | 0.17 | 0.09 | 0.00 | 0.10 | 0.00 | Уголь каменный и бурый |
| Oil Products | 0.27 | 0.21 | 0.20 | 0.30 | 0.50 | Нефтепродукты |
| Gas | 0.18 | 0.20 | 0.10 | 0.00 | 0.10 | Газ |
| Electricity | 0.25 | 0.18 | 0.10 | 0.10 | 0.10 | Электроэнергия |
| Heat | 0.72 | 0.58 | 0.60 | 0.70 | 0.60 | Тепло |
| Other | 0.31 | 0.36 | 0.10 | 0.20 | 0.20 | Другие виды |

**TABLE 7-1. Price indices and exchange rates**

**ТАБЛИЦА 7-1. Индексы цен и обменный курс**

| Year and month | National currency per U.S. dollar<br>Единиц нац. валюты за 1 доллар США | National currency per Russian ruble<br>Единиц нац. валюты за 1 российский рубль | Consumer price index (as a percent of the previous month)<br>Индекс потребительских цен (в % к предыдущему месяцу) | Producer price index (as a percent of the previous month)<br>Индекс цен производителей (в % к предыдущему месяцу) | Consumer price index (as a percent of the previous December)<br>Индекс потребительских цен (в % к декабрю прошлого года) | Producer price index (as a percent of the previous December)<br>Индекс цен производителей (в % к декабрю прошлого года) | Год и месяц |
|---|---|---|---|---|---|---|---|
| **1993** | | | | | | | **1993** |
| January | 0.84 | .. | 104.2 | 108.4 | 104.2 | 108.4 | Январь |
| February | 0.82 | .. | 102.9 | 110.3 | 107.2 | 119.6 | Февраль |
| March | 0.72 | .. | 102.4 | 104.2 | 109.7 | 124.6 | Март |
| April | 0.67 | .. | 100.3 | 99.3 | 110.1 | 123.7 | Апрель |
| May | 0.66 | .. | 99.7 | 100.0 | 109.8 | 123.7 | Май |
| June | 0.65 | .. | 102.3 | 97.8 | 112.3 | 121.0 | Июнь |
| July | 0.65 | .. | 100.8 | 101.7 | 113.3 | 123.1 | Июль |
| August | 0.64 | .. | 98.3 | 102.1 | 111.4 | 125.7 | Август |
| September | 0.62 | .. | 102.0 | 102.6 | 113.6 | 129.0 | Сентябрь |
| October | 0.61 | .. | 103.8 | 101.3 | 118.0 | 130.7 | Октябрь |
| November | 0.61 | .. | 108.8 | 102.4 | 128.4 | 133.8 | Ноябрь |
| December | 0.60 | .. | 105.1 | 101.9 | 134.9 | 136.3 | Декабрь |
| **1994** | | | | | | | **1994** |
| January | 0.59 | .. | 103.8 | 101.0 | 103.8 | 101.0 | Январь |
| February | 0.58 | .. | 103.4 | 103.8 | 107.4 | 104.8 | Февраль |
| March | 0.57 | .. | 101.7 | 101.0 | 109.2 | 105.8 | Март |
| April | 0.57 | .. | 102.7 | 100.5 | 112.2 | 106.3 | Апрель |
| May | 0.57 | .. | 100.2 | 100.4 | 112.4 | 106.7 | Май |
| June | 0.56 | .. | 102.0 | 100.2 | 114.7 | 107.0 | Июнь |
| July | 0.55 | .. | 101.1 | 100.0 | 116.0 | 107.0 | Июль |
| August | 0.55 | .. | 101.9 | 101.2 | 118.2 | 108.2 | Август |
| September | 0.55 | .. | 101.0 | 100.9 | 119.4 | 109.2 | Сентябрь |
| October | 0.54 | .. | 101.3 | 99.5 | 120.9 | 108.6 | Октябрь |
| November | 0.54 | .. | 102.0 | 101.5 | 123.3 | 110.2 | Ноябрь |
| December | 0.55 | .. | 102.4 | 100.5 | 126.3 | 110.7 | Декабрь |

## TABLE 7-1. Price indices and exchange rates
## ТАБЛИЦА 7-1. Индексы цен и обменный курс

| Year and month | National currency per U.S. dollar<br>Единиц нац. валюты за 1 доллар США | National currency per Russian ruble<br>Единиц нац. валюты за 1 российский рубль | Consumer price index (as a percent of the previous month)<br>Индекс потребительских цен (в % к предыдущему месяцу) | Producer price index (as a percent of the previous month)<br>Индекс цен производителей (в % к предыдущему месяцу) | Consumer price index (as a percent of the previous December)<br>Индекс потребительских цен (в % к декабрю прошлого года) | Producer price index (as a percent of the previous December)<br>Индекс цен производителей (в % к декабрю прошлого года) | Год и месяц |
|---|---|---|---|---|---|---|---|
| **1995** | | | | | | | **1995** |
| January | 0.55 | .. | 103.5 | 102.2 | 103.5 | 102.2 | Январь |
| February | 0.54 | .. | 103.2 | 102.5 | 106.8 | 104.8 | Февраль |
| March | 0.52 | .. | 102.6 | 100.8 | 109.5 | 105.6 | Март |
| April | 0.51 | .. | 101.9 | 100.6 | 111.7 | 106.2 | Апрель |
| May | 0.51 | .. | 101.4 | 100.0 | 113.2 | 106.2 | Май |
| June | 0.51 | .. | 101.5 | 99.7 | 114.9 | 105.9 | Июнь |
| July | 0.51 | .. | 100.3 | 101.5 | 115.2 | 107.5 | Июль |
| August | 0.53 | .. | 99.7 | 100.9 | 114.9 | 108.4 | Август |
| September | 0.54 | .. | 101.8 | 101.9 | 116.9 | 110.5 | Сентябрь |
| October | 0.53 | .. | 101.6 | 100.4 | 118.8 | 111.0 | Октябрь |
| November | 0.54 | .. | 102.0 | 103.4 | 121.1 | 114.8 | Ноябрь |
| December | 0.54 | .. | 101.7 | 101.0 | 123.1 | 115.9 | Декабрь |
| **1996** | | | | | | | **1996** |
| January | 0.54 | .. | 103.5 | 102.9 | 103.5 | 102.9 | Январь |
| February | 0.55 | .. | 101.8 | 100.9 | 105.3 | 103.8 | Февраль |
| March | 0.55 | .. | 101.5 | 100.7 | 106.9 | 104.5 | Март |
| April | 0.55 | .. | 100.5 | 101.2 | 107.5 | 105.7 | Апрель |
| May | 0.55 | .. | 100.4 | 100.8 | 108.0 | 106.5 | Май |
| June | .. | .. | .. | .. | .. | .. | Июнь |
| July | .. | .. | .. | .. | .. | .. | Июль |
| August | .. | .. | .. | .. | .. | .. | Август |
| September | .. | .. | .. | .. | .. | .. | Сентябрь |
| October | .. | .. | .. | .. | .. | .. | Октябрь |
| November | .. | .. | .. | .. | .. | .. | Ноябрь |
| December | .. | .. | .. | .. | .. | .. | Декабрь |

## TABLE 7-2. Monthly nominal wages by sector
## ТАБЛИЦА 7-2. Среднемесячная денежная зарплата по отраслям

| Sector | 1990 | 1991 | 1992 | 1993 | 1994 | 1995 | Сектора |
|---|---|---|---|---|---|---|---|
| **Nominal wages** | | | | | | | **Средняя номинальная заработная плата** |
| **Economy average** | 1.5 | 2.8 | 23.0 | 51.8 | 77.4 | 98.5 | **По народному хозяйству** |
| **Material sphere** | .. | .. | .. | .. | .. | .. | **Отрасли сферы материального производства** |
| Industry | 1.6 | 3.2 | 22.2 | 48.9 | 79.8 | 102.9 | Промышленность |
| Construction | 1.9 | 3.4 | 23.3 | 50.5 | 76.5 | 89.9 | Строительство |
| Agriculture | 1.4 | 2.4 | 17.8 | 39.7 | 58.3 | 82.8 | Сельское хозяйство |
| Transport | 1.7 | 3.0 | 39.8 | 89.8 | 119.4 | 144.9 | Транспорт |
| Communications | .. | .. | .. | .. | .. | .. | Связь |
| Trade (retail and wholesale) | 1.4 | 3.0 | 20.4 | 45.6 | 82.3 | 107.3 | Торговля (оптовая и розничная) |
| Other | .. | .. | .. | .. | .. | .. | Прочие отрасли материального производства |
| **Nonmaterial sphere** | .. | .. | .. | .. | .. | .. | **Отрасли непроизводственной сферы** |
| Municipal services | .. | .. | .. | .. | .. | .. | Жилкомхоз и бытовое обслуживание |
| Science, research and development | .. | .. | .. | .. | .. | .. | Наука и научное обслуживание |
| Education | 1.0 | 2.4 | 20.0 | 39.4 | 54.3 | 71.7 | Образование |
| Culture | 1.1 | 2.3 | 18.0 | 37.9 | 53.0 | 69.3 | Культура |
| Arts | .. | .. | .. | .. | .. | .. | Искусство |
| Health care, social security, and sports | 1.0 | 2.3 | 18.0 | 39.7 | 55.8 | 71.8 | Здравоохр., соц.обсл., физк. и спорт |
| Banking, finance, credit, insurance | 2.1 | 5.1 | 28.8 | 98.2 | 154.6 | 178.2 | Кредитование, страхование, банк. дело |
| Government | 1.8 | 3.2 | 23.0 | 54.5 | 82.4 | 107.9 | Управление |

# *Country Notes: Latvia*

**General notes:** Unless otherwise indicated, data were supplied by the Central Statistical Bureau of Latvia.

**Currency:** Unless otherwise indicated, data are in the national currency, lat. The lat was introduced on October 18, 1993 with the conversion factor of 1 lat = 200 rubles. The data for preceding years have been recalculated from rubles using this conversion factor.

**Table 1-1:** Collective farm workers include workers of agricultural statutory companies. Cooperative workers include workers of entrepreneurial companies.

**Table 2-1:** Agriculture includes hunting. Transport includes road maintenance and communication. The statistical discrepancy between total GDP by industrial origin and total GDP by expenditure category is as follows:

| Year | Statistical discrepancy (ths. of lats) |
|---|---|
| 1993 | 2692 |
| 1994 | 4556 |

**Table 2-2:** Data are in 1993 prices. See also note to Table 2-1. The statistical discrepancy between total GDP by industrial origin and total GDP by expenditure category is as follows:

| Year | Statistical discrepancy (ths. of lats) |
|---|---|
| 1992 | 2774 |
| 1993 | 2692 |
| 1994 | 2778 |
| 1995 | 2778 |

**Tables 3-2A, 3-2B, 3-3A and 3-3B:** Both exports and imports are in f.o.b. prices. Totals include trade undistributed by category.

**Tables 3-4A and 3-4B:** Both exports and imports are in f.o.b. prices. Prior to 1995, data for the Czech Republic also includes data for Slovakia. Sums of trade amounts of the CIS and non-CIS countries do not always add up to the totals because of the trade undistributed by country of origin.

**Tables 4-1 and 4-2:** Data were provided by the Ministry of Finance. For 1994-1995 data were estimated according to IMF requirements.

**Table 4-2:** In 1994, the sum of items of capital expenditure does not add up to the total.

**Table 5-2:** Data are in 1983 constant prices.

**Table 7-2:** Wages and salaries at enterprises and institutions owned by central and local government and at those with government participation. Culture includes art, recreation, and sports. The line Health care, social security, and sports shows health care and social work. The line Government shows public administration, defense, and compulsory social security.

# *Комментарии к таблицам: Латвия*

**Общее замечание:** За исключением особо отмеченных случаев, данные были получены из Центрального Статистического Бюро Латвии.

**Национальная валюта:** За исключением особо отмеченных случаев, данные приведены в национальной валюте, латах. Лат был введен 18 октября 1993 года с коэффициентом пересчета 1 лат = 200 рублей.

**Таблица 1-1:** Колхозы включают сельскохозяйственные компании. Кооперативы включают предпринимательскую деятельность.

**Таблица 1-2:** Сельское хозяйство включает охоту. Транспорт включает дорожное хозяйство и связь. Статистическое расхождение между ВВП по производству и ВВП по видам расходов составляет:

| Год | Статистическое расхождение (тысяч латов) |
|---|---|
| 1993 | 2692 |
| 1994 | 4556 |

**Таблица 2-2:** Данные приведены в ценах 1993 г. См. также примечания к Табл. 2-1. Статистическое расхождение между ВВП по производству и ВВП по видам расходов составляет:

| Год | Статистическое расхождение (тысяч латов) |
|---|---|
| 1992 | 2774 |
| 1993 | 2692 |
| 1994 | 2778 |
| 1995 | 2778 |

**Таблицы 3-2А, 3-2В, 3-3А и 3-3В:** Данные приведены в ценах фоб. Итоговые данные включают торговлю нераспределенную по категориям.

**Таблицы 3-4А и 3-4В:** Данные приведены в ценах фоб. До 1995 г. данные по Чешской Республике включают также данные по Словакии. Суммы объемов торговли стран СНГ и стран непринадлежащих к СНГ не всегда равны приведенным итоговым величинам из-за торговли нераспределенной по странам.

**Таблицы 4-1 и 4-2:** Данные были предоставлены Министерством Финансов. Данные за 1994-1995 гг. были рассчитаны по методологии МВФ.

**Таблица 4-2:** В 1994 г. сумма компонентов капитальных расходов не равна приведенной итоговой величине.

**Таблица 5-2:** Данные приведены в ценах 1983 г.

**Таблица 7-2:** В таблице приведены данные по предприятиям и организациям находящимся в частичной или полной собственности центральных и местных органов власти. Культура включает искусство, отдых и спорт. Строка Здравоохранение, социальное обслуживание и спорт показывает здравоохранение и другие отрасли социального обслуживания населения. Строка Управление показывает управление, оборону и обязательное социальное страхование.

# Lithuania / Литва

1996 Population / Численность населения в 1996 году
(thousands / тыс. человек): 3,712

Area / Территория
(thousand square kilometers / тыс. кв. км.): 65.2

Capital city / Столица :
Vilnius / Вильнюс

**Country Tables:** Tables 6-1 and 6-2 are not included because there are no recent data.

**Статистические таблицы страны:** Таблицы 6-1 и 6-2 не включены ввиду отсутствия данных за последние годы.

## TABLE 1-1. Population and employment (thousands)
## ТАБЛИЦА 1-1. Население и занятость (тысяч)

| Population or employment category | 1990 | 1991 | 1992 | 1993 | 1994 | 1995 | Население или группы занятых |
|---|---|---|---|---|---|---|---|
| **Total population** | 3,722 | 3,742 | 3,742 | 3,730 | 3,721 | 3,715 | **Население - всего** |
| Males | 1,762 | 1,772 | 1,772 | 1,765 | 1,759 | 1,755 | Мужчины |
| Females | 1,960 | 1,970 | 1,970 | 1,965 | 1,962 | 1,960 | Женщины |
| Urban population | 2,542 | 2,563 | 2,558 | 2,541 | 2,530 | 2,523 | Городское |
| Rural population | 1,180 | 1,179 | 1,184 | 1,189 | 1,191 | 1,192 | Сельское |
| Population under working age | 894 | 895 | 893 | 884 | 873 | 861 | Моложе трудоспособного возраста |
| Working-age population | 2,111 | 2,128 | 2,120 | 2,108 | 2,102 | 2,111 | Лица в трудоспособном возрасте |
| Population over working age | 717 | 719 | 729 | 738 | 746 | 743 | Старше трудоспособного возраста |
| Economically Active Population, in non-working age | 157 | 127 | 124 | 134 | .. | .. | Экономически активное население в нетрудоспособном возрасте |
| Above working age | 151 | 117 | 115 | 112 | .. | .. | Старше трудоспособного возраста |
| Below working age | 6 | 10 | 10 | 22 | .. | .. | Моложе трудоспособного возраста |
| **Total labor resources** | 2,226 | 2,219 | 2,193 | 2,191 | 2,026 | 2,081 | **Трудовые ресурсы - всего** |
| **Total employment** | 1,853 | 1,898 | 1,855 | 1,778 | 1,675 | 1,644 | **Занятое население - всего** |
| State sector employees | 1,440 | 1,333 | 1,089 | 815 | 645 | 600 | Государственный сектор |
| Leased enterprise employees | .. | .. | .. | .. | .. | .. | Арендные предприятия |
| Joint-stock company employees | .. | 224 | 328 | 475 | 552 | 564 | Акционерные общества |
| Economic association employees | .. | .. | .. | .. | .. | .. | Хозяйственные ассоциации |
| Social organization employees | .. | .. | .. | .. | .. | .. | Общественные организации |
| Joint venture employees | .. | .. | .. | .. | .. | .. | Совместные предприятия |
| Collective farm workers | 171 | 179 | .. | .. | .. | .. | Колхозы |
| Cooperative workers | 117 | 91 | .. | .. | .. | .. | Кооперативы |
| Individual labor activities | 9 | 88 | 91 | 109 | 108 | 110 | ИТД |
| Private subsidiary agricultural workers | .. | .. | .. | .. | .. | .. | Личные подсобные хозяйства |
| Private agricultural workers | .. | .. | 347 | 379 | 370 | 370 | Фермерские хозяйства |
| **Students** | 173 | 160 | 143 | 141 | 153 | 175 | **Учащиеся** |
| **Religious workers** | 1 | 1 | 1 | 1 | 1 | 1 | **Служащие религиозного культа** |
| **Working age population not employed in the national economy** | 199 | 160 | 194 | 271 | 197 | 261 | **Лица в трудоспособном возрасте, не занятые в экономике** |
| Housewives | .. | .. | .. | .. | .. | .. | Домохозяйки |
| Military personnel | .. | .. | 7 | 7 | 6 | 5 | Военнослужащие |
| Unemployed | .. | 5 | 24 | 81 | 66 | 109 | Безработные |
| **Labor force** | 1,853 | 1,903 | 1,879 | 1,859 | 1,741 | 1,753 | **Рабочая сила** |

**TABLE 1-2. Employment by sector (thousands)**
**ТАБЛИЦА 1-2. Численность занятого населения по секторам (тысяч)**

| Sector | 1990 | 1991 | 1992 | 1993 | 1994 | 1995 | Сектор |
|---|---|---|---|---|---|---|---|
| **Material sphere** | 1,373 | 1,385 | 1,390 | 1,275 | 1,217 | 1,178 | **Сфера материального производства** |
| **Agriculture and forestry** | 351 | 337 | 362 | 399 | 390 | 390 | **Сельское и лесное хозяйство** |
| Agriculture | 344 | 332 | 356 | 394 | 385 | 385 | Сельское хозяйство |
| Forestry | 7 | 5 | 6 | 5 | 5 | 5 | Лесное хозяйство |
| **Industry and construction** | 764 | 750 | 705 | 584 | 489 | 464 | **Промышленность и строительство** |
| Industry | 555 | 567 | 536 | 457 | 378 | 349 | Промышленность |
| Construction | 209 | 183 | 169 | 127 | 111 | 115 | Строительство |
| **Other** | 258 | 298 | 323 | 292 | 339 | 325 | **Другие отрасли** |
| Transport of goods | .. | .. | .. | .. | .. | .. | Грузовой транспорт |
| Road Maintenance | 62 | 76 | 124 | 100 | 92 | 95 | Дорожное хозяйство |
| Communication servicing material production | .. | .. | .. | .. | .. | .. | Связь |
| Wholesale trade | 152 | 189 | 193 | 191 | 246 | 230 | Оптовая торговля |
| Retail trade and catering | .. | .. | .. | .. | .. | .. | Розничная торговля и общепит |
| Material supply | .. | .. | .. | .. | .. | .. | Материально-техническое снабжение |
| Procurement | .. | .. | .. | .. | .. | .. | Заготовки |
| Information and computing services | 8 | 8 | 4 | .. | .. | .. | Информационно-техническое обслуживание |
| Other sectors | 36 | 25 | 2 | 1 | 1 | 1 | Другие отрасли сферы материального пр. |
| **Nonmaterial sphere** | 480 | 513 | 465 | 503 | 457 | 465 | **Сфера нематериального производства** |
| Passenger transport | 43 | 57 | .. | .. | .. | .. | Пассажирский транспорт |
| Communication | .. | .. | .. | .. | .. | .. | Связь |
| Housing | 67 | 89 | 43 | 40 | 37 | 36 | Жилищное хозяйство |
| Public utilities and personal services | .. | .. | .. | .. | .. | .. | Комм. хоз. и бытовое обслуживание |
| Health care, social security, physical culture and sports | 109 | 105 | 103 | 96 | 98 | 103 | Здравоохранение, социальное обеспечение, физкультура и спорт |
| Education | .. | .. | .. | .. | .. | .. | Образование |
| Culture and art | 185 | 189 | 138 | 136 | 140 | 142 | Культура и искусство |
| Science and scientific research | 36 | 30 | .. | .. | .. | .. | Наука и научное обслуживание |
| Credit | 12 | 11 | 14 | 21 | 25 | 21 | Кредитование |
| Insurance | .. | .. | .. | .. | .. | .. | Страхование |
| General administration and defense | 28 | 33 | 50 | 57 | 60 | 68 | Государственное управление и оборона |
| Private nonprofit institutions serving households | .. | .. | 117 | 153 | 97 | 95 | Общественные организации, обслуживающие домашние хозяйства |
| **Other, material and nonmaterial spheres** | 738 | 811 | 788 | 794 | 795 | 790 | **Остальные отрасли материального производства и нематериальной сферы** |
| **Total employment** | 1,853 | 1,898 | 1,855 | 1,778 | 1,675 | 1,644 | **Занятые - всего** |

**TABLE 1-3. Registered unemployment (thousands; end of month)**

**ТАБЛИЦА 1-3. Численность зарегистрированных безработных (тысяч; на конец месяца)**

| Year and month | Total<br>Всего | Males<br>Мужчины | Females<br>Женщины | Receiving benefits<br>Получающие пособие | Год и месяц |
|---|---|---|---|---|---|
| **1994** | | | | | **1994** |
| January | 67.3 | 34.0 | 33.3 | 18.7 | Январь |
| February | 67.7 | 34.2 | 33.5 | 17.8 | Февраль |
| March | 68.0 | 34.0 | 34.0 | 17.1 | Март |
| April | 66.1 | 32.6 | 33.5 | 16.1 | Апрель |
| May | 62.5 | 29.5 | 33.0 | 15.6 | Май |
| June | 60.0 | 27.9 | 32.1 | 15.6 | Июнь |
| July | 58.2 | 26.7 | 31.5 | 16.2 | Июль |
| August | 59.5 | 27.0 | 32.5 | 17.8 | Август |
| September | 61.3 | 27.6 | 33.7 | 19.4 | Сентябрь |
| October | 66.3 | 29.9 | 36.4 | 19.3 | Октябрь |
| November | 73.5 | 33.8 | 39.7 | 21.4 | Ноябрь |
| December | 78.0 | 36.8 | 41.2 | 23.2 | Декабрь |
| **1995** | | | | | **1995** |
| January | 90.1 | 43.0 | 47.1 | 24.7 | Январь |
| February | 100.8 | 48.2 | 52.6 | 26.6 | Февраль |
| March | 107.7 | 51.0 | 56.7 | 30.3 | Март |
| April | 107.9 | 50.2 | 57.7 | 32.0 | Апрель |
| May | 107.4 | 49.2 | 58.2 | 34.6 | Май |
| June | 104.5 | 47.1 | 57.4 | 34.9 | Июнь |
| July | 103.7 | 46.1 | 57.6 | 34.0 | Июль |
| August | 106.9 | 46.9 | 60.0 | 38.1 | Август |
| September | 110.2 | 48.0 | 62.2 | 38.4 | Сентябрь |
| October | 116.8 | 50.5 | 66.3 | 38.7 | Октябрь |
| November | 124.4 | 54.9 | 69.5 | 38.9 | Ноябрь |
| December | 127.7 | 57.4 | 70.3 | 38.4 | Декабрь |
| **1996** | | | | | **1996** |
| January | 137.4 | 63.2 | 74.2 | 40.9 | Январь |
| February | 142.3 | 66.3 | 76.0 | 40.5 | Февраль |
| March | 144.2 | 67.8 | 76.4 | 39.8 | Март |
| April | 139.6 | 65.3 | 74.3 | 41.5 | Апрель |
| May | 129.5 | 59.8 | 69.7 | 41.1 | Май |
| June | .. | .. | .. | .. | Июнь |
| July | .. | .. | .. | .. | Июль |
| August | .. | .. | .. | .. | Август |
| September | .. | .. | .. | .. | Сентябрь |
| October | .. | .. | .. | .. | Октябрь |
| November | .. | .. | .. | .. | Ноябрь |
| December | .. | .. | .. | .. | Декабрь |

# TABLE 2-1. Gross domestic product at current prices (millions of national currency)
# ТАБЛИЦА 2-1. Валовой внутренний продукт в текущих ценах (млн. национальной валюты)

| Sector of origin or expenditure category | 1990 | 1991 | 1992 | 1993 | 1994 | 1995 | Отраслевое происхождение или вид расходов |
|---|---|---|---|---|---|---|---|
| **Gross domestic product by sector of origin** | | | | | | | **Валовой внутренний продукт по отраслевому происхождению** |
| **Agriculture and forestry** | 3,576 | 8,100 | 392 | 1,221 | 1,236 | 2,106 | **Сельское и лесное хозяйство** |
| Agriculture | 3,563 | 8,100 | 390 | 1,154 | 1,135 | 1,882 | Сельское хозяйство |
| Forestry | 13 | .. | 2 | 67 | 101 | 224 | Лесное хозяйство |
| **Industry and construction** | 5,588 | 25,575 | 1,651 | 4,242 | 5,861 | 6,846 | **Промышленность и строительство** |
| Industry | 4,232 | 23,570 | 1,335 | 3,380 | 4,378 | 5,222 | Промышленность |
| Construction | 1,356 | 2,005 | 316 | 862 | 1,483 | 1,624 | Строительство |
| **Other** | 3,733 | 9,541 | 1,344 | 5,645 | 9,884 | 13,278 | **Другие отрасли** |
| Transport | 775 | 2,578 | 239 | 1,029 | 1,308 | 1,289 | Транспорт |
| Road maintenance | .. | .. | .. | .. | .. | .. | Дорожное хозяйство |
| Communication | .. | 398 | 36 | 153 | 286 | 418 | Связь |
| Wholesale trade | 631 | 3,745 | 183 | 1,864 | 4,061 | 5,934 | Оптовая торговля |
| Retail trade and catering | .. | .. | .. | .. | .. | .. | Розничная торговля и общепит |
| Material supply | 181 | 1,417 | .. | .. | .. | .. | Материально-техническое снабжение |
| Procurement | 77 | .. | .. | .. | .. | .. | Заготовки |
| Information and computing services | 45 | 29 | .. | .. | .. | .. | Информационно-вычислительное обслуживание |
| Other sectors of material production | .. | .. | .. | .. | .. | .. | Другие отрасли сферы материального пр. |
| Housing | .. | .. | .. | .. | .. | .. | Жилищное хозяйство |
| Public utilities and personal services | .. | 414 | 402 | 596 | 1,031 | .. | Ком. хоз. и бытовое обслуживание |
| Health care, social security, physical culture and sports | .. | .. | .. | .. | .. | .. | Здравоохранение, социальное обеспечение, физкультура и спорт |
| Education | .. | .. | .. | .. | .. | .. | Образование |
| Culture and art | .. | .. | .. | .. | .. | .. | Культура и искусство |
| Science and scientific research | .. | .. | .. | .. | .. | .. | Наука и научное обслуживание |
| Credit | .. | 881 | 212 | 774 | 648 | 605 | Кредитование |
| Insurance | .. | .. | 9 | 36 | 109 | 151 | Страхование |
| General administration and defense | .. | .. | 214 | 852 | 1,516 | 2,532 | Государственное управление и оборона |
| Private nonprofit institutions serving households | .. | .. | 1 | 2 | 7 | 9 | Общественные организации, обслуживающие домашние хозяйства |
| **Imputed service charge of financial intermediaries** | .. | -934 | .. | .. | .. | .. | **Условно-исчисляемая стоимость услуг финансовых посредников** |
| **Total gross value added (GVA)** | 12,897 | 42,282 | 3,387 | 11,108 | 16,981 | 22,230 | **Валовая добавленная стоимость (ВДС) - всего** |
| **Taxes on production and imports (TOPI)** | 2,006 | 6,158 | 378 | 1,134 | 1,924 | 3,320 | **Налоги на производство и импорт (НПиИ)** |
| Other taxes on production (OTOP) | 2,006 | 876 | 17 | 61 | 212 | 543 | Другие налоги на производство (ДНП) |
| **Subsidies on production and imports (SOPI)** | 2,529 | 2,105 | 55 | 265 | 270 | 275 | **Субсидии на производство и импорт (СПиИ)** |
| Other subsidies on production (OSOP) | 2,529 | 2,077 | 55 | 24 | 66 | 34 | Другие субсидии на производство (ДСП) |
| **Total GDP at factor cost (GVA-OTOP+OSOP)** | 13,420 | 38,229 | 3,064 | 10,239 | 15,327 | 19,185 | **Всего ВВП по фактр. стоимости (ВДС-ДНП+ДСП)** |
| **Net Indirect taxes (TOPI - SOPI)** | -523 | 4,053 | 323 | 869 | 1,654 | 3,045 | **Чистые косвенные налоги (НПиИ-СПиИ)** |
| **Total GDP at market prices** | 12,897 | 42,282 | 3,387 | 11,108 | 16,981 | 22,230 | **Всего ВВП в рыночных ценах** |
| **Gross domestic product by expenditure category** | | | | | | | **Валовой внутренний продукт по видам расходов** |
| **Consumption** | 9,558 | 26,127 | 2,781 | 9,494 | 15,385 | 18,574 | **Потребление** |
| Private consumption | 7,037 | 19,704 | 2,621 | 8,613 | 14,007 | 16,278 | Личное потребление |
| Government consumption | 2,522 | 6,423 | 160 | 881 | 1,378 | 2,296 | Общественное потребление |
| **Gross domestic investment** | 4,375 | 8,473 | 300 | 2,520 | 2,613 | 4,268 | **Валовые внутренние инвестиции** |
| Gross fixed investment | 3,710 | 7,178 | 987 | 2,700 | 3,500 | 3,975 | Валовое накопление основного капитала |
| Change in stocks | 665 | 1,295 | -688 | -181 | -887 | 293 | Изменения в запасах (МОС) |
| **Resource balance (net exports of GNFS)** | -1,136 | 3,571 | 306 | -906 | -1,018 | -612 | **Сальдо ресурсов (чистый экспорт ТНФУ)** |
| Exports of goods and nonfactor services | 6,989 | 12,300 | 1,077 | 9,566 | 9,361 | 12,857 | Экспорт товаров и нефакторных услуг |
| Imports of goods and nonfactor services | 8,125 | 8,729 | 771 | 10,472 | 10,378 | 13,469 | Импорт товаров и нефакторных услуг |

# TABLE 2-1A. Distribution of gross domestic product at current prices (percent)
# ТАБЛИЦА 2-1А. Распределение валового внутреннего продукта в текущих ценах ( % )



| Sector of origin or expenditure category | 1990 | 1991 | 1992 | 1993 | 1994 | 1995 | Отраслевое происхождение или вид расходов |
|---|---|---|---|---|---|---|---|
| **Gross domestic product by sector of origin** | | | | | | | **ВВП по отраслевому происхождению** |
| **Agriculture and forestry** | 27.7 | 19.2 | 11.6 | 11.0 | 7.3 | 9.5 | **Сельское и лесное хозяйство** |
| Agriculture | 27.6 | 19.2 | 11.5 | 10.4 | 6.7 | 8.5 | Сельское хозяйство |
| Forestry | 0.1 | .. | 0.1 | 0.6 | 0.6 | 1.0 | Лесное хозяйство |
| **Industry and construction** | 43.3 | 60.5 | 48.7 | 38.2 | 34.5 | 30.8 | **Промышленность и строительство** |
| Industry | 32.8 | 55.7 | 39.4 | 30.4 | 25.8 | 23.5 | Промышленность |
| Construction | 10.5 | 4.7 | 9.3 | 7.8 | 8.7 | 7.3 | Строительство |
| **Other** | 28.9 | 22.6 | 39.7 | 50.8 | 58.2 | 59.7 | **Другие отрасли** |
| Transport | 6.0 | 6.1 | 7.1 | 9.3 | 7.7 | 5.8 | Транспорт |
| Road maintenance | .. | .. | .. | .. | .. | .. | Дорожное хозяйство |
| Communication | .. | 0.9 | 1.1 | 1.4 | 1.7 | 1.9 | Связь |
| Wholesale trade | 4.9 | 8.9 | 5.4 | 16.8 | 23.9 | 26.7 | Оптовая торговля |
| Retail trade and catering | .. | .. | .. | .. | .. | .. | Розничная торговля и общепит |
| Material supply | 1.4 | 3.4 | .. | .. | .. | .. | Материально-техническое снабжение |
| Procurement | 0.6 | .. | .. | .. | .. | .. | Заготовки |
| Information and computing services | 0.4 | 0.1 | .. | .. | .. | .. | Информационно-вычислительное обслуживание |
| Other sectors of material production | .. | .. | .. | .. | .. | .. | Другие отрасли сферы матерл. произ. |
| Housing | .. | .. | .. | .. | .. | .. | Жилищное хозяйство |
| Public utilities and personal services | .. | 1.0 | 11.9 | 5.4 | 6.1 | .. | Ком. хоз. и бытовое обслуживание |
| Health care, social security, physical culture and sports | .. | .. | .. | .. | .. | .. | Здравоохранение, социальное обеспечение, физкультура и спорт |
| Education | .. | .. | .. | .. | .. | .. | Образование |
| Culture and art | .. | .. | .. | .. | .. | .. | Культура и искусство |
| Science and scientific research | .. | .. | .. | .. | .. | .. | Наука и научное обслуживание |
| Credit | .. | 2.1 | 6.3 | 7.0 | 3.8 | 2.7 | Кредитование |
| Insurance | .. | .. | 0.3 | 0.3 | 0.6 | 0.7 | Страхование |
| General administration and defense | .. | .. | 6.3 | 7.7 | 8.9 | 11.4 | Государственное управление и оборона |
| Private nonprofit institutions serving households | .. | .. | 0.0 | 0.0 | 0.0 | 0.0 | Общественные организации, обслуживающие домашние хозяйства |
| **Imputed service charge of financial intermediaries** | .. | -2.2 | .. | .. | .. | .. | **Условно-исчисляемая стоимость услуг финансовых посредников** |
| **Total gross value added** | 100.0 | 100.0 | 100.0 | 100.0 | 100.0 | 100.0 | **Валовая добавленная стоимость - всего** |
| **Total GDP at factor cost** | 104.1 | 90.4 | 90.5 | 92.2 | 90.3 | 86.3 | **ВВП по фактор. стоимости - всего** |
| **Net indirect taxes** | -4.1 | 9.6 | 9.5 | 7.8 | 9.7 | 13.7 | **Чистые косвенные налоги (НПиИ-СПиИ)** |
| **Total GDP at market prices** | 100.0 | 100.0 | 100.0 | 100.0 | 100.0 | 100.0 | **ВВП в рын. ценах - всего** |
| **Gross domestic product by expenditure category** | | | | | | | **ВВП по видам расходов** |
| **Consumption** | 74.1 | 61.8 | 82.1 | 85.5 | 90.6 | 83.6 | **Потребление** |
| Private consumption | 54.6 | 46.6 | 77.4 | 77.5 | 82.5 | 73.2 | Личное потребление |
| Government consumption | 19.6 | 15.2 | 4.7 | 7.9 | 8.1 | 10.3 | Общественное потребление |
| **Gross domestic investment** | 33.9 | 20.0 | 8.8 | 22.7 | 15.4 | 19.2 | **Вал. внутр. инвестиции** |
| Gross fixed investment | 28.8 | 17.0 | 29.1 | 24.3 | 20.6 | 17.9 | Вал. накопление осн. капитала |
| Change in stocks | 5.2 | 3.1 | -20.3 | -1.6 | -5.2 | 1.3 | Изменения в запасах (МОС) |
| **Resource balance (net exports of GNFS)** | -8.8 | 8.4 | 9.0 | -8.2 | -6.0 | -2.8 | **Сальдо ресурсов (чистый экспорт ТНФУ)** |
| Exports of goods and nonfactor services | 54.2 | 29.1 | 31.8 | 86.1 | 55.1 | 57.8 | Экспорт товаров и нефакторных услуг |
| Imports of goods and nonfactor services | 63.0 | 20.6 | 22.8 | 94.3 | 61.1 | 60.6 | Импорт товаров и нефакторных услуг |

**TABLE 2-2. Gross domestic product at constant prices (millions of national currency)**
**ТАБЛИЦА 2-2. Валовой внутренний продукт в постоянных ценах (млн. национальной валюты)**

| Sector of origin or expenditure category | 1990 | 1991 | 1992 | 1993 | 1994 | 1995 | Отраслевое происхождение или вид расходов |
|---|---|---|---|---|---|---|---|
| **Gross domestic product by sector of origin** | | | | | | | **Валовой внутренний продукт по отраслевому происхождению** |
| **Agriculture and forestry** | .. | .. | 1,310 | 1,221 | 1,154 | 1,363 | **Сельское и лесное хозяйство** |
| Agriculture | .. | .. | .. | .. | .. | .. | Сельское хозяйство |
| Forestry | .. | .. | .. | .. | .. | .. | Лесное хозяйство |
| **Industry and construction** | .. | .. | 7,196 | 4,242 | 3,933 | 4,171 | **Промышленность и строительство** |
| Industry | .. | .. | 5,911 | 3,380 | 3,185 | 3,474 | Промышленность |
| Construction | .. | .. | 1,285 | 862 | 748 | 698 | Строительство |
| **Other** | .. | .. | 7,444 | 5,645 | 6,132 | 5,981 | **Другие отрасли** |
| Transport | .. | .. | 1,146 | 1,029 | 919 | 789 | Транспорт |
| Road maintenance | .. | .. | .. | .. | .. | .. | Дорожное хозяйство |
| Communication | .. | .. | 126 | 153 | 218 | 249 | Связь |
| Wholesale trade | .. | .. | 1,451 | 1,864 | 2,320 | 2,413 | Оптовая торговля |
| Retail trade and catering | .. | .. | .. | .. | .. | .. | Розничная торговля и общепит |
| Material supply | .. | .. | .. | .. | .. | .. | Материально-техническое снабжение |
| Procurement | .. | .. | .. | .. | .. | .. | Заготовки |
| Information and computing services | .. | .. | .. | .. | .. | .. | Информационно-вычислительное обслуживание |
| Other sectors of material production | .. | .. | .. | .. | .. | .. | Другие отрасли сферы материального пр. |
| Housing | .. | .. | .. | .. | .. | .. | Жилищное хозяйство |
| Public utilities and personal services | .. | .. | 748 | 596 | 895 | .. | Ком. хоз. и бытовое обслуживание |
| Health care, social security, and sports | .. | .. | .. | .. | .. | .. | Здравоохранение, социальное обеспечение, физкультура и спорт |
| Education | .. | .. | .. | .. | .. | .. | Образование |
| Culture and art | .. | .. | .. | .. | .. | .. | Культура и искусство |
| Science and research | .. | .. | .. | .. | .. | .. | Наука и научное обслуживание |
| Credit | .. | .. | 638 | 774 | 813 | 893 | Кредитование |
| Insurance | .. | .. | 34 | 36 | 43 | 37 | Страхование |
| General administration and defense | .. | .. | 748 | 852 | 895 | 924 | Государственное управление и оборона |
| Private nonprofit institutions serving households | .. | .. | 4 | 2 | 4 | 3 | Общественные организации, обслуживающие домашние хозяйства |
| **Imputed service charge of financial intermediaries** | .. | .. | .. | .. | .. | .. | **Условно-исчисляемая стоимость услуг финансовых посредников** |
| **Total gross value added (GVA)** | .. | .. | 15,950 | 11,108 | 11,219 | 11,515 | **Валовая добавленная стоимость (ВДС) -** |
| **Total GDP at factor cost (GVA-OTOP+OSOP)** | .. | .. | .. | .. | .. | .. | **Всего ВВП по фактр. стоимости (ВДС-ДНП+ДСП)** |
| **Net indirect taxes (TOPI-SOPI)** | .. | .. | .. | .. | .. | .. | **Чистые косвенные налоги (НПиИ-СПиИ)** |
| **Total GDP at market prices** | .. | .. | 15,950 | 11,108 | 11,219 | 11,515 | **Всего ВВП в рыночных ценах** |
| **Gross domestic product by expenditure category** | | | | | | | **Валовой внутренний продукт по видам расходов** |
| **Consumption** | .. | .. | .. | .. | .. | .. | **Потребление** |
| Private consumption | .. | .. | .. | .. | .. | .. | Личное потребление |
| Government consumption | .. | .. | .. | .. | .. | .. | Общественное потребление |
| **Gross domestic investment** | .. | .. | .. | .. | .. | .. | **Валовые внутренние инвестиции** |
| Gross fixed investment | .. | .. | .. | .. | .. | .. | Валовое накопление основного капитала |
| Change in stocks | .. | .. | .. | .. | .. | .. | Изменения в запасах (МОС) |
| **Resource balance (net exports of GNFS)** | .. | .. | .. | .. | .. | .. | **Сальдо ресурсов (чистый экспорт ТНФУ)** |
| Exports of goods and nonfactor services | .. | .. | .. | .. | .. | .. | Экспорт товаров и нефакторных услуг |
| Imports of goods and nonfactor services | .. | .. | .. | .. | .. | .. | Импорт товаров и нефакторных услуг |

## TABLE 2-2A. Growth rates of gross domestic product at constant prices (percent)
## ТАБЛИЦА 2-2А. Валовой внутренний продукт - темпы прироста в постоянных ценах ( % )

| Sector of origin or expenditure category | 1990 | 1991 | 1992 | 1993 | 1994 | 1995 | Отраслевое происхождение или вид расходов |
|---|---|---|---|---|---|---|---|
| **Growth rate by sector of origin** | | | | | | | **Валовый внутренний продукт по отраслевому происхождению** |
| **Agriculture and forestry** | .. | .. | .. | -6.8 | -5.5 | 18.1 | **Сельское и лесное хозяйство** |
| Agriculture | .. | .. | .. | .. | .. | .. | Сельское хозяйство |
| Forestry | .. | .. | .. | .. | .. | .. | Лесное хозяйство |
| **Industry and construction** | .. | .. | .. | -41.1 | -7.3 | 6.1 | **Промышленность и строительство** |
| Industry | .. | .. | .. | -42.8 | -5.8 | 9.1 | Промышленность |
| Construction | .. | .. | .. | -32.9 | -13.2 | -6.7 | Строительство |
| **Other** | .. | .. | .. | -24.2 | 8.6 | -2.5 | **Другие отрасли** |
| Transport | .. | .. | .. | -10.2 | -10.7 | -14.1 | Транспорт |
| Road maintenance | .. | .. | .. | .. | .. | .. | Дорожное хозяйство |
| Communication | .. | .. | .. | 20.6 | 43.0 | 14.2 | Связь |
| Wholesale trade | .. | .. | .. | 28.5 | 24.4 | 4.0 | Оптовая торговля |
| Retail trade and catering | .. | .. | .. | .. | .. | .. | Розничная торговля и общепит |
| Material supply | .. | .. | .. | .. | .. | .. | Материально-техническое снабжение |
| Procurement | .. | .. | .. | .. | .. | .. | Заготовки |
| Information and computing services | .. | .. | .. | .. | .. | .. | Информационно-вычислительное обслуживание |
| Other sectors of material production | .. | .. | .. | .. | .. | .. | Другие отрасли сферы материального пр. |
| Housing | .. | .. | .. | .. | .. | .. | Жилищное хозяйство |
| Public utilities and personal services | .. | .. | .. | -20.3 | 50.1 | .. | Ком. хоз. и бытовое обслуживание |
| Health care, social security, and sports | .. | .. | .. | .. | .. | .. | Здравоохранение, социальное обеспечение, физкультура и спорт |
| Education | .. | .. | .. | .. | .. | .. | Образование |
| Culture and art | .. | .. | .. | .. | .. | .. | Культура и искусство |
| Science and research | .. | .. | .. | .. | .. | .. | Наука и научное обслуживание |
| Credit | .. | .. | .. | 21.3 | 5.0 | 9.8 | Кредитование |
| Insurance | .. | .. | .. | 5.6 | 19.3 | -13.1 | Страхование |
| General administration and defense | .. | .. | .. | 13.9 | 5.0 | 3.3 | Государственное управление и оборона |
| Private nonprofit institutions serving households | .. | .. | .. | -50.0 | 100.0 | -25.0 | Общественные организации, обслуживающие домашние хозяйства |
| **Imputed service charge of financial intermediaries** | .. | .. | .. | .. | .. | .. | **Условно-исчисляемая стоимость услуг финансовых посредников** |
| **Total gross value added** | .. | .. | .. | -30.4 | 1.0 | 2.6 | **Валовая добавленная стоимость (ВДС) - всего** |
| **Total GDP at factor cost** | .. | .. | .. | .. | .. | .. | **Всего ВВП по фактр. стоимости (ВДС-ДНП+ДСП)** |
| **Net indirect taxes** | .. | .. | .. | .. | .. | .. | **Чистые косвенные налоги (НПиИ-СПиИ)** |
| **Total GDP at market prices** | .. | .. | .. | -30.4 | 1.0 | 2.6 | **Всего ВВП в рыночных ценах** |
| **Growth rate by expenditure category** | | | | .. | .. | .. | **Валовой внутренний продукт по видам расходов** |
| **Consumption** | .. | .. | .. | .. | .. | .. | **Потребление** |
| Private consumption | .. | .. | .. | .. | .. | .. | Личное потребление |
| Government consumption | .. | .. | .. | .. | .. | .. | Общественное потребление |
| **Gross domestic investment** | .. | .. | .. | .. | .. | .. | **Валовые внутренние инвестиции** |
| Gross fixed investment | .. | .. | .. | .. | .. | .. | Валовое накопление основного капитала |
| **Exports of goods and nonfactor services** | .. | .. | .. | .. | .. | .. | **Экспорт товаров и нефакторных услуг** |
| **Imports of goods and nonfactor services** | .. | .. | .. | .. | .. | .. | **Импорт товаров и нефакторных услуг** |

**TABLE 2-2B. Implicit price deflators for gross domestic product (percentage change)**

**ТАБЛИЦА 2-2B. Дефляторы валового внутреннего продукта (темпы прироста в %)**

| Sector of origin or expenditure category | 1990 | 1991 | 1992 | 1993 | 1994 | 1995 | Отраслевое происхождение или вид расходов |
|---|---|---|---|---|---|---|---|
| **Price deflators by sector of origin** | | | | | | | **Дефляторы по отраслевому происхождению или виду расходов** |
| **Agriculture and forestry** | .. | .. | .. | 234.5 | 7.1 | 44.3 | **Сельское и лесное хозяйство** |
| Agriculture | .. | .. | .. | .. | .. | .. | Сельское хозяйство |
| Forestry | .. | .. | .. | .. | .. | .. | Лесное хозяйство |
| **Industry and construction** | .. | .. | .. | 335.9 | 49.0 | 10.1 | **Промышленность и строительство** |
| Industry | .. | .. | .. | 342.8 | 37.5 | 9.4 | Промышленность |
| Construction | .. | .. | .. | 306.6 | 98.3 | 17.4 | Строительство |
| **Other** | .. | .. | .. | 453.9 | 61.2 | 37.7 | **Другие отрасли** |
| Transport | .. | .. | .. | 379.4 | 42.4 | 14.7 | Транспорт |
| Road maintenance | .. | .. | .. | .. | .. | .. | Дорожное хозяйство |
| Communication | .. | .. | .. | 252.3 | 30.7 | 28.0 | Связь |
| Wholesale trade | .. | .. | .. | 692.5 | 75.1 | 40.5 | Оптовая торговля |
| Retail trade and catering | .. | .. | .. | .. | .. | .. | Розничная торговля и общепит. |
| Material supply | .. | .. | .. | .. | .. | .. | Материально-техническое снабжение |
| Procurement | .. | .. | .. | .. | .. | .. | Заготовки |
| Information and computing services | .. | .. | .. | .. | .. | .. | Информационно-вычислительное обслуживание |
| Other sectors of material production | .. | .. | .. | .. | .. | .. | Другие отрасли сферы матерл. произ. |
| Housing | .. | .. | .. | .. | .. | .. | Жилищное хозяйство |
| Public utilities and personal services | .. | .. | .. | 85.9 | 15.2 | .. | Ком. хоз. и бытовое обслуживание |
| Health care, social security, and sports | .. | .. | .. | .. | .. | .. | Здравоохранение, социальное обеспечение, физкультура и спорт |
| Education | .. | .. | .. | .. | .. | .. | Образование |
| Culture and art | .. | .. | .. | .. | .. | .. | Культура и искусство |
| Science and research | .. | .. | .. | .. | .. | .. | Наука и научное обслуживание |
| Credit | .. | .. | .. | 201.2 | -20.3 | -15.0 | Кредитование |
| Insurance | .. | .. | .. | 266.5 | 153.7 | 59.5 | Страхование |
| General administration and defense | .. | .. | .. | 250.0 | 69.4 | 61.7 | Государственное управление и оборона |
| Private nonprofit institutions serving households | .. | .. | .. | 300.0 | 75.0 | 71.4 | Общественные организации, обслуживающие домашние хозяиства |
| **Imputed service charge of financial intermediaries** | .. | .. | .. | .. | .. | .. | **Условно-исчисляемая стоимость услуг финансовых посредников** |
| **Total gross value added** | .. | .. | .. | 371.0 | 51.4 | 27.5 | **Валовая добавленная стоимость (ВДС) - всего** |
| **Total GDP at factor cost** | .. | .. | .. | .. | .. | .. | **ВВП по факторной стоимости (ВДС-ДНП+ДСП)** |
| **Net indirect taxes** | .. | .. | .. | .. | .. | .. | **Чистые косвенные налоги (НПИ-СПИ)** |
| **Total GDP at market prices** | .. | .. | .. | 371.0 | 51.4 | 27.5 | **ВВП в рыночных ценах** |
| **Price deflators by expenditure category** | | | | | | | **Дефляторы по виду расходов** |
| **Consumption** | .. | .. | .. | .. | .. | .. | **Конечное потребление** |
| Private consumption | .. | .. | .. | .. | .. | .. | Личное потребление |
| Government consumption | .. | .. | .. | .. | .. | .. | Общественное потребление |
| **Gross domestic investment** | .. | .. | .. | .. | .. | .. | **Валовые внутренние инвестиции** |
| Gross fixed investment | .. | .. | .. | .. | .. | .. | Валовое накопление основного капитала |
| **Exports of goods and nonfactor services** | .. | .. | .. | .. | .. | .. | **Экспорт товаров и нефакторных услуг** |
| **Imports of goods and nonfactor services** | .. | .. | .. | .. | .. | .. | **Импорт товаров и нефакторных услуг** |

**TABLE 3-1. Balance of payments at current prices (millions of U.S. dollars)**
**ТАБЛИЦА 3-1. Платежный баланс в текущих ценах (в миллионах долларов США)**

| Item | 1990 | 1991 | 1992 | 1993 | 1994 | 1995 | Статьи |
|---|---|---|---|---|---|---|---|
| Exports of goods and services (including workers' remittances) | .. | .. | 953.0 | 2,234.0 | 2,374.0 | 3,266.0 | Экспорт товаров и услуг (включая денежные переводы рабочих) |
| Exports of goods and nonfactor services | .. | .. | 949.0 | 2,202.3 | 2,352.0 | 3,214.3 | Экспорт товаров и нефакт. услуг |
| Merchandise (FOB) | .. | .. | 745.3 | 2,005.3 | 2,029.9 | 2,707.7 | Товары (ФОБ) |
| Nonfactor services | .. | .. | 204.0 | 197.0 | 322.1 | 506.6 | Нефакторные услуги |
| Shipment | .. | .. | 95.0 | 164.4 | 207.7 | 287.5 | Перевозки |
| Travel | .. | .. | 27.3 | 22.0 | 68.6 | 98.4 | Поездки |
| Other | .. | .. | 82.0 | 10.5 | 45.8 | 120.7 | Другие |
| Imports of goods and nonfactor services | .. | .. | 673.0 | 2,410.7 | 2,607.6 | 3,367.4 | Импорт товаров и нефакт. услуг |
| Merchandise (FOB) | .. | .. | 593.0 | 2,158.4 | 2,231.0 | 2,899.8 | Товары (ФОБ) |
| Nonfactor services | .. | .. | 80.0 | 252.4 | 376.2 | 467.0 | Нефакторные услуги |
| Shipment | .. | .. | 41.0 | 159.2 | 196.8 | 230.6 | Перевозки |
| Travel | .. | .. | 3.8 | 11.6 | 50.2 | 137.4 | Поездки |
| Other | .. | .. | 35.0 | 81.5 | 129.0 | 99.6 | Другие |
| Resource balance | .. | .. | 276.0 | -208.4 | -255.7 | -153.1 | Сальдо ресурсов |
| Net factor income | .. | .. | 4.0 | 8.0 | 8.6 | -12.9 | Чистый факторный доход |
| Factor receipts | .. | .. | 4.0 | 12.0 | 21.4 | 50.9 | Факторные поступления |
| Factor payments | .. | .. | 0.0 | 4.0 | 12.8 | 63.7 | Факторные платежи |
| Total interest due | .. | .. | 0.0 | 4.0 | 12.2 | 54.7 | Общая сумма процента к оплате |
| Other factor payments and discrepancy | .. | .. | 0.0 | 0.1 | 0.6 | 9.0 | Другие факторные платежи и стат. погр. |
| Net current transfers | .. | .. | 41.0 | 117.0 | 156.7 | 109.4 | Чистые текущие трансферты |
| Current receipts | .. | .. | 43.0 | 117.0 | 161.5 | 112.3 | Текущие поступления |
| Workers remittances | .. | .. | 0.0 | 20.5 | 0.7 | 1.1 | Денежные переводы рабочих |
| Other current transfers | .. | .. | 43.0 | 96.5 | 160.8 | .. | Другие текущие трансферты |
| Current payments | .. | .. | 2.0 | 0.0 | 4.8 | 3.0 | Текущие платежи |
| Current account balance before official grants | .. | .. | 321.0 | -83.5 | -90.0 | -57.0 | Сальдо текущего счета до офиц. безвозмезд. трансфертов |
| Official capital grants | .. | .. | .. | .. | .. | .. | Официальные кап. безвозмезные трансферты |
| Current account balance after official grants | .. | .. | 321.0 | -83.5 | -77.5 | -95.6 | Сальдо текущего счета после офиц. безвозмезд. трансфертов |
| Long Term Capital Inflows | .. | .. | 9.0 | 219.0 | 210.7 | 427.5 | Долгосрочные притоки капитала |
| Direct investment | .. | .. | 8.0 | 31.2 | 31.3 | 72.6 | Прямые инвестиции |
| Net long term borrowing | .. | .. | 1.0 | 187.2 | 174.8 | 349.0 | Чистые долгосрочные займы |
| Disbursements | .. | .. | 1.4 | 187.2 | 205.9 | 408.0 | Поступления |
| Repayments due | .. | .. | 0.0 | 0.0 | 30.3 | 59.4 | Сумма, подлежащая погашению |
| Other long-term inflows (net) | .. | .. | 0.2 | 1.0 | 4.6 | 6.2 | Другие долгосрочные притоки (чистые) |

(continued on next page)

## TABLE 3-1. Balance of payments at current prices (millions of U.S. dollars)
## ТАБЛИЦА 3-1. Платежный баланс в текущих ценах (в миллионах долларов США)

| Item | 1990 | 1991 | 1992 | 1993 | 1994 | 1995 | Статьи |
|---|---|---|---|---|---|---|---|
| Adjustment to Scheduled Debt Service | .. | .. | .. | .. | .. | .. | Регулирование долга |
| Debt service not paid | .. | .. | .. | .. | .. | .. | Невыплаченный долг |
| Interest not paid | .. | .. | .. | .. | .. | .. | Невыплаченный процент |
| Principal not paid | .. | .. | .. | .. | .. | .. | Невыплаченная сумма основного долга |
| Arrears reductions/prepayments(-) | .. | .. | .. | .. | .. | .. | Погашение просроченных платежей/выплаты авансом (-) |
| Total Other items (Net) | .. | .. | 250.0 | 163.7 | 51.5 | -100.0 | Общие другие статьи (чистые) |
| Net short-term capital | .. | .. | 200.0 | 77.5 | 97.7 | 178.8 | Чистый краткосрочный капитал |
| Capital flows not elsewhere included | .. | .. | -82.0 | -0.9 | -0.2 | -8.7 | Потоки капитала, не указанные выше |
| Errors and omissions | .. | .. | 132.0 | 87.1 | -46.1 | -270.1 | Ошибки и пропуски |
| Changes in net reserves | .. | .. | -318.0 | -299.1 | -184.7 | -231.8 | Изменения в чистых резервах |
| Net credit from IMF | .. | .. | 23.0 | .. | .. | .. | Чистый кредит МВФ |
| Reserve changes not elsewhere included | .. | .. | -341.0 | -306.0 | .. | .. | Изменения резервов, не указанных выше |
| Escrow account | .. | .. | .. | .. | .. | .. | Счет депонирования |
| Gross reserves (excluding gold) | .. | .. | .. | 350.4 | 525.3 | 757.0 | Общие резервы (исключая золото) |
| Gross reserves (including gold) | .. | .. | .. | 412.3 | 587.2 | 819.0 | Общие резервы (включая золото) |
| Nominal official exchange rate (annual average) (rf) | .. | .. | 1.9 | 4.4 | 4.0 | 4.0 | Номинальный официальный или рыночный курс (среднегодовой) |
| Nominal official exchange rate (end-of-year) (ae) | .. | .. | 3.9 | 3.9 | 4.0 | 4.0 | Номинальный официальный или рыночный курс (на конец года) |
| Manufacture unit value (percent change) | .. | .. | .. | 497.7 | 144.7 | 128.3 | Средний индекс цен на продукцию обр. пром.,% |
| Index of real effective exchange rate (IMF) | .. | .. | .. | 84.9 | 100.7 | 100.5 | Индекс реального эффективного валютного курса (МВФ) |
| Total factor payments | .. | .. | .. | 4.2 | 12.8 | 63.7 | Общая сумма факторных платежей |
| Government interest | .. | .. | 4.2 | 0.0 | 0.0 | 31.7 | Процент, выплачиваемый органами гос. управления |
| Private sector interest | .. | .. | .. | .. | .. | .. | Процент выплачиваемый частным сектором |
| Profits on direct foreign investment | .. | .. | .. | .. | .. | .. | Прибыль от прямых иностранных инвестиций |
| Official capital grants | .. | .. | .. | 0.0 | 12.9 | -39.0 | Официальные капитальные безвозмездные трансферты |
| For budgetary financing | .. | .. | .. | 0.0 | 12.9 | -40.6 | На бюджетное финансирование |
| To extrabudgetary entities | .. | .. | .. | 0.0 | 0.0 | 1.6 | На внебюджетное финансирование |
| Government net long term borrowing | .. | .. | .. | .. | .. | .. | Чистые долгосрочные государственные займы |
| Disbursements | .. | .. | 1.4 | .. | .. | .. | Поступления |
| Repayments | .. | .. | .. | .. | .. | .. | Погашения |
| Private net long term borrowing | .. | .. | .. | .. | .. | .. | Чистые долгосрочные частные займы |
| Disbursements | .. | .. | .. | .. | .. | .. | Поступления |
| Repayments | .. | .. | .. | .. | .. | .. | Погашения |

**TABLE 3-2A. Imports by commodity group (millions of U.S. dollars)**
**ТАБЛИЦА 3-2A . Импорт по товарным группам (млн. долларов США)**

| Commodity group | 1990 | 1991 | 1992 | 1993 | 1994 | 1995 | Товарные группы |
|---|---|---|---|---|---|---|---|
| TOTAL | .. | .. | .. | 2,274.6 | 2,353.4 | 3,082.6 | ВСЕГО |
| I - Live animals; animal products | .. | .. | .. | 42.5 | 37.1 | 40.0 | I - Живые животные и продукты животноводства |
| II - Vegetable products | .. | .. | .. | 41.1 | 82.2 | 94.6 | II - Продукты растительного происхождения |
| III - Animal or vegetable fats and oils and their cleavage products; prepared edible fats; animal or vegetable waxes | .. | .. | .. | 10.9 | 14.7 | 14.5 | III - Жиры и масла растительного и животного происхождения, воски |
| IV - Prepared foodstuffs; beverages, spirits and vinegar; tobacco and manufactured tobacco substitutes | .. | .. | .. | 94.2 | 101.6 | 138.5 | IV -Продукция пищевой промышленности, алкогольные и безалкогольные напитки, табак и его заменители |
| V - Mineral products | .. | .. | .. | 969.6 | 771.4 | 819.3 | V - Минеральные продукты |
| VI - Products of the chemical or allied industries | .. | .. | .. | 146.9 | 205.8 | 275.9 | VI - Продукция химической промышленности |
| VII - Plastics and articles thereof; rubber and articles thereof | .. | .. | .. | 80.5 | 73.3 | 138.9 | VII - Пластмассы и изделия из них |
| VIII - Raw hides and skins, leather, furskins and articles thereof; saddlery and harness; travel goods, handbags and similar containers; articles of animal gut | .. | .. | .. | 8.6 | 12.7 | 24.6 | VIII - Кожевенное сырьё, кожи, пушнина, меховое сырьё и изделия из них |
| IX - Wood and articles of wood; wood charcoal; cork and articles of cork; manufactures of straw, of esparto or of other plaiting materials; basketware and wickerwork | .. | .. | .. | 11.7 | 14.2 | 21.3 | IX - Древесина и изделия из древесины, древесный уголь |
| X - Pulp of wood or of other fibrous cellulosic material; waste and scrap of paper or paperboard; paper and paperboard and articles thereof | .. | .. | .. | 47.0 | 52.5 | 100.9 | X - Бумажная масса, бумажные и картонные отходы, макулатура, бумага, картон и изделия из них |
| XI - Textiles and textile articles | .. | .. | .. | 125.7 | 173.1 | 287.3 | XI - Текстиль и текстильные изделия |
| XII - Footwear, headgear, umbrellas, sun umbrellas, walking sticks, seat sticks, whips, riding crops and parts thereof; prepared feathers and articles made therewith; artificial flowers; articles of human hair | .. | .. | .. | 15.1 | 11.7 | 10.5 | XII - Обувь, головные уборы, зонты, трости и пр. |

**TABLE 3-2A. Imports by commodity group (millions of U.S. dollars)**
**ТАБЛИЦА 3-2A . Импорт по товарным группам (млн. долларов США)**

| Commodity group | 1990 | 1991 | 1992 | 1993 | 1994 | 1995 | Товарные группы |
|---|---|---|---|---|---|---|---|
| XIII - Articles of stone, plaster, cement, asbestos, mica and similar materials; ceramic products; glass and glassware | .. | .. | .. | 15.7 | 28.9 | 45.9 | XIII - Изделия из камня, гипса, цемента |
| XIV - Natural or cultured pearls, precious or semi-precious stones, precious metals, metals clad with precious metal and articles thereof; imitation jewellery; coin | .. | .. | .. | 0.9 | 1.9 | 2.0 | XIV - Жемчуг, драгоценные и полудрагоценные камни, драгоценные металлы, бижутерия, монеты |
| XV - Base metals and articles of base metal | .. | .. | .. | 165.4 | 152.7 | 204.9 | XV - Неблагородные металлы и изделия из них |
| XVI - Machinery and mechanical appliances; electrical equipment; parts thereof; sound recorders and reproducers, television image and sound recorders and reproducers, and parts and accessories of such articles | .. | .. | .. | 263.2 | 387.8 | 507.9 | XVI - Машины, оборудование, механизмы, их части и принадлежности; звуковая и теле-аппаратура, их части и принадлежности |
| XVII - Vehicles, aircraft, vessels and associated transport equipment | .. | .. | .. | 164.8 | 141.7 | 230.9 | XVII - Средства наземного, воздушного и водного транспорта |
| XVIII - Optical, photographic, cinematographic, measuring, checking, precision, medical or surgical instruments and apparatus; clocks and watches; musical instruments; parts and accessories thereof | .. | .. | .. | 28.9 | 52.7 | 76.5 | XVIII - Приборы, аппараты оптические, медицинские, измерительные и пр.; музыкальные инструменты; часы; их части и принадлежности |
| XIX - Arms and ammunition; parts and accessories thereof | .. | .. | .. | 1.6 | 1.3 | 1.0 | XIX - Оружие и боеприпасы, их части и принадлежности |
| XX - Miscellaneous manufactured articles | .. | .. | .. | 20.5 | 33.6 | 44.8 | XX - Разные промышленные товары |
| XXI - Works of art, collectors' pieces, and antiques | .. | .. | .. | 6.9 | 2.5 | 0.0 | XXI - Произведения искусства, предметы антиквариата |
| XXII - Services | .. | .. | .. | 12.9 | .. | 2.4 | XXII - Услуги |

## TABLE 3-2B Imports by commodity group (millions of national currency)
## ТАБЛИЦА 3-2B. Импорт по товарным группам (млн. национальной валюты)

| Commodity group | 1990 | 1991 | 1992 | 1993 | 1994 | 1995 | Товарные группы |
|---|---|---|---|---|---|---|---|
| TOTAL | .. | .. | .. | 9,798.2 | 9,355.5 | 12,330.3 | ВСЕГО |
| I - Live animals; animal products | .. | .. | .. | 185.5 | 147.3 | 160.1 | I - Живые животные и продукты животноводства |
| II - Vegetable products | .. | .. | .. | 174.5 | 327.5 | 378.2 | II - Продукты растительного происхождения |
| III - Animal or vegetable fats and oils and their cleavage products; prepared edible fats; animal or vegetable waxes | .. | .. | .. | 44.8 | 58.1 | 58.0 | III - Жиры и масла растительного и животного происхождения, воски |
| IV - Prepared foodstuffs; beverages, spirits and vinegar; tobacco and manufactured tobacco substitutes | .. | .. | .. | 400.8 | 403.4 | 554.0 | IV -Продукция пищевой промышленности, алкогольные и безалкогольные напитки, табак и его заменители |
| V - Mineral products | .. | .. | .. | 4,211.7 | 3,063.8 | 3,277.0 | V - Минеральные продукты |
| VI - Products of the chemical or allied industries | .. | .. | .. | 636.7 | 819.0 | 1,103.6 | VI - Продукция химической промышленности |
| VII - Plastics and articles thereof; rubber and articles thereof | .. | .. | .. | 344.1 | 291.9 | 555.6 | VII - Пластмассы и изделия из них |
| VIII - Raw hides and skins, leather, furskins and articles thereof; saddlery and harness; travel goods, handbags and similar containers; articles of animal gut | .. | .. | .. | 36.4 | 50.7 | 98.2 | VIII - Кожевенное сырьё, кожи, пушнина, меховое сырьё и изделия из них |
| IX - Wood and articles of wood; wood charcoal; cork and articles of cork; manufactures of straw, of esparto or of other plaiting materials; basketware and wickerwork | .. | .. | .. | 50.7 | 56.6 | 85.3 | IX - Древесина и изделия из древесины, древесный уголь |
| X - Pulp of wood or of other fibrous cellulosic material; waste and scrap of paper or paperboard; paper and paperboard and articles thereof | .. | .. | .. | 198.6 | 208.9 | 403.7 | X - Бумажная масса, бумажные и картонные отходы, макулатура, бумага, картон и изделия из них |
| XI - Textiles and textile articles | .. | .. | .. | 547.1 | 689.5 | 1,149.3 | XI - Текстиль и текстильные изделия |
| XII - Footwear, headgear, umbrellas, sun umbrellas, walking sticks, seat sticks, whips, riding crops and parts thereof; prepared feathers and articles made therewith; artificial flowers; articles of human hair | .. | .. | .. | 63.0 | 46.5 | 42.0 | XII - Обувь, головные уборы, зонты, трости и пр. |

**TABLE 3-2B Imports by commodity group (millions of national currency)**
**ТАБЛИЦА 3-2B. Импорт по товарным группам (млн. национальной валюты)**

| Commodity group | 1990 | 1991 | 1992 | 1993 | 1994 | 1995 | Товарные группы |
|---|---|---|---|---|---|---|---|
| XIII - Articles of stone, plaster, cement, asbestos, mica and similar materials; ceramic products; glass and glassware | .. | .. | .. | 67.0 | 115.3 | 183.8 | XIII - Изделия из камня, гипса, цемента |
| XIV - Natural or cultured pearls, precious or semi-precious stones, precious metals, metals clad with precious metal and articles thereof; imitation jewellery; coin | .. | .. | .. | 4.0 | 7.3 | 7.9 | XIV - Жемчуг, драгоценные и полудрагоценные камни, драгоценные металлы, бижутерия, монеты |
| XV - Base metals and articles of base metal | .. | .. | .. | 688.9 | 605.0 | 819.5 | XV - Неблагородные металлы и изделия из них |
| XVI - Machinery and mechanical appliances; electrical equipment; parts thereof; sound recorders and reproducers, television image and sound recorders and reproducers, and parts and accessories of such articles | .. | .. | .. | 1,142.0 | 1,543.0 | 2,031.6 | XVI - Машины, оборудование, механизмы, их части и принадлежности; звуковая и теле-аппаратура, их части и принадлежности |
| XVII - Vehicles, aircraft, vessels and associated transport equipment | .. | .. | .. | 698.2 | 563.0 | 923.2 | XVII - Средства наземного, воздушного и водного транспорта |
| XVIII - Optical, photographic, cinematographic, measuring, checking, precision, medical or surgical instruments and apparatus; clocks and watches; musical instruments; parts and accessories thereof | .. | .. | .. | 124.5 | 209.7 | 306.2 | XVIII - Приборы, аппараты оптические, медицинские, измерительные и пр.; музыкальные инструменты; часы; их части и принадлежности |
| XIX - Arms and ammunition; parts and accessories thereof | .. | .. | .. | 7.5 | 5.2 | 4.0 | XIX - Оружие и боеприпасы, их части и принадлежности |
| XX - Miscellaneous manufactured articles | .. | .. | .. | 88.8 | 133.8 | 179.3 | XX - Разные промышленные товары |
| XXI - Works of art, collectors' pieces, and antiques | .. | .. | .. | 31.2 | 10.0 | 0.0 | XXI - Произведения искусства, предметы антиквариата |
| XXII - Services | .. | .. | .. | 52.2 | .. | 9.8 | XXII - Услуги |

**TABLE 3-3A. Exports by commodity group (millions of U.S. dollars)**
**ТАБЛИЦА 3-3А. Экспорт по товарным группам (млн. долларов США)**

| Commodity group | 1990 | 1991 | 1992 | 1993 | 1994 | 1995 | Товарные группы |
|---|---|---|---|---|---|---|---|
| TOTAL | .. | .. | .. | 2,024.7 | 2,028.8 | 2,707.2 | ВСЕГО |
| I - Live animals; animal products | .. | .. | .. | 186.8 | 179.8 | 227.8 | I - Живые животные и продукты животноводства |
| II - Vegetable products | .. | .. | .. | 35.0 | 59.4 | 88.8 | II - Продукты растительного происхождения |
| III - Animal or vegetable fats and oils and their cleavage products; prepared edible fats; animal or vegetable waxes | .. | .. | .. | 1.9 | 9.2 | 28.7 | III - Жиры и масла растительного и животного происхождения, воски |
| IV - Prepared foodstuffs; beverages, spirits and vinegar; tobacco and manufactured tobacco substitutes | .. | .. | .. | 67.7 | 240.2 | 150.7 | IV -Продукция пищевой промышленности, алкогольные и безалкогольные напитки, табак и его заменители |
| V - Mineral products | .. | .. | .. | 524.8 | 339.2 | 322.4 | V - Минеральные продукты |
| VI - Products of the chemical or allied industries | .. | .. | .. | 121.6 | 216.3 | 331.2 | VI - Продукция химической промышленности |
| VII - Plastics and articles thereof; rubber and articles thereof | .. | .. | .. | 24.9 | 31.6 | 84.1 | VII - Пластмассы и изделия из них |
| VIII - Raw hides and skins, leather, furskins and articles thereof; saddlery and harness; travel goods, handbags and similar containers; articles of animal gut | .. | .. | .. | 36.6 | 27.7 | 44.3 | VIII - Кожевенное сырьё, кожи, пушнина, меховое сырьё и изделия из них |
| IX - Wood and articles of wood; wood charcoal; cork and articles of cork; manufactures of straw, of esparto or of other plaiting materials; basketware and wickerwork | .. | .. | .. | 35.4 | 82.2 | 178.2 | IX - Древесина и изделия из древесины, древесный уголь |
| X - Pulp of wood or of other fibrous cellulosic material; waste and scrap of paper or paperboard; paper and paperboard and articles thereof | .. | .. | .. | 40.8 | 24.5 | 44.6 | X - Бумажная масса, бумажные и картонные отходы, макулатура, бумага, картон и изделия из них |
| XI - Textiles and textile articles | .. | .. | .. | 195.2 | 250.5 | 398.5 | XI - Текстиль и текстильные изделия |
| XII - Footwear, headgear, umbrellas, sun umbrellas, walking sticks, seat sticks, whips, riding crops and parts thereof; prepared feathers and articles made therewith; artificial flowers; articles of human hair | .. | .. | .. | 26.4 | 21.3 | 21.7 | XII - Обувь, головные уборы, зонты, трости и пр. |

**TABLE 3-3A. Exports by commodity group (millions of U.S. dollars)**
**ТАБЛИЦА 3-3А. Экспорт по товарным группам (млн. долларов США)**

| Commodity group | 1990 | 1991 | 1992 | 1993 | 1994 | 1995 | Товарные группы |
|---|---|---|---|---|---|---|---|
| XIII - Articles of stone, plaster, cement, asbestos, mica and similar materials; ceramic products; glass and glassware | .. | .. | .. | 19.1 | 21.3 | 34.8 | XIII - Изделия из камня, гипса, цемента |
| XIV - Natural or cultured pearls, precious or semi-precious stones, precious metals, metals clad with precious metal and articles thereof; imitation jewellery; coin | .. | .. | .. | 3.4 | 8.3 | 1.5 | XIV - Жемчуг, драгоценные и полудрагоценные камни, драгоценные металлы, бижутерия, монеты |
| XV - Base metals and articles of base metal | .. | .. | .. | 106.2 | 125.6 | 235.4 | XV - Неблагородные металлы и изделия из них |
| XVI - Machinery and mechanical appliances; electrical equipment; parts thereof; sound recorders and reproducers, television image and sound recorders and reproducers, and parts and accessories of such articles | .. | .. | .. | 396.6 | 243.9 | 291.6 | XVI - Машины, оборудование, механизмы, их части и принадлежности; звуковая и теле-аппаратура, их части и принадлежности |
| XVII - Vehicles, aircraft, vessels and associated transport equipment | .. | .. | .. | 79.9 | 75.0 | 137.3 | XVII - Средства наземного, воздушного и водного транспорта |
| XVIII - Optical, photographic, cinematographic, measuring, checking, precision, medical or surgical instruments and apparatus; clocks and watches; musical instruments; parts and accessories thereof | .. | .. | .. | 34.2 | 28.6 | 27.9 | XVIII - Приборы, аппараты оптические, медицинские, измерительные и пр.; музыкальные инструменты; часы; их части и принадлежности |
| XIX - Arms and ammunition; parts and accessories thereof | .. | .. | .. | 0.3 | 0.2 | 0.0 | XIX - Оружие и боеприпасы, их части и принадлежности |
| XX - Miscellaneous manufactured articles | .. | .. | .. | 75.2 | 43.5 | 57.2 | XX - Разные промышленные товары |
| XXI - Works of art, collectors' pieces, and antiques | .. | .. | .. | 9.6 | 0.5 | 0.2 | XXI - Произведения искусства, предметы антиквариата |
| XXII - Services | .. | .. | .. | 3.1 | .. | 0.3 | XXII - Услуги |

**TABLE 3-3B. Exports by Commodity Group (millions of national currency)**
**ТАБЛИЦА 3-3B. Экспорт по товарным группам (млн. национальной валюты)**

| Commodity group | 1990 | 1991 | 1992 | 1993 | 1994 | 1995 | Товарные группы |
|---|---|---|---|---|---|---|---|
| TOTAL | .. | .. | .. | 8,707.0 | 8,077.2 | 10,826.3 | ВСЕГО |
| I - Live animals; animal products | .. | .. | .. | 792.6 | 716.8 | 911.2 | I - Живые животные и продукты животноводства |
| II - Vegetable products | .. | .. | .. | 147.0 | 237.2 | 355.0 | II - Продукты растительного происхождения |
| III - Animal or vegetable fats and oils and their cleavage products; prepared edible fats; animal or vegetable waxes | .. | .. | .. | 8.1 | 36.6 | 114.9 | III - Жиры и масла растительного и животного происхождения, воски |
| IV - Prepared foodstuffs; beverages, spirits and vinegar; tobacco and manufactured tobacco substitutes | .. | .. | .. | 286.9 | 958.6 | 601.9 | IV -Продукция пищевой промышленности, алкогольные и безалкогольные напитки, табак и его заменители |
| V - Mineral products | .. | .. | .. | 2,253.1 | 1,348.7 | 1,289.4 | V - Минеральные продукты |
| VI - Products of the chemical or allied industries | .. | .. | .. | 518.6 | 860.0 | 1,324.8 | VI - Продукция химической промышленности |
| VII - Plastics and articles thereof; rubber and articles thereof | .. | .. | .. | 108.2 | 125.8 | 336.3 | VII - Пластмассы и изделия из них |
| VIII - Raw hides and skins, leather, furskins and articles thereof; saddlery and harness; travel goods, handbags and similar containers; articles of animal gut | .. | .. | .. | 157.5 | 110.4 | 177.2 | VIII - Кожевенное сырьё, кожи, пушнина, меховое сырьё и изделия из них |
| IX - Wood and articles of wood; wood charcoal; cork and articles of cork; manufactures of straw, of esparto or of other plaiting materials; basketware and wickerwork | .. | .. | .. | 152.5 | 327.5 | 712.6 | IX - Древесина и изделия из древесины, древесный уголь |
| X - Pulp of wood or of other fibrous cellulosic material; waste and scrap of paper or paperboard; paper and paperboard and articles thereof | .. | .. | .. | 177.5 | 97.5 | 178.5 | X - Бумажная масса, бумажные и картонные отходы, макулатура, бумага, картон и изделия из них |
| XI - Textiles and textile articles | .. | .. | .. | 841.0 | 997.4 | 1,593.4 | XI - Текстиль и текстильные изделия |
| XII - Footwear, headgear, umbrellas, sun umbrellas, walking sticks, seat sticks, whips, riding crops and parts thereof; prepared feathers and articles made therewith; artificial flowers; articles of human hair | .. | .. | .. | 113.8 | 84.7 | 86.8 | XII - Обувь, головные уборы, зонты, трости и пр. |

**TABLE 3-3B. Exports by Commodity Group (millions of national currency)**
**ТАБЛИЦА 3-3B. Экспорт по товарным группам (млн. национальной валюты)**

| Commodity group | 1990 | 1991 | 1992 | 1993 | 1994 | 1995 | Товарные группы |
|---|---|---|---|---|---|---|---|
| XIII - Articles of stone, plaster, cement, asbestos, mica and similar materials; ceramic products; glass and glassware | .. | .. | .. | 83.1 | 85.0 | 139.2 | XIII - Изделия из камня, гипса, цемента |
| XIV - Natural or cultured pearls, precious or semi-precious stones, precious metals, metals clad with precious metal and articles thereof; imitation jewellery; coin | .. | .. | .. | 14.8 | 33.3 | 6.1 | XIV - Жемчуг, драгоценные и полудрагоценные камни, драгоценные металлы, бижутерия, монеты |
| XV - Base metals and articles of base metal | .. | .. | .. | 464.0 | 499.8 | 941.5 | XV - Неблагородные металлы и изделия из них |
| XVI - Machinery and mechanical appliances; electrical equipment; parts thereof; sound recorders and reproducers, television image and sound recorders and reproducers, and parts and accessories of such articles | .. | .. | .. | 1,693.4 | 969.5 | 1,166.2 | XVI - Машины, оборудование, механизмы, их части и принадлежности; звуковая и теле-аппаратура, их части и принадлежности |
| XVII - Vehicles, aircraft, vessels and associated transport equipment | .. | .. | .. | 370.2 | 298.7 | 548.9 | XVII - Средства наземного, воздушного и водного транспорта |
| XVIII - Optical, photographic, cinematograp-hic, measuring, checking, precision, medical or surgical instruments and apparatus; clocks and watches; musical instruments; parts and accessories thereof | .. | .. | .. | 147.2 | 113.9 | 111.5 | XVIII - Приборы, аппараты оптические, медицинские, измерительные и пр.; музыкальные инструменты; часы; их части и принадлежности |
| XIX - Arms and ammunition; parts and accessories thereof | .. | .. | .. | 1.3 | 0.6 | 0.2 | XIX - Оружие и боеприпасы, их части и принадлежности |
| XX - Miscellaneous manufactured articles | .. | .. | .. | 320.8 | 173.1 | 228.8 | XX - Разные промышленные товары |
| XXI - Works of art, collectors' pieces, and antiques | .. | .. | .. | 42.6 | 2.1 | 0.8 | XXI - Произведения искусства, предметы антиквариата |
| XXII - Services | .. | .. | .. | 12.8 | .. | 1.1 | XXII - Услуги |

## TABLE 3-4A. Geographical distribution of foreign trade (millions of U.S. dollars)
## ТАБЛИЦА 3-4А. Географическое распределение внешней торговли (млн. долларов США)

| Country or country group | Exports Экспорт 1990 | 1991 | 1992 | 1993 | 1994 | 1995 | Imports Импорт 1990 | 1991 | 1992 | 1993 | 1994 | 1995 | Страна или группа стран |
|---|---|---|---|---|---|---|---|---|---|---|---|---|---|
| **Total trade** | .. | .. | .. | 2,024.7 | 2,028.8 | 2,707.2 | .. | .. | .. | 2,274.6 | 2,353.4 | 3,082.6 | **Всего** |
| **CIS countries** | .. | .. | .. | 1,162.9 | 948.3 | 1,144.5 | .. | .. | .. | 1,529.3 | 1,183.3 | 1,213.1 | **Страны СНГ** |
| Armenia | .. | .. | .. | 1.5 | 2.2 | 1.5 | .. | .. | .. | 0.7 | 0.0 | 0.0 | Армения |
| Azerbaijan | .. | .. | .. | 17.9 | 9.4 | 5.2 | .. | .. | .. | 7.1 | 4.1 | 3.3 | Азербайджан |
| Belarus | .. | .. | .. | 148.1 | 133.2 | 291.1 | .. | .. | .. | 75.3 | 89.4 | 111.5 | Беларусь |
| Georgia | .. | .. | .. | 1.2 | 14.4 | 7.8 | .. | .. | .. | 2.4 | 0.0 | 0.1 | Грузия |
| Kazakstan | .. | .. | .. | 39.4 | 42.4 | 34.2 | .. | .. | .. | 44.7 | 15.1 | 13.6 | Казахстан |
| Kyrgyz Republic | .. | .. | .. | 2.5 | 3.0 | 2.4 | .. | .. | .. | 2.2 | 0.8 | 0.3 | Киргизстан |
| Moldova | .. | .. | .. | 12.9 | 12.8 | 13.5 | .. | .. | .. | 9.9 | 5.2 | 8.2 | Молдова |
| Russia | .. | .. | .. | 673.2 | 572.6 | 552.2 | .. | .. | .. | 1,209.7 | 924.9 | 957.2 | Россия |
| Tajikistan | .. | .. | .. | 4.4 | 4.3 | 2.7 | .. | .. | .. | 17.1 | 6.7 | 4.1 | Таджикистан |
| Turkmenistan | .. | .. | .. | 13.0 | 11.6 | 4.3 | .. | .. | .. | 2.2 | 1.9 | 1.2 | Туркменистан |
| Ukraine | .. | .. | .. | 232.6 | 125.1 | 203.1 | .. | .. | .. | 147.5 | 118.1 | 93.5 | Украина |
| Uzbekistan | .. | .. | .. | 16.2 | 17.3 | 26.5 | .. | .. | .. | 10.5 | 17.1 | 20.1 | Узбекистан |
| **Non-CIS countries** | .. | .. | .. | 861.8 | 1,080.5 | 1,562.7 | .. | .. | .. | 745.3 | 1,170.1 | 1,869.5 | **Остальной мир** |
| **Europe** | .. | .. | .. | 800.6 | 1,000.1 | 1,469.8 | .. | .. | .. | 676.3 | 1,085.7 | 1,738.0 | **Европа** |
| Austria | .. | .. | .. | 4.1 | 5.6 | 13.6 | .. | .. | .. | 20.5 | 14.2 | 32.9 | Австрия |
| Belgium | .. | .. | .. | 13.4 | 15.3 | 28.4 | .. | .. | .. | 15.0 | 17.2 | 38.8 | Бельгия |
| Bulgaria | .. | .. | .. | 11.9 | 7.7 | 11.1 | .. | .. | .. | 5.5 | 8.8 | 10.2 | Болгария |
| Czech Republic | .. | .. | .. | 0.1 | 12.2 | 10.0 | .. | .. | .. | 0.7 | 34.4 | 48.5 | Чешская Республика |
| Denmark | .. | .. | .. | 31.9 | 35.2 | 72.0 | .. | .. | .. | 51.1 | 61.1 | 121.2 | Дания |
| Estonia | .. | .. | .. | 51.4 | 51.7 | 60.4 | .. | .. | .. | 18.6 | 37.9 | 60.3 | Эстония |
| Finland | .. | .. | .. | 17.6 | 19.5 | 29.4 | .. | .. | .. | 29.4 | 68.6 | 109.9 | Финляндия |
| Former Yugoslavia | .. | .. | .. | 0.4 | 2.2 | 1.6 | .. | .. | .. | 2.5 | 6.3 | 8.9 | Быв. Югославия |
| France | .. | .. | .. | 16.7 | 24.1 | 45.8 | .. | .. | .. | 15.7 | 41.7 | 52.8 | Франция |
| Germany | .. | .. | .. | 137.2 | 232.4 | 389.6 | .. | .. | .. | 221.5 | 323.7 | 468.7 | Германия |
| Hungary | .. | .. | .. | 18.3 | 17.4 | 13.6 | .. | .. | .. | 11.4 | 19.7 | 30.1 | Венгрия |
| Iceland | .. | .. | .. | 1.1 | 0.2 | 3.1 | .. | .. | .. | 0.1 | 0.5 | 0.7 | Исландия |
| Ireland | .. | .. | .. | 1.0 | 1.8 | 30.5 | .. | .. | .. | 0.9 | 1.9 | 13.6 | Ирландия |
| Italy | .. | .. | .. | 46.5 | 38.6 | 52.4 | .. | .. | .. | 41.1 | 64.5 | 71.8 | Италия |
| Latvia | .. | .. | .. | 143.9 | 171.1 | 191.3 | .. | .. | .. | 32.7 | 63.9 | 107.9 | Латвия |
| Lithuania | .. | .. | .. | .. | .. | .. | .. | .. | .. | .. | .. | .. | Литва |
| Netherlands | .. | .. | .. | 56.2 | 106.0 | 132.4 | .. | .. | .. | 52.4 | 63.7 | 76.0 | Нидерланды |
| Norway | .. | .. | .. | 3.9 | 12.4 | 16.6 | .. | .. | .. | 2.9 | 15.8 | 26.9 | Норвегия |
| Poland | .. | .. | .. | 140.3 | 101.6 | 104.8 | .. | .. | .. | 50.8 | 94.4 | 125.4 | Польша |
| Romania | .. | .. | .. | 6.1 | 3.8 | 3.7 | .. | .. | .. | 0.6 | 2.3 | 1.0 | Румыния |
| Slovak Republic | .. | .. | .. | 0.1 | 2.4 | 2.1 | .. | .. | .. | 0.2 | 13.6 | 17.9 | Словацская Республика |
| Spain | .. | .. | .. | 8.5 | 17.8 | 22.4 | .. | .. | .. | 2.7 | 6.2 | 11.5 | Испания |

**TABLE 3-4A. Geographical distribution of foreign trade (millions of U.S. dollars)**
**ТАБЛИЦА 3-4А. Географическое распределение внешней торговли (млн. долларов США)**

| Country or country group | Exports Экспорт 1990 | 1991 | 1992 | 1993 | 1994 | 1995 | Imports Импорт 1990 | 1991 | 1992 | 1993 | 1994 | 1995 | Страна или группа стран |
|---|---|---|---|---|---|---|---|---|---|---|---|---|---|
| Sweden | .. | .. | .. | 35.8 | 63.1 | 68.8 | .. | .. | .. | 25.1 | 55.9 | 93.7 | Швеция |
| Switzerland | .. | .. | .. | 8.2 | 4.7 | 59.3 | .. | .. | .. | 31.1 | 28.4 | 57.3 | Швейцария |
| United Kingdom | .. | .. | .. | 32.0 | 46.9 | 84.9 | .. | .. | .. | 21.8 | 33.1 | 131.2 | Великобритания |
| Other Europe | .. | .. | .. | 14.0 | 6.4 | 22.0 | .. | .. | .. | 22.0 | 7.9 | 20.8 | Остальные страны Европы |
| **Asia** | .. | .. | .. | 39.5 | 33.4 | 56.9 | .. | .. | .. | 30.2 | 24.9 | 43.1 | **Азия** |
| Afghanistan | .. | .. | .. | 0.0 | 0.4 | 0.0 | .. | .. | .. | 0.0 | 0.0 | 0.0 | Афганистан |
| China | .. | .. | .. | 7.1 | 2.6 | 0.3 | .. | .. | .. | 0.7 | 0.6 | 1.0 | Китай |
| India | .. | .. | .. | 0.0 | 1.6 | 2.9 | .. | .. | .. | 0.8 | 2.5 | 4.2 | Индия |
| Iraq | .. | .. | .. | .. | .. | .. | .. | .. | .. | .. | .. | .. | Ирак |
| Japan | .. | .. | .. | 0.7 | 2.9 | 2.1 | .. | .. | .. | 5.6 | 5.1 | 7.0 | Япония |
| Korea, Dem. People's Rep. | .. | .. | .. | 0.0 | 0.1 | 0.1 | .. | .. | .. | 0.0 | 0.1 | 0.1 | КНДР |
| Korea, Rep. of | .. | .. | .. | 1.5 | 1.6 | 14.8 | .. | .. | .. | 1.3 | 2.2 | 5.2 | Южная Корея |
| Mongolia | .. | .. | .. | 0.0 | 0.1 | 0.0 | .. | .. | .. | .. | .. | .. | МНР |
| Syrian Arab Republic | .. | .. | .. | 0.0 | 0.3 | 0.2 | .. | .. | .. | 0.0 | 0.0 | 0.0 | Сирия |
| Turkey | .. | .. | .. | 5.2 | 3.6 | 25.7 | .. | .. | .. | 17.0 | 3.7 | 7.8 | Турция |
| Viet Nam | .. | .. | .. | 21.3 | 6.6 | 1.2 | .. | .. | .. | .. | 0.0 | 0.1 | Вьетнам |
| Other Asia | .. | .. | .. | 3.7 | 13.6 | 9.6 | .. | .. | .. | 4.8 | 10.7 | 17.7 | Остальные страны Азии |
| **America** | .. | .. | .. | 13.9 | 23.9 | 32.3 | .. | .. | .. | 35.8 | 54.3 | 84.6 | **Сев. и Южная Америка** |
| Canada | .. | .. | .. | 4.2 | 5.0 | 1.9 | .. | .. | .. | 4.9 | 2.8 | 4.6 | Канада |
| Cuba | .. | .. | .. | 0.9 | 0.6 | 0.4 | .. | .. | .. | .. | 0.0 | 0.0 | Куба |
| United States | .. | .. | .. | 5.1 | 12.9 | 20.2 | .. | .. | .. | 27.7 | 46.6 | 65.5 | США |
| Other America | .. | .. | .. | 3.7 | 5.4 | 9.8 | .. | .. | .. | 3.2 | 4.9 | 14.5 | Остальные |
| **Africa** | .. | .. | .. | 6.8 | 22.5 | 3.5 | .. | .. | .. | 0.4 | 3.6 | 1.1 | **Африка** |
| Egypt | .. | .. | .. | 0.1 | 0.9 | 0.1 | .. | .. | .. | .. | .. | 0.1 | Египет |
| Libya | .. | .. | .. | 0.0 | .. | .. | .. | .. | .. | 0.0 | .. | .. | Ливия |
| Other Africa | .. | .. | .. | 6.7 | 21.6 | 3.4 | .. | .. | .. | 0.4 | 3.6 | 1.0 | Остальные |
| **Rest of the World** | .. | .. | .. | 1.0 | 0.6 | 0.2 | .. | .. | .. | 2.6 | 1.6 | 2.7 | **Прочие страны мира** |
| Australia | .. | .. | .. | 0.5 | 0.4 | 0.2 | .. | .. | .. | 1.0 | 1.2 | 2.6 | Австралия |

**TABLE 3-4B. Geographical distribution of foreign trade (millions of national currency)**

**ТАБЛИЦА 3-4B. Географическое распределение внешней торговли (миллионов национальной валюты)**

| Country or country group | Exports Экспорт 1990 | 1991 | 1992 | 1993 | 1994 | 1995 | Imports Импорт 1990 | 1991 | 1992 | 1993 | 1994 | 1995 | Страна или группа стран |
|---|---|---|---|---|---|---|---|---|---|---|---|---|---|
| **Total trade** | .. | .. | .. | 8,707.0 | 8,077.2 | 10,826.3 | .. | .. | .. | 9,798.2 | 9,355.5 | 12,330.3 | **Всего** |
| **CIS countries** | .. | .. | .. | 4,970.8 | 3,774.0 | 4,576.4 | .. | .. | .. | 6,613.8 | 4,699.2 | 4,852.3 | **Страны СНГ** |
| Armenia | .. | .. | .. | 6.7 | 8.6 | 5.9 | .. | .. | .. | 3.1 | 0.1 | 0.1 | Армения |
| Azerbaijan | .. | .. | .. | 74.5 | 37.3 | 20.9 | .. | .. | .. | 30.1 | 16.3 | 13.0 | Азербайджан |
| Belarus | .. | .. | .. | 641.2 | 529.4 | 1,164.1 | .. | .. | .. | 325.8 | 356.1 | 446.1 | Беларусь |
| Georgia | .. | .. | .. | 5.5 | 57.4 | 31.0 | .. | .. | .. | 10.4 | 0.1 | 0.3 | Грузия |
| Kazakstan | .. | .. | .. | 167.3 | 168.9 | 137.0 | .. | .. | .. | 201.0 | 60.2 | 54.5 | Казахстан |
| Kyrgyz Republic | .. | .. | .. | 11.3 | 11.8 | 9.7 | .. | .. | .. | 10.4 | 3.2 | 1.2 | Киргизстан |
| Moldova | .. | .. | .. | 56.4 | 51.0 | 54.1 | .. | .. | .. | 41.8 | 20.6 | 32.8 | Молдова |
| Russia | .. | .. | .. | 2,884.7 | 2,280.4 | 2,207.5 | .. | .. | .. | 5,256.6 | 3,672.6 | 3,828.7 | Россия |
| Tajikistan | .. | .. | .. | 19.3 | 17.2 | 10.6 | .. | .. | .. | 72.0 | 26.7 | 16.4 | Таджикистан |
| Turkmenistan | .. | .. | .. | 56.6 | 46.1 | 17.1 | .. | .. | .. | 9.7 | 7.6 | 4.9 | Туркменистан |
| Ukraine | .. | .. | .. | 977.5 | 496.7 | 812.3 | .. | .. | .. | 609.3 | 467.6 | 373.9 | Украина |
| Uzbekistan | .. | .. | .. | 69.8 | 69.2 | 106.2 | .. | .. | .. | 43.6 | 68.1 | 80.4 | Узбекистан |
| **Non-CIS countries** | .. | .. | .. | 3,736.2 | 4,303.2 | 6,249.9 | .. | .. | .. | 3,184.4 | 4,656.3 | 7,478.0 | **Остальной мир** |
| **Europe** | .. | .. | .. | 3,449.3 | 3,984.9 | 5,878.5 | .. | .. | .. | 2,896.0 | 4,320.7 | 6,952.4 | **Европа** |
| Austria | .. | .. | .. | 17.4 | 22.4 | 54.4 | .. | .. | .. | 83.6 | 56.4 | 131.6 | Австрия |
| Belgium | .. | .. | .. | 58.9 | 61.1 | 113.6 | .. | .. | .. | 63.4 | 68.3 | 155.1 | Бельгия |
| Bulgaria | .. | .. | .. | 51.7 | 30.7 | 44.2 | .. | .. | .. | 21.5 | 35.1 | 40.8 | Болгария |
| Czech Republic | .. | .. | .. | 0.5 | 48.7 | 40.0 | .. | .. | .. | 2.6 | 137.0 | 193.8 | Чешская Республика |
| Denmark | .. | .. | .. | 130.4 | 140.4 | 287.4 | .. | .. | .. | 239.3 | 243.4 | 485.0 | Дания |
| Estonia | .. | .. | .. | 218.8 | 205.7 | 241.7 | .. | .. | .. | 77.8 | 150.9 | 241.1 | Эстония |
| Finland | .. | .. | .. | 75.8 | 77.5 | 117.4 | .. | .. | .. | 125.4 | 273.0 | 439.7 | Финляндия |
| Former Yugoslavia | .. | .. | .. | 2.0 | 8.7 | 6.4 | .. | .. | .. | 10.7 | 25.4 | 36.0 | Быв. Югославия |
| France | .. | .. | .. | 72.3 | 96.1 | 183.2 | .. | .. | .. | 67.5 | 165.8 | 211.1 | Франция |
| Germany | .. | .. | .. | 592.0 | 926.4 | 1,558.4 | .. | .. | .. | 945.3 | 1,287.7 | 1,874.8 | Германия |
| Hungary | .. | .. | .. | 79.6 | 69.4 | 54.4 | .. | .. | .. | 47.2 | 78.1 | 120.4 | Венгрия |
| Iceland | .. | .. | .. | 4.6 | 0.9 | 12.3 | .. | .. | .. | 0.5 | 1.8 | 2.8 | Исландия |
| Ireland | .. | .. | .. | 4.3 | 7.1 | 122.1 | .. | .. | .. | 3.8 | 7.6 | 54.3 | Ирландия |
| Italy | .. | .. | .. | 187.8 | 152.6 | 209.6 | .. | .. | .. | 179.7 | 257.2 | 287.1 | Италия |
| Latvia | .. | .. | .. | 635.7 | 682.0 | 765.3 | .. | .. | .. | 143.4 | 254.9 | 431.8 | Латвия |
| Lithuania | .. | .. | .. | .. | .. | .. | .. | .. | .. | .. | .. | .. | Литва |
| Netherlands | .. | .. | .. | 243.7 | 423.2 | 529.6 | .. | .. | .. | 223.9 | 253.3 | 304.1 | Нидерланды |
| Norway | .. | .. | .. | 16.8 | 49.3 | 66.2 | .. | .. | .. | 12.5 | 62.9 | 107.8 | Норвегия |
| Poland | .. | .. | .. | 608.0 | 405.1 | 419.3 | .. | .. | .. | 214.5 | 375.5 | 501.5 | Польша |
| Romania | .. | .. | .. | 26.2 | 15.2 | 14.6 | .. | .. | .. | 2.3 | 9.2 | 4.0 | Румыния |
| Slovak Republic | .. | .. | .. | 0.2 | 9.4 | 8.5 | .. | .. | .. | 0.7 | 54.1 | 71.6 | Словацкая Республика |
| Spain | .. | .. | .. | 36.3 | 71.0 | 89.6 | .. | .. | .. | 11.9 | 24.6 | 45.9 | Испания |

**TABLE 3-4B. Geographical distribution of foreign trade (millions of national currency)**

**ТАБЛИЦА 3-4B. Географическое распределение внешней торговли (миллионов национальной валюты)**

| Country or country group | Exports Экспорт 1990 | 1991 | 1992 | 1993 | 1994 | 1995 | Imports Импорт 1990 | 1991 | 1992 | 1993 | 1994 | 1995 | Страна или группа стран |
|---|---|---|---|---|---|---|---|---|---|---|---|---|---|
| Sweden | .. | .. | .. | 152.8 | 251.4 | 275.2 | .. | .. | .. | 107.2 | 222.5 | 375.0 | Швеция |
| Switzerland | .. | .. | .. | 36.2 | 18.7 | 237.3 | .. | .. | .. | 126.0 | 112.8 | 229.2 | Швейцария |
| United Kingdom | .. | .. | .. | 136.2 | 186.6 | 339.7 | .. | .. | .. | 91.5 | 132.1 | 524.5 | Великобритания |
| Other Europe | .. | .. | .. | 61.1 | 25.3 | 88.1 | .. | .. | .. | 93.8 | 31.1 | 83.4 | Остальные страны Европы |
| **Asia** | .. | .. | .. | 194.6 | 132.2 | 227.2 | .. | .. | .. | 126.1 | 98.4 | 172.2 | **Азия** |
| Afghanistan | .. | .. | .. | 0.1 | 1.5 | 0.0 | .. | .. | .. | .. | 0.1 | 0.1 | Афганистан |
| China | .. | .. | .. | 34.1 | 10.4 | 1.4 | .. | .. | .. | 3.0 | 2.6 | 4.1 | Китай |
| India | .. | .. | .. | 0.1 | 6.5 | 11.8 | .. | .. | .. | 3.0 | 9.8 | 16.6 | Индия |
| Iraq | .. | .. | .. | .. | .. | .. | .. | .. | .. | .. | .. | .. | Ирак |
| Japan | .. | .. | .. | 3.1 | 11.7 | 8.3 | .. | .. | .. | 23.5 | 20.1 | 28.2 | Япония |
| Korea, Dem. People's Rep. | .. | .. | .. | 0.0 | 0.3 | 0.3 | .. | .. | .. | 0.0 | 0.2 | 0.2 | КНДР |
| Korea, Rep. of | .. | .. | .. | 7.0 | 6.5 | 59.1 | .. | .. | .. | 5.6 | 8.7 | 21.0 | Южная Корея |
| Mongolia | .. | .. | .. | 0.0 | 0.3 | 0.0 | .. | .. | .. | .. | .. | .. | МНР |
| Syrian Arab Republic | .. | .. | .. | 0.0 | 1.0 | 0.7 | .. | .. | .. | 0.1 | 0.0 | 0.0 | Сирия |
| Turkey | .. | .. | .. | 21.7 | 14.2 | 102.6 | .. | .. | .. | 70.9 | 14.6 | 31.1 | Турция |
| Viet Nam | .. | .. | .. | 113.2 | 26.0 | 5.0 | .. | .. | .. | .. | 0.1 | 0.2 | Вьетнам |
| Other Asia | .. | .. | .. | 15.3 | 53.8 | 38.0 | .. | .. | .. | 20.0 | 42.2 | 70.7 | Остальные страны Азии |
| **America** | .. | .. | .. | 59.9 | 95.1 | 129.1 | .. | .. | .. | 149.6 | 216.4 | 338.4 | **Сев. и Южная Америка** |
| Canada | .. | .. | .. | 17.7 | 19.7 | 7.5 | .. | .. | .. | 21.3 | 11.3 | 18.6 | Канада |
| Cuba | .. | .. | .. | 3.7 | 2.6 | 1.4 | .. | .. | .. | .. | .. | 0.1 | Куба |
| United States | .. | .. | .. | 22.3 | 51.5 | 80.9 | .. | .. | .. | 115.4 | 185.7 | 262.1 | США |
| Other America | .. | .. | .. | 16.2 | 21.3 | 39.3 | .. | .. | .. | 12.9 | 19.4 | 57.6 | Остальные |
| **Africa** | .. | .. | .. | 28.3 | 88.5 | 14.2 | .. | .. | .. | 3.7 | 14.2 | 4.3 | **Африка** |
| Egypt | .. | .. | .. | 0.4 | 3.6 | 0.6 | .. | .. | .. | .. | .. | 0.3 | Египет |
| Libya | .. | .. | .. | 0.0 | .. | .. | .. | .. | .. | 0.1 | .. | .. | Ливия |
| Other Africa | .. | .. | .. | 27.9 | 84.9 | 13.6 | .. | .. | .. | 3.6 | 14.2 | 4.0 | Остальные |
| **Rest of the World** | .. | .. | .. | 4.1 | 2.5 | 0.9 | .. | .. | .. | 9.0 | 6.6 | 10.7 | **Прочие страны мира** |
| Australia | .. | .. | .. | 2.1 | 1.5 | 0.8 | .. | .. | .. | 4.4 | 4.7 | 10.3 | Австралия |

## TABLE 4-1. General government budget revenue (millions of national currency)



## ТАБЛИЦА 4-1. Доходы государственного бюджета (млн. национальной валюты)

| Type of revenue | 1990 | 1991 | 1992 | 1993 | 1994 | 1995 | Вид доходов |
|---|---|---|---|---|---|---|---|
| **Total revenue and grants** | 5,869 | 16,118 | 107,701 | 2,739 | 4,042 | 5,758 | **Всего доходов и безвозм. поступл.** |
| Grants | 292 | .. | .. | .. | .. | .. | Безвозмездные поступления |
| Total Revenue | 5,577 | 16,118 | 107,701 | 2,739 | 4,042 | 5,758 | Всего доходов |
| **Current revenue** | 5,577 | 16,118 | 107,701 | 2,739 | 4,042 | 5,758 | **Текущие доходы** |
| Tax revenue | 5,319 | 15,089 | 102,013 | 2,396 | 3,766 | 5,535 | Доход от налогов |
| Taxes on income and profits | 2,139 | 4,603 | 37,467 | 1,255 | 1,744 | 2,244 | Налоги на доходы и прибыль |
| Individual | 677 | 1,987 | 17,030 | 615 | 1,189 | 1,690 | Физические лица |
| Corporate | 1,463 | 2,616 | 20,437 | 641 | 555 | 554 | Предприятия и организации |
| Social security contributions | 1,003 | 3,677 | 24,814 | .. | .. | .. | Отчисление на соцстрах. |
| Taxes on payroll or work force | .. | .. | .. | .. | .. | .. | Налоги на заработную плату и рабочую силу |
| Taxes on the use of labor force | .. | .. | .. | .. | .. | .. | Плата за трудовые ресурсы |
| Taxes on increases in wages and salaries | .. | .. | .. | .. | .. | .. | Налог с прироста средств на оплату труда |
| Other payroll/work force taxes | .. | .. | .. | .. | .. | .. | Другие налоги на зарплату и рабочую силу |
| Taxes on property | 10 | 450 | 327 | 27 | 38 | 157 | Налоги на собственность |
| Taxes on immovable property | .. | .. | .. | 27 | 38 | 157 | Налоги на недвижимое имущество |
| Buildings | .. | .. | .. | .. | .. | 69 | Налог с владельцев строении |
| Land | .. | .. | .. | 27 | 38 | 88 | Земельныи налог |
| Estate, inheritance, and gift taxes | .. | .. | .. | .. | .. | .. | Налоги на наследство, подарки |
| Other property taxes | .. | .. | .. | .. | .. | .. | Другие налоги на имущество |
| Domestic taxes on goods and services | 2,074 | 5,777 | 37,136 | 981 | 1,430 | 2,589 | Внутренние налоги на товары и услуги |
| General sales, turnover, or value-added taxes | .. | 260 | 23,974 | 760 | 1,148 | 1,975 | Налог с продаж. с оборота или на добав. стоим. |
| Excises | 2,074 | 4,984 | 12,250 | 212 | 282 | 614 | Акцизы |
| Profits of fiscal monopolies | .. | .. | .. | .. | .. | .. | Прибыли фискальных монополий |
| Taxes on specific services | .. | .. | .. | .. | .. | .. | Налоги на особые услуги |
| Taxes on use of goods or permission to use goods or to perform activities | .. | .. | .. | .. | .. | .. | Налоги на пользование товарами или лицензии на пользование товарами и занятие деятельностью |
| Other taxes on goods and services | .. | 533 | 912 | 8 | .. | .. | Другие налоги на товары и услуги |
| Taxes on international trade and transactions | 49 | 38 | 231 | 100 | 283 | 187 | Налоги на внешнюю торговлю и операции |
| Import duties | .. | .. | .. | .. | .. | .. | Импортные пошлины |
| Export duties | .. | .. | .. | .. | .. | .. | Экпортные пошлины |
| Other | .. | .. | .. | .. | .. | .. | Другие |
| Other taxes | 42 | 544 | 2,038 | 32 | 271 | 358 | Прочие налоги |
| Nontax revenue | 259 | 1,029 | 5,688 | 343 | 276 | 223 | Неналоговые доходы |
| **Capital revenue** | .. | .. | .. | .. | .. | .. | **Капитальные доходы** |

**TABLE 4-2. General government budget expenditure by economic type (millions of national currency)**
**ТАБЛИЦА 4-2. Расходы государственного бюджета по экономическим типам (млн. национальной валюты)**

| Type of expenditure or debt holder | 1990 | 1991 | 1992 | 1993 | 1994 | 1995 | Всего расходов |
|---|---|---|---|---|---|---|---|
| **Total expenditure by economic type** | 6,345 | 15,020 | 98,992 | 2,646 | 4,355 | 6,197 | **Всего расходов по экономическим типам** |
| **Current expenditure** | 5,831 | 13,937 | 90,684 | 2,212 | 3,697 | 5,274 | **Текущие расходы** |
| Expenditure on goods and services | 2,714 | 8,610 | 57,571 | 1,638 | 3,017 | 4,385 | Расходы на товары и услуги |
| Wages and salaries | .. | .. | .. | .. | .. | 1,736 | Заработная плата |
| Employer contributions | .. | .. | .. | .. | .. | 484 | Отчисление на социальное страхование |
| Other Purchases of goods and services | .. | .. | .. | .. | .. | 2,165 | Другие покупки товаров и услуг |
| Interest payments | .. | 844 | 888 | 0 | 18 | 100 | Выплаты процентов |
| Domestic debt | .. | .. | .. | .. | .. | 98 | По внутреннему долгу |
| Foreign debt | .. | .. | .. | .. | .. | 2 | По внешнему долгу |
| Subsidies and other current transfers | 2,639 | 2,104 | 5,394 | 513 | 662 | 777 | Субсидии на другие текущие трансферты |
| Subsidies | 1,834 | 2,104 | 5,394 | 265 | 270 | 275 | Субсидии |
| Agricultural subsidies | .. | .. | .. | .. | .. | .. | Субсидии на сельское хозяйство |
| Other current transfers | 805 | .. | .. | 247 | 392 | 502 | Другие текущие трансферты |
| Other | 478 | 2,379 | 26,831 | 62 | 0 | 12 | Прочие расходы |
| **Capital expenditure** | 514 | 1,083 | 8,308 | 434 | 658 | 923 | **Капитальные расходы** |
| Acquisition of fixed capital assets | 419 | 1,083 | 8,308 | 434 | 658 | 923 | Приобретение основного капитала |
| Capital transfers | .. | .. | .. | .. | .. | .. | Капитальные трансферты |
| Other | 94 | .. | .. | .. | .. | .. | Другие капитальные расходы |
| **Surplus/deficit (-)** | -476 | 1,098 | 8,709 | 93 | -313 | -439 | **Превыш. доходов над расходами/дефицит(-)** |
| **Financing by type of debt holder** | .. | .. | .. | .. | .. | 923 | **Финансирование по типам кредиторов** |
| **Foreign (net)** | .. | .. | .. | .. | .. | .. | **Зарубежные кредиторы (сальдо)** |
| From international development institutions | .. | .. | .. | .. | .. | .. | Международные организации |
| From foreign governments | .. | .. | .. | .. | .. | .. | Правительства иностранных государств |
| Other borrowing abroad | .. | .. | .. | .. | .. | .. | Другие зарубежные кредиторы |
| **Domestic (net)** | .. | .. | .. | .. | 313 | 439 | **Внутренние кредиторы (сальдо)** |
| From monetary authorities | .. | .. | .. | .. | 239 | 438 | Органы денежного обращения |
| From deposit money banks | .. | .. | .. | .. | 38 | 1 | Депозитные денежные банки |
| Other domestic borrowing | .. | .. | .. | .. | 36 | .. | Другие внутренние кредиторы |
| *Memo items:* | | | | | | | *Справочно:* |
| Extrabudgetary surplus/ Deficit (-) not included above | .. | .. | .. | .. | 96 | 8 | Превышение доходов над расходами/дефицит (-) по внебюджетным фондам, не включенным выше |
| Total surplus/deficit (-) including extrabudgetary accounts | .. | .. | .. | .. | -217 | -431 | Итого превышение доходов над расходами/дефицит, включая счета внебюджетных фондов |

**TABLE 5-1. Agricultural production (millions of national currency, current prices)**

**ТАБЛИЦА 5-1. Сельскохозяйственная продукция (млн. нац. валюты, текущие цены)**

| Item | 1990 | 1991 | 1992 | 1993 | 1994 | 1995 | Статьи |
|---|---|---|---|---|---|---|---|
| **Total gross agricultural production** | 6,291 | 13,105 | 91,606 | 3,466 | 3,664 | 5,462 | **Валовая продукция сельского хозяйства - всего** |
| **Crops** | 2,361 | 6,226 | 52,119 | 1,634 | 1,912 | 2,800 | **Продукция растениеводства** |
| Grains | 924 | 3,033 | 27,745 | .. | .. | .. | Зерно |
| Potatoes | 463 | 1,345 | 12,460 | .. | .. | .. | Картофель |
| Vegetables | 220 | 683 | 5,690 | .. | .. | .. | Овощи |
| Fruits (excluding grapes) | 63 | 294 | 1,105 | .. | .. | .. | Фрукты (без винограда) |
| Grapes | .. | .. | .. | .. | .. | .. | Виноград |
| Tobacco | .. | .. | .. | .. | .. | .. | Табак |
| Cotton | .. | .. | .. | .. | .. | .. | Хлопок |
| Sugarbeets | 68 | 281 | 3,440 | .. | .. | .. | Сахарная свекла |
| Oilseeds | 20 | 23 | .. | .. | .. | .. | Семена масличных культур |
| Other | 603 | 568 | 1,679 | .. | .. | .. | Прочие |
| **Animal husbandry** | 3,930 | 6,879 | 39,487 | 1,832 | 1,639 | 2,500 | **Продукция животноводства** |
| Livestock | 2,217 | 4,339 | 17,185 | .. | .. | .. | Мясное животноводство |
| Cattle | 1,073 | 2,080 | 6,595 | .. | .. | .. | Крупный рогатый скот |
| Pigs | 939 | 2,000 | 9,954 | .. | .. | .. | Свиньи |
| Sheep and goats | 18 | 30 | 118 | .. | .. | .. | Овцы и козы |
| Poultry | 183 | 225 | 502 | .. | .. | .. | Птица |
| Other | 4 | 4 | 16 | .. | .. | .. | Прочие |
| Milk | 1,171 | 1,740 | 16,860 | .. | .. | .. | Молоко |
| Eggs | 118 | 368 | 2,540 | .. | .. | .. | Яйца |
| Wool | .. | .. | .. | .. | .. | .. | Шерсть |
| Other livestock | 423 | 432 | 2,902 | .. | .. | .. | Прочая |
| **Agricultural services** | .. | .. | .. | .. | 113 | 162 | **Сельскохозяйственные услуги** |

**TABLE 5-2. Agricultural production (millions of constant national currency)**

**ТАБЛИЦА 5-2. Сельскохозяйственная продукция в постоянных ценах (млн. национальной валюты)**

| Item | 1990 | 1991 | 1992 | 1993 | 1994 | 1995 | Статьи |
|---|---|---|---|---|---|---|---|
| **Total gross agricultural production** | 4,531 | 4,323 | 3,295 | 3,042 | 2,492 | 2,741 | **Валовая продукция сельского хозяйства - всего** |
| **Crops** | 1,404 | 1,527 | 1,013 | 1,237 | 864 | 1,138 | **Продукция растениеводства** |
| Grains | 413 | 44 | 264 | 323 | 251 | 243 | Зерно |
| Potatoes | 301 | 288 | 206 | 339 | 210 | 305 | Картофель |
| Vegetables | 79 | 101 | 74 | 70 | 64 | 69 | Овощи |
| Fruits (excluding grapes) | 72 | 173 | 75 | 66 | 33 | 71 | Фрукты (без винограда) |
| Grapes | .. | .. | .. | .. | .. | .. | Виноград |
| Tobacco | 47 | 42 | 32 | 48 | 24 | .. | Табак |
| Cotton | 21 | 15 | 4 | 2 | 5 | .. | Хлопок |
| Sugarbeets | 47 | 42 | 32 | 48 | 24 | 36 | Сахарная свекла |
| Oilseeds | 21 | 15 | 4 | 2 | 5 | 8 | Семена масличных культур |
| Other | 404 | 497 | 322 | 339 | 248 | 406 | Прочие |
| **Animal husbandry** | 3,127 | 2,796 | 2,282 | 1,805 | 1,628 | 1,603 | **Продукция животноводства** |
| Livestock | 1,710 | 1,494 | 1,205 | 868 | 750 | 751 | Мясное животноводство |
| Cattle | 860 | 758 | 701 | 497 | 360 | 326 | Крупный рогатый скот |
| Pigs | 666 | 575 | 401 | 292 | 301 | 335 | Свиньи |
| Sheep and goats | 9 | 9 | 7 | 6 | 6 | 6 | Овцы и козы |
| Poultry | 167 | 147 | 93 | 70 | 80 | 83 | Птица |
| Other | 8 | 5 | 3 | 3 | 3 | 1 | Прочие |
| Milk | 1,251 | 1,155 | 959 | 820 | 752 | 726 | Молоко |
| Eggs | 122 | 118 | 84 | 58 | 68 | 76 | Яйца |
| Wool | 1 | 1 | 1 | 1 | 1 | 1 | Шерсть |
| Other livestock | 43 | 28 | 33 | 58 | 57 | 49 | Прочая |
| **Agricultural services** | 826 | 797 | 525 | 267 | .. | .. | **Сельскохозяйственные услуги** |

**TABLE 5-3. Production and average yield of major agricultural crops**

**ТАБЛИЦА 5-3. Производство и урожайность важнейших сельскохозяйственных культур**

| Crop | 1990 | 1991 | 1992 | 1993 | 1994 | 1995 | Сельскохозяйственные культуры |
|---|---|---|---|---|---|---|---|
| **Production (thousands of tons)** | | | | | | | **Производство (тыс. тонн)** |
| Grain - Cleanweight | 3,265 | 3,347 | 2,225 | 2,708 | 2,138 | 1,954 | Зерно в чистом весе |
| Winter wheat | 1,176 | 841 | 826 | 884 | 537 | 612 | Пшеница - озимая |
| Spring wheat | 7 | 14 | 8 | 6 | 12 | 26 | яровая |
| Coarse grain | .. | .. | .. | .. | .. | 239 | Зерно в физическом весе |
| Rye | 470 | 345 | 342 | 434 | 313 | .. | Рожь |
| Corn | .. | .. | .. | .. | .. | .. | Кукуруза |
| Winter barley | 5 | 6 | 6 | 13 | 7 | 4 | Ячмень - озимый |
| Spring barley | 1,191 | 1,693 | 949 | 1,195 | 1,084 | 884 | яровой |
| Oats | 196 | 233 | 51 | 78 | 69 | 67 | Овес |
| Millet | .. | .. | .. | .. | .. | .. | Просо |
| Rice | .. | .. | .. | .. | .. | .. | Рис |
| Flax | 10 | 13 | 4 | 2 | 4 | 9 | Лен |
| Oilseeds | 24 | 13 | 8 | 3 | 13 | 19 | Семена масличных культур |
| Cotton (raw) | .. | .. | .. | .. | .. | .. | Хлопок - сырец |
| Cotton fiber | .. | .. | .. | .. | .. | .. | волокно |
| Sugarbeets | 912 | 811 | 622 | 855 | 462 | 692 | Сахарная свекла |
| Potatoes | 1,573 | 1,508 | 1,079 | 1,773 | 1,096 | 1,594 | Картофель |
| Pulses | .. | .. | .. | .. | .. | .. | Бобовые |
| Vegetables | 295 | 398 | 260 | 376 | 283 | 369 | Овощи |
| Fruit | 87 | 276 | 118 | 264 | 53 | 128 | Фрукты |
| Grapes | .. | .. | .. | .. | .. | .. | Виноград |
| Other | 87 | 276 | 118 | 264 | 53 | 128 | Прочие |
| Corn (silage and greenchop) | 2,171 | 1,712 | 400 | 331 | 79 | 108 | Кукуруза (на силос и зеленый корм) |
| Hay | 1,797 | 2,209 | 2,092 | 1,884 | 2,096 | 2,227 | Сено |
| **Average yield (kilograms per hectare)** | | | | | | | **Ср. урожайность (кг с га)** |
| Grain | 3,010 | 3,080 | 1,910 | 2,100 | 1,760 | 1,850 | Зерно |
| Winter wheat | 3,390 | 3,150 | 2,970 | 2,370 | 2,040 | 2,440 | Пшеница - озимая |
| Spring wheat | 2,550 | 2,980 | 1,480 | 2,090 | 1,830 | 2,540 | яровая |
| Coarse grain | .. | .. | .. | .. | .. | .. | Зерно в физическом весе |
| Rye | 2,800 | 2,500 | 2,090 | 1,880 | 1,540 | 1,780 | Рожь |
| Corn | .. | .. | .. | .. | .. | .. | Кукуруза |
| Winter barley | 3,590 | 2,960 | 2,660 | 2,310 | 1,690 | 1,610 | Ячмень - озимый |
| Spring barley | 2,990 | 3,250 | 1,560 | 2,050 | 1,760 | 1,630 | яровой |
| Oats | 2,530 | 2,870 | 820 | 1,800 | 1,270 | 1,410 | Овес |
| Millet | .. | .. | .. | .. | .. | .. | Просо |
| Rice | .. | .. | .. | .. | .. | .. | Рис |
| Flax | 440 | 750 | 180 | 380 | 450 | 710 | Лен |
| Oilseeds | 2,180 | 1,430 | 1,450 | 1,500 | 1,100 | 1,360 | Семена масличных культур |
| Cotton (raw) | .. | .. | .. | .. | .. | .. | Хлопок - сырец |
| Cotton fiber | .. | .. | .. | .. | .. | .. | волокно |
| Sugarbeets | 28,500 | 27,200 | 19,000 | 24,600 | 17,300 | 28,410 | Сахарная свекла |
| Potatoes | 14,000 | 14,200 | 9,500 | 14,500 | 9,400 | 12,800 | Картофель |
| Pulses | .. | .. | .. | .. | .. | .. | Бобовые |
| Vegetables | 17,100 | 18,400 | 11,800 | 14,700 | 9,800 | 13,970 | Овощи |
| Fruit | 2,450 | 7,800 | 3,420 | 8,410 | 1,570 | 3,590 | Фрукты |
| Grapes | .. | .. | .. | .. | .. | .. | Виноград |
| Other | 2,450 | 7,800 | 3,420 | 8,410 | 1,570 | 3,590 | Прочие |
| Corn (silage and greenchop) | 27,900 | 25,900 | 13,590 | 20,900 | 10,500 | 25,580 | Кукуруза (на силос и зеленый корм) |
| Hay | 3,800 | 3,950 | 2,540 | 2,750 | 2,740 | 3,110 | Сено |

## TABLE 5-4. Main aggregates of animal husbandry
## ТАБЛИЦА 5-4. Основные показатели животноводства

| Type of livestock or product | 1990 | 1991 | 1992 | 1993 | 1994 | 1995 | Направление животноводства или вид продукции |
|---|---|---|---|---|---|---|---|
| **Livestock (thousands of heads)** | | | | | | | **Поголовье скота (тысяч голов)** |
| Cattle | 2,322 | 2,196 | 1,701 | 1,384 | 1,152 | 1,065 | Крупный рогатый скот |
| of which: Cows | 842 | 832 | 738 | 678 | 615 | 586 | в том числе коровы |
| Pigs | 2,436 | 2,180 | 1,360 | 1,196 | 1,260 | 1,270 | Свиньи |
| Sheep and goats | 61 | 64 | 61 | 55 | 52 | 47 | Овцы и козы |
| of which: Goats | 5 | 6 | 9 | 10 | 12 | 15 | в том числе козы |
| Horses | 80 | 83 | 80 | 81 | 78 | 78 | Лошади |
| Other | 73 | 74 | 84 | 93 | 88 | 84 | Прочие |
| **Animal husbandry products** | | | | | | | **Продукция животноводства** |
| Meat (thousands of tons) | 530 | 450 | 415 | 276 | 224 | 208 | Мясо (тысяч тонн) |
| Beef | 231 | 209 | 226 | 162 | 116 | 87 | Говядина |
| Pork | 241 | 194 | 155 | 90 | 82 | 93 | Свинина |
| Lamb | 2 | 2 | 2 | 2 | 2 | 2 | Баранина |
| Poultry | 56 | 44 | 32 | 22 | 24 | 26 | Птица |
| Other | 1 | 1 | 1 | 0 | 0 | 0 | Прочие виды мяса |
| Milk (thousands of tons) | 3,157 | 2,916 | 2,421 | 2,067 | 1,896 | 1,819 | Молоко (тысяч тонн) |
| Eggs (millions) | 1,273 | 1,235 | 880 | 610 | 714 | 793 | Яйца (миллионов штук) |
| Wool (thousands of tons) | 0 | 0 | 0 | 0 | 0 | 0 | Шерсть (тысяч тонн) |

## TABLE 6-3. Primary energy supply (million tons oil equivalent) — LITHUANIA

## ТАБЛИЦА 6-3. Ресурсы первичных видов энергии (млн. тонн нефтяного эквивалента)

| Item | | 1990 | 1991 | 1992 | 1993 | 1994 | 1995 | Статьи | |
|---|---|---|---|---|---|---|---|---|---|
| **Primary production** | | | | | | | | **Производство первичной энергии** | |
| Coal and lignite (hard and brown) | | .. | .. | .. | .. | .. | .. | Уголь каменный и бурый | |
| Crude oil | | 0.00 | .. | 0.10 | 0.10 | 0.10 | 0.10 | Нефть | |
| Gas | | .. | .. | .. | .. | .. | .. | Газ | |
| Nuclear | | 3.90 | .. | 3.30 | 2.80 | 2.10 | 3.10 | Атомная энергия | |
| Hydro/geothermal | | 0.10 | .. | 0.10 | 0.10 | 0.10 | 0.10 | Гидро-геотермальная | |
| Other | | 0.16 | .. | 0.20 | 0.30 | 0.20 | 0.20 | Другие виды | |
| Total | | 4.17 | .. | 3.60 | 3.20 | 2.50 | 3.50 | Всего | |
| **Energy trade** | | | | | | | | **Торговля энергией** | |
| Coal and lignite | Exports | .. | .. | .. | .. | 0.00 | 0.00 | Уголь каменный и бурый | Экспорт |
| | Imports | 0.70 | .. | 0.60 | 0.20 | 0.30 | 0.20 | | Импорт |
| | Net imports | .. | .. | 0.60 | 0.20 | 0.30 | 0.20 | | Чистый импорт |
| Oil/oil product | Exports | 9.14 | .. | 1.10 | 3.70 | 2.20 | 1.80 | Нефть и нефтепродукты | Экспорт |
| | Imports | 16.88 | .. | 5.10 | 7.50 | 5.50 | 5.30 | | Импорт |
| | Net imports | 7.75 | .. | 4.00 | 3.80 | 3.30 | 3.50 | | Чистый импорт |
| Gas | Exports | 0.15 | .. | .. | .. | .. | .. | Газ | Экспорт |
| | Imports | 4.82 | .. | 3.20 | 1.70 | 1.70 | 2.00 | | Импорт |
| | Net imports | 4.68 | .. | 3.20 | 1.70 | 1.70 | 2.00 | | Чистый импорт |
| Electricity | Exports | 3.76 | .. | 2.40 | 1.90 | 0.50 | 0.70 | Электричество | Экспорт |
| | Imports | 1.03 | .. | 1.20 | 1.30 | 0.60 | 0.50 | | Импорт |
| | Net imports | -2.72 | .. | -1.20 | -0.60 | 0.10 | -0.20 | | Чистый импорт |
| **Total net imports** | | .. | .. | 6.60 | 5.10 | 5.50 | 5.50 | **Чистый импорт энергии-всего** | |
| **Total stock changes** | | -0.29 | .. | 0.20 | 0.30 | 0.20 | -0.30 | **Изменение запасов-всего** | |
| **Total primary energy supply** | | 13.58 | .. | 10.40 | 8.70 | 8.10 | 8.70 | **Ресурсы первичной энергии-всего** | |
| Coal and lignite | | .. | .. | 0.50 | 0.50 | 0.30 | 0.20 | Уголь каменный и бурый | |
| Oil/oil products | | 7.75 | .. | 4.40 | 3.90 | 3.50 | 3.30 | Нефть и нефтепродукты | |
| Gas | | 4.68 | .. | 3.20 | 1.70 | 1.70 | 2.00 | Газ | |
| Nuclear | | 3.90 | .. | 3.30 | 2.80 | 2.10 | 3.10 | Атомная энергия | |
| Hydro/geothermal | | 0.10 | .. | 0.10 | 0.10 | 0.10 | 0.10 | Гидро-геотермальная энергия | |
| Other | | -2.85 | .. | -1.00 | -0.30 | 0.50 | 0.00 | Другие виды | |
| **Total primary energy requirement (equals total primary energy supply)** | | .. | .. | .. | .. | 8.10 | 8.70 | **Потребность в первичной энергии-всего (равно ресурсам первичной энергии)** | |

**TABLE 6-4. Final energy consumption (million tons oil equivalent)**
**ТАБЛИЦА 6-4. Конечное потребление энергии ( млн. тонн нефтяного эквивалента )**

| | 1991 | 1992 | 1993 | 1994 | 1995 | |
|---|---|---|---|---|---|---|
| **Final energy consumption** | .. | 9.53 | 7.27 | 4.80 | 4.50 | **Конечное потребление энергии** |
| Coal & Lignite | .. | 0.42 | 0.41 | 0.30 | 0.20 | Уголь каменный и бурый |
| Oil Products | .. | 2.54 | 2.26 | 1.60 | 1.60 | Нефтепродукты |
| Gas | .. | 1.23 | 0.72 | 0.40 | 0.40 | Газ |
| Electricity | .. | 2.14 | 1.56 | 0.60 | 0.50 | Электроэнергия |
| Heat | .. | 2.77 | 2.09 | 1.70 | 1.60 | Тепло |
| Other | .. | 0.42 | 0.24 | 0.20 | 0.20 | Другие виды |
| Of which: | | | | | | В том числе |
| **Industry** | .. | 3.58 | 2.44 | 1.10 | 1.10 | **Промышленность** |
| Coal & Lignite | .. | 0.03 | 0.05 | 0.00 | 0.00 | Уголь каменный и бурый |
| Oil Products | .. | 0.72 | 0.70 | 0.20 | 0.20 | Нефтепродукты |
| Gas | .. | 0.25 | 0.16 | 0.10 | 0.10 | Газ |
| Electricity | .. | 0.98 | 0.70 | 0.30 | 0.30 | Электроэнергия |
| Heat | .. | 1.37 | 0.82 | 0.50 | 0.50 | Тепло |
| Other | .. | 0.24 | 0.01 | 0.00 | 0.00 | Другие виды |
| **Agriculture** | .. | 0.68 | 0.45 | 0.20 | 0.20 | **Сельское хозяйство** |
| Coal & Lignite | .. | 0.01 | 0.01 | 0.00 | 0.00 | Уголь каменный и бурый |
| Oil Products | .. | 0.23 | 0.24 | 0.10 | 0.10 | Нефтепродукты |
| Gas | .. | 0.03 | 0.01 | 0.00 | 0.00 | Газ |
| Electricity | .. | 0.34 | 0.16 | 0.10 | 0.10 | Электроэнергия |
| Heat | .. | 0.08 | 0.04 | 0.00 | 0.00 | Тепло |
| Other | .. | 0.00 | 0.00 | 0.00 | 0.00 | Другие виды |
| **Transport** | .. | 0.94 | 0.94 | 1.20 | 1.20 | **Транспорт** |
| Oil Products | .. | 0.87 | 0.91 | 1.20 | 1.20 | Нефтепродукты |
| Other | .. | 0.07 | 0.03 | 0.00 | 0.00 | Другие виды |
| **Households** | .. | 2.53 | 2.20 | 1.50 | 1.40 | **Домашние хозяйства** |
| Coal & Lignite | .. | 0.19 | 0.16 | 0.00 | 0.00 | Уголь каменный и бурый |
| Oil Products | .. | 0.44 | 0.29 | 0.10 | 0.10 | Нефтепродукты |
| Gas | .. | 0.34 | 0.32 | 0.20 | 0.20 | Газ |
| Electricity | .. | 0.54 | 0.33 | 0.10 | 0.10 | Электроэнергия |
| Heat | .. | 0.91 | 0.91 | 0.90 | 0.80 | Тепло |
| Other | .. | 0.11 | 0.18 | 0.20 | 0.20 | Другие виды |

# TABLE 7-1. Price indices and exchange rates

# ТАБЛИЦА 7-1. Индексы цен и обменный курс

| Year and month | National currency per U.S. dollar<br>Единиц нац. валюты за 1 доллар США | National currency per 100,000 Russian rubles<br>Единиц нац. валюты за 100,000 российских рублей | Consumer price index (as a percent of the previous month)<br>Индекс потребительских цен (в % к предыдущему месяцу) | Producer price index (as a percent of the previous month)<br>Индекс цен производителей (в % к предыдущему месяцу) | Consumer price index (as a percent of the previous December)<br>Индекс потребительских цен (в % к декабрю прошлого года) | Producer price index (as a percent of the previous December)<br>Индекс цен производителей (в % к декабрю прошлого года) | Год и месяц |
|---|---|---|---|---|---|---|---|
| **1993** | | | | | | | **1993** |
| January | 3.9 | 890.0 | 9.5 | 13.3 | 9.5 | 13.3 | Январь |
| February | 4.3 | 752.5 | 10.2 | 9.3 | 20.8 | 23.9 | Февраль |
| March | 4.7 | 730.0 | 21.4 | 10.2 | 46.5 | 36.6 | Март |
| April | 5.1 | 690.0 | 25.0 | 21.5 | 83.1 | 65.9 | Апрель |
| May | 5.1 | 591.4 | 12.7 | 16.3 | 106.4 | 93.0 | Май |
| June | 4.6 | 428.2 | 6.2 | 1.7 | 119.2 | 96.3 | Июнь |
| July | 4.3 | 413.7 | 2.9 | -1.3 | 125.6 | 93.8 | Июль |
| August | 4.0 | 405.2 | 0.9 | 2.2 | 127.8 | 98.0 | Август |
| September | 4.3 | 403.3 | 4.2 | 2.6 | 137.2 | 103.1 | Сентябрь |
| October | 4.1 | 340.8 | 7.3 | 4.6 | 154.5 | 112.4 | Октябрь |
| November | 3.9 | 330.2 | 6.8 | 3.2 | 171.8 | 119.3 | Ноябрь |
| December | 3.9 | 315.8 | 6.2 | 5.6 | 188.7 | 131.6 | Декабрь |
| **1994** | | | | | | | **1994** |
| January | 3.9 | 280.3 | 4.8 | 0.0 | 4.8 | 0.0 | Январь |
| February | 3.9 | 247.6 | 2.9 | 3.4 | 7.9 | 3.4 | Февраль |
| March | 3.9 | 229.3 | 3.3 | 2.2 | 11.4 | 5.7 | Март |
| April | 4.0 | 223.5 | 1.6 | 1.9 | 13.3 | 7.7 | Апрель |
| May | 4.0 | 213.8 | 6.3 | 6.2 | 20.4 | 14.3 | Май |
| June | 4.0 | 204.8 | 2.0 | -2.7 | 23.0 | 11.3 | Июнь |
| July | 4.0 | 197.7 | 2.1 | 1.1 | 25.6 | 12.5 | Июль |
| August | 4.0 | 189.2 | 2.2 | 3.0 | 28.4 | 15.9 | Август |
| September | 4.0 | 173.0 | 2.3 | -0.3 | 31.3 | 15.6 | Сентябрь |
| October | 4.0 | 133.5 | 2.8 | 4.5 | 35.0 | 20.8 | Октябрь |
| November | 4.0 | 127.3 | 3.6 | 4.2 | 39.8 | 25.9 | Ноябрь |
| December | 4.0 | 118.8 | 3.8 | 6.3 | 45.1 | 33.8 | Декабрь |

## TABLE 7-1. Price indices and exchange rates
## ТАБЛИЦА 7-1. Индексы цен и обменный курс

| Year and month | National currency per U.S. dollar<br>Единиц нац. валюты за 1 доллар США | National currency per 100,000 Russian rubles<br>Единиц нац. валюты за 100,000 российских рублей | Consumer price index (as a percent of the previous month)<br>Индекс потребительских цен (в % к предыдущему месяцу) | Producer price index (as a percent of the previous month)<br>Индекс цен производителей (в % к предыдущему месяцу) | Consumer price index (as a percent of the previous December)<br>Индекс потребительских цен (в % к декабрю прошлого года) | Producer price index (as a percent of the previous December)<br>Индекс цен производителей (в % к декабрю прошлого года) | Год и месяц |
|---|---|---|---|---|---|---|---|
| 1995 | | | | | | | 1995 |
| January | 4.0 | 105.5 | 5.7 | 5.2 | 5.7 | 5.2 | Январь |
| February | 4.0 | 195.4 | 3.9 | 4.9 | 9.9 | 10.3 | Февраль |
| March | 4.0 | 84.7 | 1.4 | -0.2 | 11.5 | 10.1 | Март |
| April | 4.0 | 79.8 | 1.4 | -4.7 | 13.1 | 4.9 | Апрель |
| May | 4.0 | 78.8 | 2.2 | -2.3 | 15.6 | 2.5 | Май |
| June | 4.0 | 84.5 | 1.0 | 0.2 | 16.7 | 2.7 | Июнь |
| July | 4.0 | 88.5 | 2.7 | 1.0 | 19.9 | 3.7 | Июль |
| August | 4.0 | 90.6 | 0.4 | 3.1 | 20.4 | 6.9 | Август |
| September | 4.0 | 89.5 | 2.0 | 3.5 | 22.8 | 10.7 | Сентябрь |
| October | 4.0 | 88.9 | 3.2 | 3.0 | 26.7 | 14.0 | Октябрь |
| November | 4.0 | 88.1 | 4.3 | 4.4 | 32.2 | 19.0 | Ноябрь |
| December | 4.0 | 86.7 | 2.7 | 1.3 | 35.7 | 20.6 | Декабрь |
| 1996 | | | | | | | 1996 |
| January | 4.0 | 85.4 | 3.2 | 1.6 | 3.2 | 1.6 | Январь |
| February | 4.0 | 84.0 | 2.4 | 1.0 | 5.6 | 2.6 | Февраль |
| March | 4.0 | 82.7 | 2.3 | 1.2 | 8.1 | 3.9 | Март |
| April | 4.0 | 81.6 | 1.3 | 0.2 | 9.5 | 4.1 | Апрель |
| May | 4.0 | .. | 0.3 | -0.5 | 9.7 | 3.6 | Май |
| June | 4.0 | .. | .. | .. | .. | .. | Июнь |
| July | .. | .. | .. | .. | .. | .. | Июль |
| August | .. | .. | .. | .. | .. | .. | Август |
| September | .. | .. | .. | .. | .. | .. | Сентябрь |
| October | .. | .. | .. | .. | .. | .. | Октябрь |
| November | .. | .. | .. | .. | .. | .. | Ноябрь |
| December | .. | .. | .. | .. | .. | .. | Декабрь |

## TABLE 7-2. Monthly nominal wages by sector
## ТАБЛИЦА 7-2. Среднемесячная денежная зарплата по отраслям

| Sector | 1990 | 1991 | 1992 | 1993 | 1994 | 1995 | Сектора |
|---|---|---|---|---|---|---|---|
| **Nominal wages** | | | | | | | **Средняя номинальная заработная плата** |
| **Economy average** | 283.4 | 737.0 | 5,615.0 | 189.7 | 371.0 | 516.0 | **По народному хозяйству** |
| **Material sphere** | 305.8 | 769.9 | 6,009.0 | 218.4 | .. | .. | **Отрасли сферы материального производства** |
| Industry | 303.1 | 860.4 | 6,302.0 | 208.5 | 376.0 | .. | Промышленность |
| Construction | 393.2 | 845.3 | 6,796.0 | 194.7 | 422.3 | .. | Строительство |
| Agriculture | 275.1 | 570.9 | 4,781.0 | 134.6 | 326.0 | .. | Сельское хозяйство |
| Transport | 303.5 | 703.6 | 5,981.0 | 245.8 | 450.7 | .. | Транспорт |
| Communications | 237.4 | 636.9 | 5,725.0 | 233.0 | 421.3 | .. | Связь |
| Trade (retail and wholesale) | 280.4 | 664.8 | 4,951.0 | 230.5 | 389.8 | .. | Торговля (оптовая и розничная) |
| Other | 191.6 | 701.1 | 4,971.0 | .. | .. | .. | Прочие отрасли материального производства |
| **Nonmaterial sphere** | 224.6 | 657.7 | 4,951.0 | 147.2 | .. | .. | **Отрасли непроизводственной сферы** |
| Municipal services | 273.8 | 806.3 | 6,029.0 | 220.7 | .. | .. | Жилкомхоз и бытовое обслуживание |
| Science, research and development | 332.9 | 631.2 | 4,467.0 | 169.7 | 351.5 | .. | Наука и научное обслуживание |
| Education | 184.9 | 625.2 | 4,468.0 | 129.4 | 272.0 | .. | Образование |
| Culture | 175.9 | 617.8 | 4,035.0 | 127.7 | 277.7 | .. | Культура |
| Arts | 245.9 | 562.7 | 3,933.0 | .. | .. | .. | Искусство |
| Health care, social security, and sports | 186.7 | 644.0 | 4,449.0 | 134.9 | 267.0 | .. | Здравоохр., соц.обсл., физк. и спорт |
| Banking, finance, credit, insurance | 399.7 | 1,053.8 | 9,462.0 | 501.6 | 946.8 | .. | Кредитование, страхование, банк. дело |
| Government | 381.6 | 1,035.4 | 8,901.0 | 280.6 | 692.0 | .. | Управление |

**TABLE 8-1. Money income and expenditure of the population (millions of national currency)**
**ТАБЛИЦА 8-1. Денежные доходы и расходы населения (млн. национальной валюты)**

| Type of income or expenditure | 1990 | 1991 | 1992 | 1993 | 1994 | 1995 | Вид доходов или расходов |
|---|---|---|---|---|---|---|---|
| **Income** | | | | | | | **Доходы** |
| **Total labor income** | 7,892 | 24,543 | 2,271 | 8,454 | 12,743 | 15,327 | **Всего трудовых доходов** |
| Regular wages | 5,949 | 18,979 | 1,284 | 4,141 | 7,096 | 9,532 | Заработная плата |
| Wages paid by cooperatives | 476 | .. | .. | .. | .. | .. | Заработная плата в кооперативах |
| Other wages and compensation | 183 | 373 | 659 | 3,049 | 4,611 | 4,207 | Прочие доходы типа заработной платы |
| Income paid by collective farms | 875 | 808 | .. | .. | .. | .. | Доходы от колхозов |
| Income from sale of farm products | 885 | 4,383 | 328 | 1,264 | 1,036 | 1,589 | Доходы от продажи продукции колхозов |
| **Total transfer receipts** | 2,113 | 6,754 | 580 | 1,531 | 4,020 | 3,051 | **Всего трансфертных поступлений** |
| Pensions and allowances | 1,209 | 3,836 | 334 | 912 | 1,645 | 2,323 | Пенсии и пособия |
| Scholarships | 39 | 162 | 10 | 24 | 41 | 52 | Стипендии |
| Income from the financial system (insurance, interest, etc.) | 563 | 1,352 | 138 | 378 | 945 | 642 | Доходы из финансовой системы (страховые возмещения, проценты и т.д.) |
| Other income | 303 | 1,404 | 98 | 218 | 1,389 | 33 | Прочие виды доходов |
| **Total income** | 10,006 | 31,297 | 2,851 | 9,984 | 16,763 | 18,378 | **Всего доходов** |
| **Expenditure** | | | | | | | **Расходы** |
| **Total purchases** | 8,011 | 24,062 | 2,349 | 7,674 | 12,278 | 13,845 | **Всего покупок товаров и услуг** |
| Retail goods | 7,194 | 22,079 | 2,011 | 6,433 | 10,361 | 10,868 | Товары в розничной торговле |
| Services | 818 | 1,983 | 338 | 1,241 | 1,916 | 2,977 | Услуги |
| Rent and utilities | 196 | 210 | 221 | 740 | 686 | 1,030 | Квартирная плата и коммунальные платежи |
| Transport and communications | 276 | 587 | 64 | 304 | 396 | 614 | Транспорт и связь |
| Health and other services | 191 | 976 | 30 | 197 | 782 | 1,333 | Здравоохранение и другие виды услуг |
| Cooperatives | 155 | .. | 23 | .. | .. | .. | Кооперативы |
| **Transfers and savings** | 1,212 | 6,006 | 502 | 2,310 | 4,485 | 4,534 | **Трансферты и сбережения** |
| Taxes, fees, dues, and other | 1,172 | 4,193 | 184 | 717 | 1,741 | 3,833 | Налоги, сборы, пошлины и др. |
| Savings | 7 | 1,394 | 66 | 757 | 1,355 | 416 | Сбережения |
| Other | 33 | 419 | 252 | 836 | 1,388 | 284 | Прочие |
| **Total expenditure** | 9,223 | 30,068 | 2,851 | 9,984 | 16,763 | 18,378 | **Всего расходов** |
| **Income less expenditure** | 782 | 1,229 | 0 | 0 | 0 | 0 | **Доходы за вычетом расходов** |

# *Country Notes: Lithuania*

**General Notes:** Unless otherwise indicated, the data were supplied by the Department of Statistics of the Lithuanian Government.

**Currency:** The new national currency - litas -was introduced on June 23, 1993 with the conversion rate of 100 rubles per 1 litas. Unless otherwise indicated data are in rubles up to 1992, and in litas beginning in 1993.

**Table 1-1:** Individual labor activities includes private sector employees.

**Table 1-2:** Road maintenance includes freight transportation and communications. Wholesale trade includes retail trade, catering, material supply, and procurement. Housing includes public utilities and personal services. Education is included with culture and art. Credit includes insurance.

**Table 2-1:** Data are in litas starting with 1992. Gross Value Added was is at market rather than basic prices. Sector wholesale trade includes retail trade, restaurants, and hotels. Sector public utilities and personal services includes real estate, leasing, computer services, science, other business services, private education, private health services, private sporting and leisure services, other personal services, sanitation services, and other services. Sector private non-profit institutions serving households includes also fishing, imputed household production, and exports and imports taxes. Sector general administration and defense includes government budget and social security. The sum of the subcategories within "Other" does not equal the total due to missing information. The statistical discrepancy between GDP at market prices and GDP by expenditure category is 100 mln. rubles in 1990 and 4111 mln. rubles in 1991.

**Table 2-2**: Data are in 1993 litas. See also note to table 2-1.

**Table 3-1**: The BoP for 1992 is the first compiled by Lithuania; it is experimental and thus incompatible with Bops for the following years. The base for the percentage change in manufacture unit value is June of 1993=100. The index of real effective exchange rate is annual average.

**Tables 3-2B and 3-3B**: The category services includes also other goods.

**Tables 4-1 and 4-2**: The social security fund and the extra-budgetary funds are excluded.

**Table 5-1**: Data for 1995 are preliminary.

**Table 5-2**: Data are in 1983 rubles. The figures for total gross agricultural production do not include the value of agricultural services.

**Table 5-3**: Flax is flax-fiber. Hay production includes all hay, while hay yield refers to the hay from perennial grasses only.

**Table 5-4**: Livestock is reported as of the end of each year. Meat is reported in slaughtered weight.

**Table 6-3**: The recalculation into oil-equivalent was coordinated by the Ministry of Energy.

**Table 7-1**: The price indices for 1995 were calculated excluding the prices of electricity, gas, and water. Changes in the price indices are shown instead of the price indices.

**Table 7-2**: For 1994 and 1995 the data reflect wages paid in the state sector only.

**Table 8-1**: Data are in litas beginning in 1992.

# *Комментарии к таблицам: Литва*

**Общее замечание:** За исключением особо отмеченных случаев, данные были получены из Департамента Статистики при Правительстве Литовской Республики.

**Национальная валюта:** Национальная валюта - лит - была введена 23 июня 1993 г. Коэффициент пересчета на дату введения был 1 лит за 100 рублей. За исключением особо отмеченных случаев, данные приведены в рублях до 1992 г. включительно и в литах начиная с 1993 г.

**Таблица 1-1:** Индивидуальная трудовая деятельность включает занятых в частном секторе.

**Таблица 1-2:** Дорожное хозяйство включает также грузовой транспорт и связь. Оптовая торговля включает также розничную торговлю, общественное питание, материально-техническое снабжение и заготовки. Жилищное хозяйство также включает коммунальное хозяйство и бытовое обслуживание. В культуру и искусство включено образование. Кредитование и страхование приведены вместе. В 1992 г. сумма материального и нематериального производств не равна итогу.

**Таблица 2-1:** Начиная с 1992 г. данные приведены в литах. Валовая добавленная стоимость рассчитана в рыночных ценах. Оптовая торговля включает также розничную торговлю, рестораны и гостиницы. Коммунальное хозяйство и бытовое обслуживание включают также операции с недвижимостью, сдачу в аренду, информационно-технические услуги, науку, другие предпринимательские услуги, частное образование, частные медицинские услуги, частные спортивные и туристические услуги, санитарный сервис и другие услуги. Общественные организации, обслуживающие домашние хозяйства, включают также рыболовство, домашнее производство, налоги на экспорт и импорт. Государственное управление и оборона включает государственный бюджет и систему социальной защиты. Сумма компонентов раздела Другие отрасли не совпадает с итогом ввиду отсутствия данных. Статистическое расхождение между ВВП по производству и ВВП по категориям конечного использования за 1990 г. составляет 100, а за 1991г. - 4111 млн. рублей.

**Таблица 2-2:** Данные приведены в постоянных ценах 1993 г. См. также комментарий к таблице 2-1.

**Таблица 3-1:** Платежный баланс Литвы был составлен впервые в 1992г. экспериемнтально и не сопоставим с данными за последующие годы. Средний индекс цен на продукцию обрабатывающей промышленности рассчитан к июню 1993 г. Индекс реального курса рассчитан как среднеарифметический за год.

**Таблицы 3-2В и 3-3В:** Строка Услуги включают также прочие товары, не указанные выше.

**Таблицы 4-1 и 4-2:** Данные приводятся без учёта внебюджетных фондов и фондов социальной защиты.

**Таблица 5-1:** За 1995 г. приведены предварительные данные.

**Таблица 5-2:** Данные приведены в рублях 1983 г. Валовая продукция сельского хозяйства-всего приводится без учёта стоимости сельскохозяйственных услуг.

**Таблица 5-3:** Лен включает льноволокно. Производство сена включает все виды сена; урожай сена включает только сбор многолетних трав.

**Таблица 5-4:** Поголовье скота дано на конец года. Производство мяса дается в убойном весе.

**Таблица 6-3:** Данные рассчитаны в нефтяном эквиваленте Министерством Энергетики.

**Таблица 7-1:** За 1995 г. индексы цен рассчитаны без учета цен электричества, газа и воды. Вместо индексов цен приведены изменения индексов цен.

**Таблица 7-2:** За 1994-1995 гг. данные представляют заработную плату только в государственном секторе.

**Таблица 8-1:** Начиная с 1992 г. данные приведены в литах.

# Moldova / Молдова

1996 Population / Численность населения в 1996 году
(thousands / тыс. человек): 4,334

Area / Территория
(thousand square kilometers / тыс. кв. км.): 33.7

Capital city / Столица :
Chisinau / Кишинэу

**Country Tables:** Tables 2-2 to 2-2B are not included because there are no data available.

**Статистические таблицы страны:** Таблицы с 2-2 по 2-2B не включены ввиду отсутствия данных.

## TABLE 1-1. Population and employment (thousands)
## ТАБЛИЦА 1-1. Население и занятость (тысяч)

| Population or employment category | 1990 | 1991 | 1992 | 1993 | 1994 | 1995 | Население или группы занятых |
|---|---|---|---|---|---|---|---|
| **Total population** | 4,362 | 4,361 | 4,351 | 4,348 | 4,348 | 4,339 | **Население - всего** |
| Males | 2,079 | 2,080 | 2,077 | 2,076 | 2,076 | 2,073 | Мужчины |
| Females | 2,283 | 2,281 | 2,274 | 2,272 | 2,272 | 2,266 | Женщины |
| Urban population | 2,055 | 2,047 | 2,029 | 2,022 | 2,019 | 2,002 | Городское |
| Rural population | 2,307 | 2,314 | 2,322 | 2,326 | 2,329 | 2,337 | Сельское |
| Population under working age | 1,294 | 1,288 | 1,283 | 1,263 | 1,250 | 1,230 | Моложе трудоспособного возраста |
| Working-age population | 2,397 | 2,400 | 2,396 | 2,401 | 2,411 | 2,422 | Лица в трудоспособном возрасте |
| Population over working age | 671 | 673 | 672 | 684 | 687 | 687 | Старще трудоспособного возраста |
| Economically Active Population, in non-working age | 92 | 128 | 129 | 129 | 48 | .. | Экономически активное население в нетрудоспособном возрасте |
| Above working age | 81 | 108 | 109 | 109 | 28 | .. | Старше трудоспособного возраста |
| Below working age | 11 | 20 | 20 | 20 | 20 | .. | Моложе трудоспособного возраста |
| **Total labor resources** | 2,429 | 2,463 | 2,460 | 1,954 | 1,961 | .. | **Трудовые ресурсы - всего** |
| **Total employment** | 2,071 | 2,070 | 2,050 | 1,688 | 1,681 | .. | **Занятое население - всего** |
| State sector employees | 1,300 | 1,192 | 1,124 | 776 | 680 | 567 | Государственный сектор |
| Leased enterprise employees | 73 | 115 | 116 | 77 | 48 | .. | Арендные предприятия |
| Joint-stock company employees | .. | 5 | 11 | 57 | 150 | .. | Акционерные общества |
| Economic association employees | .. | .. | 55 | 3 | 8 | .. | Хозяйственные ассоциации |
| Social organization employees | 20 | 20 | 19 | 16 | 5 | .. | Общественные организации |
| Joint venture employees | 2 | 4 | 6 | 6 | 6 | 7 | Совместные предприятия |
| Collective farm workers | 372 | 335 | 344 | 339 | 380 | .. | Колхозы |
| Cooperative workers | 85 | 52 | 39 | 131 | 123 | .. | Кооперативы |
| Individual labor activities | 4 | 4 | 4 | 4 | 4 | .. | ИТД |
| Private subsidiary agricultural workers | 144 | 274 | 276 | 225 | 223 | .. | Личные подсобные хозяйства |
| Private agricultural workers | .. | .. | 1 | 5 | 16 | 37 | Фермерские хозяйства |
| **Students** | 151 | 146 | 142 | 115 | 100 | 102 | **Учащиеся** |
| **Religious workers** | 3 | 3 | 3 | .. | .. | .. | **Служащие религиозного культа** |
| **Working age population not employed in the national economy** | 204 | 244 | 265 | 151 | 160 | .. | **Лица в трудоспособном возрасте, не занятые в экономике** |
| Housewives | .. | .. | .. | .. | .. | .. | Домохозяйки |
| Military personnel | .. | .. | .. | .. | .. | .. | Военнослужащие |
| Unemployed | .. | .. | 2 | 12 | 18 | 23 | Безработные |
| **Labor force** | 2,071 | 2,070 | 2,052 | 1,700 | 1,699 | .. | **Рабочая сила** |

## TABLE 1-2. Employment by sector (thousands)
## ТАБЛИЦА 1-2. Численность занятого населения по секторам (тысяч)

| Sector | 1990 | 1991 | 1992 | 1993 | 1994 | 1995 | Сектор |
|---|---|---|---|---|---|---|---|
| **Material sphere** | 1,552 | 1,551 | 1,533 | 1,251 | 1,288 | .. | **Сфера материального производства** |
| **Agriculture and forestry** | 678 | 743 | 749 | 730 | 767 | .. | **Сельское и лесное хозяйство** |
| Agriculture | 673 | 739 | 745 | 726 | 764 | .. | Сельское хозяйство |
| Forestry | 5 | 4 | 4 | 4 | 3 | .. | Лесное хозяйство |
| **Industry and construction** | 628 | 577 | 561 | 350 | 323 | .. | **Промышленность и строительство** |
| Industry | 456 | 424 | 415 | 245 | 232 | .. | Промышленность |
| Construction | 172 | 153 | 146 | 105 | 91 | .. | Строительство |
| **Other** | 246 | 231 | 223 | 171 | 198 | .. | **Другие отрасли** |
| Transport of goods | 56 | 53 | 51 | 37 | 57 | .. | Грузовой транспорт |
| Road Maintenance | 1 | 1 | 1 | 1 | .. | .. | Дорожное хозяйство |
| Communication servicing material production | 13 | 13 | 13 | 9 | 16 | .. | Связь |
| Wholesale trade | 3 | 5 | 4 | 3 | 3 | .. | Оптовая торговля |
| Retail trade and catering | 89 | 87 | 86 | 85 | 88 | .. | Розничная торговля и общепит |
| Material supply | 13 | 13 | 12 | 8 | 7 | .. | Материально-техническое снабжение |
| Procurement | 40 | 31 | 30 | 10 | 9 | .. | Заготовки |
| Information and computing services | 6 | 5 | 4 | 4 | 3 | .. | Информационно-техническое обслуживание |
| Other sectors | 25 | 23 | 22 | 14 | 15 | .. | Другие отрасли сферы материального пр. |
| **Nonmaterial sphere** | 519 | 519 | 517 | 437 | 393 | .. | **Сфера нематериального производства** |
| Passenger transport | 42 | 41 | 40 | 28 | .. | .. | Пассажирский транспорт |
| Communication | .. | .. | .. | .. | .. | .. | Связь |
| Housing | 56 | 65 | 66 | 12 | 9 | .. | Жилищное хозяйство |
| Public utilities and personal services | .. | .. | .. | 38 | 39 | .. | Комм. хоз. и бытовое обслуживание |
| Health care, social security, physical culture and sports | 115 | 116 | 116 | 96 | 98 | .. | Здравоохранение, социальное обеспечение, физкультура и спорт |
| Education | 232 | 224 | 223 | 166 | 168 | .. | Образование |
| Culture and art | .. | .. | .. | 25 | 23 | .. | Культура и искусство |
| Science and scientific research | 33 | 29 | 28 | 14 | 13 | .. | Наука и научное обслуживание |
| Credit | 7 | 7 | 7 | 7 | 8 | .. | Кредитование |
| Insurance | 2 | 2 | 2 | 3 | 3 | .. | Страхование |
| General administration and defense | 32 | 35 | 35 | 48 | 32 | .. | Государственное управление и оборона |
| Private nonprofit institutions serving households | .. | .. | .. | .. | .. | .. | Общественные организации, обслуживающие домашние хозяйства |
| **Other, material and nonmaterial spheres** | 765 | 750 | 740 | 608 | 591 | .. | **Остальные отрасли материального производства и нематериальной сферы** |
| **Total employment** | 2,071 | 2,070 | 2,050 | 1,688 | 1,681 | .. | **Занятые - всего** |

**TABLE 1-3. Registered unemployment (thousands; end of month)**

**ТАБЛИЦА 1-3. Численность зарегистрированных безработных (тысяч; на конец месяца)**

| Year and month | Total<br>Всего | Males<br>Мужчины | Females<br>Женщины | Receiving benefits<br>Получающие пособие | Год и месяц |
|---|---|---|---|---|---|
| **1994** | | | | | **1994** |
| January | 15.8 | 6.1 | 9.7 | 1.0 | Январь |
| February | 17.1 | 6.8 | 10.3 | 4.3 | Февраль |
| March | 17.4 | 7.0 | 10.4 | 4.4 | Март |
| April | 17.6 | 7.2 | 10.4 | 4.4 | Апрель |
| May | 17.3 | 7.0 | 10.3 | 8.0 | Май |
| June | 17.3 | 6.9 | 10.4 | 9.0 | Июнь |
| July | 18.2 | 7.2 | 11.0 | 4.0 | Июль |
| August | 19.0 | 7.4 | 11.6 | 4.6 | Август |
| September | 19.4 | 6.9 | 12.5 | 5.6 | Сентябрь |
| October | 20.1 | 7.6 | 12.5 | 5.9 | Октябрь |
| November | 20.7 | 7.7 | 13.0 | 6.0 | Ноябрь |
| December | 20.6 | 7.7 | 12.9 | 6.3 | Декабрь |
| **1995** | | | | | **1995** |
| January | 21.9 | 8.3 | 13.6 | 6.6 | Январь |
| February | 23.1 | 8.8 | 14.3 | 7.1 | Февраль |
| March | 23.4 | 8.9 | 14.5 | 7.2 | Март |
| April | 23.4 | 8.7 | 14.7 | 7.4 | Апрель |
| May | 23.0 | 8.3 | 14.7 | 7.8 | Май |
| June | 22.4 | 8.0 | 14.4 | 7.7 | Июнь |
| July | 22.5 | 8.0 | 14.5 | 7.8 | Июль |
| August | 23.1 | 8.0 | 15.1 | 8.1 | Август |
| September | 24.2 | 8.2 | 16.0 | 8.3 | Сентябрь |
| October | 24.8 | 8.5 | 16.3 | 8.0 | Октябрь |
| November | 25.1 | 8.5 | 16.6 | 7.9 | Ноябрь |
| December | 24.5 | 8.5 | 16.0 | 8.0 | Декабрь |
| **1996** | | | | | **1996** |
| January | 25.3 | 9.1 | 16.2 | 8.0 | Январь |
| February | 26.3 | 9.6 | 16.7 | 8.1 | Февраль |
| March | 27.9 | 10.8 | 17.1 | 7.7 | Март |
| April | 26.8 | 9.9 | 16.9 | 7.6 | Апрель |
| May | 26.8 | 9.9 | 16.9 | 7.5 | Май |
| June | 26.1 | 9.4 | 16.7 | 7.3 | Июнь |
| July | .. | .. | .. | .. | Июль |
| August | .. | .. | .. | .. | Август |
| September | .. | .. | .. | .. | Сентябрь |
| October | .. | .. | .. | .. | Октябрь |
| November | .. | .. | .. | .. | Ноябрь |
| December | .. | .. | .. | .. | Декабрь |

**TABLE 2-1. Gross domestic product at current prices (thousands of national currency)**
**ТАБЛИЦА 2-1. Валовой внутренний продукт в текущих ценах (тысяч национальной валюты)**

| Sector of origin or expenditure category | 1990 | 1991 | 1992 | 1993 | 1994 | 1995 | Отраслевое происхождение или вид расходов |
|---|---|---|---|---|---|---|---|
| **Gross domestic product by sector of origin** | | | | | | | **Валовой внутренний продукт по отраслевому происхождению** |
| **Agriculture and forestry** | .. | .. | .. | .. | .. | .. | **Сельское и лесное хозяйство** |
| Agriculture | .. | .. | .. | .. | .. | .. | Сельское хозяйство |
| Forestry | .. | .. | .. | .. | .. | .. | Лесное хозяйство |
| **Industry and construction** | .. | .. | .. | .. | .. | .. | **Промышленность и строительство** |
| Industry | .. | .. | .. | .. | .. | .. | Промышленность |
| Construction | .. | .. | .. | .. | .. | .. | Строительство |
| **Other** | .. | .. | .. | .. | .. | .. | **Другие отрасли** |
| Transport | .. | .. | .. | .. | .. | .. | Транспорт |
| Road maintenance | .. | .. | .. | .. | .. | .. | Дорожное хозяйство |
| Communication | .. | .. | .. | .. | .. | .. | Связь |
| Wholesale trade | .. | .. | .. | .. | .. | .. | Оптовая торговля |
| Retail trade and catering | .. | .. | .. | .. | .. | .. | Розничная торговля и общепит |
| Material supply | .. | .. | .. | .. | .. | .. | Материально-техническое снабжение |
| Procurement | .. | .. | .. | .. | .. | .. | Заготовки |
| Information and computing services | .. | .. | .. | .. | .. | .. | Информационно-вычислительное обслуживание |
| Other sectors of material production | .. | .. | .. | .. | .. | .. | Другие отрасли сферы материального пр. |
| Housing | .. | .. | .. | .. | .. | .. | Жилищное хозяйство |
| Public utilities and personal services | .. | .. | .. | .. | .. | .. | Ком. хоз. и бытовое обслуживание |
| Health care, social security, physical culture and sports | .. | .. | .. | .. | .. | .. | Здравоохранение, социальное обеспечение, физкультура и спорт |
| Education | .. | .. | .. | .. | .. | .. | Образование |
| Culture and art | .. | .. | .. | .. | .. | .. | Культура и искусство |
| Science and scientific research | .. | .. | .. | .. | .. | .. | Наука и научное обслуживание |
| Credit | .. | .. | .. | .. | .. | .. | Кредитование |
| Insurance | .. | .. | .. | .. | .. | .. | Страхование |
| General administration and defense | .. | .. | .. | .. | .. | .. | Государственное управление и оборона |
| Private nonprofit institutions serving households | .. | .. | .. | .. | .. | .. | Общественные организации, обслуживающие домашние хозяйства |
| **Imputed service charge of financial intermediaries** | .. | .. | .. | .. | .. | .. | **Условно-исчисляемая стоимость услуг финансовых посредников** |
| **Total gross value added (GVA)** | .. | .. | .. | .. | .. | .. | **Валовая добавленная стоимость (ВДС) - всего** |
| **Taxes on production and imports (TOPI)** | .. | .. | .. | .. | .. | .. | **Налоги на производство и импорт (НПиИ)** |
| Other taxes on production (OTOP) | .. | .. | .. | .. | .. | .. | Другие налоги на производство (ДНП) |
| **Subsidies on production and imports (SOPI)** | .. | .. | .. | .. | .. | .. | **Субсидии на производство и импорт (СПиИ)** |
| Other subsidies on production (OSOP) | .. | .. | .. | .. | .. | .. | Другие субсидии на производство (ДСП) |
| **Total GDP at factor cost (GVA-OTOP+OSOP)** | .. | .. | .. | .. | .. | .. | **Всего ВВП по фактр. стоимости (ВДС-ДНП+ДСП)** |
| **Net Indirect taxes (TOPI - SOPI)** | .. | .. | .. | .. | .. | .. | **Чистые косвенные налоги (НПиИ-СПиИ)** |
| **Total GDP at market prices** | 12,681 | 25,895 | 191,944 | 2,210,444 | 5,780,218 | 7,636,178 | **Всего ВВП в рыночных ценах** |
| **Gross domestic product by expenditure category** | | | | | | | **Валовой внутренний продукт по видам расходов** |
| **Consumption** | 9,715 | 18,819 | 110,311 | 1,534,474 | 4,112,115 | 5,742,406 | **Потребление** |
| Private consumption | 7,471 | 14,131 | 79,122 | 1,021,580 | 2,960,700 | 4,199,898 | Личное потребление |
| Government consumption | 2,244 | 4,688 | 31,189 | 512,894 | 1,151,415 | 1,542,508 | Общественное потребление |
| **Gross domestic investment** | 3,250 | 7,546 | 114,743 | 1,077,996 | 2,016,741 | 2,275,581 | **Валовые внутренние инвестиции** |
| Gross fixed investment | 2,426 | 4,421 | 31,108 | 277,761 | 563,286 | 748,666 | Валовое накопление основного капитала |
| Change in stocks | 824 | 3,125 | 83,635 | 800,235 | 1,453,455 | 1,526,915 | Изменения в запасах (МОС) |
| **Resource balance (net exports of GNFS)** | -284 | -470 | -33,110 | -402,026 | -348,638 | -381,809 | **Сальдо ресурсов (чистый экспорт ТНФУ)** |
| Exports of goods and nonfactor services | 6,177 | 8,361 | 72,069 | 950,596 | 2,405,951 | 3,257,246 | Экспорт товаров и нефакторных услуг |
| Imports of goods and nonfactor services | 6,461 | 8,831 | 105,179 | 1,352,622 | 2,754,589 | 3,639,055 | Импорт товаров и нефакторных услуг |

## TABLE 2-1A. Distribution of gross domestic product at current prices (percent)
## ТАБЛИЦА 2-1A. Распределение валового внутреннего продукта в текущих ценах ( % )



| Sector of origin or expenditure category | 1990 | 1991 | 1992 | 1993 | 1994 | 1995 | Отраслевое происхождение или вид расходов |
|---|---|---|---|---|---|---|---|
| **Gross domestic product by sector of origin** | | | | | | | **ВВП по отраслевому происхождению** |
| **Agriculture and forestry** | .. | .. | .. | .. | .. | .. | **Сельское и лесное хозяйство** |
| Agriculture | .. | .. | .. | .. | .. | .. | Сельское хозяйство |
| Forestry | .. | .. | .. | .. | .. | .. | Лесное хозяйство |
| **Industry and construction** | .. | .. | .. | .. | .. | .. | **Промышленность и строительство** |
| Industry | .. | .. | .. | .. | .. | .. | Промышленность |
| Construction | .. | .. | .. | .. | .. | .. | Строительство |
| **Other** | .. | .. | .. | .. | .. | .. | **Другие отрасли** |
| Transport | .. | .. | .. | .. | .. | .. | Транспорт |
| Road maintenance | .. | .. | .. | .. | .. | .. | Дорожное хозяйство |
| Communication | .. | .. | .. | .. | .. | .. | Связь |
| Wholesale trade | .. | .. | .. | .. | .. | .. | Оптовая торговля |
| Retail trade and catering | .. | .. | .. | .. | .. | .. | Розничная торговля и общепит |
| Material supply | .. | .. | .. | .. | .. | .. | Материально-техническое снабжение |
| Procurement | .. | .. | .. | .. | .. | .. | Заготовки |
| Information and computing services | .. | .. | .. | .. | .. | .. | Информационно-вычислительное обслуживание |
| Other sectors of material production | .. | .. | .. | .. | .. | .. | Другие отрасли сферы матерл. произ. |
| Housing | .. | .. | .. | .. | .. | .. | Жилищное хозяйство |
| Public utilities and personal services | .. | .. | .. | .. | .. | .. | Ком. хоз. и бытовое обслуживание |
| Health care, social security, physical culture and sports | .. | .. | .. | .. | .. | .. | Здравоохранение, социальное обеспечение, физкультура и спорт |
| Education | .. | .. | .. | .. | .. | .. | Образование |
| Culture and art | .. | .. | .. | .. | .. | .. | Культура и искусство |
| Science and scientific research | .. | .. | .. | .. | .. | .. | Наука и научное обслуживание |
| Credit | .. | .. | .. | .. | .. | .. | Кредитование |
| Insurance | .. | .. | .. | .. | .. | .. | Страхование |
| General administration and defense | .. | .. | .. | .. | .. | .. | Государственное управление и оборона |
| Private nonprofit institutions serving households | .. | .. | .. | .. | .. | .. | Общественные организации, обслуживающие домашние хозяйства |
| **Imputed service charge of financial intermediaries** | .. | .. | .. | .. | .. | .. | **Условно-исчисляемая стоимость услуг финансовых посредников** |
| **Total gross value added** | .. | .. | .. | .. | .. | .. | **Валовая добавленная стоимость - всего** |
| **Total GDP at factor cost** | .. | .. | .. | .. | .. | .. | **ВВП по фактор. стоимости - всего** |
| **Net indirect taxes** | .. | .. | .. | .. | .. | .. | **Чистые косвенные налоги (НПиИ-СПиИ)** |
| **Total GDP at market prices** | 100.0 | 100.0 | 100.0 | 100.0 | 100.0 | 100.0 | **ВВП в рын. ценах - всего** |
| **Gross domestic product by expenditure category** | | | | | | | **ВВП по видам расходов** |
| **Consumption** | 76.6 | 72.7 | 57.5 | 69.4 | 71.1 | 75.2 | **Потребление** |
| Private consumption | 58.9 | 54.6 | 41.2 | 46.2 | 51.2 | 55.0 | Личное потребление |
| Government consumption | 17.7 | 18.1 | 16.2 | 23.2 | 19.9 | 20.2 | Общественное потребление |
| **Gross domestic investment** | 25.6 | 29.1 | 59.8 | 48.8 | 34.9 | 29.8 | **Вал. внутр. инвестиции** |
| Gross fixed investment | 19.1 | 17.1 | 16.2 | 12.6 | 9.7 | 9.8 | Вал. накопление осн. капитала |
| Change in stocks | 6.5 | 12.1 | 43.6 | 36.2 | 25.1 | 20.0 | Изменения в запасах (МОС) |
| **Resource balance (net exports of GNFS)** | -2.2 | -1.8 | -17.2 | -18.2 | -6.0 | -5.0 | **Сальдо ресурсов (чистый экспорт ТНФУ)** |
| Exports of goods and nonfactor services | 48.7 | 32.3 | 37.5 | 43.0 | 41.6 | 42.7 | Экспорт товаров и нефакторных услуг |
| Imports of goods and nonfactor services | 51.0 | 34.1 | 54.8 | 61.2 | 47.7 | 47.7 | Импорт товаров и нефакторных услуг |

## TABLE 3-1. Balance of payments at current prices (millions of U.S. dollars)
## ТАБЛИЦА 3-1. Платежный баланс в текущих ценах (в миллионах долларов США)

| Item | 1990 | 1991 | 1992 | 1993 | 1994 | 1995 | Статьи |
|---|---|---|---|---|---|---|---|
| Exports of goods and services (including workers' remittances) | .. | .. | 381.3 | 437.4 | 663.5 | 865.7 | Экспорт товаров и услуг (включая денежные переводы рабочих) |
| Exports of goods and nonfactor services | .. | .. | 381.3 | 413.0 | 651.5 | 843.8 | Экспорт товаров и нефакт. услуг |
| Merchandise (FOB) | .. | .. | 368.4 | 393.0 | 619.0 | 740.6 | Товары (ФОБ) |
| Nonfactor services | .. | .. | 12.9 | 20.0 | 32.5 | 103.2 | Нефакторные услуги |
| Shipment | .. | .. | .. | 1.9 | 10.0 | 1.1 | Перевозки |
| Travel | .. | .. | 9.9 | 11.0 | 7.5 | 56.9 | Поездки |
| Other | .. | .. | 3.0 | 7.0 | 15.0 | 45.2 | Другие |
| Imports of goods and nonfactor services | .. | .. | 535.2 | 575.0 | 751.9 | 957.7 | Импорт товаров и нефакт. услуг |
| Merchandise (FOB) | .. | .. | 505.7 | 528.0 | 672.0 | 773.1 | Товары (ФОБ) |
| Nonfactor services | .. | .. | 29.5 | 47.3 | 78.9 | 184.6 | Нефакторные услуги |
| Shipment | .. | .. | 27.7 | 41.0 | 51.0 | 95.1 | Перевозки |
| Travel | .. | .. | 1.9 | 5.0 | 10.3 | 56.4 | Поездки |
| Other | .. | .. | .. | 1.0 | 18.0 | 32.5 | Другие |
| Resource balance | .. | .. | -154.0 | -162.0 | -100.4 | -113.9 | Сальдо ресурсов |
| Net factor income | .. | .. | .. | -14.6 | -15.0 | -20.5 | Чистый факторный доход |
| Factor receipts | .. | .. | .. | 24.4 | 11.0 | 20.9 | Факторные поступления |
| Factor payments | .. | .. | .. | 39.0 | 26.0 | 41.4 | Факторные платежи |
| Total interest due | .. | .. | .. | 3.6 | 17.0 | 31.2 | Общая сумма процента к оплате |
| Other factor payments and discrepancy | .. | .. | .. | 35.4 | 9.0 | 10.2 | Другие факторные платежи и стат. погр. |
| Net current transfers | .. | .. | 1.5 | 21.8 | 33.0 | 39.5 | Чистые текущие трансферты |
| Current receipts | .. | .. | 1.8 | 21.8 | 37.0 | 49.6 | Текущие поступления |
| Workers remittances | .. | .. | .. | .. | 1.0 | 1.0 | Денежные переводы рабочих |
| Other current transfers | .. | .. | 1.8 | 21.8 | 36.0 | 48.6 | Другие текущие трансферты |
| Current payments | .. | .. | 0.3 | .. | 3.9 | 10.0 | Текущие платежи |
| Current account balance before official grants | .. | .. | -152.5 | -155.0 | -82.0 | -94.7 | Сальдо текущего счета до офиц. безвозмезд. трансфертов |
| Official capital grants | .. | .. | .. | .. | 1.0 | 39.5 | Официальные кап. безвозмезные трансферты |
| Current account balance after official grants | .. | .. | -152.5 | .. | -81.0 | -55.2 | Сальдо текущего счета после офиц. безвозмезд. трансфертов |
| Long Term Capital Inflows | .. | .. | 33.1 | 123.3 | 163.0 | 194.1 | Долгосрочные притоки капитала |
| Direct investment | .. | .. | 17.4 | 0.4 | 12.3 | 63.7 | Прямые инвестиции |
| Net long term borrowing | .. | .. | 15.7 | 122.9 | 151.0 | 130.4 | Чистые долгосрочные займы |
| Disbursements | .. | .. | 15.7 | 151.3 | 169.3 | 189.5 | Поступления |
| Repayments due | .. | .. | .. | 28.4 | 17.8 | 59.1 | Сумма, подлежащая погашению |
| Other long-term inflows (net) | .. | .. | .. | .. | .. | .. | Другие долгосрочные притоки (чистые) |

(continued on next page)

**TABLE 3-1. Balance of payments at current prices (millions of U.S. dollars)**
**ТАБЛИЦА 3-1. Платежный баланс в текущих ценах (в миллионах долларов США)**

| Item | 1990 | 1991 | 1992 | 1993 | 1994 | 1995 | Статьи |
|---|---|---|---|---|---|---|---|
| Adjustment to Scheduled Debt Service | .. | .. | .. | .. | 17.8 | 18.9 | Регулирование долга |
| Debt service not paid | .. | .. | .. | .. | 17.8 | 18.9 | Невыплаченный долг |
| Interest not paid | .. | .. | .. | .. | .. | 1.1 | Невыплаченный процент |
| Principal not paid | .. | .. | .. | .. | 17.8 | 17.8 | Невыплаченная сумма основного долга |
| Arrears reductions/prepayments(-) | .. | .. | .. | .. | .. | .. | Погашение просроченных платежей/выплаты авансом (-) |
| Total Other items (Net) | .. | .. | 0.8 | 18.5 | -57.0 | -15.1 | Общие другие статьи (чистые) |
| Net short-term capital | .. | .. | 0.8 | 43.1 | 57.0 | -25.2 | Чистый краткосрочный капитал |
| Capital flows not elsewhere included | .. | .. | .. | .. | .. | .. | Потоки капитала, не указанные выше |
| Errors and omissions | .. | .. | .. | -24.6 | -114.0 | 10.1 | Ошибки и пропуски |
| Changes in net reserves | .. | .. | -1.7 | 13.4 | -32.8 | -129.5 | Изменения в чистых резервах |
| Net credit from IMF | .. | .. | .. | 87.7 | 71.3 | 64.7 | Чистый кредит МВФ |
| Reserve changes not elsewhere included | .. | .. | -1.7 | -74.3 | -104.1 | -77.4 | Изменения резервов, не указанных выше |
| Escrow account | .. | .. | .. | .. | .. | -116.7 | Счет депонирования |
| Gross reserves (excluding gold) | .. | .. | 2.4 | 76.7 | 180.0 | 257.0 | Общие резервы (исключая золото) |
| Gross reserves (including gold) | .. | .. | 2.4 | 76.7 | 180.0 | 257.0 | Общие резервы (включая золото) |
| Nominal official exchange rate (annual average) (rf) | .. | .. | 0.2 | 1.4 | 4.1 | 4.5 | Номинальный официальный или рыночный курс (среднегодовой) |
| Nominal official exchange rate (end-of-year) (ae) | .. | .. | 0.4 | 3.6 | 4.3 | 4.5 | Номинальный официальный или рыночный курс (на конец года) |
| Manufacture unit value (percent change) | .. | .. | .. | .. | .. | .. | Средний индекс цен на продукцию обр. пром.,% |
| Index of real effective exchange rate (IMF) | .. | .. | .. | .. | .. | .. | Индекс реального эффективного валютного курса (МВФ) |
| Total factor payments | .. | .. | .. | -3.2 | -17.0 | 31.5 | Общая сумма факторных платежей |
| Government interest | .. | .. | .. | -3.2 | -17.0 | 31.2 | Процент, выплачиваемый органами гос. управления |
| Private sector interest | .. | .. | .. | .. | 0.0 | 0.3 | Процент выплачиваемый частным сектором |
| Profits on direct foreign investment | .. | .. | .. | .. | .. | .. | Прибыль от прямых иностранных инвестиций |
| Official capital grants | .. | .. | .. | .. | -1.0 | -0.4 | Официальные капитальные безвозмездные трансферты |
| For budgetary financing | .. | .. | .. | .. | .. | .. | На бюджетное финансирование |
| To extrabudgetary entities | .. | .. | .. | .. | .. | .. | На внебюджетное финансирование |
| Government net long term borrowing | .. | .. | 15.7 | 69.3 | -142.0 | 119.7 | Чистые долгосрочные государственные займы |
| Disbursements | .. | .. | 15.7 | 69.3 | 9.0 | 178.8 | Поступления |
| Repayments | .. | .. | .. | .. | 151.0 | 59.1 | Погашения |
| Private net long term borrowing | .. | .. | .. | .. | .. | 10.8 | Чистые долгосрочные частные займы |
| Disbursements | .. | .. | .. | .. | .. | 10.8 | Поступления |
| Repayments | .. | .. | .. | .. | .. | .. | Погашения |

**TABLE 3-2A. Imports by commodity group (millions of U.S. dollars)**
**ТАБЛИЦА 3-2А . Импорт по товарным группам (млн. долларов США)**

| Commodity group | 1990 | 1991 | 1992 | 1993 | 1994 | 1995 | Товарные группы |
|---|---|---|---|---|---|---|---|
| TOTAL | .. | .. | .. | 628.0 | 659.3 | 840.7 | ВСЕГО |
| I - Live animals; animal products | .. | .. | .. | 4.2 | 2.4 | 8.6 | I - Живые животные и продукты животноводства |
| II - Vegetable products | .. | .. | .. | 45.8 | 26.5 | 34.1 | II - Продукты растительного происхождения |
| III - Animal or vegetable fats and oils and their cleavage products; prepared edible fats; animal or vegetable waxes | .. | .. | .. | 1.1 | 0.8 | 1.6 | III - Жиры и масла растительного и животного происхождения, воски |
| IV - Prepared foodstuffs; beverages, spirits and vinegar; tobacco and manufactured tobacco substitutes | .. | .. | .. | 18.3 | 20.6 | 34.5 | IV -Продукция пищевой промышленности, алкогольные и безалкогольные напитки, табак и его заменители |
| V - Mineral products | .. | .. | .. | 332.1 | 366.3 | 390.8 | V - Минеральные продукты |
| VI - Products of the chemical or allied industries | .. | .. | .. | 39.1 | 38.2 | 65.7 | VI - Продукция химической промышленности |
| VII - Plastics and articles thereof; rubber and articles thereof | .. | .. | .. | 8.4 | 11.0 | 21.1 | VII - Пластмассы и изделия из них |
| VIII - Raw hides and skins, leather, furskins and articles thereof; saddlery and harness; travel goods, handbags and similar containers; articles of animal gut | .. | .. | .. | 2.0 | 3.2 | 3.9 | VIII - Кожевенное сырьё, кожи, пушнина, меховое сырьё и изделия из них |
| IX - Wood and articles of wood; wood charcoal; cork and articles of cork; manufactures of straw, of esparto or of other plaiting materials; basketware and wickerwork | .. | .. | .. | 7.9 | 7.6 | 12.0 | IX - Древесина и изделия из древесины, древесный уголь |
| X - Pulp of wood or of other fibrous cellulosic material; waste and scrap of paper or paperboard; paper and paperboard and articles thereof | .. | .. | .. | 8.7 | 14.8 | 29.2 | X - Бумажная масса, бумажные и картонные отходы, макулатура, бумага, картон и изделия из них |
| XI - Textiles and textile articles | .. | .. | .. | 42.6 | 38.9 | 41.5 | XI - Текстиль и текстильные изделия |
| XII - Footwear, headgear, umbrellas, sun umbrellas, walking sticks, seat sticks, whips, riding crops and parts thereof; prepared feathers and articles made therewith; artificial flowers; articles of human hair | .. | .. | .. | 4.2 | 3.0 | 2.2 | XII - Обувь, головные уборы, зонты, трости и пр. |

## TABLE 3-2A. Imports by commodity group (millions of U.S. dollars)



## ТАБЛИЦА 3-2А . Импорт по товарным группам (млн. долларов США)

| Commodity group | 1990 | 1991 | 1992 | 1993 | 1994 | 1995 | Товарные группы |
|---|---|---|---|---|---|---|---|
| XIII - Articles of stone, plaster, cement, asbestos, mica and similar materials; ceramic products; glass and glassware | .. | .. | .. | 8.7 | 9.9 | 22.2 | XIII - Изделия из камня, гипса, цемента |
| XIV - Natural or cultured pearls, precious or semi-precious stones, precious metals, metals clad with precious metal and articles thereof; imitation jewellery; coin | .. | .. | .. | 2.3 | 0.8 | 2.3 | XIV - Жемчуг, драгоценные и полудрагоценные камни, драгоценные металлы, бижутерия, монеты |
| XV - Base metals and articles of base metal | .. | .. | .. | 28.6 | 20.6 | 33.8 | XV - Неблагородные металлы и изделия из них |
| XVI - Machinery and mechanical appliances; electrical equipment; parts thereof; sound recorders and reproducers, television image and sound recorders and reproducers, and parts and accessories of such articles | .. | .. | .. | 39.6 | 64.6 | 104.4 | XVI - Машины, оборудование, механизмы, их части и принадлежности; звуковая и теле-аппаратура, их части и принадлежности |
| XVII - Vehicles, aircraft, vessels and associated transport equipment | .. | .. | .. | 18.7 | 19.7 | 21.8 | XVII - Средства наземного, воздушного и водного транспорта |
| XVIII - Optical, photographic, cinematographic, measuring, checking, precision, medical or surgical instruments and apparatus; clocks and watches; musical instruments; parts and accessories thereof | .. | .. | .. | 3.9 | 4.1 | 6.8 | XVIII - Приборы, аппараты оптические, медицинские, измерительные и пр.; музыкальные инструменты; часы; их части и принадлежности |
| XIX - Arms and ammunition; parts and accessories thereof | .. | .. | .. | .. | .. | .. | XIX - Оружие и боеприпасы, их части и принадлежности |
| XX - Miscellaneous manufactured articles | .. | .. | .. | 11.8 | 6.3 | 4.2 | XX - Разные промышленные товары |
| XXI - Works of art, collectors' pieces, and antiques | .. | .. | .. | 0.0 | 0.0 | 0.0 | XXI - Произведения искусства, предметы антиквариата |
| XXII - Services | .. | .. | .. | 11.4 | 28.0 | 110.1 | XXII - Услуги |

**TABLE 3-2B Imports by commodity group (millions of national currency)**
**ТАБЛИЦА 3-2B. Импорт по товарным группам (млн. национальной валюты)**

| Commodity group | 1990 | 1991 | 1992 | 1993 | 1994 | 1995 | Товарные группы |
|---|---|---|---|---|---|---|---|
| TOTAL | .. | .. | .. | 909.2 | 2,692.2 | 3,784.8 | ВСЕГО |
| I - Live animals; animal products | .. | .. | .. | 6.0 | 9.8 | 39.0 | I - Живые животные и продукты животноводства |
| II - Vegetable products | .. | .. | .. | 66.4 | 109.1 | 153.1 | II - Продукты растительного происхождения |
| III - Animal or vegetable fats and oils and their cleavage products; prepared edible fats; animal or vegetable waxes | .. | .. | .. | 1.5 | 3.2 | 7.5 | III - Жиры и масла растительного и животного происхождения, воски |
| IV - Prepared foodstuffs; beverages, spirits and vinegar; tobacco and manufactured tobacco substitutes | .. | .. | .. | 26.4 | 84.4 | 155.7 | IV -Продукция пищевой промышленности, алкогольные и безалкогольные напитки, табак и его заменители |
| V - Mineral products | .. | .. | .. | 480.8 | 1,489.1 | 1,756.1 | V - Минеральные продукты |
| VI - Products of the chemical or allied industries | .. | .. | .. | 56.6 | 157.8 | 296.0 | VI - Продукция химической промышленности |
| VII - Plastics and articles thereof; rubber and articles thereof | .. | .. | .. | 12.1 | 45.1 | 95.2 | VII - Пластмассы и изделия из них |
| VIII - Raw hides and skins, leather, furskins and articles thereof; saddlery and harness; travel goods, handbags and similar containers; articles of animal gut | .. | .. | .. | 2.9 | 13.0 | 17.5 | VIII - Кожевенное сырьё, кожи, пушнина, меховое сырьё и изделия из них |
| IX - Wood and articles of wood; wood charcoal; cork and articles of cork; manufactures of straw, of esparto or of other plaiting materials; basketware and wickerwork | .. | .. | .. | 11.5 | 31.3 | 53.9 | IX - Древесина и изделия из древесины, древесный уголь |
| X - Pulp of wood or of other fibrous cellulosic material; waste and scrap of paper or paperboard; paper and paperboard and articles thereof | .. | .. | .. | 12.5 | 61.1 | 132.1 | X - Бумажная масса, бумажные и картонные отходы, макулатура, бумага, картон и изделия из них |
| XI - Textiles and textile articles | .. | .. | .. | 61.7 | 158.2 | 186.9 | XI - Текстиль и текстильные изделия |
| XII - Footwear, headgear, umbrellas, sun umbrellas, walking sticks, seat sticks, whips, riding crops and parts thereof; prepared feathers and articles made therewith; artificial flowers; articles of human hair | .. | .. | .. | 6.1 | 12.2 | 9.9 | XII - Обувь, головные уборы, зонты, трости и пр. |

**TABLE 3-2B Imports by commodity group (millions of national currency)**
**ТАБЛИЦА 3-2B. Импорт по товарным группам (млн. национальной валюты)**

| Commodity group | 1990 | 1991 | 1992 | 1993 | 1994 | 1995 | Товарные группы |
|---|---|---|---|---|---|---|---|
| XIII - Articles of stone, plaster, cement, asbestos, mica and similar materials; ceramic products; glass and glassware | .. | .. | .. | 12.7 | 40.8 | 100.1 | XIII - Изделия из камня, гипса, цемента |
| XIV - Natural or cultured pearls, precious or semi-precious stones, precious metals, metals clad with precious metal and articles thereof; imitation jewellery; coin | .. | .. | .. | 3.4 | 3.3 | 10.4 | XIV - Жемчуг, драгоценные и полудрагоценные камни, драгоценные металлы, бижутерия, монеты |
| XV - Base metals and articles of base metal | .. | .. | .. | 41.4 | 85.4 | 152.6 | XV - Неблагородные металлы и изделия из них |
| XVI - Machinery and mechanical appliances; electrical equipment; parts thereof; sound recorders and reproducers, television image and sound recorders and reproducers, and parts and accessories of such articles | .. | .. | .. | 57.4 | 264.7 | 471.3 | XVI - Машины, оборудование, механизмы, их части и принадлежности; звуковая и теле-аппаратура, их части и принадлежности |
| XVII - Vehicles, aircraft, vessels and associated transport equipment | .. | .. | .. | 27.0 | 80.9 | 98.0 | XVII - Средства наземного, воздушного и водного транспорта |
| XVIII - Optical, photographic, cinematographic, measuring, checking, precision, medical or surgical instruments and apparatus; clocks and watches; musical instruments; parts and accessories thereof | .. | .. | .. | 5.7 | 17.0 | 30.6 | XVIII - Приборы, аппараты оптические, медицинские, измерительные и пр.; музыкальные инструменты; часы; их части и принадлежности |
| XIX - Arms and ammunition; parts and accessories thereof | .. | .. | .. | .. | .. | .. | XIX - Оружие и боеприпасы, их части и принадлежности |
| XX - Miscellaneous manufactured articles | .. | .. | .. | 17.1 | 25.8 | 18.8 | XX - Разные промышленные товары |
| XXI - Works of art, collectors' pieces, and antiques | .. | .. | .. | 0.0 | 0.0 | 0.1 | XXI - Произведения искусства, предметы антиквариата |
| XXII - Services | .. | .. | .. | 25.0 | 114.7 | 494.9 | XXII - Услуги |

**TABLE 3-3A. Exports by commodity group (millions of U.S. dollars)**
**ТАБЛИЦА 3-3A. Экспорт по товарным группам (млн. долларов США)**

| Commodity group | 1990 | 1991 | 1992 | 1993 | 1994 | 1995 | Товарные группы |
|---|---|---|---|---|---|---|---|
| TOTAL | .. | .. | .. | 483.0 | 565.4 | 745.5 | ВСЕГО |
| I - Live animals; animal products | .. | .. | .. | 31.6 | 45.3 | 67.9 | I - Живые животные и продукты животноводства |
| II - Vegetable products | .. | .. | .. | 27.4 | 99.4 | 76.3 | II - Продукты растительного происхождения |
| III - Animal or vegetable fats and oils and their cleavage products; prepared edible fats; animal or vegetable waxes | .. | .. | .. | 11.9 | 11.2 | 11.1 | III - Жиры и масла растительного и животного происхождения, воски |
| IV - Prepared foodstuffs; beverages, spirits and vinegar; tobacco and manufactured tobacco substitutes | .. | .. | .. | 137.0 | 226.5 | 382.3 | IV -Продукция пищевой промышленности, алкогольные и безалкогольные напитки, табак и его заменители |
| V - Mineral products | .. | .. | .. | 72.8 | 14.8 | 8.3 | V - Минеральные продукты |
| VI - Products of the chemical or allied industries | .. | .. | .. | 12.2 | 8.0 | 8.0 | VI - Продукция химической промышленности |
| VII - Plastics and articles thereof; rubber and articles thereof | .. | .. | .. | 3.5 | 3.6 | 4.4 | VII - Пластмассы и изделия из них |
| VIII - Raw hides and skins, leather, furskins and articles thereof; saddlery and harness; travel goods, handbags and similar containers; articles of animal gut | .. | .. | .. | 3.9 | 8.8 | 14.6 | VIII - Кожевенное сырьё, кожи, пушнина, меховое сырьё и изделия из них |
| IX - Wood and articles of wood; wood charcoal; cork and articles of cork; manufactures of straw, of esparto or of other plaiting materials; basketware and wickerwork | .. | .. | .. | 1.3 | 0.3 | 0.8 | IX - Древесина и изделия из древесины, древесный уголь |
| X - Pulp of wood or of other fibrous cellulosic material; waste and scrap of paper or paperboard; paper and paperboard and articles thereof | .. | .. | .. | 12.3 | 7.7 | 8.5 | X - Бумажная масса, бумажные и картонные отходы, макулатура, бумага, картон и изделия из них |
| XI - Textiles and textile articles | .. | .. | .. | 23.6 | 29.2 | 35.1 | XI - Текстиль и текстильные изделия |
| XII - Footwear, headgear, umbrellas, sun umbrellas, walking sticks, seat sticks, whips, riding crops and parts thereof; prepared feathers and articles made therewith; artificial flowers; articles of human hair | .. | .. | .. | 4.2 | 3.0 | 3.3 | XII - Обувь, головные уборы, зонты, трости и пр. |

**TABLE 3-3A. Exports by commodity group (millions of U.S. dollars)** **MOLDOVA**

**ТАБЛИЦА 3-3A. Экспорт по товарным группам (млн. долларов США)**

| Commodity group | 1990 | 1991 | 1992 | 1993 | 1994 | 1995 | Товарные группы |
|---|---|---|---|---|---|---|---|
| XIII - Articles of stone, plaster, cement, asbestos, mica and similar materials; ceramic products; glass and glassware | .. | .. | .. | 9.9 | 5.5 | 15.4 | XIII - Изделия из камня, гипса, цемента |
| XIV - Natural or cultured pearls, precious or semi-precious stones, precious metals, metals clad with precious metal and articles thereof; imitation jewellery; coin | .. | .. | .. | 0.2 | 1.0 | 2.2 | XIV - Жемчуг, драгоценные и полудрагоценные камни, драгоценные металлы, бижутерия, монеты |
| XV - Base metals and articles of base metal | .. | .. | .. | 42.9 | 18.9 | 32.4 | XV - Неблагородные металлы и изделия из них |
| XVI - Machinery and mechanical appliances; electrical equipment; parts thereof; sound recorders and reproducers, television image and sound recorders and reproducers, and parts and accessories of such articles | .. | .. | .. | 56.7 | 54.1 | 46.4 | XVI - Машины, оборудование, механизмы, их части и принадлежности; звуковая и теле-аппаратура, их части и принадлежности |
| XVII - Vehicles, aircraft, vessels and associated transport equipment | .. | .. | .. | 19.7 | 11.0 | 12.4 | XVII - Средства наземного, воздушного и водного транспорта |
| XVIII - Optical, photographic, cinematographic, measuring, checking, precision, medical or surgical instruments and apparatus; clocks and watches; musical instruments; parts and accessories thereof | .. | .. | .. | 0.4 | 1.6 | 1.4 | XVIII - Приборы, аппараты оптические, медицинские, измерительные и пр.; музыкальные инструменты; часы; их части и принадлежности |
| XIX - Arms and ammunition; parts and accessories thereof | .. | .. | .. | .. | .. | .. | XIX - Оружие и боеприпасы, их части и принадлежности |
| XX - Miscellaneous manufactured articles | .. | .. | .. | 11.5 | 15.5 | 14.7 | XX - Разные промышленные товары |
| XXI - Works of art, collectors' pieces, and antiques | .. | .. | .. | 0.0 | 0.0 | 0.0 | XXI - Произведения искусства, предметы антиквариата |
| XXII - Services | .. | .. | .. | 21.2 | 32.8 | 103.2 | XXII - Услуги |

**TABLE 3-3B. Exports by Commodity Group (millions of national currency)**
**ТАБЛИЦА 3-3B. Экспорт по товарным группам (млн. национальной валюты)**

| Commodity group | 1990 | 1991 | 1992 | 1993 | 1994 | 1995 | Товарные группы |
|---|---|---|---|---|---|---|---|
| TOTAL | .. | .. | .. | 701.9 | 2,318.5 | 3,349.2 | ВСЕГО |
| I - Live animals; animal products | .. | .. | .. | 45.8 | 187.1 | 305.6 | I - Живые животные и продукты животноводства |
| II - Vegetable products | .. | .. | .. | 39.7 | 409.3 | 344.7 | II - Продукты растительного происхождения |
| III - Animal or vegetable fats and oils and their cleavage products; prepared edible fats; animal or vegetable waxes | .. | .. | .. | 17.3 | 46.1 | 50.3 | III - Жиры и масла растительного и животного происхождения, воски |
| IV - Prepared foodstuffs; beverages, spirits and vinegar; tobacco and manufactured tobacco substitutes | .. | .. | .. | 198.3 | 927.1 | 1,712.4 | IV -Продукция пищевой промышленности, алкогольные и безалкогольные напитки, табак и его заменители |
| V - Mineral products | .. | .. | .. | 108.1 | 61.1 | 37.6 | V - Минеральные продукты |
| VI - Products of the chemical or allied industries | .. | .. | .. | 17.7 | 32.5 | 36.2 | VI - Продукция химической промышленности |
| VII - Plastics and articles thereof; rubber and articles thereof | .. | .. | .. | 5.1 | 14.9 | 19.7 | VII - Пластмассы и изделия из них |
| VIII - Raw hides and skins, leather, furskins and articles thereof; saddlery and harness; travel goods, handbags and similar containers; articles of animal gut | .. | .. | .. | 5.6 | 36.3 | 65.4 | VIII - Кожевенное сырьё, кожи, пушнина, меховое сырьё и изделия из них |
| IX - Wood and articles of wood; wood charcoal; cork and articles of cork; manufactures of straw, of esparto or of other plaiting materials; basketware and wickerwork | .. | .. | .. | 1.9 | 1.2 | 3.7 | IX - Древесина и изделия из древесины, древесный уголь |
| X - Pulp of wood or of other fibrous cellulosic material; waste and scrap of paper or paperboard; paper and paperboard and articles thereof | .. | .. | .. | 17.9 | 31.6 | 38.3 | X - Бумажная масса, бумажные и картонные отходы, макулатура, бумага, картон и изделия из них |
| XI - Textiles and textile articles | .. | .. | .. | 34.2 | 119.8 | 157.8 | XI - Текстиль и текстильные изделия |
| XII - Footwear, headgear, umbrellas, sun umbrellas, walking sticks, seat sticks, whips, riding crops and parts thereof; prepared feathers and articles made therewith; artificial flowers; articles of human hair | .. | .. | .. | 6.1 | 12.1 | 15.0 | XII - Обувь, головные уборы, зонты, трости и пр. |

**TABLE 3-3B. Exports by Commodity Group (millions of national currency)**
**ТАБЛИЦА 3-3B. Экспорт по товарным группам (млн. национальной валюты)**

| Commodity group | 1990 | 1991 | 1992 | 1993 | 1994 | 1995 | Товарные группы |
|---|---|---|---|---|---|---|---|
| XIII - Articles of stone, plaster, cement, asbestos, mica and similar materials; ceramic products; glass and glassware | .. | .. | .. | 14.3 | 22.6 | 69.7 | XIII - Изделия из камня, гипса, цемента |
| XIV - Natural or cultured pearls, precious or semi-precious stones, precious metals, metals clad with precious metal and articles thereof; imitation jewellery; coin | .. | .. | .. | 0.3 | 3.9 | 10.1 | XIV - Жемчуг, драгоценные и полудрагоценные камни, драгоценные металлы, бижутерия, монеты |
| XV - Base metals and articles of base metal | .. | .. | .. | 62.0 | 77.4 | 145.5 | XV - Неблагородные металлы и изделия из них |
| XVI - Machinery and mechanical appliances; electrical equipment; parts thereof; sound recorders and reproducers, television image and sound recorders and reproducers, and parts and accessories of such articles | .. | .. | .. | 82.0 | 220.6 | 208.8 | XVI - Машины, оборудование, механизмы, их части и принадлежности; звуковая и теле-аппаратура, их части и принадлежности |
| XVII - Vehicles, aircraft, vessels and associated transport equipment | .. | .. | .. | 28.6 | 45.1 | 56.0 | XVII - Средства наземного, воздушного и водного транспорта |
| XVIII - Optical, photographic, cinematographic, measuring, checking, precision, medical or surgical instruments and apparatus; clocks and watches; musical instruments; parts and accessories thereof | .. | .. | .. | 0.5 | 6.6 | 6.2 | XVIII - Приборы, аппараты оптические, медицинские, измерительные и пр.; музыкальные инструменты; часы; их части и принадлежности |
| XIX - Arms and ammunition; parts and accessories thereof | .. | .. | .. | .. | .. | .. | XIX - Оружие и боеприпасы, их части и принадлежности |
| XX - Miscellaneous manufactured articles | .. | .. | .. | 16.5 | 63.2 | 66.2 | XX - Разные промышленные товары |
| XXI - Works of art, collectors' pieces, and antiques | .. | .. | .. | 0.0 | 0.0 | 0.0 | XXI - Произведения искусства, предметы антиквариата |
| XXII - Services | .. | .. | .. | 27.1 | 135.0 | 465.6 | XXII - Услуги |

**TABLE 3-4A. Geographical distribution of foreign trade (millions of U.S. dollars)**
**ТАБЛИЦА 3-4A. Географическое распределение внешней торговли (млн. долларов США)**

| Country or country group | Exports Экспорт 1990 | 1991 | 1992 | 1993 | 1994 | 1995 | Imports Импорт 1990 | 1991 | 1992 | 1993 | 1994 | 1995 | Страна или группа стран |
|---|---|---|---|---|---|---|---|---|---|---|---|---|---|
| **Total trade** | .. | .. | .. | 483.0 | 565.4 | 745.5 | .. | .. | .. | 628.0 | 659.3 | 840.7 | **Всего** |
| **CIS countries** | .. | .. | .. | 305.0 | 405.5 | 466.9 | .. | .. | .. | 444.0 | 476.0 | 568.9 | **Страны СНГ** |
| Armenia | .. | .. | .. | 0.2 | 0.2 | 2.6 | .. | .. | .. | 0.3 | 0.1 | 0.0 | Армения |
| Azerbaijan | .. | .. | .. | 31.3 | 13.0 | 5.4 | .. | .. | .. | 39.0 | 12.0 | 5.5 | Азербайджан |
| Belarus | .. | .. | .. | 17.3 | 23.7 | 26.5 | .. | .. | .. | 32.5 | 20.1 | 50.7 | Беларусь |
| Georgia | .. | .. | .. | 0.5 | 0.6 | 0.1 | .. | .. | .. | 0.5 | 0.9 | 0.1 | Грузия |
| Kazakstan | .. | .. | .. | 6.7 | 7.2 | 8.6 | .. | .. | .. | 9.4 | 3.1 | 2.5 | Казахстан |
| Kyrgyz Republic | .. | .. | .. | 1.1 | 0.4 | 0.3 | .. | .. | .. | 2.6 | 0.9 | 0.7 | Киргизстан |
| Moldova | .. | .. | .. | .. | .. | .. | .. | .. | .. | .. | .. | .. | Молдова |
| Russia | .. | .. | .. | 172.1 | 289.1 | 360.1 | .. | .. | .. | 221.7 | 309.3 | 278.0 | Россия |
| Tajikistan | .. | .. | .. | 0.8 | 0.3 | 0.1 | .. | .. | .. | 0.6 | 0.1 | 0.0 | Таджикистан |
| Turkmenistan | .. | .. | .. | 9.7 | 1.1 | 1.5 | .. | .. | .. | 5.9 | 5.0 | 0.8 | Туркменистан |
| Ukraine | .. | .. | .. | 62.9 | 68.5 | 58.9 | .. | .. | .. | 129.7 | 122.7 | 228.5 | Украина |
| Uzbekistan | .. | .. | .. | 2.4 | 1.4 | 2.8 | .. | .. | .. | 1.8 | 1.8 | 2.1 | Узбекистан |
| **Non-CIS countries** | .. | .. | .. | 178.0 | 159.9 | 278.6 | .. | .. | .. | 184.0 | 183.3 | 271.8 | **Остальной мир** |
| **Europe** | .. | .. | .. | 170.4 | 151.1 | 246.7 | .. | .. | .. | 159.6 | 144.7 | 242.7 | **Европа** |
| Austria | .. | .. | .. | 0.6 | 1.1 | 9.9 | .. | .. | .. | 2.9 | 2.1 | 7.8 | Австрия |
| Belgium | .. | .. | .. | 0.0 | 0.0 | 0.1 | .. | .. | .. | 2.8 | 4.0 | 9.4 | Бельгия |
| Bulgaria | .. | .. | .. | 16.5 | 10.4 | 21.4 | .. | .. | .. | 4.9 | 10.1 | 31.9 | Болгария |
| Czech Republic | .. | .. | .. | 1.0 | 1.6 | 0.7 | .. | .. | .. | 0.6 | 1.4 | 2.5 | Чешская Республика |
| Denmark | .. | .. | .. | 0.0 | 0.1 | .. | .. | .. | .. | 0.4 | 1.9 | 4.1 | Дания |
| Estonia | .. | .. | .. | 2.0 | 1.1 | 2.3 | .. | .. | .. | 1.8 | 1.1 | 1.7 | Эстония |
| Finland | .. | .. | .. | 0.0 | 0.1 | 0.0 | .. | .. | .. | 1.5 | 0.4 | 1.9 | Финляндия |
| Former Yugoslavia | .. | .. | .. | 0.0 | .. | 0.3 | .. | .. | .. | 0.7 | 0.2 | 0.4 | Быв. Югославия |
| France | .. | .. | .. | 0.1 | 0.1 | 1.4 | .. | .. | .. | 5.6 | 2.0 | 6.5 | Франция |
| Germany | .. | .. | .. | 14.8 | 19.7 | 45.4 | .. | .. | .. | 23.5 | 35.6 | 45.6 | Германия |
| Hungary | .. | .. | .. | 3.0 | 2.6 | 5.7 | .. | .. | .. | 7.0 | 6.9 | 8.5 | Венгрия |
| Iceland | .. | .. | .. | .. | .. | 0.1 | .. | .. | .. | .. | 0.0 | 0.2 | Исландия |
| Ireland | .. | .. | .. | 5.3 | 0.2 | 0.5 | .. | .. | .. | 0.0 | 1.1 | 0.9 | Ирландия |
| Italy | .. | .. | .. | 6.2 | 7.8 | 15.6 | .. | .. | .. | 8.6 | 8.7 | 19.3 | Италия |
| Latvia | .. | .. | .. | 1.8 | 2.9 | 4.6 | .. | .. | .. | 1.7 | 2.3 | 3.0 | Латвия |
| Lithuania | .. | .. | .. | 3.7 | 4.1 | 9.8 | .. | .. | .. | 2.0 | 4.1 | 7.3 | Литва |
| Netherlands | .. | .. | .. | 0.6 | 1.4 | 2.3 | .. | .. | .. | 10.4 | 3.2 | 6.5 | Нидерланды |
| Norway | .. | .. | .. | 0.0 | 0.0 | 0.4 | .. | .. | .. | 0.0 | 0.0 | 0.0 | Норвегия |
| Poland | .. | .. | .. | 0.7 | 2.5 | 3.0 | .. | .. | .. | 1.9 | 4.4 | 4.2 | Польша |
| Romania | .. | .. | .. | 104.0 | 83.4 | 103.7 | .. | .. | .. | 68.4 | 42.6 | 56.0 | Румыния |
| Slovak Republic | .. | .. | .. | .. | .. | 2.9 | .. | .. | .. | .. | .. | 1.9 | Словацкая Республика |
| Spain | .. | .. | .. | .. | 0.1 | 1.6 | .. | .. | .. | 4.7 | 0.3 | 1.3 | Испания |
| Sweden | .. | .. | .. | 1.0 | .. | 0.1 | .. | .. | .. | 1.2 | 2.3 | 1.2 | Швеция |
| Switzerland | .. | .. | .. | 5.9 | 2.3 | 4.1 | .. | .. | .. | 3.3 | 2.4 | 8.3 | Швейцария |
| United Kingdom | .. | .. | .. | 1.0 | 3.4 | 6.2 | .. | .. | .. | 5.1 | 2.1 | 5.5 | Великобритания |

**TABLE 3-4A. Geographical distribution of foreign trade (millions of U.S. dollars)**
**ТАБЛИЦА 3-4A. Географическое распределение внешней торговли (млн. долларов США)**

| Country or country group | Exports Экспорт 1990 | 1991 | 1992 | 1993 | 1994 | 1995 | Imports Импорт 1990 | 1991 | 1992 | 1993 | 1994 | 1995 | Страна или группа стран |
|---|---|---|---|---|---|---|---|---|---|---|---|---|---|
| Other Europe | .. | .. | .. | 2.2 | 6.2 | 4.6 | .. | .. | .. | 0.6 | 5.5 | 6.8 | Остальные стараны Европы |
| **Asia** | .. | .. | .. | 6.6 | 5.0 | 19.3 | .. | .. | .. | 4.4 | 17.8 | 16.7 | **Азия** |
| Afghanistan | .. | .. | .. | 0.0 | 0.1 | 0.0 | .. | .. | .. | 0.2 | 0.1 | .. | Афганистан |
| China | .. | .. | .. | 0.1 | 0.3 | 0.4 | .. | .. | .. | 0.7 | 5.5 | 0.2 | Китай |
| India | .. | .. | .. | .. | 0.1 | 0.3 | .. | .. | .. | 0.0 | 4.3 | 1.1 | Индия |
| Iraq | .. | .. | .. | .. | .. | .. | .. | .. | .. | .. | .. | .. | Ирак |
| Japan | .. | .. | .. | .. | .. | 0.1 | .. | .. | .. | 0.2 | 0.1 | 1.3 | Япония |
| Korea, Dem. People's Rep. | .. | .. | .. | .. | 0.0 | .. | .. | .. | .. | 0.1 | .. | 0.0 | КНДР |
| Korea, Rep. of | .. | .. | .. | .. | .. | .. | .. | .. | .. | 0.0 | 0.5 | 0.6 | Южная Корея |
| Mongolia | .. | .. | .. | .. | .. | .. | .. | .. | .. | .. | .. | .. | МНР |
| Syrian Arab Republic | .. | .. | .. | 0.1 | 0.9 | 0.1 | .. | .. | .. | 0.4 | .. | 0.0 | Сирия |
| Turkey | .. | .. | .. | 1.5 | 1.4 | 11.5 | .. | .. | .. | 0.5 | 3.4 | 6.8 | Турция |
| Viet Nam | .. | .. | .. | 0.3 | 0.0 | 1.3 | .. | .. | .. | .. | .. | 0.2 | Вьетнам |
| Other Asia | .. | .. | .. | 4.6 | 2.2 | 5.6 | .. | .. | .. | 2.3 | 3.8 | 6.5 | Остальные страны Азии |
| **America** | .. | .. | .. | 1.0 | 3.6 | 11.9 | .. | .. | .. | 20.0 | 20.0 | 11.8 | **Сев. и Южная Америка** |
| Canada | .. | .. | .. | 0.1 | 1.8 | 1.6 | .. | .. | .. | 2.0 | 0.6 | 0.6 | Канада |
| Cuba | .. | .. | .. | .. | .. | .. | .. | .. | .. | .. | .. | .. | Куба |
| United States | .. | .. | .. | 0.9 | 1.8 | 7.9 | .. | .. | .. | 14.2 | 19.2 | 10.7 | США |
| Other America | .. | .. | .. | .. | .. | 2.4 | .. | .. | .. | 3.8 | 0.2 | 0.5 | Остальные |
| **Africa** | .. | .. | .. | 0.0 | 0.2 | 0.6 | .. | .. | .. | .. | 0.6 | 0.2 | **Африка** |
| Egypt | .. | .. | .. | .. | .. | 0.1 | .. | .. | .. | .. | 0.1 | .. | Египет |
| Libya | .. | .. | .. | .. | .. | 0.1 | .. | .. | .. | .. | .. | .. | Ливия |
| Other Africa | .. | .. | .. | 0.0 | 0.2 | 0.4 | .. | .. | .. | .. | 0.6 | 0.2 | Остальные |
| **Rest of the World** | .. | .. | .. | 0.0 | 0.0 | 0.1 | .. | .. | .. | .. | 0.2 | 0.4 | **Прочие страны мира** |
| Australia | .. | .. | .. | 0.0 | 0.0 | 0.1 | .. | .. | .. | .. | .. | 0.4 | Австралия |

TABLE 3-4B. Geographical distribution of foreign trade (millions of national currency)

ТАБЛИЦА 3-4B. Географическое распределение внешней торговли (миллионов национальной валюты)

| Country or country group | Exports Экспорт 1990 | 1991 | 1992 | 1993 | 1994 | 1995 | Imports Импорт 1990 | 1991 | 1992 | 1993 | 1994 | 1995 | Страна или группа стран |
|---|---|---|---|---|---|---|---|---|---|---|---|---|---|
| **Total trade** | .. | .. | .. | 701.9 | 2,318.5 | 3,349.2 | .. | .. | .. | 909.2 | 2,692.2 | 3,784.8 | **Всего** |
| **CIS countries** | .. | .. | .. | 441.5 | 1,658.6 | 2,095.4 | .. | .. | .. | 642.8 | 1,944.6 | 2,558.5 | **Страны СНГ** |
| Armenia | .. | .. | .. | 0.3 | 0.8 | 12.0 | .. | .. | .. | 0.5 | 0.3 | 0.2 | Армения |
| Azerbaijan | .. | .. | .. | 45.3 | 52.6 | 24.0 | .. | .. | .. | 56.5 | 48.6 | 24.6 | Азербайджан |
| Belarus | .. | .. | .. | 25.1 | 96.6 | 119.3 | .. | .. | .. | 47.0 | 82.8 | 228.1 | Беларусь |
| Georgia | .. | .. | .. | 0.7 | 2.6 | 0.7 | .. | .. | .. | 0.7 | 3.9 | 0.5 | Грузия |
| Kazakstan | .. | .. | .. | 9.6 | 28.8 | 38.5 | .. | .. | .. | 13.6 | 12.4 | 11.1 | Казахстан |
| Kyrgyz Republic | .. | .. | .. | 1.6 | 1.5 | 1.1 | .. | .. | .. | 3.7 | 3.6 | 3.2 | Киргизстан |
| Moldova | .. | .. | .. | .. | .. | .. | .. | .. | .. | .. | .. | .. | Молдова |
| Russia | .. | .. | .. | 249.2 | 1,182.7 | 1,614.5 | .. | .. | .. | 321.0 | 1,260.9 | 1,249.0 | Россия |
| Tajikistan | .. | .. | .. | 1.2 | 1.2 | 0.6 | .. | .. | .. | 0.9 | 0.4 | 0.1 | Таджикистан |
| Turkmenistan | .. | .. | .. | 14.0 | 4.2 | 6.5 | .. | .. | .. | 8.6 | 19.1 | 3.4 | Туркменистан |
| Ukraine | .. | .. | .. | 91.1 | 281.8 | 265.5 | .. | .. | .. | 187.7 | 505.4 | 1,028.9 | Украина |
| Uzbekistan | .. | .. | .. | 3.4 | 5.8 | 12.7 | .. | .. | .. | 2.6 | 7.2 | 9.4 | Узбекистан |
| **Non-CIS countries** | .. | .. | .. | 260.4 | 659.9 | 1,253.8 | .. | .. | .. | 266.4 | 747.6 | 1,226.3 | **Остальной мир** |
| **Europe** | .. | .. | .. | 249.3 | 623.7 | 1,109.5 | .. | .. | .. | 231.0 | 591.0 | 1,094.6 | **Европа** |
| Austria | .. | .. | .. | 0.9 | 4.4 | 44.8 | .. | .. | .. | 4.2 | 8.5 | 35.2 | Австрия |
| Belgium | .. | .. | .. | 0.0 | 0.0 | 0.6 | .. | .. | .. | 4.1 | 16.1 | 42.5 | Бельгия |
| Bulgaria | .. | .. | .. | 23.8 | 42.6 | 96.3 | .. | .. | .. | 7.1 | 41.6 | 144.2 | Болгария |
| Czech Republic | .. | .. | .. | 1.5 | 6.5 | 3.1 | .. | .. | .. | 0.9 | 5.8 | 11.8 | Чешская Республика |
| Denmark | .. | .. | .. | 0.0 | 0.5 | .. | .. | .. | .. | 0.6 | 7.9 | 18.7 | Дания |
| Estonia | .. | .. | .. | 2.9 | 4.6 | 10.4 | .. | .. | .. | 2.6 | 4.5 | 7.5 | Эстония |
| Finland | .. | .. | .. | 0.0 | 0.2 | 0.1 | .. | .. | .. | 2.2 | 1.6 | 8.4 | Финляндия |
| Former Yugoslavia | .. | .. | .. | 0.3 | .. | 1.4 | .. | .. | .. | 1.5 | 0.9 | 1.6 | Быв. Югославия |
| France | .. | .. | .. | 0.2 | 0.4 | 6.3 | .. | .. | .. | 8.1 | 8.3 | 29.2 | Франция |
| Germany | .. | .. | .. | 21.4 | 80.9 | 204.7 | .. | .. | .. | 34.0 | 145.5 | 205.0 | Германия |
| Hungary | .. | .. | .. | 4.4 | 10.7 | 25.9 | .. | .. | .. | 10.1 | 28.6 | 38.4 | Венгрия |
| Iceland | .. | .. | .. | .. | .. | 0.7 | .. | .. | .. | .. | 0.2 | 1.1 | Исландия |
| Ireland | .. | .. | .. | 8.0 | 0.9 | 2.0 | .. | .. | .. | 0.0 | 4.4 | 4.0 | Ирландия |
| Italy | .. | .. | .. | 9.0 | 32.1 | 70.0 | .. | .. | .. | 12.4 | 35.6 | 87.0 | Италия |
| Latvia | .. | .. | .. | 2.7 | 12.0 | 20.7 | .. | .. | .. | 2.4 | 9.4 | 13.8 | Латвия |
| Lithuania | .. | .. | .. | 5.3 | 16.8 | 44.2 | .. | .. | .. | 2.9 | 17.0 | 33.0 | Литва |
| Netherlands | .. | .. | .. | 0.9 | 5.6 | 10.4 | .. | .. | .. | 15.1 | 13.0 | 29.7 | Нидерланды |
| Norway | .. | .. | .. | .. | 0.1 | 1.9 | .. | .. | .. | 0.0 | 0.1 | 0.1 | Норвегия |
| Poland | .. | .. | .. | 1.0 | 10.3 | 13.3 | .. | .. | .. | 2.7 | 18.2 | 18.8 | Польша |
| Romania | .. | .. | .. | 153.3 | 344.7 | 465.5 | .. | .. | .. | 99.0 | 171.4 | 252.0 | Румыния |
| Slovak Republic | .. | .. | .. | .. | .. | 13.1 | .. | .. | .. | .. | .. | 8.5 | Словацская Республика |
| Spain | .. | .. | .. | .. | 0.3 | 7.1 | .. | .. | .. | 6.8 | 1.0 | 6.0 | Испания |
| Sweden | .. | .. | .. | 1.5 | .. | 0.3 | .. | .. | .. | 1.7 | 9.4 | 5.6 | Швеция |
| Switzerland | .. | .. | .. | 8.6 | 9.6 | 18.3 | .. | .. | .. | 4.8 | 9.9 | 37.5 | Швейцария |

**TABLE 3-4B. Geographical distribution of foreign trade (millions of national currency)**

**ТАБЛИЦА 3-4B. Географическое распределение внешней торговли (миллионов национальной валюты)**

| Country or country group | Exports / Экспорт 1990 | 1991 | 1992 | 1993 | 1994 | 1995 | Imports / Импорт 1990 | 1991 | 1992 | 1993 | 1994 | 1995 | Страна или группа стран |
|---|---|---|---|---|---|---|---|---|---|---|---|---|---|
| United Kingdom | .. | .. | .. | 1.4 | 14.3 | 27.9 | .. | .. | .. | 7.4 | 8.8 | 24.7 | Великобритания |
| Other Europe | .. | .. | .. | 2.2 | 26.2 | 20.5 | .. | .. | .. | 0.4 | 23.3 | 30.3 | Остальные стараны Европы |
| **Asia** | .. | .. | .. | 9.6 | 20.6 | 87.2 | .. | .. | .. | 6.4 | 71.7 | 75.6 | **Азия** |
| Afghanistan | .. | .. | .. | 0.0 | 0.6 | 0.1 | .. | .. | .. | 0.3 | 0.3 | .. | Афганистан |
| China | .. | .. | .. | 0.1 | 1.2 | 1.8 | .. | .. | .. | 0.9 | 21.4 | 0.7 | Китай |
| India | .. | .. | .. | .. | 0.3 | 1.6 | .. | .. | .. | 0.0 | 17.4 | 4.8 | Индия |
| Iraq | .. | .. | .. | .. | .. | .. | .. | .. | .. | .. | .. | .. | Ирак |
| Japan | .. | .. | .. | .. | .. | 0.3 | .. | .. | .. | 0.3 | 0.3 | 5.8 | Япония |
| Korea, Dem. People's Rep. | .. | .. | .. | .. | 0.1 | .. | .. | .. | .. | 0.3 | .. | 0.0 | КНДР |
| Korea, Rep. of | .. | .. | .. | .. | .. | .. | .. | .. | .. | 0.1 | 1.9 | 2.6 | Южная Корея |
| Mongolia | .. | .. | .. | .. | .. | .. | .. | .. | .. | .. | .. | .. | МНР |
| Syrian Arab Republic | .. | .. | .. | 0.1 | 3.6 | 0.3 | .. | .. | .. | 0.5 | .. | 0.0 | Сирия |
| Turkey | .. | .. | .. | 2.1 | 6.0 | 51.9 | .. | .. | .. | 0.7 | 14.0 | 32.1 | Турция |
| Viet Nam | .. | .. | .. | 0.4 | 0.1 | 5.8 | .. | .. | .. | .. | .. | 0.7 | Вьетнам |
| Other Asia | .. | .. | .. | 6.9 | 8.7 | 25.3 | .. | .. | .. | 3.3 | 16.4 | 27.8 | Остальные страны Азии |
| **America** | .. | .. | .. | 1.5 | 14.9 | 53.9 | .. | .. | .. | 29.0 | 82.1 | 53.6 | **Сев. и Южная Америка** |
| Canada | .. | .. | .. | 0.2 | 7.5 | 7.2 | .. | .. | .. | 2.9 | 2.4 | 2.7 | Канада |
| Cuba | .. | .. | .. | .. | .. | .. | .. | .. | .. | .. | .. | .. | Куба |
| United States | .. | .. | .. | 1.3 | 7.4 | 36.0 | .. | .. | .. | 20.5 | 78.6 | 48.3 | США |
| Other America | .. | .. | .. | .. | .. | 10.7 | .. | .. | .. | 5.6 | 1.1 | 2.6 | Остальные |
| **Africa** | .. | .. | .. | 0.0 | 0.6 | 2.7 | .. | .. | .. | .. | 2.2 | 0.9 | **Африка** |
| Egypt | .. | .. | .. | 0.0 | .. | 0.5 | .. | .. | .. | .. | 0.4 | 1.1 | Египет |
| Libya | .. | .. | .. | .. | .. | 0.3 | .. | .. | .. | .. | .. | .. | Ливия |
| Other Africa | .. | .. | .. | 0.0 | 0.9 | 1.9 | .. | .. | .. | .. | 2.2 | 0.9 | Остальные |
| **Rest of the World** | .. | .. | .. | 0.0 | 0.1 | 0.5 | .. | .. | .. | .. | 0.6 | 1.6 | **Прочие страны мира** |
| Australia | .. | .. | .. | 0.0 | 0.1 | 0.5 | .. | .. | .. | .. | .. | 1.6 | Австралия |

**TABLE 4-1. General government budget revenue (thousands of national currency)**

**ТАБЛИЦА 4-1. Доходы государственного бюджета (тысяч национальной валюты)**

| Type of revenue | 1990 | 1991 | 1992 | 1993 | 1994 | 1995 | Вид доходов |
|---|---|---|---|---|---|---|---|
| **Total revenue and grants** | 4,468 | 6,403 | 44,129 | 372,400 | 1,438,500 | 2,002,000 | **Всего доходов и безвозм. поступл.** |
| Grants | 423 | 10 | .. | .. | 19,800 | .. | Безвозмездные поступления |
| Total Revenue | 4,045 | 6,393 | 44,129 | 372,400 | 1,418,700 | 2,002,000 | Всего доходов |
| **Current revenue** | 4,045 | 6,393 | 44,129 | 372,400 | 1,418,700 | 2,002,000 | **Текущие доходы** |
| Tax revenue | 2,911 | 5,525 | 42,962 | 317,300 | 1,355,800 | 1,967,100 | Доход от налогов |
| Taxes on income and profits | 1,300 | 2,188 | 14,215 | 138,100 | 548,200 | 789,300 | Налоги на доходы и прибыль |
| Individual | 306 | 501 | 3,924 | 35,600 | 130,000 | 201,700 | Физические лица |
| Corporate | 994 | 1,687 | 10,291 | 102,500 | 418,200 | 587,600 | Предприятия и организации |
| Social security contributions | .. | .. | .. | .. | .. | .. | Отчисление на соцстрах. |
| Taxes on payroll or work force | .. | .. | .. | .. | .. | .. | Налоги на заработную плату и рабочую силу |
| Taxes on the use of labor force | .. | .. | .. | .. | .. | .. | Плата за трудовые ресурсы |
| Taxes on increases in wages and salaries | .. | .. | .. | .. | .. | .. | Налог с прироста средств на оплату труда |
| Other payroll/work force taxes | .. | .. | .. | .. | .. | .. | Другие налоги на зарплату и рабочую силу |
| Taxes on property | .. | .. | .. | 14,300 | 21,700 | 104,900 | Налоги на собственность |
| Taxes on immovable property | .. | .. | .. | 14,300 | 6,400 | 11,900 | Налоги на недвижимое имущество |
| Buildings | .. | .. | .. | 200 | .. | .. | Налог с владельцев строении |
| Land | .. | .. | .. | 14,100 | .. | .. | Земельныи налог |
| Estate, inheritance, and gift taxes | .. | .. | .. | .. | 15,300 | 93,000 | Налоги на наследство, подарки |
| Other property taxes | .. | .. | .. | .. | .. | .. | Другие налоги на имущество |
| Domestic taxes on goods and services | 2,704 | 3,915 | 24,231 | 156,000 | 433,400 | 767,000 | Внутренние налоги на товары и услуги |
| General sales, turnover, or value-added taxes | 1,465 | 1,083 | 14,278 | 94,500 | 281,900 | 576,700 | Налог с продаж. с оборота или на добав. стоим. |
| Excises | 1,239 | 2,832 | 9,953 | 61,500 | 151,500 | 190,300 | Акцизы |
| Profits of fiscal monopolies | .. | .. | .. | .. | .. | .. | Прибыли фискальных монополий |
| Taxes on specific services | .. | .. | .. | .. | .. | .. | Налоги на особые услуги |
| Taxes on use of goods or permission to use goods or to perform activities | .. | .. | .. | .. | .. | .. | Налоги на пользование товарами или лицензии на пользование товарами и занятие деятельностью |
| Other taxes on goods and services | .. | .. | .. | .. | .. | .. | Другие налоги на товары и услуги |
| Taxes on international trade and transactions | .. | .. | .. | 7,000 | 29,700 | 51,300 | Налоги на внешнюю торговлю и операции |
| Import duties | .. | .. | .. | .. | 5,900 | 11,700 | Импортные пошлины |
| Export duties | .. | .. | .. | .. | .. | .. | Экпортные пошлины |
| Other | .. | .. | .. | 7,000 | 23,800 | 39,600 | Другие |
| Other taxes | -1,093 | -578 | 4,516 | 1,900 | 322,800 | 254,600 | Прочие налоги |
| Nontax revenue | 1,134 | 868 | 1,167 | 55,100 | 62,900 | 34,900 | Неналоговые доходы |
| **Capital revenue** | .. | .. | .. | .. | .. | .. | **Капитальные доходы** |

**TABLE 4-2. General government budget expenditure by economic type (thousands of natio**
**ТАБЛИЦА 4-2. Расходы государственного бюджета по экономическим типам (тысяч национальной валюты)**

| Type of expenditure or debt holder | 1990 | 1991 | 1992 | 1993 | 1994 | 1995 | Всего расходов |
|---|---|---|---|---|---|---|---|
| **Total expenditure by economic type** | 4,110 | 6,401 | 53,216 | 509,100 | 1,718,800 | 2,376,000 | **Всего расходов по экономическим типам** |
| **Current expenditure** | 3,536 | 5,618 | 44,097 | 445,900 | 1,508,900 | 2,114,700 | **Текущие расходы** |
| Expenditure on goods and services | 1,794 | 3,880 | 15,846 | 154,100 | 711,900 | 1,108,100 | Расходы на товары и услуги |
| Wages and salaries | 603 | 1,013 | 8,064 | 86,200 | 319,600 | 426,700 | Заработная плата |
| Employer contributions | 37 | 219 | 2,093 | 21,100 | 82,900 | 118,400 | Отчисление на социальное страхование |
| Other Purchases of goods and services | 1,154 | 2,647 | 5,689 | 46,800 | 309,400 | 563,000 | Другие покупки товаров и услуг |
| Interest payments | .. | 5 | 1,417 | 17,600 | 98,000 | 265,200 | Выплаты процентов |
| Domestic debt | .. | 5 | 1,417 | 17,600 | 54,400 | 172,600 | По внутреннему долгу |
| Foreign debt | .. | .. | .. | .. | 43,600 | 92,600 | По внешншму долгу |
| Subsidies and other current transfers | 1,455 | 1,390 | 7,447 | 103,900 | 183,800 | 91,000 | Субсидии на другие текущие трансферты |
| Subsidies | 1,455 | 1,390 | 7,447 | 78,700 | 183,800 | 91,000 | Субсидии |
| Agricultural subsidies | 1,455 | 1,390 | 1,827 | 50,100 | .. | .. | Субсидии на сельское хозяиство |
| Other current transfers | .. | .. | .. | 25,200 | .. | .. | Другие текущие трансферты |
| Other | 287 | 343 | 19,387 | 170,300 | 515,200 | 650,400 | Прочие расходы |
| **Capital expenditure** | 574 | 731 | 9,119 | 63,200 | 209,900 | 261,300 | **Капитальные расходы** |
| Acquisition of fixed capital assets | .. | .. | 7,205 | 63,200 | 130,400 | 159,200 | Приобретение основного капитала |
| Capital transfers | 553 | 507 | 1,106 | .. | 57,200 | 72,400 | Капитальные трансферты |
| Other | 21 | 224 | 808 | .. | 22,300 | 29,700 | Другие капитальные расходы |
| **Surplus/deficit (-)** | 358 | 2 | -9,087 | -136,700 | -280,300 | -374,000 | **Превыш. доходов над расходами/дефицит(-)** |
| **Financing by type of debt holder** | .. | .. | .. | .. | .. | .. | **Финансирование по типам кредиторов** |
| **Foreign (net)** | .. | .. | .. | .. | 222,800 | 158,500 | **Зарубежные кредиторы (сальдо)** |
| From international development institutions | .. | .. | .. | .. | .. | .. | Международные организации |
| From foreign governments | .. | .. | .. | .. | .. | .. | Правительства иностранных государств |
| Other borrowing abroad | .. | .. | .. | .. | 222,800 | 158,500 | Другие зарубежные кредиторы |
| **Domestic (net)** | .. | .. | 9,087 | 136,700 | 89,900 | 215,500 | **Внутренние кредиторы (сальдо)** |
| From monetary authorities | .. | .. | 9,087 | 89,300 | 83,000 | 113,000 | Органы денежного обращения |
| From deposit money banks | .. | .. | .. | .. | 0 | .. | Депозитные денежные банки |
| Other domestic borrowing | .. | .. | .. | 47,400 | 6,900 | 102,500 | Другие внутренние кредиторы |
| *Memo items:* | | | | | | | *Справочно:* |
| Extrabudgetary surplus/ Deficit (-) not included above | .. | .. | .. | .. | 5,600 | .. | Превышение доходов над расходами/дефицит (-) по внебюджетным фондам, не включенным выше |
| Total surplus/deficit (-) including extrabudgetary accounts | .. | .. | .. | .. | -274,700 | -374,000 | Итого превышение доходов над расходами/дефицит, включая счета внебюджетных фондов |

**TABLE 5-1. Agricultural production (millions of national currency, current prices)**

**ТАБЛИЦА 5-1. Сельскохозяйственная продукция (млн. нац. валюты, текущие цены)**

| Item | 1990 | 1991 | 1992 | 1993 | 1994 | 1995 | Статьи |
|---|---|---|---|---|---|---|---|
| **Total gross agricultural production** | 6.1 | 11.3 | 97.3 | 1,067.2 | 3,212 | 4,098 | **Валовая продукция сельского хозяйства - всего** |
| **Crops** | 3.6 | 7.4 | 64.4 | 727.2 | 2,014 | 2,615 | **Продукция растениеводства** |
| Grains | 0.4 | 1.3 | 12.1 | 209.5 | 469 | .. | Зерно |
| Potatoes | 0.1 | 0.3 | 3.7 | 57.5 | 189 | .. | Картофель |
| Vegetables | 0.4 | 0.7 | 5.8 | 65.1 | 271 | .. | Овощи |
| Fruits (excluding grapes) | 0.6 | 1.1 | 6.0 | 81.9 | 288 | .. | Фрукты (без винограда) |
| Grapes | 0.7 | 1.7 | 13.3 | 118.2 | 257 | .. | Виноград |
| Tobacco | 0.4 | 0.9 | 8.2 | 55.2 | 81 | .. | Табак |
| Cotton | .. | .. | .. | .. | .. | .. | Хлопок |
| Sugarbeets | 0.1 | 0.3 | 3.6 | 31.3 | 82 | .. | Сахарная свекла |
| Oilseeds | 0.1 | 0.1 | 2.5 | 56.5 | 55 | .. | Семена масличных культур |
| Other | 0.8 | 1.0 | 9.1 | 52.0 | 321 | .. | Прочие |
| **Animal husbandry** | 2.5 | 3.9 | 32.9 | 340.0 | 1,198 | 1,483 | **Продукция животноводства** |
| Livestock | 1.3 | 2.1 | 20.4 | 234.0 | 690 | .. | Мясное животноводство |
| Cattle | 0.6 | 0.8 | 8.5 | 109.5 | 289 | .. | Крупный рогатый скот |
| Pigs | 0.6 | 1.0 | 9.5 | 82.8 | 283 | .. | Свиньи |
| Sheep and goats | 0.0 | 0.0 | 0.2 | 9.8 | 12 | .. | Овцы и козы |
| Poultry | 0.2 | 0.3 | 2.2 | 32.1 | 105 | .. | Птица |
| Other | .. | .. | .. | .. | .. | .. | Прочие |
| Milk | 0.7 | 1.0 | 7.0 | 60.7 | 334 | .. | Молоко |
| Eggs | 0.1 | 0.2 | 1.7 | 22.9 | 108 | .. | Яйца |
| Wool | 0.0 | 0.0 | 0.5 | 4.5 | 10 | .. | Шерсть |
| Other livestock | 0.4 | 0.6 | 3.3 | 15.9 | 56 | .. | Прочая |
| **Agricultural services** | .. | .. | .. | .. | .. | .. | **Сельскохозяйственные услуги** |

## TABLE 5-2. Agricultural production (millions of constant national currency) MOLDOVA
## ТАБЛИЦА 5-2. Сельскохозяйственная продукция в постоянных ценах (млн. национальной валюты)

| Item | 1990 | 1991 | 1992 | 1993 | 1994 | 1995 | Статьи |
|---|---|---|---|---|---|---|---|
| **Total gross agricultural production** | 4.4 | 4.0 | 3.3 | 3.6 | 2.8 | 2.9 | **Валовая продукция сельского хозяйства - всего** |
| **Crops** | 2.5 | 2.4 | 2.1 | 2.6 | 1.8 | 2.0 | **Продукция растениеводства** |
| Grains | 0.3 | 0.4 | 0.3 | 0.4 | 0.2 | .. | Зерно |
| Potatoes | 0.0 | 0.0 | 0.0 | 0.1 | 0.1 | .. | Картофель |
| Vegetables | 0.4 | 0.3 | 0.2 | 0.4 | 0.2 | .. | Овощи |
| Fruits (excluding grapes) | 0.5 | 0.4 | 0.3 | 0.6 | 0.4 | .. | Фрукты (без винограда) |
| Grapes | 0.4 | 0.4 | 0.4 | 0.4 | 0.3 | .. | Виноград |
| Tobacco | 0.3 | 0.3 | 0.2 | 0.3 | 0.2 | .. | Табак |
| Cotton | .. | .. | .. | .. | .. | .. | Хлопок |
| Sugarbeets | 0.1 | 0.1 | 0.1 | 0.1 | 0.1 | .. | Сахарная свекла |
| Oilseeds | 0.1 | 0.1 | 0.1 | 0.1 | .. | .. | Семена масличных культур |
| Other | 0.3 | 0.4 | 0.4 | 0.2 | 0.3 | .. | Прочие |
| **Animal husbandry** | 1.9 | 1.6 | 1.3 | 1.0 | 1.0 | 0.9 | **Продукция животноводства** |
| Livestock | 1.1 | 0.9 | 0.6 | 0.5 | 0.4 | .. | Мясное животноводство |
| Cattle | 0.4 | 0.3 | 0.2 | 0.2 | 0.2 | .. | Крупный рогатый скот |
| Pigs | 0.5 | 0.4 | 0.3 | 0.2 | 0.2 | .. | Свиньи |
| Sheep and goats | 0.0 | 0.0 | 0.0 | 0.0 | 0.0 | .. | Овцы и козы |
| Poultry | 0.2 | 0.2 | 0.1 | 0.1 | 0.1 | .. | Птица |
| Other | .. | .. | .. | .. | .. | .. | Прочие |
| Milk | 0.6 | 0.5 | 0.5 | 0.4 | 0.4 | .. | Молоко |
| Eggs | 0.1 | 0.1 | 0.1 | 0.1 | 0.1 | .. | Яйца |
| Wool | 0.0 | 0.0 | 0.0 | 0.0 | 0.0 | .. | Шерсть |
| Other livestock | 0.0 | 0.0 | 0.0 | 0.0 | 0.1 | .. | Прочая |
| **Agricultural services** | .. | .. | .. | .. | .. | .. | **Сельскохозяйственные услуги** |

## TABLE 5-3. Production and average yield of major agricultural crops
## ТАБЛИЦА 5-3. Производство и урожайность важнейших сельскохозяйственных культур

| Crop | 1990 | 1991 | 1992 | 1993 | 1994 | 1995 | Сельскохозяйственные культуры |
|---|---|---|---|---|---|---|---|
| **Production (thousands of tons)** | | | | | | | **Производство (тыс. тонн)** |
| Grain - Cleanweight | 2,442 | 3,000 | 1,978 | 3,219 | 1,684 | 2,612 | Зерно в чистом весе |
| Winter wheat | 1,130 | 1,056 | 926 | 1,393 | 659 | 1,277 | Пшеница - озимая |
| Spring wheat | .. | .. | .. | 0 | 0 | .. | яровая |
| Coarse grain | 2,510 | 3,082 | 2,055 | 3,320 | 1,753 | 2,705 | Зерно в физическом весе |
| Rye | 2 | 3 | 2 | 3 | 3 | 5 | Рожь |
| Corn | 885 | 1,501 | 632 | 1,324 | 629 | 978 | Кукуруза |
| Winter barley | 340 | 363 | 299 | 383 | 139 | 216 | Ячмень - озимый |
| Spring barley | 98 | 86 | 129 | 126 | 207 | 140 | яровой |
| Oats | 4 | 5 | 7 | 12 | 8 | 10 | Овес |
| Millet | .. | .. | .. | .. | .. | .. | Просо |
| Rice | .. | .. | .. | .. | .. | .. | Рис |
| Flax | .. | .. | .. | .. | .. | .. | Лен |
| Oilseeds | 256 | 184 | 184 | 183 | 137 | 212 | Семена масличных культур |
| Cotton (raw) | .. | .. | .. | .. | .. | .. | Хлопок - сырец |
| Cotton fiber | .. | .. | .. | .. | .. | .. | волокно |
| Sugarbeets | 2,150 | 1,989 | 1,784 | 2,048 | 1,402 | 1,878 | Сахарная свекла |
| Potatoes | 295 | 291 | 310 | 726 | 475 | 401 | Картофель |
| Pulses | 97 | 106 | 122 | 122 | 70 | 56 | Бобовые |
| Vegetables | 1,177 | 989 | 787 | 777 | 599 | 605 | Овощи |
| Fruit | 1,841 | 1,472 | 1,335 | 2,016 | 1,335 | 1,483 | Фрукты |
| Grapes | 940 | 774 | 824 | 928 | 670 | 872 | Виноград |
| Other | 901 | 698 | 511 | 1,088 | 665 | 611 | Прочие |
| Corn (silage and greenchop) | 4,509 | 4,979 | 3,026 | 3,359 | 2,286 | 1,803 | Кукуруза (на силос и зеленый корм) |
| Hay | 356 | 409 | 278 | 306 | 223 | 227 | Сено |
| **Average yield (kilograms per hectare)** | | | | | | | **Ср. урожайность (кг с га)** |
| Grain | 3,628 | 3,949 | 2,931 | 3,831 | 2,204 | 2,988 | Зерно |
| Winter wheat | 3,940 | 3,490 | 3,290 | 4,030 | 2,190 | 3,240 | Пшеница - озимая |
| Spring wheat | .. | .. | .. | 3,952 | 2,295 | .. | яровая |
| Coarse grain | 3,729 | 4,057 | 3,040 | 3,952 | 2,295 | 3,095 | Зерно в физическом весе |
| Rye | 2,410 | 1,780 | 2,200 | 2,720 | 1,780 | 2,094 | Рожь |
| Corn | 3,420 | 4,810 | 2,440 | 3,850 | 2,210 | 2,370 | Кукуруза |
| Winter barley | 3,760 | 3,520 | 3,480 | 3,680 | 2,230 | 2,520 | Ячмень - озимый |
| Spring barley | 3,270 | 2,760 | 3,490 | 3,590 | 2,440 | 2,140 | яровой |
| Oats | 1,940 | 1,600 | 2,730 | 2,990 | 1,570 | 1,510 | Овес |
| Millet | .. | .. | .. | .. | .. | .. | Просо |
| Rice | .. | .. | .. | .. | .. | .. | Рис |
| Flax | .. | .. | .. | .. | .. | .. | Лен |
| Oilseeds | 1,594 | 1,253 | 1,248 | 1,357 | 946 | 1,267 | Семена масличных культур |
| Cotton (raw) | .. | .. | .. | .. | .. | .. | Хлопок - сырец |
| Cotton fiber | .. | .. | .. | .. | .. | .. | волокно |
| Sugarbeets | 26,383 | 24,873 | 21,611 | 24,690 | 16,903 | 20,796 | Сахарная свекла |
| Potatoes | 7,200 | 6,200 | 5,600 | 10,226 | 7,550 | 6,800 | Картофель |
| Pulses | 1,340 | 1,370 | 1,710 | 1,720 | 1,040 | 1,030 | Бобовые |
| Vegetables | 15,700 | 12,100 | 10,200 | 9,990 | 8,280 | 7,500 | Овощи |
| Fruit | 5,632 | 4,431 | 4,060 | 5,849 | 3,904 | 4,345 | Фрукты |
| Grapes | 5,380 | 4,490 | 4,870 | 5,380 | 3,970 | 4,960 | Виноград |
| Other | 5,920 | 4,370 | 3,100 | 6,100 | 3,720 | 3,670 | Прочие |
| Corn (silage and greenchop) | 14,800 | 23,800 | 9,850 | 15,200 | 8,400 | 11,550 | Кукуруза (на силос и зеленый корм) |
| Hay | 3,468 | 4,004 | 2,695 | 2,938 | 2,082 | 2,650 | Сено |

**TABLE 5-4. Main aggregates of animal husbandry**
**ТАБЛИЦА 5-4. Основные показатели животноводства**

| Type of livestock or product | 1990 | 1991 | 1992 | 1993 | 1994 | 1995 | Направление животноводства или вид продукции |
|---|---|---|---|---|---|---|---|
| **Livestock (thousands of heads)** | | | | | | | **Поголовье скота (тысяч голов)** |
| Cattle | 1,061 | 1,000 | 970 | 916 | 832 | 726 | Крупный рогатый скот |
| of which: Cows | 395 | 397 | 403 | 411 | 399 | 381 | в том числе коровы |
| Pigs | 1,850 | 1,753 | 1,487 | 1,165 | 1,061 | 1,015 | Свиньи |
| Sheep and goats | 1,282 | 1,289 | 1,357 | 1,445 | 1,507 | 1,423 | Овцы и козы |
| of which: Goats | 37 | 50 | 63 | 79 | 96 | 103 | в том числе козы |
| Horses | 47 | 49 | 51 | 55 | 59 | 61 | Лошади |
| Other | .. | .. | .. | .. | .. | .. | Прочие |
| **Animal husbandry products** | | | | | | | **Продукция животноводства** |
| Meat (thousands of tons) | 366 | 304 | 234 | 180 | 153 | 137 | Мясо (тысяч тонн) |
| Beef | 114 | 96 | 75 | 68 | 62 | 47 | Говядина |
| Pork | 177 | 145 | 114 | 79 | 61 | 60 | Свинина |
| Lamb | 7 | 5 | 4 | 4 | 5 | 5 | Баранина |
| Poultry | 66 | 56 | 39 | 26 | 24 | 24 | Птица |
| Other | 2 | 1 | 2 | 2 | 1 | 1 | Прочие виды мяса |
| Milk (thousands of tons) | 1,511 | 1,292 | 1,135 | 976 | 909 | 837 | Молоко (тысяч тонн) |
| Eggs (millions) | 1,129 | 1,061 | 813 | 618 | 515 | 563 | Яйца (миллионов штук) |
| Wool (thousands of tons) | 3 | 3 | 3 | 3 | 3 | 3 | Шерсть (тысяч тонн) |

**TABLE 6-1. Industrial production by sector (thousands of national currency)**

**ТАБЛИЦА 6-1. Промышленное производство по отраслям (тысяч национальной валюты)**

| Sector | 1988 | 1989 | 1990 | 1991 | 1992 | 1993 | 1994 | 1995 | Отрасли |
|---|---|---|---|---|---|---|---|---|---|
| **All industry** | ##### | ##### | 11,505 | 22,186 | 217,903 | 1,186,309 | 3,746,703 | 4,265,232 | **Вся промышленность** |
| **Heavy industry** | 4,046 | 4,332 | 4,576 | 8,196 | 93,571 | 479,946 | 1,784,693 | 1,782,637 | **Тяжелая промышленность** |
| Fuel and energy | .. | .. | .. | .. | .. | .. | .. | .. | Топливно-энергетическая промышленнoть |
| Electricity | 385 | 412 | 399 | 625 | 17,431 | 131,449 | 665,833 | 622,377 | Электроэнергетика |
| Fuels | .. | .. | .. | .. | .. | .. | .. | .. | Топливная промышленность |
| Ferrous and nonferrous metallurgy | 112 | 102 | 114 | 223 | 10,070 | .. | .. | .. | Металлургия |
| Chemicals and petrochemical industry | 313 | 342 | 357 | 606 | 5,511 | 6,797 | 23,294 | 22,487 | Химическая и нефтехимическая пром. |
| Machine building and metalworking | 1,827 | 1,978 | 2,046 | 3,485 | 29,727 | 170,546 | 402,625 | 391,637 | Машиностроение и металлообработка |
| Forestry, woodworking, and pulp and paper industry | 379 | 366 | 393 | 757 | 6,667 | 51,742 | 162,471 | 176,510 | Лесная, деревообрабатывающая и целлюлозо-бумажная промышленность |
| Construction materials | 454 | 431 | 453 | 949 | 8,600 | 42,334 | 168,585 | 162,610 | Промышленность строительных материалов |
| **Light industry** | 2,166 | 2,303 | 2,427 | 4,932 | 39,185 | 93,714 | 231,990 | 228,852 | **Легкая промышленность** |
| Textiles | 1,038 | 1,063 | 1,141 | 2,680 | 26,831 | 39,468 | 111,459 | 98,558 | Текстильная |
| Clothing | 684 | 779 | 833 | 1,377 | 5,872 | 24,535 | 55,368 | 48,369 | Швейная |
| Leather and shoes | 444 | 461 | 453 | 875 | 6,482 | 29,711 | 65,163 | 81,925 | Кожевенная и обувная |
| **Food industry** | 3,832 | 3,984 | 4,502 | 9,058 | 85,147 | 612,649 | 1,730,020 | 2,253,743 | **Пищевая промышленность** |
| Processed foods | 2,972 | 3,082 | 3,292 | 6,300 | 55,213 | 419,765 | 1,192,381 | 1,643,448 | Пищевкусовая |
| Meat and dairy products | 840 | 882 | 906 | 2,291 | 23,237 | 129,593 | 384,778 | 420,299 | Мясная и молочная |
| Fish | 20 | 20 | 19 | 29 | 125 | 1,406 | 5,869 | 5,500 | Рыбная |

## TABLE 6-2. Industrial production by sector in constant prices (ths. of national currency)
## ТАБЛИЦА 6-2. Промышленное производство по отраслям в постоянных ценах (тыс. национальной валюты)

| Sector | 1990 | 1991 | 1992 | 1993 | 1994 | 1995 | Отрасли |
|---|---|---|---|---|---|---|---|
| **Industrial production** | | | | | | | **Промышленное производство** |
| **All industry** | 10,884 | 9,676 | 77,185 | 77,427 | 54,043 | 52,763 | **Вся промышленность** |
| **Heavy industry** | 4,591 | 4,073 | 28,996 | 28,077 | 21,126 | 19,562 | **Тяжелая промышленность** |
| Fuel and energy | .. | .. | .. | .. | .. | .. | Топливно-энергетическая промышленноть |
| Electricity | 302 | 264 | 6,278 | 5,172 | 4,225 | 3,953 | Электроэнергетика |
| Fuels | .. | .. | .. | .. | .. | .. | Топливная промышленность |
| Ferrous and nonferrous metallurgy | 114 | 110 | .. | .. | .. | .. | Металлургия |
| Chemicals and petrochemicals | 360 | 271 | 917 | 705 | 412 | 150 | Химическая и нефтехимическая пром. |
| Machine building and metalworking | 2,278 | 2,394 | 11,430 | 12,724 | 7,692 | 7,320 | Машиностроение и металлообработка |
| Forestry, woodworking, and pulp and paper | 384 | 276 | 2,695 | 2,614 | 2,015 | 1,747 | Лесная, деревообрабатывающая и целлюлозо-бумажная промышленность |
| Construction materials | 448 | 360 | 3,111 | 2,451 | 2,421 | 2,358 | Промышленность строительных материалов |
| **Light industry** | 2,456 | 2,434 | 8,362 | 6,796 | 3,576 | 2,531 | **Легкая промышленность** |
| Textiles | 1,132 | 1,163 | 4,097 | 3,301 | 1,936 | 995 | Текстильная |
| Clothing | 863 | 867 | 1,925 | 1,502 | 879 | 855 | Швейная |
| Leather and shoe | 461 | 404 | 2,340 | 1,993 | 761 | 681 | Кожевенная и обувная |
| **Food industry** | 3,837 | 3,169 | 39,833 | 42,614 | 29,341 | 30,670 | **Пищевая промышленность** |
| Processed foods | 2,740 | 2,342 | 29,495 | 35,939 | 24,566 | 26,526 | Пищевкусовая |
| Meat and dairy products | 904 | 662 | 8,859 | 5,473 | 3,842 | 3,205 | Мясная и молочная |
| Fish | 18 | 9 | 122 | 140 | 98 | 78 | Рыбная |
| **Growth in production by sector (in percent)** | | | | | | | **Рост производства по отраслям** |
| **All industry** | 3.6 | -11.1 | -29.5 | 0.3 | -30.2 | -2.4 | **Вся промышленность** |
| **Heavy industry** | 5.1 | -11.3 | -30.4 | -3.2 | -24.8 | -7.4 | **Тяжелая промышленность** |
| Power and fuels | .. | .. | .. | .. | .. | .. | Топливно-энергетическая промышленноть |
| Electricity | -6.5 | -12.6 | -14.8 | -17.6 | -18.3 | -6.4 | Электроэнергетика |
| Fuels | .. | .. | .. | .. | .. | .. | Топливная промышленность |
| Ferrous and nonferrous metallurgy | 11.8 | -3.5 | .. | .. | .. | .. | Металлургия |
| Chemicals and petrochemicals | 3.7 | -24.7 | -40.6 | -23.1 | -41.6 | -63.6 | Химическая и нефтехимическая пром. |
| Machine building and metalworking | 4.6 | 5.1 | -37.0 | 11.3 | -39.5 | -4.8 | Машиностроение и металлообработка |
| Forestry, woodworking, and pulp and paper | 4.9 | -28.1 | -25.0 | -3.0 | -22.9 | -13.3 | Лесная, деревообрабатывающая и целлюлозо-бумажная промышленность |
| Construction materials | 4.2 | -19.6 | -48.3 | -21.2 | -1.2 | -2.6 | Промышленность строительных материалов |
| **Light industry** | 3.3 | -0.9 | -31.0 | -18.7 | -47.4 | -29.2 | **Легкая промышленность** |
| Textiles | 6.3 | 2.7 | -29.6 | -19.4 | -41.4 | -48.6 | Текстильная |
| Clothing | 4.9 | 0.5 | -35.3 | -22.0 | -41.5 | -2.7 | Швейная |
| Leather and shoe | -5.7 | -12.4 | -26.0 | -14.8 | -61.8 | -10.5 | Кожевенная и обувная |
| **Food industry** | 2.0 | -17.4 | -27.2 | 7.0 | -31.1 | 4.5 | **Пищевая промышленность** |
| Processed foods | -4.4 | -14.5 | -21.2 | 21.8 | -31.6 | 8.0 | Пищевкусовая |
| Meat and dairy products | 3.1 | -26.8 | -49.4 | -38.2 | -29.8 | -16.6 | Мясная и молочная |
| Fish | -5.3 | -50.0 | -55.6 | 14.8 | -30.0 | -20.4 | Рыбная |

**TABLE 6-3. Primary energy supply (million tons oil equivalent)**

**ТАБЛИЦА 6-3. Ресурсы первичных видов энергии (млн. тонн нефтяного эквивалента)**

| Item | | 1990 | 1991 | 1992 | 1993 | 1994 | 1995 | Статьи | |
|---|---|---|---|---|---|---|---|---|---|
| **Primary production** | | | | | | | | **Производство первичной энергии** | |
| Coal and lignite (hard and brown) | | .. | .. | .. | .. | .. | .. | Уголь каменный и бурый | |
| Crude oil | | .. | .. | .. | .. | .. | .. | Нефть | |
| Gas | | .. | .. | .. | .. | .. | .. | Газ | |
| Nuclear | | .. | .. | .. | .. | .. | .. | Атомная энергия | |
| Hydro/geothermal | | 0.059 | 0.079 | 0.100 | 0.100 | 0.000 | 0.019 | Гидро-геотермальная | |
| Other | | 0.000 | 0.000 | 0.000 | 0.000 | 0.000 | 0.058 | Другие виды | |
| Total | | 0.100 | 0.100 | 0.100 | 0.100 | 0.000 | 0.077 | Всего | |
| **Energy trade** | | | | | | | | **Торговля энергией** | |
| Coal and lignite | Exports | .. | .. | 0.100 | .. | .. | .. | Уголь каменный и бурый | Экспорт |
| | Imports | 2.570 | 2.005 | 1.000 | 1.000 | 0.400 | 0.535 | | Импорт |
| | Net imports | 2.570 | 2.005 | 0.900 | 1.000 | 0.400 | 0.535 | | Чистый импорт |
| Oil/oil product | Exports | .. | .. | 0.000 | 0.000 | .. | 0.003 | Нефть и нефтепродукты | Экспорт |
| | Imports | 4.720 | 4.288 | 2.900 | 1.800 | 1.100 | 1.058 | | Импорт |
| | Net imports | 4.720 | 4.288 | 2.900 | 1.800 | 1.100 | 1.055 | | Чистый импорт |
| Gas | Exports | .. | .. | .. | .. | .. | .. | Газ | Экспорт |
| | Imports | 3.381 | 3.261 | 2.900 | 2.600 | 1.500 | 1.531 | | Импорт |
| | Net imports | 3.381 | 3.261 | 2.900 | 2.600 | 1.500 | 1.531 | | Чистый импорт |
| Electricity | Exports | 1.714 | 1.274 | 1.100 | 1.300 | 0.000 | 0.029 | Электричество | Экспорт |
| | Imports | 1.021 | 1.014 | 1.000 | 1.100 | 0.100 | 0.454 | | Импорт |
| | Net imports | -0.693 | -0.260 | -0.100 | -0.200 | 0.100 | 0.425 | | Чистый импорт |
| **Total net imports** | | 9.978 | 9.294 | 6.600 | 5.200 | 3.100 | 3.546 | **Чистый импорт энергии-всего** | |
| **Total stock changes** | | -0.095 | 0.174 | 0.500 | 0.200 | 0.000 | 0.060 | **Изменение запасов-всего** | |
| **Total primary energy supply** | | 10.000 | 9.600 | 7.200 | 5.500 | 3.100 | 3.683 | **Ресурсы первичной энергии-всего** | |
| Coal and lignite | | 2.570 | 2.005 | 0.900 | 1.000 | 0.400 | 0.535 | Уголь каменный и бурый | |
| Oil/oil products | | 4.720 | 4.288 | 2.900 | 1.800 | 1.100 | 1.055 | Нефть и нефтепродукты | |
| Gas | | 3.381 | 3.261 | 2.900 | 2.600 | 1.500 | 1.531 | Газ | |
| Nuclear | | .. | .. | .. | .. | .. | .. | Атомная энергия | |
| Hydro/geothermal | | 0.059 | 0.079 | 0.100 | 0.100 | 0.000 | 0.019 | Гидро-геотермальная энергия | |
| Other | | -0.800 | -0.100 | 0.400 | 0.000 | 0.100 | 0.543 | Другие виды | |
| **Total primary energy requirement (equals total primary energy supply)** | | 10.000 | 9.600 | 7.200 | 5.500 | 3.100 | 3.683 | **Потребность в первичной энергии-всего (равно ресурсам первичной энергии)** | |

## TABLE 6-4. Final energy consumption (million tons oil equivalent) — MOLDOVA
## ТАБЛИЦА 6-4. Конечное потребление энергии ( млн. тонн нефтяного эквивалента )

| | 1991 | 1992 | 1993 | 1994 | 1995 | |
|---|---|---|---|---|---|---|
| **Final energy consumption** | 7.36 | 6.32 | 3.90 | 3.10 | 2.80 | **Конечное потребление энергии** |
| Coal & Lignite | 0.96 | 0.82 | 0.20 | 0.20 | 0.10 | Уголь каменный и бурый |
| Oil Products | 2.01 | 1.73 | 0.80 | 0.70 | 0.70 | Нефтепродукты |
| Gas | 0.54 | 0.46 | 0.30 | 0.30 | 0.30 | Газ |
| Electricity | 1.80 | 1.55 | 1.40 | 1.00 | 0.90 | Электроэнергия |
| Heat | 2.02 | 1.73 | 1.00 | 0.80 | 0.70 | Тепло |
| Other | 0.03 | 0.03 | 0.20 | 0.10 | 0.10 | Другие виды |
| Of which: | | | | | | В том числе |
| **Industry** | 2.27 | 1.95 | 1.10 | 0.50 | 0.50 | **Промышленность** |
| Coal & Lignite | 0.04 | 0.04 | 0.00 | 0.00 | 0.00 | Уголь каменный и бурый |
| Oil Products | 0.32 | 0.28 | 0.10 | 0.00 | 0.00 | Нефтепродукты |
| Gas | 0.17 | 0.10 | 0.10 | 0.00 | 0.10 | Газ |
| Electricity | 0.73 | 0.62 | 0.50 | 0.20 | 0.20 | Электроэнергия |
| Heat | 1.01 | 0.87 | 0.40 | 0.30 | 0.20 | Тепло |
| Other | 0.00 | 0.00 | 0.00 | 0.00 | 0.00 | Другие виды |
| **Agriculture** | 1.00 | 0.86 | 0.50 | 0.40 | 0.40 | **Сельское хозяйство** |
| Coal & Lignite | 0.01 | 0.01 | 0.00 | 0.00 | 0.00 | Уголь каменный и бурый |
| Oil Products | 0.53 | 0.46 | 0.20 | 0.20 | 0.20 | Нефтепродукты |
| Gas | 0.00 | 0.00 | 0.00 | 0.00 | 0.00 | Газ |
| Electricity | 0.30 | 0.26 | 0.20 | 0.10 | 0.10 | Электроэнергия |
| Heat | 0.16 | 0.14 | 0.10 | 0.10 | 0.10 | Тепло |
| Other | .. | .. | 0.00 | 0.00 | 0.00 | Другие виды |
| **Transport** | 1.04 | 0.89 | 0.60 | 0.40 | 0.40 | **Транспорт** |
| Oil Products | 0.92 | 0.79 | 0.50 | 0.30 | 0.30 | Нефтепродукты |
| Other | 0.12 | 0.10 | 0.10 | 0.10 | 0.10 | Другие виды |
| **Households** | 2.68 | 2.30 | 1.10 | 1.00 | 1.00 | **Домашние хозяйства** |
| Coal & Lignite | 0.90 | 0.77 | 0.10 | 0.20 | 0.00 | Уголь каменный и бурый |
| Oil Products | 0.17 | 0.15 | 0.00 | 0.00 | 0.10 | Нефтепродукты |
| Gas | 0.31 | 0.27 | 0.20 | 0.20 | 0.20 | Газ |
| Electricity | 0.54 | 0.46 | 0.40 | 0.30 | 0.40 | Электроэнергия |
| Heat | 0.73 | 0.63 | 0.30 | 0.30 | 0.30 | Тепло |
| Other | 0.03 | 0.02 | 0.10 | 0.00 | 0.00 | Другие виды |

## TABLE 7-1. Price indices and exchange rates
## ТАБЛИЦА 7-1. Индексы цен и обменный курс

| Year and month | National currency per U.S. dollar<br>Единиц нац. валюты за 1 доллар США | National currency per 000 Russian rubles<br>Единиц нац. валюты за 1000 российских рублей | Consumer price index (as a percent of the previous month)<br>Индекс потребительских цен (в % к предыдущему месяцу) | Producer price index (as a percent of the previous month)<br>Индекс цен производителей (в % к предыдущему месяцу) | Consumer price index (as a percent of the previous December)<br>Индекс потребительских цен (в % к декабрю прошлого года) | Producer price index (as a percent of the previous December)<br>Индекс цен производителей (в % к декабрю прошлого года) | Год и месяц |
|---|---|---|---|---|---|---|---|
| **1993** | | | | | | | **1993** |
| January | 0.5 | 1.0 | 155.7 | 154.0 | 155.7 | 154.0 | Январь |
| February | 0.6 | 1.0 | 127.0 | 133.0 | 197.7 | 205.0 | Февраль |
| March | 0.7 | 1.0 | 126.2 | 121.0 | 249.6 | 248.0 | Март |
| April | 0.8 | 1.0 | 114.7 | 165.0 | 286.3 | 408.0 | Апрель |
| May | 0.9 | 1.0 | 110.6 | 108.0 | 316.6 | 441.0 | Май |
| June | 1.1 | 1.0 | 133.6 | 115.0 | 423.0 | 508.0 | Июнь |
| July | 1.0 | 1.0 | 137.9 | 145.0 | 583.2 | 737.0 | Июль |
| August | 1.2 | 1.1 | 123.2 | 148.0 | 718.6 | 1,089.0 | Август |
| September | 1.4 | 1.4 | 139.3 | 144.0 | 1,001.0 | 1,568.0 | Сентябрь |
| October | 2.2 | 1.9 | 143.5 | 145.0 | 1,436.3 | 2,268.0 | Октябрь |
| November | 3.4 | 2.5 | 122.7 | 148.0 | 1,762.7 | 3,348.0 | Ноябрь |
| December | 3.7 | 2.9 | 159.2 | 134.0 | 2,807.2 | 4,483.0 | Декабрь |
| **1994** | | | | | | | **1994** |
| January | 3.7 | 2.7 | 118.9 | 157.0 | 118.9 | 157.0 | Январь |
| February | 3.8 | 2.4 | 121.6 | 123.0 | 144.6 | 190.0 | Февраль |
| March | 3.9 | 2.2 | 110.0 | 109.0 | 159.1 | 207.0 | Март |
| April | 4.1 | 2.4 | 105.0 | 106.0 | 167.1 | 220.0 | Апрель |
| May | 4.1 | 2.2 | 102.7 | 106.0 | 171.6 | 229.0 | Май |
| June | 4.1 | 2.1 | 102.7 | 102.0 | 176.2 | 234.0 | Июнь |
| July | 4.1 | 2.1 | 102.2 | 99.7 | 180.1 | 233.0 | Июль |
| August | 4.1 | 2.0 | 99.9 | 99.0 | 179.9 | 231.0 | Август |
| September | 4.2 | 1.9 | 102.5 | 103.0 | 184.4 | 233.0 | Сентябрь |
| October | 4.2 | 1.4 | 104.2 | 104.0 | 192.1 | 242.0 | Октябрь |
| November | 4.2 | 1.3 | 103.5 | 107.0 | 198.8 | 259.0 | Ноябрь |
| December | 4.3 | 1.2 | 102.9 | 102.0 | 204.6 | 265.0 | Декабрь |

## TABLE 7-1. Price indices and exchange rates
## ТАБЛИЦА 7-1. Индексы цен и обменный курс

| Year and month | National currency per U.S. dollar<br>Единиц нац. валюты за 1 доллар США | National currency per 000 Russian rubles<br>Единиц нац. валюты за 1000 российских рублей | Consumer price index (as a percent of the previous month)<br>Индекс потребительских цен (в % к предыдущему месяцу) | Producer price index (as a percent of the previous month)<br>Индекс цен производителей (в % к предыдущему месяцу) | Consumer price index (as a percent of the previous December)<br>Индекс потребительских цен (в % к декабрю прошлого года) | Producer price index (as a percent of the previous December)<br>Индекс цен производителей (в % к декабрю прошлого года) | Год и месяц |
|---|---|---|---|---|---|---|---|
| **1995** | | | | | | | **1995** |
| January | 4.3 | 1.1 | 102.9 | 110.0 | 102.9 | 110.0 | Январь |
| February | 4.4 | 1.1 | 102.3 | 104.0 | 105.3 | 114.0 | Февраль |
| March | 4.4 | 0.9 | 100.7 | 103.0 | 106.0 | 115.0 | Март |
| April | 4.5 | 0.9 | 100.6 | 101.0 | 106.6 | 116.0 | Апрель |
| May | 4.5 | 0.9 | 100.4 | 102.0 | 107.0 | 118.0 | Май |
| June | 4.6 | 1.0 | 100.2 | 101.0 | 107.3 | 120.0 | Июнь |
| July | 4.5 | 1.0 | 100.2 | 103.0 | 107.5 | 124.0 | Июль |
| August | 4.5 | 1.0 | 100.2 | 104.0 | 107.7 | 126.0 | Август |
| September | 4.5 | 1.0 | 102.6 | 103.0 | 110.5 | 130.0 | Сентябрь |
| October | 4.5 | 1.0 | 102.7 | 106.0 | 113.5 | 137.0 | Октябрь |
| November | 4.6 | 1.0 | 106.0 | 101.0 | 120.3 | 140.0 | Ноябрь |
| December | 4.5 | 1.0 | 102.9 | 102.0 | 123.8 | 141.0 | Декабрь |
| **1996** | | | | | | | **1996** |
| January | 4.5 | 1.0 | 103.5 | 102.0 | 103.5 | 102.0 | Январь |
| February | 4.6 | 1.0 | 102.5 | 103.0 | 106.1 | 106.0 | Февраль |
| March | 4.5 | 0.9 | 101.1 | 103.0 | 107.3 | 109.0 | Март |
| April | 4.6 | 0.9 | 101.1 | 101.0 | 108.4 | 110.0 | Апрель |
| May | 4.6 | 0.9 | 100.8 | 102.0 | 109.3 | 113.0 | Май |
| June | 4.6 | 0.9 | 100.1 | 102.0 | 109.4 | 115.0 | Июнь |
| July | .. | .. | .. | .. | .. | .. | Июль |
| August | .. | .. | .. | .. | .. | .. | Август |
| September | .. | .. | .. | .. | .. | .. | Сентябрь |
| October | .. | .. | .. | .. | .. | .. | Октябрь |
| November | .. | .. | .. | .. | .. | .. | Ноябрь |
| December | .. | .. | .. | .. | .. | .. | Декабрь |

**TABLE 7-2. Monthly nominal wages by sector**

**ТАБЛИЦА 7-2. Среднемесячная денежная зарплата по отраслям**

| Sector | 1990 | 1991 | 1992 | 1993 | 1994 | 1995 | Сектора |
|---|---|---|---|---|---|---|---|
| **Nominal wages** | | | | | | | **Средняя номинальная заработная плата** |
| **Economy average** | 0.2 | 0.4 | 3.5 | 31.2 | 108.4 | 143.2 | **По народному хозяйству** |
| **Material sphere** | 0.3 | 0.4 | 3.8 | 31.7 | 109.2 | 143.1 | **Отрасли сферы материального производства** |
| Industry | 0.3 | 0.5 | 4.6 | 39.8 | 153.0 | 209.7 | Промышленность |
| Construction | 0.3 | 0.5 | 3.8 | 33.4 | 149.7 | 187.5 | Строительство |
| Agriculture | 0.3 | 0.5 | 3.3 | 28.6 | 82.4 | 106.7 | Сельское хозяйство |
| Transport | 0.3 | 0.4 | 3.5 | 29.7 | 137.7 | 191.2 | Транспорт |
| Communications | 0.2 | 0.4 | 3.4 | 28.4 | 145.8 | 190.7 | Связь |
| Trade (retail and wholesale) | 0.2 | 0.4 | 2.7 | 28.2 | 105.1 | 143.2 | Торговля (оптовая и розничная) |
| Other | 0.2 | 0.4 | 3.1 | 33.1 | 136.3 | 188.0 | Прочие отрасли материального производства |
| **Nonmaterial sphere** | 0.2 | 0.3 | 3.1 | 30.1 | 106.4 | 143.4 | **Отрасли непроизводственной сферы** |
| Municipal services | 0.2 | 0.3 | 2.9 | 27.4 | 121.8 | 178.4 | Жилкомхоз и бытовое обслуживание |
| Science, research and development | 0.3 | 0.5 | 3.3 | 34.0 | 135.0 | 196.5 | Наука и научное обслуживание |
| Education | 0.2 | 0.3 | 2.9 | 25.5 | 83.8 | 108.8 | Образование |
| Culture | 0.2 | 0.3 | 3.1 | 28.7 | 87.9 | 104.6 | Культура |
| Arts | 0.2 | 0.3 | .. | .. | .. | .. | Искусство |
| Health care, social security, and sports | 0.2 | 0.3 | 2.7 | 27.5 | 102.9 | 127.4 | Здравоохр., соц.обсл., физк. и спорт |
| Banking, finance, credit, insurance | 0.4 | 0.8 | 7.7 | 96.7 | 299.6 | 494.1 | Кредитование, страхование, банк. дело |
| Government | 0.3 | 0.4 | 4.3 | 40.5 | 156.3 | 230.2 | Управление |

**TABLE 8-1. Money income and expenditure of the population (thousands of national currency)**
**ТАБЛИЦА 8-1. Денежные доходы и расходы населения (тысяч национальной валюты)**

| Type of income or expenditure | 1990 | 1991 | 1992 | 1993 | 1994 | 1995 | Вид доходов или расходов |
|---|---|---|---|---|---|---|---|
| **Income** | | | | | | | **Доходы** |
| **Total labor income** | 6,627 | 11,333 | 68,487 | 643,899 | 1,507,685 | 2,354,118 | **Всего трудовых доходов** |
| Regular wages | 4,917 | 7,844 | 49,552 | 462,452 | 1,111,147 | 1,635,365 | Заработная плата |
| Wages paid by cooperatives | 633 | 673 | 1,559 | 7,095 | 14,812 | 15,410 | Заработная плата в кооперативах |
| Other wages and compensation | 142 | 492 | 3,294 | 26,720 | 92,498 | 163,729 | Прочие доходы типа заработной платы |
| Income paid by collective farms | 994 | 1,782 | 10,222 | 103,317 | 93,054 | 127,131 | Доходы от колхозов |
| Income from sale of farm products | 574 | 1,215 | 5,419 | 51,410 | 210,986 | 427,893 | Доходы от продажи продукции колхозов |
| **Total transfer receipts** | 1,926 | 4,068 | 18,917 | 144,826 | 1,683,169 | 2,760,224 | **Всего трансфертных поступлений** |
| Pensions and allowances | 1,042 | 2,326 | 14,659 | 119,503 | 435,629 | 653,791 | Пенсии и пособия |
| Scholarships | 35 | 94 | 531 | 4,050 | 12,101 | 16,242 | Стипендии |
| Income from the financial system (insurance, interest, etc.) | 372 | 929 | 1,695 | 8,668 | 109,687 | 78,131 | Доходы из финансовой системы (страховые возмещения, проценты и т.д.) |
| Other income | 477 | 719 | 2,032 | 12,605 | 1,125,752 | 2,012,061 | Прочие виды доходов |
| **Total income** | 8,553 | 15,401 | 87,404 | 788,725 | 3,190,854 | 5,114,342 | **Всего доходов** |
| **Expenditure** | | | | | | | **Расходы** |
| **Total purchases** | 7,018 | 12,326 | 66,375 | 577,315 | 2,221,196 | 3,309,132 | **Всего покупок товаров и услуг** |
| Retail goods | 6,433 | 11,395 | 59,615 | 510,912 | 1,822,667 | 2,664,095 | Товары в розничной торговле |
| Services | 585 | 931 | 6,760 | 66,403 | 398,529 | 645,037 | Услуги |
| Rent and utilities | 135 | 197 | 1,925 | 30,627 | 145,894 | 214,137 | Квартирная плата и коммунальные платежи |
| Transport and communications | 236 | 341 | 3,250 | 24,436 | 122,242 | 259,050 | Транспорт и связь |
| Health and other services | 178 | 266 | 1,469 | 11,340 | 130,393 | 171,850 | Здравоохранение и другие виды услуг |
| Cooperatives | 36 | 127 | 116 | .. | .. | .. | Кооперативы |
| **Transfers and savings** | 1,753 | 3,124 | 12,733 | 85,843 | 677,590 | 1,429,244 | **Трансферты и сбережения** |
| Taxes, fees, dues, and other | 553 | 653 | 4,893 | 45,178 | 141,828 | 273,685 | Налоги, сборы, пошлины и др. |
| Savings | 798 | 1,966 | 5,657 | 24,083 | 432,362 | 1,047,294 | Сбережения |
| Other | 402 | 505 | 2,183 | 16,581 | 103,400 | 108,264 | Прочие |
| **Total expenditure** | 8,771 | 15,450 | 79,108 | 663,158 | 2,898,786 | 4,738,376 | **Всего расходов** |
| **Income less expenditure** | -218 | -49 | 8,296 | 125,567 | 292,068 | 375,966 | **Доходы за вычетом расходов** |

# *Country Notes: Moldova*

**General Note:** Unless otherwise indicated, data were supplied by the State Department of Statistics of the Republic of Moldova.

**Currency:** Unless otherwise indicated, data are in the national currency, leis. The lei was introduced on November 29, 1993 with the conversion factor of 1 lei = 1,000 rubles.

**Table 1-1:** Sums of items do not add up to the totals for labor resources in 1994 and for employment in 1990-1994. The line "Unemployed" shows registered unemployed. Data on labor resources and employment for 1993 through 1995 do not include Transniestria and the Bendery area.

**Tables 3-2A, 3-2B, 3-3A, and 3-3B:** The totals do not include services.

**Tables 3-4A and 3-4B:** In 1993 and 1994 the data for the Czech Republic include the data for Slovakia.

**Table 4-2:** For 1991 the sum of current and capital expenditures does not add up to the total expenditure by economic type.

**Table 5-2:** Data are in 1983 prices.

**Table 6-1:** Data for 1993 through 1995 do not include Transniestria and the Bendery area. The totals for the food industry exceed the respective sums of food industry branches by amounts of production of the flour-groat industry.

**Table 6-2:** Data for 1990 and 1991 are in 1982 prices. Starting from 1992 data are in January, 1992 prices. Data for 1993 through 1995 do not include Transniestria and the Bendery area. The totals for the food industry exceed the respective sums of food industry branches by amounts of production of the flour-groat industry.

# *Комментарии к таблицам: Молдова*

**Общее замечание:** Данные были получены из Государственного Департамента Статистики Республики Молдова.

**Национальная валюта:** За исключением особо отмеченных случаев, данные приведены в национальной валюте, леях. Лей был введен 29 ноября 1993 года с коэффициентом пересчета 1 лей = 1000 рублей.

**Таблица 1-1:** Суммы компонентов трудовых ресурсов в 1994 г. и занятого населения в 1990-1994 гг. не равны соответствующим итоговым величинам. Строка Безработные показывает зарегестрированных безработных. Данные по трудовым ресурсам и занятости за 1993-1995 гг. приведены без учета Приднестровья и района Бендер.

**Таблицы 3-2А, 3-2В, 3-3А и 3-3В:** Услуги не включены в итог.

**Таблицы 3-4А и 3-4В:** В 1993-1994 гг. данные по Чешской Республике включают данные по Словакии.

**Таблица 4-2:** В 1991 г. сумма текущих и капитальных расходов меньше общей величины расходов.

**Таблица 5-2:** Данные приведены в ценах 1983 г.

**Таблица 6-1:** Данные за 1993-1995 гг. приведены без учета Приднестровья и района Бендер. Общий объем производства в пищевой промышленности превосходит сумму приведенных компонентов на величину продукции мукомольной промышленности.

**Таблица 6-2:** Данные за 1990-1991 гг. приведены в ценах 1982 г. Начиная с 1992 г. данные приведены в ценах января 1992 г. Данные за 1993-1995 гг. приведены без учета Приднестровья и района Бендер. Общий объем производства в пищевой промышленности превосходит сумму приведенных компонентов на величину продукции мукомольной промышленности.

# Russian Federation / Российская Федерация

1996 Population / Численность населения в 1996 году
(thousands / тыс. человек): 147,976

Area / Территория
(thousand square kilometers / тыс. кв. км.): 17,075.4

Capital city / Столица :
Moscow / Москва

**Country Tables:** Tables 3-2B, 3-3B, 3-4B, 4-1 and 4-2 are not included because there are either no data available or no recent data available.

**Статистические таблицы страны:** Таблицы 3-2B, 3-3B, 3-4B, 4-1 и 4-2 не включены ввиду полного отсутствия данных либо их отсутствия за последние годы.

## TABLE 1-1. Population and employment (thousands)
## ТАБЛИЦА 1-1. Население и занятость (тысяч)



| Population or employment category | 1990 | 1991 | 1992 | 1993 | 1994 | 1995 | Население или группы занятых |
|---|---|---|---|---|---|---|---|
| **Total population** | 148,164 | 148,326 | 148,295 | 147,997 | 147,938 | 147,609 | **Население - всего** |
| Males | 69,420 | 69,542 | 69,583 | 69,473 | 69,486 | .. | Мужчины |
| Females | 78,744 | 78,784 | 78,712 | 78,524 | 78,452 | .. | Женщины |
| Urban population | 109,332 | 109,209 | 108,458 | 108,010 | 107,887 | 107,671 | Городское |
| Rural population | 38,832 | 39,117 | 39,837 | 39,987 | 40,051 | 39,938 | Сельское |
| Population under working age | 35,993 | 35,720 | 35,199 | 34,534 | 33,948 | .. | Моложе трудоспособного возраста |
| Working-age population | 83,976 | 83,892 | 83,748 | 83,767 | 84,059 | .. | Лица в трудоспособном возрасте |
| Population over working age | 28,195 | 28,714 | 29,348 | 29,696 | 29,931 | .. | Старще трудоспособного возраста |
| Economically Active Population, in non-working age | .. | .. | .. | .. | .. | .. | Экономически активное население в нетрудоспособном возрасте |
| Above working age | .. | .. | .. | .. | .. | .. | Старше трудоспособного возраста |
| Below working age | .. | .. | .. | .. | .. | .. | Моложе трудоспособного возраста |
| **Total labor resources** | 86,473 | 86,330 | 86,071 | 86,168 | 85,270 | .. | **Трудовые ресурсы - всего** |
| **Total employment** | 75,325 | 73,848 | 72,071 | 70,852 | 69,350 | .. | **Занятое население - всего** |
| State sector employees | 63,747 | 57,188 | 50,990 | 37,525 | 30,470 | .. | Государственный сектор |
| Leased enterprise employees | 2,764 | 5,590 | 2,199 | 12,502 | 15,127 | .. | Арендные предприятия |
| Joint-stock company employees | 182 | 1,068 | 4,433 | .. | .. | .. | Акционерные общества |
| Economic association employees | 100 | 795 | 916 | .. | .. | .. | Хозяйственные ассоциации |
| Social organization employees | 630 | 718 | 583 | 593 | 605 | .. | Общественные организации |
| Joint venture employees | 67 | 141 | 195 | 305 | 378 | .. | Совместные предприятия |
| Collective farm workers | 3,979 | 3,945 | 2,217 | .. | .. | .. | Колхозы |
| Cooperative workers | 2,700 | 2,901 | 2,707 | .. | .. | .. | Кооперативы |
| Individual labor activities | 128 | 342 | 161 | 1,457 | 1,600 | .. | ИТД |
| Private subsidiary agricultural workers | 1,022 | 1,078 | 1,235 | 1,185 | 1,160 | .. | Личные подсобные хозяйства |
| Private agricultural workers | 7 | 83 | 597 | 930 | 950 | .. | Фермерские хозяйства |
| **Students** | 5,642 | 5,597 | 5,568 | 5,153 | 5,322 | .. | **Учащиеся** |
| **Religious workers** | 39 | 39 | 39 | 39 | 39 | .. | **Служащие религиозного культа** |
| **Working age population not employed in the national economy** | 5,506 | 6,885 | 8,432 | 10,163 | 11,650 | .. | **Лица в трудоспособном возрасте, не занятые в экономике** |
| Housewives | .. | .. | .. | .. | .. | .. | Домохозяйки |
| Military personnel | .. | .. | .. | .. | .. | .. | Военнослужащие |
| Unemployed | .. | 61 | 578 | 3,950 | 5,171 | .. | Безработные |
| **Labor force** | .. | 73,909 | 72,649 | 74,802 | 73,655 | .. | **Рабочая сила** |

## TABLE 1-2. Employment by sector (thousands)
## ТАБЛИЦА 1-2. Численность занятого населения по секторам (тысяч)

| Sector | 1990 | 1991 | 1992 | 1993 | 1994 | 1995 | Сектор |
|---|---|---|---|---|---|---|---|
| **Material sphere** | 53,360 | 51,962 | 51,156 | 50,119 | 47,363 | .. | **Сфера материального производства** |
| **Agriculture and forestry** | 9,965 | 9,970 | 10,336 | 10,347 | 10,528 | .. | **Сельское и лесное хозяйство** |
| Agriculture | 9,728 | 9,736 | 10,101 | 10,103 | 10,278 | .. | Сельское хозяйство |
| Forestry | 238 | 234 | 235 | 244 | 250 | .. | Лесное хозяйство |
| **Industry and construction** | 31,829 | 30,895 | 29,211 | 27,945 | 25,364 | .. | **Промышленность и строительство** |
| Industry | 22,809 | 22,407 | 21,324 | 20,805 | 18,576 | .. | Промышленность |
| Construction | 9,020 | 8,488 | 7,887 | 7,140 | 6,788 | .. | Строительство |
| **Other** | 11,566 | 11,098 | 11,609 | 11,828 | 11,471 | .. | **Другие отрасли** |
| Transport of goods | 3,877 | 3,838 | 3,773 | 3,607 | 3,572 | .. | Грузовой транспорт |
| Road Maintenance | .. | .. | .. | .. | .. | .. | Дорожное хозяйство |
| Communication servicing material production | .. | .. | .. | .. | .. | .. | Связь |
| Wholesale trade | .. | .. | .. | .. | .. | .. | Оптовая торговля |
| Retail trade and catering | 5,869 | 5,626 | 5,679 | 6,374 | 6,484 | .. | Розничная торговля и общепит |
| Material supply | .. | .. | .. | .. | .. | .. | Материально-техническое снабжение |
| Procurement | .. | .. | .. | .. | .. | .. | Заготовки |
| Information and computing services | 183 | 134 | 118 | 93 | 78 | .. | Информационно-техническое обслуживание |
| Other sectors | 1,637 | 1,501 | 2,039 | 1,754 | 1,337 | .. | Другие отрасли сферы материального пр. |
| **Nonmaterial sphere** | 21,965 | 21,886 | 20,914 | 20,732 | 21,122 | .. | **Сфера нематериального производства** |
| Passenger transport | 1,941 | 1,912 | 1,859 | 1,801 | 1,783 | .. | Пассажирский транспорт |
| Communication | .. | .. | .. | .. | .. | .. | Связь |
| Housing | 3,217 | 3,159 | 2,988 | 2,982 | 3,020 | .. | Жилищное хозяйство |
| Public utilities and personal services | .. | .. | .. | .. | .. | .. | Комм. хоз. и бытовое обслуживание |
| Health care, social security, physical culture and sports | 4,238 | 4,305 | 4,227 | 4,243 | 4,394 | .. | Здравоохранение, социальное обеспечение, физкультура и спорт |
| Education | .. | .. | .. | .. | .. | .. | Образование |
| Culture and art | 7,230 | 7,273 | 7,521 | 7,239 | 7,383 | .. | Культура и искусство |
| Science and scientific research | 3,130 | 3,075 | 2,307 | 2,237 | 1,833 | .. | Наука и научное обслуживание |
| Credit | 402 | 440 | 494 | 581 | 745 | .. | Кредитование |
| Insurance | .. | .. | .. | .. | .. | .. | Страхование |
| General administration and defense | 1,806 | 1,722 | 1,519 | 1,649 | 1,659 | .. | Государственное управление и оборона |
| Private nonprofit institutions serving households | .. | .. | .. | .. | .. | .. | Общественные организации, обслуживающие домашние хозяйства |
| **Other, material and nonmaterial spheres** | 33,531 | 32,984 | 32,523 | 32,560 | 32,593 | .. | **Остальные отрасли материального производства и нематериальной сферы** |
| **Total employment** | 75,325 | 73,848 | 72,071 | 70,852 | 68,484 | .. | **Занятые - всего** |

## TABLE 1-3. Registered unemployment (thousands; end of month)
## ТАБЛИЦА 1-3. Численность зарегистрированных безработных (тысяч; на конец месяца)

| Year and month | Total Всего | Males Мужчины | Females Женщины | Receiving benefits Получающие пособие | Год и месяц |
|---|---|---|---|---|---|
| **1994** | | | | | **1994** |
| January | 893.5 | .. | .. | 707.7 | Январь |
| February | 989.3 | .. | .. | 793.6 | Февраль |
| March | 1083.4 | 386.9 | 696.5 | 889.1 | Март |
| April | 1179.9 | .. | .. | 976.0 | Апрель |
| May | 1219.3 | .. | .. | 1009.2 | Май |
| June | 1260.3 | 461.8 | 798.5 | 1044.2 | Июнь |
| July | 1324.1 | .. | .. | 1103.2 | Июль |
| August | 1392.0 | .. | .. | 1162.8 | Август |
| September | 1425.6 | 505.1 | 920.5 | 1198.7 | Сентябрь |
| October | 1475.2 | .. | .. | 1235.6 | Октябрь |
| November | 1549.6 | .. | .. | 1300.7 | Ноябрь |
| December | 1636.8 | 585.5 | 1051.3 | 1395.5 | Декабрь |
| **1995** | | | | | **1995** |
| January | 1710.4 | .. | .. | 1457.1 | Январь |
| February | 1838.9 | .. | .. | 1576.6 | Февраль |
| March | 1921.0 | 724.3 | 1196.7 | 1654.0 | Март |
| April | 1985.6 | .. | .. | 1708.8 | Апрель |
| May | 1993.1 | .. | .. | 1720.7 | Май |
| June | 2004.4 | 756.8 | 1247.6 | 1726.5 | Июнь |
| July | 2048.0 | .. | .. | 1764.2 | Июль |
| August | 2097.7 | .. | .. | 1811.7 | Август |
| September | 2104.2 | 768.6 | 1335.6 | 1820.6 | Сентябрь |
| October | 2142.1 | .. | .. | 1853.7 | Октябрь |
| November | 2227.7 | .. | .. | 1932.4 | Ноябрь |
| December | 2327.0 | 872.3 | 1454.7 | 2025.8 | Декабрь |
| **1996** | | | | | **1996** |
| January | 2417.7 | .. | .. | 2099.0 | Январь |
| February | 2567.5 | .. | .. | 2230.1 | Февраль |
| March | 2675.6 | 1062.0 | 1613.5 | 2337.2 | Март |
| April | 2771.1 | .. | .. | 2426.8 | Апрель |
| May | 2694.0 | .. | .. | 2371.6 | Май |
| June | .. | .. | .. | .. | Июнь |
| July | .. | .. | .. | .. | Июль |
| August | .. | .. | .. | .. | Август |
| September | .. | .. | .. | .. | Сентябрь |
| October | .. | .. | .. | .. | Октябрь |
| November | .. | .. | .. | .. | Ноябрь |
| December | .. | .. | .. | .. | Декабрь |

**TABLE 2-1. Gross domestic product at current prices (billions of national currency)**
**ТАБЛИЦА 2-1. Валовой внутренний продукт в текущих ценах (млрд. национальной валюты)**

| Sector of origin or expenditure category | 1990 | 1991 | 1992 | 1993 | 1994 | 1995 | Отраслевое происхождение или вид расходов |
|---|---|---|---|---|---|---|---|
| **Gross domestic product by sector of origin** | | | | | | | **Валовой внутренний продукт по отраслевому происхождению** |
| **Agriculture and forestry** | 99.6 | 192.6 | 1,409.6 | 14,402.3 | 44,704.5 | 152,189.9 | **Сельское и лесное хозяйство** |
| Agriculture | 99.1 | 191.1 | 1,385.9 | 14,137.0 | 43,776.0 | 149,627.2 | Сельское хозяйство |
| Forestry | 0.5 | 1.5 | 23.7 | 265.3 | 928.5 | 2,562.7 | Лесное хозяйство |
| **Industry and construction** | 285.4 | 655.8 | 7,782.0 | 77,663.4 | 235,951.2 | 593,860.1 | **Промышленность и строительство** |
| Industry | 228.1 | 525.9 | 6,559.2 | 65,203.0 | 177,164.4 | 467,606.5 | Промышленность |
| Construction | 57.3 | 129.9 | 1,222.8 | 12,460.4 | 58,786.8 | 126,253.6 | Строительство |
| **Other** | 217.7 | 529.7 | 10,242.2 | 77,004.5 | 323,183.2 | 891,264.1 | **Другие отрасли** |
| Transport | 52.8 | 89.0 | 1,301.0 | 12,414.8 | 48,802.0 | 185,474.6 | Транспорт |
| Road maintenance | 0.2 | 4.0 | 23.0 | 200.1 | 1,150.1 | 2,773.0 | Дорожное хозяйство |
| Communication | 7.2 | 9.9 | 115.1 | 1,252.7 | 6,451.0 | 16,968.0 | Связь |
| Wholesale trade | .. | .. | .. | .. | .. | .. | Оптовая торговля |
| Retail trade and catering | 29.5 | 150.6 | 5,321.7 | 21,955.1 | 92,866.6 | 235,771.6 | Розничная торговля и общепит |
| Material supply | 4.1 | 13.3 | 266.0 | 2,446.9 | 8,302.2 | 21,094.0 | Материально-техническое снабжение |
| Procurement | 2.7 | 5.2 | 40.6 | 597.8 | 1,578.5 | 4,691.0 | Заготовки |
| Information and computing services | 1.3 | 1.3 | 13.4 | 119.4 | 643.5 | 1,748.6 | Информационно-вычислительное обслуживание |
| Other sectors of material production | 7.6 | 16.3 | 244.1 | 1,023.8 | 3,205.3 | 8,526.1 | Другие отрасли сферы материального пр. |
| Housing | 13.0 | 23.7 | 130.6 | 4,504.7 | 19,181.1 | 72,294.7 | Жилищное хозяйство |
| Public utilities and personal services | 9.7 | 10.8 | 245.6 | 2,262.5 | 9,926.2 | 34,749.0 | Ком. хоз. и бытовое обслуживание |
| Health care, social security, physical culture and sports | 16.6 | 37.9 | 326.1 | 3,968.7 | 14,981.1 | 42,189.5 | Здравоохранение, социальное обеспечение, физкультура и спорт |
| Education | 32.3 | 52.7 | 558.6 | 6,103.5 | 26,850.7 | 49,710.5 | Образование |
| Culture and art | .. | .. | .. | .. | .. | .. | Культура и искусство |
| Science and scientific research | 16.4 | 28.5 | 182.6 | 1,860.6 | 6,148.6 | 13,493.1 | Наука и научное обслуживание |
| Credit | 5.1 | 30.5 | 894.0 | 10,029.9 | 46,295.5 | 110,044.8 | Кредитование |
| Insurance | .. | .. | .. | .. | .. | .. | Страхование |
| General administration and defense | 17.0 | 33.7 | 414.3 | 5,100.2 | 28,893.4 | 70,002.0 | Государственное управление и оборона |
| Private nonprofit institutions serving households | 2.2 | 2.6 | 34.6 | 332.0 | 1,493.9 | 3,436.0 | Общественные организации, обслуживающие домашние хозяйства |
| **Imputed service charge of financial intermediaries** | -3.1 | -30.7 | -763.0 | -9,653.8 | -44,998.3 | -107,996.4 | **Условно-исчисляемая стоимость услуг финансовых посредников** |
| **Total gross value added (GVA)** | 599.6 | 1,347.4 | 18,670.8 | 159,416.4 | 558,840.6 | 1,529,317.7 | **Валовая добавленная стоимость (ВДС) - всего** |
| **Taxes on production and imports (TOPI)** | 115.5 | 141.1 | 1,159.4 | 18,276.8 | 67,373.7 | 178,786.9 | **Налоги на производство и импорт (НПиИ)** |
| Other taxes on production (OTOP) | .. | .. | .. | .. | .. | .. | Другие налоги на производство (ДНП) |
| **Subsidies on production and imports (SOPI)** | 70.9 | 90.0 | 824.7 | 6,183.7 | 15,221.2 | 49,171.8 | **Субсидии на производство и импорт (СПиИ)** |
| Other subsidies on production (OSOP) | .. | .. | .. | .. | .. | .. | Другие субсидии на производство (ДСП) |
| **Total GDP at factor cost (GVA-OTOP+OSOP)** | 599.6 | 1,347.4 | 18,670.8 | 159,416.4 | 558,840.6 | 1,529,317.7 | **Всего ВВП по фактр. стоимости (ВДС-ДНП+ДСП)** |
| **Net Indirect taxes (TOPI - SOPI)** | 44.6 | 51.1 | 334.7 | 12,093.1 | 52,152.5 | 129,615.1 | **Чистые косвенные налоги (НПиИ-СПиИ)** |
| **Total GDP at market prices** | 644.2 | 1,398.5 | 19,005.5 | 171,509.5 | 610,993.1 | 1,658,932.8 | **Всего ВВП в рыночных ценах** |
| **Gross domestic product by expenditure category** | | | | | | | **Валовой внутренний продукт по видам расходов** |
| **Consumption** | 444.4 | 855.4 | 9,183.6 | 103,317.5 | 418,735.7 | 1,071,411.4 | **Потребление** |
| Private consumption | 305.0 | 565.6 | 6,208.2 | 65,219.1 | 247,082.8 | 684,994.0 | Личное потребление |
| Government consumption | 139.4 | 289.8 | 2,975.4 | 38,098.4 | 171,652.9 | 386,417.4 | Общественное потребление |
| **Gross domestic investment** | 194.1 | 507.2 | 6,582.1 | 53,239.4 | 176,809.5 | 465,556.1 | **Валовые внутренние инвестиции** |
| Gross fixed investment | 184.9 | 325.4 | 4,550.7 | 38,651.5 | 153,574.1 | 362,703.1 | Валовое накопление основного капитала |
| Change in stocks | 9.2 | 181.8 | 2,031.4 | 14,587.9 | 23,235.4 | 102,853.0 | Изменения в запасах (МОС) |
| **Resource balance (net exports of GNFS)** | 1.4 | 4.0 | 2,674.3 | 13,200.0 | 27,868.8 | 91,030.9 | **Сальдо ресурсов (чистый экспорт ТНФУ)** |
| Exports of goods and nonfactor services | 117.0 | 185.6 | 11,847.5 | 65,500.0 | 169,534.3 | .. | Экспорт товаров и нефакторных услуг |
| Imports of goods and nonfactor services | 115.6 | 181.6 | 9,173.2 | 52,300.0 | 141,665.5 | .. | Импорт товаров и нефакторных услуг |

**TABLE 2-1A. Distribution of gross domestic product at current prices (percent)**
**ТАБЛИЦА 2-1A. Распределение валового внутреннего продукта в текущих ценах ( % )**

| Sector of origin or expenditure category | 1990 | 1991 | 1992 | 1993 | 1994 | 1995 | Отраслевое происхождение или вид расходов |
|---|---|---|---|---|---|---|---|
| **Gross domestic product by sector of origin** | | | | | | | **ВВП по отраслевому происхождению** |
| **Agriculture and forestry** | 15.5 | 13.8 | 7.4 | 8.4 | 7.3 | 9.2 | **Сельское и лесное хозяйство** |
| Agriculture | 15.4 | 13.7 | 7.3 | 8.2 | 7.2 | 9.0 | Сельское хозяйство |
| Forestry | 0.1 | 0.1 | 0.1 | 0.2 | 0.2 | 0.2 | Лесное хозяйство |
| **Industry and construction** | 44.3 | 46.9 | 40.9 | 45.3 | 38.6 | 35.8 | **Промышленность и строительство** |
| Industry | 35.4 | 37.6 | 34.5 | 38.0 | 29.0 | 28.2 | Промышленность |
| Construction | 8.9 | 9.3 | 6.4 | 7.3 | 9.6 | 7.6 | Строительство |
| **Other** | 33.8 | 37.9 | 53.9 | 44.9 | 52.9 | 53.7 | **Другие отрасли** |
| Transport | 8.2 | 6.4 | 6.8 | 7.2 | 8.0 | 11.2 | Транспорт |
| Road maintenance | 0.0 | 0.3 | 0.1 | 0.1 | 0.2 | 0.2 | Дорожное хозяйство |
| Communication | 1.1 | 0.7 | 0.6 | 0.7 | 1.1 | 1.0 | Связь |
| Wholesale trade | .. | .. | .. | .. | .. | .. | Оптовая торговля |
| Retail trade and catering | 4.6 | 10.8 | 28.0 | 12.8 | 15.2 | 14.2 | Розничная торговля и общепит |
| Material supply | 0.6 | 1.0 | 1.4 | 1.4 | 1.4 | 1.3 | Материально-техническое снабжение |
| Procurement | 0.4 | 0.4 | 0.2 | 0.3 | 0.3 | 0.3 | Заготовки |
| Information and computing services | 0.2 | 0.1 | 0.1 | 0.1 | 0.1 | 0.1 | Информационно-вычислительное обслуживание |
| Other sectors of material production | 1.2 | 1.2 | 1.3 | 0.6 | 0.5 | 0.5 | Другие отрасли сферы матерл. произ. |
| Housing | 2.0 | 1.7 | 0.7 | 2.6 | 3.1 | 4.4 | Жилищное хозяйство |
| Public utilities and personal services | 1.5 | 0.8 | 1.3 | 1.3 | 1.6 | 2.1 | Ком. хоз. и бытовое обслуживание |
| Health care, social security, physical culture and sports | 2.6 | 2.7 | 1.7 | 2.3 | 2.5 | 2.5 | Здравоохранение, социальное обеспечение, физкультура и спорт |
| Education | 5.0 | 3.8 | 2.9 | 3.6 | 4.4 | 3.0 | Образование |
| Culture and art | .. | .. | .. | .. | .. | .. | Культура и искусство |
| Science and scientific research | 2.5 | 2.0 | 1.0 | 1.1 | 1.0 | 0.8 | Наука и научное обслуживание |
| Credit | 0.8 | 2.2 | 4.7 | 5.8 | 7.6 | 6.6 | Кредитование |
| Insurance | .. | .. | .. | .. | .. | .. | Страхование |
| General administration and defense | 2.6 | 2.4 | 2.2 | 3.0 | 4.7 | 4.2 | Государственное управление и оборона |
| Private nonprofit institutions serving households | 0.3 | 0.2 | 0.2 | 0.2 | 0.2 | 0.2 | Общественные организации, обслуживающие домашние хозяйства |
| **Imputed service charge of financial intermediaries** | -0.5 | -2.2 | -4.0 | -5.6 | -7.4 | -6.5 | **Условно-исчисляемая стоимость услуг финансовых посредников** |
| **Total gross value added** | 93.1 | 96.3 | 98.2 | 92.9 | 91.5 | 92.2 | **Валовая добавленная стоимость - всего** |
| **Total GDP at factor cost** | 93.1 | 96.3 | 98.2 | 92.9 | 91.5 | 92.2 | **ВВП по фактор. стоимости - всего** |
| **Net indirect taxes** | 6.9 | 3.7 | 1.8 | 7.1 | 8.5 | 7.8 | **Чистые косвенные налоги (НПиИ-СПиИ)** |
| **Total GDP at market prices** | 100.0 | 100.0 | 100.0 | 100.0 | 100.0 | 100.0 | **ВВП в рын. ценах - всего** |
| **Gross domestic product by expenditure category** | | | | | | | **ВВП по видам расходов** |
| **Consumption** | 69.0 | 61.2 | 48.3 | 60.2 | 68.5 | 64.6 | **Потребление** |
| Private consumption | 47.3 | 40.4 | 32.7 | 38.0 | 40.4 | 41.3 | Личное потребление |
| Government consumption | 21.6 | 20.7 | 15.7 | 22.2 | 28.1 | 23.3 | Общественное потребление |
| **Gross domestic investment** | 30.1 | 36.3 | 34.6 | 31.0 | 28.9 | 28.1 | **Вал. внутр. инвестиции** |
| Gross fixed investment | 28.7 | 23.3 | 23.9 | 22.5 | 25.1 | 21.9 | Вал. накопление осн. капитала |
| Change in stocks | 1.4 | 13.0 | 10.7 | 8.5 | 3.8 | 6.2 | Изменения в запасах (МОС) |
| **Resource balance (net exports of GNFS)** | 0.2 | 0.3 | 14.1 | 7.7 | 4.6 | 5.5 | **Сальдо ресурсов (чистый экспорт ТНФУ)** |
| Exports of goods and nonfactor services | .. | 13.3 | 62.3 | 38.2 | 27.7 | .. | Экспорт товаров и нефакторных услуг |
| Imports of goods and nonfactor services | .. | 13.0 | 48.3 | 30.5 | 23.2 | .. | Импорт товаров и нефакторных услуг |

**TABLE 2-2. Gross domestic product at constant prices (billions of national currency)**
**ТАБЛИЦА 2-2. Валовой внутренний продукт в постоянных ценах (млрд. национальной валюты)**

| Sector of origin or expenditure category | 1990 | 1991 | 1992 | 1993 | 1994 | 1995 | Отраслевое происхождение или вид расходов |
|---|---|---|---|---|---|---|---|
| **Gross domestic product by sector of origin** | | | | | | | **Валовой внутренний продукт по отраслевому происхождению** |
| **Agriculture and forestry** | .. | 95.9 | 175.3 | 1,353.2 | 13,106.1 | 42,079.8 | **Сельское и лесное хозяйство** |
| Agriculture | .. | 95.4 | 173.9 | 1,330.4 | 12,864.7 | 41,225.6 | Сельское хозяйство |
| Forestry | .. | 0.5 | 1.4 | 22.8 | 241.4 | 854.2 | Лесное хозяйство |
| **Industry and construction** | .. | 265.5 | 518.2 | 6,726.6 | 62,113.3 | 223,384.1 | **Промышленность и строительство** |
| Industry | .. | 215.1 | 431.2 | 5,601.6 | 51,771.2 | 169,888.1 | Промышленность |
| Construction | .. | 50.4 | 87.0 | 1,125.0 | 10,342.1 | 53,496.0 | Строительство |
| **Other** | .. | 213.4 | 492.6 | 9,871.4 | 74,626.0 | 311,303.1 | **Другие отрасли** |
| Transport | .. | 49.8 | 74.7 | 1,026.5 | 10,242.2 | 46,832.0 | Транспорт |
| Road maintenance | .. | 0.2 | 3.5 | 17.5 | 164.3 | 1,039.7 | Дорожное хозяйство |
| Communication | .. | 6.8 | 8.2 | 101.2 | 1,021.0 | 6,451.0 | Связь |
| Wholesale trade | .. | .. | .. | .. | .. | .. | Оптовая торговля |
| Retail trade and catering | .. | 28.6 | 145.8 | 5,183.3 | 22,613.8 | 86,365.9 | Розничная торговля и общепит |
| Material supply | .. | 3.9 | 11.1 | 228.8 | 2,079.9 | 7,887.1 | Материально-техническое снабжение |
| Procurement | .. | 2.6 | 4.1 | 36.5 | 400.5 | 1,231.2 | Заготовки |
| Information and computing services | .. | 1.2 | 1.2 | 13.0 | 117.0 | 643.5 | Информационно-вычислительное обслуживание |
| Other sectors of material production | .. | 7.2 | 13.9 | 214.8 | 809.8 | 3,045.0 | Другие отрасли сферы материального пр. |
| Housing | .. | 13.1 | 24.2 | 133.4 | 4,556.4 | 19,578.2 | Жилищное хозяйство |
| Public utilities and personal services | .. | 9.6 | 9.9 | 229.7 | 2,192.2 | 9,990.2 | Ком. хоз. и бытовое обслуживание |
| Health care, social security, and sports | .. | 16.8 | 36.7 | 326.2 | 3,929.0 | 14,867.3 | Здравоохранение, социальное обеспечение, физкультура и спорт |
| Education | .. | 32.4 | 51.9 | 536.3 | 6,073.0 | 26,628.7 | Образование |
| Culture and art | .. | .. | .. | .. | .. | .. | Культура и искусство |
| Science and research | .. | 16.1 | 21.9 | 172.3 | 1,704.3 | 5,380.5 | Наука и научное обслуживание |
| Credit | .. | 5.6 | 34.0 | 1,053.1 | 10,872.4 | 44,488.2 | Кредитование |
| Insurance | .. | .. | .. | .. | .. | .. | Страхование |
| General administration and defense | .. | 17.4 | 29.1 | 381.0 | 4,719.6 | 28,815.6 | Государственное управление и оборона |
| Private nonprofit institutions serving households | .. | 2.3 | 2.6 | 34.6 | 332.0 | 1,493.9 | Общественные организации, обслуживающие домашние хозяйства |
| **Imputed service charge of financial intermediaries** | .. | -5.5 | -34.5 | -898.8 | -10,464.7 | -43,198.4 | **Условно-исчисляемая стоимость услуг финансовых посредников** |
| **Total gross value added (GVA)** | .. | 569.3 | 1,151.6 | 17,052.4 | 139,380.7 | 533,568.6 | **Валовая добавленная стоимость (ВДС) -** |
| **Total GDP at factor cost (GVA-TOPI+SOPI)** | .. | 569.3 | 1,151.6 | 17,052.4 | 139,380.7 | 533,568.6 | **Всего ВВП по фактр. стоимости (ВДС-ДНП+ДСП)** |
| **Net indirect taxes (OTOP-OSOP)** | .. | 42.4 | 43.7 | 305.6 | 10,569.4 | 50,986.6 | **Чистые косвенные налоги (НПиИ-СПиИ)** |
| **Total GDP at market prices** | .. | 611.7 | 1,195.3 | 17,358.0 | 149,950.1 | 584,555.2 | **Всего ВВП в рыночных ценах** |
| **Gross domestic product by expenditure category** | | | | | | | **Валовой внутренний продукт по видам расходов** |
| **Consumption** | .. | 417.1 | 809.9 | 9,093.0 | 101,097.4 | 398,296.9 | **Потребление** |
| Private consumption | .. | 290.9 | 548.7 | 6,285.7 | 63,393.0 | 229,787.0 | Личное потребление |
| Government consumption | .. | 126.2 | 261.1 | 2,807.3 | 37,704.4 | 168,509.9 | Общественное потребление |
| **Gross domestic investment** | .. | 189.7 | 307.7 | 4,648.3 | 37,485.8 | 160,212.9 | **Валовые внутренние инвестиции** |
| Gross fixed investment | .. | 156.2 | 178.9 | 3,377.0 | 30,921.2 | 130,313.5 | Валовое накопление основного капитала |
| Change in stocks | .. | 33.5 | 128.7 | 1,271.3 | 6,564.6 | 29,899.4 | Изменения в запасах (МОС) |
| **Resource balance (net exports of GNFS)** | .. | 3.8 | 32.3 | 3,294.4 | 10,186.5 | 37,360.0 | **Сальдо ресурсов (чистый экспорт ТНФУ)** |
| Exports of goods and nonfactor services | .. | 29.8 | 148.5 | 11,601.5 | 65,563.6 | .. | Экспорт товаров и нефакторных услуг |
| Imports of goods and nonfactor services | .. | 26.0 | 116.2 | 8,307.1 | 55,377.1 | .. | Импорт товаров и нефакторных услуг |

**TABLE 2-2A. Growth rates of gross domestic product at constant prices (percent)**

**ТАБЛИЦА 2-2A. Валовой внутренний продукт - темпы прироста в постоянных ценах ( % )**

| Sector of origin or expenditure category | 1990 | 1991 | 1992 | 1993 | 1994 | 1995 | Отраслевое происхождение или вид расходов |
|---|---|---|---|---|---|---|---|
| **Growth rate by sector of origin** | | | | | | | **Валовый внутренний продукт по отраслевому происхождению** |
| **Agriculture and forestry** | .. | -3.7 | -9.0 | -4.0 | -9.0 | -5.9 | **Сельское и лесное хозяйство** |
| Agriculture | .. | -3.7 | -9.0 | -4.0 | -9.0 | -5.8 | Сельское хозяйство |
| Forestry | .. | 0.0 | -6.7 | -3.8 | -9.0 | -8.0 | Лесное хозяйство |
| **Industry and construction** | .. | -7.0 | -21.0 | -13.6 | -20.0 | -5.3 | **Промышленность и строительство** |
| Industry | .. | -5.7 | -18.0 | -14.6 | -20.6 | -4.1 | Промышленность |
| Construction | .. | -12.0 | -33.0 | -8.0 | -17.0 | -9.0 | Строительство |
| **Other** | .. | -2.0 | -7.0 | -3.6 | -3.1 | -3.7 | **Другие отрасли** |
| Transport | .. | -5.7 | -16.1 | -21.1 | -17.5 | -4.0 | Транспорт |
| Road maintenance | .. | 0.0 | -12.5 | -23.9 | -17.9 | -9.6 | Дорожное хозяйство |
| Communication | .. | -5.6 | -17.2 | -12.1 | -18.5 | 0.0 | Связь |
| Wholesale trade | .. | .. | .. | .. | .. | .. | Оптовая торговля |
| Retail trade and catering | .. | -3.1 | -3.2 | -2.6 | 3.0 | -7.0 | Розничная торговля и общепит |
| Material supply | .. | -4.9 | -16.5 | -14.0 | -15.0 | -5.0 | Материально-техническое снабжение |
| Procurement | .. | -3.7 | -21.2 | -10.1 | -33.0 | -22.0 | Заготовки |
| Information and computing services | .. | -7.7 | -7.7 | -3.0 | -2.0 | 0.0 | Информационно-вычислительное обслуживание |
| Other sectors of material production | .. | -5.3 | -14.7 | -12.0 | -20.9 | -5.0 | Другие отрасли сферы материального пр. |
| Housing | .. | 0.8 | 2.1 | 2.1 | 1.1 | 2.1 | Жилищное хозяйство |
| Public utilities and personal services | .. | -1.0 | -8.3 | -6.5 | -3.1 | 0.6 | Ком. хоз. и бытовое обслуживание |
| Health care, social security, and sports | .. | 1.2 | -3.2 | 0.0 | -1.0 | -0.8 | Здравоохранение, социальное обеспечение, физкультура и спорт |
| Education | .. | 0.3 | -1.5 | -4.0 | -0.5 | -0.8 | Образование |
| Culture and art | .. | .. | .. | .. | .. | .. | Культура и искусство |
| Science and research | .. | -1.8 | -23.2 | -5.6 | -8.4 | -12.5 | Наука и научное обслуживание |
| Credit | .. | 9.8 | 11.5 | 17.8 | 8.4 | -3.9 | Кредитование |
| Insurance | .. | .. | .. | .. | .. | .. | Страхование |
| General administration and defense | .. | 2.4 | -13.6 | -8.0 | -7.5 | -0.3 | Государственное управление и оборона |
| Private nonprofit institutions serving households | .. | 4.5 | 0.0 | 0.0 | 0.0 | 0.0 | Общественные организации, обслуживающие домашние хозяйства |
| **Imputed service charge of financial intermediaries** | .. | 77.4 | 12.4 | 17.8 | 8.4 | -4.0 | **Условно-исчисляемая стоимость услуг финансовых посредников** |
| **Total gross value added** | .. | -5.1 | -14.5 | -8.7 | -12.6 | -4.5 | **Валовая добавленная стоимость (ВДС) - всего** |
| **Total GDP at factor cost** | .. | -5.1 | -14.5 | -8.7 | -12.6 | -4.5 | **Всего ВВП по фактр. стоимости (ВДС-ДНП+ДСП)** |
| **Net indirect taxes** | .. | -4.9 | -14.5 | -8.7 | -12.6 | -2.2 | **Чистые косвенные налоги (НПиИ-СПиИ)** |
| **Total GDP at market prices** | .. | -5.0 | -14.5 | -8.7 | -12.6 | -4.3 | **Всего ВВП в рыночных ценах** |
| **Growth rate by expenditure category** | | | | | | | **Валовой внутренний продукт по видам расходов** |
| **Consumption** | .. | -6.1 | -5.3 | -1.0 | -2.1 | -4.9 | **Потребление** |
| Private consumption | .. | -4.6 | -3.0 | 1.2 | -2.8 | -7.0 | Личное потребление |
| Government consumption | .. | -9.5 | -9.9 | -5.7 | -1.0 | -1.8 | Общественное потребление |
| **Gross domestic investment** | .. | -2.3 | -39.3 | -29.4 | -29.6 | -9.4 | **Валовые внутренние инвестиции** |
| Gross fixed investment | .. | -15.5 | -45.0 | -25.8 | -20.0 | -15.1 | Валовое накопление основного капитала |
| **Exports of goods and nonfactor services** | .. | .. | -20.0 | -2.1 | 0.1 | .. | **Экспорт товаров и нефакторных услуг** |
| **Imports of goods and nonfactor services** | .. | .. | -36.0 | -9.4 | 5.9 | .. | **Импорт товаров и нефакторных услуг** |

## TABLE 2-2B. Implicit price deflators for gross domestic product (percentage change)
## ТАБЛИЦА 2-2B. Дефляторы валового внутреннего продукта (темпы прироста в %)

| Sector of origin or expenditure category | 1990 | 1991 | 1992 | 1993 | 1994 | 1995 | Отраслевое происхождение или вид расходов |
|---|---|---|---|---|---|---|---|
| **Price deflators by sector of origin** | | | | | | | **Дефляторы по отраслевому происхождению или виду расходов** |
| **Agriculture and forestry** | .. | 100.8 | 704.1 | 964.3 | 241.1 | 261.7 | **Сельское и лесное хозяйство** |
| Agriculture | .. | 100.3 | 697.0 | 962.6 | 240.3 | 262.9 | Сельское хозяйство |
| Forestry | .. | 200.0 | 1,592.9 | 1,063.6 | 284.6 | 200.0 | Лесное хозяйство |
| **Industry and construction** | .. | 147.0 | 1,401.7 | 1,054.6 | 279.9 | 165.8 | **Промышленность и строительство** |
| Industry | .. | 144.5 | 1,421.2 | 1,064.0 | 242.2 | 175.2 | Промышленность |
| Construction | .. | 157.7 | 1,305.5 | 1,007.6 | 468.4 | 136.0 | Строительство |
| **Other** | .. | 148.2 | 1,979.2 | 680.1 | 333.1 | 186.3 | **Другие отрасли** |
| Transport | .. | 78.7 | 1,641.6 | 1,109.4 | 376.5 | 296.0 | Транспорт |
| Road maintenance | .. | .. | .. | .. | .. | .. | Дорожное хозяйство |
| Communication | .. | 45.6 | 1,303.7 | 1,137.8 | 531.8 | 163.0 | Связь |
| Wholesale trade | .. | .. | .. | .. | .. | .. | Оптовая торговля |
| Retail trade and catering | .. | 426.6 | 3,550.0 | 323.6 | 310.7 | 173.0 | Розничная торговля и общепит. |
| Material supply | .. | 241.0 | 2,296.4 | 969.4 | 299.2 | 167.4 | Материально-техническое снабжение |
| Procurement | .. | 100.0 | 890.2 | 1,537.8 | 294.1 | 281.0 | Заготовки |
| Information and computing services | .. | 8.3 | 1,016.7 | 818.5 | 450.0 | 171.7 | Информационно-вычислительное обслуживание |
| Other sectors of material production | .. | 126.4 | 1,656.1 | 376.6 | 295.8 | 180.0 | Другие отрасли сферы матерл. произ. |
| Housing | .. | 80.9 | 439.7 | 3,276.8 | 321.0 | 269.3 | Жилищное хозяйство |
| Public utilities and personal services | .. | 12.5 | 2,380.8 | 885.0 | 352.8 | 247.8 | Ком. хоз. и бытовое обслуживание |
| Health care, social security, and sports | .. | 125.6 | 788.6 | 1,116.6 | 281.3 | 183.8 | Здравоохранение, социальное обеспечение, физкультура и спорт |
| Education | .. | 62.7 | 976.3 | 1,038.1 | 342.1 | 86.7 | Образование |
| Culture and art | .. | .. | .. | .. | .. | .. | Культура и искусство |
| Science and research | .. | 77.0 | 733.8 | 979.9 | 260.8 | 150.8 | Наука и научное обслуживание |
| Credit | .. | 444.6 | 2,529.4 | 852.4 | 325.8 | 147.4 | Кредитование |
| Insurance | .. | .. | .. | .. | .. | .. | Страхование |
| General administration and defense | .. | 93.7 | 1,323.7 | 1,238.6 | 512.2 | 142.9 | Государственное управление и оборона |
| Private nonprofit institutions serving households | .. | 13.0 | 1,230.8 | 859.5 | 350.0 | 130.0 | Общественные организации, обслуживающие домашние хозяйства |
| **Imputed service charge of financial intermediaries** | .. | .. | 2,111.6 | 974.1 | 330.0 | 150.0 | **Условно-исчисляемая стоимость услуг финансовых посредников** |
| **Total gross value added** | .. | 136.7 | 1,521.3 | 834.9 | 300.9 | 186.6 | **Валовая добавленная стоимость (ВДС) - всего** |
| **Total GDP at factor cost** | .. | 136.7 | 1,521.3 | 834.9 | 300.9 | 186.6 | **ВВП по факторной стоимости (ВДС-ДНП+ДСП)** |
| **Net indirect taxes** | .. | 20.5 | 665.9 | 3,857.2 | 393.4 | 154.2 | **Чистые косвенные налоги (НПИ-СПИ)** |
| **Total GDP at market prices** | .. | 128.6 | 1,490.0 | 888.1 | 307.5 | 183.8 | **ВВП в рыночных ценах** |
| **Price deflators by expenditure category** | | | | | | | **Дефляторы по виду расходов** |
| **Consumption** | .. | 105.1 | 1,034.0 | 1,036.2 | 314.2 | 169.0 | **Конечное потребление** |
| Private consumption | .. | 94.4 | 1,031.4 | 937.6 | 289.8 | 198.1 | Личное потребление |
| Government consumption | .. | 129.6 | 1,039.4 | 1,257.1 | 355.3 | 129.3 | Общественное потребление |
| **Gross domestic investment** | .. | 167.4 | 2,039.5 | 1,045.4 | 371.7 | 190.6 | **Валовые внутренние инвестиции** |
| Gross fixed investment | .. | 108.3 | 2,443.3 | 1,044.6 | 396.7 | 178.3 | Валовое накопление основного капитала |
| **Exports of goods and nonfactor services** | .. | 522.8 | 7,879.3 | 464.6 | 158.6 | .. | **Экспорт товаров и нефакторных услуг** |
| **Imports of goods and nonfactor services** | .. | 598.5 | 7,794.7 | 529.6 | 155.8 | .. | **Импорт товаров и нефакторных услуг** |

**TABLE 3-1. Balance of payments at current prices (millions of U.S. dollars)**
**ТАБЛИЦА 3-1. Платежный баланс в текущих ценах (в миллионах долларов США)**

| Item | 1990 | 1991 | 1992 | 1993 | 1994 | 1995 | Статьи |
|---|---|---|---|---|---|---|---|
| Exports of goods and services (including workers' remittances) | .. | .. | .. | .. | 77,700 | 98,342 | Экспорт товаров и услуг (включая денежные переводы рабочих) |
| Exports of goods and nonfactor services | .. | .. | .. | .. | 77,000 | 94,060 | Экспорт товаров и нефакт. услуг |
| Merchandise (FOB) | .. | .. | .. | .. | 69,500 | 82,638 | Товары (ФОБ) |
| Nonfactor services | .. | .. | .. | .. | 7,500 | 12,421 | Нефакторные услуги |
| Shipment | .. | .. | .. | .. | .. | 6,131 | Перевозки |
| Travel | .. | .. | .. | .. | .. | 4,312 | Поездки |
| Other | .. | .. | .. | .. | .. | 1,978 | Другие |
| Imports of goods and nonfactor services | .. | .. | .. | .. | 69,400 | 79,439 | Импорт товаров и нефакт. услуг |
| Merchandise (FOB) | .. | .. | .. | .. | 55,200 | 58,884 | Товары (ФОБ) |
| Nonfactor services | .. | .. | .. | .. | 14,200 | 20,555 | Нефакторные услуги |
| Shipment | .. | .. | .. | .. | .. | 4,114 | Перевозки |
| Travel | .. | .. | .. | .. | .. | 11,599 | Поездки |
| Other | .. | .. | .. | .. | .. | 4,842 | Другие |
| Resource balance | .. | .. | .. | .. | 7,600 | 14,621 | Сальдо ресурсов |
| Net factor income | .. | .. | .. | .. | -4,300 | -2,810 | Чистый факторный доход |
| Factor receipts | .. | .. | .. | .. | 700 | 4,282 | Факторные поступления |
| Factor payments | .. | .. | .. | .. | 5,000 | 7,093 | Факторные платежи |
| Total interest due | .. | .. | .. | .. | 5,000 | 6,624 | Общая сумма процента к оплате |
| Other factor payments and discrepancy | .. | .. | .. | .. | 0 | 469 | Другие факторные платежи и стат. погр. |
| Net current transfers | .. | .. | .. | .. | -100 | 451 | Чистые текущие трансферты |
| Current receipts | .. | .. | .. | .. | 400 | 1,047 | Текущие поступления |
| Workers remittances | .. | .. | .. | .. | .. | .. | Денежные переводы рабочих |
| Other current transfers | .. | .. | .. | .. | .. | .. | Другие текущие трансферты |
| Current payments | .. | .. | .. | .. | 500 | 596 | Текущие платежи |
| Current account balance before official grants | .. | .. | .. | .. | 3,200 | 12,261 | Сальдо текущего счета до офиц. безвозмезд. трансфертов |
| Official capital grants | .. | .. | .. | .. | 800 | 502 | Официальные кап. безвозмезные трансферты |
| Current account balance after official grants | .. | .. | .. | .. | 4,000 | 12,763 | Сальдо текущего счета после офиц. безвозмезд. трансфертов |
| Long Term Capital Inflows | .. | .. | .. | .. | -14,400 | -10,691 | Долгосрочные притоки капитала |
| Direct investment | .. | .. | .. | .. | 600 | 1,956 | Прямые инвестиции |
| Net long term borrowing | .. | .. | .. | .. | -13,200 | -12,559 | Чистые долгосрочные займы |
| Disbursements | .. | .. | .. | .. | 2,100 | 15,063 | Поступления |
| Repayments due | .. | .. | .. | .. | 15,300 | 27,622 | Сумма, подлежащая погашению |
| Other long-term inflows (net) | .. | .. | .. | .. | -1,800 | -88 | Другие долгосрочные притоки (чистые) |

(continued on next page)

## TABLE 3-1. Balance of payments at current prices (millions of U.S. dollars)
## ТАБЛИЦА 3-1. Платежный баланс в текущих ценах (в миллионах долларов США)



| Item | 1990 | 1991 | 1992 | 1993 | 1994 | 1995 | Статьи |
|---|---|---|---|---|---|---|---|
| Adjustment to Scheduled Debt Service | .. | .. | .. | .. | 16,600 | 13,092 | Регулирование долга |
| Debt service not paid | .. | .. | .. | .. | .. | 13,092 | Невыплаченный долг |
| Interest not paid | .. | .. | .. | .. | .. | 3,488 | Невыплаченный процент |
| Principal not paid | .. | .. | .. | .. | .. | 9,604 | Невыплаченная сумма основного долга |
| Arrears reductions/prepayments(-) | .. | .. | .. | .. | .. | .. | Погашение просроченных платежей/выплаты авансом (-) |
| | | .. | .. | .. | | | |
| Total Other items (Net) | .. | .. | .. | .. | -10,200 | -5,854 | Общие другие статьи (чистые) |
| Net short-term capital | .. | .. | .. | .. | -14,600 | -1,434 | Чистый краткосрочный капитал |
| Capital flows not elsewhere included | .. | .. | .. | .. | -200 | -1,133 | Потоки капитала, не указанные выше |
| Errors and omissions | .. | .. | .. | .. | 4,600 | -3,287 | Ошибки и пропуски |
| | | .. | .. | .. | | | |
| Changes in net reserves | .. | .. | .. | .. | 3,900 | -9,310 | Изменения в чистых резервах |
| Net credit from IMF | .. | .. | .. | .. | .. | .. | Чистый кредит МВФ |
| Reserve changes not elsewhere included | .. | .. | .. | .. | .. | .. | Изменения резервов, не указанных выше |
| Escrow account | .. | .. | .. | .. | .. | .. | Счет депонирования |
| | | .. | .. | .. | | | |
| Gross reserves (excluding gold) | .. | .. | .. | .. | .. | .. | Общие резервы (исключая золото) |
| Gross reserves (including gold) | .. | .. | .. | .. | .. | .. | Общие резервы (включая золото) |
| | | .. | .. | .. | | | |
| | | .. | .. | .. | | | |
| Nominal official exchange rate (annual average) (rf) | .. | .. | .. | .. | .. | .. | Номинальный официальный или рыночный курс (среднегодовой) |
| Nominal official exchange rate (end-of-year) (ae) | .. | .. | .. | .. | .. | .. | Номинальный официальный или рыночный курс (на конец года) |
| Manufacture unit value (percent change) | .. | .. | .. | .. | .. | .. | Средний индекс цен на продукцию обр. пром.,% |
| Index of real effective exchange rate (IMF) | .. | .. | .. | .. | .. | .. | Индекс реального эффективного валютного курса (МВФ) |
| | | .. | .. | .. | | | |
| Total factor payments | .. | .. | .. | .. | .. | .. | Общая сумма факторных платежей |
| Government interest | .. | .. | .. | .. | .. | .. | Процент, выплачиваемый органами гос. управления |
| Private sector interest | .. | .. | .. | .. | .. | .. | Процент выплачиваемый частным сектором |
| Profits on direct foreign investment | .. | .. | .. | .. | .. | .. | Прибыль от прямых иностранных инвестиций |
| | | .. | .. | .. | | | |
| Official capital grants | .. | .. | .. | .. | .. | .. | Официальные капитальные безвозмездные трансферты |
| For budgetary financing | .. | .. | .. | .. | .. | .. | На бюджетное финансирование |
| To extrabudgetary entities | .. | .. | .. | .. | .. | .. | На внебюджетное финансирование |
| | | .. | .. | .. | | | |
| Government net long term borrowing | .. | .. | .. | .. | .. | .. | Чистые долгосрочные государственные займы |
| Disbursements | .. | .. | .. | .. | .. | .. | Поступления |
| Repayments | .. | .. | .. | .. | .. | .. | Погашения |
| | | .. | .. | .. | | | |
| Private net long term borrowing | .. | .. | .. | .. | .. | .. | Чистые долгосрочные частные займы |
| Disbursements | .. | .. | .. | .. | .. | .. | Поступления |
| Repayments | .. | .. | .. | .. | .. | .. | Погашения |

**TABLE 3-2A. Imports by commodity group (millions of U.S. dollars)**
**ТАБЛИЦА 3-2A . Импорт по товарным группам (млн. долларов США)**

| Commodity group | 1990 | 1991 | 1992 | 1993 | 1994 | 1995 | Товарные группы |
|---|---|---|---|---|---|---|---|
| TOTAL | .. | .. | 36,984.0 | 26,807.0 | 38,661.4 | 46,680.0 | ВСЕГО |
| I - Live animals; animal products | .. | .. | 653.1 | 330.6 | 1,843.1 | 3,059.4 | I - Живые животные и продукты животноводства |
| II - Vegetable products | .. | .. | 5,159.9 | 2,107.4 | 2,511.2 | 2,534.0 | II - Продукты растительного происхождения |
| III - Animal or vegetable fats and oils and their cleavage products; prepared edible fats; animal or vegetable waxes | .. | .. | 333.6 | 119.1 | 257.1 | 697.9 | III - Жиры и масла растительного и животного происхождения, воски |
| IV - Prepared foodstuffs; beverages, spirits and vinegar; tobacco and manufactured tobacco substitutes | .. | .. | 3,385.2 | 3,374.0 | 6,090.0 | 6,951.0 | IV -Продукция пищевой промышленности, алкогольные и безалкогольные напитки, табак и его заменители |
| V - Mineral products | .. | .. | 1,000.1 | 1,072.0 | 2,519.0 | 2,837.0 | V - Минеральные продукты |
| VI - Products of the chemical or allied industries | .. | .. | 2,652.3 | 1,229.7 | 2,986.7 | 3,785.0 | VI - Продукция химической промышленности |
| VII - Plastics and articles thereof; rubber and articles thereof | .. | .. | 766.5 | 434.7 | 853.0 | 1,287.5 | VII - Пластмассы и изделия из них |
| VIII - Raw hides and skins, leather, furskins and articles thereof; saddlery and harness; travel goods, handbags and similar containers; articles of animal gut | .. | .. | 688.3 | 702.0 | 197.8 | 166.6 | VIII - Кожевенное сырьё, кожи, пушнина, меховое сырьё и изделия из них |
| IX - Wood and articles of wood; wood charcoal; cork and articles of cork; manufactures of straw, of esparto or of other plaiting materials; basketware and wickerwork | .. | .. | 46.0 | 13.8 | 91.4 | 201.0 | IX - Древесина и изделия из древесины, древесный уголь |
| X - Pulp of wood or of other fibrous cellulosic material; waste and scrap of paper or paperboard; paper and paperboard and articles thereof | .. | .. | 397.8 | 128.4 | 475.0 | 902.5 | X - Бумажная масса, бумажные и картонные отходы, макулатура, бумага, картон и изделия из них |
| XI - Textiles and textile articles | .. | .. | 3,061.0 | 2,650.0 | 2,317.9 | 2,095.0 | XI - Текстиль и текстильные изделия |
| XII - Footwear, headgear, umbrellas, sun umbrellas, walking sticks, seat sticks, whips, riding crops and parts thereof; prepared feathers and articles made therewith; artificial flowers; articles of human hair | .. | .. | 1,470.0 | 1,088.0 | 747.5 | 505.3 | XII - Обувь, головные уборы, зонты, трости и пр. |

**TABLE 3-2A. Imports by commodity group (millions of U.S. dollars)**
**ТАБЛИЦА 3-2А . Импорт по товарным группам (млн. долларов США)**

| Commodity group | 1990 | 1991 | 1992 | 1993 | 1994 | 1995 | Товарные группы |
|---|---|---|---|---|---|---|---|
| XIII - Articles of stone, plaster, cement, asbestos, mica and similar materials; ceramic products; glass and glassware | .. | .. | 227.3 | 289.0 | 434.2 | 577.3 | XIII - Изделия из камня, гипса, цемента |
| XIV - Natural or cultured pearls, precious or semi-precious stones, precious metals, metals clad with precious metal and articles thereof; imitation jewellery; coin | .. | .. | 20.0 | 111.2 | 86.6 | 428.3 | XIV - Жемчуг, драгоценные и полудрагоценные камни, драгоценные металлы, бижутерия, монеты |
| XV - Base metals and articles of base metal | .. | .. | 1,172.8 | 828.1 | 2,524.0 | 3,500.0 | XV - Неблагородные металлы и изделия из них |
| XVI - Machinery and mechanical appliances; electrical equipment; parts thereof; sound recorders and reproducers, television image and sound recorders and reproducers, and parts and accessories of such articles | .. | .. | 10,011.1 | 6,198.1 | 9,523.3 | 11,059.0 | XVI - Машины, оборудование, механизмы, их части и принадлежности; звуковая и теле-аппаратура, их части и принадлежности |
| XVII - Vehicles, aircraft, vessels and associated transport equipment | .. | .. | 3,039.0 | 2,403.9 | 2,535.1 | 2,729.0 | XVII - Средства наземного, воздушного и водного транспорта |
| XVIII - Optical, photographic, cinematographic, measuring, checking, precision, medical or surgical instruments and apparatus; clocks and watches; musical instruments; parts and accessories thereof | .. | .. | 783.6 | 536.8 | 1,586.5 | 2,077.0 | XVIII - Приборы, аппараты оптические, медицинские, измерительные и пр.; музыкальные инструменты; часы; их части и принадлежности |
| XIX - Arms and ammunition; parts and accessories thereof | .. | .. | 20.4 | 3.5 | 13.9 | 6.8 | XIX - Оружие и боеприпасы, их части и принадлежности |
| XX - Miscellaneous manufactured articles | .. | .. | 458.0 | 364.0 | 1,067.8 | 1,278.3 | XX - Разные промышленные товары |
| XXI - Works of art, collectors' pieces, and antiques | .. | .. | 0.1 | 0.2 | 0.3 | 2.1 | XXI - Произведения искусства, предметы антиквариата |
| XXII - Services | .. | .. | 1,637.8 | 2,822.3 | .. | .. | XXII - Услуги |

**TABLE 3-3A. Exports by commodity group (millions of U.S. dollars)**
**ТАБЛИЦА 3-3А. Экспорт по товарным группам (млн. долларов США)**

| Commodity group | 1990 | 1991 | 1992 | 1993 | 1994 | 1995 | Товарные группы |
|---|---|---|---|---|---|---|---|
| TOTAL | .. | .. | 42,376.0 | 44,297.0 | 66,861.8 | 79,910.0 | ВСЕГО |
| I - Live animals; animal products | .. | .. | 1,379.8 | 1,399.1 | 1,770.1 | 1,652.7 | I - Живые животные и продукты животноводства |
| II - Vegetable products | .. | .. | 95.8 | 43.2 | 381.5 | 448.8 | II - Продукты растительного происхождения |
| III - Animal or vegetable fats and oils and their cleavage products; prepared edible fats; animal or vegetable waxes | .. | .. | 17.1 | 4.2 | 74.5 | 37.2 | III - Жиры и масла растительного и животного происхождения, воски |
| IV - Prepared foodstuffs; beverages, spirits and vinegar; tobacco and manufactured tobacco substitutes | .. | .. | 160.1 | 219.1 | 557.3 | 576.3 | IV -Продукция пищевой промышленности, алкогольные и безалкогольные напитки, табак и его заменители |
| V - Mineral products | .. | .. | 21,711.1 | 20,669.2 | 30,131.0 | 33,350.0 | V - Минеральные продукты |
| VI - Products of the chemical or allied industries | .. | .. | 2,258.6 | 2,279.1 | 4,426.8 | 6,276.0 | VI - Продукция химической промышленности |
| VII - Plastics and articles thereof; rubber and articles thereof | .. | .. | 287.9 | 383.2 | 1,049.6 | 1,541.0 | VII - Пластмассы и изделия из них |
| VIII - Raw hides and skins, leather, furskins and articles thereof; saddlery and harness; travel goods, handbags and similar containers; articles of animal gut | .. | .. | 99.4 | 84.8 | 371.6 | 308.6 | VIII - Кожевенное сырьё, кожи, пушнина, меховое сырьё и изделия из них |
| IX - Wood and articles of wood; wood charcoal; cork and articles of cork; manufactures of straw, of esparto or of other plaiting materials; basketware and wickerwork | .. | .. | 1,188.6 | 1,385.0 | 1,665.0 | 2,125.0 | IX - Древесина и изделия из древесины, древесный уголь |
| X - Pulp of wood or of other fibrous cellulosic material; waste and scrap of paper or paperboard; paper and paperboard and articles thereof | .. | .. | 352.8 | 488.8 | 957.4 | 2,290.0 | X - Бумажная масса, бумажные и картонные отходы, макулатура, бумага, картон и изделия из них |
| XI - Textiles and textile articles | .. | .. | 244.0 | 187.3 | 1,225.5 | 1,091.2 | XI - Текстиль и текстильные изделия |
| XII - Footwear, headgear, umbrellas, sun umbrellas, walking sticks, seat sticks, whips, riding crops and parts thereof; prepared feathers and articles made therewith; artificial flowers; articles of human hair | .. | .. | 19.3 | 7.6 | 85.5 | 71.0 | XII - Обувь, головные уборы, зонты, трости и пр. |

**TABLE 3-3A. Exports by commodity group (millions of U.S. dollars)**
**ТАБЛИЦА 3-3А. Экспорт по товарным группам (млн. долларов США)**

| Commodity group | 1990 | 1991 | 1992 | 1993 | 1994 | 1995 | Товарные группы |
|---|---|---|---|---|---|---|---|
| XIII - Articles of stone, plaster, cement, asbestos, mica and similar materials; ceramic products; glass and glassware | .. | .. | 63.3 | 42.3 | 254.7 | 312.7 | XIII - Изделия из камня, гипса, цемента |
| XIV - Natural or cultured pearls, precious or semi-precious stones, precious metals, metals clad with precious metal and articles thereof; imitation jewellery; coin | .. | .. | 2,084.0 | 3,019.5 | 6,458.4 | 5,373.0 | XIV - Жемчуг, драгоценные и полудрагоценные камни, драгоценные металлы, бижутерия, монеты |
| XV - Base metals and articles of base metal | .. | .. | 4,761.6 | 7,254.0 | 11,241.0 | 15,577.0 | XV - Неблагородные металлы и изделия из них |
| XVI - Machinery and mechanical appliances; electrical equipment; parts thereof; sound recorders and reproducers, television image and sound recorders and reproducers, and parts and accessories of such articles | .. | .. | 1,447.6 | 1,272.3 | 3,019.8 | 3,797.0 | XVI - Машины, оборудование, механизмы, их части и принадлежности; звуковая и теле-аппаратура, их части и принадлежности |
| XVII - Vehicles, aircraft, vessels and associated transport equipment | .. | .. | 2,109.1 | 1,533.7 | 2,378.2 | 4,114.0 | XVII - Средства наземного, воздушного и водного транспорта |
| XVIII - Optical, photographic, cinematographic, measuring, checking, precision, medical or surgical instruments and apparatus; clocks and watches; musical instruments; parts and accessories thereof | .. | .. | 285.6 | 92.6 | 200.8 | 254.0 | XVIII - Приборы, аппараты оптические, медицинские, измерительные и пр.; музыкальные инструменты; часы; их части и принадлежности |
| XIX - Arms and ammunition; parts and accessories thereof | .. | .. | 3.6 | 46.2 | 463.5 | 593.3 | XIX - Оружие и боеприпасы, их части и принадлежности |
| XX - Miscellaneous manufactured articles | .. | .. | 82.8 | 82.9 | 148.1 | 120.4 | XX - Разные промышленные товары |
| XXI - Works of art, collectors' pieces, and antiques | .. | .. | 4.0 | 0.4 | 1.5 | 0.8 | XXI - Произведения искусства, предметы антиквариата |
| XXII - Services | .. | .. | 3,719.2 | 3,802.8 | .. | .. | XXII - Услуги |

**TABLE 3-4A. Geographical distribution of foreign trade (millions of U.S. dollars)**
**ТАБЛИЦА 3-4А. Географическое распределение внешней торговли (млн. долларов США)**

| Country or country group | Exports / Экспорт 1990 | 1991 | 1992 | 1993 | 1994 | 1995 | Imports / Импорт 1990 | 1991 | 1992 | 1993 | 1994 | 1995 | Страна или группа стран |
|---|---|---|---|---|---|---|---|---|---|---|---|---|---|
| **Total trade** | .. | .. | 42,376.0 | 44,297.0 | 66,862.0 | 79,910.0 | .. | .. | 36,984.0 | 26,807.0 | 38,661.0 | 46,680.0 | **Всего** |
| **CIS countries** | .. | .. | .. | .. | 13,861.0 | 14,244.0 | .. | .. | .. | .. | 10,317.0 | 13,525.0 | **Страны СНГ** |
| Armenia | .. | .. | .. | .. | 154.5 | 127.2 | .. | .. | .. | .. | 53.2 | 75.0 | Армения |
| Azerbaijan | .. | .. | .. | .. | 174.9 | 85.6 | .. | .. | .. | .. | 141.2 | 107.4 | Азербайджан |
| Belarus | .. | .. | .. | .. | 2,998.0 | 2,940.0 | .. | .. | .. | .. | 2,094.0 | 2,088.0 | Беларусь |
| Georgia | .. | .. | .. | .. | 70.4 | 48.9 | .. | .. | .. | .. | 52.6 | 57.9 | Грузия |
| Kazakstan | .. | .. | .. | .. | 1,938.0 | 2,416.0 | .. | .. | .. | .. | 1,996.0 | 2,726.0 | Казахстан |
| Kyrgyz Republic | .. | .. | .. | .. | 104.0 | 104.7 | .. | .. | .. | .. | 97.8 | 101.2 | Киргизстан |
| Moldova | .. | .. | .. | .. | 530.2 | 413.2 | .. | .. | .. | .. | 475.8 | 636.0 | Молдова |
| Russia | .. | .. | .. | .. | .. | .. | .. | .. | .. | .. | .. | .. | Россия |
| Tajikistan | .. | .. | .. | .. | 143.3 | 190.1 | .. | .. | .. | .. | 90.0 | 167.0 | Таджикистан |
| Turkmenistan | .. | .. | .. | .. | 112.0 | 93.1 | .. | .. | .. | .. | 60.4 | 60.8 | Туркменистан |
| Ukraine | .. | .. | .. | .. | 6,885.0 | 6,998.0 | .. | .. | .. | .. | 4,404.0 | 6,617.0 | Украина |
| Uzbekistan | .. | .. | .. | .. | 750.3 | 827.2 | .. | .. | .. | .. | 851.8 | 888.7 | Узбекистан |
| **Non-CIS countries** | .. | .. | 42,376.0 | 44,297.0 | 53,000.6 | 65,666.0 | .. | .. | 36,983.8 | 26,807.2 | 28,343.9 | 33,155.4 | **Остальной мир** |
| **Europe** | .. | .. | 31,527.0 | 30,021.0 | 36,916.0 | 42,102.0 | .. | .. | 23,326.0 | 14,877.0 | 20,090.0 | 24,053.0 | **Европа** |
| Austria | .. | .. | 662.9 | 1,405.0 | 884.2 | 855.2 | .. | .. | 1,042.0 | 855.2 | 979.4 | 981.5 | Австрия |
| Belgium | .. | .. | 904.5 | 1,057.0 | 1,380.0 | 1,507.0 | .. | .. | 309.9 | 466.2 | 614.4 | 866.6 | Бельгия |
| Bulgaria | .. | .. | 1,191.0 | 941.5 | 784.9 | 885.5 | .. | .. | 653.1 | 309.5 | 345.3 | 471.4 | Болгария |
| Czech Republic | .. | .. | 2,680.0 | 1,379.0 | 1,279.0 | 1,905.0 | .. | .. | 1,057.0 | 460.7 | 429.9 | 596.9 | Чешская Республика |
| Denmark | .. | .. | 451.5 | 189.7 | 217.8 | 480.6 | .. | .. | 196.5 | 189.8 | 322.7 | 483.3 | Дания |
| Estonia | .. | .. | 106.8 | 82.8 | 337.3 | 416.6 | .. | .. | 51.8 | 41.2 | 197.7 | 274.8 | Эстония |
| Finland | .. | .. | 1,596.0 | 1,364.0 | 1,891.0 | 2,365.0 | .. | .. | 1,259.0 | 723.6 | 1,628.0 | 2,041.0 | Финляндия |
| Former Yugoslavia | .. | .. | 1,043.0 | 306.6 | 310.6 | 353.0 | .. | .. | 980.0 | 494.5 | 492.0 | 596.9 | Быв. Югославия |
| France | .. | .. | 2,000.0 | 1,556.0 | 1,326.0 | 1,542.0 | .. | .. | 1,316.0 | 899.0 | 1,005.0 | 1,074.0 | Франция |
| Germany | .. | .. | 5,950.0 | 5,074.0 | 6,376.0 | 6,041.0 | .. | .. | 7,018.0 | 5,142.0 | 5,675.0 | 6,536.0 | Германия |
| Hungary | .. | .. | 1,611.0 | 2,098.0 | 1,408.0 | 1,804.0 | .. | .. | 1,112.0 | 622.3 | 761.2 | 842.1 | Венгрия |
| Iceland | .. | .. | 14.1 | 33.5 | 90.6 | 15.6 | .. | .. | 4.3 | 1.6 | 14.6 | 12.7 | Исландия |
| Ireland | .. | .. | 37.4 | 604.9 | 926.2 | 2,511.0 | .. | .. | 116.2 | 83.3 | 249.8 | 322.8 | Ирландия |
| Italy | .. | .. | 2,963.0 | 2,629.0 | 2,984.0 | 3,397.0 | .. | .. | 3,087.0 | 1,106.0 | 1,596.0 | 1,851.0 | Италия |
| Latvia | .. | .. | 142.4 | 207.6 | 627.6 | 784.4 | .. | .. | 117.3 | 77.4 | 197.4 | 391.8 | Латвия |
| Lithuania | .. | .. | 432.5 | 299.0 | 691.9 | 1,080.0 | .. | .. | 163.4 | 53.4 | 274.7 | 386.9 | Литва |
| Netherlands | .. | .. | 2,305.0 | 979.1 | 2,471.0 | 3,201.0 | .. | .. | 394.1 | 431.1 | 1,611.0 | 1,646.0 | Нидерланды |
| Norway | .. | .. | 348.0 | 284.3 | 319.3 | 335.8 | .. | .. | 271.6 | 87.6 | 110.6 | 175.2 | Норвегия |
| Poland | .. | .. | 1,667.0 | 1,311.0 | 1,414.0 | 1,995.0 | .. | .. | 1,351.0 | 528.8 | 945.8 | 1,321.0 | Польша |
| Romania | .. | .. | 606.6 | 475.0 | 474.7 | 736.2 | .. | .. | 453.3 | 101.7 | 146.3 | 131.8 | Румыния |
| Slovak Republic | .. | .. | .. | 932.4 | 1,235.0 | 1,747.0 | .. | .. | .. | 167.9 | 208.8 | 294.2 | Словацкая Республика |
| Spain | .. | .. | 564.3 | 384.8 | 200.9 | 307.7 | .. | .. | 426.1 | 174.7 | 244.7 | 241.0 | Испания |

**TABLE 3-4A. Geographical distribution of foreign trade (millions of U.S. dollars)**
**ТАБЛИЦА 3-4А. Географическое распределение внешней торговли (млн. долларов США)**

| Country or country group | Exports Экспорт 1990 | 1991 | 1992 | 1993 | 1994 | 1995 | Imports Импорт 1990 | 1991 | 1992 | 1993 | 1994 | 1995 | Страна или группа стран |
|---|---|---|---|---|---|---|---|---|---|---|---|---|---|
| Sweden | .. | .. | 710.7 | 783.0 | 855.2 | 750.8 | .. | .. | 656.0 | 313.6 | 310.5 | 546.6 | Швеция |
| Switzerland | .. | .. | 869.1 | 1,609.0 | 3,719.0 | 3,577.0 | .. | .. | 496.0 | 658.0 | 539.3 | 667.9 | Швейцария |
| United Kingdom | .. | .. | 2,325.0 | 3,353.0 | 4,259.0 | 3,095.0 | .. | .. | 601.2 | 652.7 | 895.8 | 1,099.0 | Великобритания |
| Other Europe | .. | .. | 345.2 | 988.4 | 452.8 | 413.6 | .. | .. | 193.2 | 235.2 | 294.1 | 200.6 | Остальные страны Европы |
| **Asia** | .. | .. | 8,767.0 | 10,852.0 | 10,878.0 | 15,699.0 | .. | .. | 7,999.0 | 8,148.0 | 4,657.0 | 4,580.0 | **Азия** |
| Afghanistan | .. | .. | 90.6 | 49.9 | 16.0 | 17.6 | .. | .. | 214.3 | 679.4 | 7.6 | 13.3 | Афганистан |
| China | .. | .. | 2,864.0 | 3,068.0 | 2,889.0 | 3,432.0 | .. | .. | 1,790.0 | 2,335.0 | 952.0 | 865.4 | Китай |
| India | .. | .. | 601.9 | 474.0 | 379.0 | 997.8 | .. | .. | 850.9 | 632.6 | 586.9 | 614.1 | Индия |
| Iraq | .. | .. | .. | .. | 9.0 | .. | .. | .. | 0.1 | .. | 0.0 | .. | Ирак |
| Japan | .. | .. | 1,702.0 | 2,005.0 | 2,823.0 | 3,621.0 | .. | .. | 1,697.0 | 1,367.0 | 1,114.0 | 762.6 | Япония |
| Korea, Dem. People's Rep. | .. | .. | 239.0 | 168.4 | 51.2 | 70.0 | .. | .. | 72.5 | 54.2 | 43.7 | 15.3 | КНДР |
| Korea, Rep. of | .. | .. | 265.6 | 391.2 | 567.6 | 918.8 | .. | .. | 778.2 | 305.6 | 429.1 | 502.1 | Южная Корея |
| Mongolia | .. | .. | 194.8 | 156.6 | 143.8 | 197.4 | .. | .. | 251.0 | 81.2 | 54.5 | 40.3 | МНР |
| Syrian Arab Republic | .. | .. | 194.7 | 129.6 | 86.6 | 75.4 | .. | .. | 65.9 | 92.4 | 19.0 | 11.2 | Сирия |
| Turkey | .. | .. | 661.4 | 1,078.0 | 1,014.0 | 1,661.0 | .. | .. | 482.5 | 661.2 | 400.5 | 541.5 | Турция |
| Viet Nam | .. | .. | 89.8 | 123.9 | 120.5 | 322.2 | .. | .. | 137.3 | 166.3 | 52.0 | 38.0 | Вьетнам |
| Other Asia | .. | .. | 1,863.0 | 3,207.0 | 2,778.0 | 4,386.0 | .. | .. | 1,659.0 | 1,773.0 | 997.7 | 1,176.0 | Остальные страны Азии |
| **America** | .. | .. | 1,492.0 | 2,890.0 | 4,608.0 | 6,990.0 | .. | .. | 4,894.0 | 3,286.0 | 3,055.0 | 3,975.0 | **Сев. и Южная Америка** |
| Canada | .. | .. | .. | .. | .. | .. | .. | .. | .. | .. | .. | .. | Канада |
| Cuba | .. | .. | 199.9 | 102.8 | 87.0 | 211.3 | .. | .. | 632.2 | 436.3 | 300.5 | 196.2 | Куба |
| United States | .. | .. | 762.2 | 1,997.0 | 3,561.0 | 4,537.0 | .. | .. | 2,898.0 | 2,304.0 | 2,070.0 | 2,648.0 | США |
| Other America | .. | .. | 529.9 | 790.2 | 960.0 | 2,242.0 | .. | .. | 1,364.0 | 545.7 | 684.5 | 1,131.0 | Остальные |
| **Africa** | .. | .. | 578.0 | 521.6 | 556.9 | 837.0 | .. | .. | 705.3 | 380.3 | 242.0 | 293.4 | **Африка** |
| Egypt | .. | .. | 153.1 | 169.9 | 304.9 | 393.6 | .. | .. | 258.3 | 143.7 | 61.8 | 37.2 | Египет |
| Libya | .. | .. | 112.3 | 8.7 | 0.5 | 0.1 | .. | .. | 1.1 | 0.3 | 0.1 | 0.0 | Ливия |
| Other Africa | .. | .. | 312.6 | 343.0 | 251.5 | 443.3 | .. | .. | 445.9 | 236.3 | 180.1 | 256.2 | Остальные |
| **Rest of the World** | .. | .. | 11.9 | 12.4 | 41.7 | 38.0 | .. | .. | 59.5 | 115.9 | 299.9 | 254.0 | **Прочие страны мира** |
| Australia | .. | .. | 8.0 | 10.0 | 37.6 | 29.5 | .. | .. | 52.4 | 80.9 | 191.4 | 135.0 | Австралия |

**TABLE 5-1. Agricultural production (millions of national currency, current prices)** **RUSSIAN FEDERATION**

**ТАБЛИЦА 5-1. Сельскохозяйственная продукция (млн. нац. валюты, текущие цены)**

| Item | 1990 | 1991 | 1992 | 1993 | 1994 | 1995 | Статьи |
|---|---|---|---|---|---|---|---|
| **Total gross agricultural production** | 157,407 | 260,047 | 2,706,177 | 22,763,616 | 75,226,455 | 264,725,000 | **Валовая продукция сельского хозяйства - всего** |
| **Crops** | 57,589 | 104,948 | 1,239,335 | 10,293,625 | 37,962,929 | 135,478,000 | **Продукция растениеводства** |
| Grains | .. | .. | .. | .. | .. | .. | Зерно |
| Potatoes | .. | .. | .. | .. | .. | .. | Картофель |
| Vegetables | .. | .. | .. | .. | .. | .. | Овощи |
| Fruits (excluding grapes) | .. | .. | .. | .. | .. | .. | Фрукты (без винограда) |
| Grapes | .. | .. | .. | .. | .. | .. | Виноград |
| Tobacco | .. | .. | .. | .. | .. | .. | Табак |
| Cotton | .. | .. | .. | .. | .. | .. | Хлопок |
| Sugarbeets | .. | .. | .. | .. | .. | .. | Сахарная свекла |
| Oilseeds | .. | .. | .. | .. | .. | .. | Семена масличных культур |
| Other | .. | .. | .. | .. | .. | .. | Прочие |
| **Animal husbandry** | 99,818 | 155,099 | 1,423,391 | 12,124,179 | 35,766,329 | 124,522,000 | **Продукция животноводства** |
| Livestock | .. | .. | .. | .. | .. | .. | Мясное животноводство |
| Cattle | .. | .. | .. | .. | .. | .. | Крупный рогатый скот |
| Pigs | .. | .. | .. | .. | .. | .. | Свиньи |
| Sheep and goats | .. | .. | .. | .. | .. | .. | Овцы и козы |
| Poultry | .. | .. | .. | .. | .. | .. | Птица |
| Other | .. | .. | .. | .. | .. | .. | Прочие |
| Milk | .. | .. | .. | .. | .. | .. | Молоко |
| Eggs | .. | .. | .. | .. | .. | .. | Яйца |
| Wool | .. | .. | .. | .. | .. | .. | Шерсть |
| Other livestock | .. | .. | .. | .. | .. | .. | Прочая |
| **Agricultural services** | .. | .. | 43,451 | 345,812 | 1,497,197 | 4,725,000 | **Сельскохозяйственные услуги** |

**TABLE 5-2. Agricultural production (millions of constant national currency)** **RUSSIAN FEDERATION**

**ТАБЛИЦА 5-2. Сельскохозяйственная продукция в постоянных ценах (млн. национальной валюты)**

| Item | 1990 | 1991 | 1992 | 1993 | 1994 | 1995 | Статьи |
|---|---|---|---|---|---|---|---|
| **Total gross agricultural production** | 102,085 | 97,431 | 88,280 | 84,406 | 74,265 | 67,497,613 | Валовая продукция сельского хозяйства - всего |
| **Crops** | 36,733 | 36,891 | 34,894 | 33,893 | 30,383 | 38,826,952 | Продукция растениеводства |
| Grains | 14,818 | 11,288 | 13,636 | 12,405 | 10,150 | 7,010,038 | Зерно |
| Potatoes | 5,898 | 6,564 | 7,308 | 7,194 | 6,468 | 12,577,767 | Картофель |
| Vegetables | 2,839 | 3,035 | 3,214 | 3,216 | 3,062 | 8,446,727 | Овощи |
| Fruits (excluding grapes) | 1,863 | 1,811 | 2,079 | 2,137 | 1,829 | 2,920,299 | Фрукты (без винограда) |
| Grapes | 221 | 215 | 247 | 218 | 145 | 260,073 | Виноград |
| Tobacco | 18 | 14 | 10 | 18 | 10 | 820 | Табак |
| Cotton | .. | .. | .. | .. | .. | .. | Хлопок |
| Sugarbeets | 1,600 | 1,248 | 1,313 | 1,309 | 717 | 958,020 | Сахарная свекла |
| Oilseeds | 1,439 | 1,174 | 1,153 | 1,011 | 917 | 1,224,821 | Семена масличных культур |
| Other | 8,037 | 11,542 | 5,934 | 6,385 | 7,085 | 5,428,387 | Прочие |
| **Animal husbandry** | 65,352 | 60,540 | 53,386 | 50,513 | 43,882 | 28,670,661 | Продукция животноводства |
| Livestock | 35,363 | 32,373 | 27,321 | 24,774 | 20,898 | 12,291,734 | Мясное животноводство |
| Cattle | 17,126 | 15,396 | 13,387 | 12,457 | 10,390 | 4,560,048 | Крупный рогатый скот |
| Pigs | 10,162 | 9,156 | 7,747 | 6,571 | 5,832 | 4,697,831 | Свиньи |
| Sheep and goats | 1,765 | 1,619 | 1,372 | 1,217 | 980 | 442,999 | Овцы и козы |
| Poultry | 5,802 | 5,748 | 4,449 | 4,172 | 3,393 | 2,404,993 | Птица |
| Other | 508 | 454 | 366 | 357 | 303 | 185,863 | Прочие |
| Milk | 22,100 | 20,582 | 18,745 | 18,464 | 16,741 | 11,628,360 | Молоко |
| Eggs | 4,546 | 4,513 | 4,108 | 3,859 | 3,589 | 3,072,200 | Яйца |
| Wool | 1,974 | 1,778 | 1,555 | 1,379 | 1,063 | 124,509 | Шерсть |
| Other livestock | 1,369 | 1,294 | 1,657 | 2,037 | 1,591 | 1,553,858 | Прочая |
| **Agricultural services** | .. | .. | .. | .. | .. | .. | Сельскохозяйственные услуги |

**TABLE 5-3. Production and average yield of major agricultural crops**

**ТАБЛИЦА 5-3. Производство и урожайность важнейших сельскохозяйственных культур**

| Crop | 1990 | 1991 | 1992 | 1993 | 1994 | 1995 | Сельскохозяйственные культуры |
|---|---|---|---|---|---|---|---|
| **Production (thousands of tons)** | | | | | | | **Производство (тыс. тонн)** |
| Grain - Cleanweight | 116,676 | 89,094 | 106,855 | 99,094 | 81,297 | 63,406 | Зерно в чистом весе |
| Winter wheat | 32,771 | 25,828 | 28,265 | 27,242 | 17,153 | 13,846 | Пшеница - озимая |
| Spring wheat | 16,825 | 13,071 | 17,901 | 16,305 | 14,976 | 16,273 | яровая |
| Coarse grain | 127,013 | 97,144 | 117,271 | 108,710 | 89,712 | 69,682 | Зерно в физическом весе |
| Rye | 16,431 | 10,639 | 13,887 | 9,166 | 5,989 | 4,098 | Рожь |
| Corn | 2,451 | 1,969 | 2,135 | 2,441 | 892 | 1,738 | Кукуруза |
| Winter barley | 3,137 | 2,731 | 2,662 | 2,469 | 1,039 | 1,324 | Ячмень - озимый |
| Spring barley | 24,098 | 19,443 | 24,326 | 24,374 | 26,015 | 14,462 | яровой |
| Oats | 12,326 | 10,372 | 11,241 | 11,556 | 10,757 | 8,562 | Овес |
| Millet | 1,946 | 1,040 | 1,535 | 1,128 | 482 | 488 | Просо |
| Rice | 896 | 773 | 754 | 688 | 523 | 462 | Рис |
| Flax | 71 | 102 | 78 | 58 | 54 | 69 | Лен |
| Oilseeds | 4,662 | 3,820 | 3,883 | 3,455 | 3,154 | 4,667 | Семена масличных культур |
| Cotton (raw) | .. | .. | .. | .. | .. | .. | Хлопок - сырец |
| Cotton fiber | .. | .. | .. | .. | .. | .. | волокно |
| Sugarbeets | 32,327 | 24,280 | 25,548 | 25,468 | 13,946 | 19,072 | Сахарная свекла |
| Potatoes | 30,848 | 34,329 | 38,330 | 37,650 | 33,828 | 39,909 | Картофель |
| Pulses | .. | .. | .. | .. | .. | .. | Бобовые |
| Vegetables | 10,328 | 10,425 | 10,018 | 9,827 | 9,621 | 11,275 | Овощи |
| Fruit | 2,997 | 2,746 | 3,369 | 3,193 | 2,405 | 2,511 | Фрукты |
| Grapes | 612 | 543 | 529 | 467 | 311 | 301 | Виноград |
| Other | 2,385 | 2,203 | 2,840 | 2,726 | 2,094 | 2,210 | Прочие |
| Corn (silage and greenchop) | 189,018 | 150,709 | 149,511 | 128,669 | 86,707 | 88,685 | Кукуруза (на силос и зеленый корм) |
| Hay | 30,839 | 29,321 | 24,718 | 25,175 | 22,626 | 19,919 | Сено |
| **Average yield (kilograms per hectare)** | | | | | | | **Ср. урожайность (кг с га)** |
| Grain | 1,850 | 1,440 | 1,720 | 1,630 | 1,440 | 1,160 | Зерно |
| Winter wheat | 3,370 | 2,810 | 2,620 | 2,590 | 2,210 | 1,690 | Пшеница - озимая |
| Spring wheat | 1,160 | 940 | 1,330 | 1,150 | 1,040 | 1,030 | яровая |
| Coarse grain | 2,010 | 1,570 | 1,890 | 1,780 | 1,590 | 1,270 | Зерно в физическом весе |
| Rye | 2,050 | 1,640 | 1,830 | 1,530 | 1,530 | 1,260 | Рожь |
| Corn | 2,820 | 2,680 | 2,640 | 3,050 | 1,700 | 2,700 | Кукуруза |
| Winter barley | 4,540 | 3,510 | 3,250 | 3,320 | 2,660 | 2,830 | Ячмень - озимый |
| Spring barley | 1,850 | 1,340 | 1,770 | 1,650 | 1,620 | 1,010 | яровой |
| Oats | 1,350 | 1,150 | 1,320 | 1,380 | 1,290 | 1,080 | Овес |
| Millet | 1,000 | 520 | 820 | 770 | 480 | 690 | Просо |
| Rice | 3,130 | 2,900 | 2,840 | 2,640 | 2,710 | 2,700 | Рис |
| Flax | 170 | 310 | 240 | 220 | 400 | 390 | Лен |
| Oilseeds | 1,160 | 1,030 | 990 | 910 | 790 | 910 | Семена масличных культур |
| Cotton (raw) | .. | .. | .. | .. | .. | .. | Хлопок - сырец |
| Cotton fiber | .. | .. | .. | .. | .. | .. | волокно |
| Sugarbeets | 22,100 | 17,400 | 17,800 | 19,100 | 12,600 | 17,600 | Сахарная свекла |
| Potatoes | 9,900 | 10,800 | 11,300 | 10,600 | 10,100 | 11,700 | Картофель |
| Pulses | .. | .. | .. | .. | .. | .. | Бобовые |
| Vegetables | 15,400 | 14,600 | 13,700 | 13,500 | 12,900 | 14,200 | Овощи |
| Fruit | .. | .. | .. | .. | .. | .. | Фрукты |
| Grapes | 5,070 | 4,670 | 4,840 | 4,510 | 3,470 | 3,740 | Виноград |
| Other | 3,630 | 3,340 | 4,250 | 4,060 | 2,930 | 3,020 | Прочие |
| Corn (silage and greenchop) | 18,500 | 15,500 | 15,500 | 14,400 | 11,600 | 14,300 | Кукуруза (на силос и зеленый корм) |
| Hay | 0 | 0 | 0 | .. | .. | .. | Сено |

## TABLE 5-4. Main aggregates of animal husbandry
## ТАБЛИЦА 5-4. Основные показатели животноводства

| Type of livestock or product | 1990 | 1991 | 1992 | 1993 | 1994 | 1995 | Направление животноводства или вид продукции |
|---|---|---|---|---|---|---|---|
| **Livestock (thousands of heads)** | | | | | | | **Поголовье скота (тысяч голов)** |
| Cattle | 57,043 | 54,677 | 52,226 | 48,914 | 43,297 | 39,696 | Крупный рогатый скот |
| of which: Cows | 20,557 | 20,564 | 20,243 | 19,831 | 18,398 | 17,436 | в том числе коровы |
| Pigs | 38,314 | 35,384 | 31,520 | 28,557 | 24,859 | 22,631 | Свиньи |
| Sheep and goats | 58,195 | 55,255 | 51,368 | 43,712 | 34,540 | 28,027 | Овцы и козы |
| of which: Goats | 2,953 | 3,060 | 3,186 | 3,096 | 2,773 | 2,682 | в том числе козы |
| Horses | 2,618 | 2,590 | 2,556 | 2,490 | 2,431 | 2,363 | Лошади |
| Other | .. | .. | .. | .. | .. | .. | Прочие |
| **Animal husbandry products** | | | | | | | **Продукция животноводства** |
| Meat (thousands of tons) | 10,112 | 9,375 | 8,260 | 7,513 | 6,803 | 5,796 | Мясо (тысяч тонн) |
| Beef | 4,329 | 3,989 | 3,632 | 3,359 | 3,240 | 2,734 | Говядина |
| Pork | 3,480 | 3,190 | 2,783 | 2,432 | 2,104 | 1,865 | Свинина |
| Lamb | 395 | 347 | 329 | 359 | 316 | 261 | Баранина |
| Poultry | 1,801 | 1,751 | 1,428 | 1,277 | 1,068 | 859 | Птица |
| Other | 107 | 98 | 88 | 86 | 75 | 77 | Прочие виды мяса |
| Milk (thousands of tons) | 55,715 | 51,887 | 47,236 | 46,524 | 42,176 | 39,241 | Молоко (тысяч тонн) |
| Eggs (millions) | 47,470 | 46,875 | 42,902 | 40,297 | 37,477 | 33,830 | Яйца (миллионов штук) |
| Wool (thousands of tons) | 227 | 204 | 179 | 158 | 122 | 94 | Шерсть (тысяч тонн) |

**TABLE 6-1. Industrial production by sector (millions of national currency)**

**ТАБЛИЦА 6-1. Промышленное производство по отраслям (млн. национальной валюты)**

| Sector | 1990 | 1991 | 1992 | 1993 | 1994 | 1995 | Отрасли |
|---|---|---|---|---|---|---|---|
| **All industry** | 555,698 | 1,183,224 | 17,280,900 | 120,657,400 | 356,112,200 | 975,525,316 | **Вся промышленность** |
| **Heavy industry** | 406,290 | 803,409 | 14,035,040 | 97,222,320 | 295,914,170 | 817,861,188 | **Тяжелая промышленность** |
| Fuel and energy | 62,200 | 133,767 | 4,311,731 | 30,639,990 | 101,181,210 | 282,779,915 | Топливно-энергетическая промышленноть |
| Electricity | 21,400 | 47,600 | 1,106,199 | 10,961,810 | 47,684,631 | 121,404,255 | Электроэнергетика |
| Fuels | 40,800 | 86,200 | 3,205,544 | 19,678,170 | 53,496,579 | 161,375,660 | Топливная промышленность |
| Ferrous and nonferrous metallurgy | 61,700 | 132,710 | 2,896,404 | 19,225,430 | 53,082,722 | 153,945,161 | Металлургия |
| Chemicals and petrochemical industry | 41,400 | 83,500 | 1,440,448 | 8,262,884 | 26,404,105 | 78,725,864 | Химическая и нефтехимическая пром. |
| Machine building and metalworking | 168,413 | 295,340 | 3,534,819 | 20,738,490 | 69,839,560 | 177,438,056 | Машиностроение и металлообработка |
| Forestry, woodworking, and pulp and paper industry | 31,000 | 68,900 | 822,633 | 5,227,134 | 16,334,020 | 50,500,392 | Лесная, деревообрабатывающая и целлюлозо-бумажная промышленность |
| Construction materials | 20,200 | 44,200 | 562,338 | 5,124,816 | 17,251,901 | 47,404,635 | Промышленность строительных материалов |
| **Light industry** | 65,700 | 192,251 | 1,226,765 | 6,193,436 | 11,295,351 | 24,267,485 | **Легкая промышленность** |
| Textiles | 40,300 | 133,495 | 810,351 | 3,514,512 | 5,527,229 | 12,672,263 | Текстильная |
| Clothing | 16,200 | 37,300 | 209,430 | 1,340,656 | 3,036,078 | 6,191,088 | Швейная |
| Leather and shoes | 9,000 | 21,000 | 201,339 | 1,311,037 | 2,139,000 | 4,433,341 | Кожевенная и обувная |
| **Food industry** | 72,504 | 169,940 | 1,776,510 | 15,696,810 | 44,635,144 | 119,153,170 | **Пищевая промышленность** |
| Processed foods | 30,900 | 66,700 | 829,620 | 6,602,484 | 19,104,726 | 53,582,758 | Пищевкусовая |
| Meat and dairy products | 31,000 | 86,000 | 693,311 | 7,048,041 | 19,912,903 | 51,780,334 | Мясная и молочная |
| Fish | 10,700 | 17,200 | 253,784 | 2,046,286 | 5,486,039 | 13,790,078 | Рыбная |

## TABLE 6-2. Industrial production by sector in constant prices
## ТАБЛИЦА 6-2. Промышленное производство по отраслям в постоянных ценах

| Sector | 1990 | 1991 | 1992 | 1993 | 1994 | 1995 | Отрасли |
|---|---|---|---|---|---|---|---|
| **Industrial production** | | | | | | | **Промышленное производство** |
| **All industry** | 22,906,810 | 21,074,270 | 17,280,900 | 14,844,290 | 11,741,840 | .. | **Вся промышленность** |
| **Heavy industry** | 17,754,640 | 16,511,810 | 14,035,040 | 12,070,130 | .. | .. | **Тяжелая промышленность** |
| Fuel and energy | 4,824,114 | 4,607,576 | 4,311,743 | 3,887,909 | 3,506,101 | .. | Топливно-энергетическая промышленноть |
| Electricity | 1,157,283 | 1,160,755 | 1,106,199 | 1,054,208 | 961,438 | .. | Электроэнергетика |
| Fuels | 3,666,831 | 3,446,821 | 3,205,544 | 2,833,701 | 2,544,663 | .. | Топливная промышленность |
| Ferrous and nonferrous metallurgy | 4,003,978 | 3,679,288 | 2,896,404 | 2,452,794 | 2,132,076 | .. | Металлургия |
| Chemicals and petrochemicals | 1,963,343 | 1,839,653 | 1,440,448 | 1,130,752 | 803,965 | .. | Химическая и нефтехимическая пром. |
| Machine building and metalworking | 4,675,687 | 4,208,118 | 3,534,819 | 2,933,900 | 1,936,374 | .. | Машиностроение и металлообработка |
| Forestry, woodworking, and pulp and paper | 1,058,539 | 963,270 | 822,633 | 668,801 | 469,498 | .. | Лесная, деревообрабатывающая и целлюлозо-бумажная промышленность |
| Construction materials | 723,826 | 706,454 | 562,338 | 472,364 | 335,851 | .. | Промышленность строительных материалов |
| **Light industry** | 1,925,847 | 1,752,521 | 1,226,765 | 944,609 | 511,978 | .. | **Легкая промышленность** |
| Textiles | 1,295,318 | 1,191,693 | 810,351 | 614,459 | 349,781 | .. | Текстильная |
| Clothing | 297,486 | 261,788 | 209,430 | 174,514 | 84,938 | .. | Швейная |
| Leather and shoe | 286,808 | 258,127 | 201,339 | 155,636 | 77,259 | .. | Кожевенная и обувная |
| **Food industry** | 2,348,080 | 2,125,012 | 1,776,510 | 1,616,624 | 1,288,449 | .. | **Пищевая промышленность** |
| Processed foods | 960,380 | 917,199 | 829,620 | 786,486 | 608,928 | .. | Пищевкусовая |
| Meat and dairy products | 1,061,938 | 909,457 | 693,311 | 608,461 | 506,676 | .. | Мясная и молочная |
| Fish | 325,762 | 298,356 | 253,784 | 221,677 | 172,845 | .. | Рыбная |
| **Growth in production by sector (in percent)** | | | | | | | **Рост производства по отраслям** |
| **All industry** | .. | -8.0 | -18.0 | -14.1 | -20.9 | .. | **Вся промышленность** |
| **Heavy industry** | .. | -7.0 | -15.0 | -14.0 | .. | .. | **Тяжелая промышленность** |
| Power and fuels | .. | -4.5 | -6.4 | -9.8 | -9.8 | .. | Топливно-энергетическая промышленноть |
| Electricity | .. | 0.3 | -4.7 | -4.7 | -8.8 | .. | Электроэнергетика |
| Fuels | .. | -6.0 | -7.0 | -11.6 | -10.2 | .. | Топливная промышленность |
| Ferrous and nonferrous metallurgy | .. | -8.1 | -21.3 | -15.3 | -13.1 | .. | Металлургия |
| Chemicals and petrochemicals | .. | -6.3 | -21.7 | -21.5 | -28.9 | .. | Химическая и нефтехимическая пром. |
| Machine building and metalworking | .. | -10.0 | -16.0 | -17.0 | -34.0 | .. | Машиностроение и металлообработка |
| Forestry, woodworking, and pulp and paper | .. | -9.0 | -14.6 | -18.7 | -29.8 | .. | Лесная, деревообрабатывающая и целлюлозо-бумажная промышленность |
| Construction materials | .. | -2.4 | -20.4 | -16.0 | -28.9 | .. | Промышленность строительных материалов |
| **Light industry** | .. | -9.0 | -30.0 | -23.0 | -45.8 | .. | **Легкая промышленность** |
| Textiles | .. | -8.0 | -32.0 | -24.2 | -43.1 | .. | Текстильная |
| Clothing | .. | -12.0 | -20.0 | -16.7 | -51.3 | .. | Швейная |
| Leather and shoe | .. | -10.0 | -22.0 | -22.7 | -50.4 | .. | Кожевенная и обувная |
| **Food industry** | .. | -9.5 | -16.4 | -9.0 | -20.3 | .. | **Пищевая промышленность** |
| Processed foods | .. | -4.5 | -9.5 | -5.2 | -22.6 | .. | Пищевкусовая |
| Meat and dairy products | .. | -14.4 | -23.8 | -12.2 | -16.7 | .. | Мясная и молочная |
| Fish | .. | -8.4 | -14.9 | -12.7 | -22.0 | .. | Рыбная |

## TABLE 6-3. Primary energy supply (million tons oil equivalent)

## ТАБЛИЦА 6-3. Ресурсы первичных видов энергии (млн. тонн нефтяного эквивалента)

| Item | | 1990 | 1991 | 1992 | 1993 | 1994 | 1995 | Статьи | |
|---|---|---|---|---|---|---|---|---|---|
| **Primary production** | | | | | | | | **Производство первичной энергии** | |
| Coal and lignite (hard and brown) | | 217.2 | 188.7 | 181.6 | 165.3 | 149.5 | 147.0 | Уголь каменный и бурый | |
| Crude oil | | 526.2 | 471.0 | 406.5 | 359.9 | 323.2 | 312.4 | Нефть | |
| Gas | | 597.0 | 599.7 | 597.4 | 576.5 | 566.0 | 555.0 | Газ | |
| Nuclear | | 9.2 | 9.3 | 9.3 | 9.2 | 8.2 | 7.7 | Атомная энергия | |
| Hydro/geothermal | | 14.0 | 14.1 | 14.5 | 14.7 | 14.9 | 14.8 | Гидро-геотермальная | |
| Other | | 29.0 | 29.2 | 27.8 | 23.0 | 14.7 | 15.1 | Другие виды | |
| Total | | 1392.6 | 1312.0 | 1237.1 | 1148.6 | 1076.5 | 1052.0 | Всего | |
| **Energy trade** | | | | | | | | **Торговля энергией** | |
| Coal and lignite | Exports | 39.2 | 26.2 | 24.1 | 19.1 | 16.9 | 22.3 | Уголь каменный и бурый | Экспорт |
| | Imports | 37.2 | 31.9 | 27.9 | 19.7 | 18.2 | 13.0 | | Импорт |
| | Net imports | -2.0 | 5.7 | 3.8 | 0.6 | 1.3 | -9.3 | | Чистый импорт |
| Oil/oil product | Exports | 244.1 | 225.4 | 163.7 | 165.6 | 177.2 | 172.4 | Нефть и нефтепродукты | Экспорт |
| | Imports | 52.9 | 26.0 | 11.9 | 11.8 | 16.1 | 11.8 | | Импорт |
| | Net imports | -191.2 | -199.4 | -151.8 | -153.8 | -161.1 | -160.6 | | Чистый импорт |
| Gas | Exports | 202.9 | 179.5 | 181.3 | 167.3 | 171.8 | 179.1 | Газ | Экспорт |
| | Imports | 86.1 | 20.1 | 6.5 | 11.0 | 1.4 | 3.7 | | Импорт |
| | Net imports | -116.8 | -159.4 | -174.8 | -156.3 | -170.4 | -175.4 | | Чистый импорт |
| Electricity | Exports | 7.5 | 8.0 | 7.4 | 7.3 | 2.4 | 1.7 | Электричество | Экспорт |
| | Imports | 6.1 | 5.9 | 4.7 | 4.2 | 0.1 | 0.1 | | Импорт |
| | Net imports | -1.4 | -2.1 | -2.7 | -3.1 | -2.3 | -1.6 | | Чистый импорт |
| **Total net imports** | | -311.4 | -355.2 | -325.5 | -312.6 | -332.5 | -346.9 | **Чистый импорт энергии-всего** | |
| **Total stock changes** | | -2.4 | 45.8 | -12.4 | -4.6 | -19.7 | 0.0 | **Изменение запасов-всего** | |
| **Total primary energy supply** | | 1078.8 | 1002.6 | 899.2 | 831.4 | 724.3 | 705.1 | **Ресурсы первичной энергии-всего** | |
| Coal and lignite | | 215.2 | 194.4 | 185.4 | 165.9 | 150.8 | 137.7 | Уголь каменный и бурый | |
| Oil/oil products | | 335.0 | 271.6 | 254.7 | 206.1 | 162.1 | 151.8 | Нефть и нефтепродукты | |
| Gas | | 480.2 | 440.3 | 422.6 | 420.2 | 395.6 | 379.6 | Газ | |
| Nuclear | | 21.8 | 21.3 | 21.1 | 20.8 | 20.8 | 20.9 | Атомная энергия | |
| Hydro/geothermal | | .. | .. | .. | .. | .. | .. | Гидро-геотермальная энергия | |
| Other | | 26.6 | 75.0 | 15.4 | 18.4 | 14.7 | 15.1 | Другие виды | |
| **Total primary energy requirement (equals total primary energy supply)** | | 1078.8 | 1002.6 | 899.2 | 831.4 | 724.3 | 705.1 | **Потребность в первичной энергии-всего (равно ресурсам первичной энергии)** | |

TABLE 6-4. Final energy consumption (million tons oil equivalent) — RUSSIAN FEDERATION

ТАБЛИЦА 6-4. Конечное потребление энергии ( млн. тонн нефтяного эквивалента )

| | 1991 | 1992 | 1993 | 1994 | 1995 | |
|---|---|---|---|---|---|---|
| **Final energy consumption** | 640.6 | 613.8 | 590.[illegible] | 581.7 | .. | **Конечное потребление энергии** |
| Coal & Lignite | 38.6 | 32.8 | 37.4 | 34.7 | .. | Уголь каменный и бурый |
| Oil Products | 117.0 | 112.9 | 106.3 | 98.8 | .. | Нефтепродукты |
| Gas | 108.0 | 108.0 | 125.1 | 121.7 | .. | Газ |
| Electricity | 134.1 | 124.3 | 115.3 | 107.9 | .. | Электроэнергия |
| Heat | 235.1 | 227.3 | 197.7 | 171.4 | .. | Тепло |
| Other | 7.8 | 7.7 | 8.2 | 47.2 | .. | Другие виды |
| Of which: | | | | | | В том числе |
| **Industry** | 267.1 | 248.9 | 239.6 | 212.5 | .. | **Промышленность** |
| Coal & Lignite | 4.0 | 3.9 | 8.5 | 6.8 | .. | Уголь каменный и бурый |
| Oil Products | 21.9 | 21.2 | 22.1 | 18.8 | .. | Нефтепродукты |
| Gas | 39.9 | 40.1 | 47.6 | 30.5 | .. | Газ |
| Electricity | 79.4 | 70.8 | 62.3 | 55.1 | .. | Электроэнергия |
| Heat | 121.5 | 112.5 | 97.8 | 80.5 | .. | Тепло |
| Other | 0.4 | 0.4 | 1.3 | 20.8 | .. | Другие виды |
| **Agriculture** | 45.0 | 43.8 | 53.5 | 43.4 | .. | **Сельское хозяйство** |
| Coal & Lignite | 1.2 | 1.5 | 2.7 | 3.6 | .. | Уголь каменный и бурый |
| Oil Products | 15.7 | 13.9 | 19.7 | 14.4 | .. | Нефтепродукты |
| Gas | 0.8 | 0.8 | 5.4 | 8.9 | .. | Газ |
| Electricity | 17.5 | 17.4 | 17.5 | 8.4 | .. | Электроэнергия |
| Heat | 9.2 | 8.9 | 7.8 | 7.6 | .. | Тепло |
| Other | 0.6 | 1.3 | 0.4 | 0.5 | .. | Другие виды |
| **Transport** | 135.8 | 128.5 | 101.8 | 82.6 | .. | **Транспорт** |
| Oil Products | 67.9 | 60.2 | 37.3 | 33.0 | .. | Нефтепродукты |
| Other | 67.9 | 68.3 | 64.5 | 49.6 | .. | Другие виды |
| **Households** | 173.9 | 172.3 | 175.7 | 179.8 | .. | **Домашние хозяйства** |
| Coal & Lignite | 27.3 | 26.1 | 23.5 | 13.7 | .. | Уголь каменный и бурый |
| Oil Products | 10.4 | 10.2 | 16.5 | 16.6 | .. | Нефтепродукты |
| Gas | 20.0 | 22.7 | 23.6 | 55.6 | .. | Газ |
| Electricity | 21.9 | 21.4 | 22.5 | 18.8 | .. | Электроэнергия |
| Heat | 87.9 | 84.9 | 84.6 | 67.8 | .. | Тепло |
| Other | 6.4 | 7.0 | 5.0 | 7.3 | .. | Другие виды |

## TABLE 7-1. Price indices and exchange rates
## ТАБЛИЦА 7-1. Индексы цен и обменный курс

| Year and month | National currency per U.S. dollar<br>Единиц нац. валюты за 1 доллар США | National currency per Russian ruble<br>Единиц нац. валюты за 1 российский рубль | Consumer price index (as a percent of the previous month)<br>Индекс потребительских цен (в % к предыдущему месяцу) | Producer price index (as a percent of the previous month)<br>Индекс цен производителей (в % к предыдущему месяцу) | Consumer price index (as a percent of the previous December)<br>Индекс потребительских цен (в % к декабрю прошлого года) | Producer price index (as a percent of the previous December)<br>Индекс цен производителей (в % к декабрю прошлого года) | Год и месяц |
|---|---|---|---|---|---|---|---|
| **1993** | | | | | | | **1993** |
| January | 507.0 | .. | 125.8 | 132.0 | 125.8 | 132.0 | Январь |
| February | 566.0 | .. | 124.7 | 130.0 | 156.8 | 172.0 | Февраль |
| March | 665.0 | .. | 120.1 | 119.0 | 188.4 | 204.0 | Март |
| April | 767.0 | .. | 118.7 | 121.0 | 223.6 | 247.0 | Апрель |
| May | 914.0 | .. | 118.1 | 118.0 | 264.1 | 291.0 | Май |
| June | 1,082.0 | .. | 119.9 | 116.0 | 316.7 | 337.0 | Июнь |
| July | 1,022.0 | .. | 122.4 | 128.0 | 387.6 | 431.0 | Июль |
| August | 986.0 | .. | 126.0 | 126.0 | 488.4 | 543.0 | Август |
| September | 1,059.0 | .. | 123.0 | 121.0 | 600.7 | 657.0 | Сентябрь |
| October | 1,189.0 | .. | 119.5 | 119.0 | 717.8 | 782.0 | Октябрь |
| November | 1,191.0 | .. | 116.4 | 115.0 | 835.5 | 899.0 | Ноябрь |
| December | 1,240.0 | .. | 112.5 | 111.0 | 939.9 | 995.0 | Декабрь |
| **1994** | | | | | | | **1994** |
| January | 1,434.0 | .. | 117.9 | 119.0 | 117.9 | 119.0 | Январь |
| February | 1,581.0 | .. | 110.8 | 116.0 | 130.5 | 137.0 | Февраль |
| March | 1,724.0 | .. | 107.4 | 110.0 | 140.2 | 151.0 | Март |
| April | 1,790.0 | .. | 108.5 | 110.0 | 152.1 | 167.0 | Апрель |
| May | 1,882.0 | .. | 106.9 | 107.0 | 162.7 | 178.0 | Май |
| June | 1,952.0 | .. | 106.0 | 108.0 | 172.4 | 193.0 | Июнь |
| July | 2,023.0 | .. | 105.3 | 108.0 | 181.6 | 208.0 | Июль |
| August | 2,118.0 | .. | 104.6 | 106.0 | 190.1 | 220.0 | Август |
| September | 2,346.0 | .. | 108.0 | 107.0 | 205.2 | 236.0 | Сентябрь |
| October | 3,065.0 | .. | 115.0 | 111.0 | 236.0 | 262.0 | Октябрь |
| November | 3,144.0 | .. | 114.6 | 113.0 | 270.5 | 295.0 | Ноябрь |
| December | 3,388.0 | .. | 116.4 | 113.0 | 315.1 | 333.0 | Декабрь |

## TABLE 7-1. Price indices and exchange rates
## ТАБЛИЦА 7-1. Индексы цен и обменный курс

| Year and month | National currency per U.S. dollar<br>Единиц нац. валюты за 1 доллар США | National currency per Russian ruble<br>Единиц нац. валюты за 1 российский рубль | Consumer price index (as a percent of the previous month)<br>Индекс потребительских цен (в % к предыдущему месяцу) | Producer price index (as a percent of the previous month)<br>Индекс цен производителей (в % к предыдущему месяцу) | Consumer price index (as a percent of the previous December)<br>Индекс потребительских цен (в % к декабрю прошлого года) | Producer price index (as a percent of the previous December)<br>Индекс цен производителей (в % к декабрю прошлого года) | Год и месяц |
|---|---|---|---|---|---|---|---|
| **1995** | | | | | | | **1995** |
| January | 3,836.0 | .. | 117.8 | 121.5 | 117.8 | 121.5 | Январь |
| February | 4,215.0 | .. | 111.0 | 116.9 | 130.8 | 142.0 | Февраль |
| March | 4,721.0 | .. | 108.9 | 110.7 | 142.4 | 157.3 | Март |
| April | 5,024.0 | .. | 108.5 | 114.8 | 154.5 | 180.6 | Апрель |
| May | 5,054.0 | .. | 107.9 | 108.9 | 166.7 | 196.6 | Май |
| June | 4,725.0 | .. | 106.7 | 106.1 | 177.8 | 208.5 | Июнь |
| July | 4,523.0 | .. | 105.4 | 106.7 | 187.4 | 222.5 | Июль |
| August | 4,415.0 | .. | 104.6 | 106.8 | 196.0 | 237.5 | Август |
| September | 4,472.0 | .. | 104.5 | 105.7 | 204.7 | 251.0 | Сентябрь |
| October | 4,501.0 | .. | 104.7 | 104.6 | 214.4 | 262.5 | Октябрь |
| November | 4,539.0 | .. | 104.5 | 102.9 | 224.1 | 270.0 | Ноябрь |
| December | 4,620.0 | .. | 103.2 | 101.8 | 231.3 | 275.0 | Декабрь |
| **1996** | | | | | | | **1996** |
| January | 4,689.0 | .. | 104.1 | 103.2 | 104.1 | 103.2 | Январь |
| February | 4,761.0 | .. | 102.8 | 102.7 | 107.0 | 106.1 | Февраль |
| March | 4,835.0 | .. | 102.8 | 102.6 | 110.0 | 108.8 | Март |
| April | 4,902.0 | .. | 102.2 | 102.4 | 112.4 | 111.4 | Апрель |
| May | 4,988.0 | .. | 101.6 | 101.1 | 114.2 | 112.6 | Май |
| June | .. | .. | .. | .. | .. | .. | Июнь |
| July | .. | .. | .. | .. | .. | .. | Июль |
| August | .. | .. | .. | .. | .. | .. | Август |
| September | .. | .. | .. | .. | .. | .. | Сентябрь |
| October | .. | .. | .. | .. | .. | .. | Октябрь |
| November | .. | .. | .. | .. | .. | .. | Ноябрь |
| December | .. | .. | .. | .. | .. | .. | Декабрь |

**TABLE 7-2. Monthly nominal wages by sector**

**ТАБЛИЦА 7-2. Среднемесячная денежная зарплата по отраслям**

| Sector | 1990 | 1991 | 1992 | 1993 | 1994 | 1995 | Сектора |
|---|---|---|---|---|---|---|---|
| **Nominal wages** | | | | | | | **Средняя номинальная заработная плата** |
| **Economy average** | 303 | 576 | 6,377 | 64,089 | 241,944 | 540,879 | **По народному хозяйству** |
| **Material sphere** | .. | .. | .. | .. | .. | .. | **Отрасли сферы материального производства** |
| Industry | 311 | 639 | 7,498 | 70,284 | 256,143 | 639,470 | Промышленность |
| Construction | 376 | 742 | 8,716 | 89,695 | 346,225 | 783,014 | Строительство |
| Agriculture | 289 | 473 | 4,292 | 38,668 | 120,385 | 252,569 | Сельское хозяйство |
| Transport | 349 | 678 | 9,133 | 93,878 | 354,403 | 826,563 | Транспорт |
| Communications | 257 | 552 | 5,954 | 69,334 | 299,483 | 646,925 | Связь |
| Trade (retail and wholesale) | 258 | 514 | 5,433 | 51,815 | 206,990 | 430,663 | Торговля (оптовая и розничная) |
| Other | 343 | 450 | 5,750 | 59,394 | 283,013 | 427,161 | Прочие отрасли материального производства |
| **Nonmaterial sphere** | .. | .. | .. | .. | .. | .. | **Отрасли непроизводственной сферы** |
| Municipal services | 224 | 465 | 5,384 | 60,341 | 240,764 | 598,613 | Жилкомхоз и бытовое обслуживание |
| Science, research and development | 352 | 556 | 4,273 | 47,827 | 207,303 | 406,468 | Наука и научное обслуживание |
| Education | 203 | 407 | 3,946 | 43,493 | 165,142 | 336,323 | Образование |
| Culture | 188 | 402 | 3,468 | 41,260 | 161,065 | 337,286 | Культура |
| Arts | .. | .. | .. | .. | .. | .. | Искусство |
| Health care, social security, and sports | 203 | 427 | 4,170 | 47,395 | 180,559 | 371,130 | Здравоохр., соц.обсл., физк. и спорт |
| Banking, finance, credit, insurance | 410 | 795 | 14,709 | 181,766 | 605,440 | 1,098,100 | Кредитование, страхование, банк. дело |
| Government | 364 | 538 | 5,966 | 76,553 | 303,662 | 672,707 | Управление |

**TABLE 8-1. Money income and expenditure of the population (millions of national currency)**
**ТАБЛИЦА 8-1. Денежные доходы и расходы населения (млн. национальной валюты)**

| Type of income or expenditure | 1990 | 1991 | 1992 | 1993 | 1994 | 1995 | Вид доходов или расходов |
|---|---|---|---|---|---|---|---|
| **Income** | | | | | | | **Доходы** |
| **Total labor income** | 307,094 | 553,442 | 5,400,743 | 52,425,176 | 196,028,603 | .. | **Всего трудовых доходов** |
| Regular wages | 271,511 | 475,153 | 4,732,628 | 46,372,851 | 169,847,798 | .. | Заработная плата |
| Wages paid by cooperatives | 19,371 | 21,161 | 71,002 | .. | .. | .. | Заработная плата в кооперативах |
| Other wages and compensation | 8,801 | 23,774 | 160,196 | 1,900,957 | 14,838,209 | .. | Прочие доходы типа заработной платы |
| Income paid by collective farms | 12,448 | 20,183 | 228,177 | .. | .. | .. | Доходы от колхозов |
| Income from sale of farm products | 14,334 | 34,332 | 279,742 | 4,151,368 | 11,342,596 | .. | Доходы от продажи продукции колхозов |
| **Total transfer receipts** | 76,076 | 277,013 | 1,699,204 | 27,523,816 | 168,805,505 | .. | **Всего трансфертных поступлений** |
| Pensions and allowances | 48,226 | 124,646 | 959,893 | 11,594,572 | 47,858,573 | .. | Пенсии и пособия |
| Scholarships | 1,695 | 4,593 | 33,989 | 249,964 | 809,474 | .. | Стипендии |
| Income from the financial system (insurance, interest, etc.) | 17,492 | 118,816 | 185,125 | 4,050,028 | 30,854,202 | .. | Доходы из финансовой системы (страховые возмещения, проценты и т.д.) |
| Other income | 8,663 | 28,958 | 520,197 | 11,629,252 | 89,283,256 | .. | Прочие виды доходов |
| **Total income** | 383,170 | 830,455 | 7,099,947 | 79,948,992 | 364,834,108 | 942,354,300 | **Всего доходов** |
| **Expenditure** | | | | | | | **Расходы** |
| **Total purchases** | 288,311 | 517,460 | 5,174,750 | 55,066,442 | 235,427,022 | 663,757,900 | **Всего покупок товаров и услуг** |
| Retail goods | 257,961 | 463,159 | 4,754,400 | 49,052,233 | 202,551,358 | 543,324,900 | Товары в розничной торговле |
| Services | 30,350 | 54,301 | 420,350 | 6,014,209 | 32,875,664 | 120,433,000 | Услуги |
| Rent and utilities | 8,207 | 9,132 | 66,158 | 600,122 | 4,489,406 | 16,445,984 | Квартирная плата и коммунальные платежи |
| Transport and communications | 12,396 | 21,003 | 134,693 | 2,226,800 | 12,542,537 | 45,946,915 | Транспорт и связь |
| Health and other services | 8,301 | 23,467 | 217,121 | 3,187,287 | 15,843,721 | 58,040,101 | Здравоохранение и другие виды услуг |
| Cooperatives | 1,446 | 699 | 2,378 | .. | .. | .. | Кооперативы |
| **Transfers and savings** | 75,622 | 231,633 | 957,446 | 17,473,077 | 113,017,874 | 245,451,900 | **Трансферты и сбережения** |
| Taxes, fees, dues, and other | 31,242 | 42,442 | 434,932 | 4,741,493 | 19,188,207 | 48,789,339 | Налоги, сборы, пошлины и др. |
| Savings | 28,888 | 162,872 | 337,724 | 11,370,845 | 88,233,710 | 181,978,000 | Сбережения |
| Other | 15,492 | 26,319 | 184,790 | 1,360,739 | 5,595,957 | 14,684,561 | Прочие |
| **Total expenditure** | 363,933 | 749,093 | 6,132,196 | 72,539,519 | 348,444,896 | 909,209,800 | **Всего расходов** |
| **Income less expenditure** | 19,237 | 81,362 | 967,751 | 7,409,473 | 16,389,212 | 33,144,500 | **Доходы за вычетом расходов** |

# *Country Notes: Russian Federation*

**General Note:** Unless otherwise indicated, the data were supplied by the State Committee on Statistics for the Russian Federation.

**Currency:** Ruble.

**Table 1-1:** Data are from the balance of labor resources and are reported as of the end of each year. Data for unemployed in 1991 and 1992 are calculated using a different methodology and may have a downward bias. In 1992-1994 total employment does not equal the sum of the entries. In 1994 total labor resources as well as labor force do not equal the sum of the entries. In 1993 and 1994 lease enterprises include joint-stock companies and economic associations.

**Table 1-2:** Transport includes maintenance of roads and communication servicing material production. Retail trade and catering includes wholesale trade, material supply, and procurement. Passenger transport includes communication. Housing includes public utilities and personal services. Credit includes insurance. Education is included with culture and arts.

**Table 2-1:** The sum of the entries in the breakdown of category Other is not equal to the total due to missing information. The statistical discrepancy between total GDP by industrial origin at market prices and total GDP by expenditure category is as follows:

| Year | Statistical discrepancy (bln. rubles) |
|---|---|
| 1990 | 4.3 |
| 1991 | 31.9 |
| 1992 | 565.5 |
| 1993 | 1,752.6 |
| 1994 | -12,420.9 |
| 1995 | 30,934.4 |

**Table 2-2:** Data are in previous year prices.

**Table 3-1:** Data for 1991-1993 refers to countries outside CIS. Data for 1994 are the World Bank and IMF staff estimates. Data for 1995 are from the Monthly Report of the Central Bank of the Russian Federation. Other long-term capital inflows include the balance on assets, liabilities in national currency and deposits, liabilities to enterprises in other FSU states, and miscellaneous other liabilities. Portfolio investment is included as net short-term capital, and migrant transfers are included as capital flows not elsewhere included.

**Table 3-2A:** Data for 1992 and 1993 refers to countries outside CIS. Data for 1994 and 1995 excludes services. Arms and ammunition in the table 3-3A do not include procurement for the needs of military and technical cooperation.

**Table 3-4A:** Former Yugoslavia includes Bosnia and Herzegovina, Croatia, Macedonia, Montenegro, Serbia, and Slovenia. For 1992 Czech Republic data include Slovakia.

**Table 5-1:** Beginning in 1992, total gross agricultural product includes agricultural services.

**Table 5-2:** Data for 1990-1994 are in 1983 rubles, for 1995 - in 1994 rubles.

**Table 5-4:** Data for livestock are end of year data. Meat production is expressed in weight at slaughtering.

**Table 6-2:** Data are in 1992 prices.

**Table 6-3:** Nuclear energy supply includes hydro/geothermal.

**Table 7-2:** Data include social transfers. Since 1993 culture includes art. Data for 1995 are preliminary.

**Table 8-1:** Total income for 1995 is a preliminary estimate.

# *Комментарии к таблицам: Российская Федерация*

**Общее замечание:** За исключением особо отмеченных случаев, все данные, используемые в таблицах, были получены из Государственного Комитета Российской Федерации по Статистике.

**Национальная валюта:** Рубль.

**Таблица 1-1:** Данные взяты из баланса трудовых ресурсов и приведены на конец года. Число безработных за 1991 г. и 1992 г. рассчитано различными методами и может быть занижено. В 1992-94 гг. общая численность занятых не совпадает с суммой компонентов. В 1994 г. общая численность трудовых ресурсов и рабочая сила не совпадают с суммами компонентов. В 1993-94 гг. арендные предприятия включают акционерные общества и хозяйственные ассоциации.

**Таблица 1-2:** Транспорт включает также дорожное хозяйство и связь в части обслуживания материального производства. Розничная торговля включает также оптовую торговлю, материально-техническое снабжение и заготовки. Пассажирский транспорт включает также связь. Кредитование и страхование приведены вместе. Жилищное хозяйство включает также коммунальное хозяйство и бытовое обслуживание. Образование включено в культуру и искусство.

**Таблица 2-1:** Сумма компонентов по разделу Другие отрасли не совпадает с итогом вследствие отсутствия данных. Статистическое расхождени между ВВП по производству в рыночных ценах и ВВП по видам расходов составляет в млрд. рублей:1990 г.: 4,3; 1991 г.: 31,9; 1992 г.: 565,5; 1993 г.: 1 752,6; 1994 г.: -12 420,9; 1995 г.: 30 934,4.

**Таблица 2-2:** Данные приведены в ценах предыдущего года.

**Таблица 3-1:** За 1991-93 гг. данные приводятся только для стран за пределами СНГ. За 1994 г. приводится консолидированный платежный баланс России по данным Всемирного Банка и МВФ. За 1995 г. консолидированный платежный баланс приводится по данным Центрального Банка Российской Федерации. Другие чистые долгосрочные притоки капитала включают баланс активов, пассивы в национальной валюте и во вкладах, задолженность к предприятиям других стран бывшего Советского Союза, а также прочие пассивы. Портфельные инвестиции включены в чистый краткосрочный капитал, а капитальные трансферты иностранцам включены в потоки капитала, не учтенные выше.

**Таблицы 3-2А и 3-3А:** Данные за 1992-93 гг. приводятся только для стран за пределами СНГ. Данные за 1994-95г г. приводятся без учета услуг. Раздел Оружие и боеприпасы в таблице 3-3А не включает поставки в рамках договоров о военно-техническом сотрудничестве.

**Таблица 3-4А:** Бывшая Югославия включает Боснию и Герцеговину, Македонию, Словению, Хорватию и Югославию (Сербия и Черногория). В 1992 г. данные о торговле с Чешской Республикой и со Словакией приведены вместе.

**Таблица 5-1:** Начиная с 1992 г., валовая продукция сельского хозяйства-всего включает также сельскохозяйственные услуги.

**Таблица 5-2:** Данные за 1990-94 гг. приведены в ценах 1983 г., а за 1995 г. - в ценах 1994 г.

**Таблица 5-4:** Численность скота приведена по состоянию на конец года. Производство мяса показано в убойном весе.

**Таблица 6-2:** Данные приведены в ценах 1992 г.

**Таблица 6-3:** Атомная энергетика включает гидро/геотермальную. В 1994 г. сумма компонентов производства первичной энергии не равна итогу.

**Таблица 7-2:** Данные приведены с учетом выплат социального характера. Начиная с 1993г. культура включает искусство. За 1995 г. приведены предварительные данные.

**Таблица 8-1:** За 1995 г. приведены предварительные данные о доходах.

# Tajikistan / Таджикистан

1996 Population / Численность населения в 1996 году
(thousands / тыс. человек): 5,884

Area / Территория
(thousand square kilometers / тыс. кв. км.): 143.1

Capital city / Столица :
Dushanbe / Душанбе

**Country Tables:** Tables 2-2 to 2-2B, as well as 3-2B, 3-3B, 3-4B, 5-1 and 5-2 are not included because there are either no data available or no recent data available.

**Статистические таблицы страны:** Таблицы с 2-2 по 2-2B, а также 3-2B, 3-3B, 3-4B, 5-1 и 5-2 не включены ввиду полного отсутствия данных или отсутствия данных за последние годы.

**TABLE 1-1. Population and employment (thousands)**
**ТАБЛИЦА 1-1. Население и занятость (тысяч)**



| Population or employment category | 1990 | 1991 | 1992 | 1993 | 1994 | 1995 | Население или группы занятых |
|---|---|---|---|---|---|---|---|
| **Total population** | 5,232 | 5,342 | 5,555 | 5,556 | 5,688 | 5,757 | **Население - всего** |
| Males | 2,600 | 2,652 | 2,764 | 2,766 | 2,834 | .. | Мужчины |
| Females | 2,632 | 2,690 | 2,791 | 2,790 | 2,854 | .. | Женщины |
| Urban population | 1,676 | 1,668 | 1,689 | 1,636 | 1,625 | 1,611 | Городское |
| Rural population | 3,556 | 3,674 | 3,866 | 3,920 | 4,063 | 4,146 | Сельское |
| Population under working age | 2,364 | 2,425 | 2,525 | 2,543 | 2,619 | .. | Моложе трудоспособного возраста |
| Working-age population | 2,470 | 2,509 | 2,610 | 2,601 | 2,655 | .. | Лица в трудоспособном возрасте |
| Population over working age | 398 | 408 | 420 | 412 | 414 | .. | Старше трудоспособного возраста |
| Economically Active Population, in non-working age | 55 | 55 | 111 | 118 | 134 | .. | Экономически активное население в нетрудоспособном возрасте |
| Above working age | 48 | 48 | 83 | 91 | 106 | .. | Старше трудоспособного возраста |
| Below working age | 7 | 7 | 28 | 27 | 28 | .. | Моложе трудоспособного возраста |
| **Total labor resources** | 2,469 | 2,526 | 2,669 | 2,688 | 2,746 | .. | **Трудовые ресурсы - всего** |
| **Total employment** | 1,934 | 1,969 | 1,908 | 1,854 | 1,844 | .. | **Занятое население - всего** |
| State sector employees | .. | 1,073 | 998 | 978 | 924 | .. | Государственный сектор |
| Leased enterprise employees | .. | 86 | 83 | .. | .. | .. | Арендные предприятия |
| Joint-stock company employees | .. | 2 | 26 | .. | .. | .. | Акционерные общества |
| Economic association employees | .. | 11 | .. | .. | .. | .. | Хозяйственные ассоциации |
| Social organization employees | .. | 13 | 10 | 9 | 5 | .. | Общественные организации |
| Joint venture employees | .. | 1 | 1 | 2 | 3 | .. | Совместные предприятия |
| Collective farm workers | 263 | 293 | 285 | 296 | 334 | .. | Колхозы |
| Cooperative workers | 52 | 52 | 49 | 33 | 38 | .. | Кооперативы |
| Individual labor activities | 3 | 3 | 2 | 2 | 2 | .. | ИТД |
| Private subsidiary agricultural workers | 366 | 373 | 399 | 427 | 453 | .. | Личные подсобные хозяйства |
| Private agricultural workers | .. | .. | .. | .. | .. | .. | Фермерские хозяйства |
| **Students** | 231 | 237 | 230 | 220 | 204 | .. | **Учащиеся** |
| **Religious workers** | 1 | 1 | 1 | 1 | 1 | .. | **Служащие религиозного культа** |
| **Working age population not employed in the national economy** | 299 | 318 | 530 | 596 | 697 | .. | **Лица в трудоспособном возрасте, не занятые в экономике** |
| Housewives | .. | .. | .. | .. | .. | .. | Домохозяйки |
| Military personnel | .. | .. | .. | .. | .. | .. | Военнослужащие |
| Unemployed | .. | .. | 4 | 16 | 28 | .. | Безработные |
| **Labor force** | .. | .. | 1,912 | 1,861 | 1,872 | .. | **Рабочая сила** |

## TABLE 1-2. Employment by sector (thousands)
## ТАБЛИЦА 1-2. Численность занятого населения по секторам (тысяч)

| Sector | 1990 | 1991 | 1992 | 1993 | 1994 | 1995 | Сектор |
|---|---|---|---|---|---|---|---|
| **Material sphere** | 1,473 | 1,500 | 1,459 | 1,452 | 1,490 | .. | **Сфера материального производства** |
| **Agriculture and forestry** | 833 | 881 | 892 | 949 | 1,005 | .. | **Сельское и лесное хозяйство** |
| Agriculture | 831 | 878 | 889 | 946 | 1,002 | .. | Сельское хозяйство |
| Forestry | 2 | 3 | 3 | 3 | 3 | .. | Лесное хозяйство |
| **Industry and construction** | 422 | 404 | 382 | 335 | 310 | .. | **Промышленность и строительство** |
| Industry | 261 | 257 | 250 | 219 | 205 | .. | Промышленность |
| Construction | 161 | 148 | 132 | 116 | 105 | .. | Строительство |
| **Other** | 219 | 215 | 185 | 168 | 148 | .. | **Другие отрасли** |
| Transport of goods | 54 | 55 | 48 | 40 | 40 | .. | Грузовой транспорт |
| Road Maintenance | 7 | 7 | 6 | 6 | .. | .. | Дорожное хозяйство |
| Communication servicing material production | 3 | 3 | 2 | 2 | 2 | .. | Связь |
| Wholesale trade | 79 | 79 | 72 | 69 | 89 | .. | Оптовая торговля |
| Retail trade and catering | .. | .. | .. | .. | .. | .. | Розничная торговля и общепит |
| Material supply | 16 | 17 | 15 | 9 | .. | .. | Материально-техническое снабжение |
| Procurement | 13 | 12 | 9 | 9 | .. | .. | Заготовки |
| Information and computing services | 4 | 3 | 2 | 2 | 1 | .. | Информационно-техническое обслуживание |
| Other sectors | 43 | 40 | 31 | 31 | 16 | .. | Другие отрасли сферы материального пр. |
| **Nonmaterial sphere** | 462 | 469 | 449 | 402 | 375 | .. | **Сфера нематериального производства** |
| Passenger transport | 19 | 19 | 18 | 16 | 14 | .. | Пассажирский транспорт |
| Communication | 9 | 9 | 9 | 8 | 7 | .. | Связь |
| Housing | 16 | 16 | 16 | 12 | 27 | .. | Жилищное хозяйство |
| Public utilities and personal services | 35 | 35 | 28 | 25 | .. | .. | Комм. хоз. и бытовое обслуживание |
| Health care, social security, physical culture and sports | 104 | 106 | 110 | 103 | 100 | .. | Здравоохранение, социальное обеспечение, физкультура и спорт |
| Education | 189 | 197 | 200 | 188 | 175 | .. | Образование |
| Culture and art | 28 | 25 | 19 | 18 | 17 | .. | Культура и искусство |
| Science and scientific research | 16 | 15 | 13 | 5 | 7 | .. | Наука и научное обслуживание |
| Credit | .. | .. | .. | .. | .. | .. | Кредитование |
| Insurance | 6 | 6 | 6 | 6 | 7 | .. | Страхование |
| General administration and defense | 40 | 41 | 30 | 21 | 21 | .. | Государственное управление и оборона |
| Private nonprofit institutions serving households | .. | .. | .. | .. | .. | .. | Общественные организации, обслуживающие домашние хозяйства |
| **Other, material and nonmaterial spheres** | 680 | 684 | 634 | 570 | 503 | .. | **Остальные отрасли материального производства и нематериальной сферы** |
| **Total employment** | 1,934 | 1,969 | 1,908 | 1,854 | 1,844 | .. | **Занятые - всего** |

## TABLE 1-3. Registered unemployment (thousands; end of month)

**ТАБЛИЦА 1-3. Численность зарегистрированных безработных (тысяч; на конец месяца)**

| Year and month | Total Всего | Males Мужчины | Females Женщины | Receiving benefits Получающие пособие | Год и месяц |
|---|---|---|---|---|---|
| **1994** | | | | | **1994** |
| January | 22.7 | .. | .. | 4.1 | Январь |
| February | 25.2 | .. | .. | 4.6 | Февраль |
| March | 26.8 | 15.2 | 11.5 | 4.2 | Март |
| April | 27.4 | .. | .. | 4.8 | Апрель |
| May | 27.7 | .. | .. | 6.0 | Май |
| June | 28.0 | 15.3 | 12.7 | 2.8 | Июнь |
| July | 27.7 | .. | .. | 4.8 | Июль |
| August | 27.3 | .. | .. | 4.8 | Август |
| September | 29.6 | 16.2 | 13.4 | 4.9 | Сентябрь |
| October | 30.3 | .. | .. | 5.2 | Октябрь |
| November | 30.7 | .. | .. | 5.4 | Ноябрь |
| December | 31.8 | 17.2 | 14.6 | 3.8 | Декабрь |
| **1995** | | | | | **1995** |
| January | 34.5 | .. | .. | 1.0 | Январь |
| February | 37.9 | .. | .. | 1.4 | Февраль |
| March | 30.6 | 16.8 | 13.8 | 7.6 | Март |
| April | 29.8 | .. | .. | 8.4 | Апрель |
| May | 32.1 | .. | .. | 6.6 | Май |
| June | 30.9 | 16.8 | 14.1 | 10.3 | Июнь |
| July | 29.9 | .. | .. | 13.6 | Июль |
| August | 30.7 | .. | .. | 9.9 | Август |
| September | 35.1 | 20.5 | 14.6 | 9.9 | Сентябрь |
| October | 30.5 | .. | .. | 3.6 | Октябрь |
| November | 34.7 | .. | .. | 5.0 | Ноябрь |
| December | 37.5 | 20.2 | 17.3 | 3.8 | Декабрь |
| **1996** | | | | | **1996** |
| January | 38.3 | 20.8 | 17.5 | 1.4 | Январь |
| February | 39.0 | 21.2 | 17.8 | 0.8 | Февраль |
| March | 42.1 | 21.7 | 20.4 | 4.0 | Март |
| April | 46.9 | 21.4 | 25.5 | 3.3 | Апрель |
| May | .. | .. | .. | .. | Май |
| June | .. | .. | .. | .. | Июнь |
| July | .. | .. | .. | .. | Июль |
| August | .. | .. | .. | .. | Август |
| September | .. | .. | .. | .. | Сентябрь |
| October | .. | .. | .. | .. | Октябрь |
| November | .. | .. | .. | .. | Ноябрь |
| December | .. | .. | .. | .. | Декабрь |

## TABLE 2-1. Gross domestic product at current prices (millions of national currency)
## ТАБЛИЦА 2-1. Валовой внутренний продукт в текущих ценах (млн. национальной валюты)

| Sector of origin or expenditure category | 1990 | 1991 | 1992 | 1993 | 1994 | 1995 | Отраслевое происхождение или вид расходов |
|---|---|---|---|---|---|---|---|
| **Gross domestic product by sector of origin** | | | | | | | **Валовой внутренний продукт по отраслевому происхождению** |
| **Agriculture and forestry** | .. | .. | 18,841 | 148,340 | 326,040 | 14,047 | **Сельское и лесное хозяйство** |
| Agriculture | .. | .. | 18,802 | 147,884 | .. | .. | Сельское хозяйство |
| Forestry | .. | .. | 39 | 456 | .. | .. | Лесное хозяйство |
| **Industry and construction** | .. | .. | 31,597 | 295,253 | 801,746 | 27,982 | **Промышленность и строительство** |
| Industry | .. | .. | 25,334 | 231,724 | 595,219 | 22,872 | Промышленность |
| Construction | .. | .. | 6,262 | 63,529 | 206,527 | 5,110 | Строительство |
| **Other** | .. | .. | 22,281 | 196,080 | 590,192 | 22,814 | **Другие отрасли** |
| Transport | .. | .. | 3,194 | 7,634 | 58,393 | 1,594 | Транспорт |
| Road maintenance | .. | .. | .. | .. | .. | .. | Дорожное хозяйство |
| Communication | .. | .. | .. | 1,539 | .. | .. | Связь |
| Wholesale trade | .. | .. | .. | .. | .. | .. | Оптовая торговля |
| Retail trade and catering | .. | .. | 2,238 | 23,437 | 23,741 | 2,786 | Розничная торговля и общепит |
| Material supply | .. | .. | 532 | 11,101 | 13,141 | 576 | Материально-техническое снабжение |
| Procurement | .. | .. | 696 | 6,487 | 15,097 | 644 | Заготовки |
| Information and computing services | .. | .. | 136 | 218 | .. | .. | Информационно-вычислительное обслуживание |
| Other sectors of material production | .. | .. | 528 | 5,839 | 46,834 | 1,240 | Другие отрасли сферы материального пр. |
| Housing | .. | .. | 483 | 3,030 | .. | .. | Жилищное хозяйство |
| Public utilities and personal services | .. | .. | 1,703 | 41,014 | .. | .. | Ком. хоз. и бытовое обслуживание |
| Health care, social security, physical culture and sports | .. | .. | 2,048 | 21,648 | .. | .. | Здравоохранение, социальное обеспечение, физкультура и спорт |
| Education | .. | .. | 4,468 | 44,537 | .. | .. | Образование |
| Culture and art | .. | .. | 169 | 7,548 | .. | .. | Культура и искусство |
| Science and scientific research | .. | .. | 647 | 1,238 | .. | .. | Наука и научное обслуживание |
| Credit | .. | .. | 3,141 | 2,648 | .. | .. | Кредитование |
| Insurance | .. | .. | .. | .. | .. | .. | Страхование |
| General administration and defense | .. | .. | 2,222 | 18,162 | .. | .. | Государственное управление и оборона |
| Private nonprofit institutions serving households | .. | .. | 75 | .. | .. | .. | Общественные организации, обслуживающие домашние хозяйства |
| **Imputed service charge of financial intermediaries** | .. | .. | -3,167 | -30,725 | .. | .. | **Условно-исчисляемая стоимость услуг финансовых посредников** |
| **Total gross value added (GVA)** | .. | .. | 69,551 | 608,948 | 1,717,978 | 64,843 | **Валовая добавленная стоимость (ВДС) - всего** |
| **Taxes on production and imports (TOPI)** | .. | .. | 6,612 | 129,197 | .. | .. | **Налоги на производство и импорт (НПиИ)** |
| Other taxes on production (OTOP) | .. | .. | .. | .. | .. | .. | Другие налоги на производство (ДНП) |
| **Subsidies on production and imports (SOPI)** | .. | .. | 11,676 | 59,126 | .. | .. | **Субсидии на производство и импорт (СПиИ)** |
| Other subsidies on production (OSOP) | .. | .. | .. | .. | .. | .. | Другие субсидии на производство (ДСП) |
| **Total GDP at factor cost (GVA-OTOP+OSOP)** | .. | .. | 69,551 | 608,948 | .. | .. | **Всего ВВП по фактр. стоимости (ВДС-ДНП+ДСП)** |
| **Net Indirect taxes (TOPI - SOPI)** | .. | .. | -5,064 | 70,071 | .. | .. | **Чистые косвенные налоги (НПиИ-СПиИ)** |
| **Total GDP at market prices** | 7,347 | 13,407 | 64,487 | 679,019 | 1,717,978 | 64,843 | **Всего ВВП в рыночных ценах** |
| **Gross domestic product by expenditure category** | | | | | | | **Валовой внутренний продукт по видам расходов** |
| **Consumption** | .. | .. | .. | .. | .. | .. | **Потребление** |
| Private consumption | .. | .. | .. | .. | .. | .. | Личное потребление |
| Government consumption | .. | .. | .. | .. | .. | .. | Общественное потребление |
| **Gross domestic investment** | .. | .. | .. | .. | .. | .. | **Валовые внутренние инвестиции** |
| Gross fixed investment | .. | .. | .. | .. | .. | .. | Валовое накопление основного капитала |
| Change in stocks | .. | .. | .. | .. | .. | .. | Изменения в запасах (МОС) |
| **Resource balance (net exports of GNFS)** | .. | .. | .. | .. | .. | .. | **Сальдо ресурсов (чистый экспорт ТНФУ)** |
| Exports of goods and nonfactor services | .. | .. | .. | .. | .. | .. | Экспорт товаров и нефакторных услуг |
| Imports of goods and nonfactor services | .. | .. | .. | .. | .. | .. | Импорт товаров и нефакторных услуг |

**TABLE 2-1A. Distribution of gross domestic product at current prices (percent)**

**ТАБЛИЦА 2-1А. Распределение валового внутреннего продукта в текущих ценах ( % )**

| Sector of origin or expenditure category | 1990 | 1991 | 1992 | 1993 | 1994 | 1995 | Отраслевое происхождение или вид расходов |
|---|---|---|---|---|---|---|---|
| **Gross domestic product by sector of origin** | | | | | | | **ВВП по отраслевому происхождению** |
| **Agriculture and forestry** | .. | .. | 29.2 | 21.8 | 19.0 | 21.7 | **Сельское и лесное хозяйство** |
| Agriculture | .. | .. | 29.2 | 21.8 | .. | .. | Сельское хозяйство |
| Forestry | .. | .. | 0.1 | 0.1 | .. | .. | Лесное хозяйство |
| **Industry and construction** | .. | .. | 49.0 | 43.5 | 46.7 | 43.2 | **Промышленность и строительство** |
| Industry | .. | .. | 39.3 | 34.1 | 34.6 | 35.3 | Промышленность |
| Construction | .. | .. | 9.7 | 9.4 | 12.0 | 7.9 | Строительство |
| **Other** | .. | .. | 34.6 | 28.9 | .. | .. | **Другие отрасли** |
| Transport | .. | .. | 5.0 | 1.1 | 3.4 | 2.5 | Транспорт |
| Road maintenance | .. | .. | .. | .. | .. | .. | Дорожное хозяйство |
| Communication | .. | .. | .. | 0.2 | .. | .. | Связь |
| Wholesale trade | .. | .. | .. | .. | .. | .. | Оптовая торговля |
| Retail trade and catering | .. | .. | 3.5 | 3.5 | 1.4 | 4.3 | Розничная торговля и общепит |
| Material supply | .. | .. | 0.8 | 1.6 | 0.8 | 0.9 | Материально-техническое снабжение |
| Procurement | .. | .. | 1.1 | 1.0 | 0.9 | 1.0 | Заготовки |
| Information and computing services | .. | .. | 0.2 | 0.0 | .. | .. | Информационно-вычислительное обслуживание |
| Other sectors of material production | .. | .. | 0.8 | 0.9 | 2.7 | 1.9 | Другие отрасли сферы матерл. произ. |
| Housing | .. | .. | 0.7 | 0.4 | .. | .. | Жилищное хозяйство |
| Public utilities and personal services | .. | .. | 2.6 | 6.0 | .. | .. | Ком. хоз. и бытовое обслуживание |
| Health care, social security, physical culture and sports | .. | .. | 3.2 | 3.2 | .. | .. | Здравоохранение, социальное обеспечение, физкультура и спорт |
| Education | .. | .. | 6.9 | 6.6 | .. | .. | Образование |
| Culture and art | .. | .. | 0.3 | 1.1 | .. | .. | Культура и искусство |
| Science and scientific research | .. | .. | 1.0 | 0.2 | .. | .. | Наука и научное обслуживание |
| Credit | .. | .. | 4.9 | 0.4 | .. | .. | Кредитование |
| Insurance | .. | .. | 0.0 | 0.0 | .. | .. | Страхование |
| General administration and defense | .. | .. | 3.4 | 2.7 | .. | .. | Государственное управление и оборона |
| Private nonprofit institutions serving households | .. | .. | 0.1 | .. | .. | .. | Общественные организации, обслуживаю-щие домашние хозяйства |
| **Imputed service charge of financial intermediaries** | .. | .. | -4.9 | -4.5 | .. | .. | **Условно-исчисляемая стоимость услуг финансовых посредников** |
| **Total gross value added** | .. | .. | 107.9 | 89.7 | 100.0 | 100.0 | **Валовая добавленная стоимость - всего** |
| **Total GDP at factor cost** | .. | .. | 107.9 | 89.7 | .. | .. | **ВВП по фактор. стоимости - всего** |
| **Net indirect taxes** | .. | .. | -7.9 | 10.3 | .. | .. | **Чистые косвенные налоги (НПиИ-СПиИ)** |
| **Total GDP at market prices** | 100.0 | 100.0 | 100.0 | 100.0 | 100.0 | 100.0 | **ВВП в рын. ценах - всего** |
| **Gross domestic product by expenditure category** | | | | | | | **ВВП по видам расходов** |
| **Consumption** | .. | .. | .. | .. | .. | .. | **Потребление** |
| Private consumption | .. | .. | .. | .. | .. | .. | Личное потребление |
| Government consumption | .. | .. | .. | .. | .. | .. | Общественное потребление |
| **Gross domestic investment** | .. | .. | .. | .. | .. | .. | **Вал. внутр. инвестиции** |
| Gross fixed investment | .. | .. | .. | .. | .. | .. | Вал. накопление осн. капитала |
| Change in stocks | .. | .. | .. | .. | .. | .. | Изменения в запасах (МОС) |
| **Resource balance (net exports of GNFS)** | .. | .. | .. | .. | .. | .. | **Сальдо ресурсов (чистый экспорт ТНФУ)** |
| Exports of goods and nonfactor services | .. | .. | .. | .. | .. | .. | Экспорт товаров и нефакторных услуг |
| Imports of goods and nonfactor services | .. | .. | .. | .. | .. | .. | Импорт товаров и нефакторных услуг |

## TABLE 3-1. Balance of payments at current prices (millions of U.S. dollars)
## ТАБЛИЦА 3-1. Платежный баланс в текущих ценах (в миллионах долларов США)

| Item | 1990 | 1991 | 1992 | 1993 | 1994 | 1995 | Статьи |
|---|---|---|---|---|---|---|---|
| Exports of goods and services (including workers' remittances) | .. | .. | 186.8 | 452.2 | 513.9 | .. | Экспорт товаров и услуг (включая денежные переводы рабочих) |
| Exports of goods and nonfactor services | .. | .. | 184.8 | 452.2 | 512.0 | .. | Экспорт товаров и нефакт. услуг |
| Merchandise (FOB) | .. | .. | 184.8 | 452.2 | 512.0 | .. | Товары (ФОБ) |
| Nonfactor services | .. | .. | .. | .. | .. | .. | Нефакторные услуги |
| Shipment | .. | .. | .. | .. | .. | .. | Перевозки |
| Travel | .. | .. | .. | .. | .. | .. | Поездки |
| Other | .. | .. | .. | .. | .. | .. | Другие |
| Imports of goods and nonfactor services | .. | .. | 239.6 | 660.3 | 621.1 | .. | Импорт товаров и нефакт. услуг |
| Merchandise (FOB) | .. | .. | 239.6 | 660.3 | 621.1 | .. | Товары (ФОБ) |
| Nonfactor services | .. | .. | .. | .. | .. | .. | Нефакторные услуги |
| Shipment | .. | .. | .. | .. | .. | .. | Перевозки |
| Travel | .. | .. | .. | .. | .. | .. | Поездки |
| Other | .. | .. | .. | .. | .. | .. | Другие |
| Resource balance | .. | .. | -54.8 | -208.1 | -109.1 | .. | Сальдо ресурсов |
| Net factor income | .. | .. | 2.0 | -24.2 | -21.7 | .. | Чистый факторный доход |
| Factor receipts | .. | .. | 2.0 | 0.0 | 1.9 | .. | Факторные поступления |
| Factor payments | .. | .. | 0.0 | 24.2 | 23.6 | .. | Факторные платежи |
| Total interest due | .. | .. | 0.0 | 7.4 | 23.6 | .. | Общая сумма процента к оплате |
| Other factor payments and discrepancy | .. | .. | 0.0 | 16.8 | 0.0 | .. | Другие факторные платежи и стат. погр. |
| Net current transfers | .. | .. | 0.0 | 25.4 | 15.0 | .. | Чистые текущие трансферты |
| Current receipts | .. | .. | 0.0 | 25.4 | 15.0 | .. | Текущие поступления |
| Workers remittances | .. | .. | .. | .. | .. | .. | Денежные переводы рабочих |
| Other current transfers | .. | .. | 0.0 | 25.4 | 15.0 | .. | Другие текущие трансферты |
| Current payments | .. | .. | .. | .. | .. | .. | Текущие платежи |
| Current account balance before official grants | .. | .. | -52.8 | -206.9 | -115.8 | .. | Сальдо текущего счета до офиц. безвозмезд. трансфертов |
| Official capital grants | .. | .. | .. | .. | .. | .. | Официальные кап. безвозмезные трансферты |
| Current account balance after official grants | .. | .. | -52.8 | -206.9 | -115.8 | .. | Сальдо текущего счета после офиц. безвозмезд. трансфертов |
| Long Term Capital Inflows | .. | .. | 52.4 | 85.7 | 47.1 | .. | Долгосрочные притоки капитала |
| Direct investment | .. | .. | 8.0 | 9.0 | 12.0 | .. | Прямые инвестиции |
| Net long term borrowing | .. | .. | 44.4 | 76.7 | 35.1 | .. | Чистые долгосрочные займы |
| Disbursements | .. | .. | 44.4 | 76.7 | 39.5 | .. | Поступления |
| Repayments due | .. | .. | 0.0 | 0.0 | 4.4 | .. | Сумма, подлежащая погашению |
| Other long-term inflows (net) | .. | .. | .. | .. | .. | .. | Другие долгосрочные притоки (чистые) |

(continued on next page)

## TABLE 3-1. Balance of payments at current prices (millions of U.S. dollars)
## ТАБЛИЦА 3-1. Платежный баланс в текущих ценах (в миллионах долларов США)

| Item | 1990 | 1991 | 1992 | 1993 | 1994 | 1995 | Статьи |
|---|---|---|---|---|---|---|---|
| Adjustment to Scheduled Debt Service | .. | .. | -140.0 | 155.8 | 98.3 | .. | Регулирование долга |
| Debt service not paid | .. | .. | -140.0 | 62.1 | 0.0 | .. | Невыплаченный долг |
| Interest not paid | .. | .. | .. | .. | .. | .. | Невыплаченный процент |
| Principal not paid | .. | .. | .. | .. | .. | .. | Невыплаченная сумма основного долга |
| Arrears reductions/prepayments(-) | .. | .. | 0.0 | 93.7 | 98.3 | .. | Погашение просроченных платежей/выплаты авансом (-) |
| Total Other items (Net) | .. | .. | 140.4 | -31.7 | -29.5 | .. | Общие другие статьи (чистые) |
| Net short-term capital | .. | .. | .. | .. | .. | .. | Чистый краткосрочный капитал |
| Capital flows not elsewhere included | .. | .. | 0.0 | 6.2 | 14.4 | .. | Потоки капитала, не указанные выше |
| Errors and omissions | .. | .. | 140.4 | -37.9 | -43.9 | .. | Ошибки и пропуски |
| Changes in net reserves | .. | .. | 0.0 | -2.9 | -0.1 | .. | Изменения в чистых резервах |
| Net credit from IMF | .. | .. | 0.0 | 0.0 | 0.0 | .. | Чистый кредит МВФ |
| Reserve changes not elsewhere included | .. | .. | 0.0 | -2.9 | -0.1 | .. | Изменения резервов, не указанных выше |
| Escrow account | .. | .. | .. | .. | .. | .. | Счет депонирования |
| Gross reserves (excluding gold) | .. | .. | 1.0 | 4.0 | 4.1 | .. | Общие резервы (исключая золото) |
| Gross reserves (including gold) | .. | .. | .. | .. | .. | .. | Общие резервы (включая золото) |
| Nominal official exchange rate (annual average) (rf) | .. | .. | .. | .. | .. | .. | Номинальный официальный или рыночный курс (среднегодовой) |
| Nominal official exchange rate (end-of-year) (ae) | .. | .. | .. | .. | .. | .. | Номинальный официальный или рыночный курс (на конец года) |
| Manufacture unit value (percent change) | .. | .. | .. | .. | .. | .. | Средний индекс цен на продукцию обр. пром.,% |
| Index of real effective exchange rate (IMF) | .. | .. | .. | .. | .. | .. | Индекс реального эффективного валютного курса (МВФ) |
| Total factor payments | .. | .. | .. | .. | .. | .. | Общая сумма факторных платежей |
| Government interest | .. | .. | .. | .. | .. | .. | Процент, выплачиваемый органами гос. управления |
| Private sector interest | .. | .. | .. | .. | .. | .. | Процент выплачиваемый частным сектором |
| Profits on direct foreign investment | .. | .. | .. | .. | .. | .. | Прибыль от прямых иностранных инвестиций |
| Official capital grants | .. | .. | .. | .. | .. | .. | Официальные капитальные безвозмездные трансферты |
| For budgetary financing | .. | .. | .. | .. | .. | .. | На бюджетное финансирование |
| To extrabudgetary entities | .. | .. | .. | .. | .. | .. | На внебюджетное финансирование |
| Government net long term borrowing | .. | .. | .. | .. | .. | .. | Чистые долгосрочные государственные займы |
| Disbursements | .. | .. | .. | .. | .. | .. | Поступления |
| Repayments | .. | .. | .. | .. | .. | .. | Погашения |
| Private net long term borrowing | .. | .. | .. | .. | .. | .. | Чистые долгосрочные частные займы |
| Disbursements | .. | .. | .. | .. | .. | .. | Поступления |
| Repayments | .. | .. | .. | .. | .. | .. | Погашения |

## TABLE 3-2A. Imports by commodity group (millions of U.S. dollars)
## ТАБЛИЦА 3-2А . Импорт по товарным группам (млн. долларов США)

| Commodity group | 1990 | 1991 | 1992 | 1993 | 1994 | 1995 | Товарные группы |
|---|---|---|---|---|---|---|---|
| TOTAL | .. | .. | .. | .. | .. | 799.2 | ВСЕГО |
| I - Live animals; animal products | .. | .. | .. | .. | .. | .. | I - Живые животные и продукты животноводства |
| II - Vegetable products | .. | .. | .. | .. | .. | 48.7 | II - Продукты растительного происхождения |
| III - Animal or vegetable fats and oils and their cleavage products; prepared edible fats; animal or vegetable waxes | .. | .. | .. | .. | .. | 1.4 | III - Жиры и масла растительного и животного происхождения, воски |
| IV - Prepared foodstuffs; beverages, spirits and vinegar; tobacco and manufactured tobacco substitutes | .. | .. | .. | .. | .. | 5.8 | IV -Продукция пищевой промышленности, алкогольные и безалкогольные напитки, табак и его заменители |
| V - Mineral products | .. | .. | .. | .. | .. | 596.5 | V - Минеральные продукты |
| VI - Products of the chemical or allied industries | .. | .. | .. | .. | .. | 8.3 | VI - Продукция химической промышленности |
| VII - Plastics and articles thereof; rubber and articles thereof | .. | .. | .. | .. | .. | 4.4 | VII - Пластмассы и изделия из них |
| VIII - Raw hides and skins, leather, furskins and articles thereof; saddlery and harness; travel goods, handbags and similar containers; articles of animal gut | .. | .. | .. | .. | .. | 0.0 | VIII - Кожевенное сырьё, кожи, пушнина, меховое сырьё и изделия из них |
| IX - Wood and articles of wood; wood charcoal; cork and articles of cork; manufactures of straw, of esparto or of other plaiting materials; basketware and wickerwork | .. | .. | .. | .. | .. | 7.1 | IX - Древесина и изделия из древесины, древесный уголь |
| X - Pulp of wood or of other fibrous cellulosic material; waste and scrap of paper or paperboard; paper and paperboard and articles thereof | .. | .. | .. | .. | .. | 2.1 | X - Бумажная масса, бумажные и картонные отходы, макулатура, бумага, картон и изделия из них |
| XI - Textiles and textile articles | .. | .. | .. | .. | .. | 5.6 | XI - Текстиль и текстильные изделия |
| XII - Footwear, headgear, umbrellas, sun umbrellas, walking sticks, seat sticks, whips, riding crops and parts thereof; prepared feathers and articles made therewith; artificial flowers; articles of human hair | .. | .. | .. | .. | .. | 0.6 | XII - Обувь, головные уборы, зонты, трости и пр. |

## TABLE 3-2A. Imports by commodity group (millions of U.S. dollars)
## ТАБЛИЦА 3-2А . Импорт по товарным группам (млн. долларов США)

| Commodity group | 1990 | 1991 | 1992 | 1993 | 1994 | 1995 | Товарные группы |
|---|---|---|---|---|---|---|---|
| XIII - Articles of stone, plaster, cement, asbestos, mica and similar materials; ceramic products; glass and glassware | .. | .. | .. | .. | .. | 1.0 | XIII - Изделия из камня, гипса, цемента |
| XIV - Natural or cultured pearls, precious or semi-precious stones, precious metals, metals clad with precious metal and articles thereof; imitation jewellery; coin | .. | .. | .. | .. | .. | 0.0 | XIV - Жемчуг, драгоценные и полудрагоценные камни, драгоценные металлы, бижутерия, монеты |
| XV - Base metals and articles of base metal | .. | .. | .. | .. | .. | 12.8 | XV - Неблагородные металлы и изделия из них |
| XVI - Machinery and mechanical appliances; electrical equipment; parts thereof; sound recorders and reproducers, television image and sound recorders and reproducers, and parts and accessories of such articles | .. | .. | .. | .. | .. | 87.4 | XVI - Машины, оборудование, механизмы, их части и принадлежности; звуковая и теле-аппаратура, их части и принадлежности |
| XVII - Vehicles, aircraft, vessels and associated transport equipment | .. | .. | .. | .. | .. | 4.6 | XVII - Средства наземного, воздушного и водного транспорта |
| XVIII - Optical, photographic, cinematographic, measuring, checking, precision, medical or surgical instruments and apparatus; clocks and watches; musical instruments; parts and accessories thereof | .. | .. | .. | .. | .. | .. | XVIII - Приборы, аппараты оптические, медицинские, измерительные и пр.; музыкальные инструменты; часы; их части и принадлежности |
| XIX - Arms and ammunition; parts and accessories thereof | .. | .. | .. | .. | .. | .. | XIX - Оружие и боеприпасы, их части и принадлежности |
| XX - Miscellaneous manufactured articles | .. | .. | .. | .. | .. | 12.9 | XX - Разные промышленные товары |
| XXI - Works of art, collectors' pieces, and antiques | .. | .. | .. | .. | .. | .. | XXI - Произведения искусства, предметы антиквариата |
| XXII - Services | .. | .. | .. | .. | .. | .. | XXII - Услуги |

## TABLE 3-3A. Exports by commodity group (millions of U.S. dollars)
## ТАБЛИЦА 3-3А. Экспорт по товарным группам (млн. долларов США)

| Commodity group | 1990 | 1991 | 1992 | 1993 | 1994 | 1995 | Товарные группы |
|---|---|---|---|---|---|---|---|
| TOTAL | .. | .. | .. | .. | .. | 748.6 | ВСЕГО |
| I - Live animals; animal products | .. | .. | .. | .. | .. | 0.1 | I - Живые животные и продукты животноводства |
| II - Vegetable products | .. | .. | .. | .. | .. | 0.1 | II - Продукты растительного происхождения |
| III - Animal or vegetable fats and oils and their cleavage products; prepared edible fats; animal or vegetable waxes | .. | .. | .. | .. | .. | .. | III - Жиры и масла растительного и животного происхождения, воски |
| IV - Prepared foodstuffs; beverages, spirits and vinegar; tobacco and manufactured tobacco substitutes | .. | .. | .. | .. | .. | 4.1 | IV -Продукция пищевой промышленности, алкогольные и безалкогольные напитки, табак и его заменители |
| V - Mineral products | .. | .. | .. | .. | .. | 123.8 | V - Минеральные продукты |
| VI - Products of the chemical or allied industries | .. | .. | .. | .. | .. | 0.2 | VI - Продукция химической промышленности |
| VII - Plastics and articles thereof; rubber and articles thereof | .. | .. | .. | .. | .. | 0.1 | VII - Пластмассы и изделия из них |
| VIII - Raw hides and skins, leather, furskins and articles thereof; saddlery and harness; travel goods, handbags and similar containers; articles of animal gut | .. | .. | .. | .. | .. | .. | VIII - Кожевенное сырьё, кожи, пушнина, меховое сырьё и изделия из них |
| IX - Wood and articles of wood; wood charcoal; cork and articles of cork; manufactures of straw, of esparto or of other plaiting materials; basketware and wickerwork | .. | .. | .. | .. | .. | .. | IX - Древесина и изделия из древесины, древесный уголь |
| X - Pulp of wood or of other fibrous cellulosic material; waste and scrap of paper or paperboard; paper and paperboard and articles thereof | .. | .. | .. | .. | .. | .. | X - Бумажная масса, бумажные и картонные отходы, макулатура, бумага, картон и изделия из них |
| XI - Textiles and textile articles | .. | .. | .. | .. | .. | 218.5 | XI - Текстиль и текстильные изделия |
| XII - Footwear, headgear, umbrellas, sun umbrellas, walking sticks, seat sticks, whips, riding crops and parts thereof; prepared feathers and articles made therewith; artificial flowers; articles of human hair | .. | .. | .. | .. | .. | 0.0 | XII - Обувь, головные уборы, зонты, трости и пр. |

**TABLE 3-3A. Exports by commodity group (millions of U.S. dollars)**
**ТАБЛИЦА 3-3А. Экспорт по товарным группам (млн. долларов США)**

| Commodity group | 1990 | 1991 | 1992 | 1993 | 1994 | 1995 | Товарные группы |
|---|---|---|---|---|---|---|---|
| XIII - Articles of stone, plaster, cement, asbestos, mica and similar materials; ceramic products; glass and glassware | .. | .. | .. | .. | .. | 0.1 | XIII - Изделия из камня, гипса, цемента |
| XIV - Natural or cultured pearls, precious or semi-precious stones, precious metals, metals clad with precious metal and articles thereof; imitation jewellery; coin | .. | .. | .. | .. | .. | 0.1 | XIV - Жемчуг, драгоценные и полудрагоценные камни, драгоценные металлы, бижутерия, монеты |
| XV - Base metals and articles of base metal | .. | .. | .. | .. | .. | 394.7 | XV - Неблагородные металлы и изделия из них |
| XVI - Machinery and mechanical appliances; electrical equipment; parts thereof; sound recorders and reproducers, television image and sound recorders and reproducers, and parts and accessories of such articles | .. | .. | .. | .. | .. | 2.1 | XVI - Машины, оборудование, механизмы, их части и принадлежности; звуковая и теле-аппаратура, их части и принадлежности |
| XVII - Vehicles, aircraft, vessels and associated transport equipment | .. | .. | .. | .. | .. | 2.6 | XVII - Средства наземного, воздушного и водного транспорта |
| XVIII - Optical, photographic, cinematographic, measuring, checking, precision, medical or surgical instruments and apparatus; clocks and watches; musical instruments; parts and accessories thereof | .. | .. | .. | .. | .. | .. | XVIII - Приборы, аппараты оптические, медицинские, измерительные и пр.; музыкальные инструменты; часы; их части и принадлежности |
| XIX - Arms and ammunition; parts and accessories thereof | .. | .. | .. | .. | .. | .. | XIX - Оружие и боеприпасы, их части и принадлежности |
| XX - Miscellaneous manufactured articles | .. | .. | .. | .. | .. | 2.1 | XX - Разные промышленные товары |
| XXI - Works of art, collectors' pieces, and antiques | .. | .. | .. | .. | .. | .. | XXI - Произведения искусства, предметы антиквариата |
| XXII - Services | .. | .. | .. | .. | .. | .. | XXII - Услуги |

## TABLE 3-4A. Geographical distribution of foreign trade (millions of U.S. dollars)
## ТАБЛИЦА 3-4A. Географическое распределение внешней торговли (млн. долларов США)

| Country or country group | Exports Экспорт 1990 | 1991 | 1992 | 1993 | 1994 | 1995 | Imports Импорт 1990 | 1991 | 1992 | 1993 | 1994 | 1995 | Страна или группа стран |
|---|---|---|---|---|---|---|---|---|---|---|---|---|---|
| **Total trade** | .. | .. | .. | .. | .. | 748.6 | .. | .. | .. | .. | .. | 799.2 | **Всего** |
| **CIS countries** | .. | .. | .. | .. | .. | 251.6 | .. | .. | .. | .. | .. | 478.0 | **Страны СНГ** |
| Armenia | .. | .. | .. | .. | .. | .. | .. | .. | .. | .. | .. | 0.2 | Армения |
| Azerbaijan | .. | .. | .. | .. | .. | 0.9 | .. | .. | .. | .. | .. | 0.2 | Азербайджан |
| Belarus | .. | .. | .. | .. | .. | 2.3 | .. | .. | .. | .. | .. | 0.4 | Беларусь |
| Georgia | .. | .. | .. | .. | .. | .. | .. | .. | .. | .. | .. | .. | Грузия |
| Kazakstan | .. | .. | .. | .. | .. | 7.0 | .. | .. | .. | .. | .. | 26.6 | Казахстан |
| Kyrgyz Republic | .. | .. | .. | .. | .. | 2.6 | .. | .. | .. | .. | .. | 2.7 | Киргизстан |
| Moldova | .. | .. | .. | .. | .. | .. | .. | .. | .. | .. | .. | .. | Молдова |
| Russia | .. | .. | .. | .. | .. | 95.3 | .. | .. | .. | .. | .. | 136.0 | Россия |
| Tajikistan | .. | .. | .. | .. | .. | .. | .. | .. | .. | .. | .. | .. | Таджикистан |
| Turkmenistan | .. | .. | .. | .. | .. | 2.2 | .. | .. | .. | .. | .. | 57.4 | Туркменистан |
| Ukraine | .. | .. | .. | .. | .. | 9.3 | .. | .. | .. | .. | .. | 2.2 | Украина |
| Uzbekistan | .. | .. | .. | .. | .. | 132.0 | .. | .. | .. | .. | .. | 251.4 | Узбекистан |
| **Non-CIS countries** | .. | .. | .. | .. | .. | 497.0 | .. | .. | .. | .. | .. | 321.2 | **Остальной мир** |
| **Europe** | .. | .. | .. | .. | .. | 445.3 | .. | .. | .. | .. | .. | 271.1 | **Европа** |
| Austria | .. | .. | .. | .. | .. | 9.7 | .. | .. | .. | .. | .. | 1.4 | Австрия |
| Belgium | .. | .. | .. | .. | .. | 32.7 | .. | .. | .. | .. | .. | 25.1 | Бельгия |
| Bulgaria | .. | .. | .. | .. | .. | 0.4 | .. | .. | .. | .. | .. | .. | Болгария |
| Czech Republic | .. | .. | .. | .. | .. | 2.2 | .. | .. | .. | .. | .. | 1.4 | Чешская Республика |
| Denmark | .. | .. | .. | .. | .. | .. | .. | .. | .. | .. | .. | .. | Дания |
| Estonia | .. | .. | .. | .. | .. | 2.7 | .. | .. | .. | .. | .. | 4.6 | Эстония |
| Finland | .. | .. | .. | .. | .. | 20.1 | .. | .. | .. | .. | .. | 0.0 | Финляндия |
| Former Yugoslavia | .. | .. | .. | .. | .. | 3.9 | .. | .. | .. | .. | .. | .. | Быв. Югославия |
| France | .. | .. | .. | .. | .. | 0.2 | .. | .. | .. | .. | .. | 0.6 | Франция |
| Germany | .. | .. | .. | .. | .. | 4.7 | .. | .. | .. | .. | .. | 14.2 | Германия |
| Hungary | .. | .. | .. | .. | .. | 13.5 | .. | .. | .. | .. | .. | 0.3 | Венгрия |
| Iceland | .. | .. | .. | .. | .. | .. | .. | .. | .. | .. | .. | .. | Исландия |
| Ireland | .. | .. | .. | .. | .. | 0.3 | .. | .. | .. | .. | .. | 3.8 | Ирландия |
| Italy | .. | .. | .. | .. | .. | 2.4 | .. | .. | .. | .. | .. | .. | Италия |
| Latvia | .. | .. | .. | .. | .. | 21.0 | .. | .. | .. | .. | .. | 5.1 | Латвия |
| Lithuania | .. | .. | .. | .. | .. | 9.0 | .. | .. | .. | .. | .. | 0.7 | Литва |
| Netherlands | .. | .. | .. | .. | .. | 255.1 | .. | .. | .. | .. | .. | 3.8 | Нидерланды |
| Norway | .. | .. | .. | .. | .. | 5.4 | .. | .. | .. | .. | .. | 7.9 | Норвегия |
| Poland | .. | .. | .. | .. | .. | 0.5 | .. | .. | .. | .. | .. | .. | Польша |
| Romania | .. | .. | .. | .. | .. | 2.2 | .. | .. | .. | .. | .. | 0.1 | Румыния |
| Slovak Republic | .. | .. | .. | .. | .. | 0.7 | .. | .. | .. | .. | .. | 0.0 | Словацкая Республика |
| Spain | .. | .. | .. | .. | .. | 0.7 | .. | .. | .. | .. | .. | .. | Испания |

**TABLE 3-4A. Geographical distribution of foreign trade (millions of U.S. dollars)**
**ТАБЛИЦА 3-4А. Географическое распределение внешней торговли (млн. долларов США)**

| Country or country group | Exports Экспорт 1990 | 1991 | 1992 | 1993 | 1994 | 1995 | Imports Импорт 1990 | 1991 | 1992 | 1993 | 1994 | 1995 | Страна или группа стран |
|---|---|---|---|---|---|---|---|---|---|---|---|---|---|
| Sweden | .. | .. | .. | .. | .. | .. | .. | .. | .. | .. | .. | 0.0 | Швеция |
| Switzerland | .. | .. | .. | .. | .. | 37.2 | .. | .. | .. | .. | .. | 45.3 | Швейцария |
| United Kingdom | .. | .. | .. | .. | .. | 20.7 | .. | .. | .. | .. | .. | 153.9 | Великобритания |
| Other Europe | .. | .. | .. | .. | .. | .. | .. | .. | .. | .. | .. | 2.9 | Остальные страны Европы |
| **Asia** | .. | .. | .. | .. | .. | 36.3 | .. | .. | .. | .. | .. | 11.2 | **Азия** |
| Afghanistan | .. | .. | .. | .. | .. | 0.3 | .. | .. | .. | .. | .. | 0.0 | Афганистан |
| China | .. | .. | .. | .. | .. | 5.6 | .. | .. | .. | .. | .. | 0.4 | Китай |
| India | .. | .. | .. | .. | .. | 0.2 | .. | .. | .. | .. | .. | .. | Индия |
| Iraq | .. | .. | .. | .. | .. | .. | .. | .. | .. | .. | .. | .. | Ирак |
| Japan | .. | .. | .. | .. | .. | 8.2 | .. | .. | .. | .. | .. | .. | Япония |
| Korea, Dem. People's Rep. | .. | .. | .. | .. | .. | 3.3 | .. | .. | .. | .. | .. | .. | КНДР |
| Korea, Rep. of | .. | .. | .. | .. | .. | 9.3 | .. | .. | .. | .. | .. | 0.1 | Южная Корея |
| Mongolia | .. | .. | .. | .. | .. | .. | .. | .. | .. | .. | .. | .. | МНР |
| Syrian Arab Republic | .. | .. | .. | .. | .. | .. | .. | .. | .. | .. | .. | .. | Сирия |
| Turkey | .. | .. | .. | .. | .. | 8.1 | .. | .. | .. | .. | .. | 3.9 | Турция |
| Viet Nam | .. | .. | .. | .. | .. | 0.3 | .. | .. | .. | .. | .. | 0.6 | Вьетнам |
| Other Asia | .. | .. | .. | .. | .. | 1.0 | .. | .. | .. | .. | .. | 6.2 | Остальные страны Азии |
| **America** | .. | .. | .. | .. | .. | 15.3 | .. | .. | .. | .. | .. | 30.9 | **Сев. и Южная Америка** |
| Canada | .. | .. | .. | .. | .. | .. | .. | .. | .. | .. | .. | 5.6 | Канада |
| Cuba | .. | .. | .. | .. | .. | .. | .. | .. | .. | .. | .. | .. | Куба |
| United States | .. | .. | .. | .. | .. | 14.8 | .. | .. | .. | .. | .. | 25.3 | США |
| Other America | .. | .. | .. | .. | .. | 0.5 | .. | .. | .. | .. | .. | 0.0 | Остальные |
| **Africa** | .. | .. | .. | .. | .. | 0.1 | .. | .. | .. | .. | .. | 8.0 | **Африка** |
| Egypt | .. | .. | .. | .. | .. | .. | .. | .. | .. | .. | .. | .. | Египет |
| Libya | .. | .. | .. | .. | .. | .. | .. | .. | .. | .. | .. | .. | Ливия |
| Other Africa | .. | .. | .. | .. | .. | 0.1 | .. | .. | .. | .. | .. | 8.0 | Остальные |
| **Rest of the World** | .. | .. | .. | .. | .. | .. | .. | .. | .. | .. | .. | .. | **Прочие страны мира** |
| Australia | .. | .. | .. | .. | .. | .. | .. | .. | .. | .. | .. | .. | Австралия |

## TABLE 4-1. General government budget revenue (millions of national currency)
## ТАБЛИЦА 4-1. Доходы государственного бюджета (млн. национальной валюты)

| Type of revenue | 1990 | 1991 | 1992 | 1993 | 1994 | 1995 | Вид доходов |
|---|---|---|---|---|---|---|---|
| **Total revenue and grants** | 3,436 | 6,069 | 18,648 | 177,680 | 840,834 | .. | **Всего доходов и безвозм. поступл.** |
| Grants | 1,168 | 2,900 | 0 | 0 | 0 | .. | Безвозмездные поступления |
| Total Revenue | 2,268 | 3,170 | 18,648 | 177,680 | 840,834 | .. | Всего доходов |
| **Current revenue** | 2,268 | 3,170 | 18,648 | 177,680 | 840,834 | .. | **Текущие доходы** |
| Tax revenue | 2,006 | 2,364 | 14,496 | 146,162 | 707,208 | .. | Доход от налогов |
| Taxes on income and profits | 397 | 769 | 5,778 | 45,713 | 226,910 | .. | Налоги на доходы и прибыль |
| Individual | .. | .. | .. | .. | .. | .. | Физические лица |
| Corporate | 397 | 769 | 5,778 | 45,713 | 226,910 | .. | Предприятия и организации |
| Social security contributions | 232 | .. | 0 | .. | .. | .. | Отчисление на соцстрах. |
| Taxes on payroll or work force | 250 | 334 | 1,654 | 14,445 | 51,227 | .. | Налоги на заработную плату и рабочую силу |
| Taxes on the use of labor force | 62 | .. | .. | .. | .. | .. | Плата за трудовые ресурсы |
| Taxes on increases in wages and salaries | 10 | .. | .. | .. | .. | .. | Налог с прироста средств на оплату труда |
| Other payroll/work force taxes | 178 | 334 | 1,654 | 14,445 | 51,227 | .. | Другие налоги на зарплату и рабочую силу |
| Taxes on property | 11 | 27 | 337 | 1,354 | 37,527 | .. | Налоги на собственность |
| Taxes on immovable property | 11 | 12 | 310 | 1,312 | 36,940 | .. | Налоги на недвижимое имущество |
| Buildings | 4 | 5 | 92 | 2 | 135 | .. | Налог с владельцев строении |
| Land | 7 | 7 | 218 | 1,310 | 36,805 | .. | Земельныи налог |
| Estate, inheritance, and gift taxes | .. | .. | .. | .. | .. | .. | Налоги на наследство, подарки |
| Other property taxes | .. | 15 | 27 | 43 | 587 | .. | Другие налоги на имущество |
| Domestic taxes on goods and services | 1,069 | 1,202 | 6,639 | 78,685 | 330,668 | .. | Внутренние налоги на товары и услуги |
| General sales, turnover, or value-added taxes | 1,065 | 1,198 | 4,341 | 64,137 | 234,261 | .. | Налог с продаж. с оборота или на добав. стоим. |
| Excises | .. | .. | 2,298 | 14,548 | 96,407 | .. | Акцизы |
| Profits of fiscal monopolies | .. | .. | .. | .. | .. | .. | Прибыли фискальных монополий |
| Taxes on specific services | 4 | 4 | .. | .. | .. | .. | Налоги на особые услуги |
| Taxes on use of goods or permission to use goods or to perform activities | .. | .. | .. | .. | .. | .. | Налоги на пользование товарами или лицензии на пользование товарами и занятие деятельностью |
| Other taxes on goods and services | .. | .. | .. | .. | .. | .. | Другие налоги на товары и услуги |
| Taxes on international trade and transactions | 26 | 3 | 88 | 5,965 | 60,875 | .. | Налоги на внешнюю торговлю и операции |
| Import duties | .. | .. | .. | 0 | .. | .. | Импортные пошлины |
| Export duties | 26 | 3 | 88 | 5,965 | 60,875 | .. | Экпортные пошлины |
| Other | .. | .. | 0 | 0 | .. | .. | Другие |
| Other taxes | 21 | 29 | .. | .. | .. | .. | Прочие налоги |
| Nontax revenue | 262 | 806 | 4,152 | 31,518 | 133,626 | .. | Неналоговые доходы |
| **Capital revenue** | .. | .. | .. | .. | .. | .. | **Капитальные доходы** |

## TABLE 4-2. General government budget expenditure by economic type (millions of national currency)
## ТАБЛИЦА 4-2. Расходы государственного бюджета по экономическим типам (млн. национальной валюты)

| Type of expenditure or debt holder | 1990 | 1991 | 1992 | 1993 | 1994 | 1995 | Всего расходов |
|---|---|---|---|---|---|---|---|
| **Total expenditure by economic type** | 3,186 | 5,036 | 37,454 | 336,358 | 936,167 | .. | **Всего расходов по экономическим типам** |
| **Current expenditure** | 2,374 | 4,596 | 33,889 | 274,920 | 664,266 | .. | **Текущие расходы** |
| Expenditure on goods and services | 840 | 1,566 | 9,801 | 88,171 | 219,697 | .. | Расходы на товары и услуги |
| Wages and salaries | 617 | 1,014 | 5,988 | 44,449 | 82,134 | .. | Заработная плата |
| Employer contributions | 41 | 223 | 1,449 | 12,351 | 27,093 | .. | Отчисление на социальное страхование |
| Other Purchases of goods and services | 182 | 330 | 2,364 | 31,372 | 110,470 | .. | Другие покупки товаров и услуг |
| Interest payments | .. | .. | .. | .. | .. | .. | Выплаты процентов |
| Domestic debt | .. | .. | .. | .. | .. | .. | По внутреннему долгу |
| Foreign debt | .. | .. | .. | .. | .. | .. | По внешнему долгу |
| Subsidies and other current transfers | 1,364 | 2,948 | 23,070 | 101,997 | 180,125 | .. | Субсидии на другие текущие трансферты |
| Subsidies | 783 | 747 | 12,631 | 98,684 | 176,615 | .. | Субсидии |
| Agricultural subsidies | 355 | 635 | 11,844 | .. | .. | .. | Субсидии на сельское хозяиство |
| Other current transfers | 581 | 2,201 | 10,439 | 3,313 | 3,509 | .. | Другие текущие трансферты |
| Other | 170 | 82 | 1,019 | 84,752 | 264,444 | .. | Прочие расходы |
| **Capital expenditure** | 812 | 440 | 3,565 | 61,438 | 271,902 | .. | **Капитальные расходы** |
| Acquisition of fixed capital assets | 806 | 420 | 3,338 | 51,740 | 269,286 | .. | Приобретение основного капитала |
| Capital transfers | 5 | 19 | 226 | 9,698 | 2,616 | .. | Капитальные трансферты |
| Other | .. | .. | .. | .. | .. | .. | Другие капитальные расходы |
| **Surplus/deficit (-)** | 251 | 1,034 | -18,806 | -158,678 | -95,333 | .. | **Превыш. доходов над расходами/дефицит(-)** |
| **Financing by type of debt holder** | .. | .. | .. | .. | .. | .. | **Финансирование по типам кредиторов** |
| **Foreign (net)** | .. | .. | .. | .. | .. | .. | **Зарубежные кредиторы (сальдо)** |
| From international development institutions | .. | .. | .. | .. | .. | .. | Международные организации |
| From foreign governments | .. | .. | .. | .. | .. | .. | Правительства иностранных государств |
| Other borrowing abroad | .. | .. | .. | .. | .. | .. | Другие зарубежные кредиторы |
| **Domestic (net)** | .. | .. | .. | .. | .. | .. | **Внутренние кредиторы (сальдо)** |
| From monetary authorities | .. | .. | .. | .. | .. | .. | Органы денежного обращения |
| From deposit money banks | .. | .. | .. | .. | .. | .. | Депозитные денежные банки |
| Other domestic borrowing | .. | .. | .. | .. | .. | .. | Другие внутренние кредиторы |
| *Memo items:* | | | | | | | *Справочно:* |
| Extrabudgetary surplus/ Deficit (-) not included above | .. | .. | .. | .. | .. | .. | Превышение доходов над расходами/дефицит (-) по внебюджетным фондам, не включенным выше |
| Total surplus/deficit (-) including extrabudgetary accounts | 109 | 758 | .. | .. | .. | .. | Итого превышение доходов над расходами/дефицит, включая счета внебюджетных фондов |

## TABLE 5-3. Production and average yield of major agricultural crops
## ТАБЛИЦА 5-3. Производство и урожайность важнейших сельскохозяйственных культур

| Crop | 1990 | 1991 | 1992 | 1993 | 1994 | 1995 | Сельскохозяйственные культуры |
|---|---|---|---|---|---|---|---|
| **Production (thousands of tons)** | | | | | | | **Производство (тыс. тонн)** |
| Grain - Cleanweight | 303 | 286 | 257 | 253 | 212 | .. | Зерно в чистом весе |
| Winter wheat | 134 | 141 | 156 | 159 | 104 | .. | Пшеница - озимая |
| Spring wheat | 127 | 130 | 133 | 105 | 37 | .. | яровая |
| Coarse grain | 7 | 11 | 23 | 54 | 229 | .. | Зерно в физическом весе |
| Rye | 136 | 112 | 76 | 67 | 1 | .. | Рожь |
| Corn | 2 | 2 | 2 | 1 | 18 | .. | Кукуруза |
| Winter barley | 85 | 60 | 32 | 33 | 11 | .. | Ячмень - озимый |
| Spring barley | 35 | 35 | 27 | 15 | 14 | .. | яровой |
| Oats | 11 | 12 | 12 | 15 | 2 | .. | Овес |
| Millet | 3 | 3 | 3 | 3 | .. | .. | Просо |
| Rice | 27 | 24 | 19 | 21 | 23 | .. | Рис |
| Flax | .. | .. | .. | .. | 2 | .. | Лен |
| Oilseeds | .. | .. | .. | .. | .. | .. | Семена масличных культур |
| Cotton (raw) | 842 | 826 | 513 | 524 | 529 | .. | Хлопок - сырец |
| Cotton fiber | 256 | 255 | 165 | 180 | 170 | .. | волокно |
| Sugarbeets | .. | .. | .. | .. | .. | .. | Сахарная свекла |
| Potatoes | 207 | 181 | 167 | 147 | 134 | .. | Картофель |
| Pulses | 7 | 8 | 2 | 5 | 5 | .. | Бобовые |
| Vegetables | 528 | 628 | 543 | 485 | 483 | .. | Овощи |
| Fruit | 410 | 298 | 283 | 237 | 225 | .. | Фрукты |
| Grapes | 190 | 121 | 100 | 87 | 80 | .. | Виноград |
| Other | 220 | 177 | 183 | 150 | 145 | .. | Прочие |
| Corn (silage and greenchop) | 1,222 | 1,150 | 727 | 599 | 498 | .. | Кукуруза (на силос и зеленый корм) |
| Hay | 1,521 | 1,486 | 1,212 | 1,112 | 1,014 | .. | Сено |
| **Average yield (kilograms per hectare)** | | | | | | | **Ср. урожайность (кг с га)** |
| Grain | 1,310 | 1,230 | 970 | 910 | 870 | .. | Зерно |
| Winter wheat | 930 | 980 | 860 | 850 | 880 | .. | Пшеница - озимая |
| Spring wheat | 1,090 | 1,040 | 800 | 710 | 620 | .. | яровая |
| Coarse grain | 1,310 | 1,310 | 1,040 | .. | 950 | .. | Зерно в физическом весе |
| Rye | 810 | 990 | 940 | 670 | 860 | .. | Рожь |
| Corn | 4,990 | 3,920 | 2,970 | 2,970 | 1,880 | .. | Кукуруза |
| Winter barley | 1,130 | 1,120 | 1,000 | 910 | 830 | .. | Ячмень - озимый |
| Spring barley | 830 | 960 | 790 | 680 | 540 | .. | яровой |
| Oats | 790 | 930 | 840 | 720 | 520 | .. | Овес |
| Millet | .. | .. | 860 | .. | 710 | .. | Просо |
| Rice | 2,750 | 2,530 | 1,820 | 1,710 | 1,740 | .. | Рис |
| Flax | .. | .. | .. | .. | 220 | .. | Лен |
| Oilseeds | .. | .. | .. | .. | .. | .. | Семена масличных культур |
| Cotton (raw) | 2,770 | 2,770 | 1,800 | 1,910 | 1,870 | .. | Хлопок - сырец |
| Cotton fiber | 840 | .. | .. | .. | .. | .. | волокно |
| Sugarbeets | .. | .. | .. | .. | .. | .. | Сахарная свекла |
| Potatoes | 14,300 | 14,100 | 12,800 | 11,900 | 10,800 | .. | Картофель |
| Pulses | 640 | 680 | 460 | 460 | 530 | .. | Бобовые |
| Vegetables | 19,500 | 19,300 | 16,840 | 17,860 | 15,560 | .. | Овощи |
| Fruit | .. | .. | .. | .. | .. | .. | Фрукты |
| Grapes | 7,160 | 4,450 | 3,500 | 3,010 | 1,800 | .. | Виноград |
| Other | 3,980 | 3,210 | 3,280 | 2,500 | 1,480 | .. | Прочие |
| Corn (silage and greenchop) | 22,500 | 21,600 | 16,250 | 15,410 | 13,150 | .. | Кукуруза (на силос и зеленый корм) |
| Hay | 3,290 | 3,220 | 2,890 | 2,780 | 2,280 | .. | Сено |

**TABLE 5-4. Main aggregates of animal husbandry**
**ТАБЛИЦА 5-4. Основные показатели животноводства**

| Type of livestock or product | 1990 | 1991 | 1992 | 1993 | 1994 | 1995 | Направление животноводства или вид продукции |
|---|---|---|---|---|---|---|---|
| **Livestock (thousands of heads)** | | | | | | | **Поголовье скота (тысяч голов)** |
| Cattle | 1,352 | 1,391 | 1,246 | 1,250 | 1,168 | 1,199 | Крупный рогатый скот |
| of which: Cows | 557 | 586 | 544 | 560 | 535 | 549 | в том числе коровы |
| Pigs | 183 | 128 | 56 | 47 | 33 | 33 | Свиньи |
| Sheep and goats | 2,462 | 2,484 | 2,237 | 2,081 | 1,893 | 2,707 | Овцы и козы |
| of which: Goats | 830 | 871 | 846 | 825 | 731 | 742 | в том числе козы |
| Horses | 52 | 53 | 49 | 55 | 55 | 58 | Лошади |
| Other | .. | .. | .. | .. | .. | .. | Прочие |
| **Animal husbandry products** | | | | | | | **Продукция животноводства** |
| Meat (thousands of tons) | 185 | 151 | 126 | 113 | 112 | .. | Мясо (тысяч тонн) |
| Beef | 94 | 83 | 71 | 65 | 65 | .. | Говядина |
| Pork | 15 | 9 | 5 | 2 | 1 | .. | Свинина |
| Lamb | 52 | 43 | 42 | 42 | 42 | .. | Баранина |
| Poultry | 21 | 13 | 7 | 4 | 4 | .. | Птица |
| Other | 2 | 2 | 1 | 0 | 0 | .. | Прочие виды мяса |
| Milk (thousands of tons) | 575 | 587 | 510 | 475 | 467 | .. | Молоко (тысяч тонн) |
| Eggs (millions) | 592 | 454 | 296 | 160 | 79 | .. | Яйца (миллионов штук) |
| Wool (thousands of tons) | 5 | 4 | 4 | 3 | 3 | .. | Шерсть (тысяч тонн) |

**TABLE 6-1. Industrial production by sector (millions of national currency)**

**ТАБЛИЦА 6-1. Промышленное производство по отраслям (млн. национальной валюты)**

| Sector | 1990 | 1991 | 1992 | 1993 | 1994 | 1995 | Отрасли |
|---|---|---|---|---|---|---|---|
| **All industry** | 55.0 | 123.0 | 940.0 | 7,816 | 20,022 | 86,308 | **Вся промышленность** |
| **Heavy industry** | 20.0 | 40.0 | 478.0 | 3,472 | 10,369 | 59,727 | **Тяжелая промышленность** |
| Fuel and energy | 3.2 | 5.4 | 60.0 | 703 | 1,066 | 17,886 | Топливно-энергетическая промышленноть |
| Electricity | 3.0 | 5.1 | 56.3 | 657 | 936 | 17,506 | Электроэнергетика |
| Fuels | 0.2 | 0.3 | 3.5 | 46 | 130 | 380 | Топливная промышленность |
| Ferrous and nonferrous metallurgy | 5.0 | 13.0 | 265.0 | 1,710 | 6,084 | 32,588 | Металлургия |
| Chemicals and petrochemical industry | 2.4 | 4.7 | 40.0 | 238 | 691 | 4,287 | Химическая и нефтехимическая пром. |
| Machine building and metalworking | 5.2 | 8.8 | 70.2 | 461 | 1,161 | 3,241 | Машиностроение и металлообработка |
| Forestry, woodworking, and pulp and paper industry | 0.8 | 1.9 | 8.0 | 68 | 110 | 74 | Лесная, деревообрабатывающая и целлюлозо-бумажная промышленность |
| Construction materials | 2.5 | 4.7 | 25.2 | 292 | 980 | 1,165 | Промышленность строительных материалов |
| **Light industry** | 22.7 | 58.2 | 300.0 | 2,604 | 5,603 | 14,611 | **Легкая промышленность** |
| Textiles | 18.5 | 48.3 | 271.0 | 2,353 | 5,197 | 14,033 | Текстильная |
| Clothing | 3.2 | 7.7 | 18.7 | 166 | 333 | 432 | Швейная |
| Leather and shoes | 0.9 | 2.0 | 9.4 | 80 | 62 | 146 | Кожевенная и обувная |
| **Food industry** | 8.6 | 18.5 | 110.9 | 895 | 2,082 | 5,815 | **Пищевая промышленность** |
| Processed foods | 5.8 | 12.8 | 94.2 | 730 | 1,627 | 5,155 | Пищевкусовая |
| Meat and dairy products | 2.7 | 5.5 | 16.3 | 156 | 440 | 642 | Мясная и молочная |
| Fish | 0.1 | 0.2 | 0.4 | 9 | 15 | 18 | Рыбная |

## TABLE 6-2. Industrial production by sector in constant prices
## ТАБЛИЦА 6-2. Промышленное производство по отраслям в постоянных ценах

| Sector | 1990 | 1991 | 1992 | 1993 | 1994 | 1995 | Отрасли |
|---|---|---|---|---|---|---|---|
| **Industrial production** | | | | | | | **Промышленное производство** |
| **All industry** | 181194 | 174671 | 132226 | 121912 | 90946 | 86308 | **Вся промышленность** |
| **Heavy industry** | 137550 | 131223 | 91200 | 75514 | 61091 | 59727 | **Тяжелая промышленность** |
| Fuel and energy | 22139 | 20985 | 18348 | 18893 | 18231 | 17886 | Топливно-энергетическая промышленноть |
| Electricity | 18440 | 18163 | 17146 | 18192 | 17737 | 17506 | Электроэнергетика |
| Fuels | 3699 | 2822 | 1202 | 701 | 494 | 380 | Топливная промышленность |
| Ferrous and nonferrous metallurgy | 67976 | 57100 | 46080 | 33961 | 31855 | 32588 | Металлургия |
| Chemicals and petrochemicals | 22259 | 22793 | 10462 | 6026 | 4110 | 4287 | Химическая и нефтехимическая пром. |
| Machine building and metalworking | 7075 | 7054 | 4599 | 3587 | 2525 | 2341 | Машиностроение и металлообработка |
| Forestry, woodworking, and pulp and paper | 1101 | 1244 | 781 | 618 | 175 | 74 | Лесная, деревообрабатывающая и целлюлозо-бумажная промышленность |
| Construction materials | 13821 | 13047 | 4736 | 3850 | 2672 | 1165 | Промышленность строительных материалов |
| **Light industry** | .. | .. | 18548 | 20941 | 15643 | 14611 | **Легкая промышленность** |
| Textiles | 19031 | 18841 | 16976 | 19387 | 15025 | 14033 | Текстильная |
| Clothing | 712 | 800 | 569 | 637 | 465 | 432 | Швейная |
| Leather and shoe | 1472 | 1420 | 926 | 645 | 151 | 146 | Кожевенная и обувная |
| **Food industry** | .. | .. | .. | 9576 | 6914 | 5815 | **Пищевая промышленность** |
| Processed foods | 12045 | 11611 | 8093 | 7259 | 5473 | 5155 | Пищевкусовая |
| Meat and dairy products | 10133 | 6485 | 3528 | 2180 | 1378 | 642 | Мясная и молочная |
| Fish | 138 | 145 | 94 | 120 | 64 | 18 | Рыбная |
| **Growth in production by sector (in percent)** | | | | | | | **Рост производства по отраслям** |
| **All industry** | 1.2 | -3.6 | -24.3 | -7.8 | -25.4 | -5.1 | **Вся промышленность** |
| **Heavy industry** | 2.5 | -4.6 | -30.5 | -17.2 | -19.1 | -2.2 | **Тяжелая промышленность** |
| Power and fuels | 11.4 | -5.2 | -12.6 | 3 | -3.5 | -1.9 | Топливно-энергетическая промышленноть |
| Electricity | 16.9 | -1.5 | -5.6 | 6.1 | -2.5 | -1.3 | Электроэнергетика |
| Fuels | -9.9 | -23.7 | -57.4 | -41.7 | -29.5 | -23.1 | Топливная промышленность |
| Ferrous and nonferrous metallurgy | -0.9 | -16 | -19.3 | -26.3 | -6.2 | 2.3 | Металлургия |
| Chemicals and petrochemicals | 6.9 | 2.4 | -54.1 | -42.4 | -31.8 | 4.3 | Химическая и нефтехимическая пром. |
| Machine building and metalworking | 1 | -0.3 | -34.8 | -22 | -29.6 | -7.3 | Машиностроение и металлообработка |
| Forestry, woodworking, and pulp and paper | -7.3 | 13 | -37.2 | -20.9 | -71.7 | -57.6 | Лесная, деревообрабатывающая и целлюлозо-бумажная промышленность |
| Construction materials | -5.7 | -5.6 | -63.7 | -18.7 | -30.6 | -56.4 | Промышленность строительных материалов |
| **Light industry** | -0.8 | 0.4 | -11.8 | 12.9 | -25.3 | -6.6 | **Легкая промышленность** |
| Textiles | -1.9 | -1 | -9.9 | 14.2 | -22.5 | -6.6 | Текстильная |
| Clothing | 4.7 | 12.4 | -28.9 | 11.9 | -27 | -7.5 | Швейная |
| Leather and shoe | 5.1 | -3.5 | -34.8 | -30.4 | -76.6 | -3.4 | Кожевенная и обувная |
| **Food industry** | 2.5 | -15.1 | -33 | -14.2 | -27.8 | -15.9 | **Пищевая промышленность** |
| Processed foods | 1.2 | -3.6 | -30.3 | -10.3 | -24.6 | -5.8 | Пищевкусовая |
| Meat and dairy products | 5 | -36 | -45.6 | -38.2 | -36.8 | -53.4 | Мясная и молочная |
| Fish | 14.9 | 5.1 | -35 | 28 | -46.8 | -71.8 | Рыбная |

## TABLE 6-3. Primary energy supply (million tons oil equivalent)
## ТАБЛИЦА 6-3. Ресурсы первичных видов энергии (млн. тонн нефтяного эквивалента)

| Item | | 1990 | 1991 | 1992 | 1993 | 1994 | 1995 | Статьи | |
|---|---|---|---|---|---|---|---|---|---|
| **Primary production** | | | | | | | | **Производство первичной энергии** | |
| Coal and lignite (hard and brown) | | 0.263 | 0.173 | 0.119 | 0.096 | 0.074 | .. | Уголь каменный и бурый | |
| Crude oil | | 0.194 | 0.142 | 0.082 | 0.056 | 0.034 | .. | Нефть | |
| Gas | | 0.128 | 0.107 | 0.083 | 0.056 | 0.031 | .. | Газ | |
| Nuclear | | .. | .. | .. | .. | .. | .. | Атомная энергия | |
| Hydro/geothermal | | 5.488 | 5.327 | 5.174 | 5.564 | 5.517 | .. | Гидро-геотермальная | |
| Other | | .. | .. | .. | .. | .. | .. | Другие виды | |
| Total | | .. | .. | .. | .. | .. | .. | Всего | |
| **Energy trade** | | | | | | | | **Торговля энергией** | |
| Coal and lignite | Exports | 0.127 | 0.152 | 0.103 | 0.044 | 0.029 | .. | Уголь каменный и бурый | Экспорт |
| | Imports | 0.457 | 0.375 | 0.232 | 0.019 | 0.010 | .. | | Импорт |
| | Net imports | 0.330 | 0.223 | 0.129 | -0.025 | -0.019 | .. | | Чистый импорт |
| Oil/oil product | Exports | 0.199 | .. | .. | .. | 0.010 | .. | Нефть и нефтепродукты | Экспорт |
| | Imports | 3.283 | .. | .. | .. | 0.339 | .. | | Импорт |
| | Net imports | 3.084 | .. | .. | .. | 0.329 | .. | | Чистый импорт |
| Gas | Exports | .. | .. | .. | .. | .. | .. | Газ | Экспорт |
| | Imports | 1.988 | 2.041 | 1.327 | 1.580 | 0.710 | .. | | Импорт |
| | Net imports | .. | .. | .. | .. | .. | .. | | Чистый импорт |
| Electricity | Exports | 1.841 | 1.752 | 1.819 | 2.075 | 1.679 | .. | Электричество | Экспорт |
| | Imports | 2.244 | 2.256 | 2.089 | 1.695 | 1.522 | .. | | Импорт |
| | Net imports | 0.403 | 0.504 | 0.270 | -0.380 | -0.157 | .. | | Чистый импорт |
| **Total net imports** | | .. | .. | .. | .. | .. | .. | **Чистый импорт энергии-всего** | |
| **Total stock changes** | | .. | .. | .. | .. | .. | .. | **Изменение запасов-всего** | |
| **Total primary energy supply** | | .. | .. | .. | .. | .. | .. | **Ресурсы первичной энергии-всего** | |
| Coal and lignite | | .. | .. | .. | .. | .. | .. | Уголь каменный и бурый | |
| Oil/oil products | | .. | .. | .. | .. | .. | .. | Нефть и нефтепродукты | |
| Gas | | .. | .. | .. | .. | .. | .. | Газ | |
| Nuclear | | .. | .. | .. | .. | .. | .. | Атомная энергия | |
| Hydro/geothermal | | .. | .. | .. | .. | .. | .. | Гидро-геотермальная энергия | |
| Other | | .. | .. | .. | .. | .. | .. | Другие виды | |
| **Total primary energy requirement (equals total primary energy supply)** | | .. | .. | .. | .. | .. | .. | **Потребность в первичной энергии-всего (равно ресурсам первичной энергии)** | |

## TABLE 6-4. Final energy consumption (million tons oil equivalent) — TAJIKISTAN
## ТАБЛИЦА 6-4. Конечное потребление энергии ( млн. тонн нефтяного эквивалента )

| | 1991 | 1992 | 1993 | 1994 | 1995 | |
|---|---|---|---|---|---|---|
| **Final energy consumption** | 5495.0 | 5215.0 | 4853.0 | 4167.0 | .. | **Конечное потребление энергии** |
| Coal & Lignite | 256.0 | 106.0 | 60.0 | 39.0 | .. | Уголь каменный и бурый |
| Oil Products | 130.0 | 119.0 | 141.0 | 129.0 | .. | Нефтепродукты |
| Gas | 956.0 | 319.0 | 597.0 | 349.0 | .. | Газ |
| Electricity | 3490.0 | 3813.0 | 3426.0 | 3232.0 | .. | Электроэнергия |
| Heat | 578.0 | 739.0 | 582.0 | 411.0 | .. | Тепло |
| Other | 85.0 | 119.0 | 47.0 | 7.0 | .. | Другие виды |
| Of which: | | | | | | В том числе |
| **Industry** | 3376.0 | 3302.0 | 3178.0 | 2582.0 | .. | **Промышленность** |
| Coal & Lignite | 35.0 | 15.0 | 8.0 | 6.0 | .. | Уголь каменный и бурый |
| Oil Products | 7.0 | 9.0 | 9.0 | 4.0 | .. | Нефтепродукты |
| Gas | 591.0 | 197.0 | 368.0 | 216.0 | .. | Газ |
| Electricity | 2346.0 | 2650.0 | 2324.0 | 2063.0 | .. | Электроэнергия |
| Heat | 386.0 | 408.0 | 458.0 | 291.0 | .. | Тепло |
| Other | 12.0 | 22.0 | 11.0 | 3.0 | .. | Другие виды |
| **Agriculture** | 545.0 | 225.0 | 274.0 | 247.0 | .. | **Сельское хозяйство** |
| Coal & Lignite | 3.0 | 1.0 | 1.0 | .. | .. | Уголь каменный и бурый |
| Oil Products | 90.0 | 70.0 | 105.0 | 94.0 | .. | Нефтепродукты |
| Gas | .. | .. | .. | .. | .. | Газ |
| Electricity | 276.0 | 106.0 | 145.0 | 146.0 | .. | Электроэнергия |
| Heat | 159.0 | 37.0 | 19.0 | 5.0 | .. | Тепло |
| Other | 17.0 | 11.0 | 4.0 | 2.0 | .. | Другие виды |
| **Transport** | 12.0 | 8.0 | 11.0 | 16.0 | .. | **Транспорт** |
| Oil Products | 2.0 | 5.0 | 7.0 | 16.0 | .. | Нефтепродукты |
| Other | 10.0 | 3.0 | 4.0 | 0.0 | .. | Другие виды |
| **Households** | 623.0 | 298.0 | 344.0 | 278.0 | .. | **Домашние хозяйства** |
| Coal & Lignite | 219.0 | 91.0 | 52.0 | 34.0 | .. | Уголь каменный и бурый |
| Oil Products | 0.0 | 0.0 | .. | 0.0 | .. | Нефтепродукты |
| Gas | 344.0 | 115.0 | 215.0 | 126.0 | .. | Газ |
| Electricity | 59.0 | 73.0 | 24.0 | 44.0 | .. | Электроэнергия |
| Heat | 1.0 | 19.0 | 28.0 | 74.0 | .. | Тепло |
| Other | .. | 0.0 | 25.0 | 0.0 | .. | Другие виды |

## TABLE 7-1. Price indices and exchange rates
## ТАБЛИЦА 7-1. Индексы цен и обменный курс

| Year and month | National currency per U.S. dollar / Единиц нац. валюты за 1 доллар США | National currency per 100 Russian rubles / Единиц нац. валюты за 100 российских рублей | Consumer price index (as a percent of the previous month) / Индекс потребительских цен (в % к предыдущему месяцу) | Producer price index (as a percent of the previous month) / Индекс цен производителей (в % к предыдущему месяцу) | Consumer price index (as a percent of the previous December) / Индекс потребительских цен (в % к декабрю прошлого года) | Producer price index (as a percent of the previous December) / Индекс цен производителей (в % к декабрю прошлого года) | Год и месяц |
|---|---|---|---|---|---|---|---|
| **1993** | | | | | | | **1993** |
| January | .. | .. | 119.0 | 246.1 | 119.0 | 246.1 | Январь |
| February | .. | .. | 124.4 | 183.2 | 148.0 | 450.1 | Февраль |
| March | .. | .. | 134.6 | 150.0 | 199.3 | 676.3 | Март |
| April | .. | .. | 163.9 | 141.5 | 326.6 | 956.9 | Апрель |
| May | .. | .. | 133.7 | 113.2 | 400.7 | 1,083.3 | Май |
| June | .. | .. | 117.3 | 116.0 | 470.0 | 1,256.6 | Июнь |
| July | .. | .. | 131.8 | 117.9 | 619.5 | 1,482.5 | Июль |
| August | .. | .. | 143.0 | 123.3 | 885.9 | 1,826.7 | Август |
| September | .. | .. | 136.4 | 113.1 | 1,208.3 | 2,066.0 | Сентябрь |
| October | .. | .. | 125.1 | 174.8 | 1,511.7 | 3,611.4 | Октябрь |
| November | .. | .. | 163.2 | 124.3 | 2,467.1 | 4,489.0 | Ноябрь |
| December | .. | .. | 276.9 | 135.8 | 6,831.3 | 6,096.1 | Декабрь |
| **1994** | | | | | | | **1994** |
| January | .. | .. | 76.8 | 110.9 | 76.8 | 110.9 | Январь |
| February | .. | .. | 95.6 | 111.1 | 73.4 | 123.2 | Февраль |
| March | .. | .. | 95.8 | 126.5 | 70.3 | 155.9 | Март |
| April | .. | .. | 103.1 | 102.7 | 72.5 | 160.1 | Апрель |
| May | .. | .. | 105.1 | 124.5 | 76.2 | 199.3 | Май |
| June | .. | .. | 102.7 | 125.3 | 78.3 | 249.7 | Июнь |
| July | .. | .. | 104.0 | 114.1 | 81.4 | 284.9 | Июль |
| August | .. | .. | 105.9 | 101.4 | 86.2 | 288.9 | Август |
| September | .. | .. | 103.4 | 111.0 | 89.1 | 320.7 | Сентябрь |
| October | .. | .. | 106.6 | 105.5 | 95.0 | 338.3 | Октябрь |
| November | .. | .. | 101.6 | 205.8 | 96.5 | 696.3 | Ноябрь |
| December | .. | .. | 104.7 | 117.4 | 101.3 | 817.4 | Декабрь |

## TABLE 7-1. Price indices and exchange rates
## ТАБЛИЦА 7-1. Индексы цен и обменный курс

| Year and month | National currency per U.S. dollar / Единиц нац. валюты за 1 доллар США | National currency per 100 Russian rubles / Единиц нац. валюты за 100 российских рублей | Consumer price index (as a percent of the previous month) / Индекс потребительских цен (в % к предыдущему месяцу) | Producer price index (as a percent of the previous month) / Индекс цен производителей (в % к предыдущему месяцу) | Consumer price index (as a percent of the previous December) / Индекс потребительских цен (в % к декабрю прошлого года) | Producer price index (as a percent of the previous December) / Индекс цен производителей (в % к декабрю прошлого года) | Год и месяц |
|---|---|---|---|---|---|---|---|
| **1995** | | | | | | | **1995** |
| January | .. | .. | 113.3 | 102.8 | 113.3 | 102.8 | Январь |
| February | .. | .. | 110.9 | 119.0 | 123.4 | 122.3 | Февраль |
| March | .. | .. | 117.9 | 104.6 | 145.5 | 128.0 | Март |
| April | .. | .. | 120.9 | 106.8 | 175.9 | 136.7 | Апрель |
| May | 50.5 | 1.0 | 127.9 | 106.3 | 225.0 | 145.3 | Май |
| June | 52.3 | 1.1 | 108.2 | 110.6 | 243.5 | 160.8 | Июнь |
| July | 57.0 | 1.3 | 106.7 | 99.8 | 259.8 | 160.4 | Июль |
| August | 58.0 | 1.3 | 178.1 | 107.3 | 462.7 | 172.1 | Август |
| September | 136.1 | 3.1 | 162.9 | 135.2 | 753.7 | 232.6 | Сентябрь |
| October | 196.6 | 4.4 | 156.9 | 159.8 | 1,182.6 | 371.7 | Октябрь |
| November | 265.4 | 5.9 | 123.1 | 165.2 | 1,455.8 | 614.1 | Ноябрь |
| December | 287.9 | 6.2 | 167.5 | 118.6 | 2,438.4 | 728.3 | Декабрь |
| **1996** | | | | | | | **1996** |
| January | 296.2 | 5.7 | 110.8 | 120.6 | 110.8 | 120.6 | Январь |
| February | 295.8 | 5.4 | 119.6 | 129.7 | 131.9 | 156.4 | Февраль |
| March | 280.0 | 5.4 | 116.0 | 90.4 | 152.9 | 141.4 | Март |
| April | 187.4 | 5.4 | 102.8 | 103.2 | 157.2 | 145.9 | Апрель |
| May | 278.8 | 5.4 | 100.5 | 99.7 | 158.0 | 145.5 | Май |
| June | .. | .. | .. | .. | .. | .. | Июнь |
| July | .. | .. | .. | .. | .. | .. | Июль |
| August | .. | .. | .. | .. | .. | .. | Август |
| September | .. | .. | .. | .. | .. | .. | Сентябрь |
| October | .. | .. | .. | .. | .. | .. | Октябрь |
| November | .. | .. | .. | .. | .. | .. | Ноябрь |
| December | .. | .. | .. | .. | .. | .. | Декабрь |

**TABLE 7-2. Monthly nominal wages by sector**
**ТАБЛИЦА 7-2. Среднемесячная денежная зарплата по отраслям**

| Sector | 1990 | 1991 | 1992 | 1993 | 1994 | 1995 | Сектора |
|---|---|---|---|---|---|---|---|
| **Nominal wages** | | | | | | | **Средняя номинальная заработная плата** |
| **Economy average** | 206.9 | 339.8 | 1,909.0 | 16,155.0 | 34,904.0 | 731.0 | **По народному хозяйству** |
| **Material sphere** | .. | .. | .. | .. | .. | .. | **Отрасли сферы материального производства** |
| Industry | 230.8 | 393.8 | 2,523.0 | 25,461.8 | 68,460.3 | 1,559.0 | Промышленность |
| Construction | 276.0 | 434.2 | 2,616.0 | 32,376.0 | 76,674.0 | 1,256.0 | Строительство |
| Agriculture | 177.0 | 314.8 | 1,425.0 | 11,097.0 | 18,192.0 | 464.0 | Сельское хозяйство |
| Transport | 223.0 | 323.8 | 1,611.0 | 17,916.0 | 47,377.0 | 1,072.0 | Транспорт |
| Communications | 191.0 | 329.9 | 2,083.0 | 17,299.0 | 46,661.0 | 1,102.0 | Связь |
| Trade (retail and wholesale) | 190.0 | 295.0 | 1,440.0 | 14,359.0 | 33,478.0 | 565.0 | Торговля (оптовая и розничная) |
| Other | .. | .. | .. | 19,944.0 | .. | 694.0 | Прочие отрасли материального производства |
| **Nonmaterial sphere** | .. | .. | .. | .. | .. | .. | **Отрасли непроизводственной сферы** |
| Municipal services | 160.0 | 272.9 | 1,814.0 | 16,382.0 | 38,046.0 | 651.0 | Жилкомхоз и бытовое обслуживание |
| Science, research and development | 288.0 | 435.2 | 2,534.0 | 16,568.0 | 44,508.0 | 876.0 | Наука и научное обслуживание |
| Education | 183.0 | 294.1 | 1,721.0 | 12,072.0 | 28,341.0 | 448.0 | Образование |
| Culture | 142.5 | 233.5 | 1,445.0 | 10,425.0 | 22,532.0 | 631.0 | Культура |
| Arts | 173.0 | 274.1 | 1,428.0 | 9,837.0 | 22,532.0 | 631.0 | Искусство |
| Health care, social security, and sports | 167.0 | 269.2 | 1,557.0 | 10,384.0 | 26,018.0 | 503.0 | Здравоохр., соц.обсл., физк. и спорт |
| Banking, finance, credit, insurance | 296.0 | 712.4 | 4,665.0 | 41,304.0 | 113,959.0 | 2,039.0 | Кредитование, страхование, банк. дело |
| Government | 300.0 | 419.3 | 2,994.0 | 22,576.0 | 43,106.0 | 793.0 | Управление |

**TABLE 8-1. Money income and expenditure of the population (millions of national currency)**
**ТАБЛИЦА 8-1. Денежные доходы и расходы населения (млн. национальной валюты)**

| Type of income or expenditure | 1990 | 1991 | 1992 | 1993 | 1994 | 1995 | Вид доходов или расходов |
|---|---|---|---|---|---|---|---|
| **Income** | | | | | | | **Доходы** |
| **Total labor income** | 4,254 | 7,219 | 34,734 | 356,438 | 266,401 | 10,162 | **Всего трудовых доходов** |
| Regular wages | 3,258 | 4,816 | 26,000 | 239,458 | 235,829 | 8,508 | Заработная плата |
| Wages paid by cooperatives | 203 | 180 | 773 | 6,214 | 1,933 | 57 | Заработная плата в кооперативах |
| Other wages and compensation | 137 | 319 | 933 | 11,823 | 9,325 | 427 | Прочие доходы типа заработной платы |
| Income paid by collective farms | 535 | 1,623 | 6,275 | 69,483 | 15,512 | 802 | Доходы от колхозов |
| Income from sale of farm products | 324 | 461 | 1,526 | 35,674 | 5,735 | 425 | Доходы от продажи продукции колхозов |
| **Total transfer receipts** | 1,346 | 3,290 | 8,517 | 106,040 | 114,758 | 2,622 | **Всего трансфертных поступлений** |
| Pensions and allowances | 801 | 2,046 | 6,312 | 53,451 | .. | .. | Пенсии и пособия |
| Scholarships | 44 | 103 | 490 | 3,230 | .. | .. | Стипендии |
| Income from the financial system (insurance, interest, etc.) | 249 | 320 | 504 | 3,182 | .. | .. | Доходы из финансовой системы (страховые возмещения, проценты и т.д.) |
| Other income | 252 | 821 | 1,211 | 46,177 | .. | .. | Прочие виды доходов |
| **Total income** | 5,600 | 10,509 | 43,251 | 462,478 | 381,158 | 12,784 | **Всего доходов** |
| **Expenditure** | | | | | | | **Расходы** |
| **Total purchases** | 4,631 | 7,461 | 25,298 | 250,866 | 131,806 | 6,007 | **Всего покупок товаров и услуг** |
| Retail goods | 4,207 | 6,532 | 22,033 | 222,251 | .. | .. | Товары в розничной торговле |
| Services | 424 | 929 | 3,264 | 28,615 | .. | .. | Услуги |
| Rent and utilities | 90 | 103 | 487 | 5,060 | .. | .. | Квартирная плата и коммунальные платежи |
| Transport and communications | 193 | 304 | 1,584 | 13,424 | .. | .. | Транспорт и связь |
| Health and other services | 34 | 47 | 89 | 1,012 | .. | .. | Здравоохранение и другие виды услуг |
| Cooperatives | 14 | 76 | 52 | 373 | .. | .. | Кооперативы |
| **Transfers and savings** | 963 | 2,541 | 3,472 | 82,352 | 164,726 | 1,401 | **Трансферты и сбережения** |
| Taxes, fees, dues, and other | 510 | 601 | 2,230 | 19,946 | 76,437 | 1,409 | Налоги, сборы, пошлины и др. |
| Savings | 453 | 1,881 | 934 | 61,633 | 88,289 | -8 | Сбережения |
| Other | .. | 59 | 308 | 773 | .. | .. | Прочие |
| **Total expenditure** | 5,594 | 10,002 | 28,770 | 333,218 | 296,532 | 7,408 | **Всего расходов** |
| **Income less expenditure** | 6 | 507 | 14,481 | 129,260 | 84,626 | 5,376 | **Доходы за вычетом расходов** |

# *Country Notes: Tajikistan*

**General Notes:** Unless otherwise indicated, data were supplied by the State Statistical Agency of the Republic of Tajikistan.

**Currency:** The Tajik ruble was introduced in May of 1995. The conversion factor at the time of introduction was 1 Tajik ruble per 100 Russian rubles. Unless otherwise indicated, data are in Russian rubles up to 1994 and in Tajik rubles for 1995.

**Table 1-1:** Data reflects population at the beginning of each year.

**Table 1-2:** Insurance includes credit. Wholesale trade includes retail trade and catering. In 1994 material supply and procurement are also included with wholesale trade; road maintenance is included with transportation of goods; public utilities and personal services are included with housing.

**Table 2-1:** Transport includes road maintenance and communication. Wholesale trade includes retail trade and catering. Insurance includes credit. Data for 1994 and 1995 are preliminary.

**Table 3-1:** Tajik authorities and IMF staff estimates.

**Table 5-3:** Data for grain are in clean weight.

**Table 5-4:** Data for meat are in live weight.

**Table 6-1:** All data are in Tajik rubles.

**Table 6-2:** All data are in Tajik rubles in 1995 prices.

**Table 6-3:** Coal, lignite, and oil are reported in thousand tons; gas is reported in million cubic meters; electricity is reported in million kilowatt-hours.

**Table 8-1:** Services by kind do not add up to total. The 1994 data are World Bank staff estimates. The 1995 data are for the period May-December and are preliminary.

# *Комментарии к таблицам: Таджикистан*

**Общее замечание:** За исключением особо отмеченных случаев, данные были получены из Государственного Комитета по Статистике Республики Таджикистан.

**Национальная валюта:** Таджикский рубль был введен в мае 1995 г. Коэффициент пересчета на дату введения был 1 таджикский рубль за 100 русских рублей. Данные приведены в русских рублях до 1994 г. включительно и в таджикских рублях за 1995 г.

**Таблица 1-1:** Численность населения приведена на начало года.

**Таблица 1-2:** Страхование и кредитование приводятся вместе. Оптовая торговля включает также розничную торговлю и общественное питание, а в 1994 г. сюда дополнительно включены материальное снабжение и заготовки. В 1994 г. транспорт включает также дорожное хозяйство; жилищное хозяйство включает также коммунальное хозяйство и бытовые услуги.

**Таблица 2-1:** Транспорт включает также дорожное хозяйство и связь. Страхование включает также кредитование. Оптовая торговля включает также розничную торговлю и общепит. За 1994 г. и 1995 г. приведены предварительные данные.

**Таблица 3-1:** Данные приведены по расчётам Таджикского Комитета по Статистике и сотрудников МВФ.

**Таблица 5-3:** Зерно приводится в чистом весе.

**Таблица 5-4:** Мясо приводится в живом весе.

**Таблица 6-1:** Все данные приведены в таджикских рублях.

**Таблица 6-2:** Все данные приведены в таджикских рублях, в ценах 1995 г.

**Таблица 6-3:** Данные по каменному и бурому углю и по нефти приведены в тысячах тонн, по газу - в миллионах кубических метров, по электричеству - в миллионах киловатт-часов.

**Таблица 8-1:** Сумма компонентов раздела Услуги не совпадает с итогом. Данные за 1994 г. рассчитаны сотрудниками Всемирного Банка. Данные за 1995 г. рассчитаны за май--декабрь и являются предварительными.

# Turkmenistan / Туркменистан

1996 Population / Численность населения в 1996 году
(thousands / тыс. человек): 4,198

Area / Территория
(thousand square kilometers / тыс. кв. км.): 488.1

Capital city / Столица :
Ashgabat / Ашгабат

**Country Tables:** Tables 1-3, 3-2B, 3-3B, and 3-4B are not included because there are no data available.

**Статистические таблицы страны:** Таблицы 1-3, 3-2В, 3-3В и 3-4В не включены ввиду отсутствия данных.

## TABLE 1-1. Population and employment (thousands)
## ТАБЛИЦА 1-1. Население и занятость (тысяч)



| Population or employment category | 1990 | 1991 | 1992 | 1993 | 1994 | 1995 | Население или группы занятых |
|---|---|---|---|---|---|---|---|
| **Total population** | 3,657 | 3,750 | 3,846 | 3,947 | 4,045 | 4,478 | **Население - всего** |
| Males | 1,803 | 1,850 | 1,899 | 1,950 | 1,999 | 2,219 | Мужчины |
| Females | 1,854 | 1,900 | 1,947 | 1,997 | 2,046 | 2,259 | Женщины |
| Urban population | 1,650 | 1,690 | 1,718 | 1,758 | 1,797 | 1,993 | Городское |
| Rural population | 2,007 | 2,060 | 2,128 | 2,189 | 2,248 | 2,485 | Сельское |
| Population under working age | .. | .. | .. | .. | .. | .. | Моложе трудоспособного возраста |
| Working-age population | 1,823 | 1,872 | 1,923 | 1,978 | 2,027 | 2,248 | Лица в трудоспособном возрасте |
| Population over working age | .. | .. | .. | .. | .. | .. | Старще трудоспособного возраста |
| Economically Active Population, in non-working age | 81 | 90 | 102 | .. | .. | .. | Экономически активное население в нетрудоспособном возрасте |
| Above working age | 59 | 65 | 70 | .. | .. | .. | Старше трудоспособного возраста |
| Below working age | 22 | 25 | 32 | .. | .. | .. | Моложе трудоспособного возраста |
| **Total labor resources** | .. | .. | .. | .. | .. | .. | **Трудовые ресурсы - всего** |
| **Total employment** | 1,542 | 1,571 | 1,573 | 1,642 | 1,665 | 1,673 | **Занятое население - всего** |
| State sector employees | 926 | 920 | 886 | 883 | 863 | 798 | Государственный сектор |
| Leased enterprise employees | .. | .. | .. | 61 | 75 | 77 | Арендные предприятия |
| Joint-stock company employees | .. | .. | .. | .. | .. | .. | Акционерные общества |
| Economic association employees | .. | .. | .. | .. | .. | .. | Хозяйственные ассоциации |
| Social organization employees | .. | .. | .. | 5 | 3 | 4 | Общественные организации |
| Joint venture employees | .. | .. | .. | .. | .. | .. | Совместные предприятия |
| Collective farm workers | 355 | 357 | 373 | 376 | 374 | 448 | Колхозы |
| Cooperative workers | 33 | 49 | 59 | 48 | 47 | 45 | Кооперативы |
| Individual labor activities | 2 | 2 | 2 | 2 | 2 | 3 | ИТД |
| Private subsidiary agricultural workers | 229 | 243 | 253 | 266 | 278 | 293 | Личные подсобные хозяйства |
| Private agricultural workers | .. | .. | .. | .. | .. | .. | Фермерские хозяйства |
| **Students** | .. | .. | .. | .. | .. | .. | **Учащиеся** |
| **Religious workers** | .. | .. | .. | .. | .. | .. | **Служащие религиозного культа** |
| **Working age population not employed in the national economy** | .. | .. | .. | .. | .. | .. | **Лица в трудоспособном возрасте, не занятые в экономике** |
| Housewives | .. | .. | .. | .. | .. | .. | Домохозяйки |
| Military personnel | .. | .. | .. | .. | .. | .. | Военнослужащие |
| Unemployed | .. | .. | .. | .. | .. | .. | Безработные |
| **Labor force** | .. | .. | .. | .. | .. | .. | **Рабочая сила** |

**TABLE 1-2. Employment by sector (thousands)**
**ТАБЛИЦА 1-2. Численность занятого населения по секторам (тысяч)**

| Sector | 1990 | 1991 | 1992 | 1993 | 1994 | 1995 | Сектор |
|---|---|---|---|---|---|---|---|
| **Material sphere** | 1,146 | 1,174 | 1,186 | 1,254 | 1,270 | 1,267 | **Сфера материального производства** |
| **Agriculture and forestry** | 647 | 666 | 695 | 719 | 730 | 739 | **Сельское и лесное хозяйство** |
| Agriculture | 645 | 664 | 693 | 717 | 727 | 736 | Сельское хозяйство |
| Forestry | 2 | 2 | 2 | 2 | 3 | 3 | Лесное хозяйство |
| **Industry and construction** | 321 | 327 | 318 | 341 | 335 | 322 | **Промышленность и строительство** |
| Industry | 166 | 159 | 154 | 171 | 166 | 166 | Промышленность |
| Construction | 154 | 168 | 164 | 170 | 169 | 156 | Строительство |
| **Other** | 178 | 180 | 173 | 194 | 205 | 206 | **Другие отрасли** |
| Transport of goods | 63 | 63 | 56 | 55 | 56 | 55 | Грузовой транспорт |
| Road Maintenance | .. | .. | .. | .. | .. | .. | Дорожное хозяйство |
| Communication servicing material production | .. | .. | .. | .. | .. | .. | Связь |
| Wholesale trade | .. | .. | .. | 102 | 107 | 107 | Оптовая торговля |
| Retail trade and catering | .. | .. | .. | .. | .. | .. | Розничная торговля и общепит |
| Material supply | .. | .. | .. | .. | .. | .. | Материально-техническое снабжение |
| Procurement | .. | .. | .. | .. | .. | .. | Заготовки |
| Information and computing services | .. | .. | .. | 2 | 2 | 2 | Информационно-техническое обслуживание |
| Other sectors | 115 | 117 | 117 | 35 | 40 | 42 | Другие отрасли сферы материального пр. |
| **Nonmaterial sphere** | 397 | 397 | 387 | 388 | 395 | 406 | **Сфера нематериального производства** |
| Passenger transport | .. | .. | .. | 27 | 28 | 27 | Пассажирский транспорт |
| Communication | .. | .. | .. | .. | .. | .. | Связь |
| Housing | 38 | 37 | 38 | 40 | 46 | 46 | Жилищное хозяйство |
| Public utilities and personal services | .. | .. | .. | .. | .. | .. | Комм. хоз. и бытовое обслуживание |
| Health care, social security, physical culture and sports | 86 | 87 | 82 | 97 | 96 | 97 | Здравоохранение, социальное обеспечение, физкультура и спорт |
| Education | 176 | 182 | 172 | 184 | 185 | 193 | Образование |
| Culture and art | .. | .. | .. | .. | .. | .. | Культура и искусство |
| Science and scientific research | 28 | 23 | 21 | 10 | 11 | 11 | Наука и научное обслуживание |
| Credit | .. | .. | .. | 7 | 7 | 8 | Кредитование |
| Insurance | .. | .. | .. | .. | .. | .. | Страхование |
| General administration and defense | 69 | 68 | 74 | .. | .. | .. | Государственное управление и оборона |
| Private nonprofit institutions serving households | .. | .. | .. | 23 | 22 | 24 | Общественные организации, обслуживающие домашние хозяйства |
| **Other, material and nonmaterial spheres** | 575 | 576 | 560 | 582 | 600 | 612 | **Остальные отрасли материального производства и нематериальной сферы** |
| **Total employment** | 1,542 | 1,571 | 1,573 | 1,642 | 1,665 | 1,673 | **Занятые - всего** |

## TABLE 2-1.* Gross domestic product at current prices (millions of national currency)
## ТАБЛИЦА 2-1.* Валовой внутренний продукт в текущих ценах (млн. национальной валюты)

| Sector of origin or expenditure category | 1990 | 1991 | 1992 | 1993 | 1994 | 1995 | Отраслевое происхождение или вид расходов |
|---|---|---|---|---|---|---|---|
| **Gross domestic product by sector of origin** | | | | | | | **Валовой внутренний продукт по отраслевому происхождению** |
| **Agriculture and forestry** | .. | .. | .. | 864 | 23,109 | 162,115 | **Сельское и лесное хозяйство** |
| Agriculture | .. | .. | .. | 862 | 23,092 | 161,998 | Сельское хозяйство |
| Forestry | .. | .. | .. | 2 | 16 | 117 | Лесное хозяйство |
| **Industry and construction** | .. | .. | .. | 5,858 | 18,320 | 183,775 | **Промышленность и строительство** |
| Industry | .. | .. | .. | 4,695 | 11,645 | 115,490 | Промышленность |
| Construction | .. | .. | .. | 1,163 | 6,674 | 68,285 | Строительство |
| **Other** | .. | .. | .. | 1,892 | 15,170 | .. | **Другие отрасли** |
| Transport | .. | .. | .. | 493 | 2,921 | 26,199 | Транспорт |
| Road maintenance | .. | .. | .. | .. | .. | .. | Дорожное хозяйство |
| Communication | .. | .. | .. | .. | .. | .. | Связь |
| Wholesale trade | .. | .. | .. | .. | .. | .. | Оптовая торговля |
| Retail trade and catering | .. | .. | .. | 358 | 3,590 | 20,075 | Розничная торговля и общепит |
| Material supply | .. | .. | .. | 150 | 1,267 | 11,721 | Материально-техническое снабжение |
| Procurement | .. | .. | .. | 28 | 367 | 2,616 | Заготовки |
| Information and computing services | .. | .. | .. | 3 | 50 | 459 | Информационно-вычислительное обслуживание |
| Other sectors of material production | .. | .. | .. | 43 | 47 | 427 | Другие отрасли сферы материального пр. |
| Housing | .. | .. | .. | 8 | 43 | .. | Жилищное хозяйство |
| Public utilities and personal services | .. | .. | .. | 107 | 910 | .. | Ком. хоз. и бытовое обслуживание |
| Health care, social security, physical culture and sports | .. | .. | .. | 143 | 1,003 | .. | Здравоохранение, социальное обеспечение, физкультура и спорт |
| Education | .. | .. | .. | 245 | 1,903 | .. | Образование |
| Culture and art | .. | .. | .. | 27 | 103 | .. | Культура и искусство |
| Science and scientific research | .. | .. | .. | 50 | 330 | .. | Наука и научное обслуживание |
| Credit | .. | .. | .. | 161 | 2,112 | .. | Кредитование |
| Insurance | .. | .. | .. | .. | .. | .. | Страхование |
| General administration and defense | .. | .. | .. | 74 | 522 | .. | Государственное управление и оборона |
| Private nonprofit institutions serving households | .. | .. | .. | 2 | 2 | .. | Общественные организации, обслуживающие домашние хозяйства |
| **Imputed service charge of financial intermediaries** | .. | .. | .. | -122 | -2,307 | .. | **Условно-исчисляемая стоимость услуг финансовых посредников** |
| **Total gross value added (GVA)** | .. | .. | .. | 8,492 | 54,292 | 438,581 | **Валовая добавленная стоимость (ВДС) - всего** |
| **Taxes on production and imports (TOPI)** | .. | .. | .. | 542 | 4,750 | 36,840 | **Налоги на производство и импорт (НПиИ)** |
| Other taxes on production (OTOP) | .. | .. | .. | .. | .. | .. | Другие налоги на производство (ДНП) |
| **Subsidies on production and imports (SOPI)** | .. | .. | .. | .. | .. | .. | **Субсидии на производство и импорт (СПиИ)** |
| Other subsidies on production (OSOP) | .. | .. | .. | 338 | 1,427 | 10,964 | Другие субсидии на производство (ДСП) |
| **Total GDP at market prices** | 7,582 | 14,666 | 284,197 | 8,696 | 57,625 | 464,457 | **Всего ВВП в рыночных ценах** |

*This is the first time Turkmenistan has submitted GDP estimates by industrial origin developed by the Central Statistical Office. The estimates are of an experimental nature with output valued at domestic prices. They may differ from those compiled by the World Bank and other international organizations.

**В этом году Туркменистан впервые предоставил оценки ВВП по производству, рассчитанные Государственным Комитетом по Статистике Республики Туркменистан. Расчеты носят экспериментальный характер, и весь выпуск оценен во внутренних ценах. Данные могут отличаться от публикуемых Всемирным Банком и другими международными организациями.**

**TABLE 2-1A.* Distribution of gross domestic product at current prices (percent)**

**ТАБЛИЦА 2-1А.* Распределение валового внутреннего продукта в текущих ценах ( % )**

| Sector of origin or expenditure category | 1990 | 1991 | 1992 | 1993 | 1994 | 1995 | Отраслевое происхождение или вид расходов |
|---|---|---|---|---|---|---|---|
| **Gross domestic product by sector of origin** | | | | | | | **ВВП по отраслевому происхождению** |
| **Agriculture and forestry** | .. | .. | .. | 9.9 | 40.1 | 34.9 | **Сельское и лесное хозяйство** |
| Agriculture | .. | .. | .. | 9.9 | 40.1 | 34.9 | Сельское хозяйство |
| Forestry | .. | .. | .. | 0.0 | 0.0 | 0.0 | Лесное хозяйство |
| **Industry and construction** | .. | .. | .. | 67.4 | 31.8 | 39.6 | **Промышленность и строительство** |
| Industry | .. | .. | .. | 54.0 | 20.2 | 24.9 | Промышленность |
| Construction | .. | .. | .. | 13.4 | 11.6 | 14.7 | Строительство |
| **Other** | .. | .. | .. | 21.8 | 26.3 | .. | **Другие отрасли** |
| Transport | .. | .. | .. | 5.7 | 5.1 | 5.6 | Транспорт |
| Road maintenance | .. | .. | .. | .. | .. | .. | Дорожное хозяйство |
| Communication | .. | .. | .. | .. | .. | .. | Связь |
| Wholesale trade | .. | .. | .. | .. | .. | .. | Оптовая торговля |
| Retail trade and catering | .. | .. | .. | 4.1 | 6.2 | 4.3 | Розничная торговля и общепит |
| Material supply | .. | .. | .. | 1.7 | 2.2 | 2.5 | Материально-техническое снабжение |
| Procurement | .. | .. | .. | 0.3 | 0.6 | 0.6 | Заготовки |
| Information and computing services | .. | .. | .. | 0.0 | 0.1 | 0.1 | Информационно-вычислительное обслуживание |
| Other sectors of material production | .. | .. | .. | 0.5 | 0.1 | 0.1 | Другие отрасли сферы матерл. произ. |
| Housing | .. | .. | .. | 0.1 | 0.1 | .. | Жилищное хозяйство |
| Public utilities and personal services | .. | .. | .. | 1.2 | 1.6 | .. | Ком. хоз. и бытовое обслуживание |
| Health care, social security, physical culture and sports | .. | .. | .. | 1.6 | 1.7 | .. | Здравоохранение, социальное обеспечение, физкультура и спорт |
| Education | .. | .. | .. | 2.8 | 3.3 | .. | Образование |
| Culture and art | .. | .. | .. | 0.3 | 0.2 | .. | Культура и искусство |
| Science and scientific research | .. | .. | .. | 0.6 | 0.6 | .. | Наука и научное обслуживание |
| Credit | .. | .. | .. | 1.9 | 3.7 | .. | Кредитование |
| Insurance | .. | .. | .. | 0.0 | 0.0 | .. | Страхование |
| General administration and defense | .. | .. | .. | 0.9 | 0.9 | .. | Государственное управление и оборона |
| Private nonprofit institutions serving households | .. | .. | .. | 0.0 | 0.0 | .. | Общественные организации, обслуживающие домашние хозяйства |
| **Imputed service charge of financial intermediaries** | .. | .. | .. | -1.4 | -4.0 | .. | **Условно-исчисляемая стоимость услуг финансовых посредников** |
| **Total gross value added** | .. | .. | .. | 97.7 | 94.2 | 94.4 | **Валовая добавленная стоимость - всего** |
| **Total GDP at market prices** | 100.0 | 100.0 | 100.0 | 100.0 | 100.0 | 100.0 | **ВВП в рын. ценах - всего** |

*This is the first time Turkmenistan has submitted GDP estimates by industrial origin developed by the Central Statistical Office. The estimates are of an experimental nature with output valued at domestic prices. They may differ from those compiled by the World Bank and other international organizations.

В этом году Туркменистан впервые предоставил оценки ВВП по производству, рассчитанные Государственным Комитетом по Статистике Республики Туркменистан. Расчеты носят экспериментальный характер, и весь выпуск оценен во внутренних ценах. Данные могут отличаться от публикуемых Всемирным Банком и другими международными организациями.

## TABLE 2-2. Gross domestic product at constant prices (millions of national currency)
## ТАБЛИЦА 2-2. Валовой внутренний продукт в постоянных ценах (млн. национальной валюты)

| Sector of origin or expenditure category | 1990 | 1991 | 1992 | 1993 | 1994 | 1995 | Отраслевое происхождение или вид расходов |
|---|---|---|---|---|---|---|---|
| **Gross domestic product by sector of origin** | | | | | | | **Валовой внутренний продукт по отраслевому происхождению** |
| **Agriculture and forestry** | .. | .. | .. | .. | 1,231 | 23,684 | **Сельское и лесное хозяйство** |
| Agriculture | .. | .. | .. | .. | 1,230 | 23,667 | Сельское хозяйство |
| Forestry | .. | .. | .. | .. | 1 | 17 | Лесное хозяйство |
| **Industry and construction** | .. | .. | .. | .. | 4,121 | 16,698 | **Промышленность и строительство** |
| Industry | .. | .. | .. | .. | 3,713 | 11,622 | Промышленность |
| Construction | .. | .. | .. | .. | 408 | 5,077 | Строительство |
| **Other** | .. | .. | .. | .. | 876 | .. | **Другие отрасли** |
| Transport | .. | .. | .. | .. | 149 | 2,263 | Транспорт |
| Road maintenance | .. | .. | .. | .. | .. | .. | Дорожное хозяйство |
| Communication | .. | .. | .. | .. | .. | .. | Связь |
| Wholesale trade | .. | .. | .. | .. | .. | .. | Оптовая торговля |
| Retail trade and catering | .. | .. | .. | .. | 136 | 1,734 | Розничная торговля и общепит |
| Material supply | .. | .. | .. | .. | 125 | 1,180 | Материально-техническое снабжение |
| Procurement | .. | .. | .. | .. | 20 | 382 | Заготовки |
| Information and computing services | .. | .. | .. | .. | 5 | 46 | Информационно-вычислительное обслуживание |
| Other sectors of material production | .. | .. | .. | .. | 5 | 42 | Другие отрасли сферы материального пр. |
| Housing | .. | .. | .. | .. | 2 | .. | Жилищное хозяйство |
| Public utilities and personal services | .. | .. | .. | .. | 17 | .. | Ком. хоз. и бытовое обслуживание |
| Health care, social security, and sports | .. | .. | .. | .. | 37 | .. | Здравоохранение, социальное обеспечение, физкультура и спорт |
| Education | .. | .. | .. | .. | 60 | .. | Образование |
| Culture and art | .. | .. | .. | .. | 4 | .. | Культура и искусство |
| Science and research | .. | .. | .. | .. | 28 | .. | Наука и научное обслуживание |
| Credit | .. | .. | .. | .. | 174 | .. | Кредитование |
| Insurance | .. | .. | .. | .. | .. | .. | Страхование |
| General administration and defense | .. | .. | .. | .. | 115 | .. | Государственное управление и оборона |
| Private nonprofit institutions serving households | .. | .. | .. | .. | 1 | .. | Общественные организации, обслуживающие домашние хозяйства |
| **Imputed service charge of financial intermediaries** | .. | .. | .. | .. | -131 | .. | **Условно-исчисляемая стоимость услуг финансовых посредников** |
| **Total gross value added (GVA)** | .. | .. | .. | 649 | 6,096 | 51,440 | **Валовая добавленная стоимость (ВДС) -** |
| **Total GDP at factor cost (GVA-OTOP+OSOP)** | .. | .. | .. | .. | .. | .. | **Всего ВВП по фактр. стоимости (ВДС-ДНП+ДСП)** |
| **Net indirect taxes (TOPI - SOPI)** | .. | .. | .. | .. | .. | .. | **Чистые косвенные налоги (НПиИ-СПиИ)** |
| **Total GDP at market prices** | .. | .. | .. | .. | .. | .. | **Всего ВВП в рыночных ценах** |

*This is the first time Turkmenistan has submitted GDP estimates by industrial origin developed by the Central Statistical Office. The estimates are of an experimental nature with output valued at domestic prices. They may differ from those compiled by the World Bank and other international organizations.

В этом году Туркменистан впервые предоставил оценки ВВП по производству, рассчитанные Государственным Комитетом по Статистике Республики Туркменистан. Расчеты носят экспериментальный характер, и весь выпуск оценен во внутренних ценах. Данные могут отличаться от публикуемых Всемирным Банком и другими международными организациями.

**TABLE 2-2A.* Growth rates of gross domestic product at constant prices (percent)**
**ТАБЛИЦА 2-2А.* Валовой внутренний продукт - темпы прироста в постоянных ценах ( % )**

| Sector of origin or expenditure category | 1990 | 1991 | 1992 | 1993 | 1994 | 1995 | Отраслевое происхождение или вид расходов |
|---|---|---|---|---|---|---|---|
| **Growth rate by sector of origin** | | | | | | | **Валовый внутренний продукт по отраслевому происхождению** |
| **Agriculture and forestry** | .. | .. | .. | .. | 42.4 | 2.5 | **Сельское и лесное хозяйство** |
| Agriculture | .. | .. | .. | .. | 42.6 | 2.5 | Сельское хозяйство |
| Forestry | .. | .. | .. | .. | -55.0 | 7.5 | Лесное хозяйство |
| **Industry and construction** | .. | .. | .. | .. | -29.7 | -8.9 | **Промышленность и строительство** |
| Industry | .. | .. | .. | .. | -20.9 | -0.2 | Промышленность |
| Construction | .. | .. | .. | .. | -64.9 | -23.9 | Строительство |
| **Other** | .. | .. | .. | .. | -53.7 | .. | **Другие отрасли** |
| Transport | .. | .. | .. | .. | -69.9 | -22.5 | Транспорт |
| Road maintenance | .. | .. | .. | .. | .. | .. | Дорожное хозяйство |
| Communication | .. | .. | .. | .. | .. | .. | Связь |
| Wholesale trade | .. | .. | .. | .. | .. | .. | Оптовая торговля |
| Retail trade and catering | .. | .. | .. | .. | -62.2 | -51.7 | Розничная торговля и общепит |
| Material supply | .. | .. | .. | .. | -16.5 | -6.9 | Материально-техническое снабжение |
| Procurement | .. | .. | .. | .. | -28.9 | 4.1 | Заготовки |
| Information and computing services | .. | .. | .. | .. | 63.3 | -7.6 | Информационно-вычислительное обслуживание |
| Other sectors of material production | .. | .. | .. | .. | -89.5 | -10.0 | Другие отрасли сферы материального пр. |
| Housing | .. | .. | .. | .. | -70.0 | .. | Жилищное хозяйство |
| Public utilities and personal services | .. | .. | .. | .. | -84.0 | .. | Ком. хоз. и бытовое обслуживание |
| Health care, social security, and sports | .. | .. | .. | .. | -74.3 | .. | Здравоохранение, социальное обеспечение, физкультура и спорт |
| Education | .. | .. | .. | .. | -75.6 | .. | Образование |
| Culture and art | .. | .. | .. | .. | .. | .. | Культура и искусство |
| Science and research | .. | .. | .. | .. | -43.4 | .. | Наука и научное обслуживание |
| Credit | .. | .. | .. | .. | 7.8 | .. | Кредитование |
| Insurance | .. | .. | .. | .. | .. | .. | Страхование |
| General administration and defense | .. | .. | .. | .. | 54.9 | .. | Государственное управление и оборона |
| Private nonprofit institutions serving households | .. | .. | .. | .. | -30.0 | .. | Общественные организации, обслуживающие домашние хозяйства |
| **Imputed service charge of financial intermediaries** | .. | .. | .. | .. | 7.4 | .. | **Условно-исчисляемая стоимость услуг финансовых посредников** |
| **Total gross value added** | .. | .. | .. | .. | -28.2 | -5.3 | **Валовая добавленная стоимость (ВДС) - всего** |
| **Total GDP at market prices** | .. | .. | .. | .. | .. | .. | **Всего ВВП в рыночных ценах** |

*This is the first time Turkmenistan has submitted GDP estimates by industrial origin developed by the Central Statistical Office. The estimates are of an experimental nature with output valued at domestic prices. They may differ from those compiled by the World Bank and other international organizations.

В этом году Туркменистан впервые предоставил оценки ВВП по производству, рассчитанные Государственным Комитетом по Статистике Республики Туркменистан. Расчеты носят экспериментальный характер, и весь выпуск оценен во внутренних ценах. Данные могут отличаться от публикуемых Всемирным Банком и другими международными организациями.

**TABLE 2-2B. Implicit price deflators for gross domestic product (percentage change)**
**ТАБЛИЦА 2-2B. Дефляторы валового внутреннего продукта (темпы прироста в %)**

| Sector of origin or expenditure category | 1990 | 1991 | 1992 | 1993 | 1994 | 1995 | Отраслевое происхождение или вид расходов |
|---|---|---|---|---|---|---|---|
| **Price deflators by sector of origin** | | | | | | | **Дефляторы по отраслевому происхождению или виду расходов** |
| **Agriculture and forestry** | .. | .. | .. | .. | 1,778.0 | 584.5 | **Сельское и лесное хозяйство** |
| Agriculture | .. | .. | .. | .. | 1,778.0 | 584.5 | Сельское хозяйство |
| Forestry | .. | .. | .. | .. | 1,677.8 | 580.2 | Лесное хозяйство |
| **Industry and construction** | .. | .. | .. | .. | 344.6 | 1,000.6 | **Промышленность и строительство** |
| Industry | .. | .. | .. | .. | 213.7 | 893.7 | Промышленность |
| Construction | .. | .. | .. | .. | 1,536.2 | 1,245.1 | Строительство |
| **Other** | .. | .. | .. | .. | 1,630.9 | .. | **Другие отрасли** |
| Transport | .. | .. | .. | .. | 1,867.0 | 1,057.8 | Транспорт |
| Road maintenance | .. | .. | .. | .. | .. | .. | Дорожное хозяйство |
| Communication | .. | .. | .. | .. | .. | .. | Связь |
| Wholesale trade | .. | .. | .. | .. | .. | .. | Оптовая торговля |
| Retail trade and catering | .. | .. | .. | .. | 2,549.4 | 1,057.8 | Розничная торговля и общепит. |
| Material supply | .. | .. | .. | .. | 911.2 | 893.7 | Материально-техническое снабжение |
| Procurement | .. | .. | .. | .. | 1,744.2 | 584.6 | Заготовки |
| Information and computing services | .. | .. | .. | .. | 920.4 | 893.5 | Информационно-вычислительное обслуживание |
| Other sectors of material production | .. | .. | .. | .. | 944.4 | 909.5 | Другие отрасли сферы матерл. произ. |
| Housing | .. | .. | .. | .. | 1,691.7 | .. | Жилищное хозяйство |
| Public utilities and personal services | .. | .. | .. | .. | 5,221.6 | .. | Ком. хоз. и бытовое обслуживание |
| Health care, social security, and sports | .. | .. | .. | .. | 2,633.0 | .. | Здравоохранение, социальное обеспечение, физкультура и спорт |
| Education | .. | .. | .. | .. | 3,082.3 | .. | Образование |
| Culture and art | .. | .. | .. | .. | .. | .. | Культура и искусство |
| Science and research | .. | .. | .. | .. | 1,066.1 | .. | Наука и научное обслуживание |
| Credit | .. | .. | .. | .. | 1,117.3 | .. | Кредитование |
| Insurance | .. | .. | .. | .. | .. | .. | Страхование |
| General administration and defense | .. | .. | .. | .. | 355.5 | .. | Государственное управление и оборона |
| Private nonprofit institutions serving households | .. | .. | .. | .. | 42.9 | .. | Общественные организации, обслуживающие домашние хозяства |
| **Imputed service charge of financial intermediaries** | .. | .. | .. | .. | 1,661.1 | .. | **Условно-исчисляемая стоимость услуг финансовых посредников** |
| **Total gross value added** | .. | .. | .. | .. | 790.6 | 752.6 | **Валовая добавленная стоимость (ВДС) - всего** |
| **Total GDP at factor cost** | .. | .. | .. | .. | .. | .. | **ВВП по факторной стоимости (ВДС-ДНП+ДСП)** |
| **Net indirect taxes** | .. | .. | .. | .. | .. | .. | **Чистые косвенные налоги (НПИ-СПИ)** |
| **Total GDP at market prices** | .. | .. | .. | .. | .. | .. | **ВВП в рыночных ценах** |

*This is the first time Turkmenistan has submitted GDP estimates by industrial origin developed by the Central Statistical Office. The estimates are of an experimental nature with output valued at domestic prices. They may differ from those compiled by the World Bank and other international organizations.

В этом году Туркменистан впервые предоставил оценки ВВП по производству, рассчитанные Государственным Комитетом по Статистике Республики Туркменистан. Расчеты носят экспериментальный характер, и весь выпуск оценен во внутренних ценах. Данные могут отличаться от публикуемых Всемирным Банком и другими международными организациями.

## TABLE 3-1. Balance of payments at current prices (millions of U.S. dollars)
## ТАБЛИЦА 3-1. Платежный баланс в текущих ценах (в миллионах долларов США)

| Item | 1990 | 1991 | 1992 | 1993 | 1994 | 1995 | Статьи |
|---|---|---|---|---|---|---|---|
| Exports of goods and services (including workers' remittances) | .. | .. | .. | 2,918.0 | 2,482.7 | 2,423.7 | Экспорт товаров и услуг (включая денежные переводы рабочих) |
| Exports of goods and nonfactor services | .. | .. | .. | 2,900.4 | 2,255.4 | 2,190.6 | Экспорт товаров и нефакт. услуг |
| Merchandise (FOB) | .. | 1,190.6 | 1,251.0 | 2,692.7 | 2,176.0 | 2,084.3 | Товары (ФОБ) |
| Nonfactor services | .. | .. | .. | 207.7 | 78.5 | 106.3 | Нефакторные услуги |
| Shipment | .. | .. | .. | .. | .. | .. | Перевозки |
| Travel | .. | .. | .. | .. | .. | .. | Поездки |
| Other | .. | .. | .. | .. | .. | .. | Другие |
| Imports of goods and nonfactor services | .. | .. | .. | 2,136.3 | 2,234.3 | 2,229.6 | Импорт товаров и нефакт. услуг |
| Merchandise (FOB) | .. | 483.2 | 659.3 | 1,592.0 | 1,690.4 | 1,643.6 | Товары (ФОБ) |
| Nonfactor services | .. | .. | .. | 544.3 | 543.9 | 586.0 | Нефакторные услуги |
| Shipment | .. | .. | .. | .. | .. | .. | Перевозки |
| Travel | .. | .. | .. | .. | .. | .. | Поездки |
| Other | .. | .. | .. | .. | .. | .. | Другие |
| Resource balance | .. | .. | .. | 764.1 | 21.1 | -39.0 | Сальдо ресурсов |
| Net factor income | .. | -26.6 | 13.2 | -0.7 | 62.4 | 86.7 | Чистый факторный доход |
| Factor receipts | .. | .. | .. | 17.6 | 227.3 | 215.2 | Факторные поступления |
| Factor payments | .. | .. | .. | 18.3 | 164.9 | 128.5 | Факторные платежи |
| Total interest due | .. | .. | .. | 2.5 | 24.8 | 34.5 | Общая сумма процента к оплате |
| Other factor payments and discrepancy | .. | .. | .. | 15.8 | 140.1 | 94.0 | Другие факторные платежи и стат. погр. |
| Net current transfers | .. | 1.3 | .. | 11.7 | 2.7 | -47.3 | Чистые текущие трансферты |
| Current receipts | .. | .. | .. | 11.8 | 3.4 | 26.6 | Текущие поступления |
| Workers remittances | .. | .. | .. | .. | .. | 17.9 | Денежные переводы рабочих |
| Other current transfers | .. | .. | .. | .. | .. | 8.7 | Другие текущие трансферты |
| Current payments | .. | .. | .. | 0.1 | 0.8 | 73.8 | Текущие платежи |
| Current account balance before official grants | .. | 510.6 | 425.8 | 775.1 | 86.2 | 0.6 | Сальдо текущего счета до офиц. безвозмезд. трансфертов |
| Official capital grants | .. | .. | .. | .. | .. | .. | Официальные кап. безвозмезные трансферты |
| Current account balance after official grants | .. | .. | .. | .. | .. | .. | Сальдо текущего счета после офиц. безвозмезд. трансфертов |
| Long Term Capital Inflows | .. | .. | .. | 380.3 | -38.4 | 561.2 | Долгосрочные притоки капитала |
| Direct investment | .. | .. | .. | 79.4 | 102.6 | 233.4 | Прямые инвестиции |
| Net long term borrowing | .. | .. | .. | 300.6 | -413.9 | -16.8 | Чистые долгосрочные займы |
| Disbursements | .. | .. | .. | 305.8 | 226.3 | 203.6 | Поступления |
| Repayments due | .. | .. | .. | 5.2 | 640.2 | 220.3 | Сумма, подлежащая погашению |
| Other long-term inflows (net) | .. | -0.2 | .. | 0.3 | 272.9 | 344.6 | Другие долгосрочные притоки (чистые) |

(continued on next page)

## TABLE 3-1. Balance of payments at current prices (millions of U.S. dollars)
## ТАБЛИЦА 3-1. Платежный баланс в текущих ценах (в миллионах долларов США)

| Item | 1990 | 1991 | 1992 | 1993 | 1994 | 1995 | Статьи |
|---|---|---|---|---|---|---|---|
| Adjustment to Scheduled Debt Service | .. | .. | .. | .. | .. | .. | Регулирование долга |
| Debt service not paid | .. | .. | .. | -930.9 | 673.6 | -387.0 | Невыплаченный долг |
| Interest not paid | .. | .. | .. | .. | 148.4 | -110.0 | Невыплаченный процент |
| Principal not paid | .. | .. | .. | -927.0 | 525.2 | -277.0 | Невыплаченная сумма основного долга |
| Arrears reductions/prepayments(-) | .. | -5.6 | .. | .. | 25.4 | -31.3 | Погашение просроченных платежей/выплаты авансом (-) |
| Total Other items (Net) | .. | .. | .. | .. | .. | .. | Общие другие статьи (чистые) |
| Net short-term capital | .. | .. | .. | .. | 82.4 | 129.5 | Чистый краткосрочный капитал |
| Capital flows not elsewhere included | .. | 34.3 | 20.9 | .. | .. | -12.6 | Потоки капитала, не указанные выше |
| Errors and omissions | .. | 0.1 | 38.1 | 158.1 | .. | .. | Ошибки и пропуски |
| Changes in net reserves | .. | .. | .. | .. | .. | .. | Изменения в чистых резервах |
| Net credit from IMF | .. | .. | .. | .. | .. | .. | Чистый кредит МВФ |
| Reserve changes not elsewhere included | .. | .. | .. | .. | .. | .. | Изменения резервов, не указанных выше |
| Escrow account | .. | .. | .. | -475.0 | -94.5 | -265.7 | Счет депонирования |
| Gross reserves (excluding gold) | .. | .. | .. | .. | .. | .. | Общие резервы (исключая золото) |
| Gross reserves (including gold) | .. | .. | .. | .. | .. | .. | Общие резервы (включая золото) |
| Nominal official exchange rate (annual average) (rf) | .. | 1.8 | 193.2 | 931.5 | 16.7 | 110.4 | Номинальный официальный или рыночный курс (среднегодовой) |
| Nominal official exchange rate (end-of-year) (ae) | .. | 1.7 | 414.5 | 1,191.1 | 75.0 | 200.0 | Номинальный официальный или рыночный курс (на конец года) |
| Manufacture unit value (percent change) | .. | .. | .. | .. | .. | .. | Средний индекс цен на продукцию обр. пром.,% |
| Index of real effective exchange rate (IMF) | .. | .. | .. | .. | .. | .. | Индекс реального эффективного валютного курса (МВФ) |
| Total factor payments | .. | .. | .. | -18.3 | -164.9 | 109.1 | Общая сумма факторных платежей |
| Government interest | .. | .. | .. | .. | .. | 23.3 | Процент, выплачиваемый органами гос. управления |
| Private sector interest | .. | .. | .. | .. | .. | .. | Процент выплачиваемый частным сектором |
| Profits on direct foreign investment | .. | .. | .. | .. | .. | .. | Прибыль от прямых иностранных инвестиций |
| Official capital grants | .. | .. | .. | .. | .. | .. | Официальные капитальные безвозмездные трансферты |
| For budgetary financing | .. | .. | .. | .. | .. | .. | На бюджетное финансирование |
| To extrabudgetary entities | .. | .. | .. | .. | .. | .. | На внебюджетное финансирование |
| Government net long term borrowing | .. | .. | .. | 426.8 | -383.6 | -16.5 | Чистые долгосрочные государственные займы |
| Disbursements | .. | .. | .. | 432.0 | 210.5 | 203.6 | Поступления |
| Repayments | .. | .. | .. | 5.2 | 594.1 | 220.3 | Погашения |
| Private net long term borrowing | .. | .. | .. | .. | .. | .. | Чистые долгосрочные частные займы |
| Disbursements | .. | .. | .. | .. | .. | .. | Поступления |
| Repayments | .. | .. | .. | .. | .. | .. | Погашения |

**TABLE 3-2A. Imports by commodity group (millions of U.S. dollars)**
**ТАБЛИЦА 3-2A . Импорт по товарным группам (млн. долларов США)**

| Commodity group | 1990 | 1991 | 1992 | 1993 | 1994 | 1995 | Товарные группы |
|---|---|---|---|---|---|---|---|
| TOTAL | .. | .. | .. | .. | 1,474.8 | 1,430.5 | ВСЕГО |
| I - Live animals; animal products | .. | .. | .. | .. | 78.7 | 76.1 | I - Живые животные и продукты животноводства |
| II - Vegetable products | .. | .. | .. | .. | 116.3 | 89.8 | II - Продукты растительного происхождения |
| III - Animal or vegetable fats and oils and their cleavage products; prepared edible fats; animal or vegetable waxes | .. | .. | .. | .. | 3.8 | 3.6 | III - Жиры и масла растительного и животного происхождения, воски |
| IV - Prepared foodstuffs; beverages, spirits and vinegar; tobacco and manufactured tobacco substitutes | .. | .. | .. | .. | 154.7 | 189.4 | IV -Продукция пищевой промышленности, алкогольные и безалкогольные напитки, табак и его заменители |
| V - Mineral products | .. | .. | .. | .. | 88.1 | 84.8 | V - Минеральные продукты |
| VI - Products of the chemical or allied industries | .. | .. | .. | .. | 78.7 | 107.9 | VI - Продукция химической промышленности |
| VII - Plastics and articles thereof; rubber and articles thereof | .. | .. | .. | .. | 28.4 | 46.6 | VII - Пластмассы и изделия из них |
| VIII - Raw hides and skins, leather, furskins and articles thereof; saddlery and harness; travel goods, handbags and similar containers; articles of animal gut | .. | .. | .. | .. | 4.4 | 4.6 | VIII - Кожевенное сырьё, кожи, пушнина, меховое сырьё и изделия из них |
| IX - Wood and articles of wood; wood charcoal; cork and articles of cork; manufactures of straw, of esparto or of other plaiting materials; basketware and wickerwork | .. | .. | .. | .. | 9.1 | 9.6 | IX - Древесина и изделия из древесины, древесный уголь |
| X - Pulp of wood or of other fibrous cellulosic material; waste and scrap of paper or paperboard; paper and paperboard and articles thereof | .. | .. | .. | .. | 8.8 | 8.2 | X - Бумажная масса, бумажные и картонные отходы, макулатура, бумага, картон и изделия из них |
| XI - Textiles and textile articles | .. | .. | .. | .. | 150.8 | 87.2 | XI - Текстиль и текстильные изделия |
| XII - Footwear, headgear, umbrellas, sun umbrellas, walking sticks, seat sticks, whips, riding crops and parts thereof; prepared feathers and articles made therewith; artificial flowers; articles of human hair | .. | .. | .. | .. | 42.9 | 28.8 | XII - Обувь, головные уборы, зонты, трости и пр. |

**TABLE 3-2A. Imports by commodity group (millions of U.S. dollars)**
**ТАБЛИЦА 3-2A . Импорт по товарным группам (млн. долларов США)**



| Commodity group | 1990 | 1991 | 1992 | 1993 | 1994 | 1995 | Товарные группы |
|---|---|---|---|---|---|---|---|
| XIII - Articles of stone, plaster, cement, asbestos, mica and similar materials; ceramic products; glass and glassware | .. | .. | .. | .. | 19.9 | 13.2 | XIII - Изделия из камня, гипса, цемента |
| XIV - Natural or cultured pearls, precious or semi-precious stones, precious metals, metals clad with precious metal and articles thereof; imitation jewellery; coin | .. | .. | .. | .. | 8.1 | 1.7 | XIV - Жемчуг, драгоценные и полудрагоценные камни, драгоценные металлы, бижутерия, монеты |
| XV - Base metals and articles of base metal | .. | .. | .. | .. | 87.3 | 164.2 | XV - Неблагородные металлы и изделия из них |
| XVI - Machinery and mechanical appliances; electrical equipment; parts thereof; sound recorders and reproducers, television image and sound recorders and reproducers, and parts and accessories of such articles | .. | .. | .. | .. | 241.2 | 185.5 | XVI - Машины, оборудование, механизмы, их части и принадлежности; звуковая и теле-аппаратура, их части и принадлежности |
| XVII - Vehicles, aircraft, vessels and associated transport equipment | .. | .. | .. | .. | 108.2 | 58.6 | XVII - Средства наземного, воздушного и водного транспорта |
| XVIII - Optical, photographic, cinematograp-hic, measuring, checking, precision, medical or surgical instruments and apparatus; clocks and watches; musical instruments; parts and accessories thereof | .. | .. | .. | .. | 12.1 | 14.0 | XVIII - Приборы, аппараты оптические, медицинские, измерительные и пр.; музыкальные инструменты; часы; их части и принадлежности |
| XIX - Arms and ammunition; parts and accessories thereof | .. | .. | .. | .. | 0.1 | 0.1 | XIX - Оружие и боеприпасы, их части и принадлежности |
| XX - Miscellaneous manufactured articles | .. | .. | .. | .. | 226.2 | 190.2 | XX - Разные промышленные товары |
| XXI - Works of art, collectors' pieces, and antiques | .. | .. | .. | .. | 0.0 | 0.0 | XXI - Произведения искусства, предметы антиквариата |
| XXII - Services | .. | .. | .. | .. | 7.0 | 66.4 | XXII - Услуги |

## TABLE 3-3A. Exports by commodity group (millions of U.S. dollars)



## ТАБЛИЦА 3-3А. Экспорт по товарным группам (млн. долларов США)

| Commodity group | 1990 | 1991 | 1992 | 1993 | 1994 | 1995 | Товарные группы |
|---|---|---|---|---|---|---|---|
| TOTAL | .. | .. | .. | .. | 2,145.0 | 1,880.7 | ВСЕГО |
| I - Live animals; animal products | .. | .. | .. | .. | 0.7 | 1.6 | I - Живые животные и продукты животноводства |
| II - Vegetable products | .. | .. | .. | .. | 16.6 | 3.2 | II - Продукты растительного происхождения |
| III - Animal or vegetable fats and oils and their cleavage products; prepared edible fats; animal or vegetable waxes | .. | .. | .. | .. | 11.3 | 1.9 | III - Жиры и масла растительного и животного происхождения, воски |
| IV - Prepared foodstuffs; beverages, spirits and vinegar; tobacco and manufactured tobacco substitutes | .. | .. | .. | .. | 12.0 | 4.3 | IV -Продукция пищевой промышленности, алкогольные и безалкогольные напитки, табак и его заменители |
| V - Mineral products | .. | .. | .. | .. | 1,688.3 | 1,365.4 | V - Минеральные продукты |
| VI - Products of the chemical or allied industries | .. | .. | .. | .. | 11.9 | 10.5 | VI - Продукция химической промышленности |
| VII - Plastics and articles thereof; rubber and articles thereof | .. | .. | .. | .. | 1.1 | 1.0 | VII - Пластмассы и изделия из них |
| VIII - Raw hides and skins, leather, furskins and articles thereof; saddlery and harness; travel goods, handbags and similar containers; articles of animal gut | .. | .. | .. | .. | 0.5 | 0.5 | VIII - Кожевенное сырьё, кожи, пушнина, меховое сырьё и изделия из них |
| IX - Wood and articles of wood; wood charcoal; cork and articles of cork; manufactures of straw, of esparto or of other plaiting materials; basketware and wickerwork | .. | .. | .. | .. | 0.1 | 0.2 | IX - Древесина и изделия из древесины, древесный уголь |
| X - Pulp of wood or of other fibrous cellulosic material; waste and scrap of paper or paperboard; paper and paperboard and articles thereof | .. | .. | .. | .. | 0.2 | 0.2 | X - Бумажная масса, бумажные и картонные отходы, макулатура, бумага, картон и изделия из них |
| XI - Textiles and textile articles | .. | .. | .. | .. | 380.6 | 465.2 | XI - Текстиль и текстильные изделия |
| XII - Footwear, headgear, umbrellas, sun umbrellas, walking sticks, seat sticks, whips, riding crops and parts thereof; prepared feathers and articles made therewith; artificial flowers; articles of human hair | .. | .. | .. | .. | 0.0 | 0.0 | XII - Обувь, головные уборы, зонты, трости и пр. |

**TABLE 3-3A. Exports by commodity group (millions of U.S. dollars)**
**ТАБЛИЦА 3-3А. Экспорт по товарным группам (млн. долларов США)**

| Commodity group | 1990 | 1991 | 1992 | 1993 | 1994 | 1995 | Товарные группы |
|---|---|---|---|---|---|---|---|
| XIII - Articles of stone, plaster, cement, asbestos, mica and similar materials; ceramic products; glass and glassware | .. | .. | .. | .. | 1.2 | 2.0 | XIII - Изделия из камня, гипса, цемента |
| XIV - Natural or cultured pearls, precious or semi-precious stones, precious metals, metals clad with precious metal and articles thereof; imitation jewellery; coin | .. | .. | .. | .. | .. | .. | XIV - Жемчуг, драгоценные и полудрагоценные камни, драгоценные металлы, бижутерия, монеты |
| XV - Base metals and articles of base metal | .. | .. | .. | .. | 5.6 | 3.6 | XV - Неблагородные металлы и изделия из них |
| XVI - Machinery and mechanical appliances; electrical equipment; parts thereof; sound recorders and reproducers, television image and sound recorders and reproducers, and parts and accessories of such articles | .. | .. | .. | .. | 3.3 | 2.3 | XVI - Машины, оборудование, механизмы, их части и принадлежности; звуковая и теле-аппаратура, их части и принадлежности |
| XVII - Vehicles, aircraft, vessels and associated transport equipment | .. | .. | .. | .. | 3.1 | 0.6 | XVII - Средства наземного, воздушного и водного транспорта |
| XVIII - Optical, photographic, cinematographic, measuring, checking, precision, medical or surgical instruments and apparatus; clocks and watches; musical instruments; parts and accessories thereof | .. | .. | .. | .. | 0.0 | 0.0 | XVIII - Приборы, аппараты оптические, медицинские, измерительные и пр.; музыкальные инструменты; часы; их части и принадлежности |
| XIX - Arms and ammunition; parts and accessories thereof | .. | .. | .. | .. | .. | .. | XIX - Оружие и боеприпасы, их части и принадлежности |
| XX - Miscellaneous manufactured articles | .. | .. | .. | .. | 0.4 | 0.1 | XX - Разные промышленные товары |
| XXI - Works of art, collectors' pieces, and antiques | .. | .. | .. | .. | .. | .. | XXI - Произведения искусства, предметы антиквариата |
| XXII - Services | .. | .. | .. | .. | 3.7 | 2.3 | XXII - Услуги |

**TABLE 3-4A. Geographical distribution of foreign trade (millions of U.S. dollars)**

**ТАБЛИЦА 3-4А. Географическое распределение внешней торговли (млн. долларов США)**

| Country or country group | Exports Экспорт 1990 | 1991 | 1992 | 1993 | 1994 | 1995 | Imports Импорт 1990 | 1991 | 1992 | 1993 | 1994 | 1995 | Страна или группа стран |
|---|---|---|---|---|---|---|---|---|---|---|---|---|---|
| **Total trade** | .. | .. | .. | .. | 2,145.0 | 1,880.7 | .. | .. | .. | .. | 1,467.8 | 1,364.0 | **Всего** |
| **CIS countries** | .. | .. | .. | .. | 1,650.6 | 929.5 | .. | .. | .. | .. | 685.7 | 745.3 | **Страны СНГ** |
| Armenia | .. | .. | .. | .. | 69.8 | 132.9 | .. | .. | .. | .. | 46.6 | 62.5 | Армения |
| Azerbaijan | .. | .. | .. | .. | 192.1 | 49.9 | .. | .. | .. | .. | 12.1 | 73.2 | Азербайджан |
| Belarus | .. | .. | .. | .. | 6.0 | 2.3 | .. | .. | .. | .. | 13.3 | 6.0 | Беларусь |
| Georgia | .. | .. | .. | .. | 208.4 | 53.3 | .. | .. | .. | .. | 35.5 | 22.7 | Грузия |
| Kazakstan | .. | .. | .. | .. | 283.2 | 127.4 | .. | .. | .. | .. | 42.5 | 31.4 | Казахстан |
| Kyrgyz Republic | .. | .. | .. | .. | 12.5 | 6.9 | .. | .. | .. | .. | 17.3 | 3.8 | Киргизстан |
| Moldova | .. | .. | .. | .. | 1.3 | 3.0 | .. | .. | .. | .. | 3.0 | 3.1 | Молдова |
| Russia | .. | .. | .. | .. | 113.7 | 66.8 | .. | .. | .. | .. | 154.4 | 95.8 | Россия |
| Tajikistan | .. | .. | .. | .. | 15.6 | 5.4 | .. | .. | .. | .. | 24.0 | 1.9 | Таджикистан |
| Turkmenistan | .. | .. | .. | .. | .. | .. | .. | .. | .. | .. | .. | .. | Туркменистан |
| Ukraine | .. | .. | .. | .. | 603.7 | 460.3 | .. | .. | .. | .. | 256.9 | 416.4 | Украина |
| Uzbekistan | .. | .. | .. | .. | 144.3 | 21.3 | .. | .. | .. | .. | 19.5 | 28.5 | Узбекистан |
| **Non-CIS countries** | .. | .. | .. | .. | 494.4 | 951.2 | .. | .. | .. | .. | 782.1 | 618.7 | **Остальной мир** |
| **Europe** | .. | .. | .. | .. | 287.7 | 469.2 | .. | .. | .. | .. | 352.5 | 283.0 | **Европа** |
| Austria | .. | .. | .. | .. | 9.9 | 13.0 | .. | .. | .. | .. | 29.7 | 31.2 | Австрия |
| Belgium | .. | .. | .. | .. | 0.3 | 0.4 | .. | .. | .. | .. | 2.0 | 0.5 | Бельгия |
| Bulgaria | .. | .. | .. | .. | 0.6 | 10.8 | .. | .. | .. | .. | 6.2 | 4.5 | Болгария |
| Czech Republic | .. | .. | .. | .. | 17.2 | 3.5 | .. | .. | .. | .. | 18.3 | 2.6 | Чешская Республика |
| Denmark | .. | .. | .. | .. | 0.3 | 0.2 | .. | .. | .. | .. | 0.7 | 0.0 | Дания |
| Estonia | .. | .. | .. | .. | 2.0 | 3.1 | .. | .. | .. | .. | 1.9 | 2.9 | Эстония |
| Finland | .. | .. | .. | .. | 0.4 | 0.1 | .. | .. | .. | .. | 4.4 | 1.7 | Финляндия |
| Former Yugoslavia | .. | .. | .. | .. | 0.8 | 0.0 | .. | .. | .. | .. | 22.3 | 1.8 | Быв. Югославия |
| France | .. | .. | .. | .. | 2.0 | 0.2 | .. | .. | .. | .. | 6.8 | 16.3 | Франция |
| Germany | .. | .. | .. | .. | 34.0 | 32.6 | .. | .. | .. | .. | 61.3 | 52.1 | Германия |
| Hungary | .. | .. | .. | .. | 0.2 | 0.0 | .. | .. | .. | .. | 10.6 | 0.5 | Венгрия |
| Iceland | .. | .. | .. | .. | .. | .. | .. | .. | .. | .. | .. | .. | Исландия |
| Ireland | .. | .. | .. | .. | 12.1 | 8.3 | .. | .. | .. | .. | 4.3 | 13.9 | Ирландия |
| Italy | .. | .. | .. | .. | 36.2 | 13.0 | .. | .. | .. | .. | 57.8 | 7.3 | Италия |
| Latvia | .. | .. | .. | .. | 10.6 | 0.7 | .. | .. | .. | .. | 11.1 | 1.7 | Латвия |
| Lithuania | .. | .. | .. | .. | 3.1 | 5.6 | .. | .. | .. | .. | 12.9 | 4.0 | Литва |
| Netherlands | .. | .. | .. | .. | 0.0 | 0.0 | .. | .. | .. | .. | 11.4 | 6.8 | Нидерланды |
| Norway | .. | .. | .. | .. | .. | .. | .. | .. | .. | .. | .. | .. | Норвегия |
| Poland | .. | .. | .. | .. | 2.7 | 0.0 | .. | .. | .. | .. | 4.1 | 0.6 | Польша |
| Romania | .. | .. | .. | .. | 0.7 | 0.2 | .. | .. | .. | .. | 2.3 | 0.3 | Румыния |
| Slovak Republic | .. | .. | .. | .. | 5.7 | 3.1 | .. | .. | .. | .. | 6.1 | 3.5 | Словацская Республика |
| Spain | .. | .. | .. | .. | 2.6 | 10.7 | .. | .. | .. | .. | 4.9 | 0.1 | Испания |
| Sweden | .. | .. | .. | .. | 7.6 | 17.2 | .. | .. | .. | .. | 9.5 | 1.1 | Швеция |
| Switzerland | .. | .. | .. | .. | 47.8 | 110.7 | .. | .. | .. | .. | 8.1 | 7.2 | Швейцария |
| United Kingdom | .. | .. | .. | .. | 31.8 | 43.5 | .. | .. | .. | .. | 19.1 | 17.2 | Великобритания |

**TABLE 3-4A. Geographical distribution of foreign trade (millions of U.S. dollars)**
**ТАБЛИЦА 3-4A. Географическое распределение внешней торговли (млн. долларов США)**

| Country or country group | Exports Экспорт 1990 | 1991 | 1992 | 1993 | 1994 | 1995 | Imports Импорт 1990 | 1991 | 1992 | 1993 | 1994 | 1995 | Страна или группа стран |
|---|---|---|---|---|---|---|---|---|---|---|---|---|---|
| Other Europe | .. | .. | .. | .. | 59.1 | 192.3 | .. | .. | .. | .. | 36.7 | 105.2 | Остальные страны Европы |
| **Asia** | .. | .. | .. | .. | 170.1 | 442.7 | .. | .. | .. | .. | 361.2 | 281.5 | **Азия** |
| Afghanistan | .. | .. | .. | .. | 19.3 | 9.1 | .. | .. | .. | .. | 24.2 | 6.6 | Афганистан |
| China | .. | .. | .. | .. | 1.5 | 7.1 | .. | .. | .. | .. | 4.6 | 7.7 | Китай |
| India | .. | .. | .. | .. | 2.3 | 2.2 | .. | .. | .. | .. | 6.1 | 1.3 | Индия |
| Iraq | .. | .. | .. | .. | .. | .. | .. | .. | .. | .. | .. | .. | Ирак |
| Japan | .. | .. | .. | .. | 0.0 | 164.7 | .. | .. | .. | .. | 7.4 | 7.5 | Япония |
| Korea, Dem. People's Rep. | .. | .. | .. | .. | 0.0 | 0.0 | .. | .. | .. | .. | 2.9 | 0.0 | КНДР |
| Korea, Rep. of | .. | .. | .. | .. | 0.0 | 3.5 | .. | .. | .. | .. | 3.2 | 0.6 | Южная Корея |
| Mongolia | .. | .. | .. | .. | .. | .. | .. | .. | .. | .. | .. | .. | МНР |
| Syrian Arab Republic | .. | .. | .. | .. | 0.0 | 0.1 | .. | .. | .. | .. | 3.7 | 0.2 | Сирия |
| Turkey | .. | .. | .. | .. | 78.4 | 149.6 | .. | .. | .. | .. | 181.8 | 160.4 | Турция |
| Viet Nam | .. | .. | .. | .. | .. | .. | .. | .. | .. | .. | .. | .. | Вьетнам |
| Other Asia | .. | .. | .. | .. | 67.0 | 106.4 | .. | .. | .. | .. | 127.3 | 97.2 | Остальные страны Азии |
| **America** | .. | .. | .. | .. | 35.0 | 31.9 | .. | .. | .. | .. | 68.3 | 53.7 | **Сев. и Южная Америка** |
| Canada | .. | .. | .. | .. | 0.0 | 0.0 | .. | .. | .. | .. | 3.1 | 0.0 | Канада |
| Cuba | .. | .. | .. | .. | .. | .. | .. | .. | .. | .. | .. | .. | Куба |
| United States | .. | .. | .. | .. | 35.0 | 31.9 | .. | .. | .. | .. | 56.6 | 53.5 | США |
| Other America | .. | .. | .. | .. | 0.0 | 7.2 | .. | .. | .. | .. | 8.6 | 0.2 | Остальные |
| **Africa** | .. | .. | .. | .. | 1.6 | 0.2 | .. | .. | .. | .. | 0.1 | 0.5 | **Африка** |
| Egypt | .. | .. | .. | .. | 1.6 | 0.0 | .. | .. | .. | .. | 0.0 | 0.0 | Египет |
| Libya | .. | .. | .. | .. | .. | .. | .. | .. | .. | .. | .. | .. | Ливия |
| Other Africa | .. | .. | .. | .. | 0.0 | 0.2 | .. | .. | .. | .. | 0.1 | 0.5 | Остальные |
| **Rest of the World** | .. | .. | .. | .. | .. | .. | .. | .. | .. | .. | .. | .. | **Прочие страны мира** |
| Australia | .. | .. | .. | .. | .. | .. | .. | .. | .. | .. | .. | .. | Австралия |

## TABLE 4-1. General government budget revenue (millions of national currency)
## ТАБЛИЦА 4-1. Доходы государственного бюджета (млн. национальной валюты)

| Type of revenue | 1990 | 1991 | 1992 | 1993 | 1994 | 1995 | Вид доходов |
|---|---|---|---|---|---|---|---|
| **Total revenue and grants** | 3,236 | 6,563 | 64,009 | 1,426 | 14,750 | 127,368 | **Всего доходов и безвозм. поступл.** |
| Grants | 728 | 1,409 | .. | .. | .. | .. | Безвозмездные поступления |
| Total Revenue | 2,508 | 5,154 | 64,009 | 1,426 | 14,750 | 127,368 | Всего доходов |
| **Current revenue** | 2,508 | 5,154 | 64,009 | 1,426 | 14,750 | 127,368 | **Текущие доходы** |
| Tax revenue | 1,225 | 1,975 | 34,447 | 1,077 | 14,272 | 124,930 | Доход от налогов |
| Taxes on income and profits | 258 | 992 | 15,860 | 573 | 4,242 | 37,974 | Налоги на доходы и прибыль |
| Individual | 166 | 349 | 2,985 | 88 | 842 | 4,598 | Физические лица |
| Corporate | 92 | 643 | 12,875 | 485 | 3,400 | 33,376 | Предприятия и организации |
| Social security contributions | 187 | .. | .. | .. | 3,445 | 19,887 | Отчисление на соцстрах. |
| Taxes on payroll or work force | .. | .. | .. | .. | .. | .. | Налоги на заработную плату и рабочую силу |
| Taxes on the use of labor force | .. | .. | .. | .. | .. | .. | Плата за трудовые ресурсы |
| Taxes on increases in wages and salaries | .. | .. | .. | .. | .. | .. | Налог с прироста средств на оплату труда |
| Other payroll/work force taxes | .. | .. | .. | .. | .. | .. | Другие налоги на зарплату и рабочую силу |
| Taxes on property | .. | .. | .. | .. | .. | .. | Налоги на собственность |
| Taxes on immovable property | .. | .. | .. | .. | .. | .. | Налоги на недвижимое имущество |
| Buildings | .. | .. | .. | .. | .. | .. | Налог с владельцев строении |
| Land | .. | .. | .. | .. | .. | .. | Земельныи налог |
| Estate, inheritance, and gift taxes | .. | .. | .. | .. | .. | .. | Налоги на наследство, подарки |
| Other property taxes | .. | .. | .. | .. | .. | .. | Другие налоги на имущество |
| Domestic taxes on goods and services | 780 | 983 | 18,551 | 504 | 5,855 | 61,902 | Внутренние налоги на товары и услуги |
| General sales, turnover, or value-added taxes | 780 | 983 | 17,400 | 496 | 4,305 | 38,604 | Налог с продаж. с оборота или на добав. стоим. |
| Excises | .. | .. | 1,151 | 8 | 450 | 9,474 | Акцизы |
| Profits of fiscal monopolies | .. | .. | .. | .. | .. | .. | Прибыли фискальных монополий |
| Taxes on specific services | .. | .. | .. | .. | .. | .. | Налоги на особые услуги |
| Taxes on use of goods or permission to use goods or to perform activities | .. | .. | .. | .. | .. | .. | Налоги на пользование товарами или лицензии н пользование товарами и занятие деятельностью |
| Other taxes on goods and services | .. | .. | .. | .. | 1,100 | 13,824 | Другие налоги на товары и услуги |
| Taxes on international trade and transactions | .. | .. | .. | .. | .. | .. | Налоги на внешнюю торговлю и операции |
| Import duties | .. | .. | .. | .. | .. | .. | Импортные пошлины |
| Export duties | .. | .. | .. | .. | .. | .. | Экпортные пошлины |
| Other | .. | .. | .. | .. | .. | .. | Другие |
| Other taxes | .. | .. | 36 | .. | 730 | 5,167 | Прочие налоги |
| Nontax revenue | 1,283 | 3,179 | 29,562 | 349 | 478 | 2,438 | Неналоговые доходы |
| **Capital revenue** | .. | .. | .. | .. | .. | .. | **Капитальные доходы** |

**TABLE 4-2. General government budget expenditure by economic type (millions of nationa**
**ТАБЛИЦА 4-2. Расходы государственного бюджета по экономическим типам (млн. национальной валюты)**

| Type of expenditure or debt holder | 1990 | 1991 | 1992 | 1993 | 1994 | 1995 | Всего расходов |
|---|---|---|---|---|---|---|---|
| **Total expenditure by economic type** | 3,114 | 6,048 | 92,665 | 1,809 | 16,812 | 131,282 | **Всего расходов по экономическим типам** |
| **Current expenditure** | .. | .. | .. | .. | 14,444 | 109,238 | **Текущие расходы** |
| Expenditure on goods and services | .. | .. | .. | .. | .. | .. | Расходы на товары и услуги |
| Wages and salaries | .. | .. | .. | .. | 2,823 | 18,955 | Заработная плата |
| Employer contributions | .. | .. | .. | .. | 2,375 | 18,688 | Отчисление на социальное страхование |
| Other Purchases of goods and services | .. | .. | .. | .. | .. | .. | Другие покупки товаров и услуг |
| Interest payments | .. | .. | .. | .. | .. | 1,300 | Выплаты процентов |
| Domestic debt | .. | .. | .. | .. | .. | 722 | По внутреннему долгу |
| Foreign debt | .. | .. | .. | .. | .. | 578 | По внешнему долгу |
| Subsidies and other current transfers | .. | .. | .. | .. | 1,367 | 11,343 | Субсидии на другие текущие трансферты |
| Subsidies | .. | .. | .. | .. | 1,358 | 11,343 | Субсидии |
| Agricultural subsidies | .. | .. | .. | .. | 861 | 2,550 | Субсидии на сельское хозяиство |
| Other current transfers | .. | .. | .. | .. | 9 | .. | Другие текущие трансферты |
| Other | .. | .. | .. | .. | .. | .. | Прочие расходы |
| **Capital expenditure** | .. | .. | .. | .. | 2,368 | 22,044 | **Капитальные расходы** |
| Acquisition of fixed capital assets | .. | .. | .. | .. | .. | .. | Приобретение основного капитала |
| Capital transfers | .. | .. | .. | .. | .. | .. | Капитальные трансферты |
| Other | .. | .. | .. | .. | .. | .. | Другие капитальные расходы |
| **Surplus/deficit (-)** | 122 | 515 | -28,656 | -383 | -2,062 | -3,914 | **Превыш. доходов над расходами/дефицит(-)** |
| **Financing by type of debt holder** | .. | .. | .. | .. | .. | .. | **Финансирование по типам кредиторов** |
| **Foreign (net)** | .. | .. | .. | .. | .. | .. | **Зарубежные кредиторы (сальдо)** |
| From international development institutions | .. | .. | .. | .. | .. | .. | Международные организации |
| From foreign governments | .. | .. | .. | .. | .. | .. | Правительства иностранных государств |
| Other borrowing abroad | .. | .. | .. | .. | .. | .. | Другие зарубежные кредиторы |
| **Domestic (net)** | .. | .. | .. | .. | .. | .. | **Внутренние кредиторы (сальдо)** |
| From monetary authorities | .. | .. | .. | .. | .. | .. | Органы денежного обращения |
| From deposit money banks | .. | .. | .. | .. | .. | .. | Депозитные денежные банки |
| Other domestic borrowing | .. | .. | .. | .. | .. | .. | Другие внутренние кредиторы |
| *Memo items:* | | | | | | | *Справочно:* |
| Extrabudgetary surplus/ Deficit (-) not included above | .. | .. | .. | .. | .. | .. | Превышение доходов над расходами/дефицит (-) по внебюджетным фондам, не включенным выше |
| Total surplus/deficit (-) including extrabudgetary accounts | 122 | 515 | -28,656 | -383 | -2,062 | -3,914 | Итого превышение доходов над расходами/дефицит, включая счета внебюджетных фондов |

## TABLE 5-1. Agricultural production (millions of national currency, current prices)

## ТАБЛИЦА 5-1. Сельскохозяйственная продукция (млн. нац. валюты, текущие цены)

| Item | 1990 | 1991 | 1992 | 1993 | 1994 | 1995 | Статьи |
|---|---|---|---|---|---|---|---|
| **Total gross agricultural production** | 3,491 | 7,163 | 57,795 | 1,674 | 29,068 | 106,212 | **Валовая продукция сельского хозяйства - всего** |
| **Crops** | 2,625 | 5,573 | 43,732 | 1,006 | 17,871 | 69,124 | **Продукция растениеводства** |
| Grains | 91 | 212 | 7,528 | 73 | 1,434 | 17,126 | Зерно |
| Potatoes | 10 | 31 | 165 | 1 | 93 | 1,425 | Картофель |
| Vegetables | 139 | 228 | 1,011 | 20 | 877 | 5,797 | Овощи |
| Fruits (excluding grapes) | 52 | 88 | 352 | 13 | 237 | 1,058 | Фрукты (без винограда) |
| Grapes | 112 | 254 | 1,164 | 162 | 747 | 2,988 | Виноград |
| Tobacco | .. | .. | .. | .. | .. | .. | Табак |
| Cotton | 2,000 | 4,318 | 31,910 | 568 | 12,768 | 35,037 | Хлопок |
| Sugarbeets | .. | .. | .. | .. | .. | .. | Сахарная свекла |
| Oilseeds | .. | .. | .. | .. | .. | .. | Семена масличных культур |
| Other | 222 | 443 | 1,602 | 169 | 1,715 | 5,692 | Прочие |
| **Animal husbandry** | 866 | 1,590 | 14,063 | 668 | 11,196 | 37,088 | **Продукция животноводства** |
| Livestock | 429 | 739 | 6,791 | 131 | 2,468 | 14,883 | Мясное животноводство |
| Cattle | 201 | 383 | 3,362 | 40 | 1,299 | 6,597 | Крупный рогатый скот |
| Pigs | 34 | 46 | 510 | 37 | 62 | 365 | Свиньи |
| Sheep and goats | 163 | 235 | 2,385 | 45 | 887 | 7,293 | Овцы и козы |
| Poultry | 32 | 44 | 201 | 4 | 81 | 291 | Птица |
| Other | .. | .. | .. | .. | 139 | 336 | Прочие |
| Milk | 163 | 269 | 2,694 | 172 | 1,540 | 10,728 | Молоко |
| Eggs | 34 | 71 | 359 | 48 | 216 | 4,516 | Яйца |
| Wool | 142 | 382 | 1,465 | 38 | 358 | 816 | Шерсть |
| Other livestock | 98 | 133 | .. | 153 | 6,614 | 6,145 | Прочая |
| **Agricultural services** | .. | .. | .. | .. | .. | .. | **Сельскохозяйственные услуги** |

## TABLE 5-2. Agricultural production (millions of constant national currency) TURKMENISTAN

## ТАБЛИЦА 5-2. Сельскохозяйственная продукция в постоянных ценах (млн. национальной валюты)

| Item | 1990 | 1991 | 1992 | 1993 | 1994 | 1995 | Статьи |
|---|---|---|---|---|---|---|---|
| **Total gross agricultural production** | 2,833 | 2,714 | 2,482 | 2,872 | 2,367 | 1,952 | **Валовая продукция сельского хозяйства - всего** |
| **Crops** | 2,000 | 1,865 | 1,612 | 1,860 | 1,405 | 1,107 | **Продукция растениеводства** |
| Grains | 61 | 68 | 98 | 165 | 152 | 139 | Зерно |
| Potatoes | 7 | 6 | 8 | 6 | 4 | 5 | Картофель |
| Vegetables | 122 | 116 | 94 | 245 | 132 | 90 | Овощи |
| Fruits (excluding grapes) | 28 | 32 | 27 | 28 | 26 | 20 | Фрукты (без винограда) |
| Grapes | 79 | 78 | 59 | 52 | 62 | 76 | Виноград |
| Tobacco | .. | .. | .. | .. | .. | .. | Табак |
| Cotton | 1,519 | 1,331 | 1,126 | 1,244 | 889 | 687 | Хлопок |
| Sugarbeets | 1 | .. | .. | 1 | .. | .. | Сахарная свекла |
| Oilseeds | .. | .. | .. | .. | .. | .. | Семена масличных культур |
| Other | 184 | 234 | 200 | 119 | 140 | 90 | Прочие |
| **Animal husbandry** | 833 | 849 | 870 | 1,012 | 962 | 845 | **Продукция животноводства** |
| Livestock | 391 | 387 | .. | .. | .. | .. | Мясное животноводство |
| Cattle | 181 | 183 | 187 | .. | .. | .. | Крупный рогатый скот |
| Pigs | 33 | 26 | 26 | .. | .. | .. | Свиньи |
| Sheep and goats | 148 | 154 | 171 | .. | .. | .. | Овцы и козы |
| Poultry | 29 | 25 | 21 | .. | .. | .. | Птица |
| Other | .. | .. | .. | .. | .. | .. | Прочие |
| Milk | 172 | 182 | 187 | .. | .. | .. | Молоко |
| Eggs | 31 | 29 | 28 | .. | .. | .. | Яйца |
| Wool | 136 | 139 | 141 | .. | .. | .. | Шерсть |
| Other livestock | 103 | 112 | .. | .. | .. | .. | Прочая |
| **Agricultural services** | .. | .. | .. | .. | .. | .. | **Сельскохозяйственные услуги** |

## TABLE 5-3. Production and average yield of major agricultural crops
## ТАБЛИЦА 5-3. Производство и урожайность важнейших сельскохозяйственных культур

| Crop | 1990 | 1991 | 1992 | 1993 | 1994 | 1995 | Сельскохозяйственные культуры |
|---|---|---|---|---|---|---|---|
| **Production (thousands of tons)** | | | | | | | **Производство (тыс. тонн)** |
| Grain - Cleanweight | 449 | 517 | 737 | 974 | 1,106 | 1,109 | Зерно в чистом весе |
| Winter wheat | 130 | 195 | 370 | 508 | 709 | 879 | Пшеница - озимая |
| Spring wheat | .. | 11 | 7 | 1 | 2 | 1 | яровая |
| Coarse grain | .. | .. | .. | .. | .. | .. | Зерно в физическом весе |
| Rye | .. | .. | 5 | .. | .. | .. | Рожь |
| Corn | 135 | 126 | 157 | 177 | 149 | 66 | Кукуруза |
| Winter barley | 139 | 127 | 124 | 198 | 127 | 74 | Ячмень - озимый |
| Spring barley | .. | 1 | 1 | 1 | 1 | .. | яровой |
| Oats | .. | .. | .. | .. | .. | .. | Овес |
| Millet | .. | .. | .. | .. | .. | .. | Просо |
| Rice | 42 | 54 | 64 | 88 | 114 | 89 | Рис |
| Flax | .. | .. | .. | .. | .. | .. | Лен |
| Oilseeds | .. | .. | .. | .. | .. | .. | Семена масличных культур |
| Cotton (raw) | 1,457 | 1,433 | 1,300 | 1,341 | 1,283 | 1,292 | Хлопок - сырец |
| Cotton fiber | 437 | 430 | 404 | 409 | .. | .. | волокно |
| Sugarbeets | .. | .. | .. | .. | .. | .. | Сахарная свекла |
| Potatoes | 35 | 30 | 35 | 31 | 20 | 21 | Картофель |
| Pulses | .. | .. | .. | .. | .. | .. | Бобовые |
| Vegetables | 411 | 388 | 320 | 286 | 386 | 376 | Овощи |
| Fruit | 531 | 517 | 386 | 328 | 391 | 398 | Фрукты |
| Grapes | 169 | 167 | 125 | 114 | 133 | 163 | Виноград |
| Other | 362 | 350 | 261 | 214 | 258 | 235 | Прочие |
| Corn (silage and greenchop) | 1,027 | 846 | 914 | 916 | 745 | 583 | Кукуруза (на силос и зеленый корм) |
| Hay | .. | .. | .. | .. | .. | .. | Сено |
| **Average yield (kilograms per hectare)** | | | | | | | **Ср. урожайность (кг с га)** |
| Grain | 2,360 | 2,150 | 2,170 | 2,200 | 1,830 | 1,680 | Зерно |
| Winter wheat | 2,360 | 1,900 | 940 | 1,930 | 1,650 | 1,590 | Пшеница - озимая |
| Spring wheat | 2,160 | 850 | 730 | 940 | 1,020 | 730 | яровая |
| Coarse grain | .. | .. | .. | .. | .. | .. | Зерно в физическом весе |
| Rye | .. | .. | .. | .. | .. | .. | Рожь |
| Corn | 3,100 | 3,330 | 3,640 | 3,450 | 3,200 | 2,200 | Кукуруза |
| Winter barley | 2,100 | 1,890 | 2,050 | 2,190 | 1,760 | 2,070 | Ячмень - озимый |
| Spring barley | .. | 1,620 | 1,370 | 290 | 710 | 280 | яровой |
| Oats | .. | .. | .. | .. | .. | .. | Овес |
| Millet | .. | .. | .. | .. | .. | .. | Просо |
| Rice | 2,930 | 2,830 | 2,330 | 2,270 | 2,380 | 2,290 | Рис |
| Flax | .. | .. | .. | .. | .. | .. | Лен |
| Oilseeds | .. | .. | .. | .. | .. | .. | Семена масличных культур |
| Cotton (raw) | 2,340 | 2,380 | 2,300 | 2,270 | 2,300 | 2,300 | Хлопок - сырец |
| Cotton fiber | 700 | 710 | 710 | 700 | 700 | .. | волокно |
| Sugarbeets | .. | .. | .. | .. | .. | .. | Сахарная свекла |
| Potatoes | 7,800 | 9,970 | 9,370 | 7,740 | 3,150 | 3,420 | Картофель |
| Pulses | .. | .. | .. | .. | .. | .. | Бобовые |
| Vegetables | 11,500 | 13,700 | 11,500 | 13,510 | 14,750 | 15,870 | Овощи |
| Fruit | .. | .. | .. | .. | .. | .. | Фрукты |
| Grapes | 8,180 | 8,310 | 5,970 | 5,570 | 6,550 | 7,650 | Виноград |
| Other | .. | .. | .. | .. | .. | .. | Прочие |
| Corn (silage and greenchop) | .. | .. | .. | 18,960 | 15,500 | 14,500 | Кукуруза (на силос и зеленый корм) |
| Hay | .. | .. | .. | .. | .. | .. | Сено |

## TABLE 5-4. Main aggregates of animal husbandry
## ТАБЛИЦА 5-4. Основные показатели животноводства

| Type of livestock or product | 1990 | 1991 | 1992 | 1993 | 1994 | 1995 | Направление животноводства или вид продукции |
|---|---|---|---|---|---|---|---|
| **Livestock (thousands of heads)** | | | | | | | **Поголовье скота (тысяч голов)** |
| Cattle | 829 | 899 | 1,004 | 1,105 | 1,181 | 1,200 | Крупный рогатый скот |
| of which: Cows | 331 | 360 | 416 | 478 | 534 | 567 | в том числе коровы |
| Pigs | 267 | 260 | 212 | 159 | 128 | 82 | Свиньи |
| Sheep and goats | 5,481 | 5,599 | 6,265 | 6,313 | 6,503 | 6,574 | Овцы и козы |
| of which: Goats | 337 | 350 | 440 | 463 | 522 | .. | в том числе козы |
| Horses | 19 | 19 | 21 | 22 | 25 | 26 | Лошади |
| Other | 87 | 93 | 98 | 101 | 111 | 108 | Прочие |
| **Animal husbandry products** | | | | | | | **Продукция животноводства** |
| Meat (thousands of tons) | 104 | 100 | 98 | 110 | 107 | 110 | Мясо (тысяч тонн) |
| Beef | 47 | 44 | 46 | 50 | 51 | 51 | Говядина |
| Pork | 10 | 9 | 8 | 6 | 4 | 3 | Свинина |
| Lamb | 35 | 36 | 35 | 45 | 45 | 49 | Баранина |
| Poultry | 9 | 7 | 7 | 5 | 5 | 4 | Птица |
| Other | 3 | 4 | 2 | 4 | 2 | 3 | Прочие виды мяса |
| Milk (thousands of tons) | 436 | 458 | 471 | 712 | 716 | 727 | Молоко (тысяч тонн) |
| Eggs (millions) | 328 | 300 | 292 | 267 | 270 | 270 | Яйца (миллионов штук) |
| Wool (thousands of tons) | 16 | 16 | 17 | 18 | 19 | 19 | Шерсть (тысяч тонн) |

**TABLE 6-1. Industrial production by sector (millions of national currency)**

**ТАБЛИЦА 6-1. Промышленное производство по отраслям (млн. национальной валюты)**

| Sector | 1990 | 1991 | 1992 | 1993 | 1994 | 1995 | Отрасли |
|---|---|---|---|---|---|---|---|
| **All industry** | 9.6 | 29.4 | 373.6 | 5,923 | 31,313 | 243,047 | **Вся промышленность** |
| **Heavy industry** | 4.2 | 13.1 | 253.2 | 4,474 | 19,294 | 189,088 | **Тяжелая промышленность** |
| Fuel and energy | 2.5 | 9.9 | 215.9 | 3,917 | 15,429 | 134,503 | Топливно-энергетическая промышленноть |
| Electricity | 0.5 | 1.1 | 17.5 | 328 | 2,385 | 19,136 | Электроэнергетика |
| Fuels | 2.0 | 8.7 | 198.4 | 3,589 | 13,044 | 115,307 | Топливная промышленность |
| Ferrous and nonferrous metallurgy | 0.0 | 0.0 | 0.4 | 2 | 6 | 154 | Металлургия |
| Chemicals and petrochemical industry | 0.4 | 0.8 | 11.4 | 99 | 489 | 7,094 | Химическая и нефтехимическая пром. |
| Machine building and metalworking | 0.5 | 1.3 | 8.5 | 129 | 886 | 3,531 | Машиностроение и металлообработка |
| Forestry, woodworking, and pulp and paper industry | 0.1 | 0.2 | 1.1 | 19 | 177 | 717 | Лесная, деревообрабатывающая и целлюлозо-бумажная промышленность |
| Construction materials | 0.6 | 1.2 | 14.3 | 266 | 1,960 | 8,927 | Промышленность строительных материалов |
| **Light industry** | 4.0 | 12.1 | 73.0 | 733 | 8,148 | 39,406 | **Легкая промышленность** |
| Textiles | 3.7 | 11.0 | 67.2 | 606 | 7,325 | 34,908 | Текстильная |
| Clothing | 0.5 | 0.9 | 4.4 | 60 | 579 | 2,862 | Швейная |
| Leather and shoes | 0.1 | 0.2 | 1.4 | 11 | 127 | 1,019 | Кожевенная и обувная |
| **Food industry** | 1.4 | 4.2 | 47.4 | 716 | 3,853 | 14,553 | **Пищевая промышленность** |
| Processed foods | 0.6 | 1.4 | 17.2 | 272 | 2,083 | 11,017 | Пищевкусовая |
| Meat and dairy products | 0.4 | 1.8 | 14.8 | 216 | 697 | 3,026 | Мясная и молочная |
| Fish | 0.1 | 0.1 | 0.8 | 12 | 87 | 510 | Рыбная |

**TABLE 6-2. Industrial production by sector in constant prices**

**ТАБЛИЦА 6-2. Промышленное производство по отраслям в постоянных ценах**

| Sector | 1990 | 1991 | 1992 | 1993 | 1994 | 1995 | Отрасли |
|---|---|---|---|---|---|---|---|
| **Industrial production** | | | | | | | **Промышленное производство** |
| **All industry** | .. | .. | .. | .. | .. | .. | **Вся промышленность** |
| **Heavy industry** | .. | .. | .. | .. | .. | .. | **Тяжелая промышленность** |
| Fuel and energy | .. | .. | .. | .. | .. | .. | Топливно-энергетическая промышленноть |
| Electricity | .. | .. | .. | .. | .. | .. | Электроэнергетика |
| Fuels | .. | .. | .. | .. | .. | .. | Топливная промышленность |
| Ferrous and nonferrous metallurgy | .. | .. | .. | .. | .. | .. | Металлургия |
| Chemicals and petrochemicals | .. | .. | .. | .. | .. | .. | Химическая и нефтехимическая пром. |
| Machine building and metalworking | .. | .. | .. | .. | .. | .. | Машиностроение и металлообработка |
| Forestry, woodworking, and pulp and paper | .. | .. | .. | .. | .. | .. | Лесная, деревообрабатывающая и целлюлозо-бумажная промышленность |
| Construction materials | .. | .. | .. | .. | .. | .. | Промышленность строительных материалов |
| **Light industry** | .. | .. | .. | .. | .. | .. | **Легкая промышленность** |
| Textiles | .. | .. | .. | .. | .. | .. | Текстильная |
| Clothing | .. | .. | .. | .. | .. | .. | Швейная |
| Leather and shoe | .. | .. | .. | .. | .. | .. | Кожевенная и обувная |
| **Food industry** | .. | .. | .. | .. | .. | .. | **Пищевая промышленность** |
| Processed foods | .. | .. | .. | .. | .. | .. | Пищевкусовая |
| Meat and dairy products | .. | .. | .. | .. | .. | .. | Мясная и молочная |
| Fish | .. | .. | .. | .. | .. | .. | Рыбная |
| **Growth in production by sector (in percent)** | | | | | | | **Рост производства по отраслям** |
| **All industry** | .. | 4.8 | -14.9 | 5.4 | -25.0 | -7.0 | **Вся промышленность** |
| **Heavy industry** | .. | 6.0 | -19.8 | 2.9 | -36.3 | -8.0 | **Тяжелая промышленность** |
| Power and fuels | .. | 6.8 | -22.9 | 5.7 | -39.0 | -11.1 | Топливно-энергетическая промышленноть |
| Electricity | .. | 3.8 | -1.1 | 3.8 | -14.5 | -3.4 | Электроэнергетика |
| Fuels | .. | 7.4 | -24.2 | 5.7 | -40.0 | -11.1 | Топливная промышленность |
| Ferrous and nonferrous metallurgy | .. | 20.5 | -25.5 | -7.1 | -23.1 | 120.0 | Металлургия |
| Chemicals and petrochemicals | .. | -4.9 | -35.1 | 2.4 | -46.5 | 24.6 | Химическая и нефтехимическая пром. |
| Machine building and metalworking | .. | 12.1 | -9.2 | 5.1 | -8.1 | 22.8 | Машиностроение и металлообработка |
| Forestry, woodworking, and pulp and paper | .. | 3.7 | -4.6 | -6.5 | -37.9 | 19.4 | Лесная, деревообрабатывающая и целлюлозо-бумажная промышленность |
| Construction materials | .. | 6.1 | 6.5 | 0.0 | -22.8 | -19.1 | Промышленность строительных материалов |
| **Light industry** | .. | 3.1 | 4.1 | 12.2 | -7.2 | -2.7 | **Легкая промышленность** |
| Textiles | .. | 2.2 | 4.0 | 12.4 | -8.6 | -3.0 | Текстильная |
| Clothing | .. | 8.9 | 4.6 | 20.4 | 18.2 | 1.3 | Швейная |
| Leather and shoe | .. | 11.3 | 7.1 | -21.1 | -15.6 | 13.2 | Кожевенная и обувная |
| **Food industry** | .. | 5.9 | 1.1 | -7.5 | 4.9 | -15.3 | **Пищевая промышленность** |
| Processed foods | .. | 8.4 | -2.5 | -16.7 | 9.7 | -11.9 | Пищевкусовая |
| Meat and dairy products | .. | -0.6 | 6.2 | -4.4 | 3.1 | -28.2 | Мясная и молочная |
| Fish | .. | -5.9 | 22.3 | -30.8 | -3.7 | -15.4 | Рыбная |

**TABLE 6-3. Primary energy supply (million tons oil equivalent)**

**ТАБЛИЦА 6-3. Ресурсы первичных видов энергии (млн. тонн нефтяного эквивалента)**

| Item | | 1990 | 1991 | 1992 | 1993 | 1994 | 1995 | Статьи | |
|---|---|---|---|---|---|---|---|---|---|
| **Primary production** | | | | | | | | **Производство первичной энергии** | |
| Coal and lignite (hard and brown) | | .. | .. | .. | .. | .. | .. | Уголь каменный и бурый | |
| Crude oil | | 4994.6 | 4827.3 | 4652.9 | 4301.3 | 4083.2 | 4394.0 | Нефть | |
| Gas | | 87.8 | 84.3 | 60.1 | 65.3 | 35.7 | 32.3 | Газ | |
| Nuclear | | .. | .. | .. | .. | .. | .. | Атомная энергия | |
| Hydro/geothermal | | .. | .. | .. | .. | .. | .. | Гидро-геотермальная | |
| Other | | .. | .. | .. | .. | .. | .. | Другие виды | |
| Total | | .. | .. | .. | .. | .. | .. | Всего | |
| **Energy trade** | | | | | | | | **Торговля энергией** | |
| Coal and lignite | Exports | .. | .. | .. | .. | .. | .. | Уголь каменный и бурый | Экспорт |
| | Imports | .. | .. | .. | .. | .. | .. | | Импорт |
| | Net imports | .. | .. | .. | .. | .. | .. | | Чистый импорт |
| Oil/oil product | Exports | .. | .. | .. | .. | 3501.3 | 2769.8 | Нефть и нефтепродукты | Экспорт |
| | Imports | .. | .. | .. | .. | 372.9 | 371.9 | | Импорт |
| | Net imports | .. | .. | .. | .. | .. | .. | | Чистый импорт |
| Gas | Exports | .. | .. | .. | .. | 26.1 | 24.0 | Газ | Экспорт |
| | Imports | .. | .. | .. | .. | .. | .. | | Импорт |
| | Net imports | .. | .. | .. | .. | .. | .. | | Чистый импорт |
| Electricity | Exports | .. | .. | .. | .. | 2138.8 | 1464.1 | Электричество | Экспорт |
| | Imports | .. | .. | .. | .. | .. | .. | | Импорт |
| | Net imports | .. | .. | .. | .. | .. | .. | | Чистый импорт |
| **Total net imports** | | .. | .. | .. | .. | .. | .. | **Чистый импорт энергии-всего** | |
| **Total stock changes** | | .. | .. | .. | .. | .. | .. | **Изменение запасов-всего** | |
| **Total primary energy supply** | | .. | .. | .. | .. | .. | .. | **Ресурсы первичной энергии-всего** | |
| Coal and lignite | | .. | .. | .. | .. | .. | .. | Уголь каменный и бурый | |
| Oil/oil products | | .. | .. | .. | .. | .. | .. | Нефть и нефтепродукты | |
| Gas | | .. | .. | .. | .. | .. | .. | Газ | |
| Nuclear | | .. | .. | .. | .. | .. | .. | Атомная энергия | |
| Hydro/geothermal | | .. | .. | .. | .. | .. | .. | Гидро-геотермальная энергия | |
| Other | | .. | .. | .. | .. | .. | .. | Другие виды | |
| **Total primary energy requirement (equals total primary energy supply)** | | .. | .. | .. | .. | .. | .. | **Потребность в первичной энергии-всего (равно ресурсам первичной энергии)** | |

**TABLE 6-4. Final energy consumption (million tons oil equivalent)** **TURKMENISTAN**

**ТАБЛИЦА 6-4. Конечное потребление энергии ( млн. тонн нефтяного эквивалента )**

| | 1991 | 1992 | 1993 | 1994 | 1995 | |
|---|---|---|---|---|---|---|
| **Final energy consumption** | .. | .. | .. | .. | .. | **Конечное потребление энергии** |
| Coal & Lignite | .. | .. | .. | 39.3 | 6.1 | Уголь каменный и бурый |
| Oil Products | .. | .. | .. | 1709.1 | 1613.5 | Нефтепродукты |
| Gas | .. | .. | .. | .. | .. | Газ |
| Electricity | .. | .. | .. | 6.9 | 10.3 | Электроэнергия |
| Heat | .. | .. | .. | 7.6 | 7.4 | Тепло |
| Other | .. | .. | .. | 6.3 | 4.8 | Другие виды |
| Of which: | | | | | | В том числе |
| **Industry** | .. | .. | .. | .. | .. | **Промышленность** |
| Coal & Lignite | .. | .. | .. | 0.7 | .. | Уголь каменный и бурый |
| Oil Products | .. | .. | .. | 239.6 | 355.0 | Нефтепродукты |
| Gas | .. | .. | .. | 5.3 | 3.1 | Газ |
| Electricity | .. | .. | .. | 2.8 | 2.5 | Электроэнергия |
| Heat | .. | .. | .. | 4.7 | 4.5 | Тепло |
| Other | .. | .. | .. | 3.2 | 1.3 | Другие виды |
| **Agriculture** | .. | .. | .. | .. | .. | **Сельское хозяйство** |
| Coal & Lignite | .. | .. | .. | 3.6 | 0.8 | Уголь каменный и бурый |
| Oil Products | .. | .. | .. | 695.8 | 611.1 | Нефтепродукты |
| Gas | .. | .. | .. | 0.1 | 0.1 | Газ |
| Electricity | .. | .. | .. | 0.4 | 0.4 | Электроэнергия |
| Heat | .. | .. | .. | 0.2 | .. | Тепло |
| Other | .. | .. | .. | 0.4 | .. | Другие виды |
| **Transport** | .. | .. | .. | .. | .. | **Транспорт** |
| Oil Products | .. | .. | .. | 377.8 | 312.9 | Нефтепродукты |
| Other | .. | .. | .. | .. | .. | Другие виды |
| **Households** | .. | .. | .. | .. | .. | **Домашние хозяйства** |
| Coal & Lignite | .. | .. | .. | 7.1 | 0.2 | Уголь каменный и бурый |
| Oil Products | .. | .. | .. | 9.1 | 5.0 | Нефтепродукты |
| Gas | .. | .. | .. | 0.1 | 0.1 | Газ |
| Electricity | .. | .. | .. | 1.5 | 4.4 | Электроэнергия |
| Heat | .. | .. | .. | 0.9 | 0.2 | Тепло |
| Other | .. | .. | .. | .. | .. | Другие виды |

**TABLE 7-1. Price indices and exchange rates**

**ТАБЛИЦА 7-1. Индексы цен и обменный курс**

| Year and month | National currency per U.S. dollar<br>Единиц нац. валюты за 1 доллар США | National currency per Russian ruble<br>Единиц нац. валюты за 1 российский рубль | Consumer price index (as a percent of the previous month)<br>Индекс потребительских цен (в % к предыдущему месяцу) | Producer price index (as a percent of the previous month)<br>Индекс цен производителей (в % к предыдущему месяцу) | Consumer price index (as a percent of the previous December)<br>Индекс потребительских цен (в % к декабрю прошлого года) | Producer price index (as a percent of the previous December)<br>Индекс цен производителей (в % к декабрю прошлого года) | Год и месяц |
|---|---|---|---|---|---|---|---|
| **1993** | | | | | | | **1993** |
| January | 1.0 | .. | 114.6 | 470.7 | 114.6 | 470.7 | Январь |
| February | 1.1 | .. | 241.3 | 86.7 | 276.5 | 408.1 | Февраль |
| March | 1.3 | .. | 115.1 | 93.2 | 318.3 | 380.3 | Март |
| April | 1.5 | .. | 128.0 | 103.5 | 407.4 | 393.7 | Апрель |
| May | 1.8 | .. | 114.0 | 127.4 | 464.4 | 501.5 | Май |
| June | 2.2 | .. | 155.8 | 145.8 | 723.6 | 731.2 | Июнь |
| July | 2.1 | .. | 115.4 | 119.1 | 835.0 | 870.9 | Июль |
| August | 2.0 | .. | 116.0 | 97.3 | 968.6 | 847.4 | Август |
| September | 2.0 | .. | 121.7 | 121.8 | 1,178.8 | 1,032.1 | Сентябрь |
| October | 2.4 | .. | 127.7 | 168.9 | 1,505.4 | 1,743.2 | Октябрь |
| November | 2.0 | .. | 529.1 | 111.3 | 7,964.9 | 1,940.2 | Ноябрь |
| December | 2.0 | .. | 126.2 | 111.0 | 10,051.8 | 2,153.6 | Декабрь |
| **1994** | | | | | | | **1994** |
| January | 2.0 | .. | 125.5 | 298.9 | 125.5 | 298.9 | Январь |
| February | 2.0 | .. | 118.8 | 62.0 | 149.1 | 185.3 | Февраль |
| March | 5.9 | .. | 135.0 | 78.7 | 201.3 | 145.8 | Март |
| April | 33.5 | .. | 132.2 | 96.2 | 266.1 | 140.3 | Апрель |
| May | 57.0 | .. | 115.0 | 114.5 | 306.0 | 160.6 | Май |
| June | 57.0 | .. | 115.0 | 172.4 | 351.9 | 277.0 | Июнь |
| July | 57.0 | .. | 120.0 | 96.6 | 422.3 | 267.5 | Июль |
| August | 66.0 | .. | 138.9 | 113.5 | 586.5 | 303.7 | Август |
| September | 75.0 | .. | 125.6 | 409.8 | 736.7 | 1,244.4 | Сентябрь |
| October | 75.0 | .. | 125.8 | 77.2 | 926.8 | 960.7 | Октябрь |
| November | 75.0 | .. | 115.5 | 81.1 | 1,070.4 | 779.1 | Ноябрь |
| December | 220.0 | .. | 133.4 | 81.0 | 1,427.9 | 631.1 | Декабрь |

## TABLE 7-1. Price indices and exchange rates
## ТАБЛИЦА 7-1. Индексы цен и обменный курс

| Year and month | National currency per U.S. dollar / Единиц нац. валюты за 1 доллар США | National currency per Russian ruble / Единиц нац. валюты за 1 российский рубль | Consumer price index (as a percent of the previous month) / Индекс потребительских цен (в % к предыдущему месяцу) | Producer price index (as a percent of the previous month) / Индекс цен производителей (в % к предыдущему месяцу) | Consumer price index (as a percent of the previous December) / Индекс потребительских цен (в % к декабрю прошлого года) | Producer price index (as a percent of the previous December) / Индекс цен производителей (в % к декабрю прошлого года) | Год и месяц |
|---|---|---|---|---|---|---|---|
| **1995** | | | | | | | **1995** |
| January | 220.0 | 0.0531 | 146.8 | 183.3 | 146.8 | 183.3 | Январь |
| February | 205.0 | 0.0531 | 121.1 | 277.8 | 177.8 | 509.2 | Февраль |
| March | 195.0 | 0.0431 | 118.2 | 102.5 | 210.1 | 521.9 | Март |
| April | 195.0 | 0.0391 | 111.7 | 94.5 | 234.7 | 493.2 | Апрель |
| May | 195.0 | 0.0384 | 106.7 | 87.0 | 250.4 | 429.1 | Май |
| June | 195.0 | 0.0406 | 99.6 | 130.3 | 249.4 | 559.1 | Июнь |
| July | 195.0 | 0.0428 | 105.8 | 99.5 | 263.9 | 556.3 | Июль |
| August | 195.0 | 0.0439 | 123.5 | 113.6 | 325.9 | 632.0 | Август |
| September | 347.5 | 0.0710 | 130.5 | 108.6 | 425.3 | 686.3 | Сентябрь |
| October | 500.0 | 0.1111 | 132.9 | 173.4 | 565.3 | 1,190.0 | Октябрь |
| November | 975.0 | 0.1380 | 154.7 | 121.0 | 874.5 | 1,439.9 | Ноябрь |
| December | 1,971.7 | 0.4440 | 155.7 | 89.8 | 1,361.5 | 1,293.0 | Декабрь |
| **1996** | | | | | | | **1996** |
| January | 2,562.3 | 0.5515 | 162.5 | 318.7 | 162.5 | 318.7 | Январь |
| February | 2,315.9 | 0.4850 | 125.0 | 134.2 | 203.1 | 427.7 | Февраль |
| March | 2,604.2 | 0.5400 | 119.1 | 105.3 | 241.9 | 450.4 | Март |
| April | 3,113.3 | 0.6367 | 114.8 | 164.5 | 277.7 | 740.8 | Апрель |
| May | 3,423.1 | 0.6919 | 108.5 | 143.5 | 301.3 | 1,063.1 | Май |
| June | 3,867.8 | .. | 105.4 | .. | 317.6 | .. | Июнь |
| July | 4,110.0 | .. | 103.6 | .. | 329.0 | .. | Июль |
| August | .. | .. | .. | .. | .. | .. | Август |
| September | .. | .. | .. | .. | .. | .. | Сентябрь |
| October | .. | .. | .. | .. | .. | .. | Октябрь |
| November | .. | .. | .. | .. | .. | .. | Ноябрь |
| December | .. | .. | .. | .. | .. | .. | Декабрь |

## TABLE 7-2. Monthly nominal wages by sector
## ТАБЛИЦА 7-2. Среднемесячная денежная зарплата по отраслям

| Sector | 1990 | 1991 | 1992 | 1993 | 1994 | 1995 | Сектора |
|---|---|---|---|---|---|---|---|
| **Nominal wages** | | | | | | | **Средняя номинальная заработная плата** |
| **Economy average** | 243.7 | 414.8 | 3,982.8 | 136.6 | 1,053.5 | 6,730.2 | **По народному хозяйству** |
| **Material sphere** | 266.0 | 532.5 | 4,492.2 | 148.6 | 1,235.0 | 7,184.8 | **Отрасли сферы материального производства** |
| Industry | 265.0 | 488.0 | 5,405.8 | 169.5 | 1,224.2 | 9,625.1 | Промышленность |
| Construction | 314.9 | 534.5 | 4,671.6 | 171.0 | 1,345.5 | 10,673.4 | Строительство |
| Agriculture | 274.6 | 418.9 | 4,002.0 | 116.2 | 1,510.3 | 5,502.6 | Сельское хозяйство |
| Transport | 282.4 | 494.1 | 4,590.6 | 166.3 | 1,252.8 | 10,019.4 | Транспорт |
| Communications | 243.1 | 466.8 | 4,342.8 | 155.6 | 1,384.8 | 10,161.2 | Связь |
| Trade (retail and wholesale) | 205.7 | 348.4 | 3,487.1 | 102.9 | 776.5 | 5,944.9 | Торговля (оптовая и розничная) |
| Other | 150.3 | 309.1 | 3,335.2 | 120.9 | 848.9 | 5,888.2 | Прочие отрасли материального производства |
| **Nonmaterial sphere** | 205.0 | 238.6 | 3,230.2 | 117.2 | 752.4 | 5,411.4 | **Отрасли непроизводственной сферы** |
| Municipal services | 196.4 | 326.9 | 3,081.1 | 110.5 | 812.4 | 7,305.6 | Жилкомхоз и бытовое обслуживание |
| Science, research and development | 319.5 | 374.4 | 4,469.4 | 158.8 | 1,022.3 | 9,043.2 | Наука и научное обслуживание |
| Education | 188.8 | 293.1 | 2,924.1 | 117.8 | 729.3 | 4,926.6 | Образование |
| Culture | 153.2 | 278.0 | 2,730.0 | 93.2 | 611.8 | 4,234.2 | Культура |
| Arts | 182.6 | 303.5 | .. | .. | .. | .. | Искусство |
| Health care, social security, and sports | 164.5 | 324.3 | 2,647.4 | 98.6 | 703.5 | 4,787.8 | Здравоохр., соц.обсл., физк. и спорт |
| Banking, finance, credit, insurance | 321.0 | 845.5 | 6,348.2 | 200.6 | 1,125.0 | 7,576.3 | Кредитование, страхование, банк. дело |
| Government | 305.8 | 460.4 | 4,422.7 | 154.5 | 879.9 | 6,600.6 | Управление |

**TABLE 8-1. Money income and expenditure of the population (millions of national currency)**
**ТАБЛИЦА 8-1. Денежные доходы и расходы населения (млн. национальной валюты)**

| Type of income or expenditure | 1990 | 1991 | 1992 | 1993 | 1994 | 1995 | Вид доходов или расходов |
|---|---|---|---|---|---|---|---|
| **Income** | | | | | | | **Доходы** |
| **Total labor income** | .. | .. | .. | 2,538 | 21,512 | 106,275 | **Всего трудовых доходов** |
| Regular wages | .. | .. | .. | 1,797 | 12,604 | 70,635 | Заработная плата |
| Wages paid by cooperatives | .. | .. | .. | 118 | 1,268 | 6,536 | Заработная плата в кооперативах |
| Other wages and compensation | .. | .. | .. | 90 | 160 | 315 | Прочие доходы типа заработной платы |
| Income paid by collective farms | .. | .. | .. | 588 | 8,436 | 32,257 | Доходы от колхозов |
| Income from sale of farm products | .. | .. | .. | 63 | 312 | 3,068 | Доходы от продажи продукции колхозов |
| **Total transfer receipts** | .. | .. | .. | 426 | 4,986 | 21,529 | **Всего трансфертных поступлений** |
| Pensions and allowances | .. | .. | .. | 268 | 2,020 | 16,753 | Пенсии и пособия |
| Scholarships | .. | .. | .. | 61 | 144 | 372 | Стипендии |
| Income from the financial system (insurance, interest, etc.) | .. | .. | .. | 92 | 2,762 | 446 | Доходы из финансовой системы (страховые возмещения, проценты и т.д.) |
| Other income | .. | .. | .. | 5 | 60 | 3,958 | Прочие виды доходов |
| **Total income** | .. | .. | .. | 2,964 | 26,498 | 127,804 | **Всего доходов** |
| **Expenditure** | | | | | | | **Расходы** |
| **Total purchases** | .. | .. | .. | 1,037 | 11,780 | 65,766 | **Всего покупок товаров и услуг** |
| Retail goods | .. | .. | .. | 906 | 10,214 | 53,194 | Товары в розничной торговле |
| Services | .. | .. | .. | 131 | 1,566 | 12,572 | Услуги |
| Rent and utilities | .. | .. | .. | .. | .. | .. | Квартирная плата и коммунальные платежи |
| Transport and communications | .. | .. | .. | .. | .. | .. | Транспорт и связь |
| Health and other services | .. | .. | .. | .. | .. | .. | Здравоохранение и другие виды услуг |
| Cooperatives | .. | .. | .. | .. | .. | .. | Кооперативы |
| **Transfers and savings** | .. | .. | .. | 460 | 3,761 | 34,582 | **Трансферты и сбережения** |
| Taxes, fees, dues, and other | .. | .. | .. | 143 | 1,881 | 7,582 | Налоги, сборы, пошлины и др. |
| Savings | .. | .. | .. | 276 | 654 | 8,732 | Сбережения |
| Other | .. | .. | .. | 41 | 1,226 | 18,268 | Прочие |
| **Total expenditure** | .. | .. | .. | 1,497 | 15,541 | 100,348 | **Всего расходов** |
| **Income less expenditure** | .. | .. | .. | 1,467 | 10,957 | 27,456 | **Доходы за вычетом расходов** |

# *Country Notes: Turkmenistan*

**General notes**: General Notes: Data were provided by the State Committee for Statistics of the Republic of Turkmenistan.

**Currency:** Unless otherwise indicated, data are in rubles for 1990-1992 and in manats for 1993-1995. The conversion factor at the time of manat introduction (November 1, 1993) was 500 manats per ruble.

**Table 1-1:** Line "Leased enterprise employees" shows the number of employees of small enterprises. In 1995 Collective farm workers stand for workers of farmers' associations. In 1990, 1994, and 1995 sums of employed by categories do not add up to the totals.

**Table 1-2:** Classification of employment by sector since 1993 is different from that before 1993. For example, for 1990 through 1992 other sectors of material sphere include wholesale trade, retail trade and catering, material supply, procurement, and information and computing services. For 1993 through 1995 wholesale trade includes retail trade and catering, material supply, and procurement. Transport includes communication. Housing includes public utilities and personal services. Education includes culture and art. Credit includes insurance.

**Table 2-1:** Transport includes Road maintenance and Communication.

**Table 2-2:** Data are in previous year prices. Transport includes Road maintenance and Communication.

**Table 3-3A:** The totals include exports undistributed by commodity groups.

**Table 3-4A:** The total amounts of imports do not include services. In 1995 the total amount of imports from the CIS countries includes imports undistributed by country of origin.

**Table 5-1:** For 1991 through 1993 sums of the items of animal husbandry and of livestock do not add up to the totals.

**Table 5-2:** Data are in 1983 rubles.

**Table 5-3:** Other fruits include melons and watermelons.

**Table 6-1:** Data are in manats. Data for 1990 through 1992 were converted from rubles into manats at the rate of 1 manat per 500 rubles.

**Table 6-2:** Growth rates were calculated on the basis of industrial production volume index.

**Table 6-3:** Data for oil are in thousands of tons, for gas in billions of cubic meters, and for electricity in thousands of kilowatt-hours.

**Table 6-4:** Data for coal and lignite, oil products, and other final energy consumption are provided in thousands of tons, for gas in billions of cubic meters, for electricity in billions of kilowatt-hours, and for heat in millions of gigacalories.

# *Комментарии к таблицам: Туркменистан*

**Общее замечание:** Данные были получены из Государственного Комитета по Статистике Республики Туркменистан.

**Национальная валюта:** За исключением особо отмеченных случаев, данные приведены в рублях за 1990-1992 гг. и в манатах за 1993-1995 гг. Коэффицент пересчета на дату введения маната (1 ноября 1993 г.) составлял 500 манат за 1 рубль.

**Таблица 1-1:** Строка Арендные предприятия показывает количество занятых на мелких предприятиях. В 1995 г. в строке Колхозы показаны крестьянские объединения. В 1990, 1994 и 1995 гг. суммы занятых по секторам меньше приведенных итоговых величин.

**Таблица 1-2:** Классификация занятых по отраслям начиная с 1993 г. отличается от соответствующей классификации до 1993 г. Например, в 1990-1992 гг. другие отрасли материального производства включают оптовую торговлю, розничную торговлю и общепит, материально-техническое снабжение, заготовки, а также информационно-техническое обслуживание. В 1993-1995 гг. оптовая торговля включает розничную торговлю и общепит, материально-техническое снабжение, а также заготовки. Транспорт включает связь. Жилищное хозяйство включает коммунальное хозяйство и бытовое обслуживание. Образование включает культуру и искусство. Кредитование включает страхование.

**Таблица 2-1:** Транспорт включает дорожное хозяйство и связь.

**Таблица 2-2**: Данные приведены в ценах предыдущего года. Транспорт включает дорожное хозяйство и связь.

**Таблица 3-3А**: Итог включает экспорт нераспределенный по товарным группам.

**Таблица 3-4А:** Итоговые величины импорта не включают услуги. В 1995 г. общий объем импорта из стран СНГ включает импорт нераспределенный по странам.

**Таблица 5-1:** В 1991-1993 гг. суммы компонентов продукции живодноводства и мясного живодноводства не равны соответствующим итоговым величинам.

**Таблица 5-2:** Данные приведены в ценах 1983 г.

**Таблица 5-3:** Другие фрукты включают бахчевые.

**Таблица 6-1:** Данные приведены в манатах. Данные за 1990-1992 гг. были пересчитаны из рублей в манаты с коэффициентом пересчета 1 манат = 500 рублей.

**Таблица 6-2:** Темпы прироста были рассчитаны на основе индекса физического объема производства.

**Таблица 6-3:** Нефть приведена в тысячах тонн, газ - в миллиардах кубических метров, электричество - в тысячах киловатт-часов.

**Таблица 6-4:** Уголь, нефтепродукты, а также другие виды конечного потребления энергии приведены в тысячах тонн, газ - в миллиардах кубических метров, электричество - в миллиардах киловатт-часов, тепло - в миллионах гигакалорий.

# Ukraine / Украина

1996 Population / Численность населения в 1996 году
(thousands / тыс. человек): 51,334

Area / Территория
(thousand square kilometers / тыс. кв. км.): 603.7

Capital city / Столица :
Kiev / Киев

**Country Tables:** Tables 2-2 to 2-2B, 3-2B, 3-3B, 4-1, 4-2, and 6-4 are not included because there are either no or no recent data available.

**Статистические таблицы страны:** Таблицы с 2-2 по 2-2B, 3-2B, 3-3B, 4-1, 4-2 и 6-4 не включены ввиду полного отсутствия данных либо их отсутствия за последние годы.

**TABLE 1-1. Population and employment (thousands)**
**ТАБЛИЦА 1-1. Население и занятость (тысяч)**

| Population or employment category | 1990 | 1991 | 1992 | 1993 | 1994 | 1995 | Население или группы занятых |
|---|---|---|---|---|---|---|---|
| **Total population** | 51,839 | 51,944 | 52,057 | 52,244 | 52,114 | 51,728 | **Население - всего** |
| Males | 24,007 | 24,086 | 24,167 | 24,282 | 24,236 | 24,068 | Мужчины |
| Females | 27,831 | 27,858 | 27,890 | 27,962 | 27,878 | 27,660 | Женщины |
| Urban population | 34,869 | 35,085 | 35,297 | 35,471 | 35,401 | 35,119 | Городское |
| Rural population | 16,969 | 16,859 | 16,760 | 16,773 | 16,713 | 16,609 | Сельское |
| Population under working age | 11,825 | 11,778 | 11,710 | 11,646 | 11,507 | 11,262 | Моложе трудоспособного возраста |
| Working-age population | 28,799 | 28,816 | 28,857 | 28,925 | 28,860 | 28,689 | Лица в трудоспособном возрасте |
| Population over working age | 10,960 | 11,096 | 11,235 | 11,419 | 11,493 | 11,523 | Старше трудоспособного возраста |
| Economically Active Population, in non-working age | .. | .. | .. | .. | .. | .. | Экономически активное население в нетрудоспособном возрасте |
| Above working age | .. | .. | .. | .. | .. | .. | Старше трудоспособного возраста |
| Below working age | .. | .. | .. | .. | .. | .. | Моложе трудоспособного возраста |
| **Total labor resources** | 29,706 | 29,853 | 29,544 | 29,680 | 29,378 | 30,072 | **Трудовые ресурсы - всего** |
| **Total employment** | 25,419 | 24,995 | 24,505 | 23,945 | 23,025 | 23,725 | **Занятое население - всего** |
| State sector employees | 20,653 | 20,439 | 16,661 | 15,835 | 14,017 | 11,185 | Государственный сектор |
| Leased enterprise employees | .. | .. | 1,759 | 1,623 | 1,031 | 781 | Арендные предприятия |
| Joint-stock company employees | .. | .. | .. | .. | .. | .. | Акционерные общества |
| Economic association employees | .. | .. | .. | .. | .. | .. | Хозяйственные ассоциации |
| Social organization employees | .. | .. | 35 | 30 | 25 | 32 | Общественные организации |
| Joint venture employees | .. | 21 | 41 | 72 | 85 | 102 | Совместные предприятия |
| Collective farm workers | 3,412 | 3,369 | 3,302 | 3,172 | 2,991 | 2,899 | Колхозы |
| Cooperative workers | 601 | 555 | 250 | 169 | 125 | 71 | Кооперативы |
| Individual labor activities | 54 | 59 | 1,347 | 1,416 | 2,020 | .. | ИТД |
| Private subsidiary agricultural workers | 681 | 529 | 642 | 780 | 986 | 1,744 | Личные подсобные хозяйства |
| Private agricultural workers | .. | 5 | 26 | 35 | 57 | 77 | Фермерские хозяйства |
| **Students** | 1,979 | 1,923 | 1,934 | 1,954 | 1,931 | 1,951 | **Учащиеся** |
| **Religious workers** | 18 | 18 | 20 | 22 | 21 | 19 | **Служащие религиозного культа** |
| **Working age population not employed in the national economy** | 2,290 | 2,917 | 3,085 | 3,759 | 4,401 | 4,377 | **Лица в трудоспособном возрасте, не занятые в экономике** |
| Housewives | .. | .. | .. | .. | .. | .. | Домохозяйки |
| Military personnel | .. | .. | .. | .. | .. | .. | Военнослужащие |
| Unemployed | .. | 3 | 71 | 84 | 91 | 93 | Безработные |
| **Labor force** | 25,419 | 24,998 | 24,576 | 24,029 | 23,116 | 23,818 | **Рабочая сила** |

## TABLE 1-2. Employment by sector (thousands)
## ТАБЛИЦА 1-2. Численность занятого населения по секторам (тысяч)

| Sector | 1990 | 1991 | 1992 | 1993 | 1994 | 1995 | Сектор |
|---|---|---|---|---|---|---|---|
| **Material sphere** | 18,725 | 18,225 | 17,941 | 17,454 | 16,612 | 17,341 | **Сфера материального производства** |
| **Agriculture and forestry** | 5,023 | 4,828 | 4,989 | 4,944 | 4,821 | 5,329 | **Сельское и лесное хозяйство** |
| Agriculture | 4,960 | 4,762 | 4,920 | 4,874 | 4,750 | 5,257 | Сельское хозяйство |
| Forestry | 63 | 66 | 69 | 70 | 71 | 72 | Лесное хозяйство |
| **Industry and construction** | 10,252 | 10,036 | 9,310 | 8,788 | 7,889 | 7,246 | **Промышленность и строительство** |
| Industry | 7,830 | 7,769 | 7,401 | 7,017 | 6,249 | 5,761 | Промышленность |
| Construction | 2,422 | 2,267 | 1,909 | 1,771 | 1,640 | 1,485 | Строительство |
| **Other** | 3,451 | 3,361 | 3,642 | 3,722 | 3,902 | 4,766 | **Другие отрасли** |
| Transport of goods | .. | .. | .. | .. | .. | .. | Грузовой транспорт |
| Road Maintenance | 1,145 | 1,128 | 1,025 | 1,008 | 934 | 914 | Дорожное хозяйство |
| Communication servicing material production | .. | .. | .. | .. | .. | .. | Связь |
| Wholesale trade | .. | .. | .. | .. | .. | .. | Оптовая торговля |
| Retail trade and catering | .. | .. | .. | .. | .. | .. | Розничная торговля и общепит |
| Material supply | 1,892 | 1,863 | 1,751 | 1,711 | 1,629 | 1,614 | Материально-техническое снабжение |
| Procurement | .. | .. | .. | .. | .. | .. | Заготовки |
| Information and computing services | 60 | 53 | 38 | 28 | 24 | 20 | Информационно-техническое обслуживание |
| Other sectors | 354 | 317 | 828 | 975 | 1,315 | 2,218 | Другие отрасли сферы материального пр. |
| **Nonmaterial sphere** | 6,693 | 6,771 | 6,564 | 6,491 | 6,413 | 6,384 | **Сфера нематериального производства** |
| Passenger transport | .. | .. | .. | .. | .. | .. | Пассажирский транспорт |
| Communication | 643 | 646 | 598 | 596 | 557 | 535 | Связь |
| Housing | .. | .. | .. | .. | .. | .. | Жилищное хозяйство |
| Public utilities and personal services | 994 | 997 | 898 | 840 | 820 | 820 | Комм. хоз. и бытовое обслуживание |
| Health care, social security, physical culture and sports | 1,502 | 1,521 | 1,521 | 1,532 | 1,508 | 1,516 | Здравоохранение, социальное обеспечение, физкультура и спорт |
| Education | 2,360 | 2,367 | 2,361 | 2,300 | 2,277 | 2,247 | Образование |
| Culture and art | .. | .. | .. | .. | .. | .. | Культура и искусство |
| Science and scientific research | 632 | 631 | 480 | 438 | 394 | 363 | Наука и научное обслуживание |
| Credit | .. | .. | .. | .. | .. | .. | Кредитование |
| Insurance | 129 | 134 | 144 | 162 | 176 | 181 | Страхование |
| General administration and defense | 433 | 475 | 562 | 623 | 681 | 722 | Государственное управление и оборона |
| Private nonprofit institutions serving households | .. | .. | .. | .. | .. | .. | Общественные организации, обслуживающие домашние хозяйства |
| **Other, material and nonmaterial spheres** | 10,144 | 10,132 | 10,206 | 10,213 | 10,315 | 11,150 | **Остальные отрасли материального производства и нематериальной сферы** |
| **Total employment** | 25,419 | 24,995 | 24,505 | 23,945 | 23,025 | 23,725 | **Занятые - всего** |

**TABLE 1-3. Registered unemployment (thousands; end of month)**

**ТАБЛИЦА 1-3. Численность зарегистрированных безработных (тысяч; на конец месяца)**

| Year and month | Total<br>Всего | Males<br>Мужчины | Females<br>Женщины | Receiving benefits<br>Получающие пособие | Год и месяц |
|---|---|---|---|---|---|
| **1994** | | | | | **1994** |
| January | 87.7 | 23.5 | 64.2 | 39.1 | Январь |
| February | 93.1 | 25.6 | 67.5 | 42.8 | Февраль |
| March | 98.6 | 27.1 | 71.5 | 46.8 | Март |
| April | 102.6 | 28.4 | 74.2 | 48.7 | Апрель |
| May | 101.6 | 28.3 | 73.3 | 49.8 | Май |
| June | 92.9 | 25.8 | 67.1 | 48.9 | Июнь |
| July | 91.9 | 25.0 | 66.9 | 50.9 | Июль |
| August | 91.7 | 24.4 | 67.3 | 52.0 | Август |
| September | 88.9 | 23.4 | 65.5 | 51.0 | Сентябрь |
| October | 85.9 | 22.5 | 63.4 | 48.4 | Октябрь |
| November | 82.9 | 21.4 | 61.5 | 47.4 | Ноябрь |
| December | 82.2 | 22.4 | 59.8 | 47.7 | Декабрь |
| **1995** | | | | | **1995** |
| January | 82.9 | 23.5 | 59.4 | 48.2 | Январь |
| February | 85.5 | 25.2 | 60.3 | 48.5 | Февраль |
| March | 86.6 | 25.8 | 60.8 | 50.2 | Март |
| April | 87.9 | 25.9 | 62.0 | 51.9 | Апрель |
| May | 85.4 | 24.9 | 60.5 | 51.5 | Май |
| June | 84.6 | 24.2 | 60.4 | 51.0 | Июнь |
| July | 89.2 | 24.8 | 64.4 | 53.6 | Июль |
| August | 94.6 | 25.7 | 68.9 | 57.1 | Август |
| September | 98.4 | 26.2 | 72.2 | 60.1 | Сентябрь |
| October | 103.8 | 27.0 | 76.8 | 61.6 | Октябрь |
| November | 112.6 | 29.4 | 83.2 | 65.3 | Ноябрь |
| December | 126.8 | 34.6 | 92.2 | 74.3 | Декабрь |
| **1996** | | | | | **1996** |
| January | 139.2 | 39.4 | 99.8 | 82.7 | Январь |
| February | 172.1 | 53.2 | 118.9 | 97.0 | Февраль |
| March | 199.9 | 63.6 | 136.3 | 114.7 | Март |
| April | 216.6 | 68.9 | 147.7 | 129.6 | Апрель |
| May | 219.6 | 68.7 | 150.9 | 140.5 | Май |
| June | .. | .. | .. | .. | Июнь |
| July | .. | .. | .. | .. | Июль |
| August | .. | .. | .. | .. | Август |
| September | .. | .. | .. | .. | Сентябрь |
| October | .. | .. | .. | .. | Октябрь |
| November | .. | .. | .. | .. | Ноябрь |
| December | .. | .. | .. | .. | Декабрь |

**TABLE 2-1. Gross domestic product at current prices (billions of national currency)**
**ТАБЛИЦА 2-1. Валовой внутренний продукт в текущих ценах (млрд. национальной валюты)**

| Sector of origin or expenditure category | 1990 | 1991 | 1992 | 1993 | 1994 | 1995 | Отраслевое происхождение или вид расходов |
|---|---|---|---|---|---|---|---|
| Gross domestic product by sector of origin | | | | | | | Валовой внутренний продукт по отраслевому происхождению |
| **Agriculture and forestry** | 41 | 73 | 1,049 | 31,939 | 175,418 | 718,191 | **Сельское и лесное хозяйство** |
| Agriculture | 41 | 73 | 1,047 | 31,824 | 173,113 | 706,190 | Сельское хозяйство |
| Forestry | 0 | 0 | 2 | 115 | 2,305 | 12,001 | Лесное хозяйство |
| **Industry and construction** | 72 | 164 | 2,625 | 54,324 | 510,997 | 2,315,157 | **Промышленность и строительство** |
| Industry | 58 | 137 | 2,245 | 44,042 | 421,475 | 1,821,759 | Промышленность |
| Construction | 14 | 27 | 380 | 10,282 | 89,522 | 493,398 | Строительство |
| **Other** | 47 | 92 | 1,696 | 73,264 | 61,934 | 2,031,107 | **Другие отрасли** |
| Transport | 9 | 16 | 372 | 15,812 | 76,007 | .. | Транспорт |
| Road maintenance | 1 | 1 | 20 | 750 | 9,334 | .. | Дорожное хозяйство |
| Communication | 1 | 3 | 31 | 863 | 11,921 | 648,880 | Связь |
| Wholesale trade | .. | .. | .. | .. | .. | .. | Оптовая торговля |
| Retail trade and catering | 7 | 13 | 249 | 11,318 | 61,916 | 254,297 | Розничная торговля и общепит |
| Material supply | 1 | 2 | 48 | 5,626 | 16,481 | 64,686 | Материально-техническое снабжение |
| Procurement | 1 | 2 | 32 | 1,322 | 9,179 | 29,007 | Заготовки |
| Information and computing services | 0 | 1 | 6 | 87 | 849 | 4,197 | Информационно-вычислительное обслуживание |
| Other sectors of material production | 1 | 2 | 34 | 1,420 | 8,329 | 43,631 | Другие отрасли сферы материального пр. |
| Housing | 3 | 4 | 28 | 2,728 | 17,257 | .. | Жилищное хозяйство |
| Public utilities and personal services | 3 | 4 | 39 | 1,303 | 12,503 | 125,046 | Ком. хоз. и бытовое обслуживание |
| Health care, social security, physical culture and sports | 4 | 9 | 145 | 3,996 | 35,501 | 193,444 | Здравоохранение, социальное обеспечение, физкультура и спорт |
| Education | 5 | 11 | 185 | 5,125 | 40,663 | 207,200 | Образование |
| Culture and art | 1 | 2 | 32 | 944 | 6,255 | 29,178 | Культура и искусство |
| Science and scientific research | 3 | 5 | 70 | 1,467 | 21,692 | 61,764 | Наука и научное обслуживание |
| Credit | 1 | 7 | 225 | 15,056 | 87,578 | .. | Кредитование |
| Insurance | .. | .. | .. | .. | .. | .. | Страхование |
| General administration and defense | 6 | 10 | 175 | 5,304 | 45,308 | 369,777 | Государственное управление и оборона |
| Private nonprofit institutions serving households | 0 | 0 | 3 | 143 | 1,161 | .. | Общественные организации, обслуживающие домашние хозяйства |
| **Imputed service charge of financial intermediaries** | 0 | -6 | -212 | -12,137 | -68,402 | -100,700 | **Условно-исчисляемая стоимость услуг финансовых посредников** |
| **Total gross value added (GVA)** | 160 | 323 | 5,156 | 147,390 | 1,079,947 | 4,963,755 | **Валовая добавленная стоимость (ВДС) - всего** |
| **Taxes on production and imports (TOPI)** | 35 | 45 | 729 | 31,962 | 303,602 | 1,112,324 | **Налоги на производство и импорт (НПиИ)** |
| Other taxes on production (OTOP) | 7 | 14 | 174 | 10,384 | 87,091 | 542,204 | Другие налоги на производство (ДНП) |
| **Subsidies on production and imports (SOPI)** | 21 | 56 | 680 | 20,757 | 94,552 | 240,565 | **Субсидии на производство и импорт (СПиИ)** |
| Other subsidies on production (OSOP) | .. | 1 | 2 | 62 | 1,863 | .. | Другие субсидии на производство (ДСП) |
| **Total GDP at factor cost (GVA-OTOP+OSOP)** | 153 | 310 | 4,984 | 137,068 | 994,719 | 4,421,551 | **Всего ВВП по фактр. стоимости (ВДС-ДНП+ДСП)** |
| **Net Indirect taxes (TOPI - SOPI)** | 14 | -11 | 49 | 11,205 | 209,050 | 871,759 | **Чистые косвенные налоги (НПиИ-СПиИ)** |
| **Total GDP at market prices** | 167 | 299 | 5,033 | 148,273 | 1,203,769 | 5,293,310 | **Всего ВВП в рыночных ценах** |
| **Gross domestic product by expenditure category** | | | | | | | **Валовой внутренний продукт по видам расходов** |
| **Consumption** | 123 | 214 | 3,199 | 94,925 | 816,573 | 3,692,300 | **Потребление** |
| Private consumption | 107 | 188 | 2,833 | 84,056 | 707,169 | 3,242,095 | Личное потребление |
| Government consumption | 16 | 26 | 366 | 10,869 | 109,404 | 450,205 | Общественное потребление |
| **Gross domestic investment** | 46 | 79 | 1,734 | 53,812 | 425,309 | 1,813,153 | **Валовые внутренние инвестиции** |
| Gross fixed investment | 40 | 64 | 1,381 | 36,349 | 285,820 | 1,065,500 | Валовое накопление основного капитала |
| Change in stocks | 6 | 15 | 353 | 17,463 | 139,489 | 747,653 | Изменения в запасах (МОС) |
| **Resource balance (net exports of GNFS)** | -2 | 6 | 100 | -464 | -38,113 | -212,143 | **Сальдо ресурсов (чистый экспорт ТНФУ)** |
| Exports of goods and nonfactor services | 46 | 78 | 1,207 | 38,370 | 426,002 | 2,518,776 | Экспорт товаров и нефакторных услуг |
| Imports of goods and nonfactor services | 48 | 72 | 1,107 | 38,834 | 464,115 | 2,730,919 | Импорт товаров и нефакторных услуг |

**TABLE 2-1A. Distribution of gross domestic product at current prices (percent)**

**ТАБЛИЦА 2-1А. Распределение валового внутреннего продукта в текущих ценах ( % )**

| Sector of origin or expenditure category | 1990 | 1991 | 1992 | 1993 | 1994 | 1995 | Отраслевое происхождение или вид расходов |
|---|---|---|---|---|---|---|---|
| **Gross domestic product by sector of origin** | | | | | | | **ВВП по отраслевому происхождению** |
| **Agriculture and forestry** | 24.6 | 24.4 | 20.8 | 21.5 | 14.6 | 13.6 | **Сельское и лесное хозяйство** |
| Agriculture | 24.6 | 24.4 | 20.8 | 21.5 | 14.4 | 13.3 | Сельское хозяйство |
| Forestry | 0.0 | 0.0 | 0.0 | 0.1 | 0.2 | 0.2 | Лесное хозяйство |
| **Industry and construction** | 43.1 | 54.8 | 52.2 | 36.6 | 42.4 | 43.7 | **Промышленность и строительство** |
| Industry | 34.7 | 45.8 | 44.6 | 29.7 | 35.0 | 34.4 | Промышленность |
| Construction | 8.4 | 9.0 | 7.6 | 6.9 | 7.4 | 9.3 | Строительство |
| **Other** | 28.1 | 30.8 | 33.7 | 49.4 | 5.1 | 38.4 | **Другие отрасли** |
| Transport | 5.4 | 5.4 | 7.4 | 10.7 | 6.3 | .. | Транспорт |
| Road maintenance | 0.6 | 0.3 | 0.4 | 0.5 | 0.8 | .. | Дорожное хозяйство |
| Communication | 0.6 | 1.0 | 0.6 | 0.6 | 1.0 | 12.3 | Связь |
| Wholesale trade | .. | .. | .. | .. | .. | .. | Оптовая торговля |
| Retail trade and catering | 4.2 | 4.3 | 4.9 | 7.6 | 5.1 | 4.8 | Розничная торговля и общепит |
| Material supply | 0.6 | 0.7 | 1.0 | 3.8 | 1.4 | 1.2 | Материально-техническое снабжение |
| Procurement | 0.6 | 0.7 | 0.6 | 0.9 | 0.8 | 0.5 | Заготовки |
| Information and computing services | 0.0 | 0.3 | 0.1 | 0.1 | 0.1 | 0.1 | Информационно-вычислительное обслуживание |
| Other sectors of material production | 0.6 | 0.7 | 0.7 | 1.0 | 0.7 | 0.8 | Другие отрасли сферы матерл. произ. |
| Housing | 1.8 | 1.3 | 0.6 | 1.8 | 1.4 | .. | Жилищное хозяйство |
| Public utilities and personal services | 1.8 | 1.3 | 0.8 | 0.9 | 1.0 | 2.4 | Ком. хоз. и бытовое обслуживание |
| Health care, social security, physical culture and sports | 2.4 | 3.0 | 2.9 | 2.7 | 2.9 | 3.7 | Здравоохранение, социальное обеспечение, физкультура и спорт |
| Education | 3.0 | 3.7 | 3.7 | 3.5 | 3.4 | 3.9 | Образование |
| Culture and art | 0.6 | 0.7 | 0.6 | 0.6 | 0.5 | 0.6 | Культура и искусство |
| Science and scientific research | 1.8 | 1.7 | 1.4 | 1.0 | 1.8 | 1.2 | Наука и научное обслуживание |
| Credit | 0.6 | 2.3 | 4.5 | 10.2 | 7.3 | .. | Кредитование |
| Insurance | 0.0 | 0.0 | 0.0 | 0.0 | 0.0 | .. | Страхование |
| General administration and defense | 3.6 | 3.3 | 3.5 | 3.6 | 3.8 | 7.0 | Государственное управление и оборона |
| Private nonprofit institutions serving households | 0.0 | 0.0 | 0.1 | 0.1 | 0.1 | .. | Общественные организации, обслуживающие домашние хозяйства |
| **Imputed service charge of financial intermediaries** | 0.0 | -2.0 | -4.2 | -8.2 | -5.7 | -1.9 | **Условно-исчисляемая стоимость услуг финансовых посредников** |
| **Total gross value added** | 95.8 | 108.0 | 102.4 | 99.4 | 89.7 | 93.8 | **Валовая добавленная стоимость - всего** |
| **Total GDP at factor cost** | 91.6 | 103.7 | 99.0 | 92.4 | 82.6 | 83.5 | **ВВП по фактор. стоимости - всего** |
| **Net indirect taxes** | 8.4 | -3.7 | 1.0 | 7.6 | 17.4 | 16.5 | **Чистые косвенные налоги (НПиИ-СПиИ)** |
| **Total GDP at market prices** | 100.0 | 100.0 | 100.0 | 100.0 | 100.0 | 100.0 | **ВВП в рын. ценах - всего** |
| **Gross domestic product by expenditure category** | | | | | | | **ВВП по видам расходов** |
| **Consumption** | 73.7 | 71.6 | 63.6 | 64.0 | 67.8 | 69.8 | **Потребление** |
| Private consumption | 64.1 | 62.9 | 56.3 | 56.7 | 58.7 | 61.2 | Личное потребление |
| Government consumption | 9.6 | 8.7 | 7.3 | 7.3 | 9.1 | 8.5 | Общественное потребление |
| **Gross domestic investment** | 27.5 | 26.4 | 34.5 | 36.3 | 35.3 | 34.3 | **Вал. внутр. инвестиции** |
| Gross fixed investment | 24.0 | 21.4 | 27.4 | 24.5 | 23.7 | 20.1 | Вал. накопление осн. капитала |
| Change in stocks | 3.6 | 5.0 | 7.0 | 11.8 | 11.6 | 14.1 | Изменения в запасах (МОС) |
| **Resource balance (net exports of GNFS)** | -1.2 | 2.0 | 2.0 | -0.3 | -3.2 | -4.0 | **Сальдо ресурсов (чистый экспорт ТНФУ)** |
| Exports of goods and nonfactor services | 27.5 | 26.1 | 24.0 | 25.9 | 35.4 | 47.6 | Экспорт товаров и нефакторных услуг |
| Imports of goods and nonfactor services | 28.7 | 24.1 | 22.0 | 26.2 | 38.6 | 51.6 | Импорт товаров и нефакторных услуг |

**TABLE 3-1. Balance of payments at current prices (millions of U.S. dollars)**
**ТАБЛИЦА 3-1. Платежный баланс в текущих ценах (в миллионах долларов США)**

| Item | 1990 | 1991 | 1992 | 1993 | 1994 | 1995 | Статьи |
|---|---|---|---|---|---|---|---|
| Exports of goods and services (including workers' remittances) | .. | .. | .. | 13,485 | 17,705 | .. | Экспорт товаров и услуг (включая денежные переводы рабочих) |
| Exports of goods and nonfactor services | .. | .. | .. | 13,458 | 17,647 | .. | Экспорт товаров и нефакт. услуг |
| Merchandise (FOB) | .. | .. | .. | 10,862 | 14,900 | .. | Товары (ФОБ) |
| Nonfactor services | .. | .. | .. | 2,596 | 2,747 | .. | Нефакторные услуги |
| Shipment | .. | .. | .. | 2,114 | 1,894 | .. | Перевозки |
| Travel | .. | .. | .. | 279 | 175 | .. | Поездки |
| Other | .. | .. | .. | 203 | 678 | .. | Другие |
| Imports of goods and nonfactor services | .. | .. | .. | 14,281 | 19,011 | .. | Импорт товаров и нефакт. услуг |
| Merchandise (FOB) | .. | .. | .. | 12,602 | 17,473 | .. | Товары (ФОБ) |
| Nonfactor services | .. | .. | .. | 1,679 | 1,538 | .. | Нефакторные услуги |
| Shipment | .. | .. | .. | 1,214 | 244 | .. | Перевозки |
| Travel | .. | .. | .. | 150 | 141 | .. | Поездки |
| Other | .. | .. | .. | 315 | 1,153 | .. | Другие |
| Resource balance | .. | .. | .. | -823 | -1,364 | .. | Сальдо ресурсов |
| Net factor income | .. | .. | .. | -50 | -344 | .. | Чистый факторный доход |
| Factor receipts | .. | .. | .. | 27 | 56 | .. | Факторные поступления |
| Factor payments | .. | .. | .. | 77 | 400 | .. | Факторные платежи |
| Total interest due | .. | .. | .. | .. | 303 | .. | Общая сумма процента к оплате |
| Other factor payments and discrepancy | .. | .. | .. | .. | 97 | .. | Другие факторные платежи и стат. погр. |
| Net current transfers | .. | .. | .. | 107 | 547 | .. | Чистые текущие трансферты |
| Current receipts | .. | .. | .. | 120 | 583 | .. | Текущие поступления |
| Workers remittances | .. | .. | .. | .. | 2 | .. | Денежные переводы рабочих |
| Other current transfers | .. | .. | .. | .. | 581 | .. | Другие текущие трансферты |
| Current payments | .. | .. | .. | 13 | 36 | .. | Текущие платежи |
| Current account balance before official grants | .. | .. | .. | -766 | -1,161 | .. | Сальдо текущего счета до офиц. безвозмезд. трансфертов |
| Official capital grants | .. | .. | .. | -15 | 97 | .. | Официальные кап. безвозмезные трансферты |
| Current account balance after official grants | .. | .. | .. | -781 | -1,064 | .. | Сальдо текущего счета после офиц. безвозмезд. трансфертов |
| Long Term Capital Inflows | .. | .. | .. | 1,639 | 856 | .. | Долгосрочные притоки капитала |
| Direct investment | .. | .. | .. | 198 | 151 | .. | Прямые инвестиции |
| Net long term borrowing | .. | .. | .. | 1,451 | 705 | .. | Чистые долгосрочные займы |
| Disbursements | .. | .. | .. | 1,583 | 1,109 | .. | Поступления |
| Repayments due | .. | .. | .. | 132 | 404 | .. | Сумма, подлежащая погашению |
| Other long-term inflows (net) | .. | .. | .. | 10 | .. | .. | Другие долгосрочные притоки (чистые) |

(continued on next page)

**TABLE 3-1. Balance of payments at current prices (millions of U.S. dollars)**
**ТАБЛИЦА 3-1. Платежный баланс в текущих ценах (в миллионах долларов США)**

| Item | 1990 | 1991 | 1992 | 1993 | 1994 | 1995 | Статьи |
|---|---|---|---|---|---|---|---|
| Adjustment to Scheduled Debt Service | .. | .. | .. | .. | .. | .. | Регулирование долга |
| Debt service not paid | .. | .. | .. | .. | .. | .. | Невыплаченный долг |
| Interest not paid | .. | .. | .. | .. | .. | .. | Невыплаченный процент |
| Principal not paid | .. | .. | .. | .. | .. | .. | Невыплаченная сумма основного долга |
| Arrears reductions/prepayments(-) | .. | .. | .. | .. | .. | .. | Погашение просроченных платежей/выплаты авансом (-) |
| Total Other items (Net) | .. | .. | .. | 756 | 1,027 | .. | Общие другие статьи (чистые) |
| Net short-term capital | .. | .. | .. | .. | 315 | .. | Чистый краткосрочный капитал |
| Capital flows not elsewhere included | .. | .. | .. | .. | .. | .. | Потоки капитала, не указанные выше |
| Errors and omissions | .. | .. | .. | .. | 712 | .. | Ошибки и пропуски |
| Changes in net reserves | .. | .. | .. | .. | -879 | .. | Изменения в чистых резервах |
| Net credit from IMF | .. | .. | .. | .. | -360 | .. | Чистый кредит МВФ |
| Reserve changes not elsewhere included | .. | .. | .. | .. | -459 | .. | Изменения резервов, не указанных выше |
| Escrow account | .. | .. | .. | .. | .. | .. | Счет депонирования |
| Gross reserves (excluding gold) | .. | .. | .. | 98 | 913 | .. | Общие резервы (исключая золото) |
| Gross reserves (including gold) | .. | .. | .. | 102 | 924 | .. | Общие резервы (включая золото) |
| Nominal official exchange rate (annual average) (rf) | .. | .. | .. | .. | .. | .. | Номинальный официальный или рыночный курс (среднегодовой) |
| Nominal official exchange rate (end-of-year) (ae) | .. | .. | .. | .. | .. | .. | Номинальный официальный или рыночный курс (на конец года) |
| Manufacture unit value (percent change) | .. | .. | .. | .. | .. | .. | Средний индекс цен на продукцию обр. пром.,% |
| Index of real effective exchange rate (IMF) | .. | .. | .. | .. | .. | .. | Индекс реального эффективного валютного курса (МВФ) |
| Total factor payments | .. | .. | .. | .. | .. | .. | Общая сумма факторных платежей |
| Government interest | .. | .. | .. | .. | .. | .. | Процент, выплачиваемый органами гос. управления |
| Private sector interest | .. | .. | .. | .. | .. | .. | Процент выплачиваемый частным сектором |
| Profits on direct foreign investment | .. | .. | .. | .. | .. | .. | Прибыль от прямых иностранных инвестиций |
| Official capital grants | .. | .. | .. | .. | .. | .. | Официальные капитальные безвозмездные трансферты |
| For budgetary financing | .. | .. | .. | .. | .. | .. | На бюджетное финансирование |
| To extrabudgetary entities | .. | .. | .. | .. | .. | .. | На внебюджетное финансирование |
| Government net long term borrowing | .. | .. | .. | .. | .. | .. | Чистые долгосрочные государственные займы |
| Disbursements | .. | .. | .. | .. | .. | .. | Поступления |
| Repayments | .. | .. | .. | .. | .. | .. | Погашения |
| Private net long term borrowing | .. | .. | .. | .. | .. | .. | Чистые долгосрочные частные займы |
| Disbursements | .. | .. | .. | .. | .. | .. | Поступления |
| Repayments | .. | .. | .. | .. | .. | .. | Погашения |

## TABLE 3-2A. Imports by commodity group (millions of U.S. dollars)
## ТАБЛИЦА 3-2А . Импорт по товарным группам (млн. долларов США)

| Commodity group | 1990 | 1991 | 1992 | 1993 | 1994 | 1995 | Товарные группы |
|---|---|---|---|---|---|---|---|
| TOTAL | .. | .. | .. | .. | 9,989.2 | 11,335.5 | ВСЕГО |
| I - Live animals; animal products | .. | .. | .. | .. | 61.1 | 75.5 | I - Живые животные и продукты животноводства |
| II - Vegetable products | .. | .. | .. | .. | 94.9 | 103.2 | II - Продукты растительного происхождения |
| III - Animal or vegetable fats and oils and their cleavage products; prepared edible fats; animal or vegetable waxes | .. | .. | .. | .. | 5.0 | 19.4 | III - Жиры и масла растительного и животного происхождения, воски |
| IV - Prepared foodstuffs; beverages, spirits and vinegar; tobacco and manufactured tobacco substitutes | .. | .. | .. | .. | 164.6 | 273.5 | IV -Продукция пищевой промышленности, алкогольные и безалкогольные напитки, табак и его заменители |
| V - Mineral products | .. | .. | .. | .. | 5,495.8 | 6,281.1 | V - Минеральные продукты |
| VI - Products of the chemical or allied industries | .. | .. | .. | .. | 555.4 | 614.3 | VI - Продукция химической промышленности |
| VII - Plastics and articles thereof; rubber and articles thereof | .. | .. | .. | .. | 384.7 | 412.0 | VII - Пластмассы и изделия из них |
| VIII - Raw hides and skins, leather, furskins and articles thereof; saddlery and harness; travel goods, handbags and similar containers; articles of animal gut | .. | .. | .. | .. | 52.4 | 35.1 | VIII - Кожевенное сырьё, кожи, пушнина, меховое сырьё и изделия из них |
| IX - Wood and articles of wood; wood charcoal; cork and articles of cork; manufactures of straw, of esparto or of other plaiting materials; basketware and wickerwork | .. | .. | .. | .. | 265.4 | 79.0 | IX - Древесина и изделия из древесины, древесный уголь |
| X - Pulp of wood or of other fibrous cellulosic material; waste and scrap of paper or paperboard; paper and paperboard and articles thereof | .. | .. | .. | .. | 84.1 | 206.5 | X - Бумажная масса, бумажные и картонные отходы, макулатура, бумага, картон и изделия из них |
| XI - Textiles and textile articles | .. | .. | .. | .. | 265.4 | 352.3 | XI - Текстиль и текстильные изделия |
| XII - Footwear, headgear, umbrellas, sun umbrellas, walking sticks, seat sticks, whips, riding crops and parts thereof; prepared feathers and articles made therewith; artificial flowers; articles of human hair | .. | .. | .. | .. | 38.9 | 36.1 | XII - Обувь, головные уборы, зонты, трости и пр. |

## TABLE 3-2A. Imports by commodity group (millions of U.S. dollars)

## ТАБЛИЦА 3-2А . Импорт по товарным группам (млн. долларов США)

UKRAINE

| Commodity group | 1990 | 1991 | 1992 | 1993 | 1994 | 1995 | Товарные группы |
|---|---|---|---|---|---|---|---|
| XIII - Articles of stone, plaster, cement, asbestos, mica and similar materials; ceramic products; glass and glassware | .. | .. | .. | .. | 65.5 | 92.8 | XIII - Изделия из камня, гипса, цемента |
| XIV - Natural or cultured pearls, precious or semi-precious stones, precious metals, metals clad with precious metal and articles thereof; imitation jewellery; coin | .. | .. | .. | .. | 9.2 | 69.7 | XIV - Жемчуг, драгоценные и полудрагоценные камни, драгоценные металлы, бижутерия, монеты |
| XV - Base metals and articles of base metal | .. | .. | .. | .. | 410.9 | 539.3 | XV - Неблагородные металлы и изделия из них |
| XVI - Machinery and mechanical appliances; electrical equipment; parts thereof; sound recorders and reproducers, television image and sound recorders and reproducers, and parts and accessories of such articles | .. | .. | .. | .. | 1,417.9 | 1,689.2 | XVI - Машины, оборудование, механизмы, их части и принадлежности; звуковая и теле-аппаратура, их части и принадлежности |
| XVII - Vehicles, aircraft, vessels and associated transport equipment | .. | .. | .. | .. | 410.7 | 286.6 | XVII - Средства наземного, воздушного и водного транспорта |
| XVIII - Optical, photographic, cinematographic, measuring, checking, precision, medical or surgical instruments and apparatus; clocks and watches; musical instruments; parts and accessories thereof | .. | .. | .. | .. | 123.2 | 104.2 | XVIII - Приборы, аппараты оптические, медицинские, измерительные и пр.; музыкальные инструменты; часы; их части и принадлежности |
| XIX - Arms and ammunition; parts and accessories thereof | .. | .. | .. | .. | .. | .. | XIX - Оружие и боеприпасы, их части и принадлежности |
| XX - Miscellaneous manufactured articles | .. | .. | .. | .. | 84.1 | 65.6 | XX - Разные промышленные товары |
| XXI - Works of art, collectors' pieces, and antiques | .. | .. | .. | .. | 0.0 | 0.1 | XXI - Произведения искусства, предметы антиквариата |
| XXII - Services | .. | .. | .. | .. | .. | .. | XXII - Услуги |

## TABLE 3-3A. Exports by commodity group (millions of U.S. dollars)
## ТАБЛИЦА 3-3А. Экспорт по товарным группам (млн. долларов США)

| Commodity group | 1990 | 1991 | 1992 | 1993 | 1994 | 1995 | Товарные группы |
|---|---|---|---|---|---|---|---|
| TOTAL | .. | .. | .. | .. | 9,708.2 | 11,566.5 | ВСЕГО |
| I - Live animals; animal products | .. | .. | .. | .. | 340.1 | 485.6 | I - Живые животные и продукты животноводства |
| II - Vegetable products | .. | .. | .. | .. | 81.9 | 142.7 | II - Продукты растительного происхождения |
| III - Animal or vegetable fats and oils and their cleavage products; prepared edible fats; animal or vegetable waxes | .. | .. | .. | .. | 55.6 | 91.7 | III - Жиры и масла растительного и животного происхождения, воски |
| IV - Prepared foodstuffs; beverages, spirits and vinegar; tobacco and manufactured tobacco substitutes | .. | .. | .. | .. | 560.4 | 979.4 | IV -Продукция пищевой промышленности, алкогольные и безалкогольные напитки, табак и его заменители |
| V - Mineral products | .. | .. | .. | .. | 1,015.0 | 1,220.9 | V - Минеральные продукты |
| VI - Products of the chemical or allied industries | .. | .. | .. | .. | 1,024.0 | 1,125.0 | VI - Продукция химической промышленности |
| VII - Plastics and articles thereof; rubber and articles thereof | .. | .. | .. | .. | 304.4 | 322.4 | VII - Пластмассы и изделия из них |
| VIII - Raw hides and skins, leather, furskins and articles thereof; saddlery and harness; travel goods, handbags and similar containers; articles of animal gut | .. | .. | .. | .. | 47.0 | 67.3 | VIII - Кожевенное сырьё, кожи, пушнина, меховое сырьё и изделия из них |
| IX - Wood and articles of wood; wood charcoal; cork and articles of cork; manufactures of straw, of esparto or of other plaiting materials; basketware and wickerwork | .. | .. | .. | .. | 15.9 | 31.1 | IX - Древесина и изделия из древесины, древесный уголь |
| X - Pulp of wood or of other fibrous cellulosic material; waste and scrap of paper or paperboard; paper and paperboard and articles thereof | .. | .. | .. | .. | 129.6 | 79.8 | X - Бумажная масса, бумажные и картонные отходы, макулатура, бумага, картон и изделия из них |
| XI - Textiles and textile articles | .. | .. | .. | .. | 159.4 | 314.8 | XI - Текстиль и текстильные изделия |
| XII - Footwear, headgear, umbrellas, sun umbrellas, walking sticks, seat sticks, whips, riding crops and parts thereof; prepared feathers and articles made therewith; artificial flowers; articles of human hair | .. | .. | .. | .. | 25.3 | 53.1 | XII - Обувь, головные уборы, зонты, трости и пр. |

**TABLE 3-3A. Exports by commodity group (millions of U.S. dollars)**
**ТАБЛИЦА 3-3А. Экспорт по товарным группам (млн. долларов США)**

| Commodity group | 1990 | 1991 | 1992 | 1993 | 1994 | 1995 | Товарные группы |
|---|---|---|---|---|---|---|---|
| XIII - Articles of stone, plaster, cement, asbestos, mica and similar materials; ceramic products; glass and glassware | .. | .. | .. | .. | 170.7 | 171.5 | XIII - Изделия из камня, гипса, цемента |
| XIV - Natural or cultured pearls, precious or semi-precious stones, precious metals, metals clad with precious metal and articles thereof; imitation jewellery; coin | .. | .. | .. | .. | 5.9 | 72.2 | XIV - Жемчуг, драгоценные и полудрагоценные камни, драгоценные металлы, бижутерия, монеты |
| XV - Base metals and articles of base metal | .. | .. | .. | .. | 3,513.4 | 4,189.9 | XV - Неблагородные металлы и изделия из них |
| XVI - Machinery and mechanical appliances; electrical equipment; parts thereof; sound recorders and reproducers, television image and sound recorders and reproducers, and parts and accessories of such articles | .. | .. | .. | .. | 1,372.0 | 1,360.1 | XVI - Машины, оборудование, механизмы, их части и принадлежности; звуковая и теле-аппаратура, их части и принадлежности |
| XVII - Vehicles, aircraft, vessels and associated transport equipment | .. | .. | .. | .. | 705.5 | 743.7 | XVII - Средства наземного, воздушного и водного транспорта |
| XVIII - Optical, photographic, cinematographic, measuring, checking, precision, medical or surgical instruments and apparatus; clocks and watches; musical instruments; parts and accessories thereof | .. | .. | .. | .. | 52.1 | 62.3 | XVIII - Приборы, аппараты оптические, медицинские, измерительные и пр.; музыкальные инструменты; часы; их части и принадлежности |
| XIX - Arms and ammunition; parts and accessories thereof | .. | .. | .. | .. | .. | .. | XIX - Оружие и боеприпасы, их части и принадлежности |
| XX - Miscellaneous manufactured articles | .. | .. | .. | .. | 130.0 | 52.9 | XX - Разные промышленные товары |
| XXI - Works of art, collectors' pieces, and antiques | .. | .. | .. | .. | 0.0 | 0.1 | XXI - Произведения искусства, предметы антиквариата |
| XXII - Services | .. | .. | .. | .. | .. | .. | XXII - Услуги |

**TABLE 3-4A. Geographical distribution of foreign trade (millions of U.S. dollars)**

**ТАБЛИЦА 3-4А. Географическое распределение внешней торговли (млн. долларов США)**

| Country or country group | Exports Экспорт 1990 | 1991 | 1992 | 1993 | 1994 | 1995 | Imports Импорт 1990 | 1991 | 1992 | 1993 | 1994 | 1995 | Страна или группа стран |
|---|---|---|---|---|---|---|---|---|---|---|---|---|---|
| **Total trade** | .. | .. | .. | .. | 10,272 | 11,567 | .. | .. | .. | .. | 10,745 | 11,336 | **Всего** |
| **CIS countries** | .. | .. | .. | .. | 5,619 | 6,012 | .. | .. | .. | .. | 7,838 | 7,133 | **Страны СНГ** |
| Armenia | .. | .. | .. | .. | 6 | 4 | .. | .. | .. | .. | 1 | 3 | Армения |
| Azerbaijan | .. | .. | .. | .. | 79 | 33 | .. | .. | .. | .. | 41 | 33 | Азербайджан |
| Belarus | .. | .. | .. | .. | 542 | 426 | .. | .. | .. | .. | 340 | 285 | Беларусь |
| Georgia | .. | .. | .. | .. | 9 | 11 | .. | .. | .. | .. | 3 | 5 | Грузия |
| Kazakhstan | .. | .. | .. | .. | 119 | 57 | .. | .. | .. | .. | 165 | 57 | Казахстан |
| Kyrgyz Republic | .. | .. | .. | .. | 10 | 6 | .. | .. | .. | .. | 16 | 7 | Киргизстан |
| Moldova | .. | .. | .. | .. | 489 | 130 | .. | .. | .. | .. | 172 | 39 | Молдова |
| Russia | .. | .. | .. | .. | 4,065 | 5,025 | .. | .. | .. | .. | 6,349 | 5,821 | Россия |
| Tajikistan | .. | .. | .. | .. | 4 | 6 | .. | .. | .. | .. | 7 | 4 | Таджикистан |
| Turkmenistan | .. | .. | .. | .. | 222 | 223 | .. | .. | .. | .. | 688 | 837 | Туркменистан |
| Ukraine | .. | .. | .. | .. | .. | .. | .. | .. | .. | .. | .. | .. | Украина |
| Uzbekistan | .. | .. | .. | .. | 73 | 91 | .. | .. | .. | .. | 55 | 42 | Узбекистан |
| **Non-CIS countries** | .. | .. | .. | .. | 4,653 | 5,554 | .. | .. | .. | .. | 2,908 | 4,203 | **Остальной мир** |
| **Europe** | .. | .. | .. | .. | 2,511 | 2,840 | .. | .. | .. | .. | 2,317 | 3,141 | **Европа** |
| Austria | .. | .. | .. | .. | 171 | 169 | .. | .. | .. | .. | 99 | 133 | Австрия |
| Belgium | .. | .. | .. | .. | 46 | 83 | .. | .. | .. | .. | 21 | 80 | Бельгия |
| Bulgaria | .. | .. | .. | .. | 130 | 194 | .. | .. | .. | .. | 69 | 69 | Болгария |
| Czech Republic | .. | .. | .. | .. | 126 | 71 | .. | .. | .. | .. | 128 | 95 | Чешская Республика |
| Denmark | .. | .. | .. | .. | 7 | 11 | .. | .. | .. | .. | 17 | 26 | Дания |
| Estonia | .. | .. | .. | .. | 19 | 20 | .. | .. | .. | .. | 27 | 28 | Эстония |
| Finland | .. | .. | .. | .. | 3 | 18 | .. | .. | .. | .. | 25 | 39 | Финляндия |
| Former Yugoslavia | .. | .. | .. | .. | 16 | 38 | .. | .. | .. | .. | 16 | 15 | Быв. Югославия |
| France | .. | .. | .. | .. | 37 | 35 | .. | .. | .. | .. | 65 | 87 | Франция |
| Germany | .. | .. | .. | .. | 283 | 474 | .. | .. | .. | .. | 655 | 608 | Германия |
| Hungary | .. | .. | .. | .. | 170 | 177 | .. | .. | .. | .. | 100 | 117 | Венгрия |
| Iceland | .. | .. | .. | .. | .. | 4 | .. | .. | .. | .. | 28 | 2 | Исландия |
| Ireland | .. | .. | .. | .. | 64 | 64 | .. | .. | .. | .. | 22 | 229 | Ирландия |
| Italy | .. | .. | .. | .. | 200 | 178 | .. | .. | .. | .. | 127 | 106 | Италия |
| Latvia | .. | .. | .. | .. | 94 | 76 | .. | .. | .. | .. | 70 | 84 | Латвия |
| Lithuania | .. | .. | .. | .. | 193 | 101 | .. | .. | .. | .. | 68 | 81 | Литва |
| Netherlands | .. | .. | .. | .. | 36 | 53 | .. | .. | .. | .. | 63 | 78 | Нидерланды |
| Norway | .. | .. | .. | .. | 12 | 6 | .. | .. | .. | .. | 17 | 22 | Норвегия |
| Poland | .. | .. | .. | .. | 150 | 131 | .. | .. | .. | .. | 123 | 237 | Польша |
| Romania | .. | .. | .. | .. | 72 | 72 | .. | .. | .. | .. | 26 | 25 | Румыния |
| Slovak Republic | .. | .. | .. | .. | 125 | 150 | .. | .. | .. | .. | 75 | 75 | Словацкая Республика |
| Spain | .. | .. | .. | .. | 18 | 28 | .. | .. | .. | .. | 6 | 13 | Испания |

**TABLE 3-4A. Geographical distribution of foreign trade (millions of U.S. dollars)**

**ТАБЛИЦА 3-4А. Географическое распределение внешней торговли (млн. долларов США)**

| Country or country group | Exports Экспорт 1990 | 1991 | 1992 | 1993 | 1994 | 1995 | Imports Импорт 1990 | 1991 | 1992 | 1993 | 1994 | 1995 | Страна или группа стран |
|---|---|---|---|---|---|---|---|---|---|---|---|---|---|
| Sweden | .. | .. | .. | .. | 6 | 6 | .. | .. | .. | .. | 13 | 13 | Швеция |
| Switzerland | .. | .. | .. | .. | 326 | 263 | .. | .. | .. | .. | 334 | 289 | Швейцария |
| United Kingdom | .. | .. | .. | .. | 77 | 232 | .. | .. | .. | .. | 59 | 331 | Великобритания |
| Other Europe | .. | .. | .. | .. | 131 | 189 | .. | .. | .. | .. | 65 | 259 | Остальные страны Европы |
| **Asia** | .. | .. | .. | .. | 1,558 | 1,760 | .. | .. | .. | .. | 217 | 387 | **Азия** |
| Afghanistan | .. | .. | .. | .. | 15 | 1 | .. | .. | .. | .. | 4 | 2 | Афганистан |
| China | .. | .. | .. | .. | 506 | 394 | .. | .. | .. | .. | 33 | 35 | Китай |
| India | .. | .. | .. | .. | 54 | 151 | .. | .. | .. | .. | 24 | 30 | Индия |
| Iraq | .. | .. | .. | .. | .. | .. | .. | .. | .. | .. | .. | .. | Ирак |
| Japan | .. | .. | .. | .. | 26 | 66 | .. | .. | .. | .. | 30 | 17 | Япония |
| Korea, Dem. People's Rep. | .. | .. | .. | .. | 48 | 66 | .. | .. | .. | .. | .. | 1 | КНДР |
| Korea, Rep. of | .. | .. | .. | .. | 67 | 36 | .. | .. | .. | .. | 5 | 4 | Южная Корея |
| Mongolia | .. | .. | .. | .. | 4 | 3 | .. | .. | .. | .. | 10 | 0 | МНР |
| Syrian Arab Republic | .. | .. | .. | .. | 17 | 69 | .. | .. | .. | .. | 2 | 29 | Сирия |
| Turkey | .. | .. | .. | .. | 116 | 199 | .. | .. | .. | .. | 9 | 22 | Турция |
| Viet Nam | .. | .. | .. | .. | 17 | 8 | .. | .. | .. | .. | 3 | 7 | Вьетнам |
| Other Asia | .. | .. | .. | .. | 686 | 767 | .. | .. | .. | .. | 97 | 241 | Остальные |
| **America** | .. | .. | .. | .. | 432 | 742 | .. | .. | .. | .. | 275 | 599 | **Америка** |
| Canada | .. | .. | .. | .. | 34 | 38 | .. | .. | .. | .. | 23 | 119 | США |
| Cuba | .. | .. | .. | .. | 2 | 3 | .. | .. | .. | .. | .. | .. | Куба |
| United States | .. | .. | .. | .. | 359 | 558 | .. | .. | .. | .. | 220 | 295 | США |
| Other America | .. | .. | .. | .. | 37 | 144 | .. | .. | .. | .. | 32 | 185 | Остальные |
| **Africa** | .. | .. | .. | .. | 127 | 186 | .. | .. | .. | .. | 86 | 57 | **Африка** |
| Egypt | .. | .. | .. | .. | 58 | 66 | .. | .. | .. | .. | 10 | 5 | Египет |
| Libya | .. | .. | .. | .. | .. | 0 | .. | .. | .. | .. | .. | .. | Ливия |
| Other Africa | .. | .. | .. | .. | 69 | 120 | .. | .. | .. | .. | 76 | 52 | Остальные |
| **Rest of the World** | .. | .. | .. | .. | 26 | 26 | .. | .. | .. | .. | 13 | 20 | **Прочие страны** |
| Australia | .. | .. | .. | .. | 10 | 12 | .. | .. | .. | .. | 13 | 20 | Австралия |

**TABLE 3-4B. Geographical distribution of foreign trade (millions of local currency)**

**ТАБЛИЦА 3-4В. Географическое распределение внешней торговли (миллионов национальной валюты)**

| Country or country group | Exports Экспорт 1990 | 1991 | 1992 | 1993 | 1994 | 1995 | Imports Импорт 1990 | 1991 | 1992 | 1993 | 1994 | 1995 | Страна или группа стран |
|---|---|---|---|---|---|---|---|---|---|---|---|---|---|
| **Total trade** | .. | .. | .. | .. | 309,893,500 | 1,675,934,200 | .. | .. | .. | .. | 309,888,300 | 1,699,018,200 | **Всего** |
| **CIS countries** | .. | .. | .. | .. | 169,075,700 | 843,294,300 | .. | .. | .. | .. | 221,706,000 | 1,059,445,200 | **Страны СНГ** |
| Armenia | .. | .. | .. | .. | 119,100 | 580,200 | .. | .. | .. | .. | 40,600 | 335,400 | Армения |
| Azerbaijan | .. | .. | .. | .. | 1,816,500 | 4,956,600 | .. | .. | .. | .. | 1,115,900 | 4,911,300 | Азербайджан |
| Belarus | .. | .. | .. | .. | 15,717,400 | 56,952,900 | .. | .. | .. | .. | 11,157,900 | 40,941,700 | Беларусь |
| Georgia | .. | .. | .. | .. | 197,300 | 1,680,800 | .. | .. | .. | .. | 79,100 | 790,700 | Грузия |
| Kazakhstan | .. | .. | .. | .. | 2,509,500 | 7,952,500 | .. | .. | .. | .. | 2,966,400 | 8,158,600 | Казахстан |
| Kyrgyz Republic | .. | .. | .. | .. | 154,300 | 693,100 | .. | .. | .. | .. | 190,700 | 936,600 | Киргизстан |
| Moldova | .. | .. | .. | .. | 10,404,900 | 16,596,000 | .. | .. | .. | .. | 7,705,100 | 5,462,400 | Молдова |
| Russia | .. | .. | .. | .. | 126,218,300 | 710,136,300 | .. | .. | .. | .. | 178,004,500 | 863,215,900 | Россия |
| Tajikistan | .. | .. | .. | .. | 139,800 | 756,700 | .. | .. | .. | .. | 283,500 | 584,300 | Таджикистан |
| Turkmenistan | .. | .. | .. | .. | 9,877,900 | 30,804,200 | .. | .. | .. | .. | 18,688,900 | 127,961,100 | Туркменистан |
| Ukraine | .. | .. | .. | .. | .. | .. | .. | .. | .. | .. | .. | .. | Украина |
| Uzbekistan | .. | .. | .. | .. | 1,920,700 | 12,185,000 | .. | .. | .. | .. | 1,473,400 | 6,147,200 | Узбекистан |
| **Non-CIS countries** | .. | .. | .. | .. | 140,817,800 | 832,639,900 | .. | .. | .. | .. | 88,182,300 | 639,573,000 | **Остальной мир** |
| **Europe** | .. | .. | .. | .. | 73,899,500 | 423,704,900 | .. | .. | .. | .. | 67,597,000 | 475,889,000 | **Европа** |
| Austria | .. | .. | .. | .. | 4,476,700 | 24,751,800 | .. | .. | .. | .. | 2,473,900 | 20,131,400 | Австрия |
| Belgium | .. | .. | .. | .. | 1,707,700 | 12,267,500 | .. | .. | .. | .. | 438,200 | 12,426,800 | Бельгия |
| Bulgaria | .. | .. | .. | .. | 4,312,300 | 30,622,300 | .. | .. | .. | .. | 1,907,600 | 10,680,400 | Болгария |
| Czech Republic | .. | .. | .. | .. | 3,500,200 | 10,712,800 | .. | .. | .. | .. | 3,318,700 | 14,236,700 | Чешская Республика |
| Denmark | .. | .. | .. | .. | 364,600 | 1,622,400 | .. | .. | .. | .. | 610,300 | 3,808,400 | Дания |
| Estonia | .. | .. | .. | .. | 576,900 | 3,050,300 | .. | .. | .. | .. | 2,039,100 | 4,291,700 | Эстония |
| Finland | .. | .. | .. | .. | 104,800 | 2,730,400 | .. | .. | .. | .. | 672,500 | 5,889,100 | Финляндия |
| Former Yugoslavia | .. | .. | .. | .. | 516,900 | 5,763,100 | .. | .. | .. | .. | 453,800 | 2,165,200 | Быв. Югославия |
| France | .. | .. | .. | .. | 731,800 | 5,368,300 | .. | .. | .. | .. | 1,863,500 | 13,198,000 | Франция |
| Germany | .. | .. | .. | .. | 7,612,200 | 70,978,400 | .. | .. | .. | .. | 18,530,900 | 93,239,500 | Германия |
| Hungary | .. | .. | .. | .. | 6,157,900 | 26,678,300 | .. | .. | .. | .. | 3,088,300 | 17,947,300 | Венгрия |
| Iceland | .. | .. | .. | .. | 1,000 | 617,600 | .. | .. | .. | .. | 6,700 | 351,500 | Исландия |
| Ireland | .. | .. | .. | .. | 1,115,300 | 9,270,700 | .. | .. | .. | .. | 519,900 | 32,062,800 | Ирландия |
| Italy | .. | .. | .. | .. | 4,525,200 | 26,042,700 | .. | .. | .. | .. | 2,829,700 | 15,884,900 | Италия |
| Latvia | .. | .. | .. | .. | 2,408,800 | 10,525,500 | .. | .. | .. | .. | 2,572,700 | 12,711,400 | Латвия |
| Lithuania | .. | .. | .. | .. | 4,641,200 | 14,114,800 | .. | .. | .. | .. | 1,931,800 | 12,095,400 | Литва |
| Netherlands | .. | .. | .. | .. | 887,200 | 8,379,300 | .. | .. | .. | .. | 2,466,300 | 12,113,700 | Нидерланды |
| Norway | .. | .. | .. | .. | 497,100 | 873,200 | .. | .. | .. | .. | 411,300 | 3,451,300 | Норвегия |
| Poland | .. | .. | .. | .. | 4,631,300 | 19,723,900 | .. | .. | .. | .. | 3,703,100 | 35,682,100 | Польша |
| Romania | .. | .. | .. | .. | 2,641,500 | 10,519,800 | .. | .. | .. | .. | 699,800 | 3,615,200 | Румыния |
| Slovak Republic | .. | .. | .. | .. | 4,259,500 | 22,235,500 | .. | .. | .. | .. | 2,775,400 | 11,619,400 | Словацкая Республика |
| Spain | .. | .. | .. | .. | 590,500 | 4,399,600 | .. | .. | .. | .. | 187,100 | 1,940,600 | Испания |

## TABLE 3-4B. Geographical distribution of foreign trade (millions of local currency)
## ТАБЛИЦА 3-4B. Географическое распределение внешней торговли (миллионов национальной валюты)

| Country or country group | Exports Экспорт 1990 | 1991 | 1992 | 1993 | 1994 | 1995 | Imports Импорт 1990 | 1991 | 1992 | 1993 | 1994 | 1995 | Страна или группа стран |
|---|---|---|---|---|---|---|---|---|---|---|---|---|---|
| Sweden | .. | .. | .. | .. | 151,400 | 898,400 | .. | .. | .. | .. | 465,000 | 1,972,400 | Швеция |
| Switzerland | .. | .. | .. | .. | 10,467,000 | 39,373,300 | .. | .. | .. | .. | 8,492,300 | 43,637,500 | Швейцария |
| United Kingdom | .. | .. | .. | .. | 2,177,200 | 35,479,500 | .. | .. | .. | .. | 1,817,400 | 50,859,700 | Великобритания |
| Other Europe | .. | .. | .. | .. | 4,843,300 | 26,705,500 | .. | .. | .. | .. | 3,321,700 | 39,876,600 | Остальные страны Европы |
| **Asia** | .. | .. | .. | .. | 47,980,100 | 265,050,600 | .. | .. | .. | .. | 7,010,600 | 58,323,700 | **Азия** |
| Afghanistan | .. | .. | .. | .. | 358,400 | 164,300 | .. | .. | .. | .. | 322,900 | 233,600 | Афганистан |
| China | .. | .. | .. | .. | 13,437,000 | 58,733,300 | .. | .. | .. | .. | 1,109,500 | 5,432,500 | Китай |
| India | .. | .. | .. | .. | 1,907,800 | 23,126,600 | .. | .. | .. | .. | 531,000 | 4,745,700 | Индия |
| Iraq | .. | .. | .. | .. | .. | .. | .. | .. | .. | .. | .. | .. | Ирак |
| Japan | .. | .. | .. | .. | 666,500 | 9,672,100 | .. | .. | .. | .. | 704,200 | 2,675,900 | Япония |
| Korea, Dem. People's Rep. | .. | .. | .. | .. | 1,923,500 | 9,282,700 | .. | .. | .. | .. | .. | 62,900 | КНДР |
| Korea, Rep. of | .. | .. | .. | .. | 2,705,100 | 5,391,900 | .. | .. | .. | .. | 85,700 | 514,800 | Южная Корея |
| Mongolia | .. | .. | .. | .. | 155,000 | 399,600 | .. | .. | .. | .. | 201,700 | 47,700 | МНР |
| Syrian Arab Republic | .. | .. | .. | .. | 434,800 | 11,345,500 | .. | .. | .. | .. | 51,100 | 4,980,900 | Сирия |
| Turkey | .. | .. | .. | .. | 4,314,400 | 29,600,800 | .. | .. | .. | .. | 241,900 | 3,362,800 | Турция |
| Viet Nam | .. | .. | .. | .. | 329,200 | 1,235,700 | .. | .. | .. | .. | 145,400 | 978,300 | Вьетнам |
| Other Asia | .. | .. | .. | .. | 21,748,400 | 116,098,100 | .. | .. | .. | .. | 3,617,200 | 35,288,600 | Остальные |
| **America** | .. | .. | .. | .. | 14,233,700 | 111,635,200 | .. | .. | .. | .. | 9,254,500 | 93,633,100 | **Америка** |
| Canada | .. | .. | .. | .. | 582,600 | 5,611,900 | .. | .. | .. | .. | 537,600 | 19,452,500 | США |
| Cuba | .. | .. | .. | .. | 61,700 | 470,400 | .. | .. | .. | .. | 100 | .. | Куба |
| United States | .. | .. | .. | .. | 12,348,000 | 83,060,000 | .. | .. | .. | .. | 8,035,600 | 46,527,600 | США |
| Other America | .. | .. | .. | .. | 1,241,400 | 22,492,900 | .. | .. | .. | .. | 681,200 | 27,653,000 | Остальные |
| **Africa** | .. | .. | .. | .. | 3,781,600 | 28,583,900 | .. | .. | .. | .. | 3,455,200 | 8,758,000 | **Африка** |
| Egypt | .. | .. | .. | .. | 2,091,000 | 10,027,000 | .. | .. | .. | .. | 288,700 | 809,400 | Египет |
| Libya | .. | .. | .. | .. | .. | 18,900 | .. | .. | .. | .. | .. | .. | Ливия |
| Other Africa | .. | .. | .. | .. | 1,690,600 | 18,538,000 | .. | .. | .. | .. | 3,166,500 | 7,948,600 | Остальные |
| **Rest of the World** | .. | .. | .. | .. | 922,900 | 3,665,300 | .. | .. | .. | .. | 865,000 | 2,969,200 | **Прочие страны** |
| Australia | .. | .. | .. | .. | 549,500 | 1,635,300 | .. | .. | .. | .. | 864,000 | 2,969,100 | Австралия |

## TABLE 5-1. Agricultural production (millions of national currency, current prices)



## ТАБЛИЦА 5-1. Сельскохозяйственная продукция (млн. нац. валюты, текущие цены)

| Item | 1990 | 1991 | 1992 | 1993 | 1994 | 1995 | Статьи |
|---|---|---|---|---|---|---|---|
| **Total gross agricultural production** | 61,930 | 104,958 | 1,439,117 | 54,888,000 | 358,574,000 | 1,637,412,000 | **Валовая продукция сель-ского хозяйства - всего** |
| **Crops** | 29,192 | 49,772 | 730,358 | 26,777,570 | 178,941,000 | .. | **Продукция растениеводства** |
| Grains | .. | .. | .. | .. | .. | .. | Зерно |
| Potatoes | 6,635 | .. | .. | .. | .. | .. | Картофель |
| Vegetables | 4,713 | .. | .. | .. | .. | .. | Овощи |
| Fruits (excluding grapes) | 3,907 | .. | .. | .. | .. | .. | Фрукты (без винограда) |
| Grapes | .. | .. | .. | .. | .. | .. | Виноград |
| Tobacco | .. | .. | .. | .. | .. | .. | Табак |
| Cotton | .. | .. | .. | .. | .. | .. | Хлопок |
| Sugarbeets | .. | .. | .. | .. | .. | .. | Сахарная свекла |
| Oilseeds | .. | .. | .. | .. | .. | .. | Семена масличных культур |
| Other | .. | .. | .. | .. | .. | .. | Прочие |
| **Animal husbandry** | 32,738 | 55,186 | 708,759 | 24,471,710 | 155,379,000 | .. | **Продукция животноводства** |
| Livestock | 18,442 | .. | .. | .. | .. | .. | Мясное животноводство |
| Cattle | .. | .. | .. | .. | .. | .. | Крупный рогатый скот |
| Pigs | .. | .. | .. | .. | .. | .. | Свиньи |
| Sheep and goats | .. | .. | .. | .. | .. | .. | Овцы и козы |
| Poultry | .. | .. | .. | .. | .. | .. | Птица |
| Other | .. | .. | .. | .. | .. | .. | Прочие |
| Milk | 10,380 | .. | .. | .. | .. | .. | Молоко |
| Eggs | 1,614 | .. | .. | .. | .. | .. | Яйца |
| Wool | .. | .. | .. | .. | .. | .. | Шерсть |
| Other livestock | .. | .. | .. | .. | .. | .. | Прочая |
| **Agricultural services** | .. | .. | .. | 3,638,720 | 24,254,000 | .. | **Сельскохозяйственные услуги** |

## TABLE 5-2. Agricultural production (millions of constant national currency) UKRAINE

## ТАБЛИЦА 5-2. Сельскохозяйственная продукция в постоянных ценах (млн. национальной валюты)

| Item | 1990 | 1991 | 1992 | 1993 | 1994 | 1995 | Статьи |
|---|---|---|---|---|---|---|---|
| **Total gross agricultural production** | 48,954 | 42,493 | 38,966 | 39,559 | 33,046 | 31,867 | **Валовая продукция сельского хозяйства - всего** |
| **Crops** | 21,951 | 18,191 | 18,460 | 20,651 | 15,830 | 16,390 | **Продукция растениеводства** |
| Grains | 5,921 | 4,572 | 4,486 | 5,292 | 4,049 | 3,954 | Зерно |
| Potatoes | 3,199 | 2,782 | 3,877 | 4,017 | 3,079 | 2,816 | Картофель |
| Vegetables | 1,905 | 1,858 | 1,698 | 2,150 | 1,884 | 2,145 | Овощи |
| Fruits (excluding grapes) | 1,403 | 739 | 1,027 | 1,350 | 540 | 913 | Фрукты (без винограда) |
| Grapes | 390 | 314 | 307 | 311 | 185 | 214 | Виноград |
| Tobacco | 65 | 64 | 47 | 37 | 29 | 22 | Табак |
| Cotton | .. | .. | .. | .. | .. | .. | Хлопок |
| Sugarbeets | 2,275 | 1,859 | 1,479 | 1,733 | 1,446 | 1,524 | Сахарная свекла |
| Oilseeds | 844 | 754 | 683 | 636 | 469 | 821 | Семена масличных культур |
| Other | 5,949 | 5,249 | 4,856 | 5,125 | 4,149 | 3,981 | Прочие |
| **Animal husbandry** | 27,003 | 24,302 | 20,506 | 18,908 | 17,216 | 15,477 | **Продукция животноводства** |
| Livestock | 14,710 | 13,040 | 10,735 | 9,608 | 8,318 | 7,086 | Мясное животноводство |
| Cattle | 7,760 | 6,855 | 5,750 | 5,334 | 4,617 | 3,852 | Крупный рогатый скот |
| Pigs | 4,511 | 3,903 | 3,239 | 2,949 | 2,678 | 2,339 | Свиньи |
| Sheep and goats | 184 | 157 | 143 | 124 | 114 | 92 | Овцы и козы |
| Poultry | 2,106 | 1,999 | 1,479 | 1,076 | 793 | 689 | Птица |
| Other | 149 | 126 | 124 | 125 | 116 | 114 | Прочие |
| Milk | 9,731 | 8,899 | 7,596 | 7,306 | 7,216 | 6,876 | Молоко |
| Eggs | 1,560 | 1,454 | 1,292 | 1,129 | 972 | 900 | Яйца |
| Wool | 260 | 232 | 201 | 184 | 168 | 122 | Шерсть |
| Other livestock | 742 | 677 | 682 | 681 | 542 | 493 | Прочая |
| **Agricultural services** | .. | .. | .. | .. | .. | .. | **Сельскохозяйственные услуги** |

**TABLE 5-3. Production and average yield of major agricultural crops**

**ТАБЛИЦА 5-3. Производство и урожайность важнейших сельскохозяйственных культур**

| Crop | 1990 | 1991 | 1992 | 1993 | 1994 | 1995 | Сельскохозяйственные культуры |
|---|---|---|---|---|---|---|---|
| **Production (thousands of tons)** | | | | | | | **Производство (тыс. тонн)** |
| Grain - Cleanweight | 51,009 | 38,674 | 38,537 | 45,623 | 35,497 | 33,930 | Зерно в чистом весе |
| Winter wheat | 30,348 | 21,134 | 19,473 | 21,770 | 13,720 | 15,969 | Пшеница - озимая |
| Spring wheat | 26 | 22 | 35 | 61 | 137 | 305 | яровая |
| Coarse grain | .. | .. | .. | .. | .. | .. | Зерно в физическом весе |
| Rye | 1,259 | 981 | 1,156 | 1,180 | 941 | 1,207 | Рожь |
| Corn | 4,737 | 4,747 | 2,851 | 3,786 | 1,539 | 3,392 | Кукуруза |
| Winter barley | 1,953 | 2,016 | 1,846 | 2,522 | 436 | 987 | Ячмень - озимый |
| Spring barley | 7,216 | 6,031 | 8,260 | 11,028 | 14,073 | 8,646 | яровой |
| Oats | 1,303 | 945 | 1,246 | 1,479 | 1,385 | 1,116 | Овес |
| Millet | 338 | 338 | 226 | 294 | 158 | 268 | Просо |
| Rice | 118 | 102 | 92 | 68 | 79 | 80 | Рис |
| Flax | 108 | 106 | 105 | 73 | 49 | 48 | Лен |
| Oilseeds | .. | .. | .. | .. | .. | .. | Семена масличных культур |
| Cotton (raw) | .. | .. | .. | .. | .. | .. | Хлопок - сырец |
| Cotton fiber | .. | .. | .. | .. | .. | .. | волокно |
| Sugarbeets | 44,264 | 36,168 | 28,783 | 33,717 | 28,138 | 29,650 | Сахарная свекла |
| Potatoes | 16,732 | 14,550 | 20,277 | 21,009 | 16,102 | 14,729 | Картофель |
| Pulses | 3,266 | 1,965 | 2,986 | 2,898 | 2,636 | 1,570 | Бобовые |
| Vegetables | 6,666 | 5,932 | 5,310 | 6,055 | 5,142 | 5,880 | Овощи |
| Fruit | 3,738 | 2,210 | 2,779 | 3,464 | 1,548 | 2,354 | Фрукты |
| Grapes | 836 | 673 | 657 | 666 | 395 | 457 | Виноград |
| Other | 2,902 | 1,537 | 2,122 | 2,798 | 1,153 | 1,897 | Прочие |
| Corn (silage and greenchop) | 98,372 | 88,463 | 63,042 | 77,881 | 46,170 | 61,920 | Кукуруза (на силос и зеленый корм) |
| Hay | 9,998 | 10,432 | 9,515 | 8,689 | 7,526 | 7,831 | Сено |
| **Average yield (kilograms per hectare)** | | | | | | | **Ср. урожайность (кг с га)** |
| Grain | 3,510 | 2,650 | 2,790 | 3,210 | 2,680 | 2,430 | Зерно |
| Winter wheat | 4,020 | 3,030 | 3,090 | 3,800 | 3,081 | 3,013 | Пшеница - озимая |
| Spring wheat | 3,020 | 2,170 | 2,580 | 2,750 | 2,518 | 1,692 | яровая |
| Coarse grain | .. | .. | .. | .. | .. | .. | Зерно в физическом весе |
| Rye | 2,430 | 2,010 | 2,320 | 2,370 | 1,976 | 1,998 | Рожь |
| Corn | 3,870 | 3,263 | 2,510 | 2,840 | 2,361 | 2,921 | Кукуруза |
| Winter barley | 3,717 | 3,199 | 3,011 | 3,280 | 2,268 | 2,046 | Ячмень - озимый |
| Spring barley | 3,301 | 2,402 | 2,940 | 3,200 | 2,872 | 2,140 | яровой |
| Oats | 2,683 | 1,932 | 2,530 | 2,900 | 2,294 | 1,993 | Овес |
| Millet | 1,720 | 1,800 | 1,184 | 1,490 | 883 | 1,697 | Просо |
| Rice | 4,253 | 4,430 | 3,770 | 2,890 | 3,550 | 3,640 | Рис |
| Flax | 638 | 676 | 680 | 570 | 625 | 504 | Лен |
| Oilseeds | .. | .. | .. | .. | .. | .. | Семена масличных культур |
| Cotton (raw) | .. | .. | .. | .. | .. | .. | Хлопок - сырец |
| Cotton fiber | .. | .. | .. | .. | .. | .. | волокно |
| Sugarbeets | 27,570 | 23,350 | 19,380 | 22,190 | 19,176 | 20,470 | Сахарная свекла |
| Potatoes | 11,680 | 9,490 | 11,890 | 13,690 | 10,542 | 9,623 | Картофель |
| Pulses | 2,310 | 1,440 | 2,340 | 2,340 | 2,213 | 1,447 | Бобовые |
| Vegetables | 14,900 | 12,770 | 11,010 | 13,040 | 11,529 | 12,018 | Овощи |
| Fruit | .. | .. | .. | .. | .. | .. | Фрукты |
| Grapes | 5,830 | 4,760 | 4,700 | 4,780 | 2,822 | 3,322 | Виноград |
| Other | 4,270 | 2,300 | 3,220 | 4,320 | 1,791 | 2,979 | Прочие |
| Corn (silage and greenchop) | 20,745 | 20,346 | 13,360 | 18,410 | 10,355 | 17,725 | Кукуруза (на силос и зеленый корм) |
| Hay | 2,710 | 2,870 | 2,630 | 2,470 | 2,162 | 2,195 | Сено |

## TABLE 5-4. Main aggregates of animal husbandry
## ТАБЛИЦА 5-4. Основные показатели животноводства



| Type of livestock or product | 1990 | 1991 | 1992 | 1993 | 1994 | 1995 | или вид продукции |
|---|---|---|---|---|---|---|---|
| **Livestock (thousands of heads)** | | | | | | | **Поголовье скота (тысяч голов)** |
| Cattle | 24,623 | 23,728 | 22,457 | 21,607 | 19,624 | 17,557 | Крупный рогатый скот |
| of which: Cows | 8,378 | 8,263 | 8,057 | 8,078 | 7,818 | 7,531 | в том числе коровы |
| Pigs | 19,427 | 17,839 | 16,175 | 15,298 | 13,946 | 13,144 | Свиньи |
| Sheep and goats | 7,896 | 7,259 | 6,597 | 6,118 | 4,792 | 3,209 | Овцы и козы |
| of which: Goats | 523 | 570 | 640 | 745 | 782 | 889 | в том числе козы |
| Horses | 738 | 717 | 707 | 716 | 737 | 756 | Лошади |
| Other | 6,308 | 6,196 | 6,795 | 6,891 | 6,767 | 6,367 | Прочие |
| **Animal husbandry products** | | | | | | | **Продукция животноводства** |
| Meat (thousands of tons) | 4,358 | 4,029 | 3,401 | 2,815 | 2,677 | 2,294 | Мясо (тысяч тонн) |
| Beef | 1,986 | 1,878 | 1,656 | 1,379 | 1,427 | 1,186 | Говядина |
| Pork | 1,576 | 1,421 | 1,180 | 1,013 | 916 | 807 | Свинина |
| Lamb | 46 | 40 | 35 | 31 | 44 | 40 | Баранина |
| Poultry | 708 | 654 | 498 | 362 | 265 | 235 | Птица |
| Other | 42 | 36 | 32 | 30 | 25 | 26 | Прочие виды мяса |
| Milk (thousands of tons) | 24,508 | 22,409 | 19,114 | 18,377 | 18,138 | 17,274 | Молоко (тысяч тонн) |
| Eggs (millions) | 16,287 | 15,188 | 13,496 | 11,794 | 10,154 | 9,404 | Яйца (миллионов штук) |
| Wool (thousands of tons) | 30 | 27 | 23 | 21 | 19 | 14 | Шерсть (тысяч тонн) |

## TABLE 6-1. Industrial production by sector (millions of national currency)
## ТАБЛИЦА 6-1. Промышленное производство по отраслям (млн. национальной валюты)

| Sector | 1990 | 1991 | 1992 | 1993 | 1994 | 1995 | Отрасли |
|---|---|---|---|---|---|---|---|
| **All industry** | 166,874 | 333,962 | 6,098,629 | 177,335,900 | 1,309,848,000 | 5,882,432,000 | **Вся промышленность** |
| **Heavy industry** | 113,751 | 205,652 | 4,772,789 | 128,488,500 | 1,008,269,000 | 4,714,648,000 | **Тяжелая промышленность** |
| Fuel and energy | 14,846 | 24,574 | 1,261,134 | 31,866,070 | 296,443,500 | 1,425,620,000 | Топливно-энергетическая промышленноть |
| Electricity | 5,313 | 11,816 | 390,990 | 16,720,940 | 150,032,800 | 649,419,000 | Электроэнергетика |
| Fuels | 9,532 | 12,758 | 870,144 | 15,145,130 | 146,410,700 | 776,200,000 | Топливная промышленность |
| Ferrous and nonferrous metallurgy | 20,256 | 36,271 | 1,437,702 | 32,569,330 | 278,306,500 | 1,375,240,000 | Металлургия |
| Chemicals and petrochemical industry | 10,017 | 19,825 | 405,651 | 10,114,930 | 89,863,520 | 437,483,000 | Химическая и нефтехимическая пром. |
| Machine building and metalworking | 51,228 | 88,039 | 1,133,163 | 35,105,690 | 222,509,300 | 945,002,000 | Машиностроение и металлообработка |
| Forestry, woodworking, and pulp and paper industry | 4,830 | 9,700 | 132,984 | 4,697,060 | 31,320,860 | 127,716,000 | Лесная, деревообрабатывающая и целлюлозо-бумажная промышленность |
| Construction materials | 5,741 | 12,511 | 222,402 | 8,278,878 | 52,033,940 | 232,220,000 | Промышленность строительных материалов |
| **Light industry** | 18,093 | 41,205 | 405,560 | 10,746,820 | 57,369,250 | 163,295,000 | **Легкая промышленность** |
| Textiles | 8,563 | 21,771 | 226,224 | 5,244,193 | 29,162,180 | 81,528,000 | Текстильная |
| Clothing | 6,278 | 12,575 | 97,194 | 2,084,775 | 11,038,850 | 37,507,000 | Швейная |
| Leather and shoes | 3,180 | 6,699 | 79,793 | 2,739,521 | 16,713,670 | 42,985,000 | Кожевенная и обувная |
| **Food industry** | 35,030 | 87,105 | 920,280 | 38,100,570 | 244,209,700 | 1,004,489,000 | **Пищевая промышленность** |
| Processed foods | 17,225 | 35,938 | 514,642 | 22,317,260 | 128,532,800 | 507,591,000 | Пищевкусовая |
| Meat and dairy products | 12,311 | 43,355 | 285,511 | 10,935,130 | 89,035,070 | 356,506,000 | Мясная и молочная |
| Fish | 1,509 | 2,164 | 31,320 | 1,107,787 | 6,595,606 | 230,000 | Рыбная |

## TABLE 6-2. Industrial production by sector in constant prices
## ТАБЛИЦА 6-2. Промышленное производство по отраслям в постоянных ценах

| Sector | 1990 | 1991 | 1992 | 1993 | 1994 | 1995 | Отрасли |
|---|---|---|---|---|---|---|---|
| **Industrial production** | | | | | | | **Промышленное производство** |
| **All industry** | 164,508 | 156,611 | 146,588 | 134,861 | 98,044 | 86,279 | **Вся промышленность** |
| **Heavy industry** | 113,038 | 109,381 | 102,028 | 94,731 | 70,404 | 64,538 | **Тяжелая промышленность** |
| Fuel and energy | 14,538 | 13,268 | 11,730 | 9,833 | 8,339 | 7,671 | Топливно-энергетическая промышленноть |
| Electricity | 4,972 | 4,773 | 4,467 | 4,204 | 3,678 | 3,458 | Электроэнергетика |
| Fuels | 9,566 | 8,495 | 7,263 | 5,629 | 4,661 | 4,213 | Топливная промышленность |
| Ferrous and nonferrous metallurgy | 20,234 | 17,915 | 16,066 | 12,406 | 8,865 | 8,467 | Металлургия |
| Chemicals and petrochemicals | 9,989 | 9,309 | 8,127 | 6,079 | 4,529 | 4,117 | Химическая и нефтехимическая пром. |
| Machine building and metalworking | 51,569 | 53,735 | 51,800 | 54,960 | 33,910 | 25,806 | Машиностроение и металлообработка |
| Forestry, woodworking, and pulp and paper | 4,812 | 4,922 | 4,986 | 4,847 | 3,257 | 2,690 | Лесная, деревообрабатывающая и целлюлозо-бумажная промышленность |
| Construction materials | 5,722 | 5,808 | 5,593 | 4,754 | 2,995 | 2,157 | Промышленность строительных материалов |
| **Light industry** | 18,190 | 17,860 | 19,100 | 17,400 | 9,200 | 5,806 | **Легкая промышленность** |
| Textiles | 8,554 | 7,878 | 7,871 | 6,178 | 3,114 | 1,843 | Текстильная |
| Clothing | 6,392 | 6,731 | 7,545 | 6,919 | 4,283 | 3,944 | Швейная |
| Leather and shoe | 3,169 | 3,182 | 3,580 | 3,258 | 1,678 | 1,028 | Кожевенная и обувная |
| **Food industry** | 33,280 | 29,370 | 25,460 | 22,730 | 18,441 | 15,935 | **Пищевая промышленность** |
| Processed foods | 17,001 | 15,097 | 14,402 | 13,711 | 10,804 | 9,794 | Пищевкусовая |
| Meat and dairy products | 12,218 | 10,446 | 8,294 | 6,602 | 5,499 | 3,932 | Мясная и молочная |
| Fish | 1,504 | 1,427 | 704 | 500 | 449 | 604 | Рыбная |
| **Growth in production by sector (in percent)** | | | | | | | **Рост производства по отраслям** |
| **All industry** | -0.1 | -4.8 | -6.4 | -8.0 | -27.3 | -12.0 | **Вся промышленность** |
| **Heavy industry** | -0.4 | -3.2 | -6.7 | -7.2 | -25.7 | -8.3 | **Тяжелая промышленность** |
| Power and fuels | -3.4 | -8.7 | -11.6 | -16.2 | -15.2 | -8.0 | Топливно-энергетическая промышленноть |
| Electricity | 0.7 | -4.0 | -6.4 | -5.9 | -12.5 | -6.0 | Электроэнергетика |
| Fuels | -5.4 | -11.2 | -14.5 | -22.5 | -17.2 | -9.6 | Топливная промышленность |
| Ferrous and nonferrous metallurgy | -3.6 | -11.5 | -10.3 | -22.8 | -28.5 | -4.5 | Металлургия |
| Chemicals and petrochemicals | -1.3 | -6.8 | -12.7 | -25.2 | -25.5 | -9.1 | Химическая и нефтехимическая пром. |
| Machine building and metalworking | 1.3 | 4.2 | -3.6 | 6.1 | -38.3 | -23.9 | Машиностроение и металлообработка |
| Forestry, woodworking, and pulp and paper | 2.3 | 2.3 | 1.3 | -2.8 | -32.8 | -17.4 | Лесная, деревообрабатывающая и целлюлозо-бумажная промышленность |
| Construction materials | -1.7 | 1.5 | -3.7 | -15.0 | -37.0 | -28.0 | Промышленность строительных материалов |
| **Light industry** | 0.4 | -1.8 | 6.9 | -8.9 | -47.1 | -36.9 | **Легкая промышленность** |
| Textiles | -1.6 | -7.9 | -0.1 | -21.5 | -49.6 | -40.8 | Текстильная |
| Clothing | 1.9 | 5.3 | 12.1 | -8.3 | -38.1 | -7.9 | Швейная |
| Leather and shoe | 2.9 | 0.4 | 12.5 | -9.0 | -48.5 | -38.7 | Кожевенная и обувная |
| **Food industry** | 0.8 | -11.7 | -13.3 | -10.7 | -18.9 | -13.6 | **Пищевая промышленность** |
| Processed foods | -0.2 | -11.2 | -4.6 | -4.8 | -21.2 | -9.3 | Пищевкусовая |
| Meat and dairy products | 1.9 | -14.5 | -20.6 | -20.4 | -16.7 | -28.5 | Мясная и молочная |
| Fish | 0.8 | -5.1 | -50.7 | -29.0 | -10.2 | 34.5 | Рыбная |

## TABLE 6-3. Primary energy supply (million tons oil equivalent)

## ТАБЛИЦА 6-3. Ресурсы первичных видов энергии (млн. тонн нефтяного эквивалента)

| Item | | 1990 | 1991 | 1992 | 1993 | 1994 | 1995 | Статьи | |
|---|---|---|---|---|---|---|---|---|---|
| **Primary production** | | | | | | | | **Производство первичной энергии** | |
| Coal and lignite (hard and brown) | | 111.0 | 91.9 | 91.0 | 79.2 | 65.1 | 57.7 | Уголь каменный и бурый | |
| Crude oil | | 5.3 | 5.0 | 4.6 | 4.3 | 4.3 | 4.2 | Нефть | |
| Gas | | 26.1 | 22.7 | 19.5 | 17.9 | 17.1 | 16.9 | Газ | |
| Nuclear | | 6.4 | 6.3 | 6.2 | 6.3 | 5.8 | 5.9 | Атомная энергия | |
| Hydro/geothermal | | 0.9 | 1.0 | 0.7 | 0.9 | 1.0 | 0.9 | Гидро-геотермальная | |
| Other | | 21.5 | 19.1 | 16.0 | 12.7 | 10.7 | 9.9 | Другие виды | |
| Total | | 171.2 | 146.0 | 138.0 | 121.3 | 104.0 | 95.5 | Всего | |
| **Energy trade** | | | | | | | | **Торговля энергией** | |
| Coal and lignite | Exports | .. | .. | .. | .. | 3.2 | 1.9 | Уголь каменный и бурый | Экспорт |
| | Imports | .. | .. | .. | .. | 5.6 | 13.8 | | Импорт |
| | Net imports | .. | .. | .. | .. | 2.4 | 11.9 | | Чистый импорт |
| Oil/oil product | Exports | .. | .. | .. | .. | 1.7 | 1.9 | Нефть и нефтепродукты | Экспорт |
| | Imports | .. | .. | .. | .. | 15.7 | 15.4 | | Импорт |
| | Net imports | .. | .. | .. | .. | 14.0 | 13.5 | | Чистый импорт |
| Gas | Exports | .. | .. | .. | .. | 100.0 | 138.4 | Газ | Экспорт |
| | Imports | .. | .. | .. | .. | 68571.5 | 64485.7 | | Импорт |
| | Net imports | .. | .. | .. | .. | 68471.5 | 64347.3 | | Чистый импорт |
| Electricity | Exports | .. | .. | .. | .. | 1417.4 | 4077.1 | Электричество | Экспорт |
| | Imports | .. | .. | .. | .. | 6.7 | 1.4 | | Импорт |
| | Net imports | .. | .. | .. | .. | -1410.7 | -4075.7 | | Чистый импорт |
| **Total net imports** | | .. | .. | .. | .. | .. | .. | **Чистый импорт энергии-всего** | |
| **Total stock changes** | | .. | .. | .. | .. | .. | .. | **Изменение запасов-всего** | |
| **Total primary energy supply** | | .. | .. | .. | .. | .. | .. | **Ресурсы первичной энергии-всего** | |
| Coal and lignite | | .. | .. | .. | .. | .. | .. | Уголь каменный и бурый | |
| Oil/oil products | | .. | .. | .. | .. | .. | .. | Нефть и нефтепродукты | |
| Gas | | .. | .. | .. | .. | .. | .. | Газ | |
| Nuclear | | .. | .. | .. | .. | .. | .. | Атомная энергия | |
| Hydro/geothermal | | .. | .. | .. | .. | .. | .. | Гидро-геотермальная энергия | |
| Other | | .. | .. | .. | .. | .. | .. | Другие виды | |
| **Total primary energy requirement (equals total primary energy supply)** | | .. | .. | .. | .. | .. | .. | **Потребность в первичной энергии-всего (равно ресурсам первичной энергии)** | |

## TABLE 7-1. Price indices and exchange rates
## ТАБЛИЦА 7-1. Индексы цен и обменный курс

| Year and month | National currency per U.S. dollar<br>Единиц нац. валюты за 1 доллар США | National currency per Russian ruble<br>Единиц нац. валюты за 1 российский рубль | Consumer price index (as a percent of the previous month)<br>Индекс потребительских цен (в % к предыдущему месяцу) | Producer price index (as a percent of the previous month)<br>Индекс цен производителей (в % к предыдущему месяцу) | Consumer price index (as a percent of the previous December)<br>Индекс потребительских цен (в % к декабрю прошлого года) | Producer price index (as a percent of the previous December)<br>Индекс цен производителей (в % к декабрю прошлого года) | Год и месяц |
|---|---|---|---|---|---|---|---|
| **1993** | | | | | | | **1993** |
| January | 750.0 | .. | 173.2 | 218.2 | 173.2 | 218.2 | Январь |
| February | 973.0 | .. | 128.8 | 120.8 | 223.1 | 263.6 | Февраль |
| March | 1,729.0 | .. | 122.1 | 111.6 | 272.4 | 294.2 | Март |
| April | 3,002.0 | .. | 123.6 | 118.1 | 336.7 | 347.5 | Апрель |
| May | 2,999.0 | .. | 127.6 | 152.2 | 429.6 | 528.8 | Май |
| June | 3,658.0 | .. | 171.7 | 190.1 | 727.6 | 1,005.2 | Июнь |
| July | 4,590.0 | .. | 137.6 | 131.0 | 1,014.9 | 1,316.8 | Июль |
| August | 5,970.0 | .. | 121.7 | 133.0 | 1,235.2 | 1,751.4 | Август |
| September | 5,970.0 | .. | 180.3 | 175.5 | 2,227.0 | 3,091.2 | Сентябрь |
| October | 5,970.0 | .. | 166.1 | 134.2 | 3,699.1 | 4,148.4 | Октябрь |
| November | 6,250.0 | .. | 145.3 | 133.1 | 5,374.8 | 5,521.5 | Ноябрь |
| December | 12,610.0 | .. | 190.8 | 176.9 | 10,256.0 | 9,767.5 | Декабрь |
| **1994** | | | | | | | **1994** |
| January | 12,610.0 | 9.0 | 119.2 | 134.1 | 119.2 | 134.1 | Январь |
| February | 12,610.0 | 8.0 | 112.6 | 121.3 | 134.2 | 162.7 | Февраль |
| March | 12,610.0 | 7.0 | 105.7 | 108.3 | 141.9 | 176.2 | Март |
| April | 12,610.0 | 7.0 | 106.0 | 105.4 | 150.4 | 185.7 | Апрель |
| May | 13,185.0 | 7.0 | 105.2 | 102.4 | 158.2 | 190.1 | Май |
| June | 16,607.0 | 9.0 | 103.9 | 103.0 | 164.4 | 195.8 | Июнь |
| July | 19,435.0 | 10.0 | 102.1 | 104.4 | 167.8 | 204.5 | Июль |
| August | 20,113.0 | 10.0 | 102.6 | 111.9 | 172.2 | 228.8 | Август |
| September | 24,700.0 | 11.0 | 107.3 | 112.8 | 184.8 | 258.1 | Сентябрь |
| October | 38,729.0 | 14.0 | 122.6 | 120.4 | 226.5 | 310.7 | Октябрь |
| November | 88,330.0 | 28.0 | 172.3 | 209.0 | 390.3 | 650.3 | Ноябрь |
| December | 108,855.0 | 32.0 | 128.4 | 134.4 | 501.1 | 874.0 | Декабрь |

**TABLE 7-1. Price indices and exchange rates**

**ТАБЛИЦА 7-1. Индексы цен и обменный курс**

| Year and month | National currency per U.S. dollar<br>Единиц нац. валюты за 1 доллар США | National currency per Russian ruble<br>Единиц нац. валюты за 1 российский рубль | Consumer price index (as a percent of the previous month)<br>Индекс потребительских цен (в % к предыдущему месяцу) | Producer price index (as a percent of the previous month)<br>Индекс цен производителей (в % к предыдущему месяцу) | Consumer price index (as a percent of the previous December)<br>Индекс потребительских цен (в % к декабрю прошлого года) | Producer price index (as a percent of the previous December)<br>Индекс цен производителей (в % к декабрю прошлого года) | Год и месяц |
|---|---|---|---|---|---|---|---|
| **1995** | | | | | | | **1995** |
| January | 108,155.0 | 29.0 | 121.2 | 129.2 | 121.2 | 129.2 | Январь |
| February | 121,157.0 | 29.0 | 118.1 | 111.4 | 143.1 | 143.9 | Февраль |
| March | 132,648.0 | 28.0 | 111.4 | 109.3 | 159.5 | 157.3 | Март |
| April | 131,403.0 | 26.0 | 105.8 | 105.1 | 168.7 | 165.3 | Апрель |
| May | 130,481.0 | 26.0 | 104.6 | 107.1 | 176.5 | 177.1 | Май |
| June | 142,150.0 | 30.0 | 104.8 | 108.6 | 184.9 | 192.3 | Июнь |
| July | 143,674.0 | 32.0 | 105.2 | 104.3 | 194.6 | 200.6 | Июль |
| August | 160,897.0 | 36.0 | 104.6 | 106.5 | 203.5 | 213.6 | Август |
| September | 165,340.0 | 37.0 | 114.2 | 109.9 | 232.4 | 234.7 | Сентябрь |
| October | 174,403.0 | 39.0 | 109.1 | 108.4 | 253.5 | 254.4 | Октябрь |
| November | 177,883.0 | 39.0 | 106.2 | 104.2 | 269.3 | 265.1 | Ноябрь |
| December | 179,497.0 | 39.0 | 104.6 | 102.6 | 281.7 | 272.1 | Декабрь |
| **1996** | | | | | | | **1996** |
| January | 182,800.0 | 39.0 | 109.4 | 103.4 | 109.4 | 103.4 | Январь |
| February | 188,103.0 | 40.0 | 107.4 | 102.9 | 117.5 | 106.4 | Февраль |
| March | 189,152.0 | 39.0 | 103.0 | 102.9 | 121.0 | 109.5 | Март |
| April | 187,267.0 | 38.0 | 102.4 | 101.5 | 123.9 | 111.1 | Апрель |
| May | .. | .. | 100.7 | 100.8 | 124.8 | 112.0 | Май |
| June | .. | .. | .. | .. | .. | .. | Июнь |
| July | .. | .. | .. | .. | .. | .. | Июль |
| August | .. | .. | .. | .. | .. | .. | Август |
| September | .. | .. | .. | .. | .. | .. | Сентябрь |
| October | .. | .. | .. | .. | .. | .. | Октябрь |
| November | .. | .. | .. | .. | .. | .. | Ноябрь |
| December | .. | .. | .. | .. | .. | .. | Декабрь |

**TABLE 7-2. Monthly nominal wages by sector**

**ТАБЛИЦА 7-2. Среднемесячная денежная зарплата по отраслям**

| Sector | 1990 | 1991 | 1992 | 1993 | 1994 | 1995 | Сектора |
|---|---|---|---|---|---|---|---|
| **Nominal wages** | | | | | | | **Средняя номинальная заработная плата** |
| **Economy average** | 247.3 | 474.0 | 6,649.7 | 155,400.0 | 1,377,200.0 | 7,378,000.0 | **По народному хозяйству** |
| **Material sphere** | .. | .. | .. | .. | .. | .. | **Отрасли сферы материального производства** |
| Industry | 277.7 | 548.4 | 8,296.8 | 185,617.0 | 1,539,900.0 | 7,991,000.0 | Промышленность |
| Construction | 308.7 | 579.8 | 8,089.7 | 208,626.0 | 1,977,200.0 | 9,516,000.0 | Строительство |
| Agriculture | 259.6 | 436.3 | 4,991.9 | 108,863.0 | 967,600.0 | 4,270,000.0 | Сельское хозяйство |
| Transport | 258.2 | 507.0 | 7,052.2 | 160,812.0 | 1,470,600.0 | 8,151,000.0 | Транспорт |
| Communications | 217.8 | 479.4 | 5,000.7 | 139,324.0 | 1,356,200.0 | 8,268,000.0 | Связь |
| Trade (retail and wholesale) | 224.9 | 408.8 | 5,333.7 | 120,828.0 | 1,116,300.0 | 5,618,000.0 | Торговля (оптовая и розничная) |
| Other | 147.3 | 299.4 | 3,985.8 | 115,004.0 | 1,084,700.0 | 5,590,000.0 | Прочие отрасли материального производства |
| **Nonmaterial sphere** | .. | .. | .. | .. | .. | .. | **Отрасли непроизводственной сферы** |
| Municipal services | 185.8 | 369.9 | 5,103.4 | 117,513.0 | 1,179,900.0 | 6,372,000.0 | Жилкомхоз и бытовое обслуживание |
| Science, research and development | 314.1 | 469.4 | 5,655.7 | 142,409.0 | 1,490,300.0 | 7,860,000.0 | Наука и научное обслуживание |
| Education | 176.3 | 348.7 | 4,985.6 | 111,309.0 | 1,070,600.0 | 6,881,000.0 | Образование |
| Culture | 143.2 | 297.7 | 3,978.2 | 95,066.0 | 896,700.0 | 5,412,000.0 | Культура |
| Arts | 176.6 | 351.6 | 3,741.1 | 93,624.0 | 944,900.0 | 5,242,000.0 | Искусство |
| Health care, social security, and sports | 163.1 | 339.4 | 5,212.5 | 109,810.0 | 1,091,500.0 | 7,329,000.0 | Здравоохр., соц.обсл., физк. и спорт |
| Banking, finance, credit, insurance | 366.2 | 755.5 | 11,035.4 | 453,418.0 | 3,155,900.0 | 15,333,000.0 | Кредитование, страхование, банк. дело |
| Government | 305.3 | 455.3 | 5,344.7 | 189,756.0 | 1,725,100.0 | 7,489,000.0 | Управление |

## TABLE 8-1. Money income and expenditure of the population (millions of national currency)
## ТАБЛИЦА 8-1. Денежные доходы и расходы населения (млн. национальной валюты)

| Type of income or expenditure | 1990 | 1991 | 1992 | 1993 | 1994 | 1995 | Вид доходов или расходов |
|---|---|---|---|---|---|---|---|
| **Income** | | | | | | | **Доходы** |
| **Total labor income** | 83,700 | 147,200 | 1,720,000 | 38,095,800 | 351,328,700 | 1,615,973,800 | **Всего трудовых доходов** |
| Regular wages | 67,000 | 117,200 | 1,472,600 | 30,924,300 | 293,886,200 | 1,499,416,800 | Заработная плата |
| Wages paid by cooperatives | 3,400 | 3,500 | 68,600 | 328,100 | 2,287,200 | .. | Заработная плата в кооперативах |
| Other wages and compensation | 2,400 | 5,400 | 52,000 | 2,179,400 | 17,901,400 | 6,804,400 | Прочие доходы типа заработной платы |
| Income paid by collective farms | 8,400 | 12,800 | 123,200 | 2,468,600 | 25,890,000 | 42,908,100 | Доходы от колхозов |
| Income from sale of farm products | 5,900 | 11,800 | 72,200 | 2,523,500 | 13,651,100 | 66,844,500 | Доходы от продажи продукции колхозов |
| **Total transfer receipts** | 26,200 | 56,400 | 646,300 | 24,754,300 | 187,585,600 | 753,661,400 | **Всего трансфертных поступлений** |
| Pensions and allowances | 16,700 | 34,900 | 403,100 | 13,683,800 | 104,180,100 | 477,161,100 | Пенсии и пособия |
| Scholarships | 600 | 1,500 | 14,700 | 297,200 | 2,591,800 | 9,745,900 | Стипендии |
| Income from the financial system (insurance, interest, etc.) | 5,400 | 6,500 | 32,100 | 1,452,400 | 10,354,900 | .. | Доходы из финансовой системы (страховые возмещения, проценты и т.д.) |
| Other income | 3,500 | 13,500 | 196,400 | 9,320,900 | 70,458,800 | 266,754,400 | Прочие виды доходов |
| **Total income** | 109,900 | 203,600 | 2,366,300 | 62,850,100 | 538,914,300 | 2,369,635,200 | **Всего доходов** |
| **Expenditure** | | | | | | | **Расходы** |
| **Total purchases** | 86,400 | 144,700 | 1,537,000 | 44,123,400 | 402,455,700 | 1,716,719,500 | **Всего покупок товаров и услуг** |
| Retail goods | 77,500 | 128,000 | 1,401,900 | 39,379,900 | 346,884,300 | 1,373,929,400 | Товары в розничной торговле |
| Services | 8,900 | 16,700 | 135,100 | 4,743,500 | 55,571,400 | 342,790,100 | Услуги |
| Rent and utilities | 2,100 | 2,500 | 23,400 | 1,105,600 | 11,540,500 | 135,044,500 | Квартирная плата и коммунальные платежи |
| Transport and communications | 3,500 | 5,600 | 42,200 | 1,803,600 | 24,685,300 | 130,975,600 | Транспорт и связь |
| Health and other services | 2,900 | 8,000 | 56,500 | 1,805,100 | 19,345,600 | 76,770,000 | Здравоохранение и другие виды услуг |
| Cooperatives | 400 | 600 | 13,000 | 29,200 | .. | .. | Кооперативы |
| **Transfers and savings** | 24,000 | 48,500 | 364,700 | 7,211,200 | 72,926,500 | 476,532,100 | **Трансферты и сбережения** |
| Taxes, fees, dues, and other | 7,700 | 10,100 | 160,600 | 3,005,800 | 26,121,500 | 159,800,100 | Налоги, сборы, пошлины и др. |
| Savings | 11,900 | 31,700 | 130,300 | 2,603,500 | 19,785,100 | 40,829,700 | Сбережения |
| Other | 4,400 | 6,700 | 73,800 | 1,601,900 | 27,019,900 | 275,902,300 | Прочие |
| **Total expenditure** | 110,400 | 193,200 | 1,901,700 | 51,334,600 | 475,382,200 | 2,193,251,600 | **Всего расходов** |
| **Income less expenditure** | -500 | 10,400 | 464,600 | 11,515,500 | 63,532,100 | 176,383,600 | **Доходы за вычетом расходов** |

# *Country Notes: Ukraine*

**General Notes:** Unless otherwise indicated, the data are from the Ministry of Statistics of Ukraine.

**Currency:** Unless otherwise noted the data are presented in karbovanets. The karbovanets was introduced on November 16, 1992.

**Table 1-1:** The sum of population by working age does not equal the total population. State sector employees include also consumer cooperatives employees. Individual labor activities include employed in private enterprises and other employed population not elsewhere classified.

**Table 1-2:** Employed in agriculture also include employed in private subsidiary agriculture.

**Table 2-1:** All data are in karbovanets. Wholesale trade is included with retail trade, and insurance is included with credit. For 1995, road maintenance and transportation are included in communication, housing is included with public utilities; credit, insurance, and private nonprofit institutions are included with general administration. Data for 1995 are preliminary.

**Table 3-2A and 3-3A:** The data do not reflect the movements across borders of raw materials for processing and final goods made with such raw materials.

**Table 5-2:** Data are in 1983 karbovanets.

**Table 6-2:** Data are in 1989 karbovanets.

**Table 8-1:** For 1994 and 1995, services rendered by cooperatives are included with health and other services. For 1995, income from the financial system is included with other income, and wages paid by cooperatives are included with regular wages.

# *Комментарии к таблицам: Украина*

**Общее замечание**: За исключнием особо отмеченных случаев, все данные, используемые в таблицах, были получены из Министерства Статистики Украины.

**Национальная валюта**: За исключением особо отмеченных случаев данные приведены в карбованцах. Карбованцы были введены 16 ноября 1992 г.

**Таблица 1-1:** Сумма компонентов населения в разбивке по трудоспособному возрасту не совпадает с общей численностью населения. Занятые в государственном секторе включают также занятых в потребительской кооперации. ИТД включает также занятых на частных предприятиях и другое занятое население.

**Таблица 1-2:** Занятые в сельском хозяйстве также включают занятых в личном подсобном хозяйстве.

**Таблица 2-1:** Все данные приведены в карбованцах. Розничная торговля включает также оптовую торговлю. Кредитование включает также страхование. За 1995 г. связь включает также транспорт и дорожное хозяйство; коммунальное хозяйство включает также жилищное хозяйство; государственное управление включает также кредитование, страхование и общественные организации обслуживающие домашние хозяйства. За 1995 г. приведены предварительные данные.

**Таблицы 3-2А и 3-3А:** Данные приведены без учета объемов экспорта/импорта давальческого сырья и готовой продукции из него.

**Таблица 5-2**: Данные приведены в ценах 1983г.

**Таблица 6-2:** Данные приведены в постоянных ценах 1989 г.

**Таблица 8-1:** За 1994-95 гг. раздел Здравоохранение и другие услуги включает также услуги, предоставляемые кооперативами. За 1995 г. прочие доходы включают также доходы из финансовой системы, а заработная плата включает также заработную плату в кооперативах.

# Uzbekistan / Узбекистан

1996 Population / Численность населения в 1996 году
(thousands / тыс. человек): 23,007

Area / Территория
(thousand square kilometers / тыс. кв. км.): 447.4

Capital city / Столица :
Tashkent / Ташкент

**Country Tables:** Table 5-1 is not included because there are no recent data available.

**Статистические таблицы страны:** Таблица 5-1 не включена ввиду отсутствия данных за последние годы.

# TABLE 1-1. Population and employment (thousands)
# ТАБЛИЦА 1-1. Население и занятость (тысяч)

| Population or employment category | 1990 | 1991 | 1992 | 1993 | 1994 | 1995 | Население или группы занятых |
|---|---|---|---|---|---|---|---|
| **Total population** | 20,227 | 20,613 | 21,112 | 21,608 | 22,098 | 22,467 | **Население - всего** |
| Males | 9,997 | 10,191 | 10,447 | 10,698 | 10,951 | 11,138 | Мужчины |
| Females | 10,231 | 10,422 | 10,665 | 10,910 | 11,147 | 11,329 | Женщины |
| Urban population | 8,212 | 8,274 | 8,414 | 8,489 | 8,583 | 8,663 | Городское |
| Rural population | 12,015 | 12,339 | 12,698 | 13,119 | 13,514 | 13,804 | Сельское |
| Population under working age | 8,687 | 8,886 | 9,120 | 9,322 | 9,527 | 9,656 | Моложе трудоспособного возраста |
| Working-age population | 9,948 | 10,125 | 10,356 | 10,612 | 10,866 | 11,083 | Лица в трудоспособном возрасте |
| Population over working age | 1,592 | 1,602 | 1,636 | 1,674 | 1,705 | 1,728 | Старще трудоспособного возраста |
| Economically Active Population, in non-working age | .. | .. | .. | .. | .. | .. | Экономически активное население в нетрудоспособном возрасте |
| Above working age | .. | .. | .. | .. | .. | .. | Старше трудоспособного возраста |
| Below working age | .. | .. | .. | .. | .. | .. | Моложе трудоспособного возраста |
| **Total labor resources** | 10,000 | 10,213 | 10,448 | 10,663 | 10,868 | 11,221 | **Трудовые ресурсы - всего** |
| **Total employment** | 7,941 | 8,255 | 8,273 | 8,259 | 8,150 | 8,158 | **Занятое население - всего** |
| State sector employees | 4,983 | 5,045 | 4,782 | 4,237 | 3,284 | 2,762 | Государственный сектор |
| Leased enterprise employees | 143 | 157 | 163 | 138 | 127 | 67 | Арендные предприятия |
| Joint-stock company employees | 7 | 12 | 49 | 100 | 450 | 779 | Акционерные общества |
| Economic association employees | .. | 9 | .. | .. | .. | .. | Хозяйственные ассоциации |
| Social organization employees | 20 | 23 | 23 | 28 | 21 | 38 | Общественные организации |
| Joint venture employees | 4 | 5 | 9 | 17 | 25 | 35 | Совместные предприятия |
| Collective farm workers | 1,085 | 1,186 | 1,320 | 1,600 | 1,653 | 1,562 | Колхозы |
| Cooperative workers | 224 | 132 | 56 | 37 | 55 | .. | Кооперативы |
| Individual labor activities | 13 | 10 | 40 | 107 | 218 | 250 | ИТД |
| Private subsidiary agricultural workers | 1,168 | 1,375 | 1,427 | 1,450 | 1,442 | 1,390 | Личные подсобные хозяйства |
| Private agricultural workers | 3 | 5 | 16 | 30 | 63 | 95 | Фермерские хозяйства |
| **Students** | 978 | 959 | 930 | 869 | 860 | 880 | **Учащиеся** |
| **Religious workers** | 3 | 11 | 12 | 15 | 13 | 13 | **Служащие религиозного культа** |
| **Working age population not employed in the national economy** | 1,078 | 989 | 1,233 | 1,236 | 1,410 | 1,441 | **Лица в трудоспособном возрасте, не занятые в экономике** |
| Housewives | .. | .. | .. | .. | .. | .. | Домохозяйки |
| Military personnel | .. | .. | .. | .. | .. | .. | Военнослужащие |
| Unemployed | .. | .. | .. | .. | .. | .. | Безработные |
| **Labor force** | .. | .. | .. | .. | .. | .. | **Рабочая сила** |

## TABLE 1-2. Employment by sector (thousands)
## ТАБЛИЦА 1-2. Численность занятого населения по секторам (тысяч)

| Sector | 1990 | 1991 | 1992 | 1993 | 1994 | 1995 | Сектор |
|---|---|---|---|---|---|---|---|
| **Material sphere** | 5,884 | 6,175 | 6,203 | 6,362 | 6,157 | 6,222 | **Сфера материального производства** |
| **Agriculture and forestry** | 3,120 | 3,456 | 3,595 | 3,681 | 3,608 | 3,735 | **Сельское и лесное хозяйство** |
| Agriculture | 3,115 | 3,451 | 3,590 | 3,677 | 3,604 | .. | Сельское хозяйство |
| Forestry | 5 | 5 | 5 | 4 | 4 | .. | Лесное хозяйство |
| **Industry and construction** | 1,911 | 1,855 | 1,745 | 1,779 | 1,587 | 1,503 | **Промышленность и строительство** |
| Industry | 1,201 | 1,179 | 1,147 | 1,222 | 1,067 | 1,010 | Промышленность |
| Construction | 710 | 676 | 598 | 557 | 520 | 493 | Строительство |
| **Other** | 852 | 863 | 864 | 903 | 962 | 984 | **Другие отрасли** |
| Transport of goods | 250 | 250 | 230 | 235 | 218 | 218 | Грузовой транспорт |
| Road Maintenance | .. | .. | .. | .. | .. | .. | Дорожное хозяйство |
| Communication servicing material production | .. | .. | .. | .. | .. | .. | Связь |
| Wholesale trade | .. | .. | .. | .. | .. | .. | Оптовая торговля |
| Retail trade and catering | 459 | 464 | 452 | 521 | 565 | 566 | Розничная торговля и общепит |
| Material supply | .. | .. | .. | .. | .. | .. | Материально-техническое снабжение |
| Procurement | .. | .. | .. | .. | .. | .. | Заготовки |
| Information and computing services | 14 | 12 | .. | 6 | 3 | 4 | Информационно-техническое обслуживание |
| Other sectors | 130 | 137 | 182 | 140 | 176 | 196 | Другие отрасли сферы материального пр. |
| **Nonmaterial sphere** | 2,057 | 2,080 | 2,070 | 1,897 | 1,993 | 1,936 | **Сфера нематериального производства** |
| Passenger transport | 152 | 149 | 138 | 101 | 125 | 104 | Пассажирский транспорт |
| Communication | .. | .. | .. | .. | .. | .. | Связь |
| Housing | .. | .. | .. | .. | .. | .. | Жилищное хозяйство |
| Public utilities and personal services | 194 | 189 | 187 | 172 | 184 | 185 | Комм. хоз. и бытовое обслуживание |
| Health care, social security, physical culture and sports | 468 | 488 | 497 | 467 | 486 | 483 | Здравоохранение, социальное обеспечение, физкультура и спорт |
| Education | .. | .. | .. | .. | .. | .. | Образование |
| Culture and art | 998 | 1,033 | 1,042 | 989 | 1,080 | 1,038 | Культура и искусство |
| Science and scientific research | 103 | 93 | 76 | 49 | .. | .. | Наука и научное обслуживание |
| Credit | .. | .. | .. | .. | .. | .. | Кредитование |
| Insurance | 23 | 25 | 25 | 29 | 34 | 39 | Страхование |
| General administration and defense | 119 | 103 | 104 | 90 | 84 | 87 | Государственное управление и оборона |
| Private nonprofit institutions serving households | .. | .. | .. | .. | .. | .. | Общественные организации, обслуживающие домашние хозяйства |
| **Other, material and nonmaterial spheres** | 2,909 | 2,943 | 2,934 | 2,799 | 2,955 | 2,920 | **Остальные отрасли материального производства и нематериальной сферы** |
| **Total employment** | 7,941 | 8,255 | 8,273 | 8,259 | 8,150 | 8,158 | **Занятые - всего** |

## TABLE 1-3. Registered unemployment (thousands; end of month)
## ТАБЛИЦА 1-3. Численность зарегистрированных безработных (тысяч; на конец месяца)

| Year and m | Total Всего | Males Мужчины | Females Женщины | Receiving benefits Получающие пособие | Год и месяц |
|---|---|---|---|---|---|
| **1994** | | | | | **1994** |
| January | 30.1 | .. | .. | 8.1 | Январь |
| February | 32.8 | .. | .. | 8.9 | Февраль |
| March | 33.8 | 15.4 | 18.4 | 9.1 | Март |
| April | 34.4 | .. | .. | 8.8 | Апрель |
| May | 34.2 | .. | .. | 8.2 | Май |
| June | 34.0 | 15.5 | 18.5 | 7.0 | Июнь |
| July | 33.5 | .. | .. | 6.8 | Июль |
| August | 31.2 | .. | .. | 6.5 | Август |
| September | 30.9 | 14.1 | 16.8 | 6.2 | Сентябрь |
| October | 30.5 | .. | .. | 6.5 | Октябрь |
| November | 29.6 | .. | .. | 9.2 | Ноябрь |
| December | 29.4 | 12.0 | 17.4 | 12.3 | Декабрь |
| **1995** | | | | | **1995** |
| January | 32.6 | .. | .. | 15.1 | Январь |
| February | 36.2 | .. | .. | 18.1 | Февраль |
| March | 37.9 | 16.4 | 21.5 | 20.1 | Март |
| April | 41.2 | .. | .. | 20.5 | Апрель |
| May | 41.4 | .. | .. | 18.2 | Май |
| June | 39.7 | 15.7 | 24.0 | 15.3 | Июнь |
| July | 37.7 | .. | .. | 14.7 | Июль |
| August | 35.8 | .. | .. | 13.4 | Август |
| September | 35.1 | 12.7 | 22.4 | 11.1 | Сентябрь |
| October | 34.6 | .. | .. | 10.0 | Октябрь |
| November | 33.3 | .. | .. | 11.3 | Ноябрь |
| December | 31.0 | 12.4 | 18.6 | 12.5 | Декабрь |
| **1996** | | | | | **1996** |
| January | 33.0 | .. | .. | 13.9 | Январь |
| February | 36.3 | .. | .. | 15.9 | Февраль |
| March | 37.7 | 15.5 | 22.2 | 15.9 | Март |
| April | 41.4 | .. | .. | 18.5 | Апрель |
| May | 39.9 | .. | .. | 18.4 | Май |
| June | 41.0 | 15.9 | 25.1 | 16.5 | Июнь |
| July | 40.2 | .. | .. | 17.6 | Июль |
| August | 33.9 | .. | .. | 16.4 | Август |
| September | .. | .. | .. | .. | Сентябрь |
| October | .. | .. | .. | .. | Октябрь |
| November | .. | .. | .. | .. | Ноябрь |
| December | .. | .. | .. | .. | Декабрь |

**TABLE 2-1. Gross domestic product at current prices (millions of national currency)**
**ТАБЛИЦА 2-1. Валовой внутренний продукт в текущих ценах (млн. национальной валюты)**

| Sector of origin or expenditure category | 1990 | 1991 | 1992 | 1993 | 1994 | 1995 | Отраслевое происхождение или вид расходов |
|---|---|---|---|---|---|---|---|
| **Gross domestic product by sector of origin** | | | | | | | **Валовой внутренний продукт по отраслевому происхождению** |
| **Agriculture and forestry** | 10,837 | 22,959 | 157,245 | 1,420,943 | 22,355 | 85,070 | **Сельское и лесное хозяйство** |
| Agriculture | 10,767 | 22,885 | 156,324 | 1,414,143 | 22,322 | 84,718 | Сельское хозяйство |
| Forestry | 70 | 74 | 921 | 6,800 | 33 | 352 | Лесное хозяйство |
| **Industry and construction** | 10,803 | 22,577 | 160,361 | 1,596,785 | 15,735 | 72,296 | **Промышленность и строительство** |
| Industry | 7,350 | 16,169 | 118,159 | 1,139,701 | 11,031 | 49,068 | Промышленность |
| Construction | 3,453 | 6,408 | 42,202 | 457,084 | 4,704 | 23,228 | Строительство |
| **Other** | 11,136 | 16,351 | 134,524 | 1,731,277 | 23,643 | .. | **Другие отрасли** |
| Transport | 1,735 | 2,325 | 19,720 | 245,846 | 3,362 | 25,119 | Транспорт |
| Road maintenance | .. | .. | .. | .. | .. | .. | Дорожное хозяйство |
| Communication | 185 | 312 | 3,440 | 34,635 | 406 | .. | Связь |
| Wholesale trade | .. | .. | .. | .. | .. | .. | Оптовая торговля |
| Retail trade and catering | 1,247 | 2,408 | 24,581 | 316,900 | 4,834 | 16,821 | Розничная торговля и общепит |
| Material supply | 398 | 426 | 7,113 | 68,119 | 989 | 8,876 | Материально-техническое снабжение |
| Procurement | 271 | 537 | 3,816 | 23,073 | 447 | 1,817 | Заготовки |
| Information and computing services | 48 | 68 | 324 | 3,753 | 52 | 375 | Информационно-вычислительное обслуживание |
| Other sectors of material production | 300 | 391 | 3,609 | 38,949 | 357 | 2,795 | Другие отрасли сферы материального пр. |
| Housing | 526 | 529 | 1,066 | 7,489 | 1,221 | .. | Жилищное хозяйство |
| Public utilities and personal services | 1,012 | 1,524 | 12,743 | 159,685 | 1,264 | .. | Ком. хоз. и бытовое обслуживание |
| Health care, social security, physical culture and sports | 1,200 | 1,847 | 13,430 | 153,098 | 1,352 | .. | Здравоохранение, социальное обеспечение, физкультура и спорт |
| Education | 1,793 | 2,951 | 25,444 | 341,693 | 2,757 | .. | Образование |
| Culture and art | 305 | 383 | 1,593 | 19,209 | 231 | .. | Культура и искусство |
| Science and scientific research | 286 | 564 | 3,909 | 32,301 | 459 | .. | Наука и научное обслуживание |
| Credit | 122 | 258 | 6,124 | 172,898 | 2,689 | .. | Кредитование |
| Insurance | .. | .. | .. | .. | .. | .. | Страхование |
| General administration and defense | 1,628 | 1,759 | 7,320 | 110,267 | 3,158 | .. | Государственное управление и оборона |
| Private nonprofit institutions serving households | 80 | 69 | 293 | 3,362 | 65 | .. | Общественные организации, обслуживающие домашние хозяйства |
| **Imputed service charge of financial intermediaries** | .. | -144 | -4,272 | -134,477 | -2,195 | .. | **Условно-исчисляемая стоимость услуг финансовых посредников** |
| **Total gross value added (GVA)** | 32,776 | 61,743 | 447,859 | 4,614,528 | 59,538 | 258,169 | **Валовая добавленная стоимость (ВДС) - всего** |
| **Taxes on production and imports (TOPI)** | 4,157 | 4,632 | 37,204 | 839,152 | 8,746 | 50,256 | **Налоги на производство и импорт (НПиИ)** |
| Other taxes on production (OTOP) | .. | .. | .. | .. | .. | .. | Другие налоги на производство (ДНП) |
| **Subsidies on production and imports (SOPI)** | 4,503 | 4,826 | 41,176 | 358,478 | 3,406 | 9,896 | **Субсидии на производство и импорт (СПиИ)** |
| Other subsidies on production (OSOP) | .. | .. | .. | .. | .. | .. | Другие субсидии на производство (ДСП) |
| **Total GDP at factor cost (GVA-OTOP+OSOP)** | 32,776 | 61,743 | 447,859 | 4,614,528 | 59,538 | 258,169 | **Всего ВВП по фактр. стоимости (ВДС-ДНП+ДСП)** |
| **Net Indirect taxes (TOPI - SOPI)** | -346 | -194 | -3,972 | 480,674 | 5,340 | 40,360 | **Чистые косвенные налоги (НПиИ-СПиИ)** |
| **Total GDP at market prices** | 32,430 | 61,549 | 443,887 | 5,095,202 | 64,878 | 298,529 | **Всего ВВП в рыночных ценах** |
| **Gross domestic product by expenditure category** | | | | | | | **Валовой внутренний продукт по видам расходов** |
| **Consumption** | 28,148 | 47,421 | 290,158 | 4,184,947 | 55,465 | 222,702 | **Потребление** |
| Private consumption | 19,914 | 34,635 | 201,118 | 2,930,135 | 41,692 | 160,405 | Личное потребление |
| Government consumption | 8,234 | 12,786 | 89,040 | 1,254,812 | 13,773 | 62,297 | Общественное потребление |
| **Gross domestic investment** | 10,432 | 16,506 | 194,891 | 747,369 | 11,863 | 88,349 | **Валовые внутренние инвестиции** |
| Gross fixed investment | 9,946 | 15,426 | 117,548 | 1,283,897 | 17,022 | 99,067 | Валовое накопление основного капитала |
| Change in stocks | 486 | 1,080 | 77,343 | -536,528 | -5,159 | -10,718 | Изменения в запасах (МОС) |
| **Resource balance (net exports of GNFS)** | -6,150 | -2,378 | -41,162 | 162,886 | -2,450 | -12,522 | **Сальдо ресурсов (чистый экспорт ТНФУ)** |
| Exports of goods and nonfactor services | .. | .. | .. | .. | .. | .. | Экспорт товаров и нефакторных услуг |
| Imports of goods and nonfactor services | .. | .. | .. | .. | .. | .. | Импорт товаров и нефакторных услуг |

## TABLE 2-1A. Distribution of gross domestic product at current prices (percent)
## ТАБЛИЦА 2-1А. Распределение валового внутреннего продукта в текущих ценах ( % )

| Sector of origin or expenditure category | 1990 | 1991 | 1992 | 1993 | 1994 | 1995 | Отраслевое происхождение или вид расходов |
|---|---|---|---|---|---|---|---|
| **Gross domestic product by sector of origin** | | | | | | | **ВВП по отраслевому происхождению** |
| **Agriculture and forestry** | 33.4 | 37.3 | 35.4 | 27.9 | 34.5 | 28.5 | **Сельское и лесное хозяйство** |
| Agriculture | 33.2 | 37.2 | 35.2 | 27.8 | 34.4 | 28.4 | Сельское хозяйство |
| Forestry | 0.2 | 0.1 | 0.2 | 0.1 | 0.1 | 0.1 | Лесное хозяйство |
| **Industry and construction** | 33.3 | 36.7 | 36.1 | 31.3 | 24.3 | 24.2 | **Промышленность и строительство** |
| Industry | 22.7 | 26.3 | 26.6 | 22.4 | 17.0 | 16.4 | Промышленность |
| Construction | 10.6 | 10.4 | 9.5 | 9.0 | 7.3 | 7.8 | Строительство |
| **Other** | 34.3 | 26.6 | 30.3 | 34.0 | 36.4 | .. | **Другие отрасли** |
| Transport | 5.3 | 3.8 | 4.4 | 4.8 | 5.2 | 8.4 | Транспорт |
| Road maintenance | .. | .. | .. | .. | .. | .. | Дорожное хозяйство |
| Communication | 0.6 | 0.5 | 0.8 | 0.7 | 0.6 | .. | Связь |
| Wholesale trade | .. | .. | .. | .. | .. | .. | Оптовая торговля |
| Retail trade and catering | 3.8 | 3.9 | 5.5 | 6.2 | 7.5 | 5.6 | Розничная торговля и общепит |
| Material supply | 1.2 | 0.7 | 1.6 | 1.3 | 1.5 | 3.0 | Материально-техническое снабжение |
| Procurement | 0.8 | 0.9 | 0.9 | 0.5 | 0.7 | 0.6 | Заготовки |
| Information and computing services | 0.1 | 0.1 | 0.1 | 0.1 | 0.1 | 0.1 | Информационно-вычислительное обслуживание |
| Other sectors of material production | 0.9 | 0.6 | 0.8 | 0.8 | 0.6 | 0.9 | Другие отрасли сферы матерл. произ. |
| Housing | 1.6 | 0.9 | 0.2 | 0.1 | 1.9 | .. | Жилищное хозяйство |
| Public utilities and personal services | 3.1 | 2.5 | 2.9 | 3.1 | 1.9 | .. | Ком. хоз. и бытовое обслуживание |
| Health care, social security, physical culture and sports | 3.7 | 3.0 | 3.0 | 3.0 | 2.1 | .. | Здравоохранение, социальное обеспечение, физкультура и спорт |
| Education | 5.5 | 4.8 | 5.7 | 6.7 | 4.2 | .. | Образование |
| Culture and art | 0.9 | 0.6 | 0.4 | 0.4 | 0.4 | .. | Культура и искусство |
| Science and scientific research | 0.9 | 0.9 | 0.9 | 0.6 | 0.7 | .. | Наука и научное обслуживание |
| Credit | 0.4 | 0.4 | 1.4 | 3.4 | 4.1 | .. | Кредитование |
| Insurance | 0.0 | 0.0 | 0.0 | 0.0 | 0.0 | .. | Страхование |
| General administration and defense | 5.0 | 2.9 | 1.6 | 2.2 | 4.9 | .. | Государственное управление и оборона |
| Private nonprofit institutions serving households | 0.2 | 0.1 | 0.1 | 0.1 | 0.1 | .. | Общественные организации, обслуживающие домашние хозяйства |
| **Imputed service charge of financial intermediaries** | 0.0 | -0.2 | -1.0 | -2.6 | -3.4 | .. | **Условно-исчисляемая стоимость услуг финансовых посредников** |
| **Total gross value added** | 101.1 | 100.3 | 100.9 | 90.6 | 91.8 | 86.5 | **Валовая добавленная стоимость - всего** |
| **Total GDP at factor cost** | 101.1 | 100.3 | 100.9 | 90.6 | 91.8 | 86.5 | **ВВП по фактор. стоимости - всего** |
| **Net indirect taxes** | -1.1 | -0.3 | -0.9 | 9.4 | 8.2 | 13.5 | **Чистые косвенные налоги (НПиИ-СПиИ)** |
| **Total GDP at market prices** | 100.0 | 100.0 | 100.0 | 100.0 | 100.0 | 100.0 | **ВВП в рын. ценах - всего** |
| **Gross domestic product by expenditure category** | | | | | | | **ВВП по видам расходов** |
| **Consumption** | 86.8 | 77.0 | 65.4 | 82.1 | 85.5 | 74.6 | **Потребление** |
| Private consumption | 61.4 | 56.3 | 45.3 | 57.5 | 64.3 | 53.7 | Личное потребление |
| Government consumption | 25.4 | 20.8 | 20.1 | 24.6 | 21.2 | 20.9 | Общественное потребление |
| **Gross domestic investment** | 32.2 | 26.8 | 43.9 | 14.7 | 18.3 | 29.6 | **Вал. внутр. инвестиции** |
| Gross fixed investment | 30.7 | 25.1 | 26.5 | 25.2 | 26.2 | 33.2 | Вал. накопление осн. капитала |
| Change in stocks | 1.5 | 1.8 | 17.4 | -10.5 | -8.0 | -3.6 | Изменения в запасах (МОС) |
| **Resource balance (net exports of GNFS)** | -19.0 | -3.9 | -9.3 | 3.2 | -3.8 | -4.2 | **Сальдо ресурсов (чистый экспорт ТНФУ)** |
| Exports of goods and nonfactor services | .. | .. | .. | .. | .. | .. | Экспорт товаров и нефакторных услуг |
| Imports of goods and nonfactor services | .. | .. | .. | .. | .. | .. | Импорт товаров и нефакторных услуг |

# TABLE 2-2. Gross domestic product at constant prices (millions of national currency)
# ТАБЛИЦА 2-2. Валовой внутренний продукт в постоянных ценах (млн. национальной валюты)

| Sector of origin or expenditure category | 1990 | 1991 | 1992 | 1993 | 1994 | 1995 | Отраслевое происхождение или вид расходов |
|---|---|---|---|---|---|---|---|
| **Gross domestic product by sector of origin** | | | | | | | **Валовой внутренний продукт по отраслевому происхождению** |
| **Agriculture and forestry** | .. | .. | .. | 159,553 | 1,372,889 | 22,861 | **Сельское и лесное хозяйство** |
| Agriculture | .. | .. | .. | 158,649 | 1,366,062 | 22,821 | Сельское хозяйство |
| Forestry | .. | .. | .. | 904 | 6,827 | 40 | Лесное хозяйство |
| **Industry and construction** | .. | .. | .. | 151,918 | 1,421,362 | 15,113 | **Промышленность и строительство** |
| Industry | .. | .. | .. | 113,229 | 1,064,824 | 10,601 | Промышленность |
| Construction | .. | .. | .. | 38,689 | 356,538 | 4,512 | Строительство |
| **Other** | .. | .. | .. | 133,287 | 1,754,002 | .. | **Другие отрасли** |
| Transport | .. | .. | .. | 19,225 | 244,996 | 3,645 | Транспорт |
| Road maintenance | .. | .. | .. | .. | .. | .. | Дорожное хозяйство |
| Communication | .. | .. | .. | .. | .. | .. | Связь |
| Wholesale trade | .. | .. | .. | .. | .. | .. | Оптовая торговля |
| Retail trade and catering | .. | .. | .. | 24,530 | 282,249 | 4,457 | Розничная торговля и общепит |
| Material supply | .. | .. | .. | 7,228 | 63,319 | 950 | Материально-техническое снабжение |
| Procurement | .. | .. | .. | 3,888 | 20,374 | 463 | Заготовки |
| Information and computing services | .. | .. | .. | 258 | 3,713 | 44 | Информационно-вычислительное обслуживание |
| Other sectors of material production | .. | .. | .. | 3,159 | 40,004 | 380 | Другие отрасли сферы материального пр. |
| Housing | .. | .. | .. | 811 | 7,800 | .. | Жилищное хозяйство |
| Public utilities and personal services | .. | .. | .. | 13,846 | 163,239 | .. | Ком. хоз. и бытовое обслуживание |
| Health care, social security, and sports | .. | .. | .. | 13,982 | 150,036 | .. | Здравоохранение, социальное обеспечение, физкультура и спорт |
| Education | .. | .. | .. | 25,563 | 368,288 | .. | Образование |
| Culture and art | .. | .. | .. | 1,456 | 19,561 | .. | Культура и искусство |
| Science and research | .. | .. | .. | 4,196 | 32,761 | .. | Наука и научное обслуживание |
| Credit | .. | .. | .. | 6,929 | 235,058 | .. | Кредитование |
| Insurance | .. | .. | .. | .. | .. | .. | Страхование |
| General administration and defense | .. | .. | .. | 7,934 | 119,763 | .. | Государственное управление и оборона |
| Private nonprofit institutions serving households | .. | .. | .. | 282 | 2,841 | .. | Общественные организации, обслуживающие домашние хозяйства |
| **Imputed service charge of financial intermediaries** | .. | .. | .. | -4,913 | -136,225 | .. | **Условно-исчисляемая стоимость услуг финансовых посредников** |
| **Total gross value added (GVA)** | .. | .. | .. | 439,845 | 4,412,028 | 58,847 | **Валовая добавленная стоимость (ВДС) -** |
| **Total GDP at factor cost (GVA-OTOP+OSOP)** | .. | .. | .. | 439,845 | 4,412,028 | 58,847 | **Всего ВВП по фактр. стоимости (ВДС-ДНП+ДСП)** |
| **Net indirect taxes (TOPI - SOPI)** | .. | .. | .. | -6,365 | 468,501 | 5,220 | **Чистые косвенные налоги (НПиИ-СПиИ)** |
| **Total GDP at market prices** | .. | 32,278 | 54,727 | 433,480 | 4,880,529 | 64,067 | **Всего ВВП в рыночных ценах** |
| **Gross domestic product by expenditure category** | | | | | | | **Валовой внутренний продукт по видам расходов** |
| **Consumption** | .. | .. | .. | .. | .. | .. | **Потребление** |
| Private consumption | .. | .. | .. | .. | .. | .. | Личное потребление |
| Government consumption | .. | .. | .. | .. | .. | .. | Общественное потребление |
| **Gross domestic investment** | .. | .. | .. | .. | .. | .. | **Валовые внутренние инвестиции** |
| Gross fixed investment | .. | .. | .. | .. | .. | .. | Валовое накопление основного капитала |
| Change in stocks | .. | .. | .. | .. | .. | .. | Изменения в запасах (МОС) |
| **Resource balance (net exports of GNFS)** | .. | .. | .. | .. | .. | .. | **Сальдо ресурсов (чистый экспорт ТНФУ)** |
| Exports of goods and nonfactor services | .. | .. | .. | .. | .. | .. | Экспорт товаров и нефакторных услуг |
| Imports of goods and nonfactor services | .. | .. | .. | .. | .. | .. | Импорт товаров и нефакторных услуг |

**TABLE 2-2A. Growth rates of gross domestic product at constant prices (percent)**
**ТАБЛИЦА 2-2А. Валовой внутренний продукт - темпы прироста в постоянных ценах ( % )**

| Sector of origin or expenditure category | 1990 | 1991 | 1992 | 1993 | 1994 | 1995 | Отраслевое происхождение или вид расходов |
|---|---|---|---|---|---|---|---|
| **Growth rate by sector of origin** | | | | | | | **Валовый внутренний продукт по отраслевому происхождению** |
| **Agriculture and forestry** | .. | .. | .. | 1.5 | -3.4 | 2.3 | **Сельское и лесное хозяйство** |
| Agriculture | .. | .. | .. | 1.5 | -3.4 | 2.2 | Сельское хозяйство |
| Forestry | .. | .. | .. | -1.9 | 0.4 | 21.2 | Лесное хозяйство |
| **Industry and construction** | .. | .. | .. | -5.3 | -11.0 | -4.0 | **Промышленность и строительство** |
| Industry | .. | .. | .. | -4.2 | -6.6 | -3.9 | Промышленность |
| Construction | .. | .. | .. | -8.3 | -22.0 | -4.1 | Строительство |
| **Other** | .. | .. | .. | -0.9 | 1.3 | .. | **Другие отрасли** |
| Transport | .. | .. | .. | -17.0 | -12.7 | -3.3 | Транспорт |
| Road maintenance | .. | .. | .. | .. | .. | .. | Дорожное хозяйство |
| Communication | .. | .. | .. | .. | .. | .. | Связь |
| Wholesale trade | .. | .. | .. | .. | .. | .. | Оптовая торговля |
| Retail trade and catering | .. | .. | .. | -0.2 | -10.9 | -7.8 | Розничная торговля и общепит |
| Material supply | .. | .. | .. | 1.6 | -7.0 | -3.9 | Материально-техническое снабжение |
| Procurement | .. | .. | .. | 1.9 | -11.7 | 3.6 | Заготовки |
| Information and computing services | .. | .. | .. | -20.4 | -1.1 | -15.4 | Информационно-вычислительное обслуживание |
| Other sectors of material production | .. | .. | .. | -12.5 | 2.7 | 6.4 | Другие отрасли сферы материального пр. |
| Housing | .. | .. | .. | -23.9 | 4.2 | .. | Жилищное хозяйство |
| Public utilities and personal services | .. | .. | .. | 8.7 | 2.2 | .. | Ком. хоз. и бытовое обслуживание |
| Health care, social security, and sports | .. | .. | .. | 4.1 | -2.0 | .. | Здравоохранение, социальное обеспечение, физкультура и спорт |
| Education | .. | .. | .. | 0.5 | 7.8 | .. | Образование |
| Culture and art | .. | .. | .. | .. | .. | .. | Культура и искусство |
| Science and research | .. | .. | .. | 7.4 | 1.4 | .. | Наука и научное обслуживание |
| Credit | .. | .. | .. | 13.1 | 36.0 | .. | Кредитование |
| Insurance | .. | .. | .. | .. | .. | .. | Страхование |
| General administration and defense | .. | .. | .. | 8.4 | 8.6 | .. | Государственное управление и оборона |
| Private nonprofit institutions serving households | .. | .. | .. | -3.9 | -15.5 | .. | Общественные организации, обслуживающие домашние хозяйства |
| **Imputed service charge of financial intermediaries** | .. | .. | .. | 15.0 | 1.3 | .. | **Условно-исчисляемая стоимость услуг финансовых посредников** |
| **Total gross value added** | .. | .. | .. | -1.8 | -4.4 | -1.2 | **Валовая добавленная стоимость (ВДС) - всего** |
| **Total GDP at factor cost** | .. | .. | .. | -1.8 | -4.4 | -1.2 | **Всего ВВП по фактр. стоимости (ВДС-ДНП+ДСП)** |
| **Net indirect taxes** | .. | .. | .. | 60.2 | -2.5 | -2.2 | **Чистые косвенные налоги (НПиИ-СПиИ)** |
| **Total GDP at market prices** | .. | -0.5 | -11.1 | -2.3 | -4.2 | -1.3 | **Всего ВВП в рыночных ценах** |
| **Growth rate by expenditure category** | | | | | | | **Валовой внутренний продукт по видам расходов** |
| **Consumption** | .. | .. | .. | .. | .. | .. | **Потребление** |
| Private consumption | .. | .. | .. | .. | .. | .. | Личное потребление |
| Government consumption | .. | .. | .. | .. | .. | .. | Общественное потребление |
| **Gross domestic investment** | .. | .. | .. | .. | .. | .. | **Валовые внутренние инвестиции** |
| Gross fixed investment | .. | .. | .. | .. | .. | .. | Валовое накопление основного капитала |
| **Exports of goods and nonfactor services** | .. | .. | .. | .. | .. | .. | **Экспорт товаров и нефакторных услуг** |
| **Imports of goods and nonfactor services** | .. | .. | .. | .. | .. | .. | **Импорт товаров и нефакторных услуг** |

## TABLE 2-2B. Implicit price deflators for gross domestic product (percentage change)
## ТАБЛИЦА 2-2B. Дефляторы валового внутреннего продукта (темпы прироста в %)

| Sector of origin or expenditure category | 1990 | 1991 | 1992 | 1993 | 1994 | 1995 | Отраслевое происхождение или вид расходов |
|---|---|---|---|---|---|---|---|
| **Price deflators by sector of origin** | | | | | | | **Дефляторы по отраслевому происхождению или виду расходов** |
| **Agriculture and forestry** | .. | .. | .. | 790.6 | -98.4 | 272.1 | **Сельское и лесное хозяйство** |
| Agriculture | .. | .. | .. | 791.4 | -98.4 | 271.2 | Сельское хозяйство |
| Forestry | .. | .. | .. | 652.2 | -99.5 | 780.0 | Лесное хозяйство |
| **Industry and construction** | .. | .. | .. | 951.1 | -98.9 | 378.4 | **Промышленность и строительство** |
| Industry | .. | .. | .. | 906.5 | 935.9 | 362.9 | Промышленность |
| Construction | .. | .. | .. | 1,081.4 | 1,219.4 | 414.8 | Строительство |
| **Other** | .. | .. | .. | 1,198.9 | 1,247.9 | .. | **Другие отрасли** |
| Transport | .. | .. | .. | 1,358.9 | 1,438.0 | 589.1 | Транспорт |
| Road maintenance | .. | .. | .. | .. | .. | .. | Дорожное хозяйство |
| Communication | .. | .. | .. | .. | .. | .. | Связь |
| Wholesale trade | .. | .. | .. | .. | .. | .. | Оптовая торговля |
| Retail trade and catering | .. | .. | .. | 1,191.9 | 1,612.7 | 277.4 | Розничная торговля и общепит. |
| Material supply | .. | .. | .. | 842.4 | 1,461.9 | 834.3 | Материально-техническое снабжение |
| Procurement | .. | .. | .. | 493.4 | 2,094.0 | 292.4 | Заготовки |
| Information and computing services | .. | .. | .. | 1,354.7 | 1,300.5 | 752.3 | Информационно-вычислительное обслуживание |
| Other sectors of material production | .. | .. | .. | 1,133.0 | 792.4 | 635.5 | Другие отрасли сферы матерл. произ. |
| Housing | .. | .. | .. | 823.4 | 15,553.8 | .. | Жилищное хозяйство |
| Public utilities and personal services | .. | .. | .. | 1,053.3 | 674.3 | .. | Ком. хоз. и бытовое обслуживание |
| Health care, social security, and sports | .. | .. | .. | 995.0 | 801.1 | .. | Здравоохранение, социальное обеспечение, физкультура и спорт |
| Education | .. | .. | .. | 1,236.7 | 648.6 | .. | Образование |
| Culture and art | .. | .. | .. | .. | .. | .. | Культура и искусство |
| Science and research | .. | .. | .. | 669.8 | 1,301.1 | .. | Наука и научное обслуживание |
| Credit | .. | .. | .. | 2,395.3 | 1,044.0 | .. | Кредитование |
| Insurance | .. | .. | .. | .. | .. | .. | Страхование |
| General administration and defense | .. | .. | .. | 1,289.8 | 2,536.9 | .. | Государственное управление и оборона |
| Private nonprofit institutions serving households | .. | .. | .. | 1,092.2 | 2,187.9 | .. | Общественные организации, обслуживающие домашние хозяиства |
| **Imputed service charge of financial intermediaries** | .. | .. | .. | 2,637.2 | 1,511.3 | .. | **Условно-исчисляемая стоимость услуг финансовых посредников** |
| **Total gross value added** | .. | .. | .. | 949.1 | 1,249.4 | 338.7 | **Валовая добавленная стоимость (ВДС) - всего** |
| **Total GDP at factor cost** | .. | .. | .. | 949.1 | 1,249.4 | 338.7 | **ВВП по факторной стоимости (ВДС-ДНП+ДСП)** |
| **Net indirect taxes** | .. | .. | .. | -7,651.8 | 1,039.8 | 673.2 | **Чистые косвенные налоги (НПИ-СПИ)** |
| **Total GDP at market prices** | .. | 90.7 | 711.1 | 1,075.4 | 1,229.3 | 366.0 | **ВВП в рыночных ценах** |
| **Price deflators by expenditure category** | | | | | | | **Дефляторы по виду расходов** |
| **Consumption** | .. | .. | .. | .. | .. | .. | **Конечное потребление** |
| Private consumption | .. | .. | .. | .. | .. | .. | Личное потребление |
| Government consumption | .. | .. | .. | .. | .. | .. | Общественное потребление |
| **Gross domestic investment** | .. | .. | .. | .. | .. | .. | **Валовые внутренние инвестиции** |
| Gross fixed investment | .. | .. | .. | .. | .. | .. | Валовое накопление основного капитала |
| **Exports of goods and nonfactor services** | .. | .. | .. | .. | .. | .. | **Экспорт товаров и нефакторных услуг** |
| **Imports of goods and nonfactor services** | .. | .. | .. | .. | .. | .. | **Импорт товаров и нефакторных услуг** |

## TABLE 3-1. Balance of payments at current prices (millions of U.S. dollars)
## ТАБЛИЦА 3-1. Платежный баланс в текущих ценах (в миллионах долларов США)

| Item | 1990 | 1991 | 1992 | 1993 | 1994 | 1995 | Статьи |
|---|---|---|---|---|---|---|---|
| Exports of goods and services (including workers' remittances) | .. | 685.1 | 869.3 | .. | .. | .. | Экспорт товаров и услуг (включая денежные переводы рабочих) |
| Exports of goods and nonfactor services | .. | 685.1 | 869.3 | 2,877.0 | 2,840.0 | .. | Экспорт товаров и нефакт. услуг |
| Merchandise (FOB) | .. | 677.0 | 861.0 | .. | .. | .. | Товары (ФОБ) |
| Nonfactor services | .. | 8.1 | 8.3 | .. | .. | .. | Нефакторные услуги |
| Shipment | .. | 8.1 | 8.1 | .. | .. | .. | Перевозки |
| Travel | .. | .. | 0.2 | .. | .. | .. | Поездки |
| Other | .. | .. | .. | .. | .. | .. | Другие |
| Imports of goods and nonfactor services | .. | 1,385.5 | 930.2 | 3,255.0 | 2,661.0 | .. | Импорт товаров и нефакт. услуг |
| Merchandise (FOB) | .. | 1,385.5 | 929.0 | .. | .. | .. | Товары (ФОБ) |
| Nonfactor services | .. | .. | 1.2 | .. | .. | .. | Нефакторные услуги |
| Shipment | .. | .. | .. | .. | .. | .. | Перевозки |
| Travel | .. | .. | 0.8 | .. | .. | .. | Поездки |
| Other | .. | .. | 0.4 | .. | .. | .. | Другие |
| Resource balance | .. | -700.4 | -60.9 | -378.0 | 179.0 | .. | Сальдо ресурсов |
| Net factor income | .. | .. | .. | -63.0 | -163.0 | .. | Чистый факторный доход |
| Factor receipts | .. | .. | .. | .. | .. | .. | Факторные поступления |
| Factor payments | .. | .. | .. | .. | .. | .. | Факторные платежи |
| Total interest due | .. | .. | .. | .. | .. | .. | Общая сумма процента к оплате |
| Other factor payments and discrepancy | .. | .. | .. | .. | .. | .. | Другие факторные платежи и стат. погр. |
| Net current transfers | .. | .. | 4.0 | 12.0 | 13.0 | .. | Чистые текущие трансферты |
| Current receipts | .. | .. | 4.0 | .. | .. | .. | Текущие поступления |
| Workers remittances | .. | .. | .. | .. | .. | .. | Денежные переводы рабочих |
| Other current transfers | .. | .. | 4.0 | .. | .. | .. | Другие текущие трансферты |
| Current payments | .. | .. | .. | .. | .. | .. | Текущие платежи |
| Current account balance before official grants | .. | -700.4 | -56.9 | -429.0 | 29.0 | .. | Сальдо текущего счета до офиц. безвозмезд. трансфертов |
| Official capital grants | .. | .. | 0.0 | 0.0 | 0.0 | .. | Официальные кап. безвозмезные трансферты |
| Current account balance after official grants | .. | -700.4 | -56.9 | -429.0 | 29.0 | .. | Сальдо текущего счета после офиц. безвозмезд. трансфертов |
| Long Term Capital Inflows | .. | .. | 190.7 | 771.0 | 751.0 | .. | Долгосрочные притоки капитала |
| Direct investment | .. | .. | 0.0 | 48.0 | 72.0 | .. | Прямые инвестиции |
| Net long term borrowing | .. | .. | 190.7 | 714.0 | 752.0 | .. | Чистые долгосрочные займы |
| Disbursements | .. | .. | 210.7 | 548.0 | 414.0 | .. | Поступления |
| Repayments due | .. | .. | 20.0 | -166.0 | -338.0 | .. | Сумма, подлежащая погашению |
| Other long-term inflows (net) | .. | .. | 0.0 | 9.0 | -73.0 | .. | Другие долгосрочные притоки (чистые) |

(continued on next page)

**TABLE 3-1. Balance of payments at current prices (millions of U.S. dollars)**
**ТАБЛИЦА 3-1. Платежный баланс в текущих ценах (в миллионах долларов США)**

| Item | 1990 | 1991 | 1992 | 1993 | 1994 | 1995 | Статьи |
|---|---|---|---|---|---|---|---|
| Adjustment to Scheduled Debt Service | .. | .. | .. | .. | .. | .. | Регулирование долга |
| Debt service not paid | .. | .. | .. | .. | .. | .. | Невыплаченный долг |
| Interest not paid | .. | .. | .. | .. | .. | .. | Невыплаченный процент |
| Principal not paid | .. | .. | .. | .. | .. | .. | Невыплаченная сумма основного долга |
| Arrears reductions/prepayments(-) | .. | .. | .. | .. | .. | .. | Погашение просроченных платежей/выплаты авансом (-) |
| Total Other items (Net) | .. | .. | 396.1 | .. | .. | .. | Общие другие статьи (чистые) |
| Net short-term capital | .. | .. | 396.1 | .. | .. | .. | Чистый краткосрочный капитал |
| Capital flows not elsewhere included | .. | .. | .. | .. | .. | .. | Потоки капитала, не указанные выше |
| Errors and omissions | .. | .. | .. | 103.0 | 318.0 | .. | Ошибки и пропуски |
| Changes in net reserves | .. | .. | .. | .. | .. | .. | Изменения в чистых резервах |
| Net credit from IMF | .. | .. | .. | .. | .. | .. | Чистый кредит МВФ |
| Reserve changes not elsewhere included | .. | .. | .. | .. | .. | .. | Изменения резервов, не указанных выше |
| Escrow account | .. | .. | .. | .. | .. | .. | Счет депонирования |
| Gross reserves (excluding gold) | .. | .. | .. | .. | .. | .. | Общие резервы (исключая золото) |
| Gross reserves (including gold) | .. | .. | .. | .. | .. | .. | Общие резервы (включая золото) |
| Nominal official exchange rate (annual average) (rf) | .. | .. | .. | .. | .. | .. | Номинальный официальный или рыночный курс (среднегодовой) |
| Nominal official exchange rate (end-of-year) (ae) | .. | .. | .. | .. | .. | .. | Номинальный официальный или рыночный курс (на конец года) |
| Manufacture unit value (percent change) | .. | .. | .. | .. | .. | .. | Средний индекс цен на продукцию обр. пром.,% |
| Index of real effective exchange rate (IMF) | .. | .. | .. | .. | .. | .. | Индекс реального эффективного валютного курса (МВФ) |
| Total factor payments | .. | .. | .. | .. | .. | .. | Общая сумма факторных платежей |
| Government interest | .. | .. | .. | .. | .. | .. | Процент, выплачиваемый органами гос. управления |
| Private sector interest | .. | .. | .. | .. | .. | .. | Процент выплачиваемый частным сектором |
| Profits on direct foreign investment | .. | .. | .. | .. | .. | .. | Прибыль от прямых иностранных инвестиций |
| Official capital grants | .. | .. | .. | .. | .. | .. | Официальные капитальные безвозмездные трансферты |
| For budgetary financing | .. | .. | .. | .. | .. | .. | На бюджетное финансирование |
| To extrabudgetary entities | .. | .. | .. | .. | .. | .. | На внебюджетное финансирование |
| Government net long term borrowing | .. | .. | .. | .. | .. | .. | Чистые долгосрочные государственные займы |
| Disbursements | .. | .. | .. | .. | .. | .. | Поступления |
| Repayments | .. | .. | .. | .. | .. | .. | Погашения |
| Private net long term borrowing | .. | .. | .. | .. | .. | .. | Чистые долгосрочные частные займы |
| Disbursements | .. | .. | .. | .. | .. | .. | Поступления |
| Repayments | .. | .. | .. | .. | .. | .. | Погашения |

**TABLE 3-2A. Imports by commodity group (millions of U.S. dollars)**
**ТАБЛИЦА 3-2A . Импорт по товарным группам (млн. долларов США)**

| Commodity group | 1990 | 1991 | 1992 | 1993 | 1994 | 1995 | Товарные группы |
|---|---|---|---|---|---|---|---|
| TOTAL | .. | .. | .. | .. | 2,609.5 | 2,892.7 | ВСЕГО |
| I - Live animals; animal products | .. | .. | .. | .. | 119.1 | 68.2 | I - Живые животные и продукты животноводства |
| II - Vegetable products | .. | .. | .. | .. | 647.8 | 267.5 | II - Продукты растительного происхождения |
| III - Animal or vegetable fats and oils and their cleavage products; prepared edible fats; animal or vegetable waxes | .. | .. | .. | .. | 0.6 | 12.3 | III - Жиры и масла растительного и животного происхождения, воски |
| IV - Prepared foodstuffs; beverages, spirits and vinegar; tobacco and manufactured tobacco substitutes | .. | .. | .. | .. | 147.2 | 178.7 | IV -Продукция пищевой промышленности, алкогольные и безалкогольные напитки, табак и его заменители |
| V - Mineral products | .. | .. | .. | .. | 651.9 | 78.2 | V - Минеральные продукты |
| VI - Products of the chemical or allied industries | .. | .. | .. | .. | 125.6 | 196.4 | VI - Продукция химической промышленности |
| VII - Plastics and articles thereof; rubber and articles thereof | .. | .. | .. | .. | 56.3 | 63.5 | VII - Пластмассы и изделия из них |
| VIII - Raw hides and skins, leather, furskins and articles thereof; saddlery and harness; travel goods, handbags and similar containers; articles of animal gut | .. | .. | .. | .. | 1.3 | 2.5 | VIII - Кожевенное сырьё, кожи, пушнина, меховое сырьё и изделия из них |
| IX - Wood and articles of wood; wood charcoal; cork and articles of cork; manufactures of straw, of esparto or of other plaiting materials; basketware and wickerwork | .. | .. | .. | .. | 44.2 | 31.4 | IX - Древесина и изделия из древесины, древесный уголь |
| X - Pulp of wood or of other fibrous cellulosic material; waste and scrap of paper or paperboard; paper and paperboard and articles thereof | .. | .. | .. | .. | 29.0 | 15.0 | X - Бумажная масса, бумажные и картонные отходы, макулатура, бумага, картон и изделия из них |
| XI - Textiles and textile articles | .. | .. | .. | .. | 94.5 | 84.0 | XI - Текстиль и текстильные изделия |
| XII - Footwear, headgear, umbrellas, sun umbrellas, walking sticks, seat sticks, whips, riding crops and parts thereof; prepared feathers and articles made therewith; artificial flowers; articles of human hair | .. | .. | .. | .. | 10.5 | 12.8 | XII - Обувь, головные уборы, зонты, трости и пр. |

**TABLE 3-2A. Imports by commodity group (millions of U.S. dollars)**
**ТАБЛИЦА 3-2А . Импорт по товарным группам (млн. долларов США)**

| Commodity group | 1990 | 1991 | 1992 | 1993 | 1994 | 1995 | Товарные группы |
|---|---|---|---|---|---|---|---|
| XIII - Articles of stone, plaster, cement, asbestos, mica and similar materials; ceramic products; glass and glassware | .. | .. | .. | .. | 18.6 | 20.6 | XIII - Изделия из камня, гипса, цемента |
| XIV - Natural or cultured pearls, precious or semi-precious stones, precious metals, metals clad with precious metal and articles thereof; imitation jewellery; coin | .. | .. | .. | .. | 3.0 | 0.2 | XIV - Жемчуг, драгоценные и полудрагоценные камни, драгоценные металлы, бижутерия, монеты |
| XV - Base metals and articles of base metal | .. | .. | .. | .. | 228.9 | 183.1 | XV - Неблагородные металлы и изделия из них |
| XVI - Machinery and mechanical appliances; electrical equipment; parts thereof; sound recorders and reproducers, television image and sound recorders and reproducers, and parts and accessories of such articles | .. | .. | .. | .. | 269.6 | 1,027.9 | XVI - Машины, оборудование, механизмы, их части и принадлежности; звуковая и теле-аппаратура, их части и принадлежности |
| XVII - Vehicles, aircraft, vessels and associated transport equipment | .. | .. | .. | .. | 142.1 | 219.2 | XVII - Средства наземного, воздушного и водного транспорта |
| XVIII - Optical, photographic, cinematographic, measuring, checking, precision, medical or surgical instruments and apparatus; clocks and watches; musical instruments; parts and accessories thereof | .. | .. | .. | .. | 4.0 | 139.9 | XVIII - Приборы, аппараты оптические, медицинские, измерительные и пр.; музыкальные инструменты; часы; их части и принадлежности |
| XIX - Arms and ammunition; parts and accessories thereof | .. | .. | .. | .. | .. | .. | XIX - Оружие и боеприпасы, их части и принадлежности |
| XX - Miscellaneous manufactured articles | .. | .. | .. | 8.6 | 8.6 | 146.4 | XX - Разные промышленные товары |
| XXI - Works of art, collectors' pieces, and antiques | .. | .. | .. | .. | .. | .. | XXI - Произведения искусства, предметы антиквариата |
| XXII - Services | .. | .. | .. | .. | 6.7 | 144.9 | XXII - Услуги |

**TABLE 3-2B Imports by commodity group (millions of national currency)**
**ТАБЛИЦА 3-2B. Импорт по товарным группам (млн. национальной валюты)**

| Commodity group | 1990 | 1991 | 1992 | 1993 | 1994 | 1995 | Товарные группы |
|---|---|---|---|---|---|---|---|
| TOTAL | .. | .. | .. | .. | 27,975.5 | 86,814.3 | ВСЕГО |
| I - Live animals; animal products | .. | .. | .. | .. | 1,700.0 | 1,865.6 | I - Живые животные и продукты животноводства |
| II - Vegetable products | .. | .. | .. | .. | 7,278.5 | 6,111.0 | II - Продукты растительного происхождения |
| III - Animal or vegetable fats and oils and their cleavage products; prepared edible fats; animal or vegetable waxes | .. | .. | .. | .. | 5.1 | 373.4 | III - Жиры и масла растительного и животного происхождения, воски |
| IV - Prepared foodstuffs; beverages, spirits and vinegar; tobacco and manufactured tobacco substitutes | .. | .. | .. | .. | 1,920.9 | 4,949.9 | IV -Продукция пищевой промышленности, алкогольные и безалкогольные напитки, табак и его заменители |
| V - Mineral products | .. | .. | .. | .. | 4,955.0 | 2,371.1 | V - Минеральные продукты |
| VI - Products of the chemical or allied industries | .. | .. | .. | .. | 1,317.2 | 5,674.5 | VI - Продукция химической промышленности |
| VII - Plastics and articles thereof; rubber and articles thereof | .. | .. | .. | .. | 710.0 | 1,972.3 | VII - Пластмассы и изделия из них |
| VIII - Raw hides and skins, leather, furskins and articles thereof; saddlery and harness; travel goods, handbags and similar containers; articles of animal gut | .. | .. | .. | .. | 13.0 | 78.4 | VIII - Кожевенное сырьё, кожи, пушнина, меховое сырьё и изделия из них |
| IX - Wood and articles of wood; wood charcoal; cork and articles of cork; manufactures of straw, of esparto or of other plaiting materials; basketware and wickerwork | .. | .. | .. | .. | 476.6 | 915.3 | IX - Древесина и изделия из древесины, древесный уголь |
| X - Pulp of wood or of other fibrous cellulosic material; waste and scrap of paper or paperboard; paper and paperboard and articles thereof | .. | .. | .. | .. | 297.6 | 470.0 | X - Бумажная масса, бумажные и картонные отходы, макулатура, бумага, картон и изделия из них |
| XI - Textiles and textile articles | .. | .. | .. | .. | 901.5 | 2,539.7 | XI - Текстиль и текстильные изделия |
| XII - Footwear, headgear, umbrellas, sun umbrellas, walking sticks, seat sticks, whips, riding crops and parts thereof; prepared feathers and articles made therewith; artificial flowers; articles of human hair | .. | .. | .. | .. | 58.7 | 359.9 | XII - Обувь, головные уборы, зонты, трости и пр. |

**TABLE 3-2B Imports by commodity group (millions of national currency)**
**ТАБЛИЦА 3-2B. Импорт по товарным группам (млн. национальной валюты)**

| Commodity group | 1990 | 1991 | 1992 | 1993 | 1994 | 1995 | Товарные группы |
|---|---|---|---|---|---|---|---|
| XIII - Articles of stone, plaster, cement, asbestos, mica and similar materials; ceramic products; glass and glassware | .. | .. | .. | .. | 160.2 | 664.1 | XIII - Изделия из камня, гипса, цемента |
| XIV - Natural or cultured pearls, precious or semi-precious stones, precious metals, metals clad with precious metal and articles thereof; imitation jewellery; coin | .. | .. | .. | .. | 54.2 | 5.0 | XIV - Жемчуг, драгоценные и полудрагоценные камни, драгоценные металлы, бижутерия, монеты |
| XV - Base metals and articles of base metal | .. | .. | .. | .. | 2,831.2 | 5,501.4 | XV - Неблагородные металлы и изделия из них |
| XVI - Machinery and mechanical appliances; electrical equipment; parts thereof; sound recorders and reproducers, television image and sound recorders and reproducers, and parts and accessories of such articles | .. | .. | .. | .. | 3,248.3 | 32,317.4 | XVI - Машины, оборудование, механизмы, их части и принадлежности; звуковая и теле-аппаратура, их части и принадлежности |
| XVII - Vehicles, aircraft, vessels and associated transport equipment | .. | .. | .. | .. | 1,793.2 | 6,971.6 | XVII - Средства наземного, воздушного и водного транспорта |
| XVIII - Optical, photographic, cinematographic, measuring, checking, precision, medical or surgical instruments and apparatus; clocks and watches; musical instruments; parts and accessories thereof | .. | .. | .. | .. | 37.2 | 4,540.4 | XVIII - Приборы, аппараты оптические, медицинские, измерительные и пр.; музыкальные инструменты; часы; их части и принадлежности |
| XIX - Arms and ammunition; parts and accessories thereof | .. | .. | .. | .. | .. | .. | XIX - Оружие и боеприпасы, их части и принадлежности |
| XX - Miscellaneous manufactured articles | .. | .. | .. | .. | 108.3 | 4,556.5 | XX - Разные промышленные товары |
| XXI - Works of art, collectors' pieces, and antiques | .. | .. | .. | .. | .. | .. | XXI - Произведения искусства, предметы антиквариата |
| XXII - Services | .. | .. | .. | .. | 108.8 | 4,576.8 | XXII - Услуги |

**TABLE 3-3A. Exports by commodity group (millions of U.S. dollars)**
**ТАБЛИЦА 3-3A. Экспорт по товарным группам (млн. долларов США)**

| Commodity group | 1990 | 1991 | 1992 | 1993 | 1994 | 1995 | Товарные группы |
|---|---|---|---|---|---|---|---|
| TOTAL | .. | .. | .. | .. | 2,689.9 | 3,109.0 | ВСЕГО |
| I - Live animals; animal products | .. | .. | .. | .. | 0.5 | 0.3 | I - Живые животные и продукты животноводства |
| II - Vegetable products | .. | .. | .. | .. | 50.3 | 31.9 | II - Продукты растительного происхождения |
| III - Animal or vegetable fats and oils and their cleavage products; prepared edible fats; animal or vegetable waxes | .. | .. | .. | .. | 17.3 | 14.0 | III - Жиры и масла растительного и животного происхождения, воски |
| IV - Prepared foodstuffs; beverages, spirits and vinegar; tobacco and manufactured tobacco substitutes | .. | .. | .. | .. | 45.4 | 32.6 | IV -Продукция пищевой промышленности, алкогольные и безалкогольные напитки, табак и его заменители |
| V - Mineral products | .. | .. | .. | .. | 399.0 | 450.7 | V - Минеральные продукты |
| VI - Products of the chemical or allied industries | .. | .. | .. | .. | 61.8 | 82.0 | VI - Продукция химической промышленности |
| VII - Plastics and articles thereof; rubber and articles thereof | .. | .. | .. | .. | 15.8 | 5.7 | VII - Пластмассы и изделия из них |
| VIII - Raw hides and skins, leather, furskins and articles thereof; saddlery and harness; travel goods, handbags and similar containers; articles of animal gut | .. | .. | .. | .. | 8.6 | 3.3 | VIII - Кожевенное сырьё, кожи, пушнина, меховое сырьё и изделия из них |
| IX - Wood and articles of wood; wood charcoal; cork and articles of cork; manufactures of straw, of esparto or of other plaiting materials; basketware and wickerwork | .. | .. | .. | .. | .. | .. | IX - Древесина и изделия из древесины, древесный уголь |
| X - Pulp of wood or of other fibrous cellulosic material; waste and scrap of paper or paperboard; paper and paperboard and articles thereof | .. | .. | .. | .. | 0.7 | 0.9 | X - Бумажная масса, бумажные и картонные отходы, макулатура, бумага, картон и изделия из них |
| XI - Textiles and textile articles | .. | .. | .. | .. | 1,601.8 | 1,930.7 | XI - Текстиль и текстильные изделия |
| XII - Footwear, headgear, umbrellas, sun umbrellas, walking sticks, seat sticks, whips, riding crops and parts thereof; prepared feathers and articles made therewith; artificial flowers; articles of human hair | .. | .. | .. | .. | 1.6 | 0.4 | XII - Обувь, головные уборы, зонты, трости и пр. |

## TABLE 3-3A. Exports by commodity group (millions of U.S. dollars)
## ТАБЛИЦА 3-3A. Экспорт по товарным группам (млн. долларов США)

| Commodity group | 1990 | 1991 | 1992 | 1993 | 1994 | 1995 | Товарные группы |
|---|---|---|---|---|---|---|---|
| XIII - Articles of stone, plaster, cement, asbestos, mica and similar materials; ceramic products; glass and glassware | .. | .. | .. | .. | 10.2 | 3.5 | XIII - Изделия из камня, гипса, цемента |
| XIV - Natural or cultured pearls, precious or semi-precious stones, precious metals, metals clad with precious metal and articles thereof; imitation jewellery; coin | .. | .. | .. | .. | 4.1 | 9.1 | XIV - Жемчуг, драгоценные и полудрагоценные камни, драгоценные металлы, бижутерия, монеты |
| XV - Base metals and articles of base metal | .. | .. | .. | .. | 108.6 | 175.9 | XV - Неблагородные металлы и изделия из них |
| XVI - Machinery and mechanical appliances; electrical equipment; parts thereof; sound recorders and reproducers, television image and sound recorders and reproducers, and parts and accessories of such articles | .. | .. | .. | .. | 112.5 | 41.8 | XVI - Машины, оборудование, механизмы, их части и принадлежности; звуковая и теле-аппаратура, их части и принадлежности |
| XVII - Vehicles, aircraft, vessels and associated transport equipment | .. | .. | .. | .. | 105.7 | 33.5 | XVII - Средства наземного, воздушного и водного транспорта |
| XVIII - Optical, photographic, cinematographic, measuring, checking, precision, medical or surgical instruments and apparatus; clocks and watches; musical instruments; parts and accessories thereof | .. | .. | .. | .. | 0.7 | 0.8 | XVIII - Приборы, аппараты оптические, медицинские, измерительные и пр.; музыкальные инструменты; часы; их части и принадлежности |
| XIX - Arms and ammunition; parts and accessories thereof | .. | .. | .. | .. | .. | .. | XIX - Оружие и боеприпасы, их части и принадлежности |
| XX - Miscellaneous manufactured articles | .. | .. | .. | .. | 4.3 | 4.2 | XX - Разные промышленные товары |
| XXI - Works of art, collectors' pieces, and antiques | .. | .. | .. | .. | .. | .. | XXI - Произведения искусства, предметы антиквариата |
| XXII - Services | .. | .. | .. | .. | 141.0 | 287.7 | XXII - Услуги |

**TABLE 3-3B. Exports by Commodity Group (millions of national currency)**
**ТАБЛИЦА 3-3В. Экспорт по товарным группам (млн. национальной валюты)**

| Commodity group | 1990 | 1991 | 1992 | 1993 | 1994 | 1995 | Товарные группы |
|---|---|---|---|---|---|---|---|
| TOTAL | .. | .. | .. | .. | 30,310.9 | 95,628.9 | ВСЕГО |
| I - Live animals; animal products | .. | .. | .. | .. | 3.7 | 8.4 | I - Живые животные и продукты животноводства |
| II - Vegetable products | .. | .. | .. | .. | 438.5 | 1,001.9 | II - Продукты растительного происхождения |
| III - Animal or vegetable fats and oils and their cleavage products; prepared edible fats; animal or vegetable waxes | .. | .. | .. | .. | 131.5 | 443.3 | III - Жиры и масла растительного и животного происхождения, воски |
| IV - Prepared foodstuffs; beverages, spirits and vinegar; tobacco and manufactured tobacco substitutes | .. | .. | .. | .. | 359.6 | 976.2 | IV -Продукция пищевой промышленности, алкогольные и безалкогольные напитки, табак и его заменители |
| V - Mineral products | .. | .. | .. | .. | 6,150.6 | 12,879.8 | V - Минеральные продукты |
| VI - Products of the chemical or allied industries | .. | .. | .. | .. | 691.1 | 2,549.6 | VI - Продукция химической промышленности |
| VII - Plastics and articles thereof; rubber and articles thereof | .. | .. | .. | .. | 140.6 | 172.5 | VII - Пластмассы и изделия из них |
| VIII - Raw hides and skins, leather, furskins and articles thereof; saddlery and harness; travel goods, handbags and similar containers; articles of animal gut | .. | .. | .. | .. | 44.3 | 98.9 | VIII - Кожевенное сырьё, кожи, пушнина, меховое сырьё и изделия из них |
| IX - Wood and articles of wood; wood charcoal; cork and articles of cork; manufactures of straw, of esparto or of other plaiting materials; basketware and wickerwork | .. | .. | .. | .. | 0.2 | 0.6 | IX - Древесина и изделия из древесины, древесный уголь |
| X - Pulp of wood or of other fibrous cellulosic material; waste and scrap of paper or paperboard; paper and paperboard and articles thereof | .. | .. | .. | .. | 6.3 | 27.2 | X - Бумажная масса, бумажные и картонные отходы, макулатура, бумага, картон и изделия из них |
| XI - Textiles and textile articles | .. | .. | .. | .. | 18,367.8 | 60,279.7 | XI - Текстиль и текстильные изделия |
| XII - Footwear, headgear, umbrellas, sun umbrellas, walking sticks, seat sticks, whips, riding crops and parts thereof; prepared feathers and articles made therewith; artificial flowers; articles of human hair | .. | .. | .. | .. | 11.3 | 10.5 | XII - Обувь, головные уборы, зонты, трости и пр. |

**TABLE 3-3B. Exports by Commodity Group (millions of national currency)**
**ТАБЛИЦА 3-3B. Экспорт по товарным группам (млн. национальной валюты)**

| Commodity group | 1990 | 1991 | 1992 | 1993 | 1994 | 1995 | Товарные группы |
|---|---|---|---|---|---|---|---|
| XIII - Articles of stone, plaster, cement, asbestos, mica and similar materials; ceramic products; glass and glassware | .. | .. | .. | .. | 79.2 | 104.6 | XIII - Изделия из камня, гипса, цемента |
| XIV - Natural or cultured pearls, precious or semi-precious stones, precious metals, metals clad with precious metal and articles thereof; imitation jewellery; coin | .. | .. | .. | .. | 26.2 | 285.6 | XIV - Жемчуг, драгоценные и полудрагоценные камни, драгоценные металлы, бижутерия, монеты |
| XV - Base metals and articles of base metal | .. | .. | .. | .. | 1,205.6 | 5,367.4 | XV - Неблагородные металлы и изделия из них |
| XVI - Machinery and mechanical appliances; electrical equipment; parts thereof; sound recorders and reproducers, television image and sound recorders and reproducers, and parts and accessories of such articles | .. | .. | .. | .. | 835.4 | 1,308.9 | XVI - Машины, оборудование, механизмы, их части и принадлежности; звуковая и теле-аппаратура, их части и принадлежности |
| XVII - Vehicles, aircraft, vessels and associated transport equipment | .. | .. | .. | .. | 479.5 | 974.7 | XVII - Средства наземного, воздушного и водного транспорта |
| XVIII - Optical, photographic, cinematographic, measuring, checking, precision, medical or surgical instruments and apparatus; clocks and watches; musical instruments; parts and accessories thereof | .. | .. | .. | .. | 4.9 | 25.4 | XVIII - Приборы, аппараты оптические, медицинские, измерительные и пр.; музыкальные инструменты; часы; их части и принадлежности |
| XIX - Arms and ammunition; parts and accessories thereof | .. | .. | .. | .. | .. | .. | XIX - Оружие и боеприпасы, их части и принадлежности |
| XX - Miscellaneous manufactured articles | .. | .. | .. | .. | 43.1 | 114.7 | XX - Разные промышленные товары |
| XXI - Works of art, collectors' pieces, and antiques | .. | .. | .. | .. | .. | .. | XXI - Произведения искусства, предметы антиквариата |
| XXII - Services | .. | .. | .. | .. | 1,291.5 | 8,999.0 | XXII - Услуги |

**TABLE 3-4A. Geographical distribution of foreign trade (millions of U.S. dollars)**
**ТАБЛИЦА 3-4А. Географическое распределение внешней торговли (млн. долларов США)**

| Country or country group | Exports Экспорт 1990 | 1991 | 1992 | 1993 | 1994 | 1995 | Imports Импорт 1990 | 1991 | 1992 | 1993 | 1994 | 1995 | Страна или группа стран |
|---|---|---|---|---|---|---|---|---|---|---|---|---|---|
| **Total trade** | .. | .. | .. | .. | 2,689.9 | 3,109.0 | .. | .. | .. | .. | 2,609.5 | 2,892.7 | **Всего** |
| **CIS countries** | .. | .. | .. | .. | 1,660.3 | 1,282.5 | .. | .. | .. | .. | 1,401.2 | 1,258.7 | **Страны СНГ** |
| Armenia | .. | .. | .. | .. | .. | 0.1 | .. | .. | .. | .. | 0.1 | 0.1 | Армения |
| Azerbaijan | .. | .. | .. | .. | 1.2 | 4.0 | .. | .. | .. | .. | 0.6 | 1.2 | Азербайджан |
| Belarus | .. | .. | .. | .. | 37.2 | 31.7 | .. | .. | .. | .. | 11.6 | 50.0 | Беларусь |
| Georgia | .. | .. | .. | .. | 0.4 | 0.9 | .. | .. | .. | .. | 0.3 | 0.5 | Грузия |
| Kazakstan | .. | .. | .. | .. | 370.0 | 238.1 | .. | .. | .. | .. | 148.5 | 217.8 | Казахстан |
| Kyrgyz Republic | .. | .. | .. | .. | 77.5 | 68.3 | .. | .. | .. | .. | 25.9 | 34.1 | Киргизстан |
| Moldova | .. | .. | .. | .. | 1.4 | 3.1 | .. | .. | .. | .. | 0.7 | 1.9 | Молдова |
| Russia | .. | .. | .. | .. | 476.5 | 584.8 | .. | .. | .. | .. | 764.0 | 720.0 | Россия |
| Tajikistan | .. | .. | .. | .. | 410.7 | 156.1 | .. | .. | .. | .. | 307.2 | 73.0 | Таджикистан |
| Turkmenistan | .. | .. | .. | .. | 99.3 | 150.4 | .. | .. | .. | .. | 95.7 | 98.7 | Туркменистан |
| Ukraine | .. | .. | .. | .. | 186.1 | 45.0 | .. | .. | .. | .. | 46.6 | 61.4 | Украина |
| Uzbekistan | .. | .. | .. | .. | .. | .. | .. | .. | .. | .. | .. | .. | Узбекистан |
| **Non-CIS countries** | .. | .. | .. | .. | 1,030.0 | 1,827.0 | .. | .. | .. | .. | 1,208.3 | 1,634.0 | **Остальной мир** |
| **Europe** | .. | .. | .. | .. | 615.7 | 726.6 | .. | .. | .. | .. | 490.1 | 778.2 | **Европа** |
| Austria | .. | .. | .. | .. | 41.6 | 41.1 | .. | .. | .. | .. | 27.0 | 10.1 | Австрия |
| Belgium | .. | .. | .. | .. | 7.5 | 0.3 | .. | .. | .. | .. | 15.2 | 4.3 | Бельгия |
| Bulgaria | .. | .. | .. | .. | 8.0 | 13.0 | .. | .. | .. | .. | 2.9 | 6.3 | Болгария |
| Czech Republic | .. | .. | .. | .. | 3.0 | 1.8 | .. | .. | .. | .. | 16.2 | 33.4 | Чешская Республика |
| Denmark | .. | .. | .. | .. | 2.9 | 2.3 | .. | .. | .. | .. | 1.7 | 9.9 | Дания |
| Estonia | .. | .. | .. | .. | 0.5 | 9.3 | .. | .. | .. | .. | 0.2 | 1.0 | Эстония |
| Finland | .. | .. | .. | .. | 0.3 | .. | .. | .. | .. | .. | 1.5 | 1.1 | Финляндия |
| Former Yugoslavia | .. | .. | .. | .. | .. | .. | .. | .. | .. | .. | .. | 0.1 | Быв. Югославия |
| France | .. | .. | .. | .. | 1.2 | 0.6 | .. | .. | .. | .. | 11.2 | 15.5 | Франция |
| Germany | .. | .. | .. | .. | 32.4 | 35.8 | .. | .. | .. | .. | 176.8 | 374.7 | Германия |
| Hungary | .. | .. | .. | .. | 1.5 | 1.9 | .. | .. | .. | .. | 87.5 | 145.6 | Венгрия |
| Iceland | .. | .. | .. | .. | .. | .. | .. | .. | .. | .. | .. | .. | Исландия |
| Ireland | .. | .. | .. | .. | .. | 0.8 | .. | .. | .. | .. | 1.1 | 1.5 | Ирландия |
| Italy | .. | .. | .. | .. | 26.4 | 80.9 | .. | .. | .. | .. | 23.7 | 22.1 | Италия |
| Latvia | .. | .. | .. | .. | 6.6 | 15.1 | .. | .. | .. | .. | 6.5 | 3.7 | Латвия |
| Lithuania | .. | .. | .. | .. | 16.1 | 10.4 | .. | .. | .. | .. | 7.7 | 28.4 | Литва |
| Netherlands | .. | .. | .. | .. | 153.0 | 156.8 | .. | .. | .. | .. | 51.9 | 35.5 | Нидерланды |
| Norway | .. | .. | .. | .. | .. | .. | .. | .. | .. | .. | .. | .. | Норвегия |
| Poland | .. | .. | .. | .. | 21.5 | 27.1 | .. | .. | .. | .. | 17.3 | 4.5 | Польша |
| Romania | .. | .. | .. | .. | 0.3 | 4.6 | .. | .. | .. | .. | .. | 10.0 | Румыния |
| Slovak Republic | .. | .. | .. | .. | 1.4 | 6.7 | .. | .. | .. | .. | 0.3 | 1.8 | Словацкая Республика |
| Spain | .. | .. | .. | .. | 1.0 | 1.3 | .. | .. | .. | .. | .. | 0.7 | Испания |
| Sweden | .. | .. | .. | .. | .. | .. | .. | .. | .. | .. | 12.3 | 2.8 | Швеция |
| Switzerland | .. | .. | .. | .. | 102.3 | 74.0 | .. | .. | .. | .. | 6.3 | 26.0 | Швейцария |
| United Kingdom | .. | .. | .. | .. | 175.0 | 236.6 | .. | .. | .. | .. | 18.1 | 27.9 | Великобритания |

**TABLE 3-4A. Geographical distribution of foreign trade (millions of U.S. dollars)**
**ТАБЛИЦА 3-4A. Географическое распределение внешней торговли (млн. долларов США)**

| Country or country group | Exports Экспорт 1990 | 1991 | 1992 | 1993 | 1994 | 1995 | Imports Импорт 1990 | 1991 | 1992 | 1993 | 1994 | 1995 | Страна или группа стран |
|---|---|---|---|---|---|---|---|---|---|---|---|---|---|
| Other Europe | .. | .. | .. | .. | 13.2 | 6.2 | .. | .. | .. | .. | 4.7 | 12.0 | Остальные страны Европы |
| **Asia** | .. | .. | .. | .. | 255.9 | 352.1 | .. | .. | .. | .. | 273.0 | 723.8 | **Азия** |
| Afghanistan | .. | .. | .. | .. | 4.2 | 17.2 | .. | .. | .. | .. | 0.4 | 1.4 | Афганистан |
| China | .. | .. | .. | .. | 77.0 | 35.5 | .. | .. | .. | .. | 88.1 | 23.4 | Китай |
| India | .. | .. | .. | .. | 4.2 | 5.1 | .. | .. | .. | .. | 4.1 | 13.9 | Индия |
| Iraq | .. | .. | .. | .. | .. | .. | .. | .. | .. | .. | .. | .. | Ирак |
| Japan | .. | .. | .. | .. | 5.2 | 1.6 | .. | .. | .. | .. | 23.7 | 44.8 | Япония |
| Korea, Dem. People's Rep. | .. | .. | .. | .. | 2.7 | 0.7 | .. | .. | .. | .. | 2.0 | 0.5 | КНДР |
| Korea, Rep. of | .. | .. | .. | .. | 40.1 | 146.8 | .. | .. | .. | .. | 26.4 | 429.6 | Южная Корея |
| Mongolia | .. | .. | .. | .. | 0.3 | 0.1 | .. | .. | .. | .. | .. | .. | МНР |
| Syrian Arab Republic | .. | .. | .. | .. | 0.9 | 0.1 | .. | .. | .. | .. | .. | 25.2 | Сирия |
| Turkey | .. | .. | .. | .. | 42.4 | 109.7 | .. | .. | .. | .. | 67.5 | 85.6 | Турция |
| Viet Nam | .. | .. | .. | .. | .. | 0.3 | .. | .. | .. | .. | .. | .. | Вьетнам |
| Other Asia | .. | .. | .. | .. | 78.9 | 35.0 | .. | .. | .. | .. | 60.8 | 99.4 | Остальные страны Азии |
| **America** | .. | .. | .. | .. | 21.2 | 16.4 | .. | .. | .. | .. | 101.5 | 33.2 | **Сев. и Южная Америка** |
| Canada | .. | .. | .. | .. | .. | .. | .. | .. | .. | .. | 6.8 | 2.7 | Канада |
| Cuba | .. | .. | .. | .. | 0.1 | 0.1 | .. | .. | .. | .. | .. | .. | Куба |
| United States | .. | .. | .. | .. | 20.7 | 12.7 | .. | .. | .. | .. | 94.6 | 30.4 | США |
| Other America | .. | .. | .. | .. | 0.4 | 3.6 | .. | .. | .. | .. | 0.1 | 0.1 | Остальные |
| **Africa** | .. | .. | .. | .. | 1.3 | 0.3 | .. | .. | .. | .. | 0.3 | 2.4 | **Африка** |
| Egypt | .. | .. | .. | .. | 0.3 | .. | .. | .. | .. | .. | 0.3 | 0.1 | Египет |
| Libya | .. | .. | .. | .. | .. | .. | .. | .. | .. | .. | .. | .. | Ливия |
| Other Africa | .. | .. | .. | .. | 1.0 | 0.3 | .. | .. | .. | .. | .. | 2.4 | Остальные |
| **Rest of the World** | .. | .. | .. | .. | 135.5 | 731.1 | .. | .. | .. | .. | 343.4 | 96.4 | **Прочие страны мира** |
| Australia | .. | .. | .. | .. | .. | .. | .. | .. | .. | .. | 24.4 | 3.1 | Австралия |

## TABLE 3-4B. Geographical distribution of foreign trade (millions of national currency)

## ТАБЛИЦА 3-4B. Географическое распределение внешней торговли (миллионов национальной валюты)

| Country or country group | Exports / Экспорт 1990 | 1991 | 1992 | 1993 | 1994 | 1995 | Imports / Импорт 1990 | 1991 | 1992 | 1993 | 1994 | 1995 | Страна или группа стран |
|---|---|---|---|---|---|---|---|---|---|---|---|---|---|
| **Total trade** | .. | .. | .. | .. | 30,310.9 | 95,628.9 | .. | .. | .. | .. | 27,975.4 | 86,814.3 | **Всего** |
| **CIS countries** | .. | .. | .. | .. | 15,870.2 | 38,953.9 | .. | .. | .. | .. | 12,194.9 | 38,083.6 | **Страны СНГ** |
| Armenia | .. | .. | .. | .. | 0.3 | 2.4 | .. | .. | .. | .. | 1.5 | 2.3 | Армения |
| Azerbaijan | .. | .. | .. | .. | 9.1 | 121.1 | .. | .. | .. | .. | 6.5 | 36.6 | Азербайджан |
| Belarus | .. | .. | .. | .. | 299.6 | 1,019.4 | .. | .. | .. | .. | 90.6 | 1,504.9 | Беларусь |
| Georgia | .. | .. | .. | .. | 3.7 | 28.7 | .. | .. | .. | .. | 2.2 | 13.4 | Грузия |
| Kazakstan | .. | .. | .. | .. | 2,781.9 | 6,239.7 | .. | .. | .. | .. | 1,359.3 | 6,580.1 | Казахстан |
| Kyrgyz Republic | .. | .. | .. | .. | 600.7 | 2,064.8 | .. | .. | .. | .. | 199.7 | 1,059.2 | Киргизстан |
| Moldova | .. | .. | .. | .. | 12.2 | 103.9 | .. | .. | .. | .. | 7.3 | 55.7 | Молдова |
| Russia | .. | .. | .. | .. | 6,875.9 | 18,406.3 | .. | .. | .. | .. | 6,811.1 | 21,754.0 | Россия |
| Tajikistan | .. | .. | .. | .. | 3,048.5 | 4,957.7 | .. | .. | .. | .. | 2,335.9 | 2,326.0 | Таджикистан |
| Turkmenistan | .. | .. | .. | .. | 797.1 | 4,643.1 | .. | .. | .. | .. | 744.5 | 2,982.0 | Туркменистан |
| Ukraine | .. | .. | .. | .. | 1,441.2 | 1,366.8 | .. | .. | .. | .. | 636.3 | 1,769.4 | Украина |
| Uzbekistan | .. | .. | .. | .. | .. | .. | .. | .. | .. | .. | .. | .. | Узбекистан |
| **Non-CIS countries** | .. | .. | .. | .. | 14,441.0 | 56,675.0 | .. | .. | .. | .. | 15,781.0 | 48,731.0 | **Остальной мир** |
| **Europe** | .. | .. | .. | .. | 10,938.1 | 32,232.7 | .. | .. | .. | .. | 11,472.4 | 24,277.2 | **Европа** |
| Austria | .. | .. | .. | .. | 674.3 | 1,310.9 | .. | .. | .. | .. | 181.3 | 294.4 | Австрия |
| Belgium | .. | .. | .. | .. | 127.9 | 7.8 | .. | .. | .. | .. | 139.5 | 120.6 | Бельгия |
| Bulgaria | .. | .. | .. | .. | 106.3 | 428.0 | .. | .. | .. | .. | 30.3 | 190.8 | Болгария |
| Czech Republic | .. | .. | .. | .. | 48.3 | 57.2 | .. | .. | .. | .. | 237.4 | 910.0 | Чешская Республика |
| Denmark | .. | .. | .. | .. | 50.9 | 67.4 | .. | .. | .. | .. | 8.5 | 317.0 | Дания |
| Estonia | .. | .. | .. | .. | 4.7 | 310.4 | .. | .. | .. | .. | 2.2 | 29.9 | Эстония |
| Finland | .. | .. | .. | .. | 4.0 | 0.7 | .. | .. | .. | .. | 11.7 | 35.2 | Финляндия |
| Former Yugoslavia | .. | .. | .. | .. | .. | .. | .. | .. | .. | .. | .. | 2.5 | Быв. Югославия |
| France | .. | .. | .. | .. | 10.3 | 16.4 | .. | .. | .. | .. | 196.7 | 420.3 | Франция |
| Germany | .. | .. | .. | .. | 589.6 | 1,129.7 | .. | .. | .. | .. | 2,598.7 | 11,473.6 | Германия |
| Hungary | .. | .. | .. | .. | 10.5 | 58.8 | .. | .. | .. | .. | 1,326.9 | 2,828.1 | Венгрия |
| Iceland | .. | .. | .. | .. | .. | 1.2 | .. | .. | .. | .. | .. | .. | Исландия |
| Ireland | .. | .. | .. | .. | .. | 24.8 | .. | .. | .. | .. | 15.8 | 38.8 | Ирландия |
| Italy | .. | .. | .. | .. | 426.7 | 2,500.5 | .. | .. | .. | .. | 262.9 | 664.3 | Италия |
| Latvia | .. | .. | .. | .. | 68.0 | 540.9 | .. | .. | .. | .. | 53.8 | 118.4 | Латвия |
| Lithuania | .. | .. | .. | .. | 114.3 | 275.4 | .. | .. | .. | .. | 134.3 | 892.4 | Литва |
| Netherlands | .. | .. | .. | .. | 2,605.0 | 4,721.2 | .. | .. | .. | .. | 725.8 | 1,022.2 | Нидерланды |
| Norway | .. | .. | .. | .. | .. | 0.1 | .. | .. | .. | .. | .. | .. | Норвегия |
| Poland | .. | .. | .. | .. | 260.1 | 836.6 | .. | .. | .. | .. | 280.3 | 124.9 | Польша |
| Romania | .. | .. | .. | .. | 2.0 | 128.5 | .. | .. | .. | .. | 106.4 | 344.0 | Румыния |
| Slovak Republic | .. | .. | .. | .. | 14.9 | 217.4 | .. | .. | .. | .. | 2.7 | 56.9 | Словацская Республика |
| Spain | .. | .. | .. | .. | 15.8 | 42.3 | .. | .. | .. | .. | 0.3 | 22.3 | Испания |
| Sweden | .. | .. | .. | .. | 0.2 | .. | .. | .. | .. | .. | 133.8 | 87.0 | Швеция |
| Switzerland | .. | .. | .. | .. | 2,896.1 | 12,592.8 | .. | .. | .. | .. | 4,798.5 | 3,037.8 | Швейцария |

## TABLE 3-4B. Geographical distribution of foreign trade (millions of national currency)

## ТАБЛИЦА 3-4B. Географическое распределение внешней торговли (миллионов национальной валюты)

| Country or country group | Exports Экспорт 1990 | 1991 | 1992 | 1993 | 1994 | 1995 | Imports Импорт 1990 | 1991 | 1992 | 1993 | 1994 | 1995 | Страна или группа стран |
|---|---|---|---|---|---|---|---|---|---|---|---|---|---|
| United Kingdom | .. | .. | .. | .. | 2,724.9 | 6,786.9 | .. | .. | .. | .. | 186.3 | 878.1 | Великобритания |
| Other Europe | .. | .. | .. | .. | 183.3 | 176.8 | .. | .. | .. | .. | 38.3 | 367.7 | Остальные страны Европы |
| **Asia** | .. | .. | .. | .. | 3,068.0 | 10,911.1 | .. | .. | .. | .. | 3,075.0 | 23,273.9 | **Азия** |
| Afghanistan | .. | .. | .. | .. | 59.8 | 511.9 | .. | .. | .. | .. | 4.4 | 41.1 | Афганистан |
| China | .. | .. | .. | .. | 195.0 | 1,132.3 | .. | .. | .. | .. | 844.4 | 477.3 | Китай |
| India | .. | .. | .. | .. | 46.9 | 149.1 | .. | .. | .. | .. | 85.1 | 369.5 | Индия |
| Iraq | .. | .. | .. | .. | .. | .. | .. | .. | .. | .. | .. | .. | Ирак |
| Japan | .. | .. | .. | .. | 116.8 | 53.8 | .. | .. | .. | .. | 205.2 | 1,334.0 | Япония |
| Korea, Dem. People's Rep. | .. | .. | .. | .. | 50.3 | 25.4 | .. | .. | .. | .. | 7.0 | 12.8 | КНДР |
| Korea, Rep. of | .. | .. | .. | .. | 490.2 | 4,601.8 | .. | .. | .. | .. | 338.8 | 14,527.8 | Южная Корея |
| Mongolia | .. | .. | .. | .. | 2.1 | 4.2 | .. | .. | .. | .. | 0.5 | 0.3 | МНР |
| Syrian Arab Republic | .. | .. | .. | .. | 6.6 | .. | .. | .. | .. | .. | .. | .. | Сирия |
| Turkey | .. | .. | .. | .. | 628.2 | 3,290.1 | .. | .. | .. | .. | 796.7 | 2,703.5 | Турция |
| Viet Nam | .. | .. | .. | .. | 0.4 | 9.5 | .. | .. | .. | .. | .. | .. | Вьетнам |
| Other Asia | .. | .. | .. | .. | 1,471.7 | 1,133.0 | .. | .. | .. | .. | 792.9 | 3,807.6 | Остальные страны Азии |
| **America** | .. | .. | .. | .. | 297.7 | 386.7 | .. | .. | .. | .. | 1,048.7 | 1,020.9 | **Сев. и Южная Америка** |
| Canada | .. | .. | .. | .. | .. | 0.1 | .. | .. | .. | .. | 58.7 | 83.0 | Канада |
| Cuba | .. | .. | .. | .. | .. | .. | .. | .. | .. | .. | .. | .. | Куба |
| United States | .. | .. | .. | .. | 294.1 | 378.1 | .. | .. | .. | .. | 989.0 | 936.9 | США |
| Other America | .. | .. | .. | .. | 3.6 | 8.5 | .. | .. | .. | .. | 1.0 | 1.0 | Остальные |
| **Africa** | .. | .. | .. | .. | 3.8 | 5.4 | .. | .. | .. | .. | 0.8 | 78.3 | **Африка** |
| Egypt | .. | .. | .. | .. | 3.8 | 0.4 | .. | .. | .. | .. | 0.8 | 2.2 | Египет |
| Libya | .. | .. | .. | .. | .. | .. | .. | .. | .. | .. | .. | .. | Ливия |
| Other Africa | .. | .. | .. | .. | .. | 5.0 | .. | .. | .. | .. | .. | 76.1 | Остальные |
| **Rest of the World** | .. | .. | .. | .. | 133.1 | 13,139.1 | .. | .. | .. | .. | 183.6 | 80.4 | **Прочие страны мира** |
| Australia | .. | .. | .. | .. | .. | 0.5 | .. | .. | .. | .. | 178.0 | 80.2 | Австралия |

## TABLE 4-1. General government budget revenue (millions of national currency)
## ТАБЛИЦА 4-1. Доходы государственного бюджета (млн. национальной валюты)

| Type of revenue | 1990 | 1991 | 1992 | 1993 | 1994 | 1995 | Вид доходов |
|---|---|---|---|---|---|---|---|
| **Total revenue and grants** | .. | .. | .. | .. | .. | .. | **Всего доходов и безвозм. поступл.** |
| Grants | .. | .. | .. | .. | .. | .. | Безвозмездные поступления |
| Total Revenue | 15.4 | 29.8 | 142.7 | 1,843.2 | 18,935.9 | 90,291.0 | Всего доходов |
| **Current revenue** | .. | .. | .. | .. | .. | .. | **Текущие доходы** |
| Tax revenue | 7.9 | 10.9 | 117.1 | 1,214.9 | 16,083.1 | 84,596.9 | Доход от налогов |
| Taxes on income and profits | 1.6 | 3.5 | 22.5 | 381.5 | 3,970.6 | 25,808.8 | Налоги на доходы и прибыль |
| Individual | .. | .. | .. | .. | .. | .. | Физические лица |
| Corporate | .. | .. | .. | .. | .. | .. | Предприятия и организации |
| Social security contributions | 1.1 | 0.0 | .. | 73.1 | 530.0 | .. | Отчисление на соцстрах. |
| Taxes on payroll or work force | .. | .. | .. | .. | .. | .. | Налоги на заработную плату и рабочую силу |
| Taxes on the use of labor force | .. | .. | .. | .. | .. | .. | Плата за трудовые ресурсы |
| Taxes on increases in wages and salaries | .. | .. | .. | .. | .. | .. | Налог с прироста средств на оплату труда |
| Other payroll/work force taxes | .. | .. | .. | .. | .. | .. | Другие налоги на зарплату и рабочую силу |
| Taxes on property | 0.3 | .. | 0.4 | 10.2 | 0.1 | .. | Налоги на собственность |
| Taxes on immovable property | .. | .. | .. | .. | .. | .. | Налоги на недвижимое имущество |
| Buildings | 0.0 | 0.0 | 0.0 | 0.2 | .. | .. | Налог с владельцев строении |
| Land | .. | 0.0 | 0.0 | 0.1 | 0.1 | .. | Земельныи налог |
| Estate, inheritance, and gift taxes | .. | .. | .. | .. | .. | .. | Налоги на наследство, подарки |
| Other property taxes | .. | .. | .. | 10.2 | 100.0 | .. | Другие налоги на имущество |
| Domestic taxes on goods and services | 4.0 | 5.8 | 73.7 | 527.0 | 7.9 | .. | Внутренние налоги на товары и услуги |
| General sales, turnover, or value-added taxes | 4.0 | 5.8 | 38.5 | 477.1 | 3.2 | .. | Налог с продаж. с оборота или на добав. стоим. |
| Excises | .. | .. | .. | .. | .. | .. | Акцизы |
| Profits of fiscal monopolies | .. | .. | .. | .. | .. | .. | Прибыли фискальных монополий |
| Taxes on specific services | .. | .. | .. | .. | .. | .. | Налоги на особые услуги |
| Taxes on use of goods or permission to use goods or to perform activities | .. | .. | .. | .. | .. | .. | Налоги на пользование товарами или лицензии на пользование товарами и занятие деятельностью |
| Other taxes on goods and services | .. | .. | .. | 5.0 | .. | .. | Другие налоги на товары и услуги |
| Taxes on international trade and transactions | 0.0 | 0.2 | 0.4 | 13.9 | 0.8 | 2,808.1 | Налоги на внешнюю торговлю и операции |
| Import duties | .. | .. | 0.1 | 5.4 | .. | 164.1 | Импортные пошлины |
| Export duties | .. | .. | 0.2 | 8.4 | 0.6 | 2,159.6 | Экпортные пошлины |
| Other | .. | .. | 0.1 | 0.2 | 0.2 | 484.4 | Другие |
| Other taxes | .. | .. | .. | .. | .. | .. | Прочие налоги |
| Nontax revenue | 0.2 | 2.7 | 9.7 | 65.6 | 1.2 | 2,229.6 | Неналоговые доходы |
| **Capital revenue** | .. | .. | .. | .. | .. | .. | **Капитальные доходы** |

**TABLE 4-2. General government budget expenditure by economic type (millions of national currency)**
**ТАБЛИЦА 4-2. Расходы государственного бюджета по экономическим типам (млн. национальной валюты)**

| Type of expenditure or debt holder | 1990 | 1991 | 1992 | 1993 | 1994 | 1995 | Всего расходов |
|---|---|---|---|---|---|---|---|
| **Total expenditure by economic type** | .. | .. | .. | .. | .. | .. | **Всего расходов по экономическим типам** |
| **Current expenditure** | 15.1 | 32.4 | 193.9 | 1,995.3 | 21,619.6 | 98,582.4 | **Текущие расходы** |
| Expenditure on goods and services | .. | .. | .. | .. | .. | .. | Расходы на товары и услуги |
| Wages and salaries | .. | .. | .. | .. | .. | .. | Заработная плата |
| Employer contributions | .. | .. | .. | .. | .. | .. | Отчисление на социальное страхование |
| Other Purchases of goods and services | .. | .. | .. | .. | .. | .. | Другие покупки товаров и услуг |
| Interest payments | .. | .. | .. | .. | .. | .. | Выплаты процентов |
| Domestic debt | .. | .. | .. | .. | .. | .. | По внутреннему долгу |
| Foreign debt | .. | .. | .. | .. | .. | .. | По внешнщму долгу |
| Subsidies and other current transfers | .. | .. | .. | .. | .. | .. | Субсидии на другие текущие трансферты |
| Subsidies | 3.1 | 5.3 | 2.9 | 51.5 | 216.1 | 513.0 | Субсидии |
| Agricultural subsidies | .. | .. | .. | .. | .. | .. | Субсидии на сельское хозяиство |
| Other current transfers | .. | .. | .. | .. | .. | .. | Другие текущие трансферты |
| Other | 0.3 | 7.5 | 29.4 | 310.4 | 4,933.0 | 10,994.2 | Прочие расходы |
| **Capital expenditure** | .. | .. | .. | .. | .. | .. | **Капитальные расходы** |
| Acquisition of fixed capital assets | .. | .. | .. | .. | .. | .. | Приобретение основного капитала |
| Capital transfers | .. | .. | .. | .. | .. | .. | Капитальные трансферты |
| Other | .. | .. | .. | .. | .. | .. | Другие капитальные расходы |
| **Surplus/deficit (-)** | 0.3 | -2.1 | -48.4 | -152.1 | -2,683.6 | -8,291.5 | **Превыш. доходов над расходами/дефицит(-)** |
| **Financing by type of debt holder** | .. | .. | .. | .. | .. | .. | **Финансирование по типам кредиторов** |
| **Foreign (net)** | .. | .. | .. | .. | .. | .. | **Зарубежные кредиторы (сальдо)** |
| From international development institutions | .. | .. | .. | .. | .. | .. | Международные организации |
| From foreign governments | .. | .. | .. | .. | .. | .. | Правительства иностранных государств |
| Other borrowing abroad | .. | .. | .. | .. | .. | .. | Другие зарубежные кредиторы |
| **Domestic (net)** | .. | .. | .. | .. | .. | .. | **Внутренние кредиторы (сальдо)** |
| From monetary authorities | .. | .. | .. | .. | .. | .. | Органы денежного обращения |
| From deposit money banks | .. | .. | .. | .. | .. | .. | Депозитные денежные банки |
| Other domestic borrowing | .. | .. | .. | .. | .. | .. | Другие внутренние кредиторы |
| *Memo items:* | | | | | | | *Справочно:* |
| Extrabudgetary surplus/ Deficit (-) not included above | .. | .. | .. | .. | .. | .. | Превышение доходов над расходами/дефицит (-) по внебюджетным фондам, не включенным выше |
| Total surplus/deficit (-) including extrabudgetary accounts | .. | .. | .. | .. | .. | .. | Итого превышение доходов над расходами/дефицит, включая счета внебюджетных фондов |

## TABLE 5-2. Agricultural production (millions of constant national currency)
## ТАБЛИЦА 5-2. Сельскохозяйственная продукция в постоянных ценах (млн. национальной валюты)

| Item | 1990 | 1991 | 1992 | 1993 | 1994 | 1995 | Статьи |
|---|---|---|---|---|---|---|---|
| **Total gross agricultural production** | 11,114 | 10,994 | 10,291 | 10,425 | 9,665 | 9,879 | **Валовая продукция сельского хозяйства - всего** |
| **Crops** | 7,044 | 6,672 | 6,210 | 6,152 | 5,649 | 5,966 | **Продукция растениеводства** |
| Grains | 364 | 368 | 413 | 404 | 423 | 555 | Зерно |
| Potatoes | 1,063 | 67 | 70 | 90 | 108 | 84 | Картофель |
| Vegetables | .. | 1,102 | 1,139 | 958 | 937 | 908 | Овощи |
| Fruits (excluding grapes) | .. | .. | .. | .. | .. | .. | Фрукты (без винограда) |
| Grapes | 748 | 547 | 641 | 525 | 512 | 667 | Виноград |
| Tobacco | .. | .. | .. | .. | .. | .. | Табак |
| Cotton | 4,240 | 3,854 | 3,355 | 3,373 | 3,109 | 3,107 | Хлопок |
| Sugarbeets | .. | .. | .. | .. | .. | .. | Сахарная свекла |
| Oilseeds | .. | .. | .. | .. | .. | .. | Семена масличных культур |
| Other | .. | .. | .. | .. | .. | .. | Прочие |
| **Animal husbandry** | 4,070 | 4,322 | 4,080 | 4,274 | 4,016 | 3,913 | **Продукция животноводства** |
| Livestock | .. | .. | .. | .. | .. | .. | Мясное животноводство |
| Cattle | .. | .. | .. | .. | .. | .. | Крупный рогатый скот |
| Pigs | .. | .. | .. | .. | .. | .. | Свиньи |
| Sheep and goats | .. | .. | .. | .. | .. | .. | Овцы и козы |
| Poultry | .. | .. | .. | .. | .. | .. | Птица |
| Other | .. | .. | .. | .. | .. | .. | Прочие |
| Milk | .. | .. | .. | .. | .. | .. | Молоко |
| Eggs | .. | .. | .. | .. | .. | .. | Яйца |
| Wool | .. | .. | .. | .. | .. | .. | Шерсть |
| Other livestock | .. | .. | .. | .. | .. | .. | Прочая |
| **Agricultural services** | .. | .. | .. | .. | .. | .. | **Сельскохозяйственные услуги** |

# TABLE 5-3. Production and average yield of major agricultural crops
# ТАБЛИЦА 5-3. Производство и урожайность важнейших сельскохозяйственных культур

| Crop | 1990 | 1991 | 1992 | 1993 | 1994 | 1995 | Сельскохозяйственные культуры |
|---|---|---|---|---|---|---|---|
| **Production (thousands of tons)** | | | | | | | **Производство (тыс. тонн)** |
| Grain - Cleanweight | 1,899 | 1,908 | 2,257 | 2,142 | 2,466 | 3,215 | Зерно в чистом весе |
| Winter wheat | 522 | 572 | 913 | 811 | 1,231 | 2,304 | Пшеница - озимая |
| Spring wheat | 32 | 38 | 51 | 65 | 131 | 43 | яровая |
| Coarse grain | .. | .. | .. | .. | .. | .. | Зерно в физическом весе |
| Rye | 7 | 9 | 8 | 8 | 11 | 12 | Рожь |
| Corn | 431 | 431 | 367 | 404 | 276 | 186 | Кукуруза |
| Winter barley | 358 | 293 | 335 | 263 | 258 | 307 | Ячмень - озимый |
| Spring barley | 27 | 31 | 26 | 29 | 42 | 14 | яровой |
| Oats | .. | .. | .. | .. | .. | 1 | Овес |
| Millet | 1 | 1 | 1 | 1 | 1 | 1 | Просо |
| Rice | 503 | 515 | 539 | 545 | 498 | 328 | Рис |
| Flax | .. | .. | .. | 2 | .. | .. | Лен |
| Oilseeds | .. | .. | .. | 20 | 25 | .. | Семена масличных культур |
| Cotton (raw) | 5,058 | 4,646 | 4,128 | 4,235 | 3,938 | 3,934 | Хлопок - сырец |
| Cotton fiber | 1,593 | 1,443 | 1,274 | 1,321 | 1,259 | .. | волокно |
| Sugarbeets | .. | .. | .. | 24 | 23 | 14 | Сахарная свекла |
| Potatoes | 336 | 351 | 365 | 472 | 567 | 440 | Картофель |
| Pulses | 6 | 6 | 5 | 6 | 6 | 7 | Бобовые |
| Vegetables | 2,843 | 3,348 | 3,494 | 3,039 | 2,975 | 2,725 | Овощи |
| Fruit | 1,405 | 997 | 1,141 | 941 | 908 | 1,223 | Фрукты |
| Grapes | 745 | 480 | 439 | 381 | 353 | 621 | Виноград |
| Other | 660 | 517 | 702 | 560 | 555 | 602 | Прочие |
| Corn (silage and greenchop) | 4,505 | 4,485 | 4,491 | 4,727 | 4,104 | 3,026 | Кукуруза (на силос и зеленый корм) |
| Hay | 5,425 | 5,389 | 5,474 | 4,790 | 4,070 | 2,964 | Сено |
| **Average yield (kilograms per hectare)** | | | | | | | **Ср. урожайность (кг с га)** |
| Grain | 1,880 | 1,730 | 1,860 | 1,670 | 1,620 | 1,920 | Зерно |
| Winter wheat | 1,280 | 1,180 | 1,560 | 1,270 | 1,550 | 2,050 | Пшеница - озимая |
| Spring wheat | 1,290 | 1,140 | 1,170 | 1,090 | 790 | 1,090 | яровая |
| Coarse grain | .. | .. | .. | .. | .. | 1,910 | Зерно в физическом весе |
| Rye | .. | .. | .. | 1,490 | 1,540 | 1,910 | Рожь |
| Corn | 3,960 | 3,970 | 3,710 | 3,840 | 3,380 | 3,470 | Кукуруза |
| Winter barley | 1,330 | 1,110 | 1,310 | 1,070 | 1,110 | 1,320 | Ячмень - озимый |
| Spring barley | 1,200 | 970 | 1,070 | 960 | 730 | 800 | яровой |
| Oats | .. | .. | .. | .. | 1,230 | 1,230 | Овес |
| Millet | .. | .. | .. | 580 | 1,030 | 930 | Просо |
| Rice | 3,420 | 3,220 | 2,950 | 3,010 | 2,970 | 1,950 | Рис |
| Flax | .. | .. | .. | 300 | 230 | 210 | Лен |
| Oilseeds | .. | .. | .. | 1,160 | 1,110 | 890 | Семена масличных культур |
| Cotton (raw) | 2,760 | 2,700 | 2,480 | 2,500 | 2,560 | 2,640 | Хлопок - сырец |
| Cotton fiber | 870 | 840 | 750 | 780 | 820 | .. | волокно |
| Sugarbeets | .. | .. | .. | 15,570 | 13,170 | 10,740 | Сахарная свекла |
| Potatoes | 8,000 | 8,700 | 8,300 | 9,700 | 10,130 | .. | Картофель |
| Pulses | 400 | 460 | 460 | 770 | 670 | 700 | Бобовые |
| Vegetables | 19,200 | 18,800 | 18,100 | 18,800 | 17,960 | 17,600 | Овощи |
| Fruit | .. | .. | .. | .. | .. | .. | Фрукты |
| Grapes | 7,620 | 5,090 | 4,640 | 4,020 | 3,800 | 6,510 | Виноград |
| Other | 4,700 | 3,670 | 4,930 | 3,850 | 3,870 | 4,340 | Прочие |
| Corn (silage and greenchop) | 18,900 | 18,100 | 17,800 | 18,200 | 16,200 | 15,060 | Кукуруза (на силос и зеленый корм) |
| Hay | .. | .. | .. | .. | .. | .. | Сено |

## TABLE 5-4. Main aggregates of animal husbandry
## ТАБЛИЦА 5-4. Основные показатели животноводства

| Type of livestock or product | 1990 | 1991 | 1992 | 1993 | 1994 | 1995 | Направление животноводства или вид продукции |
|---|---|---|---|---|---|---|---|
| **Livestock (thousands of heads)** | | | | | | | **Поголовье скота (тысяч голов)** |
| Cattle | 4,581 | 5,113 | 5,275 | 5,431 | 5,483 | 5,204 | Крупный рогатый скот |
| of which: Cows | 1,856 | 2,120 | 2,218 | 2,297 | 2,337 | 2,286 | в том числе коровы |
| Pigs | 716 | 654 | 529 | 419 | 350 | 208 | Свиньи |
| Sheep and goats | 9,230 | 10,110 | 10,329 | 10,391 | 10,059 | 9,322 | Овцы и козы |
| of which: Goats | 823 | 918 | 961 | 967 | 971 | 907 | в том числе козы |
| Horses | 105 | 113 | 123 | 134 | 145 | 150 | Лошади |
| Other | 36,026 | 35,200 | 26,181 | 22,485 | 19,620 | 13,495 | Прочие |
| **Animal husbandry products** | | | | | | | **Продукция животноводства** |
| Meat (thousands of tons) | 484 | 492 | 469 | 504 | 509 | 519 | Мясо (тысяч тонн) |
| Beef | 295 | 323 | 323 | 365 | 390 | 402 | Говядина |
| Pork | 51 | 44 | 36 | 27 | 20 | 15 | Свинина |
| Lamb | 67 | 62 | 68 | 74 | 73 | 83 | Баранина |
| Poultry | 67 | 60 | 39 | 36 | 24 | 16 | Птица |
| Other | 5 | 4 | 4 | 3 | 2 | 3 | Прочие виды мяса |
| Milk (thousands of tons) | 3 | 3 | 4 | 4 | 4 | 4 | Молоко (тысяч тонн) |
| Eggs (millions) | 3 | 2 | 2 | 2 | 2 | 1 | Яйца (миллионов штук) |
| Wool (thousands of tons) | 26 | 25 | 27 | 27 | 25 | 20 | Шерсть (тысяч тонн) |

**TABLE 6-1. Industrial production by sector (millions of national currency)**

**ТАБЛИЦА 6-1. Промышленное производство по отраслям (млн. национальной валюты)**

| Sector | 1990 | 1991 | 1992 | 1993 | 1994 | 1995 | Отрасли |
|---|---|---|---|---|---|---|---|
| **All industry** | 26,571 | 63,022 | 516,007 | 5,238,528 | 51,760 | 233,643 | **Вся промышленность** |
| **Heavy industry** | 11,241 | 25,820 | 293,428 | 3,123,794 | 24,718 | 150,322 | **Тяжелая промышленность** |
| Fuel and energy | 2,096 | 4,090 | 87,456 | 1,261,352 | 9,074 | 66,531 | Топливно-энергетическая промышленноть |
| Electricity | 1,017 | 1,747 | 26,716 | 419,475 | 3,387 | 34,504 | Электроэнергетика |
| Fuels | 1,079 | 2,343 | 60,740 | 841,877 | 5,687 | 32,027 | Топливная промышленность |
| Ferrous and nonferrous metallurgy | 1,166 | 6,633 | 59,604 | 484,223 | 4,165 | 26,818 | Металлургия |
| Chemicals and petrochemical industry | 1,437 | 2,697 | 26,332 | 269,850 | 1,955 | 12,813 | Химическая и нефтехимическая пром. |
| Machine building and metalworking | 4,055 | 7,302 | 78,037 | 647,897 | 4,274 | 20,739 | Машиностроение и металлообработка |
| Forestry, woodworking, and pulp and paper industry | 539 | 1,013 | 6,185 | 62,551 | 711 | 2,467 | Лесная, деревообрабатывающая и целлюлозо-бумажная промышленность |
| Construction materials | 1,352 | 2,673 | 26,294 | 294,429 | 3,094 | 15,471 | Промышленность строительных материалов |
| **Light industry** | 9,757 | 25,137 | 129,552 | 1,213,033 | 12,853 | 46,506 | **Легкая промышленность** |
| Textiles | 7,556 | 20,380 | 104,696 | 987,058 | 10,639 | 42,214 | Текстильная |
| Clothing | 1,575 | 3,317 | 15,329 | 140,877 | 1,460 | 2,928 | Швейная |
| Leather and shoes | 605 | 1,392 | 9,286 | 82,907 | 729 | 1,310 | Кожевенная и обувная |
| **Food industry** | 3,884 | 9,264 | 61,812 | 647,603 | 7,978 | 21,804 | **Пищевая промышленность** |
| Processed foods | 2,552 | 5,621 | 44,080 | 429,195 | 6,075 | 16,908 | Пищевкусовая |
| Meat and dairy products | 1,257 | 3,493 | 16,722 | 206,446 | 1,796 | 4,586 | Мясная и молочная |
| Fish | 75 | 150 | 1,010 | 11,961 | 107 | 310 | Рыбная |

**TABLE 6-2. Industrial production by sector in constant prices**

**ТАБЛИЦА 6-2. Промышленное производство по отраслям в постоянных ценах**

| Sector | 1990 | 1991 | 1992 | 1993 | 1994 | 1995 | Отрасли |
|---|---|---|---|---|---|---|---|
| **Industrial production** | | | | | | | **Промышленное производство** |
| **All industry** | .. | .. | .. | .. | 13,334 | 13,361 | **Вся промышленность** |
| **Heavy industry** | .. | .. | .. | .. | 6,834 | 6,971 | **Тяжелая промышленность** |
| Fuel and energy | .. | .. | .. | .. | 2,100 | 2,100 | Топливно-энергетическая промышленноть |
| Electricity | .. | .. | .. | .. | 688 | 691 | Электроэнергетика |
| Fuels | .. | .. | .. | .. | 1,412 | 1,409 | Топливная промышленность |
| Ferrous and nonferrous metallurgy | .. | .. | .. | .. | 1,029 | 1,019 | Металлургия |
| Chemicals and petrochemicals | .. | .. | .. | .. | 593 | 664 | Химическая и нефтехимическая пром. |
| Machine building and metalworking | .. | .. | .. | .. | 1,706 | 2,028 | Машиностроение и металлообработка |
| Forestry, woodworking, and pulp and paper | .. | .. | .. | .. | 196 | 203 | Лесная, деревообрабатывающая и целлюлозо-бумажная промышленность |
| Construction materials | .. | .. | .. | .. | 787 | 687 | Промышленность строительных материалов |
| **Light industry** | .. | .. | .. | .. | 3,260 | 3,188 | **Легкая промышленность** |
| Textiles | .. | .. | .. | .. | 2,474 | 2,484 | Текстильная |
| Clothing | .. | .. | .. | .. | 532 | 520 | Швейная |
| Leather and shoe | .. | .. | .. | .. | 247 | 184 | Кожевенная и обувная |
| **Food industry** | .. | .. | .. | .. | 2,463 | 2,495 | **Пищевая промышленность** |
| Processed foods | .. | .. | .. | .. | 1,756 | 1,838 | Пищевкусовая |
| Meat and dairy products | .. | .. | .. | .. | 672 | 628 | Мясная и молочная |
| Fish | .. | .. | .. | .. | 35 | 29 | Рыбная |
| **Growth in production by sector (in percent)** | | | | | | | **Рост производства по отраслям** |
| **All industry** | 1.8 | 1.5 | -6.7 | 3.6 | 1.6 | 0.2 | **Вся промышленность** |
| **Heavy industry** | -0.9 | 1.0 | -10.5 | 2.1 | -2.1 | 2.0 | **Тяжелая промышленность** |
| Power and fuels | 0.2 | 0.0 | -6.9 | 7.6 | 0.4 | 0.0 | Топливно-энергетическая промышленноть |
| Electricity | 0.6 | -3.2 | -6.3 | -1.7 | -3.6 | 0.4 | Электроэнергетика |
| Fuels | -0.1 | 2.2 | -7.1 | 11.9 | 2.5 | -0.2 | Топливная промышленность |
| Ferrous and nonferrous metallurgy | -6.9 | -4.5 | -14.2 | -1.4 | -10.6 | -1.0 | Металлургия |
| Chemicals and petrochemicals | -4.9 | -2.6 | -25.9 | -11.3 | -22.2 | 12.0 | Химическая и нефтехимическая пром. |
| Machine building and metalworking | -0.3 | 4.9 | 0.0 | 6.9 | 9.0 | 18.9 | Машиностроение и металлообработка |
| Forestry, woodworking, and pulp and paper | 6.0 | 7.9 | -4.1 | 7.9 | 0.0 | 3.6 | Лесная, деревообрабатывающая и целлюлозо-бумажная промышленность |
| Construction materials | 0.3 | 3.9 | -14.5 | -17.1 | -12.1 | -12.7 | Промышленность строительных материалов |
| **Light industry** | 3.7 | 2.1 | 6.9 | 3.9 | 9.1 | -2.2 | **Легкая промышленность** |
| Textiles | 2.7 | -0.7 | 6.2 | 1.9 | 10.2 | 0.4 | Текстильная |
| Clothing | 7.5 | 20.5 | 9.3 | 20.6 | 25.1 | -2.3 | Швейная |
| Leather and shoe | 6.1 | 6.4 | 9.0 | -0.5 | -21.1 | -25.5 | Кожевенная и обувная |
| **Food industry** | 5.9 | -3.2 | -14.2 | 9.9 | 3.9 | 1.3 | **Пищевая промышленность** |
| Processed foods | 10.0 | 3.7 | -9.6 | 13.4 | 10.0 | 4.7 | Пищевкусовая |
| Meat and dairy products | -0.8 | -13.0 | -25.2 | -1.4 | -7.4 | -6.5 | Мясная и молочная |
| Fish | 5.2 | 5.4 | -14.7 | -19.7 | -26.8 | -17.1 | Рыбная |

## TABLE 6-3. Primary energy supply (million tons oil equivalent)



## ТАБЛИЦА 6-3. Ресурсы первичных видов энергии (млн. тонн нефтяного эквивалента)

| Item | | 1990 | 1991 | 1992 | 1993 | 1994 | 1995 | Статьи | |
|---|---|---|---|---|---|---|---|---|---|
| **Primary production** | | | | | | | | **Производство первичной энергии** | |
| Coal and lignite (hard and brown) | | 2.2 | 2.1 | 1.6 | 1.3 | 1.3 | 1.0 | Уголь каменный и бурый | |
| Crude oil | | 2.8 | 2.8 | 3.3 | 4.0 | 5.5 | 7.6 | Нефть | |
| Gas | | 32.8 | 33.7 | 34.5 | 36.3 | 38.0 | 39.1 | Газ | |
| Nuclear | | .. | .. | .. | .. | .. | .. | Атомная энергия | |
| Hydro/geothermal | | 1.7 | 1.5 | 1.6 | 1.9 | 2.0 | 1.6 | Гидро-геотермальная | |
| Other | | .. | .. | .. | .. | .. | .. | Другие виды | |
| Total | | 39.5 | 40.1 | 41.0 | 43.4 | 46.8 | 49.3 | Всего | |
| **Energy trade** | | | | | | | | **Торговля энергией** | |
| Coal and lignite | Exports | 0.3 | 0.1 | 0.1 | 0.1 | 0.1 | 0.1 | Уголь каменный и бурый | Экспорт |
| | Imports | 0.9 | 0.9 | 0.7 | 0.2 | 0.1 | 0.0 | | Импорт |
| | Net imports | 0.6 | 0.8 | 0.6 | 0.2 | 0.0 | 0.0 | | Чистый импорт |
| Oil/oil product | Exports | 2.2 | 1.6 | 0.9 | 0.8 | 1.3 | 0.9 | Нефть и нефтепродукты | Экспорт |
| | Imports | 11.7 | 9.4 | 6.4 | 4.9 | 3.2 | 0.3 | | Импорт |
| | Net imports | 9.5 | 7.8 | 5.6 | 4.1 | 1.9 | -0.5 | | Чистый импорт |
| Gas | Exports | 8.7 | 8.7 | 7.3 | 5.9 | 4.0 | 4.5 | Газ | Экспорт |
| | Imports | 5.7 | 5.9 | 4.8 | 4.6 | 1.7 | 1.1 | | Импорт |
| | Net imports | -3.0 | -2.8 | -2.6 | -1.3 | -2.3 | -3.4 | | Чистый импорт |
| Electricity | Exports | 4.7 | 4.7 | 4.2 | 4.0 | 4.1 | 3.6 | Электричество | Экспорт |
| | Imports | 4.2 | 4.6 | 4.1 | 3.9 | 3.7 | 3.3 | | Импорт |
| | Net imports | -0.5 | -0.1 | -0.1 | -0.1 | -0.3 | -0.3 | | Чистый импорт |
| **Total net imports** | | 6.6 | 5.7 | 3.5 | 2.8 | -0.7 | -4.3 | **Чистый импорт энергии-всего** | |
| **Total stock changes** | | -1.4 | -1.0 | -1.0 | -1.7 | -3.5 | -1.7 | **Изменение запасов-всего** | |
| **Total primary energy supply** | | 44.7 | 44.8 | 43.4 | 44.5 | 42.7 | 43.4 | **Ресурсы первичной энергии-всего** | |
| Coal and lignite | | 2.8 | 2.7 | 2.4 | 1.4 | 1.2 | 1.0 | Уголь каменный и бурый | |
| Oil/oil products | | 12.4 | 10.5 | 8.7 | 7.5 | 7.0 | 7.3 | Нефть и нефтепродукты | |
| Gas | | 28.3 | 30.1 | 30.8 | 33.9 | 32.9 | 33.8 | Газ | |
| Nuclear | | .. | .. | .. | .. | .. | .. | Атомная энергия | |
| Hydro/geothermal | | 1.2 | 1.5 | 1.5 | 1.7 | 1.6 | 1.3 | Гидро-геотермальная энергия | |
| Other | | .. | .. | .. | .. | .. | .. | Другие виды | |
| **Total primary energy requirement (equals total primary energy supply)** | | 44.7 | 44.8 | 43.4 | 44.5 | 42.7 | 43.4 | **Потребность в первичной энергии-всего (равно ресурсам первичной энергии)** | |

## TABLE 6-4. Final energy consumption (million tons oil equivalent) — UZBEKISTAN
## ТАБЛИЦА 6-4. Конечное потребление энергии ( млн. тонн нефтяного эквивалента )

| | 1991 | 1992 | 1993 | 1994 | 1995 | |
|---|---|---|---|---|---|---|
| **Final energy consumption** | 34.6 | 34.1 | 35.3 | 34.1 | 34.5 | **Конечное потребление энергии** |
| Coal & Lignite | 1.3 | 1.1 | 0.6 | 0.6 | 0.3 | Уголь каменный и бурый |
| Oil Products | 7.4 | 6.6 | 5.0 | 4.7 | 4.8 | Нефтепродукты |
| Gas | 14.5 | 15.8 | 19.4 | 19.2 | 19.8 | Газ |
| Electricity | 11.4 | 10.7 | 10.2 | 9.6 | 9.6 | Электроэнергия |
| Heat | .. | .. | .. | .. | .. | Тепло |
| Other | .. | .. | .. | .. | .. | Другие виды |
| Of which: | | | | | | В том числе |
| **Industry** | 12.6 | 11.7 | 10.7 | 9.3 | 9.1 | **Промышленность** |
| Coal & Lignite | 0.4 | 0.2 | 0.1 | 0.1 | 0.0 | Уголь каменный и бурый |
| Oil Products | 0.8 | 0.7 | 0.5 | 0.5 | 0.8 | Нефтепродукты |
| Gas | 6.0 | 6.0 | 5.6 | 4.8 | 4.7 | Газ |
| Electricity | 5.5 | 4.8 | 4.5 | 3.9 | 3.7 | Электроэнергия |
| Heat | .. | .. | .. | .. | .. | Тепло |
| Other | .. | .. | .. | .. | .. | Другие виды |
| **Agriculture** | 4.8 | 4.6 | 4.2 | 4.1 | 4.3 | **Сельское хозяйство** |
| Coal & Lignite | 0.1 | 0.1 | 0.0 | 0.0 | 0.0 | Уголь каменный и бурый |
| Oil Products | 1.5 | 1.4 | 1.2 | 1.1 | 1.1 | Нефтепродукты |
| Gas | 0.2 | 0.2 | 0.3 | 0.2 | 0.1 | Газ |
| Electricity | 3.0 | 2.8 | 2.7 | 2.8 | 3.0 | Электроэнергия |
| Heat | .. | .. | .. | .. | .. | Тепло |
| Other | .. | .. | .. | .. | .. | Другие виды |
| **Transport** | 6.7 | 5.1 | 4.5 | 4.0 | 3.9 | **Транспорт** |
| Oil Products | 4.0 | 3.2 | 2.8 | 2.5 | 2.3 | Нефтепродукты |
| Other | 2.6 | 1.9 | 1.7 | 1.5 | 1.7 | Другие виды |
| **Households** | 10.5 | 12.7 | 15.9 | 16.7 | 17.2 | **Домашние хозяйства** |
| Coal & Lignite | 0.8 | 0.8 | 0.5 | 0.4 | 0.3 | Уголь каменный и бурый |
| Oil Products | 1.2 | 1.3 | 0.5 | 0.6 | 0.6 | Нефтепродукты |
| Gas | 6.1 | 8.0 | 12.2 | 13.1 | 13.7 | Газ |
| Electricity | 2.5 | 2.6 | 2.7 | 2.6 | 2.6 | Электроэнергия |
| Heat | .. | .. | .. | .. | .. | Тепло |
| Other | .. | .. | .. | .. | .. | Другие виды |

## TABLE 7-1. Price indices and exchange rates
## ТАБЛИЦА 7-1. Индексы цен и обменный курс

| Year and month | National currency per U.S. dollar<br>Единиц нац. валюты за 1 доллар США | National currency per Russian ruble<br>Единиц нац. валюты за 1 российский рубль | Consumer price index (as a percent of the previous month)<br>Индекс потребительских цен (в % к предыдущему месяцу) | Producer price index (as a percent of the previous month)<br>Индекс цен производителей (в % к предыдущему месяцу) | Consumer price index (as a percent of the previous December)<br>Индекс потребительских цен (в % к декабрю прошлого года) | Producer price index (as a percent of the previous December)<br>Индекс цен производителей (в % к декабрю прошлого года) | Год и месяц |
|---|---|---|---|---|---|---|---|
| **1993** | | | | | | | **1993** |
| January | 0.6 | .. | 127.9 | 125.2 | 127.9 | 125.2 | Январь |
| February | 0.6 | .. | 117.4 | 131.5 | 150.2 | 158.8 | Февраль |
| March | 0.7 | .. | 107.3 | 113.7 | 161.1 | 175.1 | Март |
| April | 0.8 | .. | 112.5 | 120.6 | 181.3 | 204.0 | Апрель |
| May | 1.0 | .. | 109.3 | 133.1 | 198.1 | 255.4 | Май |
| June | 1.1 | .. | 131.8 | 130.4 | 261.1 | 325.4 | Июнь |
| July | 1.0 | .. | 114.5 | 170.5 | 299.0 | 521.9 | Июль |
| August | 1.0 | .. | 116.0 | 115.6 | 346.8 | 590.4 | Август |
| September | 1.2 | .. | 108.1 | 117.4 | 374.9 | 684.3 | Сентябрь |
| October | 1.2 | .. | 129.2 | 119.9 | 484.4 | 191.0 | Октябрь |
| November | 1.2 | .. | 144.5 | 151.6 | 700.0 | 1,030.7 | Ноябрь |
| December | 1.3 | .. | 140.7 | 122.6 | 984.9 | 1,197.7 | Декабрь |
| **1994** | | | | | | | **1994** |
| January | 1.5 | .. | 125.1 | 119.0 | 125.1 | 119.0 | Январь |
| February | 1.7 | .. | 123.5 | 118.9 | 154.5 | 146.3 | Февраль |
| March | 1.8 | .. | 128.7 | 122.5 | 198.9 | 176.6 | Март |
| April | 2.6 | .. | 143.8 | 123.6 | 285.9 | 208.3 | Апрель |
| May | 4.2 | .. | 126.8 | 116.2 | 362.5 | 239.1 | Май |
| June | 6.0 | .. | 134.4 | 127.8 | 487.2 | 315.7 | Июнь |
| July | 11.0 | 0.00543 | 112.7 | 124.6 | 549.3 | 376.1 | Июль |
| August | 18.0 | 0.00598 | 107.5 | 124.3 | 590.3 | 453.2 | Август |
| September | 17.0 | 0.00618 | 119.0 | 170.8 | 702.7 | 667.6 | Сентябрь |
| October | 22.0 | 0.00735 | 120.0 | 149.4 | 843.1 | 877.7 | Октябрь |
| November | 25.0 | 0.00736 | 129.3 | 182.3 | 1,090.0 | 1,392.2 | Ноябрь |
| December | 25.0 | 0.00745 | 111.7 | 130.4 | 1,217.0 | 1,524.1 | Декабрь |

## TABLE 7-1. Price indices and exchange rates
## ТАБЛИЦА 7-1. Индексы цен и обменный курс

| Year and month | National currency per U.S. dollar<br>Единиц нац. валюты за 1 доллар США | National currency per Russian ruble<br>Единиц нац. валюты за 1 российский рубль | Consumer price index (as a percent of the previous month)<br>Индекс потребительских цен (в % к предыдущему месяцу) | Producer price index (as a percent of the previous month)<br>Индекс цен производителей (в % к предыдущему месяцу) | Consumer price index (as a percent of the previous December)<br>Индекс потребительских цен (в % к декабрю прошлого года) | Producer price index (as a percent of the previous December)<br>Индекс цен производителей (в % к декабрю прошлого года) | Год и месяц |
|---|---|---|---|---|---|---|---|
| **1995** | | | | | | | **1995** |
| January | 25.0 | 0.00662 | 115.0 | 116.2 | 115.0 | 116.2 | Январь |
| February | 25.0 | 0.00597 | 111.9 | 108.7 | 128.6 | 126.0 | Февраль |
| March | 26.8 | 0.00544 | 107.3 | 104.8 | 137.9 | 132.4 | Март |
| April | 29.2 | 0.00524 | 113.7 | 136.3 | 156.8 | 173.7 | Апрель |
| May | 30.7 | 0.00527 | 105.9 | 109.3 | 166.1 | 185.9 | Май |
| June | 28.7 | 0.00614 | 95.8 | 105.1 | 159.1 | 193.8 | Июнь |
| July | 31.4 | 0.00670 | 96.7 | 108.3 | 153.9 | 211.7 | Июль |
| August | 32.0 | 0.00711 | 100.7 | 103.4 | 155.0 | 212.8 | Август |
| September | 34.0 | 0.00747 | 105.3 | 138.9 | 163.2 | 260.1 | Сентябрь |
| October | 33.8 | 0.00759 | 109.0 | 111.9 | 177.8 | 296.0 | Октябрь |
| November | 36.0 | 0.00775 | 104.3 | 104.2 | 185.4 | 314.0 | Ноябрь |
| December | 35.8 | 0.00779 | 107.1 | 102.3 | 198.5 | 318.8 | Декабрь |
| **1996** | | | | | | | **1996** |
| January | 36.0 | 0.00772 | 110.9 | 106.9 | 110.9 | 106.9 | Январь |
| February | 36.4 | 0.00763 | 107.6 | 104.5 | 119.3 | 111.6 | Февраль |
| March | 36.4 | 0.00752 | 103.8 | 102.1 | 123.8 | 114.0 | Март |
| April | 36.9 | 0.00752 | 114.0 | 120.6 | 141.2 | 135.3 | Апрель |
| May | 37.6 | 0.00758 | 106.1 | 102.0 | 149.8 | 138.1 | Май |
| June | 37.8 | 0.00748 | 97.1 | 103.8 | 145.4 | 142.5 | Июнь |
| July | 37.9 | 0.00737 | 96.9 | 100.9 | 141.0 | 143.7 | Июль |
| August | 38.9 | 0.00733 | 101.1 | 102.2 | 142.6 | 146.8 | Август |
| September | .. | .. | .. | .. | .. | .. | Сентябрь |
| October | .. | .. | .. | .. | .. | .. | Октябрь |
| November | .. | .. | .. | .. | .. | .. | Ноябрь |
| December | .. | .. | .. | .. | .. | .. | Декабрь |

**TABLE 7-2. Monthly nominal wages by sector**

**ТАБЛИЦА 7-2. Среднемесячная денежная зарплата по отраслям**

| Sector | 1990 | 1991 | 1992 | 1993 | 1994 | 1995 | Сектора |
|---|---|---|---|---|---|---|---|
| **Nominal wages** | | | | | | | **Средняя номинальная заработная плата** |
| **Economy average** | 215.4 | 345.6 | 2,541.0 | 30,220.0 | 279.7 | 1,059.2 | **По народному хозяйству** |
| **Material sphere** | .. | .. | .. | .. | .. | .. | **Отрасли сферы материального производства** |
| Industry | 232.4 | 391.6 | 3,166.0 | 42,598.0 | 389.4 | 1,473.4 | Промышленность |
| Construction | 282.1 | 421.3 | 2,838.0 | 41,352.0 | 424.2 | 1,610.4 | Строительство |
| Agriculture | 230.7 | 378.4 | 2,569.0 | 22,892.0 | 239.8 | 800.5 | Сельское хозяйство |
| Transport | 247.9 | 391.9 | 2,055.0 | 35,923.0 | 344.2 | 1,457.9 | Транспорт |
| Communications | 200.0 | 336.8 | 2,456.0 | 33,486.0 | 340.4 | 1,506.2 | Связь |
| Trade (retail and wholesale) | 180.7 | 282.1 | 1,820.0 | 21,056.0 | 200.8 | 509.8 | Торговля (оптовая и розничная) |
| Other | 134.8 | 245.8 | 2,601.0 | 28,809.0 | 282.2 | 799.3 | Прочие отрасли материального производства |
| **Nonmaterial sphere** | .. | .. | .. | .. | .. | .. | **Отрасли непроизводственной сферы** |
| Municipal services | 163.5 | 273.6 | 2,123.0 | 29,075.0 | 242.0 | 960.2 | Жилкомхоз и бытовое обслуживание |
| Science, research and development | 275.5 | 386.7 | 2,771.0 | 35,301.0 | 337.1 | 1,291.2 | Наука и научное обслуживание |
| Education | 173.5 | 270.4 | 2,152.0 | 21,735.0 | 171.5 | 683.3 | Образование |
| Culture | 132.7 | 232.9 | 1,794.0 | 20,501.0 | 166.9 | 697.7 | Культура |
| Arts | .. | .. | .. | .. | 214.7 | 847.3 | Искусство |
| Health care, social security, and sports | 159.2 | 253.6 | 1,852.0 | 17,910.0 | 146.7 | 684.3 | Здравоохр., соц.обсл., физк. и спорт |
| Banking, finance, credit, insurance | 320.1 | 616.0 | 4,238.0 | 59,917.0 | 523.2 | 1,935.9 | Кредитование, страхование, банк. дело |
| Government | 286.3 | 373.4 | 2,700.0 | 40,242.0 | 338.6 | 1,058.3 | Управление |

**TABLE 8-1. Money income and expenditure of the population (millions of national currency)**
**ТАБЛИЦА 8-1. Денежные доходы и расходы населения (млн. национальной валюты)**

| Type of income or expenditure | 1990 | 1991 | 1992 | 1993 | 1994 | 1995 | Вид доходов или расходов |
|---|---|---|---|---|---|---|---|
| **Income** | | | | | | | **Доходы** |
| **Total labor income** | 20.5 | 34.1 | 219.4 | 3,495.3 | 31,584.4 | 96,158.0 | **Всего трудовых доходов** |
| Regular wages | 14.4 | 23.5 | 159.1 | 1,763.0 | 15,922.1 | 58,787.7 | Заработная плата |
| Wages paid by cooperatives | 1.0 | 0.7 | 1.6 | 11.0 | 90.3 | 219.3 | Заработная плата в кооперативах |
| Other wages and compensation | 0.6 | 1.4 | 6.9 | 70.4 | 622.0 | 3,838.3 | Прочие доходы типа заработной платы |
| Income paid by collective farms | 2.5 | 3.8 | 37.9 | 258.8 | 2,173.0 | 5,330.4 | Доходы от колхозов |
| Income from sale of farm products | 2.0 | 4.7 | 13.9 | 1,392.1 | 12,777.0 | 27,982.3 | Доходы от продажи продукции колхозов |
| **Total transfer receipts** | 6.0 | 15.0 | 64.0 | 751.9 | 12,827.6 | 49,485.5 | **Всего трансфертных поступлений** |
| Pensions and allowances | 3.4 | 11.9 | 53.1 | 561.2 | 6,819.5 | 23,013.2 | Пенсии и пособия |
| Scholarships | 0.2 | 0.5 | 2.8 | 24.3 | 272.7 | 1,372.2 | Стипендии |
| Income from the financial system (insurance, interest, etc.) | 1.6 | 1.6 | 6.4 | 22.9 | 249.5 | 1,617.2 | Доходы из финансовой системы (страховые возмещения, проценты и т.д.) |
| Other income | 0.8 | 1.0 | 1.7 | 143.5 | 5,485.9 | 23,482.9 | Прочие виды доходов |
| **Total income** | 26.5 | 49.1 | 283.4 | 4,247.2 | 44,412.0 | 145,643.5 | **Всего доходов** |
| **Expenditure** | | | | | | | **Расходы** |
| **Total purchases** | 19.8 | 32.8 | 166.4 | 2,668.3 | 35,507.5 | 113,148.5 | **Всего покупок товаров и услуг** |
| Retail goods | 17.9 | 30.1 | 145.4 | 2,489.0 | 32,035.3 | 97,586.1 | Товары в розничной торговле |
| Services | 1.9 | 2.7 | 21.0 | 179.3 | 3,472.2 | 15,562.4 | Услуги |
| Rent and utilities | 0.5 | 0.5 | 1.8 | 17.7 | 299.6 | 2,338.8 | Квартирная плата и коммунальные платежи |
| Transport and communications | 0.4 | 1.4 | 12.7 | 103.1 | 2,107.4 | 7,577.3 | Транспорт и связь |
| Health and other services | 0.5 | 0.7 | 6.5 | 48.3 | 788.9 | 2,919.2 | Здравоохранение и другие виды услуг |
| Cooperatives | 0.5 | 0.1 | .. | 10.2 | 276.3 | 2,727.1 | Кооперативы |
| **Transfers and savings** | 4.5 | 12.1 | 32.7 | 823.3 | 3,548.6 | 17,888.0 | **Трансферты и сбережения** |
| Taxes, fees, dues, and other | 2.3 | 2.8 | 15.9 | 171.3 | 2,245.6 | 10,961.9 | Налоги, сборы, пошлины и др. |
| Savings | 2.2 | 9.2 | 16.7 | 651.2 | 1,282.4 | 6,843.2 | Сбережения |
| Other | .. | 0.1 | 0.1 | 0.8 | 20.6 | 82.9 | Прочие |
| **Total expenditure** | 24.3 | 44.9 | 199.1 | 3,491.6 | 39,056.1 | 131,036.5 | **Всего расходов** |
| **Income less expenditure** | 2.2 | 4.2 | 84.3 | 755.6 | 5,355.9 | 14,607.0 | **Доходы за вычетом расходов** |

# *Country Notes: Uzbekistan*

**General notes**: Data were supplied by the State Committee for Statistics and Forecasting of the Republic of Uzbekistan.

**Currency:** Unless otherwise indicated, data prior to 1993 are in rubles, in 1993, in sum-coupons (1 sum-coupon = 1 ruble), and in 1994-1995, in sums. The national currency, sum, was introduced on June 27, 1994 with the conversion factor 1 sum = 1,000 sum-coupons.

**Table 1-1:** Total population is shown as of the beginning of the year. Employment data are annual averages. Sums of employment by sector and sums of items of labor resources do not add up to the totals for most of the years.

**Table 1-2:** Transport of goods includes road maintenance and communication serving the material sphere. Retail trade and catering include wholesale trade, material supply and procurement. Passenger transport includes communication. Public utilities and personal services include housing. Insurance includes credit.

**Table 2-1:** Data are in millions of rubles for 1990-1993 and in millions of sums for 1994-1995. Agriculture includes fishery. Transport includes road maintenance in 1990-1994 and road maintenance and communication in 1995. Retail trade and catering include wholesale trade. Credit includes insurance.

**Table 2-2:** Data are in previous year prices. Data are in millions of rubles for 1993-1994 and in millions of sums for 1995. Agriculture includes fishery. Transport includes road maintenance and communication. Retail trade and catering include wholesale trade. Credit includes insurance.

**Tables 4-1 and 4-2:** Data are in millions of sums.

**Table 5-2:** Data are in 1983 rubles.

**Table 5-4:** Livestock data are as of the end of the year.

**Table 6-2:** Data are in the beginning of 1994 prices.

**Table 7-1:** In 1993, the columns for consumer price indices show retail price indices. The producer price index as a percent of the previous month is estimated using the Sauerback formula, which usually produces the upward drift and is inconsistent with the producer price index as a percent of the previous December. The latter is considered to be more accurate.

**Table 8-1:** The sums of items of labor income do not add up to the totals.

# *Комментарии к таблицам: Узбекистан*

**Общее замечание:** За исключением особо отмеченных случаев, данные были получены из Государственного Комитета по Прогнозированию и Статистике Республики Узбекистан.

**Национальная валюта:** За исключением особо отмеченных случаев, данные до 1993 г. приведены в рублях, за 1993 г. в сум-купонах (1 сум-купон = 1 рубль), а за 1994-1995 гг. в сумах. Национальная валюта, сум, была введена 27 июня 1994 г. с коэффициентом пересчета 1 сум = 1000 сум-купонов.

**Таблица 1-1:** Данные по населению приведены на начало года. Данные по занятости - среднегодовые. Суммы компонентов занятого населения, а таже компонентов трудовых ресурсов не равны соответствующим итоговым величинам для большинства лет.

**Таблица 1-2:** Грузовой транспорт включает дорожное хозяйство и связь, обслуживающую материальное производство. Розничная торговля и общепит включают оптовую торговлю, материально-техническое снабжение и заготовки. Пассажирский транспорт включает связь. Коммунальное хозяйство и бытовое обслуживание включают жилищное хозяйство. Страхование включает кредитование.

**Таблица 2-1:** Данные приведены в миллионах рублей за 1990-1993 гг. и в миллионах сумов за 1994-1995 гг. Сельское хозяйство включает рыбное хозяйство. В 1990-1994 гг. транспорт включает дорожное хозяйство; в 1995 г. - дорожное хозяйство и связь. Розничная торговля и общепит включают оптовую торговлю. Кредитование включает страхование.

**Таблица 2-2:** Данные приведены в ценах предыдущего года в миллионах рублей за 1993-1994 гг. и в миллионах сумов за 1995 г. Сельское хозяйство включает рыбное хозяйство. Транспорт включает дорожное хозяйство и связь. Розничная торговля и общепит включают оптовую торговлю. Кредитование включает страхование.

**Таблицы 4-1 и 4-2:** Данные приведены в миллионах сумов.

**Таблица 5-2:** Данные приведены в ценах 1983 г.

**Таблица 5-4:** Данные по поголовью скота приведены на конец года.

**Таблица 6-2:** Данные приведены в ценах начала 1994 г.

**Таблица 7-1:** В 1993 г. вместо индекса потребительских цен приведен индекс розничных цен. Индекс цен производителей в процентах к предыдущему месяцу рассчитан по формуле Сауербека, которая обычно приводит к завышению рассматриваемого показателя и его несовместимости с индексом цен производителей в процентах к декабрю прошлого года. Последний считается более точным.

**Таблица 8-1:** Суммы компонентов трудовых доходов не равны приведенным итоговым величинам.

# Technical Notes

These technical notes explain the general data sources and methods used in the statistical handbook. Sources, methodologies, and variations in indicators specific to individual countries are discussed in the country notes that follow the country tables. The comparative tables and country tables use the same underlying data; thus the definitions and methodologies used in deriving and compiling the data are pertinent to both. For a more in-depth and authoritative discussion of the subjects addressed below, the reader is encouraged to refer to the documents and reports cited as sources of information.

## 1. POPULATION, LABOR FORCE, AND EMPLOYMENT

### Table 1-1: Population and employment

The terms below describe the components of labor force and define the various economic entities.

*Working-age* is defined as age 16 to 59 for males and age 16 to 54 for females. This concept is defined strictly by law and does not take into account a person's employment status.

*Labor resources* is a term that was used in the Soviet Union and is still in use in some of the FSU countries. It comprises those who are working and those who are able to work but are not currently working. Labor resources include the able-bodied population of working age as well as employed persons older and younger than working age. Labor resources thus include the employed population, full-time students of working age, religious workers, and able-bodied persons not employed in the economy. The last group includes housewives, the military, seasonally unemployed persons, and the truly unemployed. The concept of labor resources differs from the concept of labor force used by statistical organizations in many Western countries. Labor force is the sum of those working and those looking for work.

*The employed population* is the sum of those employed in the state sector, leased enterprises, joint-stock companies, economic associations, social organizations, joint ventures, collective farms, cooperatives, individual labor activities, private subsidiary agriculture, and private agriculture.

*The state sector* includes state owned enterprises, administration, and public institutions run by the government.

*Leased enterprises* are state enterprises that have been leased, usually to their employees. Typically, employees of an enterprise that is leased continue working in the enterprise but gain more control over operations.

*Joint-stock companies* include former state enterprises which have been corporatized. In Western business terminology, they have been "privatized".

*Economic associations* are associations of enterprises that have bonded together to operate outside the ministerial structure.

*Social organizations* are foundations, charitable organizations, and other social institutions.

*Joint ventures* are enterprises jointly owned by resident and foreign persons or entities.

*Collective farms* are collectively-owned farms. Collective farm workers, unlike state farm workers are not state employees.

*The cooperative workers* comprise those working in cooperatives producing goods and services and consumer cooperatives. *Cooperatives producing goods and services*, also referred to as private cooperatives, were legalized in 1987. With a few restrictions, they can conduct activities in nearly every sphere of production and services. Activities in this sector are distinguished from individual labor activities by the requirement that a cooperative has a minimum of three people. *Consumer cooperatives* are distinct from the newly legalized private cooperatives. Those employed in consumer cooperatives were incorporated into the state sector data around 1960 and have been included in the totals for that sector since then. In some recent breakdowns of employment, they have been included under a newly created cooperative sector.

*Private agriculture* covers small, independent farmers and is also referred to as the peasant farm economy. A small number of independent farms have always been allowed to exist, but their number has been minuscule until recent years. Regulations relating to these farms have eased in the past few years.

*Private subsidiary agriculture* covers those who are alloted small private plots and permitted to keep small numbers of livestock. Most people in private subsidiary agriculture work at this activity part-time. Although the land allocated to private subsidiary plots occupies only a small share of total agricultural land, these farms account for a large share of output of certain key commodities. Restrictions on the sector have been lifted in recent years, and its development has been encouraged.

*Individual labor activities* cover people producing handicrafts and providing services. Activities in this sector were legalized in 1986.

*Labor force* is an approximation of the international concept of labor force and is computed as the sum of the employed and unemployed populations.

**Table 1-2: Employment by sector**

*Population employed in the economy* includes workers and employees; collective farmers engaged in collective farm work; collective farmers, workers, employees, and working age members of their families engaged in private subsidiary farming; people engaged in individual labor activities; and finally, people employed in private cooperatives, joint-stock companies, social organizations, associations, and other new forms of economic organization. The annual averages are obtained as the average of twelve monthly counts.

**Table 1-3: Registered unemployment**

*Registered unemployment* refers to the number of people who qualify for the status of unemployed at state employment bureaus.

## 2. NATIONAL ACCOUNTS

The definitions and descriptions given below are brief. For a more authoritative and comprehensive explanation of national accounts, the reader is encouraged to refer to the following publications:

Organization for Economic Cooperation and Development (OECD), *National Accounts for the Former Soviet Union: Sources, Methods and Estimates*, OECD/GD (92)/175 (Paris, 1992)

Commission of the European Communities, International Monetary Fund, Organization for Economic Co-operation and Development, United Nations, and World Bank: *System of National Accounts 1993* (Brussels/Luxembourg, New York, Paris, Washington, D.C., 1993).

**Tables 2-1 and 2-2: Gross domestic product by origin and expenditure**

Table 2-1 presents gross domestic product (GDP) by sector of origin and by expenditure category in current prices; table 2-2 is in constant prices.

*Gross domestic product at market prices* represents the final result of the productive activities of resident producing units. It can be measured using two approaches:

- As the total of the value added of all resident producing units (classified by sectors or industries), plus net indirect taxes on products and imports not included in its valuation.
- As the sum of gross expenditure on the final use of goods and services valued at purchasers' prices, including exports, less imports of goods and services valued at c.i.f. (costs of insurance and freight included).

In *GDP by sector of origin* each sector's share is the value added. Value added is calculated as gross output less intermediate consumption. Gross output represents the value of those goods and services produced during a given period that are included in the production boundary of the system of national accounts (SNA). Intermediate consumption is the value of services and nondurable goods used up in production, excluding consumption of fixed capital. Some of these services are those of financial intermediaries. Since in practice it is usually difficult to allocate these services among different users, in some countries they are recorded as the intermediate consumption of a separate nominal industry, called here *Imputed service charge of financial intermediaries*. It is not included in the totals for *Other* sectors but only in the *Total gross value added.*

To derive *GDP at factor cost*, the value of indirect taxes paid out in the process of production is deducted from the total value added of industries, and the value of subsidies received in the process of production is added to the total value added. These taxes and subsidies however do not include indirect taxes (net of subsidies) on production and imports as the value added is calculated using gross output at basic prices .

To derive GDP at market prices net indirect taxes are added to GDP at factor cost. Net indirect taxes represent the excess of the total indirect taxes on production and imports over the total subsidies on production and imports.

*GDP by expenditure category* concerns the final uses of goods and services grouped into consumption, gross domestic investment, and net exports.

*Consumption* includes expenditure on consumer goods (irrespective of their durability except for purchases of dwellings) and on services by resident households, nonprofit institutions serving households (included in the tables in consumption of households), and the general government.

*Gross domestic investment* is calculated as the sum of gross fixed investment and change in inventories.

The *resource balance* or *net exports* of goods and nonfactor services represents the difference between exports of goods and nonfactor services and imports of goods and nonfactor services.

*Net Exports of goods and nonfactor services* are defined as the difference between exports and imports of goods and nonfactor services.

*Exports (imports) of goods* cover trade in "visible" goods realized as a result of business deals, deliveries according to agreements, barter exchanges, and other kinds of deliveries. Exports of goods are recorded at f.o.b. (free on board) prices that is, including the total cost up to the border of the exporting country; the imports of goods are recorded at c.i.f. prices, i.e. including the transport and insurance costs up to the border of the importing country.

*Exports (imports) of non-factor services* cover material and nonmaterial services and do not include payments or receipts of factor incomes (employee compensation, taxes or subsidies linked to production, dividends, and interest).

## 3. BALANCE OF PAYMENTS AND FOREIGN TRADE

For a complete and more authoritative explanation of concepts and definitions, please refer to: International Monetary Fund (IMF), *Balance of Payments Manual*, fifth edition (Washington D.C., 1993).

### Table 3-1: Balance of payments

The consolidated balance of payments is presented in US dollars.

The *current account* of the balance of payments refers to all transactions between resident and nonresident entities involving goods, services, income, and unrequited transfers.

*Exports of goods and services* (including workers' remittances) are the sum of exports of goods, nonfactor services, factor income receipts, and current receipts of workers' remittances. This variable is used in calculating the debt service and similar ratios.

*Exports (imports) of goods and nonfactor services* include the sum of merchandise and nonfactor services.

*Merchandise (f.o.b.)* covers exports (imports) of all goods ( with a few specified exceptions), whose ownership changes between a resident and a foreigner. The goods included are valued at their market prices and recorded for the period in which the change of ownership occurs. Also included are international transactions in nonmonetary gold, silver bullion, diamonds, and other precious metals and stones; paper money and coin not in current circulation as well as unissued securities, valued as commodities rather than at their face value; electricity, gas, and water; livestock driven across frontiers; parcel post; government exports and imports, including goods financed by grants and loans; goods transferred to or from a buffer stock organization; goods exported or imported by direct investment enterprises; migrants' personal effects; smuggled goods, whether or not detected by customs; and other unrecorded shipments, such as gifts and goods of less than a stated minimum value.

*Nonfactor services* include shipment, travel, and other nonfactor services.

*Shipment* covers freight, insurance, and other services relating to distribution.

*Travel* covers the goods and services acquired by nonresidents traveling for business or personal purposes for their own use during their stay (less than one year). International passenger services are recorded as other transportation and are not included under travel.

*Other services* include transportation, communications, financial and computer services; copyright and license payments; and other types of business services not included in shipment and travel.

The *resource balance* is calculated as the difference between exports and imports of goods and nonfactor services.

*Net factor income* is calculated as factor receipts less factor payments.

*Factor receipts* (from the rest of the world) refer to compensation of employees or similar labor-related income, dividends, interest, and rents received from the rest of the world.

*Factor payments* are payments made to the rest of the world. They include:

- *Total interest due*, which covers interest payments due on debt outstanding and disbursed, including short-term debt and IMF credit during the year specified (before rescheduling, forgiveness, and arrears accumulation).
- *Other factor payments and discrepancy* include royalty payments and gross total profit (repatriated or reinvested) on direct foreign investment. The discrepancy is the difference between the amount shown in the country's balance of payments and the World Bank's Debt Reporting System (DRS).

*Net current transfers* represent the difference between current transfer receipts and payments. The former include migrants' remittances and other current transfers, while the latter include transfers of income for which no corresponding service is rendered.

*Current account balance before official grants* is calculated as the resource balance plus net factor income plus net current private transfers.

*Official capital grants* include official unrequited transfers in the form of grant development assistance and capital transfers to finance gross capital formation or other forms of accumulation.

*Current account balance after official grants* is calculated as the sum of the current account balance before official grants and official capital grants.

*The capital account* of the balance of payments includes all transactions (actual and imputed), changes of ownership, and other specified changes in an economy's foreign financial assets and liabilities. Assets (other than monetary gold and SDRs) represent actual claims on nonresidents, while liabilities represent actual indebtedness to nonresidents.

*Long term capital inflows* are the sum of direct investment, net long-term borrowing, and other net long-term inflows.

*Adjustment to scheduled debt service* is the sum of debt service not paid plus arrears reductions and prepayments.

- *Debt service not paid* is the sum of interest and principal not paid. *Interest not paid* includes unpaid interest due to arrears, rescheduling, or forgiveness which is treated as a financing item. *Principal not paid* includes unpaid principal due to arrears, rescheduling, or forgiveness which is treated as a financing item.
- *Arrears reductions/prepayments* are cash payments over and above debt service due during the current year. Because these payments are cash outflows, they are shown as negative items. They include arrears forgiveness (reductions in interest/principal arrears) by official creditors with a counterpart entry under official capital grants.

*Total other items (net)* are calculated as the sum of net short-term capital, capital flows not elsewhere included and errors and omissions.

*Changes in net reserves* comprise the net change in a country's holdings of international reserves as a result of transactions recorded in the balance of payments current and capital accounts. They include changes in use of IMF credit, in holdings of monetary gold or SDRs, in the reserve position at the IMF, in foreign exchange assets, and in other claims on nonresidents available to the central authority. Also included as counterpart items are changes attributable to "reserve creation", monetization and/or demonetization of gold, allocation of SDRs, changes in the value of the reserves due to fluctuations in their prices (valuation change in reserves), and liabilities constituting foreign authorities' reserves (LCFARSs). An increase in net reserves (that is an increase in reserve assets or a decrease in reserve liabilities) is shown as a negative number to denote the use of foreign exchange.

*Net credit from IMF* is a member country's net drawing other than drawing against its reserve tranche position.

*Reserve changes not elsewhere included* are the total change in net reserves as defined above excluding net credit from the IMF.

The *escrow account* comprises assets set aside to guarantee future interest and principal repayments.

*Gross reserves (excluding gold)* comprises a country's holdings of Special Drawing Rights (SDRs), its reserve position in the IMF, and its holdings of foreign exchange.

*Gross reserves (including gold)* comprise gross reserves excluding gold plus the quantity of gold valued at the year-end gold price on the London market (as shown on the United Kingdom country page of the IMF's *International Financial Statistics*).

*Nominal official exchange rate (annual average)* is the period average of official or market rate.

*Nominal official exchange rate (end-of-year)* is the end-of-period official exchange rate.

*Manufactured unit value* is calculated as the weighted unit value index of exports of manufactures by industrial countries.

**Tables 3-2A and B: Imports by Commodity Group; Tables 3-3A and B: Exports by Commodity Group; Tables 3-4A and B: Geographical distribution of foreign trade**

These tables contain data on imports and exports according to the cif and fob basis respectively. A-Tables are in US dollars, B-Tables are in national currencies.The foreign trade nomenclatures are based on the Harmonized Commodity Description and Coding System (HS). For recent years foreign trade statistics are mostly customs data, which are reported in foreign currency (U.S. dollars usually). Since conversion to the national currency is performed at the date of the crossing of the customs border, the implicit trade conversion factors may differ considerably across commodity groups and trade partners, as well as from the exchange rates shown in other tables.

## 4. GOVERNMENT FINANCE

The concepts and definitions in these tables are taken from IMF, A Manual on Government Finance Statistics (Washington D.C., 1986) but have been slightly modified to take into consideration the manner in which most of the FSU government accounts have been compiled. The general government (state) budget is the consolidated account of the central and local (oblast, rayon, and municipal) governments.

**Table 4-1: General government budget revenue**

*Total revenue and grants* is calculated as the sum of total revenue and grants.

*Grants* are defined as unrequited, nonrepayable, noncompulsory receipts from other governments or international organizations in cash or in kind. These include gratuitous aid, and similar receipts, and, for 1990-1991, when the USSR existed, transfers from the all-union budget to the republican budgets.

*Total revenue* covers all receipts to the budgets of all levels (central, state, and local from enterprises and institutions and from households. It is divided into current and capital revenue.

*Current revenue* comprises tax and nontax revenue except grants, capital transfers, receipts from sales of land, intangible assets, and state and republican property.

*Tax revenue* comprises compulsory, unrequited, nonrepayable payments to government. Tax payments are classified on the basis of the item on which they are levied such as: income, payrolls, property, sales of goods and services, and external trade including social security contributions.

*Taxes on profits* include compulsory payments by enterprises and institutions (including foreign entities) based on the amount of their profits. They also include allowances from the profits of public enterprises and institutions and fixed (rental) payments.

*Social security contributions* represent the compulsory payments by enterprises of all forms of ownership and by self-employed persons to the government social security fund. Voluntary contributions paid to social security schemes by persons who are not legally required or bound to make such contributions, and contributions paid by enterprises and persons to social insurance funds outside the government are excluded.

*Taxes on payroll and work force* include taxes that are collected from employers, employees, or the self-employed either as a proportion of payroll or as a fixed amount per person and that are not earmarked for social security expenditures. Taxes included are payments for labor force, tax on the increase of the wage fund, tax on income of employees collected by employers, tax levied on single persons and families with or without children collected by employers.

*Taxes on property* cover taxes on the use, ownership, or transfer of wealth, movable and immovable property, levied at regular intervals, once and for all, or on the occasion of transfer. Included are taxes on changes in ownership of property through inheritance, gifts, or other transactions (financial and capital); one-time capital improvement taxes and special levies on capital; and recurrent taxes on immovable property- for example, building and land taxes.

*Domestic taxes on goods and services* cover all taxes and duties levied on the production, extraction, sale, transfer, leasing or delivery of goods, rendering of services, and also with respect to the use of goods, or permission to use goods and perform activities. Included are turnover taxes, sales taxes, value-added taxes, excises, taxes on the profits of fiscal monopolies, taxes on specific services, taxes on the use of goods, taxes on permission to use goods and perform activities, and other related taxes.

*Taxes on international trade and transactions* include import and export duties (taxes on imports and exports), customs duties, taxes on the profits of export or import monopolies, exchange taxes, exchange profit taxes, and taxes on travel, insurance , or investment abroad.

*Other taxes* cover taxes that cannot be allocated to any of the categories above. These are taxes on people not based on income or presumptive income (poll taxes, head taxes or capitation taxes), stamp duties, and also fines and penalties that cannot be classified as one of the taxes mentioned above. Included are taxes on urban improvement, allowances for construction and repairs of roads, passport fees, etc.

*Nontax revenues* includes all requited, nonrepayable government receipts from sources other than capital sales; all fines and penalties excluding those for noncompliance with taxes; and all voluntary, unrequited, nonrepayable, current government receipts from non-governmental sources. Therefore, this excludes government receipts from taxes, grants, borrowing, repayment of previous government lending; sales of fixed capital assets, stocks, land, and intangible assets; and gifts from nongovernmental sources for capital purposes.

*Capital revenue* covers government revenue from sales of fixed capital assets, stocks, land, and intangible assets as well as capital transfers from nongovernmental enterprises, nonprofit institutions, and individuals. Sales of intangible assets include sales of leases and concessions with respect to mineral deposits and fishing grounds, land, patents, copyrights, and trademarks.

Capital transfers cover also receipts for donations by nongovernmental sources for capital purposes, such as construction of buildings for social and cultural purposes or purchases of capital equipment. Capital transfers from other governments and international institutions are included with grants.

**Table 4-2: General government budget expenditure by economic type**

*Expenditure* is defined as government payments that are nonrepayable, that is, as payments that neither generate nor extinguish financial claims. Expenditure may be made for either current or capital purposes and may be requited or unrequited.

*Current expenditure* includes requited payments that are not connected with the acquisition of capital assets, goods or services to be used in the production of capital assets; or unrequited payments. The latter exclude the acquisition of capital assets, compensation for damage or destruction of capital assets, or increase in the financial capital of the recipients. Current expenditure is subdivided into expenditures on goods and services, interest payments on government debt, subsidies and other current transfers, and other expenditure.

*Expenditure on goods and services* represents payments in exchange for goods and services in the form of wages and salaries to employees, social security contributions, or other purchases of goods and services.

*Interest payments* are defined as payments for the use of loans obtained by the government. They do not include the repayment of debts and the commission charges paid for assistance in placing debt. They also exclude government payments of interest on loans provided to other sectors and government transfers to others for such purposes. Interest payments are shown separately for domestic and foreign debt.

*Subsidies and other current transfers* include all unrequited, nonreimbursable government payments for current purposes. They do not include transfers in kind or transfers for capital purposes.

*Other* includes other current expenditure not elsewhere classified.

*Capital expenditure* comprises payments for the acquisition of fixed capital assets, stocks, land, and intangible assets, as well as capital transfers and other capital expenditure.

*Acquisition of fixed capital assets* represents payments for purchases in the market or production within government of durable goods to be used for nonmilitary productive purposes. It includes expenditure on construction, on major repairs, and on purchases of machinery and equipment considered fixed capital goods. It does not include construction for military purposes and purchases of military equipment.

*Capital transfers* consist of unrequited government payments, neither generating nor extinguishing financial claims, made for the purposes of acquiring capital assets, compensating for the damage or destruction of capital assets, or increasing the financial capital of the recipients. They include government payments to cover construction expenses for various sectors, major repairs, acquisition of livestock, and other capital investment; compensation payments for the damage or destruction of capital assets, and for amortization of debts of other sectors; and payments to cover long-term losses of enterprises or exceptional losses due to causes beyond their control. Excluded are the government assumption of the debt of others and the cancellation of debt owed to government by other sectors with no cash transactions taking place.

*Other* includes government payments for the purchase of strategic and emergency stocks, land, and intangible assets.

*Surplus/deficit* (-) is calculated as total revenue and grants less total expenditure. With the opposite sign, it is also equal to the sum of net borrowing by the government, plus the net decrease in government cash, deposits, and securities held for liquidity purposes.

*Financing by type of debt holder* represents the total funds (foreign or domestic) obtained to cover a deficit or allocated from a surplus. The financing is equal to the surplus/deficit but with an opposite sign.

*Foreign (net)* covers lending to and repayments from nonresident governments, supranational authorities, international institutions, foreign individuals, enterprises, other entities, including commercial banks, and the acquisition or sale of equity in nonresident enterprises. Loans and credits from international development institutions include financing from the World Bank and from regional development banks, such as the Asian Development Bank, the Inter-American Development Bank, and the European Bank for Reconstruction and Development.

*Domestic (net)* includes all government financing transactions with resident individuals, enterprises, governments, and other entities. It may be affected by trading in outstanding government securities between residents and nonresidents. It covers changes in government holdings of national currency, deposits in resident financial institutions, and securities issued by residents and held by government for liquidity purposes. Borrowing *from monetary authorities* covers changes in liabilities to and claims on the central bank and other parts of the monetary system, along with other transactions equivalent in effect to credit from or to the monetary authorities though giving rise to no resulting claims. Borrowing *from deposit money banks* covers government financing from all deposit money banks, that is, financial institutions whose liabilities are primarily in the form of deposits exchangeable on sight for currency and transferable as a means of payment. *Other domestic borrowing* includes all domestic borrowing by the government from sources other than monetary authorities and deposit money banks. Implicitly, it includes domestic financing from other general government in the form of changes in the government's fixed-term contractual obligations to other parts of the general government through borrowing, repayment, securities transactions, and changes in the holdings of securities of other parts of the general government for liquidity purposes. The mutual financing among different parts of the general government would not be reflected in the consolidated total amount of financing for the general government as debits and credits from the different parts would cancel out.

*Extrabudgetary surplus/deficit (-) not included above* generally refers to accounts of government transactions that are not included in budget totals or documents and do not operate through normal budgetary procedures. Such transactions may, for example, be financed through foreign aid or special revenue not included in the budget.

*Total surplus/deficit (-) including extra-budgetary accounts* is calculated as the sum of the surplus/deficit and the extrabudgetary surplus/deficit.

## 5. AGRICULTURE STATISTICS

**Tables 5-1 and 5-2: Agricultural production** (in current and constant prices respectively)

*Total Gross agricultural production* includes the value of output produced during the year as a result of the cultivation of crops, the rearing of livestock, and their economic use.

*Crop production* includes the harvest value of all types of crops; the increase or decrease in the value of crops due to incomplete harvest; as well as expenditures on planting and cultivating orchards and other perennial plantings (except trees) until they are harvested.

*Animal husbandry* includes the value added in the process of breeding and fattening livestock and poultry; the value of output derived from the economic use of livestock (milk, wool, eggs etc.); the value of output of fur farming, dog breeding, and fish farms (fish breeding in ponds).

*Agricultural services* comprise the value of services for the improvement of land and for the protection of crops and livestock from disease, i. e. soil fertilization, other agrochemical work, zootechnical and veterinary services, irrigation, and services rendered by enterprises and organizations maintaining irrigation and environmental equipment.

**Table 5-3: Production and average yield of major agricultural crops**

Total production data are compiled on the basis of reports submitted by all state farms, collective farms, and other agricultural enterprises. Figures for production on private plots are compiled from family budget surveys. To compute average yield, the total harvest is divided by the corrected production area.

**Table 5-4: Main aggregates of animal husbandry**

The table on livestock and products of animal husbandry contains data presented in physical units.

## 6. INDUSTRY AND ENERGY STATISTICS

Note that the lists of industries/final users is not exhaustive which results in discrepancy between the sums of the breakdown and the entries for totals.

**Tables 6-1 and 6-2: Industrial production by sector** (in current and constant prices respectively)

Both total production and production by sector are sums of gross industrial output valued at enterprise wholesale prices of individual industrial enterprises. The gross output of an enterprise calculated by this method includes the value of its finished output, the value of the sold semi-finished products, and the output of ancillary industrial units, produced either with the enterprise's or with customers' raw materials. Also included are costs of major repairs performed on a contract basis and repairs on enterprise property such as utilities, subsidiary agricultural units and buildings for nonindustrial needs.

The rate of growth of industrial production (bottom half of table 6-2) is calculated at constant prices.

*Heavy industry* includes machine-building, fuel-energy industry, metallurgy (including ore extraction), chemical and petrochemical industry, timber, wood-working, pulp and paper industry, and production of construction materials.

*Light industry* includes the textiles industry (cotton, flax, hemp, jute, wool, silk, hosiery felt, and haberdashery); the clothing industry; the leather, fur, and shoe industry; and miscellaneous branches of light industry.

**Table 6-3: Primary energy supply**

*Primary production* refers to the quantity of energy extracted from natural sources, and measured after the removal of inert matter from fuels. It includes the energy consumed in this process supplied to other energy producers for transformation or other uses.

**Table 6-4: Final energy consumption**

*Final energy consumption* accounts for the use of energy products in all sectors for end-use purposes.

*Consumption by industry* excludes consumption by the energy sector and all inputs into energy conversion. Consumption in the chemical industry includes only energy used as fuel.

*Consumption by agriculture* includes fuels and energy used by agricultural equipment as well as in hunting, fishing, and forestry.

*Consumption by transport* includes all fuel consumed by road traffic as well as deliveries to ships engaged in inland and coastal water transportation and to aircraft engaged in domestic flights.

*Consumption by households* includes fuels and energy used for heat, light, and in operating electrical appliances. This category also includes free issues to employees.

## 7. PRICES AND WAGES

**Table 7-1: Exchange Rates and Price Indices**

The exchange rates are monthly averages of official exchange rates of the national banks of the respective countries.

The *wholesale prices* of industrial products are those prices at which goods are sold to enterprises and institutions. Wholesale prices presented here in most cases are measured at the enterprise level. Enterprise-level wholesale prices reflect the production cost plus the operating surplus of the enterprise. The output is valued in these prices.

*Consumer prices* reflect the prices at which goods and services are bought by households through the retail trade network, in public dining establishments, as well as by other entities and individuals providing paid services.

### Table 7-2: Monthly nominal wages by sector

*The nominal wage* is the gross amount paid to a worker or employee for work done during a fixed of period of time. The wages given for each sector are for both blue-collar and white-collar workers.

*The nominal wages by sector* are estimates based on average earnings. They are determined by dividing the wage fund by the number of workers and employees. Included in the wage fund are regular and one-time bonuses, premiums, and other payments from the material stimulation fund.

## 8. HOUSEHOLD INCOMES AND EXPENDITURES

### Table 8-1: Money income and expenditure of the population

Table 8-1 presents household monetary income and expenditures by type. It includes transactions between the population and the state. Monetary incomes are shown on a gross basis before taxes. Monetary expenditures are recorded as actual cash outlays and not as amounts owed for goods or services received.

*Income* includes all money receipts of the population in cash.

*Total labor income* is the sum of regular wages, overtime wages, other compensation, income paid by collective farms, and income from the sale of farm products.

*Total transfer receipts* are the sum of pensions and allowances, scholarships, income from the financial system, and other miscellaneous income.

*Total income* is calculated as the sum of total labor income and transfer receipts.

*Expenditure* comprises expenditures by the population incurred both in cash transactions and via transfers without actual cash transactions.

*Total purchases* are calculated as the sum of retail trade purchases and purchased services.

*Rent and utilities* include rent for dwellings and payments for hotels, hostel services, and public utilities (central heating, electricity, gas, water supply, and sewage).

*Transport and communications* cover payments for passenger and luggage transport as well as similar services rendered by transport enterprises of all types to the population while traveling; payments for postal, telegraph, and telephone services, for delivery of parcels and remittances, and for broadcasting services.

*Health and other services* include voucher payments for medical care, rest, and tourism; purchases of personal services, payments related to childcare, entertainment, legal services, bank services , education, and so on.

*Transfers and savings* include savings and compulsory payments by the population to the state budget and to various other institutions.

*Taxes, fees, dues and other* include all types of taxes and fees, stamp duties, penalties, and other payments made by the population to the state budget.

*Savings* include the increase in personal deposits balances in savings banks, and in the State (Central) Bank, as well as purchases of state bonds.

*Other* includes insurance premiums, voluntary contributions to nonprofit and cooperative institutions (including housing construction cooperatives), repayment of bank loans, purchases of lottery tickets, payments of interest on consumer credit, and decrease in consumer debt.

*Total expenditures* are calculated as total purchases and transfers plus savings.

*Income less expenditures* is calculated as the difference between total income and total expenditure. It represents the cash balance of households.

# Комментарии к показателям

В данных комментариях объясняются общие методы и источники информации, использованные при составлении настоящего сборника. Источники и методология, носящие страновую специфику, объясняются в комментариях к таблицам. Сравнительные таблицы используют ту же информацию, что и таблицы для отдельных стран. Таким образом, для них справедливы те же определения и методология. В случае возникновения дополнительных вопросов относительно используемой методологии и методов читателю предлагается ознакомиться с документами и материалами, цитируемыми и используемыми в данной публикации.

## 1. НАСЕЛЕНИЕ, ТРУДОВЫЕ РЕСУРСЫ И ЗАНЯТОСТЬ

### Таблица 1-1: Население и занятость

Приводимые ниже определения описывают категории трудовых ресурсов и форм собственности.

*Трудоспособный возраст* - для мужчин определен в рамках 16-59 лет, для женщин - 16-54 года. Верхние границы этих интервалов являются законодательно установленным пенсионным возрастом и не принимают в расчет показателей реальной занятости.

*Трудовые ресурсы* - термин использовался в Советском Союзе и до сих пор используется в некоторых странах бывшего СССР. В это понятие включаются все те, кто работает, и все те, кто находится в трудоспособном возрасте, но в настоящее время не работает. Трудовые ресурсы включают трудоспособное население в трудоспособном возрасте и занятое население старше и младше трудоспособного возраста. Таким образом, трудовые ресурсы состоят из занятого населения, студентов очного обучения в трудоспособном возрасте, служащих культа и трудоспособного населения, не занятого в народном хозяйстве. Последняя группа включает домашних хозяек, военнослужащих,сезонных рабочих, не занятых в данное время, а также полностью безработных. Концепция трудовых ресурсов отличается от концепции рабочей силы, используемой статистическими организациями многих западных стран. Рабочая сила определяется как сумма тех, кто работает, и тех, кто ищет работу.

*Занятое население* - сумма занятых в государственном секторе, на арендных предприятиях, в акционерных компаниях, в экономических ассоциациях, общественных организациях, на совместных предприятиях, в колхозах, кооперативах, индивидуальной трудовой деятельностью, в личных подсобных хозяйствах и в фермерских хозяйствах.

*Государственный сектор* - предприятия государственной формы собственности, государственный аппарат, а другие находящиеся в ведении государства учреждения.

*Арендные предприятия* - государственные или колхозные предприятия, которые были сданы в аренду, обычно коллективу. В типичной ситуации персонал арендованного предприятия продолжает на нем работать, но получает больший контроль над его деятельностью.

*Акционерные общества* включают предприятия, в т.ч. бывшие государственные, выпустившие пакеты собственных акций. Согласно западной деловой терминологии эти предприятия "приватизированы".

*Хозяйственные ассоциации* - ассоциации предприятий, объединившихся для деятельности вне министерских структур.

*Общественные организации* - фонды, благотворительные и другие общественные организации.

*Совместные предприятия* - предприятия, частично принадлежащие иностранным физическим и юридическим лицам.

*Колхозы* - сельскохозяйственные предприятия, находящиеся в коллективной собственности занятого на них персонала. Занятые в колхозах, в отличие от занятых в совхозах, не являются государственными служащими.

*Кооперативный сектор* - включает кооперативы по производству товаров и услуг и потребительскую кооперацию. *Кооперативы по производству товаров и услуг* - так же называемые частными кооперативами - были разрешены в 1987 г. С незначительными ограничениями они могут заниматься деятельностью практически во всех сферах производства и сервиса. Деятельность этого сектора экономики не следует путать с индивидуальной трудовой деятельностью, т.к. необходимым условием для образования кооператива должно быть наличие минимум трех соучредителей. *Потребительские кооперативы* - в отличие от недавно разрешенных частных кооперативов существовали всегда, а в 60-е годы отчетность по ним была включена в отчетность по государственному сектору. В некоторых недавних статистических публикациях отчетность по ним изъята из отчетности по госсектору и приплюсована к отчетности по частным кооперативам.

*Фермерские хозяйства* - мелкие, независимые фермы, также называемые крестьянскими хозяйствами. Небольшое количество крестьянских хозяйств (хуторов) существовало во все годы советской власти, но их число до недавнего времени было микроскопическим. Законодательство, касающееся этих хозяйств, было выработано несколько лет назад.

*Личные подсобные хозяйства* - сюда включены те лица (в основном сельские жители), кому разрешено иметь небольшой участок земли и небольшое количество скота в личном пользовании. Большинство занятых в ЛПХ работают на своих участках в свободное от основной работы время. Но несмотря на то, что общий размер земель под ЛПХ составляет незначительную долю сельскохозяйственных угодий, они занимают значительный вес в производстве ряда важнейших сельскохозяйственных продуктов. Ограничения на этот род деятельности были недавно отменены и его развитие ускорилось.

*Индивидуальная трудовая деятельность* - включает лиц, производящих кустарные изделия и оказывающих услуги. Законодательно разрешена в 1986 году.

*Рабочая сила* - этот показатель не полностью соответствует международным стандартам и рассчитывается как сумма занятого населения и количества безработных.

### Таблица 1-2: Численность занятого населения по секторам экономики

К населению, *занятому в экономике*, относятся рабочие и служащие, колхозники, занятые в общественном хозяйстве колхозов; колхозники и члены семей рабочих и служащих в трудоспособном возрасте, занятые в личном подсобном хозяйстве; лица, занятые индивидуальной трудовой деятельностью; лица, занятые на частных и кооперативных предприятиях, совместных предприятиях, общественных организациях (фондах), ассоциациях и во всех иных новых формах хозяйственно деятельности. Среднегодовые показатели рассчитываются как средняя показателей по 12 месяцам.

### Таблица 1-3. Численность зарегистрированных безработных

*Численность зарегистрированных безработных* показывает числленность зарегистрированных в отделениях государственной службы занятости лиц, соответствующих статусу безработного.

## 2. НАЦИОНАЛЬНЫЕ СЧЕТА

Приведенные ниже определения и понятия даются в сжатом изложении. Более подробную информацию читатель может найти в :

Organization for Economic Cooperation and Development: National Accounts for the Former Soviet Union - Sources, Methods and Estimates, OECD/GD (92)/175 (Paris,1992) - имеется русский перевод.

Commission of the European Communities, International Monetary Fund, Organization for Economic Co-operation and Development, United Nations, World Bank: System of National Accounts 1993 (Brussels/Luxembourg, New York, Paris, Washington, D.C., 1993).

### Таблицы 2-1 и 2-2: Валовый внутренний продукт

В Таблице 2-1 Валовый внутренний продукт (ВВП) по отраслевому происхождению и по категориям конечного использования приводится в текущих ценах; в Таблице 2-2 те же показатели приводятся в постоянных ценах.

*Валовый внутренний продукт* в рыночных ценах представляет собой конечный результат экономической деятельности резидентных хозяйственных единиц как сферы материального производства, так и сферы нематериальных услуг и может быть исчислен двумя методами:

- как сумма валовой добавленной стоимости всех резидентных производственных единиц (сгруппированных по секторам или отраслям) плюс чистые косвенные налоги на произведенные продукты и импорт;
- как сумма валовых расходов на конечное использование товаров и услуг (включая экспорт) в ценах покупателя минус импорт товаров и нефакторных услуг в ценах сиф (страховка и фрахт).

*ВВП по отраслевому происхождению* - вклад каждой отрасли в ВВП - оценивается по величине добавленной стоимости. Валовая добавленная стоимость определяется как разность между валовым выпуском и промежуточным потреблением. Валовый выпуск представляет собой стоимость произведенных в течение данного периода товаров и услуг, включаемых в границы производства в СНС. Промежуточное потребление - это стоимость всех товаров и услуг (за исключением основных фондов), потребленных в производстве. К промежуточному потреблению относятся и услуги финансовых посредников. Поскольку на практике их величину трудно распределить по отдельным секторам-пользователям, в некоторых странах они рассчитываются суммарно и представляются как промежуточное потребление номинальной отрасли, отсюда - *Условно-исчисленная стоимость услуг финансовых посредников*. Эти данные приводятся отдельной строкой и включаются в *Валовую добавленную стоимость, всего*, но не включаются в итог по *Другим отраслям*.

Для получения *ВВП по факторной стоимости* надо из суммы добавленной стоимости по отраслям исключить косвенные налоги (налоги на производство, взимаемые независимо от наличия прибыли), уплачиваемые в процессе производственной деятельности, и добавить субсидии, получаемые в связи с производственной деятельностью. При расчете добавленной стоимости по отраслям на основе оценки валового выпуска в основных ценах эти налоги и субсидии не включают налоги и субсидии на продукты и импорт.

Для получения ВВП в рыночных ценах надо к ВВП по факторной стоимости прибавить чистые косвенные налоги. Чистые косвенные налоги представляют собой разницу между всеми налогами на производство и импорт и всеми субсидиями на производство и импорт.

*ВВП по категориям расходов* представляет собой конечное использование товаров и услуг и включает потребление, валовое накопление и чистый экспорт (сальдо экспорта и импорта) товаров и нефакторных услуг.

*Конечное потребление* - включает расходы на потребительские товары (независимо от длительности их использования, за исключением покупок жилья) и услуги, производимые резидентными домашними хозяйствами, некоммерческими организациями, обслуживающими домашние хозяйства (здесь они отнесены к потреблению домашних хозяйств), а также сектором общего государственного управления.

*Валовое внутреннее накопление* - рассчитывается как сумма валового накопления основного капитала и изменения запасов материальных оборотных средств.

*Ресурсный баланс* (чистый экспорт товаров и нефакторных услуг) представляет собой разность между экспортом и импортом товаров и нефакторных услуг.

*Экпорт (импорт) товаров и нефакторных услуг* - сумма экспорта (импорта) товаров и экспорта (импорта) нефакторных услуг.

*Экпорт (импорт)* товаров включает торговлю товарами, реализуемыми в результате коммерческих сделок, поставок в счет соглашений, бартера и других видов поставок. Учет экспорта товаров производится по ценам фоб, то есть включая все затраты до границы страны-продавца; учет импорта производится по ценам сиф, то есть включая затраты на транспортировку и страхование.

*Экспорт (импорт) нефакторных услуг* охватывает материальные и нематериальные услуги и не включает выплаты и поступления факторных доходов (оплату труда, налоги и субсидии на производство, проценты и дивиденды).

## 3. ПЛАТЕЖНЫЙ БАЛАНС И МЕЖДУНАРОДНАЯ ТОРГОВЛЯ

Для более глубокого объяснения показателей платежного баланса необходимо обратиться к Пособию по составлению платежного баланса (IMF, Balance of Payments Manual, fifth edition, Washington, D.C., 1993).

**Таблица 3-1: Платежный баланс**

Консолидированный платежный баланс приводится в долларах США.

*Счет текущих операций* платежного баланса обобщает статистические сведения о внешнеэкономической деятельности, связанной с движением товаров, услуг, доходов и трансфертов.

*Экспорт товаров и услуг* (включая денежные переводы рабочих) - это сумма товаров и нефакторных услуг, факторных доходов и денежных переводов рабочих. Эта сумма используется для расчета показателей обслуживания внешнего долга и т.п.

*Экспорт (импорт) товаров и нефакторных услуг* - это сумма товаров и нефакторных услуг.

*Экспорт (импорт) товаров (фоб)* охватывает операции со всеми товарами (за немногими исключениями) между резидентами и нерезидентами, при которых происходит фактическая или условная смена владельца. В экспорт и импорт должны быть включены также немонетарное золото, серебряные слит-ки, бриллианты и другие ценные металлы и камни; бумажные деньги и монеты не в текущем обращении и невыпущенные ценные бумаги, которые должны оцениваться как товары, а не по своей номинальной стоимости; электричество, газ и вода; скот, перегоняемый через границы; почтовые посылки; правительственный экспорт и импорт, включая товары, финансируемые субсидиями и займами; товары, переводимые к и от владельцев организации резервного запаса; экспортируемые или импортируемые товары предприятиями с прямыми инвестициями; личные вещи мигрантов; контрабандные товары, обнаруженные или не обнаруженные таможней; другие недокументированные грузы, такие как подарки и грузы с менее, чем подлежащей объявлению минимальой стоимостью.

*Нефакторные услуги* являются второй основной категорией текущего счета. Международная торговля услугами охватывает услуги по перевозкам, поездкам, связи, финансовые и компьютерные услуги, авторские и лицензионные платежи и многие виды других деловых услуг.

*Перевозки* включают грузовые и пассажирские перевозки всеми видами транспорта и другие распределительные и вспомогательные услуги, включая аренду транспортного оборудования вместе с экипажами (на ограниченные сроки).

*Поездки* включают стоимость товаров и услуг, приобретенных у резидентов данной страны нерезидентами-путешественнниками для деловых и личных целей во время их пребывания (менее одного года) в данной стране для их личного потребления.

*Другие услуги* включают транспортные услуги, услуги связи, финансовые и другие услуги, не включенные в "перевозки и поездки".

*Сальдо ресурсов* это сумма сальдо торгового баланса и сальдо баланса нефакторных услуг.

*Чистый факторный доход* расчитывается как разница между факторными доходами и факторными платежами.

*Факторный доход* - компонент платежного баланса, характеризующий распределение доходов, созданных трудом, капиталом, собственностью (заработная плата, дивиденды, чистые проценты, рента).

*Факторные платежи* представляют платежи нерезидентам и подразделяются здесь на:

- *Общую сумму процентов к оплате*, которая включает проценты по долгам, подлежащие оплате в рассматриваемом году, включая проценты по краткосрочной задолженности и кредитам МВФ (без учета переноса сроков выплаты, списания, а также просроченной задолженности);
- *Другие факторные платежи и статистическую погрешность*, что включает плату за авторские и лицензионные права, брутто-прибыль от прямых заграничных инвестиций (вывезенную или реинвестированную). Погрешность - это разница между объемами, показанными в платежном балансе, и объемами, показанными в Системе Отчетности Должников Всемирного Банка.

*Чистые текущие трансферты* - это разница между текущими трансфертными поступлениями и текущими трансфертными платежами. *Текущие трансфертные поступления* представлены суммой денежных переводов рабочих и других трансфертов. *Текущие трансфертные платежи* представлены здесь всеми односторонними выплатами.

*Сальдо текущего счета до официальных безвозмездных трансфертов* - это сумма сальдо ресурсов, чистого факторного дохода и чистых текущих частных трансфертов.

*Официальные капитальные безвозмездные трансферты* включают официальные односторонние трансферты для финансирования капитальных вложений и других форм накопления.

*Сальдо текущего счета после официальных безвозмездных трансфертов* - это сальдо текущего счета до официальных трансфертов и официальные капитальные безвозмездные трансферты.

*Счет операций с капиталом* является разделом платежного баланса; включает все операции фактические и условно начисленные) и показывает изменения во владении в зарубежных финансовых активах и пассивах. Активы являются требованиями к нерезидентам, а пассивы - обязательствами по отношению к нерезидентам за определенный период времени. Операции с капиталом классифицируются как: прямые инвестиции, портфельные инвестиции, прочие операции с капиталом и резервы.

*Долгосрочные притоки капитала* - это сумма прямых инвестиций, чистых долгосрочных займов и других долгосрочных притоков.

*Регулирование долга* - это сумма невыплаченного долга плюс сокращение просроченной суммы погашения долга и выплаты авансом.

- *Сумма невыплаченного долга* - это сумма невыплаченных процентов и невыплаченных сумм в счет погашения основного долга. *Невыплаченные проценты* включают в себя проценты, невыплаченные в результате просрочки платежей, переноса их срока или списания. Рассматриваются как статья финансирования. *Невыплаченные суммы в счет погашения основного долга* включают в себя суммы в счет погашения основного долга, невыплаченные в результате задержки платежей, переноса их срока или списания. Рассматриваются как статья финансирования.
- *Сокращение просроченной суммы погашения долга/выплаты авансом (-)* - кассовые выплаты сверх сумм, подлежащих уплате в счет обслуживания внешнего долга в текущем году. Поскольку эти платежи представляют собой кассовый отток, они должны показываться с отрицательным знаком. Сюда же входит списание просроченных платежей (сокращение просрочки платежей по процентам/основному долгу) официальными кредиторами с соответствующей записью по статье официальных капитальных безвозмездных трансфертов.

*Общие другие статьи, сальдо* - сумма сальдо краткосрочного капитала, потоков капитала, не указанных выше, а также ошибок и пропусков.

*Изменение в чистых резервах* включает сальдо изменения внешних резервов рассматриваемой страны в результате сделок по текущему счету и счету движения капитала. Сюда входят изменения в использовании кредитов МВФ, запасах монетарного золота, специальных прав заимствования (СПЗ), резервной позиции в МВФ, активах иностранной валюты, а также иных требованиях к нерезидентам, которыми располагает центральный орган власти. Здесь же учитываются балансирующие статьи, представляющие собой изменения в результате создания резервов, т.е. монетаризация и/или демонетаризация золота, размещение СПЗ, изменение стоимости активов в результате колебания их цены (поправка на переоценку активов), а также обязательства, составляющие резервы иностранных государст. Прирост сальдо внешних резервов (т.е. увеличение резервных активов страны или сокращение ее резервных обязательств) показывается с отрицательным знаком, т.к. свидетельствует об использовании иностранной валюты.

*Чистый кредит МВФ* - чистые заимствования рассматриваемой страны помимо заимствований в пределах ее резервной позиции в МВФ.

*Изменение резервов, не указанных выше,* - общее изменение сальдо внешних резервов, как оно определено выше, за вычетом чистого кредита МВФ.

*Счет депонирования* - активы, выделенные для обеспечения предстоящих платежей по обслуживанию внешнего долга.

*Общие резервы (исключая золото)* включают СПЗ, резервную позициюв МВФ и активы в иностранной валюте.

*Общие резервы (включая золото)* представляют собой резервные активы (за исключением золота) плюс количество золота, умноженное на его цену на лондонском рынке на конец года (которая показана в Разделе "Великобритания" в International Financial Statistics).

*Номинальный официальный валютный (обменный) курс (среднегодовой)* - среднегодовое значение официального рыночного курса.

*Номинальный официальный валютный (обменный) курс (на конец года)* - официальный валютный курс на конец года.

*Средний индекс единичной стоимости продукции обрабатывающей промышленности* рассчитывается как средневзвешенный индекс единичной стоимости промышленных товаров, экспортируемых развитыми странами.

**Таблицы 3-2А и В: Импорт по товарным группам; Таблицы 3-3А и В: Экспорт по товарным группам; Таблицы 3-4А и В: Географическое распределение внешней торговли.**

В этих таблицах приводятся данные по импорту и экспорту в текущих ценах сиф и фоб соответственно, в таблицах А - в долларах США, в таблицах В - в национальной валюте. Товарные группы приводятся на основе Гармонизированной системы описания и кодирования товаров (ГС). Данные за последние годы чаще всего основаны на таможенной статистике, которая исходно представляется в конвертируемой валюте (обычно долларах США). Поскольку переоценка в национальную валюту осуществляется на дату пересечения таможенной границы, расчетный курс по внешнеторговым операциям может существенно различаться как по товарным группам, так и по торговым партнерам, а также отличаться от официального валютного курса, приводимого в других таблицах.

## 4. ГОСУДАРСТВЕННЫЕ ФИНАНСЫ

Понятия и определения в последующих таблицах разработаны Международным Валютным Фондом (см. A Manual on Government Finance Statistics. Washington DC., 1986) и несколько модифицированы с учетом существовавшей практики учета государственных финансов. Бюджетом органов власти всех уровней (государственным консолидированным бюджетом) является консолидированный бюджет органов управления всех уровней: центрального, региональных (область, автономная республика и т.л.) и местных (районных).

**Таблица 4-1: Доходы государственного бюджета**

*Всего доходов, включая безвозмездные поступления* - рассчитывается как сумма "Всего доходов" и "Безвозмездных поступлений".

*Безвозмездные поступления* представляют собой поступления от других государств или международных организаций в денежной или натуральной форме на безвозвратной и добровольной основах. Сюда включается гуманитарная помощь и т.д., а также безвозмездные поступления средств в республиканские бюджеты из союзного бюджета в период существования СССР.

*Доходы государственного бюджета* включают все поступления от предприятий и учреждений, а также от населения в бюджеты всех уровней управления. Они делятся на текущие и капитальные доходы.

*Текущие доходы* включают налоговые и неналоговые доходы (кроме безвозмездных поступлений, поступлений от продажи земли, нематериальных активов, государственного имущества, капитальных трансфертов).

*Налоговые доходы* включают различные виды налогов, то есть безвозвратных обязательных платежей органам управления, сгруппированных по объектам налогообложения: доходы, заработная плата, имущество, продажа товаров и услуг, внешняя торговля. Сюда же относятся и отчисления на социальное страхование.

*Налоги на прибыль* включают обязательные платежи предприятий и организаций (в том числе иностранных юридических лиц), размер которых устанавливается в зависимости от размера прибыли. К ним относятся также отчисления от прибыли государственных предприятий и организаций и фиксированные (рентные) платежи.

Налоги на доходы и прибыль показываются раздельно по физическим лицам и предприятиям и организациям. Налоги на корпорации, в отличие от налогов с физических лиц, налагаются на предприятие как на юридическое лицо, а не на владеющих им физических лиц.

*Отчисления на социальное страхование* включают в себя обязательные взносы предприятий всех форм собственности, а также самозанятых лиц в фонд государственного социального страхования. Сюда не включаются добровольные взносы физических лиц на социальное страхование, а также взносы предприятий и юридических лиц в негосударственные фонды социального страхования.

*Налоги на заработную плату и рабочую силу* включают налоги, взимаемые с предприятий, наёмных работников и самозанятых лиц пропорционально заработной плате или в фиксированном размере с человека, не относящиеся к расходам на социальное страхование. Сюда относятся плата за трудовые ресурсы, налог на прирост средств на оплату труда, подоходный налог, удерживаемый с граждан предприятиями, учреждениями и организациями, налог на холостяков, одиноких и малосемейных граждан, удерживаемый предприятиями.

*Налоги на собственность* включают налоги на использование, владение или передачу собственности, движимого или недвижимого имущества,которые уплачиваются регулярно, однократно или в связи с передачей. Сюда относятся налоги на имущество, переходящее в порядке наследования, дарения и прочей смены владельца (в результате финансовых или капитальных сделок), налог на операции с ценными бумагами, налог с владельцев транспортных средств, налоги на недвижимое имущество, например налог с владельцев строений и земельный налог и т.п.

*Внутренние налоги на товары и услуги* включают все налоги и пошлины, которыми облагается производство, добыча, продажа, передача, сдача в аренду или поставка товаров и предоставление услуг; налоги, взимаемые в связи с предоставлением товаров или предоставлением разрешения на использование товаров или занятие какой-либо деятельностью. Сюда включаются налог с продаж, с оборота или на добавленную стоимость, акцизы, прибыли фискальных монополий, налоги на особые услуги и др.

*Налоги на внешнюю торговлю и международные операции* включают импортные и экспортные пошлины (налоги на импорт и экспорт), таможенные пошлины, налоги на прибыли экспортных и импортных монополий, налоги на продажу и покупку иностранной валюты, поступление прибыли государственной монополии на продажу и покупку иностранной валюты, налоги на заграничные поездки, на страхование или инвестиции за границей.

*Прочие налоги* включают различные виды налогов, которые не могут быть отнесены к какой-либо из вышеупомянутых категорий (например, налоги с физических лиц, не связанные с их доходами или подушный налог; государственная пошлина, которая не может рассматриваться как ни один из вышеупомянутых видов налогов; штраф и пени за несвоевременную уплату или неуплату налогов; налоги, которые не могут быть отнесены к какой-либо вышеупомянутой категории налогов, к которым относятся, в частности, налог на благоустройство городов, отчисления на строительство и ремонт автомобильных дорог, сбор за выдачу паспорта, гербовый сбор, и т.п.).

*Неналоговые доходы* включают все возмездные и безвозмездные поступления в государственный бюджет (такие как доходы государства от собственности и предпринимательской деятельности, от продажи товаров и услуг за исключением продажи основных фондов, поступления по административным штрафам и санкциям кроме штрафов за неуплату налогов, все добровольные, безвозмездные текущие поступления из негосударственных источников). Таким образом, в эту категорию не входят налоговые поступления, безвозмездные поступления, займы, поступления по представленным ранее государственным кредитам, продажи основных фондов, резервов, земли и нематериальных активов, а также безвозмездные поступления из негосударственных источников, направленные на капиталовложения.

*Капитальные доходы* включают доходы от продажи основного капитала, запасов из государственных резервов, земли и нематериальных активов, капитальные трансферты от негосударственных предприятий, некоммерческих организаций, частных лиц. Продажа нематериальных активов включает продажу лицензий и концессий на разработку полезных ископаемых, лов рыбы и т.п., патентов, авторских прав, товарных знаков. К капитальным трансфертам относятся пожертвования из негосударственных источников, например, на строительство социально-культурных объектов, приобретение оборудования и т.п. Капитальные трансферты от других государств и международных организаций относятся к безвозмездным поступлениям.

**Таблица 4-2: Расходы государственного бюджета по экономическим типам**

*Расходы* определяются как государственные расходы, которые производятся на безвозвратной основе, то есть не связаны с возникновением или погашением финансовых требований. Эти расходы могут быть направлены как на текущие, так и на капитальные цели, они могут быть как возмещаемыми, так и безвозмездными.

*Текущие расходы* включают возмещаемые выплаты, не связанные с приобретением основного капитала, товаров и услуг для производства основного капитала, а также безвозмездные выплаты. Безвозмездные выплаты не включают приобретение капитальных активов, возмещение ущерба за повреждение основного капитала или увеличение финансовых активов получателей. В составе текущих расходов выделяются расходы на товары и услуги, выплату процентов по государственному долгу, субсидии и другие текущие трансферты и прочие расходы.

*Расходы на товары и услуги* представляют собой плату за товары и услуги и включают заработную плату работников общего государственного управления, отчисления на их социальное страхование, другие покупки товаров и услуг.

*Выплата процентов* представляет собой платежи за использование полученных от государства кредитов. Сюда не включается погашение кредитов и оплата комиссионных издержек за посредничество в получении кредита. Не включается также выплата процентов государством по кредитам, предоставленным другим секторам, или трансферты государства другим секторам на эти цели. Выплата процентов показывается отдельно по внутреннему и по внешнему долгу.

*Субсидии и другие текущие трансферты* включают другие различные безвозвратные государственные денежные выплаты для финансирования текущих расходов. Трансферты в натуральной форме и на капитальные цели здесь не учитываются.

*Прочие расходы* включают другие текущие расходы, не учтенные в описанных выше категориях.

*Капитальные расходы* - расходы на приобретение основного капитала, резервов, земли и нематериальных активов, капитальные трансферты и другие капитальные затраты.

*Приобретение основного капитала* включает расходы общего государственного управления на покупку или производство внутри данного сектора товаров длительного пользования, используемых для производственных гражданских целей. Сюда включается капитальное строительство, капитальный ремонт, приобретение оборудования и инвентаря, включаемых в основной капитал. Не включается строительство для военных целей и приобретение военной техники.

*Капитальные трансферты* представляют собой безвозмездные выплаты государства, не связанные с возникновением или погашением финансовых требований, на цели приобретения основного капитала, возмещение ущерба от его повреждения или гибели, увеличения финансового капитала получателей. Сюда включается финансирование государством капитальных вложений, затрат на капитальный ремонт, формирование основного стада, прочих капитальных затрат секторов, компенсации за повреждение и гибель основного капитала, а также погашение государством долгов других секторов и возмещение убытков предприятий, накопившимся по независящим от них причинам. В то же время признание или списание задолженности других секторов перед государством, при которых тсутствуют кассовые операции, в данной статье не учитывается.

*Другие капитальные расходы* - включают затраты государства на приобретение товаров для государственных резервов, земли и нематериальных активов.

*Превышение доходов над расходами/дефицит* рассчитывается как разность между суммарными доходами, включая безвозмездные поступления, и суммарными расходами. Эта же величина, но с противоположным знаком, равна сумме чистых заимствований государства, плюс чистое сокращение государственных кассовых остатков, вкладов и ценных бумаг, имеющих ликвидное назначение.

*Финансирование дефицита по типам кредиторов* - представляет собой все средства (внутренние или иностранные), полученные для покрытия дефицита бюджета либо, наоборот, размещение суммы превышения доходов над расходами. Величина финансирования равна превышению доходов над расходами/дефициту, но с противоположным знаком.

*Зарубежные кредиторы (сальдо)* - включает все заимствования и предоставление кредитов наднациональным органам, иностранным правительствам, международным организациям, физическим лицам, предприятиям и юридическим лицам, включая коммерческие банки, а также приобретение и продажу собственности нерезидентных предприятий. Кроме того сюда входят займы и кредиты на цели развития, полученные от таких специализированных международных организаций, как Всемирный Банк, Азиатский Банк Развития, Межамериканский Банк Развития и Европейский Банк Реконструкции и Развития.

*Внутренние кредиторы (сальдо)* - включает все финансовые операции правительства с резидентами (физическими лицами, предприятиями, органами управления, другими юридическими лицами). Сюда же относится результат торговли государственными ценными бумагами, находящимися в обращении, между резидентами и нерезидентами. Кроме того, в эту категорию включаются изменение активов национальной валюты у государства, депозитов в резидентных финансовых учреждениях, а также ценные бумаг, выпущенные резидентами и приобретенные государством в ликвидных целях.

*Органы денежного обращения* - включает изменение величины обязательств и требований по отношению к Центральному Банку и другим органам денежного обращения, наряду с иными сделками, результатом которых в конечном счете является кредитование или получение кредитов от органов денежного обращения, хотя они и не сопровождаются возникновением финансовых требований. *Депозитные денежные банки* - включает финансирование государства всеми депозитными денежными банками, т.е. финансовыми денежными учреждениями, чьи обязательства представляют собой преимущественно депозиты, которые могут как обращаться в наличность, так и использоваться в качестве средств платежа.

*Другие внутренние кредиторы* - включает все внутренние источники финансирования государства помимо органов денежного обращения и депозитных денежных банков. Фактически сюда включается внутреннее взаимное финансирование государственных органов управления всех уровней, представляющее собой изменение величины контрактных обязательств с фиксированным сроком погашения по отношению к другим органам государственного управления, в результате заимствования, выплат по долгам, продажи и покупки ценных бумаг, а также продажи и покупки одним органом управления ценных бумаг других органов управления в ликвидных целях, но не в целях экономической политики. В консолидированном бюджете взаимное финансирование государственных органов управления как источник финансирования всех государственных органов управления, естественно, устраняется.

*Превышение доходов над расходами/дефицит (-) по внебюджетным фондам, не включенным выше,* - обычно речь идет о статьях государственных доходов и расходов, которые не проходят по статьям бюджета и не осуществляются в порядке обычной бюджетной процедуры. Подобные сделки могут, например, финансироваться посредством иностранной помощи или специальных доходов, не включаемых в бюджет.

*Итого превышение расходов над доходами/дефицит, включая счета внебюджетных фондов* - рассчитывается как сумма превышения/дефицита и превышения/дефицита по внебюджетным фондам.

## 5. СЕЛЬСКОХОЗЯЙСТВЕННАЯ СТАТИСТИКА

### Таблицы 5-1 и 5-2: Сельскохозяйственная продукция (в текущих и постоянных ценах соответственно)

*Валовая продукция сельского хозяйства* включает стоимость сырых продуктов, полученных за год в результате выращивания растений и животных и их хозяйственного использования.

*Продукция растениеводства* включает стоимость валового сбора всех сельскохозяйственных культур; стоимость прироста (+) или уменьшения (-) незавершенного производства; затраты на посадку и выращивание садов и других многолетних насаждений до их плодоношения (кроме леса).

*Продукция животноводства* включает стоимость продукции выращивания скота и птицы, т.е. стоимость приплода, прироста и привеса скота и птицы; стоимость сырых продуктов животноводства, получаемых в процессе хозяйственного использования сельскохозяйственных животных (молока, шерсти, яиц и т.д.); стоимость продукции звероводства (звероводческих ферм), собаководства, рыбоводства (выращивание рыбы в прудах и других водоемах).

*Сельскохозяйственные услуги* - стоимость услуг по улучшению земель, химизации почв и другим агрохимическим работам, защите растений от болезней, вредителей сельскохозяйственных культур, зоотехническому и ветеринарному обслуживанию, орошению, а также предприятий и организаций по эксплуатации ирригационных и мелиоративных сооружений.

**Таблица 5-3. Производство и урожайность важнейших сельскохозяйственных культур**

Общее производство продукции определяется на основе отчетов, подготавливаемых колхозами, совхозами и прочими сельскохозяйственными предприятиями. Данные о производстве продукции в личных подсобных хозяйствах определяется на основе обследования семейных бюджетов. Урожайность сельскохозяйственных культур определяется путем деления всего урожая на уточненную площадь посевов.

**Таблица 6-4. Основные показатели животноводства**

В таблице представлены данные о поголовье скота и продукции животноводства в натуральных единицах измерения.

## 6. СТАТИСТИКА ПРОМЫШЛЕННОСТИ И ЭНЕРГЕТИКИ

Перечни отраслей/пользователей не являются исчерпывающими, так что их сумма не обязательно совпадает с представленными в таблицах итоговыми показателями.

**Таблицы 6-1 и 6-2: Промышленное производство по отраслям** (в текущих и сопоставимых ценах соответственно)

Общий объем продукции промышленности в целом и отдельных ее отраслей определяется как сумма данных об объеме продукции отдельных промышленных предприятий, учтенной по заводскому методу. Продукцией промышленного предприятия считается стоимость всех выработанных предприятием за отчетный период готовых изделий и реализованных на сторону полуфабрикатов (как из своего сырья и материалов, так и из сырья и материалов заказчика), а также стоимость выполненных работ по капитальному ремонту промышленного характера в соответствии с заказами со стороны или непромышленных хозяйств и организаций своего предприятия.

Темпы прироста объема промышленного производства исчисляются по данным о продукции в сопоставимых ценах (нижняя часть таблицы 6-2).

*Тяжелая промышленность* - совокупность отраслей: машиностроение, промышленность топливно-энергетическая, металлургическая (включая добычу руд), химическая и нефтехимическая, лесная, деревообрабатывающая и целлюлозно-бумажная, производство строительных материалов.

*Легкая промышленность* - совокупность отраслей промышленности, производящих товары народного потребления: текстильная промышленность (отрасли первичной обработки волокна, хлопчато-бумажная, льняная, шерстяная, шелковая, пеньково-джутовая, сетевязальная, трикотажная, валяльно-войлочная промышленность, производство текстильной галантереи); швейная промышленность; кожевенная, меховая и обувная промышленность; дубильно-экстрактовая промышленность и прочие отрасли легкой промышленности .

**Таблица 6-3. Ресурсы первичных видов энергии**

Производство первичной энергии - это количество полученной или произведенной из природных источников энергии, подсчитанное после любой операции по удалению инертных веществ, содержащихся в топливе. Сюда относится энергия, потребленная производителем в процессе производства.

**Таблица 6-4: Конечное потребление энергии**

*Конечное потребление энергии* - использование энергоносителей во всех секторах экономики с целью конечного потребления.

*Потребление в промышленности* не включает потребление энергетическим сектором. Потребление в химической промышленности включает только потребление в качестве топлива.

*Потребление на транспорте* - включает все топливо, потребленное при автомобильных перевозках, а также все поставки судам, осуществляющим перевозки по внутренним водным путям и в каботажном плавании, а также самолетам, занятым на внутренних линиях. Топливо, потребленное сельскохозяйственным оборудованием, включено в сельскохозяйственное потребление.

*Домашние хозяйства* - охватывает потребление домашними хозяйствами (включая бесплатную выдачу работникам).

## 7. ЦЕНЫ И ЗАРАБОТНАЯ ПЛАТА

**Таблица 7-1: Валютные курсы и индексы цен**

*Валютные курсы* представлены среднемесячными официальными валютными курсами по данным национальных банков соответствующих стран.

*Оптовые цены* на промышленную продукцию - это цены, по которым осуществляется реализация промышленной продукции предприятиям и организациям. Оптовые цены, представленные в предлагаемых таблицах, являются по преимуществу ценами предприятий. Они включают себестоимость продукции и прибыль, по ним производятся расчеты с промышленными предприятиями-производителями продукции и оптовой торговлей. В этих ценах рассчитывается объем промышленного производства.

*Потребительские цены* - это цены, по которым товары и услуги приобретаются населением через государственную, частную и кооперативную торговлю, предприятия общественного питания, а также у иных предприятий и частных лиц, оказывающих платные услуги.

**Таблица 7-2: Среднемесячная денежная заработная плата по отраслям**

*Заработная плата номинальная* - это суммы, начисленные рабочим и служащим за определенный период времени их работы. Заработная плата, приведенная в таблице, является средней величиной по всем занятым.

*Номинальная заработная плата по отраслям* рассчитывается путем деления фонда заработной платы на количество рабочих и служащих. Сюда же включены премии и другие выплаты из фондов материального стимулирования.

## 8. ДОХОДЫ И РАСХОДЫ ДОМАШНИХ ХОЗЯЙСТВ

**Таблица 8-1: Денежные доходы и расходы населения**

В таблице показаны денежные доходы и расходы населения по видам. Они также включают денежные потоки между государством и населением. Денежные доходы показываются в размере начисленных сумм, до выплаты всех видов налогов и удержаний.

*Доходы* включают все денежные поступления населению.

*Доходы по труду* включают заработную плату, оплату сверхурочных, доходы от колхозов и доходы от продажи сельскохозяйственной продукции.

*Трансфертные доходы* - это сумма пенсий, пособий, стипендий, доходов из финансовой системы и прочих доходов.

*Доходы всего* - это сумма доходов по труду и трансфертных доходов.

*Денежные расходы* - показываются в размере фактически выплаченных, а не подлежащих уплате сумм.

*Покупки всего* - это сумма расходов на покупку товаров и услуг.

*Квартирная плата и коммунальные платежи* включают оплату жилья, услуг гостиниц и общежитий, а также платежи за центральное отопление, воду, газ, электроэнергию, канализацию.

*Оплата услуг пассажирского транспорта* включает плату за проезд, провоз багажа и другие услуги, оказываемые населению при проезде всеми видами транспорта. *Оплата услуг связи* включает расходы на почтовую и телеграфную корреспонденцию, денежные переводы и посылки, за пользование телефоном и за радиотрансляционные точки.

*Оплата услуг здравоохранения* и других услуг включает: расходы на путевки в санатории и дома отдыха, туризм и на лечение в платных поликлиниках; оплату бытовых услуг; взносы в детские учреждения; расходы на кино, театры и другие зрелища; оплату услуг юридических консультаций, сберегательных банков, плату за обучение на курсах и т.д.

*Трансферты и сбережения* - это обязательные платежи населения в бюджет и различные организации, добровольные взносы, другие платежи, а также сбережения.

*Налоги, сборы, пошлины и другие аналогичные платежи* включают все виды налогов и сборов с населения, государственную пошлину, штрафы и другие платежи, уплачиваемые в государственный бюджет.

*Сбережения* включают прирост вкладов населения в сберегательных банках, в Государственном (Центральном) банке, приобретение облигаций, и т.д..

*Прочие расходы* включают платежи по государственному страхованию, взносы в кооперативные и общественные организации, в жилищно-строительную кооперацию, возврат банковских ссуд, приобретение лотерейных билетов, уплату процентов за товарный кредит, уменьшение задолженности по товарному кредиту и т.п.

*Расходы всего* - это сумма расходов на покупку товаров, расходов на услуги, трансферты и сбережения.

*Доходы минус расходы* - это разница между общей величиной доходов и расходов. В этой графе представлены только наличные денежные средства.

# Distributors of World Bank Publications

*Prices and credit terms vary from country to country. Consult your local distributor before placing an order.*

**ALBANIA**
Adrion Ltd.
Perlat Rexhepi Str.
Pall. 9, Shk. 1, Ap. 4
Tirana
Tel: (355 42) 274 19; 221 72
Fax: (355 42) 274 19

**ARGENTINA**
Oficina del Libro Internacional
Av. Cordoba 1877
1120 Buenos Aires
Tel: (54 1) 815-8156
Fax: (54 1) 815-8354

**AUSTRALIA, FIJI, PAPUA NEW GUINEA, SOLOMON ISLANDS, VANUATU, AND WESTERN SAMOA**
D.A. Information Services
648 Whitehorse Road
Mitcham 3132
Victoria
Tel: (61) 3 9210 7777
Fax: (61) 3 9210 7788
URL: http://www.dadirect.com.au

**AUSTRIA**
Gerold and Co.
Weihburggasse 26
A-1011 Wien
Tel: (43 1) 512-47-31-0
Fax: (43 1) 512-47-31-29
URL: http://www.gerold.co/at.online

**BANGLADESH**
Micro Industries Development Assistance Society (MIDAS)
House 5, Road 16
Dhanmondi R/Area
Dhaka 1209
Tel: (880 2) 326427
Fax: (880 2) 811188

**BELGIUM**
Jean De Lannoy
Av. du Roi 202
1060 Brussels
Tel: (32 2) 538-5169
Fax: (32 2) 538-0841

**BRAZIL**
Publicacões Tecnicas Internacionais Ltda.
Rua Peixoto Gomide, 209
01409 Sao Paulo, SP.
Tel: (55 11) 259-6644
Fax: (55 11) 258-6990
URL: http://www.uol.br

**CANADA**
Renouf Publishing Co. Ltd.
1294 Algoma Road
Ottawa, Ontario K1B 3W8
Tel: 613-741-4333
Fax: 613-741-5439
URL: http:// www.fox.nstn.ca/~renouf

**CHINA**
China Financial & Economic Publishing House
8, Da Fo Si Dong Jie
Beijing
Tel: (86 10) 333-8257
Fax: (86 10) 401-7365

**COLOMBIA**
Infoenlace Ltda.
Carrera 6 No. 51-21
Apartado Aereo 34270
Santafé de Bogotá D.C.
Tel: (57 1) 285-2798
Fax: (57 1) 285-2798

**COTE D'IVOIRE**
Centre d'Edition et de Diffusion Africaines (CEDA)
04 B.P. 541
Abidjan 04 Plateau
Tel: (225) 24-6510
Fax: (225) 25-0567

**CYPRUS**
Center for Applied Research
Cyprus College
6, Diogenes Street, Engomi
P.O. Box 2006
Nicosia
Tel: (347 2) 44-1730
Fax: (347 2) 46-2051

**CZECH REPUBLIC**
National Information Center
prodejna, Konviktska 5
CS – 113 57 Prague 1
Tel: (42 2) 2422-9433
Fax: (42 2) 2422-1484
URL: http://www.nis.cz/

**DENMARK**
SamfundsLitteratur
Rosenoerns Allé 11
DK-1970 Frederiksberg C
Tel: (45 31) 351942
Fax: (45 31) 357822

**EGYPT, ARAB REPUBLIC OF**
Al Ahram Distribution Agency
Al Galaa Street
Cairo
Tel: (20 2) 578-6083
Fax: (20 2) 578-6833

The Middle East Observer
41, Sherif Street
Cairo
Tel: (20 2) 393-9732
Fax: (20 2) 393-9732

**FINLAND**
Akateeminen Kirjakauppa
P.O. Box 128
FIN-00101 Helsinki
Tel: (358 0) 12141
Fax: (358 0) 121-4441
URL: http://booknet.cultnet.fi/aka/

**FRANCE**
World Bank Publications
66, avenue d'Iéna
75116 Paris
Tel: (33 1) 40-69-30-56/57
Fax: (33 1) 40-69-30-58

**GERMANY**
UNO-Verlag
Poppelsdorfer Allee 55
53115 Bonn
Tel: (49 228) 212940
Fax: (49 228) 217492

**GREECE**
Papasotiriou S.A.
35, Stournara Str.
106 82 Athens
Tel: (30 1) 364-1826
Fax: (30 1) 364-8254

**HONG KONG, MACAO**
Asia 2000 Ltd.
Sales & Circulation Department
Seabird House, unit 1101-02
22-28 Wyndham Street, Central
Hong Kong
Tel: (852) 2530-1409
Fax: (852) 2526-1107
URL: http://www.sales@asia2000.com.hk

**HUNGARY**
Foundation for Market Economy
112 PF 249
1519 Budapest
Tel: (36 1) 204 2951;(36 1) 204 2948
Fax: (36 1) 204 2953

**INDIA**
Allied Publishers Ltd.
751 Mount Road
Madras - 600 002
Tel: (91 44) 852-3938
Fax: (91 44) 852-0649

**INDONESIA**
Pt. Indira Limited
Jalan Borobudur 20
P.O. Box 181
Jakarta 10320
Tel: (62 21) 390-4290
Fax: (62 21) 421-4289

**IRAN**
Kowkab Publishers
P.O. Box 19575-511
Tehran
Tel: (98 21) 258-3723
Fax: (98 21) 258-3723

Ketab Sara Co. Publishers
Khaled Eslamboli Ave.,
6th Street
Kusheh Delafrooz No. 8
P.O. Box 15745-733
Tehran
Tel: (98 21) 8717819; (98 21) 8716104
Fax: (98 21) 8862479
E-mail: ketab-sara@neda.net.ir

**IRELAND**
Government Supplies Agency
Oifig an tSoláthair
4-5 Harcourt Road
Dublin 2
Tel: (353 1) 661-3111
Fax: (353 1) 475-2670

**ISRAEL**
Yozmot Literature Ltd.
P.O. Box 56055
3 Yohanan Hasandlar Street
Tel Aviv 61560
Tel: (972 3) 5285-397
Fax: (972 3) 5285-397

R.O.Y. International
PO Box 13056
Tel Aviv 61130
Tel: (972 3) 5461423
Fax: (972 3) 5461442

Palestinian Authority/Middle East
Index Information Services
P.O.B. 19502 Jerusalem
Tel: (972 2) 271219
Fax: (972 2) 271634

**ITALY**
Licosa Commissionaria Sansoni SPA
Via Duca Di Calabria, 1/1
Casella Postale 552
50125 Firenze
Tel: (55) 645-415
Fax: (55) 641-257

**JAMAICA**
Ian Randle Publishers Ltd.
206 Old Hope Road
Kingston 6
Tel: 809-927-2085
Fax: 809-977-0243

**JAPAN**
Eastern Book Service
3-13 Hongo 3-chome, Bunkyo-ku
Tokyo 113
Tel: (81 3) 3818-0861
Fax: (81 3) 3818-0864
URL: http://www.bekkoame.or.jp/~svt-ebs

**KENYA**
Africa Book Service (E.A.) Ltd.
Quaran House, Mfangano Street
P.O. Box 45245
Nairobi
Tel: (254 2) 223 641
Fax: (254 2) 330 272

**KOREA, REPUBLIC OF**
Daejon Trading Co. Ltd.
P.O. Box 34, Youida
706 Seoun Bldg
44-6 Youido-Dong, Yeongchengpo-Ku
Seoul
Tel: (82 2) 785-1631/4
Fax: (82 2) 784-0315

**KOREA, REPUBLIC OF**
Pan Korea Book Corporation
134, 1-Ka, Shinmun-Ro, Jongro-Ku
P.O. Box 11, Kwangwhamun
Seoul
Tel: (82 2) 733-2011
Fax: (82 2) 736-8696

**MALAYSIA**
University of Malaya Cooperative Bookshop, Limited
P.O. Box 1127
Jalan Pantai Baru
59700 Kuala Lumpur
Tel: (60 3) 756-5000
Fax: (60 3) 755-4424

**MEXICO**
INFOTEC
Apartado Postal 22-860, Tlalpan
14030 Mexico, D.F.
Tel: (52 5) 606-0011; 1620
Fax: (52 5) 624-2822; 2824

**NETHERLANDS**
De Lindeboom/InOr-Publikaties
P.O. Box 202
7480 AE Haaksbergen
Tel: (31 53) 574-0004
Fax: (31 53) 572-9296

**NEW ZEALAND**
EBSCO NZ Ltd.
Private Mail Bag 99914
New Market
Auckland
Tel: (64 9) 524-8119
Fax: (64 9) 524-8067

**NIGERIA**
University Press Limited
Three Crowns Building Jericho
Private Mail Bag 5095
Ibadan
Tel: (234 22) 41-1356
Fax: (234 22) 41-2056

**NORWAY**
NIC Info A/S
Book Department
P.O. Box 6125 Etterstad
N-0602 Oslo 6
Tel: (47 22) 57-3300
Fax: (47 22) 68-1901

**PAKISTAN**
Mirza Book Agency
65, Shahrah-e-Quaid-e-Azam
Lahore 54000
Tel: (92 42) 7353601
Fax: (92 42) 7585283

Oxford University Press
5 Bangalore Town
Sharae Faisal
PO Box 13033
Karachi-75350
Tel: (92 21) 446307
Fax: (92 21) 454-7640
E-mail: oup@oup.khi.erum.com.pk

**PERU**
Editorial Desarrollo SA
Apartado 3824
Lima 1
Tel: (51 14) 285380
Fax: (51 14) 286628

**PHILIPPINES**
International Booksource Center Inc.
Suite 720, Cityland 10
Condominium Tower 2
H.V dela Costa, corner Valero St.
Makati, Metro Manila
Tel: (63 2) 817-9676
Fax: (63 2) 817-1741

**POLAND**
International Publishing Service
Ul. Piekna 31/37
00-677 Warzawa
Tel: (48 2) 628-6089
Fax: (48 2) 621-7255

**PORTUGAL**
Livraria Portugal
Apartado 2681
Rua Do Carmo 70-74
1200 Lisbon
Tel: (1) 347-4982
Fax: (1) 347-0264

**ROMANIA**
Compani De Librarii Bucuresti S.A.
Str. Lipscani no. 26, sector 3
Bucharest
Tel: (40 1) 613 9645
Fax: (40 1) 312 4000

**RUSSIAN FEDERATION**
Isdatelstvo <Ves Mir>
9a, Lolpachniy Pereulok
Moscow 101831
Tel: (7 095) 917 87 49
Fax: (7 095) 917 92 59

**SAUDI ARABIA, QATAR**
Jarir Book Store
P.O. Box 3196
Riyadh 11471
Tel: (966 1) 477-3140
Fax: (966 1) 477-2940

**SINGAPORE, TAIWAN, MYANMAR, BRUNEI**
Asahgate Publishing Asia Pacific Pte. Ltd.
41 Kallang Pudding Road #04-03
Golden Wheel Building
Singapore 349316
Tel: (65) 741-5166
Fax: (65) 742-9356
e-mail: ashgate@asianconnect.com

**SLOVAK REPUBLIC**
Slovart G.T.G. Ltd.
Krupinska 4
PO Box 152
852 99 Bratislava 5
Tel: (42 7) 839472
Fax: (42 7) 839485

**SOUTH AFRICA, BOTSWANA**
*For single titles:*
Oxford University Press Southern Africa
P.O. Box 1141
Cape Town 8000
Tel: (27 21) 45-7266
Fax: (27 21) 45-7265

*For subscription orders:*
International Subscription Service
P.O. Box 41095
Craighall
Johannesburg 2024
Tel: (27 11) 880-1448
Fax: (27 11) 880-6248

**SPAIN**
Mundi-Prensa Libros, S.A.
Castello 37
28001 Madrid
Tel: (34 1) 431-3399
Fax: (34 1) 575-3998
http://www.tsai.es/mprensa

Mundi-Prensa Barcelona
Consell de Cent, 391
08009 Barcelona
Tel: (34 3) 488-3492
Fax: (34 3) 487-7659

**SRI LANKA, THE MALDIVES**
Lake House Bookshop
P.O. Box 244
100, Sir Chittampalam A. Gardiner Mawatha
Colombo 2
Tel: (94 1) 32105
Fax: (94 1) 432104

**SWEDEN**
For single titles:
CE Fritzes AB
Regeringsgaton 12
S-106 47 Stockholm
Tel: (46 8) 690 90 90
Fax: (46 8) 20 50 21

For subscription orders:
Wennergren-Williams AB
P. O. Box 1305
S-171 25 Solna
Tel: (46 8) 705-97-50
Fax: (46 8) 27-00-71

**SWITZERLAND**
Librairie Payot
Service Institutionnel
Côtes-de-Montbenon 30
1002 Lausanne
Tel: (021)-341-3229
Fax: (021)-341-3235

ADECO Van Diermen Editions Techniques
Ch. de Lacuez 41
CH1807 Blonay
Tel: (41 21) 943 2673
Fax: (41 21) 943 3605

**TANZANIA**
Oxford University Press
Maktaba Street
PO Box 5299
Dar es Salaam
Tel: (255 51) 29209
Fax (255 51) 46822

**THAILAND**
Central Books Distribution
306 Silom Road
Bangkok
Tel: (66 2) 235-5400
Fax: (66 2) 237-8321

**TRINIDAD & TOBAGO, JAMAICA**
Systematics Studies Unit
19 Watts Street
Curepe
Trinidad, West Indies
Tel: (809) 662-5654
Fax: (809) 662-5654

**UGANDA**
Gustro Ltd.
PO Box 9997
Madhvani Building
Plot 16/4 Jinja Rd.
Kampala
Tel: (256 41) 254763
Fax: (256 41) 251 468

**UNITED KINGDOM**
Microinfo Ltd.
P.O. Box 3
Alton, Hampshire GU34 2PG
England
Tel: (44 1420) 86848
Fax: (44 1420) 89889
URL: http://www.microinfo.co.uk

**VENEZUELA**
Tecni-Ciencia Libros, S.A.
Centro Cuidad Comercial Tamanco
Nivel C2
Caracas
Tel: (58 2) 959 5547; 5035; 0016
Fax: (58 2) 959 5636

**ZAMBIA**
University Bookshop
University of Zambia
Great East Road Campus
P.O. Box 32379
Lusaka
Tel: (260 1) 252 576
Fax: (260 1) 253 952

**ZIMBABWE**
Longman Zimbabwe (Pte.)Ltd.
Tourle Road, Ardbennie
P.O. Box ST125
Southerton
Harare
Tel: (263 4) 6216617
Fax: (263 4) 621670

10/07/96